Special Edition
Using
ORACLE8™/8i™

Authors

William G. Page, Jr.

David Austin

Willard Baird II

Mathew Burke

Nicholas Chase

Joe Duer

Tomas Gasper

Dan Hotka

Manish Kakade

Vijay Lunawat

Betty F. Page

Praveen Sharma

Meghraj Thakkar

Contributors to First Edition

Daniel J. Clamage

Jeff Gentry

Nathan Hughes

Ari Kaplan

Laurie J. Kirsh

Sanjay T. Mathew

Sheilah Scheurich

Michael Serbanescu

Michael Sit

que®

A Division of Macmillan Computer Publishing, USA
201 W. 103rd Street
Indianapolis, Indiana 46290

CONTENTS AT A GLANCE

SPECIAL EDITION USING ORACLE8™/8™

Copyright ©1999 by Que

International Standard Book Number: 0-7897-1975-4

Library of Congress Catalog Card Number: 99-62147

Printed in the United States of America

First Printing: June 1999

01   00   4   3

TRADEMARKS

WARNING AND DISCLAIMER

Executive Editor
Tracy Dunkelberger

Acquisitions Editor
Michelle Newcomb

Development Editor
Bryan Morgan

Managing Editor
Brice Gosnell

Project Editor
Natalie Harris

Copy Editors
Kelly Talbot
Pamela Woolf

Indexer
Johnna Vanhoose

Proofreader
Andrew Beaster

Technical Editors
Dorman H. Bazzell II
James A. Clere
Karen Edge-Clere
Tomas Gasper
Stephen P. Karniotis
Dennis R. Kennedy
Keith McKendry
Sundar Rajan

Software Development Specialist
Andrea Duvall

Interior Design
Ruth Harvey

Cover Design
Dan Armstrong
Ruth Harvey

Copy Writer
Eric Borgert

Layout Technicians
Darin Crone
Liz Johnston
Jeannie McKay

CONTENTS

ABOUT THE AUTHORS

William G. Page, Jr. began his professional career in 1982 as an Engineering, Construction, and Operations (EC&O) representative, which included the maintenance of customer information systems for the Duke Power Company in Burlington, NC. In 1987, he accepted a position as a Mathematical Statistician at the U.S. Census Bureau in Suitland, MD. Although his work initially dealt with statistical methods for the behavioral and social sciences, his career evolved toward the computer science field. He progressed through various phases of statistical, scientific, database, systems, and other programming challenges. He became proficient in a variety of programming languages, operating systems, and database systems, eventually focusing on UNIX, Sybase and Oracle. As a Principal Database Engineer with Mitretek Systems in McLean, VA, he currently focuses on Oracle and MS SQL Server, with specialties in the design and performance of database systems. He has also consulted on other information systems aspects, such as software architectures for legacy migrations, n-tiered systems, and Web-based databases. Mr. Page holds an MS degree in computer science from Virginia Tech, where he concentrated his studies in operating systems, database systems, and human factors. He intends to pursue a Ph.D. in either computer or cognitive science. His academic interests include object-oriented and relational model integration, extensions to the relational model, artificial intelligence applied to database management systems, and the information processing model of learning.

David Austin has been in the data processing profession for almost 25 years. He worked with many database architectures, including hierarchical, network, and relational, before becoming an Oracle DBA over 10 years ago. For the past 6 years, David has worked for Oracle Corporation where he is currently employed as a Senior Principal Curriculum Developer. His previous positions at Oracle include Senior Principal Consultant and Senior Principal Instructor. David, author of Using Oracle8 published by QUE/Macmillan, is a Certified Oracle8 Database Administrator. He has a B.A. with a double major in Mathematics and English and a minor in Computer Science, and an M.S. in Applied Mathematics, from the University of Colorado. He can be reached by email at daustin@us.oracle.com.

Willard Baird II has been working in data processing for fifteen years. The last ten years, he has specialized in the database arena, and he has worked with Oracle since 1991. He is a frequent speaker for the International Oracle Users Week (IOUW), and the NetSec security conference. He is an accomplished author, having written an Oracle Certification book for Macmillan publishing and various magazine articles on Oracle topics. He has created a one-day seminar on Oracle security which covers all aspects of defining and auditing an Oracle database environment. He teaches part time at the University of South Florida, where he has helped to design and organize the Advanced Database course. He has worked as an Oracle DBA for nine years in the banking industry, so he has strong experience in establishing controls and security policies, and performing security audits on an Oracle database. He can be reached by email at vw2@msn.com

Nicholas Chase has built Oracle-based Web sites for companies such as Lucent Technologies, Sun Microsystems, and Oracle. He got his first email account in 1989, and before immersing himself in the Web, he was a physicist, a high-school teacher, a low-level radioactive waste facility manager, an online science fiction magazine editor, a multimedia engineer, and an Oracle instructor. These days he is a consultant with Computer Systems Authority, helping companies make the most of the Internet. He gets through life with the help of his beautiful wife Sarah, who may never know just how important she is to him. They live in Florida with their soon-to-be-teenager, Sean. He can be reached at nick@nicholaschase.com.

Joe Duer is a technical analyst and Oracle database administrator at a technology-driven corporation based in southern Connecticut. He specializes in Web development using Oracle's Application Server and Database Server. He has developed object-oriented systems that utilize Java and C++, as well as Oracle Application Server's Java, PL/SQL, and VRML cartridges. He can be reached via email at joeduer@ix.netcom.com, and via his Web page at http://www.netcom.com/~joeduer.

Tomas Gasper is a DBA for Energizer Battery Co, in St Louis, Missouri. In past lives, he has worked as a UNIX and NT system administrator, and in application and system programming. Having worked in most aspects of IS, Tomas particularly enjoys work that involves integrating divergent systems. When not at work, he enjoys exploring the Internet and adding new capabilities to his Linux systems. Tomas can be reached via email at tgasper@highlandil.com.

Dan Hotka is Director of European Operations for Platinum Technology. He has over 21 years in the computer industry and over 15 years experience with Oracle products. He is an acknowledged Oracle expert with Oracle experience dating back to the Oracle V.4.0 days. He has co-authored the popular books *Oracle Unleashed*, *Oracle8 Server Unleashed*, and *Oracle Developer Unleashed* from Sams Publishing, is frequently published in trade journals, and regularly speaks at Oracle conferences and user groups around the world. Dan can be reached at hotka@platinum.com.

Manish D. Kakade is employed by the Electricity Metering division of Asea Brown Boveri (ABB) in Raleigh, North Carolina. At ABB, he works as a Senior Information Systems Consultant. In this position he has concentrated on Oracle database administration, back-ups and recovery, performance monitoring, and tuning, setting up the replication environment for the distributed databases. He has developed software tools and scripts to accomplish these objectives. Prior to working at ABB, he worked as a senior Oracle DBA and System administrator for Lucent Technologies, Allentown, PA, and Tata Consultancy Services, Bombay, India. In these positions, he worked with an Oracle parallel server as well as various third-party tools and systems such as Sequent, Pyramid, Sun Sparc, HP10000, Tandem, AS/400, Elxsi, etc. He has over 9 years experience in technological fields, including 7.5 years in Information Technology and 1.5 years in Machine designing. He has been involved in product design, application development, project implementation, and troubleshooting.

Vijay Lunawat is a Senior Technical Specialist with Oracle Corporation. He has bachelor's degree in Electronics Engineering. He has worked with Oracle databases for more than 11 years as a developer, database administrator, consultant, and support. A specialist in Oracle Parallel Server, he is now working with the Centers of Expertise in Oracle Support Services. He develops and frequently teaches Oracle Internals classes at Oracle Corporation. He was a contributing author for Que's *Using Oracle8* book.

Betty F. Page is employed by the U.S. Census Bureau in Suitland, MD, specializing in database systems support. She has worked in data processing for over 13 years, and with the Oracle RDBMS since 1992, as a database administrator and developer. Her main focus lately has been on her two children, ages 3 and 7 months.

Praveen Sharma is a Senior Sales consultant with Oracle Corporation in the New York Financial Services group. He has Masters degree in Information Systems and a Bachelors degree in Electrical Engineering. His responsibilities include the installation, data migration, and tuning of Oracle8 and Oracle8i databases for benchmarks and concepts. Prior to joining Oracle, he worked as an Oracle development manager and Senior Oracle developer at Hoffman la Roche and Brystol Myers Squibb, respectively. He can be reached by email at pxsharma@us.oracle.com.

Meghraj Thakkar works as a senior Software Engineer at Quest Software (Australia). Prior to this, he worked as a Technical Specialist at Oracle Corporation (USA). He has been working with various Oracle products for the past seven years. He has a master's degree in Computer Science and a bachelor's degree in Electronics Engineering. He has several industry vendor certifications, including Oracle Certified DBA (OCP), Microsoft Certified Systems Engineer (MCSE), Novell Certified ECNE, SCO UNIX ACE, and Lotus Certified Notes Consultant. He has taught several courses at the University of California, Irvine. He developed and presented a two-day course "Supporting Oracle on Windows NT" to internal Oracle employees, and presented papers at the Oracle Open World (Australia), UKOUG (UK), ECO (New York). He has co-authored several books for Macmillan Computer Publishing, including *Special Edition Using Oracle8, Oracle8 Server Unleashed, C++ Unleashed, COBOL Unleashed, Oracle Certified DBA, Using Oracle8, and Sams Teach Yourself Oracle8i on Windows NT in 24 Hours.*

DEDICATION

This book is dedicated to the ones I love: BF, LM, and BC.

ACKNOWLEDGMENTS

Thanks to Csaba Egyhazy, to James Hutchinson, and to all of my teachers who have greatly influenced me. Thanks to all of my friends at the US Census Bureau. Of course, thanks always to my family for their love, understanding, and support. - *William G. Page, Jr.*

TELL US WHAT YOU THINK!

As the reader of this book, *you* are our most important critic and commentator. We value your opinion and want to know what we're doing right, what we could do better, what areas you'd like to see us publish in, and any other words of wisdom you're willing to pass our way.

As an associate publisher for Que, I welcome your comments. You can fax, email, or write me directly to let me know what you did or didn't like about this book— as well as what we can do to make our books stronger.

Please note that I cannot help you with technical problems related to the topic of this book, and that due to the high volume of mail I receive, I might not be able to reply to every message.

When you write, please be sure to include this book's title and author as well as your name and phone or fax number. I will carefully review your comments and share them with the author and editors who worked on the book.

Fax: 317.581.4666

Email: programming@mcp.com

Mail: Associate Publisher
Que Publishing
201 West 103rd Street

INTRODUCTION

In this chapter

WHO SHOULD USE THIS BOOK

Over the past few years, the Oracle database environment has become one of the most popular database platforms in the world. Although the Oracle database is still primarily targeted at large corporations or government institutions that require massive data processing capabilities, Oracle has offered many new products that will introduce the Oracle environment to the smaller organization. With the availability of the robust Oracle database on the popular Microsoft Windows NT platform, the integration of Oracle into all types of businesses and organizations is well under way. This means that more knowledgeable and experienced IT professionals trained in Oracle technology will be needed—and not just at the Fortune 500 companies.

This book is written for the Oracle database professional. It is targeted at the intermediate to advanced Oracle Database Administrator (DBA), but it will be useful to other database professionals such as developers, designers, engineers, or architects. Within these pages you will find the information you need to enable a technology, rather than the party line on how it's "supposed" to work. End users will also find this book immensely useful, especially those users with at least some Oracle or other Relational Database Management System (RDBMS) experience. Web administrators and developers who want to store their data in properly built, maintained, and tuned Oracle databases should also consider this book. UNIX and NT System Administrators (SAs) will find this book very useful if they must administer systems serving Oracle products. Finally, technical managers who must manage DBAs and other database-related professionals working with Oracle will find much of this book invaluable in making key technical decisions related to Oracle products.

This book focuses largely on Oracle implementation and use, and on administration, development, maintenance, and tuning. However, the book also offers a solid background in relational database theory and design, which every database professional should understand. The authors of this book are experienced Oracle professionals coming from industry, government, academia, and Oracle Corporation. In addition to each chapter's content, this book offers highly useful and distilled information, including tips, notes, sidebars, guidelines, and cautions. The information contained within this book is the result of years of real-world experience in the Oracle environment. Although this book is about Oracle in general, it is focussed on Oracle's latest RDBMS product lines. In particular, it will be indispensable for those interested in learning quickly about Oracle8 and Oracle8i. This book provides a solid Oracle7 background, comprehensive coverage of Oracle8 features, and a broad overview of Oracle8i features.

WHICH VERSION TO USE: ORACLE7, ORACLE8, OR ORACLE8I

A quick discussion of the evolution of the Oracle RDBMS will help you better chart the course with which you can steer through the book. This overview must be provided because it is not uncommon to find confusion surrounding the release of Oracle8i. First, you need some clarifications. When this book refers to Oracle7, what it means is Oracle7.x, more specifically, Oracle7.3.x. When it refers to Oracle8, what it means is Oracle8.0.x. When it refers to Oracle8i, what it means is Oracle8.1.x. When it refers to simply Oracle8.x, it means both Oracle8 and Oracle8i or, in other words, both Oracle8.0.x and Oracle8.1.x. If this is confusing, imagine how the salespersons must feel.

When Oracle8 was first released, it offered some significant new features and options over Oracle7. However, the basic RDBMS Oracle7 engine was not completely rewritten. Nonetheless, it was a major migration from Oracle7 to Oracle8. As Oracle8i is now in the process of being released, its basic RDBMS engine remains largely unchanged again from Oracle8, even less so than from Oracle7 to Oracle8. Oracle8i might be thought of as a functional superset of Oracle8.

Even though they represent two different products, just as Oracle7 and Oracle8. There are parallel development paths for Oracle8 and Oracle8i such that their minor releases occur roughly at the same time. For example, after Oracle8.0.5 was released, not long afterward was seen the release of Oracle8.1.5. The next expected releases are 8.0.6 and 8.1.6. Clearly, the Oracle8.0.x technology forms the basis for Oracle8.1.x, even more so than Oracle7.3.x did for Oracle8.0.x.

Consider the following questions. What can Oracle8 do that Oracle8i cannot? Nothing because Oracle8 is a functional subset of Oracle8i. What can Oracle8i do that Oracle8 cannot? It offers many Internet-related capabilities, among other things. Most significantly, it has incorporated Java as a native database language that can act as a supplement to or replacement for SQL, and it has incorporated a Web server and development platform (WebDB). According to Oracle, the development (not support) of Oracle8.0.x might terminate with the release of 8.0.6, and after that, Oracle8.1.x will fully succeed Oracle8.0.x. In other words, Oracle8i will eventually fully succeed Oracle8.

With the advent of Oracle8i, what purposes are served by the Oracle Application Server (OAS) and other products, such as Developer, which includes Web-based development? To summarize, WebDB is only a functional subset of OAS. In other words, WebDB cannot do everything OAS can do. Further, WebDB cannot do everything Designer and Developer can do. So, although there is some product overlap, there is not enough overlap to qualify OAS and other products as obsolete. On the contrary, Oracle8i can be thought of as a total solution for small-to-medium applications (in effect, workgroup or departmental) that only require simple design and some Web development. When large applications must be properly designed and built, including complex multi-tier software architectures, products such as OAS, Designer, and Developer fulfill those enterprise needs. Hence, there remains a need for all the products because they are positioned to help with different application needs despite some functional overlap.

WHAT'S IN THIS BOOK

The book is divided into 9 parts, 41 chapters, and 2 appendices. Each part builds conceptually on the other. In particular, Part II deals with the Oracle7.x RDBMS, and Part III continues where Part II left off, explaining the major features and options of the Oracle8.x database, including an overview of Oracle8i. The following sections give you an overview of each chapter.

PART I: PRINCIPLES OF DATABASE MANAGEMENT

Chapter 1, "Database, DBMS Principles, and the Relational Model," covers what a database is and how databases have evolved over the years. It also introduces the Database Management System (DBMS) and Relational Database Management System (RDBMS). In order to explain what an RDBMS is, it also briefly covers the tenets of the Relational Model.

Chapter 2, "Logical Database Design and Normalization," covers logical Entity-Relationship Diagram (ERD) modeling, mapping ERDs to the relational model, and normalization theory. In covering normalization, a very important piece of relational design, it defines the process, gives motivation, and explains normal forms with examples.

Chapter 3, "Physical Database Design, Hardware, and Related Issues," covers many hardware, physical, and low-level issues, including application-typing of database systems, understanding quantitative estimates, denormalization and whether to use it, the storage hierarchy, RAID, understanding bottlenecks, choosing the right platform, operating system (OS) integration, and some major physical design principles.

Chapter 4, "The Oracle Solution," looks at the history of Oracle and the Oracle Corporation and whether Oracle is truly a DBMS or RDBMS; it also revisits physical design, given Oracle specifics, and considers the future of Oracle.

PART II: THE ORACLE7.X RDBMS

Chapter 5, "The Oracle Database Architecture," is an explanation of the internal data storage mechanisms of the Oracle database. Here is where information on database datafiles, tables, indexes, and other storage objects is covered, as well as detailed information on how these objects work and interact with each other.

Chapter 6, "The Oracle Instance Architecture," completes the coverage of the Oracle database server with an explanation of the memory structures and processes involved in an Oracle database. Chapters 5 and 6, when taken as a whole, provide a comprehensive explanation of the internal workings of the Oracle RDBMS.

Chapter 7, "Exploring the Oracle Environment," ventures away from the abstract topics in the first two chapters and explains exactly how Oracle is implemented and installed on a database server. The Optimal Flexible Architecture, Oracle's standard on setting up the database server to hold production databases, is also covered.

Chapter 8, "Oracle Database Administration Overview," covers what many Oracle trade books do not: an overview of the database lifecycle, definitions and responsibilities of the Database Administrator (DBA) and other database-related jobs, and an overview of the functional tasks a DBA needs to follow in order to properly build an Oracle database.

PART III: THE ORACLE8.X RDBMS

Chapter 9, "Migrating Oracle7.x to Oracle8.x," covers the three major migration methods, the migration utility, pre-migration tasks, some common problems, and post-migration tasks.

Chapter 10, "Partitioning," covers the new capabilities of Oracle to logically partition tables, partition indexes, maintain them, and provide some additional capabilities, such as integrated parallelization.

Chapter 11, "The History of Large Objects (LOBs)," reviews the history of LOBs from Oracle7 to Oracle8, the distinction between LOBs and BFILEs in Oracle8, the `DBMS_LOB` package, and many code listings as examples to their creation and use.

Chapter 12, "Object-Oriented Features," provides an object-oriented technology refresher, introduces the Oracle8 object option, and discusses many features of this new option, such as REFs, Methods, Collections, and Object Views. It includes many sample code listings.

Chapter 13, "Networking with Net8: New Features and Concepts," provides an overview of Net8 components and functionality, as well as the new Connection Manager (CMAN) utility. New features and concepts, such as connection concentration in the form of multiplexing and connection pooling, are covered, including sample configuration code listings and files.

Chapter 14, "Oracle8i Additional Topics," covers a wide array of Oracle8 new features varying in importance and depth of coverage, including the new ROWID, new password management, Recovery Manager (RMAN), and Advanced Queuing (AQ), as well as changes in constraints, National Language Support (NLS), and `SYS` security.

Chapter 15, "Oracle8i Overview," is an extremely broad and comprehensive chapter covering the Oracle8i RDBMS in contrast to the Oracle8 RDBMS. Despite its breadth of coverage, it manages to supply sufficient depth and examples in order to jump-start your Oracle8i use. Among the important new features and functionality covered are Java and all its possibilities, WebDB, the Internet File System (IFS), interMedia, availability, security, and some other features.

PART IV: PERFORMANCE TUNING

Chapter 16, "Performance Tuning Fundamentals," revisits physical design in light of tuning and covers the major tuning goals, the Return-on-Investment (ROI) strategy of tuning, and exotic solutions. This chapter also revisits application types in light of what you've learned about tuning and briefly covers the Oracle diagnostic tools available when performing database or application tuning.

Chapter 17, "Application Tuning," covers how the Oracle optimizer works, `SQL TRACE`, `TKPROF`, `EXPLAIN PLAN`, typical problems with examples, and how to efficiently rewrite queries.

Chapter 18, "Tuning Memory," covers monitoring and tuning the major Oracle memory structures, SGA and non-SGA, including the shared pool, the database buffer cache, sorting, and locks, and revisits OS integration in light of Oracle specifics.

Chapter 19, "Tuning I/O," covers tuning the various I/O aspects of Oracle, including how to monitor and tune tablespaces and datafiles, blocks and extents, rollback segments, and redo logs.

Chapter 20, "Oracle8.x Tuning Considerations," updates the previous chapters (16–19) to include Oracle8-specific tuning issues, such as dealing with partitioning, Index Organized Tables (IOTs), parallel DML (PDML), the large pool, very large memory (VLM), some Net8 coverage, and new database limits. Chapter 15, "Oracle8i Overview," also includes some Oracle8i tuning-specific information above and beyond this chapter.

PART V: MANAGING THE ORACLE DATABASE

Chapter 21, "Managing Database Storage," covers how the Oracle database objects are created and managed. This coverage includes all the Oracle storage hierarchy from tables down to blocks.

Chapter 22, "Identifying Heavy Resource Users," helps you identify users, processes, or queries causing database trouble spots and consuming inordinate amounts of database resources. The topics covered in this chapter are key to effectively monitoring and tuning your database.

Chapter 23, "Security Management," covers the complex Oracle security framework, consisting of users, roles, object and system privileges, and authentication. It also covers trusted Oracle.

Chapter 24, "Backup and Recovery," discusses that most loved and hated responsibility of the Oracle DBA: performing proper database backups. The relative merits and use of logical and physical backups, cold and online backups, and recovery methodologies are discussed.

Chapter 25, "Integrity Management," covers the concept and Oracle implementation of data access concurrency, locking, referential integrity, constraints, and triggers.

PART VI: ORACLE INTERFACES AND UTILITIES

Chapter 26, "SQL*Plus for Administrators," covers SQL*Plus from the aspect of the database administrator.

Chapter 27, "Oracle Enterprise Manager," covers the major functionality, features, and usage of the Oracle Enterprise Manager (OEM) DBA management utility, including the Performance Pack. Coverage is up-to-date with the latest version of OEM (3.x).

Chapter 28, "PL/SQL Fundamentals," is for DBAs as well as beginning developers. It gives you an overview of the PL/SQL language, including the basic language elements, control structures, and tips on design, and it also explains how to build and use procedures and packages.

Chapter 29, "Using Stored Subprograms, Packages, and the Supplied Packages," examines how to build stored subprograms and packages. It also covers the benefits of using stored PL/SQL code: faster execution, code reuse leading to shorter development cycles, better-tuned applications, ease of use, code sharing in memory, implementation and deployment of business rules, compile-time syntax checking, increased robustness, and a general simplification of client applications. It also covers the Oracle-supplied packages. Knowledge of and the capability to use these packages can make your life as a developer or DBA much easier. This chapter explains these supplied packages available to you and how to use them.

Chapter 30, "Using Import/Export," covers the usage of the Import and Export utilities and provides scenarios where these tools are used to solve real-world problems.

Chapter 31, "SQL*Loader," explores the SQL*Loader flat file load utility, as well as scenarios and real-world detailed examples.

Chapter 32, "Designer for Administrators," covers an often-overlooked area of the Oracle environment: the specific information necessary to properly administer and maintain the case repository for Designer 2000.

PART VII: ORACLE NETWORKING

Chapter 33, "Oracle Networking Fundamentals," explains networking from the Oracle standpoint and the fundamental characteristics of SQL*Net and Net8. It also covers the basic installation and configuration options of the Oracle Networking products.

Chapter 34, "The Advanced Security Option," provides information on how to configure and use the more advanced features of SQL*Net and Net8, including Oracle Names, the Advanced Security Option, including single sign-on using Public Key Infrastructure (PKI) technology (for example, x.509 certificates) and Secure Sockets Layer (SSL), as well as Fine-Grained Access Control, which permits column-level by user security granularity.

PART VIII: ORACLE APPLICATION SERVER

Chapter 35, "Oracle Application Server (OAS)," covers the fundamental architecture, installation, and administration of the Oracle Application Server (OAS) 4.x. Oracle professionals moving to Web technologies will not want to miss this chapter.

Chapter 36, "Oracle Application Server Components," gives you a detailed look at the components that make up the OAS—including the Web Listener, the Web Request Broker, the Web Request Broker engines, and the Web Server SDK.

Chapter 37, "Installing and Configuring the OAS," walks you through installing and configuring the OAS software and provides help for troubleshooting problems that occur during the installation process.

PART IX: PARALLEL AND DISTRIBUTED ENVIRONMENTS

Chapter 38, "Parallel Query Management," covers the Parallel Query Option (PQO) of the Oracle Server. This includes the use of Parallel Query in querying, DML, and loading (import or SQL*Loader).

Chapter 39, "Parallel Server Management," covers the Oracle Parallel Server (OPS) architecture, as well as when and how to use this optional product.

Chapter 40, "Distributed Database Management," builds on Part V and covers issues specific to the administration of distributed environments. Topics include distributed databases, database links, snapshots, and replication.

Chapter 41, "Replication Management," builds on the previous chapter, covering the basic, built-in snapshot replication capabilities with Oracle, Replication Manager, and Advanced Replication (AR).

APPENDICES

Appendix A, "Oracle on Solaris," offers platform-specific information for designing, configuring, administering, and tuning your Oracle database on UNIX, particularly Solaris and System V Release 4 (SVR4) systems. This includes important memory and disk settings.

Appendix B, "Oracle on Linux," although similar to the previous appendix, focuses exclusively on Linux while building upon the same concepts.

HOW TO USE THIS BOOK

Special Edition Using Oracle8/8i is a practical reference manual as well as a learning tool. You will find the information to be as valuable in your day-to-day activities as in your evening studies. Keep this book within reach because the answers to many problems typically faced by the front-line Oracle professional can be found within.

Experienced Oracle DBAs who have also been exposed to relational database theory might want to skip Part I and move directly into the heart of the book. For an Oracle7 architecture and database administration refresher, review Part II. For those well-versed in Oracle7, go directly to Part III, which is all Oracle8. For performance tuning in either Oracle7 or Oracle8, follow up with Part IV. DBAs with little experience or familiarity with the theory and concepts behind the relational database should not skip Part I. The concepts covered in Part I are fundamental for a new DBA to get off to the right start.

Treat the remaining parts as a reference for both Oracle7 and Oracle8. For a database administration reference in addition to Part II, refer to Parts V and VI. For a networking reference, refer to Part VII. For a Web server reference, refer to Part VIII. For parallel and distributed references, refer to Part IX. For platform-specific information, refer to the appendices.

Technical managers, not just DBAs, should find the entire book useful as a reference from time to time, depending on the aspect in which they need instruction or reference. For that matter, the last statement holds true for all users. You can use this book in whatever manner you desire:

> *Read it in order to learn or use it as a reference.*

There are enough supporting examples throughout the chapters to help you learn what you need to know. In fact, with its abundance of examples and clarity of explanations, this book's predecessor, the previous edition of *Special Edition Using Oracle8/8i*, has been successfully used as a freshman/sophomore level textbook in teaching Oracle.

Principles of Database Management

## CHAPTER 1

DATABASE, DBMS PRINCIPLES, AND THE RELATIONAL MODEL

In this chapter

UNDERSTANDING DATABASES

Over the years, there have been many definitions of the word *database*. For our purposes, a database is an organized collection of data serving a central purpose. It is organized in the sense that it contains data that is stored, formatted, accessed, and represented in a consistent manner. It serves a central purpose in that it does not contain extraneous or superfluous data. A phone book is a good example of a database. It contains relevant data (names) that enable access to phone numbers. It does not contain irrelevant data, such as the color of a person's phone. It stores only what is relevant to its purpose. Most often, a database's purpose is business, but it might store scientific, military, or other data not normally thought of as business data. Hence, there are business databases, scientific databases, military databases, and the list goes on and on. In addition, data can not only be categorized as to its business, but also its format. Modern databases contain many types of data other than text and numeric. For example, it is now commonplace to find databases storing pictures, graphs, audio, video, or *compound documents*, which include two or more of these types.

When discussing databases and database design in particular, it is commonplace to refer to the central purpose a database serves as its *business*, regardless of its more specific field, such as aerospace, biomedical, or whatever. Furthermore, in real life a database is often found to be very specific to its business.

In earlier days, programmers who wrote code to serve Automatic Data Processing (ADP) requirements found they frequently needed to store data from run to run. This became known as the need for *persistent storage*, that is, the need for data to persist, or be saved, from one run of a program to the next. This fundamental need began the evolution of databases. A secondary need, simple data storage, also helped give rise to databases. Online archiving and historical data are a couple of specific examples. Although files, directories, and file systems could provide most general data storage needs, including indexing variations, databases could do what file systems did and more.

Modern databases typically serve some processing storage need for departments or smaller organizational units of their parent organization or enterprise. Hence, you use the terms *enterprisewide* database to refer to the scope of the whole organization's business, *departmentwide* database to refer to the level of a department, and *workgroup* database to usually refer to some programming or business unit within a department. Most often, you find databases at the departmentwide and workgroup levels.

Occasionally, you find databases that serve enterprisewide needs, such as payroll and personnel databases, but these are far outnumbered by their smaller brethren. In fact, when several departmental databases are brought together, or *integrated*, into one large database, this is the essence of building a *Data Warehouse (DW)*. The smaller databases, which act as the data sources for the larger database, are known as *operational* databases. However, this is nothing new. An operational database is just one that produces data, which has been known for years as a *production* database. Only in the context of building a DW do you find production databases also referred to as operational databases or sometimes *operational data stores.* With the advent of Internet technology, databases and Data Warehouses now frequently serve as back ends for Web browser front ends.

When workgroup databases are integrated to serve a larger departmental need, the result is typically referred to as a *Data Mart (DM)*. A DM is nothing more than a departmental-scale DW. As you can imagine, just as with the term *database*, the term *Data Warehouse* has yielded a multitude of definitions. However, when you're integrating several smaller databases into one larger database serving a broader organizational need, the resulting database can generally be considered a DW if it stores data historically, provides decision support, offers summarized data, serves data read-only, and acts essentially as a data sink for all the relevant production databases that feed it.

Otherwise, if a database simply grows large because it is a historical database that's been storing data for a long period of time (such as a Census database), because of the type of data it must store (such as an image database), or because of the frequency with which it must store data (such as a satellite telemetry database), it is often referred to as a *Very Large Database (VLDB)*.

What qualifies as a VLDB has changed over time, as is to be expected with disk storage becoming denser and cheaper, the advent of symmetric multiprocessing machines, the development of RAID technologies, and database software growing, or *scaling*, to handle these larger databases. Currently, a general guideline is that any database of 100GB or larger can be considered a VLDB. As little as a few years ago, 10GB was considered the breakpoint.

UNDERSTANDING A DBMS

A *Database Management System (DBMS)* is the software that manages a database. It acts as a repository for all the data and is responsible for its storage, security, integrity, concurrency, recovery, and access. The DBMS has a *data dictionary*, sometimes referred to as the *system catalog*, which stores data about everything it holds, such as names, structures, locations, and types. This data is also referred to as *metadata*, which is data about data. The lifespan of a piece of data, from its creation to its deletion, is recorded in the data dictionary, as is all logical and physical information about that piece of data. A Database Administrator (DBA) should become intimate with the data dictionary of the DBMS, which serves him or her over the life of the database.

SECURING DATA

Security is always a concern in a production database and often in a development or test database, too. It is usually not a question of whether to have any security, but rather how much to have. A DBMS typically offers several layers of security in addition to the operating system (OS) and network security facilities. Most often, a DBMS holds user accounts with passwords requiring the user to *log in*, or be authenticated, to access the database.

DBMSs also offer other mechanisms, such as groups, roles, privileges, and profiles, which all offer a further refinement of security. These security levels not only provide for enforcement, but also for the establishment of business security policies. For example, only an authenticated user who belongs to an aviation group can access the aviation data. Another example is that only an authenticated user who has the role of operator can back up the database.

MAINTAINING AND ENFORCING INTEGRITY

The *integrity* of data refers to its consistency and correctness. For data to be consistent, it must be modeled and implemented the same way in all its occurrences. For data to be correct, it must be right, accurate, and meaningful.

One way a DBMS maintains integrity is by *locking* a data item in the process of being changed. A database usually locks at the database page level or at the row level. Incidentally, locking also permits concurrency, which you'll cover next.

Another way a DBMS enforces integrity is to replicate a change to a piece of data if it is stored in more than one place. The last way a DBMS enforces integrity is by keeping an eye on the data values being entered or changed so that they fall within required specifications (for example, a range check).

If proper modeling and implementation practices are followed (as is discussed later in Chapter 2, "Logical Database Design and Normalization"), the DBMS helps to automatically enforce this integrity when put in place, for example, through a trigger or constraint, both of which are defined and illustrated in Chapter 28, "PL/SQL Fundamentals." Without integrity, data is worthless. With integrity, data is information. Integrity not only enhances data, it gives data its value.

A DBMS must manage concurrency when it offers multiuser access. That is, when more than one person at a time must access the same database, specifically the same pieces of data, the DBMS must ensure that this *concurrent* access is somehow possible. *Concurrent* can be defined as simultaneous in the looser sense that two or more users access the same data in the same time period.

The methods behind how a DBMS does this are not too complex, but the actual programming behind it is. Essentially, when two or more people want to simply look at the same data without changing it, all is well. When at least one person wants to change the data and others want to look at it or change it too, the DBMS must store multiple copies and resolve all the changed copies back into one correct piece of data when everyone is done.

One aspect of concurrency management was mentioned already: locking. Generally speaking, the finer-grained (smaller) the lock, the better the concurrency (that is, more users have simultaneous access without having to wait). Rows are typically smaller than the smallest database page or block. Hence, row-level locks serve short, random data transactions better, and block-level locks serve long, sequential data transactions better.

This is how concurrency and integrity are linked. When a person wants to look at or change a piece of data, that person is performing a *transaction* with the database.

UNDERSTANDING TRANSACTIONS

A DBMS has, as part of its code, a *transaction manager* whose purpose is to manage concurrency and ensure integrity of transactions. The transaction manager has a tough job because it must enable many people to access the same data at the same time, and yet it must put the data back as though it had been accessed by one person at a time, one after the other, which ensures its correctness. Therein lies the fundamental answer as to how a DBMS must resolve all those multiple copies of data. Transactions occurring during the same time period can preserve the accuracy of the data if (and only if) they are *serializable*. Simply put, the DBMS must rearrange them so that the net result of all the changes is as if they all occurred single file.

The transaction is a unit of concurrency or work. Nothing smaller or less than a transaction can occur. That is, no one can halfway change a piece of data. All transactions must be *atomic* in that each individual transaction either completes or doesn't complete. Until modern 20th century physics came along, the atom was thought to the smallest unit of matter. Likewise, the transaction is the smallest unit of concurrency. It is all-or-nothing. A transaction that completes is said to be *committed*, and one that does not is *rolled back*.

The DBMS handles recovery using transactions as units of recovery. Normal completions, manual requests for aborts, and unexpected aborts all require the DBMS to again call on its multiple copies of data to either commit or roll back the data. A transaction log is kept by the DBMS for the purpose of rolling back and for rolling forward. A rollback is an undo operation. A rollforward is a redo operation that takes place when, for example, a committed transaction doesn't make it from memory to disk because of a hardware or software failure. The DBMS simply redoes it. Hence, the key to transaction recovery in a DBMS is that a transaction must be atomic and can be done, undone, or redone when necessary.

COMMUNICATING WITH THE DATABASE

A DBMS is no good if you can't talk to it. You might ask how one talks to a DBMS. Databases can be accessed through an *access* or *query* language. Structured Query Language (SQL) is the predominant query language today. It works mostly with the predominant type of DBMS that you will learn about shortly: the Relational DBMS (RDBMS). All communication to and from the database should pass through the DBMS, and to do this, you use SQL or something like it. DBAs use query languages to build and maintain a database, and users use query languages to access the database and to look at or change the data.

UNDERSTANDING A RDBMS

In 1970, E. F. Codd fathered the concept of the *relational model*. Before RDBMSs such as DB2 were born, hierarchic (IMS) and network (IDMS) models were commonplace. Before these models, databases were built using flat files (operating system files, not necessarily flat!) and third generation language (3GL) access routines. In fact, some customized systems are still built this way, justified or not. Many of these *legacy* databases still exist on mainframes and minicomputers. CODASYL (from the Conference on Data System Languages) was a database standard created by the Database Task Group (DBTG). This was a COBOL-based network database standard, and IDMS was one vendor implementation. Since the seventies, however, RDBMSs have come to dominate the marketplace with vendors such as Oracle, Sybase, Informix, and Ingres.

Recently, Object-Oriented (OO) DBMSs have come into the foreground and found many niche applications, such as in CAD/CAM, engineering, multimedia, and so forth. OO DBMSs filled those niches because their strengths are handling complex data types in an almost nontransactional environment. To compete, RDBMS vendors have made *universal servers* commercially available in order to offer OO/multimedia capabilities including text, audio, image, and video data types. Oracle's Universal Server is an example. In addition, *user-defined data types*, or *extensible types*, have been augmented or added to the core database servers. Oracle8 offers such capability. RDBMS products like these are considered hybrid, yet they are clearly more mainstream than ever.

Furthermore, Multi-Dimensional Databases (MDDs) have found some market share. These databases offer highly indexed data for applications with many variables that must be multidimensionally accessed and tabulated, such as behavioral science data. In traditional RDBMSs, this would be nearly impossible to implement, let alone use. Again, to compete with MDDs, RDBMS vendors offer some layered products of their own that provide superindexed data and use special techniques such as bitmapped indexes. Oracle's Express is an example of a Multi-Dimensional Database.

THE RELATIONAL MODEL

You've already learned the major responsibilities of a DBMS. In order to understand what constitutes a RDBMS, you must first cover the relational model. A relational model is one in which the following occurs:

- The fundamental pieces of data are relations.
- The operations upon those tables yield only relations (*relational closure*).

What is a relation? It's a mathematical concept describing how the elements of two sets *relate*, or correspond to each other. Hence, the relational model is founded in mathematics. For your purposes, however, a relation is nothing more or less than a table with some special properties. A relational model organizes data into tables and *only* tables. The customers, the database designer, the DBA, and the users all view the data the same way: as tables. Tables, then, are the lingua franca of the relational model.

A *relational table* has a set of *named attributes*, or columns, and a set of *tuples*, or rows. Sometimes a column is referred to as a *field*. Sometimes a row is referred to as a record. A row-and-column intersection is usually referred to as a *cell*. The columns are placeholders, having domains, or data types, such as character or integer. The rows themselves are the data. Table 1.1 has three columns and four rows.

TABLE 1.1   CAR TABLE

Make	Model	Cost
Toyota	Camry	$25K
Honda	Accord	$23K
Ford	Taurus	$20K
Volkswagen	Passat	$20K

A relational table must meet some special criteria to be part of the relational model:

- Data stored in cells must be atomic. Each cell can only hold one piece of data. This is also known as the *Information Principle*. To do otherwise does not practice good design principles, although many systems have been built that way over the years. When a cell contains more than one piece of information, this is known as *information coding*. A good example is a Vehicle Identification Number (VIN). If this were stored as one column, it would violate the information principle because it would contain many pieces of information, such as make, model, origin of plant, etc. Whether practice overrules theory is a design choice in such cases, although in most cases, this turns out to be bad news for data integrity.

- Data stored under columns must be of the same data type.

- Each row is unique. (No duplicate rows.)

- Columns have no order to them.

- Rows have no order to them.

- Columns have a unique name.

In addition to tables and their properties, the relational model has its own special operations. Rather than get deeper and deeper into relational mathematics, suffice it to say that these operations can include subsets of columns, subsets of rows, joins of tables, and other mathematical set operations such as union. What really matters is that these operations take tables as input and produce tables as output. SQL is the current ANSI standard language for RDBMSs, and it embodies these relational operations. Before SQL became dominant, a competing language was QUEL, or QUEry Language, from Ingres. Another was UDL, or Unified Data Language. ANSI, the American National Standards Institute, is a standards body with very broad scope, one that includes computer software languages such as SQL.

The primary statements that permit data manipulation, or data access, are SELECT, INSERT, UPDATE, and DELETE. Hence, any one of these data manipulation operations is a transaction, as you read earlier in the chapter.

The primary statements that permit data definition, or structural access, are CREATE, ALTER, and DROP. All these statements are replete with a slew of clauses that permit many variations with which to define and access the structure and data of the relational tables that make up your database. Hence, SQL is both a Data Definition Language (DDL) and a Data Manipulation Language (DML). A unified DDL and DML is inherently more productive and useful than two different languages and interfaces. The DBAs and the users access the database through the same overall language.

The last thing the relational model requires are two fundamental *integrity rules*. These are the *entity integrity rule* and the *referential integrity rule*. First, two definitions:

- A *primary key* is a column or set of columns that uniquely identifies rows. Sometimes, more than one column or set of columns can act as the primary key.

- A primary key that is made up of multiple columns is called a *concatenated key*, a *compound key*, or, more often, a *composite key*.

The database designer decides which combination of columns most accurately and efficiently reflects the business situation. This does not mean the other data isn't stored, just that one set of columns is chosen to serve as the primary key.

The remaining possible primary keys are referred to as *candidate keys* or *alternate keys*. A *foreign key* is a column or set of columns in one table that exist as the primary key in another table. A foreign key in one table is said to *reference* the primary key of another table. The entity integrity rule simply states that the primary key cannot be totally or partially empty, or *null*. The referential integrity rule simply states that a foreign key must either be null or match a currently existing value of the primary key that it references.

An RDBMS, then, is a DBMS that is built on the preceding foundations of the relational model and generally satisfies all the requirements mentioned. However, what happened when RDBMSs were first being sold in the late seventies through the early eighties was that SQL was being slapped on top of essentially nonrelational systems and being called relational. This triggered some corrective movements, namely, Codd's Twelve Rules (1985).

CODD'S TWELVE RULES

Codd proposed twelve rules that a DBMS should follow to be classified as *fully relational*:

1. **The information rule**   Information is to be represented as data stored in cells. As discussed earlier, the use of VIN as a single column violates this rule.

2. **The guaranteed access rule**   Each data item must be accessible by a combination of *table name + primary key of the row + column name*. If you can access a column by using arrays or pointers, for example, it violates this rule.

3. **Nulls must be used in a consistent manner**   If a Null is treated as a 0 for missing numeric values and as a blank for missing character values, it violates this rule. Nulls should simply be missing data and have no values. If values are desired for missing data, vendors usually offer the capability to use *defaults* for this purpose.

4. **An active, online data dictionary should be stored as relational tables and accessible through the regular data access language**   If any part of the data dictionary is stored in operating system files, it violates this rule.

5. **The data access language must provide all means of access and be the only means of access, except possibly for low-level access routines**   If you can access the file supporting a table through a utility other than a SQL interface, it might violate this rule. See rule 12.

6. **All views that can be updatable should be updatable**   If, for example, you can join three tables as the basis for a view but not be able to update that view, this rule is violated.

7. **There must be set-level inserts, updates, and deletes**   Currently, this is provided by most RDBMS vendors to some degree.

8. **Physical data independence**   An application cannot depend on physical restructuring. If a file supporting a table is moved from one disk to another or renamed, this should have no impact on the application.

9. **Logical data independence**   An application should not depend on logical restructuring. If a single table must be split into two, then a view has to be provided joining the two back together so that there is no impact on the application.

10. **Integrity independence**   Integrity rules should be stored in the data dictionary. Primary key constraints, foreign key constraints, check constraints, triggers, and so forth should all be stored in the data dictionary.

11. **Distribution independence**   A database should continue to work properly even if distributed. This is an extension of rule 8, except rather than only being distributed on a single system (locally), a database can also be distributed across a network of systems (remotely).

12. **The nonsubversion rule**   If low-level access is enabled, it must not bypass security or integrity rules, which would otherwise be obeyed by the regular data access language. A backup or load utility, for example, should not be able to bypass authentication, constraints, and locks. However, vendors often provide these capabilities for the sake of speed. It is then the DBA's responsibility to ensure that security and integrity, if momentarily compromised, are reinstated. An example is disabling and re-enabling constraints for a VLDB load.

If a DBMS can meet all the fundamental principles discussed in this chapter (two-part definition, six properties, relational operations, and two integrity rules) and these twelve rules, it can be designated an RDBMS. Codd summed up all this with his Rule Zero: "For a system to qualify as an RDBMS, that system must use its relational facilities exclusively to manage the database."

## CHAPTER 2

LOGICAL DATABASE DESIGN AND NORMALIZATION

In this chapter

ENTITY-RELATIONSHIP MODELING

The best thing a Database Administrator (DBA) can do for her database is to start out with a proper, logical design. Unfortunately, database design is often hurried through, done wrong, and even back-engineered after the database has been built. A well-informed and wise DBA knows that a good design improves performance rather than detracts from it, contrary to popular wisdom. Indeed, jumping directly into the physical design or further simply invites trouble, not just in terms of performance, but in data integrity. What good is a database that runs fast and houses bad data? Further, early in the design phase of a database system, creating a proper logical design enables it to tolerate physical design changes later in the production and maintenance phases. If, however, you shortcut the logical design, not only will you likely have to redesign your logical model, but you will also need to restructure your underlying physical model. The indirect cost (staff hours, downtime, and so on) can be staggering. You need to cover the principles behind logical database design and normalization before you run off and build your database.

As the relational model came to dominate over other data models during the mid-seventies, relational modeling techniques sprung up that permitted formal design capabilities. The most popular of these is the Entity-Relationship Diagram (ERD), developed by P. P. Chen in 1976. This is known as a *semantic* data model because it attempts to capture the semantics, or proper meaning, of business elements (the essence of the business). Because the relational model itself is mostly a *syntactic* model, one dealing mostly with structure, the ERD typically supplements it. In fact, ERD modeling naturally precedes relational modeling. When an ERD is complete, it is mapped to the relational model more or less directly, and later the relational model is mapped to its physical model.

An *entity* is a business element, such as an employee or a project. A *relationship* is an association between entities, such as employees working on several projects. *Attributes* are the characteristics that make up an entity, such as an employee's salary or a project's budget. Attributes are said to take on values from *domains*, or value sets. The values they take are the data used later in the relational model. These are all abstractions of a business or part of a business. ERDs can be drawn many ways. It doesn't really matter as long as you choose one and remain consistent in your meaning throughout.

For your purposes, high-level diagrams (those without attributes) are drawn using boxes for entities, with the entity name listed in the center of the box. Low-level diagrams have the entity name listed at the top in the box, with the attribute names following. Arrows are drawn between the boxes to represent the relationship types. There are three basic kinds of relationships: one-to-one, one-to-many, and many-to-many. A one-to-one relationship uses a single-headed arrow on one or both sides, depending on the kind of one-to-one relationship. A one-to-many uses a double-headed arrow. A many-to-many uses a double-headed arrow on both sides. A *pure* one-to-one relationship exists when every value of one entity is related to one and only one value of another entity, and vice versa. This type of relationship is rare. Figure 2.1 shows a one-to-one relationship. A husband is married to only one wife, and a wife is married to only one husband (without counting polygamists).

Figure 2.1
A one-to-one (1:1)
relationship.

PART

I

CH

2

A more common kind of one-to-one relationship is the *subtype* relationship. This is one of the foundations of OO analysis and design. In OO systems, this is seen as a class and a subclass (or more simply put, a class hierarchy). Figure 2.2 shows how a one-to-one subtype relationship is modeled. This diagram shows the classic example of a square being a subtype of a rectangle. The direction of the arrow indicates the direction of the *inheritance*, another OO concept related to the class hierarchy. In other words, attributes in the more general entity (the rectangle) donate attributes (such as length and width) to the more specific entity (the square). Hence, the direction of inheritance flows from general to specific.

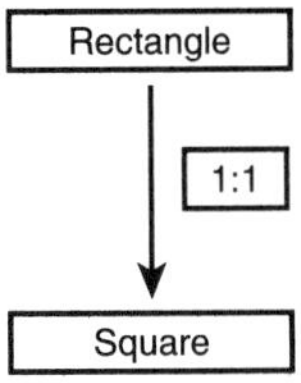

Figure 2.2
A one-to-one (1:1)
subtype relationship.

Subtype relationships are more common than pure ones, and yet both find infrequent use. As is often the case, when a designer runs across one-to-one relationships, he must ask the following questions:

- Can these two entities be combined?

- Are they one and the same for my purposes?

- Must they remain separate and distinct for some compelling business reasons?

More often than not, one-to-one entities can be combined.

The dominant relationship to be used in the relational model is the one-to-many relationship. Figure 2.3 shows a one-to-many relationship. A state has many cities, but those same cities belong to only one state. (It is true, however, that you can find a city's name reused by different states. This only means that as a designer, your choice of primary key must not be a city name. For example, it might be state name + city name. The preceding chapter contains a definition of the primary key concept and how to choose one.)

Figure 2.3
A one-to-many (1:M)
relationship.

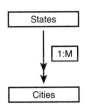

Finally, Figure 2.4 shows many employees, as discussed earlier, working on many projects—a many-to-many relationship. Notice that the underlined attributes are *identifier* attributes, representing your best current guess about what will later be the primary key in the relational model.

Figure 2.4
A many-to-many
(M:N) relationship.

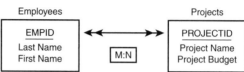

Suggestion: At this point, one of the best things you can do for yourself as a designer is to rid yourself of all your many-to-many relationships. Not that you'd actually be getting rid of them, but you can substitute two or more one-to-many relationships in their place. You want to do this because the relational model can't really handle a direct implementation of many-to-many relationships. Think about it. If you have many employees working on many projects, how do you store the foreign keys? (You can't without storing multiple values in one column, thus violating the relational requirement that data be atomic, meaning that no cell can hold more than one piece of information. This example of the Information Principle (as discussed in Chapter 1) also leads you directly to the fact that it is a special case of the First Normal Form, which is discussed shortly.) Hence, to ensure data atomicity, each many-to-many relationship is replaced by two or more one-to-many relationships.

Therefore, what you want to do is to split the many-to-many relationship so that many employees working on many projects become one employee with many assignments, and one project belongs to many assignments, with assignments being the new entity. Figure 2.5 shows this new relationship. Notice that identifier attributes have been combined.

Figure 2.5
Revised many-to-many
(M:N) relationship
using two one-to-
many (1:M and 1:N)
relationships.

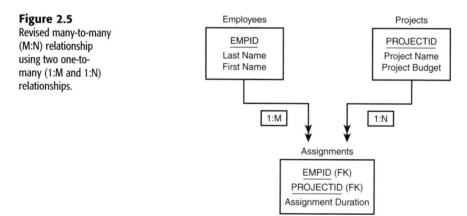

The new entity called assignment is often called an *intersection table* in the relational model because it represents the intersection of every real pairing of the two tables it relates. It is also sometimes called a *junction table* or *join table*. The intersection table is an entity that is not necessarily always a real-life abstraction of some business element, but it is the fundamental way to solve and implement the many-to-many relationships in the relational model.

MAPPING ERDS TO THE RELATIONAL MODEL

An ERD folds nicely into the relational model because it was created for that purpose. Essentially, entities become tables, and attributes become columns. Identifier attributes become primary keys. Relationships don't really materialize except through intersection tables. Foreign keys are created by always placing the primary keys from a table on a *one* side into the table on a *many* side. For example, a relationship of one state to many cities calls for you to place the state primary key in the city table to create a foreign key there, thus forging the relationship between the two.

Many automatic Computer Assisted Software Engineering (CASE) tools exist in the current market to help you accomplish this mapping. Examples include LogicWorks' ERwin and Oracle's own Designer/2000. These tools enable you to not only draw the ERDs, but also specify primary and foreign keys, indexes, constraints, and even generate standard Data Definition Language (DDL) SQL code to help you create your tables and indexes. For Oracle, you can run those scripts directly, but frequently you need to modify them, for example, to change data types or add storage parameters. These tools can also help you *reverse engineer* the logical model from an existing database that has no documentation! This is especially useful when attempting to integrate databases or when assuming DBA responsibilities of an already built database. CASE tools not only help you to design and build database systems, but they also can help you to document as well.

UNDERSTANDING NORMALIZATION

Normalization is a refinement, or extension, of the relational model. Normalization is also a process that acts upon the *first draft* relational model and improves upon it in certain concrete ways that you'll soon learn. The foundation of normalization is mathematical, like the relational model. It is based on a concept known as *functional dependency* (FD).

Although it isn't necessary to get bogged down in the mathematics of functional dependency, it is useful and instructive to at least define it for your context, the relational model. A column or set of columns, Y, is said to be functionally dependent on another column or set of columns, X, if a given set of values for X determine a unique set of values for Y. To say that Y is functionally dependent on X is the same as saying X *determines* Y, (usually written as X -> Y). Of course, the most obvious example is the primary key of a relational table uniquely determining the values of a row in that table. However, other dependencies might exist that are not the result of the primary key. The main purpose of normalization is to rid relational tables of all functional dependencies that are not the result of the primary key.

Here are the three major reasons for normalization that are usually always cited in any database analysis and design text:

- **To maintain data integrity**   This reason, perhaps above all else, is enough justification for troubling at all with normalization. Data stays correct and consistent because it's stored only once. In other words, multiple copies of the data do not have to be maintained. Otherwise, the various copies of the same data items might fall out of synchronization and might ultimately require heavy application programming control because the automatic integrity mechanisms of an RDBMS cannot be leveraged. Many legacy systems suffer this fate.

- **To build a model that is as application-independent as possible**   In other words, normalization simply furthers the notion that the relational model should be data-driven, not process-driven. For the most part, this means the database design can remain stable and intact, given changing process needs. Application programming requirements should be irrelevant in logical database design (although they mean everything to physical database design, as you'll see later.)

- **To reduce storage needs (and frequently lay the foundation for improved search performance, too)**   Except for foreign keys, full normalization rids your relational design of all redundancies. Unnecessary copies of data likewise require unnecessary secondary storage needs. In addition, the more data that exists and possibly has to be searched, the more total system time is required, and hence, the worse the performance is.

USING A NORMALIZATION EXAMPLE

In the preceding chapter, you passed quickly over how the atomic data requirement (the Information Principle) is a subset of the First Normal Form (1NF). This section re-emphasizes it and more precisely defines 1NF.

FIRST NORMAL FORM

The First Normal Form (1NF) contains no repeating groups. This is the same as saying that the data stored in a cell must be of a single, simple value and cannot hold more than one piece of information. To be very clear, the Information Principle does not permit repeating groups within a column whereas 1NF *additionally requires* that there be no repeating groups within a row, whether as repeated columns or repeated pieces of information contained within a column.

Table 2.1 lists states with cities whose populations increased at least five percent over the previous year. Because all the city information is stored in a repeating group, this table is non-normal, or not 1NF. First of all, how do you know for sure that the populations and percentages in the columns to the right of the cities belong to those cities? You could assume an order to them, of course, but this violates the fundamental relational rule that columns have no order. Worse, arrays would have to be used, and this requires end-users to know about and use a physical data structure such as an array. This surely can't make for a good user interface.

TABLE 2.1   STATES WITH CITIES HAVING >= 5% POPULATION INCREASES

STATE	ABBREV	SPOP	CITY	LPOP	CPOP	PCTINC
North Carolina	NC	5M	Burlington,	40K	44K	10%
			Raleigh	200K	222K	11%
Vermont	VT	4M	Burlington	60K	67.2K	12%
New York	NY	17M	Albany,	500K	540K	8%
			New York City,	14M	14.7M	5%
			White Plains	100K	106K	6%

To make it 1NF, move repeating groups from across columns to down rows. Table 2.2 shows the same table as in 1NF, with STATE as the primary key. However, this table still suffers from problems. To update or delete state information, you must access many rows and programmatically guarantee their consistency (the DBMS doesn't do it). To insert city information, you must add state information along with it. If you delete the last city of a state, the state information goes with it, and so on. What's the problem? You'll see in a moment.

TABLE 2.2   STATES AND CITIES IN FIRST NORMAL FORM (1NF)

STATE	ABBREV	SPOP	CITY	LPOP	CPOP	PCTINC
North Carolina	NC	5M	Burlington	40K	44K	10%
North Carolina	NC	5M	Raleigh	200K	222K	11%
Vermont	VT	4M	Burlington	60K	67.2K	12%
New York	NY	17M	Albany	500K	540K	8%
New York	NY	17M	New York City	14M	14.7M	5%
New York	NY	17M	White Plains	100K	106K	6%

To tackle the higher normalization levels, you need a *nonkey* column. The strict definition of a nonkey column is simply one that is not part of the primary key. The *broader* definition of a nonkey column is one that is not part of any candidate key. For your purposes, you'll take the strict definition. Essentially, the set of columns of a table can be thought of as having a primary key and the remainder. Any column that is part of the remainder is a nonkey column.

SECOND NORMAL FORM

The Second Normal Form (2NF) has no partial dependencies. Every nonkey column depends on the full primary key, including all its columns if it is composite. Table 2.2 does not currently comply with this criterion. City information does not depend on state information. Namely, all the city columns (CITY, LPOP, CPOP, and PCTINC) do not depend on the state name (STATE). Hence, you break them into two tables (Tables 2.3 and 2.4). It only makes sense that states and cities are separate entities, although related, and therefore should be separate tables.

TABLE 2.3   STATES IN SECOND NORMAL FORM (2NF)

STATE	ABBREV	SPOP
North Carolina	NC	5M
Vermont	VT	4M
New York	NY	17M

TABLE 2.4   CITIES IN SECOND NORMAL FORM (2NF)

CITY	ABBREV	LPOP	CPOP	PCTINC
Burlington	NC	40K	44K	10%
Raleigh	NC	200K	222K	11%
Burlington	VT	60K	67.2K	12%
New York City	NY	14M	14.7M	5%
Albany	NY	500K	540K	8%
White Plains	NY	100K	106K	6%

THIRD NORMAL FORM

The Third Normal Form (3NF) has no transitive dependencies. No nonkey column depends on another nonkey column. A table is in 3NF if all its nonkey columns are dependent on the key, the whole key, and nothing but the key. If, after eliminating repeating groups, every nonkey column is dependent on the key and the whole key, this is 2NF. Nothing but the key is 3NF. Your city table (Table 2.4) doesn't pass this test because the column PCTINC (percent increase) depends on CPOP (current population) and LPOP (last year's population). In fact, it is a function of the two. This type of column is called a *derived* column because it is derived from other, existing columns. However, all these are nonkey. The immediate solution is to drop PCTINC and calculate it on-the-fly, preferably using a view if it is highly accessed. Also, in your state table (Table 2.3), SPOP (state population) depends on ABBREV (abbreviation) because this is a candidate key, although not the primary one. Tables 2.5, 2.6, and 2.7 show your solution, which now gives you 3 tables in 3NF.

TABLE 2.5   STATES IN THIRD NORMAL FORM (3NF)

ABBREV	SPOP
NC	5 M
VT	4 M
NY	17 M

TABLE 2.6   STATE NAMES IN THIRD NORMAL FORM (3NF)

STATE	ABBREV
North Carolina	NC
Vermont	VT
New York	NY

TABLE 2.7   CITIES IN THIRD NORMAL FORM (3NF)

CITY	ABBREV	LPOP	CPOP
Burlington	NC	40K	44K
Raleigh	NC	200K	222K
Burlington	VT	60K	67.2K
New York City	NY	14M	14.7M
Albany	NY	500K	540K
White Plains	NY	100K	106K

CONTINUING THE NORMAL FORM

The Boyce Codd Normal Form (BCNF) contains no inverse partial dependencies. This is also sometimes referred to, semiseriously, as *3 1/2 NF*. Neither the primary key nor any part of it depends on a nonkey attribute. Because you took the strict definition of nonkey, 3NF took care of your candidate key problem, and your tables are already in BCNF.

Fourth Normal Form and higher: normalization theory in academia has gone many levels beyond BCNF. Database analysis and design texts typically go as high as 5NF. 4NF deals with multivalued dependencies (MVDs), whereas 5NF deals with join dependencies (JDs). Although the theory behind these forms is a little beyond the scope of this book, you should know that a table is in 4NF if every MVD is a FD, and a table is in 5NF if every JD is a consequence of its relation keys.

Normal forms as high as 7 and 8 have been introduced in theses and dissertations. In addition, alternative normal forms such as Domain Key Normal Form (DKNF) have been developed that parallel or otherwise subsume current normalization theory.

Recommendation: strive for at least BCNF, and then compensate with physical database design as necessary, which leads you to your next topic. If possible, study 4NF and 5NF, and try to reach them in your normalization efforts. Your goal as a DBA is to normalize as high as you can and yet balance that with as few entities as possible. This is a challenge because, generally, the higher the normal form, the more entities produced.

## CHAPTER 3

PHYSICAL DATABASE DESIGN, HARDWARE, AND RELATED ISSUES

In this chapter

UNDERSTANDING APPLICATION TYPES

Before you learn about physical database design and later, performance tuning, it is important to cover the major application types. First, consider the terms *transaction* and *query*. In database theory, broadly speaking, a transaction is a single, atomic SELECT, INSERT, UPDATE, or DELETE. However, with regards to application types, a transaction is generally more loosely defined as a business transaction, possibly containing multiple INSERT, UPDATE, or DELETE occurrences. In addition, DML truly refers to SELECT, INSERT, UPDATE, and DELETE. However, DML, like transaction in this context, is often used to mean only INSERT, UPDATE, and DELETE operations. In summary, DML and transaction usually mean write-only or modify-only. To distinguish the SELECT operation as read-only, the term *query* is used.

Follow these latter industry conventions for the sake of common understanding, although they are quite confusing and in fact, at conflict with their real definitions. That said, there are three main application types in the world of database systems applications:

- OLTP (Online Transaction Processing)—An OLTP system is an application that contains heavy DML, transaction-oriented activity including primarily updates but also some inserts and deletes. Classic examples are reservation systems such as those used by airlines and hotels. OLTP systems can have high concurrency. (In this case, high concurrency typically means many users simultaneously use a database system.)

- DSS (Decision Support System)—A DSS is typically a large, read-only database with historical content and is generally used for simple canned or ad hoc queries. Often a DSS grows into a VLDB, a DM, or a DW in the manner discussed in Chapter 1, "Databases, DBMS Principles, and the Relational Model." A good example of a DSS is a database behind an organization's intranet.

- Batch—A batch system is a noninteractive, automatic application that works against a database. It usually contains heavy DML and has *low concurrency*. (In this case, low concurrency typically means few users simultaneously using a database system.) The ratio of querying to transactions determines how to physically design it. Classic examples are production databases and operational databases relative to DWs.

Some less common application types include the following:

- OLAP (Online Analytical Processing)—An OLAP system offers analytical services, as the name implies. This means mathematics, statistics, aggregations, and high computation. An OLAP system doesn't always fit the OLTP or DSS molds. Occasionally, it is a cross between the two. In addition, some people simply view OLAP as an extension or an additional functional layer on top of an OLTP system or DSS. ROLAP stands for Relational OLAP. This term doesn't really add much in the way of classification, though. An OLAP tool is often tightly coupled with an MDD (discussed in Chapter 1), and sometimes it is simply layered on top of a modified RDBMS. Often, Geographic Information Systems (GIS), or spatial databases, are integrated with the OLAP databases, providing graphical mapping capabilities. A demographic database for social statistics is a good example.

- VCDB (Variable Cardinality Database)—This type of database is frequently a back-end for a processing system that causes the tables in that database to grow and shrink considerably during the processing phase that otherwise might be constant or within, for example, a 10% variability. *Cardinality* refers to the number of rows in a table at a given time. Some tables might be static lookup tables, but most are definitely highly variable in their number of records. Good examples are any databases that record short-lived activities, such as a security authorization database.

USING QUANTITATIVE ESTIMATES

Quantitative estimating of any sort is an attempt to quantify, or measure, some process or product. With databases, the two main types of quantitative estimates are *transaction analysis* (sometimes referred to as *volume analysis)* and *sizing analysis*.

TRANSACTION ANALYSIS

Transaction analysis is simply putting numbers on the database system. Different measures mean different things and apply to certain kinds of database systems. The most typical measures, or *metrics*, include the minimums, averages, or maximums of the following:

- Number of concurrent users
- Response time
- Elapsed time
- Number of transactions
- Number of concurrent programs
- Number of bytes read or written

There are many more metrics, such as the number of rows affected by an operation, but the ones in the preceding list offer some insight.

Usually, these measures have more meaning if they are expressed in the context of a given time period or activity. For example, it is usually more useful to know the maximum number of transactions per second than the cumulative number of transactions. The latter tells you little about the typical stress, or load, on the database. These numbers also mean more in the context of what kind of application your database serves.

If your application type is an OLTP system, the number of concurrent users, transactions per second, and response time are more important because concurrency is the primary issue with OLTP.

If you have a batch system, elapsed time and number of concurrent programs are perhaps most important. A DSS might require you to know the bytes read per some unit of time, among other things.

You need to ask these questions as a DBA and gather your best possible answers, for this affects your physical design and your performance tuning. In addition, these figures are largely the same measures that are used for benchmarking efforts. What you're trying to do here, though, is gather estimated, prototyped, or piloted numbers before the system is actually built in order to help build it.

SIZING ANALYSIS

Sizing is perhaps a more widely known activity, if not widely practiced often enough by all DBAs. In transaction or volume analysis, you ask "How often?" and "How much?" with regards to processes and data flow; with sizing you ask "How much?" with regards to data storage.

The fundamental thing is simply that a table with n rows of b max bytes per row needs at least $n \times b$ bytes of storage. Of course, this leaves out overhead, and this calculation varies considerably with the vendor of choice. Oracle, for example, offers a fairly complicated set of steps, as do other vendors, to help size a table, an index, or other structures. The best recommendation is to place this formula into a spreadsheet once, and you never have to do it again. Just pull it out and dust it off every time you need to do sizing for another database project. Just plug in the relevant input numbers, such as block size, block parameters, number of rows, column sizes, and so on. This way, you're able to subtotal by table, by sets of tables, by indexes, by sets of indexes, and for the whole database.

Then, a seasoned DBA adds a *fudge factor* on top of that estimate to account for any mistaken underestimates, accidental oversights, and unanticipated future changes. Something such as the final estimate size×120 percent is not unreasonable.

Remember, too, that the figure you size for is usually based on tables and indexes alone. As with all RDBMS vendors, there are many more architectural considerations (discussed in Chapter 5, "The Oracle Database Architecture," and Chapter 6, "The Oracle Instance Architecture") that add to the overall system size. Whatever final figure of bytes you come up with, remember that this is the *usable* space you need, not the amount of raw disk space. Low-level hardware and a high-level operating system can subtract from the initial unformatted (raw) size of the disk, leaving less usable space than you think.

For example, formatting can consume 15 percent of a 4GB disk. This only leaves 85 percent, or 3.4GB. If your final sizing estimate is 20GB and you don't take this into account, you purchase 5×4GB disks and yet have only 5×3.4GB, or 17GB, of usable space. You need another disk.

DENORMALIZING

Denormalization refers to dropping the level of your tables' normal forms back down a few notches for physical design, performance tuning, or other reasons.

Tip #1

> Don't do this unless you have very good reasons. A shortage of disks with no budget for new ones might be a good reason. Expecting to have poor performance without evidence, as opposed to actually having poor performance, is not a good reason. In fact, even poor performance itself does not immediately indicate the need to back off on your logical design. Your first step is performance tuning. Denormalization is always a last resort.

That said, what to do? Suppose you have 30-odd tables that make up the logical design in your database, all which are 3NF or higher (not unrealistic). However, three of these tables are virtually always joined together when they are used. Join operations themselves, with or without indexes, are resource-intensive and can consume a small machine in no time. In the interest of performance, with no other performance-tuning tricks at hand, you might want to prejoin these three tables into one table for permanent use, thereby avoiding the join for future accesses. By placing two or more normalized tables back into one, you are virtually guaranteed of reducing the normalization level or even worse, becoming fully denormalized. Of course, if this must be done, more and more procedural and application-level data integrity controls must be written to take the place of the DBMS's automatic features.

If, for example, you opt to keep both the original tables and the newly joined one, you are faced with the unenviable task of keeping them synchronized. However, if updates are very frequent, (every hour or less) and currency of the joined data is required, other methods have to be used.

Another method is to create a denormalized *view* on top of the normalized *base* tables. However, the performance of this option is the same as or worse than simply having the original three tables. Its only advantage is user interface simplicity. So, although denormalization might help in some static data cases, it usually cannot solve many dynamic data problems. A method such as Oracle's *clustering* might suffice in this type of situation if denormalization doesn't work. However, this is discussed later in detail in Chapters 5, "The Oracle Database Architecture," 16, "Performance Tuning Fundamentals," and 19, " Tuning I/O."

A final, fairly common example of denormalization is when DBAs must deal with time series. The reason why time series often must be denormalized is because time must almost always be part of the primary key of a table. This is true because most data stored is time-dependent.

A good example is a database storing satellite feed data. This data is timestamped, which is part of the primary key on most of the tables in the database. For any given table that has the timestamp as the component, all the other columns that make up the primary key, such as satellite ID, are repeated for every different timestamp. In other words, if the database downloads 100 rows of data from a single satellite every hour, then in 8 hours, you have 800 rows stored with all the other satellite information unnecessarily repeated 800 times. The wasted storage can be tremendous, especially considering you might have multiple satellites or more frequent sample rates.

PART

I

CH

3

The typical solution is to denormalize by inverting the data from row-wise to column-wise. You now have 100 timestamp columns, and you reduced the number of rows from 800 to 8, or by a factor of the sample interval of 100. Storage reduction, especially row reduction, almost always helps search performance because there are fewer rows to scan through in a table or an index. However, this type of denormalization, though often necessary, results in a table that is not normal by virtue of the timestamps being stored as repeating group columns. Hence, you are then unable to use a foreign key constraint on this former primary key component. Instead, you must resort to check constraints, procedures, triggers, and possibly supplemental application integrity handling. If anything, the lesson you should learn from this particular example is that if you must denormalize for performance, you have to pay the price in integrity management.

UNDERSTANDING THE STORAGE HIERARCHY

One of the most important things a DBA can learn about is the storage hierarchy and its associated tradeoffs. This, more than anything, helps explain a lot about physical design and performance tuning. One of the key ideas behind the storage hierarchy is *the electromechanical disadvantage*—anything that has a motor or moving parts is inherently slower than something that is solely electronic.

Figure 3.1 shows a modern interpretation of the storage hierarchy. Clearly, memory is faster than disk. As you go up the pyramid, speed increases (access time), cost increases (per unit), but storage decreases.

Figure 3.1
The storage hierarchy.

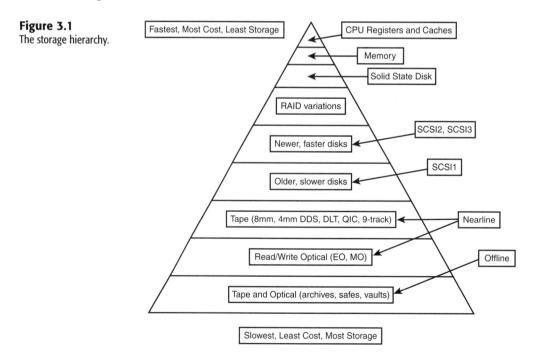

The more you want to store, the more you have to pay, especially if you want it fast. However, you can make some tradeoffs. With a historical system, you can put the older data nearline on optical disks or at least slower disks, and even older data on tape either nearline or offline. If your particular storage pyramid has everything robotically nearline, down through tape, and you have software to access it on demand, that's a Hierarchical Storage Management (HSM) system. There are vendors who specialize in this sort of hardware and software. Historical systems can afford to gravitate toward the bottom because speed is not of the essence, relative to the data currency. However, real-time systems, such as aircraft navigation and so forth, place most of their storage toward the faster elements at the top. A reasonable medium approach for many businesses is to place important, current data on RAID or fast disk and everything else on slower disk.

UNDERSTANDING RAID

RAID, or Redundant Array of Inexpensive Disks, is perhaps a misnomer. Since its inception, the disks that make up RAID have never really cost any less than regular SCSI (Small Computer Systems Interface) disks. In addition, RAID requires special hardware, software, or both to work, at added cost. So the *I* in RAID is not quite correct.

RAID is a set of disks that can work in parallel to reduce I/O time by a factor of how many disks make up the set, an important thing for databases. RAID works in parallel through a technique known as *striping*, as opposed to ordinary disk storage, which works in serial. This is simply writing a single file using stripes, or chunks of the file, across multiple disks in parallel. The stripes are some multiple size of a physical data block, the smallest unit of disk I/O. Typically, a data block is made up of 512 bytes. This is true for most UNIX systems, VMS, and DOS/NT.

RAID also offers real-time disk failure recovery, another important thing for databases. RAID can offer this level of availability through *parity* information, which is also written out to a disk or disks. Parity, checksums, and error correction are handled through certain mathematical formulas and algorithms that can reconstruct the missing data on a lost disk. RAID can offer either small or large disks in a set, which can help different database application types. For example, DSS often performs better with larger disks, whereas OLTP does better with smaller ones. RAID comes in many flavors, known as *levels*.

The RAID levels most often used in industry today are 0, 1, 3, and 5. All other levels are not used or are some variation of these four. RAID levels are offered by vendors that number 7 and higher, but these are rarely seen in practice. RAID 0 is basic striping with no parity. That is, you get the performance advantage but no parity. This is good when pure speed is the goal and availability isn't as important.

RAID 1 is known as *mirroring*, or sometimes *duplexing*, again with no parity. In mirroring, you essentially have an even set of disks, half of which contain the *real* or primary data and half of which contain the copies of that data on a diskwise basis. Actually, both disks are written to at the same time, and sometimes this can mean a performance loss when writing.

Reading, on the other hand, can actually be sped up if software is designed to read the multiple disks and merge the streams for use.

RAID 3 is striping, except with a single, dedicated parity disk. You can afford to lose one data disk and still recover it using the parity disk. However, the parity disk is a single point of failure. If it's lost it could be fatal, depending on the software or hardware and how it is written to handle this event.

RAID 5 is also striping with parity, except rather than using a single, dedicated disk, it stripes the parity along with the data across all disks. Parity information is as well protected as data, and there is no single point of failure. RAID 5, like RAID 3, can tolerate and recover from the loss of a single disk. However, neither 3 nor 5 can lose two disks and recover. Too much parity information is lost.

RAID levels 2, 4, and 6 are rarely sold or implemented in industry. The mathematics behind the parity information for these levels is too computationally intense to be practical.

A final word about RAID. With regards to striping, RAID does what can be done manually with RDBMS and OS utilities and techniques. However, it usually does a better, *finer-grained* form of striping and offers more features such as partitioning volumes (stripe sets), adjustable stripe sizes, and so forth. In addition, although the striping part of RAID can be done in a gross manner without much difficulty, you still have to manage those stripes. RAID usually excels at this and offers a single file interface in a virtual file system (VFS), leveraging OS file-level commands and utilities, as well as offering other features such as files larger than physical disk size.

Lastly, although you might be able to manage some form of striping, you have no safety net other than your standard backup and restore mechanisms. Whereas RAID gives you the tolerance to lose one disk and recover, it is too complex for you to attempt to write this software that already exists.

Tip #2

Use gross, manual RDBMS or OS striping when availability is not a major concern. Otherwise, use RAID when you need the availability it offers, want even better performance through finer-grained stripes, or need its other features such as for large files.

UNDERSTANDING BOTTLENECKS IN A DBMS

Often in the past, DBMSs have been accused of being *I/O-bound*, or disk-bound. This is the same as saying that a DBMS is bottlenecked in a system by its reading to and writing from disk. Studying the storage hierarchy you just covered, this is hardly a revelation. A disk has a much slower access speed than memory or CPU. This actually has been the case for many database applications over the years. It is especially true for DSSs, VLDBs, and DWs because huge amounts of data (GB) must be moved with single queries. However, this is not always the case. OLTP and OLAP (Online Analytical Processing) systems can often be memory-bound, or CPU-bound.

If a database hardware server has a low memory-to-disk ratio, meaning that the application is memory-poor, that database suffers considerably due to the lack of room in the memory for data and code caching. If a database application is of the OLAP type, such as a scientific database, number-crunching speed is of utmost importance. Hence, if that type of application runs on a server with a relatively weak CPU, performance is surely poor in terms of user expectations (such as response time). The lesson here is that bottlenecks in any system, database systems included, are application-specific.

Finally, in client/server database systems, the network is the slowest component of the total system, even slower than disk. For a client/server system to function efficiently, proper application segmentation must occur, and the network must not be overloaded. Further, the network must be designed, like the other resources, to minimize contention. Further still, the network hardware and software should be modernized to take advantage of the current networking capabilities. You'll revisit all these bottlenecks in Chapter 16, "Performance Tuning Fundamentals."

PART

I

CH

3

MAKING YOUR PLATFORM SELECTION

When choosing what type of hardware database server and operating system is right for your application, there are many things to consider, including the following:

- Application type—As discussed, OLTP, DSS, batch, or something else.
- Quantitative estimates—As discussed, your figures regarding transactions, volumes, and sizing.
- Current environment—Basically, what are your predominant platforms now?
- Trends—Where is the industry headed with your current environment and what are you now considering?
- Processing needs—Is your need real-time, less time-critical, or periodic? Use your transaction and volume figures to specify concurrency and load.
- Storage needs—Use your sizing figures to specify raw disk needs. Use transaction and volume figures to specify whether you need RAID.
- Staff capabilities—Is what you're considering too far from your staff's base expertise?
- Time constraints—Can you migrate or develop given your time window?
- Porting and partnerships—Does the RDBMS vendor have cozy relationships with the OS and hardware vendors?
- Integration—Similar to the preceding, but also how well do all the pieces work together, regardless of their business relationships?

The current major RDBMS vendors are Oracle, Sybase, and Informix. CA has yet to do much with Ingres, and Microsoft only offers SQL Server on NT. Smaller, desktop databases aren't considered here. Now, considering only Oracle, UNIX and Windows NT are its two major platforms. For UNIX, the platform is specifically Sun Solaris. Of course, Oracle also ports to the other flavors of UNIX. And Oracle also has some large installed bases on MVS and VMS. However, Solaris and Windows NT are its current top two porting priorities as of this writing.

As for hardware, Sun is the only *real* choice for Solaris, not counting Intel machines. Sun's machines have undergone several generations of change, yet they have all descended from their RISC-based SPARC chip. Windows NT is predominantly found on Compaq but also on DEC and HP machines. The significant thing about Windows NT on DEC is that DEC offers both Alpha and Intel machines. The recent acquisition of DEC by Compaq simplifies this supplier dilemma. Both Solaris and Windows NT can run on multiprocessing machines. However, Windows NT can only handle a limited number of processors (14), and its capability to scale flattens out at about 4 processors for Oracle. Solaris can scale very well past 20 processors, even for Oracle. Disk storage options are roughly equivalent, although some larger options are more readily available with Sun than with Compaq or HP. DEC, of course, can offer large storage like Sun.

Rather than getting further bogged down with hardware comparisons, here's a recommendation: As a set of general guidelines, consider all the options listed earlier when trying to pick a platform. If your predominant environment is DEC/VMS and you're likely to stay there for a few more years, your next platform might as well be DEC/VMS, especially if you're only planning to buy one additional machine. If you're buying for a whole department and the risk is not critical, however, it might be time to consider Windows NT or UNIX.

If you need only one machine for a relatively small database of fewer than 10GB, consider NT. On the other hand, if you only need one machine but the storage is large or high performance is required, consider UNIX. Finally, if you don't really have a predominant environment or you're just starting up new (or can treat your purchase in that respect), by all means consider both Windows NT and UNIX and let all the factors come into play except the environment factor.

A final consideration nowadays is Linux, a UNIX derivative currently enjoying some support as a direct competitor to Windows NT as both an operating system (OS) and a network operating system (NOS). Because it has yet to build up the hardware, application, and technical support around it, it remains slightly beyond the trustworthiness level required of most industrial shops. However, its popularity has possibly yet to peak, and should not be counted out.

OPERATING SYSTEM INTEGRATION AND GENERAL MEMORY/CPU RECOMMENDATIONS

Aside from secondary storage, disks, and RAID, which were emphasized when discussing the storage hierarchy, you need to consider other hardware issues and operating system (OS) components, such as memory and CPU.

Memory is often referred to as core memory, physical memory, main memory, or random access memory (RAM). These are all terms for the same thing, so here it is just *memory*.

Essentially, memory is very fast electronic storage. It stores instructions and data. For a DBMS, the most important thing is that the OS can yield some of its memory to it. Then, the DBMS can do with it what it will, which it does. This is why a DBMS is sometimes referred to as a micro-OS, an OS within an OS, or an OS on top of an OS. In essence, a DBMS takes care of itself with regards to the care and feeding of its resource needs, albeit in deference to and cooperation with the OS. This is often done through a capability known as *shared memory*, especially in UNIX. (See Appendix A, "Oracle on Solaris," for more details.)

Locking, a key component to DBMSs, is also handled through memory structures. Shared resources are secured one at a time from competing processes. A DBMS handles its own locking, does it partially with the OS, or yields locking duties to the OS.

When an OS yields some of its memory to the processes that constitute a DBMS, the DBMS takes it from there, storing in that memory space its own instructions (code caching) and data (data buffering). Without getting too much into Oracle's architecture, which is discussed in Chapters 5 and 6, look at what has been discussed. Oracle's memory access is based on the allocation of its System Global Area (SGA). The SGA contains a structure known as the database buffer cache(datacaching) and the shared pool. The shared pool contains the library cache (code caching), as well as the data dictionary cache. Undo (rollback) blocks are buffered within the data block buffers, and redo is buffered in its own redo log buffers (the log buffer) section. These components are all configurable through Oracle's parameter file, init.ora. More on this later.

RDBMSs have come a long way with regards to CPU utilization. As mentioned earlier, most database systems of the past have tended to be I/O-bound. However, with VLDBs and OLAP/MDD systems, more and more database systems are memory-bound or CPU-bound. With VLDBs, memory is a bottleneck because the amount of memory is usually too small to be of use with huge amounts of data. With heavy analytical or scientific systems or even DW systems, CPUs can be the bottleneck due to the enormous, concurrent computational demands.

With the advent and evolution of multiprocessor machines within the past 10 years, many things have changed. Very large memory is now possible ($\geq$10s of GBs). Also, CPU architectures and speeds have advanced considerably. At the time of this writing, word sizes are 32-bit and 64-bit now, with clock speeds at or near 1/2GHz, and rapdily approaching 1 GHz. These CPUs have densely pipelined architectures, permitting multiple instructions per clock tick (CPU step). The important thing is that the RDBMS software has followed suit.

Oracle and the other major RDBMS vendors have likewise rewritten their code over time to take advantage of these hardware advances. Aside from shared memory and very large memory, multiprocessing is the major advancement and refinement of recent years. Two major classes of multiprocessors exist now:

- Symmetric MultiProcessors (SMPs)
- Massively Parallel Processors (MPPs)

In SMP machines, such as those Sun offers, the CPUs use shared memory and other internal hardware items, such as buses. SMPs now have up to 64 processors. MPP machines have a shared-nothing architecture and are like micro-LANs, or Local Area Networks in a box. MPPs can have hundreds or thousands of processors.

RDBMS software now is either fully multithreaded or pseudo-multithreaded to take advantage of the processing power of the multiprocessing machines. To an operating system, an RDBMS is just one or more processes. Multithreading is a piece of software's capability to run multiple subprocesses, or threads, within its same parent process environment. Sybase and Informix, for example, are fully multithreaded. Oracle is pseudo-multithreaded when using the MultiThreaded Server (MTS) option; otherwise, it is single-threaded. A DBA simply needs to know his number of CPUs, and he can configure the Oracle MTS. Other Oracle parameters are affected by the number of CPUs (such as certain locking structures known as *latches*).

PHYSICAL DESIGN PRINCIPLES AND GENERAL HARDWARE LAYOUT RECOMMENDATIONS

What are the major principles of physical database design? Well, physical database design is actually pre-tuning, or nothing more than the second stage of tuning. (Logical database design is the first stage.) It should not be surprising, therefore, to learn that the major physical database design principles are essentially the same as the major performance tuning principles, except that you are dealing with the database before and during its construction, rather than after. There are many design principles, but the major ones always include the following:

- Divide and conquer—Partitioning, segmenting, and parallelizing are all extensions of the divide-and-conquer algorithm design approach. If a process time can be broken into pieces that can be run concurrently, it is said to be *parallelizable*. The main requirement for this is that each of the pieces of the process must be data-independent; that is, one piece can start regardless of whether any of the others have completed. An example is to split a long-running query to find a sum into two pieces, run them on separate CPUs, and then add their subtotals to get the final result. This is, in fact, what Oracle's Parallel Query capability provides.

- Preallocate and precompile—Static allocation and fixed allocation mean the same thing as preallocation. In other words, allocate your resources ahead of time, rather than let the software do it for you on-the-fly, or dynamically. This typically results in additional computational and I/O overhead, which is nearly always undesirable. Precompiled programs save substantial time over interpreted programs. DBMS caching handles a lot, but the DBA should be on the lookout for what she can also do as a supplement. For example, write generic, reusable procedures and pin them in memory. Oracle's KEEP operation does the latter. The KEEP operation is discussed further in Chapter 18, "Tuning Memory."

■ Be proactive—Anticipate the major problems. Follow the Pareto rule: Fix the 20 percent of the problems that might cause 80 percent of the trouble. This is also referred to as the 20/80 rule. A statistical way of saying this is that *performance problems aren't uniformly distributed among causes*. You want to try to predict the most major problems and either design them out of the system or at least compensate and design around them. Consider a large batch system that serially runs only a few major programs, each one inserting, updating, or deleting large amounts of data. The potential problem here is with the transaction log, especially the undo log, growing extremely large and perhaps running out of room. With Oracle, the undo log is the set of available *rollback segments*. For a DBA, the proper design would be to have at least one very large, rollback segment other than SYSTEM that is capable of handling the maximum amount of undo data generated.

■ Bulk, block, and batch—Use mass transit. Batch things together that make sense to be batched. What this means is that for things such as disk and network I/O, often the best route is to take mass transit: Group together I/O operations with the same origins and destinations. This works most often for DSS and batch systems. For example, users might frequently select a large number of rows from an extremely large table. Because these selections return so many rows, they never use any available indexing. If this is the case without the benefit of any parallelizing hardware or software, the table should exist contiguously on a single, large disk. Then you increase the database logical buffer sizes and read many physical data blocks simultaneously. In Oracle, for example, you would set DB_BLOCK_SIZE to the highest amount for your platform, for example, 8K on a Windows NT machine. You're reading as many blocks as you can with one read request. This all stems from the simple fact that in almost all electromechanical systems, startup costs are expensive. An analogous network situation is to send as much in one packet as possible because this is more cost-effective.

■ Segment the application *appropriately*—This could be considered a subheading under *divide and conquer*. It is somewhat different in that what you are emphasizing is the entire environment and the application, not just the database behind it (the backend). Consider the relative performance capabilities of the client, the network, and the server before distributing the application. Put functionality where functionality is performed logically. For example, display and presentation duties clearly belong to the client in an interactive application, whereas database events that act on database objects should be handled at the database (by the DBMS) and not by some front-end piece of software. In Oracle, use triggers and stored procedures for this design.

The major objective of physical design and tuning is to eliminate, or at least minimize, *contention*. Contention is when two or more pieces of software compete for the same resource.

Common sense tells you that something has to wait. To combat this, practice the following layout recommendations:

- Separate tables and indexes.
- Place large tables and indexes on disks of their own.
- Place frequently joined tables on separate disks, or cluster them.
- Place infrequently joined tables on the same disks if necessary (that is, if you're short on disks).
- Separate DBMS software from tables and indexes.
- Separate the data dictionary from tables and indexes.
- Separate the undo (rollback) logs and redo logs onto their own disks if possible.
- Use RAID 1 (mirroring) for undo or redo logs.
- Use RAID 3 or 5 (striping with parity) for table data.
- Use RAID 0 (striping without parity) for indexes.

As previously discussed regarding RAID, manual striping can suffice in certain cases if RAID is not available. However, in general, it is not as flexible, safe, or fast. Also, when the preceding list indicates to separate things, that means to put them on separate disks, but it can further mean to put them on separate disk controllers. The more controllers, the more ideal the performance and safety.

CHAPTER **4**

The Oracle Solution

In this chapter

REVIEWING ORACLE HISTORY

Larry Ellison is president and CEO of Oracle Corporation. In 1977, along with Robert Minor, he founded Oracle Corporation in Redwood, California. They introduced the first Relational Database Management System (RDBMS) based on the IBM System/R (Relational) model, and it was the first RDBMS to use IBM's Structured Query Language (SQL).

Today, the Oracle RDBMS is ported to almost all operating environments, including IBM mainframes, DEC VAX minicomputers, UNIX-based minicomputers, Windows NT, and several proprietary hardware-operating system platforms; it is clearly the world's largest RDBMS vendor. At the time of this writing, Oracle is the world's leading supplier of software for information management and the world's second (only to Microsoft) largest software company, with annual revenues of $7.5 billion. Oracle employs approximately 36,000 professionals worldwide.

Its initial development largely came from the IBM DB2 and SQL/DS family of products, which were direct descendants of DB2. DB2 has always been the de facto RDBMS on MVS. By contrast, Sybase and Informix, which are similar on the surface, both grew out of Ingres. With Oracle7, Oracle planted itself firmly in recent years as the premiere RDBMS vendor in both the government and private arenas, both nationally and internationally. Initially, Oracle concentrated on its RDBMS. Lately, it has launched many successful horizontal and vertical products, such as Oracle Application Server. Also, Oracle has provided many capable development tools over the years, which is perhaps one of the reasons behind its steady rise to the top. These tools, for example, include the Designer/2000 CASE tools and the Developer/2000 development package. These latter tools, now simply referred to as "Designer" and "Developer," have become increasingly Web-based, as have all of their tools, following industry precedent. In addition, Oracle Applications, including the popular Oracle Financials, bring in a robust business for Oracle to supplement their core RDBMS business.

Note

Oracle developed a host of products, which in combination are called Oracle Applications. These products include Oracle Financials, Oracle Manufacturing, Oracle Human Resources, and Oracle Automotive, among other applications. For example, Oracle has a health systems offering. Oracle also has many niche client-based tools for the Oracle RDBMS Server. These tools include Discoverer, Express, and others.

ORACLE IS A DBMS

By practical criteria, Oracle is a DBMS because it maintains a data dictionary, offers multiple layers of security, supplies means of ensuring data integrity, handles concurrency, and provides a language interface. Oracle maintains its data dictionary in its SYS and SYSTEM schemas, which are stored in the SYSTEM tablespace. Oracle offers a database-level login, OS authentication if desired, roles, privileges, and profiles. It also offers the usual ANSI SQL grant and revoke capabilities with the privileges and roles. Of course, SQL views are also available. Profiles deal more with resource usage. Integrity can be handled through *declarative integrity* for primary and foreign keys, whereby you simply state what is and what is not a key, as opposed to having to write a program to enforce it.

Oracle generates a unique index for each primary key. A user can optionally create an index for a foreign key. Oracle also offers the usual SQL constraints as well as triggers to handle other integrity issues. Locking is done at the row level by default and optionally at the block level. Row-level locking can enable greater concurrency, especially in OLTP applications. Redo logs are stored externally to the database and buffered, as mentioned earlier, in the SGA. Undo (rollback) data is stored in the database and buffered in the SGA as well.

Oracle is entry-level SQL-92 compliant, which means it meets the first level of the latest ANSI SQL standard. Oracle offers SQL*Plus, an interactive SQL command interpreter, which can also run noninteractive scripts, and a procedural programming SQL language known as PL/SQL (modeled after ADA and Pascal), which its stored procedures and triggers are written in.

Finally, Oracle also offers precompilers (for embedded SQL) and a 3GL function call interface known as the Oracle Call Interface (OCI). Yes, Oracle is a DBMS with industrial capabilities and excellent scalability. Scalability, along with providing good tools for its RDBMS, is perhaps another one of the reasons for its current popularity. Many mission-critical and production environments depend on Oracle to store and serve their data.

PART

I

CH

4

IS ORACLE AN RDBMS?

Now, you move on to the question of whether Oracle is truly an RDBMS. Well, it has been sold and used quite effectively as an RDBMS for years, of course. The only remaining question is how Oracle holds up to Codd's Twelve Rules, which you covered in the section "Codd's Twelve Rules" in Chapter 1, "Database, DBMS Principles, and the Relational Model." Not particularly well. This is no surprise because Oracle's major competitors don't fare much better.

Review Oracle's score out of 12 possible points:

> 0 = Doesn't meet criterion
>
> 1/2 = Meets some of the criterion
>
> 1 = Meets the criterion

Binary Large Objects, or BLOBs, are an early RDBMS technique used to store and manage multimedia data types. BLOBs are typically stored outside the database (in files), and pointers are placed in their corresponding column positions. BLOBs push the first two rules, that data is represented as stored in cells and that data must be accessible through table+column+primary key of the row desired. BLOBs are a data type whose physical implementation bleeds through, or is apparent, to the user. Their implementation should be transparent. However, BLOBs do not explicitly break the first two rules. Yet, Oracle (like the other vendors) gets a total rating of 1 1/2 combined for the first two rules, losing a 1/2 point for having BLOBs in the first place. Think of it as a bad conduct grade.

Oracle gets a 1/2 rating for Rule 3, the consistent treatment of NULLs, although the current implementation of NULLs in SQL is poor for all vendors and has been attacked by both Codd and another relational pioneer, C.J. Date. Codd proposes a 3-valued logic, whereas Date proposes the abolishment of NULLS altogether. The arguments are long-winded, and this is not a proper place to go into them. Suffice it to say that there are some very real data problems with the use of NULLs today in RDBMSs.

Oracle only gets a 1/2 rating for Rule 4, data dictionary accessibility through regular SQL. Yes, Oracle enables SELECT only, but INSERT, UPDATE, and DELETE are not possible. This is not to say that this should occur frequently, nor is it even desired. However, it should be possible according to Rule 4. Oracle does get passing marks for Rule 5 and Rules 7–10.

Oracle also only gets a 1/2 rating for Rules 6 and 11. For Rule 6, updatable views, Oracle7 only enabled certain (simple) views to be updatable. Oracle8 has improved this, but not 100%. For Rule 11, distributed independence, Oracle offers database links, snapshots, symmetric replication, and distributed database with two-phase commit (2PC). However, some of the networking is user-apparent, 2PC works (but not well), and replication has its own problems. The majority of the complaints center on the fact that all these capabilities require the user to know more than he or she should about the setup behind the technology.

Oracle is given a 0 rating on Rule 12, the nonsubversion rule. This is because through some of its utilities, such as SQL*Loader and Import, Oracle enables data to be stored in the database by bypassing the standard SQL route, opening up the database to potential corruption.

Final score: 8 1/2 out of 12, give or take a point or two given by someone more lenient or stringent with the ratings. The point is not the precision of the final score, but the fact that Oracle does *not* meet all of Codd's twelve rules. However, neither does Sybase nor Informix. This does not mean you cannot call Oracle an RDBMS, for surely that is what it is. It simply means that Oracle, much like its brethren, has more work to do, which is not surprising. Oracle has been improving steadily. For example, Oracle only fully passed Rule 10, stored (and declarative) integrity, with version 7.

REVISITING THE PHYSICAL LAYOUT

From physical database design, apply the general layout recommendations about the storage of the data dictionary, redo, undo, tables, and indexes. Again, you're not going to get into Oracle architecture too deeply here—just enough to do your layout.

A *tablespace* is a physical structure in Oracle that stores logical objects, or *segments*, such as tables and indexes. Tablespaces typically are stored in the OS as files. The SYSTEM tablespace, as you've seen, stores the data dictionary. TEMP stores temporary objects, such as tables and indexes, during sorts and creations. ROLL1 holds the undo storage for rollback segments. A set of redo logs is stored directly as files and not tablespaces with data files. You're just going to offer one ideal, general-purpose Oracle hardware layout, given nothing about an application. Figure 4.1 represents a minimal, possible layout.

Figure 4.1
A general purpose
Oracle physical layout

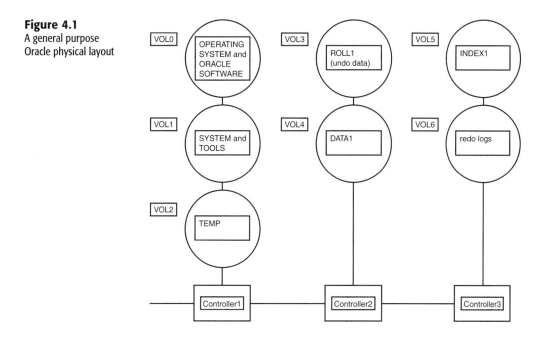

VOL stands for a volume, or set of disks. Each volume is described as follows:

- VOL0 (operating system and Oracle installation software) might be one or two disks, depending on whether it's UNIX or NT.
- VOL1 (the data dictionary) should only need to be one disk.
- VOL2 (temporary space) should only need to be one large disk, but some applications might need additional disks.
- VOL3 (undo data) should only need to be one disk.
- VOL4 (data) needs to be however large the data sizing dictates—a set of several disks using RAID 3 or 5.
- VOL5 (indexes) likewise needs to be as large as the index sizing dictates although is typically less than the total data size (a set of several disks using RAID 0).
- VOL6 (redo) can be a set of three or more disks using RAID1. At least three copies of the control files (those crucial OS files containing the database's physical, structural information) should be spread out across any of the VOLs, typically the first few.

The init.ora parameter file and password files are typically stored in their default locations under the Oracle software subdirectory. Notice that TEMP, DATA1, and INDEX1 not only are on separate disks, but are attached to different controllers on separate *I/O channels*, or buses. This is desirable for performance (and availability) reasons.

For example, if DATA1 and INDEX1 are on separate disks but are attached to the same controller, you have eliminated one bottleneck (disk contention) but created another (bus contention). You are better off than having DATA1 and INDEX1 on the same disk, but you are worse off than the configuration in Figure 4.1. In real life, your goal as a DBA is to have as many disks and controllers as possible for your hardware setup. Compromise only when absolutely necessary.

Eventually, a DBA might need to add a secondary rollback tablespace (ROLL2) for varying application needs, more data or index tablespaces, more temporary space, and so on. In sum, to correctly lay out your database, you need to know your application. You'll revisit this in Chapter 16, "Performance Tuning Fundamentals," after you've studied more architecture and performance tuning. You can then look at alternative layouts for the varying application types (such as OLTP and DSS) that you've already covered.

SIZING FOR ORACLE

In order to help you size Oracle, I've included an Oracle spreadsheet, which is based on the Oracle sizing formulas you can find in the Oracle Server Administrator's Guides. However, the formulas contained therein involve circular references, which cannot be implemented directly in a spreadsheet. I've reworked the mathematics of it and come up with some equivalent formulas that will yield the same results you need: Given reasonable assumptions, how big will your database be, in total and by tables and indexes? Simply enter the block input variables you need, which are as follows:

- *block* (DB_BLOCK_SIZE) in bytes (2048-65536)
- *pctfree* (PCTFREE) as an integer (0-100)
- *initrans* (INITRANS) as an integer (0-200+)

Then, for the Table and Index sections, for each table or index row in the spreadsheet, you only need enter the input variables, which are the following:

- *#rows* as an integer
- *raw_row* in bytes as the maximum number of bytes per row

- #cols_f as an integer as the number of fixed columns (for example, NUMBER or CHAR)
- #cols_v as an integer as the number of variable columns (for example, VARCHAR2)

Everything else is computed for number of bytes, blocks, and KB, MB, or GB per table or index; then everything is computed for the entire sum of these (the database). However, this does not take into account rollback segments, redo logs, the temporary tablespace, and other peripheral sizing elements. If desired, change the pctfree variable to function separately for the tables and indexes respectively. Notice that not only are the primary key indexes included, but also the foreign key indexes and other indexes, in particular, unique indexes. It is essential that you include *all* the indexes you expect to implement. Hopefully, this spreadsheet will be as useful a tool for you as it has been for me! This semiautomatic approach sure beats sizing by hand. The file is a Microsoft Excel 7.0 spreadsheet, with the filename orasiz.xls.

ORACLE'S FUTURE

Oracle, like other RDBMS vendors, has been incorporating OO features such as object classes (types), methods, collections (VARRAY and nested tables), security (views), and identifiers (REF) into its RDBMS. This is more apparent in Oracle8 than ever before. With Oracle7, you saw the release of Universal Server. With Oracle8, you can expect Universal Server to become more widely used. Also, with Oracle8, you gain user-defined data types (namely, object types) on the server. With the Network Computing Architecture, you gain the concept in development of data cartridges, pluggable data types with application programming interfaces (APIs). Also, expect Oracle Web development to continue to grow, especially with the availability of an improved version of Oracle Application Server, Oracle8i, Designer/2000 for the Web, Developer/2000 for the Web, and JDeveloper. With the release of Oracle8i, the distinction between what is a file system, a DBMS, and a Web server has become blurred. In fact, with the advent of Oracle8i, as some trade journals have pointed out, it becomes questionable as to whether Oracle Application Server remains relevant to the market. With the combined new capabilities of Oracle8 and 8i, you have no reason to expect less than continued market domination for the foreseeable future.

Some Oracle Milestones

1977—Oracle Corporation established

1979—Commercial RDBMS

1983—Portable RDBMS

1987—Client/Server RDBMS

1987—CASE tools

1988—Oracle 6 released

1992—Oracle7 released for UNIX

1993—Cooperative Development Environment (CDE)

continues

continued

1994—Oracle7 released for the PC

1995—Web connectivity

1996—Network Computing Architecture (NCA)

1996—Oracle Universal Server released

1997—Client/Server tools ported to the Web

1997—Oracle8 released

1999—Oracle8i released

How To Get in Touch with Oracle Corporation

Home Page: *http://www.oracle.com*

Address:

Oracle Systems Corp.

500 Oracle Parkway

Redwood Shores, CA 94065

USA

Phone Numbers:

Headquarters: (650) 506-7000

US Customer Relations: (650) 506-1500

US Sales: (800) ORACLE-1

PART II

THE ORACLE7.X RDBMS

## CHAPTER 5

THE ORACLE DATABASE ARCHITECTURE

In this chapter

DEFINING THE DATABASE

The term *database* is used both as the name for the entire database management environment and as a description (in Oracle terms) of the logical and physical data structures that make up the Relational Database Management System (RDBMS). As an Oracle professional, you define the Oracle database as the configuration files, datafiles, control files, and redo log files that make up the data processing environment, as well as the tables, indexes, and other structures contained within these objects.

THE SYS AND SYSTEM SCHEMAS

SYS and SYSTEM are two default accounts installed with every Oracle database that you should know about. The SYS schema is the owner of all the internal database tables, structures, supplied packages, procedures, and so on. It also owns all the V$ and data dictionary views and creates all the packaged database roles (DBA, CONNECT, RESOURCE, and so on). SYS is the root or administrator of an Oracle database, and because of its all-powerful nature, you should avoid doing work logged in as it. Making a simple typo when you're logged in as SYS can be devastating.

The SYS account is the only one able to access certain internal data dictionary tables. Because it owns all the data dictionary structures, it is also the schema you must log in to in order to grant explicit data dictionary object rights to other schemas. This is necessary when you're writing stored procedures or triggers using the data dictionary views and tables. The default password for the SYS account when a database is first installed is CHANGE_ON_INSTALL, and every DBA worth his or her salt follows that advice to the letter.

The SYSTEM schema is also installed upon database creation and is the default account used for DBA tasks. SYSTEM also has full rights to all database objects, and many third-party tools rely on the existence and privileges of the SYSTEM schema. The default password for the SYSTEM account is MANAGER, and like the SYS account's password, it should be changed immediately after creating a database. Many DBAs use the SYSTEM schema to perform database administration tasks, but it's preferable to create a specific user just to do DBA tasks. This ensures that a specific account is linked to a specific person and that specific user is responsible for any database modifications.

Because these schemas are well known and exist in every Oracle database, it is important to change their default passwords immediately upon database installation, securing the accounts against unauthorized access. If security is a major issue, you might also consider making it impossible to log in to these accounts and setting valid passwords only when it is necessary to log in to them.

Note

> You can make it impossible to log in to an account by issuing ALTER USER xxx IDENTIFIED BY VALUES 'password';, where 'password' is any lowercase string. This sets the stored password to the actual value you give, rather than the encrypted version Oracle would store with a normal ALTER USER xxx IDENTIFIED BY 'password'; command. It is impossible for Oracle to generate a lowercase encrypted password string, making it impossible to log in to the account.

THE COMPONENTS OF THE DATABASE

You can group the pieces of the database in two distinct categories: objects used internally by the RDBMS, which you call *system database objects*, and objects that can be accessed by any processes, which you call *user database objects*.

SYSTEM DATABASE OBJECTS

When referring to system database objects, you're looking at the database objects the RDBMS uses to support internal database functions. These objects are configured and created by the DBA or the server itself and are not explicitly used in user database transactions.

The system database objects are the following:

- The initialization parameter files
- The control files
- Online and archived redo log files
- The trace files
- The ROWID
- Oracle blocks

An explanation of each of these objects follows.

THE INITIALIZATION PARAMETER FILES

The *initialization parameter file*, or init.ora, is the primary configuration point for the RDBMS. It is nothing more than a collection of configuration keys and values, each of which controls or modifies one aspect of the operation of a database and an instance. It is an ASCII text file found in $ORACLE_HOME/dbs on UNIX servers and $ORACLE_HOME/database on NT servers. By default, it is named initSID.ora, where SID is equal to the system identifier for the database it controls. On a UNIX server, this is the filename the Oracle server looks for (where SID is equal to the value of the $ORACLE_SID environment variable) when starting the database if an init.ora file is not explicitly provided on the command line. Each Oracle database and instance should have its own unique init.ora file.

The init.ora file can include configuration values from other files using the IFILE parameter. It's also quite common in UNIX environments to link the $ORACLE_HOME/dbs/init.ora file to a file in another location to enable better control and structure of the database environment installation. Undocumented parameters (used primarily by Oracle Worldwide Customer Support) are named with a leading underscore.

The init.ora file is read when the database is started, before the instance is created or the control files are read. The values in the init.ora file determine database and instance characteristics such as shared pool, buffer cache, and redo log buffer memory allocations, background processes to automatically start, control files to read, rollback segments to automatically bring online, and so on. Changes made to parameters in the init.ora file are not recognized until the database is shut down and restarted.

The default init.ora file shipped with the Oracle RDBMS, located in the $ORACLE_HOME/dbs directory, comes preconfigured with the essential init.ora parameters and different recommended (arbitrary) values for small, medium, and large databases. This file can be copied and renamed when you're creating new databases and instances.

The configuration parameters set in the init.ora file can be viewed from within a database by querying the V$PARAMETER view. This view lists all the init.ora parameters and their values, and each one has a flag indicating whether the parameter value is the server default.

Explanations of the parameters contained within the default init.ora file are given in Table 5.1. For a more comprehensive list, consult the Oracle Server Reference manual in your server documentation set.

TABLE 5.1 COMMON INIT.ORA PARAMETERS

Parameter Name	Use
audit_trail	Enables or disables writing records to the audit trail. Note that this merely enables auditing; audit actions must be configured separately.
background_dump_dest	Destination directory for Oracle background process trace files, including alert.log.
compatible	Compatibility level of the database. It prevents the use of database features introduced at versions higher than the value of this parameter.
control_files	Control files for this database.
db_block_buffers	Number of database blocks contained in the buffer cache. db_block_buffers×db_block_size=size of database buffer cache, in bytes.
db_block_size	Size of the Oracle database block. This can not be changed after the database is created.
db_files	Maximum number of database files that can be opened.
db_name	Optional name of the database. If used, it must match the database name used in the CREATE DATABASE statement.

Parameter Name	Use
db_file_multiblock_read_count	Maximum number of database blocks read in one I/O. This is used for sequential scans and is important when tuning full table scans.
dml_locks	Maximum number of DML locks for all tables by all users of the database.
log_archive_dest	Destination of archived redo log files.
log_archive_start	Enables or disables automatic archiving. If true, the ARCH process automatically starts when the instance is started.
log_buffer	Number of bytes allocated to the redo log buffer.
log_checkpoint_interval	Number of redo log file blocks that must be filled to trigger a checkpoint.
max_dump_file_size	Maximum size in operating system blocks of Oracle trace files.
processes	Maximum number of OS processes that can connect to the database, including the background processes. This is important when tuning shared memory on a UNIX server.
remote_login_passwordfile	Specifies whether a password file is used for remote internal authentication and how many databases can use a single password file. It can be set to NONE, SHARED, and EXCLUSIVE.
rollback_segments	List of rollback segments to automatically take online at database startup.
sequence_cache_entries	Number of sequences that can be cached in the SGA. This should be set to the maximum number of sequences that will be used in the instance at any time.
shared_pool_size	Size of the shared pool, in bytes.
snapshot_refresh_processes	Number of SNP processes to start at instance startup. SNP processes are responsible for refreshing snapshots and running database jobs submitted with DBMS_JOB.
timed_statistics	Enables or disables the collecting of timing statistics for the database. Although setting this to true incurs a minimal performance overhead, it enables much greater flexibility in database tuning.
user_dump_dest	Destination directory for user trace files, including those generated by setting sql_trace to true.

THE CONTROL FILES

The *control file* is the heart of the database. It contains information on what datafiles and redo log files belong to the database, what character set the data should be stored as in the database, the status and revision of each datafile in the database, and other critical information. Most of the parameters contained in the control file are set during database creation and are relatively static. That is, they do not change from day to day. The control file is in binary format and cannot be read or edited manually.

The control file is created when the database is created. Most databases operate with multiplexed control files (as explained in the following text) and are therefore usually referred to in the plural form. The specific control files created are those specified in the CONTROL_FILES init.ora parameter. The database creation parameters specified in the CREATE DATABASE clause are stored in these files.

The database cannot be opened without the correct control files. If the control file is unavailable or corrupted for some reason, the database cannot be started and the data contained in the database cannot be accessed. For this reason, mirroring of the control files is internally supported by the Oracle server and is highly recommended. To mirror control files in a new database, merely specify more than one value for the CONTROL_FILES init.ora parameter before issuing the CREATE DATABASE command. To mirror control files in an existing database, you must shut down the database, copy the current control file to the directories where you want it to be mirrored, edit the CONTROL_FILES parameter to specify the new control file locations, and start the database.

> **Note**
>
> A good rule of thumb is to store no fewer than four copies of the control files on four separate physical disks.

Unfortunately, modifying control file parameters is not as easy as changing an initialization parameter and bouncing the database. To change any of the control file parameters, you must re-create the control files. Follow these steps to re-create your control file:

1. Back up your database. Making an error when modifying your control file can corrupt your database beyond recovery. Never perform this activity without a valid backup of the database.

2. Issue the ALTER DATABASE BACKUP CONTROLFILE TO TRACE; command from Server Manager or SQL*Plus. This creates a user trace file (located in USER_DUMP_DEST) with the commands necessary to re-create your current control file.

3. Edit the trace file generated in the preceding step. Delete all the lines in the trace file except for the CREATE CONTROLFILE statement. Set the new parameter values.

4. SHUTDOWN NORMAL the database. Move the old control files to a backup directory. Make sure none of the copies of the control files remain in the directories where Oracle looks for them at database startup, or the next step will fail.

5. STARTUP NOMOUNT the database. Run the CREATE CONTROLFILE trace file you edited. This re-creates the control files with the new parameter values.

6. Execute ALTER DATABASE OPEN;.

You can avoid ever having to re-create your control files by setting the database parameters during database creation to values higher than you'll ever need. The only thing wasted in setting these control file parameters higher than needed is a negligible amount of memory and disk space.

> **Caution**
>
> It's important that you set the CHARACTERSET parameter correctly when you create the database. Changing this parameter requires re-creating the entire database. It cannot be changed by rebuilding the control file.

The configurable control file parameters are listed in Table 5.2.

TABLE 5.2   MODIFIABLE CONFIGURATION PARAMETERS CONTAINED IN THE CONTROL FILE

Parameter Name	Description
MAXLOGFILES	Maximum number of online redo log files
MAXLOGMEMBERS	Maximum number of members per redo log file
MAXDATAFILES	Maximum number of datafiles
MAXINSTANCES	Maximum number of instances that can mount this database (parallel server)
MAXLOGHISTORY	Maximum number of archived redo log file groups to use for instance recovery (parallel server)

> **Note**
>
> To change the database name, re-create the control file as described, but change the REUSE DATABASE <old_name> line in the trace file to SET DATABASE <new_name>.

The V$CONTROLFILE view lists the control files that the Oracle server is currently reading from and writing to.

> **Tip #3**
>
> You should always keep a text copy of your control file (in addition to your ordinary binary backup copies) by issuing the ALTER DATABASE BACKUP CONTROLFILE TO TRACE statement. It can help you reconstruct your database when all else fails.

PART

II

Cʜ

5

ONLINE REDO LOG FILES

The log writer background process (LGWR) writes the contents of the (redo) log buffer to the *online redo log files*. The redo logs store all the change information for the database and are used by Oracle during database recovery. As shown in Figure 5.1, the online redo log files are made up of at least two groups of redo log files, and are written to in a circular nature.

A redo log group is active if it is currently being written to by LGWR. A log switch occurs when the current log group fills up and LGWR stops writing to it and moves on to the next one. When a log switch occurs and archive log mode is enabled for the database, the redo log group previously written to is locked by the archiver (ARCH) process and copied to disk or tape, depending on your configuration. If LGWR catches up with the ARCH process and needs to write to the group currently being written to by ARCH, all database activity is suspended until ARCH finishes writing to the log. If you see errors in your alert.log file stating that a free log group could not be latched by LGWR, this behavior is occurring in your database, indicating that you need to add more redo log groups or adjust the size of the groups.

Figure 5.1
Redo log groups with multiple members.

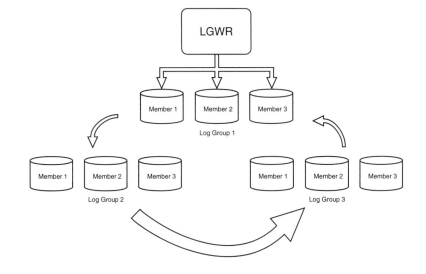

Each log group can consist of multiple members. Each member of a log group is an exact mirror of the others, and redo log entries are written to each member in parallel. If LGWR cannot write to a member of the group, it does not fail. Rather, it writes an entry in the alert.log file. By using multiple members per group, you can safeguard against database failure resulting from lost redo logs. As long as one member of the group is accessible, the database continues to function.

> **Note**
>
> The same functionality can be obtained by mirroring your redo log groups using RAID 1 (mirrored) volumes. This alleviates the overhead caused when LGWR has to update multiple log group members for each database transaction.

The V$LOG and V$LOGFILE views hold information on the online redo log files. The following query checks the status of the current logs:

```
SELECT b.member, a.bytes, a.members, a.status
FROM v$log a, v$logfile b
WHERE a.group# = b.group#
ORDER BY b.member;
```

THE TRACE FILES

All Oracle databases have at least one file where system messages, errors, and major events are logged. This file, named `sidALRT.log` (where `sid` is the system identifier for the database), is stored at the location specified by the `init.ora` parameter `BACKGROUND_DUMP_DEST`. It is the first place you should look when investigating database problems. Critical failures are always logged here, as well as database startup and shutdown messages, log switch messages, and other events.

Background and user processes also create their own trace files where problems and failures are logged. Background process trace files are stored in the `BACKGROUND_DUMP_DEST` location, whereas user trace files are stored in the directory pointed to by the `USER_DUMP_DEST` parameter setting. Setting the `USER_DUMP_DEST` directory differently than that pointed to by `BACKGROUND_DUMP_DEST` enables you to keep track of the different classes of trace files. Background process trace files are named `sidPROC.trc`, where `sid` is the system identifier for the database and `PROC` is the name of the background process (`DBWR`, `LGWR`, `SMON`, `PMON`, and so on).

User session trace files are given an `ora` prefix, followed by a sequence of unique numbers with a `.trc` file extension. User session trace files are generated when a user session causes an unrecoverable problem (such as a deadlock or a crashed server process) or when the user session is explicitly told to create them (such as when SQL tracing is enabled or an `ALTER DATABASE BACKUP CONTROLFILE TO TRACE` command is issued). To enable SQL tracing, issue `ALTER SESSION SET SQL_TRACE=TRUE` from the SQL*Plus prompt, or set the `SQL_TRACE` `init.ora` parameter to `true`. Be cautious, however, as setting `SQL_TRACE` to `TRUE` in `init.ora` causes all SQL statements that occur against the database to be written to trace files. This generates an enormous amount of trace information.

The current settings for the `BACKGROUND_DUMP_DEST` and `USER_DUMP_DEST` parameters can be queried from the `V$PARAMETER` view.

THE ROWID

For the Oracle database to retrieve information, it must be able to uniquely identify each row in the database. The internal structure the Oracle RDBMS uses for this task is called the `ROWID`, a two-byte value that stores the physical location for a row in the database. The format of the `ROWID` is as follows:

```
BBBBBBBB.RRRR.FFFF
```

`BBBBBBBB` is the block number (in hex) where the row resides in the datafile. `RRRR` is the row number (in hex) in the block where the data row exists. `FFFF` is the file number (in hex) where the block exists.

For example, a row in a table might have a `ROWID` as follows:

```
0000068C.0000.0001
```

This ROWID is in the first datafile (0001), the 68C (hex) block in that datafile, and the first row in that block (0000).

Note

You can match the file number from the preceding ROWID to the filename by querying the DBA_DATA_FILES view. In Oracle7, these file numbers are fixed, whereas in Oracle8, they are determined at database startup.

A row is assigned a ROWID when it is first created. The ROWID remains the same until the row is deleted or the segment the row is in is reorganized (through import/export, third party reorganizational tools, and so on.). Using the ROWID is the fastest method of finding a row in the database. Every table in the database contains a pseudocolumn named ROWID that can be queried to show the ROWID of each row in the table.

Because of the unique nature of the ROWID, it can be used to creatively solve many different problems. For example, one of the most common uses of the ROWID is to identify columns with duplicate values in the database. The following SQL script shows how this can be done:

```
delete from duplicate_table
where ROWID not in (select MIN (ROWID) from duplicate_table
                      group by a1, a2);
```

You can also use the value of the actual ROWIDs in queries. The following SQL script displays the number of database files a table has rows in:

```
SELECT COUNT(DISTINCT(SUBSTR(ROWID, 15, 14))) "Files"
FROM test_table;
```

ORACLE BLOCKS

The lowest level of database storage that you can manipulate is the *Oracle block*, which is the smallest unit of storage the server can address. It should not be confused with the operating system block; although an Oracle block is made up of operating system blocks, they are not the same.

Tip #4

The Oracle block should be a whole multiple of the operating system block. On UNIX, for example, this is typically 8KB. You should then set db_block_size to 8192, 16384, or so forth, such that is set to some whole multiple of 8KB.

All data access is performed in terms of the Oracle block. The size of the Oracle block is the number of bytes the RDBMS reads and writes from the datafiles in one I/O. Database object sizes and blocks in memory caches are also set in terms of Oracle blocks (although some views display storage size in bytes, this is only for readability).

Note

> The Oracle block size is set for a database upon database creation and can never be changed. If at a later time you decide that a larger (or smaller) block size is necessary, you have to rebuild the entire database from scratch.

Each Oracle block contains space for header information, future updates of data in the block, and the actual rows stored in the block. The block header contains information such as the database segments that have rows in the block, how many transactions can access the block at one time, and so on. Each block allocates a certain amount of space for future updates to the rows stored in the block. If an update occurs that causes the original row to grow, this free space is used.

The availability of a block to accept new rows is controlled by the PCTFREE and PCTUSED storage settings. The PCTFREE parameter allocates the percentage of block space to set aside for updates of data. For example, if a block has a PCTFREE value of 30%, 70% of the block space is used for new rows. When 70% of the block has been filled, Oracle takes the block off the free list and uses the remaining 30% of space to handle updates of rows within the block that require more space.

The PCTUSED parameter specifies how much space must be freed in a block (through deletions of rows within the block or updates that reduce the amount of space needed to store a row) before the block is placed back on the free list.

PCTFREE and PCTUSED work together to ensure that a block has enough space to handle future storage requirements and also to make sure that the block does not *thrash*, or in other words, spend a substantial amount of time moving back and forth from the free list. PCTFREE and PCTUSED values should *not* equal 100%, or the value of the parameters is lost. See Chapter 21, "Storage," for more information on tuning Oracle blocks.

Because it determines the number of bytes read from the datafiles during a single I/O operation, the database block size is a very important tuning consideration. Online Transaction Processing (OLTP) applications can sometimes benefit from a smaller block size (4KB or 8KB). Because these applications typically read and write small amounts of data during each transaction, smaller block sizes are more efficient in terms of I/O performance.

For warehousing or Decision Support System (DSS) databases, larger block sizes can boost performance tremendously. These types of applications are usually dealing with large amounts of data in a single transaction and are often concerned with response times measuring in minutes rather than seconds.

By setting your block size, you are adjusting the amount of data read into the buffer cache for any one I/O. When you make your decision on the optimum block size, you must keep in mind the specific types of data access your applications will be performing, as well as the amount of data you are likely to store in a single row. A database block size that is too big will read more data into the buffer cache than necessary, whereas a block size that is too small will result in row chaining.

USER DATABASE OBJECTS

User database objects are those objects that are not used exclusively by the Oracle RDBMS. They are, of course, internally managed by Oracle, but they exist to provide a set of user building blocks with which a user can build her database. User database objects include the datafiles, extents, tablespaces, and database segments. An explanation of each of these items appears in the following sections.

DATAFILES

Oracle *datafiles* exist as operating system files. Each datafile is allocated to one tablespace and holds the actual data stored in that tablespace. The datafile is an actual file in the file system and can be monitored and manipulated like any other operating system file. The data stored within the datafile is in an Oracle binary format and as such is unreadable by anything other than the Oracle RDBMS.

Datafiles are created using the CREATE TABLESPACE or ALTER TABLESPACE SQL commands. A datafile is sized according to the size specified in the create statement, not the amount of data stored in it. For example, a datafile created with a size of 10MB uses the full 10MB of space whether it contains one or one million rows.

As of Oracle 7.3, the DBA is equipped to dynamically grow and shrink Oracle datafiles. However, the datafiles cannot be shrunk smaller than the high-water mark of the datafile. Datafiles can also be taken offline individually for backups or other database operations.

You can access the DBA_DATA_FILES and V$DATAFILE views for information on the datafiles defined for the database. The following query displays the mapping between tablespaces and datafiles:

```
SELECT tablespace_name, file_name, bytes
FROM dba_data_files
ORDER BY tablespace_name, file_name;
```

EXTENTS

An *extent* is a unit of storage made up of one or more logically (that is, within Oracle) contiguous Oracle blocks. Each database segment is composed of one or more extents. Each extent in a database segment can be of the same or a different size. As of Oracle 7.3, the maximum number of extents a single database object can have is dependent on the Oracle block size.

A database segment is allocated extents upon object creation, as specified by the storage clause of the create command. When a segment can no longer fit new data into its currently allocated extents, it must allocate another extent. The size of the next extent allocated is dependent on quite a few factors, some of which are not immediately apparent. Managing the allocation of new extents is the primary concern in database space management. See Chapter 21, "Managing Database Storage," for more information.

Extent information is stored in the DBA_EXTENTS view.

TABLESPACES

A *tablespace* is a data structure used to group similarly accessed data. Each tablespace is made up of one or more datafiles. All database objects must specify a tablespace where they're to be created. The data that makes up the objects is then stored in the datafiles allocated to the specified tablespace.

Tablespaces are used to separate the I/O involved in data access. For example, one tablespace can be created to hold data objects, and another can be created to hold index objects. By allocating datafiles to these tablespaces that reside on different physical disks, you ensure that access to the index data does not interfere with accesses to the data to which the index points. See Chapter 19, "Tuning I/O," for more information.

The tablespace also plays an important part in database backup and recovery. Because a tablespace maps directly to one or more datafiles, backing up and recovering data is generally done at the tablespace (datafile) level. (The exception to this, of course, is if the backup or recovery operation is applied to the entire database.)

You can view tablespace information in DBA_TABLESPACES.

DATABASE SEGMENTS

Database segments are the user-created objects stored in the database. These largely include the data (tables) and the indexes that make up your schema.

In addition to user-created data and index segments, two types of segments generally regarded as system segments, or as administrator-created, are the temporary and rollback segments. Of course, these can be created by a user who is given the proper privileges. However, they tend to be created by the DBA and then shared by the application users and programs.

TABLES

Tables are the database segments that hold your data. Each table is composed of one or more columns, each of which is assigned a name and data type. The data type of each column defines the type and precision of data to be stored in the table. Valid Oracle column datatypes are listed in Table 5.3.

TABLE 5.3   VALID ORACLE 7.X COLUMN DATATYPES

Data type	Description	Max Size
CHAR	Fixed-length character field, padded with trailing blanks	255 bytes
VARCHAR	Variable-length character field	2KB
VARCHAR2	Variable-length character field	2KB

continues

TABLE 5.3 CONTINUED

Data type	Description	Max Size
LONG	Variable-length character data	2GB
NUMBER	Variable-length numeric data	1×10^{-130} to 9.99×10^{125}
DATE	Fixed-length date and time field B.C.E. to Dec. 31, 4712 C.E.	Jan. 1, 4712
RAW	Variable-length raw binary data	255 bytes
LONG RAW	Variable-length raw binary data	2GB
ROWID	Row ID variable type	6 bytes

Note

Oracle recommends that all variable-length character fields be defined as VARCHAR2, rather than VARCHAR, to guard against ANSI specification changes. Oracle guarantees VARCHAR2 will never change functionality in a way that will require modifications to applications to make them upward-compatible. Because VARCHAR functionality is mandated by ANSI standards boards, Oracle cannot guarantee that the functionality will not drastically change in new versions.

DBA_TABLES and DBA_TAB_COLUMNS contain information on the tables in the database.

INDEXES

Indexes are data segments created to speed up access to specific table data. An index holds the value for one or more columns of a table and the ROWID for the corresponding column values. When the Oracle server needs to find a specific row in a table, it looks up the ROWID in the index and then pulls the data directly from the table.

There are several types of indexes available in the Oracle RDBMS. By far, the most common index type is the *B*-Tree* index. This is the index type used when a standard CREATE INDEX statement is executed. A B*-Tree index is a variation on the standard search tree algorithm, wherein by traversing the index tree, you are guaranteed to find any leaf node in the same number of tree traversals. Each leaf node points to the next leaf node and the previous one, enabling fast index traversals for index range scans and the like. The B*-Tree index is guaranteed to stay balanced, and three-fourths of each node is kept empty to provide space for updates.

An in-depth explanation of the architecture of the B*-Tree index is beyond the scope of this book. However, extensive information on the subject can be found in most modern database textbooks, such as Elmasri and Navathe's *Fundamentals of Database Systems*.

A *cluster* index is the index on the column shared by tables in the cluster. Clustered tables are explained later in this section. Unlike convention indexes, cluster indexes only store the index key value once in the index, no matter how many times the index key is repeated in the table. A cluster index must be created on a cluster before any data manipulation language (DML) operations can be performed against the cluster.

The newest index type is the *bitmap* index. In a bitmap index, a bitmap is created from the column values in the indexed table and stored in the index, rather than from the actual column values. To put it another way, the index holds a bitmap for each row in the key that contains one bit for each row in the table. The bit is 1 if the value is contained within the row, and 0 if it is not. In columns with low cardinality (small number of distinct values), bitmap indexes can be much smaller and more efficient than traditional B*-Tree indexes. Table 5.4 shows a sample bitmap on a car table. The bitmap key is the color column of the table.

TABLE 5.4   BITMAP INDEX ON THE CAR TABLE

Car Color	Bitmap
Red	0 0 0 1 0 0 1 0 0 0 1 0 0 0 1 0 0 0 0 1
Green	1 0 0 0 0 0 0 1 0 1 0 0 0 1 0 0 1 0 1 0
Silver	0 0 1 0 0 0 0 0 1 0 0 0 1 0 0 1 0 0 0 0
White	0 0 0 0 1 0 0 0 0 0 0 0 0 0 0 0 0 1 0 0
Black	0 1 0 0 0 1 0 0 0 0 0 1 0 0 0 0 0 0 0 0

In this example, there are 20 rows in the table. The bitmap will be on (1) where the row in the car table matches the color. So, rows 4, 7, 11, 15, and 20 are red cars, whereas rows 2, 6, and 12 are black. The structure of the bitmap index creates much smaller indexes than a traditional B*-Tree index, but as discussed is suited only for certain types of data.

DBA_INDEXES and DBA_IND_COLUMNS contain information on all the indexes in the database.

ROLLBACK SEGMENTS

Rollback segments are the database objects that store the *before images*, or original data blocks that are changed in database transactions. They are used to provide a read-consistent view of data that has been changed but not yet committed. When a data change is made, the before image is copied into the rollback segment, and the change is made to the data blocks in the buffer cache. If another user session requests the same data, the before image stored in the rollback segment is returned (this is called a *consistent read*). When the session that is making the change commits, the rollback segment entry is marked invalid.

Multiple user sessions can share a single rollback segment. Each rollback segment is made up of at least two extents. When a transaction starts, the user session gets an exclusive lock on an available extent in an available rollback segment. Transaction information is then written to the rollback segment. If the transaction fills the first extent, it allocates another extent. If another extent is unavailable, the rollback segment automatically allocates another extent to itself, which the user session grabs. This is called *rollback segment extension*. Because

PART

II

Cн

5

extent allocation affects performance, your goal should be to enable all transactions to run without allocating new extents.

If the rollback segment is unable to allocate another extent (either because the maximum number of extents has been reached for the rollback segment or there are no more free extents in the rollback segment tablespace), an error occurs, and the transaction is rolled back. This commonly occurs in large data loads where online rollback segments do not provide sufficient space to store all the rollback information for the transaction.

See Chapter 21 for more information on creating and administering rollback segments.

The DBA_ROLLBACK_SEGS view contains information on rollback segments.

TABLE CLUSTERS

A *table cluster* is a database object that physically groups tables that are often used together within the same data blocks. The clustering of tables is most effective when you're dealing with tables that are often joined together in queries. A table cluster stores the cluster key (the column used to join the tables together), as well as the values of the columns in the clustered tables. Because the tables in the cluster are stored together in the same database blocks, I/O is reduced when working with the clusters.

HASH CLUSTERS

Hash clusters are the final option for database storage. In a hash cluster, tables are organized based upon a hash value derived by applying the hash function to the primary key values of the tables. To retrieve data from the hash cluster, the hash function is applied to the key value requested. The resulting hash value gives Oracle the block in the hash cluster where the data is stored.

Using hash clusters can significantly reduce the I/O required to retrieve rows from a table. There are several drawbacks to using hash clusters, however. See Chapter 21 for more information on creating and administering hash clusters.

THE ORACLE DATA DICTIONARY

The *data dictionary* is the repository of information on all the objects stored in the database. It is used by the Oracle RDBMS to retrieve object and security information, and it is used by the users and DBAs to look up database information. It holds information on the database objects and segments in the database, such as tables, views, indexes, packages, and procedures. It also holds information on such things as users, privileges, roles, auditing, and constraints. The data dictionary is read-only; you should *never* attempt to manually update or change any of the information in any of the data dictionary tables. It consists of four parts: the internal RDBMS (X$) tables, the data dictionary tables, the dynamic performance (V$) views, and the data dictionary views.

INTERNAL RDBMS (X$) TABLES

At the heart of the Oracle database are the so-called *internal RDBMS (X$) tables:* the tables used by the Oracle RDBMS to keep track of internal database information. The X$ tables are cryptically named, undocumented, and nearly impossible to decipher. Most of them are not designed to be used directly by DBAs or users. Nonetheless, they contain valuable information. Many undocumented or internal statistics and configurations can be found only in the X$ tables.

The easiest way to decipher what is stored in a particular X$ table is to work backward from a known data dictionary table. The SQL*Plus autotrace feature is invaluable for this work. For example, to determine where the information in V$SGASTAT is really stored, you can perform the following analysis:

1. Log in to SQL*Plus as SYS (or an account with explicit access to the X$ and V$ tables). If a PLAN_TABLE does not exist for the schema you are logged in to, create one by running the $ORACLE_HOME/rdbms/admin/UTLXPLAN.sql.

2. Issue the following SQL*Plus command: SET AUTOTRACE ON.

3. Issue a query against the table whose components you are interested in. Set the WHERE clause to a value that will never be true so that no rows are returned: SELECT * FROM v$sgastat WHERE 0 =1;.

Among other information, the autotrace returns output similar to the following:

```
Execution Plan
0   SELECT STATEMENT Optimizer=CHOOSE
1   0      FILTER
2   1         FIXED TABLE (FULL) OF 'X$KSMSS'
```

From the output of the SQL trace, you can decipher the data dictionary base tables from which the information for the view is extracted. Querying the X$ tables found in this manner often produces surprising information.

DATA DICTIONARY TABLES

The *data dictionary tables* hold information for tables, indexes, constraints, and all other database constructs. They are owned by SYS and are created by running the SQL.BSQ script (which happens automatically during database creation). They are easily identified by the trailing dollar sign at the end of their names (tab$, seg$, cons$, and so on). Most of the information in the data dictionary tables can be found in the data dictionary views, but certain applications or queries still benefit from using the information contained in the base tables.

The columns and tables of the data dictionary are well documented in the SQL.BSQ file. This file is found in the $ORACLE_HOME/dbs directory. By familiarizing yourself with the contents of SQL.BSQ, you can gain a better understanding of how the Oracle RDBMS actually stores the data dictionary and database information.

DYNAMIC PERFORMANCE (V$) VIEWS

The *dynamic performance (V$)* views are the mainstay of the Oracle DBA. These views contain runtime performance and statistic information on a large number of database functions. They are also fairly readable (as opposed to the X$ tables) and are meant to be used by the DBA to diagnose and troubleshoot problems. Documentation on most V$ views can be found in the *Oracle Reference Manual* supplied on your Oracle server media.

Note that the V$ views are actually public synonyms to the V$ views owned by SYS. This is important to note when writing stored procedures or functions that read the V$ tables. It is often necessary to reference or grant privileges to the base V$ view rather than the V$ public synonym.

DATA DICTIONARY VIEWS

The data dictionary views are views created on the X$ and data dictionary tables and are meant to be queried and used by end users and DBAs. They are divided into three categories—the DBA_, ALL_, and USER_ views. The DBA_ views contain information on all objects in the database. For example, DBA_TABLES contains information on all tables created. The ALL_ views contain information on all objects to which the user querying the table has access. The USER_ views contain information on all objects the user querying the table owns.

OTHER DATABASE OBJECTS

There are several other objects stored in the database that are not rightfully classified as segments but should be discussed nonetheless. They include views, sequences, synonyms, triggers, database links, and stored packages, procedures, and functions. They are described in the following sections.

VIEWS

Views are stored SQL statements that can be queried. A view is used for security reasons to hide certain data (such as an HR view that shows only first name, last name, and address information, but not showing social security number and salary data), and to make complicated queries easier to understand and use. Views can also be used to hide distributed database objects by creating views on remote database tables. Any statement that can be executed as a SQL query can be created as a view.

> **Note**
>
> Views can be very helpful when designing applications, because they can be used to hide complicated query logic in a table format that is much easier to query. They can be created with optimizer hints embedded in them, to ensure top query performance.

The DBA_VIEWS view holds information on views created in the database.

SEQUENCES

Sequences are database objects that are used to generate unique numbers. A sequence is created with a starting value, an increment, and a maximum value. Each time a number is recalled from a sequence, the current sequence value is incremented by one. Each sequence-generated number can be up to 38 digits long.

You use a sequence by selecting the NEXTVAL or CURRVAL pseudocolumns from it. If you have a sequence named EMP_SEQ, for example, issuing SELECT EMP_SEQ.NEXTVAL FROM DUAL; returns the next integer value of the sequence and increments the current value of the sequence by one. You can use SELECT EMP_SEQ.CURRVAL FROM DUAL; to return the current integer value of the sequence. Note that to use CURRVAL, you must have previously initialized the sequence for your user session by issuing a query on the NEXTVAL pseudocolumn of the sequence.

The most common usage of sequences is to provide unique numbers as *surrogates* for primary key columns of tables. Information on sequences is stored in the DBA_SEQUENCES view.

TRIGGERS

Triggers are stored procedures that fire when certain actions occur against a table. Triggers can be coded to fire for inserts, updates, deletes, or combinations of the three against a table and can also occur for each row that is affected or for each statement. Triggers are most often used to enforce data integrity constraints and business rules that are too complicated for the built-in Oracle referential integrity constraints. Information on database triggers can be found in the DBA_TRIGGERS view.

SYNONYMS

Synonyms are database pointers to other database tables. When you create a synonym, you specify a synonym name and the object the synonym references. When you reference the synonym name, the Oracle server automatically replaces the synonym name with the name of the object for which the synonym is defined.

There are two types of synonyms: *private* and *public*. Private synonyms are created in a specific schema and are only accessible by the schema that owns it. Public synonyms are owned by the PUBLIC schema, and all database schemas can reference them.

It's important to understand the order in which an object name is resolved within a SQL statement. If the SQL statement SELECT * FROM EMP_SALARY; is issued, the Oracle server attempts to resolve the EMP_SALARY object in the following way:

1. First, the server checks to see if a table or view named EMP_SALARY exists in the issuing user's schema.

2. If the table or view doesn't exist, Oracle checks for the existence of a private synonym named EMP_SALARY.

PART

II

CH

5

3. If this private synonym exists, the object that the synonym references is substituted for EMP_SALARY.

4. If the private synonym does not exist, the existence of a public synonym named EMP_SALARY is checked.

5. If a public synonym does not exist, Oracle returns the message ORA-00942, table or view does not exist.

Public synonyms should be used with care. Because all schemas can use public synonyms to resolve object names, unpredictable results can occur.

Information on public synonyms is stored in DBA_SYNONYMS. Note that the owner of public synonyms is listed as PUBLIC in this view.

DATABASE LINKS

Database links are stored definitions of connections to remote databases. They are used to query remote tables in a distributed database environment. Because they are stored in the Oracle database, they fall under the category of database object. More information on database links can be found in Chapter 40, "Distributed Database Management," and in the DBA_DB_LINKS data dictionary view.

> **Caution**
>
> DBA_DB_LINKS is one of the views that can store passwords in clear text, if the database link is defined with a specific UserID and password to connect to the remote database. Care should be taken when enabling end users access to this database view.

PACKAGES, PROCEDURES, AND FUNCTIONS

Stored packages, procedures, and functions are stored in the data dictionary, along with their source code. A stored procedure is a code unit that does work, can be passed arguments, and can return values. A stored function is a code unit that is passed an argument and returns one value. A package is a collection of procedures, variables, and functions, logically grouped by function. See Chapter 26, "SQL*Plus for Administrators," for more information.

You can access information on stored packages, procedures and functions through the DBA_OBJECTS and DBA_SOURCE views.

CHAPTER 6

THE ORACLE INSTANCE ARCHITECTURE

In this chapter

INTRODUCTION

When someone refers to the Oracle database, they are most likely referring to the entire Oracle database management system (DBMS). But as an Oracle professional, you must recognize the difference between the database and the instance—a distinction often confusing to non-Oracle administrators. In this chapter you explore the structure and configuration of the Oracle instance, and continue your exploration of the internals of the Oracle Relational Database Management System (RDBMS) in the next chapter by looking in-depth at the Oracle database. (To avoid confusion, the term RDBMS is used to describe the entire data management server consisting of the Oracle database and instance.) The creation of the instance is automatic and behind the scenes. The details of how and when this happens are also discussed.

DEFINING THE INSTANCE

To provide the degree of service, flexibility, and performance that Oracle clients expect, much of the work done by the database is handled by a complex set of memory structures and operating system processes called the *instance*. Every Oracle database has an instance associated with it, and unless the Oracle Parallel Server option is implemented, a database is mounted by only one instance. The organization of the instance allows the RDBMS to service many varied types of transactions from multiple users simultaneously, while at the same time providing first class performance, fault tolerance, data integrity, and security.

> **Note**
>
> This chapter defines the term *process* as any running task, operating without user intervention. Your particular OS might refer to processes as processes, or it might use other terminology, such as *tasks, jobs, threads*, and the like.

The instance structure is loosely styled after UNIX's implementation of the multitasking operating system. Discrete processes perform specialized tasks within the RDBMS that work together to accomplish the goals of the instance. Each process has a separate memory block that it uses to store private variables, address stacks, and other runtime information. The processes use a common shared memory area in which to do their work—a section of memory that can be written to and read from at the same time by many different programs and processes. This memory block is called the *System Global Area* (SGA).

> **Note**
>
> Because the SGA resides in a shared memory segment, it is also often referred to as the Shared Global Area.

You might think of the background processes as the hands of the database, handling its components directly; and you might think of the SGA as the brain, indirectly coordinating the *hands* in their information and storage retrieval as necessary. The SGA takes part in all information and server processing that occurs in the database.

Note

Single user Oracle configurations, such as Personal Oracle Lite, do not use multiple processes to perform database functions. Instead, all database functions are contained within one Oracle process. For this reason, single user is also known as single process Oracle.

CREATING THE INSTANCE

Opening an Oracle database involves three steps:

1. Creating the Oracle instance (nomount stage).
2. Mounting the database by the instance (mount stage).
3. Opening the database (open stage).

The Oracle instance is created during the nomount stage of database startup. When the database passes through the nomount phase, the init.ora parameter file is read, the background processes are started, and the SGA is initialized. The init.ora file defines the configuration of the instance, including such things as the size of the memory structures and the number and type of background processes started. The instance name is set according to the value of the ORACLE_SID environment variable and does not have to be the same as the database name being opened (but for convenience, it usually is). The next stage the database passes through is called the mount stage. The value of the control file parameter of the init.ora file determines the database the instance mounts. In the mount stage, the control file is read and accessible, and queries and modifications to the data stored within the control file can be performed. The final stage of the database is when it is opened. In this stage the database files whose names are stored in the control file are locked for exclusive use by the instance, and the database is made accessible to normal users. Open is the normal operating state of the database. Until a database is open, only the DBA is capable of accessing the database, and only through the Server Manager utilities.

In order to change the operating state of the database, you must be connected to the database as internal, or with SYSDBA privileges. When you go from a shutdown state to an open state you can step through each operating state explicitly, but when you shut down the database you can only go from the current operating state to a complete shutdown. For example, you can issue the STARTUP NOMOUNT command in the Server Manager utility. This will put your database into the nomount stage. Next, you can issue ALTER DATABASE MOUNT or ALTER DATABASE OPEN to step through the operating stages. At any operating state, if you issue a SHUTDOWN command you will completely shutdown the database. For example, you cannot go from an open state to a mount state.

An instance that does not have a database mounted is referred to as idle—it uses memory but does not do any work. An instance can only attach to one database, and unless Parallel Server is being used, a database only has one instance assigned to it. The instance is the brain of the data management system—it does all the work while the database stores all the data.

THE COMPONENTS OF THE ORACLE INSTANCE

Figure 6.1 is a visual representation of the Oracle instance. Explanations of the different components follow.

Figure 6.1
The Oracle Instance is a complex interaction of memory and background processes.

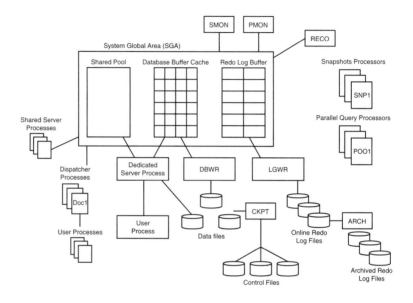

Many parameters and techniques exist to help you configure the instance to best support your applications and requirements. Configuring the instance objects for peak performance is, in most cases, a trial and error procedure—you can start with likely parameter values, but only time and monitoring give you the best possible mix of all settings and variables.

Configuring instance parameters involves changing the necessary `init.ora` parameter and *bouncing* (stopping and starting) the database. There are numerous `init.ora` parameters, and many of these are undocumented. Although you should not change or add unfamiliar initialization parameters, you can reference the internal `x$ksppi` table to view all the possible initialization parameters for a database. The `ksppinm` and `ksppdesc` columns give you the parameter name and a brief description of the parameter, respectively.

Note

Manipulating initialization file parameters without a clear understanding of the possible consequences is dangerous! There are many parameters that exist for pure diagnostic reasons, which can leave your database in an unsynchronized or corrupted state. Undocumented parameters are named with a leading underscore. Do not add or change keys or values in the `init.ora` file unless you are confident in what you are doing!

For the most part, instance configuration is primarily concerned with the objects in the SGA, and you find most of your database configuration and tuning time spent with these structures. However, there are issues and configuration options with the background processes that also need to be addressed, and you explore those parts of the instance as well.

THE SYSTEM GLOBAL AREA (SGA)

The SGA is the primary component of the instance. It holds all the memory structures necessary for data manipulation, SQL statement parsing, and redo caching. The SGA is shared, which means that multiple processes can access and modify the data contained within it at the same time. All database operations use structures contained in the SGA at one point or another. As mentioned in the previous section, the SGA is when the instance is created, during the nomount stage of the database, and is deallocated when the instance is shut down.

The SGA consists of the following:

- Shared pool
- Database buffer cache
- Redo log buffer
- Multithreaded server (MTS) structures

These are explained in the following sections.

THE SHARED POOL

The shared pool (see Figure 6.2) contains the library cache, the dictionary cache, and server control structures (such as the database character set). The library cache stores the text, parsed format, and execution plan of SQL statements that have been submitted to the RDBMS, as well as the headers of PL/SQL packages and procedures that have been executed. The dictionary cache stores data dictionary rows that have been used to parse SQL statements.

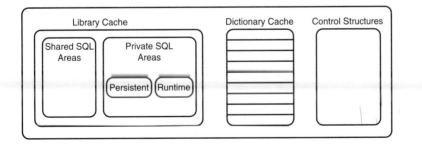

Figure 6.2
The shared pool caches information used when parsing and executing SQL statements.

The Oracle server uses the library cache to improve the performance of SQL statements. When a SQL statement is submitted, the server first checks the library cache to see if an identical statement has already been submitted and cached. If it has, Oracle uses the stored parse tree and execution path for the statement, rather than rebuilding these structures from scratch. Although this might not affect the performance of ad hoc queries, applications using stored code can gain significant performance improvements by utilizing this feature.

> **Note**
>
> For a SQL statement to use a previously cached version, it must be identical in *all* respects to the cached version, including punctuation and letter case–upper versus lower. Oracle identifies the statements by applying a hashing algorithm to the text of the statement–the hash value generated must be identical for both the current and cached statements in order for the cached version to be used.

The library cache contains both *shared* and *private* SQL areas. The shared SQL area contains the parse tree and execution path for SQL statements, whereas the private SQL area contains session specific information, such as bind variables, environment and session parameters, runtime stacks and buffers, and so on. A private SQL area is created for each transaction initiated, and it is deallocated after the cursor corresponding to that private area is closed. The number of private SQL areas a user session can have open at one time is limited by the value of the OPEN_CURSORS init.ora parameter. Using these two structures, the Oracle server can reuse the information common across all executions of an SQL statement, while session specific information to the execution can be retrieved from the private SQL area. It is important to note however, that the session-specific information contained within the User Global Area (UGA) of a user's Process Global Area (PGA), including the private SQL areas, is held in the SGA only with a Multithreaded Server (MTS) instance. Otherwise, it is held in the dedicated server.

> **Note**
>
> An application that does not close cursors as they are used continues to allocate more and more memory for the application, in part because of the private SQL areas allocated for each open cursor.

The private SQL area of the library cache is further divided into *persistent* and *runtime* areas. Persistent areas contain information that is valid and applicable through multiple executions of the SQL statement, whereas the runtime area contains data that is used only while the SQL statement is being executed.

The dictionary cache holds data dictionary information used by the RDBMS engine to parse SQL statements. Information such as segment information, security and access privileges, and available free storage space is held in this area.

The size of the shared pool is determined by the init.ora parameter SHARED_POOL_SIZE. This value is specified in bytes. You must set this value high enough to ensure that enough space is available to load and store PL/SQL blocks and SQL statements. The shared pool becomes fragmented over time from the loading and unloading of data objects, and errors can occur if there is not enough contiguous free space in the pool to load an object. You can solve this problem in the short term by issuing the SQL command ALTER SYSTEM FLUSH SHARED_POOL, but if you are regularly encountering shared pool errors during database operation, you have to increase the shared pool size.

THE DATABASE BUFFER CACHE

The operation of the database buffer cache is one of the biggest factors affecting overall database performance. The buffer cache is made up of memory blocks the same size as the Oracle blocks. All data manipulated by Oracle is first loaded into the buffer cache before being used. Any data updates are performed on the blocks in memory. For this reason, it is obviously very important to size the buffer cache correctly. Memory access is hundreds of times faster than disk access, and in an OLTP environment, most of your data operations should take place completely in memory, using database blocks already loaded into the cache.

The Oracle RDBMS swaps data out of the buffer cache according to a Least Recently Used (LRU) list. The LRU list keeps track of what data blocks are accessed and how often. When a block is accessed or retrieved into the buffer cache, it is placed on the Most Recently Used (MRU) end of the list. When the Oracle server needs more space in the buffer cache to read a data block from disk, it accesses the LRU list to decide which blocks to swap out. Those blocks at the far end of the MRU side are removed first. This way, blocks that are frequently accessed are kept in memory.

> **Note**
>
> The exception to the LRU loading rule is that data that is accessed through a full table scan is automatically placed at the bottom of the LRU list. This behavior can be overridden by specifying the table as CACHE.

Buffer blocks that have been modified are called *dirty* and are placed on the dirty list. The dirty list keeps track of all data modifications made to the cache that have not been flushed to disk. When Oracle receives a request to change data, the data change is made to the blocks in the buffer cache and written to the redo log, and then the block is put on the dirty list. Subsequent access to this data reads the new value from the changed data in the buffer cache.

The Oracle server uses deferred, multiblock writes to lessen the impact of disk I/O on database performance. This means that an update to a piece of data does not immediately update the data in the data files. The RDBMS waits to flush changed data to the data files until a predetermined number of blocks have been changed, space needs to be reclaimed from the cache to load new data, a checkpoint occurs, or DBWR times out. When DBWR is signaled to perform a buffer cache write, it moves a group of blocks to the data files.

The key to configuring the buffer cache is to ensure that the correct amount of memory is allocated for optimal caching of data. This doesn't necessarily mean allocating all possible memory resources to the buffer cache; however, as in most computer applications, there is a point of diminishing returns with increased memory allocation. There is a point of diminishing return in adding memory to obtain an increasingly better cache hit ratio. The memory you are allocating to the buffer cache could be better used in other places, such as other Oracle memory structures.

Two initialization parameters determine the size of the buffer cache—DB_BLOCK_SIZE and DB_BLOCK_BUFFERS. The DB_BLOCK_SIZE parameter is used during database creation to set the size of the Oracle block, which is explained in detail in Chapter 7, "Exploring the Oracle Environment." The DB_BLOCK_BUFFERS parameter determines the number of blocks to allocate to the buffer cache. Multiplying DB_BLOCK_SIZE × DB_BLOCK_BUFFERS gives you the total amount of memory (in bytes) of the buffer cache.

THE REDO LOG BUFFER

The redo log buffer is used to store redo information in memory before it is flushed to the online redo log files. It is a circular buffer, which means that it fills from top to bottom and then returns to the beginning of the buffer. As the redo log buffer fills, its contents are written to the online redo log files.

The redo log buffer is sized by means of the LOG_BUFFER initialization parameter. The value is specified in bytes and determines how much space is reserved in memory to cache redo log entries. If this value is set too low, processes contend with each other and the Log Writer (LGWR) (explained later in this chapter) process reading and writing to the buffer, possibly causing performance problems. This is, however, a rarity in all but the most active of databases and can be monitored using the V$SYSSTAT view. Query V$SYSSTAT$ for the *value* field with the field *name* equal to *redo log space requests*. This indicates the time user processes spent waiting for the redo log buffer.

To enforce the sequential nature of the redo log writes, the Oracle server controls access to the buffer using a *latch*. A latch a lock by an Oracle process on a memory structure—similar in concept to a file or row lock. A process must hold the redo allocation latch to be capable of writing to the redo log buffer. While one process holds the allocation latch, no other process can write to the redo log buffer using the allocation latch.

The Oracle server limits the amount of redo that can be written at one time using the value of the initialization parameter LOG_SMALL_ENTRY_MAX_SIZE. This parameter is specified in bytes, and the default value varies depending on OS and hardware. For servers with multiple CPUs, the Oracle server does not allow redo entries needing space greater than the value of the LOG_SMALL_ENTRY_MAX_SIZE parameter to be written using the redo allocation latch. Instead, processes must hold a redo copy latch. The number of redo copy latches available is equal to the value of the LOG_SIMULTANEOUS_COPIES initialization parameter. The default for LOG_SIMULTANEOUS_COPIES is the number of CPUs in the system. Using redo copy latches, multiple processes can simultaneously write to the redo log buffer.

You can monitor the redo allocation and copy latches using the V$LATCH dynamic performance view. (See Chapter 18, "Tuning Memory," for more information on tuning the redo latches.)

THE ORACLE BACKGROUND PROCESSES

Within any given second, an Oracle database can be processing many rows of information, handling hundreds of simultaneous user requests, and performing complex data manipulations, all while providing the highest level of performance and data integrity. To accomplish these tasks, the Oracle database divides the grunt work between a number of programs, each of which operates in large part independently of one another and has a specific role to play. These programs are referred to as the Oracle *background processes*, and are the key to effectively handling the many operational stresses placed upon the database. A complete understanding of the background processes and the tasks they perform helps you analyze performance problems, pinpoint bottlenecks, and diagnose trouble spots in your database.

The Oracle background processes are as follows:

- SMON and PMON
- DBWR
- LGWR
- Dnnn
- ARCH
- CKPT
- RECO
- SNPn
- LCKn
- Pnnn
- Snnn

Also of interest are the user and server processes, which handle user transactions against the database, and the Parallel Query (Pnnn) processes, which perform parallel query operations for the database. Although these are not classified as Oracle background processes, it is important to understand the role they play in the Oracle environment. A discussion of each of these processes follows.

PART

II

CH

6

SMON AND PMON

For one reason or another, connections into the Oracle database might crash, hang, or otherwise abnormally terminate. End users might shut down their client machine without logging out of the database application, or a network or system failure unrelated to the database might cause an automated database job to fail. The Oracle server must be capable of transparently resolving the problems resulting from these kinds of failures.

Together SMON and PMON are the background processes responsible for automatically resolving database system problems. PMON, the Process Monitor, performs automatic cleanup of terminated or failed processes, including clearing the orphaned sessions left from an abnormally terminated process, rolling back uncommitted transactions, releasing the locks held by disconnected processes, and freeing SGA resources held by failed processes. It also monitors the server and dispatcher processes, automatically restarting them if they fail.

SMON, the System Monitor, plays a smaller but nonetheless very important role. Upon database startup, SMON is the process that performs automatic instance recovery. If the last database shutdown was not clean, SMON automatically rolls forward the operations that were in progress, and rolls back the uncommitted transactions. SMON is also the process that manages certain database segments, reclaiming temporary segment space no longer in use, and automatically combining contiguous blocks of free space in data files.

> **Note**
>
> SMON only combines free space in tablespaces where the default storage parameter—used when creating tablespaces or tables—pctincrease is not 0. Set the pctincrease to at least 1 if you want SMON to automatically handle this operation.

SMON and PMON are two of the required background processes. The database does not start if either of these two processes fail on startup.

DBWR

DBWR, or the mandatory Database Writer process, is responsible for writing the dirty blocks from the database buffer cache to the data files. Rather than write out each block as it is modified, DBWR waits until certain criteria are met, and in batch reads the dirty list and flushes all the blocks found in it to the data files. This provides a high level of performance and minimizes the extent to which the database is I/O bound.

DBWR flushes the dirty blocks when

- a checkpoint occurs,
- the dirty list reaches a specified length, determined by half of the value for the init.ora parameter DB_BLOCK_WRITE_BATCH,
- the number of used buffers reaches the value of the init.ora parameter DB_BLOCK_MAX_SCAN, or
- a DBWR timeout occurs (about every three seconds).

Configuring the DBWR background process is fairly straightforward, and the default values for settings are in many cases sufficient for a small- or medium-sized database. Larger, more active or specialized databases often have special needs, however, that force the manual configuration of some of the DBWR parameters.

In most installations, there is one DBWR process to handle all the write activity of the database. You can, however, start more than one DBWR process if you find DBWR is incapable of keeping up with the demands of the database. The init.ora parameter DB_WRITERS, which defaults to 1, sets the number of DBWR processes that are created at startup. In most cases, the decision to use more than one DBWR process is only made when the OS on which the Oracle server is being run does not support a synchronous I/O. If this is the case, multiple DBWR processes should be created. Some suggest that you should use as many DBWR processes as physical disks used to store data files on; others suggest setting the number to be equal to the number of data files in the database. Experiment with adding and subtracting DBWR processes until your best performer is reached.

The database buffer cache also uses latches to control access to the memory structure. The LRU latch controls the replacement of buffers in the buffer cache. In very active servers with multiple CPUs, there might be contention for these latches. If this happens, set the parameter DB_BLOCK_LRU_LATCHES to a number equal to the number of latches to create for the buffer cache. This number cannot be greater than twice the number of CPUs and is automatically set to the number of CPUs in the system.

Another init.ora parameter that affects DBWR behavior is DB_BLOCK_CHECKPOINT_BATCH. This parameter sets the maximum number of blocks DBWR writes with each checkpoint (see the section below on the checkpoint process, CKPT, for more information). By increasing this number, you can decrease the number of times DBWR must flush the buffer cache. Increasing this number too much, however, might cause an unacceptable delay when DBWR finally does flush the buffer.

A third parameter to keep in mind is DB_BLOCK_CHECKSUM. This is a Boolean parameter that, when enabled, causes each database block to be written with a checksum value attached. When the block is subsequently read, the checksum is computed and compared with that stored in the database. If the values are different, an error is raised. This is a valuable parameter when troubleshooting data corruption problems, but should not be enabled all the time because of the performance hit taken from calculating and storing the checksum for each I/O operation.

LGWR

LGWR, or Log Writer, is the fourth and final mandatory background process. Log Writer is the process that writes redo log entries from the redo log buffer in the SGA to the online redo log files. LGWR performs this write when a commit occurs, the inactivity timeout for LGWR is reached, the redo log buffer becomes one-third full, or DBWR completes a flush of the data buffer blocks at a checkpoint. LGWR also handles multiple user commits simultaneously, if one or more users issue a commit before LGWR has completed flushing the buffer on behalf of another user's commit.

It is important to note that Oracle does not regard a transaction as being complete until LGWR has flushed the redo information from the redo buffer to the online redo logs. It is LGWR's successful writing of the redo log entries into the online redo logs, and not the changing of the data in the data files, which returns a success code to the server process.

The LGWR process is rarely a source of performance problems for the database. In addition, few options are available for custom configuration of LGWR. Most of the configuration necessary involves the redo log buffer and memory structures supporting that buffer, rather than the LGWR process itself.

The exception to this, however, deals with the secondary task of the LGWR process, performing the operations necessary to conduct a database checkpoint. The LGWR performs this task unless the CKPT process is activated. A checkpoint causes process and I/O time to be spent by both LGWR and DBWR. More frequent checkpoints decrease the recovery time necessary if a database failure occurs, as well as reducing the work necessary to perform each individual checkpoint. You must weigh both of these factors when deciding on the correct checkpoint interval. Several parameters govern the occurrence of database checkpoints.

LOG_CHECKPOINT_INTERVAL and LOG_CHECKPOINT_TIMEOUT are two parameters that can change the checkpoint interval—that is, the time or situation necessary for a database checkpoint to be triggered. LOG_CHECKPOINT_INTERVAL, when set, causes a checkpoint to be triggered when a number of OS blocks (not Oracle blocks) is written to redo. LOG_CHECKPOINT_TIMEOUT, when set, causes a checkpoint to occur after the interval (in seconds) specified for the parameter.

These parameters should be used with care. If LOG_CHECKPOINT_INTERVAL is used, it should be set so that the number of OS blocks that trigger a checkpoint are relative to the size of the redo log group. Remember that when a redo log group fills, a checkpoint is triggered. Be careful that you do not set a LOG_CHECKPOINT_INTERVAL value that causes more checkpoints to occur than necessary or forces checkpoints when they are not needed. For example, consider a redo log group of 3MB, and a LOG_CHECKPOINT_INTERVAL set to 2.5MB. When 2.5MB are written to the redo logs, the LOG_CHECKPOINT_INTERVAL value causes a checkpoint to occur. In addition, when the redo log group fills (after only 0.5MB have been written), another checkpoint occurs. In essence, two checkpoints will occur right after each other.

You can also control the frequency of checkpoints by sizing your redo log groups accordingly. If you size your logs so that a log switch occurs every hour, you only have one checkpoint an hour from redo log group switches. However, if your groups are sized so that checkpoints occur every five minutes, you waste a lot of process and I/O time performing the related checkpoints.

A final parameter that is of use is the Boolean LOG_CHECKPOINTS_TO_ALERT. This places a stamp in the alert.log file for the database whenever a checkpoint occurs and is valuable when trying to pinpoint the exact checkpoint interval.

DISPATCHER PROCESSES (Dnnn)

As mentioned previously, server processes can be either dedicated to a user process or shared among user processes. Using shared servers requires configuring the Multithreaded Server (MTS), as discussed in Chapter 37, "Installing and Configuring the OAS". When using shared server processes, at least one dispatcher process must be present, and more can be present depending on the needs of the environment. The dispatcher process passes user requests to the SGA request queue and returns the server responses back to the correct user process.

The number of dispatcher processes is controlled using a number of init.ora parameters. The MTS_DISPATCHERS parameter specifies the protocol the dispatcher uses as well as the number of dispatchers to start that use the protocol. Multiple protocol groups can be configured using multiple MTS_DISPATCHERS lines. A typical MTS_DISPATCHER line might look like this:

```
MTS_DISPATCHERS = "tcp, 4"
MTS_DISPATCHERS = "spx, 2"
```

Multiple protocol groups can also be configured within the same MTS_DISPATCHERS parameter, like so

```
MTS_DISPATCHERS = ("tcp, 4", "spx, 2")
```

The MTS_MAX_DISPATCHERS parameter controls the maximum number of dispatcher processes allowed for the RDBMS. (See Chapter 34, "The Advanced Security Option," for more details on configuring the MTS services.)

ARCH

The archiver process is responsible for copying full online redo logs to the archived redo log files. This only occurs when the database is operating in ARCHIVELOG mode. Archivelog mode is required for point-in-time recovery. It also permits "hot" backups. While the archiver is copying the redo log, no other processes can write to the log. This is important to keep in mind, because of the circular nature of the redo logs. If the database needs to switch redo logs but the archiver is still copying the next log in the sequence, all database activity halts until archiver finishes. Also note that if ARCH is for some reason unable to finish copying the log, it waits until the error stopping it from finishing the write is resolved.

It is important to note that the ARCHIVE_LOG_START parameter in the init.ora file must be set to TRUE for ARCH to automatically start when a database opens. Placing the database in archivelog mode is in itself not enough to cause ARCH to automatically start. If you do configure archivelog mode and don't automatically start the ARCH process, the database hangs when all online redo logs fill, waiting for you to manually archive the online logs.

CKPT

CKPT, the checkpoint process, is an optional background process that performs the checkpoint tasks that LGWR would normally perform—namely updating the data file and control file headers with the current version information. Enable this process to reduce the amount of work on LGWR when there are frequent checkpoints occurring, frequent log switches, or many data files in the database.

Setting the CHECKPOINT PROCESS parameter to TRUE enables the CKPT process. All other parameters related to checkpoints that are described also hold true when the CKPT process is running.

PART

II

CH

6

> **Caution**
>
> With Oracle 8.x, the CHECKPOINT_PROCESS parameter is obsolete because it is already integrated into the RDBMS with a setting of TRUE. If you include it in your Oracle 8.x init.ora file, your instance will fail to start.

RECO

RECO, the recovery process, is responsible for recovering failed transactions in distributed database systems. It is automatically started when the database is configured for distributed transactions (that is, when the DISTRIBUTED_TRANSACTIONS init.ora parameter is set to a value greater than zero). The RECO process operates with little or no DBA intervention when an in-doubt transaction occurs in a distributed system. The RECO process attempts to connect to the remote database and resolves the in-doubt transaction when a database connection is successful. (See Chapter 40, "Distributed Database Management," for more information on RECO and the two phase commit.)

SNPn

SNPn, the snapshot process, handles the automatic refreshing of database snapshots and runs the database procedures scheduled through the DBMS_JOB package. The init.ora parameter JOB_QUEUE_PROCESS sets how many snapshot processes are started, and JOB_QUEUE_INTERVAL determines how long (in seconds) the snapshot processes sleep before waking to process any pending jobs or transactions.

LCKn

In a parallel server environment, multiple instances mount one database. The lock process is responsible for managing and coordinating the locks held by the individual instances. Each instance in the parallel server installation has 1–10 lock processes assigned, and each instance must have the same number. This process has no purpose in a non-parallel server environment. See Chapter 39, "Parallel Server Management," for more information on the Lock background process.

Pnnn

Parallel query processes are named Pnnn. The Oracle server starts and stops query processes depending on database activity and your configuration of the parallel query option. These processes are involved in parallel index creations, table creations, and queries. There are always as many processes started as specified in the PARALLEL_MIN_SERVERS parameter, and there are never more than as specified by PARALLEL_MAX_SERVERS.

For more information on configuring the parallel query processes, see Chapter 38, "Parallel Query Management."

USER AND SERVER PROCESSES (Snnn)

Applications and utilities access the RDBMS through a user process. The user process connects to a server process, which can be *dedicated* to one user process or shared (with MTS) among many. The server process parses and executes SQL statements that are submitted to it and returns the result sets back to the user process. It is also the process that reads data blocks from the data files into the database buffer cache.

Each user process is allocated a section of memory referred to as the Process Global Area (PGA). The contents of the PGA differ depending on what type of connection is made to the database. When a user process connects to the database via a dedicated server process, user session data, stack space, and cursor state information is stored in the PGA. The user session data consists of security and resource usage information; the stack space contains local variables specific to the user session; and the cursor state area contains runtime information for the cursor, including rows returned and cursor return codes. If, however, the user process connects through a shared server process, the session and cursor state information is stored within the SGA. Although this does not increase the memory requirements for the database as a whole, it does require a larger SGA to hold the extra session information.

Anatomy of a Transaction

To gain a better understanding of how all the preceding components of the instance interact, look at a typical transaction as it moves through the instance structures.

A transaction begins when a user session connects to a server session using an SQL*Net driver. This connection can be a dedicated connection with its own server process or a shared connection handled through a dispatcher process. The server session hashes the SQL statement passed to it and compares that hash number with the hash numbers of statements already saved in the shared SQL area. If an exact duplicate of the statement is found in the shared pool, the parsed form of the statement and the execution plan that are already stored are used. If a match is not found in the shared pool, the server session parses the statement.

Next, the server session checks to see whether the data blocks necessary to complete the transaction are already stored in the database buffer cache. If the blocks are not in the cache, the server session reads the necessary blocks from the data files and copies them into the cache. If the transaction is a query, the server session returns the results of the query to the user session (performing the data block read and copy as many times as necessary to return all data).

For a transaction that modifies data, there are more steps involved. For this example, assume the transaction is an update. After the necessary data blocks are read into the buffer cache, the blocks in memory are modified. Modifying cached blocks marks them as dirty, and they are placed on the dirty list. Redo information is also generated, and is stored in the redo log cache.

The transaction continues until one of several things happens. If the transaction is relatively short lived (for example, an update to one row of sales data), it finishes and the user commits, which signals LGWR to flush the redo log buffer to the online redo log files. If the transaction is fairly long and complex, any of the following can happen:

- The redo generated causes the redo log buffer to become one-third full. This triggers a redo log buffer flush by LGWR.

- The number of blocks placed on the dirty list reaches a threshold length. This triggers DBWR to flush all the dirty blocks in the database buffer cache to the data files, which in turn also causes LGWR to flush the redo log buffer cache to disk.

- A database checkpoint occurs. This triggers a database buffer cache flush, as well as a redo log cache flush.

- The number of available free buffers in the buffer cache drops below the threshold value. This also causes a database buffer cache flush.

- An unrecoverable database error occurs. This forces the transaction to be terminated and rolled back and an error reported back to the server session.

While the transaction is processing with redo being generated to the redo cache and flushed, the online redo logs gradually fill. When the current log fills, LGWR begins writing to the next log group, while ARCH copies the redo log to disk or tape. Because the transaction never records as successful until all redo log information is written from the redo log buffer to the online redo logs, both LGWR and ARCH must be capable of completing their respective tasks without error.

MONITORING THE INSTANCE

For the majority of the time, the SGA and Oracle background processes operate without administrator intervention. However, there are times when problems must be diagnosed and fixed. There are several methods available to the DBA to monitor and track the behavior of the instance and its associated structures.

USING THE TRACE FILES

The best place to find information about instance problems is in the trace files of the processes themselves. These trace files are written to the location defined in the USER_DUMP_DEST or BACKGROUND_DUMP_DEST, depending on the specific process and the error encountered. When a background process is terminated or abnormally aborts an operation, it usually produces a trace file containing the error message(s) causing the failure, dumps of the current process stacks, currently executing cursors, and any other information pertinent to the problem. Although some of this information is useful to you as a DBA, it is more important to collect and forward these trace files to Oracle worldwide customer support consultants who might be able to help you diagnose your problems. They have tools available to pinpoint exactly where the problem occurs. Background process failures also usually write an entry into the alert.log file for the database or to their own separate trace files located in the directory specified by the init.ora parameter background_dump_dest.

TRACKING THROUGH THE OPERATING SYSTEM

Background processes can also be tracked through the OS using system commands. In a UNIX environment, each background process is a separate task and can therefore be tracked separately. It is often very valuable to look at OS memory and CPU utilization of processes (using such tools as sar, ps, vmstat, and top) to identify performance problems or runaway queries. Sometimes the only way to resolve a hung or broken server or user processes is by terminating them at the OS level. Use caution, however, when attempting to modify or terminate any other Oracle background process. Most background processes will crash the entire database if abnormally terminated.

In an NT server environment, tracking the background processes is a little trickier. This is because the entire Oracle instance is implemented on the NT OS as a single background process called a *service*. The individual background processes are implemented as threads belonging to the service. Although there are plenty of utilities available on NT to track and monitor the behavior of processes, thread administration tools are fairly uncommon. One solution is to use the Performance Monitor utility that ships with the NT OS to monitor, among other things, the memory consumption and context switches of all the threads belonging to the service. By converting the SPID column from the following query from decimal to hexadecimal, you can match the NT thread ID with the background process from the Oracle side.

```
SELECT spid, name FROM V$process, V$bgprocess WHERE addr = paddr;
```

See Appendix C, "Oracle on Windows NT," for more information on tuning and tracking NT background threads.

USING THE V$ TABLES TO MONITOR INSTANCE STRUCTURES

Numerous dynamic performance views are available to the DBA to display instance information. These views are invaluable when attempting to discover the current state of the database instance and troubleshoot problems related to the instance.

MONITORING DATABASE CONNECTIONS

Both user and background processes that are connected to the instance can be monitored using the V$ views. The V$process view displays information about all processes that are connected to the database, including background and user processes. V$bgprocess contains a list of all possible background processes, with an additional column, PADDR, which contains the hexadecimal address of running background processes (or 00 for those that are not running).

The columns of interest to you from the V$process table are as shown in Table 6.1:

TABLE 6.1   V$process **TABLE COLUMNS**

Column	Usage
ADDR	Oracle address of the process
PID	Oracle process ID
SPID	OS system process ID
USERNAME	OS process owner
SERIAL#	Oracle process serial #
TERMINAL	OS terminal identifier
PROGRAM	OS program connection
BACKGROUND	1 for background process, NULL for user process

The columns of interest to you from the V$bgprocess table are as shown in Table 6.2.

TABLE 6.2   V$bgprocess **TABLE COLUMNS**

Column	Usage
PADDR	Oracle process address (same as ADDR column of V$process)
NAME	Name of the background process
DESCRIPTION	Description of the background process
ERROR	Error state code (0 for no error)

You can display the addresses and names of all running background processes by joining the V$process and V$bgprocess table, as in the following query:

```
SELECT spid, name
FROM V$process, V$bgprocess
WHERE paddr(+) = addr;
```

Information about user sessions that are connected to the database are stored in the V$session view. The V$session view contains many fields, and a great deal of valuable information can be accessed from this view.

The columns of interest from the V$session view are as shown in Table 6.3.

TABLE 6.3   V$session **COLUMNS**

Column	Usage
SID	Session identifier
SERIAL#	Session serial #
PADDR	Address of parent session
USER#	Oracle user identifier (from the SYS.USER$ table)

Column	Usage
USERNAME	Oracle username
COMMAND	Current command in progress for this session. For number to command translations, see the sys.audit_actions table.
STATUS	Status of the session (ACTIVE, INACTIVE, KILLED)
SERVER	Type of server connection the session has(DEDICATED, SHARED, PSEDUO, or NONE)
OSUSER	OS Username the connection has been made from
PROGRAM	OS Program making the connection into the database
TERMINAL	Type of terminal the connection is made from
TYPE	Type of session (BACKGROUND or USER) SQL_HASH_VALUE and SQL_ADDRESS. Used to uniquely identify the currently executing SQL statement

The following query displays important information on connected processes. It also demonstrates the manner in which the process views relate to each other:

```
col bgproc format a6 heading 'BGProc'
col action format a10 heading 'DB Action'
col program format a10
col username format a8
col terminal format a10

SELECT
 b.name bgproc, p.spid, s.sid, p.serial#, s.osuser,
 s.username, s.terminal,
 DECODE(a.name, 'UNKNOWN', '-----', a.name) action
FROM
 V$process p, V$session s, V$bgprocess b,
 sys.audit_actions a
WHERE
 p.addr=s.paddr(+) AND b.paddr(+) = s.paddr AND
 a.action = NVL(s.action, 0)
ORDER BY
 sid;
```

By querying the V$access view, you can display information on what database objects users are currently accessing. This is useful when trying to figure out what a third-party application or undocumented procedure is doing and can also be useful to resolve security problems. By using a DBA account to run an application or procedure that is giving you security problems, you can determine the exact objects to which security should be granted.

Finally, the V$mts view contains tracking information for shared server processes. This view contains columns for maximum connections, servers started, servers terminated, and servers highwater.

MONITORING THE SHARED SQL AREA

Often it is useful to be able to look into the RDBMS engine and see what SQL statements are being executed. The V$sqlarea view contains information on SQL statements in the

PART

II

CH

6

shared SQL area, including the text of SQL statements executed, the number of users accessing the statements, disk blocks and memory blocks accessed while executing the statement, and other information.

> **Note**
>
> The `disk_reads` and `buffer_gets` columns that are found in `V$sqlarea` track the number of blocks that are read from disk and from the buffer cache. These two columns are quick and easy ways to find queries that are utilizing large amounts of database resources.

The `V$open_cursor` view is also useful to investigate cursors that have not yet been closed. The following query displays all open cursors for a given user's SID:

```
SELECT b.piece, a.sql_text
FROM V$open_cursor a, V$sqltext b
WHERE
  a.sid = &SID and
  a.address = b.address and
  a.hash_value = b.hash_value
ORDER BY
  b.address, b.hash_value, b.piece asc;
```

The `V$sqltext` view can also be used to determine what SQL statements are passed to the database engine. Unlike `V$sqlarea`, which only stores the first 80 characters of the SQL statement, this view holds the entire SQL statement. The `V$sqltext_with_newlines` view is identical to `V$sqltext`, except that the newline characters in the SQL statements have been left in place.

> **Note**
>
> The SQL statements stored in `V$sqltext` are split into pieces. To retrieve the entire statement, you have to retrieve all the parts of the SQL statement and order by the `PIECE` column.

MONITORING THE SGA

There are two `V$` views available that provide information about the operation of the SGA. The `V$sga` view displays the size (in bytes) of each major component of the SGA, including the redo log cache, the database buffer cache, and the shared pool. The `V$sgastat` contains much more interesting information. Within this view you find the specific size for each individual memory structure contained in the SGA, including the memory set aside for stack space and PL/SQL variables and stacks. You can also query this view to find the amount of free memory available in the SGA:

```
SELECT bytes FROM V$sgastat WHERE name = 'free memory';
```

MONITORING THE LIBRARY AND DICTIONARY CACHE

Two views exist that contain information regarding the library and data dictionary cache. V$librarycache contains library cache performance information for each type of object in the library cache. The V$rowcache view contains performance information for the data dictionary cache. (See 38 for more information on these views and the information contained in them.)

MONITORING THE PARALLEL QUERY PROCESSES

The V$pq_sysstat and V$pq_tqstat views contain information on the parallel server processes and their behavior. Query V$pq_sysstat to display current runtime information on parallel query servers, such as the number of query servers busy and idle and dynamic server creation and termination statistics. The V$pq_tqstat view contains information on queries that have previously run that used parallel query servers. (See Chapter 38 for more information on tracking the parallel servers.)

MONITORING THE ARCHIVER PROCESSES

Archiver activity is stored in the V$archive view. You can retrieve information on the archived logs written by ARCH from this view. (For an explanation of the columns in this view, see Chapter 39.)

MONITORING THE MULTITHREADED SERVER PROCESSES

The Vmts, Vdispatcher, and V$shared_server views contain information on the status of the MTS processes and memory structures. V$mts contains tracking information on the shared server processes such as the number of servers started, terminated, and the highwater value for running servers. V$dispatcher contains information on the dispatcher processes running. From this view you can query the name, supported protocol, number of bytes processed, number of messages processed, current status, and other runtime information relating to the dispatcher processes. The V$shared_server view provides the same type of information for the shared server processes running.

(See Chapter33, "Oracle Networking Fundamentals," for more information on setting up and tuning the shared server and dispatcher processes.)

CHAPTER

7

EXPLORING THE ORACLE ENVIRONMENT

In this chapter

CREATING THE ORACLE ENVIRONMENT

The Oracle database is a powerful yet complicated data storage and retrieval system capable of supporting enormous workloads while maintaining high levels of performance, security, and data integrity. An integral part of a successful database is the manner in which the software is installed and configured on the database server. This chapter examines the role the server software and configuration plays in the database environment and deciphers the sometimes confusing aspects of the Oracle server installation. This chapter also explores strategies for creating your Oracle server environment, as well as your first Oracle database. Finally, it looks at what you can do to familiarize yourself with an unfamiliar Oracle database.

When configuring a server to house the Oracle software, you must take several key factors into consideration. These include the flexibility of the design, the ease of administration, and the simplicity of the structure. If you design your environment with these points in mind, you will be rewarded with an environment conducive to your uptime and performance goals, as well as avoid the problems and anxiety that a poorly designed server structure can create.

DESIGNING AN OPTIMAL FLEXIBLE ARCHITECTURE

The Oracle standard for creating and configuring your Oracle environment is named the Optimal Flexible Architecture, or OFA Standard. It is a set of rules and guidelines that enables you to easily create and configure a production level Oracle server. As the name states, the OFA Standard was created to give you the most flexible Oracle environment without sacrificing usability, ease of administration, or simplicity of design.

Mr. Cary Millsap of Oracle Corporation wrote the OFA Standard in the early 1990s. The definitive white paper on the structure can be found at `http://www.europa.com/ ~orapub/index.html`. Mr. Millsap's article goes into much more detail than is described here. His white paper deals with configuring the entire environment, whereas you are concerned with the creation and configuration of the operating system directory structures and naming conventions used to support the Oracle database. Mr. Millsap's OFA Standard paper is required reading for any Oracle DBA or systems integrator interested in the best practices for implementing an Oracle installation.

Mr. Millsap sums up the purpose of the OFA Standard Recommendations with his statement that "A good standard should act as a strong floor, without becoming a ceiling that inhibits 'creative magic'." The OFA Standard Recommendations are just those— recommendations. Your specific environment will have requirements and specifications that are best met with methods not included in (or contrary to) the OFA Standard. However, close study of the OFA Standard reveals many best practice methods that would only be obvious through difficult trial, error, and experience.

CREATING TOP-LEVEL DIRECTORIES

The first step in configuring your environment is to decide on the naming and creation of the OS mount points and top-level directories of your Oracle installation. As with many configuration items, the implementation varies from UNIX to NT, but the general concepts remain the same. The first OFA rule relates to this topic and is the following:

> OFA Rule 1—Name all mount points that will hold site-specific data to match the pattern /pm, where p is a string constant chosen not to misrepresent the contents of any mount point, and m is a unique fixed-length key that distinguishes one mount point from another.

In other words, create top-level mount points that are unique, but do not have meaning in and of themselves. The character portion (p) should be short and simple—one or two characters are ideal. The numbered portion distinguishes the mount points from each other. Each mount point should have the same named portion and be of the same length (for example, u01, u02, and u03 or ora01, ora02, and ora03).

On an NT server, the different drives and volumes are already separated according to drive letters. This makes the usage of mount point names as described previously unnecessary. Use a directory named orant (the default Oracle name) on each drive to denote Oracle applications and files.

Tip #5	To minimize confusion, UNIX naming conventions are used throughout this explanation. However, unless otherwise indicated, all the structure and naming conventions given are applicable to both UNIX and NT environments.

Using mount points without site-specific, application-specific, or hardware-specific connotations enables great flexibility when reconfiguring your system. Consider the following example: Bob, a novice DBA, names mount points on his UNIX system that refer to the physical disks each mount point volume is attached to. This makes it very easy for Bob to balance his datafile I/O over drives. By glancing at the pathname, he can tell that his main data tablespace is on DISK01, whereas his index tablespace is on DISK05. But, as it always happens, Bob's database grows, forcing him to add more disks and new hardware. Bob wants to take advantage of his new RAID controller to stripe and mirror some volumes, which means he must reorganize his entire drive subsystem to accomplish these goals. Unfortunately, this also means that if he wants to keep his naming convention, he must rename his mount points and change all his backup scripts, applications, and so on to point to the new paths. Bob could have avoided this hassle by using directory names yourthat are unique but that by themselves have no meaning.

USING APPLICATION DIRECTORIES

One of the benefits gained from implementing an OFA-compliant configuration is the ease in which multiple applications and multiple versions of the same application can be installed, using the same directory structure. In an OFA environment, each application has its own home directory that stores the binaries, configuration files, and the like that are necessary for running the application. The next two OFA rules relate to this, and are as follows:

> OFA Rule 2—Name application home directories matching the pattern /pm/h/u, where pm is a mount-point name, h is selected from a small set of standard directory names, and u is the name of the application or application owner.

> OFA Rule 3—Store each version of Oracle Server distribution software in a directory matching the pattern h/product/v, where h is the application home directory of the Oracle software owner, and v represents the version of the software.

A sample implementation of this rule is given in the following directory template:

```
/[mount_point]/APP/[application_name]/PRODUCT/[version]/application home
```

In this example, you see that application home directories are stored in the APP subdirectory directly underneath your mount point. You next use a generic name to identify the directory under which the application is stored. The PRODUCT directory and version then follow. A sample hierarchy using this naming convention follows:

```
/u01
    app
        finance
            [...]
        qse
            [...]
        oracle
            admin
            product
                7.1.6
                    [...]
                7.3.3
                    [...]
                8.0.3
                    [...]
```

Although this method might seem more complicated than necessary, the resulting flexibility and ease of administration is well worth it. As you can see, under this mount point you have three applications installed—finance, qse, and oracle. finance and qse are third party or homegrown applications, and the directory structures underneath the main directories follow the same format as shown in the Oracle hierarchy. In the oracle application directory, you see the product and admin subdirectory. Within the product subdirectory are three versions of the Oracle software—7.1.6, 7.3.3, and 8.0.3. Any change or new installation of Oracle software can be made to one version without fear of interaction with any other version.

Separating the versions in this manner is very important when performing testing and cutover of new Oracle versions. Obviously you need the capability to easily install a new version of the software without impacting your production installation. After your new version is tested, cutover to the new version is a simple matter of setting the correct environment variables to the new directory. The old version can then be deleted at your leisure.

MANAGING DATABASE FILES

One of the needs that necessitated the creation of the OFA guidelines was the difficulty DBAs faced when simultaneously administering many databases. A method to organize administrative information and data into a manageable and predictable format was needed. The admin directory you saw earlier is used to store files related to administering the database and goes a long way in improving the capability of a single person to keep track of many databases. Your next OFA rule is related to this structure:

> OFA Rule 4—For each database with db_name=d, store database administration files in subdirectories of /h/admin/d, where h is the Oracle software owner's login home directory.

The following chart shows a sample admin directory structure:

```
/u01/app/oracle/admin
          PROD
               bdump
               udump
               cdump
               pfile
               sql
               create
```

The subdirectories in the admin directory are explained in Table 7.1.

TABLE 7.1   admin DIRECTORIES

Directory Name	Usage
bdump	Background dump files (value of BACKGROUND_DUMP_DEST)
udump	User dump files (value of USER_DUMP_DEST)
cdump	Core files (UNIX only)
pfile	init.ora and any other database initialization parameters
sql	Database administration SQL files
create	Scripts used to create the initial database and database objects

init.ora files, trace and dump files, alert.log, and so forth are all stored in this central administrative directory. This eases administering the large amounts of data produced by an Oracle database. You can add directories to store other data as the need arises.

> **Note**
>
> On UNIX platforms, create a link of the `init.ora` file from the `$ORACLE_HOME`/dbs directory to the `admin/pfile` directory. This ensures the Oracle default configuration is intact and enables you to benefit from the OFA structure. On NT platforms, either you have to specify the full pathname to the `init.ora` file when starting the database and create an OFA-compliant structure, or you have to store the `init.ora` files in the default `$ORACLE_HOME/database` directory to keep the default Oracle configuration intact.

NAMING CONVENTIONS

When managing multiple databases on one database server, a file naming convention is important. The OFA standard gives the following rule for naming database files:

OFA Rule 5—Name Oracle database files using the following patterns:

```
/pm/q/d/control.ctl - control files
/pm/q/d/redon.log - redo log files
/pm/q/d/tn.dbf - data files
```

These naming conventions are defined as follows:

- *pm* is a mount point name
- *q* is a string denoting the separation of Oracle data from all other files
- *d* is the `db_name` of the database
- *n* is a distinguishing key that is fixed-length for a given file type
- *t* is an Oracle tablespace name

Never store any file other than a control, redo log, or data file associated with a database d in */pm/q/d*.

Deviation from this standard depends on your personal preference, but the naming convention ideas should not be ignored. Use a meaningful filename extension, include the tablespace name in data file names, and keep all datafiles in their own exclusive directories.

A template for an alternative naming standard that keeps the original naming conventions could be *tn_*SID*_n*.ext, where *tn* is an abbreviation for the tablespace the datafile is for, SID is the database the datafile belongs to, and n is the datafile number.

Try to keep the tablespace abbreviation brief and, if possible, keep it a set number of letters. This produces uniform reports. Also, the number portion for redo log files should indicate both the log group and member—using a combination of numbers and characters, such as 01a (first log group, first member) and 02c (second log group, third member), works well. Names using the alternative notation are shown in Table 7.2.

TABLE 7.2   DATABASE FILE EXAMPLES

File Name	Explanation
syst_PROD_01.dbf	First SYSTEM tablespace datafile for the PROD database
ctrl_TEST_02.ctl	Second controlfile for the TEST database
redo_PPRD_01a.log	First member of the first redo log group for database PPRD
redo_PPRD_02c.log	Third member of the second redo log group for database PPRD
data_PROD_02.dbf	Second data tablespace datafile for the PROD database
initTEST.ora	Initialization parameter file for the TEST database

As you can see, investing the extra time in implementing a naming convention for your database files results in names that have no guesswork involved. You can immediately determine their function by glancing at the name.

The OFA rule also dictates that database datafiles, redo log files, and controlfiles should be stored in a dedicated directory off the mount point. The following shows a directory structure that complies with this recommendation, containing data for four databases:

```
/u01
    app
    oradata
        PROD
            [...]
        PPRD
            [...]
        DEVL
            [...]
        TEST
            [...]
```

All datafiles, log files, controlfiles, and archived redo log files are stored in the directory under the oradata subdirectory. Each database has its own directory, and *only* database files are stored in these directories.

PUTTING IT ALL TOGETHER

A wise person once said that the great thing about standards is the variety from which to choose. This is especially apt when describing the OFA guidelines. There is no one perfect solution for creating an Oracle server environment because no two environments are the same.

The following are sample OFA implementations on both UNIX and NT. These are meant to give you ideas and get you started. You might find specific points that, when reworked, serve your particular needs better than those presented. Explanations of each section are also given.

PART

II

CH

7

LISTING 7.1   UNIX SAMPLE OFA IMPLEMENTATION

```
/    Root Directory
    u01                                            u01 Mount Point
app                                        Application Directory
oracle                                     Oracle Application Directory
        admin                                Administrative Directory
        PROD                               PROD Database Directory
        pfile                         Initialization Parameter Files
        bdump                         Background Dump Files
        udump                         User Dump Files
        cdump                         Core Files
        create                          Database Creation Scripts
        sql                     SQL Scripts
        PPRD                              PPRD Database Directory
            [...]                              Same Directory Structure as PROD
        TEST                              TEST Database Directory
            [...]                              Same Directory Structure as PROD
        product                              Application Files Directory
            7.1.3                            Version 7.1.3 Files
                [...]                        ORACLE_HOME for version 7.1.3
            8.0.3                            Version 8.0.3 Files
                [...]                        ORACLE_HOME for version 8.0.3
        qse                                  QSE Application Directory
            admin                              Administrative Directory
                [...]                          Directories for QSE Administration
            product                            Application Files Directory
                [...]                          QSE Versions and Files
        oradata                                    Oracle Database Files Directory
            PROD                               PROD Database Files
            PPRD                               PPRD Database Files
            TEST                               TEST Database Files
    u02                                        u02 Mount Point
        oradata                                    Oracle Database Files Directory
            PROD                               PROD Database Files
            PPRD                               PPRD Database Files
            TEST                               TEST Database Files
[...]
```

LISTING 7.2   NT SAMPLE OFA IMPLEMENTATION

```
C:                                         Drive Designator
    oracle                                    Oracle Software Directory
        home                                  Oracle Home Directory
            [...]                             ORACLE_HOME Contents
        oradata                               Oracle Database Files
            PROD                             PROD Database Files Directory
                [...]                        PROD Database Files
            PPRD                             PPRD Database Files Directory
                [...]                        PPRD Database Files
        admin                                Oracle Administrative Directories
            PROD                             PROD Administrative Directory
                [...]                        Same Structure as UNIX
            PPRD                             PPRD Administrative Directory
                [...]                        Same Structure as UNIX
```

```
D:                                      Drive Designator
     oracle                              Oracle Software Directory
        oradata                          Oracle Database Files
            PROD                         PROD Database Files Directory
                [...]                    PROD Database Files
            PPRD                         PPRD Database Files Directory
                [...]                    PPRD Database Files
     [...]
```

One of the crucial factors in making the OFA standards work is the separation of application and database files. The admin and oradata directories are created to keep all database-specific files separate from the Oracle software. This is necessary to fulfill one of the promises discussed earlier: the simple and transparent cutover to new software versions.

The final OFA rule from Mr. Millsap's paper you are going to discuss follows:

> OFA Rule 6   Refer to explicit path names only in files designed specifically to store them, such as the UNIX /etc/passwd file and the Oracle oratab file; refer to group memberships only in /etc/group.

If followed, this rule helps you avoid a common pitfall everyone steps into: creating an application on-the-fly that becomes a common tool used everyday and breaks as soon as any system reconfiguration is performed. Avoid using hard-coded directory names in a shell script, batch file, or application program. When working with the Oracle tools, this is easier than it sounds; any directory or value you might need to work with is probably already implemented as an environment variable or Registry key.

CONFIGURING THE ORACLE ENVIRONMENT

The Oracle server is a complex set of interacting programs and processes. The software environment involved is likewise complicated and often difficult to understand. Various parameters exist to control the behavior of the Oracle programs, set the locations for configuration or shared files, define the language and character set to use, and perform myriad other tasks. On a UNIX machine, these parameters are stored as environment variables that are usually loaded from the supplied coraenv or oraenv files called from the user's login script. On a 16-bit Windows computer, the parameters are stored in the oracle.ini file. On 32-bit Windows computers (Windows 95, Windows NT, and so on), these configuration parameters are stored in the Registry.

The environment variable files or Registry keys are created the first time an Oracle product is installed on a machine. Subsequent software installations add to and update these configurations. Systems programmers or DBAs also modify these configurations by hand to tune, troubleshoot, and customize the Oracle environment. A full description of the software configuration parameters can be found in your operating system-specific Oracle documentation. Take a few minutes to familiarize yourself with the various parameters for your operating system; many problems can be solved with careful tweaking of these parameters.

> **Note**
>
> Don't confuse the Oracle configuration parameters with the initialization parameters of a database. The Oracle configuration parameters apply to the Oracle software installed on a computer, whereas the initialization parameters configure a single database.

There are several environment variables with which you should be immediately familiar, as they play an important role in the operation of the Oracle server. ORACLE_HOME defines the base path for the Oracle software. It is explained in detail later in this chapter. ORACLE_SID is set to the default database SID (System Identifier) for your session. Many tools use the ORACLE_SID to determine what database to connect to. It is important you always know what values these variables are set to—having wrong values for either of these can result in performing operations on the wrong database or using the wrong version of the Oracle tools.

UNDERSTANDING THE ORACLE SOFTWARE ENVIRONMENT

When you install Oracle software on a server or client computer, an Oracle directory structure is created to store the binary executables, shared libraries, configuration files, trace files, and so on used by the Oracle programs. This directory tree is semistandard across different server platforms and versions of Oracle software. Both server and client software is stored in the same directory.

> **Tip #6**
>
> On UNIX machines, do not mix different versions of the Oracle software in the same Oracle directories. On Windows machines, do not mix 16- and 32-bit versions of the Oracle software in the same Oracle directories.

Oracle software is usually installed on the server using an operating system account created specifically for the task. This userID, by default named oracle, must have complete rights to all the Oracle directories (including those used for software installation and Oracle datafile storage) and files. In an OFA-compliant server configuration, this user's home directory is the /mount/app/oracle directory. It is important that the oracle account is secured from unauthorized access. In most environments, access to this account compromises the security of the entire database environment.

The following sections explain the components of the Oracle directory structure. In particular, you look at what the Oracle home is, how server structures differ between UNIX and NT platforms, and how different versions of Oracle software can coexist on UNIX and NT platforms.

ORACLE_HOME SWEET HOME

The top of the Oracle directory tree is referred to as the Oracle home. It is defined on the server as an environment variable or Registry setting named ORACLE_HOME and is a mandatory configuration parameter. Many Oracle executables use the ORACLE_HOME variable to locate shared code, configuration files, and so on. For example, on a UNIX server, an Oracle program might look for a configuration file in `$ORACLE_HOME/network/admin`, rather than in `/u01/app/oracle/network/admin`.

> **Note**
>
> Some Oracle environment variables, such as `TNS_ADMIN`, override the default `ORACLE_HOME` directories used to locate files.

The `ORACLE_HOME` directory should be set up on database login by either the user login script, Registry values, or `.INI` file values, depending on your architecture. Other environment values, such as `LD_LIBRARY_PATH` (on UNIX systems) and `PATH`, should refer to the `ORACLE_HOME` variable previously set. This enforces one of your OFA rules where hard-coded directory values are only set in one administrative location.

RUNNING MULTIPLE VERSIONS OF ORACLE ON UNIX

When a database is started, the value of the `ORACLE_HOME` variable determines what version of the Oracle server executable and libraries is used to open the database. By manipulating and controlling the value of `ORACLE_HOME`, you can define what version of the Oracle software is used. This is how multiple versions of Oracle databases can be run simultaneously on the same server. The following shows a sample Oracle directory structure (on a UNIX server):

```
/u01/app/oracle/product
              7.1.6
                 bin
                 rdbms
                 [...]
              7.3.3
                 bin
                 rdbms
                 [...]
              8.0.3
                 bin
                 rdbms
                 [...]
```

In this example, three versions of the Oracle database are installed in an OFA-compliant directory structure. At any one time, multiple databases running multiple versions of the server executables can be operating. If a DBA logs in and sets her `ORACLE_HOME` to `/u01/app/oracle/product/7.1.6`, the database she starts runs the version 7.1.6 server executables. If the DBA logs in and sets her `ORACLE_HOME` to `/u01/app/oracle/product/8.0.3`, she uses the 8.0.3 server executables.

There are two versions to keep in mind when working with the Oracle environment:

- The version of the software (server executables and libraries) itself
- The version of the database

These versions are separate and distinct from each other. Oracle does not perform version checking between the server executables and the database. For example, you will not receive errors from starting a database at version 7.1.6 with the version 7.3.3 software. When multiple versions of Oracle are installed on the same server, care must be taken to not mix the software and Oracle versions.

> **Note**
>
> In a UNIX environment, by default the ORACLE_HOME and related environment variables are set on database login by prompting the user for the preferred SID, looking up that SID in the oratab file, and setting the ORACLE_HOME to the value found for that SID in oratab. In a Windows environment, ORACLE_HOME is read from the Registry or .INI file.

Running Multiple Versions of Oracle on NT

Because of the architectural differences between UNIX and NT servers, running multiple versions of Oracle server software on NT servers is handled differently from the way it is on its UNIX counterpart. An instance on an NT server is implemented as a service with the background processes created as multiple threads spawned by the service process. The service gets all its configuration information from the Windows NT Registry. Because there is only one Registry with one set of values on an NT server, there can be only one ORACLE_HOME defined on the server at any one time. This means running multiple versions of Oracle software on an NT server cannot be handled by manipulating the ORACLE_HOME environment variable.

To circumvent this design and enable multiple Oracle versions to exist on a single NT server, all the version-specific directories, executables, and files have the major version number appended to them. For example, the Oracle server executable of a version 7.2.3 database on an NT server is named oracle72.exe, whereas the 7.3.3 version is named oracle73.exe. Likewise, the RDBMS directory is named rdbms72 or rdbms73, and Oracle utilities such as tkprof or Export are named tkprof72 on a 7.2 database or exp73 for database version 7.3.

> **Note**
>
> Because of this naming convention, having multiple minor versions of the Oracle software installed at the same time is unsupported. For example, Oracle version 7.3.2 and version 7.3.3 software both have the same suffix of 73 on their directories and files, and they would therefore be incapable of coexisting on the same NT server. Because of the confusion and the potential for accidents this causes, however, avoid running multiple versions of NT on the same server when possible.

Oracle supplies a utility to switch Oracle homes on 16-bit Windows clients and versions of Windows95 and NT machines. This is not the same as operating with multiple ORACLE_HOME directories. All this program does is to change all directory references in the init.ora or Registry from one location or another. This does enable you to install and test software inmultiple ORACLE_HOME directories, but it does not enable programs to run from separate ORACLE_HOME directories simultaneously.

16-bit Windows software uses the `oracle.ini` file to set the Oracle software configuration variables. 32-bit Windows software uses the `HKEY/LOCAL_MACHINE/SOFTWARE/ORACLE` Registry key to set Oracle environment variables. Because of this, both 16- and 32-bit versions of Oracle software can coexist on a 32-bit Windows operating system. It is recommended that you use different `ORACLE_HOMES` (`orawin` and `orawin95` or `orant`, by default), managed separately by their respective `.INI` file and Registry settings, to avoid problems with shared coded discrepancies between the versions.

Programs and drivers written for 16-bit Oracle software are unable to operate with 32-bit versions, and vice versa. You'll often see this in relation to programs that use SQL*Net, such as ODBC drivers, as well as third party programming tools that rely on Oracle-supplied libraries and DLLs. In these situations, simultaneously running the 16- and 32-bit versions of the Oracle software is the only way to keep everything working smoothly.

THE ORACLE_HOME DIRECTORIES

As stated before, the `ORACLE_HOME` variable points to the top level of the Oracle software directory tree. `ORACLE_HOME` contains other directories, each of which contains Oracle files or more directories. The directories located within `ORACLE_HOME` are fairly standard in all Oracle installations, and each directory contains files for specific programs or functionality. Table 7.3 lists some of the important directories found in an Oracle installation, as well as their purposes.

TABLE 7.3   IMPORTANT ORACLE_HOME DIRECTORIES AND USAGE

Directory Name	Usage
BIN	Oracle executables and shared DLLs
DBS	Oracle server files and default directory for `init.ora` files
DATABASE	Starter database and default Oracle database files (NT)
RDBMS	Database files
RDBMS/ADMIN	SQL scripts to create system database objects, roles and views
RDBMS/TRACE	Default database dump directory
NETWORK	Oracle networking files
NETWORK/ADMIN	SQL*Net configuration files
NETWORK/TRACE	Default SQL*Net dump directory
PLSQL	PL/SQL configuration files and SQL scripts
DOC	Online documentation
SYSMAN	Oracle Enterprise Manager files
PLUS	SQL*Plus files

PART

II

CH

7

In general, the `admin` directories contain SQL scripts related to the creation of administrative objects related to whatever product directory they are in. The most interesting directory to the DBA is `$ORACLE_HOME/rdbms/admin`. Here you'll find the SQL scripts that are run to create the system database objects, packages, procedures, and so on. `$ORACLE_HOME/network/admin` holds all the files necessary to configure SQL*Net communications. `$ORACLE_HOME/dbs` holds `sql.bsq`, the SQL file run during database creation to create the data dictionary tables.

OTHER IMPORTANT CONFIGURATION FILES

There are a few other files you should be aware that are installed with the Oracle server installation. The `oratab`, `oraenv`, and `coraenv` files are only found on UNIX servers. `oratab` is a text file that holds a line for each database on the system. Each line consists of the database SID, the Oracle home for that particular database, and a flag indicating whether the database should be automatically started or shut down. Several supplied Oracle programs and scripts, such as `dbstart` or `dbshut`, use this file to identify the databases located on the server as well as their versions. `dbstart` and `dbshut` also use the automatic startup flag to choose the databases on which to perform their actions.

`oraenv` and `coraenv` are script files that define and set the environment variables necessary to run Oracle programs and tools in the UNIX environment. `oraenv` is for Bourne shell (sh) or Korn Shell (ksh) environments, whereas `coraenv` is for environments using cshell (csh). `oraenv` and `coraenv` also access the `oratab` file to determine the proper `ORACLE_HOME` to set based on the value for the database SID entered on login. These files are the place to start researching when you begin customizing your UNIX Oracle environment.

On NT servers, you should be aware of the password file, which is created by the `oradim` utility, for each database. This file contains the password for the internal user account— the account used when starting or shutting down the database. The password file, named `oraSID.pwd` or `pwdSID.ora`, is flagged, hidden, and stored in the `$ORACLE_HOME/database` directory. It is used with certain security configurations to authenticate remote DBAs to the database. In addition, on NT, this password file is internally synchronized with the controlfiles for that SID.

CREATING YOUR FIRST DATABASE

Now that you have gained knowledge about the Oracle environment as well as the specifics regarding the Oracle database and instance, its time to look at the process involved in creating an Oracle database from scratch.

Creating an Oracle database consists of a number of discrete steps:

1. Creating the initialization parameter file and administration directory for the new database
2. Creating the instance
3. Creating the database

4. Running postdatabase creation procedures

5. Creating the supporting database objects

6. Securing the default accounts

7. Updating system files to recognize the new database

Each of these steps is examined in the following sections.

CREATING THE INITIALIZATION PARAMETER FILE

The first step in creating a new database is to copy the default init.ora file (found in $ORACLE_HOME/dbs on UNIX platforms and $ORACLE_HOME/database on NT servers) to a file that uniquely identifies the parameter file as belonging to a specific database. This file contains parameter settings specific to the new database. Oracle's default naming convention for the init.ora files is initSID.ora, where SID is the system identifier you have chosen for the new database. The Oracle tools will look for a file of this name (using the value of ORACLE_SID to fill in the SID portion of the filename) if a parameter file is not explicitly specified on startup. Edit the copied file, and replace the default parameter values with values that make sense. At the very least, make sure the controlfile parameter, db_block_size, and db_name parameters are correct.

Now is also a good time to create the directories that will hold your Oracle datafiles, the background and user trace files, and whatever other administrative directory structures you use. Consult the section "Designing an Optimal Flexible Architecture" earlier in this chapter for details on this configuration.

CREATING THE INSTANCE

Instance creation is one of the most misunderstood tasks related to Oracle database administration. As previously discussed, the instance is specifically that portion of the Oracle RDBMS consisting of the background processes and memory structures contained within the server's memory address space. Creating and working with instances is significantly different between UNIX and NT platforms. The following sections discuss the different steps involved with each environment.

CREATING AN INSTANCE ON UNIX

On UNIX platforms, the Oracle instance is not a permanent structure but rather is created each time the database is started, using the parameters in the init.ora file specified at database startup. The instance is named using the value of the ORACLE_SID environment variable. The exact time instance creation occurs is in the state known as nomount. When you start up nomount, you are doing nothing more than allocating the SGA and starting the server's background processes. Depending on your UNIX platform, the instance name (or SID, as defined by the ORACLE_SID value) might also be a part of the background process task names.

CREATING AN INSTANCE ON NT

Creating and working with an instance on an NT server is substantially more involved than on a UNIX server. Because of the NT architecture, all UNIX daemon processes are implemented using NT services. A service must be defined and stored within the NT Registry before it can be activated. So, for each NT database you have, you must create an associated service to host the instance for the database. Unlike the UNIX server, an NT Oracle instance is represented by a physical operating system construct that is persistent regardless of whether the instance is started.

In most installations, each database has two NT services assigned to it. Only one of these services, the OracleServiceSID, is required for database operation. The OracleServiceSID service is created with the initialization parameter file embedded in its definition. This is how NT knows which init.ora file to look to when creating the instance, as well as what database (using the controlfile parameter in init.ora) the instance is for. The other service, OracleStartSID, is provided as a convenient way to automatically start your instance and database when the NT server starts. When the OracleStartSID service is started, it automatically starts OracleServiceSID and opens the database to which OracleServiceSID points. Creating the OracleStartSID service is discussed later in this chapter.

The services necessary to run the Oracle instance are created using the oradim utility. Remember that oradim, like all other major Oracle on NT executables, will have the first two digits of the Oracle version appended to it, as in oradim80.exe. oradim has two methods of operation—through a GUI interface and using the command line. Those used to NT will probably prefer the GUI interface, whereas UNIX administrators will be glad the command line interface is available. Invoking oradim with no arguments will automatically start the GUI interface. The GUI interface can be used to create the initial service and instance, whereas the command line option enables greater control and more powerful administration options.

One thing to note about oradim is that it does not output error messages to stdout, or the screen. Rather, all errors will be written to the oradim.log file located in the $ORACLE_HOME/rdbms directory. This is a minor inconvenience that will hopefully be changed in future Oracle versions. The reason for this error handling design is beyond all comprehension.

When you invoke the oradim GUI, you are presented with two screens containing database parameters for you to fill in. Follow the instructions, and oradim creates the Oracle services, creates the database, and runs catalog.sql and catproc.sql (discussed in the section "Running Postdatabase Creation Procedures"). Be sure to change the default values given for the database name, instance name, datafile, and parameter files.

Running the character oradim is where things get interesting. From the command line, you can create, edit, and delete existing Oracle services. For experienced Oracle DBAs, the command line version of oradim is often preferred over GUI because of the higher level of control and functionality. For this example, you will assume the command line version of oradim is used.

The basic `oradim` command line uses the following format:

```
oradim -command -sid SID [flags]
```

`oradim` commands are described in Table 7.4.

TABLE 7.4 `oradim` COMMAND LINE OPTIONS

Command	Function
NEW	Create a new database instance service
EDIT	Edit an existing instance service
STARTUP	Start up an instance and/or database
SHUTDOWN	Shut down an instance and/or database
DELETE	Delete instance services

An important thing to realize is that the instance services are completely independent of their associated databases. A database can exist on an NT server without an associated instance service. Also, the version of `oradim` used when creating the service specifies the version of the Oracle server executable (`oracle.exe`) that will be run when starting the instance.

To create an Oracle service, issue the following command:

```
oradim -new -sid [sid_name]
-pfile [init.ora directory]
-intpwd [internal password]
-startmode auto
```

This creates the `OracleServiceSID` and `OracleStartSID`, with the SID value equal to whatever you made the `sid_name`. The `startmode` of auto creates the `OracleStartSID` file. The `pfile` parameter gives the location of the `init.ora` file used to configure the instance started with the `OracleServiceSID` service.

For more information and examples on using the `oradim` command, refer to your Oracle NT Operating System Specific documentation.

CREATING THE DATABASE

After the instance is configured, you can create the database. This is where you actually issue the CREATE DATABASE command. The CREATE DATABASE command creates the system datafile and tablespace, controlfiles, initial redo log groups, the system rollback segment, and the internal database tables necessary for the operation of the Oracle database.

The CREATE DATABASE command syntax can be found in the *Oracle Server Reference Manual*. It is important to correctly size the datafile specified in the CREATE DATABASE command. This datafile is assigned to the SYSTEM tablespace. Because hard drive space is relatively inexpensive, size the file two to three times larger than what you expect to use (at least 50–100MB). Allocate more space if the database will make heavy usage of stored packages, procedures,

PART

II

CH

7

functions, and triggers, as the code for these objects is stored in the SYSTEM tablespace and can use up quite a bit of space. Set your MAX parameters high as well. The defaults, which are used if you do not explicitly state values for MAXDATAFILES, MAXLOGFILES, and so on, are generally too low. The only drawback here is the controlfile will be a few KB larger than it needs to be—hardly a drawback at all. Also, be sure you specify the correct value for CHARACTERSET. This is one of the parameters that is nontrivial to change after database creation.

Before running the CREATE DATABASE command, ensure the controlfile parameter in the init.ora is set properly and your ORACLE_SID is set to the proper database name. If you've set the db_name init.ora parameter, make sure it is the same as the SID value of your Oracle service. Store the text of the CREATE DATABASE SQL statement in a text file. This reduces the likelihood of errors due to typos and provides a level of self-documentation. Also, be sure that the OracleServiceSID service is started by running the Services applet in the NT Control Panel and making sure OracleServiceSID is running.

On UNIX, run svrmgrl. On NT systems, run svrmgr23.exe for 7.3.x systems, or svrmgr30.exe for 8.0.x systems. Connect internal to the database. For 7.3.x, you get a message stating you have "connected to an idle instance." This indicates that the instance is running, but no database has been attached to it. However, note for 8.0.x, you only receive "connected" as the message, even though, indeed, the instance is idle! Start up the database nomount by issuing the command:

```
startup nomount pfile=[init.ora file path and name];
```

When the database starts, run your CREATE DATABASE script. The time it takes for this command to complete depends mostly on how large you've made your system datafile. When the create command finishes, your database opens automatically. At this point, you have a working (albeit a bare) Oracle database.

RUNNING POSTDATABASE CREATION PROCEDURES

Immediately after creating your database, there are two Oracle-supplied SQL scripts you must run:

- catalog.sql
- catproc.sql

The oradim GUI tool automatically executes these scripts after creating the database. Both of these scripts are found in $ORACLE_HOME/rdbms/admin. catalog.sql creates the data dictionary views and V$ view synonyms, whereas catproc.sql runs the scripts necessary to install the Procedural Option, or PL/SQL objects, and its supporting database structures. Failing to run either of these two scripts will result in strange and unpredictable errors.

Another script you might want to run is pupbld.sql. This creates the product user profile tables. These are Oracle-supplied tables that can be used to limit access of Oracle programs to the database. The product user profile tables are rarely used today due to the many third party applications that access the database using native or ODBC drivers and that do not check these tables for resource limits. If you do not create these tables, however, whenever a user other than SYSTEM logs in to the database through SQL*Plus, he gets an annoying error message on his screen. Log in as SYSTEM when creating these tables.

Finally, if this database will be involved in replication, you need to run $ORACLE_HOME/rdbms/admin/catrep.sql. This script creates the procedures and objects necessary to support the replication options.

Tip #7	A very useful tip for the build database process is to start a spool file before you run your database creation scripts and then review it for errors when the scripts have finished. This will help you to catch errors before you get too far.

CREATING THE SUPPORTING DATABASE OBJECTS

Now that you have a skeleton database, you can begin creating the supporting objects that will enable your database to support a production level workload. The key to creating the supporting objects is flexibility and manageability. If you keep these two goals in mind, your database installation will be a success.

The first thing you need to do is create a rollback segment to be used when creating the rest of your supporting database objects. When created, your database has one system rollback segment, created in the system tablespace. This rollback segment is only used for transactions involving objects in the system tablespace and cannot be dropped or taken offline. Create a temporary rollback segment using the following command:

```
create rollback segment rbs_temp
storage (initial 10k next 10k minextents 3 maxextents 121)
tablespace system;
```

Bring the rollback segment online by issuing this command:

```
alter rollback segment rbs_temp online;
```

Now, create your production tablespaces. At a minimum, create the tablespaces listed in Table 7.5.

TABLE 7.5   SOME SAMPLE DATABASE TABLESPACES

Tablespace Name	Purpose
TEMP	Stores temporary database segments
TOOLS	Stores third party or in-house database tool objects
RBS	Stores rollback segments
RBS_02	Stores large rollback segments for bulk data loads
USER_DATA	Default tablespace for end users
USER_INDEX	Index tablespace for end users

Your objective in creating these tablespaces is to separate operational and application data and functions. The TEMP, RBS, and RBS_02 tablespaces hold objects necessary for the Oracle database to function, whereas TOOLS, USER_DATA, and USER_INDEX hold user data. See Part IX of this book, Performance Tuning, for more information on separating data, I/O, and functionality using tablespaces.

Also, create your production rollback segments. Create at least two rollback segments in the RBS tablespace to support OLTP transactions. These segments should be relatively small, with many extents. Name them RBS##— for example, RBS01, RBS02, and RBS03. Create one rollback segment in the RBS_02 tablespace for bulk data loads. This segment should be large with fewer extents. Call this rollback segment RBS_LOAD##—for example RBS_LOAD01. Bring the OLTP rollback segments online and place their names in the rollback_segments init.ora value list.

When you have finished these tasks, drop the temporary rollback segment you created earlier by issuing the following command:

```
drop rollback segment rbs_temp;
```

SECURING THE DEFAULT ACCOUNTS

A new database always has two default system accounts—SYS and SYSTEM. The initial password for SYS is CHANGE_ON_INSTALL, and the password for SYSTEM is MANAGER. Change these immediately. It would be frightening to know how many databases can be broken into by logging in as SYS or SYSTEM.

Also, if you have installed the demo tables, consider changing the scott userID's password from the commonly known tiger to something else.

UPDATING THE SYSTEM CONFIGURATION FILES

Finally, you need to register your new database in all the configuration files on your system. If this is the first database on the system, you'll want to set your ORACLE_SID variable to reflect this. On an NT server, you need to create this value before you can set it. If you are on a UNIX server, you'll want to update oratab to reflect the new database information. Also, put the database in the tnsnames.ora and listener.ora files so they are reachable via SQL*Net.

At this point (assuming all the previous steps were completed successfully), you have a fully functional Oracle database to start your development, testing, or playing.

EXPLORING THE ORACLE DATABASE

Anyone who works with Oracle for any length of time sooner or later faces the task of administering, troubleshooting, or working within a database environment that is completely unfamiliar to her. It is important to be able to quickly familiarize yourself with the custom configurations and setup of a foreign environment. This ensures that your time is spent handling the critical tasks at hand, rather than wasting it on time-consuming and trivial items such as what rollback segments you can use for your data load, what tablespace to store your user data in, and so on.

In the following sections, you'll look at how to extract information about the database from the database. The information in these pages coupled with the information covered in the previous sections will enable you to complete your picture of an unfamiliar database environment (and perhaps even your own).

LOOKING AT THE DATABASE

The first order of business is to get a handle on the database and its objects. This includes looking at the datafiles, tablespaces, redo logs, and rollback segments, as well as memory allocations to the various caches and what background processes are running. Database jobs stored in the job queue and the users and security privileges assigned to database users are also of interest.

The V$database and V$thread data views are useful to locate information on the database and instance, respectively. V$database shows you the database name and archiving mode (whether the database is running archivelog or noarchivelog mode). V$thread is specifically a Parallel Server view, but it is useful as it gives the instance name (more of an issue on an NT server than in the UNIX environment). You can also query V$instance for the database open time. In Oracle8, V$instance contains the startup_time field, which displays the instance start time. If you are using Oracle7, the following query transforms the V$instance startup information into a usable format:

```
SELECT TO_CHAR (TO_DATE (a.value, 'J')
+ b.value/86400, 'HH24:MI:SS DD-MON-RR')
start_time
FROM v$instance a, v$instance b
WHERE a.key = 'STARTUP TIME - JULIAN'
AND b.key = 'STARTUP TIME - SECONDS';
```

The output of this query looks similar to the following:

```
START_TIME
------------------
22:48:37 06-MAR-98
```

In Oracle7, this rather elaborate query is necessary because the Julian date portion of the startup time is stored in one column in V$instance, whereas the time portion of the date is stored in a separate field in seconds.

Note

V$thread contains an OPEN_TIME field that might be different than the time displayed in V$instance. This is because one field displays the time the instance was created, whereas the other shows the time the database was opened and made available for access.

You can list the active controlfiles by querying `V$controlfile`. Rollback segment information as stored in `dba_rollback_segs`, `V$rollstat`, and `V$rollname`. `dba_rollback_segs` shows information on all rollback segments in the database, whereas the `V$` views only list those rollback segments that are currently online. The following query makes sense of the online rollback segment information:

```
SELECT a.segment_name, a.tablespace_name,
b.bytes, b.extents,
c.shrinks, c.extends, c.hwmsize
FROM dba_rollback_segs a, dba_segments b, v$rollstat c
WHERE a.segment_id = c.usn
AND a.segment_name = b.segment_name;
```

This query produces output similar to the following:

```
SEGMENT_NAME        TABLESPACE_NAME
BYTES     EXTENTS
SHRINKS     EXTENDS     HWMSIZE
------------     ---------------
----------- ----------
----------- ---------- ----------
RBS01               ROLLBACK_DATA
102400          2
1         3     100352
RBS02               ROLLBACK_DATA
102400          2
0         0     100352
RBS03               ROLLBACK_DATA
102400          2
1         1     100352
SYSTEM              SYSTEM
204800          4
0         0     202752
```

Information on the redo logs is stored in the `V$log` and `V$logfile` views. The following query displays pertinent information on the redo logs created for the database:

```
SELECT member, bytes, members, a.status
FROM v$log a, v$logfile b
WHERE a.group# = b.group#
ORDER BY member;
```

The output of this query looks similar to the following:

```
MEMBER                                          BYTES     MEMBERS STATUS
-------------------------------------------- ---------- ---------- ---------
C:\ORADATA\PPRD\REDO_PPRD_01A.LOG               204800          1 CURRENT
C:\ORADATA\PPRD\REDO_PPRD_02A.LOG               204800          1 INACTIVE
```

Mapping your datafiles and tablespaces is important. Query `dba_data_files` for this information. You can query information specific to your tablespaces from `dba_tablespaces` and datafile-specific information from `V$datafile`.

Query V$sgastat for information on instance memory allocations. The following query might be helpful:

```
SELECT name, bytes
FROM v$sgastat
WHERE name in
('free  memory', 'fixed_sga', '
db_block_buffers', 'log_buffer',
'dictionary cache', 'library cache','sql area');
```

The results of this query run on a very small database are shown:

```
NAME                              BYTES
------------------------------    ----------
free memory                       2287676
fixed_sga                           35208
db_block_buffers                   409600
log_buffer                           8192
dictionary cache                   226376
library cache                      247636
sql area                           466040
```

V$bgprocess can be used to quickly list the running background processes. The following query helps:

```
SELECT name FROM v$bgprocess WHERE paddr <> '00';
```

The dba_jobs table holds information on pending jobs scheduled through the DBMS_JOBS package. You can list the scheduled database jobs with the following query:

```
SELECT log_user, job, what,
to_char(last_date, 'DD-MON-YY') l1, last_sec l2,
to_char(next_date, 'DD-MON-YY') n1, next_sec n2, failures
FROM dba_jobs
ORDER BY next_date DESC, next_sec DESC;
```

User information is stored in dba_users. Information on granted privileges is stored in the dba_tab_privs, dba_sys_privs, and dba_role_privs tables. You can also query role_tab_privs, role_sys_privs, and role_role_privs to display information on privileges granted to roles. More information on monitoring security information can be found in Chapter 23, "Security Management."

LOOKING AT THE DATABASE SEGMENTS

Now that you know where database configuration information is stored, look at the user data objects information. Database segments you are interested in include tables, indexes, views, clusters, and other data-storing objects.

The DBA_TABLES, DBA_INDEXES, DBA_SEGMENTS, DBA_SEQUENCES, and DBA_OBJECTS data dictionary views provide information on the various database segments stored in the database.

The format and information in the views are fairly self-explanatory. DBA_OBJECTS is interesting because it stores creation and last modification (timestamp) information on all objects stored in the database, and DBA_SEGMENTS is useful because it stores the size and number of extents used by each database segment. Please refer to Chapter 21, "Managing Database Storage," for more in-depth information on how to access and use information from these views.

PART

II

CH

7

LOOKING AT MISCELLANEOUS DATABASE OBJECTS

Your exploration of the database is not complete without looking at several other structures, including the stored PL/SQL objects, triggers, synonyms, and database links.

Sources for the packages, procedures, and functions are stored in the `sys.source$` table. When you create the object, all the blank lines are stripped and each line is stored as a separate record in this table. You can query `dba_source` to easily retrieve the text of stored packages, procedures, and functions. The following query produces the source code for an indicated stored object:

```
SELECT text
FROM dba_source
WHERE name = upper('&Object_Name')
ORDER BY line;
```

Information on triggers is stored in the `dba_triggers` table. Because the trigger body is stored as a long value, you need to set your `longsize` to an adequate value when querying on this column from SQL*Plus. In this view, the `TRIGGER_TYPE` column is either `row` or `statement`, and `TRIGGERING_EVENT` stores the type of trigger—`before insert`, `after update`, and so on.

`dba_synonyms` lists information on the synonyms in the database. Note that public synonyms have `PUBLIC` as their owner. Query `dba_db_links` for information on the defined database links. One word of caution on `dba_db_links`: If the link is defined with a user and password to connect to, the password is stored in `cleartext`.

EXPLORING AN UNFAMILIAR ENVIRONMENT

Now, put some of the information covered in this chapter into a familiar frame of reference. Suppose you are a contract DBA and have just arrived at a new site. The previous DBA has already departed the scene and amazingly enough, has left no supporting documentation of his system configuration. What can you do?

The following two sections explore possible courses of action—one on a UNIX server, and one on an NT server. They should give you ideas and reinforce the information presented earlier in the chapter.

EXPLORING THE UNIX ENVIRONMENT

Your primary interest is to determine how the Oracle software has been installed and configured and what databases are on the system. The first step is obtaining access to the OS account used to install the Oracle software. Next, you need to locate possible `ORACLE_HOME` directories. If there is only one `ORACLE_HOME` on the system, this should already be set by your login sequence. Check the `ORACLE_HOME` environment variable for this value. Also, find and check the `oratab` file to determine if database and `ORACLE_HOME` information is contained within. This is not a guaranteed comprehensive list. However, the `oratab` file is manually updated, and up-to-date information is not a requirement to operate the database. Another alternative is to search for the Oracle server executable (oracle), or the rdbms and dbs directories. These are standard in all Oracle server installations. Make a careful list of all possible Oracle directories.

Next, determine what databases are on the server. In each of the Oracle home directories you found, check the dbs directory. All the configured databases should have an initSID.ora file in this directory. The file might be linked to a different administrative directory, but the listing of these files shows you all the databases that are configured. Again, this does not necessarily mean that all these databases exist. The creation as well as the deletion of the init.ora files is, for the most part, manually done by the DBA. It is also no guarantee that the init.ora files are in the dbs directory. As this is where these files are looked for by default by Oracle programs, it is likely you'll find them here.

Check your user and system login script and determine whether custom modifications have been made to the Oracle environment. Check to see whether coraenv or oraenv are being called from the login script and whether these files have been modified in any way. If coraenv or oraenv are not being called, determine where the Oracle environment variables are being set. Check the system startup scripts (rc files and the like) to see what programs or daemons are automatically started on system boot. Don't forget to check the crontab file or system scheduler for the Oracle owner and administrator to determine what automated jobs are scheduled and running. Finally, examine your UNIX kernel parameters to see how the memory and kernel have been configured for your Oracle install. The location and method of setting these parameters varies between UNIX vendors. Check your OS documentation for more details.

Tip #8	Use the UNIX find command to automatically locate files that you are otherwise having a hard time finding manually. Consult your UNIX system's online man (manual) pages for proper syntax.

EXPLORING THE NT ENVIRONMENT

On an NT server, figuring out the specific configuration of the Oracle environment is a little more straightforward than on a UNIX server. This is because fewer aspects of the configuration are left completely to the DBA's whimsy. Your first step in deciphering an NT environment is to look at the Oracle Registry values. Using regedit, look at the HKEY_LOCAL_MACHINE\software\oracle key. The string values tell you the ORACLE_HOME location, among other useful information. Next, open the Services applet in the Control Panel, and look for any Oracle services. There is one Oracle service for each database on the system. There might be an Oracle start service for each database as well. Also, look for any other Oracle services that are installed—TNS Listener, Web Server, and so on.

All configuration values of interest are stored in the Oracle Registry key. The init.ora parameter files for the database are in $ORACLE_HOME/database. This is also the default directory to store database datafiles. You might find them here. Use the Windows NT Explorer to help you locate files. Be sure to check the NT Task Manager and job scheduler to see what jobs might be or have been running.

PART

II

CH

7

## CHAPTER 8

ORACLE DATABASE ADMINISTRATION OVERVIEW

In this chapter

In this chapter, you review exactly what a database administrator (DBA) is and does, what makes up the database lifecycle, the steps a DBA should follow to build an Oracle database, and the maintenance duties of an Oracle DBA. Much of this chapter might also apply to DBAs supporting nearly any other RDBMS, just so long as they can figure out the appropriate "mappings" from their RDBMS to the Oracle RDBMS. This is as it should be because database theory and technology, including administration, apply to all RDBMSs. As was alluded to in Chapter 4, "The Oracle Solution," RDBMSs, including Oracle, have all fallen short in different ways and to varying degrees in the faithfulness of their particular implementation of the relational model. To paraphrase Chris Date, "The vendors have let us down."

WHAT IS THE DATABASE LIFECYCLE?

A software *lifecycle* is a way of describing how software is created and evolves. A cliché often used to describe a piece of software's full lifecycle is "cradle to grave," meaning from the beginning to the end. All software lifecycles, including database software, travel through a series of *phases*. These phases are discrete processes that move the software development process further along. In other words, they describe the progress of the lifecycle. These phases are sequentially and iteratively dependent. For example, speaking in generalities, if Phase A precedes B, then B depends on A, and further, B might provide *feedback* to A in an iterative, loopback fashion. To simply show the precedence and dependency, you can use A -> B. To additionally show the feedback, you need only draw an arc from B back to A.

There are many models that provide various methods of notating (graphically or otherwise) a software lifecycle. One of the most classic software lifecycle models is the waterfall model. Other models exist, such as the spiral model. First, let's look at a description of a basic software lifecycle, which is a simplification of the waterfall model:

```
Analysis -> Design -> Implementation -> Maintenance
```

This model is a baseline for all software development. Now it's time to briefly cover what each of the phases represents.

THE ANALYSIS PHASE

The Analysis phase represents the comprehensive collection and documentation of user requirements, in addition to an analysis of what those requirements mean operationally. Hence, quite often the Analysis phase is also known as the Requirements Analysis phase. Different clients offer varying levels of cooperation as to their requirements. Some go to excruciating detail in their hardcopy statements of work, whereas others might simply provide vague, verbal directions. Generally, though, the focus is to outline the *functional* requirements of the system to be built, which might or might not include specifications dealing with items such as a user interface or performance considerations. A *specification* is simply another word for requirement. When a programmer wants to begin designing his program, he must review the "specs."

THE DESIGN PHASE

The Design phase primarily includes algorithm design, but also input/output considerations, such as formatting and display if a program is to be interactive or precision if a program is to be scientific. To begin coding without a design is akin to beginning a long drive without having a planned route. In any event, many important choices are made during the Design phase that impact not only functionality and presentation, but also pure performance. It is without a doubt that the proper choice of data structures and algorithm can make or break the subsequent performance of that program.

THE IMPLEMENTATION PHASE

The Implementation phase is essentially the coding of the program or system. After you have a proper choice of data structures, algorithms, and other such building blocks, you can begin programming in the chosen language. Within the programming itself, there, too, are many choices to be made. For example, which control flow structure would be best to implement a particular algorithm? In addition, within this phase, you also make choices that represent implicit or explicit tradeoffs, such as storage for speed (or vice versa). Quite often at this point in software development, practicality overrules theoretical concerns. For example, you might have to use certain types of programming interfaces, not because they are somehow better or faster, but because they are standardized in one way or another. Of course, implementation can be said to include other phases known as Test and Deployment.

THE TEST PHASE

The Test phase is just what you might think. In the Test phase, for example, you might test all the individual components of the system (*unit testing*) and then all of them together in an *end-to-end* (start-to-finish) *test*, also known as an *integrated* or *system test*. You make a change, and then you go back (*regress*) and retest everything (or, at least, everything that could have been impacted). You compare outputs to outputs to ensure that the functionality has not been lost. Other ways of testing are *load testing* and *performance testing*. To load test a system, you run the test with the smallest expected number of users and then increase that number to approach the maximum number of expected users, comparing *metrics* from each of the runs to see what effect, if any, increasing the concurrency has on your system performance. Another way of load testing is to increase the volume of data flowing through your system, as opposed to increasing the number of users accessing it. In many cases, you look at both.

To performance test, you establish what your performance goals are, in many cases simply by asking the client if this has not already been articulated by him. Generally, you consider one of three performance measures, or metrics: *elapsed time*, *response time*, and *throughput*. Elapsed time, also known as *wall time* or *clock time*, is how long a process takes to run in terms of finish time minus start time. This is useful for batch systems. Response time is how long it takes for a process to initially get a response to a request. Hence, this measure is useful for interactive systems, such as DSS systems. Throughput is a measure of how many pieces of work, usually business-defined "transactions," can pass through a system per unit time. For example, transactions per second is a measure of throughput, and this measure is useful for OLTP systems. Performance tests can be defined as part of functional requirements.

THE DEPLOYMENT PHASE

The Deployment phase occurs after a system has passed all its testing phases and is ready to be *deployed*, or installed, to all its endpoint systems, clients, and servers. The process of installing all the supporting hardware and software and, of course, the application software itself in runtime form is what deployment is all about. As soon as everything is deployed, it might be briefly retested and then effectively "turned over" to the responsible user after some *Transition* phase (wherein the contractors, if the project was *outsourced*, possibly supply some onsite support of the application software), depending on the contract specifications. After deployment, the product now enters the Maintenance phase.

THE MAINTENANCE PHASE

The Maintenance phase is where most software spends its life. It has been estimated that most software spends 70% or more of its time in the Maintenance phase. Hence, for this reason alone, this is perhaps the most important phase because wrong decisions at this point in software development could, over time, sink an otherwise correctly functioning piece of software. Decisions here involve many issues related to "open" systems such as portability and interoperability, which might affect a piece of software's long-term livelihood. Maintenance, as you might expect, also involves many systems integration issues, such as replacing existing hardware and software components over time, removing certain other components, and introducing new ones over time for various reasons. As you can imagine, the more components that are involved, the more complex the integration can be because many interactions are involved. As with the Implementation phase, standardized interfaces become increasingly more important as predictable behavior is what is desired. With systems integration, an old cliché holds true: "The more moving parts, the more likely there will be problems (and failures)." One of the reasons behind some of the integration problems is *heterogeneity*. That is, if many or all of the different parts come from different vendors, the likelihood of a *seamless* (that is, without any major incompatibilities) integration is small.

Now that you have covered the general software development lifecycle, consider the database-specific one. What database-specific activities relate to the general software model? The following are some answers:

- Analysis—The Conceptual Model (or Business Model) begins to take shape.
- Design—The Conceptual Model is refined. The Logical Design includes the initial mapping of the Conceptual Model to the Relational Model and the Entity Relationship Diagram (ERD). Normalization takes place. Then the Physical Design is mapped out. Also, the design of the database front-end and back-end programming can begin as soon as the Logical Design is complete.
- Implementation—To a database system, this is known as *the Build*, in which the DDL builds the structure of the database, and *the Load*, in which DML or vendor utilities

initially load the data into the database, if an initial load is appropriate (as opposed to loading it over time). Also, for a database system, the coding of the program can begin or continue from the Design phase.

- Test—After the database is built and loaded and the programs have been written, all can be tested, unit-wise and integrated.
- Deployment—With many modern systems, deployment means installing software on PCs (clients) and servers (Web servers and database servers).
- Maintenance—This is really no different from any other software system, except that it pertains more to data-centered software than process-centered software.

WHAT IS A DBA?

Frequently, my students ask me to delineate the differences between all the database professions currently available in the marketplace. Of course, the DBA is the central database position, around which all other positions revolve. Before considering only what a DBA is, first consider all the major database-related positions commonly found in the job market:

- Designer
- Architect
- Engineer
- Developer
- Programmer
- Operator
- Administrator (DBA)

First, consider the *Designer*. The Designer, as you might think, gathers the initial user requirements (if they have not already been gathered). She then analyzes, refines, and extrapolates them to fit the standardized database model inputs, such as conforming them to the relational model. The initial brainstorming sessions with the users and subsequent analyses help formulate what is typically known as *the Conceptual Model*, which we very briefly touched upon in Chapter 1, "Principles of Database Management," and Chapter 2, "Logical Database Design and Normalization." The conceptual model might also be referred to as the business model, containing not only the data model of the business at hand, but also *the business rules*, which will later manifest themselves as constraints, procedures, and triggers in any given RDBMS implementation. The Designer's scope of responsibility, as you might guess, spans the Requirements Analysis, Logical Design, and Physical Design phases.

An *Architect*, sometimes referred to as a Database Systems Architect or an Information Systems Architect, has very broad responsibility for the design and engineering of all the hardware, software, and networking components that comprise the enterprise. Hence, the Architect is part Designer, part Engineer, and in his career might have functioned as some or all of the other database-related positions. An Architect generally has many years of experience (for example, 10–15 or more) in not only database technology positions, but also in information technology in general.

An *Engineer*, in contrast to an Architect, typically has a more narrow responsibility, focussing only on database technology or only on one department or division within an organization. His scope might be more narrow in either its technology or organizational breadth. However, an Engineer is typically a Database Administrator or Developer with many years of experience (for example, 5–10 or more) and has sufficient experience and insight into fields both closely related to database technology and perhaps those more on the periphery.

A *Developer* sometimes means the same thing as a Programmer, but you can make a distinction. A database Developer typically works with front-end programs that supply interactive input (for example, Oracle Forms) and output (for example, Oracle Reports). Hence, the interactive nature of database Development finds many Developers working on such things as Microsoft Visual Basic, Microsoft Access, Sybase (PowerSoft) PowerBuilder, and Borland Delphi. All these programs are about building Graphical User Interfaces (GUIs), such as those typically following the Microsoft Windows interface design or Web browsers. Those based on Microsoft Windows are sometimes loosely referred to as the client applications in a client/server paradigm, or they are sometimes even more loosely referred to simply as client/server. Those based on Web browsers and Web technology are simply referred to as Web-based. Unfortunately, this loose categorization is misleading because Web-based systems are simply a special case of client/server systems. Developers, then, are responsible for building front-end, GUI-database, input/output programs. However, the actual amount of program coding that they produce is very little because it is almost all generated by the front-end tools themselves. When developers must actually write code, they still usually only have to write in fairly high-level languages, referred to as fourth generation languages (4GL), including macro and script languages. Many of these tools rely on either ODBC technology or native vendor RDBMS protocols, such as Oracle SQL*Net or Sybase Open Client (DB-Lib and Net-Lib).

A database *Programmer*, in contrast to a Developer, actually does write quite a bit of code, most often in SQL and vendor-based, control-flow, SQL-based 4GLs, such as Oracle PL/SQL and SQL Server Transact-SQL (T-SQL). However, you will also frequently find database Programmers writing in embedded SQL or native application programming interfaces (APIs), such as the Oracle Call Interface (OCI) or Sybase Open Client. As such, you will of course find these database Programmers often well-versed in languages such as C, C++, and Java, and therefore, they are not much different than their predecessors who happened to write in COBOL and FORTRAN and access file systems as opposed to databases. In fact, in many cases, these programmers are one and the same, being experienced ones who have simply updated their skills.

An *Operator* might be thought of as an operations support (also known as operations and maintenance, or O & M) technician. He is typically responsible for the maintenance of certain hardware and software on a periodic basis. You will find Operators staffed around the clock in shifts to support 24×7 or otherwise critical systems. The typical duties of an Operator, especially in relation to database support, generally have to do with backup and recovery. Quite often, an Operator is the person responsible for the tape (and optical) archives, including database archives. With modern tape (and optical) robotic devices (stackers, jukeboxes, and so on), Operators are no less important in that arena, although perhaps less busy, because those devices themselves require quite a bit of care and feeding, despite their "lights out" sales pitches. Apart from tertiary storage duties, such as "hanging tapes," Operators might also fulfill the roles of "hanging cable" (physically installing network cables), laying power distribution cables under computer room floors, attaching secondary storage devices (hard disks), building the racks that support multiple computers, or even setting up some computer devices out of the box.

Finally, you come to the DataBase *Administrator*, or *DBA*. This is the central database-related position, generally thought of as a progression above that of a Programmer, but below that of Engineer. A DBA often goes on to become an Engineer or even an Architect yet often was already a Developer, Programmer, or Operator. A DBA, along with operating system *System Administrators* (SAs) typically delegates maintenance and operations tasks to Operators. Also, DBAs must work closely with Developers and Programmers in building a complete, well-integrated database system, with the DBAs concentrating on the "back-end," and the Developers/Programmers concentrating on the "front-end." In addition, a DBA might have either been or might become a Designer. Either way, the DBA must also work extremely closely with the Designer to bridge the gap from Design to Build (Implementation).

In the real world, you will often find talented people playing multiple roles. For example, one person might be a Designer, Developer/Programmer, and a DBA. In some situations, you will find one person functioning as both a DBA and an SA. In other organizations, all the above professions are separate and distinct job positions. How one person might come to function in multiple roles can be due to many things, including the overall breadth and depth of a person's technical talents or a company's unwillingness or shortsightedness to understand the need for the different roles. In addition, sometimes a company simply either cannot afford all the multiple positions relative to the company's size or the database's (lack of) importance. Also, what is increasingly more often the case is that the companies are simply unable to hire and fill all the multiple positions because there has been and still is a shortage of database-related professionals relative to the number of available positions. This tends to not only drive the potential salaries up for any single position, but it also inflates them further for those persons capable of fulfilling more than one role.

As opposed to DBAs in general, now look at what an Oracle DBA is and does in some more detail.

THE ADMINISTRATIVE STEPS IN BUILDING A DATABASE

For an Oracle DBA, there are several "administrative steps" in building an Oracle database, and many of them would apply with a little modification to any other vendor's database. Over time, I have had many colleagues and students with varying database backgrounds, both generally with any databases and specifically with Oracle, ask what the major steps in building an Oracle database that a DBA should follow are. This is not an unreasonable question at all because very often it is glossed over as to the proper order of things. Quite often, many references and resources gloss over the high-level sequencing of the tasks in favor of low-level specifics. For example, you find out how to edit and change parameters in an `init.ora` file, but where does it fit into the "big picture"? In hopes of getting the overall sequence of events across, the following list explains these steps in sufficient detail, but not in too much depth:

1. Install the Oracle software (RDBMS, Networking, Client, and so on).
2. Edit the initialization parameter file (`init.ora`).
3. Create the Oracle instance.
4. Create the Oracle database, including the system tablespace and redo logs.
5. Create the data dictionary (that is, run the `cat` scripts).
6. Create the remaining tablespaces and rollback segments.
7. Create the tables.
8. Add the primary and unique keys disabled.
9. Enable the primary keys and unique keys (creates indexes).
10. Add the foreign keys (enabled).
11. Create foreign key indexes and indexes for other appropriate columns.
12. Add check constraints and write triggers as appropriate.
13. Write procedures, functions, and other code (that is, Pro*C) as appropriate.

Although some of these steps can be separated further (or even combined), in my experience in building Oracle databases, I find this separation of DBA (and partly, Developer) duties to be highly flexible and scalable.

1. When installing the Oracle software, you must take into consideration not only your current needs or initial database state, but your future needs and anticipated growth. To that end, using a variation of the Optimal Flexible Architecture (OFA) will be very useful. For further information on the OFA, which includes directory and filename suggestions for organization and convention, please refer to Chapter 7, "Exploring the Oracle Environment," and Appendix A, "Oracle on Solaris," as they both contain overviews of implementing an OFA database.

2. Of course, unless you install and expect to use the default Oracle instance and database (ORCL), you need to create your own. To do this, your first act must be to edit the initialization parameter file (`init.ora` or `init<SID>.ora`). You edit it to specify at the very

minimum your db_name and control_files, but perhaps also other things such as the size of db_block_size. Later, you will also have to re-edit your init.ora file when you have created your rollback segments you want to use on a permanent basis to have with the open on startup with rollback_segs. Plus, there are many other things you might adjust or enable here, such as archive log mode.

3. To create the instance, then, is to first create a custom-edited init.ora file containing control file specifications. On UNIX, when you start up nomount within svrmgrl, you have "created" your instance. On UNIX, you will be able to connect internal by belonging to a UNIX group named *dba*. In NT, you will use the Oracle NT Instance Manager (oradim80.exe), either in command-line or GUI mode, to create your instance, and this will also create a password file and associated service (with a startup file). When you create the NT instance, you specify a password for internal so that you can connect internal within svrgmr30.exe. Refer to Chapter 7, "Exploring the Oracle Environment," and Appendix B, "Oracle on Windows NT," for further information regarding Oracle on NT, and refer to Chapter 7 and Appendix A for further information regarding Oracle on UNIX.

4. The next task you have is to create your database while in the nomount state. When you write your create database script, at a minimum you will specify the creation of your system tablespace and initial redo logs. However, you should also take this opportunity to set such things as MAXDATAFILES and MAXLOGFILES as high as expected. An initial system rollback segment is created, which you can later discard. On database creation, your init.ora parameters are read, and your control files are created in the specified locations.

5. Here, you will run the basic Oracle-supplied packages that you would generally run for any Oracle database: catalog.sql, catproc.sql, pupbld.sql, and perhaps a few others, such as utlexcpt.sql, utlxpln.sql, or catrep.sql, as your application might dictate. This essentially establishes your administrative access and views (for SYS, SYSTEM, and other users) into the Oracle data dictionary (X$ tables). The V$ views, DBA_ tables, and USER_ tables are created.

6. You can then create your remaining user tablespaces that will serve your interactive users and application needs. At this point you will have properly sized your tables (and indexes) and should be able to come up with reasonable tablespace sizes based on your estimates. Refer to Chapter 4, "The Oracle Solution," in the section "Sizing for Oracle". Remember to set PCTINCREASE to 1 if you want SMON to be able to automatically coalesce the tablespace fragementations. In addition, it is here you will need to also create your expected user and application rollback segments. When you have done so, remember to go back and re-edit the init.ora rollback_segs parameter as mentioned.

7. Now, again using your sizing inputs, you are ready to create your empty tables. Your considerations should include overriding the storage parameters of the tablespaces, as well as considering what datatypes are most appropriate for the data that they must hold. With VLDBs, for example, logical compression can be very important.

Remember to keep heavily joined and other simultaneously heavily accessed tables separated not only onto different tablespaces, but preferably onto different disks. Refer to Chapter 3, "Physical Database Design, Hardware, and Related Issues," Chapter 4, "The Oracle Solution," Chapter 16, "Performance Tuning Fundamentals," and Chapter 19 "Tuning I/O," for further information regarding I/O layout and tuning guidance.

8. In Oracle, remember that to add a primary key enabled (the default) will automatically create an index in the default tablespace of the owner. This is almost always not a good idea. Hence, define all your primary keys initially disabled. What holds true for primary keys holds true for unique keys also.

9. Enable all your primary keys separately with physical parameters specified. This keeps the logical definitions separate from the physical layout. This is always a good idea, especially for VLDBs (Very Large DataBases) and portability concerns. Again, unique keys can be treated the same way.

10. In Oracle, adding foreign keys enabled (the default) does not automatically create indexes anywhere for them. This is important to know because when large tables are joined, foreign keys can be a performance detriment.

11. Create indexes for those foreign keys participating in large table joins because without them, the parent table is locked *at the table level*. With them, either row-level locks or no locks are acquired, as with an ordinary table access. In addition, index those columns of large tables that are expected to be accessed heavily with SELECTS as part of the column list or the WHERE clause.

12. The addition of constraints and triggers makes a relational database complete in terms of data integrity. Without them, aside from primary and foreign key constraints, you really only have just another database. With these additional constructs, you can add business rules, such as domain integrity enforcement (for example, valid value ranges for a column), and data flow dependencies (for example, when an employee is to be inserted into a database, his identifying information is inserted first into one table, and his other information is inserted last into the remaining tables that define an employee). Remember, constraints, when enabled, check every row for every access, which is a *very* expensive proposition. To identify any constraint violations (*exceptions*), you would typically enable them after any bulk loading or large modifications and then disable them. Triggers are triggered by a modification to the table on which they are defined, and then can act on any other table (or simply do some computational or file processing). However, they can not act upon the table on which they are defined, in direct contrast to check constraints, which can only act upon the table ("check" the columns) on which they are defined. Constraints are simply DDL statements, and triggers are defined through DDL, but the body is essentially a procedure body (DML).

13. Procedures, functions, cursors, and embedded SQL do what constraints and triggers cannot. Procedures and functions, for example, do not depend on a modification event of a single table. They can be run independently of any given table modifications. Cursors enable record-at-time access within procedures, functions, or embedded SQL, when

set-based access is otherwise somehow inadequate (and it sometimes is). Embedded SQL provides tight integration, especially with cursors, with a 3GL such as C. Armed with all these programmatic tools, an Oracle DBA or Developer/Programmer can fulfill nearly any database-related programming tasks. As you might expect, here is where the DBA leaves off and the Developers/Programmers pick up, although, in theory, they could have already have begun designing and writing this code as early as when the Logical Design was complete. (They just couldn't have compiled it because the database had yet to be built.)

What makes these steps scalable to large systems is that, except for the first three, each of the remaining steps might correspond to one or more SQL*Plus scripts. For example, you might have the scripts in Table 8.1.

TABLE 8.1   SCALABLE BUILD SCRIPTS

Step	Script	Description
(4)	crdb.sql:	Creates the database
(5)	runcat.sql:	Runs the cat scripts (creates the catalogs)
(6)	tspaces.sql:	Creates the tablespaces
(6)	rollback.sql	Creates the rollback segments
(7)	tables.sql	Creates the tables
(8)	addpk.sql	Adds the primary keys disabled
(8)	adduk.sql	Adds the unique keys disabled
(9)	enablepk.sql	Enables the primary keys (and creates their indexes)
(9)	enableuk.sql	Enables the unique keys (and creates their indexes)
(10)	addfk.sql	Adds the foreign keys enabled
(11)	crfk.sql	Creates the foreign key indexes
(12)	addck.sql	Adds the check constraints
(12)	trig.sql	Creates the triggers
(13)	procs.sql	Creates the procedures
(13)	funcs.sql	Creates the functions

Why does this separation help at all? It helps on many levels. First, it organizes things systematically. So, for example, when you go to build your database, you build it one step at a time, and if something fails, you know *precisely* where you were when it failed (in the middle of one step). Often, you need only fix what you can and simply rerun that step, as opposed to dropping everything and returning back to the beginning of some very large "create everything" script. Hence, these steps help you *modularize* your database build, which is desirable for many reasons, not the least of which is troubleshooting the build. Further, these steps tend to separate logical definitions from physical layouts. This means that when changes to one or the other (most likely to the physical, usually) are made, you only have to modify one script and not two for every logical–physical pair of scripts, such as tables–tablespaces, `addpk–enablepk`, and so on. In addition, as desired, these scripts could, of course, be broken down even further into different groups of areas within an application if the total application were sufficiently large enough to warrant it. A final motivation is to consider porting, and hence, rebuilding, this database on another platform with a different physical layout. These steps and scripts will definitely facilitate such a migration, even more so than exporting and importing objects.

One final note: Where do you think you would place a bulk load operation (between what steps)? Well, one natural place to load data, as from SQL*Loader for example, would be right after you create your tables, but before you create your keys, indexes, and constraints. This would likely be after Step 7 but before Step 8. Why not load after Step 8 onward? Having enabled keys, indexes, and constraints can slow down a bulk loading operation considerably. What about data integrity? When you go to enable your keys and constraints, you will find any and all integrity and constraint violations at that time. You can then repair the data and reload incrementally or fully as necessary. That way, you sacrifice neither speed nor integrity.

SUMMARY

You have reviewed the general software development lifecycle and how a database-specific software lifecycle looks mapped onto the general model. You see that it is not too much different. However, there are some differences from the viewpoint of the DBA. For example, in the design, you focus more on modeling data rather than processes, although the latter are equally important, especially for the Developers and Programmers. In the implementation, you focus more on building the database structure, as opposed to writing code, although again the latter is the crux of the Programmers' work, if not also the Developers.

You also considered which major database professions are available and how they differ, not only in skill level and experience, but as to where they fit in the database lifecycle relative to their colleagues. As you can see, most of these professions can lead from one to another over time, and hence, there is quite a bit of room for career growth in the database field.

Next, you consider what an Oracle DBA must do in enough detail to understand the build phase of the database lifecycle with a focus on flexibility and scalability. Quite often, books and other sources skirt right over this proper sequence of events and miss seeing the forest for the trees. This chapter attempts to explicitly address this situation by enumerating the major build steps for an Oracle DBA to follow and by highlighting their reusability and how they loosely are coupled, separable, and lend themselves as scripts. For even more in-depth coverage of DBA duties, please refer to Part V, "Managing the Oracle Database," and Part VI, "Oracle Interfaces and Utilities." The chapters contained within Part V help you manage storage, resource utilization, security, backup/recovery, and integrity. In addition, the chapters contained within Part VI cover the basic Oracle utilities with which you can more effectively manage your Oracle databases, including SQL*Plus, PL/SQL, and especially Oracle Enterprise Manager (OEM). The last utility is a GUI tool that puts much administrative power in the hands of a DBA, equalling the work of many SQL*Plus scripts or PL/SQL programs.

PART

III

THE ORACLE8.x RDBMS

CHAPTER 9

MIGRATING ORACLE7.X TO ORACLE 8.X

In this chapter

This chapter will discuss the three major methods of migrating an Oracle7.x database to an Oracle8.x database. It will concentrate on the Migration Utility method, discuss the pre-migration tasks that must accompany any migration method, consider common problems, and briefly overview some of the likely post-migration tasks.

THE THREE MAJOR METHODS

The three major methods of migrating from an Oracle7 database to an Oracle8 database are the following:

- The Migration Utility—An Oracle8 supplied tool that can be used in a GUI or command-line mode, which facilitates an *in-place* database migration from an Oracle7 (7.1.6 or greater) database to an Oracle8 database.

- Export/Import—This is the same technique used to perform an ordinary (same version to same version) full database backup and recovery using the proprietary Oracle binary format of export and import, except in the case of migration an Oracle8 database, it is imported from a full Oracle7 database export.

- COPY or CTAS—This method copies an entire database, one table at a time, via a SQL*Net (Net8) COPY command or via a DDL Create Table As Select (CTAS) command, from an Oracle7 database to an Oracle8 database.

Table 9.1 outlines the advantages and disadvantages of each approach.

TABLE 9.1   ADVANTAGES AND DISADVANTAGES OF MIGRATION METHODS

Method	Advantages	Disadvantages
Migration Utility (In-Place Migration)	Oracle-supplied and supported. Mostly automated. Relatively fast. Relatively space-efficient.	Source Oracle7 database must be version 7.1.6 or greater. Full migration only. Migration is destructive (to the source Oracle7 database).
Export/Import	Any Oracle7 source database. Partial migration possible Side benefit of defragmentation. Migration is nondestructive.	Relatively slow. Full database exports often limited by OS file or partition limits. Unless direct-to-tape, requires space for a full database export file on disk.
COPY or CTAS	Any Oracle7 source database. Partial migration possible. Side benefit of defragmentation. Migration is nondestructive.	Relatively slow. Significant manual effort required. Both source and target databases must be OPEN.

Now briefly look at these comparative advantages and disadvantages. Before or during migration, new Oracle8 base tables and V$ views are added. In addition, some Oracle7 base tables and V$ views are modified. Updating the structures of the datafile headers, control files, and redo log files also must take place. Any method must accomplish this either before or during the actual transfer of the Oracle7 data to the Oracle8 database.

Now review the two methods with which most Oracle7 database administrators should already be familiar: export/import and copy/ctas. With the export/import method, the required Oracle7 to Oracle8 conversions occur automatically when the Oracle8 import utility imports from an Oracle7 export file. Perhaps the greatest benefit of using the export/import method is administrative familiarity with the tools, whereas perhaps the greatest detriment is the large space requirement for a full database export file. However, with export/import, "piecemeal" migration is possible, although you are only trading space for time in that it will take longer overall to complete the migration. However, this author would argue that in most cases, the speed of the migration is not the utmost concern. Instead, it is the success of the migration that is the prime concern in most installations.

The copy/ctas method is arguably as familiar to Oracle7 DBAs as is export/import. However, this method is rarely used as a primary backup and recovery method, especially for VLDBs. More often, it is used by users as their own method of backups outside the standard backup methods, such as export/import or RMAN. Perhaps the greatest benefit of the copy/ctas method is the simplicity of the operations, whereas perhaps the greatest detriment is the time it takes to migrate. This latter condition is the case because tables must be copied, more or less one-at-a-time, compounded by the fact that both databases must remain up until the copies are complete. Again, like export/import, the migration can be done in stages, but this only extends the time to migrate even further. In the case of copy/ctas, as opposed to export/import, the time it takes to migrate is more important because it has the potential to interfere with normal operation time windows. As a side note, INSERT INTO...SELECT can be used as an alternative to CREATE TABLE AS SELECT, the only difference being that the target tables are already created.

One could argue that at least a fourth method exists: the Unload/Load method. With this method, you spool all your Oracle7 table data out to flat (ASCII) files and then load them with SQL*Loader into your new Oracle8 database. This method has the benefit of being able to unload the data offline, like export, before being reloaded; hence, it is inherently an asynchronous method. However, it is also inherently the most time-consuming manually, and for all but the smallest or simplest databases, this author would argue that this is not really a feasible alternative.

THE MIGRATION UTILITY (MIG AND MIG80)

Because the Migration Utility is new to Oracle8 and offers perhaps the best overall solution, especially for large databases in terms of space and time efficiency, an entire section is devoted to it.

HIGH-LEVEL STEPS

The high-level steps in using the Migration Utility method are summarized in the following list:

1. Install the Migration Utility.
2. Prepare for migration (see the section, "Pre-Migration Tasks")

3. Install the Oracle8 software.

4. Run the Migration Utility.

5. Prepare the Oracle7 database for conversion.

6. Convert the Oracle7 database to Oracle8.

7. Perform final housekeeping (see the last section, "Post-Migration Tasks").

LOW-LEVEL TASKS

Next you'll spend some time delineating the low-level tasks that must be followed in using the Migration Utility method. Look at each one in sufficient detail:

1. Run the Oracle installer (`orainst`), and choose "Install Migration Utility O7 -> O8". This utility is then copied into the Oracle7 `$ORACLE_HOME/bin` subdirectory. It also installs an associated message file, a new version of `migrate.bsq` in the `$ORACLE_HOME/dbs` subdirectory, and installs required NLS files as necessary.

2. Conceptually and strategically prepare for migration by following the tasks outlined in the next section, "Pre-Migration Tasks." Implementation-wise, the single most important thing to do is to make sure to get a successful, full Oracle7 database backup before proceeding. If possible, take two full backups, perhaps with varying modes such as one full cold and one full export. Leave the instance shut down.

3. Run the Oracle installer (`orainst`) and install the Oracle8 software with the Install/Upgrade option. This latter option prevents the installer from creating a new instance and database.

4. The instance should still be down from Task 2. Run the Migration Utility installed in Task 1 in the Oracle7 `$ORACLE_HOME/bin` subdirectory. This executable is named either `mig` on UNIX or `mig80` in NT. Before running `mig`, know its main parameters:

   - `check_only`—If `FALSE` (the default), space usage is calculated, and the actual migration takes place. If `TRUE`, only space usage is calculated. This is the equivalent of a `noexec` option with the main output being whether space is determined to be sufficient in the migration database (source and target, in this case).

   - `no_space_check`—When set to `TRUE`, no space check is performed, and `check_only` is ignored. If `FALSE` (the default), `check_only` is obeyed.

   - `dbname`—The name of the old source database (`db_name` in `init.ora`) to migrate.

   - `new_dbname`—The name of the new target database (`db_name` in new `init.ora`); can be the same as the old one; the default is `DEFAULT`.

   - `pfile`—The name of the `init.ora` file for the old source database.

   - `spool`—The relative or absolute path of the filename in double quotes to which to log output.

Caution

> Because the Oracle8 data dictionary is about 50% larger than that of Oracle7, it is important to either manually add a datafile to the SYSTEM tablespace, or at least set AUTOEXTEND on those datafiles already supporting it (assuming there is space at the OS level). Another alternative is to manually resize (AUTOEXTEND) the existing datafile(s) of the SYSTEM tablespace.

Run the mig executable from the OS command-line prompt, qualified by a parameter list as in *<parameter1>* = *<value1>* *<parameter2>* = *<value2>* and so forth. On NT you run mig80 at an MS-DOS prompt, and on UNIX you run mig at your shell prompt. Assuming the Oracle bin directory is in your system startup image path, an example might look like the following:

```
C:\>MIG80 DBNAME=MYDB NEW_DBNAME=MYNEWDB SPOOL=MYLOG
```

The migration utility will run the ASCII migrate.bsq script file, which in turn creates a migrate user wherein it builds views to support the migration process. When it is done, it will leave in place a log file (from the SPOOL option) in its specified location (or default) and a binary conversion data file (conv<SID>.dbf) in the Oracle7 ORACLE_HOME/dbs subdirectory.

5. Prepare the Oracle7 database for *conversion*, which is the separate, critical stage that occurs right after running the migration utility. To prepare the Oracle7 database, remove (move or rename) the Oracle7 control files because new Oracle8 control files will be created in their place. Ensure that all other files, datafiles and redo log files are intact.

   Also, prepare the OS environment by resetting the ORACLE_HOME OS variable (Registry on NT or shell environment variable on UNIX) to the new Oracle8 directory location. Then, reset the Oracle binary executable path (Image Path in proper NT Registry subtree or shell PATH variable in UNIX if necessary, although the ORACLE_HOME variable should have taken care of this on UNIX). Also, reset your ORACLE_SID if this has changed. Set the ORA_NLS33 parameter if necessary.

   Edit your new Oracle8 init.ora file to include the parameter setting of compatible = 8.0.0 (or higher). Also, remove any obsolete Oracle7 parameters. (Please refer to your server manual for the most recent list) Ensure your parameter settings for control_files=() and other file locations, such as bdump and cdump, are correct (that is, do not contain any Oracle7 path references)

   Copy the conversion data file (conv<SID>.dbf) from the Oracle7 $ORACLE_HOME/dbs subdirectory to the Oracle8 $ORACLE_HOME/dbs subdirectory.

6. Convert your database. *This is the point of no return.* In other words, after you run convert and your database either successfully converts or not, it cannot be reverted to the Oracle7 state without a full cold restore. To do this, run the following in svrmgrl (UNIX) or svrmgr30 (NT):

```
svrmgrl> connect internal
svrmgrl> startup nomount
svrmgrl> alter database convert;
svrmgrl> alter database open resetlogs;
```

7. Performing the final housekeeping chores entails several things, including dropping the migrate user (with the cascade option) created when the migration utility is run, and running the `catalog.sql` and `catproc.sql` scripts. However, a new script is supplied, `cat8000.sql`, which, when run, will do all the aforementioned chores for you.

The Migration Utility GUI is the counterpart to the command-line version, `mig`. It can be accessed and run from the Oracle installer (`orainst`) and is done just after the migration utility is installed. Select the following options: "Install," "Migrate from Oracle7 to Oracle8," "Run Migration Utility," and "Migration Utility: Oracle7 to Oracle8.x.x.x.x." You will then be prompted for what would otherwise be the command-line `mig` options, such as `check_only`. If you choose the option to only check for space requirements, then just like the command-line version, you will have to rerun the utility to perform the actual migration (without that option chosen). So, with the GUI in place of the command-line version, you would perform Tasks 1 and 2, but not 3 because the GUI will install the Oracle8 software *and* migrate the data.

PRE-MIGRATION TASKS

There are some important things you must plan and do before rushing off to run the Migration Utility, though, and the following list of steps summarizes your pre-migration checklist:

- Review the new Oracle8 features.
- Choose your migration method.
- Estimate hardware and software resource needs.
- Acquire necessary resources.
- Develop acceptance criteria (with which to test).
- Develop a migration schedule.
- Back up the source Oracle7 database.

To help you review the new Oracle8 features, read all of Part III, "The Oracle8.x RDBMS," which includes the chapters following this one, 10 through 15. In it you can decide whether migration to Oracle8 is an appropriate move for your installation at this time. On the other hand, factors other than new functionality and enhancements come into play when making the decision to migrate. In particular, one of the most important is Oracle's policy of "desupporting" older versions of Oracle on a very progressive basis. For example, all of Oracle7 is scheduled to be desupported by the end of calendar year 2000. In particular, Oracle7.3.3 and earlier were desupported as of December 31, 1998, and Oracle7.3.4, the terminal (final) release of Oracle7, is scheduled to be desupported by December 31, 2000. (However, this latter date has already been moved twice.)

It is important to consider space and time requirements when deciding which migration method to choose. In addition, consider how critical your database and its uptime requirements (if any) are. If your database must be highly available and is very large, the migration utility is probably the best approach, especially if used in a testbed fashion several times before actually proceeding with the production migration. On the other hand, if your database is relatively small or is not as critical, either the export/import or copy/ctas option are fine choices. In that case, the only reason to use the migration utility might be to gain experience with the utility itself, which is not necessarily a bad reason if other larger, more critical databases are to follow the migration path.

To estimate your hardware and software resource needs, review your space and time requirements from the previous task of choosing your migration method. Except for the increased storage needs of the Oracle8 SYSTEM tablespace and binaries, which is constant regardless of the migration method, you will find that the migration utility (in-place) method will require the least amount of extraneous, or processing, space. This is true because no intermediate transitional structures are required. Also, you will find it to be the fastest method because the time to migrate is proportional to the number of database objects to migrate and not the total database size. Lastly, with the migration utility method, only one of everything is needed: one machine, one server, one instance, one database, and so forth. This is evident because the old database is migrated "in-place" to become the new database.

The most outstanding resource requirement with the export/import method is the need for the relatively large amount of space for the full database export file. However, this can be exported directly to tape, at least in UNIX, and this moves the online storage need to an offline storage need. With the copy/ctas method, what is required storage-wise is that the database objects in the new database will require at least as much (a little bit more, in fact, due to the new ROWIDs and other factors) storage as they did in the old database. For both export/import and copy/ctas methods, they will require almost two of everything: two instances, two databases, and perhaps even two machines, if, for example, the source database already consumes most of its machine's resources. Relative to the migration utility, for VLDBs, the export/import and copy/ctas methods are expensive proposals.

When you have determined your resource needs, given your chosen migration method, acquire those resources. Install and configure the secondary machine to mirror the primary machine's environment, resource allocations, and utilizations as closely as possible. If two machines are acquired and one machine clearly has more power and resources than the other, work it so that the target Oracle8 instance winds up on that box, unless for some reason that is not feasible or acceptable.

ACCEPTANCE CRITERIA

Acceptance criteria can include a series of tests. These tests are described in Table 9.2.

TABLE 9.2 ACCEPTANCE CRITERIA

Test	Description
Migration	Migrate a subset or a clone of the source database. Subsets can be easily tested with the export/import methods, but a clone database will be needed to test the migration utility without the need of some kind of backup/restore.
Minimal	Test the minimal functionality of the application on the target database after the migration.
Functional	Test the full functionality of the application on the target database after the migration. In other words, all possible functional path combinations are walked through.
Integration	Test the entire system by testing all the external components (interfaces) that interact with the core application built on the target database.
Performance	Before the migration, baseline the performance of all, or at least key, functional components of the application. After, run the same functional components (the benchmarks), and measure the same performance aspects. Compare the "after" to the "before," with the idea that the "after" (Oracle8) should perform at least as well as, perhaps better, than the "before" (Oracle7).
Load	Also known as a volume test or stress test. This type of test can be combined with the performance test by varying the number of users and/or the volume of data. Again, compare before and after performance to see that the "after" performs at least as good, if not better.

Given the chosen migration method, the size, criticality, and uptime of your database, as well as other factors, decide on a realistic migration schedule. If your database is small or is non-critical, simply migrate on the weekend or even during the workweek if possible. However, if your database is on the other end of the extreme, or is simply "high-profile" or has high "visibility" within your company, consider doing an *offline migration*, if possible. For example, if your database has a 24×7 uptime requirement, how can you upgrade? Well, if you can take a full cold backup and restore it onto another machine (that is, make a clone database), then by all means do that and migrate the clone. However, if you cannot lose the transactional activity from the time of the backup through the time of the upgrade, you might want to consider, if possible, creating a standby or replicated database, and upgrade that secondary database, thereby not losing any transactional activity. If the upgrade fails, you need only re-clone and update your secondary database.

Backing up your source Oracle7 database before a migration to Oracle8 should go without saying. However, it can't, because many DBAs still do not take it seriously enough. Your worst case scenario, however, can be realized if you choose the migration utility method, fail, and have no good backup to restore.

COMMON PROBLEMS

One common problem is resource limits: insufficient space in the SYSTEM tablespace. As mentioned, Oracle8 needs about 1.5 times the amount of Oracle7. Also, ORACLE_HOME/bin under Oracle8 will take about 3 times the space under Oracle7.

Partial usage of ROWIDs is another common problem. Refer to Chapter 14, "Oracle8i Additional Topics," but suffice it to say that partial ROWID usage in Oracle7 applications will not port to Oracle8 without rewriting them using the new Oracle8 DBMS_ROWID package to accommodate the new Oracle8 ROWID structure.

Migration invalidates all code objects. All table data distribution statistics (for the cost-based optimizer) are lost. Some indexes might get marked as unusable.

The GUI migration utility (orainst) uses only the US7ASCII character set, as opposed to the command-line version which might specify any.

The ROWIDs of Oracle7 tables in read-only tablespaces are not converted to the new Oracle8 ROWIDs (because they are read-only!). The workaround is to temporarily change the tablespaces to read-write (regular), SELECT * from each read-only table in those tablespaces (to force the ROWID conversions with a full table scan), and then change them back to read-only. Without doing this, the tables in read-only tablespaces otherwise have to undergo a temporary ROWID conversion every time they are read!

POST-MIGRATION TASKS

Aside from obvious post-migration activities, those of backing up the newly migrated Oracle8 database and testing the acceptance criteria you developed in pre-migration, there are a few other important items. These include (performance) tuning your new Oracle8 database, as well as installing unbundled (optional) products such as the Object Option. Most of the administrative scripts on which you rely will have to be modified to help you monitor and manage storage and growth, as well as performance, effectively given the new Oracle8 data structures, objects, and views. Your Oracle7 applications will likely have to be modified, if for no other reason then to take advantage of some of the new features of Oracle8. As mentioned earlier, those applications relying on partial ROWID manipulations will have to be rewritten. Lastly, if SQL*Net connection strings are not fully ported as-is to Net8, reliant applications will have to be modified accordingly.

PART

III

CH

9

PARTITIONING

In this chapter

Partitioning is perhaps the single most important new feature of the Oracle8 RDBMS. Although some form of it existed with Oracle7, it has been enhanced and incorporated more fully into the RDBMS engine with the release of Oracle8. The term *partitioning* is overloaded. In other words, it has many meanings with regards to database theory and other vendors, such as Informix. However, what you of course deal with here is the specific Oracle capability of partitioning tables and indexes.

WHAT IS PARTITIONING?

Oracle first had the capability of partitioning with *partition views* in Oracle7. Partition views helped to physically divide data storage on disk according to some user-defined business rules, conditions, or specifications. In essence, tables and indexes were able to be divided up based on the values of a given column. For example, if a state column contained two character abbreviations for states, a table could be divided by storing all the states that make up the different regions of the country (for example, East Coast) on separate disks.

This was done using check constraints, which were made to be *mutually exclusive*. That is, all the different subsets of values for a given column, when divided out, could not overlap. (Think about it: If they could overlap, you would be able to store a single row on more than one disk, but how would Oracle know which one to use?) In addition to manually setting up the mutually exclusive partitions, you would set the initialization parameter, `partition_view_enabled`, to TRUE. This would inform the optimizer to investigate for all the tables the possibility that they might happen to be partitioned such that the WHERE clause under consideration might need to access only one or a few of the partitions, as opposed to having to access all the partitions making up the entire table. This efficiency is most notable for large tables undergoing full table scans, but it can also be realized in other situations. For example, it can be efficient with large index scans or medium-sized table or index accesses. The optimizer behavior of being able to "skip" partitions, given partition boundary knowledge, is known as *partition elimination*. Listing 10.1 shows how a partition view might have been set up in Oracle7.

LISTING 10.1   CREATING A PARTITION VIEW IN ORACLE7

```
SQL> create table EAST_REGION (STATEID,…) …;
SQL> create table WEST_REGION (STATEID,…) …;
SQL> create table NORTH_REGION (STATEID,…) …;
SQL> create table SOUTH_REGION (STATEID,…) …;

SQL> create view NATIONAL as
2 select * from EAST_REGION union all
3 select * from WEST_REGION union all
4 select * from NORTH_REGION union all
5 select * from SOUTH_REGION union all;

SQL> alter table EAST_REGION
2 add constraint CKSTATE check
3 (STATE_ID between 1 and 13);
…
SQL> alter table SOUTH_REGION
2 add constraint CKSTATE check
3 (STATE_ID between 39 and 50);
```

The Oracle7 capability of partition views was enhanced and incorporated into Oracle8, and now, no initialization parameter such as *partition_view_enabled* is needed to inform the optimizer. In addition to the initialization parameter in Oracle7, partitions were implemented using constraints and views. An entire partitioned table, in fact, was a view that was in actuality the union of all those horizontal fragments created and stored by the constraints. The horizontal fragments themselves were in actuality tables.

This situation is different with Oracle8 in that partitioning is a new physical layer in the Oracle database storage architecture, residing between the table and its extents. A table is mapped to a set of partitions, which are in turn mapped one-to-one to a set of extents, with each of those extents mapped to one or more tablespaces having one or more datafiles each. Figure 10.1 compares the addition of a partitioned table to a non-partitioned table.

Figure 10.1
Comparison of a
Non-Partitioned and
Partitioned Table

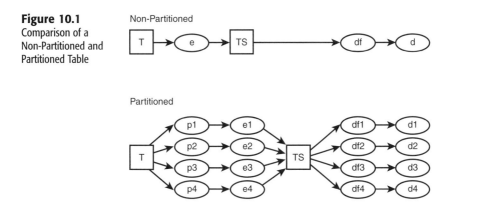

Legend: T=Table, e=extent, TS=Tablespace, df=datafile, d=disk, p=partition

Further, partitioning is now part of the Oracle extended SQL Data Definition Language (DDL). Partitioning, being a part of the language, has much importance. It means that the optimizer is "partition aware" and can take advantage of partition elimination without the need for such things as an initialization parameter. Tables and indexes can be partitioned.

PARTITIONING STRATEGIES

There are several partitioning strategies. Database objects, such as tables or indexes, can be partitioned, as with Oracle7 or Oracle8, using ranges of column values. This is generally known as *key partitioning* because, more often than not, the column is an index or key in the table. Oracle7 enables the ranges to be specified using BETWEEN...AND or the inequalities <= or >=. Oracle8 requires you to use the new language LESS THAN, as you will soon see.

There are other types of partitioning which Oracle does not currently implement. These include *hash partitioning* and *expression partitioning*. As you can see, key partitioning is a special case of expression partitioning. Why would anyone need expressions other than those supplied by Oracle7 or Oracle8? Currently with Oracle, you can only take contiguous subsets of sequential ranges of a column to partition a table. Suppose, for pure performance reasons, you want to use some sort of MOD or RANDOM function to distribute the data equally in some manner unrelated to the value of any particular column. In general, this undermines the partition elimination advantages normally gained, but in some cases it might be beneficial. For example, partitioning might be used as an alternative to Oracle striping and RAID. Figure 10.2 is an illustration to that effect. See how the distribution of rows is highly affected by the method of division.

Figure 10.2
Illustration of RAID, Striping, and Partitioning

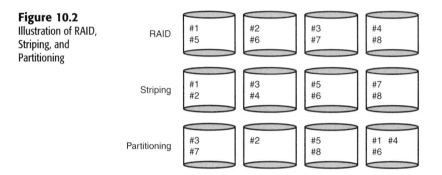

It turns out that at some cost you can emulate expression partitioning in Oracle by using key partitioning and an additional column per table. For example, suppose you want to partition your 500 million row Oracle table randomly. You can add a column to your table containing uniquely computed random numbers for each row and then apply the Oracle8 key partitioning using the LESS THAN keywords. You can do this because you control the range or random numbers generated; because you only need some range of numbers to do key partitioning, you are in business. The drawback, of course, is that you have one additional column you have to drop on a very large table.

With Oracle7 or 8, you normally use parallel queries in conjunction with partition views or partitioning. You generally set the degree of parallelism equal to some multiple of the number of tables making up a partition view in version 7 or equal to the number of partitioning making up a table in version 8. Not only do you gain the optimizer advantage of partition elimination, but you also gain the advantage of being able to query in parallel those remaining partitions that were unable to be eliminated. Hence, as with a parallel query, you normally use partitioning in applications that store large amounts of data. These applications tend to be very large databases, data marts, or data warehouses. However, online transaction processing systems can also benefit, as they might also themselves be very large databases.

ORACLE8 PARTITIONING: SOME EXAMPLES

In Oracle8, a table or index can have up to 64,000 partitions. The *partition key* is the column on which the table or index is partitioned. A partition key, like a primary key, can be composite, having up to 16 columns. Neither clusters nor large objects (LONG or RAW, for example) are supported in partitioned tables. A non-partitioned (regular) table can have either partitioned or non-partitioned indexes. Likewise, a partitioned table can have either partitioned or non-partitioned indexes. However, aside from simple capability, issues such as manageability and performance also impact your physical design. Listing 10.2 shows an example of an Oracle8 partitioned table.

LISTING 10.2   CREATING A PARTITIONED TABLE IN ORACLE8

```
SQL> create table EMPS
2 (EMPID number(5), EMPNAME varchar2(30), EMPADDR varchar2(75))
3 partition by range (EMPID)
4 (partition P1 values less than (10001),
5 partition P2 values less than (20001),
6 partition P3 values less than (30001),
7 partition P4 values less than (40001),
8 partition P5 values less than (50001));
```

PART

III

CH

10

In Listing 10.2, if you have 50,000 employees numbered 1-50,000, you would have created five separate partitions of the EMPS table with 10,000 employees stored in each.

Individual partitions of a table can have varying tablespaces and storage parameters, as Listing 10.3 shows:

LISTING 10.3   PARTITIONED TABLE TABLESPACES AND PARAMETERS

```
SQL> create table DEPTS
1 (DEPTID number(2), DEPTNAME varchar2(20),
2 DEPTBUDGET number(9)
3 partition by range (DEPTID)
4 (partition P1 values less than (51)
5 tablespace T1 storage (initial 10M next 10M),
6 partition P2 values less than (101)
7 tablespace T2 storage (initial 20M next 20M));
```

The VALUES LESS THAN clause specifies an exclusive upper boundary for that partition. For example, in Listing 10.3, partition P1 can hold DEPTIDs up to 50, but not 51 or higher. Hence, the LESS THAN in the VALUES LESS THAN clause means *strictly less than*. Each partition automatically establishes a constraint on that partition. For example, an attempt to insert a row with DEPTID = 101 causes an ORA-14400 error, "Inserted partition key is beyond highest legal partition key," because your highest enabled value is 100 for the highest partition (P2). To avoid this, you can use the keyword MAXVALUE as shown in Listing 10.4, which is a simple modification of Listing 10.3:

LISTING 10.4   PARTITIONED TABLE USING MAXVALUE

```
SQL> create table DEPTS
1 (DEPTID number(2), DEPTNAME varchar2(20),
2 DEPTBUDGET number(9)
3 partition by range (DEPTID)
4 (partition P1 values less than (51)
5 tablespace T1 storage (initial 10M next 10M),
6 partition P2 values less than (maxvalue)
7 tablespace T2 storage (initial 20M next 20M));
```

The only difference is that the value of 101 is replaced by the keyword MAXVALUE in the highest partition P2. Additionally, NULL values can not be used in the VALUES LESS THAN clause, and when rows having NULL values for the partition key are inserted, they are collated (sorted) as greater than all literal values but not greater than MAXVALUE.

EXAMPLES USING PARTITION KEYS

As mentioned previously, a partition key can be made up of multiple columns (that is, be composite). The order of comparison is left to right, and if MAXVALUE is used, all values following the MAXVALUE usage *are ignored*. Composite partitioning can make sense when there is a composite primary key on a table or when you want to partition by primary key and foreign key combinations on frequently joined tables. Listing 10.5 gives an example of partitioning a table that has a primary key, and Listing 10.6 gives an example of partitioning a table on a primary key and foreign key combination.

LISTING 10.5 PARTITIONING BY PRIMARY KEY

```
SQL> create table EMPS
2 (SSN number(9), SEQNO number(3),
2 EMPNAME varchar2(30), EMPADDR varchar2(75))
3 primary key (SSN, SEQNO)
4 partition by range (SSN, SEQNO)
6 (partition P1 values less than (333333334,334),
7 partition P2 values less than (666666668,668),
8 partition P3 values less than (1000000000,1000));
```

LISTING 10.6 PARTITIONING BY PRIMARY AND FOREIGN KEY COMBINATION

```
SQL> create table EMPS
2 (EMPID number(5), EMPNAME varchar2(30),
3 EMPADDR varchar2(75), DEPTID number(2))
4 primary key (EMPID, DEPTID)
5 foreign key (DEPTID) references DEPTS
6 partition by range (EMPID,DEPTID)
7 (partition P1 values less than (10001,21),
8 partition P2 values less than (20001,41),
9 partition P3 values less than (30001,61),
10 partition P4 values less than (40001,81),
11 partition P5 values less than (50001,101));
```

PARTITIONING INDEXES

There are four main types of indexes available to use with partitioned or non-partitioned tables. They are the following:

1. Non-partitioned (regular)
2. Global prefixed
3. Local prefixed
4. Local nonprefixed

In order to understand these index types, first learn some background information. Recall that partitioned or non-partitioned tables can have partitioned or non-partitioned indexes; the only real restriction on index partitioning is that a clustered index might not be partitioned. An index is considered *prefixed* if the leftmost columns of that index are of exactly the same order and number as those in the partition key. In addition, the index columns can be a superset of the partition key, but not a subset.

A *global* index can only be prefixed, but its partition distribution is normally different from its associated table. If a global nonprefixed index is desired, use a regular index instead. Oracle chose not to implement this capability because the overhead of its usage would be of worse performance than a regular index. Global indexes are *not* maintained by Oracle. That is, specific relationships (value range correspondence) among the index partitioning and the table partitioning are *not* maintained by Oracle after being set up. The major disadvantage of a global index is that the Oracle optimizer cannot take advantage of partition elimination with a global index. On the other hand, global indexes offer an option for partitioning the index on value ranges other than those of the associated table. This can be useful in a multiple index situation such as that found with Data Warehousing and the MultiDimensional Databases associated with OnLine Analytical Processing applications. Also, when storage is at a premium, global indexes are attractive options because they might require fewer partitions than their associated tables. Listing 10.7 gives an example of a partitioned table and an associated global prefixed index.

LISTING 10.7 A PARTITIONED TABLE'S GLOBAL PREFIXED INDEX

```
SQL> create table EMPS
2 (EMPID number(5), SSN number(9), EMPNAME varchar2(30), EMPADDR varchar2(75))
3 partition by range (EMPID)
4 (partition P1 values less than (33334),
5 partition P2 values less than (66668),
6 partition P3 values less than (100000));

SQL> create index EMPS_IDX
2 on EMPS (EMPID, SSN)
3 global
4 partition by range (EMPID)
5 partition P2 values less than (50001),
6 partition P3 values less than (100000));
```

A *local* index can be either prefixed or not. However, there is a one to one correspondence between the index partitions and their associated table partitions. That relationship, when set up, is considered *equi-partitioned* and thereafter is maintained by Oracle. The Oracle optimizer can take advantage of partition elimination and as such can potentially provide a substantial performance boost comparable to striping and RAID, as mentioned earlier. Hence, the major advantages of local indexes are the automatic equi-partition maintenance and the associated optimizer-aware potential performance gain. About the only disadvantage associated with a local index is its restrictive requirement of having to have the same partition scheme as its associated table, whether prefixed or not. For multiple index needs, this might require too much complexity of management. Also, the associated interleaved storage needs can become a difficult problem.

Listing 10.8 gives an example of a partitioned table and an associated local prefixed index. Listing 10.9 gives an example of a partitioned table and an associated local nonprefixed index. Notice that in both cases there are no PARTITION BY RANGE or VALUES LESS THAN clauses because Oracle knows this is a local index and will equi-partition it according to the exact same table specifications. (The LOCAL keyword informs Oracle.) Contrast Listings 10.8 and 10.9 to Listing 10.7 to see the differences between local and global, as well as between local prefixed and local nonprefixed.

Note

Although local index partitions differ only by their choice of index columns, in effect determining whether they are prefixed, global index partitions differ by the choice of value ranges.

LISTING 10.8   A PARTITIONED TABLE AND AN ASSOCIATED LOCAL PREFIXED INDEX

```
SQL> create table EMPS
2 (EMPID number(5), SSN number(9),
3 EMPNAME varchar2(30), EMPADDR varchar2(75))
4 partition by range (EMPID)
5 (partition P1 values less than (33334),
6 partition P2 values less than (66668),
7 partition P3 values less than (100000));

SQL> create index EMPS_IDX
2 on EMPS (EMPID, SSN)
3 local
4 (partition IP1,
5 partition IP2,
6 partition IP3);
```

LISTING 10.9   A PARTITIONED TABLE AND AN ASSOCIATED LOCAL NONPREFIXED INDEX

```
SQL> create table EMPS
2 (EMPID number(5), SSN number(9),
3 EMPNAME varchar2(30), EMPADDR varchar2(75))
4 partition by range (EMPID)
5 (partition P1 values less than (33334),
6 partition P2 values less than (66668),
7 partition P3 values less than (100000));

SQL> create index EMPS_IDX
2 on EMPS (SSN)
3 local
4 (partition IP1,
5 partition IP2,
6 partition IP3);
```

MAINTENANCE OPERATIONS

There are two basic statements that perform all partition operations. They are ALTER TABLE and ALTER INDEX. The partition extensions to the ALTER TABLE statement are the following:

DROP PARTITION

ADD PARTITION

RENAME PARTITION

MODIFY PARTITION

TRUNCATE PARTITION

SPLIT PARTITION

MOVE PARTITION

EXCHANGE PARTITION

The partition extensions to the ALTER INDEX statement are the following:

DROP PARTITION

RENAME PARTITION

REBUILD PARTITION

MODIFY PARTITION

SPLIT PARTITION

PARALLEL

UNUSABLE

PART

III

CH

10

Most of these partition operations should be familiar and self-explanatory to experienced Oracle DBAs because they generally "look and feel" like ordinary table or index operations such as DROP TABLE or DROP INDEX. However, you will take a closer look at the ones that are unique to partitions (SPLIT, MOVE, EXCHANGE, and UNUSABLE). Listing 10.10 gives you an example of a SPLIT.

LISTING 10.10   THE SPLIT PARTITION MAINTENANCE OPERATION

```
SQL> alter table EMPS split partition P3
1 at ((75000))
2 into (partition P3, partition P4);
```

What happens in Listing 10.10 is that partition P3 retains all the rows with EMPID values less than 75000 (but greater than whatever was in P2) and that the new partition P4 stores all those rows with values equal to or greater than 75000. As you can see, SPLIT always produces one additional new partition.

Listing 10.11 gives you an example of the MOVE operation. As you can see, this is simply moving a partition from one tablespace to another.

LISTING 10.11 MOVING PARTITIONS

```
SQL> alter table EMPS move partition P3
1 tablespace T3;
```

Listing 10.12 shows you one type of EXCHANGE statement. EXCHANGE converts a partition to a non-partitioned table and a non-partitioned table to a partition. EXCHANGE is likely to be used when you want to migrate Oracle7 partition views (discussed earlier) to Oracle8 partitioned tables.

LISTING 10.12 CONVERTING PARTITIONS TO NON-PARTITIONED TABLES

```
SQL> alter table EMPS8 exchange partition P1
1 with table EMPS7
2 including indexes
3 without validation;
```

Listing 10.12 also shows you that you can optionally include indexes (with certain restrictions) and not be required to validate the value ranges of the rows being moved. The default is to exclude indexes and require validation.

An index partition can become marked *Index Unusable* (IU) by Oracle, meaning that you have to rebuild at least those IU partitions making up the index in question, if not the whole index.

The 6 maintenance operations that mark an index IU are the following:

1. SQL*Loader or Import Partition with the option to bypass the index
2. Direct-path SQL*Loader that partially fails
3. ALTER TABLE TRUNCATE PARTITION
4. ALTER TABLE SPLIT PARTITION
5. ALTER TABLE MOVE PARTITION
6. ALTER INDEX SPLIT PARTITION

PARALLEL CAPABILITIES

There are three major parallel capabilities that can work with partitioning to enhance performance:

- Parallel Query (PQ), also known as the Parallel Query Option (PQO)
- Parallel Data Definition Language (PDDL)
- Parallel Data Manipulation Language (PDML)

Parallel Query operates only slightly differently on partitioned tables from the way it does on non-partitioned tables. On non-partitioned tables, table scans are parallelized only if the number of rows in the table is greater than or equal to an internal threshold that is checked at compile time. By contrast, on partitioned tables, tables scans are parallelized only if the sum of the sizes of the *relevant* partitions is greater than or equal to that same internal threshold, which is checked not only at compile time, but also at runtime if necessary, due to partition restriction by the query itself. Partitions are said to be relevant if they are not skipped on partition elimination by the optimizer when reviewing the partition value ranges (boundaries) relative to the query needs. With PQ, parallelism is by ROWID range, regardless of table partitioning.

Parallel Data Definition Language is limited to a small set of DDL commands that can be parallelized:

- CREATE INDEX
- CREATE TABLE AS SELECT
- ALTER TABLE MOVE PARTITION
- ALTER TABLE SPLIT PARTITION
- ALTER INDEX REBUILD PARTITION

Aside from the addition of the partition-specific operations, this type of parallelism in Oracle8 is the same as it was in Oracle7.

Parallel Data Manipulation Language might be a little confusing, but basically, when Oracle refers to DML in general, it is referring to INSERT, UPDATE, and DELETE operations and *not* to SELECT operations. Although in database textbooks and literature outside of Oracle, the acronym DML stands for Data *Manipulation* Language. Oracle, however, would rather have you think of it as Data *Modification* Language. If you think of DML as modification and Query as SELECT, it makes sense on Oracle's terms that PQ handles SELECT parallelization, whereas PDML handles INSERT, UPDATE, and DELETE parallelization.

As you might imagine, there is generally less opportunity, especially with OLTP and DSS systems, for PDML to have as big an impact on performance as PQ. However, sometimes there are isolated cases of processing or highly volatile tables that grow and shrink rapidly within those application types. In addition, batch databases tend to be made up of many of these volatile tables. Further, these types of tables tend to be very large in some applications. When these latter conditions seem to apply to your organization, PDML should benefit you as much or more so than PQ.

As with PQ, the benefit of PDML relies on the number of rows in the tables to be accessed, the number of disk drives across which those tables span, the number and type of controllers that serve those disks, the number of CPUs, and other software or hardware factors. For example, Oracle uses partitions to datafiles to device mapping to help divide and allocate the PDML statement work to its slaves. Also, as with PQ, PDML provides a fail-safe level. As with all true transaction-oriented RDBMSs, if the work of one PDML slave fails, all slaves roll back so that the entire PDML statement fails, guaranteeing the atomicity of the transaction. This operates much like a local 2PC (two-phase commit) operation. With PDML, UPDATE and DELETE operations require tables to be partitioned, but INSERT...SELECT does not require it, as with SELECT and PQ.

Note

There is *no* initialization parameter to enable PDML. To do so, you must use ALTER SESSION ENABLE PARALLEL DML. However, the optimizer might choose to *not* parallelize the DML due to other restrictions. Every statement during an enabled PDML session must be followed by a COMMIT or ROLLBACK to prevent the error "ORA-12830: Must COMMIT or ROLLBACK after executing parallel INSERT / UPDATE / DELETE is returned." Also, if the first DML statement in a transaction (PL/SQL code block) fails to be executed in parallel, all subsequent statements are executed serially, despite hints or default table degrees.

Additional Considerations

Aside from PDML, which is a major piece of functionality associated with partitioning in Oracle8, many other features and examples of functionality are related to these new partitioning capabilities. Partition-extended table names are one enhancement which accompanies partitioning. This language extension is nonstandard (that is, not ANSI), so you have to use views to wrap code that used them to facilitate standardization. Listing 10.13 gives an example of using a partition-extended table name.

Listing 10.13   A Partition-Extended Table Name

```
SQL> select * from EMPS partition (p1);
```

Partition locks add another layer of granularity to Oracle7's locking scheme in order to support a concept that Oracle coins *partition independence*. Partition independence simply means that you can treat partitions in Oracle8 pretty much the same as you treated tables in Oracle7. This way, a DBA can do some maintenance to one partition without affecting users' access to the other partitions. Naturally, the partition level lock exists as a locking layer between the table level and row levels. In summary, the benefit of partitioning independence is independent administration of such things as backup and recovery. This can also be viewed as a high availability feature in that one partition can fail while the others remain accessible.

Caution

One caution I advise in using partitioning is that you cannot update a partition key column that would cause the row to be moved from one partition to another. In Oracle8 partitioning, *there is no automatic row migration*. If you did try such an update, you would receive the error "ORA-14402: Updating partition key column would cause a partition change." Unfortunately with Oracle8, the DBA has to migrate rows manually.

Now assume you have an employees table (EMPS) that is partitioned on employee identification (EMPID) and has two partitions, P1 and P2, with P1 holding values less than 51 and P2 having everything 51 and above. Listing 10.14 gives you an example of two update statements. The first works. However, the second fails with an ORA-14402 error, as noted in the preceding caution. One way to solve this is to do an insert and delete, but this is inefficient for bulk operations. In that case, you are better off using the partition operations discussed earlier or unloading and reloading your partitions.

LISTING 10.14   PARTITION UPDATE STATEMENTS

```
SQL> update EMPS set EMPID = 67
2 where EMPID = 66;
/* This works ok, since this particular employee stays in partition P2 */

SQL> update EMPS set EMPID = 67
2 where EMPID = 33;
/* This will not work, since it would cause this particular employee to move
from partition P1 to P2.  Hence, it will generate an ORA-14402 error. */

SQL> insert into EMPS partition (P2)
2 values (33, …);
SQL> delete from EMPS
2 where EMPID = 67;
```

PART

III

CH

10

A final consideration is the new ROWID format for Oracle8 as opposed to Oracle7. With Oracle8, the ROWID was extended to mainly accommodate partitioning, which you see in this chapter, but to also accommodate the object option that is discussed in Chapter 11, "The History of Large Objects (LOBs)." This new ROWID format is discussed in depth in Chapter 13, "Networking With Net8: New Features and Concepts."

## CHAPTER 11

LARGE OBJECTS

In this chapter

THE HISTORY OF LARGE OBJECTS (LOBs)

The first attempts by Relational Database Management Systems (RDBMSs) to store and retrieve large objects were crude. The interesting thing is that although those first attempts were crude, they did get the job done at some elementary level. This probably explains why those early methods still exist today under different names by different vendors.

The early attempts made by most RDBMS vendors were the external storage datatype method, known generally to the database world as the Binary Large Object (BLOB), not to be confused with the internal Oracle8 BLOB datatype to be discussed in a later section. This was the conventional way to manage large, unstructured data. What does large mean? That actually depends on the RDBMS vendor, but in general it means larger than their largest variable character could support. For example, with Oracle7, that largest variable was varchar2(2000). Rdb/VMS, Sybase, and Oracle all had some variation on the BLOB. Although stored internally (logically within the table), Oracle7 had LONG and LONG RAW, which are compared later in this chapter in the section "Oracle7 vs. Oracle8 Structures" with the new Oracle8 datatypes. What does unstructured mean? In general, it means data that might represent prose (alphanumeric) information, such as comments, remarks, memos, résumés, open-ended answers to survey questions, and so forth. Those familiar with dBASE would have used a MEMO field in dBASE terms. But it also means data that is multimedia, including things such as graphics, engineering drawings, images, video, audio, and so forth.

In other words, BLOBs were created to store data which had no regular structure but that could reliably be broken down into non-null columns for every row in a table. In fact, if this data were somehow attached to the right-hand side of an otherwise normalized table, the table would then look irregular, due to the varying lengths of data enabled per row. Those familiar with C/C++ would quickly recognize this as a "ragged array". Naturally, for most relational database designers, this would not do: to store the data inside the database, attached to a particular table and ruining an otherwise normalized design. The immediate remedy, which is still used today among all the RDBMS vendors, was the BLOB, which would be stored outside the database in an operating system file. All that would be stored in any table would be the column name, and pointers to the associated external files per every row under that column. The table then had the illusion of being "normal" because the pointers themselves had the same datatype (that being fully proprietary and specific to that particular RDBMS vendor's implementation).

DISADVANTAGES TO USING PROPRIETARY IMPLEMENTATIONS

Proprietary datatypes in an RDBMS, like most vendor extensions to the relational model, were not (and still aren't) a good idea. Why? If for no other reason, portability is then partially or fully sacrificed. Case in point: One company's application was fully developed in Sybase using TEXT columns (one type of Sybase BLOB) and then had to abandon a fully operational Sybase environment for one reason or another. That company then had to reimplement everything in Oracle. Guess what? Yes, all the Sybase proprietary BLOBs (TEXT columns) had to be replaced with Oracle proprietary BLOBs (LONG columns).

What other disadvantages exist besides the proprietary datatype itself? For one, as you might expect, a proprietary datatype means nonstandard, which means non-ANSI SQL, which in turn means no standard language support for the datatype. Hence, along with a proprietary datatype, you must accompany it with a proprietary language to store, retrieve, and otherwise manipulate it. In other words, it needs its own set of DDL and DML operations, which, in fact, is the case for all the vendors. So the company which had to port from Sybase to Oracle not only had to just replace datatypes, but also had to rewrite code, generally an option of last resort in any porting operation.

Are there any other disadvantages besides the datatype itself and its associated operations? Certainly. There are other vendor-specific environment and behavioral modes of operations that generally require you to work either in a "BLOB-enabled" mode or not. Quite often, too frequently in fact, you can find vendors, including Oracle, not permitting BLOB operations or access in many everyday, routine operations. Those who have worked with LONGs in Oracle7 understand this point very well.

Perhaps the most fundamental problem with BLOBs is that they aren't "first class citizens" of the database. This means that, although they are peripherally stored and retrieved, they otherwise do not interact with the rest of the database data or components in any meaningful way. One way of thinking about this situation is that BLOBs really only represent the addition of simple operating file system capabilities to the RDBMS and nothing more nor less. The ramifications with regard to the relational model cannot be ignored. Generally, these early BLOBs were under little or no concurrency control, meaning locking did not mean the same thing at all relative to database pages or rows. In addition, the optimizer was not "aware" of these BLOBs and could not generate any kind of query plans including them. On a related point, things like indexes and ordinary character datatype substring operations were not enabled on BLOBs. Many other things you might want to do as a DBA or developer or might want the RDBMS to handle were not possible with BLOBs. Hence, with Oracle8, the early BLOBs of Oracle7 have been reincarnated in another form, but Oracle has made some progress toward making BLOBs become more useful columns in their implementation of the relational model.

ORACLE7 VS. ORACLE8 STRUCTURES

In Oracle7, the LONG and LONG RAW datatypes were internal BLOBs. They had all the "bad" characteristics of BLOBs, except that they were internal. In Oracle8, Large Objects (*LOBs*) can be internal or external. Table 11.1, "Oracle7 vs. Oracle8 Large Objects," summarizes some of the differences between Oracle7 LONGs and Oracle8 LOBs.

TABLE 11.1   ORACLE7 VS. ORACLE8 LARGE OBJECTS

Oracle Version	7 (LONGs)	8 (LOBs)
Maximum Size	2GB	4GB
Internal or External	Internal	Both
Access	Sequential	Random
SELECT Return Value	Pointer	Data
Columns per Table	One	Many

It is highly instructive to contrast the older LONGs with the newer LOBS. With Oracle7 LONGs, there were essentially only two LONG types: LONG character and LONG RAW binary. Oracle7 LONGs enabled up to 2GB of data to be stored "in the table" itself, could only be accessed sequentially, could only be stored in one column per table, and SELECT statements returned the actual data directly.

With Oracle8, LOBs enable up to 4GB of data stored either inside or outside the table, can be accessed randomly (directly), can be stored in more than one column per table, and SELECT statements return a pointer (a *locator*) to the data (whether stored inside or outside the table).

LOBs

In Oracle8, there are four kinds of LOBs: BLOBs, CLOBs, NCLOBs, and BFILEs. They are summarized as follows:

- BLOBs—Internal binary LOBs
- CLOBs—Internal character LOBs
- NCLOBs—Internal fixed-width multibyte character LOBs
- BFILEs—External binary file

As you might have noticed, Oracle8 BFILEs are the direct descendants of the early RDBMS BLOBs (again, not to be confused with Oracle8 BLOBs) that were stored as pointers inside the database to operating system files outside the database.

LOBs are made up of two parts: the data (the *value*) and the pointer to the data (the *locator*). A LOB column does not hold the value, only its locator, although the value is stored with the table itself. Further, programs must declare local variables of the locator type in order to use LOBs. You will see later in this chapter that the PL/SQL interfaces use locators like operating system file handles. When LOBs (except for BFILEs) are created, the locator is stored in the column, and the value is stored in the *LOB segment*, which is part of the table inside the database. When a BFILE is created, the locator is stored in column as usual, but the value is stored in an operating system file outside the database.

Internal LOBs (BLOBs, CLOBs, and NCLOBs, but not BFILEs) can, as you have learned, be a column in a table, a SQL variable, or a PL/SQL variable. Most importantly, with regards to faithfulness to the implementation of the relational model, internal LOBs are subject to modified concurrency control, redo logging, and backup/recovery mechanisms. This represents progress over the early RDBMS BLOBs. Oracle8 BLOBs are functionally similar to Oracle7 LONG RAWs. Likewise, CLOBs are functionally similar to LONGs. However, NCLOBs are new. They were created to handle National Character (NC) sets, and hence, the name NC + LOBs = NCLOBS. Lastly, there is no implicit conversion between these different internal LOB types.

CREATING TABLES USING LOBS

The `CREATE TABLE` statement is used as you normally would use it to create a table that might include some LOBs. The locator and the empty value are created on `INSERT`. The PL/SQL `DBMS_LOB` package or Oracle Call Interface (OCI) can be used to load the LOBs. Deleting a row containing a LOB not only deletes the locator, but also its associated value (as one would hope). An `UPDATE` statement might update a full LOB value, but cannot update just pieces of it (such as a substring operation on a character datatype). Also, when a LOB is created on `INSERT`, a LOB index segment, in addition to the LOB (value) segment, is automatically created to index the pieces of the LOB value for random access. Hence, every LOB creation creates two segments: a LOB (value) segment and a LOB index segment.

LOB STORAGE MANAGEMENT

How is internal LOB storage managed? The granularity of storage and concurrency is known as a *chunk*, which is comprised of one or more Oracle blocks (as set by `db_block`). The default chunk size is one block. In effect, a chunk is a chain (linked list) of blocks. The blocks within a chunk are logically contiguous, although contiguity is not required given a linked list data structure. This knowledge can be used to coordinate other database aspects, such as setting the `db_file_multiblock_read_count` equal to the chunk size can be a performance enhancement. The LOB index maintains the linked list of chunks so that they can be accessed directly; without it, they could only be accessed sequentially. The LOB index is a simple inverted list of chunk values to chunk addresses. *Versioning* is a mechanism by which multiple versions of the same LOB can occupy the LOB segment to varying degrees. The `pctversion` storage parameter indicates what percentage of LOB segment space is dedicated to storing all (old) versions except the current one. If old versions of the current LOB surpass `pctversion`, then Oracle attempts to reclaim space from the oldest versions until the old versions occupy less than or equal to `pctversion`. Versioning takes place at the chunk level.

Two other storage parameters, `cache`/`nocache` and `logging`/`nologging`, control whether the I/O utilizes the SGA database buffer cache and redo logging mechanisms, respectively. The default combination, `nocache` and `nologging`, is best for general performance. As usual, use `cache` when repeated reuse of the LOB is expected, and use `logging` when it is critical changes to the LOB must not be lost. This is not particularly different from ordinary objects.

PART

III

CH

11

How is internal LOB concurrency managed? It turns out that the chunk, like the block, is not only the unit of storage (and I/O) and versioning, but also the unit of concurrency. Read-consistency is handled very much like it is with the other ordinary Oracle datatypes. The main differences with LOBs are that the granularity is a chunk rather than a block, and read-consistent LOB data (old chunks representing old versions) is stored within the LOB segment and not within a rollback segment or the database buffer cache. Generally speaking, if high update activity to the LOB must occur within the same time frame as high select activity, then the pctversion should probably be relatively high to enable more uninterrupted concurrency. What would be an interruption? Again, as with normal read-consistency, a user might encounter an ORA-1555 error "Snapshot too old." Basically this would mean you would need more rollback space (more single segment storage or more segments). With the LOB segment, you can increase the storage amount or simply just increase the pctversion if that would be sufficient. As a point of contrast, if there is low update activity or if high update activity occurs at times different from high select activity, the pctversion is not as critical and can be set lower.

BFILEs

File systems and third generation languages formed the foundation of preRDBMS, and even preDBMS, information storage and retrieval systems, or information systems for short. However, their very shortcomings were the reasons for the drive toward DBMSs and ultimately toward RDBMSs. However, despite lacking the major subsystems of modern RDBMSs, file-based information systems still flourish to some degree in many sectors, in particular, certain file-based information systems that might benefit from the old BLOB-style approach of external storage and retrieval (in Oracle8, BFILEs). The likely candidates would not be transaction-oriented, would not critically depend on data integrity, and would perhaps form the basis of some loosely structured or unstructured historical application, such as a memo or resume archive serving an intranet.

Oracle8 enables the creation, association, and securing of BFILE objects. However, everything else with BFILEs must be done through the DBMS_LOB package or OCI. BFILEs are read-only. Hence, they are good choices to be stored on optical disks (CDROMs) that serve historical applications as aforementioned. The data must already exist as an operating system file, and Oracle must have read privileges on the file (and directory access, of course, to get to the file). As with the dropping of tablespaces, which leaves datafiles resident in the operating system as operating system files, the deletion of BFILE objects does not delete their associated operating system files. As Oracle DBAs are aware, they must either delete them themselves or get an operating System Administrator (SA) to do it.

As mentioned, when a BFILE is created, its locator is stored in a column in some table, whereas its value is the associated external operating system file itself. The BFILE locator stores information other than just the filename; it includes the directory and other information relating to its status. In a "normalized" table, each row and column intersection can contain a unique value (although it can also contain previously used values as in a foreign key). Likewise, each BFILE column can point to a different file per each row. As with the other internal LOBs, the DBMS_LOB package and the Oracle8 OCI provide stream I/O access to the BFILE. Unlike normal block I/O, which takes place between ordinary objects (for example, tables) and the SGA, BFILE I/O (through DBMS_LOB or the OCI) is *direct*, similar to direct path loading with SQL*Loader. In other words, it bypasses the SGA.

Database subsystems such as concurrency control, redo logging, and backup/recovery mechanisms are not available in Oracle8 with BFILEs. In addition, security is problematic in that BFILE security within an Oracle8 database essentially depends on the operating system security defined on it. For example, to secure a BFILE, an SA or DBA must set directory and file access control (read permission for Oracle), enable application access permissions outside of Oracle, allocate enough storage for initial storage and anticipated growth for the file, and consider operating system or hardware addressing limits such as maximum file size per single physical disk, single logical volume, or absolute (uncondi-tional) maximum. As an example, Solaris 2.2 enabled access (through its I/O interfaces) to files up to 2GB, as did many earlier UNIX implementations. However, with Solaris 2.3, "large" files and file systems were enabled, of sizes greater than 2GB (for example, 4GB or 9GB, which corresponded to the largest single disk sizes available at the time).

To help administer access to BFILEs in Oracle8, the *directory* database object was created. This directory object is really just an *alias*, or synonym, for an operating system directory. Hence, the directory object is *virtual*. These internal Oracle directories can be secured, sup-plying the only real way to secure access to a BFILE through an internal Oracle mechanism (as opposed to operating system security). Users can be granted access privileges to these directories, and they can be used in PL/SQL or OCI. A DBA or user with CREATE ANY DIRECTORY privilege in Oracle8 can create a directory. Privileges are then granted and revoked as with any other ordinary database objects.

BFILE access is checked at runtime, and the runtime errors which might occur are the following:

- Insufficient user privileges.
- Directory does not exist.
- File does not exist.

When a BFILE or directory is created, the existence of the proper privileges, directory names, and filenames are not checked (at compile time).

EXAMPLES USING LOBS AND BFILES

Look at some LOB and BFILE examples:

LISTING 11.1   CREATING A TABLE WITH A CLOB AND A BLOB

```
SQL> create table candidates (
   2 pk number(9),
   3 name varchar2(40),
   4 address varchar2(80),
   5 resume CLOB,
   6 photo BLOB );
SQL> declare
   2    r CLOB;
   3    p BLOB;
   4 Begin
   5   SELECT resume into r from candidates where pk = 12345;
   6   SELECT photo into p from candidates where pk = 12345;
   7 End;
```

The preceding code (Listing 11.1) creates a table with a CLOB (resume) and a BLOB (photo). This CREATE statement creates five segments: the table itself and two each for the two LOBs. Then, a very simple PL/SQL block declares a local variable CLOB (r) and a local variable BLOB (p) in order to retrieve the locators of the corresponding LOBs in the database.

LISTING 11.2   CREATING A TABLE WITH LOBS, BLOBS, AND CLOBS

```
SQL> create table landscape_plans (
   2 front_yard BLOB,
   3 back_yard BLOB,
   4 contract CLOB,
   5 plan_name varchar2(20),
   6 plan_budget number(9)
   7 LOB (front_yard, back_yard, contract)
   8 store as (
   9 storage (initial 1M next 1M pctincrease 0)
  10 chunk 32
  11 pctversion 30
  12 nocache    /* default */
  13 nologging    /* default */
  14 index (
  15 storage (initial 128K next 128K)
  16 )        /* end LOB clause */
  17 );          /* end create table */
```

The preceding code (Listing 11.2) creates a table with three LOBs, two BLOBs and one CLOB. The chunk size is set to 32 blocks. (You also might want to set the db_file_multiblock_read_count to 32 in the init.ora parameter initialization file.) The pctversion is set to 30 percent, enabling old LOB versions to occupy up to 30 percent of the total LOB segment. The defaults are nocache and nologging and are specified here as an illustration. The index clause for the LOB follows, specifying somewhat smaller extent sizes (about a tenth) than those used for the actual LOB.

LISTING 11.3 CREATING A TABLE WITH BFILES

```
SQL> create table background_check (
   2 employee_id number(5),
   3 hire_date date,
   4 photo BFILE,
   5 thumbprint BFILE );
```

The preceding code (Listing 11.3) creates a table with two BFILEs, one for a picture (photo) of the employee, and one for thumbprint. Notice that you don't actually have (or need) any additional storage parameters, as the BFILE storage is actually more in the operating system domain.

LISTING 11.4 CREATING DIRECTORIES FOR LOBS

```
# mkdir /user/data/bfiles/thumbprints    /* UNIX or DOS */
# mkdir /user/data/bfiles/photos

SQL> create directory thumbprints as '/user/data/bfiles/thumbprints';

SQL> create directory photos as
 '/user/data/bfiles/photos';
```

The preceding code (Listing 11.4) shows how directories for the thumbprint and photo LOBs got created at the operating system (OS) level and within Oracle8.

THE DBMS_LOB PACKAGE

The following summarizes the DBMS_LOB procedures and functions as they look called within another piece of code, along with a functional description:

APPEND (LOBs only)

Sample Syntax: APPEND(d,s)

Comments: Appends s to d.

COMPARE

Sample Syntax: result:=COMPARE(b1,b2,n,o1,o2)

Comments: Compares b1 to b2 (including BFILEs) for n bytes starting at offset o1 in b1 and offset o2 in b2. A result of 0 means equal, -1 if b1 is less, and 1 if b2 is less.

COPY

Sample Syntax: `COPY(d,s,n,do,so)`

Comments: Copies d to s for n bytes starting at offset do in d and offset so in s.

ERASE (LOBs ONLY.)

Sample Syntax: `ERASE(b,n,o)`

Comments: Erases b for n bytes starting at offset o.

FILECLOSE (BFILEs ONLY.)

Sample Syntax: `FILECLOSE(b)`

Comments: Closes an open BFILE b.

FILECLOSEALL (BFILEs ONLY.)

Sample Syntax: `FILECLOSEALL`

Comments: Closes all currently open BFILEs.

FILEEXISTS (BFILEs ONLY.)

Sample Syntax: `result:=FILEEXISTS(b)`

Comments: Returns 1 if the actual file of BFILE b exists in the operating system, 0 otherwise.

FILEGETNAME (BFILEs ONLY.)

Sample Syntax: `FILEGETNAME(b,d,f)`

Comments: Given a BFILE b (locator), returns the directory d and filename f for it.

FILEISOPEN (BFILEs ONLY.)

Sample Syntax: `FILEISOPEN(b)`

Comments: Determine if a BFILE b is open.

FILEOPEN (BFILEs ONLY.)

Sample Syntax: `FILEOPEN(b,m)`

Comments: Open a BFILE b in mode m (for example, `file_readonly`).

LOADFROMFILE

Sample Syntax: `LOADFROMFILE(b,l,n,bo,lo)`

Comments: Copies a BFILE b into LOB l for n bytes starting at offset bo in b and offset lo in l.

GETLENGTH

Sample Syntax: `length:=GETLENGTH(l)`

Comments: Returns the length of a LOB `l`. If the LOB is empty, the length returned will be `0`.

INSTR

Sample Syntax: `position:=INSTR(l,p,o,n)`

Comments: Returns the position `p` in LOB `l`, starting the search at offset `o` and for the n(th) occurrence of `p`.

READ

Sample Syntax: `READ(l,n,o,b)`

Comments: Reads up to `n` bytes of data from LOB `l`, starting at offset `o` and returning the bytes read into the buffer `b`. Currently the return buffer `b` is of type RAW or VARCHAR2, and can only handle 32K.

SUBSTR

Sample Syntax: `s:=SUBSTR(l,n,o)`

Comments: Returns a substring `s` of the LOB `l` of up to `n` bytes starting at offset `o`. Like READ, the return value is of type RAW or VARCHAR2 and can only return up to 32K.

TRIM (LOBs ONLY.)

Sample Syntax: `TRIM(l,n)`

Comments: Right TRIMs (reduces) the LOB `l` to length `n`.

WRITE

Sample Syntax: `WRITE(l,n,o,b)`

Comments: Writes up to `n` bytes from buffer `b` to the LOB `l`, starting from offset `o`. Like READ and SUBSTR, WRITE can only write up to 32K from a RAW or VARCHAR2 buffer `b`.

In addition to these, there are "constructor" type functions that create empty LOBs. They are `EMPTY_CLOB()` and `EMPTY_BLOB()`, which create, as you might expect, an empty CLOB and an empty BLOB, respectively.

PART

III

CH

11

SOME MORE EXAMPLES

Listing 11.5 gives an example inserting an empty BLOB and updating it with a copy of an existing BLOB value.

LISTING 11.5   INSERTING AND UPDATING A BLOB

```
SQL> create table inventory (
   2 ID number(9),
   3 cost number(6),
   4 picture BLOB );

SQL> insert into inventory values (
   2 123456789,
   3 5900,     /* $59.00 */
   4 empty_blob() );

SQL> update inventory
   2 set picture = (
   3   select picture from inventory
   4   where ID=999999999 )
   5 where ID=123456789;
/* This copies the picture belonging
to item 999999999 to our new item 123456789. */
```

Notice you did not require any special locking to accomplish this copy. This is because you did a wholesale copy. However, to use the DBMS_LOB routines to move data, you need to lock your rows with SELECT FOR UPDATE statements, as Listing 11.6 shows. Listing 11.7 shows how to disassociate a LOB value from a row by using an empty LOB function

LISTING 11.6   USING LOBs TO MOVE DATA

```
SQL> create table memo_archive (
   2 ID number(9),
   3 memo CLOB );

SQL> declare
buffer varchar2(80);
   3   local_memo CLOB;
   4 begin
   5   buffer:="For Official Use Only";
   6   select memo into local_memo
   7   from memo_archive where ID=873561495
   8   for update;
   9   dbms_lob.write(local_memo,length(buffer),65536,buffer);
  10   commit;
  11 end;
  12 /
```

LISTING 11.7 USING AN EMPTY LOB FUNCTION

```
SQL> update memo_archive
  2 set memo=empty_clob()
  3 where ID=371620603;
```

This leaves the LOB locator intact, but simply nullifies the LOB value (sets it to the "empty string" or "null string").

SOME FINAL ISSUES

BLOBs and BFILEs are measured in bytes, whereas CLOBs and NCLOBs are measured in characters. Although for CLOBs, one byte equals one character, this is not true for multibyte character sets and NCLOBs. This is important when considering the *offset* arguments passed to many of the DBMS_LOB procedures and functions. The offsets are set to one by default, meaning the first byte in a BLOB or BFILE and the first character in a CLOB or NCLOB.

Some issues arise in dealing with IMPORT/EXPORT. IMPORT converts CLOBS and NCLOBS from the character set of the export dump file into the character set (or national character set) of the target database. Make sure your NLS parameters are set correctly. BFILE files are not exported by EXPORT, although the locators and directories are. After importing, manually move the operating system files, and reassociate the BFILEs to their new directories.

PART

III

CH

11

## CHAPTER 12

OBJECT-ORIENTED FEATURES

In this chapter

BACKGROUND

Object-oriented DBMSs (OODBMSs), that is, those DBMSs that are not predominantly relational (RDBMSs), are direct descendants of object-oriented programming languages such as Actor and SmallTalk. The need for persistent storage, one of the fundamental reasons that helped to drive the emergence of DBMSs and RDBMSs to supersede 3GL/file-based information systems, also helped to drive the emergence of OODBMSs to supersede object-oriented programming language information systems. Interestingly enough, one of the general arguments in favor of object-oriented systems is that they provide more powerful semantic modeling, and at a higher level, than relational data modeling derivatives, such as Entity Relationship Diagramming (ERD) variations. Yet, at the same time, one of the arguments against object-oriented systems is that they hearken a return to 3GL/file-based information systems in that their implementations and language elements occasionally dip to very low levels (a la C/C++ pointers). In essence, they resort to *navigational or procedural* queries, which are also strongly similar to prerelational systems such as COBOL-based hierarchical and network DBMSs, contrasted to RDBMS SQL-based systems whose queries are largely *descriptive or declarative*.

Relational vendors such as Oracle are not to be left out, so consider Oracle8 and its current *object-relational* implementation. As with any RDBMS vendor, you must consider several things in order to help you evaluate its object-oriented capabilities, such as the following:

- Faithfulness to object-oriented concepts and constructs
- Object-oriented to relational mapping of concepts and constructs
- Emulation, full, or hybrid implementation
- Performance degradation or enhancement
- Capability to use existing RDBMS subsystems

One of the major reasons to want an RDBMS with an object-oriented interface such as Oracle8 is so that object-oriented application programs can communicate directly to the object-oriented portion of the RDBMS as opposed to having to handle the object-relational mapping (decomposition and recomposition) dynamically within the code. As an example, consider embedded SQL, where SQL, a set-based language, has to interface with a host 3GL such as C, which is record-based. This undesirable situation, remedied through constructs such as *cursors* and software such as *precompilers* (for example, Pro*C), is known as an *impedance mismatch*. The situation with an application based on an object-oriented programming language interfacing with an RDBMS is similar.

Oracle8 specifically helps to alleviate the object-oriented development and RDBMS back-end situation by providing some powerful built-in object-oriented capabilities, such as the following:

- Relationships as datatypes
- Inheritance

- Collections as datatypes, including nesting (containers)
- User-defined (extensible) datatypes
- Improved large objects (LOBs)

With Oracle8, as with any OODBMS or object-relational DBMS (ORDBMS), you can not only leverage your investment in object-oriented development, but you can also take advantage of object-oriented modeling, which is at a higher level of abstraction than relational modeling. In other words, you can model things as whole items that reflect a closer correspondence to the "real" world. For example, you can have a complex object known as a CAR in your OODBMS, which would likely be several tables in an RDBMS, such as MAKE, MODEL, ENGINE, PARTS, and so forth. As a commentary on the "naturalness" of object-oriented modeling versus relational modeling,consider the following scenario contrasting the two:

With object-oriented technology, it is like waking up in the morning and putting on your clothes. In the evening, you simply take them off for their next use. Very natural. However, with relational technology, you must gather all the fabric for your clothes, sew them together, and then put them on. In the evening, you must pull them apart, seam by seam, to store them for their next sewing and subsequent use.

Although humorous and not fully accurate, this example has some truth in it. This idea was basically taking a jab at having to join things in an RDBMS that were broken apart in the first place through normalization. Relational designers know this to be the case, and this is why such things as denormalization exist.

What are some of the perceived benefits of object-oriented technology, especially relative to relational technology but also in general? Some of the more important have already been discussed, but here's a list of most of the major strengths of object-orientation:

- Modeling: business-level abstractions
- Reusability: lifecycle code reuse can be very cost effective
- Complexity: no datatype limitations; multimedia data; nesting
- Extensibility: user-defined datatypes to reflect the modeling
- Performance: typically hawked as an advantage over RDBMSs

As summarized earlier, Oracle8 meets many of these needs by providing specific capabilities such as inheritance, collections, containers, and user-defined datatypes. Performance, however, is hard to determine. Much depends on the logical and physical overall design of the database. However, appropriate application segmentation, coupled with experimental, iterative testing (benchmarks) as is usual with any performance tuning effort, can provide answers as to whether Oracle8 using object-orientation or Oracle8 alone better meets your specific application performance requirements.

OBJECT-ORIENTED TECHNOLOGY

One of the major problems with object-oriented technology, believe it or not, has always been the lack of a standard definition among the object-oriented community as to what is an *object*. Contrast that with relational technology, which has virtually never had any discrepancies among the relational community as to what is a relation. The fact that the definition of an object (and, in fact, almost all the other object-oriented terminology) has eluded standardization has always been the major stumbling block that has prevented object-oriented technology from coming into its own, so to speak.

In any event, for your purposes, Oracle8 defines an *object* as an instance of an object type, an *object type* being the basic object-oriented modeling building block typically directly referring to a real world, business item. So, similar to a row in a table, an object is the data, whereas the object type is the structure, much like any other data structure (a record, for example). An Oracle8 object type is equivalent to an *object class* in many other object-oriented languages and systems. An Oracle8 object type has two components:

- Attributes—Essentially datatypes or other object types, not unlike attributes (columns) in a relation (table) or fields in a record; sometimes referred to as the *structural* part of the object type.

- Methods—PL/SQL (or C) subprograms that make up the allowable set of operations on the object type; sometimes referred to as the *behavioral* part of an object type.

INHERITANCE, POLYMORPHISM, AND OTHER ISSUES

Other important concepts in object-oriented technology include *inheritance* and *polymorphism*. Inheritance is the capability for one object type to include attributes or methods from another object type. The direction is from the general to the specific, exactly like subtypes in the relational model. An example is that you might have an employee object type and a manager object type (a subtype of the employee type). All employees have names, addresses, social security numbers, and so forth. Also, all employees are hired, paid, rated, and so forth. All the preceding represent some of the general, or common, attributes that can be inherited from the employee object type to the manager object type. This means a couple of things relating to efficiency, not just conceptual understanding: One, the common attributes and methods to all employees (including managers) need only be stored once, and two, the manager object type need only store attributes and methods specific to itself, such as signature_authority (an attribute) or rate_an_employee (a method). So, inheritance can be based on attributes (structural) or methods (behavioral).

The situation that was just described, a manager object type inheriting attributes and methods from an employee type, is known as *single* inheritance. Of course, there is another kind of inheritance, known as *multiple* inheritance. Single inheritance can be in the form a hierarchical model in which a child might have at most one parent. Multiple inheritance permits a more general model: the network (or lattice) model. That is, children can have multiple parents, as in the real world. To contrast with your employee→manager single inheritance, consider a multiple inheritance scheme in which managers are also corporate officers: employee→manager←officer. The arrow notation specifies the direction of inheritance, from the general (parent) to the specific (child).

Polymorphism, like inheritance, can be structural or behavioral. Consider an object type such as employee where you do not also have a manager object type. Instead, an employee is simply an employee and not a manager. How do you get a manager type out of an employee type? In reality, this is an old programming construct known by different terms in different programming languages, but this will be described here as a *variant record* for generality. A variant record is one that can hold some common (inherited) data and also some extra fields, depending on the record type being inputted. This situation is analogous to a non-normal table that might hold both employees and managers. How about the methods? Similar to the attributes, the methods might be *visible* depending on the object being instantiated (employee or manager).

What was just described is really general structural polymorphism. How about behavioral polymorphism? In object orientation, when a method is invoked, you say that you have sent it a *message* (to execute). When you send a message to the method, it might execute differently, depending on what object type it currently belongs to or more specifically, what instances are affected. For example, if you call the hire method, it *constructs* (creates) a new employee or a manager. Although you call only one hire method, there are actually two different implementations to construct an instance (instantiate an object): by filling in the common employee attributes for employees, or by filling in the common employee attributes and specific manager attributes for managers. An object-oriented system can implement this *variant program* through simple IF/THEN logic within a single program or through *vectoring*, which is IF/THEN logic plus a call to the one necessary program out of all possible programs. Polymorphism is also referred to as *overloading*. *Late-binding* (runtime binding) makes polymorphism possible in modern languages and systems. In object-orientation, every object type always has at least one method—its own constructor method.

One other important concept is that of an *object ID (OID)*, which represents a universally unique identifier that represents an object after it is constructed. It is meant to be unique across all object-oriented systems and languages, even those outside of Oracle. The generation of an OID in Oracle8 is a secret of the Oracle Corporation, but the uniqueness seems to be linked somehow to CD-ROM distribution. For those familiar with ethernet in local area networking, an OID should be unique just like an ethernet card's ethernet address, which is "burned in" at the factory. This concept of an ID that is unique even outside its own system is something altogether different from a primary key or surrogate key in the relational model. However, it is something like a primary key in a distributed database, which must be unique across more than one system.

What are some of the things you might expect from Oracle8 or any ORDBMS? You might want something such as *object views*, which compose (integrate) multiple relational tables. In addition to customized (user-defined) data as you have already covered, you might want some prebuilt, complex, business datatypes that serve specific niche needs (for example, spatial). A client-side object cache might also be desirable for performance and flexibility of access. You also don't want to lose the strong points of an RDBMS: integrity, concurrency, and security.

ORACLE8 OBJECT OPTION

What, then, has Oracle8 given you by way of object-oriented technology? Oracle extended its already complex and multipurpose RDBMS with the following:

- Object types—Essentially, records or classes as already discussed
- Object views—As you might have wanted, something to put together your many normalized tables into one business item
- Object language—Extensions to the Oracle SQL and PL/SQL languages
- Object APIs—Objects supported through Oracle precompilers (for example, Pro*C), PL/SQL, OCI
- Object portability—Through the Object Type Translator (OTT), which can, for example, port an Oracle8 object type to a C++ class

However, despite these advancements, Oracle8 does not support multiple inheritance, polymorphism, or constraints on object attributes (such as referential integrity).

The Oracle8 Open Type System (OTS) is a repository for all Oracle8 object types, as well as external object types from other languages or systems. Within OTS, there is a datatype hierarchy that has as its foundation the built-in Oracle8 datatypes that you know and love from Oracle7. However, Oracle8 also adds large objects (see Chapter 11, "The History of Large Objects (LOBs)") in the form of BLOB, CLOB, NCLOB, and BFILE, collection types in the form of VARRAY (variable array) and nested TABLE, and object IDs in the form of REF (reference). Also, user-defined datatypes can be built on any of the built-in datatypes plus previously user-defined datatypes. The only exceptions are that they cannot be built on LONG, LONG RAW, ROWID, or %TYPE. When you create a user-defined object type in Oracle8, you can use it for many purposes thereafter, including the following:

- As a column of a relational table
- As an attribute within another object type
- As part of an object view of relational tables
- As the basis for an object table
- As the basis for PL/SQL variables

Extended Oracle SQL to manage object types, as you might expect, includes the following:

- CREATE TYPE
- ALTER TYPE
- DROP TYPE
- GRANT/REVOKE TYPE

Like columns in a table, attributes within an object type must be unique but can be reused in other object types. Like columns in a table, you always access attributes within an object through its name. No capabilities exist for positional or offset access. Any given object type can be *simple, composite, or self-referencing*. A simple object type is just that. A composite object type, as you might expect, contains at least one other object type. A self-referencing object type contains at least one attribute that references the object type itself.

LISTING 12.1   CREATING AN EMPLOYEE OBJECT TYPE

```
SQL> create type employee_type as object (

    1 ssn number(9),
    2 name varchar2(35),
    3 address varchar2(70),
    4 resume CLOB );
```

LISTING 12.2   USING AN OBJECT TYPE AS A COLUMN IN A RELATIONAL TABLE

```
SQL> create table manager_candidates (

    1 position varchar2(40),
    2 vacancy CLOB,
    3 employee employee_type );

SQL> insert into manager_candidates values (

    1 'Technical Manager',empty_clob(),
    2 employee_type(123456789,'John Doe','123 Maple St :
    3 Metropolis : NY : 12762',empty_clob() ) );

SQL> select mc.employee.name from manager_candidates mc

    1 where mc.employee.ssn = 123456789;
```

Notice you must use an alias and dot notation to retrieve an attribute value of an object within a table. Also notice how that when you did the insert, you called the constructor method named `employee_type` for the object type named `employee_type`. All constructors have the same name as their corresponding object type. Listing 12.3 gives you another example of what you can do with an object type, this time creating an object table.

LISTING 12.3

```
SQL> create table employee of employee_type;
```

Creating this object table also creates a column that will hold the object ID (OID, or REF) for an object instance (row). This is to be contrasted with creating a relational table that happens to have an object type in a column position. An object type within a relational table has no OID.

THE REF ATTRIBUTE

A relationship within the Oracle8 object world is really no different from what it was within the Oracle relational world: It specifies how objects relate to one another. Oracle8 only supports a one-to-one unidirectional relationship, which might or might not be sufficient to model your business. When you declare an attribute within an object type as a REF, it represents a reference to some other object type, and this is essentially a relationship. A REF represents an object relationship. A REF is also essentially a pointer, or a "handle" for an object. You can limit the *scope* of what a REF actually references. The notion of scope is to be included in SQL3, the latest revision to the ANSI SQL standard, which includes some object-oriented features.

Like a surrogate key in RMT (Relational Model Two), an object reference (REF) in Oracle8 is a system-generated value, unique among all objects (everywhere), and points to some persistent object. A REF actually references an object, a row (instance) in an object table, not really the object type. A REF for a given object is the combination of that object's OID + the object's table ID + the object table's database ID. Listing 12.4 shows you how to create an object type containing a REF attribute to your already created employee_type, create an object table based upon that object type, and insert a row (instantiate an object).

LISTING 12.4

```
SQL> create type insured_employee_type as object (

    1 control_number number(9),
    2 contract CLOB,
    3 employee_ref ref employee_type );

SQL> create table insured_employee (

    1 of insured_employee_type
    2 scope for (employee_ref) is employee );

SQL> insert into insured_employee

    1 select control_sequence.nextval,
    2 empty_clob(),
    3 ref(e) from employee e
    4 where e.ssn=123456789;
```

METHODS

An object type can have zero or more MEMBER methods. A MEMBER method, or just "method", is a subprogram that can operate on the data (that is, the attributes) within any object type, not just the one in which it's defined. Of course, a method is simply either a PL/SQL procedure or function.

Just as with any PL/SQL packaged subprogram, you create an interface, or *specification*, and an implementation, or *body*, for each method. When you access a method, you use dot notation (object.method). Listing 12.5 gives an example of method creations (specification and body) within an object type, followed by some PL/SQL code that calls that method.

LISTING 12.5

```
SQL> create type auto_type as object (
   1 vin varchar2(80),
   2 make varchar2(30),
   3 model varchar2(40),
   4 member function getcost
   5 return number,
   6 pragma restrict_references
   7 (getcost, WNPS) );

SQL> create type body auto_type (
   1 member function getcost
   2 return number is
   3 begin
   4 return (cost);
   5 end; );

/* create object table and insert some data */

SQL> declare
   1 a auto_type;
   2 c number;
   3 begin
   4    select value(a)
   5    into a
   6    from auto a
   7    where a.vin=1VWF673FB9093871AF21;
   8    c:=a.getcost();
   9    /* do something with c */
  10 end;
```

Notice that the function is set to WNPS with a pragma directive. WNPS stands for "Writes No Package State," which means that the function is set so that it cannot modify any parameters within itself (and otherwise produce a *side effect*). To compare or order object types, you can define a MAP or an ORDER function to compare two objects. When you use these comparison functions, you are specifying the object sorting semantics (that is, a collating sequence) to be used for conditions and sorting. Please refer to the Oracle8 or Oracle8i CD-ROM documentation for further implementation details.

COLLECTIONS (VARRAY AND NESTED TABLE)

A collection is an ordered or unordered group of things. A VARRAY is ordered, whereas a nested TABLE is unordered. A nested TABLE is in the latest ANSI standard, but the VARRAY is nonstandard. Any master-detail (that is, one-to-many) relationship can help contrast these two kinds of collections. A master list of items in some order could use a VARRAY, and each line item detail for each master line could use a nested TABLE within the VARRAY.

Caution	Parallel Query, Parallel DML, Replication, and Distributed Database functionality is not supported for collections.

An Oracle8 VARRAY, like most arrays, has an implicit order. Each element in the array has an offset position from the start of the array and can be directly accessed by that offset (also known as a subscript or index). VARRAY data is stored inline (within the table row), unless the cell storage exceeds 4KB (at which point it is stored outside the database). Each VARRAY, like most arrays, has a *count* and a *limit*. The count is how many elements are currently stored in the VARRAY, whereas the limit is the maximum number of elements that can be stored. You can access individual elements through subscripting within PL/SQL and 3GL, but not within plain SQL.

A nested table is well suited for master-detail (that is, one-to-many) relationships, as mentioned. A nested table in Oracle8 is actually a user-defined type, or TABLE *type*, that can be used within a table as a column, within an object type as an attribute, or as a PL/SQL variable. Nested tables are stored outside the host table in a *storage table*, using a STORE AS clause. Nested tables have some advantages and disadvantages. Advantages include the capability to index them (as opposed to object tables) and joins are not necessary (similar to clusters). One disadvantage is that although you have a form of cascade delete (master row delete will delete all detail rows), referential integrity constraints are not possible.

Listing 12.6   Creating and Using Both a varray and a Nested table (table Type)

```
/* VARRAY */
SQL> create type tax_type as object (
    1 year date,
    2 taxes_paid number );
SQL> create type tax_array_type as VARRAY(3)
    1 of tax_type;
SQL> create type client_type as object (
    1 cid number,
    2 name varchar2(35),
    3 address varchar2(80),
    4 taxes tax_array_type );
SQL> create table clients of client_type;
/* nested TABLE */
SQL> create type child_type as object (
    1 child_id number,
    2 child_name varchar2(35) );
SQL> create type child_nest_type as TABLE
    1 of child_type;
```

```
SQL> create table parent (

  1  parent_id number,
  2  parent_name varchar2(35),
  3  parent_address varchar2(80),
  4  children child_nest_type )
  5  NESTED TABLE children store as child_nest_store;
```

In general, use VARRAY collections for situations when you would have used an array in programming, and use nested TABLE collections when you would have used a record (within a record) in programming. These Oracle8 collection structures are analogous to those programming data structures.

OBJECT VIEWS

Object views of relational tables offer advantages to users and developers such as bridging object-oriented front-end applications to relational back-end stores, accommodating multiple object-oriented front-end schemes to one relational back-end model, and the parallel development of new object-oriented applications and current relational applications. The latter item is one way of saying that object views facilitate migration to object-oriented technology. To the user, the entire system appears as if it were object-oriented–based, but in reality, the data is relational. However, that fact is transparent. Of course, because object views are a special case of views in general, they offer the same general advantage views offer: varying views of the same data for different users and different purposes.

The general order to create object views properly is the following:

- Create tables
- Create object types
- Create object views
- Create INSTEAD OF triggers

An INSTEAD OF trigger is more or less what it sounds like. It is a trigger that enables you to insert, update, or delete the relational tables on which an object view is based, rather than attempt to modify the object view directly (which cannot be done).

LISTING 12.7   THE STEPS FOR CREATING AN OBJECT VIEW

```
SQL> create table depts (

  1  deptid number,
  2  deptbudget number );

SQL> create table branches (

  1  branchid number,
  2  branchbudget number,
  3  deptid number );
```

continues

LISTING 12.7 CONTINUED

```
SQL> create type funding_type as object (

  1 deptid number,
  2 deptbudget number,
  3 branchid number,
  4 branchbudget number );

SQL> create or replace view funding_objv as

  1 select funding_type
  2 (deptid,deptbudget,branchid branchbudget) funding,
  3 from depts d, branches b
  4 where d.deptid = b.deptid;

SQL> create to replace trigger funding_trig INSTEAD OF

  1 insert on funding_objv for each row
  2 begin
  3 insert into depts values
  4 (:new.funding.deptid, :new.funding.deptbudget);
  5 insert into branches values
  6 (:new.funding.branchid, :new.funding.branchbudget,
  7 :new.funding.deptid);
  8 end;
  9 /
```

## CHAPTER 13

NET8 NEW FEATURES AND CONCEPTS

In this chapter

Oracle8 has renamed SQL*Net 2.x to Net8 8.x. Accompanying this name change is a group of important functional enhancements that, if configured properly, can yield better scalability and performance. These enhancements include multiplexing, connection pooling, concentration, naming service changes, connectivity changes, security changes, and overall performance. Administration has also been improved.

OVERVIEW

Net8 is server backward compatible to SQL*Net 2.1, but not client forward compatible. That is, a Net8 listener can service Net8 and SQL*Net 2.x clients, but a SQL*Net 2.x listener can service only clients of the same version or lower (not higher, and therefore, not Net8 clients).

Scalability is enhanced through the availability of multiplexing, connection pooling, concentration, and enhanced naming services. Connectivity now supports foreign data sources and Level 2 Open Database Connectivity (ODBC), which has support for stored procedure calls. Security is enhanced through the Advanced Security Option (ASO), which permits single sign-on through X.509 digital certificates based on public key technology. ASO also includes basic point-to-point ("over the wire") encryption between clients and servers. Both clients and servers are mutually authenticated with digital certificates, providing single sign-on verification, which is generally recognized as superior in most cases to other external authentication technologies. Performance is enhanced through the availability of a TNS Raw interface, client-side name caching like UNIX-style DNS, and an optimized dispatcher code path.

Administration has been improved by providing native OEM and OEM applet integrated support. Configuration can be centralized for a distributed arrangement as well as local. Oracle Names offers enhanced dynamic discovery. Oracle8 Net8 clients can have profiles. There is a Net8 wizard available for configuration. Lastly, a default configuration is automatically supplied for small-scale systems.

CONNECTION MANAGER (CMAN)

The Connection Manager (CMAN) is a new networking feature that works only with the MultiThreaded Server (MTS) option. It *concentrates* requests from multiple clients and multiplexes them into one physical communication. In addition to concentration, CMAN can perform several functions, including acting as a firewall that can authorize transmissions or a bridge to convert between protocols.

With the firewall capability, CMAN can create access control lists (ACLs) of authorized clients and filter (enable or deny) transmissions across CMAN based on source (host or client), destination host, and database (SID).

With the protocol bridge capability, CMAN effectively replaces the former MultiProtocol Interchange (MPI), enabling hosts (clients and servers) using different networking protocols to communicate with one another.

Multiplexing involves combining multiple logical sessions into one physical link. In essence, the physical link is shared among the sessions, of which no single session ever utilizes the physical link 100% of the time. The first session establishes the physical link, which is then time-shared by all subsequent sessions. When all sessions are closed, the physical link is closed.

Why is multiplexing beneficial? As with the MTS option, multiplexing permits a greater concurrency of sessions than would be possible without it. The number of concurrent sessions is limited by OS limits such as the OS ceilings on file descriptors, semaphores, processes, threads, and sockets. Without the MTS option, typically only a few hundred (200–300) concurrent sessions are possible. With it, a few thousand concurrent sessions are possible, increasing overall productivity-per-unit time (that is, *throughput*). This scalability of *load* is possible, as mentioned, because all sessions are not always 100% busy. In other words, they are all idle at some point or another. The *overlap* of their idleness across time provides the opportunity for the concurrency. This is why applications with long-running SQL statements, complex SQL statements, or those SQL statements otherwise having a high percentage of computational time will gain the most from MTS and Net8 multiplexing. Therefore, the MTS option and Net8 multiplexing breaks the main bottlenecks in a potentially highly concurrent environment: the OS and the network. CMAN is responsible for managing multiplexing, with the MTS option providing the foundation on which it works.

Connection pooling, like multiplexing, is ideal for highly concurrent applications having a high percentage of computational time. That computational time might include searching, sorting, formatting, or other such CPU-intensive activities, and so it is also known as "think time." Connection pooling functions work best with a switchboard with a limited number of empty slots that is intentionally less than the number of incoming calls. A set number of *ports* is established. Based on UNIX networking, a port is the combination of a hardware address (for example, a host IP address) and a software address (for example, a UNIX socket). What connection pooling does is to remove the overhead of idle sessions.

When you read of connections and sessions, the terms generally mean the same thing in this context, although they do have subtly different meanings. As an aside, a connection is an established network link between machines (clients and servers), whereas a session is an established program link.

In any event, connection pooling temporarily disconnects idle sessions and passes their connection to new sessions wanting to connect or previously idle sessions wanting to reconnect. Connection pooling ensures that as many non-idle sessions are concurrently active as possible. It enables a new session to be established even if that session number surpasses the ceiling specified by the DBA.

OTHER NEW FEATURES AND CONCEPTS

Net8 supports both the two-tier (client/server) and now the N-tier configurations of distributed systems. In either configuration, multiple listeners can be *load balanced*. In other words, multiple sessions can be distributed nearly equally across multiple listeners accessing the same or multiple databases.

The two-tier, client/server configuration was, of course, supported by older versions of SQL*Net. It is characterized by synchronous remote procedure calls (RPCs) over a persistent connection-based protocol (such as TCP). The client blocks (goes into a suspended, or wait, state) until results are returned from server, and the RPC fails if the server does not respond (for example, is down). Because in a traditional client/server arrangement the connection is persistent, or dedicated, the network utilization is wasted if the RPC performs a lot of computation.

With the N-tier model, asynchronous message queuing can utilize connectionless protocols such as UDP. Clients place their message on the queue and either terminate or go on to other processing; they do not wait, and the message is handled by the server when the server becomes available (and so it never fails). When real-time needs are critical, messaging is not the preferred method. However, when high throughput is important, in the face of high concurrency, this model is preferred.

TNS Raw is essentially the capability to communicate across a low-level protocol without using Net8 headers whenever possible. A basic client/server connection utilizes TNS Raw calls transparently. In other words, no settings require configuration on either the client or the server by the user or the DBA to use it. TNS Raw automatically works when possible, for example, when no security services (that is, ASO) are required. With TNS Raw, there is greater packet efficiency (or density), in that more data is transmitted per packet because the space for the control information normally carried by Net8 headers now can carry data. Furthermore, less total data, in terms of packets, is transmitted for the same session. When TNS Raw is transparently utilized, two Net8 upper-level header-processing layers are bypassed, resulting in less total network processing time and less overall response time.

NEW SECURITY CAPABILITIES

With the Advanced Security Option (ASO), Net8 transmissions can be encrypted with your choice of encryption algorithm (RSA or DES) and key size (number of bits). CMAN supports ASO encryption so that when a protocol bridge exists, the encryption stream is not broken. ASO also provides single sign-on security through standards-based X.509 digital certificates. Digital certificates are based on public key infrastructure (PKI) technology. Each certificate is "signed" with an entity's private key, hence the term *digital signature*. With PKI technology, enforcement can be one-way (server only) or two-way (server and client), the latter also referred to as *strong* authentication. ASO also can provide external authentication adapters to plug in to Net8 that can be used as alternatives or supplements to digital certificates. These additional external authentication methods include ticket-based technologies (Kerberos, Sesame, DCE), token-based (SecurID), and biometrics (fingerprint, retina, and so on).

There are really two parts, then, to ASO. The part of ASO providing transmission (Net8) encryption replaces its predecessors, the Advanced Networking Option (ANO) and Secure Network Services (SNS). The part of ASO corresponding to encrypted authentication methods, such as digital certificates, supersedes Security Server, which existed as a bundled product with the early releases of Oracle8. ASO was launched with the release of Oracle8i, although it was still not fully available, as was Oracle8i, at the time of this writing.

NEW SERVICES, TOOLS, AND APIS

Oracle Names is a directory service providing name-to-address resolution for Net8 services. With Net8, Oracle Names has enhanced or new features that are all more or less based on the UNIX-based Domain Name Services (DNS) technology:

- Dynamic resolution—Net8 services can self-register with a Names Server.
- Client discovery—Clients can retrieve the list of Names Servers at installation time.
- Client caching—A client-side cache of names can be maintained as opposed to resolving a name upon each request.

The installer locates or asks for a Names Server. The Names Server is contacted, and a list of all Names Servers known to it is downloaded. The client asks each server on that list for its lists of servers and orders the results by response time (which the DBA can re-sort later if desired). This ordered response list becomes the initial client-side cache (or local names cache), stored in the .SDNS.ORA file. Other external naming services (even non-database), such as NIS, NDS, and CDS, can be integrated. For example, the native hostname adapter can use an OS naming service such as Sun Microsystem's Network Information Service (NIS, formerly known as "the Yellow Pages" on UNIX) in place of an Oracle Names Server. If the protocol is TCP/IP, there is one listener per database, and no security services (that is, ASO) are required.

Administration has been simplified through OEM applets, which can be used with OEM or by themselves. Although the Network Manager software is obsolete, the Net8 Assistant takes its place for server-side (listener) configuration. However, Net8 automatically configures itself on a TCP/IP environment. If all defaults are accepted, the listener does not require a listener.ora file. With Names Server, client profiles are created and edited with the Client Profile Editor, which can be shared among users (that is, clients). The Net8 client automatically loads the client profile data from the Names Server, which holds the profiles.

PART

III

CH

13

There is a Net8 wizard that automates initial client configuration. It is called up at installation time, handles the initial creation of the client-side Names Server cache, provides the choice of an existing or default client profile (from the Names Server), and enables editing of the configuration files. Also, Net8 Easy Config is simply renamed from SQL*Net Easy Config as the client-side configuration tool.

Net8 can use tracing through Oracle Trace, which has several benefits. Oracle Trace is a program external to Net8 and therefore has a smaller executable "footprint" than previous

SQL*Net tracing code. It can trace from point-to-point, in effect, from client-to-server. There is the Trace Assistant, which can extract and display errors from the trace file, extract packet type and information sent by a client or received by a server, and maintain statistics on packets.

Finally, Net8 also offers an open application programming interface (API), known as the Net8 OPEN API, that permits portability. Applications built on Net8 networking can be easily ported when moving from one protocol to another because the Net8 approach is protocol independent. Appropriate low-level calls embedded within Net8 itself can be replaced by relinking with the appropriate protocol adapter libraries. However, the high-level Net8 calls embedded within the application do not have to be changed.

CONFIGURING SOME NEW FEATURES

On the server-side, just as there is a `lsnrctl` listener control program and a corresponding `listener.ora` configuration file, there is an analogous `cmctl` connection manager control program and an analogous `cman.ora` configuration file. On the client-side, however, the same configuration file, `tnsnames.ora`, remains the only one that would be modified. You can perform most all the same commands within `cmctl` as in `lsnrctl`, such as `start`, `stop`, `status`, and `version`. In addition to `cmctl`, there are two processes which `cmctl` controls: the connection manager gateway, or `cmgw`, and the connection manager administrator, or `cmadm`. `cmgw` is analogous to the actual listener process. It is the communications hub and is primarily responsible for all the connection concentration duties as well as the duties associated with the other new features. `cmadm` is primarily responsible for managing address information and registration in conjunction with the Oracle Names server. `cmctl` refers internally to `cmgw` as `cm` and `cmadm` as `adm` when they are used as arguments to `start` and `status`. Only `cm` is an argument to `stop` because when `cmgw` terminates, `cmadm` automatically terminates, too.

Concentration (multiplexing and connection pooling) and bridging are enabled by editing each client's `tnsnames.ora` file *and* by editing the `init.ora` file. Establishing a firewall is done by editing the `cman.ora` file. Enabling listener load balancing is done by editing the `init.ora` file. Enabling the MTS option, of course, is done by editing the `init.ora` file, also.

MULTIPLEXING AND CONNECTION POOLING

Multiplexing is set up on each client and the server. Suppose the `cman.ora` file contains the following:

```
cman=(address=(protocol=tcp)(host=cman)(port=1610))
```

In this case, the `tnsames.ora` on each client would be edited to look like this:

```
mysid=(description=
    (address_list=
        (address=(protocol=tcp)(host=myserver)(port=1521))
        (address=(protocol=tcp)(host=cman)(port=1610))
        (connect_data=(sid=mysid))
        (source_route=yes)
    ))
```

On the server, the next line in the MTS section of your `init.ora` would be set like the following:

```
MTS_DISPATCHERS="(PROTOCOL=TCP)(POOL=YES)(MULT=YES)"
```

When enabling connection pooling or multiplexing, note that this setting is different from SQL*Net 2.x. When not using those Net8 features, the settings remain the same. Notice that you enable these concentration features for an entire protocol and that you are not specifying any initial startup amount of dispatchers.

When multiplexing is enabled on each client and the MTS option is enabled (in the `init.ora` file), the associated feature of connection pooling is also then available. *Connection pooling* is, in effect, a more specialized type of multiplexing. Both features cannot exist without MTS being enabled. Both are types of connection *concentration*.

BRIDGING

Multiprotocol support is also primarily set up on each client. The `tnsames.ora` on each client would be edited to look like the following:

```
mysid=(description=
    (address_list=
        (address=(protocol=spx)(service=cman))
        (address=(protocol=tcp)(host=myserver)(port=1521))
        (connect_data=(sid=mysid))
        (source_route=yes)
    ))
```

FIREWALL

Filtering support is set up on the server. The `cman.ora` file might be edited to look like this:

```
cman_rules=(rules_list=
(rule=
(src=good_host2)(dst=myhost)(srv=mysid)(act=accept))
(rule=
(src=bad_host1)(dst=myhost)(srv=mysid)(act=reject))
)
```

Actual IP addresses with or without wildcards can be used for the SRC and DST specifications, such as (`SRC=234.136.*.*`).

LISTENER LOAD BALANCING

To enable listener load balancing, in the MTS section of your `init.ora` file, set the following:

```
MTS_MULTIPLE_LISTENERS=TRUE
```

PART

III

CH

13

CMAN Profile

To set particular CMAN operating parameters, edit `cman.ora` file to include some or all of the following `cman_profile` segment:

```
cman_profile=
    (parameter_list=        /* DEFAULTS   */
    (maximum_relays=512)    /* 8          */
    (log_level=1)           /* 0          */
    (tracing=yes)           /* NO         */
    (relay_statistics=yes)  /* NO         */
    (show_tns_info=yes)     /* NO         */
    (use_async_call=yes)    /* YES        */
    (authentication_level=1) /* 0         */
    )
```

The following table briefly summarizes the descriptions of each parameter with maximums, if applicable:

TABLE 13.1   CMAN Operating Parameters

Parameter	Description
maximum_relays	Maximum number of concurrent connections (the maximum is 1024); contrast with the SESSIONS init.ora parameter
log_level	0 means no logging; 1–4 are increasingly detailed levels of logging.
tracing	yes or no; if yes, Oracle Trace must be turned on.
relay_statistics	yes or no; yes records number of IN/OUT bytes and packets, among other things.
show_tns_info	yes or no; if yes and log_level is greater than 0, TNS events are recorded in the log file
use_async_call	yes or no; if no, calls will be synchronous
authentication_level	0 or 1; if 1, reject clients not using ASO security services

Sample Configuration Files

As mentioned before, to enable the advanced concentration features of multiplexing and connection pooling, you first need the MTS option enabled, meaning you must reconfigure the `init.ora` file. The MTS options and addressing are closely integrated with the configuration of the `tnsnames.ora` and `listener.ora` files. In addition, the configuration of CMAN is closely integrated with the configuration of the `listener.ora` and all the clients' `tnsnames.ora` files. Following is a set of sample segments of files, one each of `init.ora`, `tnsnames.ora`, `listener.ora`, and `cman.ora`. (These examples are not using the Oracle Names service.) Pay attention to the bold sections, which are most pertinent to the close integration among all these files. MTS, listener load balancing, multiplexing, connection pooling, bridging, firewall, and CMAN profile features are enabled. The examples follow:

INIT.ORA
```
/* To enable MTS, multiplexing, connection pooling and listener load balancing */
/* This is just the MTS section of an init.ora file */
MTS_SERVICE=MYSID
MTS_SERVERS=10
MTS_MAX_SERVERS=100
MTS_DISPATCHERS="(protocol=tcp)(pool=yes)(mult=yes)"
MTS_DISPATCHERS="(protocol=spx)(pool=yes)(mult=yes)"
MTS_DISPATCHERS="(protocol=ipc)(pool=yes)(mult=yes)"
MTS_MAX_DISPATCHERS=100
MTS_LISTENER_ADDRESS=
"(address=(protocol=tcp)(host=myhost)(port=1521))"
MTS_LISTENER_ADDRESS=
"(address=(protocol=tcp)(host=cman)(port=1610))"
MTS_LISTENER_ADDRESS=
"(address=(protocol=spx)(service=cman))"
MTS_LISTENER_ADDRESS=
"(address=(protocol=ipc)(key=mysid))"
MTS_MULTIPLE_LISTENERS=TRUE
```

Also, you might need to set the **SESSIONS** parameter, which tells the instance the maximum number of active sessions to enable with concentration features (multiplexing or connection pooling) turned on.

TNSNAMES.ORA
```
/* To enable multiplexing, connection pooling, and bridging */

mysid=(description=
    (address_list=
        (address=(protocol=tcp)(host=myhost)(port=1521))
        (address=(protocol=tcp)(host=cman)(port=1610))
(address=(protocol=spx)(service=cman))
        (address=(protocol=ipc)(key=mysid))
        (connect_data=(sid=mysid))
        (source_route=yes)
    ))
```

LISTENER.ORA
```
/* The foundation of all the addressing */

listener=(address_list=
(address=(protocol=tcp)(host=myhost)(port=1521))
(address=(protocol=tcp)(host=myhost)(port=1526))
(address=(protocol=spx)(service=cman))
    (address=(protocol=ipc)(key=mysid))
    sid_list_listner=
        (sid_list=
            (sid_desc=mysid)
(sid_desc=another_sid))
    )
```

CMAN.ORA
```
/* To enable firewall and set the CMAN profile */

cman=(address_list=
(address=(protocol=spx)(service=cman))
(address=(protocol=tcp)(host=cman)(port=1610))
)
```

```
cman_rules=(rules_list=
(rule=
(src=good_host2)(dst=myhost)(srv=mysid)(act=accept))
(rule=
(src=bad_host1)(dst=myhost)(srv=mysid)(act=reject))
)

cman_profile=
    (parameter_list=
    (maximum_relays=512)
    (log_level=1)
    (tracing=yes)
    (relay_statistics=yes)
    (show_tns_info=yes)
    (use_async_call=yes)
    (authentication_level=1)
```

CHAPTER 14

ORACLE 8.x ADDITIONAL TOPICS

In this chapter

There are several new features, or enhancements, found in Oracle8.x. These include all types of enhancements; however, performance enhancements are primarily covered in Chapter 20, "Oracle8.x Tuning Considerations." This chapter primarily covers the new ROWID format, new password management functionality, the Recovery Manager, and Advanced Queuing. However, it also briefly covers the changes in constraints, national language support, and SYS security.

NEW ROWID

The new ROWID format in Oracle8.x was changed to mainly accommodate the new features of partitioning and objects, as well as increased database limits (see Chapter 18, "Tuning Memory") providing for more database files and tablespaces than in Oracle7.x. The ROWID is the foundation of all storage addressing in Oracle, hence the importance of this fundamental change.

The ROWID is used to uniquely identify a row in a regular Oracle index (B-tree) and is used throughout the Oracle8 kernel. In Oracle7.x, the ROWID included a file number, block number, and a row number, and it used only one number consistently to identify the datafile. In other words, in Oracle7.x, file numbers were absolute. In Oracle8.x, file numbers are relative. An Oracle8.x datafile has two parts to its file number:

- An absolute component unique within the database (as in Oracle7.x), represented by the column FILE_NO in dba_data_files.
- A relative component unique only within a tablespace, represented by the column RELATIVE_FNO in dba_data_files.

Because the file number is relative to a tablespace, the new ROWID must also store some indication of the segment reference. In Oracle8.x, this is the data object number, which identifies a table or a partition. From determining this segment, Oracle8 can then determine the containing tablespace, as with dba_tablespaces.

The data object number can be determined, for example, from the column DATA_OBJECT_ID in dba_objects. This data object number is *not* an object identifier (see Chapter 10, "Partitioning"). It is included in every block and is unique. When a table is truncated or a partition is moved, the *version* of the data object number is incremented. In this way, Oracle8 can verify that the number in the block matches (that is, is the correct version), and can also compare it to rollback blocks to ensure the proper versioning, too.

The new ROWID format uses base-64 encoding, and is 18 characters wide. This means there are 64^{18} possible rows in any given Oracle8 database. The components of the new Oracle8.x ROWID are laid out in Table 14.1.

TABLE 14.1   NEW ROWID COMPONENTS

Data Object #	Relative File #	Block #	Slot #
OOOOOO	FFF	BBBBB	SSS

From left-to-right, the first six characters represent the data object number, the next three represent the relative file number within a tablespace, the next six represent the block number within the file, and the last three represent the (row) slot number within the block. Contrasted to Oracle7.x, the real differences are the data object number and the relative file number.

Contrast this with the Oracle7.x ROWID format in Table 14.2

TABLE 14.2   OLD ROWID COMPONENTS

Block #	Row #	File #
BBBBBBBB.	RRRR.	FFFF

From left-to-right, the first eight characters represent the block number within the file, the next four represent the row number within the block, and the final four represent the absolute file number. These types of ROWIDs are sufficient for most situations, except for cases involving Global indexes on partitioned tables because partitions can span multiple tablespaces.

How can some of the differences between the Oracle7.x ROWID and the Oracle8.x new ROWID be summarized? Table 14.3 helps somewhat.

TABLE 14.3   ROWID VERSIONS COMPARISON

Version	Description	Bytes	Display	File Nos.
7.x	restricted	6	2 dots	absolute
8.x	extended	10	no dots	relative

The tablespace-relative addressing is the foundation of Oracle's support of VLDBs. Oracle8 uses 10 bytes to store this new ROWID, as opposed to 6 bytes for Oracle7.x. When relative ROWID is sufficient, the *restricted* ROWID is used. When absolute ROWID is required, as with Global indexes on partitioned tables, the *extended* (full) ROWID is used. Restricted ROWIDs are sufficient for nonpartitioned indexes on nonpartitioned tables, equipartitioned indexes on partitioned tables, and chaining and migration pointers across blocks. Extended ROWIDs are necessary for Global indexes on partitioned tables, kernel use, and stored forms of ROWID.

When retrieving Oracle7 ROWIDs from Oracle8, the ROWIDs appear in restricted format, as they always did in Oracle7.x. However, when retrieving Oracle8 ROWIDs from Oracle7, you need to use the DBMS_ROWID package to interpret the extended format. Oracle7 tables can be exported to Oracle8, but Oracle8 tables containing the new ROWID format cannot be

PART

III

CH

14

exported to Oracle7. Further, if ROWIDs are kept in any stored form, they will need to be recomputed after import because their contents will be otherwise obsolete and in need of updating.

Application portability issues arise only if the application either partially stores or retrieves ROWID rows. On the other hand, those applications using ROWIDs on the whole should be unaffected. When Oracle7 tables are either exported or migrated (using the Migration Utility) to Oracle8, stored ROWID column widths are automatically widened to accommodate the new, wider Oracle8 ROWIDs. The aforementioned DBMS_ROWID package is created by the dbmsutil.sql script, which is called by the catproc.sql script. Table 14.4 lists the functions and return values of the DBMS_ROWID package. Listing 14.1 shows an example of converting a restricted ROWID to an extended ROWID.

TABLE 14.4   DBMS_ROWID PACKAGE FUNCTIONS

Function	Returns
rowid_create	a new ROWID
rowid_info	type and components
rowid_type	type (0=restricted, 1=extended)
rowid_object	data object number (segment)
rowid_relative_fno	relative file number
rowid_block_number	block number
rowid_row_number	row (slot) number
rowid_to_absolute_fno	absolute file number
rowid_to_extended	extended ROWID
rowid_to_restricted	restricted ROWID
rowid_verify	0=can be extended, 1=cannot

LISTING 14.1   EXAMPLE OF CONVERTING A RESTRICTED ROWID TO AN EXTENDED ROWID

```
SQL> select * from mytable where mykey=12;
mykey myROWID             myvalue
----- ------------------- -------
   12 00000001A.0011.0009     102
SQL> update mytable set myrowid-
  1 dbms_rowid.rowid_to_extended(myrowid, 'JOHN', 'MYTABLE', 0)
  2 where mykey=12;
SQL> select * from mytable where mykey=12;
mykey myROWID             myvalue
----- ------------------- -------
   12 AAAAbCAACAAAAAbAAAA     102
```

The ROWID_to_extended function takes in an old (restricted) ROWID, owner, table, and conversion_type. The conversion_type is either 0 for a stored (internal) conversion or 1 for a displayed (external) conversion. It returns a new (extended) ROWID as per our earlier function list.

PASSWORD MANAGEMENT ENHANCEMENTS

The new enhancements offered for password management in Oracle8 include account locking, aging and expiration, a history mechanism, and complexity verification (proactive checking). To enable password management, run the utlpwdmg.sql script. You can set up profiles and assign users to them. However, unlike resource limits, which can be turned on or off with the resource_limit parameter in the init.ora file, password limits are always enforced.

With account locking, Oracle8 automatically locks an account after a specified number of failed login attempts. This number can be set on a user or group basis. The account is unlocked after a timeout period, or it is manually unlocked. It can be manually locked as needed, in which case it can be unlocked only manually (and not through a timeout).

With password aging and expiration, you can specify an expiration period, or lifetime, that corresponds to how long a password remains valid. You can also specify a grace period that enables a user so much time to change her password after it expires. You can manually expire or pre-expire, accounts, which makes sense for newly created users who have only the grace period amount in which to change their passwords. These characteristics can be set on a user or group basis. For example, Group A might have an expiration period of 90 days with a grace period of 5 days, but Group B might have an expiration period of 30 days with a grace period of 1 day. In addition, user C might have individual expiration and grace periods of 60 days and 10 days, respectively.

With the password history mechanism, a user can not reuse any password used within the past time interval, which is specified in that user's profile. Again, it is important to remember that, unlike resource limits, this and other password limits are always enforced (until modified).

Proactive password checking is provided through a default SYS PL/SQL function. You can replace that function with your own PL/SQL function of increased sophistication. The default function provides complexity verification by checking that each password is the following:

1. At least four characters in length
2. != userID
3. At least one character each of the following: alphabetic, numeric, and punctuation
4. Different from the last password by at least three characters

Your own password checking function is created in the SYS schema, is attached to a user or group profile, and must adhere to the following specification:

```
myfunction (
  p_userid IN varchar2(30),
  p_new_password IN varchar2(30),
  p_old_password IN varchar2(30) )
return boolean;
```

The CREATE PROFILE and ALTER PROFILE statements handle all the settings of the aforementioned password limits. The default password settings for the CREATE PROFILE statement are shown in Table 14.5.

TABLE 14.5   CREATE PROFILE DEFAULT PASSWORD SETTINGS

Setting	Default	Units
failed_login_attempts	3	Number
password_life_time	60	Days
password_reuse_time	180	Days
password_reuse_max	Unlimited	Number
password_lock_time	1	Number
password_grace_time	10	Days
password_verify_function	Default	Function

Most of these settings have been explained in the previous paragraphs. Now, you'll look at some that might be unclear. The password_reuse_max represents the maximum number of password changes before a password can be used again. The default is unlimited, but password reuse is nonetheless controlled by password_reuse_time. Both can be set to unlimited; however, only one can be actually set to a number. In this respect, they are mutually exclusive settings.

The password_lock_time specifies the number of days that an account is locked after the specified number of failed login attempts. Hence, with the default settings, a user account will be locked for one day if the user fails to log in after three attempts. Lastly, the actual name of the default password_verify_function is simply verify_function.

Listing 14.2 gives you an example of creating a profile for setting password limits and then creating a user to have that profile.

LISTING 14.2   EXAMPLE OF CREATING A PASSWORD PROFILE FOR A USER

```
SQL> create profile secure90 limit
   2 password_life_time 90
   3 password_reuse_time 366
   4 password_grace_time 5;
SQL> create user john
   2 identified by all4one?
```

```
     3 default tablespace scratch
     4 temporary tablespace temp2
     5 quota 10M on scratch
     6 password expire
     7 profile secure90;
```

Notice the CREATE USER statement above pre-expired the account for new user john. The
CREATE USER and ALTER USER statements enable you to attach your custom profiles to a
particular user. You could also do this with groups instead. Also, the ALTER USER statement
would be used to manually lock or unlock an account as in the following:

```
SQL> alter user john
   2 account lock ¦ unlock;
```

DBA_USERS and USER_USERS contain new columns that reflect these new password management
features, as shown in Table 14.6.

TABLE 14.6   THE NEW USER PASSWORD MANAGEMENT FEATURES

New Column	Meaning
account_status	locked, expired, or open
grace_date	date of change + password_grace_time
lock_date	date of lock
expiry_date	date of creation + password_life_time

Also, DBA_PROFILES lists the password settings and contains a new column, resource_type,
specifying kernel or password. A new view, user_password_limits, contains the columns
resource_name and limit.

RECOVERY MANAGER (RMAN) CONCEPTS

Recovery Manager (RMAN) is an administrative piece of software that manages backup,
recovery, and restoration for Oracle8. RMAN can be standalone or distributed. RMAN
uses a PL/SQL interface to the Oracle8 server that invokes the three main functions:
BACKUP, RECOVER, and RESTORE. RMAN uses a control repository known as the *recovery
catalog*. As of 8.0.4, third-party storage subsystems such as EMC/Epoch, Legato, IBM, and
so forth can be integrated into the RMAN solution. Tape drives, for example, used with
robotic, multiple tape units such as those from Exabyte, can be used in a parallel fashion.

The four fundamental pieces of the RMAN architecture are the RMAN interface (an OEM
applet graphical user interface or a command-line interpreter, which is available with OEM
versions 1.4 and greater), the BACKUP/RECOVER/RESTORE server functionality, the recovery catalog,
and the storage subsystem (operating system, third party, or both).

Why use RMAN to manage your Oracle8 backups? It automates many of the administrative
backup functions and duties. Backups can take place at many levels: database, tablespaces,

PART

III

CH

14

or datafiles. Datafiles can be specified for backing up based on user-defined tolerances. Most important, true incremental backups are possible. In other words, backups at any level can be executed to back up changed blocks only. Further, unused blocks are not backed up. Backups can be easily scheduled and controlled. Storage subsystem handling is also administered more easily, and its operations might be parallelized as mentioned. In addition, RMAN can integrate with established third-party hardware and software vendors, also as mentioned.

There are two main RMAN interfaces: a command-line interpreter (CLI) or an OEM graphical user interface (GUI). The CLI is an application similar to SQL*Plus and can be likewise interactively or noninteractively executed. The GUI is integrated within OEM and offers an API library that can be linked with another third-party application (such as a storage subsystem).

THE RECOVERY CATALOG

The recovery catalog, created by the `catrman.sql` script, is normally stored in a dedicated database, much like the OEM repository. The *recovery database* is the database that houses the recovery catalog. A *target database* is any application or user database that is a target database for RMAN to back up. The recovery catalog must be backed up as with any of your other application databases. To back up the recovery database, you reverse the roles of it and one target database so that for the backup of the recovery database, it is momentarily a target database, and some other target database is the recovery database. Hence, this means that there are really at least two recovery catalogs—one for all the user databases and at least one other for the recovery catalog itself.

Tip #9	For availability, you would typically place the primary RMAN repository in a separate (recovery) database on a separate machine from your core application (target) databases. In addition, you could create an RMAN repository in one application database just for the handling the primary RMAN repository. This way, you could lose any particular database and be able to recover it, including the recovery database itself.

The recovery catalog maintains information in its database repository about datafile backup sets, archivelog backup sets, backup pieces, datafile copies, archived redo logs, archived redo log copies, control file information of the target databases (that is, their physical structure), and the universe of available backup commands.

RMAN statically stores control file information about all its target databases. When a backup operation takes place, RMAN communicates what needs to be backed up to the Oracle8 server serving the target database, which, as you know, already has the backup functionality within its kernel. That is, RMAN initiates and manages the backups, but each targeted database actually backs up itself. Hence, when the structure of any target database changes (for example, a datafile is added or renamed), that information must be updated at the recovery catalog before the next backup operation takes place. Almost all the necessary information to update the recovery catalog is found in the control files of the target databases except for rollback segment information, which must be selected from the data dictionaries of the databases (implying that the target databases must be *open*).

However, RMAN can operate without a recovery catalog, as is appropriate when you have only one or a few databases to back up or if tablespace point-in-time recovery (PTR) is not essential. Why can't you have PTR? Rollback information would have been stored in the recovery catalog, having been queried from the target database, but without a recovery catalog, there can be no PTR. Other limitations to operating without a recovery catalog include not being able to use stored scripts (which would be stored in the catalog) and automatic recovery when control files are lost or damaged is not fully possible (only partially so).

RMAN COMMANDS AND FUNCTIONALITY

Recovery Manager, as mentioned, relies on (target) server backup functionality. This functionality resides in database packages that include all the necessary backup, recover, and restore subprograms. RMAN's predecessor, External (or Enterprise) Backup Utility (EBU), could only call third-party tools. Integration was at the highest programmatic level. Now RMAN can control both the operating system (OS) and third party storage subsystems through API functionality. Integration is at the lowest functional level.

The RMAN commands include the capability to register a target database, reset the state of a target database (even to a previous backed up version), and update the recovery catalog when a target database has changed (even the state of a previously backed up control file). *Synchronization* of the catalog is the periodic updating of target database information: all the control files and rollback information. This is important, not only because there might have been structural changes, but also because log file activity is now recorded in the control files. In Oracle8.x, the control files grow, now keeping track of log file switches and archived redo log file copies. Hence, disciplined synchronization becomes very important.

RMAN offers the capability to use the BACKUP, RECOVER, and RESTORE commands directly or embedded within scripts. An RMAN script is called by the RUN command. The CREATE SCRIPT command is used to create the script (and store it in the recovery catalog). For safety, keep an OS copy of each of your backup scripts (in the event of the loss of your recovery catalog, for example). REPORT and LIST commands offer log output of recovery catalog information and RMAN status. REPORT reports on datafiles that might need backup files based on user tolerances related to redundancy, increments, or time; backup files that might be deleted; and backup files that are unrecoverable. LIST lists information about user-specified datafiles in backup sets or having copies, partially or fully matching the search criteria.

RMAN TERMINOLOGY

Backup sets are sets of either datafiles (and possibly controlfiles) or archivelog files. In other words, multiple files are written to a single backup set. This is in contrast to an *image copy*, in which a single file is simply copied. Files backed up in backup sets must be restored (and extracted) before they can be used, whereas image copies can be used directly, simply by renaming the lost datafile. Full or incremental backups to backup sets are supported.

Parallelism can be specified to match the number of available tape drives. Backup sets can be *staged* from disk to tape and vice versa on a recovery. Datafiles can be stored in backup sets across multiple tapes (a multitape volume), and are multiplexed in a round robin fashion, with a user-specified number of blocks per datafile at a time. Controlfile blocks are written in full first, if included, and are not interleaved with datafile blocks. Backup sets can be written to disk or tape.

A *backup piece* is a single file belonging to a backup set. This file can contain blocks from more than one datafile and can be manifested as an OS file or tape volume. A backup set is the sum of all its backup pieces.

An image copy can only be written to disk, and as mentioned, there is a single file that is one-to-one with the source file. If the sum of all your image copies comprise your entire database, then you have a full cold backup. You can also register foreign backups, that is, those image copies not created by RMAN.

A *full* backup contains all the blocks of all the specified datafiles to be backed up. An *incremental* backup contains only those blocks modified since the last backup. *Cumulative* incremental backups are possible, but they waste space and time, so their benefit diminishes with the number accumulated. You can also take a full backup as a baseline, which is subsequently ignored by all successive incrementals. A *multilevel* incremental is just like the UNIX ufs backup scheme. Level 0 represents a full backup, and you can then specify up to 7 more levels of incrementals. For example, level 2 might represent weekly incrementals and level 1 daily incrementals. An incremental in this scheme only backs up since the last incremental of the same level or lower. For example, level 2 backs up only what has changed since the last level 2, 1, or 0. Multilevel incrementals enhance recovery because you only need restore at most one incremental from any given level.

Tags are character strings (up to 30 characters) that can be assigned to backup sets or image copies. Tags are symbolic names long used by storage subsystems to help users have a mnemonic reference to some storage unit, such as a tape volume or disk partition. Its use is no different with RMAN. Tags can span backup sets and image copies. In other words, tags are not necessarily unique per a backup set or image copy. Although potentially problematic, this can be useful in grouping certain backup sets that make up common sense whole units, such as one tablespace.

Parallelization of backup and restore operations is handled internally by RMAN, which establishes multiple, concurrent user sessions, one per device. RMAN multiplexes individual commands occurring within the user sessions. Hence, although statement execution is serial within RMAN (like SQL*Plus), parallelization is attained by virtue of the multiple user sessions. Datafiles are grouped by RMAN when multiplexing them to a backup set, although a user can specify the groupings. RMAN supports PTR of any tablespace except SYSTEM. In order to accomplish the latter, Oracle requires that the database be cloned and be done only with technical support assistance.

Backup essentially requires the database to be open (to obtain the rollback information). However, restore only requires an instance to be started. Both backup and restore check for, record, and report block corruption. They also do checksums for fractured block detection. A fractured block is one that happened to be read by the backup operation while it was being modified, and hence it must be reread to obtain a consistent version.

As mentioned, in Oracle8.x, controlfiles now grow, based on log switches and archivelog file copies. However, the growth can be controlled by setting the init.ora parameter con-trol_file_record_keep_time, which is set to the number of days to keep the oldest reusable entry or record. A reusable entry is a line in the controlfile that can be reused, in contrast to the Oracle7.x controlfile, which had no reusable entries. If you set this parameter to 0, entries are reused whenever they are needed, and they are not aged.

All the pertinent data dictionary views that hold RMAN backup and recovery information are prefixed as V$BACKUP_*. These include the following:

    V$BACKUP_CORRUPTION

    V$BACKUP_DATAFILE

    V$BACKUP_REDOLOG

    V$BACKUP_SET

    V$BACKUP_PIECE

    V$BACKUP_MEMBER

    V$BACKUP_RESTORE_STAT

    V$BACKUP_PARMS

Monitor these for RMAN activity in addition to V$ARCHIVED_LOG and V$DATAFILE.

ADVANCED QUEUING (AQ) CONCEPTS

There are two main types of execution in a distributed environment: *immediate* (synchronous) or *deferred* (asynchronous). In most cases, immediate action is what is called for in many distributed systems. But in others, such as replication-based distributed systems, deferred action is appropriate. Queuing is a mechanism that implements deferred action. *Queues* are First-In, First-Out (FIFO) or First Come, First Serve (FCFS) data structures in which the first thing in is the first one to get serviced and exit. That is, things are handled based purely on the order in which they arrived. However, variations on the pure queue exist that are all more or less based on the concept of *prioritization*. A unit of work in queue is referred to as a *job*. A job is said to *wait* in a queue to be *serviced*, or processed. *Persistent* queuing guarantees that, even if there were a system failure, all jobs in the queue would be processed upon successful restart of the system. Job control and workflow management are two areas well fit for queuing. Transaction Processing (TP) monitors and Message-Oriented Middleware (MOM) either rely on or emulate queuing functionality. Oracle8.x supplies Advanced Queuing (AQ) capability without the need for third-party software.

A *message* is the smallest job that can be processed. Like a network packet, it contains user data and control information. A single transaction can *create* (produce) or *process* (consume)

PART

III

CH

14

multiple messages. ENQUEUE creates messages, and DEQUEUE enables messages to be processed. A *message queue* is a queue, or collection, of messages. Multiple message queues can be created for various reasons, such as to functionally separate some insular messaging tasks from others, to separate independent messaging activity, and perhaps to increase throughput in the process. A *queue table* is simply an Oracle table that can hold multiple message queues.

Some of the more important features of Oracle8.x AQ include the following:

- Message ordering and prioritization
- Objects as user data
- Reply and exception queues
- Transactional or nontransactional message
- Multiple recipients of a message
- Message grouping

Much of the user and administrative functionality of Oracle AQ is supplied through the system packages dbms aq and dbmsaqadm. dbms aq holds the two basic procedures, enqueue and dequeue. Users must be granted the aq_user_role. The *payload* of a message is its user data. Look at the enqueue and dequeue specifications:

```
enqueue (
queue_name          IN    varchar2,
enqueue_options     IN    enqueue_option_t,
message-properties  IN    message_properties_t,
payload             IN    <object_type ¦ raw>,
msgid               OUT    raw )

dequeue (
queue_name          IN    varchar2,
dequeue_options     IN    dequeue_option_t,
message-properties  OUT    message_properties_t,
payload             OUT    <object_type ¦ raw>,
msgid               OUT    raw )
```

Because payload can be specified as an object type, it can essentially by anything an object type can be, which is quite broad (see Chapter 10). The enqueue_options, dequeue_options, and message_properties are all predefined record types. A queue name uniquely identifies a queue. msgid uniquely identifies a message. Please refer to the Oracle8.x documentation, which covers in depth all the enqueue and dequeue options. For now, though, take a look at simple enqueue and dequeue calls:

```
dbms_aq.enqueue (
queue_name => 'john.jq1',
payload => employee_type
msgid => msgh );

dbms_aq.dequeue (
queue_name => 'john.jq1',
payload => employee_type
msgid => msgh );
```

With the enqueue call, a message having msgid, msgh, and payload of an object of employee_type is queued up in the queue table jq1 owned by john. The subsequent dequeue call dequeues that same message. All the defaults for the enqueue_options, dequeue_options, and message_properties are taken. Also, notice the use of the => parameter assignment operator.

Tip #10	An AQ timer process, or *time manager (tm)*, is required when any messages have associated time-based properties, such as delays, expirations, or retention intervals. Set the init.ora parameter AQ_TM_PROCESSES to 1, and this will start up one time manager process. Currently, it can only be set to 1, but in future releases, it might be increased to enable multiple time managers.

The DBMS_AQADM package contains the subprograms that manage the creation and control of the queues and queue tables, as well as managing subscribers and starting/stopping the time manager process. You must have AQ_ADMINISTRATOR_ROLE to execute these procedures:

```
CREATE_ ¦ DROP_ QUEUE_TABLE
CREATE_ ¦ DROP_ ¦ ALTER_ ¦ START_ ¦ STOP_ QUEUE
START_ ¦ STOP_ TIME_MANAGER
ADD_ ¦ REMOVE_ ¦ QUEUE_ SUBSCRIBER(S)
```

SYS must first execute the *grant_type_access* procedure to give access to the AQ administrator on the AQ object types. The AQ administrator can then further grant privileges as necessary to users. Look at simple create and drop queue tables:

```
dbms_adqam.create_queue_table (
queue_table => 'jq1',
queue_payload => employee_type );

dbms_adqam.create_queue_table (
queue_table => 'jq1');
```

As you can see, with defaults taken, these statements can be quite simple. However, as with the enqueue and dequeue operations, there are many options that can be specified in executing many of the DBMS_AQADM procedures, especially those dealing with creation. As an example, one last key concept left to cover is that of a subscriber. A *subscriber* is a user who is enabled to dequeue from a queue that permits multiple consumers per message, an option on queue table creation. To cover all the possible options available with the DBMS_AQ user and DBMS_AQADM administrative packages would be beyond the scope of this book. However, suffice it to say that Oracle has supplied a very robust, yet complex, queuing mechanism integrated with its database engine.

The DBA_QUEUE and USER_QUEUE tables hold table queue information. Likewise, the DBA_QUEUE and USER_QUEUE hold queue information. There is also an AQ$*<queue_table>* view available for each queue table.

CONSTRAINTS, NATIONAL LANGUAGE SUPPORT, AND SYS SECURITY

In Oracle8.x, constraint checking can be *deferred* until the end of a transaction, meaning that the server checks that the constraint is satisfied only at commit time. If the constraint is violated during the transaction, there is no problem. If it is violated at commit time, the whole transaction is rolled back.

This is in contrast to *immediate* constraint checking, in which the server checks the constraint at the end of each statement. If the statement violates the constraint, the statement is rolled back, not the whole transaction.

Also, instead of constraints being just disabled or enabled, they can be *enforced*. An enforced constraint is one that enforces all new modification statements but ignores the currently existing data (which might, in fact, violate the constraint).

Although perhaps not a good idea, Oracle8.x now enables unique and primary key constraints to be handled using non-unique indexes, if desired.

With national language support (NLS), the NCHAR column is new. It is a fixed width character, multibyte datatype capable of holding up to 2000 characters. The NVARCHAR2 is to varchar2 as NCHAR is to char. However, NVARCHAR2 can hold up to 4000 characters. Lastly, to store or retrieve NCHAR or NVARCHAR2 datatypes, prefix the actual value with a literal N, not in quotes.

In Oracle8.x, unless you belong to the OSDBA group or you have the SYS password/internal password, you will not be able to connect to the SYS schema without the SYSDBA role. Those users having system privileges using the ANY qualifier (such as SELECT ANY TABLE) will not be able to access the SYS schema in Oracle8.x as they had been able to in Oracle7.x. In Oracle8.x, you have to have SELECT_CATALOG_ROLE or EXECUTE_CATALOG_ROLE to select or execute SYS objects.

ORACLE8I OVERVIEW

In this chapter

Oracle8i, the latest version of the Oracle RDBMS, is a portable and highly scaleable database for developing, deploying, and managing applications within the enterprise and on the Internet. It was designed to support very large and high volume transaction processing and data warehousing applications.

The major new feature of Oracle8i is the inclusion of Java and Internet capabilities in the database. Integrated with the database server is a Java Virtual Machine (JVM), called Oracle JServer, so developers can now create applications in Java, PL/SQL, C, or OCI. It enables developers to write stored procedures, database functions, or triggers in Java. Because Java is platform independent, applications developed in it can be easily deployed on any server that supports Java without rewrites or recompiles. Another major feature of Oracle8i is the Internet File System (iFS), which enables the database to store and manage relational and nonrelational data files. Oracle8i comes with Oracle interMedia which can manage and access multi-media data (audio, video, image, text, and spatial). Oracle8i also includes Oracle WebDB, a Web development environment that enables developers to build dynamic, data-driven Web sites with a standard Web browser and the Oracle8i database.

JAVA CAPABILITIES IN ORACLE8I

Figure 15.1 illustrates the reference Java Virtual Machine (JVM) architecture. Having Java in the database makes it easier, faster, less costly, and highly productive to develop and deploy intranet/Internet applications. The Java programming language enables the developer to take advantage of a multitude of development tools readily available for use. Also Java code is safe to execute in a database server in contrast to languages such as C or C++ because it doesn't enable the manipulation of pointers to memory locations. The Oracle8i Java VM's memory manager automatically allocates and frees memory so that it minimizes the problem of memory bounds causing data corruption in the database.

Figure 15.1
The Oracle8i Java
Virtual Machine
Architecture

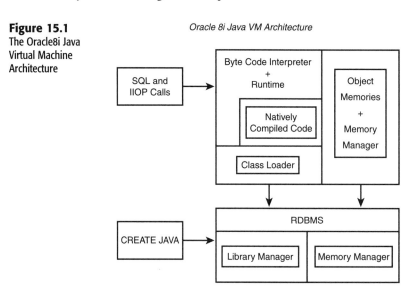

Oracle 8i Java VM Architecture

Before Oracle8i, there were no enterprise-class Java servers integrated into an RDBMS available for developing large-scale applications. Most application server and database server vendors have used the Java VM from JavaSoft (JDK) to run server-side Java applications. The Java VM from JavaSoft was developed as a client-side VM running in a single-user environment, and it does not provide the high scalability needed for enterprisewide applications. Oracle's Java VM is highly integrated with the database to meet the needs of mission-critical applications. The Oracle8i JVM includes integrated Java Database Connectivity (JDBC) drivers and SQLJ translators and offers the following features: high performance, scalability, high availability, manageability, and compliance with standards and Java runtime support. The JVM is compliant with the JDK 1.1.6 specification and supports all the standard JDK libraries.

The JVM has efficient memory management capabilities and reduces required user memory to between 80–150KB for typical Java sessions. It runs in the same process and address space as the database kernel itself, sharing a number of memory heaps and having direct access to the database's buffer cache for optimal performance. Because the JVM allocates its shared memory pool from the database's SGA, a larger SGA needs to be configured to accommodate the JVM. The Oracle Multithreaded Server architecture, which can scale to tens of thousands of concurrent users, (available since the Oracle7 release) is where the Java VM has been integrated into the server. MTS is based on an architecture where database listeners route user connections to a group of dispatchers that interact with server processes to handle database connections. The intent of Oracle8i is to support the very large number of concurrent users in Internet applications. The Java VM was designed to run Java applications faster, more securely, and more reliably. Because the JVM is integrated into the database, it can be ported across all the many hardware and operating systems platforms that Oracle supports, thereby fulfilling the Java promise of "write once, run anywhere".

MAJOR COMPONENT OF THE JAVA VIRTUAL MACHINE

The major components of the JVM are the following:

- *Library Manager* provides the facilities to load, store, and manage Java programs in the database. Users can import or export Java objects in three forms: source, binaries and resources, or archives.

- *Class Loader* locates, loads, and initializes local DBMS-stored Java classes on request from the Java VM. It reads the .class file information and produces all the data structures needed by the Java VM to execute Java code.

- *Memory Manager* (Garbage Collector) is responsible for automatically managing the Java VM's memory heaps and allocating and collecting object memories efficiently. Memory is allocated in standard chunks called object memories. Each object memory is a pool of memory that is allocated and collected as a single unit, and within each unit all the objects share a common lifetime and format.

- The *Java-Through-C Compiler*, NCOMP, is a native compiler embedded in the Java VM. It translates standard Java .class binaries, generating specialized C programs that are then compiled to C executables.

■ *Java stored procedures and triggers* can be compiled with the Java native compiler and stored in the database as database objects similar to PL/SQL stored procedures. Procedures written in Java can call procedures written in PL/SQL and vice/versa. Because stored procedures execute in the database, they minimize the network traffic between applications and the database, thereby increasing performance. You can now use Java in all the contexts in which you traditionally used PL/SQL. An overview of the Java stored procedures architecture is illustrated in Figure 15.2.

Figure 15.2
Java Stored Procedures in Oracle8i

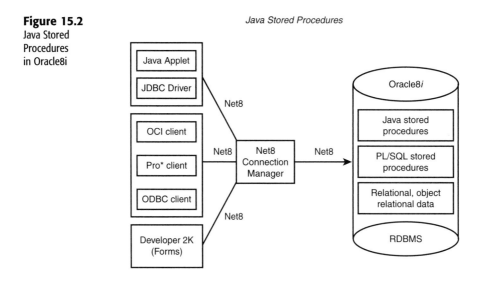

Java Stored Procedures

WRITING JAVA STORED PROCEDURES

The steps required to write Java stored procedures are the following:

1. Write your Java code.
2. Load and resolve it.
3. Publish the code.
4. Run it.

First, you write and test your Java program, and then you load it into the Oracle8i JVM and resolve all references. The Java programs loaded into the database are stored as *library units* in a database schema similar to the way PL/SQL program units are stored.

The following example is a simple Java program called student.java that prints the line "Student List" to the computer screen:

```
public class student {
  public static void main (string args[]) {
    system.out.print ("Student List");

  }
}
```

Once you get that simple example to compile and run, you will know that your environment is set up correctly.

You can load Java source, binaries, or resource files in two ways. One way is with a new DDL command in SQL*Plus:

```
"CREATE JAVA {SOURCE ¦ CLASS ¦ RESOURCE}"
```

Using this statement you can input the Java code from a binary file or by use of a LOB column in the database.

The second way is by using the LOADJAVA utility provided by Oracle8i. This utility automates the steps in loading the Java into the database. It loads Java files into a database table called create$java$lob$table, then runs the SQL "CREATE JAVA ..." command. The LOADJAVA utility can also take a resolve specification as an argument to resolve its external references. There is also a DROPJAVA utility for dropping Java programs stored in the database library units.

When you specify the resolve option, LOADJAVA uses the SQL ALTER JAVA CLASS ...RESOLVE statement to resolve external references now in uploaded Java classes otherwise the ALTER JAVA statement executes implicitly at run time.

The following is an example of syntax for resolving a Java class. This loads the exam.jar file into user SCOTT's schema, then resolves external references:

```
loadjava -user scott/tiger -resolve exam.jar
```

The loadjava can also take a resolver specification that lists one or more items, each consisting of a name spec and a schema spec that it searches in the order listed.

The following iis an example of using the LOADJAVA utility with a RESOLVER specification to load the student.class file into user PETER schema in database sid MYSID. It searches for class names that begin with home.java in schema PETER, then searches in schema PUBLIC:

```
loadjava -user peter/page@tysons1:5521:mysid
        -resolver '(("/home/java/*" PETER) (* PUBLIC))' student.class
```

The following is an example of using a binary file on the operating-system level to load Java code:

```
/* Create a directory on the server's file system. */
SQL> CREATE DIRECTORY b_dir
   2 as '/home/user/oracle8/student';
Statement processed.

/* Then load the Java class file using the "CREATE JAVA CLASS ..." command. */
SQL> CREATE OR REPLACE JAVA CLASS
   2 USING BFILE (b_dir, 'student.class');
Statement processed.
```

After the Java program has been loaded into the database, the code needs to be published. This is done by registering the program with SQL, though only the top-level Java entry point needs to be registered. The top-level Java entry point is the Java class or method that SQL initially calls with SQL. The Java code can be published by using call specifications,

CALL-spec, a PL/SQL subprogram spec-annotated to show that a Java method implements the subprogram.

The following is an example of CALL-spec for the appr-bonus Java method of class employee.emp:

```
SQL> CREATE OR REPLACE PROCEDURE A_BONUS
     (C_SAL IN NUMBER, BONUS NUMBER)
2>    AS LANGUAGE JAVA
3>    NAME 'employee.emp.appr_bonus (float,float,float)';
4>    /
5>    Statement processed.
```

The final step is to run your Java code by having SQL call it. This can be done in two ways:

One way uses the CALL statement:

```
SQL> VARIABLE CSAL NUMBER
SQL> VARIABLE BONUS NUMBER
SQL> EXECUTE :CSAL := 20000;
Statement processed.
SQL> EXECUTE :BONUS := 100;
Statement processed.
SQL> CALL A_BONUS (:CSAL, :BONUS);
Statement processed.
```

The other way is ito call a Java stored function from a SQL query:

```
CALL-spec for s_grade Java method of class student.stud -

SQL> CREATE OR REPLACE FUNCTION SGRADE (GRAD IN NUMBER)
       RETURN VARCHAR2
2>    AS LANGUAGE JAVA
3>    NAME 'student.stud.s_grade (float) return java.lang.String';
4>    /
Statement processed.
```

The following example uses a SQL DML statement to call the Java stored function SGRADE:

```
SQL> SELECT SNAME,GRAD, SGRADE(GRAD) FROM STUD;
```

PL/SQL can call Java stored procedures directly by simply invoking the PL/SQL CALL-spec.

The following is an example of PL/SQL calling a Java stored procedure directly:

```
DECLARE
    sal     number;
    bonus   number;
BEGIN
...
A_BONUS (sal, bonus);
...
END;
```

Tip #11	In Java, a Remote Method Invocation (RMI) call is simply a specialized Remote Procedure Call (RPC). Oracle8i uses RMI as the transport protocol over Internet Inter-ORB Protocol (IIOP). As you might expect, this "retrofitting" of an already existing technology is a logical extension of object-oriented and network programming. However, the topics of network and distributed programming, object-oriented programming, and Java are beyond the scope of this book, so please refer to the appropriate Que books for more in-depth explanations and examples.

SQLJ: THE ORACLE8I JAVA PREPROCESSOR

SQLJ, a new programming syntax, is Oracle's preprocessor for JDBC; it could be thought of as PRO*Java. It enables developers to embed SQL statements into Java programs similar to Oracle's other pre-compilers (that is, PRO*C). SQLJ only supports static SQL versus Pro*C, which supports static and dynamic SQL. Oracle developed SQLJ with numerous partners, including IBM, Tandem(now Compaq), and Sun, and it was adopted as an ANSI standard in December 1998. It was designed to be used independently of the target database so it should be possible to take an Oracle SQLJ stored procedure and run it on another vendor's database if the vendor supports SQLJ.

Programmers write a Java program with embedded SQL statements then run it against a SQLJ translator, which replaces the SQL statements with calls to the SQLJ runtime. Then any Java compiler can be used to compile the generated Java program. SQLJ consists of a translator and a runtime component. The translator checks the syntax and semantics of the embedded SQL and produces a .java source file and one or more SQLJ profiles. SQLJ profiles contain details about your SQL operations and the types and modes of data being accessed. SQLJ then automatically invokes a Java compiler that produces a .class file from the .java file. There is also the customizer component that SQLJ automatically invokes to adapt the SQL profiles for the specific database to connect to. By default, the Oracle customizer is used to add support for Oracle-specific extended features. The SQLJ runtime environment consists of a SQLJ runtime library that is Java and which in turn calls a JDBC driver that connects to the appropriate database.

Figure 15.3 illustrates the SQLJ development process.

There are basically four steps to developing a SQLJ application:

1. Translate SQLJ code using the SQLJ translator, which generates Java source files with calls to the SQLJ runtime.
2. Compile the Java source files using a Java compiler.
3. Customize the Java .class files.
4. Run the application using the SQLJ runtime library.

Figure 15.3
The SQLJ
Development
Process

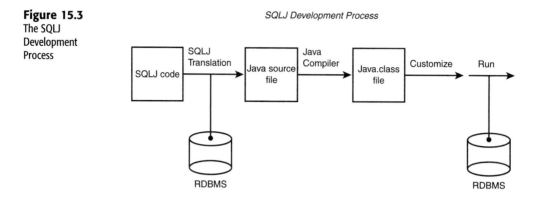

SQLJ Development Process

Here is an example of embedding a SQL `select` statement in a SQLJ program. The symbol `#sql` prefixes the SQL statement, which follows contained inside curly braces:

```
#sql { select deptno into :deptno from emp where empid = :emp };
```

The only requirements for running a SQLJ program are the SQLJ runtime library, a JDBC driver, and a Java Virtual Machine where the programs will execute. An advantage SQLJ has over JDBC is that it does syntax and semantics checking of SQL at translation time, rather than runtime. Though you do not have to choose between SQLJ or JDBC, these APIs are interoperable.

SAMPLE SQLJ CODE VERSUS JDBC CODE

Following are SQLJ and JDBC program fragments for the same SELECT statement. SQLJ code is shorter because it uses host variables to pass arguments to SQL statements, whereas JDBC uses separate statements to bind each argument and to retrieve each result:

```
###SQLJ

java.sql.DATE a; int b; string c;
...
#sql   { SELECT col1 INTO :a FROM EMP WHERE col2 = :b and col3 = :c };

###JDBC

java.sql.DATE a; int b; string c;
...
PreparedStatement x = connection.prepareStatement
  ("SELECT col1 FROM EMP WHERE col2 = ? and col3 = ?");
x.setint(1, b);
x.setstring(2, c);
ResultSet y = x.executeQuery();
y.next();
a = y.getDate(1);
y.close();
x.close();
```

ENTERPRISE JAVABEANS SUPPORT

Enterprise JavaBeans (EJB) are basically distributed Java components that implement a set of predefined Java interfaces designed for transaction processing functionality. They enable developers to design and package applications in components that can be assembled with components written by other developers. Component-based programming has become more popular due to the prospect of reusable application code, easy assembly of applications by wiring components from different vendors, and flexibility of deployment. More organizations are using component-based development for new applications because traditional applications do not lend themselves to code reuse. Benefits include better design and code reuse and that it is easier to maintain and easier to deploy across tiers in a multi-tiered environment. JavaBeans are already being widely used to assemble GUI-based applications, though mainly as client-side applications. Unlike client-side components, server-side components (such as EJBs) are typically transactional, and they encapsulate business logic and need to run in a server environment.

Oracle has chosen EJB as their architecture for component-based distributed computing. There are three models currently for server-side components: EJB, CORBA, and DCOM. The JavaBeans specification, created by JavaSoft extends Java to support cross-platform object technology. Distributed Component Object Model (DCOM) is Microsoft's component model for building components that interoperate on a desktop to work across a network. DCOM is an extension of the Component Object Model (COM), that has been part of the Windows operating systems for many years as the underlying framework that makes OLE and ActiveX possible. The Common Object Request Broker Architecture (CORBA) 3.0 is the latest specification, released in December 1999 by the Object Management Group. This model specifies a transport mechanism, Internet Inter-ORB Protocol (IIOP), that allows different operating systems running on different hardware to interoperate. It also specifies a neutral language, Interface Definition language (IDL) where developers specify the interfaces to objects. For more discussion on how CORBA is relevant to Oracle, see the section later in this chapter, "Java and CORBA."

An EJB executes inside a container. A container provides an operating system process or thread in which to execute the components. Some types of containers are a Web server, a transaction processing (TP) monitor or a database system.

DEVELOPING AND DEPLOYING ENTERPRISE JAVABEANS

Briefly, the following steps are involved in developing and deploying Enterprise JavaBeans:

A developer needs to define four items for client applications to be able to invoke methods of the bean that contain the business logic:

- Define the remote interface—The remote interface lists all the methods or public interfaces of the bean that clients can call.

  The following is an example of a remote interface for the STOCK bean:

```
public interface Stock extends javax.ejb.EJBObject
{
  float getPrice () throws java.rmi.RemoteException;
void buy (float amount) throws java.rmi.RemoteException;
}
```

- Define the home interface—The home interface serves as a mechanism for clients to be able to create an instance of the bean.

  The following is an example of home interface for the stock bean:

  ```
  public interface StockHome extends javax.ejb.EJBHOME
   {
   Stock create () throws java.rmi.RemoteException, javax.ejb.CreateException;
   }
  ```

- Define the bean—The bean itself is standard Java code that implements the business logic.

  The following is an example of the bean itself:

  ```
  public class StockBean implements javax.ejb.SessionBean
  {
  public float getPrice ()
   {  ADD ANY BUSINESS LOGIC HERE ...
   }
  public void buy (float amount)
    {  ADD ANY BUSINESS LOGIC HERE ...
    }
  ```

- Define the bean deployment descriptor—This ties together all the components of the bean. The syntax looks like a Java class and begins with a `SessionBean` statement.

  Here is an example of creating a deployment descriptor for the STOCK Bean:

  ```
      SessionBean StockBean {
          BeanHomeName = "bn=myStock";
      Attribute
          RemoteInterfaceClassName = Stock;
    Attribute
          HomeInterfaceClassName = StockHome;
       ...}
  ```

After these steps have been done, you need to compile and package your Java code.

You compile the EJB, its remote interface, and its home interface to Java classes with the following statement:

```
% javac  StockBean.java  Stock.java  StockHome.java ...
```

Then, you package the class files in an EJB package (a Java archive, or JAR file) with the following statement:

```
% jar  cf  Stock.jar  *.class
```

Next, you add the EJB deployment descriptor to the bean with the CREATEEJB tool provided by Oracle:

```
% createejb  Stock.jar -desc  Stock.dsc
```

Finally, you deploy the EJB onto the Oracle8i server using the DEPLOYEJB tool provided by Oracle.

The following example deploys the EJB in the user SCOTT schema and creates a jar file:

```
% deployejb -u scott -p passwd -s <servicename> -gen Stockclient.jar
Stock.jar
```

After successfully deploying the EJB, you can then activate it from a client application.

JAVA AND CORBA

The CORBA (Common Object Request Broker Architecture) is an object-oriented protocol that makes it possible for distributed programs written in different programming languages to communicate over a network, including the Internet. CORBA is a standards-based distributed component model proposed by the Object Management Group (OMG). It is a standard for building, deploying, and managing distributed object applications that are interoperable across platforms. CORBA 2.0 (and greater) objects communicate using OMG's Internet Inter-ORB Protocol (IIOP). IIOP is another OMG standard for communication between and among distributed objects running on the Internet, intranets, and enterprise computing environments. CORBA components written in different languages and running on different platforms can transparently communicate and interoperate. So, the client and server code can be written in any language, not just Java, and are compiled into native machine code. Oracle8i uses Java as its CORBA implementation language. Oracle8i integrates a Java-based, CORBA 2.0-compliant Object Request Broker (ORB) that provides users with the ability to call into and out of the database using IIOP. This ORB is based on code from the Inprises VisiBroker for Java. Oracle8i comes with a complete set of tools for developing CORBA applications. Using these tools, you can compile IDL specifications, or load Java source files or classes into the database.

ORACLE'S JAVA DEVELOPMENT TOOL: JDEVELOPER

JDeveloper 2.0 is a Windows-based Java programming tool with an integrated project navigator, a code editor, a debugger, and a compiler. SQLJ translator and debugger are also an embedded part of JDeveloper.

JDeveloper was designed for developers building multi-tiered Java applications. Developers can create, debug, and deploy Java stored procedures, Enterprise JavaBeans, SQLJ and CORBA objects, and HTML Web applications. The Project Navigator enables developers to manage multiple projects that can be destined for different tiers within one session. There are many code generation wizards to aid in the rapid development of applications. The Enterprise JavaBeans wizard can automatically create new EJBs. Servlets and Java Server Pages (JSP) can be easily generated with the aid of the Servlet wizard and the JSP wizard. The Data Form wizard guides in creating single-table or master-detail forms. A developer can use the PL/SQL-to-Java wizard to generate Java class definitions from selected stored procedures. Several JDBC drivers are provided with JDeveloper for accessing other databases, though it is most tightly integrated with Oracle.

INTERNET FILE SYSTEM (iFS)

Users can now store Web pages, documents, spreadsheets, word-processing files, images, and other traditional files directly within the database with the new Internet File System, or iFS. It appears as another file system and can be accessed just like any other network directory. The iFS organizes its contents into folders, and they appear to clients the way any folder or directory should. The difference is that files stored in iFS have all the reliability and security provided by the Oracle database. It eases the job of system administrators because they only have to maintain, administer, back up, and restore a single system rather than several separate ones.

Beside providing easier file storage in the database, the iFS provides for integration of relational and non-relational data. Users can access the iFS from multiple protocols, providing universal access to their data. Authorized users can search and view any of their files stored in iFS from any computer through a standard Web browser, Microsoft Windows Explorer, FTP client, or email client. Advanced searching capabilities are available through ConText technology. The iFS is written in Java, as are the specialized parsers and renderers it uses. The iFS uses XML, the next generation markup language for the Internet, to "parse" and "render" files. This enables the database to convert the contents of known file types to XML files using a file filter. Following this, the XML can be stored in a table in the database. Rendering converts the stored XML to the file format (HTML, XML, or the original file format) as requested by the client. Users can move files into or out of iFS easily by dragging and dropping through Windows Explorer. They can be edited directly within the iFS by double-clicking them and launching the appropriate application. When a user adds or updates a file, iFS uses ConText technology to build a keyword index based on the contents and external properties of the file (author, title, date, and so on). Afterwards, the iFS can perform the search quickly using the preconstructed index.

Key features of the iFS include the following:

- Advanced searches—Files are automatically indexed on content and file properties providing for relational queries and ConText-based queries.
- Check-in, checkout (CICO)—Documents are locked when checked out until they are checked back in.
- Access Control List (ACL) Security—Security and privileges are based on ACL model.
- Versioning—Multiple versions of documents are enabled.
- Change Notification—Email notification available upon insertion, update, or deletion of files.
- Automatic Expiration—Files can be purged after a certain time period.
- Quotas—Quotas can be set to control space usage.
- XML support—This is supplied through document parsing and rendering.
- Universal access—This is provided via SMB, HTTP, FTP, SMTP, IMAP4, and POP3 protocols.
- Java, CORBA, PL/SQL Programming APIs—APIs are available for writing applications based on the iFS.

ORACLE INTERMEDIA

Oracle interMedia contains five management modules to handle multimedia in the database. Oracle interMedia Text, built on Oracle's ConText technology, enables users to search text using advanced retrieval and natural language queries. Oracle interMedia Image manages two-dimensional, static, digital images and supports basic manipulation functions, such as scaling and cropping. Users can store and retrieve images in interMedia Image without being experts in image file formats as it supports most desktop publishing image file formats including the following: TIFF, JPG, BMP, TARGA, PCX, PICT, GIF, CALS Raster, SUN, Flashpix, and RPIX.

Oracle interMedia Video and interMedia Audio enable browser-based audio and video input from different sources, such as Oracle VideoServer, Oracle8i, and Web sites. The following industry standard audio and video formats are supported by interMedia: AIF, AIFF-C, AUFF, WAV, QuickTime, AVI, MPEG, and Real Networks. Applications can query and retrieve multimedia data in the same fashion as traditional relational data. Oracle interMedia Locator handles location queries, such as finding stores, distribution points, and events based on spatial data given, such as location or distance from an address. Because interMedia is fully integrated into Oracle8i, developers have access to advanced text searching capabilities through standard SQL calls rather than a proprietary interface.

Oracle interMedia Text uses text indexes, which can be created on almost any database column or object to perform searches. Text queries are executed against the index within the database and return a hitlist of matching documents. All text indexes are stored and managed by the database, though the documents searched by interMedia can be stored in the file system or anywhere on the Web at a URL address. InterMedia can handle mixed queries (full text and structured data in the database) using a single SQL command. For example, you can search for documents containing the word "Internet" and combine other information stored in the database such as author, date, or document type. The SQL CONTAINS function enables users to run text search queries from any tool or environment that supports SQL or PL/SQL. InterMedia provides full-text searching capabilities that include exact word or phrase searching, Boolean specifications, proximity, wildcards, thesaurus word equivalence, case-sensitivity, and section searching. It has the capability to identify the thematic content of documents using a Theme-base of around half a million words. Also "about" searching, searching for documents about a subject or theme, can be done using the optimal combination of full-text, language-based and theme-based techniques available.

The following example will search the column bdate. Then the results are combined with the CONTAINS function, which searches the text index for documents that contain the word "Internet" and are about the subject Browser:

```
SELECT author, isbn, bdate from books
 WHERE bdate > '01-MAR-1999' AND
 CONTAINS ( btext, 'Internet AND ABOUT (Browser)' ) > 0;
```

Oracle interMedia uses object data types, similar to JAVA or C++ classes, called ORDAudio, ORDImage, and ORDVideo to describe audio, image, and video data. An instance of these data types consists of attributes such as metadata, media data, and methods. *Metadata* is information about the data, and *media data* is the actual audio, image, or video. *Methods* are procedures that can be performed on the object, such as `store`, `deliver`, or `compress`. The media data can be stored in the database as a BLOB type, or it can be stored outside and easily imported into the database. The media data could be stored in other sources like BFILEs (operating system file of large objects), HTTP server-based URLs, specialized media servers such as Oracle VideoServer, or user-defined sources. The metadata and methods for these object data types are always stored and managed in the database. InterMedia enables media data to be located through standard queries on relational data (for example, student name) and object metadata (for example, student photo). When located, media data can be accessed using SQL like any other relational data through the `ORDAudio`, `ORDImage`, and `ORDVideo` data types.

Oracle interMedia Locator supports online geocoding facilities for locator applications and proximity queries. It is built using components from Oracle8i Spatial and supports geocoding, storage, and retrieval of geocoded data in Oracle8i databases. Geocoding uses points to represent addresses and locations of interest (for example, postal codes, latitude/longitude). In combination with third-party geocoding and mapping tools, interMedia can perform within distance queries on geocoded data. After the data is geocoded, interMedia can calculate distances and graphically represent sites in applications. For example, you can query the database to locate the gas station nearest to your work site, or you can find all hotels within a one-mile radius of Walt Disney World and return a plotted map of the locations.

ORACLE WEBDB

Oracle WebDB provides a complete Web development environment that includes an HTML server so it can process HTTP requests and serve Web pages. There is no need to install software on every user's machine, to remotely manage files using FTP, or to perform complex software upgrades. The only client software needed to develop and deploy applications is a Web browser, Netscape Navigator 3.1 or later or Microsoft Internet Explorer 4.0 or later. WebDB was designed to be easy to use, easy to access, and easy to administer. It is a collection of PL/SQL procedures contained entirely within an Oracle database (version 7.3.3 or later). It also includes a lightweight listener that acts as a Web server and a PL/SQL interface to the database. WebDB combines an HTML interface with a complete set of browser-based HTML tools for developing Web applications. Rapid development is facilitated by the use of simple wizards that guide users through the whole process of building components (that is, forms, reports, charts, menus, calendars, and hierarchies). The wizard, in effect, writes the PL/SQL code for you, or you can bypass the wizard and write your own code. When a developer creates a component, it is given a URL. Deployment with WebDB is as easy as adding that URL to HTML text. Figure 15.4 gives you an example of a chart wizard.

Figure 15.4
The WebDB Chart
Wizard Screen

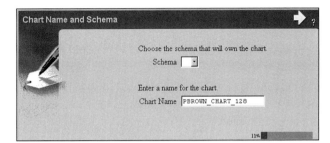

All the tools necessary to administer, manage, and configure the database are included in
WebDB. Administrators can manage privileges and listener settings or monitor end-user
and database activity from the browser. Any database object (tables, partitions, redo logs,
and so on) can be created, viewed, edited, or dropped through the Web browser. WebDB
has advanced performance-tracking facilities that help in resolving performance problems.
User components you can monitor include response times, requests by component name,
requests by day and hour, requests by browser type, requests by IP address. Figure 15.5
illustrates a chart that can be generated showing the number of component requests, by user.

Figure 15.5
A WebDB Chart
Showing Requests
by Database User

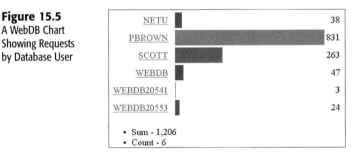

A Web site created using WebDB is divided into sections called *corners*. Corners contain
items related to a specific topic. The site administrator assigns owners to the corners who
are responsible for management of that area. Corner owners can grant different types of
access (such as add, edit, and delete) to the contents of their corner to other users. Content
authors can update their corner of the Web site using a point-and-click interface without
needing any other software. This decentralizes management of content while maintaining
centralized control of the Web site.

ORACLE8I AVAILABILITY AND RECOVERABILITY

Oracle8i advanced features and enhancements that strive to provide 24×365 availability include Parallel Server improvements, a new fast-start fault recovery, online backup, recovery, and reorganization, and Transparent Application Failover.

Oracle Parallel Server enables multiple Oracle instances running on nodes of a cluster to concurrently access a single database. This shared access helps remove any single point of failure so that during a system crash in one node, work can continue on any other node. In Oracle8i, Parallel Server can be scaled to support thousands of users with the use of Cache Fusion clustering architecture and cluster load balancing. *Cache Fusion* uses dedicated, high-speed interconnects to pass data directly between nodes for virtually unlimited scalability. This technology enables the buffer cache of one node in a cluster to ship data blocks directly to the buffer cache of another node, thereby reducing disk I/O. *Cluster load balancing* dynamically connects users to system modes that are least utilized, thereby reducing user access times and increasing the number of users that can be served.

The *automated and read-only standby database* enables Oracle to automatically maintain one or more copies of a production database for disaster recovery. The standby database is initially created by copying the production database, and the copy can reside in the same site or in a different one. After creation of the standby, updates and changes to the production database are propagated to the standby database so that the databases are synchronized. The standby database is then put in sustained recovery mode. As archived redo logs are generated on the production database, they are transferred to the standby via a Net8 connection. After being received by the standby database, they are automatically applied, thereby synchronizing the two databases. This eliminates the need for manually maintaining a standby database, though that is still an option. If a networking error or out of space problem prevents the log file from being successfully created, the database will, after a user specified interval, automatically retry the archiving operation. Previously, the standby database could not be opened or used without subsequently recreating another copy of the production database. In Oracle8i, DBAs can now open the standby database in read-only mode. This provides a way to query and generate reports against the standby while off-loading some processing against the production database. While in this mode, the standby can continue to automatically receive the archive redo logs from the production database, and the queued logs are then applied when the standby is returned to sustained or manual recovery mode.

Online Data Reorganization and Defragmentation is another new feature. Oracle8i now enables users full access to the database during data reorganization and index build and rebuilds . DBAs can perform maintenance while tables and indexes are completely online and without interrupting any changes being made to the base table.

Users can continue to access and update the base table while the index is being created. Any changes to the base table and index during the build are recorded in a journal table and applied to the new index at the end of the operation. Indexes can also be rebuilt online, providing for high database availability. As with index creation, the rebuild uses a journal table to record changes made to the base table during the rebuild operation. Online index defragmentation or coalescing is like online index rebuilding, except defragmentation doesn't require additional storage space. The index defragmentation process collapses into a single block adjacent to index blocks that have less than one block of data.

Oracle8i enables Index-Organized Tables(IOTs) to be moved and reorganized while available to users. Changes made to the table are recorded in a journal table and merged with the table at the end of the process. These online reorganizations can be done on a single IOT or on a single partition in a partitioned IOT.

Fast-start fault recovery is a new feature designed to make system fault recovery as quick as possible and limit the down time. It is very fast, and recovery time can be bounded by the administrator. After a system crash, the database normally does a roll-forward of committed changes and a rollback of uncommitted changes. Oracle8i has a new fast-start checkpointing architecture where the checkpoint process continuously writes modified blocks to disk. The DBA specifies a limit on how long roll-forward will take instead of how often checkpoints should occur. The rollback processing is intended to be eliminated by use of a technology called nonblocking roll back. Now, new transactions can start right after roll-forward finishes. Then, if a new transaction accesses a row locked by a dead transaction, only the changes that block its progress are roll-backed. Also, the database is capable of rollbacking dead transactions in parallel.

Extended Backup and Recovery with Recovery Manager performance improvements. Recovery Manager is a utility that manages the processes of creating and restoring backups of the database. It now has an integrated media management API that can direct the backup software to perform the copy operation on the database's behalf. It will also do cross checks on its catalog against the media management software catalog and marks deleted backups as expired. Recovery Manager can enable DBAs to preview a restore/recovery operation to see what will happen before the operation starts. Also, Recovery Manager can now multiplex backup sets to multiple I/O devices. Oracle8i with Transparent Application Failover can augment recovery from system crashes. Client programs can automatically reconnect when a database connection is broken. Also, any queries being processed at the time of the crash can automatically be restarted, and data returned to the program will resume from the point the failure occurred.

SECURITY

Oracle8i provides a secure platform on which to deploy and execute distributed Java applications. Procedures, CORBA servers, and Enterprise JavaBeans components can be accessed via the Internet standard Secure Sockets Layer (SSL) over Oracle's Net8 and CORBA's IIOP. Oracle8i offers a single sign-on that enables users to authenticate themselves once in an intranet/Internet environment, alleviating the problem of having too many passwords. This public key infrastructure (PKI), based single sign-on, uses X.509 (version 3) certificates for authentication over SSL. Oracle Wallet Manager is a tool provided by Oracle to protect and manage user certificates, keys, and trustpoints.

Oracle8 introduced enterprise roles, one or more global roles spanning one or more data servers, centrally administered and maintained. Oracle8i improves on this by storing and managing user information in a source called Internet directory, instead of a proprietary data store. The Internet directory is compliant with the Lightweight Directory Access Protocol (LDAP) version 3 standard. Single station administration is available through enhancements made to the Oracle Enterprise Security Manager tool. Now, from a single console, administrators can create a user in multiple Oracle8i databases or create enterprise roles that span multiple databases. Oracle8i introduces the single enterprise user, creating one account per user for the entire organization instead of creating multiple accounts per user. Now, you have fewer user accounts to manage, and security is easily enforced through use of the Internet directory.

Enforced, flexible, fine-grained access control, along with a secure application context, is offered in Oracle8i. It is enabled by associating one or more security policies with tables or views. A finer level of granularity in accessing data is now possible with fine-grained access control. Different policies for different types of access (that is, select, update, and delete) can be enabled. Now you can specify who has access to particular rows of a table, separating data access down to an individual level. Access can be based on a user (for example, a user's role, whether the user is a manager or employee) or on the application (for example, whether the user is accessing a human resources application or is a customer creating a new order).

In the following example, the table ACCOUNT has a policy that bank customers can see only their own account. A customer accesses the table by issuing the following:

```
SELECT * FROM ACCOUNT;
```

The SELECT statement causes the database to call the policy function and then transparently and dynamically rewrites the query by appending the WHERE clause:

```
SELECT * FROM ACCOUNT WHERE ID = (SELECT ID FROM CUSTTAB WHERE CNAME =
USERENV('user'));
```

Secure application contexts are offered in Oracle8i on which to base the fine-grain access control policies. Application contexts are user-defined, as are their attributes, and each application can have its own context with different attributes. For example, a human resources application can have a security policy based on employee number, department, and position attributes. Accordingly, the database will enforce this by enabling a user in a manager position to only update records for an employee in his department.

OTHER FEATURES

Oracle Enterprise Manager Release 2.0 is the latest version of the systems management tool provided with Oracle8i. Some of the features provided are the capability to manage from virtually anywhere, the capability to manage everything in the enterprise, and "set and forget" management, which minimizes the manual administering of systems. It is a Java-based application and can be accessed from any Web browser. Administrators can manage multiple machines from one centralized console. The repository is now a shared common repository and is available to multiple OEM administrators. Initially, there is one default superuser, SYSMAN, who can create other superusers and administrators and who assigns the appropriate responsibilities and privileges to the other administrators. Each new administrator is given a console password that gives access to the console systems required to perform management tasks. Because each administrator has specific responsibilities, they can define permission levels for other administrators for the groups, jobs, and events they create. Permission levels include none, view, modify, or full.

LogMiner is a database analysis tool that lets DBAs use SQL to read, analyze, and interpret the redo log files. Logminer requires access to the data dictionary of the database being analyzed and works with redo log files from Oracle release 8.0 forward. The log files being analyzed are mapped to a dynamic performance view (V$logmnr_contents). Each row in this table represents information on a logical operation performed in the database. For each of these operations, REDO and UNDO SQL statements are given that describe the changes made in the database. The SQL REDO statement shows the original operation done on the database, and the SQL UNDO statement shows statements that can rollback the changes.

This example shows the query to find what changes Benlin made to the SAVINGS table.

```
select sql_redo, sql_undo from v$logmnr_contents where  username = 'Benlin' and
seg_name = 'SAVINGS';
```

The query returns the following, which shows Benlin first deleted his savings record and then re-created this record with a higher amount. The statements to rollback the changes made by Benlin are shown in the SQL_UNDO column.

SQL_REDO	SQL_UNDO
delete * from savings where id = 999 and rowid = 'QSDFJKKJKAA';	insert into savings (name, id, amt) values ('benlin', 999, 10);
insert into savings (name, id, amt) values ('benlin', 999, 500);	delete * from savings where id = 999 and rowid = 'QSDFJKKJKAA';

The *Database Resource Manager* is a new tool in Oracle8i that allocates and manages CPU resources among database users and applications. Previously, all users and applications had equal access to the database. Now you can allocate more resources to the more important tasks. Using this tool, users and groups of users are assigned to resource consumer groups. The administrator establishes a resource plan that specifies how resources are allocated among the different resource consumer groups. Subplans, providing for further subdivision of resources, can be defined within a resource consumer group. A maximum of eight levels can be defined for allocating resources. Changes made in the Database Resource Manager can be dynamically altered on a database without having to shutdown and restart the system. Administrators can have many different resource plans and resource consumer groups, all of which are stored in the data dictionary.

Also, the *automatic degree of parallelism* (ADOP) feature has been integrated into the Database Resource Manager to optimize system utilization. This feature limits the degree of parallelism for parallel query operations.

Partitioning enables users to split tables and indexes into more manageable units. The Oracle8.0 release introduced *range* partitioning for tables where data is split based on a range of values called a partition key. In Oracle8i, now there is hash partitioning and composite partitioning. *Hash* partitioning enables you to evenly stripe data across devices whereby rows are split by a hash of the partition key. *Composite* partitioning is a combination of range and hash. First, data is partitioned by a range of values. Then, each partition is sub-partitioned into several hash partitions. Oracle8i also includes support for object-relational and LOB column types. Partitions can be backed up and recovered independently from other partitions of the same table or index without hindering access to unaffected partitions.

Materialized views, a new database object type, is an optimization feature for creating, maintaining, and using *summary tables*. A summary table, also called an aggregate table, is where summary and join operations are precomputed and the results are stored in the database. By accessing the summary table instead of computing the aggregate from data every time, performance is much improved. Administrators can specify how and when these tables should be refreshed (that is, synchronously, when new data is loaded, weekly, and so on). Also, a summary advisor wizard is available to help administrators in the creation and maintenance of summary tables.

Transportable tablespaces enable you to move tablespaces between databases without doing a full export/import. DBAs can copy the datafiles of tablespaces between identical systems (hardware architecture), thereby transferring data quickly and easily. The tablespace to transport must be self-contained, meaning there are no references pointing from inside the tablespace to outside of the tablespace. There is a PL/SQL procedure called `transport_set_check` provided to check whether a set of tablespaces is self-contained.

First, the tablespace to be moved is put into read-only mode to ensure that the data captured is a consistent image. Then an export is run of the metadata for the tablespace; this is fast because the amount of data is very small. Next, the datafiles for the tablespace are copied to the new system using any operating system facilities. At the new system, an import is done of the metadata for the tablespace, and again this is fast, due to the amount of data. This is also another way to perform point-in-time recovery on a tablespace. By moving a good copy of the tablespace into the production database, recovery can be quickly achieved.

Locally-managed (bitmapped) tablespaces are a new tablespace type that improve space management in the database and minimize extent fragmentation. An *extent* is a logical unit of storage made up of one or more contiguous data blocks. Before Oracle8i, management of free and used extents was done through the data dictionary tables. Now, you have the option of using bitmaps in the tablespace to indicate used and free blocks, thereby minimizing access to the data dictionary. These tablespaces are created using the `CREATE TABLESPACE` command with the `EXTENT MANAGEMENT LOCAL` clause.

This type of tablespace will automatically size all new extents at standard sizes using either an `autoallocate` or `uniform` option. Under the `autoallocate` option, the system will automatically create variable extent sizes. You can specify the size of the initial extent then the system will determine the size of additional extents. Under the `uniform` option, all extents created are the same size. If you do not specify the EXTENT MANAGEMENT clause, the default is EXTENT MANAGEMENT DICTIONARY, indicating that the tablespace will be managed by the system through the data dictionary.

> **Note**
>
> If you use the LOCAL clause, you cannot use DEFAULT storage_clause, MINIMUM EXTENT, or TEMPORARY parameters in the CREATE TABLESPACE command.

Following is an example of creating a locally managed tablespace TS where every extent allocated is 64K and each bit in the bitmap indicates 32 blocks (assuming a block size of 2K):

```
SQL> create tablespace TS
  2 datafile '/u01/oracle/mysid/ts.dbf' size 10M
  3 extent management local uniform size 64K;
```

Temporary tables can now be created in a user's temporary tablespace. They last only for the duration of a transaction or session and are available only to the session that inserts data into them. Temporary tables cannot be partitioned, index-organized, clustered, or containing columns of nested table or varray type. These tables cannot have any foreign key constraints defined.

The following statement creates a temporary table, stocks:

```
SQL> CREATE GLOBAL TEMPORARY TABLE stocks
    (stockname varchar2
      stockprice float);
```

The Drop column command gives the capability to drop a column from a table without having to re-create the table and its associated indexes and constraints.

This SQL statement will remove the column descriptor for col_1 and the data associated with col_1 from each row in the table census. All indexes or constraints defined on this column are also dropped:

```
SQL> ALTER TABLE census DROP col_1;
```

SUMMARY

Oracle8i, with its new features and enhancements, is an ideal platform for Internet computing. Oracle8i will enable over tens of thousands of Internet users to connect to a single instance of the Oracle8i database by leveraging server-side SQLJ and the integrated Java Virtual Machine in the database. Because the JVM is integrated in Oracle8i, it inherits the reliability, portability, scalability, throughput, and performance of the database. Developers can substitute Java procedures for PL/SQL procedures, or they can coexist. Tools provided, such as WebDB, improve ease of use and Web application deployment. The iFS option makes multiprotocol access to the same information across platforms easy for all users of the system. And the interMedia product enables open, standard SQL access to text and multimedia content in applications.

PART IV

PERFORMANCE TUNING

## CHAPTER 16

PERFORMANCE TUNING FUNDAMENTALS

In this chapter

REVISITING PHYSICAL DESIGN

Chapter 3, "Physical Database Design, Hardware, and Related Issues," stated that physical (and logical) designs are the first steps in tuning a database. This is indeed true. One of the first steps in many tuning books is to tune the design. By following proper logical and physical design, you have done just that. If all has gone well, your design should enable your database to perform at more than an acceptable level to begin with. However, there are two things that always creep up with database systems: *growth* and *changing application requirements*.

If your database is relatively static, is made up of mostly lookup tables, or for any other reason experiences very little or very slow growth, this factor is not a problem. If, on the other hand, your database is like most others, it will grow over time by some substantial percentage, such as 10 percent or more. Then, despite initially good logical and physical designs, you might periodically need to tune the database to accommodate or otherwise compensate for this growth. In addition, all database systems have fallen prey to the phenomenon of applications, which are in perpetual redefinition. Here is an example you might have come across:

Manager: "The application doesn't work. It's running too slowly. What's wrong with the database?"

Programmer: "The code hasn't changed."

DBA: "The database hasn't changed."

What could be the problem, then? In this instance, the *usage* has probably changed. This is really only another fancy way of saying that the application requirements have changed. For example, suppose the application originally was intended to enable read-only access to seven tables individually. However, if the application is now being used to join four more tables with some or all these seven tables to gather more information than originally requested, some tuning might be necessary. In fact, some physical redesign, also known as physical restructuring, might be required.

You can restructure a database physically to improve performance and still permit the application to function as desired. This is possible with Oracle, as with other vendors, because Oracle obeys Codd's Rule 8: physical data independence. So the answer might have been found by consulting with the user:

User: "The application doesn't work? Oh yeah. We're using some different tables now."

There is one other thing, aside from growth and changing application requirements, that requires a DBA's performance tuning skills. *the poorly designed database.*

With growth and changing application requirements, you had assumed the database was well-designed. Unfortunately, as many DBAs can attest, this is often not the case. Many times, a DBA takes over a database system that another DBA has left, is called in to fix the performance of someone else's database system, or is confronted with a database system that is the result of a legacy migration. In cases such as these, what is needed before performance tuning proper is a logical and physical analysis and redesign. It might be that the database doesn't need much redesign, or it might be that it needs a complete overhaul.

In either case, when that design has been ironed out, the DBA can move on to performance tuning proper. However, after the redesign, it might be best to simply put the application to use and do some performance monitoring first. After all, with proper design (or redesign) comes initially good performance. It might very well be that no new additional tuning is required for some time to come. (In practice, I have personally found this to be the case.)

UNDERSTANDING WHY YOU TUNE

Why tune? You have just answered this question. The current database system is not performing acceptably, based on user-defined criteria, for one of the following reasons:

- Poor design
- Growth
- Changing application requirements (possibly including a redefinition of what acceptable performance is)

When might database tuning efforts not be fully effective? When components that are external to the database, yet vital to the entire client/server application performance, fail to perform acceptably, database tuning might not help without the corresponding tuning of these other application infrastructure pieces. Except for the most isolated, stand-alone, batch production database applications, most modern database systems are client/server-based.

The main components *external* to the backend database are the backend operating system (or OS), the network, and the client OS. The major examples are the following:

- Very weak clients (PCs)
- Network saturation
- Very weak, saturated, or poorly tuned OSs

Clients (PCs) might be weak in the sense that they have older CPUs (486 or less), relatively little memory (16MB or less), or little storage (1GB or less). This especially holds true if the application is *"heavyweighted* toward the client" and thus requires a fat client. A *fat client* is one in which a large portion of the application processing is segmented onto the client. A *thin client* is obviously the opposite of this, with most of the processing taking place at the server end. Unless an application requires only dumb terminal access or thin clients, weak clients will not suffice. Thin clients, however, will suffice for the Internet computing paradigm, in which Web browsers are the only requirement on the client side.

A network is considered to be *saturated* by varying definitions. To be saturated means that a system component has reached maximum possible throughput. A 10Mbps ethernet is considered saturated when it reaches 30% of its bandwidth. Networking specialists handle this in different ways, including resegmenting the network locally, adding more network segments, or changing to a broader-band network media type, such as a 100Mbps Fiber Distributed Data Interface (FDDI). In any case, you have gone well off the beaten path of database tuning.

An OS can be very weak, just like a client. It is only weak relative to the applications it must support. But in general, modern database servers that have 32-bit processors, 4 processors, 256MB memory, and 10GB of disk space can be considered weak. An OS can be saturated in various ways, just as a network can. Under heavy load (many concurrent users or huge amounts of data being moved), an OS's CPU, I/O, and memory can be saturated.

Another way of putting this is that when a component is saturated, the system is bottlenecked on that component. Hence, if the CPU of a UNIX machine is saturated, such as with a utilization of 85% or more, the UNIX system is said to be bottlenecked on the CPU, or simply CPU-bound.

Lastly, an OS might just need some retuning. If, for example, a DSS requires only very large files to be stored on disks, a system administrator (SA) can tune the UNIX file system so that it optimally stores very large files in contiguous chunks.

Tuning a database system is heavily intertwined with tuning the OS, as you'll see in Chapter 17, "Application Tuning," Chapter 18, "Tuning Memory," Chapter 19, "Tuning I/O," and Chapter 20, "Oracle8.x Tuning Considerations." It is a good thing to be both an SA and a DBA because you don't have to ask permission to do this or that. You just do it. However, in practice, DBAs often have to fight battles with SAs and management over resource allocation and tuning issues. My recommendation is to gather quantifiable proof through Oracle diagnostic tools, discussed later in this chapter (see the section "Using Oracle Diagnostic Tools") and in Chapters 17 to 20, and use those figures to justify your resource needs.

KNOWING THE TUNING PRINCIPLES

Now is a good time to enumerate the major performance tuning principles you find in almost any performance tuning reference.

What are the major performance tuning principles? They are as follows:

1. Divide and conquer.
2. Preallocate, prefetch, and precompile.
3. Triage. (Be proactive.)
4. Bulk, block, and batch.
5. Segment the application *appropriately*.

If these look familiar, they should. They are the physical design principles discussed in Chapter 3, with a slight twist on Numbers 2 and 3. Now look at a few scenarios regarding how these principles apply to performance tuning per se, and not just physical database design.

TUNING PRINCIPLE 1

Divide and conquer is the principle. In essence, you want to use parallel techniques as a remedy for a bottleneck.

Follow along with this scenario: If performance monitoring shows that the database system has a heavy concentration of physical reads and writes to one particular disk, that disk is a bottleneck. The physical and logical structures of Oracle, for example, need to be separated to enable parallel access. As often is the case, what is happening here is that an application has several users or processes trying to access the same tables or tablespaces on that disk. Frequently, tables that must be joined together exist on the same disk. This makes for poor performance.

The OS must access the disk on Oracle's behalf for some blocks of the table's data, perform this cycle again for the second table, and repeat the whole process for all the blocks of both tables until Oracle has joined the two. What happens at the hardware level is that the read/write head of the disk must read the requested sectors (physical data blocks) of the first table, reposition itself to read the requested sectors of the second table until a match is found, and then repeat. Access time (in milliseconds) of a disk consists of seek time and latency (rotational delay). Seek time is the repositioning that was mentioned, when the read/write head must move inward and outward along the radius of the disk to find the track containing the requested sectors. Seek time dominates the *latency*, or the time it takes for the disk to spin around to access the sectors.

The important thing is that joining two or more tables on the same disk requires a high proportion of seeks to reads. As a DBA, your goal is to reduce the number of seeks. You want to minimize contention and get rid of this bottleneck. To do this, you separate the tables that are being joined onto different disks. This same methodology holds true for tables that coexist on the same disk and can be simultaneously accessed even though they aren't being joined together. The result is the same: bottleneck. The solution is the same: separate them.

By the way, RAID is susceptible to this scenario just as easily as a standard disk. At first, it might not seem possible that RAID, especially levels 1, 3, and 5 (which were discussed in Chapter 3), could suffer this same type of problem. Quite clearly, striping a single table across several disks (a RAID volume) undoubtedly increases performance. However, if this table is stored on the same RAID volume with tables that must be joined with it or at least are accessed concurrently, you have the same problem: bottleneck. Again, the solution is the same: separate them.

The reason you still have the bottleneck is not so clear at first glance, but think about it. Chunks of all the tables (stored in the data files of their respective tablespaces) are striped across all the disks of that RAID volume. Although no single table exists in its entirety on any one disk, chunks of all tables coexist on all the disks. Hence, you have the same problem on a smaller scale. Rather than separating joined or otherwise simultaneously accessed tables onto different disks as with standard disk setups, you separate the tables onto different RAID volumes.

TUNING PRINCIPLE 2

Preallocate, prefetch, and precompile is the principle. Do work ahead of time whenever possible.

Follow along with this scenario: Suppose you have a database system that is particularly volatile. It grows and shrinks considerably and frequently. In fact, as an application type, it can be called an VCDB. When accessing the database during the nongrowth period, performance is reasonable. However, during its growth phase, performance is very poor, especially early on.

What is likely happening here is that dynamic growth is slowing down the online system. In Oracle terms, this is known as *dynamic extension*. Rows are being updated or inserted such that Oracle must extend, or allocate the next extent for a table as designated by the storage clause when either created or altered, or take the tablespace default. In either case, the table had enough space from creation time up until this most recent growth period and then had to extend to accommodate it. Of course, simply having a table extend in Oracle is not the end of the world. Far from it. It is, in fact, a normal course of events.

However, when a table is frequently extending, especially for large amounts of data, and causing online access to suffer, it's a major problem. Concurrent users shouldn't have to suffer. For database systems of this type, which require frequent or very large data extents, preallocation is best. You want to create your table with sufficient storage to begin with, that is, to handle the maximum expected peak size. In the storage clause of your table (or tablespace) create statement, set your INITIAL and NEXT extent sizes, and then set MINEXTENTS so that INITIAL + ((MINEXTENTS - 1) x NEXT) equals the maximum expected peak size of the table.

TUNING PRINCIPLE 3

Triage is the principle. Attack the most important problems first to get the greatest return on investment.

Follow along with this scenario: You have a slow batch system. When you do production runs, the system crawls. Upon reviewing the SQL code that makes up the application, you seem to have several very inefficient programs that could be rewritten. To do so might take about two months. You then analyze performance monitoring statistics and find that rollback shows high contention, apparently because you are running several concurrent programs simultaneously to help speed up the runs. You fix the rollback by adding more segments, but you gain little increase in your elapsed times. What to do?

No matter how well you tune the back end, the front end (or application code) dominates the total time usage of a client/server system, not accounting for networking and other issues. You must tune the application first and then tune the database. The investment of two months is well worth it when the production runs finish faster than ever.

If this can't be done for some reason, other database efforts such as logical or physical restructuring can be done as a temporary measure. But this truly shouldn't be done at all; you'd be changing your good database design because of a poor application design. You wouldn't gain much with that approach.

TUNING PRINCIPLE 4

Bulk, block, and batch is the principle. When appropriate, group things together that are processed together and don't compete with one another for resources.

Follow along with this scenario: Your DSS provides real-time, read-only information to external analysts via the Internet. You have a Web page as a front end to your database system. Concurrency is sometimes medium-high (up to 100 users), but does not seem to cause problems. What you have had complaints about is the throughput from selecting from large tables.

You have a classic case here. When selecting most or all the rows from a table, the optimizer must choose a full table scan over any indexes as its access path. This in itself cannot be avoided if that is what the user desires, and this type of access is part of the application requirements. What can you do to speed things up? Well, you can initially set your DB_BLOCK_SIZE to 8KB on your UNIX system. You can then increase this to 16KB or 32KB. The larger the block, the more cost effective your reads are. In other words, you get more rows of data per block with each read. Hence, you can make the reads more efficient by increasing block size for large data retrievals.

You can also consider increasing DB_FILE_MULTIBLOCK_READ_COUNT and DB_BLOCK_BUFFERS as necessary. Reading more blocks simultaneously and increasing block buffering should also help in DSS cases, but you'll learn more about these later in Chapters 18 and 19.

TUNING PRINCIPLE 5

Segmenting the application appropriately is the principle. Assign the various pieces of the application to the appropriate places (the client, the middle tier, or the server).

Follow along with this scenario: You have a client/server database system that does order entry and control. However, the order entry screens themselves tend to run slowly on the PCs. Response time is poor, and the application seems to burden the client because a single entry might take seconds (which is slow, in terms of response time).

This could be anything. You first need to examine how the application is partitioned. It turns out that most of the data validation is done in the front end code, and this might be the culprit because it accounts for a large majority of the lines of code. Most of the front end code algorithms go like this:

1. Clerk logs in to the database.
2. Clerk reads data from some tables.
3. Clerk enters data into the screen.
4. Clerk waits while the frontend validates entered data in some tables with other tables.
5. Clerk logs out if done or repeats Steps 2 through 4 if not.

The problem with this is that the clerk's transaction is active the entire time, and it interactively validates data among tables from the front end. This validation process (step 4) should take place on the server, noninteractively. It belongs there because it deals directly with the data. Processes should normally be located as close as possible to the data on which they operate, unless there is some compelling reason to do otherwise (such as that the server is underpowered). A standard way to segment the preceding application is to divide it into three major steps: read (the input data) with a transaction, change locally (interactively) without a transaction, and write back the changes (the output data) with a transaction. This *application segmenting* is also known as *transaction chopping*. If done correctly, it should result in a substantial reduction in response time.

TUNING GOALS

There are different ways of determining the goals of a performance tuning effort. A DBA should consider them all. Consider your application type, which was discussed in Chapter 3 and will be discussed again later in this chapter (see the section "Revisiting Application Types"). Database systems can be sampled on various quantitative measures, which were also discussed in Chapter 3, and will be discussed in the section "Understanding Benchmarks" later in this chapter. The most important of these are the following:

■ Throughput—Work per unit time, as measured by transactions per second (tps); higher is better.

■ Response time—The time it takes for an application to respond, as measured in milliseconds or seconds; lower is better.

■ Wall time—The elapsed time a program takes to run; lower is better.

In any system, throughput and response time usually run counter to one another as tuning goals. If response time is high (bad), throughput might be high (good). If throughput is low (bad), response time might be low (good).

Common sense helps when sorting out these two conflicting measures. The more users that are concurrently using a system within a certain amount of time, the more likely it is that each user will experience longer delays than normal, but the number of transactions going through the system will be greater. On the other hand, if you decrease the number of concurrent users accessing the system within a certain time window, each user will enjoy faster response time at the expense of fewer overall transactions completing in that duration.

Typically, OLTP systems want low response time or high throughput, in terms of transactions per second, depending on the application needs. A DSS wants low response time. However, a DSS might also want high throughput in terms of blocks read or written per unit time. This type of throughput is not necessarily counterproductive to high concurrency and low response times. A batch (production) system typically wants lower wall times. For example, everyone likes for the payroll application to complete on time!

Always consider the two central tuning goals:

- *Maximize your return on investment*. Invest your time and effort wisely by working on the problems most likely to yield the most improvement.
- *Minimize contention*. Bottlenecks are characterized by delays and waits; eliminate or reduce these whenever possible.

Finally, consider the following general-purpose database tuning goals:

- Minimize the number of blocks that need to be accessed; review and rewrite code as necessary.
- Use caching, buffering, and queuing whenever possible to compensate for the electromechanical disadvantage (memory is faster than disk); prefetch.
- Minimize the data transfer rates (the time it takes to read or write data); fast disks, RAID, and parallel operations help do this.
- Schedule programs to run as noncompetitively as possible; they might run concurrently and yet still be noncompetitive for the most part.

PART

IV

CH

16

USING THE RETURN ON INVESTMENT STRATEGY

The return on investment (ROI) strategy is a top-down, cost-effective way of viewing the performance tuning process. It helps you find the best way to approach the tuning of your particular application. You have seen ROI turn up before as one of the major performance tuning principles (triage) and as one of the two major performance tuning goals. Now you take it to heart and use it as a high-level, step-by-step methodology for performance tuning.

You want to do performance tuning in the order that gives you the greatest gain for your time and effort. In the ROI strategy that follows, notice that steps 1 through 3 amount to logical and physical design, which were covered in Chapter 1, "Database, DBMS Principles, and the Relational Model," and Chapter 2, "Logical Database Design and Normalization." Logical design is DBMS vendor independent. Hence, there are no Oracle specifics when dealing with logical design (not counting logical design tools). You'll revisit application types in the next section and apply some Oracle-specific recommendations for physical design and performance tuning recommendations for these applications. In the later chapters, you'll revisit these performance tuning recommendations for Oracle more closely, looking at tuning the application, tuning memory, and tuning I/O.

Steps 4 and 5 amount to tuning the application, which you'll cover in Chapter 17. Steps 6 and 7 amount to tuning memory and are included in Chapter 18. Steps 8 and 9 amount to tuning I/O and appear in Chapter 19. Steps 10 and 11 deal with components even more external to the database than the OS: the network and the client. Step 12 offers some advanced and less common solutions that should be tried only after standard methods have been applied and the desired performance gains have not been realized (steps 1 through 11). Chapters 17, 18, and 19 contain Oracle specifics to help you do proper performance tuning.

For now, review the steps in a little more detail, in descending order of return on investment.

STEP 1: DO A PROPER LOGICAL DESIGN

As covered in Chapter 2, you can reduce storage. In practice, this often means more tables with fewer rows per table. In turn, this means the capability for faster searching. The fewer rows that are stored and must be searched through, regardless of the searching technique, the quicker you'll be able to find what you're looking for.

STEP 2: DO A PROPER PHYSICAL DESIGN

In Chapter 3, you saw a general-purpose hardware layout. In the later section, "Step 12: If All Else Fails, Consider More Exotic Solutions," you'll see some more application-specific twists to this general hardware layout.

STEP 3: REDESIGN IF NECESSARY

If, at any stage of a database's life cycle, the design comes into question, consider redesigning it if resources and management permit. Sometimes the best way to correct a database without extensive tuning efforts is a re-analysis and redesign. For example, consider redesign when there is no initial design, when there is a hurried design, or when multiple databases might need to be integrated.

STEP 4: WRITE EFFICIENT APPLICATION CODE

A program only runs as fast as the algorithms of which it's composed. If some SQL code uses an inefficient search or sort routine, despite the best efforts of the Oracle's optimizer, the application runs slowly through no fault of the database itself. If you come into a job, and the code is already written but has been written poorly, consider the next step rather than trying to fix pieces at a time.

STEP 5: REWRITE CODE IF NECESSARY

If application code efficiency comes into question and if resources and management permit, re-analyze and rewrite code more efficiently. Be aware of the Oracle optimizer and Oracle SQL *rewriting rules* for more efficient code. A database application is no different from any ordinary piece of software. It can be written well or written poorly. After design issues, the application is the single largest tuning opportunity for return on investment. Without a doubt, time and effort should be spent here.

STEP 6: TUNE DATABASE MEMORY STRUCTURES

In Chapter 6, "The Oracle Instance Architecture," you saw that the SGA houses all the tunable, shared memory structures. When deemed necessary, Oracle can offer substantial improvements through the tuning of its database buffer cache. This cache buffers all database blocks that are accessed by Oracle, on the way to it (read) or from it (write). Also, the shared pool caches SQL code via the library cache component and caches the data dictionary through the aptly named data dictionary cache. Further rollback is cached via the aforementioned database buffer cache, although it's not separately tunable. But the redo log buffer is a separately defined, tunable area in the SGA. Sufficiently sizing all these memory structures reduces contention and combats the electromechanical disadvantage.

STEP 7: TUNE OS MEMORY STRUCTURES IF NECESSARY

In Windows NT, there isn't as much to tune by way of memory usage as what must be tuned in larger, multiuser OSs such as VMS and UNIX. In UNIX, for example, the named Oracle user (usually "oracle") must typically have unlimited shell process limits. This must be done manually or within a login script. The UNIX swap area functions as an area for OS temporary storage, user temporary storage, and the OS virtual memory backing store. Hence, in UNIX, the swap area can be a bottleneck, especially on a database server.

In Oracle on UNIX, the SA and DBA must work together so that UNIX provides enough shared memory and semaphores to give the Oracle processes enough *breathing room* to operate efficiently. See Appendix A, "Oracle on Solaris," and Appendix B, "Oracle on Windows NT," for further discussion of these vital topics.

STEP 8: TUNE DATABASE I/O

Database I/O is, of course, affected by both RDBMS and OS memory structures. But what Step 8 means is tuning the I/O by relocating database logical and physical structures to reduce contention. Of course, a DBA does both, especially if she follows these steps in proper order.

For example, if you reach this point in tuning, you will have already tuned the database buffer cache. Now you simply continue by essentially refocusing on the physical design. That is, you physically do more redesigning, if necessary, with database I/O exclusively in mind. Your physical redesign will be far more specific than that done previously. You want to improve I/O time estimates in the direction desired, such as reducing the wall time of applications with heavy inserts.

STEP 9: TUNE OS I/O IF NECESSARY

The OS fulfills all read and write requests by all processes, including Oracle background processes such as DBWR and LGWR. An OS typically buffers these requests, performs the reads or writes, and then returns the acknowledgment and data back to the process upon completion. File systems are data structures that contain metadata about the files they manage, such as the location of each file's starting sector address, its sector length, its directory tree location, its attributes (such as permissions, size, timestamps, and so on), and other information.

In UNIX, file systems also have their own logical block sizes, which correspond to something greater than or equal to a physical block size (512 bytes), usually 8KB by default. The Oracle block size should be at least 8KB or a multiple of it, such as 16KB.

Other important OS and Oracle I/O tuning issues include read-ahead capabilities, asynchronous I/O, multiblock reads, RAID stripe sizes, disk geometry issues, controller issues, and many more. If the DBA is not also the SA, which is most often the case, he must work cooperatively with the SA to appropriately integrate Oracle and OS I/O parameters.

STEP 10: TUNE THE NETWORK IF NECESSARY

As discussed in the "Understanding Why You Tune" section, a saturated network can cancel out improvements made by database tuning. A DBA must ensure, through proactive means such as the use of network monitoring software if necessary, that her client/server system's overall application performance is not suffering unduly because of network load or other network ailments. Network administrators, like SAs, must work closely with DBAs to resolve these issues.

STEP 11: TUNE THE CLIENTS IF NECESSARY

Local Area Network (LAN) administrators and general-purpose network administrators (including their WAN responsibilities) typically are responsible for the hardware and software of networked clients, or PCs. These administrators, along with the DBAs, must correctly size and configure the clients, upgrading if necessary, to enable client/server database applications to function within acceptable performance criteria. For example, when Oracle has been tuned and can service a query (when received across a network from a client) in subsecond time, it makes no difference if the network delay is on the order of several seconds from client to server, and vice versa.

STEP 12: IF ALL ELSE FAILS, CONSIDER MORE EXOTIC SOLUTIONS

"Exotic solutions" include Oracle's MultiThreaded Server (MTS), transaction processing (TP) monitors, Oracle's Parallel Query and other parallel capabilities, Oracle's clustering capability, Oracle's bitmapped indexing, MPP machines, solid state disks, memory-resident (RAM) disks, hardware accelerators, and queuing systems.

This section briefly covers some of these solutions now because they won't be covered in later chapters.

ORACLE'S MULTITHREADED SERVER (MTS)

As discussed in Chapter 3, Oracle's MTS is a pseudo-multithreaded solution to help counter a high number of concurrent users or programs accessing a single database. MTS is essentially a low-cost form of TP monitor that's goal is to enable a high number of concurrent users and to service them all, thereby maximizing throughput (not response time). However, MTS moves as much Process Global Area (PGA) memory into the SGA as possible, thereby sharing more memory and reducing the overhead (its *state* information) in maintaining each individual process.

TRANSACTION PROCESSING (TP) MONITORS

In contrast, a TP monitor goes one step further by *not* maintaining the full process state information and persistent connections as is done by an ordinary OS or RDBMS, including MTS. Overhead per process is further reduced. Typical concurrency thresholds for OSs and RDBMSs are around 200 or so users. This means that after most operating and database systems reach this number, their performance drops precipitously. This is known as *thrashing* and is symptomatic of too high a degree of multiprogramming or too many users.

TP monitors can help by permitting 1,000 or so concurrent users where only a few hundred were possible before. This is why TP monitors typically *sit in front of* an RDBMS. They are said to *live* in the middle tier between the backend (the RDBMS) and the frontend (the client, or PC). Two major commercial offerings at the time of this writing are Novell/BEA's Tuxedo and IBM/TransArc's Encina.

ORACLE'S PARALLEL QUERY OPTION (PQO)

As mentioned briefly in Chapter 3, Oracle's Parallel Query (PQ) can speed up queries by the divide-and-conquer principle. However, Oracle also permits parallel index creation, parallel SQL*Loader loads, and parallel import/exports. All these capabilities cut actual wall time by several factors, which is always a boon to DBA work. PQ can benefit any user, although the latter parallel operations tend to mostly help the DBA because she is the one who does (or should do) these tasks the most.

ORACLE'S CLUSTERING

With Oracle, you can use an index cluster or a hash cluster to bring two or more tables together that are frequently joined or otherwise accessed together. Clustering essentially incorporates child tables into their parent table *at the physical level*. In other words, the primary key of a parent table not only stores its single, unique row data (as it usually would) for a particular primary key value, but it also stores the repeating groups made up of the rows of its child tables that reference the value through their foreign keys. Hence, the data remains normalized at the logical level but can be thought of as being denormalized at the physical, or storage, level. This is entirely acceptable and doesn't bypass or break any Relational Model principles or normalization theory. Clusters can be indexed (B*-trees) or hashed. Chapter 19 will discuss this further.

ORACLE'S BITMAPPED INDEXES

Oracle also offers bitmapped indexes, which are normally associated with OLAP systems but are often used with other systems, DSS in particular. Bitmapped indexes are good alternatives to the conventional indexes (B*-trees) for those that are to be based on columns with a small subset of distinct values. They take up less space than regular indexes and are efficient with complex where clauses. Therefore, they are popular choices for DSS and OLAP systems, with their large amounts of data and high analytical demands. If a system is moderately or highly updated, however, bitmaps are not a good choice.

The way these indexes work is that all the distinct values down a column are inverted across an index column with a bit (a 0 or 1) for each row to represent whether that column equals a given distinct value. Table 16.1 shows a simple table, STUDENT, with two columns, STU-DENT_ID and SEX, and three rows. This table shows you how a bitmapped index works. You'll learn about the implementation and usage of bitmaps in Chapter 17.

TABLE 16.1 BITMAPPED INDEX ON THE *STUDENT* TABLE

STUDENT_ID	SEX	SEX='M'	SEX='F'
719250751	M	1	0
298674071	F	0	1
347691027	M	1	0

MASSIVELY PARALLEL PROCESSOR (MPP) MACHINES

MPP machines were quickly covered in Chapter 3 also, as were SMP machines. Both machine types are multiprocessors, and both offer vast amounts of computational power. Aside from architectural differences, the difference in power between the two is one of degree rather than of kind. Basically, MPP machines offer more processors, hundreds or thousands, whereas SMP offers a hundred or fewer. Mid-range and low-end SMPs have become commodities, whereas high-end SMPs and MPPs are not as prevalent.

Modern UNIX and UNIX-variant multiprocessors can safely surpass mainframe power. What this means to most database systems is added parallel computational power. This can work in unison with such things as PQ. Unfortunately, most database systems cannot take advantage of *all* this power simply because they might be I/O-bound instead of processor-bound. More likely, the actual software architecture that makes up the RDBMS kernel, such as multithreaded scalability, cannot scale enough past 20 processors or so to leverage the vast power beyond that count. Currently, this appears to be true of Oracle, Sybase, and Informix.

Varying hardware solutions exist, some of which are based on relatively old technology and some of which are based on newer advances. The older camp includes RAM disks. If an OS permits this type of arrangement, what you have is a section of core (and virtual) memory that acts as a separate disk. Of course, if the power goes out, the disk is lost unless the contents are copied to a more permanent store (namely, disk). Some DOS versions permitted this, and it worked well for smaller xBase databases, such as dBase. UNIX still enables this sort of thing. Sun Solaris, in particular, enables the configuration of temporary file systems that are, in effect, UNIX RAM disks.

In any case, the use of these disks is problematic for database systems, not just counting hardware crashes or power loss. You also might have a case where, for whatever reason, the RAM disk is unavailable and the RDBMS must timestamp the data located on that disk. Result: a database in need of recovery! Bad news. However, if the system proves highly reliable, in practice, I have personally seen an increase in performance by a factor of ten due to an appropriate use of such a disk. In Oracle, one possibility is to store TEMP on a RAM disk.

SOLID-STATE DISKS

Solid-state disks are relatively new, even though the idea and prototypes behind them have been around for 15 years or so. They just haven't been commercially available until the last five years or so. Hardware SMP vendors, such as Sun, and third-party suppliers offer such disks now.

A solid-state disk is essentially a specialized, permanent memory card. The obvious benefit is that the electromechanical disadvantage is all but eliminated because there's no disk access time to factor in. Access time is near the core memory speeds. The disadvantages are the high price, proprietary/compatibility issues, and the lack of a long production cycle behind these products. This latter issue almost always means the technology is still relatively new and unstable.

HARDWARE ACCELERATORS

Hardware accelerators are specialized I/O cards that supply abundant cache space, specialized firmware, and sometimes specialized microprocessors to *accelerate* the I/O channels they support (hence the name). They have been commercially available for a few years longer than solid-state disks but have not found much success. Their prices have been reasonable, but again there are proprietary/compatibility issues. Because they don't replace disks but only augment them, the stability of their technology is not quite as important as solid-state disks. In any case, they have proven fairly reliable when properly configured. Database Execrator (DBE) is one example.

QUEUING SYSTEMS

Queuing software, such as IBM's Message Queuing Middleware (MQM) series, offers asynchronous message passing capabilities. This breed of software is also sometimes referred to as Message Oriented Middleware or MOM. What this software does is basically what a queue should do: buffer things in a First-In, First-Out (FIFO) manner. This is sometimes required instead of or in addition to TP monitors to help defray the overhead in servicing the numerous users of high-concurrency systems.

In addition to FIFO buffering, this type of software often guarantees delivery of the client request to the server. Hence, this software speeds things up indirectly by not only buffering client/server requests in a networked system, but by preventing unnecessary retransmissions of the same requests.

REVISITING APPLICATION TYPES

Chapter 3 covered the three major application types (OLTP, DSS, and batch), and mentioned some lesser ones (OLAP, VCDB). Now reconsider Oracle tuning recommendations for these different types, and look at some new, application-specific twists on the general hardware layout that was presented. First, compare and contrast OLTP and DSS, the two major application types.

OLTP ISSUES

An OLTP system has high concurrency (a large number of interactive users) and is update-intensive (has large amounts of insert, update, and delete statements). Because OLTP applications can grow or shrink significantly due to inserts and deletes, the extents in the tablespaces supporting the most volatile tables and indexes should be pre-allocated to their maximum expected size. Dynamic extension only hurts performance in this case. Basically, you must plan for capacity and implement your findings now, long before you reach those maximums.

You must have enough redo and rollback to handle the transaction needs. If transactions are relatively short or modify relatively small amounts of data, you need many smaller rollback segments. Because you have many concurrent users, you need many rollback segments to minimize contention. You should likewise have many redo logs to handle frequent check-pointing if the system has this critical need. The rollback segments and redo logs should be separated and can be sized using Oracle diagnostic tools (see the section "Using Oracle Diagnostic Tools").

Database check constraints and referential integrity constraints cost less overall in terms of computing time, compared to placing this logic in the application code. In any case, make sure that the application code is as reusable as possible to promote sharing. Oracle uses the library cache of its shared pool to efficiently reuse this code when called multiple times. For OLTP, the application process overhead should be reduced by using bind variables instead of literals. If there are fewer symbols within a statement to parse, there is a better chance of shared statements, given less parsing.

In addition, with OLTP systems, you need more indexes because you are trying to access relatively small amounts of data in a more or less random fashion within tables. However, you don't want so many indexes that you actually wind up slowing the application down. As a rule of thumb, establish indexes on all your primary and foreign keys, and add others sparingly. Remember, updating and rebuilding indexes is very costly, and high DML (insert, update, and delete) activity triggers just this sort of index restructuring.

As mentioned earlier in the section "Step 12: If All Else Fails, Consider More Exotic Solutions," the MultiThreaded Server (MTS) option might be used when your database system is under extremely heavy load or on a daily basis if required. Remember, though, that the primary goal of MTS is to improve throughput of highly concurrent systems, and many OLTP systems are concurrent to varying degrees. However, maximizing throughput often increases response time delays. So using MTS is a matter of policy. That is, if high throughput defines good performance to you, use it. If you want low response times, don't.

DSS ISSUES

With DSS, the databases are often large, historical, and read-only. Hence, queries (selects) are the meat of DSS activity. Oracle's Parallel Query can be used to speed up particularly slow queries that can be paralleled through some physical (tablespace and data file) restructuring. As mentioned before, you want to read as many rows as possible with one Oracle block read. You want to maximize your block reads by reading multiple, sequential blocks, because DSS queries typically trigger full table scans, which are sequential by nature. So set the DB_BLOCK_SIZE and DB_FILE_MULTIBLOCK_READ_COUNT parameters as high as possible. These parameter settings are explained further in Chapter 19.

However, here are some words of caution:

- Make sure that your extent sizes are multiples of `DB_FILE_MULTIBLOCK_READ_COUNT`.
- Make sure that `DB_FILE_MULTIBLOCK_READ_COUNT` is a multiple of `DB_BLOCK_SIZE`.
- If you're using RAID, ensure that your RAID stripe size is a multiple of your extent size and that the preceding two cautions still hold true.

You have three methods for using indexes with DSS. Because most queries return full table scans of large tables, you might wonder why you should use indexes at all with a DSS. (In fact, not using them is Method 1.) The three methods are as follows:

- *Method 1*: Don't use any indexes at all, especially if you never have any highly selective queries or can't afford the additional storage required to create conventional indexes on every table.
- *Method 2*: Keep only a few indexes on those tables that are selective by a small percentage of your DSS queries.
- *Method 3*: Use bitmap indexing, as briefly discussed in the section "Step 12: If All Else Fails, Consider More Exotic Solutions." Because DSS queries tend not to be highly selective most of the time and would otherwise trigger full table scans even if conventional indexes existed, use bitmap indexes as an alternative.

Of course, in reality a DBA will probably use all these methods from time to time.

Don't use bind variables in DSS application code. Why? This is in direct contrast to the OLTP recommendation because with OLTP, you want to minimize application process overhead (parsing). However, with relatively long-running DSS queries, parsing is a much smaller percentage of the overall query time. You want to ensure that the optimizer chooses the best access plan. If bind variables are used, the optimizer cannot call on its stored statistics (via the `ANALYZE` command) to pick the best way to access the data. Any selectivity that could have been gained through literals, which would help reduce the scale of the intermediate tables and final output returned, would be negated.

With OLTP, you wanted many relatively small rollback segments. With DSS and long-running queries, similar to long-running batch production systems, you want one or two large rollback segments. This is only to enable read-consistent, concurrent views of large amounts of rollback data. Although if the DSS were 100% read-only, this would be a non-issue. In practice, I have found there are virtually no 100% read-only systems.

Other Considerations for both OLTP and DSS

Additional considerations are the Oracle block-level parameters `INITRANS` and `PCTFREE` for both OLTP and DSS. For OLTP, set `PCTFREE` relatively low (or just leave it at the default) because each block must have room to grow and change. With mostly read-only DSS, set `PCTFREE` high because the data in the blocks will remain mostly static. For OLTP, you want to set `INITRANS` relatively high because a high number of concurrent users will otherwise trigger dynamic transaction header slot expansion, and consequently block-level reorganizations, possibly escalating up to the extent levels.

With DSS, there's little chance of concurrent users having to wait due to locking because most transactions will be selects, not to mention the large amount of blocks a DSS stores. Hence, set INITRANS to some medium level if your DSS also supports a moderate level of insert, update, or delete. Otherwise, it can be left at the default.

UNDERSTANDING BENCHMARKS

A benchmark is just a criterion that is representative of an application's real work. Chapter 3 mentioned that quantitative measures as a result of transaction analysis can also be used as benchmarks. The performance of an application on its benchmark run is measured by some specifically chosen quantitative measures. With benchmark runs, you usually have preset conditions or configurations that you keep constant (the *initial conditions*, or *dependent variables*) while changing one variable (an *independent variable*) at a time between runs. This enables you to study the impact of these variables separately. Hence, benchmarking is just a variation on the scientific, or experimental, method. If done properly, you can assess cause and effect or, at the very least, correlation of effects. Your hypothesis is that changing the independent variable (for example, block size) will affect the dependent variables (for example, throughput).

Benchmarking can provide various benefits. Usually, benchmarking is associated with simulation. A simulation of a system is a functioning prototype that mimics the real work of that system to predict its performance or test its functionality. However, benchmarks also offer the capability to run baselines, which are the relevant quantitative measures you take right after you release a production system or right before you begin your performance tuning effort. It gives the DBA a basis for comparison, to test whether his or her performance tuning changes have caused any improvement!

The best-known of the database system benchmarks are those prepared by the Transaction Processing Performance Council (TPC). This council has produced numerous benchmarks, but the first ever created were simply representative bank teller operations (TPC-A and TPC-B). For these benchmarks, a small database is created, including a bank table, a branch table, and an account table. The operations include updates to these tables and inserts to a history table. Performance is measured in terms of transactions per second (tps), a quantitative measure of throughput. Because TPC-A and TPC-B were released several years ago, the TPC has come out with newer benchmarks, TPC-C and TPC-D, aimed at benchmarking different kinds of applications.

TPC-A (1989) tests an OLTP environment with high concurrency and significant I/O, using one relatively simple, multitasked transaction. (A transaction is multitasked when it performs more than one single select, insert, update, or delete.) The TPC uses the term *transaction type* to refer to a specific, multitasked transaction. In TPC-A, the transaction has multiple updates and an insert.

TPC-B (1990) is basically the same thing as TPC-A, except that it removes the high concurrency requirement. It is used as a database *stress test*, essentially just testing significant I/O. Yet this distinction is vague when using virtual terminals in simulation software, so often these two benchmarks are reported together or in lieu of one another.

TPC-C (1992) is an OLTP benchmark involving a mix of five different, more complex transaction types and nine database entities. By contrast, TPC-A and TPC-B use a single transaction type and four database entities. The business is now based on a supplier database with an order entry system, as opposed to a bank teller application.

TPC-D (1995) is a DSS benchmark that focuses especially on heavy, real-world transactions. It includes 17 complex queries against large amounts of data. This is the latest TPC benchmark offering. TPC-D is geared toward heavyweight queries that run for long periods of time, in contrast to the lighter-weight TPC-A and TPC-B and the relatively middleweight TPC-C.

When performed in an unbiased, independent environment, these benchmarks provide a basis for comparison between RDBMS software vendors. The database systems can be compared both tuned and untuned. The application is the same, so if the networking is the same and the platform (hardware and OS) is very much the same, the only variable remaining is the RDBMS software. It's often the case that no two vendors will compete on the same platform with the same benchmark (at least within the same time period).

With good simulation software, such as LoadRunner, virtual users and processes can be made to simulate apparent load on a database system during the benchmark. The number of concurrent users can be increased incrementally, as can the number of transactions per user. Either way, the total number of transactions is increased, and you can effectively create and observe a database stress test. When the runs are validated and the statistics (tps) are gathered, you can explore the ROI strategy and use the performance tuning fundamentals as necessary to attack the general problem of tuning, even if done on a simulated system.

USING ORACLE DIAGNOSTIC TOOLS

Your major Oracle diagnostic tools are as follows:

- `SQL_TRACE` and `TKPROF`
- `EXPLAIN PLAN`
- The `V$` dynamic performance views and Server Manager line mode
- Server Manager Monitor (GUI)
- The Performance Pack of Enterprise Manager
- `utlbstat/utlestat` and `report.txt`
- Third-party products

USING `SQL_TRACE` AND `TKPROF`

To tune applications, you can use `SQL_TRACE` and `TKPROF`. You must set the `init.ora` parameter `TIMED_STATISTICS=TRUE` to get timing information. The timing is good to 1/100 of a second. Real-time database systems might have to use alternative timing methods, such as writing your own timer or sampling the real-time OS clock on which the database system resides. You can optionally set the `USER_DUMP_DEST` to the directory of your choice and also set

MAX_DUMP_FILE_SIZE to the maximum number of bytes you want your trace file to grow. Set SQL_TRACE=TRUE at either the system level (for all sessions) through the init.ora parameter or at the session level through ALTER SESSION SET SQL_TRACE=TRUE;.

Execute the application, and then set SQL_TRACE back to FALSE if desired. In effect, you're not planning on running the application for timing purposes again in the near future. Use TKPROF to format the trace file. (The TKPROF utility is run from the command line.) Statistics gathered include the query execution cycle component times (parse, execute, and fetch) and logical versus physical reads. The usage, syntax, and interpretation of SQL_TRACE and TKPROF will be covered in detail in Chapter 17.

USING EXPLAIN PLAN

Another application tuning tool is EXPLAIN PLAN. You must run utlxpln.sql to create the PLAN_TABLE, or create it yourself interactively. EXPLAIN PLAN FOR <SQL statement>; will explain the execution plan for that SQL statement without executing it. (This is similar to the NO EXEC option with some other interpreted languages.) You can use this with or without SQL_TRACE and TKPROF. I recommend you review the code first (read it), run SQL_TRACE with TKPROF next, and then use EXPLAIN PLAN last if you're still having difficulty with an application that's performing poorly. This will be addressed in Chapter 17, along with how the Oracle optimizer works, which will help explain how EXPLAIN PLAN works.

USING THE V$ DYNAMIC PERFORMANCE VIEWS

To help tune memory (see Chapter 18) and tune I/O (see Chapter 19), all the Oracle products, such as SQL*DBA, Server Manager, and Enterprise Manager, rely on the V$ dynamic performance views. These views are grouped into instance, database, memory, disk, user, session, and contention aspects of performance. They are based on the internal X$ base tables. DESCRIBE V$FIXED_TABLE and SELECT the columns you want from the V$FIXED_TABLE table to get a listing of the V$ views. The X$ tables are typically not queried directly. Their names and contents change from version to version and within versions.

The V$ views are called dynamic because they are populated at instance startup and are truncated at shutdown. The V$ views (and X$ tables) also form the basis of the standard Oracle tuning scripts, utlbstat/utlestat, which query them using SQL scripts and format the output that is returned. Therefore, if utlbstat/utlestat do not give you what you want, you can use Server Manager and the V$ views to either supplement or supplant those utilities. The least common denominator for all Oracle platforms, older and newer, are SQL scripts, V$ views, and either SQL*DBA or Server Manager line mode (svrmgrl on UNIX, and svrmgr23.exe on NT, for example). This means that if you have developed your own performance scripts, you can run them within these command-line utilities. In addition to these, there's always SQL*Plus, of course.

USING THE SERVER MANAGER MONITOR

The Server Manager Monitor, which is becoming obsolete because of the advent of Enterprise Manger, offers several screens relating to performance. These screens monitor the MultiThreaded Server, logical and physical I/O, process information, locks and latches, shared pool information, and rollback information. The screens are updated in real-time and as mentioned, are based on the V$ views and X$ tables.

Using the Performance Pack of Enterprise Manager

Enterprise Manager's Performance Pack is extremely useful. It offers several components that can save a lot of time over command-line methods and scripting, especially for experienced DBAs or those who know precisely what to look for. Enterprise Manager enables you to quickly get to that information. The statistics are based on the V$ views and X$ tables but are reformatted into a much more readily digestible GUI form.

The components in the Performance Pack help analyze your logical and physical design. They also monitor locks, a variety of performance issues (throughput, redo, rollback, I/O, memory, and so on), the top user sessions with regards to resource consumption, your tablespace storage (data files, fragmentation, and so on), and application events through tracing.

Using utlbstat/utlestat AND report.txt

The most commonly used Oracle diagnostic utilities by far are the utlbstat/utlestat pair. A DBA runs utlbstat before running his or her application or simulation. The utlbstat.sql script builds the beginning tables necessary to collect and store the performance data. Then the DBA runs utlestat.sql, which builds the ending tables and the difference tables, computes the performance differences (the *deltas*) between the utlbstat run and this utlestat run (in effect, the application duration), formats the output data (including comments and some explanations), and writes it to the default file, report.txt. This file must be interpreted by the DBA, either directly or indirectly (by taking some of the output values given and using them as inputs into simple formulas).

Interpretation of this data means comparing these final figures to more or less established guidelines, keeping the ROI strategy in mind, and categorizing the findings as acceptable or not for that given area of performance. The output in report.txt nearly covers all the bases, either directly or indirectly. So a DBA must simply apply the ROI strategy, the established guidelines, and his or her application knowledge, and determine whether the memory performance is acceptable, the I/O performance is acceptable, and so forth.

Using Third-Party Products

This chapter presented a fairly high-level overview of the major Oracle diagnostic tools. Third-party performance monitoring tools exist, and they have relatively large market shares within the installed Oracle customer base. Some examples include offerings from BMC, Platinum, and Compuware. You'll use utlbstat/utlestat and report.txt as your diagnostic tools for Chapters 18 and 19. Of course, you'll use EXPLAIN PLAN and SQL_TRACE with TKPROF for the next chapter.

PART

IV

Cʜ

16

CHAPTER **17**

APPLICATION TUNING

In this chapter

MOTIVATION

Tuning the application really amounts to tuning your SQL statements within your application. If your application has a graphical user interface (GUI) front end, tuning the application still amounts to tuning analogs of SQL statements. In other words, all the GUI-level actions can be mapped to one or more SQL statements (SELECT, INSERT, UPDATE, DELETE, and so on) of varying complexity. In any case, your Return-on-Investment (ROI) strategy tells you that you must tune the application first, if at all possible, and then resort to tuning all the aspects of the database last.

Subjective estimates have shown applications being responsible, on average, for 80 percent of the total system (application plus database) performance, leaving only 20 percent for the database. I agree with the idea behind this claim, as you have just covered. However, I tend not to agree with the numbers that make up this claim. In my experience, I have seen systems that fulfill these estimates and systems that exhibit the opposite situation—the opposite situation being the database accounting for most, if not all, of the performance.

What this really means to DBAs is that the performance of systems can be labeled situational, relative, or application-specific. This should sound familiar, especially in regards to discussions of application types. Yet, one absolute rule does hold true, and I whole-heartedly advocate that DBAs pay close attention to the first rule of tuning:

> *The application should always be tuned first.*

This holds true for two reasons: 1. The majority of database systems existing today owe most of their performance to their applications. 2. Even if this does not hold true for your individual system, as a DBA you must categorize the system's application type—even if this does not hold true for your individual system. This means that you must review the application, in specific, the types of transactions—the access code and the SQL code. Even if your application code is programmed as efficiently as possible from a database access point of view, you must still understand how the programs interact with your database.

How do you accomplish the task of reviewing the application? If the application is reasonably small—in terms of lines of code or number of separate program units (modules)—then manually reviewing everything is possible. On the other hand, if the application is large, full manual review would most likely be out of the question. Principle 3, Triage, of your Performance Tuning Fundamentals (see Chapter 16, "Performance Tuning Fundamentals"), gives you direction. You can focus on those modules or sections of code that tend to account for most of the resource and time consumption.

First, you attempt to fix the 20 percent of the application code that accounts for 80 percent of the system performance. (Then you can work on the remaining code to squeeze out the rest of the performance potential, if you have the time and personnel to do so.) How do you actually do this? The sections following the next one discuss the Oracle tools that you need. But first, the next section gives you the necessary background to use those tools—an understanding of the Oracle optimizer and how it works.

UNDERSTANDING THE OPTIMIZER

An *optimizer* is a piece of software and a part of an RDBMS that is responsible for optimizing, or formulating the most efficient way for a given SQL statement to access the data. To do this, the optimizer chooses a sequence of access paths that provide the (hopefully) fastest way for Oracle to get to the data and then builds the execution plan based on those access paths. An *access path* is a physical way to the data. An *execution plan* is the sequence of Oracle executable steps that follow the chosen access paths.

The technology behind the Oracle optimizer, as with many other RDBMS vendors, has advanced considerably over the past few years. Ironically, the optimizer still might not always provide the best way ("the optimal way") to access data. In older versions, the programmer had to be careful about how she coded her SQL statements. With the knowledge that the ordering within a SQL statement could drastically affect how it would perform, programmers had to do a lot of manual optimization. Likewise, the DBA had to be aware of this situation. The better the optimizer, the less optimization responsibility is on the users, programmers, and DBAs. Even with the current field of RDBMS optimizers, programmers still need to know optimization techniques and apply them when possible. However, programmers don't need to be quite as expert about the optimizer as before. DBAs should always remain aware of the optimizer technology, optimization rules, and proper optimizer usage.

PART

IV

CH

17

Optimizers come in two flavors:

- Rule-based—A rule-based optimizer chooses the access paths based on a static, RDBMS vendor-specific rank ordering of those access paths that are the fastest ways to the data. Although the rankings are vendor-specific, it is relatively easy to compare and map analogous access paths between the output of different vendors' optimizers.

- Cost-based—A cost-based optimizer chooses the access paths based on some data-distribution statistics stored internally, usually within the RDBMS data dictionary. Typically, the DBA must periodically run some RDBMS commands to maintain these statistics.

Oracle7.x and higher optimizers offer both rule-based and cost-based optimization capabilities within the same optimizer. Oracle6.x optimizer offers rule-based optimization, but it does not have a fully automatic cost-based optimization. All these versions offer a programmer an override known as a *hint*. It is not a true override in the sense that the optimizer does not always follow the hint. Consider a hint a suggestion to the optimizer. If no syntax errors exist, the optimizer should generally follow it. A hint is placed *inline*, meaning directly in the SQL statement code. Listing 17.1 shows a SELECT statement that suggests to the optimizer to use the INDEX on the table from which it is selecting:

LISTING 17.1 AN EXAMPLE OF A QUERY WITH A HINT

```
SQL> SELECT /*+ INDEX */ EMPLOYEE_ID
  2> FROM EMPLOYEES
  3> WHERE EMPLOYEE_ID = 503748;
```

Notice the hint immediately follows the SQL command (SELECT). The hint comment, like any regular SQL*Plus comment, begins with a /* and is immediately followed by a plus sign (+), which makes /*+ the start of a hint comment. The usual */ ends the hint comment. Also, consider how the optimizer knows which index to use if more than one exists, especially if for some reason, more than one exists on EMPLOYEE_ID. In the previous example, only /*+ INDEX */ is stated, and it is assumed that only one (primary key) index exists for this table. Hence, for this listing, there is no ambiguity. In cases where there is ambiguity, you need to include the table and index name in the hint to give the optimizer specific information. Hints are discussed in more detail in the following sections.

> **Note**
>
> The optimizer accepts only one hint per statement or statement block. The optimizer ignores any additional hints. Further, the optimizer ignores any misspelled hints. There is no reported error, and you have to use Explain Plan, discussed later in its own section, to determine whether your hint was followed.

RANKING ACCESS PATHS

The Oracle optimizer access paths, ranked by fastest to slowest, top to bottom, are shown in Table 17.1.

TABLE 17.1 ORACLE OPTIMIZER ACCESS PATHS, RANK-ORDERED

Rank	Access Path
1	Single row by ROWID
2	Single row by cluster join
3	Single row by hash cluster key with unique or primary key
4	Single row by unique or primary key
5	Cluster join
6	Hash cluster key
7	Indexed cluster key
8	Composite key
9	Single-column indexes
10	Bounded range search on indexed columns
11	Unbounded range search on indexed columns
12	Sort-merge join
13	MAX or MIN of indexed columns
14	ORDER BY on indexed columns
15	Full table scan

Source: Oracle Corporation

When the Oracle optimizer is following the rule-based strategy, it uses the fastest access paths that fit the given query. For example, Listing 17.2 shows the same query from Listing 17.1 without the hint, and it has been modified with a > WHERE clause.

PART

IV

CH

17

LISTING 17.2   AN EXAMPLE OF A QUERY WITHOUT A HINT AND AN UNBOUNDED RANGE SEARCH

```
SQL>   SELECT EMPLOYEE_ID
       2> FROM EMPLOYEES
       3> WHERE EMPLOYEE_ID >     500000;
```

If Oracle were using rule-based as its strategy and a primary key index existed on EMPLOYEE_ID on the table EMPLOYEES, it would use Access Path #11 (unbounded range search on indexed columns) for Listing 17.2 because the WHERE clause is unbounded. In other words, a WHERE clause is unbounded when it has a greater than (> or >=) operator and no corresponding less than (< or <=) operator, or vice versa. The range is not known until execution time.

If the WHERE clause is bounded (in effect, it has both operators), the finite range is known at parse time. To make an unbounded WHERE clause bounded, you could use the literal maximum (if you knew it), or at least the theoretical maximum for that column according to your business rules. However, you probably wouldn't want to use the MAX operator in addition to your original unbounded range search—if you look at the rank ordering, using MAX is #13, which is below your objective of improving an unbounded search (#11) to a bounded one (#10). Using the MAX operator with your original unbounded range search would only slow you down. But using the actual maximum, perhaps if statically known, would do the trick. Follow these do's and don'ts that are illustrated in Listing 17.3:

- Do use an actual maximum value (literal) known ahead of time. This is illustrated in the first query of Listing 17.3 (678453).

- Do use a theoretical business maximum value (literal) known ahead of time if the actual is not known. This is illustrated in the second query of Listing 17.3 (999999).

- Don't use the MAX SQL aggregate function because it only slows things down. This is illustrated in the third query of Listing 17.3.

LISTING 17.3   REWRITING AN UNBOUNDED SEARCH TO MAKE IT BOUNDED

```
SQL>   SELECT EMPLOYEE_ID
       2> FROM EMPLOYEES
       3> WHERE EMPLOYEE_ID > 500000 AND EMPLOYEE_ID <=678453;

SQL>   SELECT EMPLOYEE_ID
       2> FROM EMPLOYEES
       3> WHERE EMPLOYEE_ID > 500000 AND EMPLOYEE_ID <=999999;

SQL>   SELECT EMPLOYEE_ID
       2> FROM EMPLOYEES
       3> WHERE EMPLOYEE_ID > 500000 AND EMPLOYEE_ID <=MAX(EMPLOYEE_ID);
```

ANALYZING QUERIES TO IMPROVE EFFICIENCY

Not surprisingly, this general field of attempting to reformulate or rewrite queries to improve their efficiency is known as *query rewriting*. Query rewriting is covered in more detail later in this chapter in the sections "Identifying Typical Problems" and "Rewriting Queries." The previous examples are standard fare and easy to understand. For example, to get the maximum (MAX) of a set of values in a column, it seems to take close to the amount of time of a full-table scan—regardless of whether the column was indexed. As you can see by the rank ordering of the MAX access path, this seems to be the case. However, there are far less understandable and more exotic ways of rewriting queries that are not as obvious.

Now that you've studied the rule-based optimization, what about cost-based optimization? Review the following two queries given in Listings 17.4 and 17.5.

LISTING 17.4   FIRST OF TWO SIMILAR QUERIES ON THE SAME TABLE

```
SQL>    SELECT EMPLOYEE_ID
        2> FROM EMPLOYEES
        3> WHERE EMPLOYEE_TYPE='VICE PRESIDENT';
```

LISTING 17.5   SECOND OF TWO SIMILAR QUERIES ON THE SAME TABLE

```
SQL>    SELECT EMPLOYEE_ID
        2> FROM EMPLOYEES
        3> WHERE EMPLOYEE_TYPE='PROGRAMMER';
```

Now, suppose you have a relatively large software company and you have 6 vice presidents and about 2000 programmers out of about 6000 total employees. The two preceding queries explain the difference between rule-based and cost-based query optimization and why cost-based optimization is preferred. Assuming you have a non-unique index on the column EMPLOYEE_TYPE, rule-based optimization chooses Access Path #9 (single-column indexes) for both queries. On the other hand, cost-based optimization—given the data distributions that programmers account for 1/3 of the total number of rows and that vice presidents account for only 1/1000—chooses to use the non-unique index for the query in Listing 17.4, but it is intelligent enough to opt for the full-table scan (the worst case Access Path #15) for the query in Listing 17.5. The intelligence comes from the stored knowledge of the data distribution.

If the optimizer must access a significant fraction of all the rows of a table, a full-table scan is actually more efficient than an index scan. This is because the process of scanning an index for a row and then retrieving that particular row requires at least two read operations per row and sometimes more—depending on how many distinct data values are in the index. However, the full-table scan only needs one read operation per row. Multiply this times many rows, and it is pretty clear why an index is slower when accessing a large amount of a table, compared to just reading through the entire table, as with the query in Listing 17.5. Aside from the total number of read operations, another major reason why a full-table scan is better than an index on retrieving large parts of a table is that most of the necessary reads are sequential or nearly sequential. Obviously, to read from an index, then read from a table, then back to the index, then back to the table, and so forth, cannot be sequential, whether the table and index are on the same disk or are spread out in good tuning fashion. The index slows things down for queries and data like the query in Listing 17.5.

The index clearly outperforms a full-table scan for the queries and data like in Listing 17.4. This is because you only need to retrieve a small number of rows (6) and your total number of read operations is only 12 (2×6). By comparison, you still must perform 6,000 read operations (the entire table) with a full-table scan because a full-table scan has no knowledge of where individual pieces of data are stored. It must check every row. In fact, queries and data in Listing 17.4 are classic examples of the need for an index, especially if executed often enough. The best way to sum up the discussion of these two similar queries with different data counts is that these queries show how a user or programmer could not know that, given rule-based optimization, query and data like that in Listing 17.5 could perform better by using cost-based optimization.

SPECIFYING OPTIMIZER MODE

The next obvious question is how to specify the optimizer mode in Oracle. You have learned about rule-based and cost-based optimization so far. You can specify your desired form of optimization at the instance, session, or statement levels. To specify at the instance level, set the `init.ora` parameter, `OPTIMIZER_MODE`, to one of the following values:

- `CHOOSE`—When set to this value, the optimizer chooses the cost-based mode if statistics are available (have been run by the DBA). Otherwise, it resorts to rule-based optimization.

- `RULE`—The optimizer uses the rule-based approach.

- `FIRST_ROWS`—The optimizer chooses the cost-based approach (again if statistics are available) to minimize response time. That is, to minimize the time to present the first rows to the screen. Use this mode if you have a highly interactive, screens-based application, such as many OLTP and smaller DSS systems are.

- `ALL_ROWS`—The optimizer chooses cost-based mode (again if statistics are available) to minimize throughput, that is, to minimize the total number of rows passing through the system per unit of time (transactions per second). Use this if you have a batch or large DSS system.

To specify at the session level, issue the following DDL statement:

```
SQL> ALTER SESSION SET OPTIMIZER_GOAL=<value>;
```

The `value` is one of the previously mentioned optimizer modes (`CHOOSE`, `RULE`, `FIRST_ROWS`, `ALL_ROWS`). The result is only good for the session, and hence, must be reissued in a future session if desired.

To specify at the statement level, use hints as discussed earlier. The hints can be any of the optimizer mode values (`CHOOSE`, `RULE`, `FIRST_ROWS`, `ALL_ROWS`), or they can be one of the access paths shown in Table 17.2.

TABLE 17.2   BASIC ACCESS PATHS FOR HINTS

Access Path	Description
ROWID	Uses ROWID scan for retrieval
CLUSTER	Uses a cluster key scan
HASH	Uses a hash index scan
INDEX	Uses an index scan
INDEX_ASC	Uses an index scan and scans in ascending order
INDEX_DESC	Uses an index scan and scans in descending order
AND_EQUAL	Uses multiple indexes and merges their resultsi
ORDERED	Uses the order of the tables in the FROM clause to be the order of the join
USE_NL	Uses the nested loops method for joining tables
USE_MERGE	Uses the sort-merge method for joining tables
FULL	Uses a full table scan

TABLE 17.3   ADDITIONAL ACCESS PATHS FOR HINTS (VERSION 7.3 AND LATER)

Access Path	Description
CACHE	Tells Oracle to treat the table as a cached table, keeping its blocks in the SGA after a full scan for later quick access
HASH_AJ	Specifies type of join to use during an antijoin (Oracle7.3 and later)
MERGE_AJ	Specifies type of join to use during an antijoin
NO_MERGE	Tells Oracle not to merge the view's SQL syntax with the syntax of a query that uses the join
NO_CACHE	Marks blocks as "least recently used" so they get removed from SGA soon
NONPARALLEL	Allows to disable parallelism of a query
ROWID	Uses TABLE ACCESS BY ROWID operation
STAR	Uses a composite key/start query execution path when resolving a join
USE_CONTACT	Forces OR conditions in the WHERE clause to be compounded as UNION ALL
USE_HASH	Uses a hash join

Also, to use any of the cost-based optimization modes (FIRST_ROWS, ALL_ROWS), the DBA must run the statistics periodically to keep the stored data distributions up-to-date. A DBA can either take all statistics or take some statistics with a (simple random) sample. To take all statistics means to do a full-table scan. To take a sample means to access some fraction less than the total number of rows. A DBA issues the following DDL statement to take all statistics:

```
SQL> ANALYZE TABLE <table_name> COMPUTE STATISTICS;
```

This works fine for relatively small tables—less than a million rows. But for large tables, DBAs might want to opt for taking a sample. Statistically, as long as the sample is large enough relative to the total number of rows, it is sufficiently accurate not to require taking all statistics. To take a sample, a DBA issues the following DDL statement:

```
SQL> ANALYZE TABLE <table_name> ESTIMATE STATISTICS;
```

This statement causes the sampling (by default) of up to 1,064 rows, regardless of how large the actual table might be. A DBA might specify percentage by issuing this:

```
SQL> ANALYZE TABLE <table_name> ESTIMATE STATISTICS SAMPLE 10 PERCENT;
```

This samples 10 percent, rounded to some whole number of rows, of the total number of rows in the table. For example, this samples 600 rows to use for estimates out of your 6,000 row EMPLOYEES table. A DBA might also specify the actual sample size, by issuing something like the following:

```
SQL> ANALYZE TABLE <table_name> ESTIMATE STATISTICS SAMPLE 2000 ROWS;
```

Clearly, this samples precisely 2,000 rows of the specified table.

PART

IV

CH

17

Caution

If you specify a percentage greater than 50 (or a number of rows greater than 50 percent), the ANALYZE command resorts to a full-table scan COMPUTE rather than your specified ESTIMATE.

With Oracle versions 7.3 and higher, the ANALYZE command has an added FOR clause. With this clause, you can name specific columns with FOR COLUMN. For example, if only a few columns have changed since the last ANALYZE run or if you want to reduce the ANALYZE run time, specify FOR INDEXED COLUMNS ONLY, which does exactly what it says by not taking statistics on non-indexed columns.

A DBA should run ANALYZE on a regular, periodic basis. However, what might be sensible for one application might not be for another. For example, a DSS that is uploaded from three feeder batch systems on a monthly basis only needs to have those tables analyzed (with COMPUTE) that have been loaded, and then only immediately following the load or at some reasonable time before their next usage. In contrast, a high activity OLTP system— such as one that handles flight reservation information—might need to have nearly all its tables, which might be modified on a minute-by-minute basis, analyzed (with ESTIMATE) on a short interval, such as every hour or less. These types of systems are probably mirrored and one production copy should be analyzed offline while the other continues to serve, and then vice versa. In general, ANALYZE your tables as frequently as possible or on intervals when your tables change most so that the Oracle optimizer can best serve your application needs. Do it interactively if necessary, but most often these ANALYZE runs can be scheduled or triggered by DML events and therefore can be written by using noninteractive scripts or stored procedures.

UNDERSTANDING OPTIMIZATION TERMS

To wrap up the section on optimization, look at a few commonly used definitions that, as a DBA, you should understand. A *histogram* is nothing more or less than a special type of bar chart. When you ANALYZE...COMPUTE or ANALYZE...ESTIMATE, you store the data distributions of the columns for that table. A data distribution is a function that maps frequencies (counts, or subtotals) or percentages of distinct values. In Oracle, those data distributions are stored numerically but can be displayed as histograms if you write a program to do so.

The *selectivity*, or sometimes, the selectivity factor, of an index is the number of total distinct values in a column of data values divided by the total (nondistinct) values. The higher the selectivity factor is, the better. In addition, the higher the selectivity, the better the justification for creating and using an index on that column is. Usually, fewer distinct values means less selectivity. (This makes sense because that number is the numerator of the selectivity formula.)

For example, normally a column that stores gender type (such as Male or Female) or categorical types with few distinct possibilities (such as marital status, with Single, Married Divorced, or Widowed) is not selective and normally will not provide a good basis for an index usage. One exception is when one or more of the distinct values in these types of columns is extremely rare in occurrence and happens to be queried often (used frequently in WHERE clauses). Suppose, for example, that marital status is used as a column for a senior citizens table where the value Single is fairly rare, occurring less than 10 percent of the time. It also happens that the Single value is often queried. Hence, an index will do nicely for these queries, although it is of no help in querying on the other values. Further, a bitmapped index would work well here. The decision of when to use an index and what type of index to use is covered in the section "Identifying Typical Problems" later in this chapter.

An optimizer chooses to read and return data from an index when it is available, as opposed to having to go fetch it from the table. This optimizer preference is known as *index coverage* and usually results in better performance, although occasionally it can result in poorer performance. Suppose, for example, you have a composite index on LAST_NAME, FIRST_NAME, and MIDDLE_INITIAL in an EMPLOYEE table. You can run the following query to find all the employees with the LAST_NAME SMITH:

```
SQL> SELECT LAST_NAME
   2> FROM EMPLOYEES
   3> WHERE LAST_NAME = 'SMITH';
```

In this case, the query is said to be *covered by the index*. In other words, all the columns requested in the SELECT clause of the SELECT statement are stored (not only in the table but) in the index. For obvious reasons, the optimizer normally prefers to use the index alone over using both the index and the table. Why get water from two wells when one supplies all you need? However, index coverage can have an undesirable side effect, which is discussed in the section "Identifying Typical Problems."

Lastly, one of the most important rules of thumb you should know as a DBA with regards to query tuning is *the 5 percent rule*. This applies to Oracle7.x but not older versions. If, given available statistics from an ANALYZE run, the optimizer finds the expected number of rows to be returned greater than 5 percent, it opts for a full-table scan. With 6.x and 5.x, this percentage was 15 percent and 20 percent, respectively. Often, this is still called the 20 percent rule, although the actual percentage no longer applies to modern Oracle versions. This is vital information for a DBA to be aware of, for the optimizer might make the wrong (less than optimal) choice at times, given your knowledge of the application, and you would need to override it (with a hint or by rewriting the query, for example).

SQL TRACE AND tkprof

The SQL TRACE facility, along with the tkprof formatting program, provides the capability to generate and review performance statistics for individual SQL statements. You enable SQL TRACE at the instance or session level. However, there are a few init.ora parameters you must enable to use SQL TRACE in either case. If not already set, set the following parameters:

```
TIMED_STATISTICS=TRUE
USER_DUMP_DEST=<directory>
MAX_DUMP_FILE_SIZE=<size in operating system blocks>
```

Clearly, you want TIMED_STATISTICS on if you want SQL TRACE to be able to collect timing information. USER_DUMP_DEST should be specified, unless you want the trace files to be stored in the default operating-system–specific location. In addition, MAX_DUMP_FILE_SIZE should be set sufficiently high to hold all the generated trace files. To enable SQL TRACE at the instance level (that is, for all sessions), set the following init.ora parameter:

```
SQL_TRACE=TRUE
```

All sessions will generate trace files. In addition to instance specifics, name trace files with session specifics to be able to distinguish which ones belong to which sessions and to ensure that enough space is in USER_DUMP_DEST to hold all those files. Or, run the trace files in isolation, sequentially if possible, so there will be no confusion. To enable SQL TRACE at the session level, issue the following DDL statement:

```
SQL> ALTER SESSION SET SQL_TRACE=TRUE;
```

The SQL TRACE only generates statistics for the duration of the session. Now, to be able to read the information created by SQL TRACE, you must use tkprof. You run the tkprof program at the operating system level (command line). The abbreviated syntax to do this is the following:

```
tkprof <tracefile> <outputfile>
```

An example in UNIX might look like the following:

```
hostname% tkprof ora_1776.trc ora_1776.out
```

In this example, tkprof reformats the trace file (ora_1776.trc) into a readable, user-defined output file (ora_1776.out). An example of what the tkprof output might look like for the following SQL statement is shown in Listing 17.6:

```
SELECT * FROM EMPLOYEES WHERE DUTY >= 10;
```

LISTING 17.6 AN EXAMPLE OF FORMATTED tkprof OUTPUT

```
Call       count   cpu     elapsed   disk   query   current   rows
Parse      1       0.17    0.35      0      0       0         0
Execute    1       0.00    0.01      0      0       0         0
Fetch      1       0.06    0.10      13     304     0         3679
Misses in library cache during parse: 1
Misses in library cache during execute: 1
Optimizer mode: CHOOSE
Parsing user id: 8
```

So what does all this information mean, and how can it help you tune your application? Well, as with most diagnostic tools, information is supplied, but interpretation, at least automatic interpretation, is not. First, examine each of the columnar statistics in your output file and what they mean, as discussed in Table 17.4.

TABLE 17.4 DESCRIPTION OF tkprof STATISTICS

Statistic	Description
count	The number of Parse, Execute, or Fetch calls.
cpu	The actual cpu time in seconds (if Parse = 0.00, the statement was in the library cache).
elapsed	The actual clock (or wall) time in seconds (should always be greater than or equal to cpu time).
disk	Oracle blocks read from the datafiles; also known as *physical reads*.
query	Oracle buffers read for consistent read from the rollback buffer cache, stored in the database buffer cache; also known as *consistent gets*.
current	Oracle buffers read in current mode from the database buffer cache; also known as *db block gets*.
rows	The number of rows accessed by the main driving (or outer) statement; shown for Fetch for SELECT statements, otherwise shown for Execute (DML).

Note the number of logical reads equals *query+current*. How should you interpret this? Your goals, as an application developer, programmer, or DBA should be to do the following:

1. Reduce the number of logical reads to as little as possible. Make sure you are accessing exactly what you need to access *and nothing more*. In other words, don't access tables or rows within tables unless you absolutely must. Take shortcuts whenever possible. For

example, suppose an EMPLOYEES table contains a foreign key on DEPT_ID to a DEPARTMENTS table and to a lookup table known as DEPT_NAMES. Now suppose a common query is to retrieve the DEPT_NAME given the DEPT_ID when retrieving an EMPLOYEES row using the following:

```
SQL>   SELECT E.LAST_NAME, E.FIRST_NAME, N.DEPT_NAME
   2>  FROM EMPLOYEES E, DEPARTMENTS D, DEPT_NAMES N
   3>  WHERE E.DEPT_ID = D.DEPT_ID
   4>  AND D.DEPT_ID = N.DEPT_ID;
```

This yields the desired result, but the DEPARTMENTS table never had to be accessed. This is especially true if proper integrity and referential constraints are defined and maintained. In particular, DEPT_ID in DEPT_NAMES should also be a foreign key to the DEPARTMENTS table. Hence, you would never have a DEPT_ID existing in the DEPT_NAMES table that did not first exist in the DEPARTMENTS table. To reduce unnecessary accesses, this could be simplified to the following:

PART

IV

CH

17

```
SQL>   SELECT E.LAST_NAME, E.FIRST_NAME, N.DEPT_NAME
   2>  FROM EMPLOYEES E, DEPT_NAMES N
   3>  WHERE E.DEPT_ID = N.DEPT_ID;
```

2. Reduce the physical reads/logical reads ratio to as close to 0 as possible. First, ensure that the first goal of reducing the total logical reads is addressed. Second, make sure you are accessing what you need to access in the most efficient manner possible. Use what you've learned so far in this chapter. Plus, the remaining sections will aid you by providing more examples and scenarios. Third, if you've absolutely covered the first two tasks, increase your database buffer case in your SGA and if necessary, purchase more core memory. This is discussed further in Chapter 18, "Tuning Memory." On average, your ratio should be less than .10 for most statements. In the tkprof output example for a SELECT statement, the ratio is 13/304, or about .04. This is a good ratio. In fact, it corresponds to a 96 percent (100–.04) database buffer cache's hit ratio.

3. Reduce the logical reads/rows to as close to 0 as possible. For every logical read, you want to read as many rows as possible. Hence, the smaller the ratio is, the more efficient your reads are. This is an aspect of *block efficiency*, which is discussed in Chapter 19, "Tuning I/O." Clearly, if the ratio seems too high, for example only 1:8 (0.125) or larger, the db_block_size should probably be increased because it appears to be too low relative to the large row sizes. In the previous tkprof example, the ratio is good (13/879), of about .015, or smaller than 1:67. This means about 1000 rows for every 15 blocks read is retrieved, or about 67 rows per block. (If you were using a 16K Oracle db_block_size, this is about 246 bytes per row.)

tkprof offers several other command-line options in addition to the abbreviated example just presented. The most useful are discussed in Table 17.5. Interpreting execution plans is covered in more detail in the following section, "Understanding EXPLAIN PLAN."

TABLE 17.5   SOME tkprof COMMAND-LINE OPTIONS

Option	Description
explain=user/password	Enables you to run an EXPLAIN PLAN as a *user*; extremely useful because it provides the execution plans for each of the statements in the trace file.
record=file	Enables you to specify a *file* in which to save the statements in the trace file; useful to save scripts with for individual statement testing.
sys=NO	Suppresses recursive calls traced back through the SYS user; this is useful because even though you can view these calls by default, they can't really be modified to help performance in any way—leaving them out simplifies the amount of output you have to filter through.

To display all the options on the screen, type *tkprof help=YES* at the command line.

Caution

The explain tkprof command line option provides plans at tkprof runtime and is not based on the SQL TRACE run, so these two sets of output might not agree.

The following list summarizes using SQL TRACE and tkprof:

1. Use these facilities mostly when you have multiple concurrent applications and want to pinpoint your most resource-intensive applications. Target those that appear to be most inefficient for your priority-tuning efforts.

2. Turn on SQL TRACE in init.ora or with ALTER SESSION.

3. Run your applications.

4. Turn off SQL TRACE (if you're not expecting to reuse it soon).

5. Run tkprof to format your trace files into readable output files.

6. Interpret the results.

7. Tune your application or database as indicated. This often means rewriting the queries.

8. Go back to Step 2 and repeat until you are satisfied with Step 6.

UNDERSTANDING EXPLAIN PLAN

Whereas the SQL TRACE facility and tkprof program can provide useful statistics and execution plan information given many statements run in a single application sequence, EXPLAIN PLAN can give execution plan information for a-statement-at-a-time without having to run the statement. This is extremely useful in analyzing individual problem queries, especially if the queries are long-running queries. Why run a query and wait for the execution plan output via SQL TRACE or tkprof when you could have it immediately by using EXPLAIN PLAN? Hence, Oracle also supplies this immensely useful utility.

How do you use EXPLAIN PLAN? First, run the script to create the PLAN_TABLE that stores the EXPLAIN PLAN output. This is usually $ORACLE_HOME/rdbms<version>/admin/utxlplan.sql on UNIX, although the directories and filename might change from platform to platform. The location is similar on NT. After you run this script, it should have created the PLAN_TABLE under your schema (assuming you have the proper privileges).

Second, run EXPLAIN PLAN for the statement on which you want to generate the execution plan information, such as with the following query:

```
SQL>    EXPLAIN PLAN
        2> SET STATEMENT_ID='STMT_1'
        3> FOR
        4> SELECT EMPLOYEE_ID
        5> FROM EMPLOYEES
        6> WHERE EMPLOYEE_ID=243218;
```

Use the following SELECT statement from the PLAN_TABLE to get the output you need:

```
SQL>    SELECT OPERATION, OPTIONS, OBJECT_NAME, ID, PARENT_ID, POSITION
        2> FROM PLAN_TABLE
        3> WHERE STATEMENT_ID='STMT_1'
        4> ORDER BY ID;
```

The output then looks like the following:

Operation	Options	OBJECT_NAME	ID	PARENT_ID	Position
SELECT STATEMENT			0		2
TABLE ACCESS	BY ROWID	EMPLOYEES	1	0	1
INDEX	RANGE SCAN	EMPL_IDX	2	1	1

Source: Oracle Corporation

You can also generate a tree-walk, if you prefer. To get an indented, text graph representation, use the following SQL code:

```
SQL>    SELECT LPAD(' ',2*LEVEL-1) || OPERATION || ' ' || OPTIONS || ' ' ||
OBJECT_NAME || ' ' || DECODE(ID, 0, 'COST= '|| POSITION) "QUERY PLAN"
        2> FROM PLAN_TABLE
        3> START WITH ID=0 AND STATEMENT_ID='STMT_1'
        4> CONNECT BY PRIOR ID=PARENT_ID;
```

The output should look like the following:

```
Query Plan
- - - - - - - - - - - - - - - - - - - - - - - - - - - - - - - - - - - - - - -
SELECT STATEMENT         COST=2
    TABLE ACCESS BY ROWID EMPLOYEES
        INDEX RANGE SCAN EMPL_IDX
```

This is frequently more useful for large queries that generate large execution plans. The indentations represent another level down in the execution tree, parent to child. The preceding example contains three levels, and the cost is equal to two. The most important thing, however, is the verification that you expected the optimizer to use the index and it did. If it did not, you would need to review the various possibilities as to why it didn't, such as the number of rows returned, the index not being highly selective, and so forth. Attempt to fix this situation; then rerun EXPLAIN PLAN and see if you fixed the problem. This iterative use of EXPLAIN PLAN in verifying what you think should be going on with the optimizer is the most notable use of EXPLAIN PLAN.

The following summarizes using EXPLAIN PLAN:

1. Use EXPLAIN PLAN in place of SQL TRACE or tkprof when you have only one or a few queries in your application, when you have isolated your major performance problems down to one or a few queries, when your queries mostly run sequentially, or when you simply cannot afford the iterative execution time spent waiting for each SQL TRACE/tkprof run.

2. Run $ORACLE_HOME/rdbms<version>/admin/utxlplan.sql.

3. Use EXPLAIN PLAN for your current query.

4. Select text or tree output from the resulting PLAN_TABLE.

5. Interpret the results. Verify your expectations of the optimizer's behavior.

6. Tune the query as indicated. This often means rewriting it.

7. Go back to Step 3 and repeat until you are satisfied with Step 5.

IDENTIFYING TYPICAL PROBLEMS

The root of most application-tuning problems is improper index usage. In the first section, you'll take a look at some of the rules for proper index usage. In the second section, you'll consider typical application problems, those directly and indirectly related to indexing, as well as some unrelated to indexing.

THE PROPER USE OF INDEXES

Typically, most application-tuning problems occur when deciding whether to use indexes. Over time, indexes have been both underused and overused. My experience has shown both extremes among DBAs of varying expertise. The best thing you can say about indexing is that you must use it correctly. The following is a list of tips for using indexes properly:

- Index columns frequently used in WHERE clauses.
- Index columns frequently used to join tables.
- Index columns with high selectivity (near 1).
- Use bitmapped indexes for columns with low selectivity (near 0).

In addition to the preceding tips, you can do several more things to make your database more efficient through the use of indexes.

For example, use hash indexes for columns with high selectivity (near 1) *and* that are nearly always accessed through *point* queries—also known as *exact match* queries. These are queries with equality comparisons, such as WHERE *x* = *y* or WHERE *s* = 'abc' Use regular (B*Tree) indexes for almost all other columns, which tend to be accessed with a substantial percentage of *range* (search) queries, bounded or unbounded. These are queries with inequality comparisons, such as WHERE *x* > *y* or WHERE *s* LIKE *c*%.

Don't index columns that must be updated frequently. Also, try to refrain from indexing any columns on tables with high insert and delete activity. Either of these cases causes continual reorganization of the B*Tree structure and eventually, poor performance due to index fragmentation. Primary and foreign keys are exceptions.

Index primary and foreign keys. Oracle creates a unique index on defined primary keys whether you create one or not. However, the Oracle default is to not create an index on a foreign key, unless you explicitly do it with a CREATE or ALTER command. Do so because this enhances performance by not locking the parent table when the child tables are being accessed through DML.

Add additional columns to form composite indexes when sensible. This takes advantage of the optimizer's preference for index coverage that was discussed earlier. Oracle, unlike Sybase for example, uses a more restricted form of index coverage. Oracle imposes the restriction so that columns can be retrieved from the index only if they form a leading column of that (composite) index. Suppose a table has a composite index on columns *a+b+c*. The optimizer would use the index for a WHERE clause by using *a*, *a+b*, or *a+b+c*, but not *b*, *c*, *b+c*, nor *a+c*. For Oracle, index coverage can only occur for left-hand ordered subsets (prefixes) of the composite index.

Don't index columns that are nearly always used in WHERE clauses with functions or operators (except for MIN or MAX). The optimizer will not use the index in this case. Alternatively, create a derived column or rewrite the query, using hints or tricks to bypass this behavior. Use EXPLAIN PLAN to verify your results.

Don't index columns that are primarily used for negative or NULL comparisons. The Oracle optimizer will not use indexes based on the following comparison operations in WHERE clauses:

- IS NULL

- IS NOT NULL

- !=

Alternatively, rewrite the query in the positive vein using the = or IN operators. If using NULL comparisons, you might need to consider using defaults.

Be wary of using indexing with views and complex subqueries. It is difficult to predict what will occur given the various layers of these types of statements. You must use EXPLAIN PLAN over and over to be sure of what these queries are doing. If you cannot get your queries to behave as you need, consider rewriting them by collapsing the subqueries into one larger query or breaking them apart into many, sequential subqueries. Also, consider abandoning the views or possibly materializing them.

Finally, don't forget to index *appropriately* (see the previous steps), and don't index for the sake of indexing. In my experience, I have seen databases with tables having indexes on nothing, and I have seen databases with tables having indexes on everything. Indexes on nothing are typically never a good thing because you should always have a primary key index. Indexes on everything are typically not beneficial either because quite often this is symptomatic of either a poor requirements analysis, poor database design, or poor application design.

Now that the major indexing guidelines have been covered, you can go over some of the more typical problems found in application tuning.

TYPICAL PROBLEMS IN APPLICATION TUNING

Almost all the typical problems in application tuning deal with some form of inefficient SQL coding or inappropriate use of indexes. This section discusses several of these problems.

One problem that can appear is known as the *index coverage anomaly*. An interesting thing about index coverage can occur. If, as it turns out, the number of rows returned by this query is some large number, as might be with a low selectivity index, then a full-table scan would be more efficient. However, if ANALYZE has not been run, the optimizer resorts to rule-based optimization and chooses the index access path over the full-table scan. Unless the DBA keeps statistics up-to-date, the optimizer might choose poorer access paths through no fault of its own.

Another problem that can occur is known as the *unnecessary multipass* or *multiloop*. Look at the following queries:

```
SQL> SELECT A FROM T WHERE A > 9;

SQL> SELECT B/A FROM T WHERE B < 3 AND A > 9;
```

Clearly, this could be done in one pass through table T:

```
SQL> SELECT A , B/A FROM T WHERE B < 3 AND A > 9;
```

Using unnecessary functions or NULL comparisons is another possible difficulty. As already discussed regarding the proper use of indexes, the optimizer will not use the index in these cases, so don't do something like the following:

```
SQL> SELECT A FROM T WHERE X < MAX(X);
```

As covered earlier, you want to use literals and bound this range search to something like the following:

```
SQL> SELECT A FROM T WHERE X >= 0 AND X < 999999;
```

Also, if possible, convert NULL enabled columns to a default basis:

Use

```
SQL> SELECT A FROM T WHERE X > 0;
```

instead of

```
SQL> SELECT A FROM T WHERE X != 0;
```

or

```
SQL> SELECT A FROM T WHERE X IS NOT NULL;
```

because neither of the two latter statements uses an index on the X column, if that was what was intended.

Don't forget to index foreign keys. This causes the child table to lock the parent table when the child table is being inserted, updated, or deleted, and vice versa. If you do index all your foreign keys, an update to the child does *not* lock the parent and an update to the parent only acquires a row-level lock as necessary.

Don't select information from a table when it could be somehow otherwise derived. One cardinal application-programming rule in dealing with databases is the following:

PART

IV

CH

17

> **Note**
>
> Trading off computation for storage is almost always a good thing in a database application.

This is true because most database applications tend to be I/O bound. Compression is an example of such a benefit. As another example, suppose you are computing sales taxes based on a single, flat tax rate (or even a few levels of tax rates). The taxes table will likely be a mostly static lookup table, the rate being usually constant within a given tax period (for example, one year). The following example shows how to use a function rather than to access a stored, derived column unnecessarily.

Don't use the following:

```
SQL> SELECT (P.COST + (P.COST * T.RATE)) "COST WITH TAX"
  2> FROM PRICES P, TAXES T
  3>  WHERE P.PART_ID = T.PART_ID
```

Instead, use something like this:

```
SQL> SELECT (COST * 1.06) "COST WITH TAX"
  2> FROM PRICES;
```

This says something about the original design in that you might not have needed the TAXES table. However, putting that issue aside, you certainly don't need to access the tax rate column (RATE) to be able to apply that multiplier. This is especially true because you are relying on a constant (a simple, hard-coded, literal replacement). This only works well if the developers have sufficient domain (business) knowledge and if the amount of knowledge is relatively small and well known by all developers. In any case, this example shows how a simple function can replace a table access. Please be aware, however, that this technique of hard-coding is considered poor programming design, but that your aim is better application performance. Often, these two are at crossroads, and this last example is no exception. You must decide which of all your goals is most important for you to achieve.

Don't trigger unnecessary full-table scans and cause the cumulative percentage problem. Why scan a table when you don't need to? Easier said than done. You must generally be on the lookout for queries that might launch a full-table scan, in other words, queries that don't use an index as intended or somehow cause a full-table scan in another way. Also, don't forget about the 5 percent rule. If the optimizer expects more than 5 percent (in version 7.x and above) to be returned from a query, it resorts to a full-table scan. This can occur when multiple WHERE conditions combine to sum up past that amount with something like the following:

```
SQL> SELECT A FROM T WHERE X = 1 AND Y = 2 AND Z = 3;
```

If statistics show X = 1 having 3 percent, Y = 2 having 2 percent, and Z = 3 having 2 percent, the optimizer will see the cumulative percentage as 7 percent and opt for the full-table scan. If desired, you can break these two queries apart, especially for large tables, and get better performance with the same results:

```
SQL> SELECT A FROM T WHERE X = 1;
SQL> SELECT A FROM T WHERE Y = 2 AND Z = 3;
```

The optimizer uses the indexes on X, Y, and Z because the first query shows only 3 percent and the second, only 4 percent.

Use DISTINCT, ORDER BY, and UNION carefully. These operations cause the creation of temporary tables and add the additional overhead of sorting on-the-fly. As a DBA, you can tolerate few of these concurrently, unless you have infinite resources. Think of many of these occurring at once as having the same performance drain incurred from issuing many CREATE INDEX statements at once. If you must use DISTINCT, use it infrequently, and store the output for future use. If you must use ORDER BY, try to have an index on that column. If you must use UNION, use UNION ALL (which does not eliminate duplicates). This latter solution works in most cases, as long as you have all your primary keys defined and enabled.

Note

In any application tuning, consider translated SQL statements because the application front end might be written in other SQL. ODBC driver translations do not always produce an optimized query for many reasons. Just watch for such occurrences and set the ODBC trace on so you see the translated SQL that might be preventing the use of an index.

REWRITING QUERIES

Well, you've already rewritten numerous queries in the last and previous sections. Now, concentrate on rewriting queries with a few examples of how you can really tune SQL to high efficiency. Aside from the many techniques discussed already, two of the best are the following:

- Using set operators
- Using Boolean conversions

The field of rewriting queries is highly mathematical, yet eminently practical. When you hear of rewriting queries, it means rewriting them to speed them up, rather than to fix them. The latter is more along the lines of getting it right the first time and maintenance programming. What you're interested in here is raw speed, often at the expense of readability and maintainability. Hence, some organizational choices are to be made before venturing into this area.

USING SET OPERATORS

You've already seen that UNION can be a performance hit. What you should be more interested in is using MINUS or INTERSECT. These can actually help performance. Observe the following query:

```
SQL> SELECT ACCOUNT_ID
   2> FROM JOBS_COMPLETED
   3> WHERE ACCOUNTS_ID NOT IN (ACCOUNTS_PAID);
```

It can be rewritten as follows:

```
SQL> SELECT ACCOUNT_ID FROM JOBS_COMPLETED
   2> MINUS
   3> SELECT ACCOUNT_ID FROM ACCOUNTS_PAID;
```

Both of these queries give the same functional result: They return those accounts that have their jobs completed but have *not* been fully paid. However, using EXPLAIN PLAN will likely reveal that the total logical reads for the first are much higher than for the second. In Oracle, at least, using the MINUS operator is very efficient.

INTERSECT is like the complement of MINUS, except that MINUS is an asymmetrical (one-way) operator, and INTERSECT is a symmetrical (two-way) operator. That is, a symmetrical operator works the same on both directions. UNION is symmetrical. If you reversed which table you selected from using MINUS in the previous example, you would get a different answer. You would get all the accounts that have been paid but have *not* had their jobs completed (which might or might not be a typical business practice). For another example, to find all accounts that have had their jobs completed *and* have been fully paid, use the following:

```
SQL> SELECT ACCOUNT_ID FROM JOBS_COMPLETED
   2> INTERSECT
   3> SELECT ACCOUNT_ID FROM ACCOUNTS_PAID;
```

USING BOOLEAN CONVERSIONS

A Boolean expression is one that evaluates to TRUE or FALSE. The WHERE clause of a SQL statement is an example of a Boolean expression. You can take advantage of this fact by coming up with functions that convert WHERE clauses (Boolean expressions) to numeric values, such as 1 for TRUE and 0 for FALSE. How can this help? Consider the following queries to obtain varying tax rates given four types of marital status (S=Single, M=Married, D=Divorced, and W=Widowed):

```
SQL> SELECT SINGLE_TAX "TAX" FROM TAXES WHERE STATUS='S';
SQL> SELECT MARRIED_TAX "TAX" FROM TAXES WHERE STATUS='M';
SQL> SELECT DIVORCED_TAX "TAX" FROM TAXES WHERE STATUS='D';
SQL> SELECT WIDOWED_TAX "TAX" FROM TAXES WHERE STATUS='W';
```

Again, putting aside the issue of database design because this *might* be a poorly designed table, you can see that you must make four full-table scans of the TAXES table to get the information you need. This is a good example because you're dealing with more than two distinct values. Can you do better? First, you need a Boolean conversion. In other words, you need a function to return SINGLE_TAX when STATUS='S', MARRIED_TAX when STATUS='M', and so forth. Oracle provides just such a function, DECODE. If you carefully walk through the following query, you see that it fully replaces the previous four queries, provides the same functional result, and yet *requires only one table scan*.

```
SQL> SELECT DECODE(STATUS, 'S', 1, 0)*SINGLE_TAX +
  2>     DECODE(STATUS, 'M', 1, 0)*MARRIED_TAX +
  3>     DECODE(STATUS, 'D', 1, 0)*DIVORCED_TAX +
  4>     DECODE(STATUS, 'W', 1, 0)*WIDOWED_TAX
  5>     "TAX"
  6> FROM TAXES;
```

This is an incredible efficiency gain. However, as you can tell, the readability and maintainability suffer. In addition, using the DECODE function might not always work. You might have to use other contrived functions. In this case, what you needed was an associative array, and DECODE just happened to provide that type of functionality. Obviously, the hard work is reviewing at the original query to come up with a function that gives you an equivalent answer.

INTRODUCING NEW INDEX FEATURES FOR ORACLE8

A few new features have been added to Oracle8 regarding indexing that will no doubt be useful for future application development. These are discussed in the remainder of this chapter.

USING INDEX PARTITIONING

Oracle8 enables you to *partition*, or physically divide, indexes along a partition key. This means partitioning an index along the same columns that make up the index. Partitions can be stored on separate tablespaces with separate storage parameters. Hence, partitions are "subtables". The following is an example:

```
SQL8>  CREATE INDEX EMPL_IDX ON EMPLOYEES(EMPLOYEE_ID)
    2> PARTITION BY RANGE (EMPLOYEE_ID)
    3> (PARTITION ip1 VALUES LESS THAN (499999)
    4> TABLESPACE empl_idx1,
    5> PARTITION ip2 VALUES LESS THAN (1000000)
    6> TABLESPACE empl_idx2);
```

USING EQUI-PARTITIONED, LOCAL INDEXES

In Oracle8, if you create an index as LOCAL, Oracle automatically *equi-partitions* it. That is, it uses the same partition key, the same number of partitions, and the same partition boundaries as the partitioned table it references. A *local* index is one in which all the index keys in one partition point to all the data in one table partition. There is a one-to-one mapping. A *global* index is one in which this does not hold true. This ensures that a table and its index are equi-partitioned. Aside from higher availability similar to striping, equi-partitioning with a local index enables the optimizer to be partition-aware. The following is an example:

```
SQL8>  CREATE INDEX EMPL_IDX ON EMPLOYEES(EMPLOYEE_ID)
    2> LOCAL
    3> (PARTITION ip1 TABLESPACE empl_idx1,
    4> PARTITION ip2 TABLESPACE empl_idx2);
```

USING A PARTITION-AWARE OPTIMIZER

As just mentioned, if you create equi-partitioned, local indexes, the optimizer can generate query plans by using partition knowledge. Therefore, it can parallelize some operations.

USING INDEX-ONLY TABLES

In Oracle8, you can now create an *index-only* table. This is also known as an *in-place index*. Essentially, the table is physically sorted, rather than logically sorted with a B*Tree. This has the obvious performance benefit of removing the logical reads from the B*Tree to the table because the data and the index are one and the same. Again, you would normally use the primary key as the indexing column. An example is as follows:

```
SQL8>  CREATE TABLE EMPLOYEES
    2> (EMPLOYEE_ID NUMBER(6) CONSTRAINT empl_pk PRIMARY KEY,
    3> <column, column, ...>)
    4> ORGANIZATION INDEX TABLESPACE empl_dat1;
```

The ORGANIZATION INDEX clause tells Oracle8 this is an index-only table.

USING REVERSE KEY INDEXES

A *Reverse key* index is one in which the order of the individual column bytes is reversed (not the column order). Reverse key indexes have proven useful in improving Oracle Parallel Server (OPS) performance. Use the REVERSE keyword on CREATE INDEX to create one for OPS usage.

PART

IV

CH

17

TUNING MEMORY

In this chapter

In Oracle, *tuning memory* usually means tuning the Shared Global Area (SGA). This includes monitoring and tuning the shared pool (the data dictionary and library caches) and the database buffer cache. Tuning memory is closely intertwined with tuning the application and tuning I/O, because one of the primary goals in tuning—reducing or eliminating contention—must involve all aspects of the tuning process. For example, this book covers tuning rollback segments and redo logs under tuning I/O, yet both have memory components that must be tuned, such as the rollback buffer area and the redo log buffer. However, because the major emphasis with each is I/O contention, they are covered under tuning I/O. You must also tune other memory-based structures such as locks and latches, and some of those are covered in this chapter. Sorting is another memory issue. When you sort anything, whether it is as a result of a CREATE INDEX, an ORDER BY, a join, or so forth, the ideal situation is to do as much as possible in memory and then resort to disk only as necessary. Finally, as a DBA, you must be an active participant in the integration with and tuning of the operating system (OS).

Unless it comprises part of a specialized database machine, any RDBMS, Oracle included, must request memory from the OS. The OS handles most of the memory management at the lower level, such as shared memory, for the RDBMS. Depending on the RDBMS, it can handle some more of the higher-level functions, such as locking. As examples, consider Sybase and Oracle with regard to memory management. Sybase opts for using a large shared memory segment and managing itself through low-level OS system calls. Oracle chooses this same approach. Sybase natively handles its own locking and interprocess communications, within its multithreaded process. Oracle, on the other hand, manages some of its locking and interprocess communications internally, yet also relies on the OS to do some of the work. These methods of handling memory are a direct result of the architecture of the RDBMS. In either case, the RDBMS, in and of itself a micro-operating system, must integrate closely with the OS for it to have its resource requests handled efficiently. This holds true not only for memory, but for all resources, including I/O. There are few exceptions. Raw disk space in UNIX is one notable exception (see Appendix A, "Oracle on Solaris"). For now, turn your attention to actually collecting data and diagnosing memory problems.

UTLBSTAT/UTLESTAT

As you learned in Chapter 16, "Performance Tuning Fundamentals," the UTLBSTAT and UTLESTAT scripts lay the foundation for all your diagnostic work. You often supplement these with manual queries or customized scripts of the V$ dynamic performance views, such as V$SYSSTAT, but this is precisely where (along with the X$ tables) these two scripts gather their information in the first place. By using these from one job to the next, you help ensure a common denominator to communicate with other Oracle DBAs and consultants regarding the performance of a particular system.

As you've seen, these scripts are usually found in the $ORACLE_HOME/rdbms<version>/admin subdirectory. Before you actually use them, set TIMED_STATISTICS=TRUE in your init.ora parameter file or ALTER SESSION SET TIMED STATISTICS=TRUE at your session level. Log in to svrgmrl (server manager line mode, versions 7.1 and later). Next, CONNECT / AS SYSDBA (or CONNECT INTERNAL). Then, run utlbstat.sql.

This creates your beginning collection tables and views (in the SYS schema); these objects have names with BEGIN in them. The beginning statistics are then selected and stored there. Next, run your application, if it is not already running. Your goal as a DBA is to capture your system statistics during its peak activity. When the peak has tapered, or after some reasonable period of time, run utlestat.sql. This interval of time need not be overly long, but should be sufficient. For example, if your peak load activity lasts 2 hours (120 minutes) each day, sample at least 20% of this, or about 24 minutes, preferably toward the middle of the interval. (Also, remember, your database must remain up at all times during this sample run. This should not be a problem, however, because you are trying to sample from a live, peak-loaded, production database, and you hope the database stays up anyway!) This creates your ending and differences collection tables and views. The ending objects have names with END in them. The ending statistics are then selected and stored there. The differences between the beginning and ending statistics (the *deltas*) are stored in the differences tables. Finally, utlestat.sql selects from the differences objects, formats the data, and stores the information in the file report.txt. Then, the hard work begins—interpretation.

INTERPRETING RESULTS

No two consultants agree on every last detail when it comes to tuning Oracle, but they *should* agree on most things. It has often been said that performance tuning is part science, part art. I generally agree with this assessment, but try not to turn this type of work into a priesthood. In other words, interpretation is the part that is mostly art, because that part requires human beings to make value judgments on the relative strengths and weaknesses of a system.

Interpretation can be, and has been, semi- or fully automated, using sophisticated parsers and programs. However, the undeniable reality is that despite how programmed this process can be, it nevertheless remains partly subjective. Although it can be programmed, do the same two tuners or programmers use the same rules or guidelines as to what level of performance is "good" or "bad"? Most assuredly not. Furthermore, this considers only general purpose tuning, if there is such a beast. When you bring to bear the problem of application specifics, these so-called fully automatic, performance-tuning software programs quickly lose their usefulness.

Now I'll sum up how to use UTLBSTAT/UTLESTAT properly and tune your database system:

1. Set TIMED STATISTICS=TRUE either at the instance or session level.
2. Log in to svrmgrl (server manager line mode) and CONNECT / AS SYSDBA (or CONNECT INTERNAL).
3. Run $ORACLE_HOME/rdbms<version>/admin/utlbstat.sql at the beginning of your monitoring period, which should be some duration of normal, peak activity.
4. Run $ORACLE_HOME/rdbms<version>/admin/utlestat.sql at the end of your monitoring period.
5. Interpret your results in report.txt by using reasonable guidelines (which I'll cover soon).

6. Make recommended changes or fixes (if any); this could be anything from changing an `init.ora` parameter to reorganizing your physical design.

7. Repeat process beginning with step 3 until satisfied with step 5.

Reviewing the Report File

The file `report.txt` contains a large variety of information to help you tune the application, memory, and I/O. At the high level, it has statistics on the shared pool (the data dictionary and library caches), the database buffer cache, per transaction/login data, per tablespace/file I/O, and wait events. You can use all these statistics or some of them.

Tip #12	Make sure the individual statistics you use are relevant to your application. In the final analysis, your users are the true test of whether your application's performance is "good."

Some statistics offer different views on the performance of the same item and should agree. When they don't agree, interpretation becomes more subjective and application-specific. For example, suppose you have three statistics that report the performance in different ways about the library cache. Furthermore, what if two out of three show "good" performance according to accepted guidelines, but the remaining one shows "poor" performance. Does this mean your application's performance is good? It truly depends on what type of application you have and what each statistic means in relation to it. For example, if the two statistics showing good performance mean more to a batch system, and you have an OLTP system, those particular measures are misleading.

Tuning the Shared Pool

As you learned in Chapter 6, "The Oracle Instance Architecture," the shared pool consists largely of two main structures:

- The *data dictionary cache*
- The *library cache*

The areas that store parsed SQL statements for later reuse are the shared SQL areas. The private SQL areas are those areas associated with cursor durations within applications. Tuning the shared pool is where tuning memory and tuning the application overlap considerably. This chapter augments the previous chapter (Chapter 17, "Application Tuning")

The shared pool is a cache structure. Like all other cache structures, it is a memory-resident data structure.

A *cache* is a special type of buffer. Whereas a buffer is a "dumb" mechanism, simply providing temporary storage for data on its way between fast memory and slow disk, a cache is a "smart" mechanism, retaining memory as to whether it has that information, or part of it, so that it can avoid as many unnecessary trips to the disk as possible. When an I/O request is made, the cache checks to see whether it already has it in memory. If it does, it answers the request itself, returning the requested data. This is known as a *hit*. If it does not, a trip to the disk is warranted. This is known as a *miss*.

For almost all cache mechanisms, the guideline for effective performance is to have a 90%+ *hit ratio*, which can be defined as $100 \times (1.00 - (\text{sum(misses)} / \text{sum(requests)}))$, where sum(requests) = sum(misses) + sum(hits). For example, if your cache has 4 misses and 46 hits, your hit ratio is $100 \times (1.00 - (4/50)) = 100 \times (1.00 - (.08))$, or 92%, which is very good. Caches are generally managed by a Least Recently Used (LRU) algorithm, which ensures that, at any given time, the Most Recently Used (MRU) data is held in cache, and the LRU data is aged out."

When Oracle parses a SQL statement, it allocates a SQL area in the *library cache* for it by applying a mathematical formula to the alphanumeric text of the SQL statement and using the result to store (and later find) it in the cache. In other words, it uses a *hash function*. As you might expect, in order for a statement to be reused by another, the statements must be identical. For example, the following are not identical in the eyes of Oracle when storing them in the library cache:

```
SELECT * FROM EMPLOYEES;
SELECT      * FROM EMPLOYEES;
SELECT * FROM employees;
```

Although to you and me, they are functionally identical, they are not hash-identical. In order for them to be hash-identical, there can be no white space (spaces, tabs, indents, or nonprintable control characters) or differences in case. Furthermore, the following two statements cannot reuse the same hashed SQL area parse plan:

```
SELECT * FROM EMPLOYEES WHERE EMPLOYEE_ID=927354;
SELECT * FROM EMPLOYEES WHERE EMPLOYEE_ID=746293;
```

PART

IV

CH

18

This is true because of the use of the literals 927354 and 746293 in the WHERE clause. Because the input of the alphanumeric statement in the hash function is different, they cannot possibly hash to the same library cache location. How to win? Well, except for DSS as discussed earlier, you should use bind variables. *Bind variables* enable SQL statements to be general enough to be reused and yet have parametric values rather than constants:

```
SELECT * FROM EMPLOYEES WHERE EMPLOYEE_ID=:EMPID;
```

This type of statement can be reused and is typically found in embedded SQL application code, where :EMPID is the bind variable—in this case, a host 3GL variable, such as a C integer. The value of the C variable can now take on 927354, 746293, and so forth, and yet be reused in the library cache.

GUIDELINES FOR IMPROVING THE PERFORMANCE OF THE LIBRARY CACHE

Minimize unnecessary parse calls from within applications. Parsing is CPU-intensive. Because caching and buffering are involved, it is also memory intensive as a by-product. Cursor opening and closing should be carefully placed in the application to facilitate reuse of the private SQL areas for multiple SQL statements. The DBA might have to increase the init.ora parameter OPEN_CURSORS as necessary to allow for the sufficient allocation of cursor space (private SQL areas). To determine whether your application might be inefficient in this regard, run SQL TRACE/TKRPOF (Chapter 17) and examine whether the count column for Parse is near the value for Execute (or Fetch). If so, the application is then reparsing for almost every execute (or fetch).

Maximize reuse of those statements that must be parsed. As mentioned, SQL statements must be identical to be reused. One way to help do this is to adopt a standard way of coding that all application developers must follow, such as "always code SQL statements in uppercase." You could go one step farther and have a program pass through all your development code and enforce such a thing, in case developer compliance was poor. Furthermore, except for DSS applications, use bind variables when appropriate. These almost always make sense because they generalize your application, as opposed to having literal values hard-coded. This pays for itself in maintainability, if not library cache reuse.

Pin frequently used program objects in memory. In Oracle, a cursor, trigger, procedure, or package can be held in memory using a special shared pool package, DBMS_SHARED_POOL. To create this package, run the $ORACLE_HOME/rdbms<version>/admin/dbmspool.sql script. You might also need to run $ORACLE_HOME/rdbms<version>/admin/prvtpool.sql. Check the version on your platform to see whether this is the case. To pin a program object in memory, use the following:

```
SQL> EXECUTE DBMS_SHARED_POOL.KEEP('<object_name>');
```

To unpin it:

```
SQL> EXECUTE DBMS_SHARED_POOL.UNKEEP('<object_name>');
```

To determine whether the object was successfully pinned:

```
SQL> SELECT SUBSTR(NAME,1,25), KEPT FROM V$DB_OBJECT_CACHE;
```

If the object was pinned, the KEPT column has a YES value; otherwise, it says NO.

Minimize fragmentation in the library cache. Your application suffers ORA-04031 errors (not enough contiguous free space) unless you guard against fragmentation. One way is to pin frequently used large objects in memory. For less frequently used objects, which might be large, reserve some space. You can do this by setting the init.ora parameters SHARED_POOL_RESERVED_SIZE and SHARED_POOL_RESERVED_MIN_ALLOC. You set aside a shared pool "reserved area" for your large objects. Essentially, you guarantee that your necessary large objects will find space. Set SHARED_POOL_RESERVED_SIZE to what would be the maximum number of bytes of your largest objects simultaneously loaded. Set SHARED_POOL_RESERVED_MIN_ALLOC to the minimum number of bytes an object can be in order to use your reserved area specified by SHARED_POOL_RESERVED_SIZE. To determine the size of a particular object you want to include in your reserved area, use the following:

```
SQL> SELECT SUBSTR(NAME,1,25) "NAME", SHARABLE_MEM
    2> FROM V$DB_OBJECT_CACHE
    2> WHERE NAME='<object_name>';
```

Also, to determine the size you need to set SHARED_POOL_RESERVED_SIZE to, use this:

```
SQL> SELECT SUM(SHARABLE_MEM)
  2> FROM V$DB_OBJECT_CACHE
  3> WHERE SHARABLE_MEM >= <SHARED_POOL_RESERVED_MIN_ALLOC>;
```

Hence, to execute the previous query, you must have some rough idea as to what classifies, at a minimum, as a "large object." So, you want to take the following steps:

1. Set SHARED_POOL_RESERVED_MIN_ALLOC to your specification.

2. Set SHARED_POOL_RESERVED_SIZE to the output of the last query, plus some additional percentage (for example, 10%).

Also, you can set CURSOR_SPACE_FOR_TIME to TRUE to prevent SQL areas associated with cursors from aging out of the library cache before they have been closed by a program.

Caution

Do not change CURSOR_SPACE_FOR_TIME from its default value of FALSE if any of the following apply to your situation:

- RELOADS in V$LIBRARY_CACHE always shows a 0 value.
- You are using Oracle Forms or SQL*Forms.
- You use any dynamic SQL.

PART

IV

CH

18

Aside from the many application-based memory issues and tuning methods that you have just learned, you can look at what utlbstat.sql/utlestat.sql (report.txt) offers. A sample of report.txt is included on the CD-ROM. In particular, you can look at the first section in report.txt, Library cache statistics. Specifically, ensure that the GETHITRATIO for the SQL AREA LIBRARY is in the 90s, preferably the high 90s. If you didn't run utlbstat.sql/utlestat.sql, you can also use the following:

```
SQL> SELECT GETHITRATIO
  2> FROM V$LIBRARYCACHE
  3> WHERE NAMESPACE='SQL AREA';
```

However, this method is a running average since the last instance startup and includes ramp-up times. *Ramp-up* is the initialization process any system goes through when it first starts up. The statistics gathered during this period are misleading and not useful because they largely reflect the physical reads necessary to fill all the various Oracle buffers and caches. Hence, sometimes this is also called *caching up*. As you learned earlier, you want to sample statistics during your peak load times. When a system is running at peak activity for some time, that system is said to be *in equilibrium*. If you run utlbstat.sql after peak activity has been reached and then run utlestat.sql just before peak activity ceases, you have a valid sample. Hence, selecting from the V$ dynamic performance views can be misleading, especially if you sample them early in the instance lifetime. The longer the instance remains up, the better the V$ views' statistics are because the peak and normal activities outweigh the initial startup period more and more. To be fair, the same can be said of utlbstat.sql/utlestat.sql.

If the GETHITRATIO is less than .90, apply the guidelines for improving the performance of the library cache. This typically means application code can be rewritten more efficiently.

Again, from the first section of report.txt, the Library cache statistics, calculate the RELOADS/PINS ratio for the SQL AREA LIBRARY.

If the RELOADS/PINS ratio is greater than .01, increase the size (in bytes) of the *total* shared pool, by setting the init.ora parameter, SHARED_POOL_SIZE. Remember, this sets the entire shared pool, including not just the library cache but also the data dictionary cache.

From the Latch statistics section of report.txt, ensure that the HIT_RATIO for LATCH_NAME = 'library cache' is in the high 90s. Other measures for measuring high latch contention, which can be an indication of poor library cache (and total shared pool) performance, are the following:

From the System wide wait events section of report.txt, check the (wait) Count column for Event Name = 'latch free'.

Also run the following query:

```
SQL> SELECT COUNT(*) "LIBRARY_LATCH_WAITS"
  2> FROM V$SESSION_WAIT W, V$LATCH L
  3> WHERE W.WAIT_TIME = 0
  4> AND W.EVENT='latch free'
  5> AND W.P2 = L.LATCH#
  6> AND L.NAME LIKE 'library%';
```

If any of the following are true, apply the guidelines for improving the performance of the library cache, and if necessary, increase the SHARED_POOL_SIZE setting:

- The HIT_RATIO for LATCH_NAME = 'library cache' is < .98
- The (wait) Count for Event Name='latch free' is > 10
- The LIBRARY_LATCH_WAITS is > 2

The *data dictionary cache* portion of the shared pool, as you might expect, holds the caching structure for the Oracle data dictionary. The SHARED_POOL_SIZE parameter is the only way to indirectly size the data dictionary cache itself. The following are the objects held in the SYS and SYSTEM schemes (the SYSTEM tablespace):

- X$ tables
- V$ views
- DBA_ views
- User_ views

Sizing, diagnosing, and tuning the library cache so that it performs well should have the side effect of helping the performance of the data dictionary cache because they both coexist in the shared pool. They are not separately configurable.

There are a couple of ways to measure data dictionary cache performance. One is to query the V$ROWCACHE view:

```
SQL> SELECT SUM(GETMISSES)/SUM(GETS) "DC_MISS_RATIO"
    2> FROM V$ROWCACHE;
```

The other way is to use the data dictionary section of report.txt. Compute the sum of all the GET_MISS and divide that by the sum of all the GET_REQS to get a similar DC_MISS_RATIO.

If either of these two methods yield a DC_MISS_RATIO > .15, increase the SHARED_POOL_SIZE (and retest).

MULTITHREADED SERVER ISSUES

You should also briefly consider the MultiThreaded Server (MTS) and the allocation of server memory versus client (user) memory. Just as there is an SGA, there is a User Global Area (UGA), which contains user session information, sort areas, and private SQL areas. Normally, the default Oracle RDBMS instance (referred to as the *dedicated server*) results in a one-to-one mapping of user processes to server processes. With MTS, the UGA is moved up into the shared pool. The remaining process-specific memory is retained in the Process Global Area (PGA) and holds information that cannot be shared. In this way, the total amount of memory required in using MTS is not really more than the dedicated server, just redistributed. However, you have to increase SHARED_POOL_SIZE. To help size the UGA that is relocated to the SGA, run the following query:

PART

IV

CH

18

```
SQL> SELECT SUM(VALUE)
    2> FROM V$SESSTAT SE, V$STATNAME SN
    3> WHERE SN.NAME = 'max session memory'
    4> AND SE.STATISTIC# = SN.STATISTIC#;
```

This yields the maximum amount of UGA session memory used since instance startup. You might want to sample this over time and take the maximum of the maximums. Then increase SHARED_POOL_SIZE by this amount.

> **Note**
>
> In Oracle8, use 'session uga memory max' for the previous query.

With MTS, you have some control over the distribution of server versus user memory. Two init.ora parameters that affect user memory are

- SESSION_CACHED_CURSORS
- CLOSE_CACHED_OPEN_CURSORS

If desired, set SESSION_CACHED_CURSORS to your expected maximum number of session cursors to be cached in the users' memory area. As long as reparsing is kept low, this helps offload server memory requirements at the expense of increasing user memory. Optionally, set this parameter when statements are *frequently* reused.

The default setting for CLOSE_CACHED_OPEN_CURSORS is FALSE, meaning that cursors are not closed on COMMIT. Optionally, set this to TRUE if most SQL statements are *rarely* reused.

Caution

Make sure your settings for CURSOR_SPACE_FOR_TIME and CLOSE_CACHE_OPEN_CURSORS do not conflict. For example, setting both to TRUE or both to FALSE seems to be the best approach.

Next, turn your attention to the database buffer cache.

Tuning the Database Buffer Cache

Perhaps the single most important tuning change you can make to improve the performance of your Oracle system is to properly set the size of your database buffer cache. The *database buffer cache* is the cache structure in the SGA and holds copies in memory of the Most Recently Used (MRU) Oracle data blocks. The two parameters that size this area are

- DB_BLOCK_SIZE
- DB_BLOCK_BUFFER

DB_BLOCK_SIZE is the size of an Oracle block. This can range from 2KB (2,048 bytes) up to 64KB (65,536 bytes) on UNIX platforms. For performance, generally the higher the better. If your database has already been created with a relatively small block size (such as the default 2KB), consider rebuilding it if that is feasible for your application. If so, do the following:

1. Shut the instance down.
2. Do a full export of your database (if feasible).
3. Increase DB_BLOCK_SIZE in your init.ora.
4. Start up the instance.
5. Reimport your database as SYS.

If your database is too large to be able to use export/import, ensure you have ASCII files of your table data (select them if necessary, or use a third-party tool). Rerun your DDL create scripts. Use SQL*Loader to reload the tables, in parallel if possible.

DB_BLOCK_BUFFERS is the number of Oracle blocks to be held in memory. Each buffer equals one block. This should be sufficiently high to yield an efficient cache hit ratio, but not so high as to cause operating system paging. The last thing you want is to have your SGA being paged in and out of memory by the OS. Paging is Oracle's primary job when it comes to the DB_BLOCK_BUFFERS, and you don't want the OS paging underneath Oracle. It pages them in on demand. Hence, your database buffer cache, along with the shared pool, should fit comfortably in real (available core) memory, and not be close to it or larger than it. Reasonable sizes are 1/2 to 3/4 of total system memory. For example, on a 1GB UNIX system, you might want to set it so that your SGA takes about 3/4, or 750MB. You must be careful to take into account other

Oracle and non-Oracle application memory requirements, user memory requirements, and the operating system requirements. The size of the database buffer cache is

`DB_BLOCK_BUFFERS x DB_BLOCK_SIZE`

The database buffer cache is somewhat of a misnomer. Recall that a cache is a special type of buffer. Hence, *buffer cache* is actually redundant, not to mention a little confusing. (Maybe Oracle could have called it the database block cache?) In any case, all you really need to understand is that it caches the Oracle blocks. It is different from the shared pool in that it caches data and not programs.

The Oracle RDBMS server *always* reads Oracle blocks into the database buffer cache before passing them on to user processes. A user process, or application, always reads from (and writes to) the database buffer cache. The following are the steps in the buffer management of an I/O request:

1. User selects data (requests block).
2. Server looks in database buffer cache for it.
3. If it finds it (through the hash function) in the LRU list, it returns it.
4. If it doesn't find it, it reads in the block from the datafile on disk and attaches it (using the hash function) to the MRU or LRU end of the LRU list as appropriate.
5. If user does not modify it, it's finished.
6. If user does modify it, DBWR writes the block (dirty buffer) back to its location in the datafile on disk.

Indexes are accessed one block at a time. Full table scans can have multiple blocks read with one request. Set the number of blocks (batch size) by setting

`DB_FILE_MULTIBLOCK_READ_COUNT = <the number of blocks to be read>`

Buffers can be free (clean), dirty, current, or read-consistent (rollback). A *free buffer* is one that has yet to be used since instance startup, or one that has been used and is now available. A *dirty buffer* is one that has been used, but has not been *flushed*, or written out by DBWR on checkpoint. A *current buffer* is one used in service of an INSERT, UPDATE, or DELETE. By their very nature, current buffers more often than not become dirty. *Read-consistent* buffers serve SELECT statements and rollback. Blocks read in service of full table scans are placed at the Least Recently Used (LRU) end of the LRU buffer chain. However, you can cache whole tables on the MRU end of the chain.

How do you tune the database buffer cache? Because memory I/O is several magnitudes faster than disk I/O (nanoseconds versus milliseconds), you want I/O requests to be satisfied by memory as often as possible. Namely, you want blocks to be found frequently (more than 90% of the time) in the database buffer cache, as opposed to having to fetch them from disk. You also want to minimize LRU latch contention. The LRU buffer chain, or list, is locked through latch mechanisms, just like those used throughout the Oracle kernel, and in the library cache in particular. As with any latch approach, you must have enough because latches (also known as *spin locks*) contain no queuing mechanisms as with semaphores.

As mentioned in tuning the library cache, the cache hit ratio for almost any cache structure should be greater than or equal to 90% to be considered good. Again, this is the ratio of hits to requests. In other words, this is the number of times Oracle data blocks satisfy an I/O request, divided by the total number of I/O requests. A hit is when the block is in cache, and a miss is when it is not (and must be read from disk). There are at least two ways to measure the database buffer cache hit ratio. One way is to run the following query:

```
SQL> SELECT 1-(P.VALUE/(D.VALUE+C.VALUE))  "CACHE HIT RATIO"
  2> FROM V$SYSSTAT P, V$SYSSTAT C, V$SYSSTAT D
  3> WHERE P.NAME='physical reads'
  5> AND D.NAME='db block gets'
  4> AND C.NAME='consistent gets';
```

Here 'physical reads' is the number of blocks read from disk, 'db block gets' is the number of blocks read from current copies of blocks in cache, and 'consistent gets' is the number of read-consistent (rollback) copies of blocks in cache. Hence, the database buffer cache hit ratio formula is really

```
1 - (physical reads / logical reads)
```

The number of logical reads equals the number of current copies read plus the number of consistent copies read. The number of physical reads represents the number of misses. The number of logical reads represents the number of requests. From report.txt under the Statistics section, you also can gather the physical reads, db block gets, and consistent gets. Use the same formula to compute the cache hit ratio.

If the database buffer cache hit ratio is less than .90, increase DB_BLOCK_BUFFERS and rerun utlbstat.sql/utlestat.sql. Increasing this parameter, as with most init.ora parameters, requires an instance shutdown and startup. However, it does not cause a major headache, such as changing the DB_BLOCK_SIZE would when the database has been built.

There is a way in Oracle to test the effect of adding more buffers. Why would you want to do this as opposed to simply increasing DB_BLOCK_BUFFERS? It is often the case that you need to add more buffers to your database buffer cache, but don't have enough real memory to support it. Hence, this technique can be used as a justification for purchasing more memory. To do this, shut down the instance and set

```
DB_BLOCK_LRU_EXTENDED_STATISTICS =  <n>
```

where <n> is the number of buffers you want to add.

Then start up the instance again. Let your application run normally for a reasonable amount of time, just as you would for utlbstat.sql/utlestat.sql. The table X$KCBRBH contains the information you need to make a prognosis. Do the following query:

```
SQL> SELECT SUM(COUNT)
  2> FROM X$KCBRBH
  3> WHERE INDEX < <n>;
```

This returns the number of additional cache hits you would gain by adding these <n> buffers. To then determine what your new hypothetical database buffer cache hit ratio would be, add the <n> to the original equation:

```
1 - (physical reads - <n>) / (logical reads)
```

As you can see, this results in a higher cache hit ratio because the numerator being subtracted from 1 is smaller as long as <n> is greater than 0. As an example, suppose from report.txt you have physical reads = 40000, consistent gets = 100000, and db block gets = 30000. Then, your cache hit ratio, before adding any buffers is

```
1 - (40000/(100000+30000) ) = 1 - (40000/130000) = 1 - (.31) = .69
```

which is woefully below .90. Suppose you want to try adding 10,000 more buffers. You set your extended statistics on and queried your X$KCBRBH table, and it indicated that you would gain 30,000 more hits. Your new, hypothetical cache hit ratio (with accompanying improved performance) would then be

```
1- ((40000 - 30000) / (130000)) = 1 - (10000 / 130000) = 1 - (.08) = .91
```

which is a considerable improvement. Of course, this example has well-rounded numbers, but it should be sufficient to emphasize the point that it is very useful when you have run out of core memory and need a justification to purchase more, in particular to bolster the database buffer cache. As might not be immediately apparent, the hardest thing is to determine what number of buffers to add to give you the additional gain in the number of hits you need. I suggest that you try moving up in percentages; first add 10%, then go up or down depending on the result. There is a counterpart way of testing the effect of subtracting "unnecessary" buffers. However, any DBA knows that an unnecessary buffer is a mythical beast, so this book won't cover this technique because it is rarely, if ever, used.

You can consider specific system wait events as other guidelines to help measure the performance of the database buffer cache. You can gather 'buffer busy waits' and 'latch free' from the System wide wait events section of report.txt or from V$SYSTEM_EVENT and V$SESSION_WAIT, as shown earlier in tuning the library cache. Also, examine 'free buffer inspected' from V$SYSSTAT or report.txt. In particular, a latch contention problem can be indicated if any of the following are much greater than 0:

- Buffer busy waits
- Latch free
- Free buffer inspected

The init.ora parameter DB_BLOCK_LRU_LATCHES is set by default to 1/2 the number of CPUs on an SMP machine. If this seems insufficient based on the previous measures, increase it up to twice the number of CPUs.

PART
IV

CH
18

Caution

Don't increase DB_BLOCK_LRU_LATCHES unless you have evidence indicating to do so, and then increment it only in degrees—for example, from 1/2 (# CPUs) to 3/4 (# CPUs) and so forth. If a heavier workload is predicted than was sampled for, you can increase this a little more.

As mentioned, you can counteract the phenomenon of full table scan blocks being placed at the LRU end of the LRU list if you cache whole tables at the MRU end. How do you do this? Either use CREATE TABLE with the nondefault CACHE clause or embed a CACHE hint in the first query that references the table. Set the init.ora parameter CACHE_SIZE_THRESHOLD to the maximum number of blocks allowed to be cached per table. You should generally use these techniques when you expect to frequently reuse the same tables, such as with lookup tables. Be careful not to cache too many tables, thereby defeating the purpose of the cache itself. The situation can deteriorate rapidly, especially if most non-lookup, large tables don't get a chance to get at least partially cached.

If you run the $ORACLE_HOME/rdbms<version>/admin/catparr.sql script, it creates the V$CACHE view, along with other views germane only to Oracle Parallel Server (OPS). However, the V$CACHE view can be very useful because it offers a mapping of blocks to datafiles by object. Hence, you can determine which objects, such as tables, have blocks currently in the database buffer cache. This can tell you, for example, whether your attempts to cache your lookup tables worked. The view is not dynamic, as many of the V$ views are, so you must rerun the catparr.sql script whenever you CREATE new objects or ALTER your current objects' storage parameters.

TUNING SORTS

Sorting is the process of putting something in a particular order, such as alphabetical or numerical, ascending or descending, and so forth. As with any RDBMS, Oracle requires sorting to take place for various reasons, sometimes implicitly due to the nature of a SQL statement, and other times explicitly through a user request. In any case, sorting consumes significant amounts of CPU time, memory, and disk.

Your first best strategy is to avoid unnecessary sorts when possible. However, when this cannot be done, which is more often the case, sorting needs to be tuned so that the sorts perform optimally. Sorting can take place fully in memory, and that is the desired case. However, it is more likely to spill over to disk sorting, especially with large tables, which can be extremely time-consuming despite even the best physical design of a database.

Your second best strategy is to sort in memory as much as possible and sort on disk only when absolutely necessary. Of course, this implies allocating sufficient temporary disk space (in effect, the TEMP tablespace), and separating this space physically from the rest of the Oracle datafiles, rollback segments, and redo logs.

WHAT TRIGGERS SORTS?

The CREATE INDEX statement obviously requires a sort operation on the index key to enable the building of the B*Tree structure. ALTER INDEX ... REBUILD likewise requires the same sort. However, you can choose to sort the data at the operating system level and then create the index with the NOSORT option. This doesn't usually buy you anything, unless you happen to already have a sorted copy of the data, because you are only trading RDBMS sorting for

OS sorting, which isn't much of a trade. Other options include using a fast, third-party sorting utility, such as SyncSort, or using Oracle's Parallel Query Option (PQO) to use SQL*Loader and load the data in parallel, unsorted.

ORDER BY and GROUP BY usually require sorts. However, an ORDER BY on an indexed column uses the already sorted index in most circumstances. To verify this without the need for execution, use EXPLAIN PLAN as previously discussed in Chapter 17. The DISTINCT qualifier must use a sorting technique (again, unless it is used on a column already with a unique index) to eliminate duplicate column values. Likewise, a UNION must eliminate duplicate rows. (However, a UNION ALL, by definition, allows duplicate rows, so because it doesn't eliminate duplicates, it doesn't require sorting. If primary keys are enforced on the two UNIONable tables, there won't be any duplicates to start with, so the UNION ALL is a recommended substitute for the UNION operation.) INTERSECT and MINUS require some duplicate elimination, though experience nowhere near the burden of a UNION operation. Similarly, IN and NOT IN can require sorting, especially if they are in support of nested subqueries. A join operation requires sorts of whatever tables do not already have existing indexes on the join key. The more usual situation, though, is for tables to be joined on primary keys (already having unique indexes), thereby negating the need for sorting any of the tables. The following list sums up the SQL commands or operators that can trigger sorts:

- CREATE INDEX, ALTER INDEX ...REBUILD
- ORDER BY, GROUP BY
- DISTINCT
- UNION, INTERSECT, MINUS
- IN, NOT IN

PARAMETERS FOR SORTS

The two primary init.ora parameters affecting sort operations are

- SORT_AREA_RETAINED_SIZE: The maximum amount of memory to be used for an in-memory sort
- SORT_AREA_SIZE: The maximum amount of memory to be used for an external disk sort operation, involving the allocation of a temporary segment

If a sort operation requires more than SORT_AREA_RETAINED_SIZE for an in-memory sort, it attempts to perform the sort within SORT_AREA_SIZE for an external disk sort, allocating a temporary segment in the process. If the sort operation requires further memory, it splits the sort burden into multiple *sort runs* and allocates multiple temporary segments for that purpose. The server process sorts one segment at a time and returns the merger of the sorted segments as the result. These memory allocations are not stored in the SGA shared pool, except when using MTS. Instead, they are part of the UGA. If you are using MTS, they are part of the SGA shared pool because the UGA is relocated there anyway.

PART

IV

CH

18

Using EXPLAIN PLAN (see Chapter 17), you can see that many SQL statements can require multiple sorts within their execution plans. The sort that is currently executing is known as the *active sort*. A *join sort* is a sort in support of a join operation. Any active sort requires SORT_AREA_SIZE. Any join sort requires SORT_AREA_RETAINED_SIZE. These settings hold true only for the dedicated server. For PQO, each parallel query server requires SORT_AREA_SIZE. However, two *sets* of parallel servers can be working at once. So, for PQO, set the following values:

- SORT_AREA_SIZE x 2 x (degree of parallelism)
- SORT_AREA_RETAINED_SIZE x (degree of parallelism) x (number of sorts > 2)

For PQO, the optimal value is 1MB. Higher values haven't yielded better performance. In general, set SORT_AREA_SIZE = SORT_AREA_RETAINED_SIZE, except for MTS, which requires some special considerations.

Tip #13	For MTS, set SORT_AREA_RETAINED_SIZE much smaller than SORT_AREA_SIZE. As a guideline, you can set the following: SORT_AREA_RETAINED_SIZE = (SORT_AREA_SIZE / the number of expected concurrent sorts), but not less than 1/10 (SORT_AREA_SIZE).

Temporary (sort) segments must be created when a sort cannot take place fully in memory. That is, as discussed, when the sort operation's memory requirements exceed the setting of SORT_AREA_RETAINED_SIZE, it then requires the allocation of a temporary segment and attempts to work within SORT_AREA_SIZE. A true temporary tablespace (versions greater than or equal to 7.3) segment cannot contain any permanent objects and consists solely of a single sort segment. Temporary tablespaces are created with the CREATE or ALTER TABLESPACE <tablespace_name> TEMPORARY ... syntax. Again, these temporary tablespaces are made up of one segment, created initially by the first sort requiring it. This segment grows in extents as sort concurrency and operation sizes increase.

Be careful how you set the INITIAL and NEXT extent parameters. A useful guide can be to set INITIAL = NEXT = (<max size as prescribed by datafile or disk> / <number of expected concurrent sorts>). The number of expected concurrent sorts can be calculated roughly as equal to twice the number of concurrent queries. This is a case when you don't want one large extent sized just below the datafile size, which would normally be a good recommendation for general use (permanent) tablespaces, as you will see later in Chapter 19, "Tuning I/O." Also, set INITIAL = NEXT = some multiple of SORT_AREA_SIZE plus at least one block for the overhead of the extent header because you wouldn't want any single sort requiring more than one extent. At the same time, you can afford to have a few sorts stored in the same extents, due to the random nature of concurrent access. Set PCTINCREASE to 0 because you don't want any surprises, such as increasingly large NEXT extents. Besides, because concurrency again plays a factor here; having equal-sized extents is a fair approach, barring actual sizing techniques, and it works well with random size requirements (no single sort need is too far from the average).

In the SGA, a memory structure known as the Sort Extent Pool (SEP) includes the extents that make up the single sort segments belonging to the temporary tablespaces. When sort space is requested by a process, this pool offers *free extents* (those that have been allocated and used by an earlier running process, and are now free but not deallocated) to be reused, much like the capability of reusing buffers in the database buffer cache. Furthermore, the V$SORT_SEGMENT contains information such as number of users, extents, and blocks using the temporary sort segments. You can use this to determine efficiency (hits) and help size your extents properly.

Tip #14	Remember to redefine users' default tablespaces. Use the ALTER USER syntax or Enterprise Manager to do it. TEMP has traditionally been the main temporary tablespace and has often been used to store permanent (processing) objects. However, create as many temporary tablespaces as you might need (such as three or four), and allocate them to different user groups according to varying processing requirements. This can help eliminate contention among users and Oracle itself. As an example, reserve TEMP for Oracle. Then create and assign TEMP2, TEMP3, and so forth to belong to various user or process groups.

Oracle offers the capability of having sorts bypass the database buffer cache. This is called *sort direct writes*. Of course, you still need SORT_AREA_SIZE bytes, but each sort operation can have its own memory buffers and write them directly to disk. The size of the buffers is set by the init.ora parameter SORT_WRITE_BUFFERS (2–8), and the number of buffers is set by SORT_WRITE_BUFFER_SIZE (32–64KB). Each regular (serial) sort operation requires a Sort Direct Writes Buffer of

```
(SORT_WRITE_BUFFERS x SORT_WRITE_BUFFER_SIZE) + SORT_AREA_SIZE
```

For PQO, each (parallel) sort requires

```
((SORT_WRITE_BUFFERS x SORT_WRITE_BUFFER_SIZE)
+ SORT_AREA_SIZE) x 2 x (degree of parallelism)
```

The init.ora parameter, SORT_DIRECT_WRITES, determines the sorting behavior regarding using the database buffer cache or not. If set to AUTO, the default, and if SORT_AREA_SIZE >= 10 x Sort Direct Writes Buffer, the Sort Direct Writes Buffer is used. If set to FALSE, sort writes are buffered in the database buffer cache before being written back out to disk. These are normal sort buffer writes. If set to TRUE, sort writes are always sort direct writes. VLDBs, DSSs, and Data Warehouses should normally have this set to TRUE (or at least left at the default AUTO).

OTHER FINE-TUNING PARAMETERS FOR SORTS

The following are other fine-tuning parameters that impact sort performance:

- SORT_READ_FAC
- SORT_SPACEMAP_SIZE

SORT_READ_FAC is a ratio representing the amount of time to read one Oracle block divided by the block transfer rate. It must be <= DB_FILE_MULTIBLOCK_READ_COUNT. The formula to set it is

```
(average seek time + average latency time
+ block transfer time) / (block transfer rate)
```

This parameter takes into account operating system and hardware (disk) device characteristics for sort reads. However, what if you used mixed disks having, of course, mixed access times (access time = seek time + latency time)? Do you take the least-common-denominator approach and set this to the characteristics of the slowest disk?

> **Caution**
>
> Unless you have a very homogeneous hardware (disk) configuration, and have intimate hardware expertise, I would advise you to *not* set this parameter. If done improperly, it can hurt much more than help.

SORT_SPACEMAP_SIZE represents the size in bytes of the *sort space map*, which is a map per sort (*per context*) of the multiple sort run addresses. The formula to set it is

```
(total sort bytes / SORT_AREA_SIZE) + 64
```

total sort bytes requires that you know the size in bytes of the columns being sorted, multiplied by the number of rows. You can use the entire table size in bytes, but this is an overestimate (not necessarily a bad thing).

Query the V$SYSSTAT view as follows:

```
SQL> SELECT M.VALUE / D.VALUE "Memory Sort Ratio"
    2> FROM V$SYSSTAT M, V$SYSSTAT D
    3> WHERE M.NAME = 'sorts (memory)'
    4> AND D.NAME = 'sorts (disk)';
```

From report.txt, the Statistics section, compute the Memory Sort Ratio as the total of 'sorts (memory)' divided by the total of 'sorts (disk)'.

If either method of computing Memory Sort Ratio yields a ratio less than .95, you need to increase SORT_AREA_SIZE (and SORT_AREA_RETAINED_SIZE) by at least the deficit percentage, which is calculated as .95 minus Memory Sort Ratio. For example, if your Memory Sort Ratio is .78, your deficit percentage is .95 − .78 = .17. This implies that you need to increase your sort parameters by at least 17%.

TUNING THE MULTITHREADED SERVER (MTS)

This section, rather than rehashing the architecture of the MTS, offers a series of brief explanations and guidelines to help you tune your MTS configuration, especially regarding memory performance optimization. As a refresher, recall that the MTS relocates session user memory, the User Global Area (UGA), to the SGA shared pool, where it is shared by many sessions. Generally, you would use the MTS when you want to increase the throughput (for example, in terms of transactions per second) of a database system, and specifically when the system is under heavy (concurrent) load. In other words, MTS is intended for an OLTP system with many hundreds of concurrent users, at least greater than 200.

> **Caution**
>
> If you were to use MTS for a system that is not as heavily loaded as described, the overhead of using MTS would outweigh its minimal benefits. That is, for lightly loaded systems, MTS can actually hurt performance. So, use MTS as advised mainly for heavily loaded OLTP systems.

> **Tip #15**
>
> Set MTS_SERVERS = 1/100 (*the number of concurrent transactions*), where *the number of concurrent transactions* equals the number of concurrent users times the number of transactions per user. Set MTS_MAX_SERVERS = 1/10 (MTS_SERVERS). Increase these in increments of magnitude. Similarly, set MTS_DISPATCHERS = MTS_SERVERS and MTS_MAX_DISPATCHERS = MTS_MAX_SERVERS.

To monitor and tune shared servers, use the following:

```
SQL> SELECT BUSY / (BUSY+IDLE) "Shared Servers Busy"
    2> FROM V$SHARED_SERVER;

SQL> SELECT SERVERS_HIGHWATER
    2> FROM V$MTS;
```

For dispatchers:

```
SQL> SELECT BUSY / (BUSY+IDLE) "Dispatchers Busy"
    2> FROM V$DISPATCHER;

SQL> SELECT SUM(WAIT)/SUM(TOTALQ) "Dispatcher Waits"
    2> FROM V$QUEUE
    3> WHERE TYPE = 'DISPATCHER';

SQL> SELECT COUNT(*) "Number of Dispatchers"
    2> FROM V$DISPATCHER;
```

PART

IV

CH

18

If Shared Servers Busy is greater than .50, or the SERVERS_HIGHWATER is close to or equal to MTS_MAX_SERVERS, increase MTS_MAX_SERVERS. If the Dispatchers Busy is greater than .50, the Dispatcher Waits is greater than 0, or the Number of Dispatchers is close to or equal to MTS_MAX_DISPATCHERS, increase MTS_MAX_DISPATCHERS. Usually, if you increase one, you should probably also increase the other.

TUNING LOCKS

As with the section "Tuning the MultiThreaded Server (MTS)," this section won't go into much detail rehashing the software engineering and functional details of Oracle's locking mechanisms. (See Chapter 25, "Integrity Management," for the background information on Oracle locking.) Rather, you will look at some brief background and useful tuning advice. Locks in Oracle, as with any RDBMS, are memory-based structures. Like latches, they are made up of two basic logical structures: a gate and a queue. If you have only the gate, you have a latch. If you have a gate and a queue, along with a queuing process, you have a lock.

The central goals of tuning are to not have unnecessary waiting, not experience deadlock, and not actually run out of locks during critical processing. The *granularity* of Oracle's locks is row-level. That is, for INSERT, UPDATE, and DELETE statements, locks are held at row level by default. SELECT statements (queries) hold no locks by default, unless explicitly specified in the code. DDL also holds locks, but the capability to performance-tune them is limited; so instead, concentrate on the dominant issue of performance-tuning DML locking.

> **Note**
>
> Transactions hold locks until they commit or roll back.

Locks can cause unnecessary waits as a direct result of poor application coding with regard to locking. Unnecessary lock waits can be caused by coding locks at unnecessarily high granularity—for example, locking a table when you need only a row. If the code involves unnecessarily long transactions, this causes undue lock waits. An example is a persistent client/server connection held for the duration of a transaction. Many times, this type of coding can be chopped into two or more transactions of shorter duration. Finally, if code is not committed (or rolled back) on a regular basis, the locks remain unduly held. When coding, ensure the following:

- Hold locks only when necessary.
- Hold locks at the lowest possible level.
- Keep transactions as short as possible.
- Commit (or roll back) as frequently as possible.
- Chop client/server transactions where possible.

This is where tuning locks overlaps with tuning the application. When coding, ensure that you hold locks only when necessary, hold locks at the lowest possible level, keep transactions short as possible, commit (or rollback) as frequently as possible, and chop client/server transactions where possible.

> **Tip #16**
>
> Create indexes on all your foreign keys to eliminate unnecessary parent-child locking.

To monitor locking, run the $ORACLE_HOME/rdbms<version>/admin/catblock.sql as SYS to create locking views. Then you can gather session wait information from the tables DBA_OBJECTS, DBA_WAITERS, DBA_BLOCKERS, V$SESSION, and V$LOCK. What you can also do is run the $ORACLE_HOME/rdbms<version>/admin/utllockt.sql script to get most of this same information. Examine Count for Event Name = 'enqueue' under System wide wait events. If any of these sources of information suggest that locking is unnecessarily high, apply the previous guidelines. Use the ALTER SESSION KILL syntax to kill sessions if necessary. If deadlock occurs, a trace file is dumped. Examine it to determine which sessions and what types of locks caused the deadlock. Then eliminate unnecessary locking and reorder your processing if necessary.

If it appears you need to increase the number of locks to alleviate lock waits or because you have already hit the default ceiling, you might need to increase ENQUEUE_RESOURCES. ENQUEUE_RESOURCES is a function of DML_LOCKS, DDL_LOCKS, other parameters, and platform specifics. You can ALTER TABLE DISABLE LOCKS to speed up certain guaranteed exclusive runs, but I wouldn't normally recommend it. Also, you can set DML_LOCKS = 0 to help speed up an overall instance, but this can have undesirable side effects. Oracle apparently still somehow manages concurrency without the use of heavy-weight locks, but the mechanism can be subject to integrity problems; therefore, I again would not recommend this.

Tip #17	Set DML_LOCKS = (*the maximum number of concurrent users*) x (*the number of tables*). You can also explicitly set ENQUEUE_RESOURCES, but this resets upon resetting DML_LOCKS anyway. For example, if you have U users and T tables, you should set DML_LOCKS = (U x T), plus perhaps some additional percentage, such as 10%.

OPERATING SYSTEM INTEGRATION REVISITED

Without getting too platform-specific, look briefly at some of the common operating system memory issues associated with tuning memory in Oracle. Platform specifics can be found in Appendix A, "Oracle on Solaris," and Appendix B, "Oracle on Windows NT." The major operating system integration memory issues are

- Shared memory
- Semaphores
- Interprocess communication
- Virtual memory
- Memory file systems

Shared memory is a mechanism used by virtually all RDBMS vendors, particularly on UNIX. Shared memory permits multithreading and memory sharing among processes. Oracle uses the latter approach with its SGA, by sharing it among all sessions for that instance. The MTS also depends heavily on this resource to simulate multithreading at the interprocess level.

Caution	The Oracle SGA should fit comfortably well within the shared memory given to it by the operating system. Otherwise, you have unnecessary paging and swapping, which can cripple a system.

Semaphores are true locking mechanisms. Oracle uses them as the basis for *enqueue* resources, such as DML locks. Again, they are made up of a (global memory) gate and a queue, along with a set of queuing operations. Oracle's locking operations map to operating system low-level semaphore operations.

Interprocess communication refers to the native operating system communication protocols that allow processes to communicate. These can be implemented as sockets, streams, named pipes, or other mechanisms. Because Oracle is not fully multithreaded, it depends heavily on the operating system interprocess operations. Oracle's intersession communications are mapped to these low-level operations. When using SQL*Net, the IPC protocol refers to and uses the default operating system interprocess communication method.

Virtual memory is a special type of cache. It is an extension of real memory to the disk. The hit ratio of virtual memory can be calculated just as with any cache. Virtual memory must be sufficient to handle all the total memory needs of the operating system itself and all applications, including Oracle. When real memory is paged or swapped, it is sent to virtual memory (disk). The actual disk supporting virtual memory is called *the backing store*. Again, you don't want the Oracle SGA to be paged or swapped there, nor any of the major Oracle background processes to be swapped out.

Memory file systems are file systems held entirely in real or virtual memory. Sometimes these are called RAM disks (as with DOS) or temporary file systems (as with UNIX). In any case, they, of course, outperform ordinary disk file systems by some orders of magnitude. Because they can be at least partly held in memory and take advantage of virtual memory caching, at least some, if not most, of their operations are to and from memory. Oracle can sometimes use these as an exotic performance tuning solution. For example, you could create an Oracle temporary tablespace (or permanent tablespace) on an operating system memory file system. They could also be used, for example, to store lookup tables.

CHAPTER 19

TUNING I/O

In this chapter

In general, tuning I/O (Input/Output) can be thought of simply as an extension or refinement of physical design. When you initially do your physical design, you are working from your best quantitative estimates. If you reach the stage in which you must tune I/O because performance is unacceptable, you work from actual measurements of your application as it runs for some peak periods of time. Tuning I/O in Oracle consists mainly of tuning the underlying physical structures of the segments (tables and indexes) that make up a database. These include tablespaces—made up of extents, in turn made up of blocks—and datafiles, which are the operating system (OS) entities supporting these Oracle physical structures. These and other Oracle structures are covered in depth in Chapter 5, "The Oracle Database Architecture," so this chapter won't go too deeply into their definitions and functions, except to reemphasize certain relevant concepts along the way.

I/O means reads and writes. In database terms, more specifically for DML, SELECT operations are the reads and INSERT, UPDATE, and DELETE operations are the writes. A DDL, (a CREATE, ALTER, or DROP) is always a writing operation. Hence, reading from and writing to any Oracle structure is considered an I/O issue for the purposes of this chapter. For example, issuing a SELECT statement generates a read from one or more indexes and/or from one or more tables. It also generates some minimal redo log information. Issuing an INSERT, UPDATE, or DELETE generates reads *and* writes from one or more indexes and/or tables, roll back data, and redo log information. This last fact leads to a more subtle, general fact: Reading is simply reading, but writing is reading *and* writing. How can you write information to a block that has yet to be read into the database buffer cache? Aside from the direct path capability of SQL*Loader, you can't.

So, when you consider tuning I/O in Oracle, not only do you consider tuning tablespaces, extents, blocks, and datafiles, but you also consider tuning rollback segments and redo logs (because user DML generates all these kinds of I/O). Hence, the sections following cover each of these kinds of I/O: tablespaces and datafiles, extents and blocks, rollback segments, and redo logs. Similar to previous tuning chapters on memory and application issues, you will encounter overlaps of tuning I/O with tuning memory and tuning I/O with tuning the application.

Remember, any I/O operation requires reading Oracle data blocks into the database buffer cache before any further activity can take place. This is an example of where tuning memory and tuning I/O overlap. Consider a different idea: Suppose you have an OLTP application that heavily reads and writes from only a few tables out of several. Those tables need to be placed in separate tablespaces, and further, on separate disks. This is an example of where tuning the application and tuning I/O overlap. A high level look at tuning tablespaces and datafiles is a good place to start your study.

TUNING TABLESPACES AND DATAFILES

As you know from Chapter 5, tablespaces are Oracle structures for physical storage. A tablespace stores a collection of segments: tables and indexes. A tablespace maps to one or more datafiles at the OS level. You learned the concept of application typing in Chapters 3,

"Physical Database Design, Hardware, and Related Issues," and 16, "Performance Tuning Fundamentals," and how this affects your physical design. Recall that in order to have a proper physical layout, tablespaces (and their datafiles) are separated as much as possible on different disks. Separating tablespaces on different disks can eliminate, or at least reduce, disk contention.

Disk contention occurs when you have multiple users or programs attempting to access the same disk at the same time. For example, if you have two tables that must be joined together very often, such as DEPARTMENTS and EMPLOYEES tables, their tablespaces should usually be separated on two different disks because attempting to access either the tables or the indexes on the same disk results in the same contention for the resource. Ideally, then, these four segments will exist in four tablespaces residing on four different disks. Other methods, such as clustering, enable these segments to coexist on the same disk. You will explore Oracle's version of the clustering technique, referred to as one of the exotic solutions, in Chapter 10, "Partitioning."

PARTITIONING TABLESPACES

As you learned in Chapter 3 and Chapter 10, you want your Oracle physical layout so that the following will occur:

- SYSTEM resides on a separate disk.
- TEMP resides on at least one separate disk.
- DATA1 to DATA*N* reside on up to *N* separate disks.
- INDEX1 to INDEX*N* reside on up to *N* separate disks.
- ROLLBACK resides on at least one separate disk.
- redo log1 to redo log*N* reside on up to *N* separate disks.

Remember that on initial creation, a user's default tablespace and default temporary tablespace point to SYSTEM! Change these if they were not created properly by doing the following:

```
SQL> ALTER USER <user>
    2> DEFAULT TABLESPACE <tablespace>
    3> TEMPORARY TABLESPACE TEMP;
```

To determine whether DATA (or INDEX) tablespaces can coexist, you need to classify tables by their level of activity, in addition to *typing* the application.

For example, suppose you have a DSS application in which during normal operation all tables are read-only (except when they are bulk loaded). Does this mean that you can put all the tables on only one disk? Not at all! In fact, consider that there might be, for the sake of illustration, 10 tables that are heavily read out of, for example, 40 tables. Of those 10, 7 are accessed concurrently, and 4 of those are almost always joined in usage. You should ideally have *at least* 9 disks for the data alone!

How do you arrive at this figure? You need 7 separate disks because 7 are accessed concurrently, including the 4 tables frequently being joined. You need at least one more for the remaining three (10–7) heavily read tables that are not concurrently accessed, and you need at least one more for the remaining 30 (40–10) tables—that is, if one disk could hold all those 30 tables! In any case, like application typing, this is activity classification: classifying tables by their frequency of access or in other words, how active they are. If a table is very active, it is said to be *hot*. The same holds true for active columns within a table, which are also called hot. A *warm* table or column is one that is simply less active, relative to a hot component. Thus, cold components are those that are infrequently accessed. You might also see the nomenclature Low/Medium/High activity used. In summary, in addition to typing your application, classify your tables as the following:

H   High activity, or hot

M   Medium activity, or warm

L   Low activity, or cold

Although a simple classification, this helps immensely with your physical layout and performance tuning. For example, high DML activity tables cause high fragmentation. If stored on their own, separate tablespaces or disks, this isolates them from causing unnecessary fragmentation of lower activity tables. When your classification job is done, follow these simple guidelines for tablespace partitioning and table/index placement:

- Place each of the hot tables/indexes on its own, separate tablespace/disk.

- Place each of the warm tables/indexes on its own, separate tablespace/disk.

- Place groups of cold tables/indexes on their own, separate tablespaces/disks.

- Always place joined tables/indexes on their own, separate tablespace/disks.

- Keep data and index tablespaces separate.

- Put your hottest tablespaces on your fastest disks and your coldest on the slowest.

- If necessary, because of disk space limitations, place warm and cold tables/indexes on the same tablespaces/disks, taking into consideration concurrent access issues. (For example, you might not want to place a warm, interactively accessed table on the same tablespace as a cold, batch-accessed table that is used for a long processing duration of several hours.)

- If *not* concurrently accessed, place "like" tables/indexes on the same tablespaces/disks.

- An elaborate extension of the previous guideline: If necessary, because of disk space limitations, *interleave* hot, warm, and cold table placements. In other words, know your access patterns, types of usage, and concurrency levels for all your tables. Armed with this knowledge, if you're tight on disk space, you might, for example, place two hot tables not concurrently accessed together on the same tablespace/disk, place a hot index with a cold table in different tablespaces on the same disk, or place all three types of tables *and* indexes in six different tablespaces on the same disk under the right conditions! Recommendation: *Don't* do this unless you absolutely have to. This is a last ditch effort for database systems extremely low on disk space.

Clustering provides an optional storage method for storing frequently joined tables.

CLUSTERING

A *cluster* is a special type of tablespace in which parent-child, or master-detail, types of hierarchical relationships can be *physically nested*. For example, if an employee can work in only one department, it is a logical, one-to-many relationship from a DEPARTMENTS table to an EMPLOYEES table. The EMPLOYEES table has a foreign key, DEPTID, back to the DEPARTMENTS table primary key, DEPTID. You can create a cluster like so:

```
SQL> CREATE CLUSTER DEPTS_EMPS (DEPTID NUMBER (9))
   2> SIZE 256
   3> TABLESPACE DATAn
   4> STORAGE (...);

SQL> CREATE TABLE DEPARTMENTS
   2> (DEPTID NUMBER(9) PRIMARY KEY, ...)
   3> CLUSTER DEPTS_EMPS (DEPTID);

SQL> CREATE TABLE EMPLOYEES
   2> (EMPID NUMBER (9) PRIMARY KEY, ...
   3> DEPTID NUMBER (9) REFERENCES DEPARTMENTS)
   4> CLUSTER DEPTS_EMPS (DEPTID);
```

The optional SIZE argument specifies how many bytes are expected to be exhausted by the *cluster key* (in this case, DEPTID) and all its associated rows. Table 35.1 is a textual representation of how the DEPTS_EMPS cluster is physically organized:

TABLE 19.1 THE DEPTS_EMPS CLUSTER

DEPARTMENTS (before clustering):

DEPTID	DEPTNAME	etc.
1	PERSONNEL	
2	ACCOUNTING	

EMPLOYEES (before clustering):

EMPID	EMPNAME	DEPTID	etc.
1	William Day	1	
2	James Hutch	1	
3	Ely Jones	1	
4	Peter Page	2	
5	Tom Edwards	2	

continues

TABLE 19.1   CONTINUED

The DEPARTMENTS and EMPLOYEES tables after clustering:

DEPTID	DEPTNAME	etc.		
	EMPID	EMPNAME	etc.	
1	PERSONNEL			
	1	William Day		
	2	James Hutch		
	3	Ely Jones		
2	ACCOUNTING			
	4	Peter Page		
	5	Tom Edwards		

The "etc." refers to other nonkey columns in the DEPARTMENTS and EMPLOYEES tables. As you can see, the EMPLOYEES table is physically nested within the DEPARTMENTS table so that whenever these two tables are accessed by a join on DEPTID, the data is already organized in that fashion and much more readily available than would ordinarily be the case with two non-clustered tables. Use ordinary indexes (B*Tree structures) for most cases, in particular those involving any substantial range retrievals (bounded or not). However, if your application queries are almost always point queries (exact matches, equality comparisons), you might want to use *hash indexing*.

A hash index is one that takes as input a column value and using a specialized internal hash function, computes an output that is the physical address of that row (in effect, the ROWID). If a column is of a NUMBER datatype, is uniformly distributed, and is not composite, you might choose to use it, rather than the internal hash function, to create the hash index. For example, if you re-create the DEPTS_EMPS cluster using a hashed index, the syntax is as follows:

```
SQL> CREATE CLUSTER DEPTS_EMPS (DEPTID NUMBER (9))
     2> SIZE 256
     3> HASH IS DEPTID HASHKEYS 29
     3> TABLESPACE DATAn
     4> STORAGE (...);
```

The HASH IS option tells Oracle to use the DEPTID column instead of the internal hash function. The HASHKEYS argument tells how many hash buckets to create to hold the hash cluster key index (DEPTID) output values. This argument should be set equal to the number of distinct cluster key values, rounded up to the next highest prime number. In this case, suppose you have 25 departments (DEPTID). You round up to 29, the next highest prime number. For further information on how to size and manage hash clusters and indexes, please refer to the Oracle *Server Administrator's Guide*.

MONITORING

You have seen guidelines and clustering to help alleviate contention for hot tablespaces, but how do you tell which tablespaces are hot? You learned in Chapter 3 that if you have good quantitative estimates from your early modeling specifications, namely good transaction analysis figures, you have a head start and can use those figures to guide your initial physical layout.

If, for example, 3 tables out of 20 incur 150 transactions per second (tps) on average, and your remaining tables incur only less than 30 tps, you can safely say that those first 3 tables are your hot tables, relative to the others, and therefore should be separated from the rest, along with their indexes. After you're past deployment, however, and into production usage, you need monitoring techniques that give you actual, low-level I/O figures, such as physical reads and writes per second, rather than high-level estimates, such as tps.

You have your usual two Oracle standbys to help do the monitoring: the V$ dynamic performance views and the report.txt output from properly "bookended" utlbstat.sql/utlestat.sql runs. These utilities are explained in Chapter 18 "Tuning Memory". You can also use OEM/PP to examine FILE I/O. You need to examine V$DATAFILE and V$FILESTAT views:

```
SQL> SELECT NAME, PHYSRDS, PHYSWRTS
  2> FROM V$DATAFILE DF, V$FILESTAT FS
  3> WHERE DF.FILE# = FS.FILE#;
```

Also examine PHYS_READS and PHYS_WRITES from the I/O section of report.txt. The sum of the physical reads and the physical writes is the total I/O for that file or tablespace. Consider the sum of all the files for all the tablespaces by each disk. If using the V$ views method, select the information twice, *bookending* your statistics collection: first, after your application has reached peak capacity, and last, just before your application is expected to decline. This mimics the utlbstat.sql/utlestat.sql approach. Using either method, sum your beginning and ending total I/Os *by disk*. Subtract the beginning I/Os from the ending I/Os. Subtract your beginning time from the ending time of your statistics-gathering runs. Convert your time figure to seconds. Divide your *deltas*, the elapsed I/Os, by the elapsed time between the beginning and the ending.

Here's an example: Disk #3 contains Files #6 and #7 and shows beginning figures of 1,200 physical reads, 400 physical writes at 11:00 am. Its ending figures are 31,000 physical reads, 17,000 physical writes at 11:20 pm. This is equal to

((31000 - 1200) + (17000-400)) / (11:20 - 11:00) =

(29800 + 16600) / (20 minutes) =

(46400) / (1200 seconds) =

38.67 I/Os per second

This shows under 40 I/Os per second for this disk, which is desirable because this is widely considered a saturation point for most modern disks. However, if all the other disks, for example, are much less than 40 I/Os per second, you still want to offload this disk to help balance the I/O. You don't want simply to reduce each disk in isolation, but also to balance the I/O as much as possible—in effect, spread it out across all disks.

Guideline: If any given disk approaches or exceeds 40 I/Os per second, you likely need to offload some of its burden to other disks. In the best case, this means moving tables, or worse, possibly moving tablespaces and their corresponding datafiles. After that, you need to consider interleaving, clustering, striping, or if necessary, buying more disks. Your goal is to even out all the disk I/Os so that they are each at 40 I/Os per second or less, given your application's peak load requirements, and to equalize all the disk I/Os per second as much as possible so that all disks are evenly burdened.

TUNING BLOCKS AND EXTENTS

Oracle blocks are organized by extents, and extents comprise tablespaces. They are the physical foundation of the storage of tablespaces. Hence, the more efficiently you can access the data in them and manage their growth, the better your performance will be.

USING PREALLOCATION

From Chapter 16, "Performance Tuning Fundamentals," you learned that dynamic allocation incurs too much overhead and hurts I/O performance. Static preallocation is preferred in almost all cases. You can statically preallocate a segment (table or index) or a tablespace. Generally, you choose one way or the other. If you preallocate the tablespace, you should already have a good idea of the sizes of your tables and how they will map to the extents. If you set tablespace defaults and then preallocate your tables, you have a little more flexibility in mixing tables of different extent requirements in the same tablespace. However, remember that you don't want to mix tables of too many different extent sizes (not more than three, as a general guideline) because this effectively engineers fragmentation, which is undesirable.

Rather than review all the storage terminology and parameters given in Chapter 5, "The Oracle Database Architecture," and Chapter 21, "Managing Database Storage," briefly look at the two different approaches for the same tablespace storing the same two tables. Suppose you have two tables requiring a maximum of 100MB each. Create a tablespace of 256MB to enable some additional growth, with a single datafile. The first approach, preallocating the tablespace, looks like the following:

```
OQL> CREATE TABLESPACE TS1
  2> DATAFILE '/data1/file1.dat' SIZE 256M
  3> DEFAULT STORAGE (INITIAL 100M NEXT 100M
  4> MINEXTENTS1);

SQL> CREATE TABLE T1 (a number(9), ..., z number(9))
  2> TABLESPACE TS1;

SQL> CREATE TABLE T2 (a number(9), ..., z number(9))
  2> TABLESPACE TS1;
```

The second approach, preallocating the tables, looks like this:

```
SQL> CREATE TABLESPACE TS1
   2> DATAFILE '/data1/file1.dat' SIZE 256M;

SQL> CREATE TABLE T1 (a number(9), ..., z number(9))
   2> TABLESPACE TS1
   3> STORAGE (INITIAL 100M NEXT 10M
   4> MINEXTENTS 1);

SQL> CREATE TABLE T2 (a number(9), ..., z number(9))
   2> TABLESPACE TS1
   3> STORAGE (INITIAL 100M NEXT 10M
   4> MINEXTENTS 1);
```

Preallocating the tables individually gives you a finer-grained control not only over the growth but also over the performance associated with this tablespace. Why allocate 100M if one of the tables happens to extend when you need only allocate 10M? In general, the finer the unit of storage preallocated, the better the performance, for many of the reasons discussed in Chapter 10.

USING ORACLE STRIPING

You've encountered striping before in the discussions regarding physical design and RAID in Chapter 3. This section shows you how to do *manual striping*, also known as *Oracle striping*.

Oracle striping is essentially a form of preallocation of extents so that each extent takes up (nearly) all its corresponding datafile, which is conveniently located on a separate disk. Of course, the drawback is that you should have a very good idea of what your maximum growth might be for the long term, or you should at least know what your peak size is for the medium term. However, the benefits are generally worth the effort, helping to parallel many of your I/O operations to your high-activity tablespaces. Suppose you have one very high activity table that you want to stripe. It has a peak size of less than 600MB, and you have three available disks with which to stripe it. The syntax looks like the following:

PART

IV

CH

19

```
SQL> CREATE TABLESPACE TS1
   2> DATAFILE '/data1/file1.dat' SIZE 200M,
   3> DATAFILE '/data2/file2.dat' SIZE 200M,
   4> DATAFILE '/data3/file3.dat' SIZE 200M;

OQL> CREATE TABLE T1 (a varchar2(25), ..., z varchar2(25))
   2> TABLESPACE TS1
   3> STORAGE (INITIAL 198M NEXT 198M
   4> MINEXTENTS 3 PCTINCREASE 0);
```

Setting `PCTINCREASE` to `0` is necessary to override the default setting (50). Now you have stored a table across three different disks by manually preallocating the necessary (maximum) extent sizes at slightly less (1 percent as a general guideline) than the corresponding datafile sizes. The table is effectively striped across the disks. The stripe unit is one Oracle extent of 198MB each. Compared to RAID striping, this is a very large stripe unit because RAID stripe units are usually measured in multiples of KB or less. However, it is nonetheless effective and requires no additional hardware or software. On the other hand, if you have incorrectly sized the table, or especially if the grow-shrink behavior of the table is erratic, the maintenance for this approach quickly becomes unwieldy. This is when you want to turn to RAID as a replacement for Oracle striping, if striping is still desired despite all else.

As we briefly covered in Chapters 3 ("Physical Database Design, Hardware, and Related Issues") and 4 ("The Oracle Solution"), for datafiles supporting table or rollback tablespaces, RAID 3 or 5 is a good choice. RAID 0 is a good choice for indexes. RAID 1 is a good choice for redo logs. RAID can be used instead of Oracle striping, as just mentioned, but it can also be used in addition to Oracle striping. For example, in the previous example of a table striped across the datafiles, each of those datafiles might be striped on an individual RAID volume (set of disks), rather than simply being stored on a single (non-RAID) disk. This approach can provide substantial performance gains, but requires complex and often constant DBA management, so choose your strategy wisely. Remember that although RAID 1, 3, and 5 can tolerate single disk losses, RAID is not a substitute for a good backup system!

AVOIDING FRAGMENTATION

One of your major goals is to avoid unnecessary fragmentation. One way to do this is by proper sizing, through estimation or measurement, and correct preallocation of extents. Also, avoid mixing tables of varying levels of activity, sizes, and known extent requirements in the same tablespaces. *Extent fragmentation* occurs when extents are allocated and deallocated within a tablespace. Extent fragmentation occurs in two ways: through free space fragmentation or through simple table fragmentation. *Free extents* are those that have never been allocated or that have been deallocated after their segment has been dropped. When a pattern of isolated pockets of free extents scattered throughout the tablespace occurs, this is known as *Swiss cheese* fragmentation or *bubbling*. When a pattern of contiguous pockets of free extents occurs in runs throughout a tablespace, this is known as *honeycomb* fragmentation. In either case, you have *free space fragmentation*. When a table dynamically extends beyond its initial creation extents, this is said to be *table fragmentation*.

Although fragmentation is usually considered primarily a space issue, like all things in a database system, it has its effects on performance. Whether directly or indirectly, extent fragmentation triggers dynamic extension, which you do not want occurring unnecessarily, from the standpoint of performance. If, in the lifetime of a tablespace, segment creation and dropping has created a swiss cheese effect, it detracts from performance by necessitating I/Os from multiple extents. Generally speaking, this usually isn't so bad. However, in the worst case, it can substantially slow down system performance. For example, suppose your PQO is configured based on precise data arrangements to help speed up full table (sequential) scans to a very large, hot table. After some time, that table becomes extent-fragmented. The PQO configuration becomes slower and slower because it was initially configured based on load-balancing the extents. In addition, what was initially a set of sequential reads from contiguous disk locations has become groups of sequential reads from various (random) disk locations, requiring more seek activity!

Use the following to help determine the degree of your table fragmentation:

```
SQL> SELECT SEGMENT_NAME, EXTENTS
   2> FROM DBA_EXTENTS
   3> WHERE EXENTS > 4
   4> ORDER BY EXTENTS;
```

If any segments are returned, consider these too fragmented (unless you have planned these extents as part of Oracle striping or as part of a VLDB table, for example). To rectify this, do one of two things:

■ Create a second table with new storage parameters, selecting from the first. Disable referencing constraints. Drop the first. Rename the second to what the first was called. Re-enable referencing constraints. Re-create any indexes and grant privileges as necessary.

■ Export the table with the compress option. Disable referencing constraints. Drop it. Import it back. Re-enable referencing constraints. Re-create any indexes and grant privileges as necessary.

Use the following to help determine the degree of your free space fragmentation:

```
SQL> SELECT TABLESPACE_NAME, COUNT(TABLESPACE_NAME)
   2> FROM DBA_FREE_SPACE
   3> ORDER BY TABLESPACE_NAME
   4> GROUP BY TABLESPACE_NAME
   5> HAVING COUNT(TABLESPACE_NAME) > 10;
```

If any tablespaces are returned, consider these too fragmented. Issue the ALTER TABLESPACE <tablespace_name> COALESCE statement (for Oracle versions 7.3 and higher) to help rectify this. Rerun the query later. If some tablespaces are still returned and the fragmentation is high, (greater than 5× the number of segments), you might want to follow the previous guidelines for each table, if feasible. Drop all the tables. Drop the tablespace. Delete the datafiles. Re-create the tablespace. Re-create all the tables. Rerun your query to gather a benchmark against which to compare your future growth.

PART
IV
CH
19

Tip #18	In order for SMON to be able to coalesce the free space of a tablespace, whether automatically or through the ALTER command, that tablespace must have its PCTINCREASE > 0. However, this can lead to undesirable, geometric growth of a table in the tablespace, unless the tables override the PCTINCREASE setting. Recommendation: Set PCTINCREASE to 1 for tablespaces and to 0 for tables.

Block fragmentation can occur two ways: through migrated rows or through chained rows. *Migrated rows* are rows that have been updated within a block but have increased in size so that they exceed the free space remaining in its original block. They are reassigned to another block (off the freelist), and a pointer is maintained in the original block. *Chained rows* are those that are inserted or updated and whose size is such that it cannot fit in the free space of any block. They are split across blocks using pointers. Chained rows can be avoided by proper sizing and setting of DB_BLOCK_SIZE. Migrated rows can be avoided by enabling enough update room (100–(PCTFREE+PCTUSED)). To determine the degree of your chained or migrated rows, run the following:

```
SQL> ANALYZE TABLE T1 COMPUTE STATISTICS;
SQL> SELECT TABLE_NAME, CHAIN_CNT
    2> FROM DBA_TABLES
    3> WHERE CHAIN_CNT > 0
    4> ORDER BY CHAIN_CNT;
```

This gives you an ordered listing of the tables having chained or migrated rows. To help repair the situation for migrated rows, you can drop and re-create the table. If the table is very large, you can run the utlchain.sql to create the CHAINED_ROWS table. Then run the following:

```
SQL> ANALYZE TABLE T1 LIST CHAINED ROWS;
```

The ROWIDs of the migrated rows are stored in CHAINED_ROWS. You can use this to select the migrated rows from your table and place them into a temporary table. Then delete them from your original table. Insert them back into your original table from the temporary table.

Related topics to fragmentation performance issues include the High Water Mark, Freelists, and Table/Index Reorganization. The *High Water Mark (HWM)* is the number of blocks that have been used in that segment to date. DELETE does not lower the HWM. Oracle must read the unused blocks below the HWM during full table scans. Although it does not reset the HWM for the current segment, you can reclaim wasted space for other segments using the following:

```
SQL> ALTER TABLE T1 DEALLOCATE UNUSED;
```

In addition, TRUNCATE TABLE <table name> does reset the HWM for the table and all indexes, as opposed to DELETE FROM <table_name>.

Freelists are linked lists of the free blocks, containing one or more lists per segment. Examine freelist wait events in V$WAITSTAT or use the System wide wait events section of report.txt. If any of the freelist events are much greater than 0 or much greater than your baselined figures, consider adding freelists or freelist groups to your hot tables. They must be re-created to do so.

Consider re-creating your tables if there is a lot of free space, on average, in the blocks below the HWM. After analyzing your table and computing or estimating statistics, examine the following:

```
SQL> SELECT TABLE_NAME, AVG_SPACE
    2> FROM DBA_TABLES
    3> WHERE AVG_SPACE > (.10 * BLOCKS)
    3> ORDER BY AVG_SPACE;
```

In other words, if your table has greater than 10 percent free space in its blocks below the HWM, drop and re-create the table by using import/export or a temporary table select/rename method.

Indexes that belong to heavily updated tables should bear inspection. They often need re-creating. One general guideline is that if the index size approaches 1/3 of the actual table size, drop and re-create the index. Another general guideline is that if the number of levels of the index exceeds three, the index might be too high. ANALYZE your indexes and examine the INDEX_STATS table to gather information. If necessary, drop and re-create the desired indexes or use the ALTER INDEX <index_name> REBUILD statement.

INITRANS is a fine-tuning parameter affecting I/O performance at the block level. INITRANS sets the number of initial transaction slots per block. This should represent the number of concurrent users or program accesses to the block. This is set at the table level. If your application has high concurrency requirements, set INITRANS correspondingly high to avoid excessive dynamic creation of transaction slots. The byte overhead is low, and the performance gain is worthwhile.

TUNING ROLLBACK SEGMENTS

Rollback segments are more-or-less random I/O components. They are written to con-currently (by DBWR), are buffered in the database buffer cache, and are stored in specialized tablespaces. Rollback segments can experience contention among themselves and between themselves and other database I/O components, such as data tablespaces. They provide the capability of undoing the effects of uncommitted transactions. Hence, they are generally referred to as the *undo logs*, or the undo part of a general purpose transaction log, with regard to all RDBMSs. Undo data means the read-consistent Oracle blocks found in either the database buffer cache in memory or in the rollback segment itself on disk. They are used for transaction rollback, instance recovery, and shared read capabilities. They are allocated to transactions in a circular fashion.

The major performance-tuning goal is to reduce contention. In other words, you want to minimize transaction waits for rollback segments, especially in a high-concurrency environment, which many OLTP systems are. Contention for rollback segments can best be avoided by creating a sufficient number of properly sized segments. Rollback segments hold transaction tables in their headers. Concurrent transactions contending for the same rollback segment show up as contention for the transaction table (undo header) itself. How can you detect this contention? Use the following:

```
SQL> SELECT CLASS, COUNT
     2> FROM V$WAITSTAT
     0> WHERE CLASS LIKE '%undo%'
     3> AND COUNT > 0;
```

You can alternatively use this:

```
SQL> SELECT USN, WAITS
     2> FROM V$ROLLSTAT
     3> WHERE WAITS > 0;
```

PART

IV

CH

19

You can also examine UNDO_SEGMENT where TRANS_TBL_WAITS > 0 from the rollback section of report.txt. You can also review the System wide wait events section of report.txt for '%undo%' events, or select these events from the view V$SYSTEM_EVENT. Also, if you encounter the ORA-01555: snapshot too old error, you have run out of rollback. You need either more segments, larger segments, or both.

If ORA-01555 occurs frequently or transaction table wait events are much greater than 0, this indicates contention. Specifically, for very large databases or for very high query concurrent databases (such as some DSS systems), if either of the WAITS / GETS from V$ROLLSTAT or TRANS_TBL_WAITS / TRANS_TBL_GETS ratios are > 1% (.01), there might be a rollback contention problem. Allocate the number of rollback segments as the number of concurrent users and programs divided by 4, up to a maximum of 50.

Other rollback segment tuning recommendations follow. Set NEXT = INITIAL for rollback segments. PCTINCREASE is always 0 for rollback segments. Set MINEXTENTS to >= 20 so that INITIAL * MINEXTENTS is about one percent below the tablespace (datafile) size to prevent dynamic extension, subject to increasing concurrency at the beginning of the rollback segments' lifespans. Set OPTIMAL = INITIAL * MINEXTENTS to prevent unnecessary shrinkage of the rollback segment. You can measure the amount of undo generated by transactions through the V$TRANSACTION view. Look at SUM(USED_UBLK) and MAX(USED_UBLK) at peak load times to determine the total and the maximum amount of undo during that interval. Set INITIAL to >= MAX(USED_UBLK) after several samplings. For additional fine tuning, set the init.ora parameters PROCESSES, TRANSACTIONS, and TRANSACTIONS_PER_ROLLBACK_SEGMENT appropriately. See the Oracle *Server Administrator's Guide* for further detail on these parameters. However, these parameters have minimal effects relative to allocating the proper numbers and sizes of your rollback segments.

Small transactions (usually found in OLTP systems) are those that generate small amounts of undo information. For this situation, use up to 50 rollback segments as per the previous guideline and commit as frequently as possible within the applications. Large transactions (usually found in batch systems) require single, large rollback segments. For this environment, you don't necessarily need many rollback segments, just larger ones. To ensure that a particularly long-running (large) transaction uses a particularly large rollback segment, use the following:

```
SQL> SET TRANSACTION USE ROLLBACK SEGMENT <rollback_segment>;
```

Set the init.ora parameter DISCRETE_TRANSACTIONS_ENABLED to TRUE if you have many small transactions that cause limited changes, such as updating only a few rows within one block at a time or inserting a single row at a time. See the Oracle *Server Administrator's Guide* for the detailed transaction criteria and prerequisites before using this parameter.

Tuning Redo Logs

Redo logs are sequential I/O components. In addition, they are written to (by LGWR) only one at a time, are buffered in a separate portion of the SGA (the log buffer), and are stored as OS files. So there is no contention for redo logs, only contention between redo logs and other database I/O components, such as data tablespaces. Redo logs serve only instance recovery (roll forward), as opposed to rollback segments, which serve additional purposes. The LGWR process writes to the redo logs (in effect, does a log flush) when one of the following occurs: a commit, a DBWR data flush (checkpoint), a checkpoint timeout occurs (at LOG_CHECKPOINT_INTERVAL), or the log buffer exceeds 1/3 full. They are allocated to LGWR in a circular fashion, and a log switch always triggers a checkpoint.

Some major performance tuning goals are to minimize the following:

- Checkpoints as much as possible for the given application
- Redo wait events as much as possible
- Redo latch contention issues

The following are recommendations to configure checkpointing mechanism:

1. Have >= 2 groups of >= 2 members on separate I/O channels (disks and controllers), each member the same size.

2. Set CHECKPOINT_PROCESS to TRUE in init.ora to offload the file header synchronization duties from the LGWR process to the CKPT process.

3. Leave the init.ora parameter LOG_CHECKPOINT_TIMEOUT set to 0.

4. Set LOG_CHECKPOINT_INTERVAL equal to the size of one redo log in OS blocks plus one OS block. Here is an example: all the redo log members are sized at 1MB, and 1MB = 1024KB = 2048 OS blocks (512 bytes per OS block). So set LOG_CHECKPOINT_INTERVAL to 2048 + 1, or 2049. This, plus having LOG_CHECKPOINT_TIMEOUT set to 0, enables checkpoints to occur only at log switch boundaries, generally a desirable performance enhancement.

PART

IV

CH

19

Caution

Very heavy OLTP environments need many large redo logs to support this type of configuration. Otherwise, you might need to reduce your checkpointing activity from nearly every minute to only once per log switch event, perhaps every 15–30 minutes.

Caution

If using ARCHIVELOG mode, ensure that your longest running transaction, the one generating the most redo information, will not consume the total of all your available redo log members. Otherwise, as whenever redo log switching outstrips archiving, your database will halt!

How do you monitor and tune redo wait events and redo latch contention issues? Examine the Statistic section of report.txt for 'redo log space requests' and the System wide wait events section of report.txt for 'log file space/switch'. These events can also be reviewed using the V$SYSSTAT and V$SYSTEM_EVENT views, respectively.

If either of these events are much greater than 0, this indicates that LOG_BUFFER is sized too small. Increase it by five percent or more, let your application run for some time, and query these measures again. Repeat this process until these events are at or very near zero.

Use the statistic 'redo size' Total from the Statistic section of report.txt, or the VALUE from V$SYSSTAT, to help you determine how to size your redo appropriately. This statistic is the total redo information generated for that sample interval.

Tip #19	Reduce the amount of (unnecessary) redo information generated by using SQL*Loader in Direct Path mode. If you're archiving, also specify UNRECOVERABLE. If you have PQO, specify UNRECOVERABLE for your parallel table and index create statements.

Redo copy latches, such as all latch (or 'spin lock') structures, are memory-based mechanisms that provide 'no-queue' locking of the redo LOG_BUFFER. There is actually only one redo allocation latch, and a process might hold it exclusively (described as a WAIT or WILLING_TO_WAIT request or status) while it writes and others wait; instead, it might release it (described as a NOWAIT or IMMEDIATE request or status) and hold a redo 'copy' latch while it writes, which enables another process to own the one redo allocation latch. How can you measure the contention for this resource? Use the V$LATCH view and compute the MISSES/GETS ratio where NAME is like 'redo%'. Similarly, compute the MISSES/GETS and NOWAIT_MISSES/NOWAIT_GETS ratios from the two latch sections of report.txt. Additionally, from the report.txt, observe the HIT_RATIO and NOWAIT_HIT_RATIO figures, which are the inverses of the misses-to-gets ratios just computed.

Note	If the any of the misses-to-gets ratios are much greater than 1 percent (.01) or either of the two hit ratios are much less than 99 percent (.99), there might be too much redo latch contention. To help remedy this, increase the init.ora parameter, LOG_SIMULTANEOUS_COPIES, which is set by default to the number of CPUs, up to twice the number of CPUs. To reduce locking times and promote Shortest Job First (SJF) allocation, which is optimal, reduce the size of the init.ora parameter LOG_SMALL_ENTRY_MAX_SIZE. It represents a threshold. If a process's redo information is less than this—that is, if it generates relatively small redo log entries—it can exclusively hold the one redo allocation latch (and quickly write its information and free up the latch faster than larger processes, thereby increasing concurrency). Examine its value using SHOW PARAMETER in SVRMGRL. Reduce it by a percentage (5 percent or 10 percent) at a time. Repeat the process until the amount of redo contention is acceptable.

ORACLE8 NEW I/O FEATURES

In addition to the Oracle8 new index features covered in Chapter 17, "Application Tuning," such as index-only tables and equi-partitioned objects, there are some other Oracle8 new features that offer opportunities for I/O performance gains. These include partition-extended table names and direct load INSERTs.

PARTITION-EXTENDED TABLE NAMES

Table partitioning, as discussed with regard to equi-partitioned objects (tables and indexes, equally partitioned along the same value sets), offers an alternative to partition views. Partition views (Oracle 7) using PQO must be manually created by horizontally fragmenting a single, long table into many smaller tables, creating a view to unite them all, creating constraints on the value sets within each smaller table, and setting the init.ora parameter PARTITION_VIEW_ENABLED to TRUE. Partitioned tables (Oracle 8) are created as shown in Chapter 29, "Partitioning," by partitioning a chosen column. However, rather than having a view made up of a union of tables, you have a table made up of a union of partitions. In addition, you can reference the partitions directly, with certain restrictions:

```
SQL> SELECT * FROM T1 PARTITION (P1);
```

In addition, Oracle8 provides the capability of migrating previously created Oracle7 partition views to Oracle8 partitioned tables.

DIRECT LOAD INSERTS

With direct load INSERTs, INSERTs can take advantage of the same Direct Path mode of SQL*Loader capability, which bypasses the database buffer cache, generates no redo information, and writes directly to the datafiles. Furthermore, in Oracle8, you can put a table, index, or tablespace in No-logging mode. This additionally enhances your direct load INSERTs. Direct Load INSERTs trade off space for performance because they insert rows above the HWM of a segment. This wastes space, but it is not a major issue if a segment is often close to full, does not experience major grow-shrink patterns, and (especially) has a tablespace to itself. For hot tables, this capability might be used in conjunction with planned, periodic reorganization.

PART

IV

CH

19

CHAPTER 20

ORACLE8.x TUNING CONSIDERATIONS

In this chapter

Whereas Chapter 16 applies regardless of any specific vendor RDBMS software or version, and most of what is in Chapters 17-19 applies to both the Oracle7.x and the Oracle8.x RDBMS, this chapter applies almost exclusively to the Oracle8.x RDBMS. You will examine I/O, memory, and networking improvements with regards to performance.

PARTITIONING

Of course, the major I/O performance enhancement with the Oracle8.x RDBMS over the Oracle7.x RDBMS is surely partitioning. In Chapter 10, "Partitioning," you discovered some of the differences between Oracle7.x partition views and Oracle8.x partitioning, and it is relatively clear that the Oracle8.x incarnation has certain performance advantages. Whereas Oracle7.x partition views rely on multiple tables and views of those tables unioned, there is no native language support because there are really no new structures. Hence, the I/O granularity in terms of all things (locking, optimization, and so on) remains at the table level. In contrast, with Oracle8.x, partitions are not only new storage constructs, but are accounted for natively at the language, and therefore optimization, levels.

One of the major performance advantages with partitions is partition elimination. Review this concept. If a table is partitioned on some column (the partition key), any given query (that is, SELECT statement) can possibly be satisfied by the rows in only one of those partitions. An example is that you have partitioned employees on a column such as pay grade. If you want to examine one pay grade, you need only access one partition to retrieve those requested rows. The Oracle optimizer knows this because it can match the range of values you requested against those ranges of values you previously used to (horizontally) partition the rows of the table. Partition elimination can potentially speed up performance by as much as n times if there are n partitions to search.

Of course, partitioning is a divide-and-conquer physical design strategy (refer to Chapter 3, "Physical Database Design, Hardware, and Related Issues"), just like RAID and Oracle "manual" striping. If there are n partitions to access and process parallelization accompanies this data parallelization (for example, Parallel Query), the speed up can approach n times. However, the overhead of recombination subtracts from the overall performance speed up by some factor for all the aforementioned methods. You will further discover some Oracle process parallelization methods, Parallel Query (Oracle7.x and Oracle8.x) and Parallel Data Manipulation Language (Oracle8.x), later in this chapter in the section "Parallel Data Manipulation Language (PDML)."

Another consideration with partitioning is that it adds a level of locking granularity between a table and a row. This is almost always helpful to add a granularity of locking, especially if it is at a level lower than that of a table. Consider the overhead of a multitude of row locks, say approximately 1/5 of the total number of rows, when a single partition lock might do. Hence, when row-level locks are needed, they are granted. But when a partition-level lock is acquired instead of a table lock, then you have saved not only the overhead of many row locks, but also provided for more concurrent access to the nonlocked partitions. Table locks are determined at parse time and then are acquired at execution time. Partition locks are both determined and acquired at execution time in place of table locks whenever possible.

In Oracle8.x, there is a *logging/nologging* attribute, which is applicable during some SQL statements at the tablespace, table, index, or partition level. The nologging attribute supersedes the *unrecoverable* option in Oracle7.x. However, for backward compatibility, the unrecoverable option is still currently supported. The nologging attribute is specified on a database object, whereas the unrecoverable option was associated with a statement. For example, all `INSERT` operations (serial or parallel) generate no redo log entries with nologging in effect on the objects which would be affected. As another example, `CREATE TABLE` and `CREATE INDEX` can use nologging on their affected objects as they would have used unrecoverable in their statements. Further, `INSERT...SELECT` and `CREATE TABLE AS SELECT` are potential operations which could take advantage of the nologging attribute.

Direct load operations are supported in a parallel fashion, as you will discover further under the "Parallel Data Manipulation Language (PDML)" section later in this chapter; however, they can also be serial. A direct load is akin to SQL*Loader direct path mode. Direct loads are only for `INSERT` operations. They use temporary segments to insert into, and from which they then append directly above the high water mark (HWM) of the target object. The HWM is adjusted to its new level for the object, and the newly inserted rows are given `ROWID`s. This type of load is in contrast to the regular way of inserting; that is, having to go through the SGA associated freelist before writing to the datafiles underlying the target objects. `INSERT /*+ APPEND */` supplies an optimizer hint to use direct loads, and this is the mechanism used to enable direct loading on objects. If direct load is not desired, nothing special need be done, unless for some reason you want to fully insure it—then use the `NOAPPEND` hint.

INDEX ONLY TABLES (IOTS)

With ordinary Oracle indexes based on a B-tree variation data structure, you basically have the index, which is essentially a sorted subset of the table in question, and the table itself. With Oracle8.x, you can have Index-Only Tables that are essentially tables which are themselves their own index, too. That is, the table and the index structure are one and the same. As a point of comparison, Sybase has always clustered indexes in which a table is physically sorted as opposed to logically sorted by another index structure (*nonclustered index* in Sybase terms). Hence, Oracle Index-Only Tables are analogs of Sybase clustered indexes, and regular Oracle indexes are analogs of Sybase nonclustered indexes.

Why do you need Index-Only Tables? Regular Oracle indexes (B-trees) are quite efficient for most database applications if used correctly. However, they do have some drawbacks. First, they store the indexed columns redundantly. Hence, performance is inversely proportional to key size. Second, B-trees always require at least two logical reads (and usually more): one to read the index and one to read the table. How can this situation be improved? A natural extension is the Index-Only Table (IOT).

There are some considerations and restrictions in using these IOTs, however. An Index-Only Table can only be physically sorted once, and it is restricted to the primary key. As you can imagine, then, an IOT must have a primary key. An Oracle Index-Only Table (like a Sybase clustered index) is an RDBMS example of an inverted index or inverted list, which

PART

IV

CH

20

were data structures used in 3GL and file processing systems predating modern DBMSs. Also, IOTs can be neither partitioned nor replicated. Perhaps the most important issue when considering the usage of an IOT is the fact that it has no ROWIDs! For example, because there are no ROWIDs, creating other indexes on an IOT is not possible. (This is in contrast to Sybase, which does enable secondary indexes on a clustered index table.) IOTs cannot be part of an index cluster or hash cluster. Further, unique constraints other than the primary key cannot be enforced because with Oracle, unique constraints (like primary keys) are enforced through indexing.

Listing 20.1 gives you an example of creating an Index-Only Table.

LISTING 20.1   CREATING AN INDEX-ONLY TABLE

```
SQL> create table employee
  1 (eid number,
  2 ename char(35),
  3 eaddr varchar2(80),
  4 resume CLOB)
  5 primary key (eid)
  6 organization index
  7 tablespace data1
  8 pctthreshold 90
  9 overflow tablespace data2;
```

Notice several things with the CREATE statement. You are creating an Index-Only Table (employee) on the primary key (eid) in a given tablespace (data1) and specifying that it is an IOT by using the organization index clause. You further specify that if any rows exceed 90% of your Oracle block size (db_block_size), you are to store the nonkey columns of those rows in the overflow tablespace (data2). The overflow area functions much like an overflow area for chained rows, which contain overflow pointers to overflow segments. An IOT column in the dba_tables and user_tables views has a new IOT column, which is set to IOT, IOT_OVERFLOW, or NULL (for regular, or non-IOT, tables).

PARALLEL DATA MANIPULATION LANGUAGE (PDML)

Recall that you briefly covered some of the aspects of parallelism with partitions in Chapter 10. This chapter goes into a little more depth and not specifically limiting itself to partitioned parallelism. There are three main types of parallelism granularity, and each is applicable to its own set of SQL statements, as is demonstrated in Table 20.1.

TABLE 20.1   PARALLELISM GRANULARITY FOR SQL STATEMENTS

Type	SQL Statements	Remarks
ROWIDs	SELECT	Within a table or partition
Partitions	UPDATE, DELETE	At the partition level
Slaves	INSERT...SELECT	At the table level

The Parallel Query (PQ) architecture is the same in Oracle8.x as it was in Oracle7.x. However, now it is possible to parallelize some INSERT, UPDATE, and DELETE operations in addition to the parallelization of SELECT by PQ. This new DML capability (remember: Oracle refers to DML as INSERT, UPDATE, and DELETE) is called Parallel Data Manipulation Language (PDML). PQ can parallelize within a partition, whereas PDML can only parallelize at the partition or table levels.

Parallelization by ROWIDs is handled for SELECT statements by Parallel Query. It is irrelevant whether a table is partitioned because the parallelism is at a lower level of granularity than the partition (ROWID). This means that multiple PQ slaves can read from a single table or a single partition. However, no PQ slave can span more than one partition.

Parallelization by partitions or slave processes is handled for UPDATE, DELETE, and INSERT... SELECT operations by PDML. First, consider UPDATE and DELETE operations. When the subject tables are partitioned, the parallelism is by partitions for UDPATE and DELETE with only one slave permitted per partition. When the subject tables are not partitioned, UPDATE and DELETE cannot be parallelized.

Regardless of whether the subject tables are partitioned, INSERT...SELECT is parallelized by distributing the new rows (without ROWIDs) by volume across INSERT slave processes. Multiple slaves insert above the high water mark concurrently in a direct load fashion, as you saw in the earlier performance considerations regarding direct loading in the "Partitioning" section in this chapter. There can be multiple slaves per table or partition, as the case might be.

As you might recall from Chapter 10, you enable PDML at the session level, as opposed to PQ, which is typically enabled at the instance level, although controllable at the session level also. Parallel hints within your SQL code, as were done for PQ, are done the same way for PDML. Also, the precedence rules still apply for determining the degree of parallelism. In addition to considering the number of CPUs on the system and the number of partitions to be accessed (if partitioned), PDML, like PQ, will pick only one of the following *parallel directives* to determine the degree of parallelism with which to execute the subject SQL statement:

1. Hint-specified degree
2. Table default degree
3. Table with largest degree (hint or default) in a join

PART
IV

CH
20

Listing 20.2 gives you a subtle example of an INSERT...SELECT with hints. Assume the tables T1 and T2 both have default degrees of 8. What will be the overall degree of parallelism Oracle picks to execute this statement?

LISTING 20.2   USING HINTS IN AN INSERT...SELECT STATEMENT

```
SQL> INSERT /*+ parallel(T1,4) */
INTO T1
SELECT /*+ parallel (T2,6) */ column1, column2, column3
FROM T2;
```

The overall degree of parallelism will be 4 because the INSERT hint is considered first and overrides not only table default degrees (8), but also the SELECT hint (6). The table with the largest degree associated with it (here, both T1 and T2 with 8 each) does not apply because there is no join involved.

Finally, how can you monitor PDML activity to help you adjust out degrees of parallelism, as you would normally do with PQ? The PDML_ENABLED column has been added to the V$SESSION view and will specify YES or NO, corresponding of course to whether PDML is enabled for that session. The row DML Parallelized has been added to the V$PQ_SESSTAT view, enabling you to see how many DML operations have been parallelized cumulatively for that session. Also, V$PQ_SYSSTAT now contains a new row, DML Initiated, representing all the cumulative instances DML initiated across all sessions. Note, too, that in V$PQ_SYS-STAT, all the other "old" rows apply as sums of both the PQ and the PDML activity. For example, "Servers Highwater" will represent the most slave processes ever started by either PQ or PDML. As this section has focused mostly on PDML, please refer to Chapter 38, "Parallel Query Management", for more in-depth coverage of PQ alone.

Why is PDML a performance enhancement with Oracle8.x? Well, just as *n*-way data parallelization (that is, partitioning) can help lay the foundation for an *n* times speed up, it is process parallelization (PQ and PDML) that actually supplies the other missing half of the "parallelization equation." Hence, accompanying either RAID, striping, or especially partitioning with Oracle8.x, PQ and PDML can facilitate an *n* times speed up.

THE LARGE POOL AND VERY LARGE MEMORY

As of 8.0.2, the Large Pool is an optional new memory area within the SGA. It can be used to support UGA (session-specific) memory reallocations by the MultiThreaded Server (MTS), or even XA, to support I/O slaves' memory allocations such as those used by DBWR and LGWR (db_writer_processes, dbwr_io_slaves, and lgwr_io_slaves), and memory allocations by backup and restore operations.

By creating a Large Pool to be separate from, for example, the Shared Pool, MTS does not have to grow within the shared pool, thereby shrinking the available room for the library (SQL) cache. This is because the Shared Pool is not dynamically reallocated, and both MTS and SQL caching (along with data dictionary caching) compete for that same memory resource. However, within the statically allocated Shared Pool, both MTS and SQL caching are dynamically allocated memory structures. To help alleviate this situation, you can allocate a Large Pool to be mainly used by MTS and leave the Shared Pool to mainly handle SQL caching. This breaks up the Shared Pool bottleneck and prevents the grow-shrink cycle of contention within it.

I/O slaves, as well as backup and restore processes, can allocate memory in the hundreds of KB. Under heavy contention, the Shared Pool might not be able to keep up with these processes, and they might therefore become memory-starved. Essentially, they remain in long wait states, not progressing or progressing very little at a time. The Large Pool can also alleviate this situation by removing some of the contention burden from the Shared

Pool. Because the large pool does not have an LRU list, as you would expect in a caching situation, it has less overhead and simply acts more as a large, lightweight buffer.

The relevant `init.ora` parameters are listed in Table 20.2.

TABLE 20.2   `init.ora` PARAMETERS

Parameter	Description
large_pool_size*	Size of the large pool
large_pool_min_alloc*	Minimum allocation from large pool
shared_pool_size	Size of the shared pool
shared_pool_reserved_size	Size of reserved list for large objects
shared_pool_reserved_min_alloc	Minimum allocation from reserved list

* New to Oracle8.x.

Remember to figure in the Large Pool as part of the overall memory allocated to the SGA by Oracle.

Although Very Large Memory is a capability that existed in later versions of 7.3.x, it was relatively overlooked by the user community and therefore underused. It should find much more use with Oracle8.x, and this is why it is covered in this chapter, as opposed to Chapter 18, "Tuning Memory".

Oracle Very Large Memory capability was largely conceived because of memory addressing limitations of the Windows NT operating system. Although Windows NT can run on 64-bit machines such as AlphaServers, it is nonetheless a 32-bit operating system with 32-bit addressing limitations, among other restrictions. For example, with a 32-bit machine, conceivably 2 to the 32nd power, or 4GB, of memory should be addressable. However, Windows NT reserves 2GB for itself ("system addressability"), leaving 2GB of memory for user threads ("user addressability"). Please note, however, that the Enterprise Edition of NT needs only to reserve 1GB, thereby effectively adding 1GB to the maximum user addressability (making it 3GB).

However, not all NT machines have 4GB or more of physical memory installed. How, then, can Oracle operate on an NT machine with, for example, only 2GB (or less) of physical memory? In reality, NT will grow downward from the uppermost memory-addressing region, permitting user threads, such as Oracle, to grow upward. The problem, of course, then becomes whether NT and Oracle will be able to get all that they require dynamically, without "stepping on each others' feet," so to speak. In fact, what usually happens on such systems is that either NT or Oracle begins swapping and thrashing as opposed to ordinary paging, and under these types of conditions, this often causes fatal crashes due to memory (lack of) resource errors.

How does VLM work? Another way of asking this is how does a user process go about accessing existing physical memory not directly addressable by the operating system at hand? The answer is: *indirectly*. Lotus, Intel, and Microsoft many years ago created a specification for getting around the then so-called "640KB or the 1MB barrier" of DOS physical memory access. They succeeded in creating what is now known as the LIM specification for *expanded memory*. What they did was to use some of the upper memory of DOS (the 384KB above the first 640KB), which was directly addressable, to store the addresses of memory above 1MB. In essence, they used addressable memory to function as indirect addressing or in other words, as a memory paging table. The LIM specification opened the door to applications such as the Lotus 1-2-3 spreadsheet to access memory of several MB. Although this technology is now obsolete, first with the advent of extended memory and later with the advent of Microsoft Windows memory addressing, it was extremely innovative at the time.

How does LIM compare to VLM? Oracle VLM is predicated on the exact same notion of expanding memory access through indirection. Although the actual implementation is different, the concept is functionally the same. *Memory donor* processes are pseudo-user threads, which Oracle VBLM uses to expand the access of its memory addressability beyond 2GB on a 4GB NT machine. With Oracle VLM, the limit of memory addressability is whatever the physical memory is installed, minus the 1 or 2GB NT requires. Tests conducted by Oracle have shown performance improvements of between one and two orders of magnitude; or in other words, between 10× and 100× sped up. (This is extremely good, considering the theoretical maximum gain, without overhead, is about three orders of magnitude.)

How to get VLM to work? One parameter in the `init.ora` file is applicable: `use_indirect_data_buffers`. Set this to `TRUE`, and Oracle can use memory not only outside of its normal SGA allocation, but beyond the 4GB addressable period by NT or any other user threads. In other words, this enables Oracle VLM. Additional `init.ora` parameters might be required or needed to be adjusted. Please refer to your Oracle8 Server Tuning Guide or Oracle8 Tuning Guide which will contain even more specific implementation details. The following is a summary of some useful Oracle VLM information:

- Permits indirect access to all of physical memory beyond NT reach
- Is bundled with Oracle Enterprise Edition
- Runs transparently on NT 4.0, NT 4.0 Enterprise Edition, and NT 5.0
- No application code changes are required
- Has shown as much as 2–3 orders of magnitude performance increase

NETWORKING ENHANCEMENTS

One major functional enhancement with regard to networking can impact performance in a positive way. The construct known as the *external procedure* is now available. An external procedure is some piece of code external to PL/SQL or SQL. It can be useful in that it already does some very complex or unique processing, such as some kinds of scientific programming. In other words, many legacy routines exist which function perfectly well, and aside from Oracle integration, there is no other reason to rewrite them. To reuse existing working code is a faster way to develop than to rewrite code.

Not only might reusing external routines rather than rewriting them be the fastest way to develop, it might also be the case that the routines themselves are in fact faster than you could ever write in PL/SQL anyway. For example, they can be written in some compact and fast 3GL language such as C. Further, C can also "wrap" assembler code, which is about as fast as any application code is going to get, assuming it is properly coded.

The steps that occur when an external process is called from within PL/SQL are the following:

1. PL/SQL calls an external process using an *alias library*.
2. PL/SQL passes this request to the Net8 listener.
3. The listener starts the `extproc` dedicated process.
4. `extproc` loads the external shared library.
5. `extproc` executes the external procedure on behalf of PL/SQL.

An alias library is an internal Oracle library that maps to an external (operating system) shared library. To create (associate) an alias library, simply use the extended DDL, as in the following example:

```
SQL> create or replace library libm
2    is '/usr/share/libm.so';
```

What privileges does a user need to be able to create or use these alias libraries? To create one, an administrator or user needs CREATE LIBRARY or CREATE ANY LIBRARY. Users of the external process will need the EXECUTE privilege on the alias library itself. The accuracy of your CREATE LIBRARY statement is checked only at runtime, not at creation time. Hence, ensure that the shared libraries actually do exist precisely as the absolute (includes full path) filename specified. To review the state of the libraries, you can select from USER_LIBRARIES or ALL_LIBRARIES.

The `extproc` process started by the listener lasts only for the duration of the session bounding an external process *callout*. Each session uses a different `extproc` process to execute the external processes requested. You must configure the listener to associate the instance. A separate listener is recommended to prevent corruption of the SGA due to memory leaks from external programs or their interaction with PL/SQL. An `extproc` entry within TNSNAMES.ORA is as any other entry. However, the name of the `extproc` alias must be extproc_connection_data, which is predefined on installation. Simply uncomment it, edit it if necessary, and use it. The following is an example of an extproc entry:

```
extproc_connection_data =
(
DESCRIPTION =
(ADDRESS = (PROTOCOL = ipc) (KEY = mysid) )
(CONNECT_DATA = (SID = mysid) )
)
```

DATABASE LIMITS

Database limits periodically increase, and they tend to increase whenever a new release of RDBMS software comes out. Historically, many RDBMS vendors have had some of their own shortcomings, and different RDBMSs have had different weaknesses. However, it appears that Oracle8.x has some ceilings that are unlikely to be reached by most applications, even most VLDBs, any time soon.

Table 20.3 gives the new datatype maximums.

TABLE 20.3 DATATYPE MAXIMUMS

Datatype	Maximum Bytes
CHAR(n)	n <= 2000
VARCHAR(n)	n <= 4000
VARCHAR2(n)	n <= 4000
NCHAR(n)	n <= 4000

In addition to increasing the maximum number of bytes per some datatypes, what other database object maximums exist? Table 20.4 provides just that information.

TABLE 20.4 DATABASE OBJECT MAXIMUMS

Object	Maximum Number
Database size	512 PB (Petabytes)
Tablespaces per database	~ 2 billion
Datafiles per tablespace	1022
Columns per table	1000
Indexed columns per table	32

SUMMARY

Now review what you have covered, and briefly, how this relates to performance. You have covered the Oracle8.x enhancements (concepts and/or constructs), along with some description and relevance to performance that are detailed in Table 20.5.

TABLE 20.5 ORACLE ENHANCEMENTS

Enhancement	Description	Importance
Partitioning	Data parallelization	RAID-like speed up
IOTs	Inverted list	Half the logical I/Os
PDML	Process parallelization	Factorial speed up
Large Pool	Offload the Shared Pool	More scalable
VLM	Indirect memory access	Access above 4GB on NT
Extproc	External process	Callouts to C
Ceilings	Datatypes and objects	Mainly for VLDBs

All these enhancements are a significant improvement over Oracle7.x. However, taken altogether, Oracle should be able to store and retrieve from VLDBs and Data Warehousing systems with much more native parallelization (data and code) capabilities than ever before.

PART

V

Managing the Oracle Database

CHAPTER 21

MANAGING DATABASE STORAGE

In this chapter

ADMINISTERING DATABASE OBJECTS

An Oracle database has many different components that consume disk and system resources. As you will see, each resource has unique storage characteristics and requires unique handling and care. In the following sections, you'll look at database segments and their unique storage concerns. I'll talk about the segments themselves, such as tables, clusters, indexes, rollback segments, and temporary segments, as well as the internal methods used by the Oracle database to store them.

MANAGING ORACLE BLOCKS

The smallest unit of storage addressable by the Oracle server is the Oracle block. All database segments are composed of Oracle blocks, and the block structure is the same whether the segment is a table, index, cluster, or other object. Designing a database with optimal characteristics starts with the proper configuration and administration of the Oracle blocks.

Each Oracle block is made up of the following three sections:

- Block header
- Data storage
- Free space areas

The block header contains information about the block—what type of segment data is stored in the block, what segments have data in the block, the address of the block, and pointers to the actual rows stored in it. The header size is composed of a fixed part and a variable part, and a block header in general uses 85 to 100 bytes in the block.

Within the Oracle block, managing the data storage and free space areas are directly related to each other. The data area is where the rows are actually stored in the block. The reserved free space area is a region, defined as a percentage of the total available space, that is reserved to store information for future updates of rows stored in the block. Managing the data and reserved block areas are the main concern of Oracle block administration, and are discussed later in the chapter.

UNDERSTANDING PCTFREE AND PCTUSED

PCTFREE and PCTUSED are two storage parameters applied to segments that are often misunderstood, but the concept is actually quite simple (despite Oracle's somewhat poor choice of semantics). When Oracle writes information to the database, it must first find one or more blocks within a segment's allocated extents in which to store the information. Oracle maintains a list of blocks that are free for each segment (this is also known as a *free list*). Oracle uses the combination of PCTFREE and PCTUSED parameters to determine when blocks do and do not have sufficient space to accept new information.

Tip #20	In many cases, Oracle's default settings for *PCTFREE* and *PCTUSED* work quite well. However, it is important to always be observant and keep in mind the implications of the default settings. In particular, regularly watch out for *row migration*.

If the percentage of free space in a block is greater than the *PCTFREE* parameter, it is added to the segment's free list so that it can be used to store new information (for instance, a new row in a table or a new index node for an index segment). When the percentage of free space has fallen below *PCTFREE*, the block is considered "full," and Oracle removes it from a segment's freelist. Should the percentage of space used in a block fall below *PCTUSED*, Oracle then adds the block to the segment's free list so that it can again be used to store new information. This method allows Oracle to keep enough extra space for rows to grow without having to span more than one block. Keeping rows confined to a single block helps keep your database running at peak performance.

The values of *PCTFREE* and *PCTUSED* should never equal 100%. If a segment is configured this way, it is possible that a block will continually be taken off of and placed on the free list by every minor data manipulation. The overhead incurred by the database engine handling can easily be avoided by leaving a margin of at least 20% between *PCTFREE* and *PCTUSED*. The Oracle defaults of 10 for *PCTFREE* and 40 for *PCTUSED* illustrate this margin.

PCTFREE and *PCTUSED* are specified in the storage clause of a database segment. You can query their current values using the *dba_tables*, *dba_clusters*, or *dba_indexes* data dictionary views. Using *PCTFREE* and *PCTUSED*, you can fine-tune the storage characteristics of individual segments to meet their particular storage needs. For example, a table that will never be updated (a main-frame database extract used for reporting, or tables held in read-only tablespaces) can be safely set with a *PCTFREE* of 0. This saves you space in each block—for a 4KB block and *PCTFREE* setting of 10, approximately 800 bytes per block is available for data that would have been reserved. For a 500MB table, you could realize savings of around 50MB for implementing this one minor change. On the other hand, a table containing columns that are guaranteed to be updated in the future can be set with a higher *PCTFREE* to avoid row chaining or migration. Row chaining and migration is discussed in detail in the "Understanding Database Fragmentation" section of this chapter.

Figure 21.1 shows how *PCTUSED* and *PCTFREE* work together to control space utilization inside the block. In the example, assume that *PCTFREE* is set to 10% and *PCTUSED* is set to 40%. Number 1 shows that new data can be added into this block until less than 20% free space remains. This is because 20% of the space after block overheads is reserved for future updates via the *PCTFREE* parameter. Number 2 shows that when the *PCTFREE* limit is reached, the remaining free space can only be used for updates of existing data—no new inserts are permitted in this block. Number 3 shows the block being placed back on the free list as a result of deletions or updates and the used space in the block falling below 40% (the *PCTUSED* setting of the table). Number 4 shows that when the used space falls below *PCTUSED*, new insertions are now possible in the block. As insertions are made inside the block, the used space starts increasing, again touching the upper limit, and the cycle begins again.

Figure 21.1
The relation between
PCTFREE and
PCTUSED.

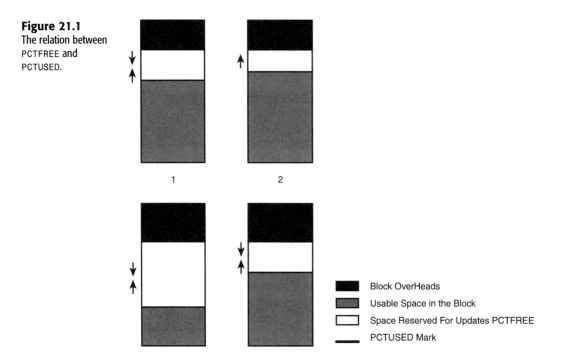

- Block OverHeads
- Usable Space in the Block
- Space Reserved For Updates PCTFREE
- PCTUSED Mark

INDEXES AND PCTUSED/PCTFREE

It is worth noting that indexes, because of their structural nature, use *PCTUSED* and *PCTFREE* somewhat differently than tables. These parameters apply only when an index is initially created and have no further function during future updates. *PCTFREE*'s setting, therefore, allows an index structure to be initially built with enough room in the leaf blocks to allow additional keys to be added without having to repeatedly split existing leaf blocks to accommodate new keys. Because row deletes cannot happen during an index build, indexes do not benefit from any *PCTUSED* setting.

Tip #21	When creating a new index against an existing table, if the table is expected to grow considerably in the near term future, consider specifying a low *PCTFREE* value when creating the index.

MANAGING TABLE STORAGE

Table size (roughly a function of row width×number of rows) is probably the best metric for determining storage needs. A table's space requirements are roughly the product of average row length and number of rows. When DBAs discuss the approximate *size* of the databases in their care, the number of rows is often used as a metric. Although this by itself does not provide a lot of information for planning long term storage needs, it does tend to give you some insight as to the magnitude of the database size.

Tables are generally the starting point for most storage management; they act as a yardstick of sorts that determines the storage needs of most other database components. For this reason, understanding the nature of the data contained in database tables (data types, number of null columns, and so on) proves to be beneficial to the savvy DBA.

A table's size increases as new rows are inserted or existing rows are updated with larger values. The average length of a row and the number of rows are the main factors influencing a table's size.

Sizing a table is a conceptual task and should be done in the design phase, before the table is created. Issues, such as expected growth and storage parameter values, should be handled when deciding sizing parameters.

Consider the following CREATE TABLE example:

```
create table employee (              /* PART 1 */
  emp_no     char(4),
  emp_name   varchar2(30),
  age        number,
  dept_id    char(4)
)
  tablespace EMPLOYEE_TS             /* PART 2 */
  storage ( initial 10M
            next    10M
            pctincrease 0
            minextents 1
            maxextents  50
    freelists 1)
 pctfree 10;
```

The CREATE TABLE statement is made up of two parts: Part 1 (as labeled) is the mandatory table definition, where you indicate the key attributes such as columns, datatypes, and constraints. Part 2 deals with sizing issues related to the table and is what you are interested in. Let's look at an explanation of these sizing parameters:

- TABLESPACE—What tablespace the table will be created in. If omitted, the table is created in the default tablespace for the owner.

- INITIAL—The size of the initial extent allocated for the table.

- NEXT—The size of the next extent allocated for the table, if the initial extent is completely filled with table rows.

- PCTINCREASE—Percentage to oversize the third (if minextents is set to one) and subsequent extents of the table. Originally created as a way to "lazily" handle extending tables, this parameter can quickly make life difficult for the unwary DBA. For example, a table with PCTINCREASE of 50 (the default), an INITIAL setting of 10M, and a NEXT of 10M have a first extent of size 10M, a second extent of size 10M, a third extent of 15M (10M×150%), a fourth extent of 22.5M, and so on. Calculate the size of the eleventh extent and you'll see a value of 0 or 1 is recommended for this parameter.

- MINEXTENTS—The number of extents allocated at creation time. For tables this is almost always 1—rollback segments have different requirements, as discussed later, in "Managing Rollback Segments."

- *MAXEXTENTS*—The maximum number of extents the table can allocate. Although versions 7.3 and later of the Oracle RDBMS enable you to have unlimited extents allocated, it is useful to give this parameter a value if only to alert you of an object wildly overextending.

- *PCTFREE*—The amount of space reserved in each block of the segment for future updates of existing rows.

- *PCTUSED*—The point at which a block in the segment is placed back onto the free list. Both *PCTFREE* and *PCTUSED* are discussed in the previous section.

- *FREELISTS*—Specifies the number of freelists to be stored in the freelist group of the table, index, or cluster. This defaults to one, and should be increased only if many simultaneous updates to a single block of the table are expected.

MANAGING INDEXES

Indexes can be the most difficult type of segment to manage. Many application programmers (as well as DBAs) try to solve any database performance issue by asking for more indexes. Remember that more indexes almost always hurts update performance and might not always provide better *SELECT* performance. Keep close tabs on your indexes and remove any that are not being used.

Tip #22	Use Oracle's *EXPLAIN PLAN* facility to determine whether an added index had the desired effect on queries.

Many unnecessary indexes can, over time, creep into your database and cause performance problems. Oracle almost always prefers performance to disk space thriftiness. Keep a record of every non–primary key index and the application the index has been created for, as well as the particular function or problem the index was created to solve. It is not unusual for several indexes to be created for a specific application; without documentation, you might find yourself supporting indexes created for applications that no longer exist.

MONITORING ROLLBACK SEGMENTS

Rollback segments are a bit different than other segments such as indexes and tables. Because rollback segments are dynamic in nature, DBAs should generally focus on making sure each rollback segment and associated tablespace has sufficient space for growth without the use of too many extents.

MONITORING TEMPORARY TABLESPACES AND SEGMENTS

Like rollback segments, the temporary tablespaces in an Oracle database require special monitoring. Temporary segments are held only as long as the transaction creating the segment is active. Therefore, high-water marks are your metric, rather than how much space is being used at any one point in time. The goal is ensuring that enough space exists for the largest transaction the system will have to process.

UNDERSTANDING DATABASE FRAGMENTATION

One of the most common problems facing database administrators deals with fragmentation of database objects. Fragmentation wastes space, causes performance problems, and makes administration of database objects more difficult than necessary. The term database fragmentation, however, is a class of problems, rather than a problem in and of itself—there are several problem areas that fall under the generic term of database fragmentation, including fragmented database objects, fragmented tablespaces, chained rows, and migrated rows.

Tip #23	DBAs should be particularly conscious of how database applications perform their tasks. Developers often create temporary tables or data rows that are deleted prior to the end of a program. This practice can cause fragmentation without leaving many clues. DBAs are encouraged to be at least casually familiar with how database applications are designed.

Database fragmentation is usually the result of rows being inserted, updated, and deleted, and objects being created and dropped. Thus, a newly created database is not fragmented. It's only after you've run one or more active applications on your database that you begin to see evidence of database fragmentation.

In the following sections, I'll look at four types of database fragmentation and outline ways you can fix your database, as well as prevent this from happening in the first place.

UNDERSTANDING FRAGMENTED TABLESPACES

Tablespaces become fragmented through the erratic and unplanned dropping and recreating of database objects within the tablespace. Tablespace fragmentation occurs when *bubbles* of free space become trapped between used extents in a tablespace. This happens when objects that reside in the tablespace are dropped. These bubbles of trapped space can be reused, but only if an object is created that fits in the space left by the object.

Note	Tablespaces do not become fragmented through any row-level activity. This is a common—but completely false—misconception.

For example, assume there are four tables in a tablespace: customer, employee, stock, and company. Each of these objects is composed of one extent of 10MB each. The configuration of this tablespace looks like Figure 21.2. Note the free extent of 10MB at the end of the tablespace, and how closely packed these objects are. This is the goal, and what you should attempt to obtain at the end of the day.

PART

V

CH

21

Figure 21.2
Tablespace
configuration before
fragmentation.

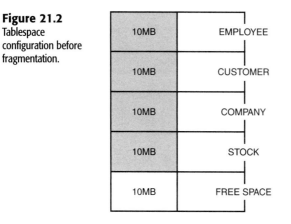

Of course, you can't have this situation for long. Assume that due to performance requirements, you have to move the customer table into a different tablespace. The tablespace will now look like Figure 21.3. Notice the 10MB hole in the tablespace. If you need to create another object with a size less than or equal to 10MB, there is no problem. But assume you need to create a policy table in this tablespace, having storage parameters of an initial extent of 15MB and a next extent of 10MB. This tablespace has 20MB of total free space, but the maximum size of any free extent is only 10MB; therefore, your creation of the policy table will fail.

Figure 21.3
Fragmentation in
the tablespace after
dropping one table.

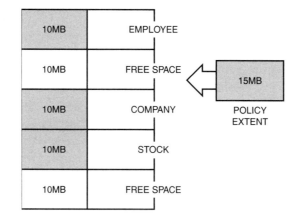

This example shows the problem occurring on a very small scale, with only one object in the tablespace being dropped. Consider a busy real life development environment, however, where objects are dropped and different-sized objects are created almost continually. This activity results in non-contiguous bubbles of free space forming all over the tablespace—similar to that depicted in Figure 21.4. The total free space of the tablespace seems quite adequate at first glance, but no large contiguous free space extents are in the tablespace, which severely limit your ability to make use of the free space.

Figure 21.4
A completely frag-
mented tablespace.

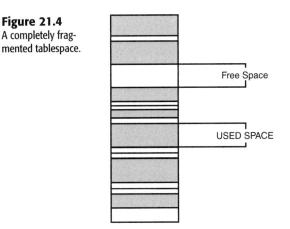

The Oracle RDBMS does try to help the DBA slightly with space allocation and management. Consider the same scenario above with four tables in the tablespace. Now suppose
you drop two of the tables, both of which reside in the "middle" of the tablespace. This
gives you a tablespace structure as shown in Figure 21.5. If the same request for a 15MB
table is processed, the SMON background process automatically coalesces the two 10M
extents into one 20MB extent, and uses it to fulfill the object creation. *SMON* also coalesces
space automatically, if the *PCTINCREASE* for the tablespace is set to a non-zero value.

Figure 21.5
Fragmentation in
tablespace after
dropping two tables.

10MB	EMPLOYEE
10MB	FREE SPACE
10MB	FREE SPACE
10MB	STOCK
10MB	FREE SPACE

You can also manually coalesce the space in a tablespace with the following command:

```
alter tablespace armslivedb01_ts coalesce;
```

The following script creates a view you can use to identify problem segments in your tablespaces. Query this view by *tablespace_name* to get an idea where space problems might be
occurring, as well as to see how fragmented individual objects are in the tablespace.

```
CREATE OR REPLACE VIEW ts_blocks_v AS
SELECT tablespace_name, block_id, bytes, blocks, '== free space ==' segment_name
```

```
FROM dba_free_space
UNION ALL
SELECT tablespace_name, block_id, bytes, blocks, segment_name
FROM dba_extents;

Select * from ts_blocks_v;
TABLESPACE_NAME        BLOCK_ID   BYTES      BLOCKS    SEGMENT_NAME
-------------------    --------   ---------  -------   ----------------
PROG_PLAN_IDX_08         34562    221962240   27095 == free space ==
BMC_SMGT_TS               339    102088704   12462 == free space ==
DBA_TEST                 42372    533700608   65149 == free space ==
BPW_DATA_01             111667    133808128   16334 == free space ==
BPW_IDX_01              155439    299515904   36562 == free space ==
AUDIT_01                 84231        40960       5 SQLAB_COLLECTION
AUDIT_01                     2      1064960     130 TB_225AUDIT
AUDIT_01                  2692       532480      65 TB_237AUDIT
BPW_DATA_01             105737     41943040    5120 TB_G026CAPACITY
BPW_DATA_01             105702       286720      35 TB_G016RESOURCE
BPW_DATA_01             105667       286720      35 TB_G006NSU
BPW_DATA_01             105602       532480      65 TB_7056SUBST_AUDIT
BPW_DATA_01             105567       286720      35 TB_64S6MSG_TYPE_CODESET
BPW_DATA_01             101982     29368320    3585 TB_64R6CAPACITY_CONSTRAINT
BPW_DATA_01               1092       286720      35 TB_5317INV_RI
```

Tablespace fragmentation can lead to the following problems:

- It can cause space in the tablespace to be trapped and unable to be effectively used.

- It can cause administrative problems when it becomes necessary to re-create fragmented objects.

Note

Advances in both RDBMS and disk technology have, to some extent, minimized the impact of fragmented tablespaces on overall system performance. It is however, still necessary to minimize tablespace fragmentation for the most optimal system performance as well as to make the most efficient use of disk space.

Tip #24

When examining database fragmentation, be sure to always check for row chaining or migration. Both of these problems can easily be overlooked, yet cause measurable performance problems.

DEALING WITH FRAGMENTED TABLESPACES

The best way to deal with tablespace fragmentation is to avoid it. This can be done but requires careful planning and administrative overhead. If you are faced with cleaning up fragmented tablespaces, the easiest way is to export the offending objects in the tablespace, drop the objects, and import them back. This not only coalesces your free space, but Export also coalesces your database objects into one extent.

To prevent fragmentation

- Group objects with similar space and growth characteristics together.
- If possible, size their extents the same, so that all objects can share extents deallocated or regained from dropping objects.
- Keep each segment's *PCTINCREASE* at 0.

Following these tips will eliminate extents of all different sizes being created and then being unusable by future database segments.

> **Note**
>
> Beginning in Oracle7.3, setting the default *PCTINCREASE* greater than 0 on a tablespace will cause *SMON* to automatically coalesce adjacent free extents. Unless your database system absolutely cannot spare the CPU time or disk I/O, you should set this parameter to at least 1.

Finally, the following script shows you how much free space is available in each tablespace in your database, as well as the size of the largest free extent, and the number of free extents in each tablespace. This is a good place to start when looking for problems—if you see 500MB of free space in a tablespace, but have a largest free extent of 15MB, you have an obvious problem.

```
SELECT tablespace_name, sum(bytes) "Free Bytes", max(bytes) "Largest Extent",
       count(block_id) "# Extents"
FROM dba_free_space
GROUP BY tablespace_name;
```

UNDERSTANDING OBJECT FRAGMENTATION

Fragmented tablespaces are a sure way to give any DBA space allocation headaches. The more insidious and easily missed fragmentation problems, however, are at the object level. In object-level fragmentation, the object might look fine and healthy at the tablespace level, having a single extent, but some probing inside those extents can reveal a different story.

A common occurrence is that a DBA sees space allocation problems in an often-modified tablespace, and rebuilds the tablespace and all its objects. Subsequently, the database performance can increase. This increase in performance is attributed to the tablespace fragmentation being eliminated, but it could very well be the elimination of object-level fragmentation that gives you the performance boost.

| Tip #25 | While technically not fragmentation, many *DELETE* operations can produce sparsely filled blocks that have not yet met the *PCTUSED* criteria to be placed back on the free list. Most operations intended to cure a database of object fragmentation will also fix the sparse block problem. |

Object fragmentation can lead to the following problems:

- Additional read calls made to the database which can cause response time to increase.
- Wasted space due to holes of free space inside table and index blocks.
- Read performance drops. Because data is no longer closely packed together, the physical disk drives must seek and read data from a larger disk surface area than is necessary.

Object fragmentation is the umbrella term for three specific types of fragmentation: row migration, row chaining, and overextended segments (objects having a large number of extents or almost near the *maxextents* parameter). I discuss each of these in the following sections.

UNDERSTANDING ROW MIGRATION

Row migration occurs when an update to a row makes the length of the row larger than the space available to it in the block. When this happens, a portion of the row is migrated to a new data block. The address of this new location is stored in the original row location. When Oracle needs to read this row, it first reads the original location and finds some data along with a pointer to another block where the rest of the row's data can be found. See Figure 21.6 for a pictorial representation.

Figure 21.6
An example of row migration in blocks.

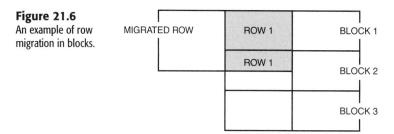

There are two problems with row migration:

- Oracle has to perform at least one additional I/O read every time it has to fetch a migrated row. It must read each block that contains either a portion of the row's data or a pointer to another block that contains the row's data.
- Oracle also has to store additional pointers along with row data to accommodate the row migration mechanism. While usually not substantial, this wastes some disk space.

> **Note**
>
> You can legitimately ask why Oracle performs row migration instead of moving the entire row to a new block. Moving a row's location would be quite expensive from a time and locking perspective as the row's *ROWID* (which is loosely tied to its physical location) is stored in indexes and other areas in the database. For each *ROWID*, Oracle would have to have a reverse index to all references of a *ROWID* so they could be efficiently updated. Clearly this would cause considerable overall system overhead that simply isn't necessary.

UNDERSTANDING ROW CHAINING

Row chaining occurs when a row is too long to fit in any one data block. This results in the row being stored in a chain of one or more data blocks. Row chaining often occurs with large rows containing *LONG*, *LONG RAW*, or *LOB* datatypes. Refer to Figure 21.7 for more on chained rows in a table.

Figure 21.7
Row length greater than the block size, causing row chaining.

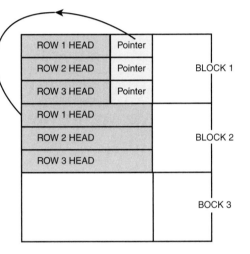

ELIMINATING CHAINED AND MIGRATED ROWS

Chained and migrated rows can pose a serious problem to the overall performance of your database installation. You can check for chained and migrated rows by issuing the following SQL statement:

```
analyze table customer list chained rows into chained_rows;
```

To create the *chained_rows* table, execute *utlchain.sql*, located in the *$ORACLE_HOME/rdbms/admin* directory. When you run *utlchain.sql*, a table called *chained_rows* will be created, which you use as the destination of the SQL statement.

This command stores the *ROWID* and table of all chained and migrated rows in the database into the *chained_rows* table. Query the *chained_rows* table directly to find specific information on the rows and tables.

Because migrated rows occur only when a row is updated to a larger value, you can eliminate all migrated rows by performing the following steps:

1. Create a temporary table to hold the migrated rows. Use a SQL statement such as the following:

```
CREATE TABLE temp_emp AS
SELECT * FROM emp WHERE rowid in
(SELECT rowid FROM chained_rows
WHERE table_name = 'EMP');
```

2. Delete the rows stored from the preceding statement from the master table:

```
DELETE FROM emp WHERE rowid in
(SELECT head_rowid FROM chained_rows
WHERE table_name = 'EMP');
```

3. Insert the rows from the temporary table:

```
INSERT INTO emp SELECT * FROM temp_emp;
```

This procedure eliminates all migrated rows. By deleting the rows referenced in *chained_rows* and rerunning the *analyze* statement, you can positively identify all rows that are chained.

One problem with this solution (particularly on large tables) is that you waste all the space in the old blocks where these chained rows were originally stored. The inserted rows don't fit there and so all the deleted rows leave blocks of free space in the table where the old rows were placed. There are two main disadvantages to this type of row packing:

- A lot of free space in the table might never be used, depending on the *PCTUSED* setting, and therefore space is wasted.

- When this table is read via a full table scan, there could be a performance penalty (although this is generally unlikely) because a greater number of blocks must be read.

An alternative to this is to store the data from the table into a temporary table, truncate the table, and insert the data back in. You could also use export, drop the table, and then use import to re-create the table. The latter solution is the most straightforward and thorough, but is also the most time consuming.

Sizing of *PCTFREE* is important when trying to avoid row migration. A rough calculation you can use to derive the *PCTFREE* is to assume a table has an average row length *x* bytes, and that *y* bytes are going to be updated after the original insertion. Given these requirements, the derivation for *PCTFREE* would be as follows:

```
PCTFREE=100*y/x
```

Applying practical values, if you have a table of row length 100 bytes and 21 bytes that are going to be updated later, the value of *PCTFREE* would be 100×21/100, which would give you 21%.

Row chaining is much more difficult to fix. The only solution is to either shorten the row length of a table or increase the size of the database block. The former option usually requires the redesigning of a table's structure whereas the latter requires a full database export, re-creation, and full import. Neither of these options are very attractive, but could be necessary if chained rows in a table are causing performance issues.

| Tip #26 | Before taking any drastic steps to eliminate row chaining, look at the data types used in the offending table. Some of Oracle's newer data types (such as *VARCHAR2*) are far more space-conscious than their older counterparts (*CHAR*) and would require little to no application changes. |

MANAGING ROLLBACK SEGMENTS

Management of the database rollback segments can be much more complex than other segments in the database. It is therefore important that the operational intricacies of the rollback segments be understood before you can look at strategies for managing these sometimes troublesome objects.

Rollback segments are used to provide *read consistency* (explained later in this chapter), transaction rollback, and database recovery (covered in Chapter 24, "Backup and Recovery"). They store the *before image* of data involved in a transaction. If the transaction wants to undo the changes made, the information in the rollback segments can be used to restore the database to its prior state. This is referred to as *transaction rollback*.

Rollback segments, like any other segments, are located in a tablespace and composed of extents. Every database has a *SYSTEM* rollback segment, located in the system tablespace and created when the database is created. Its use by normal users is not permitted and cannot be taken offline or dropped. You should create additional rollback segments for the normal functioning of the database in a tablespace dedicated to rollback segments. It is common for rollback segments to extend and contract, which is not the type of activity you want to happen in table, index, or system tablespaces.

Rollback segments must be tuned to handle concurrent transactions as well as transactions of different sizes. Typically, you need more rollback segments with more extents on systems with more concurrent transactions. The larger your transactions (for example, updating a large quantity of rows) the larger your rollback segments need to be. Because rollback segments usually are allowed to grow and then shrink back to the *OPTIMUM* storage parameter value, special care must be taken to make sure you truly know how much space a rollback segment needs.

Tip #27	Oracle's Snapshot Too Old error message is usually caused by either too few and/or too small rollback segments.

UNDERSTANDING ROLLBACK SEGMENT OPERATION

Transactions either explicitly ask for or are implicitly assigned to a particular rollback segment. Multiple transactions can concurrently write to any given rollback segment or extent within the segment. Blocks, however, are dedicated to one particular transaction. Oracle uses existing extents and blocks allocated to a rollback segment in a circular fashion. As needed (and permitted by applicable storage parameters), new extents are allocated to accommodate active transactions. When transactions end, however, their rollback information is not removed (remember that rollback segments are written to circularly). This is to accommodate other existing transactions that might still rely on the old versions of changed data for a read consistent view of the database.

See Figure 21.8 for a depiction of this rollback segment extension.

PART

V

CH

21

Figure 21.8
Allocation of extents inside rollback segments.

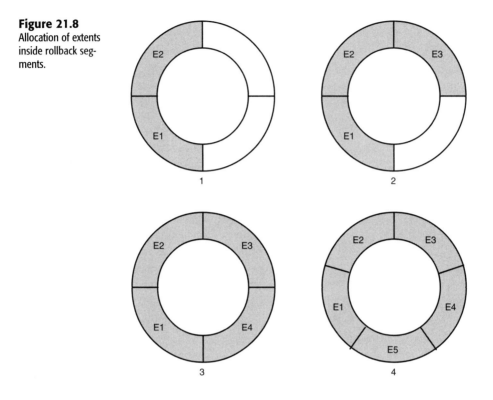

In Figure 21.8, diagrams 1 through 3 show the order in which Oracle uses existing extents; diagram 5 shows Oracle adding an extent to the rollback segment. Diagram 1 shows Oracle actively using extents E1 and E2 with E3 and E4 being idle. Diagrams 2 and 3 show Oracle using the remaining extents for transaction rollback information. Diagram 4 shows Oracle allocating another extent, E5, to accommodate active transactions. Unless Oracle needs to allocate another extent for active transactions, the next extent to be used will be E1 again.

> **Note**
>
> Extensions can fail if the `maxextents` for a rollback segment is reached or there is no more space in the tablespace to allocate to the rollback segment.

Dynamic extension of a rollback segment is a costly operation and causes a performance hit. It can also cause space problems, if the rollback segments are not carefully placed in the overall database configuration. Rollback segments should be allocated to tablespaces reserved for rollback segment use. All rollback segments contained in any given tablespace should be sized exactly the same—because of the frequent extension and deallocation of extents; fragmentation problems as previously discussed are sure to be a problem if mismatched extent sizes are configured.

Tip #28

> Many times, specific rollback segments with specially designed sizes are created for specific transaction classes (such as DSS and OLTP). Because these will be unusually sized rollback segments, they should be stored in their own tablespace to minimize fragmentation.

Here are some general concepts regarding the extension and allocation of the extents in rollback segments:

- A single extent in the rollback segment can be written to by multiple transactions, but each block within the extent must contain information for only one transaction.

- A single transaction can only be assigned a single rollback segment, no matter how many rollback segments might exist in the system.

- Oracle uses a round-robin policy to determine what rollback segment a transaction should use unless it explicitly asks for a particular rollback segment. Although this attempts to keep each rollback segment handling around the same number of transactions, it makes it impossible to guess what rollback segment is going to be allocated to a transaction.

- The allocated extents are used in increasing order of block ID in the rollback segment. If the fifth and seventh extent are free in a rollback segment, for example, the fifth extent is always allocated before the seventh.

- Every rollback segment (like most segments) must have a minimum of two extents.

SIZING ROLLBACK SEGMENTS

When sizing rollback segments, keep in mind that they should be sized large enough that the system will not immediately need to reuse blocks recently released by a finished transaction. Other concurrent transactions might still need to use rollback information generated by a completed update/insert/delete transaction for a read consistent view of the database.

Consider a long running report that gives information about the salary details of all the employees in a company. Literally, this report traverses every record of the *Employee* table and obtains some associated information from other reference tables. Assume that an HR employee issues the report at 3:00 p.m. At 4:00 p.m., another user in payroll decides the salary increments for employees need to be processed for the year (an obvious example of poor communication between departments), and issues the job that performs this maintenance. This process modifies the records of most employees in the company, and commits this information immediately. See Figure 21.9 for a graphical representation.

Tip #29

> Rollback segment use is impacted by which type of update activities a transaction runs. Generally, *DELETE*s consume the most rollback space, followed by *UPDATE*s, and then *INSERT*s.

Figure 21.9
Long-running query
and batch job.

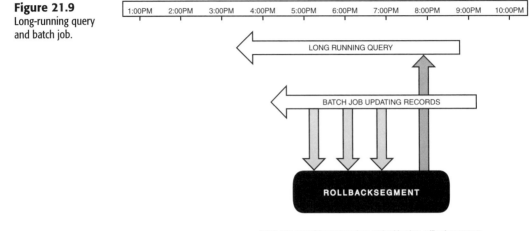

Batch jobs commiting transactions and writing into rollback segments
and the query reading commited information from rollback segment to
obtain a read = consistent snapshot of data.

Meanwhile, your original HR report is still chugging along. It comes to a point where an employee record that it needs to retrieve has had the salary changed by the salary increment process. At this point, what should Oracle do? Should the report deliver the salary details that are committed and are current, or should it return the old salary that was recorded before the increment?

If the report gets information that is current, that would mean some employees in the report have the pre-increment salary and some have the post-increment salary, which would make the report inconsistent and useless. This is where the importance of rollback segments becomes apparent. Through Oracle's transaction processing mechanism, the before update images of all rows changed in the salary increment processing program are written to the rollback segments. When the report program reaches a record that has been changed, it can determine, using the block control information (the SCN, or system change number), that it needs to look to the rollback segment to find information as it was when the report began running.

Note that the proper processing of this situation is entirely reliant on the transaction having sufficient rollback space, so that information written to the rollback segment is not overwritten by subsequent transactions. If the information the transaction needs does get overwritten, you will get the all too common and hateful Snapshot Too Old error.

The preceding example is one aspect to be considered when sizing rollback segments. From the discussion, it's clear there should be enough space in the rollback segments to store these inactive or committed data transactions that might be needed by other long-running queries.

You can avoid problems with long-running queries by

- Allocating sufficiently large enough rollback segment space to accommodate the most likely transaction concurrency scenarios.
- Following a scheduling policy whereby long-running queries are to be run at a different time of day than short OLTP transactions.
- Creating a large rollback segment that is used only by long-running batch jobs.

Tip #30	Use the SET TRANSACTION USE ROLLBACK SEGMENT statement to explicitly use a particular rollback segment at the beginning of transaction.

```
set transaction use rollback segment RB1;
```

USING THE OPTIMAL PARAMETER

When creating the rollback segment, the target size of the rollback segment can be defined using the OPTIMAL storage parameter. The OPTIMAL parameter specifies the size to which rollback segments should shrink to, when possible.

Let's look at a sample create rollback segment statement:

```
create rollback segment r05
tablespace rbs
storage ( initial 10M
          next      10M
          optimal  20M
          minextents 2
          maxextents 100);
```

The RDBMS tries to maintain the size of this rollback segment at the specified optimal value of 20MB. The size is always interpreted to be rounded up to the extent boundary, which means that the RDBMS tries to keep the fewest number of extents, such that the total size is greater than or equal to the size specified in OPTIMAL.

Whenever a rollback segment begins writing to another extent, Oracle checks whether the segment is larger than the OPTIMAL size and, if so, whether the next extent is completely idle. If both checks are true, Oracle deallocates the extent and continues on to the next subsequent extent (which can also be deallocated if the same criteria is met). When attempting to deallocate the inactive extents, the oldest ones are first deallocated.

The OPTIMAL command is seen by some as a brother to the PCTINCREASE storage parameter—the lazy DBA's way to administer. Although it does make rollback segment administration slightly easier, it can also prove to do more harm then good.

Caution	If you find your rollback segments are continuously shrinking because of the OPTIMAL clause, it is likely that your rollback segments are improperly sized. If this extent allocation and deallocation is common, it can become a performance concern.

PART

V

CH

21

PERFORMING LOAD TESTS TO OBTAIN ROLLBACK ESTIMATES

To correctly size the rollback segments you need to have an idea of the amount of undo information that is going to be generated by larger transactions. Typically, every rollback segment should be large enough to accommodate the largest transaction's rollback needs, while not being so large that they waste inordinate amounts of space (The only exception to this is if you have special-purpose rollback segments as previously discussed). In order to get a reasonable estimate of the size of the undo generated, perform a load test on a sample transaction that generates a large amount of undo information using Listing 21.1.

Tip #31	If you do not know what SQL statements a particular job is issuing against the database (and do not have source code available), considering use Oracle's tracing facility to gather exact the SQL statements to tune for.

For the test you are performing, ensure that no other active transactions are generating undo information. The steps involved in generating a load test follow:

1. Create two tables to hold your statistical information: *stat$undo_begin* and *stat$undo_end*.

2. Assume that the load test is performed on rollback segment, *R01*. After connecting to the database, issue a set transaction command to ensure that all the undo data belonging to this transaction is written into rollback segment *R01*.

3. Capture the initial amount of data written to the rollback segment *ro1* to the table *stat$undo_begin* by using the *v$rollstat* table.

4. Issue the test transaction statements.

5. After the transaction completes, again obtain the amount of data written to the rollback segment *R01* to the snapshot end table *stat$undo_end*.

6. Now that you have the snapshot start and snapshot end values in the tables, it's simply a matter of subtracting the two values to obtain the amount of data written to rollback segment *R01*. These values can be used to determine sizing needs of your rollback segments.

Listing 21.1 is the script for performing the preceding steps.

LISTING 21.1   PERFORMING LOAD TESTS TO OBTAIN ROLLBACK ESTIMATES

```
REM
REM Create the set up tables
REM
create table stats$undo_begin (writes number);
create table stats$undo_end   (writes number);
REM
REM Capture the initial number of write for rollback seg RO1.
REM Replace RO1 with the name of your rollback segment.
REM
```

```
insert into stats$undo_begin
    select sum(writes) from v$rollstat
    where usn = ( select usn from v$rollname where
                  name = 'RO1');
REM
REM Alter the current session so that it uses the test rollback
REM segment only.  Replace R01 with the name of your rollback segment.
REM
commit;
set transaction use rollback segment RO1;
REM
REM Run the long running batch job which generates largest undo data.
REM Replace the name of your batch job script with 'large_batch_job'
REM
@large_batch_job;
REM
REM Capture the writes generated at the end of the batch job.
REM Replace R01 with the name of your rollback segment.
REM
insert into stats$undo_end
    select sum(writes) from v$rollstat
    where usn = ( select usn from v$rollname where
                  name = 'RO1');
REM
REM Get the amount of data that has been generated as redo for the
REM transaction under tesst
REM
select (e.writes - b.writes ) undo_generated
    from stats$undo_begin b, stats$undo_end e;
UNDO_GENERATED
        898998
```

In the output shown in Listing 21.1, the undo generated by the batch job is 898998 bytes. This script can be used as a starting point to appropriately size rollback segments.

IDENTIFYING STORAGE PROBLEMS

When a database is up and running, you sometimes need to revisit the issue of how large each major component of the database is. Of primary concern is making sure that table-spaces are large enough to hold the segments they contain. Tables, indexes, and clusters all grow over time, and you need to make sure that an *INSERT* or *UPDATE* will not fail during production hours because the tablespace is out of room.

When I discuss the space *allocated* for a segment, I refer to the space reserved for a segment. This does not imply that the segment is actually using *all* the space (although, it is almost always using some portion of it). For example, suppose you say that table *ABC* has 90MB allocated to it in two extents of 50 and 40MB respectively. Table *ABC* is actually *using* between 50 and 90MB. When the first extent is exhausted, the *NEXT* parameter in the table definition dictates that another 40MB is allocated even if only 10KB is actually needed at the moment. *ABC* would not need to look for more space until the remaining 39.99MB were filled. Although this design might seem somewhat odd to some DBAs not from a mainframe data processing environment, it is a key element in Oracle's performance characteristics.

DBAs using Oracle's Enterprise Manager will find the job of assessing their database's current storage situation much easier than their command-line counterparts. Storage Manager is the portion of the Enterprise Manager suite that provides a GUI interface to the most commonly needed storage information. Figure 21.10 shows a sample window of Storage Manager.

Figure 21.10
An example of Oracle's Storage Manager.

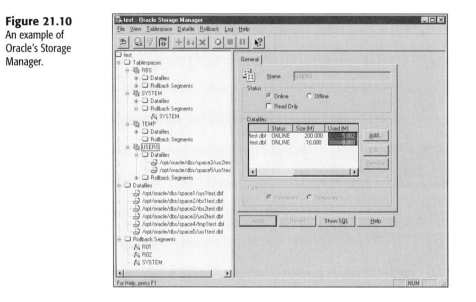

Your database need not reside on a Windows NT machine to use Storage Manager. Oracle's Net8 networking component enables a Windows system running Storage Manager to work with databases on remote machines. The remote machines can reside on a local or wide area network and can be any Oracle supported platform.

Experienced DBAs will find Storage Manager—like quite a few of Oracle's Windows-based GUI tools at the time of this writing—to be missing several important capabilities needed for effective storage management. Storage Manager is a useful tool simplifying many day-to-day tasks, but it is no substitute for the command-line interface.

EXPLORING TABLESPACES

Your exploration of the database tablespaces usually involves deciphering the total size of the tablespace, as well as what datafiles are used by the tablespace. The DBA_DATA_FILES table contains all the relevant information about datafiles. Because a tablespace's size is the sum of its datafile parts, you can determine a tablespace's size from the DBA_DATA_FILES table also.

Here's an example:

```
COLUMN TABLESPACE_NAME FORMAT A10
COLUMN FILE_NAME FORMAT A35
SELECT TABLESPACE_NAME, FILE_NAME, BYTES, STATUS FROM DBA_DATA_FILES
ORDER BY TABLESPACE_NAME;
TABLESPACE FILE_NAME                                     BYTES STATUS
```

```
RBS      /u02/oradata/test/rbs1test.dbf    20971520 AVAILABLE
RBS      /u02/oradata/test /rbs2test.dbf   20971520 AVAILABLE
SYSTEM   /u01/oradata/test/sys1test.dbf    20971520 AVAILABLE
TEMP     /u04/oradata/test/tmp1test.dbf    10485760 AVAILABLE
USERS    /u05/oradata/test/usr1test.dbf    20971520 AVAILABLE
```

You see a row for each datafile in the database, which shows the tablespace it belongs to, its size (in bytes), and its status. The status field should almost always be *AVAILABLE*.

You often want to check on your tablespaces to make sure you have plenty of free space available, in case a segment needs to grow. This is not as simple a question as it would at first seem. In order to answer this question, you need to know the following:

- How large the tablespace is
- How much aggregate free space remains
- What the largest free extent is
- Whether any one segment can grow by at least one extent
- How fragmented the tablespace is

You need to start with how large a tablespace is. Totaling the sizes of associated datafiles provides you with that information fairly easily. For example:

Tip #32	It is often convenient to write a script that automatically gathers storage information about each database and emails it to the appropriate DBA staff.

```
SELECT TABLESPACE_NAME,SUM(BYTES) FROM DBA_DATA_FILES GROUP BY TABLESPACE_NAME

TABLESPACE SUM(BYTES)
---------- ----------
RBS          41943040
SYSTEM       20971520
TEMP         10485760
USERS        20971520
```

The next problem is to determine how much free space, in aggregate, is in the tablespace. Oracle keeps a list of all free extents in the database in the *DBA_FREE_SPACE* table. By totaling the sizes of free extents in your tablespace of interest, you see how much free space remains. This example shows the amount of free space in each tablespace in the database.

```
SELECT TABLESPACE_NAME, SUM(BYTES) FROM DBA_FREE_SPACE
GROUP BY TABLESPACE_NAME;

TABLESPACE SUM(BYTES)
---------- ----------
RBS          29343744
SYSTEM       11552768
TEMP         10483712
USERS         9439232
```

Knowing the largest free extent in each tablespace helps you make sure that any of the segments can grow by at least one extent. Even though tablespace *USERS* can have 9MB of free space, it can be split in three pieces, each having only roughly 3MB. This is important to know because there might be a table with a *NEXT* extent value of 5MB. If this is so, Oracle would fail to allocate the additional extent, because there are no free extents of at least 5MB available. Again, you turn to the *DBA_FREE_SPACE* table, except now you're looking for the largest free extent, as shown in this example:

```
SELECT TABLESPACE_NAME, MAX(BYTES) FROM DBA_FREE_SPACE
       GROUP BY TABLESPACE_NAME;

TABLESPACE MAX(BYTES)
---------- ----------
RBS          20969472
SYSTEM        4096000
TEMP         10483712
USERS         9439232
```

By looking at the output from the last two SQL statements, you can see that the *USERS* tablespace does indeed have all 9MB in one piece. Notice though that the *SYSTEM* tablespace's largest free extent is only 4MB, yet it has 11MB free in total.

Now you need to look at all of the segments contained in the tablespaces. Recall that the *NEXT* storage parameter always indicates the size of the next extent a segment asks for. At the very least, you should make sure that any one segment can grow by at least one extent. This minimizes the chance that you are in imminent danger of running out of space. You'll want to look at the *DBA_SEGMENTS* table because it considers all segments in a database no matter what type they are. This example lists any segments (along with additional information) that cannot grow at least one extent in the database:

```
    COLUMN SEGMENT_NAME FORMAT A30
SELECT SEGMENT_NAME,SEGMENT_TYPE,OWNER,A.TABLESPACE_NAME "TABLESPACE_NAME",
INITIAL_EXTENT,NEXT_EXTENT,PCT_INCREASE, B.BYTES "TABLESPACE MAX FREE SPACE"
FROM DBA_SEGMENTS A,
(SELECT TABLESPACE_NAME,MAX(BYTES) "BYTES" FROM DBA_FREE_SPACE
GROUP BY TABLESPACE_NAME) B
WHERE
A.TABLESPACE_NAME = B.TABLESPACE_NAME AND NEXT_EXTENT > B.BYTES;

SEGMENT_NAME
-----------------------------------------------------------------------------
SEGMENT_TYPE       OWNER                           TABLESPACE_NAME
-----------------  ------------------------------  ----------------------------
INITIAL_EXTENT NEXT_EXTENT PCT_INCREASE TABLESPACE MAX FREE SPACE
-------------- ------------ ------------ -------------------------

TEST1
TABLE              TGASPER                         USERS
        512000   41943040           50                     9439232
```

In this example, you can see that a table *TEST1* in the *TGASPER* schema would not be able to allocate another extent because the *NEXT_EXTENT* parameter is set to 40MB and you can see that the *USERS* tablespace's largest free extent is 9MB. Because 40MB is also larger than the amount of free space in the tablespace, you would need to add more space to the tablespace to allow *TEST1* to grow. Even if enough aggregate free space exists, you would still probably add more space to allow *TEST1* to grow by 40MB or change the *NEXT_EXTENT* parameter in *TEST1* to fit within the largest free extent size.

Tip #33	If a tablespace reaches a point where there is a large discrepancy between the largest free extent and total free space, it is probably time to consider reorganizing the tablespace.

Caution	Exercise caution when setting the *PCTINCREASE* parameter. In the previous example, you see that the *PCTINCREASE* value is set to 50. This means that each successive extent will be 50% larger than the last. Your segments can, quite quickly, try to allocate obnoxiously large extents. Proper planning usually allows you to keep *PCTINCREASE* set to a fairly low value. Many sites' policies demand that *PCTINCREASE* be set to 0 for all segments.
	Regardless of how you set *PCTINCREASE* on segments, you will almost always want to set the default *PCTINCREASE* value for the tablespaces to 1. In Oracle versions 7.3 and later, *SMON* automatically coalesces adjacent free segments when this parameter is not 0.

Tablespace fragmentation can become a serious problem particularly in development or test systems where different segments are frequently created and dropped. I previously discussed that this activity causes tablespace fragmentation by creating *bubbles* of space, caught in the tablespace that are too small to be used by most segments.

You should regularly evaluate the degree to which your tablespaces are fragmented. Excessive fragmentation prevents segments from growing because all the free space is broken up into small and unusable pieces. As a temporary solution, you can add more space to a tablespace. This opens up a large single extent, which at least allows segments to grow and keep your database operational. Regular defragmentation is recommended for optimum performance and disc space efficiency.

Fortunately, newer versions of Oracle have provided a fairly basic yet very useful storage management tool for DBAs called Storage Manager. Storage Manager is a GUI-based tool that enables DBAs to quickly check critical storage issues related to objects and tablespaces.

Although Storage Manager is not a replacement for all the information gathering discussed here, it does offer a quick way to check allocated and total free space in a tablespace.

After you start Storage Manager, expand the Tablespaces tree entry by double-clicking it. You'll see all your tablespaces shown in the right-hand window along with graphs indicating the size of each tablespace and the total amount of free space. Figure 21.11 shows an example of this information.

PART

V

CH

21

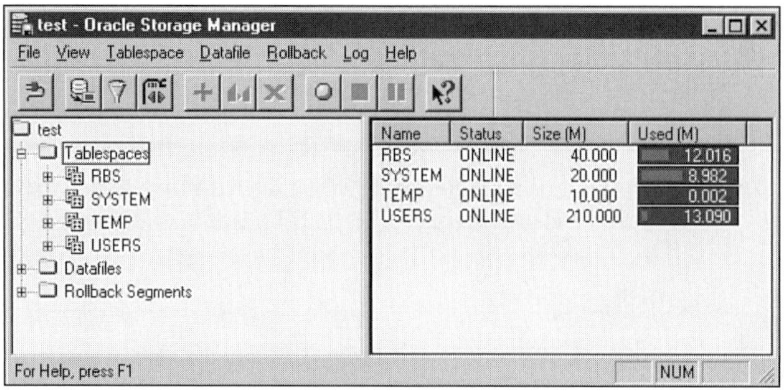

Figure 21.11
Storage Manager
providing quick
tablespace storage
information.

Remember that the free space shown is a total of all free extents in the tablespace. If Storage Manager indicates that tablespace *USERS* has roughly 197MB free, this does not necessarily mean that all 197MB are contiguous.

CHECKING ON TABLES

Your check-up on a database table involves assessing the total allocated size as well as the space actually used. You'll also have an interest in the number of extents allocated by the table. One or two extents with a low space used–to–allocated ratio would imply that the *INITIAL* and *NEXT* extent values can be set too high. Dozens of extents might indicate that the *NEXT* extent parameter is set too low.

You can determine the total allocated space of a table by totaling the sizes of all related extents. Extent information can be found in the *DBA_EXTENTS* table. This example demonstrates how you can easily compute the allocated space of each table in a given tablespace (*USERS* for this example):

```
    SELECT TABLESPACE_NAME,SEGMENT_NAME,SUM(BYTES),COUNT(*) EXT_QUAN
FROM DBA_EXTENTS
         WHERE TABLESPACE_NAME='USERS' AND SEGMENT_TYPE='TABLE'
GROUP BY TABLESPACE_NAME,SEGMENT_NAME;
TABLESPACE SEGMENT_NAME                    SUM(BYTES)   EXT_QUAN
---------- -----------------------------  ----------   ----------

USERS      EMP                                102400          1
USERS      DEPT                                10240          1
USERS      INOUT_LOG                         4096000        100
USERS      PHONE_LOG                         2048000          1
USERS      HOURS                            1024000          2
```

You can see for each table (in the *SEGMENT_NAME* column) the total amount of allocated space (in bytes) as well as the quantity of extents (in the *EXT_QUAN* column) allocated for the table. Notice that the *INOUT_LOG* table has allocated 4MB in 100 extents. This implies that the *NEXT* storage parameter is set too low.

Your last evaluation of tables focuses on determining a space used–to–allocated ratio. Recall that Oracle allocates space according to the values of the *INITIAL* and *NEXT* storage parameters. Therefore, you cannot be certain that a table actually *needs* all the space allocated to it.

Be aware that the ratio you calculate is only an estimate, but it is still useful for computing the actual space used by a table.

Oracle provides a method for computing table statistics through the *ANALYZE TABLE* statement. For each table in your database, you should regularly compute or at least estimate statistics. Use commands similar to this example that analyzes the *PHONE_LOG* table:

```
ANALYZE TABLE PHONE_LOG COMPUTE STATISTICS;
```

When this command is run, the *DBA_TABLES* view reflects the statistics gathered for the *PHONE_LOG* table. In *DBA_TABLES*, there are *BLOCKS* and *EMPTY_BLOCKS* columns that indicate the number of blocks used and not used respectively. Be aware that these columns assume that when a block is used, it will always be used. If a table contains one million rows and 700,000 are then deleted, the *BLOCKS* and *EMPTY_BLOCKS* values will not change.

The following SQL statement displays the space used by the *PHONE_LOG* table as a percentage of the space allocated:

```
SELECT BLOCKS/(BLOCKS+EMPTY_BLOCKS)*100 USED_PCT FROM DBA_TABLES WHERE
     TABLE_NAME='PHONE_LOG';
USED_PCT
----------
 15.397996
```

Here you can see that although the *PHONE_LOG* table has 2MB allocated to it, only 15% is actually used to hold the table. Unless you expect this table to grow substantially in size over the next year or so, you might want to consider dropping and reloading this table with only 700KB or so allocated to it.

Tip #34	Although it is necessary to run an individual *ANALYZE TABLE* command for each table, the job of generating a script to compute statistics for the entire database can be made much easier by using the *DBMS_UTILITY.ANALYZE_SCHEMA* stored procedure.

OPTIMIZING CLUSTER STORAGE

Cluster check-ups are mostly limited to identifying excessive extents. Optimizing storage for clusters is even more important than tables because their efficiency (or lack thereof) will be seen in more than just one table. You can compute the number of extents for each cluster by using this SQL statement:

```
    COLUMN SEGMENT_NAME FORMAT A20
    SELECT OWNER, SEGMENT_NAME,COUNT(*)
       FROM DBA_EXTENTS WHERE SEGMENT_TYPE='CLUSTER'
GROUP BY SEGMENT_NAME,OWNER;
```

The *COUNT(*)* column shows the number of extents for each cluster. Ideally, you will want just one extent per cluster. More than a dozen or so can indicate an *INITIAL* and/or *NEXT* storage parameter value that is set too low.

Unfortunately, Oracle does not provide you an easy way to determine what percentage of the allocated blocks are being used in a cluster. Although answers to questions such as these lurk in the *x$* tables, you are advised against relying on these tables unless specifically directed otherwise by Oracle.

Your best option is to recalculate the optimum storage parameters as if you intend to re-create a cluster and compare your newly computed optimum values with the cluster's current settings. If these values differ substantially, your best option is probably to re-create the cluster with correct storage parameters. To do so, follow these steps:

1. Perform a logical backup.

2. Drop the cluster and associated tables

3. Re-create the dropped objects with correct storage parameters.

4. Reload the rows into the dropped tables from the logical backup taken in step 1.

When this procedure has finished, you are ready to allow users back onto the database system.

CHECKING INDEXES

As they do with clusters, most DBAs find that a periodic storage health check simply verifies that the number of extents is within reason. Just as with clusters, you'll use a simple SQL statement for a check-up:

```
COLUMN SEGMENT_NAME FORMAT A20
SELECT OWNER, SEGMENT_NAME,COUNT(*)
    FROM DBA_EXTENTS WHERE SEGMENT_TYPE='INDEX'
GROUP BY SEGMENT_NAME,OWNER;
```

Indexes can be highly sensitive to excessive extent quantity. Try to keep the number of extents down to half a dozen or so for most indexes. Ideally, of course, just one extent will be used.

WATCHING THE GROWTH OF ROLLBACK SEGMENTS

Working with rollback segments is discussed in depth in a previous section, "Managing Rollback Segments." From a storage management perspective, however, you are interested in knowing how large your rollback segments are growing. Recall that by specifying an *OPTIMAL* storage parameter size, a rollback segment can automatically shrink in size after a transaction completes. Oracle does, however, keep a high-water mark that indicates how large each rollback segment has grown, how many times it has extended, and how many times it has shrunk, since the instance was started. To see the high-water mark (in bytes) for each rollback segment, use this SQL statement:

```
SELECT N.NAME, OPTSIZE, HWMSIZE
    FROM V$ROLLNAME N, V$ROLLSTAT S WHERE N.USN=S.USN;
```

For each rollback segment, you are able to see the optimal size as well as the maximum size (so far) in the *OPTSIZE* and *HWMSIZE* columns respectively. If *OPTSIZE* is blank, *HWMSIZE* is the current size of the rollback segments (and no shrinking will occur).

Frequently, you will create a set of rollback segments for production hours and a set of rollback segments for batch jobs (and perhaps a few extra for special job requirements). You will always need enough space in the appropriate tablespaces to contain all the rollback segments at the optimal size. In addition, enough space must be free in the tablespaces to accommodate the *HWMSIZE* for each set of rollback segments, which could be active at any given time.

For instance, suppose you have *RP01*, *RP02*, and *RP03* rollback segments used during production hours and *RB01*, *RB02* are used for batch processing during evening hours. The result of the previous SQL query is

```
NAME                              OPTSIZE    HWMSIZE
--------------------------------  ---------  ---------
RP01                               10240000   20480000
RP02                               10240000   40960000
RP03                               10240000   10240000
RB01                              102400000  102400000
RB02                               51200000   61440000
```

The total optimum size for all rollback segments is roughly 180MB (meaning, this is the absolute smallest size the rollback segments will ever be). You assume that batch and production jobs are never run together, so at any given time, either the production or batch rollback segments remain at their optimum size. Therefore, during production, you can conclude that the largest amount of space needed by the rollback segments was 220MB (totaling the *HWMSIZE* column for production rollback segments and the *OPTSIZE* column for batch rollback segments). During batch hours, the rollback segments' largest space needed was 190MB (since the instance was last started).

Tip #35

If *V$ROLLSTAT* shows too many shrinks/extends, you might want to schedule a script to extract the contents of *V$ROLLSTAT* to determine whether there is a particular time when rollback segments are shrinking or extending. Many times, a particular job can be isolated that simply needs to be assigned to its own rollback segment.

Do not take these calculations literally. Always provide plenty of cushion space beyond what you have calculated to be the maximum needed so far. Remember that values in *V$* views always reset when the instance has been restarted.

MANAGING TEMPORARY TABLESPACE

Keeping tabs on the temporary tablespaces (where sorts occur) can be a rather tricky proposition. Temporary tablespaces are used exclusively for Oracle's internal needs. Segments are created and destroyed on a fairly routine basis in most installations automatically. Storage management issues with temporary tablespaces are usually limited to knowing the size of the tablespaces, and the maximum amount of temporary storage used at any one time.

PART
V

CH

21

The size of the temporary tablespace should be relatively constant and not subject to great fluctuations—although large queries involving sorting, index creation of large tables, and other major transactions can allocate an abnormal amount of temporary segments.

Tip #36	Remember that Oracle will many times perform a sort as a necessary step to other functions such as joins and *GROUP BY* clauses. Don't assume that Oracle isn't using a temporary tablespace because no explicit sorts are requested.

To monitor temporary segments, check for all segments that are of type *TEMPORARY* in *DBA_SEGMENTS*. The following query can help:

```
SELECT owner, segment_name, tablespace_name, bytes, extents
FROM dba_segments
WHERE segment_type = 'TEMPORARY'
```

Always be on the lookout for errors in the alter log file or errors returned to applications indicating that the temporary tablespace is either too small or does not allow enough extents for a transaction to complete. In the latter case, solving this problem will usually entail either setting *MAXEXTENTS* higher (or unlimited) or increasing the *NEXT* extent storage parameter.

ADMINISTERING A GROWING DATABASE

Careful monitoring of your database usually enables you to spend some time carefully planning for future growth. Most databases require a balance of performance, fault tolerance, and ease of maintenance. You need to provide the path for database growth, while simultaneously maintaining acceptable performance levels and ensuring the uptime and integrity of the database and its data.

Database growth usually focuses on segment and tablespace growth. Growing tablespaces is a matter of adding one or more datafiles to each tablespace in need of more storage, or resizing datafiles already allocated to the tablespace. Although segments automatically grow, there comes a practical and system limitation, which dictates that you should consolidate all the segment's data into a single extent. The need for consolidation depends largely on the data contained in the segment. Lookup tables rarely grow and rarely need attention. Tables containing data, in contrast, can require regular consolidation because they grow on a regular basis.

Tip #37	Oracle can also be configured to allow datafiles to automatically grow, however this should never be done as a substitute for standard growth monitoring and management. Unless you truly understand the growth profile of your database, the use of auto growing datafiles is discouraged.

In this section, I look at the issues surrounding the maintenance of a growing database environment and suggest possible courses of action to ensure that the database services you provide can handle the demands placed on them.

CORRECTING EXCESSIVE TABLE GROWTH

The Oracle RDBMS handles regular table growth by allocating additional extents to the table segment. You periodically will find tables that are growing much faster than anticipated, however, and such tables can benefit from a complete reorganization. Correcting an overextended table involves the following steps:

1. Compute the total size of the table (summing the sizes of all extents).
2. Perform a logical backup of the table.
3. Drop the table.
4. Re-create the table with an initial extent of at least the size from step 1. You should make the initial extent size large enough to contain the current data plus an extra amount of space to accommodate another 6 to 12 months of growth.
5. Import the table's data from the logical backup taken in step 2.

This is commonly referred to as *reorganizing* (reorg) the table. The preceding steps can be performed one of two ways—using export/import to create the logical backups, or by using a `CREATE TABLE AS SELECT` statement. For smaller tables, `CREATE TABLE AS SELECT` is often quicker and easier to perform.

Tip #38	It might be helpful in your organization to plan regular database reorg times. This should allow you to always reorg the segments most out of line with their designed storage needs.

The main problem with performing a table reorganization is handling foreign key constraints dependent on the table. Oracle does not allow you to drop a table that has enabled foreign keys accessing the table. There are two ways to circumvent this problem:

- Drop the foreign keys against the table, reorganize the table, and re-create the foreign keys.
- Disable all foreign keys referencing the table to be reorganized, alter the next extent storage parameter for the table, truncate the table, reload the data, and re-enable the disabled foreign keys.

Although the first method is less work, the second is preferred because the integrity definitions are not lost. It is also preferred because grants and other database structures are not lost from the truncate, as they are when the table is dropped. Oracle does not allow you to drop the table, even if you disable the foreign keys—this restriction does not apply to truncating the table. Size the next extent so that all the database rows fit in the two extents, and allocate enough space to allow for future growth. When finished, you will have a table with two extents—an initial extent of the same size as it was when created, and a second extent containing your remaining table data and growth space.

CONSOLIDATING CLUSTERS

Because clusters and tables are similar in their storage nature, your procedure for consolidating their respective data into single extents varies only slightly. Follow these steps to consolidate clusters:

1. Compute the total allocated size of the cluster itself as well as the associated tables. The cluster's total size should roughly match that of the cumulative total sizes of the member tables.

2. Perform a logical backup of the cluster (to include all associated tables).

3. Drop the cluster and associated tables.

4. Re-create the tables first, then the cluster with an initial extent size sufficient to contain all the data for each segment plus enough surplus space to accommodate 6 to 12 months of growth.

5. Reload the cluster from the logical backup in step 2.

Clusters are relatively similar in nature to tables and the points mentioned previously apply to clusters as well.

CONSOLIDATING INDEXES

An index is very easy to consolidate into a single extent. Because there is no real data that must be saved first and then reloaded, there are only three steps:

1. Compute the total needed for the index.

2. Drop the index.

3. Re-create the index with an initial extent large enough to contain all of index's data as well as enough extra space to accommodate 6 to 12 months of growth.

Alternatively, use the `ALTER INDEX REBUILD` command to re-create an index with new storage parameters. This is especially helpful on very large indexes, or primary key indexes that cannot be easily dropped. Be sure to look into the `UNRECOVERABLE` and `PARALLEL` clauses to speed index rebuild time.

> **Caution**
>
> `ALTER INDEX REBUILD` builds a new copy of an existing index and does not delete the original until the new index is fully built. Although this has index construction time benefits and minimizes the impact on users, it requires that you have enough free tablespace to accommodate both the original and new indexes. Also, using it too much can badly fragment an index tablespace.

MANAGING TABLESPACE GROWTH

Handling tablespace growth used to be solved by adding a datafile to the tablespace, with the `ALTER TABLESPACE ADD DATAFILE` command. Although fairly routine, this is a procedure not easily implemented in a hands-off or scripted manner, and thus requires the full attention of a DBA to perform. Although not a problem in a planned storage upgrade, this could be a problem when your production system runs out of temp space, and the DBA (most likely you) is in another time zone.

Luckily, Oracle addressed this problem in version 7.3 and beyond of the database. You now have two valuable features with which to help manage tablespaces and datafiles—resizable datafiles and automatic datafile extension. Although not a replacement for vigilant space monitoring and planned routines, these new features deserve a valuable place in any Oracle DBA's arsenal.

To resize a datafile, issue the following command:

```
alter database datafile [datafile name] resize [new_size];
```

> **Caution**
>
> Many operating systems and associated tools (backup software, for instance) have limitations on file sizes. Be sure you are familiar with your operating system's limitations before resizing a datafile or turning on the datafile autoextending feature of Oracle.

For example, the following statement resizes a datafile in the *user_data* tablespace to 20MB:

```
alter database datafile '/u01/oradata/PROD/user_PROD_01.dbf' resize 20M;
```

You can resize a datafile to as large as the OS volume the datafile is stored on can handle. When resizing a tablespace to reclaim lost space, however, a tablespace can only be resized to a size greater than the tablespace's high-water mark. Consider the following tablespace map:

Table1	5MB
Free Space	10MB
Table2	15MB
Free Space	125MB
Table3	15MB
Free Space	100MB

In this example, you have three tables in the tablespace taking up 35MB total. The tablespace itself is 265MB in length, but the only space you could reclaim would be the last 100MB.

With *autoextending datafiles*, Oracle automatically allocates a predetermined amount of space to a datafile when that datafile fills to capacity. The syntax of the command is as follows:

```
ALTER DATABASE DATAFILE [file_spec]
AUTOEXTEND ON NEXT [increment_size] MAXSIZE [max_size,UNLIMITED];
```

increment_size defines how much space to add to the datafile when it fills. *MAXSIZE* sets the maximum size of the datafile. An example of this command follows:

```
ALTER DATABASE DATAFILE '/u02/oradata/DEVL/temp_DEVL_01.dbf'
AUTOEXTEND ON NEXT 10M MAXSIZE 500M;
```

Tip #39	*AUTOEXTEND* can also be enabled when creating the tablespace, by placing the *AUTOEXTEND* parameter and values immediately after the datafile specification.

AUTOEXTEND is especially useful for temporary and rollback segment tablespaces. It is a great tool in avoiding transaction failures because there is no more space for a temporary segment or rollback segment to extend. But be wary of an *UNLIMITED MAXSIZE*—you can find yourself filling an entire OS volume with your temporary tablespace datafile, because of a runaway query that should have been canceled in the first place, when it started allocating all of your temporary space.

OS File system Fragmentation

Oracle DBAs are fairly accustomed to dealing with database fragmentation but often forget the implications of OS fragmentation. Most Oracle sites create tablespaces with datafiles, which are stored on a file system native to the operating system. File systems can quickly and easily have most of the free space badly fragmented. When Oracle tries to create a datafile of several megabytes, it usually depends on the OS to actually allocate the space it needs on a physical device. If the OS cannot find contiguous free space, it allocates multiple sections of free space until it has found enough aggregate space to hold a datafile. Because of this, more read/write head movement is required to access data in the new datafiles.

From a performance standpoint, keeping Oracle's segments fragmentation low does absolutely no good if the datafiles have been scattered all over a disk drive by the operating system. Methods of defragmenting a file system vary widely from operating system to operating system. Windows NT, unlike many UNIX implementations, enables file systems to be defragmented with the database and system up and running. Several third-party products are on the market to perform this function. *On-the-fly defragmenting*, as this is called, should be scheduled to run during times with the least amount of database activity. As always, be prepared for disaster by having a recent backup ready.

TROUBLESHOOTING

EXTENT LIMITATIONS

Oracle is reporting an error "Unable to extend…"

Oracle might not be able to extend a segment due to insufficient contiguous space in the segment's tablespace or too many extents. Remember the *MAXEXTENTS* parameter on a segment can limit the number of extents allowed, or you might have reached Oracle's internal extent limits (determined by database block size). If too many extents are causing you problems, you should probably focus on reducing the number of extents rather than increasing the extent limits imposed on your segment.

FRAGMENTATION FROM TEMPORARY TABLES

The application developers insist that it is necessary for a batch program to create and drop temporary tables to perform the necessary functionality. This activity, though, causes some tablespaces to become badly fragmented in short order.

Try to determine exactly which programs will create temporary segments and change them to create the segments all on one or more tablespaces dedicated to temporary segments (which should all have the default *PCTINCREASE* set to 1 or more). At the end of a batch cycle, all temporary segments should have been cleaned off of the temporary tablespace and *SMON* will coalesce all of the now free extents into one large free extent.

PROJECT: MONITORING DATABASE GROWTH

Remember when your database was first created? You had everything set up just right; space was optimally allocated, no hint of data fragmentation was evident, and your queries ran almost instantly. Now, a few years (months?) later, tablespaces consist of datafiles placed wherever you have space, free disk storage is tight, and performance is barely acceptable; you have to clean up the mess.

If left unchecked, databases can easily grow out of control. In this section, I'll discuss techniques you can use to get a handle on your database and monitor its growth. With this information, you'll have the ability to plan disk allocation and database growth—before your users call to let you know that they're "unable to allocate 64 bytes in tablespace *PAYROLL_DATA_01*". I'll also look at some useful tuning information that will help you keep your database healthy and responsive.

The CD-ROM includes several different files that make up a full database size tracking system. By running the *GETSTATS.SQL* program (found on the CD-ROM) on a regular basis (daily, ideally), you'll collect a detailed history and trend information about every segment and tablespace in your database. The software system is optimized to minimize the overhead of storing this history information; it only stores changes in storage statistics. For instance, a segment's storage information is only recorded when it allocates another extent. While this comes at the cost of runtime performance, by scheduling queries against the tracking system after hours, you minimize the performance impact on your system.

Before running GETSTATS.SQL to gather statistics, you'll need to create the repository tables and supporting views and stored procedures. To do this, log in to the database as a user with DBA privileges (this schema will be used to hold the repository objects) and run the following SQL scripts:

1. *CREATE_TABLES.SQL*
2. *CREATE_FUNCTIONS.SQL*
3. *CREATE_VIEWS.SQL*

All the information contained in the tracking system is stored in the *SPACEHIST* and *PROCDATES* tables. *SPACEHIST* contains the size history of segments in your database whereas *PROCDATES* stores every day for which statistics exist. Because *SPACEHIST* only records changes, you'll need to use a view to make sense of the information. The view *V_SPACEHIST* provides a look at the data contained in your tracking tables, trended across the time duration you run *GETSTATS.SQL* on.

The *V_SPACEHIST* view contains a row for each segment on each date in *PROCDATES*. *V_SPACEHIST* is defined as follows:

```
SAMPLE_DATE         DATE
OWNER               VARCHAR2(20)
SEGMENT_TYPE          VARCHAR2(20)
SEGMENT_NAME           VARCHAR2(20)
TABLESPACE            VARCHAR2(20)
BYTES               INTEGER
EXTENTS               INTEGER
NEXT_EXTENT           INTEGER
```

The following describe the columns for *V_SPACEHIST*:

- *SAMPLE_DATE* contains the date for which the segment's statistics were valid.
- *INSTANCE* is the database name that contains the segment.
- *OWNER* is the owner of the segment.
- *SEGMENT_TYPE* defines the type of the segment being examined.
- *SEGMENT_NAME* specifies the segment's name.
- *TABLESPACE* indicates the name of the tablespace containing the segment.
- *BYTES* is the number of bytes allocated to the segment. This value is computed by summing the bytes of all extents allocated for the segment.
- *EXTENTS* is the number of extents for the segment.
- *NEXT_EXTENT* the value of the *NEXT_EXTENT* parameter.

If you were to query *V_SPACEHIST* without a *WHERE* clause, rows would be returned for every segment you have tracked statistics on, for every day these statistics were collected. Looking at all the information contained in this view is probably not too useful. Fortunately, you can use SQL's powerful querying capabilities to gather the information you need.

Tip #40	There are also many turnkey solutions for tracking database growth information from vendors such as BMC and Platinum.

"A picture is worth a thousand words" accurately describes how a graphical representation of data is often much more meaningful than the rows it represents. For instance, if you wanted to know when in the last six months your database grew from 2.7GB to 6GB, you could examine a couple hundred lines from a SQL query or look at a single graph showing the same information, and know instantly when peak growth occurred.

An ODBC connection and spreadsheet software are all the tools you need to build concise yet informative graphs depicting storage usage in your database. As you can see in Figure 21.12, the Microsoft Excel spreadsheet chart shows a period of time when the database grew as a whole. With this information, you might want to drill down to segment-level data, using the *V_SPACEHIST* view. By graphing the data first, you can instantly identify which period of time you need to focus your investigation on.

Figure 21.12
Graphing the information from the V_SPACEHIST view can quickly identify times of peak growth.

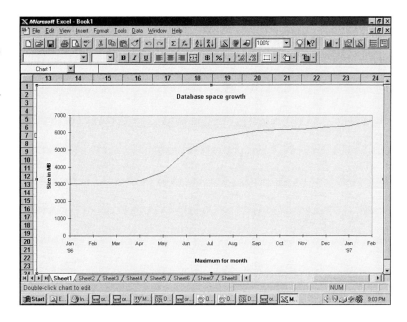

Many times, a sudden change in database growth is due to an increase in the number of users or an application change, which results in more data being stored. When a database is established, DBAs are many times out of the information loop, and your database size might be growing rapidly without you knowing it. By collecting storage statistics regularly, you'll know when irregular growth has occurred and will have the opportunity to take preventative measures before a serious problem develops.

Suppose, for example, you run *GETSTATS.SQL* every night and once a week you would like to see a chart showing growth for your production database over the last six months. You would start with a SQL statement similar to the following:

```
SELECT sample_date, SUM(bytes)
   FROM v_spacehist WHERE sample_date > (SYSDATE) - 180
GROUP BY sample_date;
```

Because the *V_SPACEHIST* view contains *OWNER* and *TABLESPACE* information for each segment it tracks, you can narrow your focus to track growth for specific users or tablespaces. This example provides 90 days of growth information for all segments owned by the user *TGASPER*:

```
SELECT sample_date, SUM(bytes) FROM v_spacehist
WHERE owner = 'TGASPER' AND  sample_date > (SYSDATE - 90)
GROUP BY sample_date;
```

Monitoring growth for a specific tablespace is just as easily accomplished, as shown in this example:

```
SELECT sample_date, SUM(bytes) FROM v_spacehist
WHERE  tablespace = 'USERS' AND sample_date > (SYSDATE - 180)
GROUP BY sample_date;
```

PART

V

CH

21

Unless you are in a unique environment, your database will grow over time. When you initially design systems, you plan for anticipated future growth. Regular monitoring of your database helps make sure that unanticipated growth doesn't catch you off guard.

CHAPTER **22**

IDENTIFYING HEAVY RESOURCE USERS

In this chapter

Every database administrator has faced a situation wherein the database starts dragging and becomes slow suddenly for some reason. This can happen in a well-tuned database and can catch you unaware. At this time, it takes the skill of the DBA to spot the defaulting user and do what is needed to make the difference in the performance of the database. A number of times I have had the opportunity to pinpoint a session that was eating up all system resources, causing the overall performance of the database to drop. The defaulting user could be the user who had executed a large query having a few tables and missed a few key column joins in the SELECT clause, or it could be an unoptimized statement. The aim of this chapter is to equip the DBA with the skills necessary to identify such users with relative ease. This chapter provides the methods and techniques to identify the resource-intensive users and does not get into the details of remedying the problems. The details as to how to treat them are covered in other performance-tuning sections of the book.

RESOURCES THAT MAKE THE DIFFERENCE

There are a number of approaches that you can take to identify heavy resource users. The approach followed here first takes an overview of the environment. If something wrong is sensed, further probing is done into the area to get into the user details. The resources that you would be looking at here are CPU, file I/O, and memory. If the CPU is heavily loaded and is kept fully busy by some user doing a lot of CPU-intensive work, it can drag the system down. Similarly, heavy file I/O can also cause the system performance to drop. Heavy requirements for memory by some processes can lead to paging and swapping, which can severely hamper the performance of the system. You should concentrate on these three resources. Basically, every process that gets executed on the server tries to acquire the following resources:

- CPU—Every process needs to have some slice of the CPU time for executing its job. Some processes grab a lot of CPU time, and others finish a lot earlier. The limited amount of available CPU power must be shared between the Oracle processes on the system and the internal operating system (OS) processes. Obviously, CPU-intensive users are users that consume a lot of CPU time.

- File I/O—Every time a process needs to access data, it first searches the buffer cache if the data is already brought in by some previous process. If the data is already present in the buffer cache, the read is completed very fast. If the data required is not present in the cache, the data has to be read from the disk. A physical read has to be performed. Such reads from the disk are very expensive because the time it takes for reading from the disk is approximately 50 times higher than the time it takes to read from the cache. When the system starts becoming I/O-intensive, the system performance might start degrading, as all the processes would be doing most of the time is waiting for the data to be returned from the disk.

  The resource about which I am talking here is time. There is greater time being consumed as a result of heavy disk file accesses, and time is the essence of life. Ultimately, the use of all resources will boil down to one resource—time.

- Memory—Shortage in this resource due to high usage of memory by some processes could also be one of the possible reasons for performance degradation. On UNIX systems, efficient use of memory is made by using the concept of *virtual memory*. In a virtual memory system, only the most-used pages are kept in the physical memory; the rest or currently inactive pages are kept on the swap space and are brought in on request. When memory falls short on a system due to low physical memory or high demands on memory by processes, then, to cater to this memory requirement, the system first starts paging. If there is still a shortage of memory, the system resorts to swapping physical processes, which can substantially degrade system performance. Paging and swapping are discussed in the later section "Resource Memory".

When there is heavy use of these resources, the system experiences a drop in performance. Therefore, it is very important to locate how much of these resources is allocated to each user. To identify heavy resource consumption, you concentrate on one resource at a time and try to identify the individual resource consumption by processes.

WINDOWS NT PERFORMANCE MONITORING

Oracle8i for Windows NT includes the following three Performance Monitoring Tools:

- Oracle8 data dictionary views
- Windows NT Performance Monitor
- Oracle8 Performance Monitor

ORACLE8 DATA DICTIONARY VIEWS

There are sets of data dictionary views that contain a wealth of information regarding database performance. There are two general categories of data dictionary views: *static* and *dynamic*. Static views contain information about the overall structure of the database, such as the names, location of database files, user information, storage utilization, redo log and control file information, and so on. Dynamic views, known as V$tables, reflect realtime performance information, such as physical I/O, memory utilization, user activities, and more.

WINDOWS NT PERFORMANCE MONITOR

Windows NT does not have very many tunable parameters. For example, in UNIX, a system administrator can modify a large number of kernel parameters that directly affect system performance. Windows NT, on the other hand, does not enable the kernel to be touched at all. Windows NT is supposed to be self-tuning in that it contains a number of adaptive algorithms that dynamically adjust performance while the system is running.

Most of the performance information for the Windows NT OS can be found in the Windows NT Performance Monitor (PerfMon). PerfMon is a flexible graphical tool that you can use to collect realtime performance information about Windows NT. It also generates numeric values for each counter that is selected. These values are displayed in the lower portion of the chart display. You can use that information to determine what parts of the system are experiencing performance bottlenecks and take steps to eliminate these problems. Windows NT treats almost everything in the entire operating system as an Object.

ORACLE8 PERFORMANCE MONITOR

The Oracle8 Performance Monitor is a series of customized PerfMon counters that can be used to measure Oracle database performance. This Performance monitoring tool takes the information from data dictionary views and displays it graphically. The counters are all based on SQL statements issued against the data dictionary. You can see the SQL statements issued by Oracle8 PerfMon in the PERF81.ORA file, which is located in the ORANT\DBS directory. When you click on the Oracle8 Performance Monitor Icon, a connection to the database is established automatically. The username, password and other information for this connection is located in the Windows NT Registry. To see this information, run the Registry editor program (REGEDT32.EXE). Open the HKEY_LOCAL_MACHINE key, and then navigate to SYSTEM\CurrentControlSet\Service\Oracle80\Performance, as shown below. Then, change the value for the username, password, or host name by double-clicking on them (see Figure 22.1). The default values are system/manager@orcl.

Figure 22.1
Registry Entries for
Oracle8 Performance
Monitor Tool

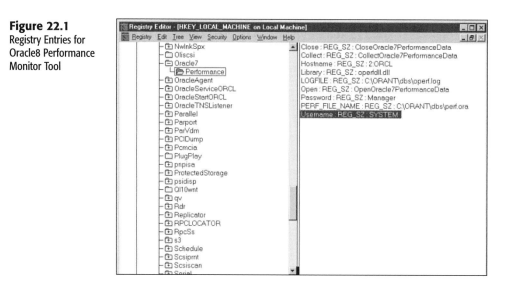

Performance Monitor counters for Oracle8 are shown in Table 22.1.

TABLE 22.1 PERFORMANCE MONITOR COUNTERS

Object	Counters
Oracle8 Buffer Cache	%phyreads/gets
Oracle8 Dictionary Cache	%getmisses/gets
Oracle8 Data files	phyrds/sec;phywrts/sec (each instance is an individual data file)

Object	Counters
Oracle8 DBWR stats 1	buffers scanned/second;LRU scans/second
Oracle8 DBWR stats 2	checkpoints/sec; timeouts/sec
Oracle8 Dynamic Space Management	recursive calls/sec
Oracle8 Free List	%freelist waits/requests
Oracle8 Library Cache	%reloads/pins
Oracle8 Redo Log Buffer	redo log space requests
Oracle8 Sorts	sorts in memory/sec; sorts on disk/sec

CPU

UNIX is a multiprocessing operating system; that is, the UNIX operating system is capable of managing multiple processes simultaneously. Every process that has to execute a job using the CPU waits in the queue called the *run queue* for a CPU time slice to execute its job. When it is the process's turn, the process is allocated a time slice in which to execute its job. A well-tuned CPU should not have many processes waiting in the run queue to execute processes, but it should be adequately busy. The next sections identify processes that are consuming an excessive amount of CPU resource. While doing this exercise, bear in mind that on a lightly loaded system, one process can literally hog all the CPU, which is perfectly normal and should be no reason for alarm. When you are trying to identify heavy CPU users, you must see to it that at any point in time there is a sufficient number of jobs running on the system and that there is a performance problem. It is only under this condition that you proceed with the approach mentioned here because as specified previously, a system with a low load has its few users consuming a lot of the CPU time, which is really normal.

TAKING A CPU OVERVIEW

Before you identify which user is causing a CPU resource problem, you must have a general overview of how the CPU is behaving. On UNIX systems, you can determine CPU behavior by using the sar -u command. The sar -u command output has three columns of interest as shown in the Table 22.2

TABLE 22.2   IMPORTANT COLUMNS IN sar -u COMMAND OUTPUT

Column Name	Description
usr	Percentage of CPU time spent in servicing user requests.
sys	Percentage of time spent by CPU attending system calls.
wio	Percentage of time spent by the CPU waiting for completion of I/O from the disk. If this percentage is regularly high, it might indicate a possible bottleneck on the disks or inefficiencies in the I/O system.
Idle	Percentage of time the CPU was idle.

A well-tuned or healthy CPU generally has the user CPU time double the system CPU time; that is, the CPU is spending more time servicing user requests as compared to servicing system calls.

A sample output of the sar command is shown later. The basic format of the command is as follows:

```
sar -u n t
```

n is the interval for which the monitoring is to be done, and t is the number of times for which the monitoring is to be performed. Following is an example of the output of the sar CPU Utilization command:

```
$ sar -uM 2 10

HP-UX arms1 B.10.10 U 9000/819    09/04/97

19:53:57    cpu     %usr    %sys    %wio    %idle
19:53:59      0       38       9      40       12
              1       43      10      37       10
         system      40      10      39       11
19:54:01      0       51      14      29        6
              1       45      17      33        6
         system      48      15      31        6
19:54:03      0       42       8      44        6
              1       44       6      42        8
         system      43       7      43        7
19:54:05      0       52      10      34        4
              1       34      17      42        6
         system      43      14      38        6
19:54:07      0       30      14      45       11
              1       37      10      46        7
         system      34      12      46        9
19:54:09      0       44      10      38        8
              1       44       6      43        6
```

If the CPU overview shows a lot of idle time, it could possibly mean that the CPU is not utilized to the fullest extent possible. If the %wio, %usr, and %sys columns have low values and the idle has a high value, it means there is nothing running on the system.

If the system time spent by the CPU is higher then the user time, this also needs to be checked. Overall, you should aim to get the user CPU time to be double or more than the system CPU time; otherwise, you need to probe further. In the preceding output, the %wio column shows a high value; that means that in the current scenario, there is no problem with the CPUs, but there could be a bottleneck on the disks. You might further need to execute the sar -d command to find out which disk is facing the I/O load.

As mentioned earlier, every process that has to be executed on the system waits in the queue called the run queue. If there are too many jobs waiting on the run queue, it is an indication there are heavy resource-intensive jobs running on the system and the CPU cannot cope with the demands of the system. The following is a sample assessment of the run queue and also another good starting point to see whether the CPUs are bogged down with processes running on the system:

```
$ sar -qu 2 10

HP-UX arms1 B.10.10 U 9000/819    09/06/97

17:35:37 runq-sz %runocc swpq-sz %swpocc
         %usr    %sys    %wio    %idle
17:35:39  1.0     25     0.0       0
          39      11     43        6
17:35:41  0.0      0     0.0       0
          46      10     40        5
17:35:43  1.0     25     0.0       0
          17       5     55       24
17:35:45  1.0     25     0.0       0
          38       9     42       10
17:35:47  1.0     25     0.0       0
          39       9     45        8
17:35:49  0.0      0     0.0       0
          36       6     52        6
17:35:51  1.0     25     0.0       0
          22      10     51       16
17:35:53  1.0     25     0.0       0
          44       7     46        3
17:35:55  2.0     25     0.0       0
          41       8     45        6
17:35:57  0.0      0     0.0       0
          25       8     50       17

Average   1.1     18     0.0       0
Average   35       8     47       10
```

Table 22.3 explains the meaning of the different columns in the output.

TABLE 22.3   EXPLANATION OF COLUMNS IN THE sar -qu OUTPUT

Column Name	Column Description
runq-sz	The size of the run queue. It does not include processes that are sleeping or waiting for I/O to complete; it does include processes that are in memory and are waiting to be run.
%runocc	The percentage of time the run queue is occupied by processes waiting to be executed.
swpq-sz	The average length of the swap queue during the interval the monitoring was done. Processes that are ready to be run but have been swapped out are included in this count.
%swpocc	The percentage of time the swap queue of processes that can be run (processes swapped out but ready to run) was occupied.

From the previous output, you can see that the size of the run queue is only 1; that means that during the monitoring interval, only one process was waiting for the CPU in the queue. During the interval, the run queue percentage is occupied only 25 percent of the time. You can conclude that at this point the CPU is very lightly loaded. Typically, be on the lookout for a run queue in excess of 5 or 6. If the queue gets larger than these values, either reduce the number of running processes, increase the number of CPU, or upgrade the existing CPU. You can identify which processes are waiting for CPU resources or loading the CPU by using the techniques mentioned in the next section.

FINDING HEAVY CPU USERS

There are several ways to find heavy CPU users on a system. You can either use the operating system tools to identify heavy CPU usage users or use the information stored in the Oracle system tables. In this section, you examine both options. In fact, both routes can be used to tally up and find a heavy CPU user on the system.

USING THE ORACLE ROUTE

The Oracle dynamic system performance table provides a vast wealth of information about what is happening on the system. The V$SYSSTAT and V$SESSTAT views are two of the dynamic performance views that you use to find the information you require.

A general listing of the value stored in V$SYSSTAT is given in the Listing 22.1, shown next. The information you are interested here is CPU usage, but this view can be used for a number of other monitoring purposes.

```
SQL> select * from v$sysstat order by class,statistic#;
```

The following listing is the output of the above SQL statement:

LISTING 22.1   USING V$SYSSTAT TO FIND SYSTEM STATISTICS

STATISTIC# NAME	CLASS	VALUE
0 logons cumulative	1	2051
1 logons current	1	68
2 opened cursors cumulative	1	72563
3 opened cursors current	1	636
4 user commits	1	289212
5 user rollbacks	1	7299
6 user calls	1	2574300
7 recursive calls	1	4726090
8 recursive cpu usage	1	1334927
9 session logical reads	1	205058382
10 session stored procedure space	1	0
12 CPU used by this session	1	4896925
13 session connect time	1	6.2794E+11
15 session uga memory	1	8599758248
16 session uga memory max	1	169781672
20 session pga memory	1	311833920
21 session pga memory max	1	324695784
101 serializable aborts	1	0
133 bytes sent via SQL*Net to client	1	206511175
134 bytes received via SQL*Net from client	1	174496695
135 SQL*Net roundtrips to/from client	1	2588500
136 bytes sent via SQL*Net to dblink	1	0
137 bytes received via SQL*Net from dblink	1	0

```
138 SQL*Net roundtrips to/from dblink        1           0
 84 redo entries                             2     2040536
 85 redo size                                2   502002531
 86 redo entries linearized                  2           0
 87 redo buffer allocation retries           2        2391
 88 redo small copies                        2     1807035
 89 redo wastage                             2    76782505
 90 redo writer latching time                2         888
 91 redo writes                              2      183133
 92 redo blocks written                      2      576689
 93 redo write time                          2      502618
 94 redo log space requests                  2          66
 95 redo log space wait time                 2        2635
 96 redo log switch interrupts               2           0
 97 redo ordering marks                      2           0
 22 enqueue timeouts                         4          25
 23 enqueue waits                            4          57
 24 enqueue deadlocks                        4           0
 25 enqueue requests                         4      707487
 26 enqueue conversions                      4        7259
 27 enqueue releases                         4      707376
 37 db block gets                            8     5809539
 38 consistent gets                          8   202261999
 39 physical reads                           8   124879028
 40 physical writes                          8      367214
 41 write requests                           8       25221
 42 summed dirty queue length                8       37479
 43 db block changes                         8     3994241
 44 change write time                        8       56399
 45 consistent changes                       8      822006
 46 redo synch writes                        8       23407
 47 redo synch time                          8      103518
 48 exchange deadlocks                       8           0
 49 free buffer requested                    8   123453575
 50 dirty buffers inspected                  8       42044
 51 free buffer inspected                    8       86462
 52 commit cleanout failure: write disabled  8           0
 53 commit cleanout failures: hot backup in  8           0
    progress

 54 commit cleanout failures: buffer being w 8         164
    ritten

 55 commit cleanout failures: callback failu 8        2769
    re

 56 total number commit cleanout calls       8      547911
 57 commit cleanout number successfully comp 8      538392
    leted

 58 DBWR timeouts                            8       10503
 59 DBWR make free requests                  8       38615
 60 DBWR free buffers found                  8    18186694
 61 DBWR lru scans                           8       42222
 62 DBWR summed scan depth                   8    20000100
 63 DBWR buffers scanned                     8    20699788
```

continues

LISTING 22.1 CONTINUED

```
STATISTIC# NAME                                            CLASS      VALUE
---------- ----------------------------------------- ---------- ----------
        64 DBWR checkpoints                                  8        998
        70 recovery blocks read                              8          0
        71 recovery array reads                              8          0
        72 recovery array read time                          8          0
        73 CR blocks created                                 8     125716
        74 Current blocks converted for CR                   8      14791
        99 background checkpoints started                    8         18
       100 background checkpoints completed                  8         18
        28 global lock gets (non async)                     32          1
        29 global lock gets (async)                         32          0
        30 global lock get time                             32          0
        31 global lock converts (non async)                 32          0
        32 global lock converts (async)                     32          0
        33 global lock convert time                         32          0
        34 global lock releases (non async)                 32          0
        35 global lock releases (async)                     32          0
        36 global lock release time                         32          0
        78 next scns gotten without going to DLM            32          0
        79 Unnecessary process cleanup for SCN batch        32              0
           ing

        80 calls to get snapshot scn: kcmgss               32    2619387
        81 kcmgss waited for batching                       32          0
        82 kcmgss read scn without going to DLM             32          0
        83 kcmccs called get current scn                    32          0
        65 DBWR cross instance writes                       40          0
        66 remote instance undo block writes                40          0
        67 remote instance undo header writes               40          0
        68 remote instance undo requests                    40          0
        69 cross instance CR read                           40          0
        98 hash latch wait gets                             40          0
       118 table scans (short tables)                       64     366085
       119 table scans (long tables)                        64      10819
       120 table scans (rowid ranges)                       64         15
       121 table scans (cache partitions)                   64          0
       122 table scans (direct read)                        64         15
       123 table scan rows gotten                           64  904956876
       124 table scan blocks gotten                         64  129018277
       125 table fetch by rowid                             64   31893640
       126 table fetch continued row                        64     506029
       127 cluster key scans                                64     135034
       128 cluster key scan block gets                      64     363979
       129 parse time cpu                                   64      34740
       130 parse time elapsed                               64      55148
       131 parse count                                      64     532516
       132 execute count                                    64    2390178
       139 sorts (memory)                                   64      40412
       140 sorts (disk)                                     64        268
       141 sorts (rows)                                     64   49141580
```

```
142 session cursor cache hits                    64           0
143 session cursor cache count                   64           0
 11 CPU used when call started                  128     4896911
 14 process last non-idle time                  128  6.2794E+11
 17 messages sent                               128      160593
 18 messages received                           128      160593
 19 background timeouts                          128       31883
 75 calls to kcmgcs                              128       90759
 76 calls to kcmgrs                              128     4168092
 77 calls to kcmgas                              128      306090
102 transaction lock foreground requests        128           0
103 transaction lock foreground wait time        128           0
104 transaction lock background gets            128           0
105 transaction lock background get time        128           0
106 transaction tables consistent reads - un    128      143669
    do records applied

107 transaction tables consistent read rollb    128         131
    acks

108 data blocks consistent reads - undo reco    128      678275
    rds applied

109 no work - consistent read gets              128   194428691
110 cleanouts only - consistent read gets       128       25194
111 rollbacks only - consistent read gets       128       86452
112 cleanouts and rollbacks - consistent rea    128       54180
    d gets

113 rollback changes - undo records applied     128       14117
114 transaction rollbacks                       128        1520
115 immediate (CURRENT) block cleanout appli    128       73789
    cations

116 immediate (CR) block cleanout applicatio    128       79374
    ns

117 deferred (CURRENT) block cleanout applic    128      264576
    ations

144 cursor authentications                      128       95248
```

The statistic you are interested is CPU used by this session having a statisticm# value of 12:

```
12 CPU used by this session                      1     4896925
SQL> select * from v$sysstat WHERE name = 'CPU used by this session' order by
class,statistic#
```

Now the value of CPU used by this session is in hundredths of a second. Convert the value into minutes by modifying the query as follows:

```
col name format a35
col value format 999.99 heading "Time in ¦ Mins"
select statistic#,name,class ,value/60/100 value
from v$sysstat
where statistic# =  12
/
```

The following listing is the output of the above SQL statement.

```
STATISTIC# NAME                                      CLASS     Mins
---------- ------------------------------------- ---------- --------
        12 CPU used by this session                   1    817.56
```

This output shows that the RDBMS with all its background and foreground server processes has consumed approximately 817 minutes of CPU time since startup. This is again information at an overall level. You now want to find which session has consumed how much of the CPU resource.

There is another dynamic performance view called V$SESSTAT. Basically, the only difference between the two is that V$SYSSTAT stores the summary level information, and V$SESSTAT stores information at the session level; V$SESSTAT can be called the child table of V$SYSSTAT. You can use the information in V$SESSTAT to find out which session is consuming the maximum CPU.

You do that by using the script in Listing 22.2.

LISTING 22.2 SCRIPT AND OUTPUT TO PRODUCE CPU USAGE REPORT

```
col prog format a10
col value format 9999.99 heading "Time In¦    Mins"

Select a.sid,
             spid,
             status,
             substr(a.program,1,10) prog,
             a.terminal,
             osuser,
             value/60/100 value
From    v$session a,
             v$process b,
             v$sesstat c
Where   c.statistic# = 12
And     c.sid       = a.sid
And     a.paddr     = b.addr
Order by value desc;
The following is the output of the above SQL statement.
  Time In
     SID SPID      STATUS   PROG        TERMINAL    Schema     Mins
---------- --------- -------- ---------- ----------- -------- --------
      45 11145     INACTIVE C:\ARMS\BS Windows PC TIFFANY    95.87
      95 12370     INACTIVE C:\WINDOWS Windows PC SUSANE     22.99
      47 9778      INACTIVE C:\ARMS\BS Windows PC LIN        10.22
      22 9295      ACTIVE   C:\ARMS\DE Windows PC INGEMAR     3.96
```

```
 37 14427     INACTIVE C:\ARMS\CS Windows PC SHARON          .50
107  9454     INACTIVE sqlplus@ar ttyp2       MARK       .34
 65 16959     INACTIVE C:\ARMS\CS Windows PC APEKSH         .32
 35 17077     INACTIVE C:\ARMS\CS Windows PC TEUTA      .30
 34 18995     INACTIVE C:\ARMS\CS Windows PC KASTURI        .23
 23  578      INACTIVE C:\ARMS\CS Windows PC REEHER         .20
 33 16965     INACTIVE C:\ARMS\CS Windows PC JULIE          .20
 71 16973     INACTIVE C:\ARMS\CS Windows PC AMY        .19
 92 16989     INACTIVE C:\ARMS\CS Windows PC BARRETT         .17
 82 8004      INACTIVE C:\ARMS\CS Windows PC GABRIELLE         .17
 96 17090     INACTIVE C:\ARMS\CS Windows PC MANISH         .16
 20 5466      INACTIVE C:\ARMS\CS Windows PC BURTNER        .16
 29 17033     INACTIVE C:\ARMS\CS Windows PC DAVID          .14
 43 16953     INACTIVE C:\ARMS\CS Windows PC ADITI          .13
 77 16947     INACTIVE C:\ARMS\CS Windows PC GARY       .12
 54 8971      INACTIVE C:\ARMS\CS Windows PC RANDY          .11
```

From Listing 10.2, you can conclude that session 45 and 95 are the top CPU users on the system, consuming 95 and 22 minutes, respectively. The only problem with this output is that it reflects cumulative statistics since start of the session rather than statistics in an interval.

To elaborate, if session A has used 50 minutes of CPU time over 8 hours and session B has used 30 minutes of CPU time over 1 hour, this output will report that session A is a higher CPU user than session B—which is not actually true because the rate of CPU usage by session B far exceeds the rate of CPU usage of session A. This output does give a fairly accurate overview of the top CPU users on the system, however.

If you want to be more accurate, you have to capture statistics over an interval. Select a time period on the system that is the busiest period of the day. Then capture the CPU usage of the session and store it in a temporary table. After a time period equal to the busy interval has elapsed again, capture the CPU usage of every session using V$SESSTAT and store it in a temporary table. The information captured in the two snapshots stored in the temporary table can be used to find the rate of CPU usage and the total CPU usage by individual session during the interval. This can be accomplished by the script in Listing 22.3.

LISTING 22.3 CREATE THE TEMPORARY TABLES TO STORE SNAPSHOT INFORMATION

```
REM Table to store the start snapshot values
Create table stat$cpu_begin
(sid number,
cpid varchar2(9),
schemaname varchar2(30),
cpu_usage number(10),
program varchar2(48),
time_stamp date);
REM Table to store the end snapshot values
Create table stat$cpu_end
(sid number,
spid varchar2(9),
schemaname varchar2(30),
cpu_usage number(10),
program varchar2(48),
time_stamp date);
```

After the tables are created, the first snapshot can be taken using the script in Listing 22.4.

LISTING 22.4 SCRIPT TO CAPTURE THE INITIAL CPU STATISTICS IN THE stat$cpu_begin TABLE

```
Insert Into stat$cpu_begin
Select a.sid,
       b.spid,
       a.schemaname,
       value,
       a.program,
       sysdate
From   v$session a,
       v$process b,
       v$sesstat c
Where  c.statistic# = 12
And    c.sid        = a.sid
And    a.paddr      = b.addr;
```

Similarly, after the busy period is over, you could again run the script shown in Listing 22.5 and populate the table stat$cpu_end.

LISTING 22.5 SCRIPT TO CAPTURE THE END CPU STATISTICS IN THE stat$cpu_end TABLE

```
Insert Into stat$cpu_end
Select a.sid,
       b.spid,
       a.schemaname,
       value,
       a.program,
       sysdate
From   v$session a,
       v$process b,
       v$sesstat c
Where  c.statistic# = 12
And    c.sid        = a.sid
And    a.paddr      = b.addr;
```

You are now ready to produce the heavy CPU user report along with the rate of CPU usage. This report is more accurate because it reports on the rate of CPU usage, which is a more important factor in determining a heavy resource user. This report shows the CPU consumption rate of each session at a minutes-per-hour level. This snapshotting technique irons out the discrepancies in Listing 22.5. Shown next in Listing 22.6 is the script required to generate the CPU usage report.

LISTING 22.6 SCRIPT TO PRODUCE THE CPU USAGE REPORT USING SNAPSHOTTING

```
Break on sid on spid on tot_usg on mins_per_hr
Select e.sid,
   e.spid,
      e.cpu_usage,
         b.cpu_usage,
```

```
            to_char((e.cpu_usage - b.cpu_usage)/(6000),'9999.99')   tot_usg_mins
,
            to_char( ((e.cpu_usage - b.cpu_usage)/(6000))/( (e.time_stamp - b.ti
me_stamp)*24),'99.99')  mins_per_hr
         From    stat$cpu_end e, stat$cpu_begin b
         Where  b.sid =  e.sid
         And    b.spid = e.spid
          order by mins_per_hr;
```

Note

This SQL code works on the basis of statistics captured using the V$SESSTAT view for the statistic that has the value 12 (CPU used by this session). There can sometimes be a problem using this if this value is incremented by Oracle on exit of the user call just before returning to the client process. Therefore, if you are monitoring a batch job that has a user call that has not yet returned, the CPU usage value might not be updated in the V$SESSTAT, and you might get inaccurate results. Be aware of this when you are using the previous SQL listings. Accurate results can be achieved if the monitoring interval is large, assuming all sessions will have the V$SESSTAT updated at some point during the interval.

Now that you have identified which session is causing the CPU resource to be used heavily, you can determine what the session is executing for the CPU to be used so heavily.

The script shown in Listing 22.7 can be used to find the SQL statement the session is currently executing. This gives a fair indication of which program the session is executing, what is the current section of code, and whether any query optimization needs to be performed on the SQL.

LISTING 22.7   SCRIPT TO FIND THE CURRENT SQL STATEMENT THE SESSION IS EXECUTING

```
set head off
set long 9000
set linesize 100
set pagesize 30
set feedback off
set wrap on
set verify off

select sql_text
from v$sqltext , v$session
where sid = 45
and v$sqltext.address = v$session.sql_address
order by piece

The following listing is the output of the above SQL statement.

SQL_TEXT
----------------------------------------
Select * from employee where emp_id =800
```

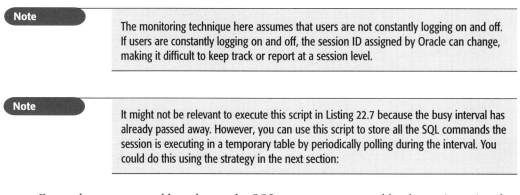

Note

The monitoring technique here assumes that users are not constantly logging on and off. If users are constantly logging on and off, the session ID assigned by Oracle can change, making it difficult to keep track or report at a session level.

Note

It might not be relevant to execute this script in Listing 22.7 because the busy interval has already passed away. However, you can use this script to store all the SQL commands the session is executing in a temporary table by periodically polling during the interval. You could do this using the strategy in the next section:

Create the temporary table and store the SQL statements executed by the session using the script in Listing 22.8.

LISTING 22.8   SCRIPT TO CREATE SQL EXECUTION HISTORY TABLE stat$session_hash

```
Create table stat$session_hash
(sid number,
spid varchar2(9),
schemaname varchar2(30),
hash_value number,
time_stamp date,
num_occ     number);
```

After the table is created, you can run the script in Listing 22.9 to create the procedure sp_stat$sample_hash, which stores all SQL's executed by different sessions during the monitoring interval in the SQL execution history table stat$session_hash.

LISTING 22.9   SCRIPT TO CREATE PROCEDURE sp_stat$sample_hash

```
Cursor c_stat$session is
      Select sid,
             spid,
             schemaname,
             sql_hash_value
      From v$session a,
           v$process b
      Where a.paddr = b.addr;

v_stat$session     c_stat$session%RowType;
v_stat$session_hash stat$session_hash%RowType;
e_next                          exception;

Begin

      Open c_stat$session ;

      Loop

      Begin
```

```
        Fetch c_stat$session
        Into  v_stat$session;

        Begin

            Select *
            Into   v_stat$session_hash
            From   stat$session_hash
            Where  sid = v_stat$session.sid
            And    spid = v_stat$session.spid
            And    hash_value = v_stat$session.sql_hash_value;

            Insert Into stat$session_hash
            values
            (v_stat$session.sid,
             v_stat$session.spid,
             v_stat$session.schemaname,
             v_stat$session.sql_hash_value,
             sysdate,
             1
            );

        Exception
        When No_Data_Found Then
        Update stat$session_hash
        Set num_occ = num_occ + 1
        Where  sid = v_stat$session.sid
        And    spid = v_stat$session.spid
        And    hash_value = v_stat$session.sql_hash_value;

        When Others Then
        Raise e_next;

        End;

    Exception

    When e_next Then
    Null;

    When Others Then
    Null;

    End;

    Commit;

    End Loop;

    Close c_stat$session;

End;
```

This procedure (sp_stat$sample_hash) can be run intermittently during the monitoring interval. After the begin and end CPU usage information and the SQL execution history is captured, you can generate a report of the heavy CPU users along with the SQL statements that each session was executing during the period of the snapshot. This report can then be used to tune the SQL statements that cause the heavy usage of the CPU. Listing 22.10 gives the script for generating the heavy CPU usage report along with the hash value of the SQL statements that were executed by the sessions.

LISTING 22.10   SCRIPT TO PRODUCE CPU USAGE REPORT WITH THE HASH VALUE OF SQL STATEMENTS EXECUTING DURING THE MONITORING INTERVAL

```
Break on sid on spid on tot_usg_mins on mins_per_hr

Select e.sid,
  e.spid,
  to_char((e.cpu_usage - b.cpu_usage)/(6000),'9999.99')   tot_usg_mins,
  to_char( ((e.cpu_usage - b.cpu_usage)/(60100))/( (e.time_stamp - b.time_stamp
)*24),'99.99')  mins_per_hr,
        hash_value,
        num_occ
        From    stat$cpu_end e, stat$cpu_begin b , stat$session_hash c
        Where   b.sid =  e.sid
        And     b.spid = e.spid
        And     e.sid  = c.sid
        And     e.spid = c.spid
        order by mins_per_hr;
```

The following listing is the output of the above SQL statement.

SID	SPID	Tot Usg In Mins	Mins Per Hr	HASH_VALUE	NUM_OCC
23	9461	29.04	9.68	-1.447E+09	7
24	9776	25.38	8.46	1739700154	1
				-1.306E+09	5
				1014890971	1
34	11525	22.41	7.47	573420945	7
35	9459	17.55	5.85	1739700154	2
				1561770773	1
35	9459	10.32	3.44	2113573249	1
59	9531	.00	.00	1739700154	6
56	10010	.00	.00	573420945	7
53	11114	.00	.00	-2.056E+09	7
52	10014	.00	.00	1739700154	3
105	9533	.00	.00	573420945	7
86	9529	.00	.00	573420945	7
				1907631373	1
73	9527	.00	.00	573420945	7
62	9541	.01	.00	-1.306E+09	5
109	16988	.00	.00	1848020776	7
52	10014	.00	.00	-1.306E+09	1

From this output, you can easily determine that sessions 23 and 24 are the top CPU users with a minutes-per-hour CPU usage of 9.68 and 8.46 minutes, respectively. Using the sql_hash_value and the V$SQLTEXT view, you can determine the SQL statement that caused such a high amount of CPU to be used and take suitable action. The column num_occ in Listing 22.10 shows the number of times the SQL statement was executed during the monitoring interval.

Note

> Most likely, the SQL statements that cause more CPU to be used are full table scans or SQL statements causing more physical reads on the system. When data is required that is not already present in the data block buffer, a miss occurs, and the data must be read from the physical device. The miss of data causes the buffer manager to allocate space for data to be read in the buffer cache if free space is not available. The buffer manager then moves blocks of data to be written out to be moved into the dirty list so that they are subsequently written out to the disk. The processing requirements of the buffer manager make the physical read a CPU-intensive operation as compared to data that is read directly from the cache.

USING THE OPERATING SYSTEM ROUTE

To find heavy CPU users on UNIX systems, you can use the top command. The top command lists the heaviest CPU users in descending order of wait times. When the top CPU user is found, you can find what the user is actually doing. Listing 22.11 is a sample output of the top command.

LISTING 22.11   SAMPLE OUTPUT OF THE top COMMAND

```
%top
System: arms1                                 Sat Aug 30 16:35:57 1997
Load averages: 0.59, 0.61, 0.69
20 processes: 18 sleeping, 2 running
Cpu states:
CPU   LOAD   USER   NICE    SYS   IDLE  BLOCK  SWAIT   INTR   SSYS
0     0.56  34.6%   0.0%   1.4%  64.0%   0.0%   0.0%   0.0%   0.0%
1     0.61  57.6%   0.0%   1.2%  41.3%   0.0%   0.0%   0.0%   0.0%
---   ----  -----  -----  -----  -----  -----  -----  -----  -----
avg   0.59  46.2%   0.0%   1.2%  52.7%   0.0%   0.0%   0.0%   0.0%

Memory: 25956K (10740K) real, 37996K (19316K) virtual, 15364K free  Page# 1/14

CPU  TTY   PID USERNAME  PRI NI   SIZE   RES  STATE   TIME %WCPU  %CPU COMMAND
1     ? 28586 manish     238 20  9164K 1072K run   157:22 90.13 89.97 oracleor
1     ?  1020 oracle     154 20  8712K  616K sleep   0:10  1.47  1.46 oracleor
1     ?  1900 oracle     154 20  8692K  588K sleep   0:05  1.10  1.09 oracleor
1     ?  1988 oracle     154 20  8620K  528K sleep   0:04  0.55  0.55 oracleor
0     ?   822 oracle     154 20  8764K  656K sleep   0:24  0.51  0.51 oracleor
1     ?  1793 oracle     154 20  8636K  524K sleep   0:01  0.43  0.43 oracleor
1     ?    50 root       100 20     0K    0K oloop 226:02  0.37  0.37 notior
0     ?   304 root       154 20    24K   24K sleep 258:04  0.33  0.33 syncer
0     ?     0 root       127 20     0K    0K sleep  86:40  0.30  0.30 swapper
0    p2  2204 evett      178 20   720K  312K run     0:00  0.92  0.27 top
1     ? 29494 oracle     154 20  8772K  660K sleep   0:28  0.23  0.23 oracleor
```

From this output, it is evident that PID 28586 and USERNAME manish is the heavy CPU user. Note that from the USER, SYS, and IDLE values, you can see that the system shows a value of 46% USER and SYS   1.2% and the rest is idle. This means that the system is purely servicing user requests, which is a good sign. Although the user is the top CPU user, it's not a cause for alarm because on a lightly loaded system if there is a single process that requires a lot of CPU, it will hog the CPU.

A key thing to look for is the load averages on the system. The first line shows the load averages on the system as 0.59, 0.61, and 0.69. The 0.59 is the load average over the last 1 minute, 0.61 is the load average over the last 5 minutes, and 0.69 is the load average over the last 15 minutes. The load averages give a fair idea of how the load was on the system and is now over the last 15 minutes, which can be very useful information when the CPU loads suddenly surge and the system performance seems to be deteriorating. When the load average suddenly increases, you can infer that this could be due to some resource-intensive process on the system. System loads of 2 or 3 indicate light system loads, and loads of 5 or 6 indicate medium system loads. Other information to look for is the %CPU column, which indicates the percentage of CPU time used by the particular process. If this figure is high, it is a clear indication of the process being very CPU-intensive.

You can also ascertain heavy users by using the ps command itself. The ps command contains a column that shows the amount of time the CPU spends in servicing the particular process. You can sort the output of ps in descending order of CPU time and again find out the top CPU resource user.

LISTING 22.12 OBTAINING CPU USAGE USING THE ps COMMAND

```
$ ps -ael ¦ sort -n -r -k 13
 F S   UID   PID  PPID  C PRI NI    ADDR   SZ   WCHAN TTY     TIME COMD
 1 R   105 28586 28585 89 200 20 3903a00 1741     - ?    192:21 oracle
 1 S   104 14171     1  0 154 20 3937a00 1711 36f8b38 ?   152:29 oracle
 3 S     0     3     0  0 128 20 2529100    0  3c2050 ?   122:09
➥statdaemon
 3 S     0     0     0  0 127 20   40c8b0    0  3c2050 ?    86:47 swapper
 3 S     0     2     0  0 128 20  2155e80    0  40e990 ?    32:19 vhand
 1 S     0   459   458  0 127 20  2718180    2 7ffe6000 ?  32:05 netfmt
 1 S     0  1016     1  0 154 20  2874180    9  40e0a8 ?    22:52 spserver
 1 S     0   787     1  0 154 20  280e880  180  40e0a8 ?    21:01 dced
 1 S     0   681     1  0 154 20  27cef80   85  40e0a8 ?    15:47 snmpdm
 1 S   104  1339     1  0 154 20  2845980  195  40e0a8 ?    14:18 tnslsnr
 3 S     0    12     0  0 138 20   254de00    0 391cf40 ?   12:00
➥vx_sched_threa
 3 S     0    54     0  0 100 20   254d980    0     - ?      6:24 nvsisr
 1 S   125 13379     1  0 156 20  3330200 1535 461a84 ?      5:21 oracle
 3 S     0     4     0  0 128 20  2529380    0  40e4dc ?      4:09
➥unhashdaemon
 1 S   125 13383     1  0 156 20  3739d80 1529 461a94 ?      4:41 oracle
 1 S   104 21303     1  0 154 20  2948d80 1846 3e55438 ?     4:02 oracle
```

Listing 22.12 shows that PIDs 28586 and 14171 are the top CPU resources. 28586 has used 192.21 minutes of CPU time, and 14171 has used 152.29 minutes of CPU time since the time the process started.

Note

> The processes might be inactive, so beware of sessions that have consumed a lot of CPU resources during the early part of the day and are now idle. To determine whether the process is idle, run the same command repeatedly and check whether the CPU time is increasing. Active sessions can be identified by looking at the second column S in Listing 22.12. The value R indicates it is running. Even here, a process with state S could currently be sleeping because it's waiting for something and then go into the run state. Keep all this in mind in order to identify a currently active top CPU resource. Alternatively, the snapshot technique as shown in the Oracle route can be used for identifying. Finally, the administrator can use the values used from the Oracle route and the values used from the operating system route to zero in on the heavy resource user.

After the `pid` is identified, you can find the `sid` of the process and can further use the oracle view V$SQLTEXT to find what process is currently executed. This can be done with the script in Listing 22.13.

LISTING 22.13 SCRIPTS TO OBTAIN THE `pid` FROM THE `sid` AND TO OBTAIN THE SQL STATEMENT THE SESSION IS EXECUTING

```
REM Find the sid of the Unix process using the process id
Select sid
From   v$session a,
       v$process b
Where  a.paddr = b.addr
And    b.spid   = <pid> ;

REM Find the SQL the user is currently executing
Select sql_text
From   v$sqltext a ,
       v$session b
Where       a.hash_value = b.sql_hash_value
And     b.sid        = <sid>
Order By piece;
```

In the Windows NT OS, you can monitor the processor object and use the % Processor Time counters to produce a chart of CPU utilization over a period of time. You can create line charts or bar charts of the data.

Heavy disk usage can cause CPU performance problems. When disks are performing heavy I/O, the CPU becomes bogged down by handling I/O interrupts. You can monitor this in PerfMon (Windows NT OS) by looking at Processor: interrupts/sec and Processor: %interrupttime.

If the CPU spends an inordinate amount of time handling interrupts, it can cause serious performance slowdowns. Also, you can check processor utilization time (Processor: %processor time), as shown in Figure 22.2. If the amount is more than 90 percent for a sustained period of time, you have a CPU bottleneck.

Figure 22.2
Monitoring Processor
Utilization Time Using
Oracle8 Performance
Monitor

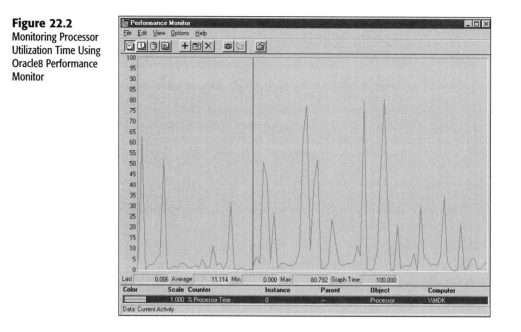

FILE I/O (DISK ACCESS)

When data is required by a particular user program, the OS first checks to see whether this data is currently available in the cache and if so, how it will be used. If the data is not found in the cache, this data has to be read from the disk. The process of reading data from the disk is highly expensive when compared to reading data from the cache because the memory is much faster as compared to disk access. Disk operations greatly hinder the throughput of processes.

Performance of the disk access-based process depends on factors such as the number of I/O controller cards, the software, the speed of the disk, and so forth.

When a process requests data, the following are the brief events that occur to retrieve the requested data:

1. The I/O controller locates the address of the data on the right disk; this is known as the *queuing* delay. Typically, there are other outstanding requests of data to be read from the disk at the given point in time. The time spent in the queue is dependent on the OS and the system load on the disk. The requests that are outstanding on the disk are sorted in such a way that the disk head does not have to do too much back-and-forth movement. This sorting of requests might result in the requests spending more time in the queue, but the seek time is reduced.

2. When the location of the data is found, the disk arm—or to be precise, the disk head— must be positioned over the correct disk on the right track. The time delay that occurs here is called the *seek time*.

3. The disk head then reads the data of the disk as the disk rotates below the disk head. After the disk head is positioned over the right track, it has to wait for the disk to rotate so that the relevant sectors of the data are right under the disk head and the read/write can be completed. This period is commonly referred to as the *rotational latency*.

4. The data read in by the disk head is then transferred to the controller. This final part of the I/O is referred to as the *data transfer time*. Finally, the data is transferred over the I/O back plane and is routed to the process that made the request for the data.

The total time required to retrieve data from the disk can roughly be said to be the following

```
Queue Time + Seek Time + Rotational Latency + Data Transfer Time
```

As can be clearly seen, disk access involves mechanical and rotational motion of the disk and can be a bottleneck on the system if there are frequent I/O calls on the same disk concurrently by multiple users. Finally, the I/O rate of the disk governs the total throughput of the disk, resulting in users queuing on the disk.

As in the CPU usage section, this section shows you how to identify users doing a lot of file access after you take an overview of the system.

TAKING AN I/O OVERVIEW

Before you proceed to find heavy I/O users, you must determine whether any of the file systems are heavily accessed currently. If this is true, only then do you proceed to locate these users.

As before, take a snapshot of the system for a small period of time, and then obtain the interval output. By looking at the output, it is very easy to evaluate whether there is any heavy I/O going on.

Listing 22.14 can be run to take a quick overview of the system. In this listing, there are two tables, stat$begin_file and stat$end_file, which are used to store the start and end file I/O statistic details. Using the difference between the two snapshots and the time between the two you can compute the rate of file access. Run Listing 22.14 to store the file I/O statistics at the start of the snapshotting interval.

LISTING 22.14 SCRIPTS TO CREATE TEMPORARY TABLES AND INSERT VALUES IN THE stat$begin_file TABLE

```
REM
REM Start IO : Script to Capture File I/O Statistics at the beginning of the
interval.
REM
Drop View stats$file_view;
Create View stats$file_view As
  Select ts.name     ts,
  i.name      name,
  x.phyrds pyr,
  x.phywrts pyw,
```

continues

LISTING 22.14 CONTINUED

```
 x.readtim prt,
 x.writetim pwt,
 x.phyblkrd pbr,
 x.phyblkwrt pbw,
 sysdate      st_time
From v$filestat x, ts$ ts, v$datafile i,file$ f
Where i.file#=f.file#
And ts.ts#=f.ts#
And x.file#=f.file#;

Drop Table stats$begin_file;

Create Table stats$begin_file   Tablespace tools
Storage(Initial 10K Next 10K Pctincrease 10 ) As
Select *
From stats$file_view
Where 0 = 1;

Drop Table stats$end_file;
Create Table stats$end_file   Tablespace tools
Storage(Initial 10K Next 10K Pctincrease 10 )As
Select *
From stats$begin_file;

Insert Into stats$begin_file
Select *
From stats$file_view;
```

After the desired interval when the performance of the system is to be analyzed is over, run the end I/O script to capture the statistics at the end of the interval. The end I/O script captures and stores statistics in stat$end_file and generates the I/O report. Listing 22.15 is the script for the end I/O and obtains the I/O usage report.

LISTING 22.15 SCRIPT TO POPULATE stat$file_end TABLE AND GENERATE THE I/O USAGE REPORT

```
REM
REM End IO : Script to Capture File I/O Statistics at the end of the interval.
REM
Set Term Off
Insert Into stats$end_file
Select *
From stats$file_view;

Drop Table stats$files;
Create Table stats$files  Tablespace tools
Storage(Initial 10K Next 10K Pctincrease 0)As
Select b.ts table_space,
b.name file_name,
e.pyr-b.pyr phys_reads,
e.pbr-b.pbr phys_blks_rd,
e.prt-b.prt phys_rd_time,
```

```
e.pyw-b.pyw phys_writes,
        e.pbw-b.pbw phys_blks_wr,
e.pwt-b.pwt phys_wrt_tim,
      (e.st_time -b.st_time)*24*60*60 tot_tim
From stats$begin_file b, stats$end_file e
Where b.name=e.name;

Drop Table stats$begin_file;
Drop Table stats$end_file;
Set Term On
Clear Screen
Set Pause On
Set Pagesize 24
Set Feedback off
Col table_space Format a17
Col file_name Format a55
Col phys_writes Format 9999999 Heading 'PHY_WRS'
Col phys_reads  Format 9999999 Heading 'PHY_RDS'
Col phys_rd_time Format 999999 Heading  'PHY_RDT'
Col phys_wrt_tim Format 999999999  Heading 'PHY_WRT'
Col phys_blks_rd Format 999999999 Heading 'BLKS_RD'
Col phys_blks_wr Format 9999999    Heading 'BLKS_WR'
Col ios_sec Format 999 Heading 'IOS_SEC'

REM
REM Generate IO Overview Report
REM
Select table_space,
      file_name,
phys_reads,
phys_writes,
phys_blks_rd,
phys_blks_wr,
phys_rd_time,
phys_wrt_tim,
(phys_reads + phys_writes)/tot_tim ios_sec
From stats$files
Order By ios_sec Desc
```

The following listing is the output of the above SQL statement.

```
TABLE_SPACE        FILE_NAME
----------------   ------------------------------------------------------------
PHY_RDS  PHY_WRS    BLKS_RD  BLKS_WR PHY_RDT   PHY_WRT IOS_SEC
--------  --------  ---------  -------- -------  -------- -------
ARMSLIVEDB04_TS    /u03/oradata/ora7/armslive/armslivedbu04.dbf
  23100       34      23100       34   17644       106      93

ARMSLIVEIDX02_TS   /da11/oradata/ora7/armslive/armsliveidxa07.dbf
  16886        0      16886        0     912         0      68

ARMSLIVEIDX11_TS   /u14/oradata/ora7/armslive/armsliveidx19.dbf
   3461      542       3461      542    1288      2946      16

ARMSLIVEDB04_TS    /u03/oradata/ora7/armslive/armslivedbu02.dbf
   2521       38       2521       38    2131       255      10
```

continues

LISTING 22.15   CONTINUED

```
RBS2                    /db07/oradata/ora7/rbs4ora7.dbf
        1       982          1       982       3       7890        4

ARMSLIVEIDX03_TS        /db04/oradata/ora7/armslive/armliveidxb01.dbf
      870        51        870        51     323        124         4

ARMSLIVETMP01_TS        /db06/oradata/ora7/armslive/armslivetmpb01.dbf
      866         1      24729         1    1402          2         3

ARMSLIVEDB12_TS         /u03/oradata/ora7/armslive/armslivedbu19.dbf
      157       323        157       323      32       1065         2

ARMSLIVEDB11_TS         /u09/oradata/ora7/armslive/armslivedbu16.dbf
       87       331        273       331      30       1693         2

ARMSLIVEIDX10_TS        /u16/oradata/ora7/armslive/armsliveidx17.dbf
      137        25        137        25      69         66         1

SYSTEM                  /u01/oradata/ora7/syst1ora7.dbf
       63        23         79        23      31        204         0

SYSTEM                  /u01/oradata/ora7/syst2ora7.dbf
       34        12         37        12      11         90         0

ARMSLIVEDB02_TS         /db06/oradata/ora7/armslive/armslivedb06.dbf
        7        32          7        32       1        203         0
```

From this I/O overview report, it is evident that there is some I/O activity on the system and the tablespace most affected by this is ARMSLIVEDB04_TS. The tablespace has an I/O rate of around 93 read/writes per second. Depending on the speed of the disk or the I/O rate the disks can support, it can be ascertained whether the value obtained is high or not. Having observed that there is a high activity on the system, you can now proceed to identify the user causing this high I/O to be generated.

You can also have a sample overview at the operating system level on a UNIX system using the sar command. The sar command shown in Listing 22.16 samples the disk activity for an interval of 5 seconds for 3 times.

LISTING 22.16   sar COMMAND USED FOR MONITORING DISK I/O STATISTICS

```
$ sar -d 5 3

HP-UX arms1 B.10.10 U 9000/819     08/30/97

19:43:00   device   %busy   avque   r+w/s   blks/s   avwait   avserv
19:43:05   c0t5d0   76.05    1.94     169     2711     8.76     5.94
           c0t4d0    9.58    0.95      12      192     8.86     9.04
           c0t3d0    8.18    0.50       6      102     4.77    12.28
           c3t6d0    7.58    0.50      28      447     5.20     3.12
           c4t6d1   15.77    1.30      28      450     8.44    14.35
           c4t5d0    6.19    0.50       5       77     5.02    12.64
```

	c3t4d0	7.19	0.50	9	150	5.27	7.68
	c3t5d0	0.40	0.50	0	6	3.80	9.32
19:43:10	c0t6d0	0.20	0.50	0	1	6.42	11.56
	c0t5d0	72.60	1.79	186	2980	8.59	5.09
	c0t4d0	6.20	0.50	7	115	5.48	8.48
	c0t3d0	8.60	0.50	7	112	5.19	13.32
	c3t6d0	6.20	0.50	27	438	5.12	2.42
	c4t6d1	15.40	1.52	25	394	9.70	16.09
	c4t5d0	3.60	0.50	3	42	4.40	14.15
	c3t4d0	5.00	0.50	6	99	5.63	7.49
19:43:15	c0t5d0	73.20	1.86	184	2947	9.44	5.38
	c0t4d0	12.00	0.50	14	221	5.05	9.26
	c0t3d0	8.60	0.50	6	99	5.39	12.99
	c3t6d0	6.40	0.50	27	435	5.31	2.33
	c4t6d1	14.40	1.33	23	365	10.21	14.72
	c4t5d0	4.20	0.50	3	51	5.38	13.08
	c3t4d0	9.60	0.50	13	202	4.76	7.91
Average	c0t5d0	73.95	1.86	180	2879	8.93	5.46
Average	c0t4d0	9.26	0.66	11	176	6.53	9.01
Average	c0t3d0	8.46	0.50	7	104	5.11	12.88
Average	c3t6d0	6.73	0.50	28	440	5.21	2.63
Average	c4t6d1	15.19	1.38	25	403	9.38	15.03
Average	c4t5d0	4.66	0.50	4	56	4.97	13.14
Average	c3t4d0	7.26	0.50	9	150	5.12	7.74
Average	c3t5d0	0.13	0.50	0	2	3.80	9.32
Average	c0t6do	0.07	0.50	0	0	6.42	11.56

This sar command was fired at the same time the I/O overview snapshot script was executed. In this command, disk c0t5d0 has a read/write rate of 180, and it clearly indicates the heavy I/O access on that disk. The sar output is detailed; it shows the await, which is the time spent in the queue, and the avserv, which is the sum of the seek time plus the rotational latency plus the disk transfer time. This information can be pretty useful. Using both of these techniques, you can identify the disk and files that are heavily accessed.

Now find users using a lot of I/O resources. At the operating system level, it is difficult to find the users doing a lot of I/O; therefore, you derive your information using Oracle system tables.

FINDING HEAVY I/O USERS

To identify heavy resource users, you can use the V$SESS_IO view. This view stores information about the I/O statistics for the sessions. For every session, there is one row corresponding to it in this view. The explanation of the columns in the view V$SESS_IO is giving in Table 22.4.

TABLE 22.4   COLUMN DESCRIPTION OF THE VIEW V$SESS_IO

Column Name	Description
SID	The session identifier (Database Name)
BLOCK_GETS	The number of block gets for the session
CONSISTENT_GETS	The number of consistent gets for this session using the consistent get mechanism

continues

TABLE 22.4 CONTINUED

Column Name	Description
PHYSICAL_READS	The number of physical reads for this session
BLOCK_CHANGES	The number of block changes for this session
CONSISTENT_CHANGES	The number of consistent changes for this session

As shown in the previous section, you can use the snapshotting technique on this view, storing the start and end snapshot values captured during a monitoring interval in a temporary table and then using the difference to find the users doing a lot of file access. Use the difference in the PHYSICAL READS column to find users doing lots of data accessing from the disk. The difference in the BLOCK_GETS column can be used to identify users performing a lot of buffer reads. Similar scripts can be developed as shown in the CPU section earlier.

The most common events in the database that might cause heavy disk access are sorts to disk (which can cause bottlenecks on the temporary tablespace), full table scans, and heavy index reads.

You can identify sessions currently doing a sort by using the script in Listing 22.17.

LISTING 22.17 SCRIPT TO IDENTIFY SESSIONS CURRENTLY DOING A SORT

```
Select sid
From v$session_wait
Where event = 'db file scattered read'
And    p1 = <file id>;
```

The p1 column in V$session_wait contains the *file id* on which the event is performed. Now, you can replace *file id* by the file# value found from dba datafiles for files belonging to the temporary tablespace. Select the file# column from dba_data_files for temporary tablespaces in the database and replace the *file id* variable in the Listing 22.17.

After the sid value is found, the current SQL statement executed by the session can be found using V$SQLTEXT view and the script in Listing 22.17. If excessive disk sorts are performed on the database, consider increasing the value of the init.ora parameter SORT_AREA_SIZE.

To identify a session currently doing a full table scan and waiting for a multiblock read call to return or whose last wait was for a multiblock read, you can use the script in Listing 22.18. Listing 22.18 immediately identifies all sessions that are doing full table scans.

LISTING 22.18 SCRIPT TO FIND SESSIONS CURRENTLY DOING FULL TABLE SCANS

```
col sql_text format a40

select sid,sql_text
From v$session a, v$sqlarea b
Where a.sql_hash_value = b.hash_value
```

```
And sid in
 (Select sid
                From v$session_wait
                Where event like  'db file scattered read')
 /
```

The following listing is the output of the above SQL statement.

```
SID          SQL_TEXT
----------  -------------------------------------------
      100 select ord_id from cust_ord where crea_u
          ser_id like  'BSMJG%'
 102 select emp_id,name  from employee where
          salary > 1003;
```

To identify SQL statements that are doing a lot of physical reads and accessing large number of buffers, you can use the V$SQLAREA view, as in Listing 22.19 You can replace the value of buffer_gets and disk_reads in Listing 22.19 by a value that you think is appropriate.

LISTING 22.19   SCRIPT TO IDENTIFY SESSIONS DOING EXCESSIVE PHYSICAL READS OR ACCESSING A LARGE NUMBER OF BUFFERS

```
set pagesize 100
col sql_text format a50

select substr(sql_text,1,200) sql_text, buffer_gets, disk_reads
from v$sqlarea
where buffer_gets > 10000
or disk_reads > 10000000
order by disk_reads desc;
```

The following listing is the output of the above SQL Script.

SQL_TEXT	BUFFER_GETS	DISK_READS
Select RTrim (cust_ord.brand_id) ,RTrim (ord_id) ,Nvl (cust_ord.pmt _mthd_id ,'12') ,Nvl (card _num ,'0') ,To_Char (Nvl (card_exp_dt ,sysdate) ,'mmyy') ,Nvl (pp_amt ,0.00) ,Nvl (ord_amt ,	20488669	13025204
Select count (*) From cust_ord ,cmpn_pmt_type Whe re auth_stat = f and cust_ord.pmt_mthd_id In (Oo lect pmt_mthd_id From pmt_mthd Where pmt_mthd_typ in ('R' ,'D')) and cust_ord.cmpn_id =cmpn_pmt_t	13136493	12952619
SELECT TITLE_ID,CNTRY_ID FROM CUST_ORD_ADR WHER E RTRIM(UPPER(ORD_ID)) = RTRIM(UPPER(:b1)) AND RT RIM(UPPER(ADR_ID)) = RTRIM(UPPER(:b2))	10469659	10453418
update cust_ord set ord_stat = '07', chng_user_id = 'stat19', chng_dt = sysdate where ord_id in (select c.ord_id from cust_ord a, cust _ord_line b, cust_ord_itm c where a.ord_id	24942696	3454225

It's likely that most of these SQL statements are doing full table scans, causing a lot of reads to be done. The SQL statements should be optimized by adding secondary performance indexes where possible or by using other tuning techniques.

In the Windows NT OS, you have to execute the following DISKPERF command from the Windows NT prompt to enable the disk counters to gather statistics for disk reads and writes:

```
DISKPERF -YE
```

This impacts on system overhead; that is why, by default, this counter is disabled. You have to reboot the system to get the correct readings of logical disk counters.

The DB_BLOCK_SIZE parameter impacts on disk I/O.DB_BLOCK_SIZE should be equal to or in multiple of NT Cluster size. DB_BLOCK_SIZE should never be smaller than the NT cluster size. Cluster size is the smallest atomic unit of I/O that Windows NT can read or write at a single time. For instance, if DB_BLOCK_SIZE is 4K and NT cluster size is 1K, then Windows NT needs to perform four I/Os every time Oracle needs to read from disk. It's not acceptable.

DISK QUEUES

A disk drive can only support one request at a time. A disk queue can form when there are other processes waiting for the disk. You will see performance problems if the disk is overloaded with queues. The PerfMon counter Physical Disk: Disk Transfers/sec lets you see the disk transfer rate over time. The disk queue (for both reads and writes) can also be viewed by charting physical Disk: Avg. Disk Queue Length, as shown in Figure 22.3.

Figure 22.3
Monitoring Physical
Disk Performance

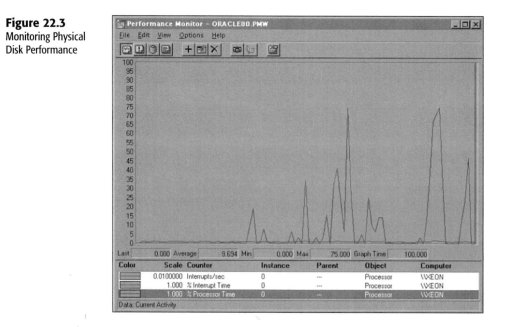

Precautions to be taken to minimize the I/O problems include the following:

- Spread the I/O load across multiple spindles by using more disk drives and disk controllers.
- Keep Oracle online redo logs on separate, nonstriped disks away from the data files.
- Upgrade the hardware with faster disks, faster controllers, and faster I/O buses, for example, from IDE disks to SCSI or from SCSI to fast/wide SCSI.

MEMORY

UNIX systems use virtual memory for memory management. With virtual memory processes, it is possible that the sum of the sizes of all the processes on the system exceeds the physical memory available on the system. Virtual memory is implemented using paging and swapping, the two memory management policies on UNIX. Virtual memory makes it possible to enable the size of a process to be greater than the amount of physical memory that is available for it.

Main memory (RAM) stores data required for program execution. When data is no longer required for execution, this data is stored in secondary storage on the disk, making room for other active processes. This secondary storage area to which entire processes are moved from main memory on the disk is termed as *swap space*.

In *paging*, a single page of memory is transferred to the swap space, that is, a portion of the entire process. In *swapping*, the entire process is transferred to the swap space. Paging frees a small amount of memory, and swapping frees a large amount of memory. The concept behind these memory management policies is that the most required pages of memory of a process are kept in the physical memory, and the rest is stored in the secondary storage area, the swap space.

When a process requires more memory, inactive pages in physical memory can be paged out and space is freed on the physical memory. When space is freed on the physical memory side, pages that reside in the secondary memory can now be brought to the physical memory (RAM). Paging occurs when UNIX moves a single page of memory to the swap space; therefore, only a portion of the process gets moved to the swap space. Swapping, on the other hand, moves the entire process to the swap space. Thus, swapping frees up lots of physical memory, but it's more expensive than paging. The key indicators to an ideal memory situation is that under full load the system is paging lightly and should be not swapping at all.

On most systems, the following pattern is observed: When the system is lightly loaded, there is no paging or swapping; when the system is moderately loaded, paging starts; and when the system gets heavily loaded, paging stops and swapping begins on the system, on account of the heavy memory requirement and the low availability of physical memory. Swapping is the most expensive of the memory operations.

In a virtual memory system, the memory address used by processes on the system is not the physical memory address, but one called the *virtual address*. This virtual address is translated by the Memory Management Unit (MMU) into the physical memory address.

When a process needs a page of memory, it references that page using the virtual address. This virtual address is translated by the MMU to locate the actual physical address. This translated address can map into an area in physical memory (RAM) or it can map into the secondary storage (swap) address.

If the physical page is located on RAM, the process can use it immediately. If it is located on the disk, a *page fault* is generated by the MMU, and the operating system then reads this page into a free page in physical memory; this is called a *page in* operation. If there is a severe short-age of memory, the reading of this page could cause some other pages in physical memory to be written to the disk. This is commonly referred to as a *page out*. After the page is read in by the operating system, the new address of the page is conveyed to the MMU and the operating system then restarts the instruction. Paging causes only pages of physical memory to be moved to the disk; swapping causes the entire process to be moved to disk in order to free memory resources. If there is severe memory shortage on the system, swapping can become very high.

Both *page outs* and *page ins* are expensive with regard to the performance of the system because a disk read/write is very expensive when compared to using data that is directly available on the cache. Therefore, if a process generates a lot of page faults due to frequent requests for new pages of data on a system where physical memory is scarce, the process definitely runs slowly.

In systems using virtual memory, only a portion of the memory used by a process resides in the physical memory. This portion of the memory is called the *working set* of the process. Because at any given point in time the process is not going to use all its pages, it's more economical to keep the currently used page in the physical memory. During the course of the operation of the process, the process might require pages that are currently not in the physical memory. This causes a page fault, but it is perfectly normal to have some page faults during the course of the operation of the process because it is definitely not feasible to have all the memory pages that the process requires to be located on the main memory. The operating system will always try to keep all the pages of the *working set* in main mem-ory. This technique for using memory maximizes the memory throughput of a system, keeping in mind that there are many concurrent processes running on the system that are actively making concurrent demands for memory.

The actual physical memory usage of a process is never constant, and it is very difficult to determine due to its variable nature. On the other hand, the virtual memory requirements of the process can be more easily ascertained. The physical memory consumed by a process varies based on a number of factors such as system load, what the process is doing, and so forth. For example, if a process is running on a heavily loaded system because there are lots of other processes requiring physical memory pages, the actual amount of the pages allocated in physical memory to this process will be very close to the working set size of the process. On the other hand, if the same process is run on a lightly loaded system where there are not many concurrently active processes running, the actual number of physical pages allocated to the process will be much more than the working set requirement of the process. Similarly, during the course of the operation of a process, the working set of the process changes, so the amount of physical memory allocated also changes. All this makes it very difficult to predict programs that consume large physical memory because memory allocation is completely situation-based. To simulate the physical memory requirement of a process, you must also simulate the load on the system because the physical memory usage of a process that is running in isolation on the system is much higher than one that is running on the peak load. Remember these key points:

- For monitoring the memory usage of a process on the system, you must take into account the system load. As mentioned in the CPU section, it is perfectly normal for a process on a lightly loaded system to hog a lot of physical memory and occupy a very conservative size on a heavily loaded system.

- To check whether the physical memory is sufficient for all processes running on the system, the best test is to do the following:

    1. Load your system to the top or to the peak load.

    2. Check for the overall memory behavior (as shown in the next section) to see whether there are any signs of paging or swapping. Ignore a small amount of paging because it is natural for processes to page as the working set of the process changes. However, if there are excessive signs of page outs or swapping, it is an indication that the amount of physical memory available on the system is less or that you might have to reschedule the timing of some of your memory-intensive processes.

Before you explore monitoring memory usage, analyze how the memory usage of a single process is broken down in the following section.

PROCESS MEMORY BREAKUP

Every process on a UNIX system is broken down into two broad regions: the text pages and the data pages. The *text* segment contains the machine instructions that the process executes. The *data* segment contains all the other information that the process requires during its execution. The text pages are marked as read-only because they contain the machine instructions and are paged from the file system. Processes executing the same program will share the same text page, thus optimizing memory usage. For example, if ten users work on Oracle Forms, all of them share the executable or the text page of the Oracle Forms executable.

On the other hand, the data pages are marked read/write. They are private to the process, and they are paged from the paging area (swap); that is, every process has its own private data page and as the number of processes increases, the requirement for private pages also increases--unlike the case with shared text pages. The fundamental difference is that if a text page is paged out because of memory shortage, the physical page of memory the text page is currently occupying can be overwritten by the new information; but if a data page is overwritten or paged out, that page must be written or copied to disk before the overwriting of the physical page can begin. The reason behind this is simply that text pages are never modified, and the image of the text page can always be obtained from the file system.

A UNIX process is actually divided into six regions: text, stack, heap, BSS, initialized data, and shared memory.

Text, as mentioned, is shared between processes and is paged from the file system. It contains the machine instructions, and they are marked read-only.

The *stack* is private to the process, is paged from the swap area, and contains the runtime execution stack. The runtime stack contains function and procedure activation records apart from function and procedure parameters. The stack pages are marked as read/write. The size of the stack can grow.

The *heap* contains the data pages that are allocated to the process as it runs. The heap is a private process region and its size can grow very large during program execution. The heap pages are marked as read/write, and these pages are paged from the swap area.

The *BSS* segment is also private to the process. It's marked as read/write, its size remains static during the execution of the process, and the pages of the BSS segment are marked as read/write. The size of this segment remains fixed during the execution of the program. This segment is used to store statically allocated uninitialized data, and these pages are paged from the swap area.

The *initialized data* segment is private to the process. It's marked as read/write, it is paged from the swap, and the size remains constant during the execution of the process.

Shared memory segments, as the name says, are pages that are shared between processes. They are marked as read/write. Shared pages are allocated using the `shmget()` system call. Processes are attached to share pages by using the `shmat()` system call. Shared pages are paged from the swap, and the size of the shared memory segment remains fixed when the allocation is done.

TAKING A MEMORY OVERVIEW

Before you probe into the finer details of individual processes using memory, you must first take an overview of the system. The key thing to look for when taking a memory overview of the system is excessive paging and swapping on the system. If memory is scarce on the system, then when a process is allocated a time slice of the CPU, it uses the CPU time for swapping and paging and does nothing else that could be very drastic to the performance of the system. High paging and swapping activity on the system severely hampers the performance of the system and must be prevented as much as possible by either adding extra physical memory or by rescheduling processes.

On UNIX systems, `vmstat` and `sar` are utilities that can be used to monitor the system memory usage. The disadvantage of both these tools is that they enable memory to be monitored only at an overall level and do not give the per process memory usage breakdown. Shown in Listing 22.20 is the output of the `vmstat` command.

LISTING 22.20 OUTPUT OF THE vmstat COMMAND USED FOR MONITORING MEMORY USAGE

```
vmstat -S 2 10
procs        memory           page     faults                 cpu
r  b  w   avm  free  si so  pi po  fr de  sr   in   sy   cs us sy id
1 111 0  5152 2885   0  0   0  0   0  0   0 1028 3068 1121 19  8 73
1 111 0  5152 2885   0  0   0  0   0  0   0 1004 2778 1074 17  5 78
2 117 0  4986 2885   0  0   0  0   0  0   0 1022 2666 1097 18 10 72
2 117 0  4986 2885   0  0   0  0   0  0   0 1008 2618 1129 22  7 71
0 111 0  5644 2842   0  0   0  0   0  0   0  994 2742 1079 27 10 64
0 111 0  5644 2841   0  0   0  0   0  0   0 1016 2974 1210 24 14 63
0 111 0  5644 2927   0  0   0  0   0  0   0 1029 4388 1438 21  9 70
0 109 0  5816 2927   0  0   0  0   0  0   0  997 3656 1359 12  8 81
0 109 0  5816 2927   0  0   0  0   0  0   0  953 3135 1255 16  5 79
```

The important columns of interest are in Table 22.5.

TABLE 22.5 IMPORTANT COLUMNS IN THE vmstat OUTPUT

Column Name	Description
procs	Number of processes in various states as shown below
r	Number of processes in run mode
b	Number of processes in block mode
w	Number of processes swapped and waiting for processing resources
memory	Reports on real and virtual memory
avm	Average active memory
free	Size of the free list in pages
page	Reports on the page faults in the interval
si	Number of pages swapped in
so	Number of pages swapped out
pi	Number of kilobytes paged in (check out)
po	Number of kilobytes paged out
cpu	Reports on CPU usage
us	Percentage of time spent servicing user requests
sy	Percentage of time spent servicing system calls
id	Idle time

As you can see, the vmstat command is quite comprehensive and gives almost an entire overview of the system from memory usage, process states, and the CPU usage percentages.

In this output, key things to look for as far as memory usage is concerned are the columns po, so, b, and w.

If the po (page outs) and so (swap outs) values are high, it indicates a severe memory shortage on the system. In Listing 22.20, there are no page outs occurring on the system. There is approximately 2885×4KB (4KB is the size of the memory page), which is 11.26MB, of free memory available on the system.

If you look at the preceding output, you see that the b column indicates a high number of blocked processes. I did some further investigation by using the sar -d command and found that the high number of blocked processes was due to some heavy I/O occurring on a few disks, and the processes were blocked on account of the I/O that was waiting to be completed. If the vmstat output shows a high number of pagings or swappings, you must identify the heavy resource users.

FINDING HEAVY MEMORY USERS

Monitoring the individual usage of memory on UNIX systems can be pretty tricky. Most of the utilities, such as vmstat and sar, report the memory usage at a system level and do not report the per process memory usage. Another reason why the actual physical memory usage is not easy to access is the fact that each process is divided into text and data, and the text pages are shared between processes, whereas the data pages are private to the process. If the process is attached to a shared memory segment, this offset must be subtracted to obtain the actual private memory (the memory used by the process). As the text page is shared, this is reported in the virtual memory usage of all the processes. Therefore, if you add the virtual memory usage of all the processes on the system, the figure obtained will be much larger than the actual virtual memory used by all the processes.

Nevertheless, you can make an assumption that when monitoring memory on an Oracle system, all the processes share the same text (that is, Oracle executable) page. If all the processes are using the same executable, the offset text memory usage of all the processes is the same. The rest of the memory is the private memory used by the process. On UNIX systems, the ps command with the -l option can be used to determine the per process memory usage of each individual process. The -l option reports the memory usage under the sz column of the ps output. The ps command shown in Listing 22.21 can be used to monitor memory usage of Oracle processes (foreground and background) on the system. The sz column reports the size of the physical page of the core image of the process. It includes the text, data, and the stack space. The output in Listing 22.21 shows the ps command sorted in descending order of the sz column, which is the seventh column in the output. This output gives a fair idea of the text + data + stack usage of all the Oracle processes.

> **Note**
>
> The SZ column mentioned previously refers to text plus data plus stack memory usage. This size of the text page of the Oracle executable can be determined by using the size command on the Oracle executable. After the text page size of the executable is obtained, theoretically, if you subtract the value obtained from the virtual memory size using the ps -ael command, you would get the actual per-process virtual memory usage of the process. However, sometimes the SZ column in the ps -el command does not report the actual text page size; it reports only the page that is required by the process. This happens because of the demand-paging algorithm, wherein only the most required pages of text are used by the process and the rest are brought as required from the file system.
>
> You can use the size column report in the top command because the top command reports the total text-page size rather than the actual used-page size when it reports on the virtual memory in the SIZE column. In the Listing 22.21, the size of the virtual memory used by the process ID 25623 is 8640K, which includes the complete text page.

LISTING 22.21   OBTAINING THE VIRTUAL MEMORY SIZE USING THE top COMMAND OUTPUT

```
System: arms1                              Tue Sep  9 19:41:51 1997
Load averages: 4.87, 4.74, 4.44
211 processes: 204 sleeping, 7 running
Cpu states:
CPU   LOAD    USER    NICE    SYS    IDLE   BLOCK   SWAIT    INTR    SSYS
0     4.98    88.1%   0.0%    11.9%  0.0%   0.0%    0.0%     0.0%    0.0%
1     4.75    79.2%   0.0%    20.8%  0.0%   0.0%    0.0%     0.0%    0.0%
---   ----    -----   -----   -----  -----  -----   -----    -----   -----
avg   4.87    83.2%   0.0%    16.8%  0.0%   0.0%    0.0%     0.0%    0.0%
Memory: 53592K (15892K) real, 72336K (25548K) virtual, 11848K free   Page# 1/20
CPU  TTY    PID USERNAME  PRI NI    SIZE    RES  STATE    TIME %WCPU  %CPU COMMAND
0     ? 25623 arms       240 20   8640K    548K run      7:34 43.47 43.39 oracleor
1     ? 18128 oracle     241 20   9184K   1024K run    177:07 31.29 31.23 oracleor
0     ? 19523 oracle     240 20   9644K   1552K run     60:48 26.19 26.15
oracleor
```

> **Note**
>
> If I try to find the size value using the ps command, the following is obtained:
>
> ```
> $ ps -ael | grep 256,23
>   1 R    105 25623 25622 254 241 20   3909b00 1524        - ?
> ➡9:20 oracle
> ```
>
> The ps command shows that the size of the virtual memory is 1524*4K =6096K, which is much less than the top command 8640K value because the text page size used is actually much lower than the total text page size.
>
> Keep this in mind when computing actual memory usage of the individual processes.

The following output in Listing 22.22 determines the pid of the Oracle processes. When the pid is obtained using the SQL statements in the previous sections, the sid of the processes can be found, and further investigation can be done at the session level. This is described in the following output.

LISTING 22.22   ps COMMAND USED FOR FINDING THE MEMORY USAGE BY PROCESSES

```
$ ps -eal ¦ grep oracle ¦ sort -n -r -k 10
 1 R   129 28060 28058 248 240 20  3932f00 2400      - ?  15:24 oracle
 1 R   104 28049     1 246 239 20  3941080 2001      - ?  10:55 oracle
 1 S   104 25751     1   0 156 20  38e1f80 1939  461b34 ?  19:02 oracle
 1 S   104 15018     1   0 154 20  37c2980 1915  3d90e38 ? 198:25 oracle
 1 S   104 25861     1  59 148 20  3807d00 1711  2194bac ?  32:42 oracle
 1 S   104 25743     1   0 156 20  3e38380 1658  461b1c ?  23:52 oracle
 1 S   104 14103     1   0 154 20  2829900 1653  3d4e338 ? 109:12 oracle
 1 R   104 25739     1 255 241 20  37c2d80 1623      - ? 142:21 oracle
 1 S   104 27772     1   0 156 20  372ba80 1603  461b04 ?   9:11 oracle
 1 S   105 22744 22743   0 154 20  3941e80 1578  3d61da2 ?  38:59 oracle
 1 S   129 25731 25727   0 154 20  335f700 1538  38c47a2 ?   0:00 oracle
 1 S   104 19722     1   0 154 20  2845380 1525  3d6cb38 ?   0:05 oracle
 1 S   129 28055 28053   0 154 20  3780f00 1522  3dda0a2 ?   0:00 oracle
 1 S   125 25629     1   0 156 20  3738680 1511  461aa4 ?   0:01 oracle
 1 S   104  7258     1   0 154 20  38e6100 1498  391e838 ?   0:00 oracle
 1 S   125 25623     1   0 156 20  294f600 1493  461a8c ?   0:38 oracle
 1 S   125 25621     1   0 156 20  2576080 1490  461a84 ?   1:15 oracle
 1 S   125 25627     1   0 156 20  3807300 1483  461a9c ?   0:03 oracle
 1 S   125 25625     1   3 156 20  3937000 1483  461a94 ?   2:00 oracle
 1 S   125 25649     1   0 156 20  2958980 1478  461af4 ?   0:10 oracle
 1 S   125 25647     1   0 156 20  3903b00 1478  461aec ?   0:10 oracle
 1 S   125 25645     1   0 156 20  2845a80 1478  461ae4 ?   0:11 oracle
 1 S   125 25643     1   0 156 20  3354400 1478  461adc ?   0:13 oracle
 1 S   125 25641     1   0 156 20  391d700 1478  461ad4 ?   0:13 oracle
 1 S   125 25639     1   0 156 20  3739b80 1478  461acc ?   0:13 oracle
 1 S   125 25637     1   0 156 20  2852780 1478  461ac4 ?   0:14 oracle
 1 S   125 25635     1   0 156 20  2888580 1478  461abc ?   0:15 oracle
 1 S   125 25633     1   0 156 20  3663e80 1478  461ab4 ?   0:15 oracle
 1 S   125 25631     1   0 156 20  3e40c80 1478  461aac ?   0:15 oracle
 1 S   125 25619     1   0 156 20  27fb500 1477  461a7c ?   0:01 oracle
```

The memory usage of individual processes can also be monitored using the V$SESSTAT system view. To understand which part of memory you are looking at, you will now look into how memory is organized in the Oracle SGA. The SGA is a shared segment that comprises the shared pool, the block buffers, and the redo log buffers. The shared pool is the area in the SGA that contains constructs such as shared SQL areas and the data dictionary cache.

For every SQL statement that is executed on the server, there is a shared part (*shared SQL area*) and a private part (*private SQL area*). Two users executing the same SQL code use the same shared SQL area, but each of the users has an individual private SQL area.

The shared SQL area contains the parse tree and the execution plan for every SQL statement. The size of the area depends on the complexity of the statement. The size of every such SQL area can be determined by using the sharable_memory column of the V$SQLAREA view, which contains all the SQL areas in the shared pool. Every session that executes the same SQL shares the same shared SQL area.

The private SQL area is the memory area that contains data such as binding information and runtime buffers. Every session that executes a SQL statement has its own individual private SQL area for every SQL statement that it executes. To summarize, for multiple sessions that are executing the same SQL statement, there is one shared SQL area, and there are multiple private SQL areas owned individually by each of the sessions. The private SQL area is further divided into a persistent area and the runtime area.

The area of memory in which you are required to monitor memory usage is the *Program Global Area (PGA)*. The PGA contains data and control information for a single process. The PGA is also referred to as the *Process Global Area*. The contents of the PGA vary depending on the type of connection, dedicated or multithreaded.

In both architectures, the PGA always contains the *stack space*, which is the memory used to store the session variables, arrays, and other information.

In a *dedicated server option*, the PGA stores additional information related to the user's session; that is, the private SQL area and other session information is stored here. In a *multithreaded option*, this information is located in the SGA.

You can monitor the PGA usage and assess the per user memory requirement on the system. The PGA memory usage can be done by using the V$SESSTAT view. The statistic# value=20 corresponds to PGA memory usage. To monitor heavy memory users, use the script in Listing 22.23.

LISTING 22.23   FINDING PGA MEMORY USAGE USING V$SESSTAT

```
col value format 99999 heading "Memory ¦Kb"

Select sid,
  value/1024 value
  From v$sesstat
  Where statistic# =20
  Order By value desc
```

The following is the output of the above SQL statement.

```
     Memory
     SID      Kb
---------- -------
      31    1165
     153     754
     142     733
     101     COC
      70     362
      73     336
      26     306
      60     298
      82     297
      53     297
 123     275
      44     272
     110     270
```

Having ascertained the session that consumes a high amount of PGA, you can proceed with the steps mentioned in the previous sections to find what each session is doing.

Windows NT OS can address a maximum of 4GB memory; out of that 2GB is reserved f
or the operating system, and the remaining 2GB is for other applications.

For finding the memory available in your Windows NT server, open the Windows NT
Explorer and choose Help, About Windows NT. The following window appears on your
screen, which shows the memory available in kilobytes.

Figure 22.4
Memory Available
In The System

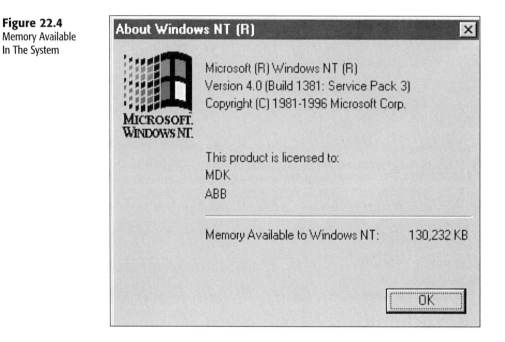

BUFFER CACHE

The most important factor of memory (SGA) is to tune the database buffer cache so that
users will be able to read information from memory as much as possible, instead of from
disk. If buffer cache is tuned effectively, it ensures that the database does not become I/O
bound and, therefore, slower. You can query the V$SYSSTAT table to get realtime perfor-
mance information about buffer cache usage, or you can use the Oracle8 Performance
Monitor. The Oracle8 buffer cache %phyrds/gets counter shows the cache miss ratio,
which shows the percentage of database reads that involved physical disk activity.

The current miss ratio, which showed in fig 22.5 is 1.9 percent. It should not go above 20
percent, as you should always keep cache hit ratio more than 80 percent.

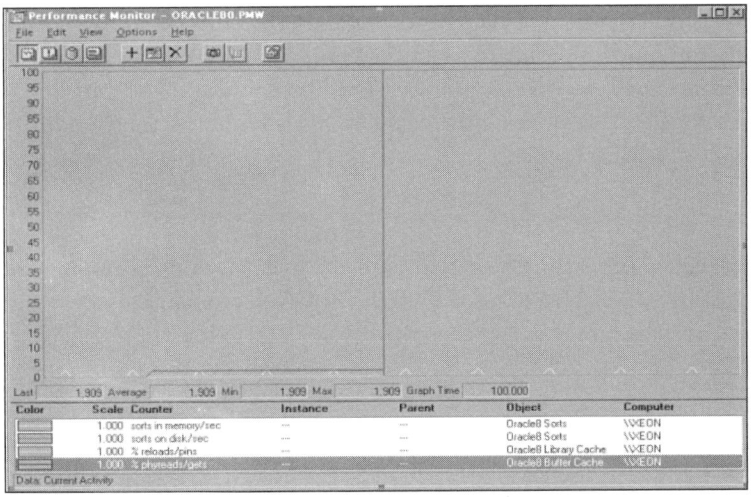

Figure 22.5
Monitoring The Cache
Miss Ratio

You can execute the following query to get realtime performance information about buffer cache usage:

```
select trunc((1-(sum (decode (name, 'physical reads',value,0)))/
    (sum(decode(name,'db block gets',value,0)) +
    (sum(decode(name,'consistent gets',value,0)))))
    )*100) "Buffer Hit Ratio"
from v$sysstat;
```

SHARED POOL

The shared pool is composed of library cache and data dictionary cache.

LIBRARY CACHE

The library cache contains all recently executed SQL statements, such as stored procedures, functions, packages, triggers, and PL/SQL blocks.

Execute the following query to determine the performance of the Library Cache by getting the value of hit ratio:

```
select sum ( pinhits - reloads )/sum ( pins ) "HIT RATIO",
    sum (reloads) / sum (pins) "RELOAD PERCENT"
from v$librarycache;
```

The following is the output of the above SQL statement.

```
HIT RATIO  RELOAD PERCENT
---------  --------------
.99729584     .00005962
```

The preceding example's figures of a hit ratio of 99.729% and a reload percent of 0.0059% are acceptable. You should try to keep the hit ratio above 85 percent, whereas the reload percent should be 2 percent or less. The library cache reload percent can be viewed in Oracle8 PerfMon by using the counter Oracle8 Library cache:%reloads/pins, displayed in the preceding example.

DATA DICTIONARY CACHE

The data dictionary cache is central to efficient database operation. The V$ROWCACHE table contains information about it. Without it, Oracle would have to get metadata information from disk each time a query is parsed.

Execute the following query to determine the cache miss ratio:

```
select sum(gets) "Dict. Gets",
    sum(getmisses) "Get Misses",
    sum(getmisses)/sum(gets)*100 "Ratio (Ideal <15%)"
from v$rowcache;
```

The following is the output of the above SQL statement.

```
Dict. Gets Get Misses Ratio (Ideal <15%)
---------- ---------- ------------------
    204324        960          .46984202
```

For optimum performance, the dictionary cache miss ratio should be at or below 15 percent. You can also use the Oracle8 PerfMon counter Oracle8 Data Dictionary Cache: %getmisses/gets to get the same information.

RECURSIVE CALLS

Recursive calls crop up whenever a table, index, or rollback segment requires more space in the database. They affect the performance of the data dictionary cache. Oracle has to issue recursive calls behind the scenes to update the data dictionary with information about the new extents when database objects have no more room available and will incur dynamic extension.

Execute the following query to determine the amount of recursive calls:

```
select * from v$sysstat
where name = 'recursive calls'
/
```

You can also use the Oracle8 PerfMon and chart the counter Oracle8 Dynamic Extension: recursive calls/sec, as shown in Figure 22.6.

Figure 22.6
Monitoring Recursive
Calls of The Database

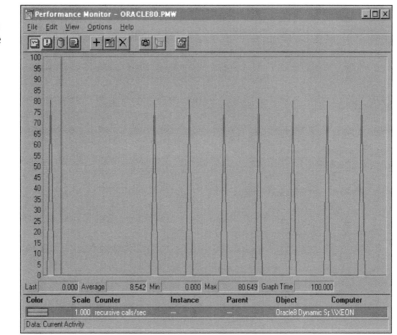

PAGING

In memory, a page is the smallest amount of I/O that Windows NT can work with at a time. When an application program requires more memory, Windows NT looks for pages in memory that have not been used recently. It then performs page-outs, moving inactive pages to a specially designated file on disk, in order to make room for more active pages. If one or more pages in the page file are required again, Windows NT performs page-ins, moving these pages from the page file back into memory. Default page size for Intel-based NT systems is 4K and for Alpha-based NT systems is 8K.

You can see the page-ins and page-outs by viewing the Memory:Pages Input / sec and Memory:Pages Output / sec in the Windows NT PerfMon, as shown in Figure 22.7.

The Oracle8 initialization parameter PRE_PAGE_SGA can be used to keep the SGA in memory as much as possible. When PRE_PAGE_SGA is set to YES, Windows NT tries its hardest to keep the pages that constitute the SGA in physical memory as much as possible, and it avoids writing SGA pages to the paging file. The Windows NT paging file PAGEFILE.SYS resides on the C: drive by default. The total size of the page files should be at least as large as physical memory.

Figure 22.7
Monitoring Windows
NT Paging Activity

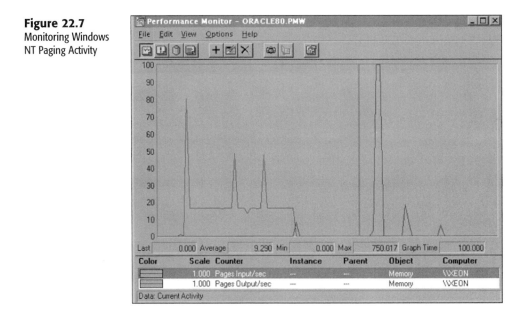

PAGE FAULTS

The total number of pages in physical memory that a program uses while it runs is referred to as that process's *working set*. If a process needs to access a page that is not currently in its working set, a page fault occurs. This can be either a soft fault (where the required page is found elsewhere in memory) or a hard fault (where the required page is on disk and has to be read into memory).

To quickly identify the processes that have most page faults, use Windows NT Task Manager, as shown in Figure 22.8.

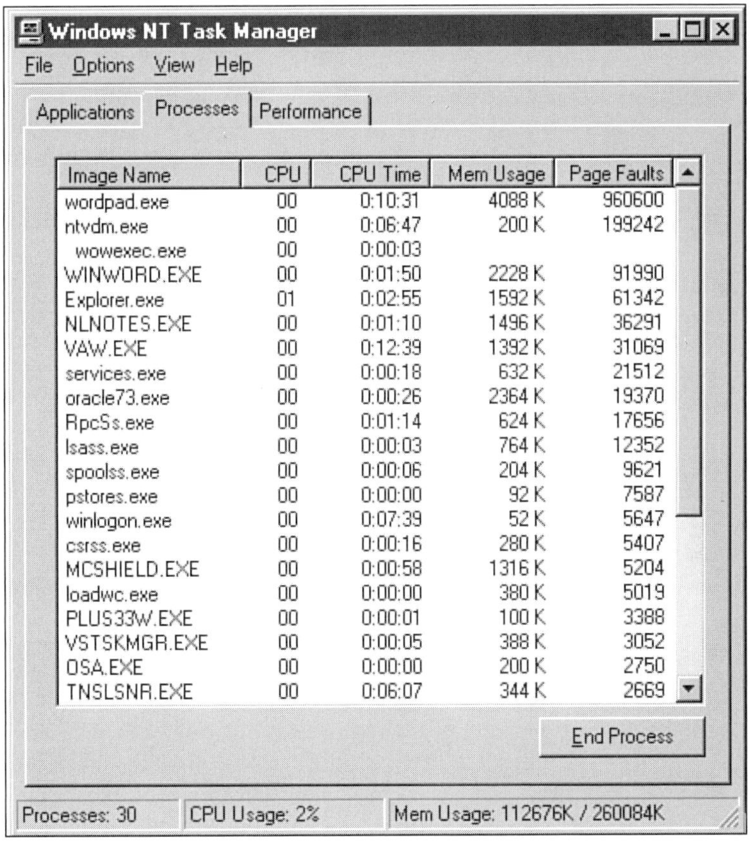

Figure 22.8
Using Task Manager
To Identify Page Faults

Image Name	CPU	CPU Time	Mem Usage	Page Faults
wordpad.exe	00	0:10:31	4088 K	960600
ntvdm.exe	00	0:06:47	200 K	199242
wowexec.exe	00	0:00:03		
WINWORD.EXE	00	0:01:50	2228 K	91990
Explorer.exe	01	0:02:55	1592 K	61342
NLNOTES.EXE	00	0:01:10	1496 K	36291
VAW.EXE	00	0:12:39	1392 K	31069
services.exe	00	0:00:18	632 K	21512
oracle73.exe	00	0:00:26	2364 K	19370
RpcSs.exe	00	0:01:14	624 K	17656
lsass.exe	00	0:00:03	764 K	12352
spoolss.exe	00	0:00:06	204 K	9621
pstores.exe	00	0:00:00	92 K	7587
winlogon.exe	00	0:07:39	52 K	5647
csrss.exe	00	0:00:16	280 K	5407
MCSHIELD.EXE	00	0:00:58	1316 K	5204
loadwc.exe	00	0:00:00	380 K	5019
PLUS33W.EXE	00	0:00:01	100 K	3388
VSTSKMGR.EXE	00	0:00:05	388 K	3052
OSA.EXE	00	0:00:00	200 K	2750
TNSLSNR.EXE	00	0:06:07	344 K	2669

Windows NT Task Manager

File Options View Help

Applications | Processes | Performance

End Process

Processes: 30   CPU Usage: 2%   Mem Usage: 112676K / 260084K

The following are some remedies to solve the excessive paging problem:

- Make the Windows NT paging file larger.
- Stop unnecessary Windows NT services.
- Confirm that the entire SGA fits into physical memory.
- Remove network protocols that are not being used.
- Increase the memory size.

CHAPTER 23

SECURITY MANAGEMENT

In this chapter

Oracle8i has a very impressive suite of new security features. The tenets of security are C.I.A.: Confidentiality, Integrity, and Availability. Oracle has enhanced security in all these areas. The security principle that is the foundation for Oracle's security model is based on the least privilege principle. This principle says that a user should only have the privileges needed to perform his duties. This allows for a granular approach to developing a security policy. These features can be broken down into two broad categories: database security and security for a database used for Internet processing. An Oracle database used for the Internet includes all the typical database security plus support for Internet standard security options. The Internet database requires special security. Both Internet and standard database security issues will be discussed and explained in this chapter.

USER AUTHENTICATION

Users must be identified and authenticated before they are enabled access to your database. Users will be identified by Oracle, but they can be authenticated in three different ways: database, external, or enterprise authentication. Additionally, database and Web servers can be authenticated. This will be discussed later in the section "Oracle8i Internet Security Features."

DATABASE AUTHENTICATION

Database authentication is used when a user is created and a password is specified. This is a good approach for small user communities when there are no additional security products available. The other types of authentication require the reserved word *external* to be used in place of the user password.

When a user is created, a password must be selected for the user. Applying rules on a user password is called *password management*, and a company should have guidelines for passwords. A strong password is one that is not easily guessed, is longer then five bytes, and is not a word found in the dictionary. If the password is in a dictionary, a computer vandal might be able to guess the password by using a "brute force attack." (A *brute force attack* is one in which a computer vandal uses a userID and writes a program to try different passwords that are generated from a dictionary.) A password also should expire after a certain length of time and not be reused by the same user.

Oracle now has the capability of providing password management when using database-level authentication. This is accomplished by setting parameters on a profile and assigning that profile to a user. A *profile* is a database entity that specifies resource limits, and when a profile is assigned to a user, it enforces those limits on the user. A profile can be created using the Enterprise Manager or SQL*Plus. The database must have resource limits turned on for the profile resource limits to take affect. You do this by setting the RESOURCE_LIMIT parameter in the init.ora file to TRUE. A profile can limit the number of sessions, the CPU usage per session, the number of CPU calls, the logical reads, the logical reads per call, idle time, and connect time. The profile can prevent computer vandals from utilizing all the resources from a computer in a denial-of-service attack.

The profile can now enforce password management rules, which are options that you can elect to be used:

- Locking of a user account—When a user has multiple failed logins, the account can be locked for a specified period of time.

- Password Lifetime and Expiration—A given password will now have a specified time limit for use and then will expire and have to be changed. A grace period will be given to a user after the password expires; if the user does not change the password, the account is locked. The database/security administrator can also set the password to an expired state.

- Password History—The password history option checks each newly specified password to ensure that a password is not reused for the specified amount of time or for the specified number of password changes. The database administrator can configure the rules for password reuse with CREATE PROFILE statements.

- Password Complexity Verification—Complexity verification checks the strength of a password to make it harder for a computer vandal to defeat it. The default password complexity verification routine requires that each password does the following:

  - Be a minimum of four characters in length

  - Does not equal the userID

  - Includes at least one alphabetic character, one numeric character, and one punctuation mark

  - Does not match any word on an internal list of simple words, such as welcome, account, database, user, and so on

  - Differs from the previous password by at least three characters

- Database Administrator Authentication—Database administrators require a more secure authentication scheme due to the privileged nature of their tasks (such as shutting down or starting up a database). Additional authentication can be implemented using the operating system and/or a password file.

- Operating system—If the operating system provides a way of segmenting users into groups such as UNIX or NT, Oracle will recommend DBAs be placed in a special group. This enables Oracle to have additional authentication via the group ID to know that a user is a DBA.

- Using a Password File to authenticate DBAs—A password file for DBAs is optional and can be set up using the ORAPWD password utility. The password file will restrict administration privileges to only the users who know the password and have been granted a special role. The roles are SYSOPER and SYSDBA:

  - SYSOPER enables you to perform STARTUP, SHUTDOWN, ALTER DATABASE OPEN/MOUNT, ALTER DATABASE BACKUP, ARCHIVE LOG, and RECOVER and includes the RESTRICTED SESSION privilege.

  - SYSDBA contains all system privileges with ADMIN OPTION, and the SYSOPER system privilege; it enables you to perform CREATE DATABASE and time-based recovery.

USING ORAPWD

The ORAPWD utility is executed at the command prompt of an operating system. Use the following steps:

1. Create the password file using the ORAPWD utility:

    ORAPWD FILE=filename PASSWORD=password ENTRIES=max_users

    FILE= is the actual filename for the password file, PASSWORD= is the password that must be used to sign on to the database as a DBA, and ENTRIES= is the maximum number of users that can have the DBA privilege.

2. Set the REMOTE_LOGIN_PASSWORDFILE initialization parameter to a valid value. This parameter has three valid values: NONE, SHARED, and EXCLUSIVE. The NONE value causes Oracle to behave as if the password file does not exist; this is the default value. The EXCLUSIVE value does the following:

    - Restricts the password file to one database.
    - Enables users to be granted the roles SYSDBA and SYSOPER.

    The SHARED value enables a password file to be used by multiple databases. However, the only users recognized by a SHARED password file are SYS and INTERNAL, and you cannot add users to a SHARED password file.

3. Users can be added to the password file by using the GRANT command to assign the database administration privilege to the appropriate user, as long as the password file is in EXCLUSIVE mode. The following are examples:

    GRANT SYSDBA TO jefferson
    GRANT SYSOPER TO smith

Note

Use the REVOKE command to remove users from the password file.

USING SYSDBA

The privilege SYSDBA enables the user to perform the same operations as OSDBA. Likewise, the privilege SYSOPER enables the user to perform the same operations as OSOPER.

Privileged users are able to connect to the database by using a command similar to this:

CONNECT jefferson/password@prddb.hq.com AS SYSDBA

The use of a password file does not prevent OS-authenticated users from connecting if they meet the criteria for OS authentication.

If you want to list password file members, the view V$PWFILE_USERS shows all the users that have been granted SYSDBA and SYSOPER system privileges for a database.

EXTERNAL AUTHENTICATION

External authentication relies on an operating system or network authentication service. This places control outside of Oracle for password management and user authentication, although Oracle still identifies the user. A database password is not required for this type of login. To use this option, set the parameter OS_AUTHENT_PREFIX in the database init.ora file. This tells Oracle that any user that has the same prefix as this value is to be authenticated externally. For example, if the value is set to ops$ and you have two users named ops$jones and smith, Oracle does not require a password from ops$jones, but it does require one from smith. This parameter can be set to any prefix you want and even can be set to a null string by specifying an empty set of double quotes. The init.ora parameter REMOTE_OS_AUTHENT must be set to true (the default is false) to enable Oracle to use the username from a nonsecure connection. This keeps a potential computer vandal from masquerading as a valid user.

Network authentication is accomplished with the Oracle Advanced Security (OAS) option and can authenticate users with the following technologies:

- Network Authentication Services(such as Kerberos and SESAME)—Enable a central source for password management and can enforce single sign-on using third-party software. A user is created on each database that she will use and database privileges are assigned to that user, but the password is the reserved word *external*. This tells Oracle to identify the user only and enable an external source to authenticate the password. OAS uses an authentication server that has usernames, passwords, and hostnames to verify the password. If the password is authenticated, the user is enabled access to the Oracle database.

- Token Devices—A token is a physical device that a user must have to establish a connection to the database. The token could be a one-time numeric password that is generated on a device the size of a thick credit card. This numeric password must be used in conjunction with a short numeric personal identification number (PIN). The Oracle server has an additional security service added to the configuration that is keeping track of the token's password. Another method is the challenge/response. A number is sent to the user (challenge) and the user enters the number on a device, which gives another number (response) that is used as the password.

- Biometric Devices—Uses a physical characteristic that is unique to the individual, currently a fingerprint scan device that can be used with OAS. The user fingerprint must first be recorded on the system, and then the user specifies the Oracle service and places her finger on the fingerprint reader. The finger placed on the reader will be compared with the fingerprint on the database.

ENTERPRISE AUTHENTICATION

Enterprise Authentication enables a central source for password management and can enforce single sign-on using Oracle Security Service (OSS). The user is called a *global user* and must be created on each database that he will use with the password *globally*. This tells Oracle to identify the user only and enable an OSS to authenticate the password and convey user enterprise authorizations. If the password is authenticated, the user is enabled access to the Oracle database. OSS interfaces with Oracle Enterprise Manager to centralize security role management and enterprise authorizations. This enables the user to have global identities that are centrally managed.

ENTERPRISE ROLES

Enterprise roles are a container for one or more global roles. Enterprise roles are now stored in an Internet Directory or they can be stored in a Lightweight Directory Access Protocol (LDAP)-complaint directory server.

Global roles are different from database roles because they enable you to assign authorization information to (global) users across multiple databases. When a global user logs on to a database, the global roles are dynamically assigned to that user. Global roles must first be assigned to a global user in the Oracle Security Server and then have privileges associated with each global role on the database Server. The privileges associated with a global role can differ between databases.

TABLESPACE ASSIGNMENT AND USAGE

When the user is created, you must tell Oracle where you want to store objects that the user creates in the database; if a storage clause does not specify where to place the objects, this is called the user's *default tablespace*. The default tablespace should be specified to prevent database objects, such as tables or indexes, from being created in the system tablespace; if the user will never have the privilege to create an object in the database, you can let it default to system. If the user will be creating objects in the system tablespace, tablespace fragmentation or an out-of-space condition could be the result. The temporary tablespace is really a sort-work area and is used by SQL statements (such as ORDER BY and GROUP BY). The temporary tablespace is also used when a user builds an index. You should specify a temporary tablespace other then the system tablespace, due to the increased contention with the data dictionary.

A tablespace quota limits the size of database objects that users create in a tablespace. The default is to have no quota size limitation, but if a user has allocated database objects in a tablespace and you want to restrict the use of that tablespace, set the quota for that user to 0 for that tablespace. With this restriction in place, the current objects in that tablespace cannot be allocated any more space, but they remain in the tablespace.

DATABASE PRIVILEGE MANAGEMENT

A privilege can be either an object privilege or system privilege. There are over 60 distinct system privileges that enable users to perform administrative activities on the database (see Table 23.1).

TABLE 23.1   SYSTEM PRIVILEGES

Privilege	Actions Enabled
ANALYZE	
ANALYZE ANY	Analyze any table, cluster, or index in the database.
AUDIT	
AUDIT ANY	Audit any schema object in the database.
AUDIT SYSTEM	Enable and disable statement and privilege audit options.
CLUSTER	
CREATE CLUSTER	Create a cluster in own schema.
CREATE ANY CLUSTER	Create a cluster in any schema; behaves similarly to CREATE ANY TABLE.
ALTER ANY CLUSTER	Alter any cluster in the database.
DROP ANY CLUSTER	Drop any cluster in the database.
DATABASE	
ALTER DATABASE	Alter the database; add files to the operating system via Oracle, regardless of operating system privileges.
DATABASE LINK	
CREATE DATABASE LINK	Create private database links in own schema.
INDEX	
CREATE ANY INDEX	Create an index in any schema on any table.
ALTER ANY INDEX	Alter any index in the database.
DROP ANY INDEX	Drop any index in the database.
LIBRARY	
CREATE LIBRARY	Create callout libraries in own schema.
CREATE ANY LIBRARY	Create callout libraries in any schema.
DROP LIBRARY	Drop callout libraries in own schema.
DROP ANY LIBRARY	Drop callout libraries in any schema.
PRIVILEGE	
GRANT ANY PRIVILEGE	Grant any system privilege (not object privileges).

continues

PART

V

CH

23

TABLE 23.1 CONTINUED

Privilege	Actions Enabled
PROCEDURE	
CREATE PROCEDURE	Create stored procedures, functions, and packages in own schema.
CREATE ANY PROCEDURE	Create stored procedures, functions, and packages in any schema. (This requires that the user also have ALTER ANY TABLE, BACKUP ANY TABLE, DROP ANY TABLE, SELECT ANY TABLE, INSERT ANY TABLE, UPDATE ANY TABLE, DELETE ANY TABLE, or GRANT ANY TABLE privileges.)
ALTER ANY PROCEDURE	Compile any stored procedure, function, or package in any schema.
DROP ANY PROCEDURE	Drop any stored procedure, function, or package in any schema.
EXECUTE ANY PROCEDURE	Execute any procedure or function (standalone or packaged), or reference any public package variable in any schema.
PROFILE	
CREATE PROFILE	Create profiles.
ALTER PROFILE	Alter any profile in the database.
DROP PROFILE	Drop any profile in the database.
ALTER RESOURCE COST	Set costs for resources used in all user sessions.
PUBLIC DATABASE LINK	
CREATE PUBLIC DATABASE LINK	Create public database links.
DROP PUBLIC DATABASE LINK	Drop public database links.
PUBLIC SYNONYM	
CREATE PUBLIC SYNONYM	Create public synonyms.
DROP PUBLIC SYNONYM	Drop public synonyms.
ROLE	
CREATE ROLE	Create roles.
ALTER ANY ROLE	Alter any role in the database.
DROP ANY ROLE	Drop any role in the database.
GRANT ANY ROLE	Grant any role in the database.
ROLLBACK SEGMENT	
CREATE ROLLBACK SEGMENT	Create rollback segments.
ALTER ROLLBACK SEGMENT	Alter rollback segments.
DROP ROLLBACK SEGMENT	Drop rollback segments.

Privilege	Actions Enabled
SESSION	
CREATE SESSION	Connect to the database.
ALTER SESSION	Issue ALTER SESSION statements.
RESTRICTED SESSION	Connect when the database has been started using STARTUP RESTRICT. (The OSOPER and OSDBA roles contain this privilege.)
SEQUENCE	
CREATE SEQUENCE	Create a sequence in own schema.
CREATE ANY SEQUENCE	Create any sequence in any schema.
ALTER ANY SEQUENCE	Alter any sequence in any schema.
DROP ANY SEQUENCE	Drop any sequence in any schema.
SELECT ANY SEQUENCE	Reference any sequence in any schema.
SNAPSHOT	
CREATE SNAPSHOT	Create snapshots in own schema. (User must also have the CREATE TABLE privilege.)
CREATE SNAPSHOT	Create snapshots in any schema. (User must also have the CREATE ANY TABLE privilege.)
ALTER SNAPSHOT	Alter any snapshot in any schema.
DROP ANY SNAPSHOT	Drop any snapshot in any schema.
SYNONYM	
CREATE SYNONYM	Create a synonym in own schema.
CREATE ANY SYNONYM	Create any synonym in any schema.
DROP ANY SYNONYM	Drop any synonym in any schema.
SYSTEM	
ALTER SYSTEM	Issue ALTER SYSTEM statements.
TABLE	
CREATE TABLE	Create tables in own schema. Also enables grantee to create indexes (including those for integrity constraints) on table in own schema. (The grantee must have a quota for the tablespace or the UNLIMITED TABLESPACE privilege.)
CREATE ANY TABLE	Create tables in any schema. (If grantee has CREATE ANY TABLE privilege and creates a table in another user's schema, the owner must have space quota on that tablespace. The table owner need not have the CREATE [ANY] TABLE privilege.)

PART

V

CH

23

continued

TABLE 23.1   CONTINUED

Privilege	Actions Enabled
TABLE	
ALTER ANY TABLE	Alter any table in any schema and compile any view in any schema.
BACKUP ANY TABLE	Perform an incremental export using the export utility of tables in any schema.
DROP ANY TABLE	Drop or truncate any table in any schema.
LOCK ANY TABLE	Lock any table or view in any schema.
COMMENT ANY TABLE	Comment on any table, view, or column in any schema.
SELECT ANY TABLE	Query any table, view, or snapshot in any schema.
INSERT ANY TABLE	Insert rows into any table or view in any schema.
UPDATE ANY TABLE	Update rows in any table or view in any schema.
DELETE ANY TABLE	Delete rows from any table or view in any schema.
TABLESPACE	
CREATE TABLESPACE	Create tablespaces; add files to the operating system via Oracle, regardless of the user's operating system privileges.
ALTER TABLESPACE	Alter tablespaces; add files to the operating system via Oracle, regardless of the user's operating system privileges.
MANAGE TABLESPACE	Take any tablespace offline, bring any tablespace online, and begin and end backups of any tablespace.
DROP TABLESPACE	Drop tablespaces.
UNLIMITED TABLESPACE	Use an unlimited amount of any tablespace. This privilege overrides any specific quotas assigned. If revoked, the grantee's schema objects remain, but further tablespace allocation is denied unless enabled by specific tablespace quotas. This system privilege can be granted only to users and not to roles. In general, specific tablespace quotas are assigned instead of granting this system privilege.
TRANSACTION	
FORCE TRANSACTION	Force the commit or rollback of own in-doubt distributed transaction in the local database.
FORCE ANY TRANSACTION	Force the commit or rollback of any in-doubt distributed transaction in the local database.
TRIGGER	
CREATE TRIGGER	Create a trigger in own schema.
CREATE ANY TRIGGER	Create any trigger in any schema associated with any table in any schema.
ALTER ANY TRIGGER	Enable, disable, or compile any trigger in any schema.
DROP ANY TRIGGER	Drop any trigger in any schema.

Privilege	Actions Enabled
USER	
CREATE ANY USER	Create users; assign quotas on any tablespace, set default and temporary tablespaces, and assign a profile as part of a CREATE USER statement.
BECOME ANY USER	Become another user. (Required by any user performing a full database import.)
ALTER USER	Alter other users: change any user's password or authentication method, assign tablespace quotas, set default and temporary tablespaces, assign profiles and default roles in an ALTER USER statement. (Not required to alter own password.)
DROP USER	Drop another user.
VIEW	
CREATE VIEW	Create a view in own schema.
CREATE ANY VIEW	Create a view in any schema. To create a view in another user's schema, you must have CREATE ANY VIEW privileges, and the owner must have the required privileges on the objects referenced in the view.
DROP ANY VIEW	Drop any view in any schema.

You should give these privileges only to users who administer the database. Object privileges enable access to and maintenance of database objects; this category of privileges is for end-users. An object privilege (see Table 23.2) can be administered directly to the user, or the privilege can be granted to a role and then the role granted to the user.

TABLE 23.2   OBJECT PRIVILEGES

Object	SQL Statement Enabled
ALTER	ALTER object (table or sequence)
DELETE	DELETE FROM object (table or view)
EXECUTE	EXECUTE object (procedure or function); references to public package variables
INDEX	CREATE INDEX ON object (tables only)
INSERT	INSERT INTO object (table or view)
REFERENCES	CREATE or ALTER TABLE statement defining a FOREIGN KEY integrity constraint on object (tables only)
SELECT	SELECT...FROM object (table, view, or snapshot); SQL statements using a sequence
UPDATE	UPDATE object (table or view)

UNDERSTANDING SECURITY ROLES

A *role* is a database entity that is a named group of privileges. This creates a many-to-one relationship between privileges and roles, where you have many privileges to one role. A role is a database entity that is unique within the database and not owned by a user. You can create a role with the CREATE ROLE statement, and it cannot be the same name as a user. Users can also create roles if they have create role privileges. When you create a role, it becomes part of your default role set.

ROLE AUTHORIZATION

The use of a role can be authenticated by a password. This does enhance the security of the role and will keep the user who does not know the password from enabling the role. Unfortunately, the password for the role has to be hard coded in the application somewhere. The SET ROLE command enables the role dynamically when a role has been granted to a user but is not part of her default role set. The default role set is automatically enabled whenever a user creates a session in Oracle. With prior releases of Oracle, this was the best way to keep the user from trying to access the data from anything but the application. For example, a user might have access to the PAYROLL tables via the PAYROLL_role. If this role is part of her default role set, she could use software other then the payroll application to modify data. Even with the SET ROLE command, a user can still defeat this advanced security feature. Oracle now has added the functionality of a secure application role. These new type of roles can only be enabled through a trusted package. The trusted package verifies that the user is not connected directly to the database, but instead is using the application. The syntax for creating a secure application role is as follows:

```
CREATE ROLE payroll_role IDENTIFIED  USING payroll_pkg.admin;
```

The role is payroll role, and it is using the trusted package payroll pkg.admin.

ROLE AUTHORIZATION BY THE OPERATING SYSTEM

The following statement creates a role named ACCTS_REC and requires that the operating system authorize its use:

```
CREATE ROLE role IDENTIFIED EXTERNALLY;
```

Operating system role authentication is possible only when the operating system can dynamically link operating system privileges (OSP) with applications. When a user starts an application, the operating system grants an OSP to the user. The granted OSP corresponds to the role associated with the application. At this point, the application can enable the application role.

If a role is authorized by the operating system, you must configure information for each user at the operating system level. This operation is operating system-dependent.

The database has a soft limit of how many roles a user can have as part of the default role set. If the user has more roles than that limit, he will receive an error when logging in. If this error occurs, check MAX_ENABLED_ROLES in the init.ora; it might need to be increased.

A role might also be granted to another role, enabling all the privileges of the granted role to be inherited.

UNDERSTANDING ADMINISTRATION

Administrators should have only the authority they need to administer the database. The primary administration tasks in a database environment can be broken into two main areas: security administration and database administration. A *security administrator* creates, alters, and drops users and maintains security roles and user profiles, but he does not have DBA privileges, such as starting and stopping a database.

When you grant a role to a user who will administer the privileges of the role, you must do so with the ADMIN option. This option enables users to perform administration activities, such as altering or dropping the role and granting the role to other users with the ADMIN option. This option should not be given to anyone other then administrators.

PART

V

CH

23

THE ORACLE ENTERPRISE SECURITY MANAGER

The Oracle Enterprise Security Manager enables an administrator to manage all aspects of Oracle database security throughout the enterprise using one tool. This tool will allow you to create a user, assign them the default tablespace and temporary tablespace and their password. Once the user is created, then privileges can be assigned to them. Non-enterprise roles can also be created and maintained here as well as global roles. This single console enables you to create a user in an Internet Directory, create a user in multiple Oracle8i databases, and create and administer enterprise roles. For more information on this product, see Chapter 27, "Oracle Enterprise Manager."

MONITORING DATABASE ASSETS

Oracle can audit and record activity that occurs on the database. You enable auditing by using the AUDIT SQL command and disable auditing using the NOAUDIT SQL command. There are three categories of audit actions: login attempts, object accesses (specific statements on specific objects), and database actions (specific system privilege and statements without regard to object).

Any command, successful or unsuccessful, can be audited in these categories. To create the audit system views, run the CATAUDIT.SUL file script as the user SYS and set the init.ora parameter AUDIT_TRAIL. You can set AUDIT_TRAIL to write to the database or to an operating system file: AUDIT_TRAIL=DB writes to the database, and AUDIT_TRAIL-OS writes to an operating system file. You must restart the Oracle instance for the new init.ora parameter to take effect. If you set the parameter AUDIT_TRAIL to DB, all audited activity is written to the SYS.AUD$ table. You should modify the tablespace storage parameter of the SYS.AUD$ table from the system tablespace to a tablespace created for auditing purposes. You can issue all the audit commands from SQL*WORKSHEET or SQL*Plus.

AUDITING LOGINS

The AUDIT ANY privilege is required to issue audit commands. To audit logins, use the AUDIT SESSION command. This command can audit all successful and unsuccessful attempts to establish a connection with the database. To audit only unsuccessful attempts, use the AUDIT SESSION WHENEVER NOT SUCCESSFUL command. To audit only successful attempts, use the AUDIT SESSION WHENEVER SUCCESSFUL command. You can generate audit reports if the audit data is stored in the SYS.AUD$ TABLE. To report on login attempts, use the DBA_AUDIT_SESSION view:

```
SELECT
os_username, /* O/S user name*/
username,   /* Oracle user name */
to_char(timestamp,'DD-MON-YY HH24:MI'), /* Login time */
to_char(logoff_time, 'DD-MON-YY HH24:MI') /* Logoff time */
FROM dba_audit_session
ORDER BY os_username;

OUTPUT TO QUERY
OS_USERNAME   USERNAME   TIMESTAMP            LOGOFF
JOHNES        JOHNES     24-MAR-97 18:00    14-FEB-97 18:05
```

AUDITING DATABASE ACTIONS

By auditing database actions, you can audit at the statement and system privilege level, without regard to a specific database object. The statement AUDIT *statement* feature of the audit facility enables you to audit more then one SQL statement. For example, using the audit statement ROLE audits the CREATE ROLE, ALTER ROLE, SET ROLE, and DROP ROLE SQL statements. To audit system privileges, you must specify the privilege. The system privilege ALTER DATABASE is not included in the statement audit option, but you can still audit it because it is a system privilege. Some of the statement audit options use the same name as the system privileges. You can use the AUDIT statement for a user, session, or access. You can further define it to audit only successful or unsuccessful statements. A list of statements that can be audited are shown in Table 23.3.

TABLE 23.3 STATEMENT AUDIT OPTIONS

Statement	Option
OPTION	SQL STATEMENT
ALTER SYSTEM	ALTER SYSTEM
CLUSTER CLUSTER	CREATE CLUSTER, ALTER CLUSTER, TRUNCATE CLUSTER, DROP
DATABASE LINK	CREATE DATABASE LINK, DROP DATABASE LINK
INDEX	CREATE INDEX, ALTER INDEX, DROP INDEX
NOT EXISTS	All SQL statements that return an Oracle error because the specified structure or object does not exist

Statement	Option
PROCEDURE	CREATE [OR REPLACE] FUNCTION, CREATE [OR REPLACE] PACKAGE, CREATE [OR REPLACE] PACKAGE BODY, CREATE [OR REPLACE] PROCEDURE, DROP PACKAGE, DROP PROCEDURE
PUBLIC DATABASE	CREATE PUBLIC DATABASE LINK, DROP PUBLIC
LINK	DATABASE LINK
PUBLIC SYNONYM	CREATE PUBLIC SYNONYM, DROP PUBLIC SYNONYM
ROLE	CREATE ROLE, ALTER ROLE, SET ROLE, DROP ROLE
ROLLBACK SEGMENT	CREATE ROLLBACK SEGMENT, ALTER DROPBACK SEGMENT, DROP ROLLBACK SEGMENT
SEQUENCE	CREATE SEQUENCE, DROP SEQUENCE
SESSION	Connects and Disconnects
SYNONYM	CREATE SYNONYM, DROP SYNONYM
SYSTEM AUDIT	AUDIT, NOAUDIT
SYSTEM GRANT	GRANT *system privileges/role* TO *user/role* REVOKE *system privileges/role* FROM *user/role*
TABLE	CREATE TABLE, ALTER TABLE, DROP TABLE
TABLESPACE	CREATE TABLESPACE, ALTER TABLESPACE, DROP TABLESPACE
TRIGGER	CREATE TRIGGER, ALTER TRIGGER, ENABLE or DISABLE, ALTER TABLE with ENABLE, DISABLE, and DROP clauses
USER	CREATE USER, ALTER USER, DROP USER
VIEW	CREATE [OR REPLACE] VIEW, DROP VIEW

AUDITING DML ON DATABASE OBJECTS

You can audit a specific schema object using the following syntax:

```
AUDIT object_opt ON schema.object
  BY SESSION/ACCESS WHENEVER NOT/SUCCESSFUL;
```

You can specify an object option, such as insert or update, or you can use the keyword ALL to specify all object options.

```
AUDIT insert,update
ON scott.emp_table
WHENEVER NOT SUCCESSFUL;

AUDIT ALL
  ON scott.emp_table
  WHENEVER NOT SUCCESSFUL;
```

Administering Auditing

If you choose to store the audit records on the database, it is a good idea to run reports on the audit table on a daily basis and then delete the data to conserve space. The audit table should have restricted access, and all activity against the SYS.AUD$ table should be recorded by using the following statement:

```
AUDIT INSERT, UPDATE, DELETE, SELECT
ON sys.aud$
BY ACCESS;
```

Auditing can create excessive overhead on a database, so be very selective. The BY SESSION clause in the audit statement causes Oracle to write a single record for all SQL statements of the same type that were used in the same session. The BY ACCESS clause in the audit statement causes Oracle to write one record for each audited statement. If you audit data definition language (DDL) statements, Oracle automatically uses BY ACCESS, no matter which clause is specified. To maintain a secure environment, you should implement a policy to decide which actions to audit.

The following AUDIT SQL statement shows how to use some of the more restrictive options:

```
AUDIT statement_opt/system_privileges
  BY user (optional)
  BY session/access WHENEVER NOT/SUCCESSFUL;
```

The next code sample shows how to audit statements relating to roles and a session:

```
AUDIT role;
AUDIT session whenever not successful;.
```

Protecting Data Integrity

You can protect data integrity through the use of secure user connections and encryption algorithms. Passwords can now be encrypted when users sign on to an Oracle database. The password is encrypted using a modified DES (data encryption standard) algorithm. Encryption is turned on by setting an environment variable on the client machine and the init.ora parameter on the database server. You must set the client machine's environment variable ORA_ENCRYPT_LOGIN to TRUE.

> **Note**
>
> This variable varies depending on the operating system. You must also set the DBLINK_ENCRYPT_LOGIN init.ora parameter to TRUE on the database server.

Oracle encrypts the password of a userID when a database session is initiated, but it does not encrypt the altering of the password.

Computer vandals can compromise data integrity by modifying the data or DML that travels on a network, which can result in a logical-corrupt database. When the integrity of a database is in question, it is very costly and time-consuming to restore.

Encrypting all your data is the perfect solution to potential security breaches because if the data is being passively monitored by computer vandals, they can't use the data and will probably look for easier prey. Oracle's Advanced Security (OAS) provides this additional level of security and more. The OAS currently offers two encryption algorithms, RSA and DES, with different key lengths. For use in the U.S. and Canada, 56-bit RSA RC4, 56-bit DES, and 128-bit RSA are available; for export outside the U.S. and Canada, 40-bit RSA RC4 and 40-bit DES40, 3DES, are available. Data integrity is protected by using cryptographic checksums using the MD5 algorithm or SHA (Secure Hashing Algorithm). This ensures that the data is not tampered with between the time it leaves a client workstation and the time it arrives at the database server.

ORACLE8I INTERNET SECURITY FEATURES

Oracle8i Advanced Security Option provides an impressive set of security features that are designed with Internet standards in mind. Today's architecture is multi-tiered and possibly connected via many networks. This creates a daunting security challenge. There are thin clients connecting to application servers and then application servers connecting to database servers. The database server must be able to trust that not only the user is who he says he is, but the application server is who it says it is as well. These types of authentication can occur using two methods: passwords and digital certificates. Passwords have already been discussed in the prior section entitled "User Authentication," so that leaves digital certificates to be addressed here.

USING DIGITAL CERTIFICATES

A digital certificate can be used to authenticate a user or a machine. The type of certificate is X.509 version 3, an Internet standard-based Public Key Infrastructure (PKI). A certificate contains the following:

- Distinguished name of the certificate owner
- The distinguished name of the certificate authority
- The certificate owner's public key
- Range of dates that the certificate is valid
- Public key of the certificate owner
- Signature of issuer
- Serial number of the certificate

These certificates must be used with the Secure Sockets Layer protocol (SSL). SSL also provides data encryption across the network and data integrity checking. Encryption is key to keeping data private. The data integrity checking defeats a computer vandal from modifying the data while it is en route to the database (see Figure 23.1). The Oracle Certificate Authority or another certificate authority, publishes wallets in an Oracle Directory server or another LDAP directory structure. Oracle uses an "Oracle Wallet" to store the certificate and private key. The Oracle Wallet Manager is a central tool for managing the contents of the wallets.

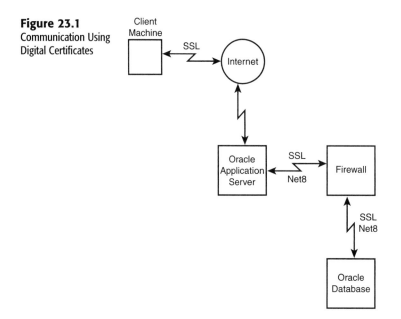

Figure 23.1
Communication Using
Digital Certificates

ADVANCED AUTHENTICATION USING THE RADIUS (REMOTE AUTHENTICATION DIAL-IN USER SERVICE) PROTOCOL

Now that every machine or user can have a digital certificate, Oracle can use a stronger means of authentication then a password. The RADIUS protocol has become an Internet standard, and Oracle8i Advanced Security Option now works with any RADIUS-compliant security server. This protocol supports passwords, tokens, biometrics and smartcards.

FIREWALL SUPPORT

A firewall is used to prevent the public Internet traffic from entering into the private network of a company. It is also used to protect the servers that communicate to servers that are connected to the Internet (see Figure 23.2). Most leading firewall vendors now have proxies to enable NET8 and SQL*NET traffic to pass through the firewall, thus providing protection for the database server from a computer vandal attack. A computer vandal might try an attack on the database server operating system, but if the firewall is only enabling NET8 and SQL*NET traffic, this will be impossible, so the database server is secure.

Figure 23.2
Firewall Support

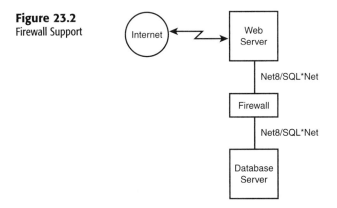

FINE-GRAINED ACCESS CONTROL (VIRTUAL PRIVATE DATABASE)

A virtual private database guarantees a user can only look at data that she has been given access to. This enables an existing production database to be accessed over the Internet with Oracle's assurance that the end user can only see her data. This security is kept at the database server level. This prevents it from being bypassed by client software, such as a report writer. A virtual private database is defined by associating tables or views to a security policy. Any access to the table or view after the policy has been implemented causes the data server to call a function that is enforcing the policy. This function returns code that is added to the WHERE clause before the SQL statement is executed. This additional code contains the access rules that have been used to help secure the data. You can define different policies for different DML for the same table (for example, INSERT of the employee table can have a different policy then a DELETE of the employee table). These SQL statements are fully parsed and optimized and will be in the SHARED POOL, to be used by other users when applicable.

THE DATABASE RESOURCE MANAGER

The Database Resource Manager manages how much CPU and the degree of parallelism multiple instances can acquire from the operating system. This is a great security and admin istration feature. From a security standpoint, it can be used to prevent denial of service attacks against a production environment that is used for the Internet. It is an administration plus if that database shares system resources with other databases that are not used for the Internet. There are four mechanisms for managing database resources:

1. Resource consumer groups are assigned at the user level, and all their sessions are part of that consumer group.

2. Resource plans contain resource consumer groups or other resource plans; they also include a specification on how to partition resources.

3. Resource allocation methods are a policy to be followed by a particular resource. Resource allocation methods are used by resource plans and resource consumer groups.

4. Resource plan directives let an administrator assign members to a particular plan and then manage the resources that the members use.

By creating an Internet resource group and restricting the amount of resources for that group, the administrator can better manage their production environment that is connected to the Internet. He can prevent one resource group from executing first and then consuming all the computing resources on the operating system.

HARDWARE SECURITY

Computer hardware needs to be stored in a restricted area where access is limited and where appropriate fire control mechanisms are in place. The electricity should be clean, meaning not subject to power surges or outages. Clean electricity is usually provided by an uninterrupted power supply (UPS).

RECOVERING LOST DATA

In your security plan, you must specify how to recover data lost due to a security breach. There is a saying: "Your system is only as good as your last backup and your ability to recover." That sums up my philosophy on database recovery. Following are some good questions to ask yourself regarding backups:

- How is the backup media physically secured?
- Is the backup media shipped offsite when the backup is complete in case of a situation in which the data center is lost?
- Is the backup media replaced in accordance with the manufacturer's guidelines?
- Is the backup hardware cleaned regularly?
- Is the backup verified as readable and available for recovery?
- Is there a backup log that shows which backup media was used for a particular day and how many times the media has been used for backup?

There are two ways to back up an Oracle database. The first is by using an operating-system backup called a *physical backup*; the second is by using the Oracle Export utility, which creates a *logical backup*.

OPERATING SYSTEM BACKUP

An operating-system backup requires a utility that is specific to the operating system and that enables the DBA to restore the database by using an operating-system restore utility. You can perform the operating-system backup with the database down (a *cold backup*) or with it up (a *hot backup*). A hot backup is used in shops that require high database availability. A hot backup enables tablespaces to be backed up while online and available for transaction processing, or while offline and unavailable. A cold backup must include all Oracle data files, control files, and online redo log files (for reference, I call these files the operating-system backup file set). A hot backup is considered a partial backup because it backs up only the files requested.

You can operate the database in ARCHIVELOG mode and in NOARCHIVELOG mode. The ARCHIVELOG mode means that as the online redo logs are filled, their contents are archived, which frees the current redo log. The archive redo logs are used to recover the transactions recorded on them or to redo them in the event of a database recovery. To perform a hot backup, the database must be in ARCHIVELOG mode. The NOARCHIVELOG mode means that online redo logs are not archived when they are full, but they are written over by the latest transaction. Therefore, only the current redo logs are available for recovery. If you don't archive, you must make a backup of the operating-system file set, and when the database is restored, you must restore all the files in the operating-system backup file set.

A cold backup has the virtue of having the least amount of steps in the restore process, which usually means the least chance of error, and it is faster than a hot backup.

PART

V

CH

23

LOGICAL BACKUP

A logical backup using the Oracle Export utility creates a file that has the information to re-create data structures and the data contained in the database. This information can be stored on a disk device or tape media. A logical backup takes longer than a physical backup and might require additional work in preparing the database for recovery. There are three Export modes:

- *User mode*, which backs up all objects owned by a user
- *Table mode*, which backs up specific tables owned by a user
- *Full database mode*, which backs up all objects of the database

You can control the Export utility using a parameter file to perform custom backups of data on the database. You can perform an export at three levels of data collection: incremental, cumulative, and complete. An *incremental export* backs up only data that has changed since the last incremental export. A *cumulative export* exports data only from tables that have changed since the last cumulative export; this export is used to condense the incremental exports. A *complete export* exports all data contained in a database. You should execute a complete export on a limited basis, due to the large volume of data collected.

Exports can be very flexible, but a regular schedule is important. It is a good idea to do a complete export on the first day of the month, an incremental export every day, and a cumulative report every weekend.

BACKUP AND RECOVERY

In this chapter

BACKUP STRATEGY

As most people have learned at some point in their computing lives, data backups are an absolutely essential ingredient in almost any computer system they depend on. Disk head crashes, circuitry failure, and even catastrophic loss of data centers are all facts of life that DBAs must plan for. Fortunately, Oracle is a very robust database system with years of field-proven backup and recovery techniques that can keep your data safe when the inevitable happens. As a professional DBA, you are expected to keep your system running like a well-oiled machine. You must also take measures to ensure that the data contained in your RDBMS is safe from all sorts of threatening hazards.

Imagine that it's two weeks prior to end-of-year processing and your database system has just lost a disk drive. The CEO and CFO are both standing in your office. They want to know how long it will be before the system is back up, and they remind you that they can't lose any data from the financial system. This chapter is designed to give you the information you'll need to tell them: "It won't be long," and "of course there won't be any loss." You'll also learn some common non-emergency uses of the backup system.

Tip #41	Advertise to your user and management population what backups can and cannot do along with how long it will typically take to recover the system. By involving everyone early on, you will hopefully be able to keep everyone's expectations in line with reality.

It's also worth pointing out that in this context, backups are used for data recovery both in emergency situations and in controlled situations in which you are simply moving data from one instance to another, switching machines, or just reorganizing a database.

The emphasis of this chapter is on helping you to decide, plan, and test your backup strategy. The ease with which you're able to recover your database is directly related to the effort you put into your backup strategy. If you are in an uncomfortable recovery situation, you should work with Oracle support for your specific recovery needs because the specific details vary on a case-by-case basis. As you design, implement, and use your backup strategy, please keep these important points in mind:

- Plan your backup *and* recovery strategy. Plan how you'll use your backups to recover your database.

- Test your backup and recovery strategy on a regular basis (and especially important with new staff members).

- Be sure operating system (OS)level backups are still taken off the database server. Database backups do not safeguard *init.ora* files, Oracle installations, or OSs.

- Perform appropriate backups of the database before and after significant modifications. This is particularly important if modifications include dropping segments or tablespaces.

- Tablespaces containing very dynamic data need to be backed up more frequently than more static tablespaces.

- Keep older backups on hand. You might not find that a table or row was deleted for months or sometimes years.

- Export your databases regularly for added protection.

- Consider distributed database backups for high-availability applications.

UNDERSTANDING PHYSICAL AND LOGICAL DATA LOSS

Data loss can be classified as either *physical* or *logical*. Physical data loss is the loss of components at the OS level of a database, such as data files, control files, redo logs, and archive logs. This might be caused by a disk drive crash, someone accidentally deleting a data file, or a configuration change that overwrites any critical database file. Logical data loss is a loss of database-level components, such as tables, indexes, or table records. This can be caused by someone accidentally dropping the wrong table, an application going awry, or a shortsighted *WHERE* clause in a *DELETE* statement. Not surprisingly, Oracle enables both physical data and l ogical data backups. Although each backup solution *could* be used as a substitute for the other, you'll find out that an effective backup plan must include both to fully protect you from data loss.

The physical data backup is a copy of the following:

- Data files
- Control files
- Applicable archived redo logs

If you lose a disk drive or need to move some of the data files around, this is the most straightforward approach to recovery. Physical backups are usually run at scheduled intervals to protect against the physical loss of a database. Indeed, if you want to ensure that you can recover the system to the last commit, you must have a physical backup as a base, as well as the archive and redo logs that have accumulated since the last physical backup.

Physical backups are further categorized into *cold* and *hot* backups. Cold backups are used when you have the option of shutting down the database long enough to back up the system. Hot backups provide a physical backup when the database is open and available for use by users. This enables an Oracle database to operate 24 hours a day, 7 days a week (24/7) and still be backed up at regular intervals. Unless you absolutely must have your database running in a 24/7 cycle, you are much better off using cold backups. As you will see, hot backups are not for the meek and must be thoroughly tested before you rely on them.

Please be aware that the term *cold backup* is synonymous with *offline backup*, as is *hot backup* with *online backup*.

Backup Frequency and *ARCHIVELOG* Mode

Two essential parts of planning backups are choosing the proper backup frequency for your database and deciding whether to run in ARCHIVELOG mode.

When choosing a backup interval, always ask yourself, "How much data can I afford to lose?" If your database is not running in ARCHIVELOG mode, you could lose all transactions since your last backup. If your business needs enable the database to lose one week's worth of transactions, you need to backup the database at least once per week.

You can't lose any transactions in production OLTP systems. Running in ARCHIVELOG mode is highly desirable (when practical) because it enables you to fully recover your database to the last commit, even if your last physical backup was two days ago.

Even with ARCHIVELOG mode enabled, you must still make regular physical backups of the system. You must have all the archived redo logs since the last physical backup to fully recover a database. A regular physical backup reduces the amount of space needed to store archived redo logs, as well as reducing the risk of losing transactions because of a lost or damaged archived redo log.

Physical backups should be used for recovery on the same machine, Oracle version, and instance from which they originated. Therefore, physical backups should be considered nonportable. They are usually only useful for safeguarding data on the same machine and instance against data loss.

One exception to this rule is when you want to completely transfer a database from one system to another. As long as both machines are of the same architecture, OS version, and Oracle version, you can just copy the physical components of a database from system A to system B. If any of these conditions are not met or if you are just in doubt, use a logical backup to move your data.

A logical data backup is usually a collection of SQL statements to re-create the database objects (the database itself, tables, indexes, grants, roles, and so on), as well as the individual records, in an ASCII format.

Oracle's logical backup system should be used when you need to move specific data between instances, or when you need to copy all an instance's data between differing system architectures, OS versions, or Oracle versions. Logical backups are usually run by the DBA on an as-needed basis, although there is certainly a need for somewhat regular logical backups in addition to physical backups.

Tip #42

Oracle's traditional backup tools usually make poor candidates for archiving old data out of a database system (particularly if the data can be loaded into a non-Oracle system). Third party tools from vendors such as BMC and Platinum offer greater flexibility and portability for these special case logical backups.

In developer environments, application developers should work with DBAs to plan a logical backup strategy. Typically, two copies of the database exist, one that is production and another that is used by the developers to debug their applications. The development database should be synchronized with the production database periodically.

Examples

Now, look at some practical real-world problems. You *must* have your database running in *ARCHIVELOG* mode and the archiver must be running for you to recover your system to the last commit. The following sections list common backup needs and the recommended backup methods. The remainder of this chapter covers the actual mechanics of the backup and recovery methods provided by Oracle.

To help illustrate the correct usage of each backup system, the following provide several corresponding examples.

Physical Backups

Physical backups are the most critical backups taken. They are needed to guarantee that a database can be restored with minimal or no loss of data in the event of a physical database loss or corruption.

Cold Physical Backups   Cold physical backups provide the easiest and most straightforward means of protecting a database from physical damage or loss. Examples of appropriate uses of cold physical backups are the following:

- A database has been created on a database server and you want to make sure a backup is taken on a routine basis. The database does not need to be available during the backup process.

- The system administrator will be upgrading your disks from 4GB each to 9GB each. You need to back up the system and restore it in the same directory structure on the new drives.

Hot Physical Backups   Hot physical backups provide the same protection from physical database damage. The backup process can be run with the database open and available to users. Situations where hot physical backups may be needed include the following:

- Your business needs demand that the database be available to your user community 24 hours a day, 7 days a week.

- Research has shown that your database requires a full day of processing to reach a high cache hit ratio. On particularly large databases on systems with many gigabytes of memory dedicated to Oracle, it might take several hours of processing before Oracle has cached the full working set of data. Even though the system might be able to shut down during the night, morning performance is much better if the database is not shut down at night.

- Whereas your user community only needs the system for 12 hours a day, nearly the entire remaining 12 hours are spent on batch processing; there is simply not enough downtime for both batch processing and system backups.

LOGICAL BACKUPS

Logical backups enable database object level recovery and are a necessary component of an overall backup strategy to guarantee that an inadvertent change to the database (such as *DELETE*, *DROP*, or *UPDATE*) can be recovered from.

FULL LOGICAL BACKUP   Full logical backups will export the entire database to an Oracle format file that is portable between Oracle versions, operating systems, and hardware platforms. Specific situations that might require a full logical backup include the following:

- You do not have another physical system for a test bed, but you do have a production and test instance on the same machine and you want to synchronize them occasionally.

- The new server was just installed and will be replacing your old machine. Your old and new database servers are different platforms (for example, Sun and HP).

LOGICAL BACKUP OF A SPECIFIC TABLE   Oracle's logical backup facility will provide for backups to be taken of specific tables. This functionality is useful if the following situations occur:

- You need to move table *ABC* from the *JSMITH* schema to the *TGASPER* schema.

- You will be dropping table *ABC*, although you want to save a backup copy of it just in case.

LOGICAL BACKUP OF A SPECIFIC USER   Logical backups can be made of one or more specific users (or schemas). You might want to use this capability when the following happen:

- You have just been told that user *JSMITH* can be dropped. This user owns several tables, and you think there is a chance that someone might want them later, so you want to back up just the *JSMITH* schema.

- There is an application using tables contained entirely in a single schema. You are planning to upgrade the application and must run a script to "update" the tables and indexes for the new version to work correctly.

Tip #43

These specific cases illustrate which backup methods are appropriate for the different situations you will encounter throughout your database's life. Don't rely on a single backup method. Although most DBAs understand the need for physical backups, many do not run logical backups regularly. This makes them vulnerable to an inadvertent *DROP* command. Remember that *DROP* commands are immediate; *there is no rollback*. With help from Oracle Support, it is possible to use your physical backups to recover a dropped table. This is a very time-consuming and expensive process that probably can be avoided by having a logical backup on hand. Remember that the system does not need to be shut down for logical backups.

> Making a logical backup is very important to do before you run a SQL script that you have not thoroughly examined. *DROP* or *DELETE* commands might lurk unexpectedly, just waiting to zap your database!
>
> If you run hot backups as your physical backup, you should also run cold backups when you have the opportunity. Because of the complexity of hot backups, it gives many DBAs (myself included) a warm fuzzy feeling to know that they have a fairly recent cold backup in their back pockets. You can never have enough backups.

USING LOGICAL BACKUPS

Oracle provides you with logical backups through the *EXP* facility (*IMP* is used for logical recovery). You can use *EXP* either entirely in batch mode, entirely interactively, or interactively with some keywords specified. Before getting into the operational aspect of *EXP*, look at the available keywords. Running *exp HELP=Y* shows all them, as seen in Listing 24.1.

LISTING 24.1   EXP KEYWORDS

```
oreo:./815/bin$ exp help=y
Keyword  Description (Default)          Keyword      Description (Default)
---------------------------------------------------------------------------
USERID    username/password            FULL         export entire file (N)
BUFFER    size of data buffer          OWNER        list of owner usernames
FILE      output file (EXPDAT.DMP)     TABLES       list of table names
COMPRESS import into one extent (Y)    RECORDLENGTH length of IO record
GRANTS    export grants (Y)            INCTYPE      incremental export type
INDEXES   export indexes (Y)          RECORD       track incr. export (Y)
ROWS      export data rows (Y)         PARFILE      parameter filename
CONSTRAINTS export constraints (Y)     CONSISTENT   cross-table consistency
LOG       log file of screen output    STATISTICS   analyze objects (ESTIMATE)
DIRECT    direct path (N)              TRIGGERS     export triggers (Y)
FEEDBACK display progress every x rows (0)
QUERY     select clause used to export a subset of a table
```

The keywords shown in listing 24.1 are explained in the following text.

USERID is the userID/password that *EXP* will use to log in to the database to perform the export. At the minimum, you must have the *CONNECT SESSION* privilege enabled to use *EXP*. If you intend to export another user's objects, you must have the *EXP_FULL_DATABASE* privilege. A DBA user, of course, can do anything.

Tip #44	You can use *EXP* with remote databases using the usual *USERID/PASSWORD@REMOTE_NAME* convention.

FULL specifies whether you are exporting the *entire* database. It defaults to *N*.

BUFFER is used to determine how many rows will be loaded into memory before committing to the export file. The default value is OS-dependent. The larger your buffer, generally the faster your export will run (and the more system memory will be used). You can compute the number of rows that will fit into the buffer as follows:

```
rows=buffer_size/maximum_row_size
```

If the table contains a *LONG* column, only one row will be in the buffer at one time.

OWNER lists the schemas you want to export. Use this keyword if you are exporting full schemas. If *ROWS=N*, only the SQL code needed to regenerate a schema will be exported—no table rows.

FILE is the name of the export file. You should use a filename that is reasonably descriptive of the data contained. In some OSs (UNIX in particular), you can export directly to a tape device. This is particularly useful for large database backups when you don't have enough disk space anywhere for the export file.

> **Caution**
>
> When you specify a filename for the *FILE* keyword, be aware that these files can be rather large, depending on what you are exporting. In OSs such as UNIX, you can export directly to tape, which eliminates this problem. If this is not an option, you will have to break up your export into small enough pieces to fit in either several different filesystems or in one location so that each piece can be moved off to tape before the next piece is created in a subsequent *EXP* run. You might want to run *EXP* during off hours to reduce the impact of a full filesystem.

TABLES lists individual tables you want to export. If *ROWS=N*, only the SQL code needed to regenerate the specified tables is exported; no rows are exported.

COMPRESS has many implications when it is time to import the data. *COMPRESS=Y* will cause *IMP* to construct the initial extent of a new object to be large enough to hold all the object's data. For instance, if a table has four extents and each one is 20MB in size, the initial extent of the new table will be approximately 80MB. If *COMPRESS=N*, the new table will have four 20MB extents, just as the original did.

> **Caution**
>
> Although *COMPRESS=Y* is very useful when you are trying to reorganize a table (to reduce the number of extents, thereby improving performance), you need to do some homework before using this option. Suppose you have a table, *ORDERS*, that has these extent sizes: 30MB, 100MB, 1000MB, 1500MB, 1500MB, and 1000MB. The total size of this table is a little more than 5GB. Now suppose your machine only has disk drives of 2GB and 4GB. The largest single extent your system could have is 4GB, yet Oracle expects to find a 5GB extent. The import process will not work because Oracle is unable to allocate a 5GB extent. Before using *COMPRESS=Y*, use the following SQL statement on each table you intend to export:
>
> ```
> SELECT SUM(BYTES) FROM DBA_EXTENTS WHERE SEGMENT_NAME=<table name>
> AND OWNER=<table owner>
> ```
>
> Using this statement helps make sure you can accommodate the table in a single extent.

RECORDLENGTH is used for moving export files to an Oracle database on another operation system. If you are moving from system A to system B, you must know what the record size is on system B. This information is found in the OS documentation supplied by Oracle.

GRANTS indicates to *EXP* whether to export *GRANTS* associated with objects being exported.

INCTYPE specifies a *COMPLETE*, *CUMULATIVE*, or *INCREMENTAL* backup. You must use a *USERID* with *EXP_FULL_DATABASE* because this option is only useful with *FULL=Y*. In most OLTP production environments, this capability is seldom used.

> **Note**
>
> A *CUMULATIVE* or *INCREMENTAL* export exports an entire table if it has changed. *EXP* does not just export changed rows. If you do choose to use this option, be sure you regularly perform a *COMPLETE* export to keep your baseline export current.

PART

V

CH

24

INDEXES indicates if you want to export the indexes on the tables being exported.

RECORD specifies whether Oracle keeps track of a *COMPLETE*, *CUMULATIVE*, or *INCREMENTAL* export. This is useful in the following case:

You normally run a *COMPLETE* on Sunday and *CUMULATIVE* exports on Monday through Friday. Tuesday night you plan to reload the test system with a *COMPLETE* export of the production system. If *RECORD=Y* when you exported the production system Tuesday night, Wednesday's *CUMULATIVE* export is based on Tuesday night's *COMPLETE* instead of Sunday's. Basically, *RECORD=N* is used if you are running an export on the database out of sequence with your normally scheduled exports.

ROWS indicates whether you want to export the data contained in the tables you are exporting. If *ROWS=N*, only the SQL code needed to re-create the table is exported.

PARFILE is the filename of a parameter file containing any valid keyword settings used for *EXP*. Here's an example of a parameter file:

```
TABLES=CUSTOMER,VEDOR
OWNER=SUSAN
COMPRESS=N
RECORD=N
```

As you can see, there's nothing fancy about a parameter file. It only has a keyword and value on each line. This is particularly useful if you have a standard export you need to run periodically because you don't need to worry about forgetting to set a keyword.

CONSTRAINTS indicates whether you want to export constraints associated with the objects you are exporting.

CONSISTENT is useful if you are exporting tables while they are also being updated. *CONSISTENT=Y* ensures that each table in the export is consistent to a single point in time. If *EXP* encounters an updated row while exporting a table, it uses the rollback information and exports the old version. If a new row is inserted, *EXP* ignores it. Do not use *CONSISTENT=Y* unless it is needed because *EXP* keeps a rollback segment during the entire export. Because this also places extra load on your database, it is an option best used during off hours.

If you encounter a Snapshot Too Old error, you probably need to run your export during a period of lighter system load. You might even need to run it with the database open in *RESTRICT* mode to keep users from updating the database during your export. You might also need to export while in *RESTRICT* mode if you need a consistent view of several tables. *CONSISTENT=Y* only provides read consistency on a per-table basis.

LOG is a filename where you want to save the export messages and errors. Normally, *EXP* just displays this information on your screen. However, because the information might race by too quickly for you to read, you probably want to save your *EXP* log output to file. All the messages and errors are shown on your screen, even when you specify a *LOG* filename.

Tip #45	If you are using a UNIX system, you can redirect the *EXP* screen output to */dev/null* if you would rather not see the messages fly by on your monitor. If *EXP* is displaying a large amount of information, it usually runs faster if you redirect the output to */dev/null*. This is because it is much faster for UNIX to simply throw away the information than send it to your screen.

STATISTICS specifies how statistics are generated when the exported file is imported. The options are *COMPUTE*, *ESTIMATE*, or *NONE*. If your export is large, setting *STATISTICS* to *ESTIMATE* or *NONE* saves you time (*NONE* saves the most). You can always use the *ANALYZE TABLE* command later to generate the statistical data.

DIRECT is a recent enhancement of *EXP*. It greatly improves exporting performance by reading the data blocks directly (rather than going through the normal database engine). Generally, if you have this option, you should use it! Your exports run *much* faster.

TRIGGERS indicates whether trigger PL/SQL code will be exported along with the table. The default is *Y*, which is probably best for most uses.

FEEDBACK is a recent addition to *EXP*. If you set *FEEDBACK=n* (where *n* is some positive integer) *EXP* display a period (.) for every *n* rows it exports. Setting *FEEDBACK=0* disables this feature.

QUERY was introduced with Oracle8i. It enables you to only export a subset of a table based on a *SELECT* clause. Refer to the Oracle utility reference manual for a complete description of this new keyword.

You can enter as many keywords as you want in any order on the command line. Use the following syntax:

```
exp [<keyword>=<value>[,<value>,…] [<keyword>=<value>[,<value>…] …]]
```

Generally, I prefer to use *EXP* entirely in batch mode because I can easily repeat the command, either unchanged or with minor modifications. If *EXP* needs more information than you provided on the command line, such as the userID/password, it prompts you to enter it. To run *EXP* entirely interactively with no keywords, just type in **exp**" at your system's command prompt. *EXP* prompts you for all the information it needs.

FULL LOGICAL BACKUPS

EXP is particularly well-suited for full logical database backups. The only requirements are that you must have the *EXP_FULL_DATABASE* privilege and you must have enough storage space for the export file. Here's an example of a full logical backup being written to the default output filename:

```
exp USERID=SYSTEM/MANAGER FULL=Y
```

The next example shows a full logical backup being saved directly to tape on a UNIX system:

```
exp USERID=SYSTEM/MANAGER FULL=Y FILE=/dev/rmt0
```

Having a recent full logical backup on hand gives a DBA a safety net of sorts if an object (user, table, index, and so on) is inadvertently dropped, corrupted, or changed. Although it does not bring your beloved object back to its state when it was dropped, you do at least have the object restored.

LOGICAL BACKUPS OF SPECIFIC USER SCHEMAS

EXP easily supports the backup of specific user schemas. Exporting a specific group of users will, by default, include the user definition, all tables, indexes, constraints, grants, and associated data. This is particularly useful if a user's *USERID* must change, or if a user is to be dropped and you simply want to keep a copy on hand. You can specify either a single user or a group of users. Here's an example of the command line needed to export the *TGASPER* schema to the standard output filename:

```
exp  USERID=SYSTEM/MANAGER OWNER=TGASPER
```

Now suppose you're cleaning up old user accounts and you'll be dropping the *JSMITH*, *JKLEIN*, *MJONES*, and *BGEORGE* accounts. Being the prudent DBA that you are, you never *really* delete anything. You're prepared if someone comes back to you next month and says, "I really, *really* need the *XYZ* table from the *JKLEIN* account. I know we asked you to delete that schema, but we're in a real pickle if we can't get the data from that table." This command shows exporting multiple user schemas to a UNIX tape device:

```
exp USERID=SYSTEM/MANAGER OWNER=JSMITH,JKLEIN,MJONES,BGEORGE FILE=/dev/rmt0
```

Now you're prepared.

PART

V

CH

24

Tip #46	Whenever you are exporting information to tape that will be subsequently deleted from the database, you might want to test the export tape before actually deleting the information from the database.

LOGICAL BACKUPS OF SPECIFIC TABLES

Exporting a set of tables is handled very much the same way that user exports are handled. You have the option of exporting a single table or a set of tables by listing the names of the tables with the *TABLES* keyword. The following example exports the *ABC* and *XYZ* tables from the *BGEORGE* schema to the default output file:

```
exp USERID=SYSTEM/NANAGER OWNER=BGEORGE TABLES=ABC,XYZ
```

Backing up specific tables is useful if you need to move specific tables between schemas in the same or different Oracle instances, for instance. You might also want to keep a logical backup of a table before dropping it from the system.

Tip #47	Whether you call it experience or paranoia, I'm always reluctant to really drop anything without first making a logical backup of it. Your environment might or might not call for such measures, but be aware that it is very time-consuming and difficult to restore a dropped object.

Note	*EXP* lacks some key capabilities that many DBAs familiar with other RDBMSs might find surprising. *EXP* does not enable you to export information based on a *SQL WHERE* clause. Rather, it only enables you to export full objects, full schemas, or the whole database. Oracle's export file is, practically speaking, a proprietary format. You do not have access to the raw text data or the SQL code used to regenerate a database, tables, grants, and so on. There are many third-party tools on the market that do provide these missing capabilities.

USING COLD PHYSICAL BACKUPS

Cold physical backups are the DBA's tool of choice for protecting the database system as a whole from all sorts of data-destroying demons. Regular cold backups, along with a good set of archived and current redo logs, enable you to recover to any point in time—even to the very last commit just before that disk drive bearing failed.

Prior to the advent of the Windows NT desktop environment, cold physical backups were performed almost entirely with OS-level utilities such as *tar* (UNIX). The only database interaction was shutting down the database and restarting it afterwards. In the UNIX world, this still holds true. Because Windows NT machines are not command-line–oriented, Oracle created a product called Backup Manager, which enables you to use a standard Windows NT GUI program to perform physical backup and recovery. Beginning in Oracle8, Oracle introduced a new backup and recovery system called Recovery Manager (or *RMAN*, for short). This system, although somewhat complex, can be used for virtually all backup and/or recovery needs.

> **Note**
>
> Do not confuse this Recovery Manager with Oracle's NT Recovery Manager; the names are very similar, but they are entirely different products.

Each backup system has a different set of peculiarities that, although ultimately performing the same function, is very different in its approach. The command-line and desktop backup methods each have their own subsection in the hot and cold physical backup sections. Because *RMAN* was designed to be a more singular physical backup tool, its use is covered in a later section entitled "Using Recovery Manager (*RMAN*) for Physical Backups."

Regardless of your environment or method, a cold physical backup should include the following elements of your database:

- Control files
- Data files
- Redo log files
- Archive log files

Command-Line–Driven Cold Physical Backups

UNIX DBAs might feel somewhat abandoned by Oracle because of its lack of GUI tools for administering functions such as backup and recovery. But if you do a little work perfecting some scripts, backup and recovery in the command-line world can be more flexible and trouble-free than is possible through Backup Manager.

A cold physical backup usually involves making a file-level copy of all the necessary database elements (configuration files, data files, control files, redo logs, and archive logs). Before starting your backup process, you need to make sure that your database can stay offline l ong enough to back it up completely. If you don't have enough time, you should consider hot backups.

The basic steps required to perform a cold backup are as follows:

1. Build a list of the OS-level files you'll need to back up.
2. Shut down the database with either *NORMAL* or *IMMEDIATE* options.
3. Perform the OS-level backup of the file list from Step 1.
4. Start up the database normally.

> **Caution**
>
> Do not back up the system after an abrupt shutdown. Only back up the database after it has been shut down using either *IMMEDIATE* or *NORMAL* mode.

In addition, when you have backed up your archive log files, you might remove them from the system (but be sure keep archive log files somewhere for a longer period of time). I generally like to keep the last seven days' worth of archive logs on the system. Assuming you back up your database every night, this ensures that you can still recover the database even if your backup has failed for the last seven days. Consider the Thanksgiving weekend. Most companies are closed Thursday through Sunday. If on Wednesday your backup script fails for some reason (or the backup drive simply decides to take the holiday off also), you might not know that anything has failed until Monday morning. Even if you have a 24/7 operations staff, they might not monitor the backups as closely as you do. By keeping the last seven days' worth of archive log files on the system, you can still recover the database if it failed sometime Monday afternoon.

Tip #48	For truly mission critical databases, it is important to keep archive logs at least as long as the time between either full *ANALYZE*s or exports of the database. The reason for this is if a bad block develops, you can recover the data file back to a known good point in time (when your last database analysis or export showed it to be completely valid) and use the archive logs to roll the system forward until the last commit. After you have run an *ANALYZE TABLE VALIDATE STRUCTURE* statement against all tables in the database without error, you can consider your database free of any bad blocks and older archive logs will not be needed to recover from bad blocks.

BUILDING YOUR FILENAME LIST

No matter how hard they try, DBAs never seem to be able to keep a solid handle on the full set of files that comprise their databases. This is unfortunate because a cold backup can be almost worthless if it is not a complete set of database files. Before you shut down the database, it might be worthwhile to just double-check everything to make sure you have a full list of the files you'll need to back up.

When the database is started, you are either explicitly or implicitly reading an *init<instance>.ora* file. You must back up this file. You should also take a look at this file to see if there is an *ifile* line, which basically tells Oracle to *include* another file while reading *init.ora*. If there is a filename listed for the *ifile* keyword, you must back up that file, also.

To generate a list of control files being used by the database, you can either look at the applicable *init.ora* file or run this SQL statement:

```
SELECT VALUE FROM v$PARAMETER WHERE NAME='control_files';
```

Oracle returns a comma-delimited listing of control files.

A listing of all database data files can be obtained with this SQL statement:

```
SELECT FILENAME FROM DBA_DATA_FILES;
```

Oracle returns a query result listing all the OS-level filenames used for tablespaces within the database.

If the database is shut down normally, the redo logs contain no information that Oracle needs. Technically, they do not need to be backed up for your cold backup to be useful—but you'd still have to create new ones during recovery, so you might want to back them up anyway. This SQL statement results in a listing of redo log files:

```
SELECT MEMBER FROM V$LOGFILE;
```

Archive logs are usually automatically written out by the archiver process to a single directory. The `log_archive_dest` keyword in the `init.ora` file is set to the destination directory where the archive logs will be written. You can also use this SQL statement to obtain the same information:

```
SELECT VALUE FROM V$PARAMETER WHERE NAME='log_archive_dest';
```

Tip #49	In a large database, keeping track of individual files can be very time-consuming and prone to error. Your best defense against both problems is a good organizational structure of files. When possible, use Oracle's OFA (Optical Flexible Architecture) guidelines for a consistent and easy to maintain file structure.
	With OFA organization, you can quickly identify all the critical pieces of a database that need to be backed up. OFA also has the benefit of helping the DBA make sure that control files, redo logs, and other redundant database components are mirrored on more than one physical device.

SHUTTING DOWN ORACLE

You don't need to do anything special here. Just shut down the database normally. Do not use *SHUTDOWN ABORT*. Use either *SHUTDOWN NORMAL* or *SHUTDOWN IMMEDIATE*.

PERFORMING THE BACKUP

Here's where the rubber meets the road. With the list of files you have either on hand or from Step 1 (Building Your Filename List), you're ready to back up the database. Using your OS-level tool of choice, you need to back up the files, in any order, to a backup device (usually tape).

For UNIX, the tools of choice tend to be *tar*, *cpio*, or *vdump*, with *tar* being the most universal.

Start up Oracle as you normally would.

Tip #50	Although cold backups tend to be time-consuming, you have several options to help reduce the time your database must be down.
	If you have lavish amounts of disk space, you can simply perform a file copy of the configuration files, data files, control files, redo logs, and archive logs to a temporary area on disk. Then you can start up your database again and then start the backup of the temporary area to tape. You'll need at least twice the amount of disk space needed for the database, but it will dramatically decrease the time needed to do your backup.
	Consider adding multiple tape units to your system. With many OSs, you can run multiple instances of the backup program at the same time. This enables you to back up several different areas of the database simultaneously. In practice, four tape drives will usually back up a database in one third the time it takes a single tape drive.

DESKTOP DRIVEN COLD BACKUPS

Remember when computers were completely text-driven, using arcane commands that made little sense? Just as the GUI interface has simplified word processing, spreadsheets, email, and even system administration, it has provided many useful capabilities to the DBA. Oracle's Backup Manager serves as a one-stop–shopping utility for Oracle backups. What used to be done with scripts and numerous OS-based utilities can now be done with a single program supplied and supported by Oracle. Figure 24.1 shows the versatile yet simple interface of the Backup Manager.

Figure 24.1
Oracle's Backup Manager for Windows NT has a simple GUI.

Backup Manager's interface is fairly simple to use. Please note that the Backup Manager window might be slightly different from what you see in Figure 24.1. It might only provide you with options that are applicable to the database state (running/not running, archive/noarchivelog mode).

The only work you need to do outside of this utility is to determine where to store your offline backup. Backup Manager will enable you to back up either to a directory on disk or to a tape drive. Notice that in the lower-left corner of Figure 24.1, Backup Manager tells you exactly how much space will be needed to back up the database. You'll need either a directory or a tape device with enough capacity for the backup function to work properly.

Performing a cold physical backup involves the following steps:

1. Be sure the database is up and running normally. (See the following Caution.)
2. Start Backup Manager.

3. Choose the Offline–Full Database option from the Select Backup Type Box.

4. Choose to back up either to disk or tape by selecting either Tape or Disk in the Destination box. If you back up to tape, you also need to indicate which tape device to use. Otherwise, you need to indicate which directory you would like to back up to.

5. Click on the Backup button. Backup Manager does the rest.

6. Restart the database.

Caution

Do not back up to the same physical devices that your database resides on.

Caution

Because cold backups are usually made while the database is offline, it might seem odd to make sure that the database is running in Step 1. This is because Backup Manager needs to access the database before it shuts it down for a backup so it can build a list of database files it needs to back up. Starting Backup Manager without the database running might result in an incomplete backup set.

PART

V

CH

24

Tip #51

Backup Manager will not perform an offline backup if there are open sessions (including Server Manager). If you have difficulty keeping sessions from opening in Oracle, you can open the database in `RESTRICT` mode before starting Backup Manager. Don't forget to close your Server Manager session!

Backup Manager does not back up the `init.ora`, `config.ora`, or `archive log` files. Although these files would typically be backed up during normal OS backup procedures, you should double-check with the system administrator to ensure that these very important files are backed up regularly.

USING HOT PHYSICAL BACKUPS

The databases DBAs are entrusted with maintaining can often be the lifeblood of a company. They are sometimes called on to be available 24 hours a day, 7 days a week. In this environment, nothing short of an industrial strength RDBMS will suffice. Oracle is such a database, with a track record spanning many years and many different environments.

Hot backups require you to have a higher level of expertise and comfort level with both Oracle and the supporting OS. Because of the added complexity of hot backups, you must also invest more time and effort in testing your backup strategy. No hot backup system should be considered reliable until you have recovered from a multitude of failures *on a test system*. Before embarking on a hot backup project, be sure that the added availability time is worth the additional costs and headaches.

Before continuing, you should make sure you're familiar with cold backups. You'll be building on the topics discussed in the previous section when discussing hot backups. In particular, this section takes your knowledge of cold backups and adds the complexity of backing up your database while it is up and running. Oracle provides two hot backup methods, one for the command-line UNIX world and one for the desktop (Windows) world. Because of this, hot backups are discussed for each method separately.

UNDERSTANDING THE REASONING

A very common question from system administrators and DBAs alike is "Why are hot back-ups such a big deal? We back up the OS with users on it without any problems, so we can just back up Oracle data files with users on the system. Right?" Wrong. Explaining the complexities of hot backups requires a brief discussion of how Oracle stores information and changes.

Recall that Oracle's atomic storage unit is the *block* (that's size is configurable when the database is created). There is data in the block, along with a block header that stores information about the data contained therein.

As a normal cold backup proceeds, each data file is copied bit-by-bit to the backup device. If the database is online, your trouble spot is the case in which both the backup program and Oracle are working on the same block. Suppose the backup program has just finished backing up the header portion of a particular block when Oracle writes new data and updates the header. After the backup finishes backing up the block in question, it has an old header with new data. It has a corrupt block that Oracle does not know what to do with.

Oracle's solution is to implement a special mode, known as *backup* mode, that is enabled and disabled on a tablespace-by-tablespace basis. When it's enabled and Oracle updates a block, an entire copy of the changed block is written to the redo logs. This is in contrast to Oracle's normal procedure of just writing the specific changes to the redo logs.

An online backup of the Oracle data files will still have the corrupt data blocks, but valid copies exist in the redo logs (and ultimately in the archive logs). In a recovery situation, a data file is restored and Oracle uses the redo/archive logs to "patch" the data files with valid blocks. Thus, the end result is a valid and consistent database. This system is illustrated in Figure 24.2.

Figure 24.2
Oracle's backup mode enables the patching of possibly corrupted data blocks during recovery.

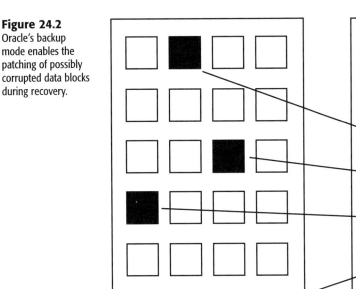

Backup Begins

Backup Ends

COMMAND-LINE–DRIVEN HOT PHYSICAL BACKUPS

Hot backups in the command-line–based UNIX world are usually accomplished through a combination of SQL and OS-based scripts. The specifics vary from OS to OS, but here's the sequence of operations:

1. Build a list of tablespaces to be backed up.
2. For each tablespace in that list, do the following:
   a. Build a list of data files.
   b. Place the tablespace in backup mode.
   c. Back up data files in the list from Step 2a to a backup device.
   d. Take the tablespace out of backup mode.
3. Use Oracle to produce a "backupable" control file.
4. Back up the control file from Step 3 to a backup device.
5. Force a log switch.
6. Wait for the redo log to be archived.
7. Back up the archive log directory to a backup device.

Building a List of Tablespaces

A simple SQL statement will generate a list of tablespaces in an Oracle database:

```
SELECT TABLESPACE_NAME FROM DBA_TABLESPACES;
```

Building a List of Data Files for a Tablespace

You'll need a list of data files for the tablespace so you know exactly which files to back up:

```
SELECT FILE_NAME FROM DBA_DATA_FILES WHERE TABLESPACE_NAME='<tablespace name>';
```

Placing Tablespaces in Backup Mode

Before backing up a tablespace's data files, it needs to be placed in backup mode using the following SQL statement:

```
ALTER TABLESPACE <tablespace name> BEGIN BACKUP;
```

Backing Up Data Files to Backup Device

This is largely an OS issue. You would be wise to use SQL*Plus to generate a list of files that should be backed up for each tablespace. The CD-ROM included with this book has a working script for UNIX that illustrates this procedure.

Taking Tablespaces Out of Backup Mode

Just as you used the SQL statement to place the tablespace in backup mode, you'll use a similar statement to take it out of backup mode:

```
ALTER TABLESPACE <tablespace name> END BACKUP;
```

Generating a "Backupable Control File"

Because having an Oracle instance running necessarily means that the control files are open and prone to updates at any time, you need Oracle to produce a copy of the control files that is guaranteed to be consistent and will not be updated. The following SQL statement will do just this:

```
ALTER DATABASE BACKUP CONTROL FILE TO <output filename> REUSE;
```

<output filename> should be any valid filename that specifies where you would like the control file copy to be written. *REUSE* just means that if the file already exists, it should be written over instead of aborting.

Forcing a Log Switch

Oracle marks in the redo logs when a backup on a tablespace begins and ends. Because you do not back up redo logs, you need to archive the current redo log (which has the "end of backup" marker in it for the tablespace you just backed up). That way, when you back up the archive log directory, you'll also be backing up the logs with "begin backup" and "end backup" for each tablespace. The log switch is accomplished as follows:

```
ALTER SYSTEM SWITCH LOGFILE;
```

WAITING FOR THE SWITCHED REDO LOG TO BE ARCHIVED

Normally when a log switch occurs, Oracle's archiver process immediately copies the current redo log to the archive log directory. This takes time, and Oracle does not tell you when the redo log has been successfully archived. Generally, a fixed delay of two to five minutes is placed in the backup script, which should be long enough under most conditions. However, if your redo logs are particularly large or you archive to a slow medium (such as optical disc), you should make sure that your delay gives Oracle plenty of time to archive a redo log.

BACKING UP THE ARCHIVE LOG DIRECTORY TO A BACKUP DEVICE

Just as you did in the cold backup section, you need to back up the directory containing the archive logs to a backup device.

<table>
<tr><td>Tip #52</td><td>Because Oracle writes a full block to the redo logs for each write operation instead of just the changed information, the redo logs fill up much faster when tablespaces are in the backup mode. You should try to schedule your online backups when there is the least activity on your database. Pay particular attention to scheduled batch jobs. They tend to be very write-intensive and can easily be overlooked because they are often run by automatic schedulers.</td></tr>
</table>

PART

V

CH

24

DESKTOP-DRIVEN HOT PHYSICAL BACKUPS

DBAs supporting Oracle in a Windows NT environment will find hot backups to be much easier than their command-line counterparts. Again, you'll use Oracle's Backup Manager to perform the actual backups. When you start Backup Manager while the database is running, a window similar to that in Figure 24.3 is displayed.

Figure 24.3
Backup Manager can be used for performing hot backups.

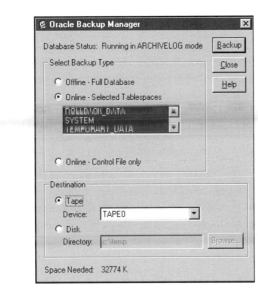

You need to decide where to place your backup of the database. You can either back up to a directory on disk or to a tape drive. Fortunately, Backup Manager indicates how much space will be needed to back up the database in the manner you have selected. This information will help you decide where to back up the database. Follow these steps to perform an online backup of your database:

1. Make sure your Oracle database is running normally.

2. Start Backup Manager.

3. Choose the Online–Selected Tablespaces option in the Select Backup Type box.

4. Select the tablespaces you want to back up. For a full backup, you must select all the tablespaces. After you have done this, the amount of space needed to back up the selected tablespaces will appear in the lower-left corner.

5. In the Destination box, choose whether to back up to tape or disk. If you choose to back up to disk, also supply the name of the directory where you want the database backup to be stored.

6. Click on the Backup button.

7. When the backup finishes, choose the Online–Control File Only option in the Select Backup Type box.

8. In the Destination box, choose the Disk Directory option and supply a directory name where you want to store the control file backup. Although you *could* back up to tape, the small size of control files usually does not make this a worthwhile option.

After this procedure completes, your database has been successfully backed up. Backup Manager has finished backing up your database and has taken all tablespaces out of *BACKUP* mode.

> **Caution**
>
> Backup Manager does not back up the `init.ora`, `config.ora`, or `archive log` files used to start your database. Although these files would typically be backed up during normal OS backup procedures, you should double-check with the system administrator to ensure that these very important files are backed up regularly.

USING RECOVERY MANAGER (RMAN) FOR PHYSICAL BACKUPS

Oracle8's introduction of Recovery Manager (*RMAN*) is most likely the beginning of a completely new way of performing backups on Oracle databases. It offers all the hot and cold backup capabilities from within both command-line and GUI user interfaces. *RMAN* works with both disk and tape backup media and offers the following advantages over traditional OS-based physical backup methods:

- Hot backups do not incur the redo log generation rates normally associated with traditional *BEGIN/END* backup methodologies.

- Database blocks are checked for corruption as an integral part of the backup process. This can often eliminate the need for frequent *ANALYZE TABLE VALIDATE STRUCTURE* statements against the entire database.

- Incremental physical backups are supported.

- Multi-threaded backups are supported (Enterprise edition only).

- *RMAN* offers an integral cataloging system that can help minimize confusion when trying to identify needed backup tapes.

RMAN clearly offers many advantages over traditional backup methods. Many users, however, shy away from its use for the following reasons:

- Although Oracle has gone to great lengths to make *RMAN* as straightforward as possible, the degree of flexibility it must provide also can make it a bit cumbersome to work with for simple backup needs.

- Being a newer product that has the potential to lose valuable data, some organizations might want to use it only in more limited and less critical systems before relying on it totally.

- Backups are not something to be changed without extensive testing; organizations with solidly written existing scripts might be reluctant to embrace a new and relatively young backup system until its advantages outweigh the initial implementation costs.

The use of *RMAN* can nearly occupy a book by itself. In this section, you will be introduced to a basic full system backup process. For further information, refer to Oracle's "Recovery Manager Concepts" chapter in the Oracle8 Backup and Recovery Guide. The examples shown will use the command-line version of *RMAN*. The GUI version is accessible via Enterprise Manager's Backup Manager software.

Before using Recovery Manager, it is necessary to establish a recovery catalog on a database other than the one that is to be backed up. The reason for having the recovery catalog on a different database (and, hopefully, a different node) is to make sure that the catalog is available when the cataloged database is not (such as when recovering from media failure). If you have more than one database node, Mars and Venus, for example, you might want to use Mars's database to hold Venus's catalog and vice versa.

| Caution | Although *RMAN* does not require the use of a catalog, it is highly recommended that one be used. |

RMAN typically requires two command-line arguments to be issued (see the sample *RMAN* session in this section for examples of these arguments' use):

■ *TARGET* specifies a *userID/password[@dbname* that has administrative authority on the database *RMAN* is to be used on.

■ *RCVCAT* specifies a *userID/password@dbname* that is used to store the recovery catalog for the target database. This should always be on a different database (and host, if possible) than the target database.

Using Recovery Manager for the first time requires the following initial steps be taken:

1. Choose a database on which to store the recovery catalog.

2. On the database chosen in Step 1, create a user *RMAN* with your choice of password. *GRANT CONNECT* and *RESOURCE* to *RMAN*. Make sure to choose an appropriate default and temporary tablespace.

3. Log in to the catalog database as *RMAN* and run the *CATRMAN.SQL* script found in the same directory as *CATALOG.SQL* and *CATPROC.SQL*.

4. You must register the database to be backed up in the catalog as shown in the following example.

```
[tgasper@oreo tgasper]$ rman target=sys/manager rcvcat=rman/rman@remote_db

Recovery Manager: Release 8.0.5.0.0 - Production

RMAN-06005: connected to target database: TST8
RMAN-06008: connected to recovery catalog database

RMAN> register database;
RMAN-03022: compiling command: register
RMAN-03023: executing command: register
RMAN-08006: database registered in recovery catalog
RMAN-03023: executing command: full resync
RMAN-08029: snapshot controlfile name set to default value: ?/dbs/snapcf_@.f
RMAN-08002: starting full resync of recovery catalog
RMAN-08004: full resync complete
RMAN> exit;
```

You are now ready to use *RMAN* to backup your database. The following example shown from within *RMAN* will perform a cold database backup if the database is not open (it must, however, be mounted) and a hot backup if the database is open. Hot backups, as with the traditional backups, can only be done on database systems running in *ARCHIVELOG* mode.

```
RMAN> run {
2> allocate channel c1 type disk;
3> backup full filesperset 3
4> (database format 'rm_%p%d.%s');
5> }

RMAN-03022: compiling command: allocate
RMAN-03023: executing command: allocate
RMAN-08030: allocatedRMAN-08500: channel c1: sid=13 devtype=DISK
```

```
RMAN-03022: compiling command: backup
RMAN-03023: executing command: backup
RMAN-08008: channel c1: starting datafile backupset
RMAN-08502: set_count=3 set_stamp=362111548
RMAN-08010: channel c1: including datafile 1 in backupset
RMAN-08011: channel c1: including current controlfile in backupset
RMAN-08010: channel c1: including datafile 2 in backupset
RMAN-08013: channel c1: piece 1 created
RMAN-08503: piece handle=rm_1TST8.3 comment=NONE
RMAN-08008: channel c1: starting datafile backupset
RMAN-08502: set_count=4 set_stamp=362111606
RMAN-08010: channel c1: including datafile 4 in backupset
RMAN-08010: channel c1: including datafile 3 in backupset
RMAN-08013: channel c1: piece 1 created
RMAN-08503: piece handle=rm_1TST8.4 comment=NONE
RMAN-03023: executing command: partial resync
RMAN-08003: starting partial resync of recovery catalog
RMAN-08005: partial resync complete
RMAN-08031: released channel: c1

RMAN> exit;
```

RESTORING FROM LOGICAL BACKUPS

When you created logical backups, you used the *EXP* utility supplied by Oracle. Because the export is in a proprietary format, there is only one (official) complimentary utility, *IMP*. Despite the name, *IMP* will not import data from other systems. The appropriate utility for this is SQL*Loader.

IMP follows the same syntax as *EXP*, and many of the options are identical. Listing 24.2 shows the output of *IMP HELP=Y*.

LISTING 24.2 IMP HELP=Y OUTPUT

Keyword	Description (Default)	Keyword	Description (Default)
USERID	username/password	FULL	import entire file (N)
BUFFER	size of data buffer	FROMUSER	list of owner usernames
FILE	output file (EXPDAT.DMP)	TOUSER	list of usernames
SHOW	just list file contents (N)	TABLES	list of table names
IGNORE	ignore create errors (N)	RECORDLENGTH	length of IO record
GRANTS	import grants (Y)	INCTYPE	incremental import type
INDEXES	import indexes (Y)	COMMIT	commit array insert (N)
ROWS	import data rows (Y)	PARFILE	parameter filename
LOG	log file of screen output		
DESTROY	overwrite tablespace data file (N)		
INDEXFILE write table/index info to specified file			
FEEDBACK display progress every x rows(0)			

The common keywords that can be used in conjunction with the *IMP* program are as described in the following text.

USERID is the userID/password that *IMP* uses to log in to the database to perform the import. At the minimum, you must have the *CONNECT SESSION* privilege enabled to use *IMP*. If your export file is a full export, you must have the *IMP_FULL_DATABASE* privilege to import it. A DBA user can do anything, of course.

Tip #53	You can use *IMP* with remote databases using the usual *USERID*/*PASSWORD@REMOTE_NAME* convention.

FULL specifies whether you are importing the *entire* database. It defaults to *N*.

Tip #54	You can always choose *FULL=N* when working with an export file that was exported with *FULL=Y*.

BUFFER is used to determine how many rows will be loaded into memory before writing to the database. The default value is OS-dependent. The larger your buffer, generally the faster your import will run (and the more system memory that will be used). You can compute the number of rows that will fit into the buffer as follows:

```
rows=buffer_size/maximum_row_size
```

If the table contains a *LONG* column, only one row will be in the buffer at one time.

FROMUSER defines the names of the source schemas in the export file. Unless you are also using the *TOUSER* keyword, the objects will be imported into identically named schemas in the database. If a schema named in *FROMUSER* does not exist (and no *TOUSER* was specified), objects will be imported into the *USERID* schema running *IMP*.

FILE is the name of the export file (or of the tape device).

TOUSER is the name of an existing user schema in the database into which the database objects can be loaded. This keyword compliments the *FROMUSER* keyword. Generally, this is used for importing objects into schemas named differently from the schemas that were exported.

SHOW, when set to *Y*, displays the contents of the export file; nothing is actually committed to the database.

TABLES is a list of one or more tables that should be imported. If this omitted, all tables are imported.

IGNORE, set to *Y*, enables the export to just continue if an object cannot be created. This is useful if you are importing rows into a table that already exists.

Tip #55	If you intend to import into preexisting tables with constraints, you might want to temporarily disable them because data might be loaded into tables in any order. When the backup is finished, you can re-enable the constraints.

RECORDLENGTH is used for moving export files to an Oracle database on another operation system. Basically, if you are moving from system A to system B, you must know what the record size is on system B. This information is found in the OS documentation supplied by Oracle.

GRANTS determines if permission settings are imported with objects.

INCTYPE accepts either *RESTORE* or *SYSTEM* as input. *SYSTEM* imports the system's objects (that is, *only SYSTEM* schema objects) from the last incremental export file. *RESTORE* imports user objects that have changed since the last time you ran an export.

INDEXES indicates if indexes for imported tables should also be imported.

COMMIT indicates if *IMP* should make multiple commits while importing each table. If *COMMIT=N*, a single commit occurs after each table is loaded. *COMMIT=Y* reduces the chance that rollbacks will overflow. The advantage to *COMMIT=N* is that if the import fails on a particular table, a rollback will occur that will completely empty the table. This is desirable because it returns the table to the state it was in before the import, thereby making it easy to restart the import without risk of duplicate records.

ROWS determines if the rows of imported tables are also loaded. Setting *ROWS=N* is useful if all you want to do is move a schema definition with no data in the tables.

PARFILE is used identically with *IMP* as it is with *EXP*.

LOG is used to log all output normally sent to the terminal to a file. Provide a standard file-name where you want the output to be logged. Using this option will not prevent output from being displayed to the screen.

DESTROY is valid when a full export is being imported. When a new tablespace is created, *DESTROY=Y* effectively enables any existing data files to be overwritten. This is useful if you are replacing an instance entirely. However, if you are creating a duplicate copy of a database on the same machine, you want to use *DESTROY=N*. You don't want to destroy your original database! In this case, you create all the necessary tablespaces manually and then perform the import.

INDEXFILE is the name of a file where the SQL code that's needed to create the indexes in the export file is written. When it's used, no changes to the database are performed. This is useful if you want to change the initial or next extent values in your new system. If you will be manually creating indexes from this output, be sure to import with *INDEXES=N* to prevent them from automatically being created.

Just as with *EXP*, you can supply as many keywords as you want with *IMP*. If *IMP* needs more information than you provided, it will prompt you for it. To run fully interactively, just type **imp** on the command line.

You will either be performing a full import or a partial import. The former completely re-creates a database on a target instance. Obviously your export file must have all the information in it that you'll need to import. You can always import a subset of the data in an export file. These two different modes will be covered separately in the following sections.

Fully Restoring from a Logical Backup

A full logical restore is typically used to re-create a copy of an existing system on either the same machine or a different machine. Because export files are platform-independent, they are the tool of choice for this operation. Export files are also fairly version-independent. In fact, a logical backup/restore is often recommended when you are upgrading Oracle versions.

The only requirement for a successful restore is that a database instance exists. All tablespaces, users, profiles, tables, indexes, and so on will be re-created with *IMP*.

Tip #56	Enabling *IMP* to create tablespaces could present a serious problem. The tablespaces will be re-created with identically named data files (including their paths). You might want to have the same tablespaces on different databases, but you will also likely need to have different data file filenames, have them located in different directories, or make them different sizes, or a different platform might not be able to use the same filename format at all. In these cases, you want to manually create tablespaces on the target system. This SQL statement gives you some guidance with each tablespace name and its size (in bytes): `SELECT TABLESPACE_NAME,SUM(BYTES) FROM DBA_DATA_FILES GROUP BY TABLESPACE_NAME;`

The following SQL statement will help you decide on tablespace sizes. It indicates the amount of space (bytes) in each tablespace that has not been allocated to a segment (table, index, and so on):

`SELECT TABLESPACE_NAME,SUM(BYTES) FROM DBA_FREE_SPACE GROUP BY TABLESPACE_NAME;`

Caution	If you are copying one instance into another on the same machine, you *must* manually create tablespaces on the target instance. If you don't, *IMP* might destroy the data files in your original database instance when it tries to create tablespaces in the target instance.

The syntax of a typical full logical restore is fairly simple. The following is an example:

`imp USERID=SYSTEM/MANAGER FULL=Y IGNORE=Y FILE=<export filename>`

Here, you're assuming that an instance is already running and that the appropriate tablespaces already exist.

Partial Restores with Logical Backups

In most cases, you will be using the *IMP* utility to restore a particular set of objects (or user schemas) to your database. You should have the appropriate tablespaces, rollback segments, and users set up before attempting to use *IMP* to restore a portion of the database. Keep in mind that if a tablespace does not exist or cannot hold the object being imported, it will be loaded into the user's default tablespace. Also, when importing, if a *FROMUSER* listed user does not exist on the current database, the user specified in *USERID* will be used to store the objects.

EXAMPLE 1

Recall the scenarios that were proposed when demonstrating why a DBA should use logical backups. After each brief recount, the *IMP* command line needed to restore the objects/schemas in question will be shown.

Suppose you need to rename the user *SKLEIN* to *SJONES*. You already exported the original user schema to a file. The new userID *SJONES* has been created, and you are ready to restore the objects from the old schema to the new:

```
imp USERID=SYSTEM/MANAGER FILE=SKLEIN2SJONES.DMP FROMUSER=SKLEIN TOUSER=SJONES
```

EXAMPLE 2

You were asked last week to drop the user *TGASPER* from the database. You did so after running a *FULL=Y* export of the database (after hours, of course). Now marketing needs to look at the tables that were in the *TGASPER* schema. You have just re-created the *TGASPER* schema and are ready to import the objects:

```
imp USERID=SYSTEM/MANAGER FILE=/dev/rmt0 FROMUSER=TGASPER
```

EXAMPLE 3

A common application uses tables in the APAS schema for its configuration information. Last month, version 2.3 was upgraded to version 3.0. At that time, the tables *STACONF* and *USRCONF* were no longer needed. Being the shrewd DBA that you are, you exported those tables before dropping them. Version 3.01 just came out and—you guessed it—they need the *USRCONF* table back:

```
imp USERID=SYSTEM/MANAGER FILE=table_STACONF.dmp TABLE
```

Without a doubt, you will have to deal with far more complex import/export issues. Hopefully, you have a fairly good idea what to expect from *EXP* and *IMP*. If at all possible, always try out your imports on a test instance before attempting them on the production system—especially if you use *IGNORE=Y*. You could conceivably damage a database table beyond repair with an incorrect import. Remember that you're paying for Oracle's support program. Be sure to use it in dealing with import/recovery issues if you have any doubts.

USING PHYSICAL RECOVERY

Many DBAs would agree that physical recovery can be the most stressful and difficult part of their jobs. Like physical backups, a good portion of recovery has traditionally been OS-centric. Both the Windows NT Recovery Manager and Recovery Manager (*RMAN*) can replace much of the OS portion of the recovery process. No matter which platform you use, most of the same issues and sequences apply. Physical recovery can encompass far more than this book can cover. There are generally four situations in which performing physical recovery is required:

- You need to make a copy of the current database on another system (using the same version of the OS and Oracle). (Note: This could also be done with a logical backup/restore using the *FULL=Y* keyword.)

- You need to restore the database or any portion of it in case a disk upgrade or change in filesystem partitioning occurs.

- One or more data files has been damaged or lost.

- You need to restore the database to a previous state.

The first two situations are really the same procedure: You need to restore missing files (maybe all them) from a cold backup. In effect, you're physically re-creating the database. This topic is covered in this chapter's "Physically Re-creating a Database" section.

Recovering from lost data files is an issue you face when a disk drive fails, data files are accidentally deleted, or you are unable to access data for whatever reason. Because you don't want to lose any data, you will use a *complete recovery*.

Restoring to some point in the past is also a form of complete recovery, except that you must take a "one step forward and two steps back" approach. This is known as an *incomplete recovery*.

Tip #57	If you are working on your production system and need to perform any type of recovery, you should always, if possible, shut down the database and make a cold backup of everything before you even think about recovering the database. This is just in case something goes wrong, and you end up with a completely ruined database. Furthermore, a good rule of thumb is to try a recovery. If it fails, call Oracle. DBAs can quickly get themselves way in over their heads by experimenting with recovery techniques.

PHYSICALLY RE-CREATING A DATABASE

DBAs often need to create an exact duplicate of a database on another machine. As part of general maintenance, it is not unusual to upgrade database disk drives or to rebuild the file systems containing database files. In either case, you need to "take a picture" of the system (in other words, do a cold backup). You then either copy all the files to another machine or restore them to the same machine when the system administrators finish their maintenance work.

Tip #58	If physical restores are being used to create another copy of an existing system, keep in mind that the database name itself will not change even if the SID changes. Refer to Oracle note 15390.1 or Oracle Support for assistance in changing the database name of an existing database.

All you need to do is restore the cold backup to either the original machine (when the mainte-nance is finished) or a new machine, and then start the database. Remember that all your data, redo logs, archive logs, and control files should go into exactly the same directory location where they were originally. Because of the cold backup/restore, Oracle will wake up in it's new environment unaware that anything has happened since it was shutdown. Therefore, it will expect to find all the components where they were before.

Tip #59	If you need to change the location of a few files, use the *ALTER DATABASE RENAME FILE* statement described in the section "Renaming and Moving Database Files." If you need to change the location of many database files, it is usually best to create a script to do the job or use a logical backup and recovery. It is very tedious and error-prone to change the location of many database files one at a time in Server Manager.

PART

V

CH

24

On a command-line system, the recovery is completely OS-based. You need to restore all the following database files:

- *init<instance>.ora*
- *config<instance>.ora*
- Redo logs
- Control files
- Data files
- Archived redo logs

You will restore these files using whatever backup/restore utilities are available on your machine.

If you only lost a few files during maintenance, you can restore just the lost files *provided that you have not restored the database after your cold backup*. After you have all the files are in place, start the database through Server Manager.

In the Windows NT environment, Oracle provides NT Recovery Manager to restore the data files. Before running NT Recovery Manager, make sure the appropriate *init<instance>.ora* file exists. Remember to put it on the same drive letter and directory path where it was originally.

When you start NT Recovery Manager, you see a window similar to Figure 24.4.

Figure 24.4
Oracle's NT Recovery Manager provides a convenient GUI interface for recovering databases.

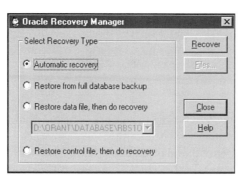

To restore the database, complete the following steps:

1. Select Restore from full database backup option.

2. Click on the Recover button.

3. NT Recovery Manager now needs to know where to find the backup files (generated by Oracle Backup Manager). Enter the name of the directory where the backup files are located, or select the tape device where the backup tape has been mounted.

4. If you are recovering from disk, make sure <latest backup> is indicated in the Backup: field.

5. Click OK. The restore will now commence.

6. Start the database.

Tip #60

If you are using Oracle in a Windows NT environment and find the GUI utilities do not offer a particular recovery option, remember you still have nearly all the command-line recovery-oriented tools available to UNIX DBAs.

COMPLETE RECOVERY

Complete recovery will bring your databases back to life without losing any transactions if a data file is lost. Complete recoveries use the redo and archive log files to prevent the loss of data if a data file is lost or damaged. It is imperative that control files, redo logs, and archive logs do not reside on the same physical disk as data files. Losing archive logs or redo logs as well as data files will prevent you from recovering without data loss (this is known as an *incomplete recovery*).

The idea of a complete recovery is to restore an older (and valid) copy of a lost data file from a warm or cold backup and then reapply all the changes that have occurred since the restored data file was backed up. *Rolling forward*, a technique used by many RDBMSs (including Oracle) to provide complete recovery, means "replaying" the actions contained in the redo and archive logs. Oracle keeps a master odometer, known as a *sequence number*, recorded in both data files and control files. By looking at the control files, Oracle knows what sequence number all the data files should have recorded. If a particular data file does not contain the current sequence number, Oracle knows that it is not current and is in need of recovery before the database can open.

By looking at the sequence number in a data file in need of recovery, Oracle knows where it needs to begin replaying transactions. Oracle will expect to find at least one set of current redo logs, as well as all the archive log files it will need in the archive log directory (set in the *init<sid>.ora* file). Therefore, you should only delete files from the archive log directory that were recorded before the beginning of the last backup. If you're missing any archive logs or you've lost all copies of your redo logs, you might have to perform an incomplete recovery—you won't be able to recover to the last commit.

Tip #61	If you happen to have archive log files in several different directories, Oracle will prompt you when it cannot find a particular archive log file in the default directory (if you are using command line recovery). At this point, you will be able to supply the complete path to where the archive log file in question can be found.

When you have experienced the loss of a data file, you need to shut down the database (if it hasn't shut itself down). If necessary, use *SHUTDOWN ABORT*. If you have experienced a hardware failure, you'll need to fix the problem before continuing.

COMMAND-LINE ENVIRONMENTS

Now that the OS is back up and running, inspect the damage. When you know which data files were lost, you (or the system administrator) should restore them to the same location where they were originally. Do not recover any redo logs or control files from a backup, even if some were lost.

If you lost a control file, you can replace it by just making a copy of a current control file. All the control files are listed in the *init<sid>.ora* file for your instance.

Oracle will use the copies of redo logs that still exist in different locations on the system to compensate for the lost redo log(s). You'll recover lost redo log files after the data files are fixed.

Before continuing, double-check that you have all the archive logs since the last backup was started. They should all be in the archive log directory (or at least on the system in one or more other directories). Now you're ready to roll forward the old data files to the last commit:

1. Start Server Manager.

2. Start up the database just as you normally would.

3. When the database tries to open, Oracle will discover that one or more of the data files have an outdated sequence number. Oracle will stop and wait for you to recover the database. You should now type in the following:
   ```
   RECOVER AUTOMATIC DATABASE;
   ```

4. When the recovery is complete, the outdated data files will have been rolled forward.

5. Shut down the database normally. If you lost a redo log file, you can replace it with a current and valid copy of a redo log file from the same group number. By querying *V$LOG*, you can determine what files are in the same redo log group.

6. Make a cold backup of the database.

7. Start up the database normally.

WINDOWS NT ENVIRONMENTS

This procedure describes the same recovery procedure as described in the preceding section for the Windows NT OS. Although you can recover a Windows NT Oracle database using the same command-line utilities described in the preceding section, it is much easier and more straightforward to use Oracle's GUI tools.

You need to identify which files were lost. Keeping a list of all data files on the database is helpful when you're completely recovering a database with NT Recovery Manager. Whenever you add a data file to the database, NT Recovery Manager should be started and then closed. NT Recovery Manager builds a list of data files, control files, and redo logs every time it is started and the database is running. By doing this, you can browse through NT Recovery Manager's list of data files to determine which files are lost or damaged. You should still keep a paper copy of the data files in your NT-based Oracle instances.

In the Windows NT environment, Oracle's NT Recovery Manager takes care of almost everything related to a complete recovery (assuming all goes well). Before starting, you should double-check that you have all the archive logs since the beginning of the last backup. These files should all be in the archive log directory specified in the *init<instance>.ora* or *config<instance>.ora* file. If you backed up your database to disk, you need to make sure the backup files are online. Otherwise you need to have the backup tape handy.

Follow these steps to recover your Windows NT Oracle database:

1. Try to start up Oracle normally through Server Manager. It will fail, but this is to be expected because of the missing or damaged files.

2. Start Oracle NT Recovery Manager.

3. Choose the Restore data file, and then do the recovery option.

4. Click on the Files button. A window similar to the one in Figure 24.5 should now appear.

5. Click the Control Files radio button.

6. Remove any control files listed by clicking each control file filename and then the Remove button.

7. Click the Log Files button.

8. Remove any redo log files listed by clicking the filename of each redo log file and then the Remove button.

9. Click the Data Files radio button.

10. Remove any data files listed that *do not* need recovery. The only files listed should be those that are missing or damaged.

11. Click OK.

12. Click Recover.

13. Select where your database backup can be found. Choose either Restore from tape or Restore from disk. If you choose a disk location, be sure that the directory shown in the Directory field is where your backup files are and that <latest backup> is shown in the Backup: field.

14. Click OK.

15. NT Recovery Manager might issue some warnings about shutting down the database while another session is open. Just click OK on any that pop up.

16. Start up the database normally.

Figure 24.5
Select database files
to recover with NT
Recovery Manager.

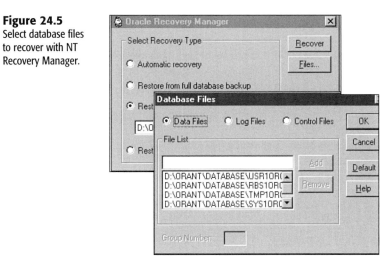

NT Recovery Manager will automatically roll forward the data files from the last backup using the redo and archive logs. If you need to recover any missing redo log files, complete the following steps:

1. Shut down the database.

2. Replace the missing redo log file by copying a file from the same group number.

3. Restart the database.

If you need to recover any missing control files, complete the following steps:

1. Shut down the database.
2. Replace the missing control log file with a copy of one of the current control files.
3. Restart the database.

RECOVERY MANAGER (RMAN)

Recovery Manager can offer a complete environment from which to perform physical database recovery. Because Recovery Manager maintains a backup catalog, it can track precisely what backup sets are needed for a given recovery scenario. Recovery Manager can virtually eliminate the OS-level work previously needed to recover a database. Recovery Manager offers many restore/recovery options including the following:

- Full database or tablespace point in time recovery
- Individual data file recovery
- Individual tablespace recovery
- Restoration of data files to different locations
- Complete restores of a database

As with backups, Recovery Manager offers a wide array of restore/recovery options that are beyond the scope of this section. Please refer to Oracle's Backup and Recovery Guide for a complete description of Recovery Manager's capabilities.

> **Note**
>
> Remember that for *RMAN* to be able to recover a database, it *must* be started in *NOMOUNT* mode. This differs from most other recovery systems that either enable or require the database to be completely offline.

EXAMPLE   In the following example, you have a UNIX system that has just crashed and in the process destroyed a data file. Now, the database, of course, will not start because Oracle cannot validate all the data files. In this example, the following is true:

- BT's catalog has been registered in another Oracle8 database, TST8 (and TST8 is registered properly with Net8).
- BT is running in *ARCHIVELOG* mode with all recent archive logs online in the destination directory specified in the *initBT.ora* file.
- A proper backup cycle has been established using *RMAN*.

> **Caution**
>
> Even though *RMAN* is very well designed to avoid further damaging an already damaged database, you should *always* shut down Oracle and perform a full OS-level backup of all Oracle components before beginning any recovery process.

In the sample session below, you can see that the BT database is being started in Server Manager. Notice that Oracle has identified that file #2 is missing. Oracle also displays the filename associated with file #2, however, *RMAN* only needs the file number to restore the correct data file:

```
[tgasper@oreo BT]$ svrmgrl

Oracle Server Manager Release 3.0.5.0.0 - Production

(c) Copyright 1997, Oracle Corporation.  All Rights Reserved.

Oracle8 Release 8.0.5.0.0 - Production
PL/SQL Release 8.0.5.0.0 - Production

SVRMGR> connect internal;
Connected.
SVRMGR> startup
ORACLE instance started.
Total System Global Area                        4758800 bytes
Fixed Size                                        48400 bytes
Variable Size                                   4227072 bytes
Database Buffers                                 409600 bytes
Redo Buffers                                      73728 bytes
Database mounted.
ORA-01157: cannot identify data file 2 - file not found
ORA-01110: data file 2: '/u02/oradata/BT/BT_data1.dbf'
SVRMGR> exit
```

Tip #62	When a database is in *MOUNT* mode, you can query the fields *FILE#* and *NAME* in the view *V$DATABASE* to see a complete list of data files and their associated file numbers. You can then check, at the operating system level, to see exactly what files have been lost and will need to be restored in *RMAN*.

Knowing that you need to restore file #2 to continue, the next sample session shows *RMAN* being used to restore the missing file from backup and bring it completely up-to-date with the *RECOVER DATABASE* command. Notice how the catalog schema owner and database is specified with the *RCVCAT* keyword when *RMAN* is run from the command line:

```
[tgasper@oreo BT]$ rman

Recovery Manager: Release 8.0.5.0.0 - Production

RMAN>

Recovery Manager complete.
[tgasper@oreo BT]$ rman target=sys/change_on_install rcvcat=rman/rman@tst8

Recovery Manager: Release 8.0.5.0.0 - Production

RMAN-06005: connected to target database: BT
RMAN-06008: connected to recovery catalog database

RMAN> run {
2> allocate channel c1 type disk;
3> restore (datafile 2);
4> recover database;
5> release channel c1;
6> }
```

```
RMAN-03022: compiling command: allocate
RMAN-03023: executing command: allocate
RMAN-08030: allocated channel: c1
RMAN-08500: channel c1: sid=10 devtype=DISK

RMAN-03022: compiling command: restore

RMAN-03022: compiling command: IRESTORE
RMAN-03023: executing command: IRESTORE
RMAN-08016: channel c1: starting datafile backupset restore
RMAN-08502: set_count=1 set_stamp=362157796
RMAN-08019: channel c1: restoring datafile 2
RMAN-08509: destination for restore of datafile 2: /u02/oradata/BT/BT_data1.dbf
RMAN-08023: channel c1: restored backup piece 1
RMAN-08511: piece handle=BT.FULL.BTxxxxxx.1.1L
RMAN-08024: channel c1: restore complete
RMAN-03023: executing command: partial resync
RMAN-08003: starting partial resync of recovery catalog
RMAN-08005: partial resync complete

RMAN-03022: compiling command: recover

RMAN-03022: compiling command: recover(1)

RMAN-03022: compiling command: recover(2)

RMAN-03022: compiling command: recover(3)
RMAN-03023: executing command: recover(3)
RMAN-08054: starting media recovery
RMAN-08055: media recovery complete

RMAN-03022: compiling command: recover(4)

RMAN-03022: compiling command: release
RMAN-03023: executing command: release
RMAN-08031: released channel: c1

RMAN> exit
```

In this example, you are only restoring one data file and are subsequently recovering the database. You could, however, add as many RESTORE commands as needed to restore all missing data files. You could also have omitted the RECOVER DATABASE command and handled the final roll-forward yourself from within another Server Manager session.

INCOMPLETE RECOVERY

When you completely recover a database, your intention is to avoid losing any committed transactions. To do this, you must have all the archive logs since the beginning of the last backup, as well as current redo logs. If you do not have all these files, you must perform an incomplete recovery—you must bring the database up with some transactions lost.

Tip #63	Before starting an incomplete recovery, it is usually wise to check with Oracle support to make sure you really have no other option. Special circumstances can many times enable a complete recovery that ordinarily is not possible.

Generally, this type of recovery is something to be avoided. However, there are instances when you need to restore a database to what it was at some point in the past.

EXAMPLE

Suppose a bank is being investigated by auditors for covering up money laundering. The auditors probably want to look at the bank's databases as they were during the money laundering but before the cover-up. A DBA can, with the right set of hot or cold backups and archive logs in place, take the database back in time, so to speak. The auditors could then examine the database as it was during the laundering operation and expose the crime.

COMMAND-LINE ENVIRONMENTS

If an archive log file is missing, Oracle will stop the recovery process and prompt you to place the missing file in the archive log directory. Because you do not have this log file available, for whatever reason, you need to tell Oracle to open the database with what it has recovered so far. Oracle cannot skip an archive log and continue restoring with subsequent logs. Listing 24.3 shows an example of trying a complete recovery of a database with a lost data file. The example system is missing an archive log file, log #303.

LISTING 24.3 ORACLE SERVER MANAGER ARCHIVE LOG

```
[tgasper@oreo dbs]$ svrmgrl
Oracle Server Manager Release 3.0.5.0.0 - Production
(c) Copyright 1997, Oracle Corporation.  All Rights Reserved.
Oracle8 Release 8.0.5.0.0 - Production
PL/SQL Release 8.0.5.0.0 - Production
SVRMGR> connect internal;
Connected.
SVRMGR> startup
ORACLE instance started.
Total System Global Area                    2260240 bytes
Fixed Size                                     48400 bytes
Variable Size                                1728512 bytes
Database Buffers                              409600 bytes
Redo Buffers                                   73728 bytes
Database mounted.
ORA-01113: file 2 needs media recovery
ORA-01110: data file 2: '/u01/oradata/BT/BT_users1.dbf'
SVRMGR> recover automatic database;
ORA-00279: change 68782 generated at 04/07/99 00:47:34 needed for thread 1
ORA-00289: suggestion : /u01/app/oracle/admin/BT/arch/archT0001S0000000303.ARC
ORA-00280: change 68782 for thread 1 is in sequence #303
ORA-00278: log file '/u01/app/oracle/admin/BT/arch/archT0001S0000000303.ARC'
 no longer needed for this recovery
ORA-00308: cannot open archive log
'/u01/app/oracle/admin/BT/arch/archT0001S0000000303.ARC'
ORA-27037: unable to obtain file status
Linux Error: 2: No such file or directory
Additional information: 3
Specify log: {<RET>=suggested ¦ filename ¦ AUTO ¦ CANCEL}
```

Oracle is now waiting for you to tell it what to do next. Because your complete recovery failed, you must now begin an incomplete recovery. First, cancel the current recovery by typing **CANCEL**. Now shut down the database normally.

The tablespace *USERS* uses *BT_users1.dbf*, which Oracle cannot completely recover because of the missing archive logs. Unfortunately, your life just got much more complicated. Now would be a good time to let the spouse know you will not be home for a while because there is no way to bring the *BT_users1.dbf* file back to a consistent state relative to the rest of the database. Your only safe alternative (from a data consistency standpoint) is to restore all the data files from your last backup and to apply archive logs through log #302. You will be losing all the transactions that have occurred after log #302. Here are the steps you'll need to follow:

1. Restore all the data files from your last backup.
2. Try to start the database normally.
3. When Oracle says it is in need of recovery, enter this SQL statement:
   ```
   RECOVER AUTOMATIC DATABASE;
   ```
4. Oracle will stop recovering when it cannot find the archive log file you are missing.
5. Cancel the recovery by entering **CANCEL**.
6. Cause an incomplete recovery with this SQL statement:
   ```
   RECOVER DATABASE UNTIL CANCEL;
   ```
7. Reply with **CANCEL** at the prompt.
8. Force the database open with this SQL statement:
   ```
   ALTER DATABASE OPEN RESETLOGS;
   ```
8. Immediately shut down the database.
9. Make a cold backup.
10. Restart the database normally.

Tip #64

Recovery Manager (*RMAN*), introduced in Oracle8, does offer the capability to do point-in-time recovery of a single tablespace without having to roll back the entire database. As with most complex restore operations, you should consult with Oracle support before using tablespace point-in-time recovery.

Caution

Make sure you make a cold backup any time you open the database with *RESETLOGS*. If you do not, any archive log files will be useless because *RESETLOGS* makes the current archive log files incompatible with a pre-*RESETLOGS* backup of the database.

Through a lot of work, you can restore the data contained in the *USERS* tablespace up to log #302 and logically move it into the database without losing any data in other tablespaces. Doing this, though, might create referential integrity problems with your data.

Although the specific procedures for this are beyond the scope of this book, here's the general plan:

1. Restore your last backup of the system to a test machine. You'll need to re-create redo logs manually.

2. Copy all the archive logs through #302 to the test machine.

3. Recover the database with the `RECOVER DATABASE UNTIL CANCEL` command.

4. Step through all the archive logs until you reach #302. After #302, cancel the restore.

5. Open the database with the `RESETLOGS` option.

6. Perform a logical backup of all the tables in the `USERS` tablespace.

7. Re-create the `USERS` tablespace on your failed system.

8. Logically restore the tables exported in Step 6 back to the instance that lost the `USERS` tablespace in the first place.

In a situation such as this, it is best to bring Oracle Support into the process. Their expertise will provide all the details relevant to your particular recovery situation. If you do intend to pursue this course of action, call Oracle Support before you attempt any type of recovery—*do not attempt an incomplete recovery.*

Renaming and Moving Database Files

There are many times when you need to either rename files in your database or move them from one location on the server to another. Oracle does enable you to do all this, but there are very specific steps that should be followed. The most important of these steps is that you should do all this type of work during off hours. You will need to shut down the database to perform many of these operations. Be aware that dropping a redo log file, changing a control file entry, or performing other operations within Oracle will not physically remove or rename files in the OS. You must perform these operations manually at the OS level.

Tip #65	Any time more than one or two database files are to be moved, it is advisable to use scripts that have been proofread (and checked on a test system, ideally) to perform both the OS and Oracle tasks.

Control Files   The location of control files are kept in the appropriate `init.ora` or `config.ora` file with the `control_files` keyword. To move control files, complete the following steps:

1. Shut down the database.

2. Copy or move a control file to the new location.

3. Edit the appropriate `init<sid>.ora` file. There is a list of control files following the `control_files` keyword. You might change the location or name of a control file, delete a control file from the list, or add a location to a new control file.

4. Start up the database.

REDO LOG   Redo logs must be changed from within either SQL*Plus or Server Manager. Technically, you can perform this operation while the database is up and running, but it is still advisable to do it when you are sure there is no activity on the system. To move or rename redo logs, complete the following steps:

1. Shut down the database.
2. Start the database in *EXCLUSIVE* mode. The following example shows this operation from within Server Manager:
   ```
   STARTUP EXCLUSIVE;
   ```
3. Use this SQL statement to find out the group number of the files you want to change:
   ```
   SELECT * FROM V$LOGFILE;
   ```
   Keep a note of the group number you are working with.
4. Now, determine which redo log group is active:
   ```
   SELECT * FROM V$LOG;
   ```
5. The active redo log group is indicated by *CURRENT*, shown in the *STATUS* column from the query run in Step 4. If a file you need to move is currently in an active group, switch Oracle to the next redo log group:
   ```
   ALTER SYSTEM SWITCH LOGFILE;
   ```
6. Now drop the redo log group. In the example, you're dropping the #2 log group. In your system, use the number you wrote down from Step 3.
   ```
   ALTER DATABASE DROP LOGFILE GROUP 2;
   ```
7. Create the redo log file group with the files in the location you want. In this example, you will re-create group #2 with two files (you should *always* have at least two files in each redo log group). You will use 1MB for each file. Obviously, your group number, actual filenames, and size will vary according to your site requirements.
   ```
   ALTER DATABASE ADD LOGFILE GROUP 2
   ```
   ```
   ('/u03/oradata/test/log2atest.log','/u04/oradata/test/log2btest.log') size 1M;
   ```
8. Shut down the database and restart it normally.

DATA FILES   Data files are fairly easy to move around. You'll usually use Server Manager and an OS utility to actually move or rename data files. If you are relocating files as part of a physical recovery, just place the data files where you want them to be. Here's how to change your data file locations/names:

1. Shut down the database if it is running.
2. With an OS utility, move or rename the files to the new locations or names. Be sure to keep track of *exactly* where files were and where they are now.
3. Start the database in *MOUNT* mode. The following example shows this operation from within Server Manager:
   ```
   STARTUP MOUNT;
   ```

4. For each changed file, set the new filenames in Oracle. The following example changes Oracle internally so that it will look in the right location for a data file. Here, you have moved the *rbs1test.dbf* file from the */u01/oradata/test* file system to the */u02/oradata/test* file system.

```
ALTER DATABASE RENAME FILE
'/u01/oradata/test/rbs1test.dbf' TO
'/u02/oradata/test/rbs1test.dbf';
```

5. Now shut down and restart the database. If it fails to start up because of a missing data file, you'll need to find out where the file went and use Oracle's *RENAME* facility so that Oracle finds the file it needs.

WINDOWS NT ENVIRONMENTS

Unfortunately, Oracle's NT Recovery Manager does not gracefully handle incomplete recoveries. For this reason, the task of incomplete recovery using Oracle's NT Recovery Manager is a task best handled with assistance from Oracle Support. Incomplete recoveries are delicate procedures, and at this point you can ill afford to take the chance that NT Recovery Manager will issue a SQL statement that will render your database permanently unusable.

PART
V
CH
24

> **Caution**
>
> Even with Oracle's expert help, never begin any recovery process without first having a complete backup of the broken database. Just in case the recovery process goes awry, you'll have something to fall back to and start over from.

TESTING STRATEGIES

In this chapter, you have covered a very large amount of material related to backing up and recovering Oracle databases. Most DBAs find that every site has requirements for backup and recovery that make them unique. Because you rely so heavily on your backup and recovery solutions, you must make certain that they can truly be relied on. An untested backup and recovery solution is worse than nothing at all—it gives you a false sense of security.

The ideal situation is when you have a completely identical machine to the one you want to protect that you can use to test backup and recovery scenarios. You should start out by cloning the production system to your test system (with the databases shut down, of course). By simulating various failures (shutting the power off to disk drives, deleting files, corrupting redo log files, and so on) and having to recover from them, you'll get invaluable hands-on experience that you could never get by reading any book or attending any seminar. If you can simulate a load on the system while performing these operations, you'll get the best possible experience along with complete reassurance that your backup and recovery solution will protect you against almost any failure.

If you, like most DBAs, don't have a complete system to use for your testing, create an instance on a machine that is most similar to the one you need to protect. It is best to pick a machine that does not already have Oracle instances. This minimizes the chance that you'll damage a working Oracle database. Copy as much of the production database to this test instance as space permits. Simulate the filesystem/disk layout as closely as possible. Use the same backup and recovery procedures you would use on the production system when simulating failures and trying to recover from them.

Tip #66	No matter how you test your backup and recovery solution, make sure you document the exact procedures you follow. Also document where you have difficulty and what your resolution is. Any time you experience a failure on your production system, add that scenario to your failure/recovery exercises. If it happens once, it'll probably happen again. Whenever a new DBA joins your staff, have him or her perform the same disaster and recovery exercises.

Troubleshooting

Aborted Warm Backups

During a warm backup of the database, the system crashed and had to be rebooted. Now the Oracle server indicates it must perform some media recovery even though nothing was lost.

Oracle is saying the data files need to be recovered because they are still in backup mode. (This can be confirmed by querying the *V$BACKUP* view.) Fear not, no actual recovery is needed. Simply use the *ALTER DATABASE DATAFILE END BACKUP* statement for each file that is still in backup mode. Shut down the database and start up normally.

Table Constraints on Imports

When importing data into an existing set of tables, various constraints (such as foreign key relationships) do not enable the data to be imported.

To ease imports, it is sometimes convenient to use the *ALTER TABLE DISABLE CONSTRAINT* statement to temporarily disable constraints such as foreign or unique keys. Be aware that when the *ALTER TABLE ENABLE CONSTRAINT* statement is issued to re-enable constraints after the import process completes, Oracle will first confirm that all data meets the constraints before actually enabling them. This can take quite some time on larger tables.

Project: Varying Implications of Damaged Archive Logs

When attempting to perform a complete recovery, Oracle indicates that one of the archive log files is corrupt or missing and cannot be used. You want to make as complete a recovery as possible.

Usually, you now have some very difficult choices. You can do one of the following:

- Stop the recovery process now and follow the instructions for an incomplete recovery to start the database. This will result in the loss of transactions since the bad archive log was created.

- Restore the database to the original failure point when you lost one or more data files and then drop the lost or damaged data files from the database. You'll lose any data in the lost data files, but if you can recover the information lost from the data file from a logical backup or another copy of the database system, this might be the most appealing. All the remaining data will be completely current.

If you choose the 2nd option, while the database is in a mounted and non-open state, you can use the *ALTER DATABASE DATAFILE OFFLINE* statement to take the lost or damaged data file offline as shown in the following example:

```
SQL> ALTER DATABASE DATAFILE '/u01/oradbs/PRD/PRD_custindx1.dbf' OFFLINE;
```

By taking the data file offline, you'll be able to open the database and inspect the damage. After opening the database, query *DBA_DATA_FILES* to obtain the file number for the lost or damaged data file as shown in the following example:

```
SQL> select file_id,file_name from dba_data_files where
  2  file_name = '/u01/oradbs/PRD/PRD_custindx1.dbf';

   FILE_ID FILE_NAME
---------- --------------------------------------------------
         3 /u01/oradbs/PRD/PRD_custindx1.dbf
```

You can see here that the lost file has a file number of 3. Now, by querying *DBA_EXTENTS*, it is possible to see which segments have been affected by the failure as shown in the following example:

```
SQL> select owner,segment_name,segment_type from dba_extents
  2  where file_id = 3

OWNER            SEGMENT_NAME                SEGMENT_TYPE
---------------- --------------------------- ----------------
PRDSYS           MCUST_AKEY1                 INDEX
PRDSYS           MCUST_AKEY2                 INDEX
DBAUSR           AUDIT_PKEY                  INDEX
PRDSYS           INVTRY_IDX3                 INDEX
PRDSYS           INVTRY_AKEY1                INDEX
BATCHUSR         JOBRESULT_PKEY              INDEX
BATCHUSR         JOBRESULT_IDX1              INDEX
```

Here, you can see that the only segments that were affected by the lost data file were indexes—which can always be rebuilt from the original tables. In effect, even though you did lose information, you did not lose information that could not be rebuilt.

To reconstruct the system at this point, follow these steps:

1. Drop the indexes shown from the preceding query. Before doing do, you might want to make sure you have the DDL code necessary to rebuild the indexes later.

2. Use the `ALTER DATABASE DATAFILE OFFLINE DROP` statement to drop the damaged data file.

3. Re-create the data file in Oracle.

4. Re-create the lost index objects.

As a general rule, you should consult with Oracle support before attempting any unordinary recovery methods. Generally speaking, Oracle is an extremely robust database design that can be very accommodating when you need to get everything possible from a damaged database.

You can use Table 24.1 as a guideline for the recoverability aspects of common Oracle objects in the event of a completely lost data file.

TABLE 24.1 RECOVERABILITY PROSPECTS FOR LOST FILES

Oracle object	Recoverability
Tables	If multiple extents hold data, it is usually possible to query all the rows that are not held in the extents affected by the data file loss. Oracle support should be consulted if this is necessary.
Indexes	As shown previously, indexes are completely recoverable. Simply drop the indexes in the database, re-create the storage area affected, and re-create the indexes.
Rollback Segments	Although it is technically possible to start Oracle and drop active rollback segments, it is highly advisable to consult with Oracle support to make certain you are aware of the implications in your particular situation. Dropping damaged active rollback segments and continuing database operations can be very risky and should be avoided if at all possible.
Temporary Segments	These generally should not pose a serious problem. You should generally be able to re-create any lost temporary tablespace data files without causing any data integrity issues. Any affected transactions will, of course, be rolled back and will have to be resubmitted.

INTEGRITY MANAGEMENT

In this chapter

As the size of the database and the number of users on the system increases, complexity in terms of internal resource contention also increases, thus leading to performance problems. The general symptoms of such internal contention are that there is enough free memory and the CPU is not very busy, but there are still performance problems on the system. Such symptoms would make a novice administrator wonder what is happening on the system. The aim of this chapter is to empower the administrator to identify such contention issues. The resources that are addressed in this chapter are locks and latches.

Database contention can be split into two main categories, both of which are discussed in detail later in this chapter.

- Locks   Used to restrict other users' access to data.
- Latches   An internal mechanism used by oracle to manage and maintain memory locks.

IMPLEMENTING LOCKS

- Data Consistency

    The Oracle locking mechanism ensures that the data returned by a query is consistent with the time at which the query began. Therefore, a user performing a query sees a static picture of the data even if other users are changing it. This provides data consistency.

- Data Concurrency

    Locks are used to prevent destructive interaction between users accessing the same object. The locking mechanism of Oracle enables many users to safely access data at the same time. This provides data concurrency.

- Data Integrity

    Transactions hold locks until they perform a commit or rollback. This provides data integrity.

Locks might never be required for a single user database, but when you work in a multiuser environment, it is important to have a mechanism in place that will automatically cater to data concurrency, consistency, and integrity issues. Oracle maintains the integrity, concurrency and consistency of data by using an internal locking mechanism. How Oracle maintains each of these is discussed in the following sections.

Oracle automatically caters to these issues by acquiring different types of locks on behalf of the user to enable or prevent simultaneous access to the same resource by different users and ensuring that data integrity is not violated. The term *resource* here means user objects such as tables and rows. When implementing locks, one of the key issues to keep in mind is that it should not be a bottleneck on the system, preventing concurrent access to data. Oracle will therefore automatically acquire locks at different levels, depending on the database operation being performed, to ensure maximum concurrency. For example, when a user is reading data of a row, other users should be enabled to write to the same row. No user should be enabled to drop the table, however. These issues relating to which transaction should be enabled what level of access to an object or data are implemented using the different locking levels, which will be covered in the next section.

NEED FOR LOCKING

Before you actually get into the intricacies of locking, examine the various scenarios in which locking becomes really important. The following are a few of the instances that explain why data consistency and concurrency are so important:

- A user is modifying data in a table, and at the same time another user is trying to drop the same table. Oracle prevents this from happening by acquiring a table-level lock for the first user. The second user, who wants to drop the table, waits for the Table Lock to be released by the first user, after which she can drop the table.

- User A is trying to read some data within a transaction, which was modified and committed by user B after user A's transaction started. User A reads the committed data of User B. This means that the data read within the same transaction is not consistent to a point in time. Oracle ensures data read within a transaction is consistent with the point in time when the transaction started. Oracle implements transaction-level read consistency using the system change number (SCN).

  A System Change Number (SCN) is a data structure that defines a committed version of the database at a given point in time. An SCN can be thought of as Oracle's logical clock. They increase in numeric value with each commit. For example, if a transaction does an UPDATE and commits, it will be assigned an SCN value of, say, 500. The next transaction that commits will receive an SCN value of 501 or greater.

- One user modifies the data, and another user modifies the same row before the first user has committed the transaction; therefore, the changes made by the first user are lost. Oracle prevents this from happening by acquiring a row-level exclusive lock on the table's row and causing the second user to wait.

- One user reads data off another user's data that is not yet committed; that is, user A reads a row that user B is changing before user B's changes are committed. Oracle prevents this from happening by enabling user A to read the old data, that is, the data before user B modified it. Oracle does this by obtaining the data from the rollback segments.

PART

V

CH

25

LOCKING CONCEPTS

Oracle will automatically decide—depending on the context—what lock needs to be applied for the given situation to provide the maximum level of data concurrency using the lowest level of restriction. Oracle has two levels of locking: share and exclusive.

Share locks are implemented with higher concurrency of data access in mind. If a shared lock is acquired, other users can share the same resource. A number of transactions can acquire a shared lock on the same resource, but this is not true in the case of exclusive locks. For example, multiple users can read the same data at the same time.

Exclusive locks prevent simultaneous sharing of the same resource. For example, if one transaction acquires an exclusive lock on a resource, no other transaction can alter or modify that resource until the time the lock is released. Here again, sharing the resource is enabled. For example, if a table is locked in exclusive mode, it will not prevent other users from selecting from the same table.

You can use the levels of locking to enable concurrent access and at the same time ensure data integrity. Oracle achieves this goal by applying the lowest level of restriction. Oracle will automatically lock either the individual row or the entire table, depending on what is needed. Oracle uses the following general guidelines to implement the level of locking it needs to apply:

- If a user is trying to read data from a row, another user should be enabled to write to the same row.

- If a user is updating the data of a row, other users should be able to read data of the same row at the same time.

- If two users are updating the same table, they should be prevented only when they are trying to access the same row.

One of the most important types of functionality that is implemented using locking mechanisms is data consistency. Oracle ensures data consistency at two levels: statement level and transaction level.

Statement-level read consistency means any statement that starts executing will see committed data that was available before the statement started executing. All changes, committed or uncommitted, made to data while the statement is executing are invisible to other sessions, that started prior to the commit session. Oracle provides statement-level read consistency by ensuring that only committed data before the SCN observed at the time when the statement started executing is available to other sessions (for an example, please see the Table 25.1).

TABLE 25.1 ONLY COMMITTED DATA BEFORE THE SCN OBSERVED AT THE TIME WHEN THE STATEMENT STARTED EXECUTING IS AVAILABLE TO OTHER SESSIONS

Time	Session-1	Session-2	Session-3
10:00	Transaction starts		
10:01		Transaction starts	
10:02	Read consistent. (Can't see the transactions committed by session-2)	Transaction commits and ends transaction.	
10:03			Transaction starts
10:04	Still read consistent.		Can see committed data by session-2.
10:05			Transaction commits and ends transaction.
10:06	Read consistent. (Can't see the transactions commited by session -2 & session -3)		

Transaction-level read consistency means that all data seen within the same transaction is consistent to the point of time. Oracle ensures transaction-level read consistency by using the SCN mechanism and by acquiring exclusive table and row locks when needed.

Oracle implements read consistency by using the data available in the rollback segments. When a query enters the execution stage, the current SCN is determined. As it starts reading data of data blocks, the SCN of the block is compared with the observed SCN. If the blocks SCN has a value greater than SCN at the start of the query, it means that the data in those blocks has changed after the query has started executing. If this data is read from the data blocks, it is not consistent with the point in time the query started. Oracle uses the rollback segments to reconstruct the data, as rollback segments will always contain the old data—except in case of high update activity on the system where the old data in the rollback segments could potentially be overwritten.

LOCKING TYPES

Oracle automatically acquires different types of locking, depending on the operation and the resource on which it has to acquire the lock.

There are four classes of Oracle locks:

Data locks(DML Locks) are acquired on tables and are used to protect data, or rather, ensure integrity of data.

Dictionary locks(DDL Locks) are used to protect the structure of objects—for example, the structural definition of tables and view indexes. A dictionary lock is automatically acquired by Oracle on behalf of any DDL transaction requiring it.

Internal locks and latches protect internal database structures. Latches are discussed in greater detail in the section entitled "Implementing Locks with Latches".

Distributed locks and *Parallel Cache Management* (PCM) locks are used in Parallel Server (see Part IX, "Parallel and Distributed Environments").

DATA (DML) LOCKS

PURPOSE OF DML LOCKS   The purpose of DML locks is to guarantee the integrity of data being accessed concurrently by multiple users. DML locks prevent the destructive interference of simultaneous DML operations.

For example, DML locks ensure that a specific row in a table can be updated by only one transaction at a time. They also ensure that a table cannot be dropped if an uncommitted transaction contains an insert into the table.

DML statements use two types of lock structures:

1. The transaction gets a shared lock on a table.
2. The transaction gets an exclusive lock on each of the rows it is changing.

The following examples show shared and exclusive types of locks:

- If three users try to update the same row at the same time, all of them get the Shared Table Lock, but only the user who has requested the lock first gets the row lock.
- A row that is being modified is always locked exclusively so that other users cannot modify that row until the transaction holding the lock is committed or rolled back.

MODES OF DML LOCKS The following list shows the Oracle locking modes used for DML.

1. Row Share (RS):

   A Row Share lock is a shared Table Lock. It is an exclusive lock on rows queried.

2. Row Exclusive (RX):

   A Row Exclusive lock generally indicates that the transaction holding the lock has made one or more updates to rows in the table.

3. Share Lock (S):

   If a transaction holds a Share Table Lock, it prevents other transactions from performing DML operations on the table.

4. Share Row Exclusive (SRX):

   If a transaction holds an SRX Table Lock, it prevents other transactions from performing DML or SELECT ....FOR UPDATE statements.

5. Exclusive (X):

   An Exclusive lock is the most restrictive mode of table lock, allowing the transaction that holds the lock exclusive write access to the table.

> **Note**
>
> You can increase the number of locks available for an instance by increasing the value of the parameters DML_LOCKS and ENQUEUE_RESOURCES. In the V$LOCK view, the Row Locks and the Table Locks are indicated by the values TX and TM respectively in the Lock Type column. However, the Mode column of V$LOCK view contains the value SX for both types of locks.

DDL LOCKS (DICTIONARY LOCKS)

DBAs need to be aware of Data Definition Language (DDL) locks and their impact on transactions. The knowledge of DDL locks will help you to diagnose and resolve locking problems. A DDL lock protects the definition of a schema object while that object is acted on or referenced by an ongoing transaction.

For example, when a user creates a procedure, Oracle automatically acquires DDL locks for all the objects referenced in the procedure definition.

FUNCTIONS OF DDL LOCKS   The following list describes the functionality of DDL Locks.

- DDL locks prevent objects referenced in the procedure from being altered or dropped before the procedure compilation is complete.
- DDL locks only affect individual schema objects that are modified or referenced during DDL operations. They do not lock the whole data dictionary.
- DDL locks cannot be implemented explicitly.

DIFFERENT MODES OF DDL LOCKS   The following list describes the Oracle locking modes used for DDL.

1. **Exclusive DDL Locks:** This lock is granted when statements such as CREATE, ALTER, and DROP are issued on an object.

   Feature of Exclusive DDL Locks:
   - Users cannot get an Exclusive DDL lock on the table if another user holds any level of lock. For example, an ALTER TABLE statement will fail if another user has an uncommitted transaction on the table.

2. **Share DDL Locks:** This lock is granted when statements such as GRANT and CREATE PACKAGE are issued on an object.

   Features of Shared DDL Locks:
   - A Shared DDL lock does not prevent similar DDL statements or any DML statement from being issued on an object, but it prevents another user from altering or dropping the referenced object.
   - Another feature of a Shared DDL lock is that it lasts for the duration of DDL statement execution and until an implicit commit occurs.

3. **Breakable Parse DDL Locks:** A statement or PL/SQL object in the library cache holds a lock for every object it references.

   Features of Breakable Parse DDL Locks:
   - The Breakable Parse DDL lock checks whether the statement should be invalidated if the referenced object changes.
   - A Breakable Parse DDL lock persists as long as the associated SQL statement remains in the shared pool. It checks to see whether the statement should be invalidated if the object changes.

TABLE LOCKS (TM)

Table Locks are acquired when a transaction issues the statements in Table 25.1. Table Locks are acquired by Oracle on behalf of the transaction to reserve DML access on the table and to prevent conflicting DDL operations on the table. For example if a transaction has a Table Lock on a table, then it will prevent any other transaction to acquire an exclusive DDL lock on the table, which is required to drop or alter the table.

TABLE 25.2   STATEMENTS AND TABLE LOCKS ACQUIRED

Statement	Type	Mode
INSERT	TM	Row Exclusive(3) (RX)
UPDATE	TM	Row Exclusive(3) (RX)
DELETE	TM	Row Exclusive(3) (RX)
SELECT FOR UPDATE	TM	Row Share(2) (RS)
LOCK TABLE	TM	Exclusive(6) (X)

Table 25.1 shows the different modes in which Table Locks(TM)are acquired by the RDBMS when specific statements are issued. The Type column has a value such as TM, and the mode column has a value of 2, 3, or 6. The value TM indicates a Table Lock; the value 2 indicates a row share (RS) lock, 3 indicates a row exclusive lock (RX), and 6 indicates an exclusive (X) lock. For example, The value TM of Type column and value 3 of Mode column, would be stored in the V$lock table, against the session that issued the statement when the corresponding statement is issued, so you need to be familiar with these values. V$lock is the table in which Oracle lists the locks currently held by the Oracle server, which is discussed in detail with examples in the section "Analyzing V$lock."

For example, when an INSERT statement is issued, the Type column in V$lock will have the value TM for the session, and the mode column will have the value 3, which means row exclusive (RX) lock. For additional details, refer to the section "Analyzing V$lock". For all statements except the Lock table, there will be two entries in the V$lock table: one corresponding to the Table Lock (TM) and another entry corresponding to the Transaction Lock (TX). For statements such as insert update, deleting a TM Lock is acquired only to prevent conflicting DDL operations on the locked objects, which means that when a user is inserting into a table, he or she acquires a TM Lock in mode 3 (RX)). If another user is trying to drop the same table, it will have to acquire a TM Lock in mode 6 (Exclusive). The TM 3) (RX) lock will prevent the TM (6) (X) session from acquiring the lock and the second session will remain waiting. Table 25.2 illustrates lock modes acquired by a session and lock modes permitted.

TABLE 25.3   LOCKING MODES AND OPERATIONS PERMITTED

SQL Statement	Table Lock Mode	Permitted Lock Modes
Select * from tname...	none	RS,RX,S,SRX,X
Insert Into tname...	RX	RS,RX
Update tname...	RX	RS*,RX*
Delete From tname	RX	RS*,RX*
Select...From tname For Update Of...	RS	RS*RX*S*,SRX*
Lock Table In	RS	RS,RX,S,SRX

SQL Statement	Table Lock Mode	Permitted Lock Modes
ROW SHARE MODE		
Lock Table In ROW EXCLUSIVE MODE	RX	RS,RX
Lock Table In SHARE MODE	S	RS,S
Lock Table In SHARE ROW EXCLUSIVE MODE	SRX	RS
Lock Table In EXCLUSIVE MODE	X	None
RS: Row Share	SRX: Share Row Exclusive	
RX: Row Exclusive	X: Exclusive	
S: Share		

If another transaction has already acquired a lock on the row, a wait will occur.

Transaction Locks (TX): This type of lock is acquired when a transaction issues the statements in Table 25.3. Transaction Locks are always acquired at the row level. TX Locks exclusively lock the rows and prevents other transactions to modify the row until the transaction holding the lock rollbacks or commits the data.

TABLE 25.4   TRANSACTION LOCKS STATEMENTS

Statement	Type	Mode
INSERT	TX	Exclusive(6) (X)
UPDATE	TX	Exclusive(6) (X)
DELETE	TX	Exclusive(6) (X)
SELECT FOR UPDATE	TX	Exclusive(6) (X)

For TX Locks to be acquired, the transaction must first acquire a TM Lock on the table. For example, when an insert statement is issued (refer to Table 25.1), a TM Lock in mode 3 (RX) has to be acquired. After the TM Lock in RX mode is acquired, the transaction will have to acquire a TX in exclusive (X) mode (see Table 25.3). The TX Lock will be prevented from being acquired only if another transaction has a TX Lock on the same row, and the TM Lock will be prevented if there is already a TM Lock in exclusive (X) mode on the table.

The other modes are 4 (Share) and 5 (Share Row Exclusive), but these locking modes do not occur commonly on the database and hence do not merit much discussion.

MANUAL LOCKING

If you want to perform a global update of column values within a table and you want the transaction to have exclusive access to the table, so that the transaction does not have to wait for other transactions to complete operations on the table. You can achieve this by locking the table manually to prevent other transactions from acquiring a lock on the table.

Example: `LOCK TABLE <Table Name> IN <mode>`

You can lock tables explicitly in different modes:

- Row Share
- Share
- Share Row
- Share Row Exclusive
- Row Exclusive

The Share mode (4) lock is acquired when a user issues the following statement:

```
e.g. SQL> LOCK TABLE <table name> IN SHARE MODE;
     Table(s) Locked.
```

The Share Row Exclusive mode (5) lock is acquired when a user issues the following:

```
SQL> Lock table <table name> in SHARE ROW EXCLUSIVE MODE;
     Table(s) Locked.
```

Now you can update the column values without contention from other transactions.

Very few applications actually have to use these statements; therefore, they are not considered really important when compared to other day-to-day, more frequently occurring locking types.

DATABASE DEADLOCKS

A *deadlock* is a situation when two or more users wait for the same data locked by each other.

Most database deadlocks occur within a table index. A SELECT statement of a single row from a database might cause more than one lock entry to be placed in the storage pool. An individual row receives a lock, but each index node that contains the value for that row will also have locks assigned.

The shared locking scenario of Oracle ensures that all database integrity is maintained and that updates do not inadvertently overlay prior updates to the database. There are some disadvantages to maintaining shared locks. In Oracle, each lock requires 4 bytes of RAM storage within the Oracle Instance storage pool, and large SQL SELECT statements can create storage shortage conditions that can cripple an entire database. For example, suppose a SELECT statement that retrieves 1000 rows into the buffer will require 4000 bytes of locking space. This condition causes database deadlock.

ANALYZING V$lock

Oracle stores all information relating to locks in the database in the dynamic status table V$lock. This section analyzes various scenarios in the database when resources are locked and examines the V$lock table to see how Oracle reports the lock.

The following is a description of the structure of V$lock:

```
ADDR RAW(4)
KADDR RAW(4)
SID NUMBER
TYPE VARCHAR2(2)
ID1 NUMBER
ID2 NUMBER
LMODE NUMBER
REQUEST NUMBER
CTIME NUMBER
BLOCK NUMBER
```

The important columns of interest, which would be of use when analyzing locking situations, are as follows:

- sid   This is the session identifier.

- Type   This is the type of lock acquired or waiting by the session. Example values are the following:

PART

V

CH

25

```
TX Transaction
    TM DML or Table Lock
    MR Media Recovery.
    ST Disk Space Transaction
```

As said previously, this chapter covers only TX and TM Locks.

- lmode/request   This column contains the mode of the lock. The possible values are the following:

```
0    None
1    Null
2    Row Share              (RS)
3    Row Exclusive          (RX)
4    Share                   (S)
5    Share Row Exclusive (SRX)
6    Exclusive              (X)
```

If the column lmode contains a value other than 0 or 1, it indicates that the process has acquired a lock. If the request column contains a value other than 0 or 1, it indicates that the process is waiting for a lock. If lmode contains a value 0, it indicates that the process is waiting to acquire a lock.

- The following Select statement is a quick way to check whether there are any sessions waiting to acquire locks on any table:

```
Select count(*)
From v$lock
where lmode = 0
```

If the Select statement returns a value that is greater than zero, there are locks sessions on the systems currently waiting to acquire locks.

- id1   Depending on the type of lock, the value in this column can have different meanings. If the type of lock is TM, the value in this column is the ID of the object that is to be locked or is waiting to be locked, depending on the context. If the type of lock is TX, the value in this column is the decimal representation of the rollback segment number.

- id2   If the type of lock is TM, the value in this column is zero. If the type of the lock is TX, it is the representation of the wrap number—that is, the number of times the rollback slot has been reused.

Using this information, you can now examine various scenarios and analyze the values stored in this table in different cases. The next section covers detailed case analyses of commonly occurring locks on the database and how to read this information from V$lock view.

CASE 1: A TABLE LOCKED EXCLUSIVELY

For purposes of discussion, assume that the table that is going to be locked is the employee table and the session ID is 28. Assume that one user issues the following statement:

```
Lock table employee in exclusive mode;
```

This statement will lock the table in exclusive mode. If a table is locked exclusively by a user, the only SQL statement that can be used on the table by another user is the select statement. Insert, update, delete or any DDL operation on this table by the other users will not be permitted until the lock is released.

For examining the records in the V$lock table, use the following select statement:

```
Select sid,
       type,
       lmode,
       request,
       id1,
       id2
From v$lock
where sid = 28;
```

When you execute the select statement, you get the following output:

```
    SID TY      LMODE    REQUEST       ID1         ID2
- - - - - - - - - - - - - - - - - - - - - - - - - - - - - - - - - - -
     28 TM          6          0      7590           0
```

Note the following observations:

- There is only one entry in the V$lock.

- The lock acquired is a TM (Table) Lock.

- The lmode column contains the value 6, which indicates that a table-level exclusive lock has been acquired by the session.

- The id1 column contains the value 7590, which is the object id of the employee table. The id2 column, as expected for TM Locks, has a value of 0. To obtain the description of the object, you can use the sys.obj$ table. You can use the following select statement:

```
Select name
        From sys.obj$
        where obj#      =       7590;

        Name
        --------
        Employee
```

- The request column contains the value 0, which indicates that the lock has been acquired by this session.

CASE 2: SESSION UPDATING A ROW OF AN EXCLUSIVELY LOCKED TABLE

In Case 2, the table is locked exclusively by a session while another session is trying to update a row of the same table. Here is the SQL issued by the session trying to update the table:

```
Update employee
Set Name = 'MANISH'
where emp_id    =       '1086';
```

In this case, the entry for the first session in V$lock remains the same as in Case 1, but the entries for the second session are very interesting. Assume the session ID of the second session is 29. Now assume you execute the following select statement:

```
Select sid,
      type,
      lmode,
      request,
      id1,
      id2
From v$lock
where sid in (28,29);
```

This is the output:

SID	TY	LMODE	REQUEST	ID1	ID2
28 TM	6	0	7590	0	
29 TM	0	3	7590	0	

The following are the observations in this case:

- The entry for session 28 remains the same as in Case 1.
- There is one entry for session 29. This entry is for a TM Lock. Note the value of lmode is 0, and the value of request is 3. This means that session 29 is waiting to acquire a Table Lock on the table. A Table Lock has to be first acquired by session 29 to flag that it is currently using this table. This will prevent any other sessions from issuing any DDL statements on this table. This Table Lock is basically acquired to flag or mark the table as used by the session. The id1 column here again indicates the object id of the table, which has to be locked.

PART

V

CH

25

- The Transaction (TX) Lock has not yet been acquired by session 29; only after the TM Lock is acquired can session 29 acquire the TX Lock, provided no other session is accessing or updating the same row.

Now if session 28 rolls back or commits the transaction, session 29 can acquire the lock it is waiting for. If you examine the entries in V$lock for session 29, you get two records after session 28 has committed the transaction. This is the output:

```
SID TY      LMODE    REQUEST      ID1        ID2
- - - - - - - - - - - - - - - - - - - - - - - - - - - - - - -
    29 TM       3        0         7590          0
    29 TX       6        0       327680      10834
```

The following are the observations:

- The lock entry for session 28 in V$lock is no longer present, as it has committed the transaction.
- Session 29 is now able to successfully acquire the TM Lock, and the value 3 in the request column moves to the lmode column, indicating the lock has been acquired by the session.
- Session 29 also acquires another lock on the table; this is the Transaction or TX Lock. The value in the Type column for this entry is TX, and the value of lmode is 6, which is the Transaction Lock.
- The value in id1, 327680, is the number of the rollback segment. To obtain the name of the rollback segment, you can use the V$rollname view. The following select statement will give the name of the rollback segment where session 29 starts writing the rollback information.

```
        Select name
        From v$rollname
        where usn    =    trunc(327680/65536)

    NAME
        - - - - - - - - - - - - - -
        RB03
```

Therefore, session 29 starts writing the rollback information in rollback segment RB03.

- Whenever a session has to acquire a TX Lock, it first has to acquire a TM Table Lock. After the Table Lock is acquired, the session acquires the TX Lock, provided no other session has already acquired the TX Lock on the same row. In summary, the session has to acquire two locks.

CASE 3: A SESSION TRYING TO UPDATE AN UPDATED ROW BY ANOTHER SESSION

This particular locking case is the most common scenario in everyday locking situations. When two sessions simultaneously try to update the same row, the session that first updates the row gets the lock, and the second session will wait behind the first session to acquire the lock. The lock acquired by the first session will be released only when the first session commits or rolls back the transaction.

In this example, session 29 (the first session) has updated the employee name in a record of the employee table to TOM and has not yet committed the change. Session 30 (the second session) now tries to update the same row. To analyze V$lock, you can use the same select statement as in the last example, but replace the sid column with the relevant sid values:

```
SID TY     LMODE    REQUEST      ID1       ID2
-------------------------------------------------
29 TM        3          0        7590        0
29 TX        6          0      327680     10834
30 TM        3          0        7590        0
30 TX        0          6      327680     10834
```

Based on the output of the select statement, the following observations can be made:

- Session 29 (the first session) will have two records locks in V$lock: a TM Lock and the TX Transaction Lock.

- Session 30 will have one entry in this table corresponding to the TM Table Lock. In this particular case, session 30 is able to acquire the TM Lock immediately because no other session has locked the table exclusively.

- Session 30 has another record corresponding to the Transaction Lock (TX). This entry will have the request column with a value of 6. This means Session 30 is waiting to acquire a row exclusive lock. The value in the id1 and id2 columns will have the same value as the id1 and id2 values corresponding to session 29.

- This is the most common locking scenario when one row is locked by one session and another session is trying to update the same row.

- If session 29 now rollbacks or commits the transaction as in Case 2, session ID 30 can acquire the lock, and the value in the request column for the lock entry will move into the mode column, indicating that the lock has been acquired.

MONITORING LOCKS ON THE SYSTEM

Now that you are familiar with the concepts of locking and the associated system tables, it should be easy to detect locks on the scripts. With the information in the previous section, the user will be able to write his or her own lock detection scripts, but some lock monitoring scripts are given here nevertheless. This section will contain some useful scripts for detecting and monitoring locks.

The script in Listing 25.1 will help give you an idea of the number of objects locked in the database. It will report on all objects that are currently locked with their lock modes, and it will also report all the sessions waiting to acquire any locks.

PART

V

CH

25

LISTING 25.1   SIMPLE SCRIPT TO CHECK LOCKS ON THE SYSTEM

```
Select s.username,
       s.sid,
       l.type,
       l.id1,
       l.id2,
       l.lmode,
       l.request,
       p.spid PID
From v$lock l,
     v$session s,
     v$process p
Where s.sid = l.sid
And    p.addr = s.paddr
And    s.username is not null
Order By id1, s.sid,request;
```

USERNAME	SID	TY	ID1	ID2	LMODE	REQUEST	PID
MARK	39	TM	4573	0	3	0	19271
MANISH	41	TM	4573	0	2	0	20155
KASTURI	116	TM	4573	0	2	0	19914
ADITI	125	TM	4573	0	2	0	19906
ADITI	95	TM	12547	0	2	0	19906
JYOTI	95	TM	15397	0	3	0	20364
KASTURI	116	TM	15397	0	2	0	19914
ADITI	39	TM	15397	0	2	0	19906
MANISH	41	TX	65548	91271	6	0	20155
ADITI	125	TX	65548	91271	0	6	19906
MARK	39	TX	196626	107701	6	0	19271
JYOTI	95	TX	262156	118264	6	0	20364
KASTURI	116	TX	327699	200758	6	0	19914

All the locks are of the type TM (2,3) and TX (6). As previously mentioned, these are the most commonly acquired locks in any database.

A quick scan through the output leads to the following conclusions:

- There are three table objects—4573, 12547, and 15397—that are currently locked in the database.
- Session 39 is locking 4573 in row exclusive mode.
- Session 41 is locking object 4573 in row share mode.
- Session 116 is locking object 4573 in row share mode.
- Session 125 is locking object 4573 in row share mode.
- Session 95 is locking object 12547 in row share mode.
- Session 95 is locking object 15397 in row exclusive mode.

- Session 116 is locking object 15397 in row share mode.

- Session 39 is locking object 15397 in row share mode.

- Sessions 95, 116, 125, 39, and 41 each have a Transaction Lock (TX). The most important observation is that session 125 has a nonzero value in the request column, which means that it is waiting for a lock. Because the id1 and id2 values on the TX entry for session 41 and 125 match, you can infer that transaction 41 is locking out transaction 125. The common resource between transaction 125 and 41 is object ID 4573, so you can infer from this that session 41 has locked a particular row in object 4573, and session 125 is trying to lock the same row—hence, it's waiting.

This output was easy to interpret because there was only one common resource between 125 and 41, and it was easy to narrow down to which resource was causing the lock problem. In a majority of cases, there will be more than one resource, which is common between two sessions, and of course, one of them will be locked. In such cases, it would be difficult to use the previous output to interpret which resource is locked. In that case, you have to use the view V$sqltext, which stores the text of SQL statements belonging to the shared SQL cursors in the System Global Area (SGA). Using the previous output, find the session ID of the session that is waiting to acquire the lock, and then use the next select statement to interpret which resource the session is trying to lock and is waiting for, as follows:

```
Select sqltext
from v$sqltext a,v$session b
where a.address = b.sql_address
and    a.hash_value = b.sql_hash_value
and    b.sid      = 125
order by piece;
```

The output from the SQL statement above is as follows:

```
SQL_TEXT
--------------------------------------------------------
update employee set sname = 'JYOTI' where emp_id = '100';
```

This means that session 41 has already locked the employee record 100, and session 125 is trying to lock the same row. Thus, using the previous lock monitor report and the SQL statement in execution makes it easy to pinpoint which resource is locked.

GENERIC SQL SCRIPTS

This section will present several generic scripts to assist you in determining lock information in the database.

Listing 25.2 is a generic script that displays SQL Text, the SID, and the object name of the locks currently being held in the database.

LISTING 25.2   DISPLAY INFORMATION ON DATABASE LOCKS

```
Set pagesize 60
Set linesize 132
select s.username username,
    a.sid sid,
    a.owner¦¦'.'¦¦a.object object,
    s.lockwait,
    t.sql_text SQL
from v$sqltext t,
    v$session s,
    v$access a
where t.address = s.sql_address
and     t.hash_value = s.sql_hash_value
and     s.sid = a.sid
and     a.owner != 'SYS'
and     upper(substr(a.object,1,2)) != 'V$'
/
```

The output from the SQL statement above is as follows:

```
USERNAME      SID      OBJECT        LOCKWAIT  SQL
- - - - - - - - - - - - - - - - - - - - - - - - - - - - - - - - - - - - - - - - - - - - - - - - - - - - - - -
SHARON         8     MARK.CONFIG     E0034C98  update mark.config set irn=12 where
➥irn=4
KASTURI        12    KASTURI.EMP     E0034A5C  update kasturi.emp set tabno=10
➥where tabno=5
ADITI          99    DAVID.CHANNEL   E0034D99  update david.channel set c_irn=3
➥where c_irn=1
```

Listing 25.3 is a generic script generates a fairly easy-to-read report of locks being held (or waiting) in the database.

LISTING 25.3   GENERATE REPORT ON LOCKS HELD IN THE DATABASE

```
select B.SID,
    C.USERNAME,
    C.OSUSER,
    C.TERMINAL,
        DECODE(B.ID2, 0, A.OBJECT_NAME,'Trans-'¦¦to_char(B.ID1)) OBJECT_NAME,
            B.TYPE,
        DECODE(B.LMODE,0,' —Waiting— ',
                        1,'Null',
                        2,'Row Share',
                        3,'Row Excl',
                        4,'Share',
                        5,'Sha Row Exc',
                        6,'Exclusive','Other') "Lock Mode",
        DECODE(B.REQUEST,0,' ',
                          1,'Null',
                          2,'Row Share',
                          3,'Row Excl',
                          4,'Share',
                          5,'Sha Row Exc',
                          6,'Exclusive','Other') "Req Mode"
    from    DBA_OBJECTS A,
```

```
    V$LOCK B,
    V$SESSION C
where A.OBJECT_ID(+) = B.ID1
and B.SID = C.SID
and C.USERNAME is not null
order by B.SID, B.ID2;
```

The output from the SQL statement above is as follows:

```
Sess          Op Sys               OBJ NAME or
ID  USERNAME User ID   TERMINAL TRANS_ID        TY Lock Mode    Req Mode
- - - - - - - - - - - - - - - - - - - - - - - - - - - - - - - - - - - - - - - -
   7 JYOTI    jla       JLA      TRANSMISSION    TA Row Excl
   8 JOHN     jxl       JXL      TABLE_CONFIG  TM Row Excl
   9 BONITA   bog       BOG      DEPT_SCHED      TX -Waiting— Exclusive
  10 MANISH   mdk       MDK      AUDIT         TX Exclusive
  12 MARK     mdb       MDB      INDEX_BLOCKS     TM Row Excl
```

Another useful view is V$session_wait, which lists the events for which active sessions are waiting. The event that is registered in V$session_wait is enqueue. Therefore, if you query V$session_wait for a session that is locked or that you think is locked, you get the output in Listing 25.2.

The following are statements issued in SQL*PLUS to format the output of the query on V$session_wait:

LISTING 25.4 FINDING LOCKS ON A SESSION USING V$session_wait

```
col  event format a8
col  p2text format a5
col  p2 format 999999
col  p3text format a5
col  p3 format 999999
col  wait_time format 999999999
col  secs format 99999
col  state format a8
col  seq# format 99999
set pagesize 24
set verify off

select event, p2text,p2 ,p3text,p3,seq#,wait_time,state,seconds_in_wait secs
from v$session_wait
where    sid  = 126|
```

The output from the SQL statement above is as follows:

```
EVENT    P2TEX     P2 P3TEX     P3  SEQ#  WAIT_TIME STATE     SECS
- - - - - - - - - - - - - - - - - - - - - - - - - - - - - - - - - - - - - -
enqueue  id1    65548  id2    91271  6845          0 WAITING    850
```

Columns p2 and p3 contain the values id1 and id2, which are the values that can be obtained from V$lock. The output also reports the number of seconds the session has remained locked.

> **Note**
>
> When trying to interpret the output from V$session wait, always remember to check the value of the state column because it is a very important parameter. The possible values in this column are:
>
> - Waiting—Indicates the session is currently waiting for the event. When the value is Waiting in the state column, the seconds_in_wait column will contain the actual time in milliseconds for which the session waited for the event.
>
> - Waited unknown time—This value is shown when the TIMED_STATISTICS parameter is set to false.
>
> - Waited short time—Indicates that the session waited for a very brief period.
>
> - Waited known time—Indicates that the session has acquired the event that it was waiting for. The wait_time column will actually contain the time for which the session waited.

Another important view, V$sysstat, contains all the important statistics of the entire system. You can use V$sysstat to get an overview of the number of times any session has waited for a lock.

Use the following SQL:

```
select decode(class,1,'User',
                    2,'Redo',
                    4,'Enqueue',
                    8,'Cache',
                    16,'OS',
                    32,'Par Ser',
                    64,'SQL',
                    128,'Debug') class1   ,
statistic#,name,value
from v$sysstat
WHERE name = 'enqueue waits';
```

The output from the SQL statement above is as follows:

```
Class    S#N Name                                       Value
-------------------------------------------------------------
Enqueue   23 enqueue waits                              19989
```

From this SELECT statement, you can conclude that there were 19989 waits for lock on the system. Note that this counter gets incremented when the lock is released; if a session is currently waiting for a lock, the value is not reflected in the counter. If the value of enqueue waits is too high, the application needs review—and possible rescheduling—of concurrently running jobs that access the same resources.

Listing 25.5 is a generic script generates a report of users (sessions) waiting for locks.

LISTING 25.5 GENERATE REPORT ON USERS WAITING FOR LOCKS

```
column username format   A15
column sid       format   9990      heading SID
column type      format   A4
column lmode     format   990       heading 'HELD'
```

```
column request  format  990      heading 'REQ'
column id1         format  9999990
column id2 format   9999990
break on id1 skip 1 dup
spool tfslckwt.lst
SELECT sn.username,
    m.sid,
    m.type,
        DECODE(m.lmode, 0, 'None',
                    1, 'Null',
                    2, 'Row Share',
                    3, 'Row Excl.',
                    4, 'Share',
                    5, 'S/Row Excl.',
                    6, 'Exclusive',
                lmode, ltrim(to_char(lmode,'990'))) lmode,
        DECODE(m.request, 0, 'None',
                1, 'Null',
                    2, 'Row Share',
                    3, 'Row Excl.',
                    4, 'Share',
                    5, 'S/Row Excl.',
                    6, 'Exclusive',
                    request, ltrim(to_char(m.request,'990'))) request,
        m.id1,
    m.id2
FROM      v$session sn,
    v$lock m
WHERE (sn.sid = m.sid AND m.request != 0)
        OR (    sn.sid = m.sid
                AND m.request = 0 AND lmode != 4
                AND (id1, id2) IN (SELECT s.id1, s.id2
                    FROM v$lock s
                        WHERE request != 0
                    AND s.id1 = m.id1
                        AND s.id2 = m.id2)
            )
ORDER BY id1, id2, m.request;
spool off
clear breaks
```

PART

V

CH

25

The output from the SQL statement above is as follows:

USERNAME	SID	TYPE	HELD	REQ	ID1	ID2
SYSTEM	12	TX	Exclusive	None	131087	2328
SCOTT	7	TX	None	Exclusive	131087	2328
AMY	8	TX	Exclusive	None	131099	2332
MANISH	10	TX	None	Exclusive	131099	2332
BOLDT	12	TX	None	Exclusive	131099	2332

Listing 25.6 is a generic script displays locks and gives the SID and the serial number to kill; the report generated by this script gives information on sessions that are holding locks and gives the information needed to kill using the ALTER SYSTEM KILL SESSION command.

LISTING 25.6   DISPLAYING INFORMATION ON SESSIONS HOLDING LOCKS

```
set linesize 132 pagesize 66

break on Kill on username on terminal
column Kill heading 'Kill String' format a13
column res heading 'Resource Type' format 999
column id1 format 9999990
column id2 format 9999990
column lmode heading 'Lock Held' format a20
column request heading 'Lock Requested' format a20
column serial# format 99999
column username  format a10  heading "Username"
column terminal heading Term format a6
column tab format a35 heading "Table Name"
column owner format a9
column Address format a18
select  nvl(S.USERNAME,'Internal') username,
        nvl(S.TERMINAL,'None') terminal,
        L.SID¦¦',¦¦S.SERIAL# Kill,
        U1.NAME¦¦'.'¦¦substr(T1.NAME,1,20) tab,
        decode(L.LMODE,    1,'No Lock',
                           2,'Row Share',
                           3,'Row Exclusive',
                           4,'Share',
                           5,'Share Row Exclusive',
                           6,'Exclusive',null) lmode,
        decode(L.REQUEST,1,'No Lock',
                           2,'Row Share',
                           3,'Row Exclusive',
                           4,'Share',
                           5,'Share Row Exclusive',
                           6,'Exclusive',null) request
from    V$LOCK L,
        V$SESSION S,
        SYS.USER$ U1,
        SYS.OBJ$ T1
where   L.SID = S.SID
and     T1.OBJ# = decode(L.ID2,0,L.ID1,L.ID2)
and     U1.USER# = T1.OWNER#
and     S.TYPE != 'BACKGROUND'
order by 1,2,5 ;
```

The output from the SQL statement above is as follows:

```
Username   Term   Kill String   Table Name           Lock Hld  Lock Req
---------------------------------------------------------------------
SAMUEL     ttyr6  7,5159        SAMUEL.TABLE_CONFIG  Row Excl
YA-MEI     ttyr5  8,941         SCOTT.SCHEDULE       Row Excl
BARRETT    ttyq3  6,8885        SYS.CLUSTERS         Exclusiv
                                SCOTT.ACCOUNT        Row Excl
```

Execute the following command for an example demonstrating how to kill a session:

```
ALTER SYSTEM KILL SESSION '6,8885';
```

It will kill Barrett's Locked sessions.

Another useful script can be found in the $ORACLE_HOME/rbms/admin directory. This script is called utllockt.sql, and it prints the lock information in a tree format. This makes the information easier to read and makes it easier to decipher who is locking the resources.

AVOIDING LOCKS: POSSIBLE SOLUTIONS

This section provides some general practices to avoid locking.

Some applications use control tables to generate the next serial number. A typical example of this type is the next order number in an order table. There would be a control table storing the last order number generated. Any program that needs to generate a new order number would select from this table the last order number generated and then increment it by one. After the last order number is incremented, it is updated back to the control table.

In a multiuser environment where there could be many sessions trying to enter an order in the database, the control table could be a bottleneck. Consider a case where one session selects the last order number from the control table and after updating the incremented order number, hangs before committing for some reason; the whole application could come to a standstill with users queuing behind this hung session. Another bottleneck created by this type of order number generation occurs when one session updates the incremented order number back to the control table and then does some additional processing before committing. The time for which the control table record is locked will be the time for which the processing lasts. The additional processing time after capturing the next serial number from the control table will greatly limit the throughput of the system.

There are several possible solutions to these problems:

- Reduce the time between updating the last order number to the control table and the commit; that is, as soon as the next serial number is obtained, it should be immediately committed to the database, thus enabling other sessions to access the record.

- Consider using sequences. The advantages are many. The use of sequences greatly simplifies the application code. In the previous logic, a select and an update need to be performed. However, after the select is done from the sequence, the sequence number automatically gets incremented, thus having I/O advantage. The locking bottleneck is completely removed because Oracle automatically increments the sequence number internally for you. The disadvantage is that the last number generated cannot be rolled back after being used, thereby leading to holes.

Batch processing jobs inherently select a bulk of records from a table on which processing is to be done, perform some processing on them, and then update them back with new values. It's very important to lock these records before the program does the processing because the batch job could select old values from the table while another session comes and updates the record. Therefore, when the batch job has to update the results back to the table at the end of processing, it will find that another session has updated the record already. To prevent this from happening, the records are locked in advance while selecting themselves. The pseudo-PL/SQL code for this would look like Listing 25.7.

LISTING 25.7   BATCH PROCESSING PSEUDOCODE

```
Begin
Declare c_emp for
     Select * from emp
     <Where Clause >
For Update;

v_emp c_emp%RowType;

Begin
Open c_emp;
Loop;
Begin

    Fetch c_emp into v_emp;

    —Do some processing —
    Update c_emp
    Set sal = X,
        incr = Y
    Where emp_id = v_emp.emp_id;
    End;
End Loop;
Commit;
Close c_emp;
End ;
End ;
```

In this code, notice that the entire set of records to be processed is locked; it needs to be locked before processing so that another session cannot update these records while they are still being processed. The disadvantage in this code is that even after the records get processed, they are locked until all the records are processed. If the processing time is very long, the time for which these records are locked will prevent concurrent access to these by any other session. Depending on the demand for these records at the given point in time, this locking strategy might prove to be a performance bottleneck.

Alternative code that could be used to combat this situation is given in Listing 25.8.

LISTING 25.8   BATCH PROCESSING PSEUDOCODE FOR MAXIMUM CONCURRENCY

```
Begin
    Declare c_emp for
         Select rowid  from emp
         <Where Clause >;

    v_emp c_emp%RowType;
    r_emp emp%RowType;

    Begin
    Open c_emp;
    Loop;
    Begin
```

```
        Fetch c_emp into v_emp;

        Select *
        Into    r_emp
        From    emp
        Where rowid = v_emp.rowid;
        <Where Clause >
        For Update;
        —Do some processing —
        Update emp
        Set sal = X,
            incr = Y
        Where rowid = v_emp.rowid
        <Where Clause >;

        Commit;

        End;
    End Loop;

    Close c_emp;
    End ;
End ;
```

Notice in Listing 25.8 that the outer cursor is just selecting all the rows from the table. The outer cursor feeds values to the inner select, and the inner select will lock only one row at a time with the for update clause. The commit in Listing 25.8 is now moved inside the loop; therefore, after every row is updated, the commit is issued, thus maximizing concurrent access to the table for other users. You might be tempted to move the commit in the script in Listing 25.7 inside the loop. Unfortunately, if this is done in Oracle6.0, the cursor also gets closed, resulting in termination of the PL/SQL loop. All the relevant rows in the table are locked as soon as the cursor is opened by the open clause. When the commit is issued, the cursor loses its context and will display the following message:

ORA-01002: fetch out of sequence

Therefore it's necessary to code in the style shown previously.

Care should be taken when using tables with row-level triggers on them. For example, a table can have a row-level trigger such that when a record of the table is updated, the trigger on the table might cause other tables to be updated. This can cause a lot of locks to be implicitly acquired on the system by a single update statement.

User education can help in avoiding locks. A number of times I have noticed that users who think that their process has hung for some reason switch off their terminal in order to reset the process (particularly in client/server applications). Another category of users is the type who leaves the terminal logged on when taking a lunch break or when leaving the desk. This could lock some tables in the system and could cause other users to wait behind this user. Users need to be made to understand that switching off a terminal does not reset the process, and the process is still active on the server side. Similarly, users should be encouraged to log off inactive terminals. This can help to increase concurrency and keep users from locking up.

LOCKING AND DISTRIBUTED DATABASES

Distributed databases must handle inherent updating problems when a transaction attempts to simultaneously update two distributed databases, known as Two-Phase Commit (2PC). This is shown in the following SQL statements:

```
APPLY UPDATE A (DB1)
APPLY UPDATE B  (DB2)
IF A = OK AND B = OK
    COMMIT A
        < = At this point deadly exposure occurs.
    COMMIT B
ELSE
    ROLLBACK A
    ROLLBACK B
```

Here, after successfully executing UPDATE statements, the system will issue the COMMIT statements to A and B. The point of exposure occurs when a failure happens after the COMMIT of A and before the COMMIT of B. It causes a major loss of integrity for which there is no automated recovery. The only solution to this problem is to terminate the transaction and manually roll back the updates to A and B.

The following techniques can be used for releasing the locks into the database:

- Use the command to kill the session, which holds the Lock ALTER SYSTEM KILL SESSION 'sid,serial#';.

- Ask the Lock holder to COMMIT or ROLLBACK.

- Kill the userID from the UNIX prompt with kill -9 <UserID>.

- In a Two-Phase commit transaction, use ROLLBACK FORCE or COMMIT FORCE.

- Kill the user session from Server Manager Menu mode or from Enterprise Manager.

DETAILED LOCKING INFORMATION SCRIPT:

Listing 25.9 is a detailed locking information script provides fully decoded information regarding the locks currently held in the database.

LISTING 25.9   RETRIVING DECODED INFORMATION ON DATABASE LOCKS

```
set lines 200
set pagesize 66
break on Kill on sid on  username on terminal
column Kill heading 'Kill String' format a13
column res heading 'Resource Type' format 999
column id1 format 9999990
column id2 format 9999990
column locking heading 'Lock Held/Lock Requested' format a40
column lmode heading 'Lock Held' format a20
column request heading 'Lock Requested' format a20
column serial# format 99999
column username  format a10  heading "Username"
column terminal heading Term format a6
```

```
column tab format a30 heading "Table Name"
column owner format a9
column LAddr heading "ID1 - ID2" format a18
column Lockt heading "Lock Type" format a40
column command format a25
column sid format 990
rem     L.SID¦¦',','¦¦S.SERIAL# Kill,
select
nvl(S.USERNAME,'Internal') username,
        L.SID,
        nvl(S.TERMINAL,'None') terminal,
        decode(command,
0,'None',decode(l.id2,0,U1.NAME¦¦'.'¦¦substr(T1.NAME,1,20),'None')) tab,
decode(command,
0,'BACKGROUND',
1,'Create Table',
2,'INSERT',
3,'SELECT',
4,'CREATE CLUSTER',
5,'ALTER CLUSTER',
6,'UPDATE',
7,'DELETE',
8,'DROP',
9,'CREATE INDEX',
10,'DROP INDEX',
11,'ALTER INDEX',
12,'DROP TABLE',
13,' — -',
14,' — -',
15,'ALTER TABLE',
16,' — -',
17,'GRANT',
18,'REVOKE',
19,'CREATE SYNONYM',
20,'DROP SYNONYM',
21,'CREATE VIEW',
22,'DROP VIEW',
23,' — -',
24,' — -',
25,' — -',
26,'LOCK TABLE',
27,'NO OPERATION',
28,'RENAME',
29,'COMMENT',
30,'AUDIT',
31,'NOAUDIT',
32,'CREATE EXTERNAL DATABASE',
33,'DROP EXTERNAL DATABASE',
34,'CREATE DATABASE',
35,'ALTER DATABASE',
36,'CREATE ROLLBACK SEGMENT',
37,'ALTER ROLLBACK SEGMENT',
38,'DROP ROLLBACK SEGMENT',
39,'CREATE TABLESPACE',
40,'ALTER TABLESPACE',
41,'DROP TABLESPACE',
42,'ALTER SESSION',
```

PART

V

CH

25

continues

LISTING 25.9   CONTINUED

```
43,'ALTER USER',
44,'COMMIT',
45,'ROLLBACK',
46,'SAVEPOINT',
47,'PL/SQL EXECUTE',
48,'SET TRANSACTION',
49,'ALTER SYSTEM SWITCH LOG',
50,'EXPLAIN',
51,'CREATE USER',
52,'CREATE ROLE',
53,'DROP USER',
54,'DROP ROLE',
55,'SET ROLE',
56,'CREATE SCHEMA',
57,'CREATE CONTROL FILE',
58,'ALTER TRACING',
59,'CREATE TRIGGER',
60,'ALTER TRIGGER',
61,'DROP TRIGGER',
62,'ANALYZE TABLE',
63,'ANALYZE INDEX',
64,'ANALYZE CLUSTER',
65,'CREATE PROFILE',
66,'DROP PROFILE',
67,'ALTER PROFILE',
68,'DROP PROCEDURE',
70,'ALTER RESOURCE COST',
71,'CREATE SNAPSHOT LOG',
72,'ALTER SNAPSHOT LOG',
73,'DROP SNAPSHOT LOG',
74,'CREATE SNAPSHOT',
75,'ALTER SNAPSHOT',
76,'DROP SNAPSHOT',
84,'-',
85,'TRUNCATE TABLE',
86,'TRUNCATE CLUSTER',
87,'-',
88,'ALTER VIEW',
89,'-',
90,'-',
91,'CREATE FUNCTION',
92,'ALTER FUNCTION',
93,'DROP FUNCTION',
94,'CREATE PACKAGE',
95,'ALTER PACKAGE',
96,'DROP PACKAGE',
97,'CREATE PACKAGE BODY',
98,'ALTER PACKAGE BODY',
99,'DROP PACKAGE BODY',
command||' - ???') COMMAND,
        decode(L.LMODE,1,'No Lock',
                2,'Row Share',
                3,'Row Exclusive',
                4,'Share',
                5,'Share Row Exclusive',
```

```
                   6,'Exclusive','NONE') lmode,
         decode(L.REQUEST,1,'No Lock',
                   2,'Row Share',
                   3,'Row Exclusive',
                   4,'Share',
                   5,'Share Row Exclusive',
                   6,'Exclusive','NONE') request,
l.id1||'-'||l.id2 Laddr,
l.type||' - '||
decode(l.type,
'BL','Buffer hash table instance lock',
'CF','Cross-instance function invocation instance lock',
'CI','Control file schema global enqueue lock',
'CS','Control file schema global enqueue lock',
'DF','Data file instance lock',
'DM','Mount/startup db primary/secondary instance lock',
'DR','Distributed recovery process lock',
'DX','Distributed transaction entry lock',
'FI','SGA open-file information lock',
'FS','File set lock',
'IR','Instance recovery serialization global enqueue lock',
'IV','Library cache invalidation instance lock',
'MB','Master buffer hash table instance lock',
'MM','Mount definition gloabal enqueue lock',
'MR','Media recovery lock',
'RE','USE_ROW_ENQUEUE enforcement lock',
'RT','Redo thread global enqueue lock',
'RW','Row wait enqueue lock',
'SC','System commit number instance lock',
'SH','System commit number high water mark enqueue lock',
'SN','Sequence number instance lock',
'SQ','Sequence number enqueue lock',
'ST','Space transaction enqueue lock',
'SV','Sequence number value lock',
'TA','Generic enqueue lock',
'TD','DDL enqueue lock',
'TE','Extend-segment enqueue lock',
'TM','DML enqueue lock',
'TT','Temporary table enqueue lock',
'TX','Transaction enqueue lock',
'UL','User supplied lock',
'UN','User name lock',
'WL','Being-written redo log instance lock',
'WS','Write-atomic-log-switch global enqueue lock',
'TS',decode(l.id2,0,'Temporary segment enqueue lock (ID2=0)',
                    'New block allocation enqueue lock (ID2=1)'),
'LA','Library cache lock instance lock (A=namespace)',
'LB','Library cache lock instance lock (B=namespace)',
'LC','Library cache lock instance lock (C=namespace)',
'LD','Library cache lock instance lock (D=namespace)',
'LE','Library cache lock instance lock (E=namespace)',
'LF','Library cache lock instance lock (F=namespace)',
'LG','Library cache lock instance lock (G=namespace)',
'LH','Library cache lock instance lock (H=namespace)',
'LI','Library cache lock instance lock (I=namespace)',
'LJ','Library cache lock instance lock (J=namespace)',
'LK','Library cache lock instance lock (K=namespace)',
```

continues

LISTING 25.9 CONTINUED

```
'LL','Library cache lock instance lock (L=namespace)',
'LM','Library cache lock instance lock (M=namespace)',
'LN','Library cache lock instance lock (N=namespace)',
'LO','Library cache lock instance lock (O=namespace)',
'LP','Library cache lock instance lock (P=namespace)',
'LS','Log start/log switch enqueue lock',
'PA','Library cache pin instance lock (A=namespace)',
'PB','Library cache pin instance lock (B=namespace)',
'PC','Library cache pin instance lock (C=namespace)',
'PD','Library cache pin instance lock (D=namespace)',
'PE','Library cache pin instance lock (E=namespace)',
'PF','Library cache pin instance lock (F=namespace)',
'PG','Library cache pin instance lock (G=namespace)',
'PH','Library cache pin instance lock (H=namespace)',
'PI','Library cache pin instance lock (I=namespace)',
'PJ','Library cache pin instance lock (J=namespace)',
'PL','Library cache pin instance lock (K=namespace)',
'PK','Library cache pin instance lock (L=namespace)',
'PM','Library cache pin instance lock (M=namespace)',
'PN','Library cache pin instance lock (N=namespace)',
'PO','Library cache pin instance lock (O=namespace)',
'PP','Library cache pin instance lock (P=namespace)',
'PQ','Library cache pin instance lock (Q=namespace)',
'PR','Library cache pin instance lock (R=namespace)',
'PS','Library cache pin instance lock (S=namespace)',
'PT','Library cache pin instance lock (T=namespace)',
'PU','Library cache pin instance lock (U=namespace)',
'PV','Library cache pin instance lock (V=namespace)',
'PW','Library cache pin instance lock (W=namespace)',
'PX','Library cache pin instance lock (X=namespace)',
'PY','Library cache pin instance lock (Y=namespace)',
'PZ','Library cache pin instance lock (Z=namespace)',
'QA','Row cache instance lock (A=cache)',
'QB','Row cache instance lock (B=cache)',
'QC','Row cache instance lock (C=cache)',
'QD','Row cache instance lock (D=cache)',
'QE','Row cache instance lock (E=cache)',
'QF','Row cache instance lock (F=cache)',
'QG','Row cache instance lock (G=cache)',
'QH','Row cache instance lock (H=cache)',
'QI','Row cache instance lock (I=cache)',
'QJ','Row cache instance lock (J=cache)',
'QL','Row cache instance lock (K=cache)',
'QK','Row cache instance lock (L=cache)',
'QM','Row cache instance lock (M=cache)',
'QN','Row cache instance lock (N=cache)',
'QO','Row cache instance lock (O=cache)',
'QP','Row cache instance lock (P=cache)',
'QQ','Row cache instance lock (Q=cache)',
'QR','Row cache instance lock (R=cache)',
'QS','Row cache instance lock (S=cache)',
'QT','Row cache instance lock (T=cache)',
'QU','Row cache instance lock (U=cache)',
'QV','Row cache instance lock (V=cache)',
'QW','Row cache instance lock (W=cache)',
```

```
'QX','Row cache instance lock (X=cache)',
'QY','Row cache instance lock (Y=cache)',
'QZ','Row cache instance lock (Z=cache)','????') Lockt
from    V$LOCK L,
        V$SESSION S,
        SYS.USER$ U1,
        SYS.OBJ$ T1
where   L.SID = S.SID
and     T1.OBJ#  = decode(L.ID2,0,L.ID1,1)
and     U1.USER# = T1.OWNER#
and     S.TYPE != 'BACKGROUND'
order by 1,2,5
/
```

IMPLEMENTING LOCKS WITH LATCHES

Oracle implements locks using various techniques mentioned in the previous section. Using latches is one of them. Latches, unlike locks, are acquired internally and released by Oracle. Latches cannot be acquired explicitly by issuing a statement. Basically, latches are used to control access to shared code paths. A latch is a type of a lock that can be very quickly acquired or freed. Latches are used to prevent more than one process from executing the same piece of code at a given time.

FUNCTIONING OF LATCHES

Latches are used to control access to shared structures. Latches are implemented using semaphores at the operating system level. Latches are locks that are held for a very small amount of time.

Before a process gets access to a shared structure protected by a latch, it has to first acquire the latch. This latch could currently be free (that is, no other process is accessing the latch), in which case the process gets the latch immediately. This process will hold the latch for the period of time it requires and will then relinquish the latch. This is the simplest and the typical case.

Consider the case in which a particular latch is already acquired by a process. Another process trying to acquire the latch has two options, depending on the type of latch it is trying to acquire. Associated with latches, there are two types.

- Immediate
- Willing to wait

If the process tries to acquire the latch in *immediate* mode and it is already held by another process, the process will not wait to acquire the latch if the latch is not available immediately. It will continue by taking a different action.

In *willing to wait* mode, if the process fails to acquire the latch in the first try, it will wait and try again. If the system has multiple CPUs, this unsuccessful process will start spinning on the latch and try to acquire it. The number of times the process spins on the latch is defined by the init.ora parameter spin_count. With every spin, it will try to acquire the latch; if it does not, it spins again and this goes on until the number of spins reaches spin_count value. The process will then go to sleep for a specified amount of time, wake up again, and repeat the previous sequence of steps as shown in Figure 25.1.

Figure 25.1
Process spinning on a latch

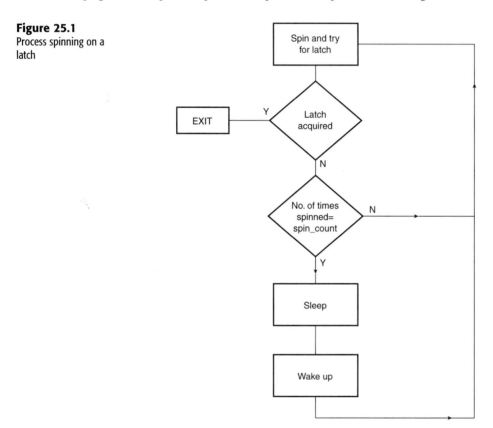

ANALYZING VIEWS RELATED TO LATCHES

This section discusses data dictionary views, which can be used to obtain more information about latches on the system. Only the important columns in these views are discussed here. V$latch and V$latchholder are two very important views associated with latches:

- V$latch—This view contains all important statistics related to the performance of various latches on the system. Table 25.5 gives the description of important columns of view V$latch.

- V$latchholder—If the system is currently having latch contention problems, this view can be used to determine which session is currently holding the latch.

TABLE 25.5   V$latch

Column Name	Description
immediate_gets	The number of requests for the latch that were successful in obtaining the latch immediately (immediate mode only).
immediate_misses	The number of requests for the latch that were not successful in obtaining the latch immediately (immediate mode only).
gets	The number of successful requests for latches that were willing to wait for the latch.
misses	The number of unsuccessful requests for latches that were willing to wait for the latch.
sleeps	The number of times a process that was willing to wait for the latch requested the latch and when it did not get it, had to sleep.
spin_gets	The number of times the latch was obtained without sleeping but just spinning.
Sleep1-10	Every time a process sleeps, the value in this column is incremented—for example, if a process had to sleep three times before it acquired the latch, the sleep3 column would be incremented by 1.

CHECKING FOR LATCH CONTENTION

If the system is facing latch contention problems, the scripts Listing 25.10 and Listing 25.11 can be useful in finding out which latch is badly hit. All scripts query the V$latch table to find the latch details. Shown next is the description of the V$latch:

```
ADDR                        RAW(4)
 LATCH#                     NUMBER
 LEVEL#                     NUMBER
 NAME                       VARCHAR2(64)
 GETS                       NUMBER
 MISSES                     NUMBER
 SLEEPS                     NUMBER
 IMMEDIATE_GETS             NUMBER
 IMMEDIATE_MISSES           NUMBER
 WAITERS_WOKEN              NUMBER
 WAITS_HOLDING_LATCH        NUMBER
 SPIN_GETS                  NUMBER
 SLEEP1                     NUMBER
 SLEEP2                     NUMBER
 SLEEP3                     NUMBER
 SLEEP4                     NUMBER
 SLEEP5                     NUMBER
 SLEEP6                     NUMBER
 SLEEP7                     NUMBER
 SLEEP8                     NUMBER
 SLEEP9                     NUMBER
 SLEEP10                    NUMBER
 SLEEP11                    NUMBER
```

PART

V

CH

25

The following script should be run from SQL*Plus.

LISTING 25.10   SCRIPT TO IDENTIFY LATCH PERFORMANCE ON THE SYSTEM

```
col name heading "Name" format a20
col pid heading "HSid" format a3
col gets heading "Gets" format 999999990
col misses heading "Miss" format 99990
col im_gets heading "ImG" format 99999990
col im_misses heading "ImM" format 999990
col sleeps heading "Sleeps" format 99990

select  n.name name, h.pid pid , l.gets gets , l.misses misses,
l.immediate_gets im_gets, l.immediate_misses im_misses, l.sleeps sleeps
from v$latchname n , v$latchholder h , v$latch l
where l.latch# = n.latch#
and l.addr = h.laddr(+)
```

The output from the SQL statement above is as follows:

Name	HSid	Gets	Miss	ImG	ImM	Sleeps
cached attr list		0	0	0	0	0
modify parameter values		931	0	0	0	0
messages		736117	44	0	0	80
enqueue hash chains		1257100	145	0	0	163
trace latch		0	0	0	0	0
cache buffers lru chains		**197351761**	**2092**	**66288289**	**20919**	**4020**
cache buffer handles		2348	0	0	0	0
multiblock read objects		2139864	700	1	0	900
cache protection latch		0	0	0	0	0
shared pool		1261081	207	0	0	208
library cache		7867103	11803	376	0	11854
redo allocation		1306657	501	0	0	760
redo copy		34	0	463290	71	47

In this output, the HSID column indicates the session ID of the session currently holding the latch. If the number of misses as a percentage of the gets is more than 1 percent, the latch needs some attention.

Using the V$session wait view is another way to check whether a session hung for a long time is waiting for a latch. The query in Listing 25.11 can be used.

LISTING 25.11   USING V$session_wait TO IDENTIFY LATCH CONTENTION

```
select event, p1text,p1 ,p2text,p2 ,seq#,wait_time,state
from v$session_wait
where    sid  = '&&1'
and event = 'latch free';
```

The output from the SQL statement above is as follows:

```
EVENT          P1TEXT      P1 P2TEXT    P2      SEQ# WAIT_TIME STATE
- - - - - - - - - - - - - - - - - - - - - - - - - - - - - - - - - - - - - - - - - - - - -
latch free     address     3 number    11      1181         0 WAITING
```

If the wait_time column has a value of 0, the session is currently waiting for the latch.

The P2 column indicates the number of the latch. The name of the latch can be found by using V$latchname:

```
Select name
From v$latchname
Where latch# = 11;
cache buffers chains
```

Listing 25.12 is a report generation script that lists information critical to determining if a database instance is experiencing latch contention. Latch contention ratios should remain less than or equal to one percent. Here is the script.

LISTING 25.12   LISTING INFORMATION FOR DETERMINING LATCH CONTENTION

```
ttitle -
    center    'Latch Contention Report'   skip 3

col name form A25
col gets form 999,999,999
col misses form 999.99
col spins form 999.99
col igets form 999,999,999
col imisses form 999.99

select name,
    gets,
    misses*100/decode(gets,0,1,gets) misses,
    spin_gets*100/decode(misses,0,1,misses) spins,
    immediate_gets igets,
    immediate_misses*100/decode(immediate_gets,0,1,immediate_gets) imisses
from v$latch
order by gets + immediate_gets
    /
```

PART

V

CH

25

The output from the SQL statement above is as follows:

```
                    Latch Contention Report

NAME                          GETS  MISSES  SPINS      IGETS IMISSES
- - - - - - - - - - - - - - - - - - - - - - - - - - - - - - - - - - - - - - - - - - - - -
cached attr list                 0    .00    .00          0    .00
trace latch                      0    .00    .00          0    .00
cache protection latch           0    .00    .00          0    .00
KCL freelist latch               0    .00    .00          0    .00
redo copy                        0    .00    .00          0    .00
archive control                  0    .00    .00          0    .00
KCL name table latch             0    .00    .00          0    .00
```

continues

continued

```
lock element parent latch          0      .00      .00              0      .00
loader state object freelist       0      .00      .00              0      .00
process queue                      0      .00      .00              0      .00
error message lists                0      .00      .00              0      .00
query server freelists             0      .00      .00              0      .00
query server process               0      .00      .00              0      .00
virtual circuits                   0      .00      .00              0      .00
virtual circuit queues             0      .00      .00              0      .00
virtual circuit buffers            0      .00      .00              0      .00
global tx hash mapping             0      .00      .00              0      .00
device information                 0      .00      .00              0      .00
parallel query alloc buffer        0      .00      .00              0      .00
parallel query stats               0      .00      .00              0      .00
process queue reference            0      .00      .00              0      .00
global transaction                 0      .00      .00              0      .00
global tx free list                0      .00      .00              0      .00
cost function                      0      .00      .00              0      .00
instance latch                     0      .00      .00              0      .00
NLS data objects                   1      .00      .00              0      .00
cache buffer handles              42      .00      .00              0      .00
latch wait list                   70      .00      .00              0      .00
multiblock read objects          124      .00      .00              0      .00
library cache load lock          326      .00      .00              0      .00
sort extent pool                 867      .00      .00              0      .00
ktm global data                  867      .00      .00              0      .00
process allocation               680      .00      .00            680      .00
sequence cache                 2,128      .00      .00              0      .00
user lock                      2,676      .00      .00              0      .00
session switching              4,120      .00      .00              0      .00
modify parameter values        5,005      .00      .00              0      .00
cache buffers lru chain       41,770      .00      .00         31,613      .00
dml lock allocation          116,700      .00      .00              0      .00
transaction allocation       177,154      .00      .00              0      .00
undo global data             206,727      .00      .00              0      .00
enqueue hash chains          271,775      .00      .00              0      .00
messages                     592,041      .00      .00              0      .00
shared pool                  860,906      .00      .00              0      .00
enqueues                   1,151,391      .00      .00              0      .00
list of block allocation   1,558,054      .00      .00              0      .00
session allocation         1,688,085      .00      .00              0      .00
system commit number       1,859,249      .00      .00              0      .00
redo allocation            2,009,258      .01      .00              0      .00
row cache objects          2,501,694      .00      .00             42      .00
session idle bit           4,167,221      .00      .00              0      .00
library cache             13,734,618      .00      .00             41      .00
cache buffers chains      43,694,786      .00      .00      6,832,121      .00
```

Listing 25.13 is a script gives the ratios of various sleeps of the latches.

LISTING 25.13 RETRIEVING LATCH SLEEP RATIOS

```
col name form A18 trunc

col gets form 999,999,990
col miss form 90.9
```

```
col cspins  form A6 heading 'spin¦sl06'
col csleep1 form A5 heading 'sl01¦sl07'
col csleep2 form A5 heading 'sl02¦sl08'
col csleep3 form A5 heading 'sl03¦sl09'
col csleep4 form A5 heading 'sl04¦sl10'
col csleep5 form A5 heading 'sl05¦sl11'
col Interval form A12
set recsep off

select a.name,
    a.gets gets,
     a.misses*100/decode(a.gets,0,1,a.gets) miss,
      to_char(a.spin_gets*100/decode(a.misses,0,1,a.misses),'990.9')¦¦
      to_char(a.sleep6*100/decode(a.misses,0,1,a.misses),'90.9') cspins,
     to_char(a.sleep1*100/decode(a.misses,0,1,a.misses),'90.9')¦¦
      to_char(a.sleep7*100/decode(a.misses,0,1,a.misses),'90.9') csleep1,
     to_char(a.sleep2*100/decode(a.misses,0,1,a.misses),'90.9')¦¦
      to_char(a.sleep8*100/decode(a.misses,0,1,a.misses),'90.9') csleep2,
     to_char(a.sleep3*100/decode(a.misses,0,1,a.misses),'90.9')¦¦
      to_char(a.sleep9*100/decode(a.misses,0,1,a.misses),'90.9') csleep3,
     to_char(a.sleep4*100/decode(a.misses,0,1,a.misses),'90.9')¦¦
      to_char(a.sleep10*100/decode(a.misses,0,1,a.misses),'90.9') csleep4,
     to_char(a.sleep5*100/decode(a.misses,0,1,a.misses),'90.9')¦¦
      to_char(a.sleep11*100/decode(a.misses,0,1,a.misses),'90.9') csleep5
from v$latch a
where a.misses <> 0
order by 2 desc
/
```

The output from the SQL statement above is as follows:

```
spin    sl01  sl02  sl03  sl04  sl05
NAME                     GETS  MISS sl06   sl07  sl08  sl09  sl10  sl11
-----------------------------------------------------------------------
cache buffers chai  43,696,090  0.0   0.0 #####  0.0   0.0   0.0   0.0
                                      0.0   0.0   0.0   0.0   0.0   0.0
library cache       13,738,029  0.0   0.0  97.1  0.0   2.9   0.0   0.0
                                      0.0   0.0   0.0   0.0   0.0   0.0
session idle bit     4,167,650  0.0   0.0 #####  0.0   0.0   0.0   0.0
                                      0.0   0.0   0.0   0.0   0.0   0.0
row cache objects    2,502,963  0.0   0.0 #####  0.0   0.0   0.0   0.0
                                      0.0   0.0   0.0   0.0   0.0   0.0
redo allocation      2,010,038  0.0   0.0 #####  0.0   0.0   0.0   0.0
                                      0.0   0.0   0.0   0.0   0.0   0.0
system commit numb   1,859,423  0.0   0.0 #####  0.0   0.0   0.0   0.0
                                      0.0   0.0   0.0   0.0   0.0   0.0
session allocation   1,688,269  0.0   0.0 #####  0.0   0.0   0.0   0.0
                                      0.0   0.0   0.0   0.0   0.0   0.0
enqueues             1,152,139  0.0   0.0 #####  0.0   0.0   0.0   0.0
                                      0.0   0.0   0.0   0.0   0.0   0.0
messages               595,209  0.0   0.0 #####  0.0   0.0   0.0   0.0
         0.0   0.0   0.0   0.0   0.0   0.0
enqueue hash chain     272,103  0.0   0.0   0.0  0.0 #####  0.0   0.0
                                      0.0   0.0   0.0   0.0   0.0   0.0
cache buffers lru       41,778  0.0   0.0 #####  0.0   0.0   0.0   0.0
                                            0.0   0.0   0.0   0.0   0.0   0.0
```

TUNING SOME IMPORTANT LATCHES

Of all the latches shown in Listing 25.14, a few important and proper steps can be taken to tune them. The latches that will be covered in this section are cache buffers lru chain, redo allocation, redo copy, and library cache.

Listing 25.14 shows all the latches possible on the database.

LISTING 25.14   LISTING OF ALL LATCHES

```
LATCH#          NAME
-------------------------------
       0 latch wait list
       1 process allocation
       2 session allocation
       3 session switching
       4 session idle bit
       5 cached attr list
       6 modify parameter values
       7 messages
       8 enqueues
       9 enqueue hash chains
      10 trace latch
      11 cache buffers chains
      12 cache buffer handles
      13 multiblock read objects
      14 cache protection latch
      15 cache buffers lru chain
      16 system commit number
      17 archive control
      18 redo allocation
      19 redo copy
      20 KCL freelist latch
      21 KCL name table latch
      22 instance latch
      23 lock element parent latch
      24 loader state object freelist
      25 dml lock allocation
      26 list of block allocation
      27 transaction allocation
      28 sort extent pool
      29 undo global data
      30 ktm global data
      31 sequence cache
      32 row cache objects
      33 cost function
      34 user lock
      35 global tx free list
      36 global transaction
      37 global tx hash mapping
      38 shared pool
      39 library cache
      40 library cache load lock
```

```
41 virtual circuit buffers
42 virtual circuit queues
43 virtual circuits
44 NLS data objects
45 query server process
46 query server freelists
47 error message lists
48 process queue
49 process queue reference
50 parallel query stats
51 parallel query alloc buffer
52 device information
```

cache buffers lru chain

The `cache buffers lru chain` latch is responsible for protecting the access paths to `db block` buffers in the buffer cache. The buffer cache size defined by the `init.ora` parameter `db_block_buffers` resides in the SGA and contains the cached copy of data read from data files. When processes need to read data, the presence of the data in this buffer as a result of the data being read in by some process makes the read very I/O-efficient.

The buffer cache is organized in two lists: the dirty list and the LRU list. The *dirty list* contains the buffers that have been modified but not written to the disk yet. The LRU list is comprised of the pinned buffers, the dirty buffers that have not yet been moved to the dirty list, and the free buffers. The *pinned buffers* are buffers that are currently accessed by other processes. The *dirty buffers* contain buffers that are to be written to the disk, and they then subsequently get moved to the dirty list. The *free buffers* are the buffers that are available for use.

When a process needs to read data from the disk that is not already present in the cache, it needs a free buffer to read the new data. It scans the LRU list to check for free buffers. If there are excessive requests for free buffers in the buffer cache, there will be high access to the LRU list causing contention for the cache buffer LRU chain.

The contention for this latch can be minimized by the `init.ora` parameter `db_block_lru_latches`, which is available in Oracle8. By increasing the `db_block_lru_latches` value, the contention can be minimized for this latch. The maximum value for this parameter is double the number of CPUs.

The basic reason for contention for this latch is a high request for free buffers. You can optimize the SQL statements to minimize the high demand for free buffers or increase the `db_block_buffer` parameter to increase the number of free buffers available on the system.

PART

V

CH

25

Note

> Note that the SGA must fit into a contiguous chunk of real memory, so if the buffer cache is enlarged, you must ensure that there is enough contiguous memory available on the system to service the increase.

redo allocation AND redo copy

The `redo allocation` and `redo copy` latches control the write access to the redo log buffer. When a process requires writing to the redo log buffer, one of these latches is to be acquired by the process. If the size of the redo log information written to the redo log buffer is less than the `log_small_entry_max_size` parameter, the process will use the `redo allocation` latch. If the size is greater than this value, the process is copied using the `redo copy` latch.

A quick way to check whether there is any contention on the redo log buffer is to check whether there are any waits associated with writing to the redo log buffer. This can be done by using the system view `V$sysstat`:

```
Select name, value
From v$sysstat
Where name = 'redo log space requests';
```

The output from the SQL statement above is as follows:

```
Name                                           Value
- - - - - - - - - - - - - - - - - - - - - - - - - - - - - - - - - - - - - - - - - -
redo log space requests                          12
```

The size of the redo log buffer will have to be increased if the number of waits is too high.

CONTENTION FOR THE `redo allocation` LATCH   The contention for `redo allocation` can be reduced on a multi-CPU system by forcing the process to use the `redo copy` latch instead. Because there can be multiple `redo copy` latches, the copy will be done more efficiently. The number of `redo copy` latches is defined by the `init.ora` parameter `log_simultaneous_copies`. The maximum number of available latches on the system is double the number of CPUs. For a single CPU system, this value is `0`, and the `redo allocation` latch will be used. If there is a contention for the `redo allocation` latch, the value of `log_small_entry_max_size` can be decreased from its current value so that the `redo copy` latch is used.

CONTENTION FOR THE `redo copy` LATCH   If the system is facing contention for the `redo copy` latch, it can be decreased by either increasing the value of `log_small_entry_max_size` (so that the `redo allocation` latch is used) or increasing the value of `log_simultaneous_copies` (so that it increases the number of `redo copy` latches available).

The `init.ora` parameter `log_entry_prebuild_threshold` can be increased so that the data that is written to the redo log buffer is grouped and written out. By increasing the parameter, a number of write operations can be grouped so that they can be written out in one operation, thereby reducing requests for these latches and thus contention.

LIBRARY CACHE

This latch is primarily concerned with control of access to the `library cache`. The `library cache` includes shared SQL area, private SQL areas, PL/SQL procedures packages, and other control structures. Shared SQL area contains SQLs that are shared among multiple sessions. By increasing the sharing of these SQLs, contention to this latch can be avoided.

Contention for this latch occurs when there is a lot of demand for space in the `library cache`. Very high parsing on the system and heavy demand to open a new cursor because of low sharing among processes are some of the common causes of contention for this latch.

Contention for this latch can be avoiding by using code that can be shared by multiple sessions. For example, the RDBMS treats the following two SQLs differently:

```
select name from employee where emp_id = 100;
Select name from employee where emp_id = 100;
```

Though both the SQL statements look the same, the hash values of these statements are different. One of the statements has `Select` with the "s" in upper case and the other one has `select` in lower case. Therefore, when this statement is issued, the RDBMS will parse both the statements individually as different statements, thus causing load on the latches. This situation can be avoided by developing coding standards wherein indentation and case standards are implemented so that every SQL statement written would have the same hash value as far as possible. Note even putting in more empty spaces causes one `select` statement to be considered different from another causing increased parsing.

Using bind variables in SQL statements can increase the sharing of the same clauses. For example, consider the two cases, not using bind variables:

```
Select sal from employee where emp_id = 100;
Select sal from employee where emp_id = 200;
```

Now, consider them using bind variables:

```
Select sal from employee where emp_id  := emp_id;
```

By using bind variables, both the previous `select` statements in the first case can share the same `select`, which is stored in the `library cache`, thus reducing unnecessary parsing and reducing load on the latch. Using bind variables prevents multiple copies of the same `select` statement from being formed in the shared pool.

Parsing can be reduced in the shared pool or by pinning frequently used objects such as procedures and packages. The advantage of pinning these objects is that these will never be flushed out of the shared pool and subsequently the parse time is reduced. Objects that are used very frequently can be identified by the following query:

```
Select name ,executions
From v$db_object_cache
Where executions > <threshold limit>
order by 2 desc;
```

These high-execution objects can be pinned in the shared pool using

```
dbms_share_pool.keep('object_name','P');.
```

To check the objects in the shared pool that are not pinned, execute the following query:

```
Select name,type,kept,sharable_mem
From v$db_object_cache
Where kept = 'NO'
Order by sharable_mem desc;
```

Fragmentation of the shared pool can also cause high demand for these latches. A fragmented shared pool means the net free memory available in the shared pool might be large, but the total contiguous memory available might not be the same. Therefore, when an object like a large PL/SQL object with a very high memory requirement is to be located in the shared pool, it will cause a lot of smaller chunks of allocated memory areas to be flushed. These would then have to be parsed again when a user makes the request for the same SQL again. The primary cause of fragmentation is large PL/SQL objects. Fragmentation can be avoided by increasing sharing among SQL statements by use of bind variables and pinning of large PL/SQL objects using the techniques mentioned above.

ORACLE INTERFACES AND UTLILITIES

SQL*Plus for Administrators

In this chapter

This chapter discusses SQL*Plus, an interactive program used to access an ORACLE database. It is also the Database Administrator's best friend and an indispensable tool.

In addition to SQL*Plus, a database administrator (DBA) can interface with the database and use SQL*Plus commands (but only a subset of the commands) in two other tools:

- Server Manager
- Worksheet utility in the Enterprise Manager

Note

From release 8.1.3 all Server Manager commands are available in SQL*Plus. Oracle is planning to discontinue Server Manager and supply one integrated tool to do all DBA and SQL commands. (see the section entitled "New Features in Oracle8.1.x")

Because SQL*Plus is such a vast subject, which cannot be dealt with in a single chapter, I will concentrate mainly on features of interest to DBAs, EXECUTE, AUTOTRACE, and various new features, and lesser-known and lesser-used features (COPY command, disabling commands).

ADMINISTERING SQL*PLUS

There are two files, `glogin.sql` and `login.sql`, that are used to administer SQL*Plus. The `glogin.sql` file is the global setup file, and login.sql is intended for individual use. These two files contain SQL*Plus commands and/or SQL statements that are executed every time an ORACLE user invokes SQL*Plus. The `glogin.sql` file is read and executed first, followed by the user's `login.sql` file.

The `glogin.sql` file is located in the `$ORACLE_HOME/sqlplus/admin` directory. The ORACLE DBA may customize this file to include SQL*Plus commands, SQL statements, and PL/SQL blocks that will be executed by every SQL*Plus user at the beginning of his or her SQL*Plus session. The `glogin.sql` file is also known as a *Site Profile*.

Note

Under Windows 95/NT 4.0, the `glogin.sql` file is located in the directory `%ORACLE_HOME%\PLUS`*nn*, where *nn* represents the version of SQL*Plus installed on your machine. For example, if SQL*Plus 3.3 is installed, the directory name will be `%ORACLE_HOME%\PLUS33`.

USING SQL*PLUS ENVIRONMENT VARIABLES

There are two environment variables that are used by SQL*Plus:

- SQLPATH
- editor

SQL*Plus uses the environment variable SQLPATH to identify the directory where the login.sql file is located. In other words, SQL*Plus will look in every directory defined in SQLPATH for login.sql, starting with the local directory (the directory you were in when you started SQL*Plus).

For example, if you want SQL*Plus to look for login.sql first in the local directory, then in your home directory, and then in another directory, set SQLPATH as follows:

```
$ SQLPATH=".:$HOME:<other_directory>"; export SQLPATH    —(Bourne/Korn shell)
$ set SQLPATH=(. $HOME <other_directory>)         — C shell
```

Under Windows95/NT 4.0, SQLPATH is defined in the Registry. The default value is $ORACLE_HOME\DBS (set during installation). The value for ORACLE_HOME is C:\ORAWIN95 for Windows95 and C:\ORANT for NT 4.0 (replace C: with the name of the disk drive where you installed ORACLE, if you did not install it on your C: drive).

> **Note**
>
> Under Windows 95/NT 4.0, the login.sql file is located in directory %ORACLE_HOME%\DBS, the default value for SQLPATH.

To set or change the value of SQLPATH under Windows95/NT 4.0, follow these steps:

1. Select Run from the Start menu.
2. Enter **regedit.exe/regedit32.exe** (for Windows95/NT, respectively).
3. Click OK.
4. Double-click on HKEY_LOCAL_MACHINE.
5. Double-click on SOFTWARE.
6. Double-click on ORACLE.
7. Double-click on SQLPATH.
8. The Edit String dialog box appears. In the Value Data field enter the new value for SQLPATH.
9. Click OK.
10. From the Registry menu, select Exit.
11. Reboot your machine for the new value to take effect (or log out and log back in Windows NT 4.0)

> **Note**
>
> SQLPATH is also used by SQL*Plus to identify the location of SQL scripts that you run from SQL*Plus.

There is another environment variable that can be set in glogin.sql or login.sql. This environment variable is named _editor. It defines the editor you can use to edit SQL*Plus commands.

To set the value of editor to the vi text editor, enter the following line in `glogin.sql` or `login.sql`:

```
define _editor=vi
```

> **Note**
>
> In Oracle8.1.x it is possible to change editors on-the-fly.
> Go to Edit -> Editor -> Define editor and enter Notepad or vi.

If you use any other text editor, replace `vi` with the appropriate name. For more information on using different editors, see the section "Using Your Operating System Editor in SQL*Plus," later in this chapter.

INVOKING/ACCESSING SQL*PLUS

To invoke SQL*Plus from the operating system prompt, use the following command:

```
$ sqlplus [[-S[ILENT]] [logon] [start]]¦-?
```

The `-S[ILENT]]` parameter is used when running SQL*Plus from a shell script, because it suppresses all the information that SQL*Plus displays when invoked, such as the SQL*Plus banner, prompt messages, and the command prompt.

The `[logon]` section requires the following syntax:

```
username[/password] [@connect_string]¦/¦/NOLOG
```

The `[start]]` clause enables you to start SQL*Plus and run a command file containing any combination of SQL*Plus commands, SQL statements, and/or PL/SQL blocks. In addition, you can pass arguments to the command file. The `start` clause requires the following syntax:

```
@file_name[.ext] [arg...]
```

If you do not enter the username and/or the password, SQL*Plus prompts you to enter them.

After you successfully access SQL*Plus, you can enter three type of commands at the SQL*Plus prompt (`SQL >`):

- SQL commands/statements for working with database objects and manipulating the data stored in the database
- PL/SQL (Procedural Language/SQL) blocks for working with database objects and manipulating the data stored in the database
- SQL*Plus commands for setting options, editing, storing, and retrieving SQL commands and PL/SQL blocks, and for formatting the output of queries

To submit a SQL command to SQL*Plus, enter a semicolon (;) at the end of the command and press Enter. SQL*Plus executes the command, displays the results of the query, and returns you to the prompt.

To end a PL/SQL block, enter a period (.) on a line by itself. To submit a PL/SQL block for execution, terminate it with a slash (/) on a line by itself and press Enter.

EDITING SQL COMMANDS

If you make a mistake when entering a SQL command and want to correct it, or if you want to run the last command with only a minor change, you are lucky! SQL*Plus stores the most recently entered SQL statement in a buffer, appropriately called the *SQL buffer*. SQL*Plus provides a set of commands to retrieve and edit SQL statements and PL/SQL blocks stored in the buffer.

Note that SQL*Plus commands are not saved in the buffer. Therefore, they cannot be retrieved and modified. However, there is a way to store SQL*Plus commands in the buffer. This method is discussed in the section "Entering and Editing SQL*Plus Commands," later in this chapter.

Table 26.1 lists the commands used to view, edit, and run the contents of the SQL*Plus buffer:

TABLE 26.1 SQL*PLUS COMMANDS USED WITH THE SQL BUFFER

Command	Abbreviation	Action
APPEND *text*	A *text*	Add *text* to the end of a line
CHANGE *old/new*	C *old/new*	Change *old* text with *new* in a line
CHANGE */text*	C */text*	Delete *text* from a line
CLEAR BUFFER	CL BUFF	Delete all lines
DEL	(NONE)	Delete current line in buffer
INPUT	I	Add one or more lines to the buffer
INPUT *text*	I *text*	Add a line consisting of *text*
LIST	L	Lists the contents of the SQL*Plus buffer
LIST *n*	L *n* or *n*	Lists line *n*
LIST *	L *	Lists the current line
LIST *m n*	L *m n*	Lists lines *m* to *n*
LIST *LAST*	L *LAST*	Lists the last line in buffer

PART

VI

CH

26

With the exception of the LIST command, all other editing commands affect only a single line in the buffer. This line is called the *current line*. It is marked with an asterisk when you list the SQL command or PL/SQL block. When you run the LIST command, the current line will always be the last line in the buffer. Also note that the semicolon (;) that ends a SQL command is not saved in the buffer, as shown in Listing 26.1.

Listing 26.1 SQL Statement Stored in Buffer

```
SQL> LIST
    1  SELECT empno, ename, deptno, job, sal, comm
    2  FROM emp
    3* WHERE comm IS NOT NULL
```

If you get an error message, the line containing the error becomes the current line so that you can edit it right away to correct the error(s). Listing 26.2 shows a listing with an error.

Listing 26.2 Line with Error Becomes Current Line

```
SQL> SELECT empno, empname, deptno, job, sal, comm
    2  FROM emp
    3  WHERE comm IS NOT NULL;
SELECT empno, empname, deptno, job, sal, comm
                *
ERROR at line 1:
ORA-00904: invalid column name
```

ENTERING AND EDITING SQL*PLUS COMMANDS

SQL*Plus commands, such as DESCRIBE, entered directly at the SQL*Plus prompt are not saved in the SQL buffer. Therefore, you cannot retrieve the last SQL*Plus command entered to edit and/or rerun it. The result of trying to list a SQL*Plus command from the buffer is shown in Listing 26.3.

Listing 26.3 SQL*PLUS Commands Are Not Buffered

```
SQL> DESCRIBE EMP
 Name                   Null?       Type
 - - - - - - - - - - - - - - - - - - - - - - - - - - - -
 EMPNO                  NOT NULL    NUMBER(4)
 ENAME                              VARCHAR2(10)
 JOB                                VARCHAR2(9)
 MGR                                NUMBER(4)
 HIREDATE                           DATE
 SAL                                NUMBER(7,2)
 COMM                               NUMBER(7,2)
 DEPTNO                 NOT NULL    NUMBER(2)
SQL> LIST
No lines in SQL buffer.
```

To store SQL*Plus commands in the buffer, enter INPUT with no text and press Enter. SQL*Plus prompts you with a line number where you can enter the commands. When you are finished entering the commands, enter a blank line by pressing the Return key. Listing 26.4 shows an example.

LISTING 26.4 STORING SQL*PLUS COMMANDS IN THE BUFFER

```
SQL> INPUT
     1  DESCRIBE EMP
     2
SQL> L
     1* DESCRIBE EMP
```

Note

See SQL*Plus commands table for the abbreviation "L" which stands for "List".

You cannot execute the command from the buffer, but you can save it in a file, which you can retrieve and run later in SQL*Plus. A failed attempt at running a SQL*Plus command from the buffer but then successfully saving it to a file is shown in Listing 26.5.

LISTING 26.5 SAVE SQL*PLUS COMMANDS TO FILES

```
SQL> RUN
     1* DESCRIBE EMP
DESCRIBE EMP
*
ERROR at line 1:
ORA-00900: invalid SQL statement
SQL> SAVE test
Created file test
SQL> GET test
     1* DESCRIBE EMP
```

The newly created file is saved in the directory pointed to by the SQLPATH environment variable.

USING YOUR OPERATING SYSTEM EDITOR IN SQL*PLUS

The editing capabilities offered by SQL*Plus are poor and not intuitive compared to other text editors. (For instance, one cannot use the arrow, HOME or END keys.) Therefore, many users prefer to create their command files using editors they feel comfortable with, then run these files in SQL*Plus using the START or @ commands.

If you would rather work with your operating system editor than use the editing capabilities of SQL*Plus, you can do that in SQL*Plus by using the EDIT command. The syntax of the EDIT command is:

```
EDIT [file_name[.ext]]
```

This will open the file_name with the editor defined by the variable _editor in the glogin.sql or login.sql file. If you want to use a different editor in your SQL*Plus session, you can redefine the _editor variable with the SQL*Plus command DEFINE:

```
DEFINE _editor=emacs
```

PART
VI
CH
26

If the *editor* variable is not defined, the EDIT command tries to use the default operating system editor (for example, Notepad in Windows 95).

When you issue the EDIT command, you invoke an editor from within SQL*Plus without leaving it, which is convenient.

If you do not supply a filename when running the EDIT command, SQL*Plus will save the contents of the SQL buffer in a file and open that file with the editor. By default, the name of the file is afiedt.buf, and it is created in the current directory or the directory defined in the SQLPATH environment variable. You can, when opening the editor, use the full pathname for the file you want to edit, for example: EDIT C:\MYDIR\MYFILE.SQL

```
SQL> EDIT
Wrote file afiedt.buf
```

You can change the name of the file where SQL*Plus saves the contents of the buffer by setting the appropriate value in the editfile variable, as shown in Listing 26.6.

LISTING 26.6   EDITED FILES HAVE A DEFAULT NAME

```
SQL> SHOW editfile
editfile "afiedt.buf"
SQL> SET editfile "buffer.txt"
SQL> SHOW editfile
editfile "buffer.txt"
```

If you do not enter a filename when running the EDIT command and the SQL buffer is empty, SQL*Plus returns a notification message, like the one shown in Listing 26.7.

LISTING 26.7   EMPTY BUFFERS HAVE NOTHING TO SAVE

```
SQL> CLEAR BUFFER
buffer cleared
SQL> EDIT
Nothing to save.
```

The default extension for the filename is .sql. So, if you do not specify a file extension, SQL*Plus will look for a file named file_name.sql. If you want to edit a file with an extension other than .sql, you have to explicitly specify the extension. You can also change the default value for the file extension through the SUFFIX variable, as shown in Listing 26.8.

LISTING 26.8   CHANGING THE DEFAULT SUFFIX

```
SQL> SHOW SUFFIX
suffix "SQL"
SQL> SET SUFFIX sh
SQL> SHOW SUFFIX
suffix "sh"
```

> **Note**
>
> The SUFFIX variable applies only to *command files*, not to spool (output) files. Depending on the operating system, the default extension for spool files is .lst or .lis.

RUNNING SQL*PLUS/SQL COMMANDS

You can run SQL commands and PL/SQL blocks three ways:

- From the command line
- From the SQL buffer
- From a command file (informally known as a SQL script)

To execute a SQL command or a PL/SQL block from the buffer, SQL*Plus provides the RUN command and the / (forward slash) command. The syntax of the RUN command is

```
R[UN]
```

The RUN command lists and executes the SQL command or PL/SQL block currently stored in the buffer.

Let's assume that the buffer contains this query:

```
SELECT empno, ename FROM emp
```

If you ran the query using the RUN command, it would look like Listing 26.8.

LISTING 26.8   RUNNING A QUERY WITH THE *RUN* COMMAND

```
SQL> RUN
     1* SELECT empno, ename FROM emp
EMPNO      ENAME
- - - - - - - - - - - - - - - - - - -
      7369 SMITH
      7499 ALLEN
      7521 WARD
      7566 JONES
      7654 MARTIN
      7698 BLAKE
      7782 CLARK
      7788 SCOTT
      7839 KING
      7844 TURNER
      7876 ADAMS
      7900 JAMES
      7902 FORD
      7934 MILLER
 14 rows selected.
```

RUN displays the command from the buffer and returns the results of the query. In addition, RUN makes the last line in the buffer the current line.

The / command is similar to the RUN command. It executes the SQL command or PL/SQL block stored in the buffer, but it does not display the contents of the buffer, as shown in Listing 26.9.

LISTING 26.9 RUNNING A QUERY WITH THE / COMMAND

```
SQL> /
EMPNO      ENAME
-------------------
     7369 SMITH
     7499 ALLEN
     7521 WARD
     7566 JONES
     7654 MARTIN
     7698 BLAKE
     7782 CLARK
     7788 SCOTT
     7839 KING
     7844 TURNER
     7876 ADAMS
     7900 JAMES
     7902 FORD
     7934 MILLER
14 rows selected.
```

Note

Unlike the RUN command, the / command does not make the last line in the buffer the current line.

To run a SQL command, a SQL*Plus command, or a PL/SQL block from a command line, there are two commands:

- START
- @ ("at")

The syntax of the START command is

```
START file_name[.ext] [arg1 arg2...]
```

The file_name[.ext] represents the command file you wish to run. If you omit the extension, SQL*Plus assumes the default command-file extension (usually .sql).

SQL*Plus searches in the current directory for a file with the filename and extension that you specify in your START command. If no such file is found, SQL*Plus will search the directory or directories specified in the SQLPATH environment variable for the file. You could also include the full pathname for the file, for example: C:\MYDYR\MYFILE.SQL.

You can include any SQL command, SQL*Plus command, or PL/SQL block that you would normally enter interactively into a command file. An EXIT or QUIT command used in a command file exits SQL*Plus.

The arguments section ([arg1 arg2...]) represents values you want to pass to parameters in the command file. The parameters in the command file must be specified in the following format: &1, &2, ...(or &&1, &&2, ...). If you enter one or more arguments, SQL*Plus substitutes the values into the parameters in the command file. The first argument replaces each occurrence of &1, the second replaces each occurrence of &2, and so on.

The START command defines the parameters with the values of the arguments. If you run the command file again in the same SQL*Plus session, you can enter new arguments or omit the arguments to use the current values of the parameters. To run a command file named DELTBL.SQL, you enter the following:

```
SQL> START DELTBL
```

The @ ("at") command functions very much like the START command. The only difference is that the @ command can be run both from inside a SQL*Plus session and at the command-line level when starting SQL*Plus, whereas a START command can be run only from within a SQL*Plus session. To start a SQL*Plus session and execute the commands from a command file, enter

```
$ sqlplus [username/password] @file_name[.ext] [arg1 arg2...]
```

If the START command is disabled, this will also disable the @ command. The section "Restricting a User's Privileges in SQL*Plus," later in the chapter, contains more information on disabling SQL*Plus commands.

USING THE EXECUTE COMMAND

Starting with SQL*Plus 3.2, there is a new command, EXECUTE, that enables the execution of a single PL/SQL statement directly at the SQL*Plus prompt, rather than from the buffer or a command file. EXECUTE's main usage is for running a PL/SQL statement that references a function or a stored procedure, as shown in Listing 26.10.

PART

VI

CH

26

LISTING 26.10 USE EXECUTE WITH STORED PROCEDURES

```
SQL> VARIABLE id NUMBER          — Define a bind variable
SQL> EXECUTE :id := ADD_CASES(10);
PL/SQL procedure successfully completed.
SQL> PRINT id
        ID
----------
        10
SQL> EXECUTE :id := ADD_CASES(3);
PL/SQL procedure successfully completed.
SQL> PRINT id
        ID
----------
         0
```

The value returned by the stored procedure ADD_CASES is stored in the bind variable :id.

SAVING SQL*PLUS/SQL COMMANDS

You can save the SQL*Plus or SQL command stored in the buffer in an operating system file (called command file), using the SAVE command. The syntax of the SAVE command is

```
SAV[E] file_name[.ext] [CRE[ATE] ¦ [REP[LACE] ¦ APP[END]]
```

The file_name[.ext] is the name of the operating system file where you want to store the contents of the SQL buffer. To name the file, use the file-naming conventions of the operating system where SQL*Plus is running. If you do not provide an extension for the file, SQL*Plus uses the default extension, .sql. You could also specify a path as part of the file name. If you do not specify a path, the SAVE command will use the directory named in the SQLPATH environment variable as the path for the file.

The CRE[ATE] parameter creates the file. If the file already exists, you will receive an error message.

The REP[LACE] parameter replaces an existing file with the contents of the SQL buffer. If the file does not exist, SAVE...REPLACE creates it.

The APP[END] parameter appends the contents of the SQL buffer at the end of the file. If the file does not exist, SAVE...APPEND creates it.

RETRIEVING SQL*PLUS/SQL COMMANDS

To retrieve SQL*Plus or SQL commands, use the GET command. The syntax of the command is

```
GET file_name[.ext] [LIS[T] ¦ NOL[IST]]
```

The GET command loads an operating system file—file_name—that contains SQL*Plus and/or SQL commands, into the SQL buffer, so that you can edit the commands in the file or run them. The default extension for the file is .sql.

The LIS[T] parameter lists the contents of the file as SQL*Plus loads the file in the buffer. LIST is the default. The NOL[IST] parameter does not list the contents of the file.

If you do not specify the full path for the filename in the GET command, SQL*Plus searches for it first in the current directory, then in the directories listed in the environment variable SQLPATH.

| Tip #67 | If you use Windows 95/NT, you can have SQL*Plus look in a specific directory for your command files by starting the application in that directory. To do this, change the Windows shortcut Start In property to the directory that contains the files. Files that you open, create, or save without specifying a directory path will be opened, created, or saved in the directory in which you start SQL*Plus. |

USING THE SQL*PLUS COPY COMMAND

Although its effectiveness has been somewhat reduced since ORACLE introduced the CREATE TABLE...UNRECOVERABLE AS SELECT... in version 7.2, the COPY command is still one of the most useful SQL*Plus commands; yet it is not understood very well, and therefore not used very often. The COPY command can be used for several functions:

- Copying one or more tables, or an entire schema, from a local database to a remote database or to another local database. This can be used to move an entire schema from one database to another without using Export/Import utilities and is especially helpful when the export file is larger than the operating system file limit.

- Copying specific rows (based on a query) from one table to another table in a remote or local database.

- Copying the contents of a table containing a LONG column to another table. This is the only way to do this, because a LONG column cannot be used in a SELECT statement.

- Copying tables from an Oracle database to a non-Oracle database.

The syntax of the COPY command is:

```
COPY {FROM username[/password]@database_specification¦ TO
username[/password]@database_specification¦ FROM
username[/password]@database_specification TO
username[/password]@database_specification} {APPEND¦CREATE¦INSERT¦REPLACE}
destination_table [(column, column, column ...)] USING query
```

The username[/password] represents the Oracle username and password you wish to COPY FROM and TO. In the FROM clause, username/password identifies the source of the data; in the TO clause, username/password identifies the destination. If you do not specify a password in either the FROM clause or the TO clause, SQL*Plus will prompt you for it. SQL*Plus will not display the user's response to these prompts.

The database_specification is a database link name, a Net8 service name or a SQL*Net V2 service name. A database_specification clause must be provided in the COPY command. In the FROM clause, database_specification represents the database at the source; in the TO clause, database_specification represents the database at the destination.

The destination_table is the table you want to create or to which you want to add data and [(column, column, column, ...)] specifies the names of the columns in destination_table.

If you specify columns, the number of columns must be the same as the number of columns selected by the query. If you do not specify any columns, the copied columns will have the same names in the destination table as they had in the source table if COPY creates destination_table.

The USING query parameter specifies a SELECT statement that extracts the rows and columns that the COPY command copies.

PART

VI

CH

26

The FROM username[/password]@database_specification section defines the username, password, and database that contains the data to be copied. If you omit the FROM clause, the source defaults to the database to which SQL*Plus is connected. You must include a FROM clause to specify a source database other than the default.

The TO username[/password]@database_specification section specifies the database containing the destination table. If you omit the TO clause, the destination defaults to the database to which SQL*Plus is connected. You must include a TO clause to specify a destination database other than the default.

Several parameters control how the COPY command copies data from one table to another. The parameters are the following:

- APPEND inserts the rows from the query into the destination table if the table exists. If the destination table does not exist, COPY creates it. APPEND inserts the rows even if the table is empty (contains no data).

- CREATE inserts the rows from the query into the destination table after first creating the table. If the destination table already exists, COPY returns an error.

- INSERT inserts the rows from the query into the destination table. If the destination table does not exist, COPY returns an error. When using INSERT, USING query must select one column for each column in the destination table.

- REPLACE replaces the destination table and its contents with the rows extracted by the query. If the destination table exists, COPY drops it and replaces it with a table containing the copied data. If the destination table does not exist, COPY creates it.

Three SQL*Plus SET variables control the behavior of the COPY command:

- LONG
- COPYCOMMIT
- ARRAYSIZE

LONG determines the length of LONG columns that you copy. If any LONG columns contain data longer than the value of LONG, COPY truncates the data.

By default, SQL*Plus performs a commit at the end of each successful COPY command. If you set the SQL*Plus SET variable COPYCOMMIT to a positive integer value *n*, SQL*Plus performs a commit after copying every *n* batch of records. The SET variable ARRAYSIZE determines the size of a batch.

Note

When using the COPY command, some operating environments (most notably VAX/VMS, OpenVMS) require that database specifications be placed in double quotation marks.

> **Note**
>
> If any of the column names specified in the (column, column,...) clause of the COPY command contains lowercase letters or blanks, the column name must be enclosed in double quotation marks.

> **Note**
>
> Be careful when using the COPY command to copy tables that contain NUMBER columns ! These columns become DECIMAL with a precision of 38 in the destination database.

USING SQL TO CREATE SQL

There are many situations in which the DBA or a regular user needs to perform SQL statements on many database objects (tables, indexes, and so forth). For example, the DBA may periodically need to load data from a PRODUCTION database into a DEVELOPMENT or TEST database. Before loading the data, he or she may need to delete the data from all the tables in the DEVELOPMENT or TEST database. Doing it on a table-by-table basis could be very tedious, especially if there are a few hundred tables in the database. One simple and fast solution in this situation is to use SQL*Plus to create the required SQL statements, save them into an operating system file and run the file from SQL*Plus.

For example, to delete all the rows from all the tables belonging to user SCOTT, SYSTEM can use the SQL in Listing 26.11.

LISTING 26.11   SQL GENERATES SQL

```
SQL> CONNECT SYSTEM
Enter password: *******
Connected.
SQL> SET PAGESIZE 0
SQL> SET HEADING OFF
SQL> SET FEEDBACK OFF
SQL> SET VERIFY OFF
SQL> SET ECHO OFF
SQL> SPOOL DELTBL.SQL
SQL> SELECT 'DELETE '||TABLE_NAME||';'
  2    FROM DBA_TABLES
  3   WHERE OWNER='SCOTT';
DELETE ACCTS;
DELETE ACCT_ADDRS;
DELETE BONUS;
DELETE CITIES;
DELETE COMPANY_SUMMARY;
DELETE CUSTOMER;
DELETE DEPT;
DELETE DUMMY;
DELETE EMP;
DELETE FUNDS;
DELETE FUND_CONTRIB;
DELETE FUND_XACT;
DELETE F_EMPCOMP;
```

LISTING 26.11   CONTINUED

```
DELETE F_XACT_TYPE;
DELETE INVINFO;
DELETE INVREQUEST;
DELETE ITEM;
DELETE ORD;
DELETE ORDER_HISTORY;
DELETE PRICE;
DELETE PRODUCT;
DELETE SALES_REVENUE;
DELETE SALGRADE;
DELETE STOCK_HISTORY;
SQL> SPOOL OFF
```

When you run the file above you get the file DELTBL.SQL as follows:

```
DELETE ACCTS;
DELETE ACCT_ADDRS;
DELETE BONUS;
DELETE CITIES;
DELETE COMPANY_SUMMARY;
DELETE CUSTOMER;
DELETE DEPT;
DELETE DUMMY;
DELETE EMP;
DELETE FUNDS;
DELETE FUND_CONTRIB;
DELETE FUND_XACT;
DELETE F_EMPCOMP;
DELETE F_XACT_TYPE;
DELETE INVINFO;
DELETE INVREQUEST;
DELETE ITEM;
DELETE ORD;
DELETE ORDER_HISTORY;
DELETE PRICE;
DELETE PRODUCT;
DELETE SALES_REVENUE;
DELETE SALGRADE;
DELETE STOCK_HISTORY;
```

Running DELTBL.SQL by issuing the command @DELTBL.SQL will delete the rows in the tables shown. Other commands are used to format the output and create the command file:

- SET PAGESIZE 0 turns off all page formatting information, such as column headings, titles, the initial blank line, page breaks, and so on.

- SET HEADING OFF turns off the display of column headings (you could use either SET HEADING OFF or SET PAGESIZE 0).

- SET FEEDBACK OFF suppresses the display of the number of rows returned by the query.
- SET VERIFY OFF does not display the text of a SQL command before and after SQL*Plus replaces substitution variables with values.
- SET ECHO OFF suppresses the listing of the SQL commands in the DELETE.SQL file as these are executed.
- SPOOL DELTBL.SQL starts spooling and saving commands entered at the SQL*Plus prompt and query results into a file named DELTBL.SQL. The commands and query results continue to be displayed on the terminal. If you do not specify a file extension, SQL*Plus uses the default extension for output files (.lst or .lis).
- SPOOL OFF stops pooling and closes the DELTBL.SQL file.

If SYSTEM wants to delete the rows from all of SCOTT's tables, all he has to do is run the DELTBL.SQL file in SQL*Plus, which can be done as follows:

```
SQL> @DELTBL
```

RESTRICTING A USER'S PRIVILEGES IN SQL*PLUS

ORACLE provides database administrators with a tool that enables them to disable specific SQL and SQL*Plus commands in the SQL*Plus environment. This is done on a per-user basis. This tool is, in fact, a table, PRODUCT_USER_PROFILE, owned by user SYSTEM. The table description for PRODUCT_USER_PROFILE is given in Table 26.2; Table 26.3 describes the purpose of the individual columns in the PRODUCT_USER_PROFILE table.

TABLE 26.2 THE *PRODUCT_USER_PROFILE* TABLE DEFINITION

Name	Null?	Type
PRODUCT	NOT NULL	VARCHAR2(30)
USERID		VARCHAR2(30)
ATTRIBUTE		VARCHAR2(240)
SCOPE		VARCHAR2(240)
NUMERIC_VALUE		NUMBER(15,2)
CHAR_VALUE		VARCHAR2(240)
DATE_VALUE		DATE
LONG_VALUE		LONG

TABLE 26.3   PURPOSE OF *PRODUCT_USER_PROFILE* TABLE COLUMNS

Column	Purpose
PRODUCT	Must contain the product name (in this case SQL*Plus). No wildcard (%) or NULL values are allowed in this field.
USERID	Must contain the name (in uppercase) of the user for whom you wish to disable the command. To disable a command for several users, use wildcard (%) or enter multiple rows. To disable a command for all the users, insert a wildcard (%) by itself in this field.
ATTRIBUTE	Must contain the name (in uppercase) of the SQL or SQL*Plus command to be disabled (for example, ALTER). No wildcard value is allowed in this column.
SCOPE	SQL*Plus ignores this column. A NULL should be entered in this column. This column is reserved for use by products other than SQL*Plus.
NUMERIC_VALUE	SQL*Plus ignores this column. A NULL should be entered in this column. This column is reserved for use by products other than SQL*Plus.
CHAR_VALUE	Must contain the string "DISABLED".
DATE_VALUE	SQL*Plus ignores this column. A NULL should be entered in this column. This column is reserved for use by products other than SQL*Plus.
LONG_VALUE	SQL*Plus ignores this column. A NULL should be entered in this column. This column is reserved for use by products other than SQL*Plus.

Running the script PUPBLD.SQL as the SYSTEM user creates the PRODUCT_USER_PROFILE table. The location of this file varies from platform to platform. For example, for Personal Oracle under Windows 95, the PUPBLD.SQL file is located in directory C:\ORAWIN95\DBS (C:\ORAWIN95 is the default ORACLE_HOME directory for Oracle products under Windows 95). On UNIX platforms, the file is located in directory $ORACLE_HOME/sqlplus/admin.

The PUPBLD.SQL command file is run during the installation of ORACLE software and the creation of the starter database (in the script crdb on UNIX platforms and buildall on Windows 95/NT). If you do not create the starter database during the installation process, you have to run the PUPBLD.SQL script as user SYSTEM to create the PRODUCT_USER_PROFILE table.

If the PUPBLD.SQL is not run, every time a user logs on to SQL*Plus, he or she will receive the following warning message:

```
Warning: Product user profile information not loaded !
Error in disabling roles in product user profile.
```

DISABLING A SQL COMMAND

To disable a SQL or SQL*Plus command for a given user, the SYSTEM user must insert a row that matches the column and values shown in Table 26.4.

TABLE 26.4   VALUES NEEDED TO RESTRICT SQL*PLUS COMMANDS

Column	Value
PRODUCT	SQL*Plus
USERID	Username of user being restricted
ATTRIBUTE	Command name being restricted
CHAR_VALUE	DISABLED
SCOPE	NULL
NUMERIC_VALUE	NULL
DATE_VALUE	NULL
LONG_VALUE	NULL

For example, to disable user SCOTT's access to the operating system from SQL*Plus, log on to SQL*Plus as SYSTEM and execute the SQL statement in Listing 26.12.

LISTING 26.12   DISABLE HOST COMMAND FOR USER SCOTT

```
INSERT INTO
product_user_profile
(product, userid, attribute, scope, numeric_value,
 char_value, date_value, long_value)
VALUES
('SQL*Plus', 'SCOTT', 'HOST', NULL, NULL, 'DISABLED', NULL, NULL);
```

SQL*Plus reads restrictions from the PRODUCT_USER_PROFILE table when a user accesses SQL*Plus and enforces them for the duration of the user's session.

Note   If any changes affecting a user are made to the PRODUCT_USER_PROFILE table, they will not affect a user's current session. The user will see the effect of these changes the next time he logs on to SQL*Plus.

REENABLING A SQL COMMAND

To reenable a command, delete the row containing the restriction. Listing 26.13 reenables the command that was disabled in Listing 26.12.

LISTING 26.13   REENABLE HOST COMMAND FOR USER SCOTT

```
DELETE [FROM] product_user_profile
WHERE userid='SCOTT' and attribute='HOST';
```

The following SQL*Plus commands (listed in alphabetical order) can be disabled using the PRODUCT_USER_PROFILE table:

- COPY
- EDIT
- EXECUTE
- EXIT
- GET
- HOST (or your operating system's alias for HOST, such as ! on UNIX or $ on VMS)
- QUIT
- PASSWORD
- RUN
- SAVE
- SET (see the following note)
- SPOOL
- START (see the following note)

Note

Disabling the SQL*Plus SET command will also disable the SQL SET ROLE and SET TRANSACTION commands.

Note

Disabling the SQL*Plus START command will also disable the SQL*Plus @ and @@ commands.

The following SQL commands can be disabled:

- ALTER
- ANALYZE
- AUDIT
- CONNECT
- CREATE
- DELETE
- DROP
- GRANT
- INSERT
- LOCK
- NOAUDIT

- RENAME
- REVOKE
- SELECT
- SET ROLE
- SET TRANSACTION
- TRUNCATE
- UPDATE

You can also disable the following PL/SQL commands:

- BEGIN
- DECLARE

Note

Disabling BEGIN and DECLARE does not prevent the use of the SQL*Plus EXECUTE command. EXECUTE must be disabled separately.

DISABLING SET ROLE

The SQL command SET ROLE enables an application user to access privileges granted through an application role, which can cause security problems. To prevent application users from accessing application roles in SQL*Plus, a DBA can use the PRODUCT_USER_PROFILE table to disable the SET ROLE command. This restricts a SQL*Plus user to only those privileges associated with the roles enabled when he or she started SQL*Plus.

DISABLING ROLES

To disable a role for a specific user, insert a row in PRODUCT_USER_PROFILE containing the user's username in the UserID column, ROLES in the Attribute column, and the role name in the Char_Value column.

Note

If you enter PUBLIC or % in the UserID column when disabling a role, you disable that role for all the users. % or PUBLIC should only be used for roles which are granted to PUBLIC.

The Oracle user SYSTEM owns the PRODUCT_USER_PROFILE table. When SYSTEM logs on, SQL*Plus does not read the PRODUCT_USER_PROFILE table. Thus, no SQL*Plus restrictions apply to user SYSTEM.

Caution

The product-level security provided by PRODUCT_USER_PROFILE is enforced only by SQL*Plus, not the Oracle RDBMS.

TRACING SQL STATEMENTS

Before SQL*Plus 3.3, obtaining statistics about the execution of SQL statements in SQL*Plus was very limited. The only commands available for this purpose are SET TIME and SET TIMING.

The SET TIME command controls how SQL*Plus displays the current time. The ON parameter displays the current time before each SQL*Plus prompt and the OFF parameter suppresses the display of the current time. The syntax of the SET TIME command is

```
SET TI[ME] [OFF ¦ ON]      (OFF is the default).
```

Listing 26.14 shows an example of using the SET TIME command.

LISTING 26.14 ESTIMATING RUNTIME

```
SQL> SHOW TIME
time OFF
SQL> SET TIME ON
01:17:57 SQL> SELECT t1.dname, t2.ename, t2.sal, t2.job
01:18:11    2  FROM dept t1, emp t2
01:18:23    3  WHERE t1.deptno = t2.deptno;

DNAME           ENAME            SAL  JOB
--------------------------------------------------
RESEARCH        SMITH            800  CLERK
SALES           ALLEN           1600  SALESMAN
SALES           WARD            1250  SALESMAN
RESEARCH        JONES           2975  MANAGER
SALES           MARTIN          1250  SALESMAN
SALES           BLAKE           2850  MANAGER
ACCOUNTING      CLARK           2450  MANAGER
RESEARCH        SCOTT           3000  ANALYST
ACCOUNTING      KING            5000  PRESIDENT
SALES           TURNER          1500  SALESMAN
RESEARCH        ADAMS           1100  CLERK
SALES           JAMES            950  CLERK
RESEARCH        FORD            3000  ANALYST
ACCOUNTING      MILLER          1300  CLERK
14 rows selected.
01:18:43 SQL>
```

By subtracting the time displayed at the last line entered (01:18:23) from the time displayed at the first prompt after the query execution (01:18:43), the user can get an estimate of the time it took to execute the query (includes the time required to enter the WHERE clause).

The runtime calculated using this method does not reflect the true speed with which Oracle executes a query, because this elapsed time includes the overhead of displaying the query to the SQL*Plus interface. The actual time to run the query is much shorter.

The SET TIMING command controls the display of execution time statistics. The syntax of the SET TIMING command is

```
SET TIMI[NG] [OFF ¦ ON]                 (OFF is the default)
```

The SET TIMING ON command displays the execution time statistics for each SQL or PL/SQL block executed in SQL*Plus. SET TIMING OFF suppresses the display of the timing statistics.

Listing 26.15 shows an example of using the SET TIMING command.

LISTING 26.15 TIMING EXECUTION

```
SQL> SHOW TIMING
timing OFF
SQL> SET TIMING ON
SQL>  SELECT t1.dname, t2.ename, t2.sal, t2.job
    2  FROM dept t1, emp t2
    3  WHERE t1.deptno = t2.deptno;
DNAME            ENAME            SAL   JOB
-------------------------------------------------
RESEARCH         SMITH            800   CLERK
SALES            ALLEN           1600   SALESMAN
SALES            WARD            1250   SALESMAN
RESEARCH         JONES           2975   MANAGER
SALES            MARTIN          1250   SALESMAN
SALES            BLAKE           2850   MANAGER
ACCOUNTING       CLARK           2450   MANAGER
RESEARCH         SCOTT           3000   ANALYST
ACCOUNTING       KING            5000   PRESIDENT
SALES            TURNER          1500   SALESMAN
RESEARCH         ADAMS           1100   CLERK
SALES            JAMES            950   CLERK
RESEARCH         FORD            3000   ANALYST
ACCOUNTING       MILLER          1300   CLERK
14 rows selected.
real: 2690
```

As shown in Listing 26.14 and 26.15, the SET TIME and SET TIMING commands provide very basic, and not very precise, timing statistics for SQL statements and/or PL/SQL blocks executed in SQL*Plus. No information about the execution/access path used by the optimizer was available directly in SQL*Plus prior to SQL*Plus 3.3.

A new feature, called AUTOTRACE, is available starting with SQL*Plus 3.3 and higher. It enables a SQL*Plus user to see the execution plan of DML statements (SELECT, INSERT, UPDATE, and DELETE) while in SQL*Plus, without having to use the regular facilities (SQL TRACE, EXPLAIN PLAN, and the TKPROF utility) that ORACLE provides to trace the execution of SQL statements.

To enable this feature, the DBA must run, as user SYS, a SQL script called PLUSTRCE.SQL. The location of the PLUSTRCE.SQL file is operating system–dependent. The PLUSTRCE script does the following:

- Creates a role named PLUSTRACE
- Grants SELECT privilege on the tables V$SESSTAT, V$STATNAME, and V$SESSION to the PLUSTRACE role
- Grants the role PLUSTRACE to the DBA role with ADMIN OPTION

To enable the AUTOTRACE capability for a user, three conditions must be met:

- The user must have been granted the PLUSTRACE role by any user who has been granted the DBA role.

- The user must have created a PLAN_TABLE in his or her own schema. The user runs the utlxplan.sql script to do this. The script is located in the directory $ORACLE_HOME/rdbms/admin on UNIX platforms and in the directory %ORACLE_HOME%\Rdbms8x\Admin under Windows 95/NT.

- The SET system variable AUTOTRACE must be set appropriately.

After these steps are performed, the user can get a report on the execution path used by the optimizer and the execution statistics after the successful running of any DML statement (SELECT, INSERT, DELETE, UPDATE). The output of the report is controlled by the AUTOTRACE system variable.

The allowed settings for the AUTOTRACE system variable and the result of using them are listed in Table 26.5.

TABLE 26.5 AUTOTRACE VALUES

Value	Result
SET AUTOTRACE OFF	The default. No report is generated.
SET AUTOTRACE ON EXPLAIN	The trace report shows only the execution path; no execution statistics.
SET AUTOTRACE ON STATISTICS	The trace report shows only the execution statistics; no execution path.
SET AUTOTRACE ON	The trace report shows both the execution path and the execution statistics.
SET AUTOTRACE TRACEONLY	Same as SET AUTOTRACE ON; however, the result of the query is not shown.

UNDERSTANDING THE EXECUTION PLAN

The execution plan shows the access paths the optimizer is using when executing a query. The execution plan output is generated using the EXPLAIN PLAN command. Each line displayed in the execution plan has a sequential line number. The line number of the parent operation is also displayed. The execution plan consists of four columns (for standard queries, only three columns are displayed; the fourth column is displayed only in the case of distributed queries or queries run using the Parallel Query Option (PQO)).

The name of the columns, the order in which they're displayed, and their description are shown in Table 26.6.

TABLE 26.6   EXECUTION PLAN COLUMN DESCRIPTIONS

Column Name	Description
ID_PLUS_EXP	Displays the line number of each execution step
PARENT_ ID_PLUS_EXP	Displays the relationship between a step and its parent
PLAN_ PLUS_EXP	Displays each step of the report; for example, TABLE ACCESS (FULL) OF 'DEPT'
OBJECT_NODE _PLUS_EXP	Displays the database link(s) or parallel query servers used (only when running distributed queries or queries using the Parallel Query Option (PQO)

The default column formats are usually set in the Site Profile (the glogin.sql file).

The format of the columns can be altered using the SQL*Plus command COLUMN. You can change the width of a column, rename it, or stop it from being displayed. For example, to prevent the ID_PLUS_EXP column from displaying, enter

```
SQL> COLUMN ID_PLUS_EXP NOPRINT
```

The second part of the statement-tracing report displays the statement-execution statistics. They show the system resources required to execute the query and their usage. Unlike the execution path, the default format of the statistics report cannot be changed.

USING THE AUTOTRACE FEATURE

This section shows in detail the steps required to enable user SCOTT to use the AUTOTRACE facility in SQL*Plus.

First, user SYSTEM logs on to SQL*Plus and grants user SCOTT the PLUSTRACE role (SYS has previously run the $ORACLE_HOME/sqlplus/admin/plustrce.sql script that creates the PLUSTRACE role in the database). Listing 26.16 shows this being done.

PART

VI

CH

26

LISTING 26.16   GRANTING PLUSTRACE ROLE

```
SQL>

C:\>sqlplus system

SQL*Plus: Release 8.1.3.0.0 - Beta on Sun Mar 7 09:25:09 1999

(c) Copyright 1998 Oracle Corporation.  All rights reserved.

Enter password:

Connected to:
Oracle8 Enterprise Edition Release 8.1.3.0.0 - Beta
With the Partitioning and Objects options
PL/SQL Release 8.1.3.0.0 - Beta
SQL> GRANT plustrace TO scott;
Grant succeeded.
```

Next, user SCOTT logs on to SQL*Plus and creates the PLAN_TABLE (required by the EXPLAIN PLAN command) into his schema by running the script $ORACLE_HOME/rdbms80/admin/ utlxplan.sql, as shown in Listing 26.17.

LISTING 26.17   CREATING PLAN_TABLE

```
SQL> CONNECT scott
Enter password: *****
Connected.
SQL> @$ORACLE_HOME/rdbms80/admin/utlxplan
Table created.
SQL> L
  1   create table PLAN_TABLE (
  2       statement_id     varchar2(30),
  3       timestamp        date,
  4       remarks          varchar2(80),
  5       operation        varchar2(30),
  6       options          varchar2(30),
  7       object_node      varchar2(128),
  8       object_owner     varchar2(30),
  9       object_name      varchar2(30),
 10       object_instance  numeric,
 11       object_type      varchar2(30),
 12       optimizer        varchar2(255),
 13       search_columns   numeric,
 14       id               numeric,
 15       parent_id        numeric,
 16       position         numeric,
 17       cost             numeric,
 18       cardinality      numeric,
 19       bytes            numeric,
 20       other_tag        varchar2(255),
 21*      other            long)
```

The L[IST] command lists the contents of the SQL buffer, which contains the last SQL command executed the CREATE TABLE plan_table statement from the ORACLE_HOME/rdbms80/admin/utlxplan.sql script.

Next, SCOTT enters and executes the query he wants to trace. Listing 26.18 shows an example.

LISTING 26.18   TRACING A QUERY

```
SQL>  SELECT t1.dname, t2.ename, t2.sal, t2.job
   2   FROM dept t1, emp t2
   3   WHERE t1.deptno = t2.deptno;
DNAME             ENAME              SAL   JOB
- - - - - - - - - - - - - - - - - - - - - - - - - - - - - - - -
RESEARCH          SMITH              800   CLERK
SALES             ALLEN             1600   SALESMAN
SALES             WARD              1250   SALESMAN
RESEARCH          JONES             2975   MANAGER
SALES             MARTIN            1250   SALESMAN
```

```
SALES          BLAKE          2850    MANAGER
ACCOUNTING     CLARK          2450    MANAGER
RESEARCH       SCOTT          3000    ANALYST
ACCOUNTING     KING           5000    PRESIDENT
SALES          TURNER         1500    SALESMAN
RESEARCH       ADAMS          1100    CLERK
SALES          JAMES           950    CLERK
RESEARCH       FORD           3000    ANALYST
ACCOUNTING     MILLER         1300    CLERK
14 rows selected.
```

To get information on both the execution path and the execution statistics, SCOTT has to set the AUTOTRACE variable appropriately. Listing 26.19 shows the commands used to set AUTOTRACE on and run the previous query from the buffer.

LISTING 26.19   TRACING THE QUERY IN THE BUFFER

```
SQL> SET AUTOTRACE ON
SQL> /
Execution Plan
----------------------------------------------------------
    0      SELECT STATEMENT Optimizer=CHOOSE
    1    0   NESTED LOOPS
    2    1     TABLE ACCESS (FULL) OF 'EMP'
    3    1     TABLE ACCESS (BY ROWID) OF 'DEPT'
    4    3       INDEX (UNIQUE SCAN) OF 'DEPT_PRIMARY_KEY' (UNIQUE)
Statistics
----------------------------------------------------------
      0   recursive calls
      2   db block gets
     43   consistent gets
      0   physical reads
      0   redo size
    726   bytes sent via SQL*Net to client
    376   bytes received via SQL*Net from client
      3   SQL*Net roundtrips to/from client
      0   sorts (memory)
      0   sorts (disk)
     14   rows processed
```

To trace the same statement without displaying the query data:

```
SQL> SET AUTOTRACE TRACEONLY
SQL> /                    — slash command: doesn't display query text
14 rows selected.
Execution Plan
----------------------------------------------------------
    0      SELECT STATEMENT Optimizer=CHOOSE
    1    0   NESTED LOOPS
    2    1     TABLE ACCESS (FULL) OF 'EMP'
    3    1     TABLE ACCESS (BY ROWID) OF 'DEPT'
    4    3       INDEX (UNIQUE SCAN) OF 'DEPT_PRIMARY_KEY' (UNIQUE)
Statistics
----------------------------------------------------------
```

PART

VI

CH

26

continues

continued

```
  0  recursive calls
  2  db block gets
 43  consistent gets
  0  physical reads
  0  redo size
726  bytes sent via SQL*Net to client
376  bytes received via SQL*Net from client
  3  SQL*Net roundtrips to/from client
  0  sorts (memory)
  0  sorts (disk)
 14  rows processed
```

Tip #68

The TRACEONLY option is particularly useful when you are tuning a query that returns a large number of rows.

The client referred to in the execution statistics is SQL*Plus. SQL*Net refers to the generic interprocess communication between client (SQL*Plus) and the server (ORACLE RDBMS), whether SQL*Net is installed and used or not.

SQL*PLUS RELEASE 8.1 ENHANCEMENTS

SQL*Plus Release 8.1 gives the user the ability to do the following:

- Access all Oracle8i data types and user defined data types
- Access all new SQL features introduced in Oracle8i
- SQL*Plus Release 8.1 has all features present in release 8.0

Also, there are Server Manager functions which are now made available from SQL*Plus. Some of these functions are: startup, shutdown, show parameter, show sga, archive log, recover database, and connect internal.

There is a new command named ARCHIVE LOG. The ARCHIVE LOG command allows redo log files to be archived. It also displays information about redo log files.

For example:

```
SQL> connect internal
Connected.
SQL> archive log list
Database log mode              No Archive Mode
Automatic archival             Enabled
Archive destination            D:\ORANT\oradata\orcl2\archive
Oldest online log sequence     2
Current log sequence           5
SQL>
```

You can now use the RECOVER command to recover a database from SQL*Plus. The RECOVER command performs media recovery on tablespaces, datafiles or the entire database.

For example:

```
SQL> recover database
ORA-00283: recovery session canceled due to errors
ORA-01124: cannot recover data file 1 - file is in use or recovery
ORA-01110: data file 1: 'D:\ORANT\ORADATA\ORCL2\SYSTEM01.DBF'
```

The SET command now has an INSTANCE clause. The INSTANCE clause changes the default instance for your session to the specified instance. The SET command now has a LOGSOURCE clause. The LOGSOURCE clause specifies the location from which archive logs are retrieved during recovery.

You can now see init.ora parameters from SQL*Plus by using the SHOW PARAMETERS command.

For example:

```
SQL> show parameters block

NAME                                     TYPE     VALUE
- - - - - - - - - - - - - - - - - - - - - - - - - - - - - - - - - - - - - - - - -
db_block_buffers                         integer  1000
db_block_checking                        boolean  TRUE
db_block_checksum                        boolean  FALSE
db_block_lru_latches                     integer  1
db_block_max_dirty_target                integer  1000
db_block_size                            integer  2048
db_file_multiblock_read_count            integer  8
hash_multiblock_io_count                 integer  1
sort_multiblock_read_count               integer  2
```

You can see SGA (system global area) information from sql*plus.

For example:

```
SQL> show sga

Total System Global Area     20396276 bytes
Fixed Size                      63732 bytes
Variable Size                18210816 bytes
Database Buffers              2048000 bytes
Redo Buffers                    73728 bytes
SQL>
```

You can start the database from SQL*Plus using STARTUP, with the options to mount and open a database.

For example:

```
SQL> startup
ORACLE instance started.
Total System Global Area     20396276 bytes
Fixed Size                   63732 bytes
Variable Size                18210816 bytes
Database Buffers             2048000 bytes
Redo Buffers                 73728 bytes
Database mounted.
Database opened.
SQL>
```

PART

VI

CH

26

You can shutdown a database from SQL*Plus using SHUTDOWN. The SHUTDOWN command shuts down an Oracle instance that is currently running. It also optionally closes and dismounts a database.

For example:

```
SQL> shutdown immediate
Database closed.
Database dismounted.
ORACLE instance shut down.
SQL>
```

SQL*Plus is the single tool most commonly used to interact with an Oracle database and to perform administrative functions like startup, shutdown, or recover a database. It is an interactive tool which lets users create, modify, delete, or query database objects like tables, views, indexes, and constraints. It also allows users with appropriate privileges to create new users and grant them privileges or modify exiting users. Users with appropriate privileges can delete users and their privileges from SQL*Plus. In Oracle8i, all Server Manager commands are merged with SQL*Plus so that DBAs can use this tool to effectively manage their databases.

ORACLE ENTERPRISE MANAGER

In this chapter

UNDERSTANDING THE ENTERPRISE MANAGER ARCHITECTURE

Enterprise Manager is much more than just a set of database administration tools. This product provides a framework for an enterprisewide distributed system management solution. For example, a database administrator can physically reside in Los Angeles and manage databases in New York, London, and Tokyo from the same integrated console. A set of centrally located Oracle tables forms a repository to store information necessary to support the activities of each administrator. This repository is maintained by the new Management Server and can reside anywhere on the network or on the local Windows 95/98 or Windows NT workstation supporting the Enterprise Manager client.

Enterprise Manager is open and extendible. Tool Command Language (Tcl), pronounced "tickle," is a nonproprietary and widely used scripting language characterized by ease of use and extensibility. Tcl is used to submit commands to remote operating systems and databases for execution. The implementation of Tcl used by Enterprise Manager, known as OraTcl, includes extensions that enable functions you need to fully manage an Oracle database environment:

- Start and stop Oracle databases
- Execute SQL
- Access operating system resources and functions
- Access Simple Network Management Protocol (SNMP) Management Information Base (MIB) variables describing Oracle databases
- Access non-Oracle SNMP-enabled devices and services

> **Note**
>
> To become familiar with Tcl, review the Enterprise Manager Tcl scripts found in `%ORACLE_HOME%\SYSMAN\SCRIPTS\TCL`.

SNMP is an open standard used by remote intelligent agents to communicate with non-Oracle software and hardware. Originally, SNMP was designed to communicate with network devices, but it is now used to communicate with applications as well. Use of the SNMP standard enables integration of a variety of third-party software and hardware with Enterprise Manager. Application developers integrate applications within the console using Object Linking and Embedding (OLE) or calls to one of the published Application Program Interfaces (APIs) specific to Enterprise Manager. To top it off, when information moves over the network between the console and the remote intelligent agents, it can be secured with Oracle Secure Network Services using the Net8 Advanced Networking Option (ANO). This level of security makes it possible to administer remote databases over the Internet.

All these components and technologies are tied together with an architecture that makes use of a graphics-oriented console client linked to remote intelligent agents that communicate with the databases (see Figure 27.1). In addition to the messages between the communication daemon and the intelligent agents, the application components such as the Database Administration Tools communicate directly with remote databases by using SQL over Net8. Tasks performed by the application components directly on remote databases in real time do not use the communication daemon. The communication daemon uses either native TCP/IP or Net8 Transparent Network Substrate (TNS) connections to communicate with remote intelligent agents to perform core console functions such as job scheduling and event management.

Figure 27.1
The Enterprise Manager architecture provides centralized database management.

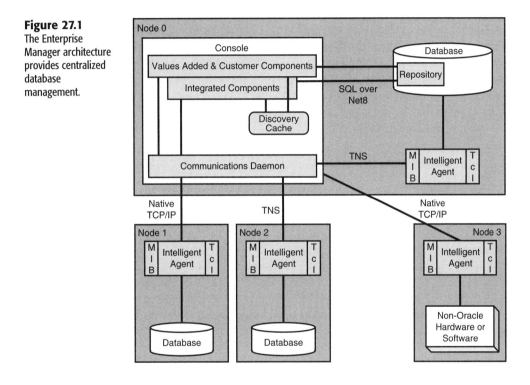

The *discovery cache* is a large buffer that is used to store metadata describing the services and nodes managed by the console. Metadata is collected the first time an object is accessed, and the data is stored in the discovery cache for the remainder of the session. When metadata in the discovery cache is accessed, there is no need to repeat queries to determine the structure of remote databases. As a result, response time improves, and unnecessary resource utilization is avoided. At the end of a session, the data is stored in the repository so that it will be available for the next session. Custom applications can also access the discovery cache.

The intelligent agents autonomously execute and manage remote activities. After the communication daemon instructs a remote agent to execute a particular script at a given time, the script executes independently from the console. If the console is unavailable when it is time for a remote job to run, the agent manages the execution and buffers up to 500 returned messages. The agent passes this information back to the console when it becomes available and re-establishes communication. Similarly, intelligent agents handle remote event monitoring and responses independent of the console.

Most installations of Enterprise Manager do not take full advantage of the architecture. In some ways, this is a tribute to the flexibility of the product to support real-time database administration using components such as Schema Manager without depending on the entire architecture. Sites that already use robust third-party systems management tools, such as BMC Patrol, CA-Unicenter, Compuware EcoTools, or Platinum ProVision, duplicate existing functions while increasing administrative overhead and system workload if the entire framework is implemented. Sites that are not using such tools might find Enterprise Manager, which is bundled with Oracle8i Server at no extra cost, a suitable substitute (value-added products, such as the Diagnostics Pack, are available at an additional charge).

Due to the limited scope of Enterprise Manager and currently available add-on tools to extend its capabilities, it is not a substitute for a robust systems management product whose scope extends well beyond database management. Particularly in large enterprises where the operations staff benefits from the efficiencies of a common user interface and approach to tasks across many platforms, database technologies, and other managed technology, a more comprehensive solution might add value. In any case, it is likely that there is a place for at least some of the components of Enterprise Manager in any Oracle database environment.

GETTING STARTED

Enterprise Manager has a robust architecture, but it is easy to start using it. After the software is installed, tools such as Schema Manager, which does not require a repository or remote intelligent agent, are immediately functional. The repository enables some functions such as data accumulation for performance analysis and capacity planning. This repository makes some activities easier, such as logging in to the console, by storing preferred credentials between sessions. Because stored information varies from one administrator to the next, each administrator should have a separate repository. Only one instantiation of Enterprise Manager can connect to a repository at any given time.

The best place to start exploring and gain immediate benefit from Enterprise Manager is using the following Database Administration Tools:

- Instance Manager
- Schema Manager
- SQL Worksheet
- Security Manager
- Storage Manager

These five tools can be accessed in four ways. The first is directly from the Windows taskbar. For example, from the Start menu on the taskbar, choose Programs, Oracle-*Oracle Home*, DBA Management Pack, and then Instance Manager to start the Instance Manager.

The second way to access the database administration applications is from the Enterprise Manager console application launch palette. Before you can use the console, it is necessary to build a repository. Unlike earlier releases of Enterprise Manager, the process of repository construction is performed automatically. The first time the console starts with a given userID, Repository Manager describes the sub-components that are necessary to start the console. When you respond OK to the prompt, Repository Manager creates a repository for itself, Enterprise Manager, and Software Manager, and it starts the Discover New Services Wizard. If there are nodes on the network that already have Oracle Intelligent Agent configured, this wizard communicates with the remote nodes to populate the navigation tree on the console. Because this function can be performed at any time, you can skip it for a fast start.

Caution

Because a repository is built automatically during the first login, you must be careful to avoid creating a repository for a system user, such as SYSTEM, in the SYSTEM tablespace. A repository in the SYSTEM tablespace might cause fragmentation and space constraints that adversely impact performance and manageability.

After the Enterprise Manager console opens, use the Database Administration Tools from the Applications toolbar to explore the Instance Manager, the Schema Manager, and other Database Administration Tools. The remaining tools—Backup Manager, Data Manager, and Software Manager—can only be accessed from here in the console.

The third way to access the Database Administration Tools is also from within the console on the menu bar by selecting Tools, Applications.

Enterprise Manager is now ready to use, but there are no databases or listeners known to Enterprise Manager unless the Discover New Services Wizard took advantage of remote intelligent agents to automatically discover and define them. To add databases and nodes representing systems, from the menu bar choose Navigator, Service Discovery, and Manually Define Services to start the Service Definition Wizard. The wizard guides database administrators through the process of defining listeners and databases to Enterprise Manager. Database Administration Tools are now accessible, in the fifth and final way by right-clicking on one of the newly added databases in the upper-left Navigator window. From the mouse menu, select Related Tools to see a context-sensitive list of tools available to access the selected database (see Figure 27.2).

Figure 27.2
Context-sensitive menus enable Schema Manager access to the database through the console.

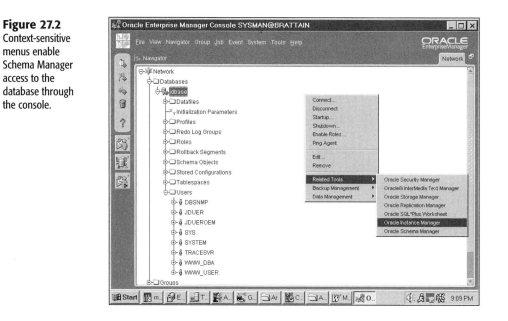

USING THE CONSOLE FUNCTIONS

When database administrators become familiar with Enterprise Manager, console functions are not usually the attraction of the product. Most database administrators become interested in the product because of the Database Administration Tools and the Diagnostics and Tuning Packs. However, a significant portion of these components are crippled or do not function at all without the Event Management and Job Scheduling components working with remote intelligent agents:

- Backup Manager cannot perform backups or recoveries without Job Scheduling.

- Data Manager cannot perform imports, exports, or loads without Job Scheduling.

- Software Manager cannot distribute software without Job Scheduling.

- Trace Manager cannot collect performance data for analysis without Job Scheduling.

- The defragmentation and coalescence functions of Tablespace Manager require Job Scheduling.

- The Advanced Events that come with the Diagnostics and Tuning Packs depend on Event Management.

Use the information in this section to implement the full architecture so that the promise of Enterprise Manager is fulfilled. The focus on implementation and configuration of the integrated console functions found in this book is intended to enable database administrators to take full advantage of all the other useful functions that depend on the console components.

The Enterprise Manager Console centralizes control of the database environment. Whether managing a single database or a global enterprise, the console provides consolidated management. There are four primary console functions, each of which is represented in a pane in the console window:

- Navigator
- Group
- Event Management
- Job Scheduling

The Navigator provides a tree structure representing all databases, servers, Net8 listeners, Web servers, and groups of these components. Context-sensitive access to the Database Administration Tools is only a few mouse clicks away. Group (formerly called Map) provides a way to geographically track the status of systems and drill down into systems to examine listeners and databases. In conjunction with the event functionality, Map shows system status at a glance.

Event management and job scheduling are dependent on the availability of remote intelligent agents. The Event Management component communicates with remote intelligent agents to track activities and conditions on remote systems. Using this capability, Enterprise Manager sends mail, pages people, or runs a job to correct a fault or capture diagnostic information for later analysis. If a job runs to resolve or prevent a fault, the Job Scheduler component handles the task. In addition, the Job Scheduler can launch, monitor, and report completion of a series of activities on remote systems.

UNDERSTANDING THE INTEGRATED CONSOLE FUNCTIONS

Some console functions apply to all the other components of Enterprise Manager to enforce security, make applications available, manage the four panes of the console window, and manage the communication daemon.

SECURITY

Security functionality for Enterprise Manager is managed from the console and is accessible from the menu by selecting System, Preferences. The database administrator can store the passwords necessary to access the services managed by Enterprise Manager. When many userIDs with different passwords are required to administer a large environment, you often resort to writing them down on slips of paper or in notebooks. It is impossible to remember 20 userIDs and the associated continually changing passwords. The user preferences at least enable database administrators to store passwords in a secured environment where they will not accidentally fall into the wrong hands.

LAUNCH PALETTES

Launch palettes are small toolbars on the left side of the console. The Launch palettes are accessed and managed from the menu bar by selecting View and then Show/Hide Toolbar. The default installation of Enterprise Manager without value-added or custom products provides only the Application palette.

You can activate the Enterprise Manager toolbar by choosing View, Show Toolbar from the menu bar. The toolbar consists of five sections of buttons for related tasks (see Figure 27.3). These tasks manage which application panes are visible, provide drag-and-drop help, manage map images, create and remove events, and create and remove jobs.

Figure 27.3
The Enterprise Manager toolbar (far left) provides tools for the map, event, and job console panes.

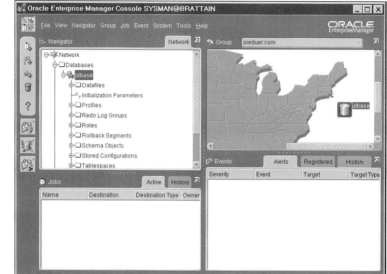

SURFING DATABASES WITH NAVIGATOR

Navigator is the most widely used part of the Enterprise Manager console. It behaves much like the Windows Explorer, so the interface is intuitive and immediately usable. Right-clicking on any object reveals a mouse menu to create new tree views, access Navigator functions, or use related Database Administration Tools.

From the Navigator menu, select Split View to create a reference point for the top of a tree in a new view easily accessible using tabs at the top of the Navigator window. In a complex database or operating environment, the tree views make accessing the parts of the environment of interest more efficient (see Figure 27.4). Filters provide an alternative method of limiting branches of the tree to objects of interest. For example, if all general ledger objects begin with "GL_", a filter value of GL_% will limit objects below the filter in the tree structure to those that belong to the general ledger system.

Figure 27.4
Navigator provides
a way to get to and
manipulate any object
in any database.

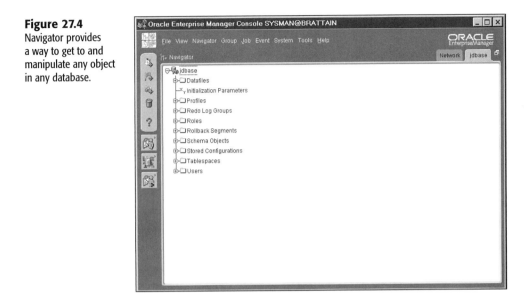

The same menu enables the database administrator to create new objects of the same type or delete existing objects. Some object changes are possible directly from Navigator using Quick Edit whereas more complex changes might require accessing one of the Database Administration Tools that operate on the selected object by selecting Related Tools.

Tip #69	Because the mouse menu is context-sensitive, the operations available vary widely across different objects.

Navigator is also the source of components for Group. To add an object to a map, simply drag the object from Navigator to Map and drop it where you want it on the map.

Using Navigator, a single administrator can access every object in every database, create new objects, and delete existing objects without writing a single SQL statement. Navigator easily becomes the database administrator's primary interface to manually query and alter databases and their objects.

PART
VI

CH
27

VISUALIZING THE DATABASE WORLD WITH GROUP

Map provides a geographically oriented means to monitor the status and basic information concerning databases, nodes, listeners, and Web servers, as well as groups of these four objects. Maps of Asia, Europe, Japan, the United States, and the world are provided with the product, but any bitmap file (*.BMP) is a valid map. The map doesn't even have to be geographical. Consider organizational charts, business process flows, and network diagrams as alternative maps. The capability to quickly switch between maps from the Console toolbar enables many views of the enterprise.

Used in conjunction with remote intelligent agents, Group indicates the status of each object on the map with a small signal flag. Green signal flags mean all is well. Yellow flags indicate that some condition requires attention, and red indicates a serious problem. The event management component of Enterprise Manager enables the database administrator to define conditions and thresholds necessary to trigger changes in status indicated by the signal flags. Double-clicking on a map object starts a view-only Quick Edit of the object. Database Administration tools, usually started from the Console, can be directly started specific to an object if the object is selected on the map.

AUTOMATING ADMINISTRATION TASKS WITH JOB

The Enterprise Manager Job Scheduling component, known as Job, provides a way for database administrators to automate tasks at specific times or based on events in the operating environment. Scheduling is especially valuable in complex environments with many systems. Job can perform any tasks requiring operating systems commands or SQL. The remote agent handles actual execution independent of the Enterprise Manager console.

Tip #70	Job is not usable if Oracle Intelligent Agent is not installed and configured.

Job comes with a variety of predefined tasks ready to configure and schedule. The process for creating a job is best explained using an example. To schedule an export of a remote database, start by selecting Job, Create Job from the Enterprise Manager menu bar. The resulting window contains five tabs: General, Tasks, Parameters, Schedule, and Permissions.

Starting with General, give the job a name and description. Then, select the destination type and a destination. To perform a database export, the destination type should be "Database." Next, move to the Tasks tab. There are over a dozen database and system building block tasks available to configure a job. Select the Export task from the Available Task list and move it to the Job Tasks list. More complex jobs are composed of multiple tasks arranged in the required order.

Next, select the Parameters tab, where configuration information for each task in a job is managed. For your export, select the Details button to start the Export Wizard, and determine whether you will export the entire database or specified users and tables. (see Figure 27.5).

Figure 27.5
Many task building blocks are available to create a job, each with their own parameters.

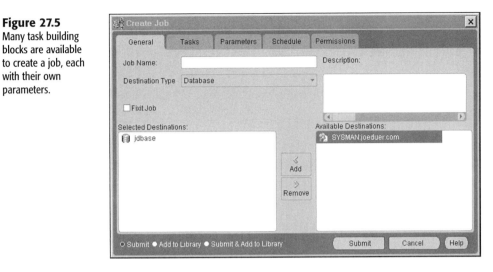

Tip #71

If there are no objects in the Available Objects list, go to Navigator and create a database group in the Database Groups folder. The database groups make up the available object list.

The export job is now ready to schedule. Select the Schedule tab and define when the job should run. Pressing the Submit button saves the job; it is ready to run at the specified time. The job name and description are displayed in the Jobs console window when the Job Library tab is selected. Information on active and complete jobs is available from other tabs.

Job is an easy-to-use and well-organized job scheduling system that gives database administrators the capability to automate tasks on diverse systems directly from the Enterprise Manager console. However, it is no substitute for the more robust job scheduling components of the comprehensive systems management packages that provide features such as job restart and job triggers based on the existence of a file on remote systems. The key to using Job to its full potential is to understand your job scheduling requirements. If you are currently using cron to schedule all your UNIX-based jobs, Job is a huge improvement. If you are thinking about implementing a more robust job scheduling process for your entire operation as part of an enterprisewide systems management strategy, you might find other products more suitable.

PART
VI
CH
27

RESPONDING TO CHANGE WITH EVENT MANAGEMENT

The Event Management System (EMS) is the Enterprise Manager component that monitors the health and welfare of remote databases and the services that make them available to applications. Unlike Job, which triggers tasks on a specific schedule, EMS works with remote intelligent agents to constantly monitor for unusual conditions, known as events, and then manage the events based on specifications defined by the database administrator. Events can trigger a job to take preventative or corrective action to keep a system available and to collect information for later analysis. If events are serious enough, Map is notified to change the visual signal flags on the graphical display. EMS can even send mail or use pagers to notify individuals of events.

Like Job, EMS uses the communication daemon on the local client and remote intelligent agents on each system to monitor and respond to events. The intelligent agents actually monitor system resources, so the events are managed 24 hours a day without the direct participation of the Enterprise Manager console. Without Oracle Intelligent Agent installed and configured, Job is not usable.

To begin monitoring a remote resource for a particular event, the event must be registered in EMS. A variety of predefined events come ready to configure and register. The process to begin monitoring is best explained using a simple example. To monitor the availability of a remote listener, start by selecting Event, Create Event Set from the Enterprise Manager menu bar. The resulting window contains three tabs: General, Tests, Parameters, and Permissions.

Starting with General, give the event a name and description and select the destination type. To monitor a database, the destination type should be Database. Next, move to the Tests tab. Select the UpDown event from the Available Event list and move it to the Selected Event list. More complex event sets are composed of multiple events as shown in Figure 27.6.

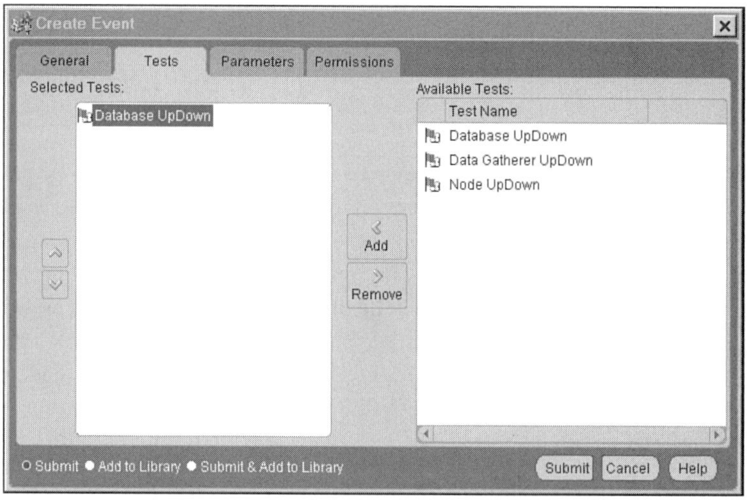

Figure 27.6
Many predefined events are available for monitoring databases.

Next, select the Parameters tab, where configuration information is managed for each selected event in an event set. There are no parameters required for this type of test. To monitor a database, simply make sure you have set the Frequency information on the General tab to determine how often the remote intelligent agent should check on the database and press the Submit button to complete the event set.

The event set is now registered. You can doublecheck that it is by going to the Events pane of the Enterprise Manager and clicking on the Registered tab.

> If there are no destinations on the Available Destinations list, you will need to go to Navigator and create a database group in the Database Groups folder. The database groups make up the available destination list. Defining groups based on the responsible administrators simplifies notification setup in the Event Management System when event sets are registered.

EMS is now configured to monitor the selected databases based on the event set configuration and respond to the event.

Like Job, EMS is a solid component of Enterprise Manager that opens the door to enterprisewide systems management. Before expending the effort to fully configure Enterprise Manager for event monitoring, make sure that the tool meets all your requirements. For a pure Oracle database focus, it probably does, but if you require an integrated solution that covers areas outside database monitoring or requires monitoring for multiple database technologies, you might want to purchase a more comprehensive tool.

USING THE DATABASE ADMINISTRATION TOOLS

Although the Enterprise Manager Navigator console components provide access to various objects in the Oracle database environment, the detailed administration is accomplished with the Database Administration Tools. The user interface of the tools is based on the familiar Windows Explorer tree structure, making all the tools intuitive and easy to use. When objects are selected on the left side of the application window, a display on the right side of the window describes the object or, for folders, the objects in the folder.

The toolbars provide easy access to key functions in each application. As each object is selected in the navigation tree, the appropriate buttons are activated to enable operations on the selected objects. Some applications have their own wizards on the toolbar to perform functions specific to their subject area. Toolbar functions found in most of the Database Administration Tools include database connection requests, navigation tree refresh, folder filtering, object creation and removal, and drag-and-drop help.

A significant consideration when deciding how to use the Database Administration Tools revolves around how database design tools are used in the development process. If the database design is managed in a tool such as Oracle Designer, Computer Systems Advisors Silverrun, Logic Works Erwin, or Powersoft PowerDesigner, using Schema Manager to change objects in the production schema is just as counterproductive as using native DDL. Schema Manager is not a replacement for database design tools. However, Schema Manager is still useful for building objects such as temporary tables outside the scope of the production database design. Developers use the tools to create objects for testing before changes are introduced into the database design.

MANAGING INSTANCES

Database administrators manage the availability and configuration of databases, as well as the instance sessions and transactions, using Instance Manager. All the configuration information stored in the INIT<SID>.ORA configuration files is accessible directly from Instance Manager (see Figure 27.7). Sessions and in-doubt transactions are monitored and managed on the right side of the application window based on the objects selected in the tree navigator on the left side of the window.

Figure 27.7
Instance tuning parameters are altered for implementation.

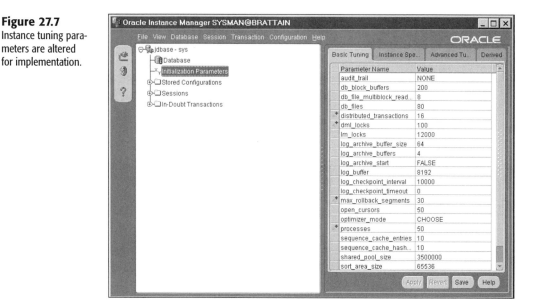

Instance Manager provides a variety of functions related to the management of database availability. The database administrator can shut down and start up database instances, mount and open databases, and toggle archive logging on and off. Automatic archival can be temporarily turned on (until the instance is cycled) or several types of manual archival can be triggered. Information on the status of the database, its logging status, and SGA configuration is available by selecting the database object in the navigation window.

Tip #72

If the database management functions found on the menu bar by selecting Database are grayed out and inaccessible, it is because the connected user is not authorized to perform these functions. If you want to perform these tasks, reconnect to the database as SYSOPER or SYSDBA.

Selecting the Sessions folder in the navigation window provides session information. In addition, access to the instance to new sessions is restricted or enabled using the Sessions selection from the menu bar. Sessions can be disconnected either immediately or after the current transaction is complete. Selecting the In-Doubt Transactions provides information about these transactions, which can be forced to commit or rollback.

Instance configuration information is also managed by the Instance Manager. Parameters that are dynamically updateable in the database take effect immediately. Other changes take effect the next time the database is cycled. Multiple configurations are stored in the Windows Registry for access and review. Any configuration can be exported to a file or automatically propagated to remote systems.

Tip #73	Stored configurations help track changes to each database. If all configuration changes are made and stored in Instance Manager, you can always see your change history online. The date of implementation and the person making the change should be recorded as part of the configuration name and description. Hopefully, future releases will store configurations in the repository instead of the Windows Registry of the local workstation.

MANAGING SCHEMAS

Schema Manager is perhaps the most comprehensive and widely used of the Database Administration Tools. Schema Manager administers clusters, constraints, database links, functions, indexes, packages, partitions, privileges, procedures, queues, refresh groups, sequences, snapshot logs, snapshots, synonyms, tables, triggers, views (see Figure 27.8), and the relationships these objects have to each other.

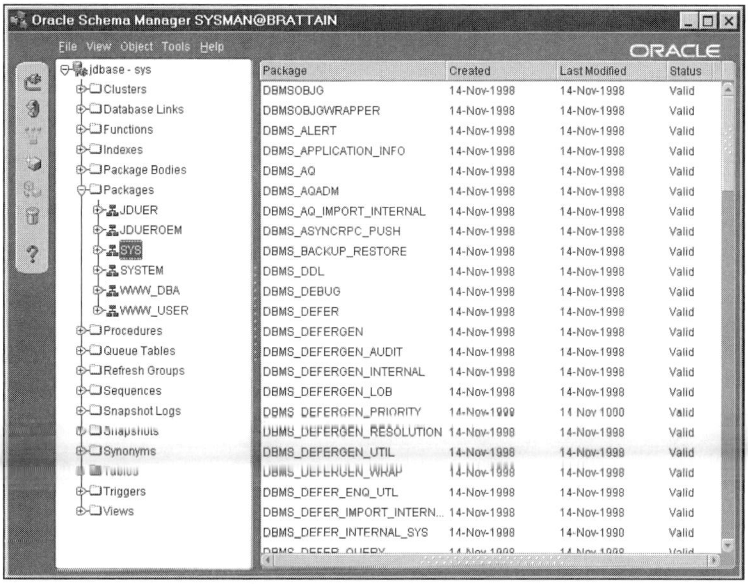

Figure 27.8
Schema Manager shows the dependencies of a view.

Schema Manager provides a variety of capabilities related to managing schema objects. The database administrator can create any managed object and can even use existing objects as templates. When an object is selected in the navigation tree, Schema Manager creates or assigns object privileges, synonyms, and indexes related to the selected object. Partitions can be removed from a selected table.

As powerful as Schema Manager is, it is one of the simplest Database Administration Tools to use. Listing 27.1 shows the result of a simple operation to clone the SYS.OBJ$ table and its indexes as recorded by Schema Manager.

LISTING 27.1   OBJ$_TBL.SQL—DDL TO CREATE OBJ$ AND ITS INDEXES

```
REM  Schema Manager recorded SQL to create a duplicate copy of SYS.OBJ$
REM and its indexes and constraints.
CREATE TABLE "JGENTRY".TEST
(OBJ# NUMBER NOT NULL, DATAOBJ# NUMBER NULL, OWNER# NUMBER NOT NULL,
NAME VARCHAR2(30) NOT NULL, NAMESPACE NUMBER NOT NULL,
SUBNAME VARCHAR2(30) NULL, TYPE# NUMBER NOT NULL, CTIME DATE NOT NULL,
MTIME DATE NOT NULL, STIME DATE NOT NULL, STATUS NUMBER NOT NULL,
REMOTEOWNER VARCHAR2(30) NULL, LINKNAME VARCHAR2(128) NULL,
FLAGS NUMBER NULL, OID$ RAW(16) NULL, SPARE1 NUMBER NULL,
SPARE2 NUMBER NULL,SPARE3 NUMBER NULL, SPARE4 VARCHAR2(1000) NULL,
SPARE5 VARCHAR2(1000) NULL,
SPARE6 DATE NULL,  CHECK (OBJ# IS NOT NULL),  CHECK (OWNER# IS NOT NULL),
CHECK (NAME IS NOT NULL),  CHECK (NAMESPACE IS NOT NULL),
CHECK (TYPE# IS NOT NULL), CHECK (CTIME IS NOT NULL),
CHECK (MTIME IS NOT NULL), CHECK (STIME IS NOT NULL),
CHECK (STATUS IS NOT NULL)) PCTFREE 10 PCTUSED 40 INITRANS 1 MAXTRANS 255
STORAGE (INITIAL 10K NEXT 100K MINEXTENTS 1 MAXEXTENTS 2147483645
PCTINCREASE 0) TABLESPACE "USER_DATA"
CREATE UNIQUE INDEX "JGENTRY"."I_OBJ1" ON  "JGENTRY"."TEST" ("OBJ#")
TABLESPACE "USER_DATA" PCTFREE 10 INITRANS 2 MAXTRANS 255
STORAGE (INITIAL 10K NEXT 24K MINEXTENTS 1 MAXEXTENTS 121 PCTINCREASE 50
FREELISTS 1)
CREATE UNIQUE INDEX "JGENTRY"."I_OBJ2" ON  "JGENTRY"."TEST"
("OWNER#", "NAME", "NAMESPACE", "REMOTEOWNER", "LINKNAME", "SUBNAME")
TABLESPACE "USER_DATA" PCTFREE 10 INITRANS 2 MAXTRANS 255
STORAGE ( INITIAL 10K NEXT 100K MINEXTENTS 1 MAXEXTENTS 2147483645
PCTINCREASE 0 FREELISTS 1)
CREATE INDEX "JGENTRY"."I_OBJ3" ON  "JGENTRY"."TEST" ("OID$")
TABLESPACE "USER_DATA" PCTFREE 10 INITRANS 2 MAXTRANS 255
STORAGE ( INITIAL 10K NEXT 10K MINEXTENTS 1 MAXEXTENTS 121 PCTINCREASE 50
FREELISTS 1)
EXIT;
```

The entire content of OBJ$_TBL.SQL was generated using the create like operation on four existing objects, changing the schema names and tablespaces, and reassigning the column order to the indexes (which is not retained by the create like operation on an index).

MANAGING SECURITY

Security Manager provides database administrators with a means to manage access privileges and object privileges within Oracle8i (see Figure 27.9). The database administrator can easily create, alter, and drop security objects and associate privileges, roles, quotas, and profiles to users and other roles.

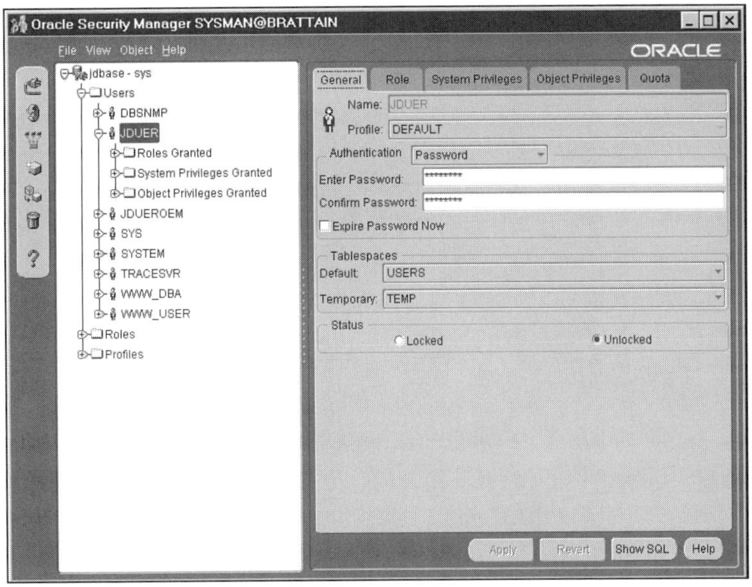

Figure 27.9
Notice the
Administrator toolbar
on the left side of the
Security Manager
screen.

Security Manager is so easy to use that it could be provided to end-user security administrators to administer application security. These end-user security administrators have ADMIN OPTION granted for the roles and object privileges within their sphere of responsibility. Custom application components to perform this function are avoidable by the proper use of roles, application user training, and Security Manager. Application users enjoy direct and timely management of data they own, and database and security administrators can spend time on more productive pursuits.

MANAGING STORAGE

Storage Manager provides database administrators with a means to manage and monitor tablespaces, data files, and rollback segments within Oracle8i. The database administrator can easily create, alter, and drop storage (see Figure 27.10). The interdependencies of storage objects are shown from the perspective of any of the three storage objects. Storage Manager adds rollback segments and data files to tablespaces, takes tablespaces online and offline, and takes them into and out of read only mode. Individual data files and rollback segments can also be taken online and offline. Storage Manager can also shrink rollback segments.

The graphic display of storage utilization at a glance enables database administrators to track down storage problems quickly and respond to them all within the same tool.

PART

VI

CH

27

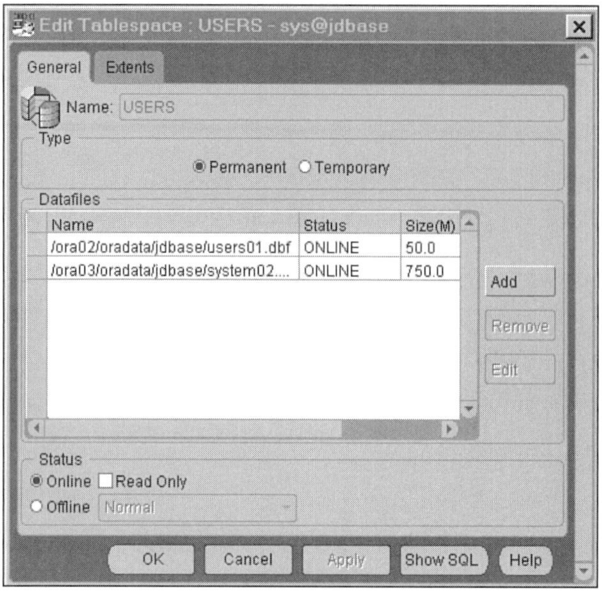

Figure 27.10
Create a tablespace
while displaying
storage utilization.

EXECUTING SQL

SQL Worksheet is the Database Administration Tool answer to Server Manager and SQL*Plus. Targeted at database administrators, it provides a means to submit SQL, PL/SQL, DBA commands, and SQL scripts. With a robust command history and retrieval capability, it provides some of the capabilities that endeared the now obsolete SQL*DBA application to database administrators. Divided into a top output pane and bottom input pane, both of which are scrollable, commands are entered in the input pane, and results scroll across the top output pane.

An input pane toolbar provides several useful and convenient functions. Buttons are used to create new scripts, open scripts, and save scripts. Another button executes the currently open script. The remaining three buttons display the command history and enable the user to scroll through the previously used commands. Previously issued commands are pulled into the input window for execution from the command history display in a separate window. A button associated with the output pane enables the database administrator to save the output to a file.

MANAGING RECOVERABILITY

Backup Manager provides two subsystems for managing recovery and backup of Oracle8i databases: Operating System Backup and Oracle8i Recovery Manager. The Operating System Backup doesn't provide a comprehensive solution for Oracle8i (it is Oracle7-oriented). Oracle8i Recovery Manager is a comprehensive recovery and backup solution including features such as a point-in-time database recovery, scripting, and control file recovery. An optional recovery catalog provides a repository for metadata describing backup and recoveries.

| Tip #74 | To use Backup Manager, Job must be configured and available with a remote intelligent agent operational on the system where the target database resides. |

Wizards that guide the database administrator through the steps necessary to perform recovery and backup are available. Alternatively, database administrators can create backup sets and jobs for image copies manually.

MANAGING DATA

Data Manager assists database administrators to perform imports, exports, and table loads. This tool provides an easy-to-use interface that generates parameter files passed on to SQL*Loader and the import/export utilities for execution. In order to perform these functions on remote systems, Job must be configured and available with a remote intelligent agent operational on the system where the target database resides. Data Manager can operate on local databases without Job.

The navigation tree in Data Manager is user-oriented, with tables and partitions filling the two levels of the hierarchy below user. Export, import, and load operations each have their own wizard to prepare the input parameters necessary to run the utilities. In order to use the load function, a load control file must be prepared in advance of using the utility.

Data Manager is a great way for the novice DBA to become familiar with the three utilities that move data into and out of a database. The wizards are a good training before later exposure to the native utilities and their arcane parameters.

MANAGING SOFTWARE

Software Manager provides a method for database administrators to distribute Oracle software and related configuration information across a network of computers by using an easy-to-use central client interface working with remote intelligent agents. Multiple software distribution servers provide a means to scale up the solution for large installations. Software Manager provides an inventory of software installed in Oracle Home directories on the target remote systems.

A software distribution process is built into Software Manager. Certain systems are designated software distribution hosts. These hosts are the sources for software to distribute to the target systems. Software releases are defined on the software distribution servers based on the product installation files found on Oracle software distribution media or in installation staging areas. Software packages based on components of one or more releases on a distribution server are then bundled, ready for distribution and installation. Installations that require responses are dealt with using response files. The software packages are then submitted for installation on the target remote systems using Job, which is required to use Software Manager.

PART

VI

CH

27

USING THE DIAGNOSTICS PACK

The Enterprise Manager Diagnostics Pack is a value-added component of Enterprise Manager that provides tools for performance monitoring and tracking, session monitoring, trace management, and lock management. Good database performance tuning requires more than a point-in-time snapshot of system information. Performance management is a method, not a tool or skill, that requires access to key performance metrics for different times of the day, week, and month over a period of time. Ideally, the result of performance management is not corrective action based on an immediate problem, but preventative action based on trends detected through an ongoing analysis process. The Diagnostics Pack provides tools necessary to capture, store, and analyze performance data to meet this objective.

Tip #75	Note that there is an additional cost for licensing the use of the Enterprise Manager Diagnostics Pack. You shouldn't install this component unless it is properly licensed.

MONITORING AND TRACKING PERFORMANCE

The centerpiece of the Diagnostics Pack is the Performance Manager. This tool provides real-time performance monitoring and the capability to record performance characteristics for later analysis. A set of predefined metrics in the form of charts and tables enables a quick start to use the tool without up-front development. Database administrators can add new measurements to meet specialized needs that aren't met by the standard charts provided with Performance Manager.

Performance Manager has built-in charts for collection and analysis of contention, global database statistics, I/O, workload levels, memory, and parallel server information. Anything else collectable with a SQL statement is the basis for new charts as required for specialized analysis and tuning.

Performance Manager is a comprehensive tool, but it is also easy to use. Performance collection displayed in flexible graphic detail can be created in just a few minutes.

TRACING DATABASE ACTIVITY

Trace Manager is a comprehensive tool for collecting data for performance management, capacity planning, and workload management. By using the provided Application Programming Interface (API), Trace Manager can even collect information from third-party and custom applications. The Enterprise Manager Job component schedules collection of trace data on systems with remote agents. Job must be configured before using Trace Manager. The tool also uses its own repository and an Oracle Expert repository, which it builds the first time it is accessed by a user who hasn't used Expert or Trace.

To configure Trace Manager, it is necessary to create collections and discover Trace-enabled products. When configured, collections are launched to pull data from Trace-enabled software.

Oracle Trace is a flexible tool with many data collection capabilities enabled from both the remote application code and the Trace Manager. The documentation in the current release consists of two volumes totaling 275 pages. Setup requires the Enterprise Manager console with Job configured, the Trace and Expert repositories on the client, remote intelligent agents on a node where Trace-enabled programs reside, Trace Collection Services on remote nodes (usually linked with the remote application), and Trace Formatter tables on remote nodes. Each application might require configuration as well. For example, at a minimum, Oracle8i must have the `ORACLE_TRACE_ENABLE` parameter set to `TRUE` before it will produce trace data. The setup is not trivial and should not be taken lightly. However, Trace is the key to providing the data necessary to take full advantage of the Enterprise Manager Diagnostics Pack.

MONITORING SESSIONS

TopSessions enables database administrators to monitor database sessions and kill them if necessary due to inactivity or over-utilization of resources. This tool monitors all sessions or only the most active based on consumption of specified resources such as memory or I/O. Filtering provides a means to narrow the focus on sessions of interest when analyzing activity.

Tip #76

Before running TopSessions for Oracle8i, run `%ORACLE_HOME%/SYSMAN/SMPTSInn.SQL` to ensure that tables required to perform all the functions are in place with appropriate permissions. Be aware that this script can not run "as is" and requires some editing to alter the `ORACLE_HOME` drive and name. It is still necessary to log in as `SYS` to explain access plans.

TopSessions can drill down into sessions to display exhaustive session statistics on redo, enqueue, caching, the operating system, parallel server, SQL, and other miscellaneous information. Examining active or open cursors reveals the SQL code executed by each cursor and the access plan the SQL code is using for execution. Locking information, including identification of blocking locks held by the session, is also available.

Tip #77

TopSession can identify locks for a particular session, but for in-depth analysis of the entire locking picture, the tool to use is Lock Manager. Lock Manager displays either all locks held on the database or only blocking or waiting locks. Offending sessions can be killed directly from Lock Manager.

USING CAPACITY PLANNER AND LOCK MANAGER

The Capacity Planner of the Diagnostics Pack is used to collect and store database and operating system statistics in a repository that can be later analyzed. This is a new feature added to the Diagnostics Pack in version 2.0.

You define what type of statistics are collected by defining a *collection view*, and this data is analyzed and summarized by the Capacity Planner by the use of an *analysis view*.

The Capacity Planner can be executed in one of two modes: *Repository* mode is used to store the collected system statistics in the repository database for later analysis; *standalone* mode does not require a connection to a repository, but not all functionality is available in this mode.

The last Diagnostics Pack utility you will learn about is the Lock Manager. The Lock Manager (also new for 2.0) is a great utility for monitoring database locks and troubleshooting problem blocking and waiting conditions.

The one prerequisite for using Lock Manager is having the lock views present in the database. These views are:

- V$LOCK
- V$SESSION
- DBA_OBJECTS

The Lock Manager window displays the lock information by session ID, but it can be sorted in many different combinations.

USING THE TUNING PACK

Another Oracle pack that you can license at additional cost is the *Tuning* pack. The utilities included in the Tuning pack are the Tablespace Manager, Oracle Expert, and SQL Analyze.

These utilities help the DBA tune databases by looking at the storage usage and requirements of database tablespaces, the dynamic performance of the database itself, and the structure of SQL statements executed by the database. Each of these utilities is covered in more detail in the sections that follow.

MANAGING TABLESPACES

Tablespace Manager provides detailed information on storage utilization in tablespaces, data files, and rollback segments. A color-coded map of each piece of storage enables the database administrator to visualize the storage used by every database object, how many extents are used, and where the extents are placed in both the tablespace and data files. This information is invaluable when tracking down I/O contention or tracking the progress of large database loads and index builds.

In addition to the graphical display, there are two other tabs in the right application pane. The Space Usage tab displays the space utilization statistics, such as the row count and the average row length. The Extent Information tab shows information such as the extent count for the selected object and the data file where the selected extent resides.

Tip #78

> Most of the information under the Space Usage tab is produced by the ANALYZE SQL command. For objects with no statistics, generate statistics using ANALYZE or the Tablespace Analyzer Wizard. If the database is tuned for rules-based optimization and the CHOOSE optimization mode is employed, generating statistics might have an adverse performance impact. Likewise, if cost-based optimization is implemented and statistics are not available, performance might severely suffer.

Using Job, Tablespace Manager employs four wizards to change and analyze storage configurations. All four wizards submit jobs to the Enterprise Manager Job Scheduling component to perform the requested tasks. The Tablespace Analyzer Wizard analyzes selected tables, partitions, clusters, and indexes using the ANALYZE SQL command. The Tablespace Organizer Wizard defragments tables, partitions, and clusters using export and import utilities and rebuilds the indexes. It can also detect space that has not been used at the end of segments. The Defragmentation Wizard duplicates Tablespace Organizer defragmentation capabilities, but it is easier and quicker to use because it uses default options. The Coalesce Wizard combines adjacent free space into a single block. This is a particularly important technique for active operational databases where object sizes change frequently and temporary objects are routinely created and dropped. Unless a selected object contains adjacent free blocks, this wizard is disabled.

Using Oracle Expert

Like Oracle Trace, Oracle Expert is an elaborate product with its own user's guide consisting of 160 pages in the current release. Expert is more than just a product; it is the implementation of a performance management methodology. Whereas other Diagnostics Pack components provide information for database administrators to analyze, Expert applies a set of rules to the data to develop conclusions and make recommendations to improve performance. Expert considers trends that develop over time as well as current system conditions. As new database releases become available, the rules are updated to make recommendations on how to take advantage of new advanced features. As a result, Expert doubles as a mentor to help database administrators learn more about performance management and Oracle8i.

Unfortunately, performance tuning is often neglected in favor of day-to-day requirements until serious performance problems impact the production database environment. Expert provides a means to automatically sift through performance data that might consume a large percentage of even a skilled database administrator's time. Expert doesn't replace the database administrator as a performance tuner. It does free the database administrator from the mundane task of screening mountains of data to find potential problems. With Expert, the performance-tuning focus becomes how to deal with what Expert finds and enhancing Expert with more rules based on the experience and knowledge of the database administrator. Performance tuning becomes more efficient, effective, and rewarding.

To start an Expert tuning session, from the menu, select File, New and start telling Expert about the areas it should analyze. The scope of the tuning session is defined based on requirements for instance tuning, application tuning, and storage structure tuning.

PART

VI

CH

27

The profile of the system is defined based on the type of workload (OLTP, DSS, or Batch), downtime tolerance, peak logical write rates, and application information. After the scope is defined, choose the Collect tab to define what data and how much data to collect for analysis. When the collection parameters are defined at the minimum level necessary to meet the tuning session scope, click the Collect button to acquire the required data. Before applying this process to a production database, practice in a test environment until the impact of the various options is understood and the amount of time consumed performing the specified activities is quantified.

Next, select the View/Edit tab to provide more detailed specifications for the tuning session. This is where the specific tuning rules and thresholds are defined. Experienced tuners might want to alter some of the hundreds of rules based on the profile of the target database and personal knowledge and experience. For inexperienced tuners, it is an opportunity to see what Expert believes is good and bad.

From the Analyze tab, click the Perform Analysis button to begin the analysis process. After analysis is complete, select the Recommendation tab to get advice from Expert. If recommendations are deemed reasonable, use the Implement tab to generate implementation scripts and new parameter files. Run the scripts and implement the new parameters to put Expert advice to work. If the advice does not seem correct, this can often be traced back to a rule that might require modification for the target database environment. Recollecting data is not required to develop new recommendations based on rule changes. Simply alter the rules to better reflect the environment of the target database and rerun the analysis.

Expert provides the opportunity to aggregate the collected wisdom at Oracle Corporation and add the experience and knowledge of the local database administration team to a structured methodology for performance management. Although most installations do not use this component of Enterprise Manager, it is probably most useful where it is least used—in small organizations with limited database tuning experience. Progressive database administrators in such environments should find a friend in Expert after even a short period of time using the tool.

USING SQL ANALYZE

The last Tuning Pack utility you will learn about is SQL Analyze. SQL Analyze is a tool that will enable you to performance tune any troublesome SQL statement.

After you start up SQL Analyze, you use TopSQL to find and analyze SQL statements and then pick out the ones you feel need tuning. Then, generate EXPLAIN PLAN and statistics on how the statement performs. After you review the statistics, you can tune the statement. To help you in tuning the statement, you can use the Hint and Tuning wizards. These wizards can add optimization hints, set the access path for tables used by the statement, and define the join order if your statement does a join.

After you have fine-tuned the poorly performing statement, execute it again and compare the results.

USING THE ENTERPRISE VALUE-ADDED PRODUCTS

Oracle provides several other value-added products that integrate with Enterprise Manager. Each meets specialized requirements for areas such as Web server management and processing of biometrics information such as fingerprints.

Replication Manager is useful for environments that make heavy use of Oracle8i replication features. Oracle Rdb for NT provides tools to manage the Rdb database that Oracle acquired from Digital Equipment Corporation (DEC) several years ago. Oracle Fail Safe manages high availability environments implemented on Windows NT clusters. Oracle Biometrics works with specialized hardware to administer fingerprint identification used with the Advanced Networking Option (ANO). Oracle also integrates Web Server Manager and Security Server Manager with Enterprise Manager as value-added applications.

Using the Oracle Enterprise Manager Software Developer's Kit (SDK), developers build their own applications integrated with Enterprise Manager to meet the specific needs of their environment. Several third-party applications are integrated with the Oracle Enterprise Manager. The functionality of these applications ranges from systems management functions, such as transaction processing management connected through Oracle XA, to specialized vertical market applications, including a computerized medical record system. More third-party applications are under development.

Among the newer packs available with Enterprise Manager version 2.0 are the following:

- Change Management Pack—This pack helps the DBA manage object definition changes across multiple databases.
- Management Pack for Oracle Applications—The job of managing the multiple tier Oracle Applications environment is made simpler by this pack. The Management Pack for Oracle Applications extends the Oracle Enterprise Manager to provide for monitoring, capacity planning, and troubleshooting Oracle Applications.
- Standard Management Pack—This pack is a group of general utilities to help the DBA troubleshoot problems, track changes, and tune database indexes.

SUMMARY

In this chapter, you learned all about Oracle Enterprise Manager. You were introduced to each of the many components and utilities that comprise Enterprise Manager, such as Schema Manager, Security Manager, and Tablespace Manager. You also learned about the additional features that come with the optional software packs, such as the Diagnostics and Tuning packs.

By utilizing all these features to the maximum, the DBA can sleep soundly at night knowing that the databases are being watched carefully by a qualified software sentry.

PART

VI

CH

27

PL/SQL FUNDAMENTALS

In this chapter

UNDERSTANDING PL/SQL

PL/SQL is a Procedural Language extension to Oracle's version of ANSI standard SQL. SQL is a non-procedural language; the programmer only describes what work to perform. How to perform the work is left to the Oracle Server's SQL optimizer. In contrast, PL/SQL, like any third-generation (3GL) procedural language, requires step-by-step instructions defining what to do next.

Like other industry-standard languages, PL/SQL provides language elements for variable declaration, value assignment, conditional test and branch, and iteration. Like C or Pascal, it is heavily block-oriented. It follows strict scoping rules, provides parameterized subroutine construction, and like Ada, has a container-like feature called a package to hide or reveal data and functionality at the programmer's discretion. It is a strongly typed language; data type mismatch errors are caught at compile and runtime. Implicit and explicit data type conversions can also be performed. Complex user-defined data structures are supported. Subroutines can be overloaded to create a flexible, modular environment.

Additionally, because it is a procedural wrapper for SQL, the language is well integrated with SQL. Certain language features enable it to interact with the Oracle RDBMS, performing set and individual row operations. The more you know about writing SQL the better designed your PL/SQL programs will be.

PL/SQL provides a feature called Exception Handling to synchronously handle errors and similar events that may occur during processing. You'll learn how to embed exception handlers in your PL/SQL code to deal with error conditions, such as NO_DATA_FOUND or DUP VAL ON INDEX, gracefully.

PL/SQL is not an objected-oriented language. It does have some features found in languages such as Pascal and Ada. If you're familiar with the syntax of Pascal, you will have no trouble learning PL/SQL. Unlike languages such as C and Pascal, pointers are not supported. PL/SQL is primarily a back-end development tool, where it interacts strictly with database tables and other database objects. Interaction with the operating system and external software components is handled through the supplied database packages.

PL/SQL is 100% portable across all Oracle platforms. Because its data types are based on the database server's, the language is completely machine-independent. You do not need to learn various flavors for UNIX, Windows NT, NetWare, and so on. A PL/SQL program will compile and run on any Oracle Server with no modifications required.

This portability also extends to 3GL programming languages. PL/SQL provides a standardized interface to various languages such as C and COBOL via the Oracle-supplied precompilers. The precompilers support the ANSI standard for embedded SQL.

With Oracle8i, Oracle has focused on integrating the RDBMS with the Internet. In addition to your capability to write PL/SQL applications that can be accessed by any browser in the world via Oracle Application Server, Oracle8i adds the capability to make an HTTP request directly from a PL/SQL procedure. Oracle has also put a great deal of work into interoperability between PL/SQL and Java stored in the database to the point where one can call the other seamlessly.

UNDERSTANDING THE PL/SQL ENGINE

Before you look at PL/SQL as a language, you need to understand it in the executing environment.

FITTING INTO THE CLIENT/SERVER ENVIRONMENT

In a client/server configuration, the real bottleneck is typically the network. Connect a couple hundred users to the Oracle server via your compiled C, C++, Delphi, or COBOL program, and you'll have a very sluggish network system. The solution is to combine complex program segments, especially those performing reiterative or related SQL statements, into PL/SQL blocks. These blocks can be embedded in an OCI (Oracle Call Interface) program, or executed even more efficiently by moving them into the database itself as stored functions, procedures, and packages. Figure 28.1 shows the typical interaction between client applications with the Oracle server.

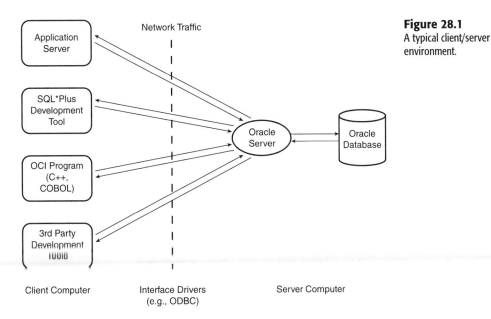

Figure 28.1
A typical client/server environment.

PL/SQL is executed by the PL/SQL engine. This engine is part of the database server. Figure 28.2 illustrates internally how a PL/SQL block is handled.

Figure 28.2
The PL/SQL engine is a component of the Oracle database server.

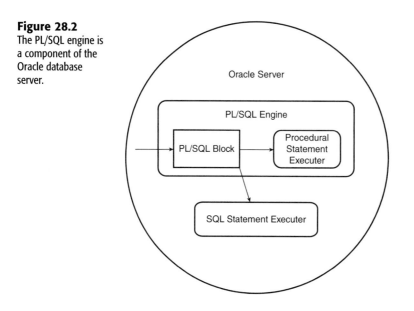

Whatever tool you use, such as Oracle SQL*Plus, the tool must submit the PL/SQL source text to the Oracle Server. The PL/SQL engine scans, parses, and compiles the code. The compiled code is then ready to be executed. During execution, any SQL statements are passed to the SQL Statement Executor component for execution. The SQL Statement Executor performs the SQL or DML statement. The data set retrieved by the query is then available to the PL/SQL engine for further processing.

One advantage of using a PL/SQL block to perform a set of SQL statements, versus sending them individually, is the reduction in network traffic. Figure 28.3 illustrates this idea.

Figure 28.3.
Grouping several SQL statements into one PL/SQL block reduces network traffic.

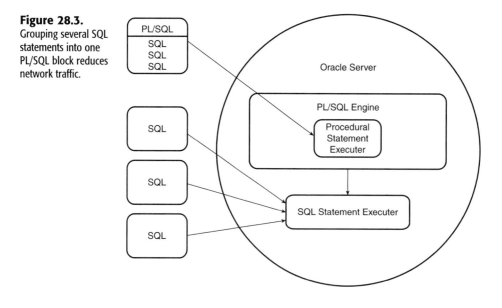

This alone can substantially improve an application's performance. Additionally, the SQL/DML statements can be treated as a single transaction. If the entire transaction succeeds, then all the modifications to the database can be committed. If any part fails, the entire transaction can be rolled back. Because complex logic can be included in the PL/SQL block, and thereby executed on the server, client program size and complexity is reduced.

EXECUTING STORED SUBPROGRAMS

A further refinement involves storing compiled, named PL/SQL blocks in the database. PL/SQL blocks will be referred to collectively in this chapter as stored subprograms or just subprograms. "Named" simply means the name of the subprogram that is included with its code, just like any C function or Pascal subroutine. Figure 28.4 illustrates how the PL/SQL engine calls stored subprograms.

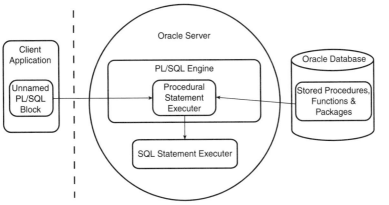

Figure 28.4
The PL/SQL engine runs stored subprograms.

These subprograms can perform complex logic and error handling. A simple anonymous or unnamed block (a block of PL/SQL code that isn't labeled with a name), embedded in a client application, can invoke these subprograms. This capability is generally referred to as a Remote Procedure Call (RPC). Subprograms can also call other subprograms. Because these subprograms are already compiled, and hopefully well tuned by the developer, they offer a significant performance improvement, as well as reduce application development by providing reusable building blocks for other applications or modules.

SHARED SQL AREAS WITHIN THE SYSTEM GLOBAL AREA

The System Global Area (SGA) is a large chunk of memory allocated by the operating system to the Oracle Server. Within this memory, the Server maintains local copies of table data, cursors, user's local variables, and other sundry items.

When you compile any PL/SQL program, whether a named or unnamed block of code, the source and object code are cached in a shared SQL area. The space allocated to each PL/SQL block is called a cursor. The server keeps the cached program in the shared SQL area until it gets aged out, using a Least Recently Used algorithm. Any SQL statements inside the PL/SQL block are also given their own shared SQL area. When a named subprogram is compiled, its source code is also stored in the data dictionary.

The code contained in a subprogram is reentrant; that is, it is shareable among connected users. When an unnamed PL/SQL block is submitted to the server for execution, the server determines whether it has the block in cache by comparing the source text. If the text is exactly identical, character for character, including case, the cached, compiled code is executed. The same is true for SQL statements; if the query text is identical, the cached, parsed code can simply be executed. Otherwise, the new statement must be parsed first. By sharing executable code, a server-based application can achieve substantial memory savings, especially when hundreds of clients are connected.

PRIVATE SQL AREAS

If several users are executing the same block of code, how does the server keep their data separated? Each user's session gets a private SQL area. This hunk of memory contains a private copy of the variable data included in the subprogram. A private SQL area is also allocated for any SQL statements within the PL/SQL block. Figure 28.5 represents the scheme.

Figure 28.5
Shared and private SQL areas within the SGA.

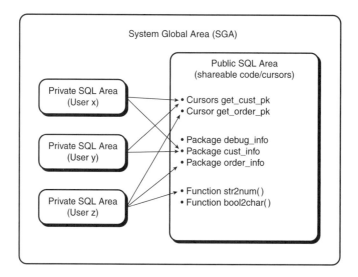

The first time a stored subprogram is referenced, it must be loaded from the database into the SGA. Once loaded, it is available to every user. As long as it continues to be referenced by any user (not necessarily the one who first called it), the subprogram will remain in memory. Packages work the same way, except that a whole set of subprograms may be included in the package. The initial load may take longer, but now all these subprograms are available; there is no further disk hit. When a set of subprograms are expected to be invoked, you're better off having them all load at once. Packages offer this mechanism.

FITTING INTO THE CLIENT ENVIRONMENT

The PL/SQL engine may also be embedded in certain Oracle tools, such as SQL*Forms 4.5 and other Oracle Developer development tools. The main advantage here is programming in a familiar language. The client program can perform the computations contained in the local PL/SQL block, and send the SQL to the server or invoke stored PL/SQL portions. Again, this supports code reuse and simplifies the client program by handling portions of complex logic directly on the database server.

SERVER-SIDE VERSUS CLIENT-SIDE DEVELOPMENT

The developer must consciously decide how much complexity to hide on the server versus how much to keep in the client program. After years of developing client/server applications, the author suggests some guiding principles to follow:

- Reduce network traffic. Push some functionality onto the server. The network is typically the bottleneck in any client/server application.

- Develop standard code. Standard code can be reused on new applications or when adding on to existing applications. This leverages past development effort.

- Strive for low coupling and high cohesiveness. Coupling occurs when one module is dependent on the specific contents of another module, such as when you use global variables instead of passing in parameters. Cohesiveness means putting like elements in the same place, such as bundling all math functions into one math library.

- Hide implementation details. This reduces client program complexity and decouples functionality from implementation. Decoupling is removing or avoiding module dependencies. When implementing top-down design, for example, defer the actual "how-to" by pushing implementation details down to the lower levels.

- Write modules in a generic manner. The more specific a module is, the less reusable it is. Look for patterns and common traits. This does not mean cram several different activities into a single module.

- Handle business rules in a consistent, centralized manner. This makes them more visible and reusable on future projects. If your business rules are ever-changing and spread out over many client program modules, you will have to locate and revise them all over the place—a process that is neither efficient nor maintainable.

Tip #79	Clamage's Rule of Maintainability: A highly maintainable program module is one that requires little or no changes when the requirements for that module changes. An unmaintainable program is one that requires substantial modifications in order to incorporate new requirements. The above principles will help guide you toward the goal of building highly maintainable software.

Use stored subprograms to implement these principles. By providing standard libraries of stored subprograms, multiple and future client applications can take advantage of earlier, completed development. For example, business rules can be implemented as stored subprograms. If a rule changes, for example, how to compute a sales commission, just modify and recompile the appropriate stored program. Any dependent client programs need not change or even be recompiled, provided the stored subprogram's interface remains unchanged.

Packages are a good way to increase a subprogram's generality by allowing the subprogram name to be overloaded. Overloading simply means giving the same subprogram name to a set of code, usually with different data types or different numbers of arguments in the parameter list. For example, the addition operator is overloaded in nearly all computer languages to handle both integer and floating point arithmetic.

ADDING PL/SQL TO YOUR TOOLBOX

Stop for a minute and think about how you can use PL/SQL in your everyday tasks. You may not be involved in application development. As a DBA, you have to perform steady maintenance on the database. You can use PL/SQL to make your life easier.

ENERGIZE YOUR SQL SCRIPTS

Some SQL*Plus scripts can actually generate another script, such as listing the number of rows for every table in a tablespace. However, the scripts could be rewritten in PL/SQL, compiled, and stored in the database; thereby running much faster, without writing the intermediate script to a file.

Writing these kinds of scripts is also somewhat difficult; a PL/SQL script is more straightforward and easier to document and maintain. Additionally, a compiled PL/SQL program is readily shared among DBAs (especially if you're in a "24×7" shop). Instead of searching the hard drive for scripts, everyone will always know where they are and how to run them.

Stored subprograms can take parameters, which makes them extremely flexible. You can even write SQL*Plus front ends for them, collect user input and pass these values in, without having to know the order and types of the parameters.

SIMPLIFYING DATABASE ADMINISTRATION

You probably have a good set of SQL scripts that give you information about your database in action. But after you understand PL/SQL, you'll envision a whole new set of programs that give you additional information on database performance, storage, user load, locks, and so on. PL/SQL eliminates the restrictions and limitations of plain SQL scripts.

You can automate many tasks, running them at set intervals by using the supplied packages. You can send system or application data to external performance monitors (written, perhaps, in C++ or Delphi) and use their powerful reporting and graphing features to display this information in real-time.

Some tools, such as Visual Basic, are easy to use. With the additional capabilities of PL/SQL, you can develop visual tools to simplify tasks such as running EXPLAIN PLAN and graphically viewing indexes and constraints on tables. Several upscale third-party tools were developed this way.

GETTING BETTER INFORMATION WITH LESS HASSLE

You can write PL/SQL programs that use the data dictionary, for example, to show detailed index information for any particular table, even if it's in another schema. This is great if you're not logged on as SYS or SYSTEM and you need some data dictionary information, and you don't want to have to reconnect. This is especially helpful to developers, who always need to access that kind of information. You can reverse-engineer any database object using PL/SQL, rebuilding a syntactically correct statement to re-create the object. This will save you the trouble of manually updating your scripts every time you alter a table or grant a new privilege.

If composing a large, complex SQL statement is difficult, you can break it up into smaller parts and run them together in a PL/SQL script. This is preferable to trying to join more than seven tables, after which the SQL Executor seems to bog down. Multi-table joins can be improved dramatically by doing the Master table lookups separately. Plus, it's easier to validate the output of a script when you know the reusable code in it is already working correctly.

DESIGNING BETTER DATABASE APPLICATIONS

You can use PL/SQL in stored procedures and packages to build better applications. A concerted effort to design and build reusable PL/SQL modules will reap long term benefits. With some thoughtful design and planning, you can do the following:

- Leverage the effort in one application when building the next one.
- Spread the cost of building several related applications across all of them.
- Provide consistent interfaces to underlying tables and other objects.
- Simplify and optimize data access.
- Reduce application maintenance and deployment costs.
- Enforce coding standards.

Using PL/SQL is easy and fun. It has a relatively short learning curve as languages go. Experiment to determine what works well or at all. If you follow the steps detailed in this section, you should become productive in just a few days and, after only a few months, master PL/SQL sufficiently enough to achieve some sophisticated results.

GETTING STARTED WITH PL/SQL

This section details some things the DBA must do before you can do much with PL/SQL. The architecture of the application environment in which you'll be working will also be explored.

Before you can really get into writing PL/SQL programs, you or your DBA must first do the following:

- Grant you (that is, your Oracle account name) the CREATE PROCEDURE privilege so you can create subprograms in your own schema. For new applications, you might want to create a special user name and schema (a particular tablespace).

- Grant you directly (not via a Role) SELECT, INSERT, UPDATE, or DELETE privileges on any database objects (for example, tables and sequences) in whatever schema for which you may be writing PL/SQL programs. A stored subprogram or package can only reference objects that the owner of the subprogram (you) has access rights to directly (not via a role).

- Make sure the appropriate Oracle-supplied packages have been compiled, and you have EXECUTE privilege on them. You will find them in the directory <ORACLE_HOME>/rdbms<version>/admin/ where <ORACLE_HOME> is the Oracle home directory (shown either in the UNIX shell variable of the same name or in the Windows Registry) and <version> is the database version. The names of the package scripts have the general form of dbms*.sql. For example, on the author's Windows NT machine, dbmssql.sql is in c:\oraNT\rdbms80\admin.

- Make sure there is sufficient storage available for your stored subprograms and packages. These objects make additional data dictionary entries in the SYSTEM tablespace. The DBA may create a default tablespace for your own local copies of tables and indexes, so you aren't messing with Production objects.

- Make sure the shared and private SQL areas in the System Global Area (SGA) are sufficiently large to handle the anticipated load from running PL/SQL scripts and subprograms.

- Make sure you have access to the SQL*Plus application or a suitable third-party tool.

Once these things are in place, you're ready to start developing PL/SQL programs!

UNDERSTANDING THE SCHEMA OF THINGS

In abstract terms, a schema is a logical collection of related database objects, such as tables, indexes, and views. A schema is a developer's-eye view of the database objects of interest, such as are shown on an Entity-Relationship Diagram (or ERD).

In an Oracle database, a schema is a logical collection of objects stored within one or more tablespaces. Because it is a logical collection, several applications can share schemas, or cross schema boundaries into other schemas. The relational organization of schema objects is strictly as the DBA and developers see it, which is why a "roadmap," such as an ER diagram, is critical to the success of any database-related software development. A tablespace, in turn, is a logical storage area that maps to one or more physical files out on disk. Figure 28.6 illustrates this organization.

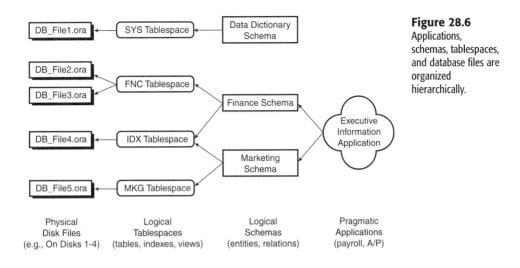

Figure 28.6
Applications, schemas, tablespaces, and database files are organized hierarchically.

Typically, a schema has exactly one owner (that is, an Oracle user account) responsible for creating, altering, and dropping these objects. This owner then grants access privileges to other users, either directly or via roles. If you're not the owner of these objects, you qualify references to the objects by specifying which tablespace they are in using dot notation, as with SELECT CUST_NAME FROM MKG.LEADS.

Managing Your PL/SQL Code

After they have been thoroughly tested and validated in your own development schema, your stored PL/SQL programs are likely to become objects managed by the schema owner. In a complex development environment with many developers, it becomes critical to determine who is the owner of the source code and where it is kept. When a module is being worked on, it is in a state of flux. The developer can make significant changes to a private copy, some of which may be backed out later. It's strongly recommended that you use a Code Management System (CMS) to control the one official version of the source code. When the module has been thoroughly tested and accepted for Production, the new version is placed in the CMS, and the schema owner can compile the new version. The quickest way to shoot yourself in the foot is to lose track of which copy is the one known good version. In the long run, just keeping different subdirectories for different versions is a poor code management strategy.

There is no correspondence between schemas and tablespaces; one or more schemas may be stored in a single tablespace, or one schema may be broken up into separate tablespaces. In practice, it is generally a good idea to store a schema in its own set of tablespaces, along with a good set of documentation. For example, tables may be stored in one tablespace and indexes in another. Conceptually, both tablespaces are included in the same schema.

Tip #80

PL/SQL developers should have their own default tablespaces to play around in, preferably on a non-Production database. You can create your own private tables and indexes with

PART

VI

CH

28

continues

continued

> which to experiment. This way, if you inadvertently corrupt a temporary, local copy of a Production table, who cares? Whereas the alternative could result in an abrupt end in your career (at least as far as your current workplace goes). Additionally, any stored programs or packages you compile are strictly local to within your schema (stored in the data dictionary alongside subprograms belonging to other schemas), so you can make experimental changes to Production code in a safe development environment.

Caution

> The caveat to this scheme is to take care with object references. If it's in your default schema, you don't need to qualify the reference with the schema name; otherwise, you must qualify it in order for it to be properly found. You can use synonyms for unqualified objects in PL/SQL code to provide the qualifier.

As a pragmatic consideration, some applications may easily cross schema boundaries, whereas core applications might focus on one schema. For example, a marketing application may have been developed to automate this one department. Later, upper management may request a high-level view of the entire enterprise, requiring a new application to obtain data from several schemas. The work you do in one application may be reused in another, so always keep an eye toward making PL/SQL modules generic enough to be used in multiple contexts.

YOUR BASIC PL/SQL DEVELOPMENT ENVIRONMENT

PL/SQL code is developed using your favorite text editor and the Oracle-supplied SQL*Plus application, or one of the several fine third-party development toolkits. If you're in a UNIX environment, it's a good idea to have a couple of sessions up—one running a text editor such as vi or emacs, and another session running SQL*Plus. If you're running Windows, you can use Notepad (or a real programmer's editor) and have a SQL*Plus session up.

Caution

> Under Windows 3.x, while SQL*Plus is running any SQL or PL/SQL, your entire Windows environment is effectively locked up. Be sure to save any text changes before running something in SQL*Plus. If you find you need to kill a long-running query, you'll feel better knowing you're not in peril of losing any work.

Oracle has thoughtfully provided some standard runtime libraries to perform certain valuable activities, such as standard I/O, timing, data exchange between active sessions, dynamic SQL creation, and other sophisticated low-level operations. As your programming needs increase in complexity, you will use these supplied packages more frequently.

ACCESSING THE DATA DICTIONARY

The data dictionary is exposed to the different users through various views. These views have the same name with different prefixes. These views can be broken down into the following categories (in no particular order):

- General catalog and object information
- Storage information for objects such as tablespaces, segments, and extents
- Procedures, packages, triggers, and their source code
- Tables, columns, clusters, and indexes
- Views, synonyms, and sequences
- Users, roles, profiles, privileges
- Locks and auditing information
- Performance information
- Distributed database information
- Export information

For the privileged DBA user, the most appropriate views to use are prefixed with DBA_. These views provide information about every database object in all schemas, generally organized by schema owner. For everybody else, there are the ALL_ views and the USER_ views. Additionally, the performance views (beginning with V$) are publicly accessible.

OBJECTS IN YOUR SCHEMA

The USER_ views display only those database objects owned by the currently connected user (you). If you created it, you'll find it listed here. For example, the view USER_SOURCE contains the source code for your stored subprograms and packages.

OBJECTS IN SOMEONE ELSE'S SCHEMA

The ALL_ views display only those database objects either owned by you or those objects in other schemas to which you have been granted access. In the latter case, these privileges may have been granted either directly or via a role; however, only those objects granted privileges directly to you will be accessible from within your PL/SQL code. For example, ALL_TABLES contains all of your tables, plus anyone else's tables for which you've been granted access.

For example, the view ALL_SOURCE contains all of your source code, as well as just the package headers of someone else's stored packages that were granted the EXECUTE privilege to you. The reason for this distinction is that you only need to know how to correctly call someone else's packaged subprograms; you can't modify them anyway, so you don't need to see the implementation details.

When you execute a subprogram owned by someone else, it is normally executed with their privileges, not yours. In Oracle8i, however, developers have the option of specifying that a subprogram is run with "invoker's rights" rather than "definer's rights".

OBJECTS IN THE DBA'S SCHEMA

The DBA is privileged; she has access to every database object within all schemas in the data dictionary. Stored subprograms are a suitable way to expose this information to all users, without giving them anything approaching DBA privileges—provided, of course, that

PART

VI

CH

28

the DBA compiles these subprograms. For example, the view DBA_OBJECTS contains information about every database object (including those owned by SYSTEM and SYS) of all types of objects (such as tables, indexes, sequences, and so on). By writing and compiling a few simple PL/SQL stored procedures, the DBA can make this information available to those who need it in an easily deployable manner.

LANGUAGE TUTORIAL

The best way to learn a new language is to jump right in! The following section presents PL/SQL in a tutorial manner, starting with the basics and moving swiftly through the various language features. If you're familiar with any other computer language like Pascal, FORTRAN, C, or COBOL, you won't have any trouble. It is strongly recommended that you try out the code that's presented here and on the accompanying CD as you follow along.

Mark Twain once wrote, "The nice thing about making a mistake is that you recognize it when you make it again." In this section you will take his advice and make plenty of mistakes. You'll look at common compilation and runtime errors, and the (often terse) error messages the Server hands back. You will deliberately run some buggy code here and there just so you can have the pleasure of debugging it. Then, when you're on your own, and an error message pops up, you won't be totally confused.

CODING CONVENTIONS

PL/SQL is not case sensitive; all text is converted to uppercase (except those in literal strings). Therefore, you cannot use case to distinguish variables and other user-defined elements. For readability, all code in this section has been standardized to follow some simple casing rules in order to distinguish these elements in the source code:

- All reserved words, Oracle-supplied packages, built-in functions, user-defined constants, Oracle and user-defined data types, and schema names are in uppercase.
- User-defined cursors, variables, packages, Oracle and user-defined subprograms, table and column names are in lowercase.
- Parameter list variables are capitalized (for example, Pname where P is for Parameter).

You can follow these or whatever conventions you desire. Just be consistent. Code in this section is documented heavily with inline comments, indents are carefully placed (usually two spaces at a time, never tabs), and whitespace is used to align statements more cleanly and keep lines of text under 80 characters.

PL/SQL is a free-form textual language; any amount of white space, such as spaces, newlines, and tabs, act as delimiters and are otherwise ignored. One or more statements can be on one line, or a statement can be broken up on several lines. In general, statements are ended with a semicolon (;). There is no limit placed on the number of characters per line, or the number of lines per module. However, there are operating system-dependent restrictions on the overall size of a source code module.

Caution

Previous versions of the Oracle Server imposed limitations on the size of a PL/SQL module, depending on the operating system. On NetWare 3.x it is limited to 32KB. For most flavors of UNIX and Windows NT, the module size is restricted to 64KB. Violating this limit can crash your database server or the server machine itself. This restriction has been removed in Oracle8i.

SPECIAL CHARACTERS

Some characters have particular meanings in a PL/SQL program. Most are obvious, such as math symbols and relational operators. Others, such as Association and Host Variable Indicator, are less obvious. These will be explored in later sections. Table 28.1 lists these characters (in some cases, pairs) and a brief description.

TABLE 28.1   SPECIAL CHARACTERS ORGANIZED BY TYPE

Type	Character	Description
Arithmetic Operators	+	Addition and Unary Positive
	-	Subtraction and Unary Negation
	*	Multiplication
	/	Division
	**	Exponentiation
Relational Operators (used in Boolean expressions)	=	Equivalence
	<	Less Than
	>	Greater Than
	<>	Not Equal
	!=	Not Equal (alternate)
	~=	Not Equal (alternate)
	^=	Not Equal (alternate)
	<=	Less Than or Equal
	>=	Greater Than or Equal
Expressions and Lists (used in statements, data type declarations, parameter list declarations, variable and table references)	:=	Assignment
	(	Start List or Subexpression
	)	End List or Subexpression
	,	Separates List Items (as in parameter lists)
	..	Range Operator (used in FOR-IN loops)
	||	String Concatenation
	=>	Association (used in parameter lists)
	;	Statement End
	%	Cursor Attribute or Object Type
	.	Member Specifier for Qualified References
	@	Remote Database Indicator
	'	Start/End of Character String
	"	Start/End of Quoted Identifier
	:	Host Variable Indicator
	&	Bind Variable Indicator
Comments and Labels	—	Single Line Comment
	/*	Start Multiline Comment
	*/	End Multiline Comment
	<<	Start Label
	>>	End Label

PART

VI

CH

28

Notice that there are several ways you can say "Not Equal" in PL/SQL. For consistency, one form (!=) is used throughout this tutorial. In case you were wondering, Modulo arithmetic is handled by a built-in function.

> **Note**
>
> Comments cannot be nested. Anything typed after a single-line comment is ignored. Anything typed between multiline comment delimiters is ignored.

PL/SQL's BLOCK STRUCTURE

The PL/SQL block is the fundamental programming construct. Programming in blocks lends itself to a top-down, structured modularity and a straightforward, logical organization.

An unnamed PL/SQL block has three sections: the Declaration and Body sections, and optionally, the Exception section:

```
DECLARE
  -- declarations
BEGIN
  -- executable code
EXCEPTION
  -- exception handlers
END;
```

Actually, the Declaration section is optional, too, but you can't do much more than some one-liners without declaring variables! All user-defined variables, constants, data types, cursors, functions, and procedures are declared in the Declaration section. If none are to be defined, you may omit this section.

For example, consider the familiar "Hello, World!" example used in many programming language books (see Listing 28.1).

> **Note**
>
> Refer to Chapter 26, "SQL*Plus For Administrators," if you want more information on the SET statement.

LISTING 28.1 *hello.sql*—HELLO WORLD PROGRAM

```
SET SERVEROUTPUT ON
BEGIN
  DBMS_OUTPUT.enable;
  DBMS_OUTPUT.put_line('Hello, World!');
END;
/
```

Line 1 tells SQL*Plus to write out whatever the server returns to it.

Lines 2 and 5 provide the scope of the current block.

Line 3 turns on the outputting mechanism. (This is optional in versions 7.3 and later.)

Line 4 prints the string 'Hello, World!'

Line 6 executes the unnamed PL/SQL block. fundamental

The server responds with the following:

```
Hello, World!
PL/SQL procedure successfully completed.
SQL>
```

Nothing is returned to the screen until just after the procedure completes. This is because the server is processing the PL/SQL block (most probably across the network) and it returns any messages only when it is completely finished.

Literal strings are always enclosed in single quotes. Before we go on, let's talk a little bit about literals.

LITERALS

Literals are fixed strings, numbers, and Boolean values. They cannot be modified at runtime; they are strictly read-only values. Single-character and string literals are specified with enclosing single quotes. Here are some examples of string literals:

- ' '—a single blank character
- 'Hello, World!'
- 'This string contains ''embedded'' single quotes'
- 'Double quotes are "okay" too'
- '12345'—this is a string, not an integer, literal
- '01/01/1900'—looks like a date
- '~!@#$%^&*()_-+=|\{}[]:;<>,.?/'—literals can contain special characters
- '' ''—this specifies a string containing the 3 characters ' ' (single quote, space, single quote)

Character and string literals are treated as a CHAR type (fixed-length character string). It can be assigned to any CHAR or VARCHAR2 variable. PL/SQL is only case sensitive within a string literal.

A numeric literal can have any integer or floating-point value, for example:

12345	Integer literal
-12345.0	Floating-point literal
12345.67890	Floating-point literals can have any arbitrary precision
100.	This is a floating-point literal, too, with zero precision
1.2345E2	You can use scientific notation!
1.2345E-2	
0.12345 or .12345	Leading zero is optional

It is good programming practice to declare fundamentalconstants to contain literal values that are used throughout a program. You can give them meaningful names. Additionally, they are more maintainable; if a literal value must be changed, it need only be modified in one place. This technique avoids the unmaintainable "magic number" syndrome, where special values are used that nobody can remember why. Listing 28.2 shows an example.

LISTING 28.2 `circle.sql`—USING CONSTANTS TO MAKE CODE MORE MAINTAINABLE

```
DECLARE
  PI CONSTANT REAL := 3.14159265359;
  circumference REAL;
  area REAL;
  radius REAL := &Radius;
BEGIN
  circumference := PI * radius * 2.0;
  area := PI * radius**2;
  DBMS_OUTPUT.put_line('Radius = ' || TO_CHAR(radius) ||
                       ', Circumference = ' || TO_CHAR(circumference) ||
                       ', Area = ' || TO_CHAR(area));
END;
```

When you run this program, SQL*Plus first prompts you for a value for the bind variable specified with the ampersand (line 5). Here's what happens:

```
Enter value for radius: 3.5
old   5:    radius REAL := &Radius;
new   5:    radius REAL := 3.5;
Radius = 3.5, Circumference = 21.99114857513, Area = 38.4845100064775
PL/SQL procedure successfully completed.
```

Notice that the bind variable is not a PL/SQL variable; it is a placeholder for the value you must supply. Also, it's not necessary to turn on the server's output again, or re-enable output, if you've been following along since the first example. Once these things are turned on, they stay on for the duration of your session (unless you deliberately turn them off or reconnect).

Note how the constant variable PI is specified and receives its value in its declaration. You could also use the keyword DEFAULT in place of the assignment operator ":="; it means the same fundamentalthing in the context of a declaration.

The Boolean literals TRUE and FALSE are also supported (note they are not enclosed in single quotes). They can be used in any Boolean expression and assigned to any Boolean variable.

The truth table in Table 28.2 illustrates all binary Boolean combinations for the relational operators AND, OR, and XOR (eXclusive OR) and unary negation (NOT or ~) for the values TRUE, FALSE, and NULL. The relational operator XOR is not supported in PL/SQL; however, the PL/SQL built-in function XOR() performs this operation.

TABLE 28.2 TRILOGIC TRUTH TABLE FOR *AND, OR, XOR, NOT*

p	q	p AND q	p OR q	p XOR q	NOT p
TRUE	TRUE	TRUE	TRUE	FALSE	FALSE
TRUE	FALSE	FALSE	TRUE	TRUE	FALSE
TRUE	NULL	NULL	TRUE	NULL	FALSE
FALSE	TRUE	FALSE	TRUE	TRUE	TRUE
FALSE	FALSE	FALSE	FALSE	FALSE	TRUE
FALSE	NULL	FALSE	NULL	NULL	TRUE
NULL	TRUE	NULL	TRUE	NULL	NULL
NULL	FALSE	FALSE	NULL	NULL	NULL
NULL	NULL	NULL	NULL	NULL	NULL

As an example, take a look at Listing 28.3.

LISTING 28.3 `booly.sql`: USING BOOLEANS

```
DECLARE
  T CONSTANT BOOLEAN NOT NULL := TRUE;   — must have a value
  x BOOLEAN;
  y BOOLEAN;
BEGIN   — illustrate Booleans
  x := 1 = 2;   — this expression evaluates to false
  y := XOR(T, x);   — and this evaluates to true
  IF (x) THEN   — test for true fundamental
    DBMS_OUTPUT.put_line('x = TRUE');
  ELSIF (NOT x) THEN   — test for false
    DBMS_OUTPUT.put_line('x = FALSE');
  ELSE   — x must be null
    DBMS_OUTPUT.put_line('x is NULL');
  END IF;
  IF (y) THEN   — test for true
    DBMS_OUTPUT.put_line('y = TRUE');
  ELSIF (NOT y) THEN   — test for false
    DBMS_OUTPUT.put_line('y = FALSE');
  ELSE   — y must be null
    DBMS_OUTPUT.put_line('y is NULL');
    DBMS_OUTPUT.put_line('Booly for you!');
  END IF;
END;
/
```

The server responds with the following:

```
x = FALSE
y = TRUE
PL/SQL procedure successfully completed.
```

There are no functions that convert a Boolean value to a string or a string back to a Boolean; you will write them later. Note on line 2 how you specify that a variable must not be NULL. This has limited value in this context, but the syntax is supported. Be aware that there is a slight overhead associated with variables declared NOT NULL.

Experiment with the value of T and x and rerun the block to see what you get (the SQL*Plus command EDIT will allow you to edit the text and rerun it). If you leave off the default assignment, you'll get fundamentalthe following:

> **Note** See Chapter 26 for more details on the EDIT command.

```
ERROR at line 1:
ORA-06550: line 2, column 3:
PLS-00322: declaration of a constant 'T' must contain an initialization
assignment
ORA-06550: line 2, column 5:
PL/SQL: Item ignored
```

You have encountered your first compiler error. The ERROR at line 1 tells you that the entire unnamed block had an error. This is because the whole block is shipped over to the server as a single transaction. The next error message is helpful and tells you that you forgot to initialize the constant variable. In fact, all constants must be initialized, even if it's to NULL, which would be perfectly valid without the NOT NULL clause. The ORA-06550 says that the Oracle Server experienced some sort of PL/SQL compilation error (it is left to the PL/SQL compiler to describe the actual error).

And if you drop the CONSTANT and initialization, but leave the NOT NULL, you'll get the following:

```
ERROR at line 1:
ORA-06550: line 2, column 5:
PLS-00218: a variable declared NOT NULL must have an initialization assignment
```

At runtime, when the block is entered, a variable is initialized to the specified value. If no assignment is prescribed, then by default the variable is assigned a NULL value. Try leaving off the CONSTANT, NOT NULL and initialization, and you'll get the following:

```
x = FALSE
y is NULL
Booly for you!
```

The variables receive their values at runtime, and not at compile time, because like automatic (or stack) variables in other languages, they don't actually exist until the block is in scope. This means that they are de-allocated when the block is out of scope, and reallocated when the block is reentered. Be aware of this overhead for procedures and functions that are invoked multiple times. In fact, take advantage of it. Because variables are initialized to NULL by default, if they do require an initial non-NULL value, this is a good place fundamentalto do it.

When a variable is declared CONSTANT, its value cannot be changed at runtime. To attempt to do so would raise an exception. Also, the type and length of the initializing literal must match that of the variable. For example, if a declaration for a variable x was CHAR(4) :=

"NO GOOD!", an exception would be raised at runtime (not at compile time). As you saw earlier, constants must be assigned a value in their declaration, even if the desired value is NULL. Otherwise, a compile error occurs.

A variable can be declared NOT NULL to indicate that it may never hold a NULL value. Such a variable must be initialized to some non-NULL value in its declaration. Note the correct placement of the CONSTANT and NOT NULL keywords before and after the data type, respectively.

Here are some more examples of valid and invalid initializing statements:

```
DECLARE
   price        NUMBER(5,2) := 19.92;    -- valid initialization
   discount     NUMBER(3,3) := .0625;    -- gets rounded to .063
   max_quantity INTEGER(4) := 50000;     -- runtime error!
   max_discount CONSTANT REAL := 0.75;   -- valid
   min_discount CONSTANT REAL;           -- compile error! not initialized
   disc_type    VARCHAR2(1) := NULL;     -- valid and redundant
   disc_name    CONSTANT CHAR(20) := NULL;  -- valid but of dubious value
   quantity     INTEGER NOT NULL := 0;   -- correct usage
   item_name    VARCHAR2(30) DEFAULT 'Hammer';  -- alternate assignment
```

BRANCHING

While you're looking at it, let's enumerate all the syntactical flavors of the IF/THEN statement.

USING CONDITIONAL (IF/THEN/ELSE) LOGIC   Your basic conditional test-and-branch logic has the following form:

```
IF (some condition is true) THEN  -- test condition
   ...     -- condition was true, do this stuff
ELSE      -- condition was false
   ...     -- so do this stuff instead
END IF;  -- end of test
```

For the record, the first block of statements after the IF...THEN is called the antecedent, while the block following the ELSE is called the consequent. You can have multiple statements inside the THEN, ELSE, and ELSIF blocks. If you want, you can put BEGIN...END statements inside the antecedent or consequent. The consequent is, of course, optional. Notice that the block is ended with END IF. It's a good habit to always comment the top and end of a conditional statement, especially a fundamentallong one, so you know what it's for

```
IF (some condition is true) THEN  -- test for some condition
  BEGIN
    ...
  END;
ELSE  -- condition was false
  DECLARE  -- define some local variable
    x NUMBER;
  BEGIN
    ...
  END;
END IF;  -- test for some condition
```

The preceding variable x won't even be created unless the consequent is executed. You can use this to limit the use of local variables to only the block that needs them and save a little memory.

How you choose to indent this is up to you, but consider indenting one block inside another block.

You can nest these statements to any depth. You can perform some very complex logic in this manner.

The conditional expression is computed using short-circuit evaluations. This means that if the first part of a complex OR expression evaluates to TRUE, or the first part of an AND expression evaluates to FALSE, evaluation stops immediately and there is no need to evaluate further. Most other languages also support short-circuit evaluation. Such expressions are always evaluated left to right, with expressions in parentheses taking higher precedence.

TESTING FOR THE NULL CONDITION   The special literal value NULL can be assigned to variables of any data type. It represents an unknown value. You must use the special syntax IS NULL and IS NOT NULL to test for its existence and absence, respectively. The tests

```
IF (x = NULL)  THEN ... and
IF (x != NULL) THEN ...
```

will always fail. The correct way is

```
IF (x IS NULL)     THEN ... and
IF (x IS NOT NULL) THEN ... .
```

USING SEQUENTIAL IF LOGIC   Sometimes you need to test a series of values, one right after another. It would be inefficient to code a series of IF/THEN statements if an earlier one might fundamental succeed, and all the subsequent ones would be expected to fail, as follows:

```
IF (val = '0') THEN  -- is value a digit?
  ...
END IF;  -- zero?
IF (val = '1') THEN  -- maybe a 1?
  ...
END IF;  -- 1?
  ...
IF (val = '9') THEN  -- maybe a 9?
  ...
END IF;  -- end of test
```

You could use nested IF/ELSE statements, but this becomes pretty ugly, what with all the indentation. Instead, use ELSIF to make your code more efficient. As soon as one of the conditions is true, its antecedent is executed and the entire block is exited:

```
IF (val = '0') THEN  -- is value a digit?
  ...
ELSIF (val = '1') THEN
  ...
ELSIF (val = '2') THEN
  ...
ELSIF (val = '9') THEN
```

```
    ...
ELSE   -- not a number
    ...
END IF;   -- end of test
```

Tip #81

PL/SQL doesn't have a `SWITCH` statement (as in C), nor a `CASE` statement (as in Pascal), nor a computed `GOTO` (like FORTRAN). Simulate these constructs with the sequential `IF`.

Listing 28.4 shows a simple example written to estimate the author's 1996 fundamental Federal tax liability (from IRS Publication 15, Circular E, Employer's Tax Guide, Rev. January 1997).

LISTING 28.4 *fedtax.sql*—SEQUENTIAL *IF* LOGIC USED TO DETECT VALUE RANGES

```
SET SERVEROUTPUT ON;
-- assumes annual payroll, married
DECLARE
num_wh NUMBER := &num_witholding;
wh_amount NUMBER;
gross NUMBER := &annual_gross_salary;
liab NUMBER;
adj_gross NUMBER;
BEGIN
  DBMS_OUTPUT.ENABLE;
  wh_amount := num_wh * 2550;   -- annual allowance
  adj_gross := gross - wh_amount;
  IF adj_gross <= 6425 THEN
    liab := 0;
  ELSIF adj_gross <= 44250 THEN
    liab := (adj_gross - 6425) * 0.15;
  ELSIF adj_gross <= 89675 THEN
    liab := 5673.75 + (adj_gross - 44250) * 0.28;
  ELSIF adj_gross <= 151850 THEN
    liab := 18392.75 + (adj_gross - 89675) * 0.31;
  ELSIF adj_gross <= 267900 THEN
    liab := 37667 + (adj_gross - 151850) * 0.36;
  ELSE   -- over max
    liab := 79445 + (adj_gross - 267900) * 0.396;
  END IF;   -- test adjusted gross
  DBMS_OUTPUT.PUT_LINE('FEDERAL TAX LIABILITY: ' || TO_CHAR(liab));
END;
/
```

When you run the function, you are prompted for the bind variable values, and fundamental the server returns the following:

```
Enter value for num_witholding: 4
old    2: num_wh NUMBER := &num_witholding;
new    2: num_wh NUMBER := 4;
Enter value for annual_gross_salary: 60000
old    4: gross NUMBER := &annual_gross_salary;
new    4: gross NUMBER := 60000;
FEDERAL TAX LIABILITY: 7227.75
PL/SQL procedure successfully completed.
```

The parentheses around the expression to be tested are optional. They are recommended, however, especially for complex expressions.

UNCONDITIONAL BRANCHING   PL/SQL supports unconditional branching with GOTO. You specify the target of the jump with a label, just like in BASIC and Assembler. You may jump anywhere within the present block or the enclosing block. Generally, the use of GOTO is frowned upon, as it leads to unstructured code. Such programs usually become unmaintainable rather quickly. The syntax is illustrated in Listing 28.5.

LISTING 28.5   *okgoto.sql*—USING *GOTO*

```
BEGIN
  BEGIN
    GOTO MID;    -- forward reference OK because it's in scope
  END;
  <<MID>>
  NULL;
END;
/
```

The label MID is denoted by the enclosing double angle brackets. Notice that the label is not terminated by a semicolon.

This compiles successfully. However, Listing 28.6 illustrates a different fundamentalscenario.

LISTING 28.6   *badgoto.sql*—IMPROPER USE

```
BEGIN
  GOTO MID;    -- invalid!
  BEGIN
    <<MID>>
    NULL;
  END;
END;
/
```

You get a compilation error because the label is out of scope:

```
ERROR at line 1:
ORA-06550: line 2, column 8:
PLS-00201: identifier 'MID' must be declared
ORA-06550: line 2, column 3:
PL/SQL: Statement ignored
```

The outer block does not know about the existence of anything inside an inner block.

Notice the NULL statement. This is a perfectly valid statement that only acts as a placeholder. You can't have a label immediately before any flavor of END statement (as in END IF). You'll get a compilation error. You remedy this problem by using the NULL statement.

You cannot jump from one block to another block at the same level inside an enclosing block, as with Listing 28.7.

LISTING 28.7 *bad2goto.sql*— CANNOT BE USED BETWEEN BLOCKS AT THE SAME LEVEL WITHIN AN ENCLOSING BLOCK

```
BEGIN
  BEGIN
    GOTO OTHER;   -- invalid!
  END;
  BEGIN
    <<OTHER>>      -- out of scope
    NULL;
  END;
END;
/
```

This restriction also holds true for conditional statements. You can't jump fundamentalfrom the antecedent to the consequent (see Listing 28.8).

LISTING 28.8 *bad3goto.sql*—YOU CAN'T JUMP BETWEEN THE ANTECEDENT AND CONSEQUENT

```
BEGIN
  IF (TRUE) THEN -- always do the antecedent
    GOTO CONSEQUENT;
  ELSE  -- consequent
    <<CONSEQUENT>>
    NULL;
  END IF;  -- of jump example
END;
/
```

This time Oracle senses you're doing something weird and gives you the following:

```
ERROR at line 3:
ORA-06550: line 3, column 5:
PLS-00375: illegal GOTO statement; this GOTO cannot branch to label 'CONSEQUENT'
ORA-06550: line 4, column 3:
PL/SQL: Statement ignored
```

Also, Oracle won't detect infinite loops, as with the following:

```
BEGIN
  <<INFINITE_LOOP>>
  GOTO INFINITE_LOOP;
END;
```

Caution

This tiny bit of code will throw your SQL*Plus session into an infinite loop! You'll have to ask your DBA to kill the session if you are foolish enough to do this, especially in a

PART
VI

CH
28

continues

continued

> Windows 3.x environment, which will promptly lock up until the session is killed. If you're running Windows 95 or Windows NT you can blow away the SQL*Plus session, losing some resources (such as allocated memory or available handles in use by the session) on your machine in the fundamentalprocess.

LABELS AND SCOPING RULES   The scope of a variable declaration is local to the enclosing block. The variable can generally only be referenced within the confines of the block or sub-block in which it is defined. Variables declared in the parameter list of a subprogram may only be referenced from within that subprogram. Additionally, any variables declared within the body of a subprogram are strictly local to that subprogram. It's okay for an inner block to rename a variable; it is still a new and different variable from the one in the outer scope.

At runtime, when a block goes out of scope, the variables, cursors, and similar constructs local to it are deallocated. When the block is again in scope, the variables are re-created and initialized to whatever values were specified in their declaration. You'll take a closer look at this later on in the section on stored procedures.

The general rule of thumb to use when deciding where best to place a declaration is to constrict the scope to only those blocks that will ever need to reference it. The object will therefore only exist when absolutely needed, conserving memory. Balance this memory-conserving heuristic with any need for object persistence or time savings required by allocating objects once up front.

An inner block may reference an object in an enclosing block through the use of labels. This is a poor programming practice and you should instead use a different variable name, or pass the variable in on the stack to a subroutine. However, the language does support labels, so if you feel compelled to use this feature, follow these steps:

1. Insert a label at the start of the outer block.

2. Use dot notation within the inner block to refer to variables defined by the outer block.

3. The label is the qualifier needed to reference the outer variable of the same name as an inner one.

Listing 28.9 illustrates the correct and incorrect use of qualifying fundamentallabels.

LISTING 28.9   *badlabel.sql*—USE AND ABUSE OF LABELS TO DIFFERENTIATE BLOCKS

```
<<OUTER_BLOCK>>      -- this label names the outer block
DECLARE
  x NUMBER;   -- available to both inner and next blocks
  y NUMBER;
BEGIN
  <<INNER_BLOCK>>   -- might as well label the inner one too
  DECLARE
    x NUMBER;   -- only available to this block
  BEGIN  -- inner block
    x := OUTER_BLOCK.x;   -- qualified reference to outer block variable
    y := 0;   -- an unqualified reference to outer block variable
```

```
   END INNER_BLOCK;
   <<NEXT_BLOCK>>
   DECLARE
      x NUMBER;
   BEGIN  -- next block
      x := INNER_BLOCK.x;  -- THIS IS ILLEGAL!!
      x := OUTER_BLOCK.x;  -- this is OK
   END NEXT_BLOCK;
      x := INNER_BLOCK.x;  -- THIS IS ALSO ILLEGAL!!
 END OUTER_BLOCK;
```

You get the following errors:

```
ERROR at line 1:
ORA-06550: line 17, column 22:
PLS-00219: label 'INNER_BLOCK' reference is out of scope
ORA-06550: line 17, column 5:
PL/SQL: Statement ignored
ORA-06550: line 20, column 20:
PLS-00219: label 'INNER_BLOCK' reference is out of scope
ORA-06550: line 20, column 3:
PL/SQL: Statement ignored
```

Note that you cannot go in the other direction; namely, you cannot try to refer to an inner block's variable in the outer block. Why not? Because it doesn't exist. The variable in the inner block isn't created until you're actually within the inner block, and is immediately deallocated upon exiting the inner block, so that there is no opportunity for the outer fundamental block to refer to it.

Likewise, a subroutine nested inside of a subprogram uses the name of the subprogram with dot notation to refer to a variable defined at the level of the enclosing subprogram. But it is always a better coding practice to pass the needed value in on the parameter list, or simply do not reuse variable names in inner blocks. The fewer informal or unusual references, the easier it'll be to maintain your code.

It is okay to have nested blocks without labeling them. You can even create new variables in the sub-blocks. Nested blocks are useful when, for example, you're performing an operation that might generate an exception and you need to localize the exception handler to within the enclosing block.

You've already seen a few identifiers—the variables, data types, packages, and procedures. Now you need to become aware of a few general rules about naming them.

IDENTIFIERS

Identifiers are lexemes representing programming items, such as variables, constants, user-defined data types, cursors, exceptions, database tables, columns, procedures, functions and packages. An identifier must begin with a letter and may contain up to 30 letters, numbers, underscores, dollar signs ($), or pound signs (#) only.

Valid Identifiers	Invalid Identifiers
PI	3D-array
length_of_string	function_header
char$	var name
RQGetSegment	area/height
local##time	$HOME

Identifiers cannot contain embedded blanks, hyphens, or slashes, but you can use double quotes around identifiers to distinguish them from other lexemes, such as when a table's column name is the same as a PL/SQL reserved word. For example, EXCEPTION is a PL/SQL reserved word, yet it's not reserved in SQL and therefore might have been used as a column name. In fundamentalorder to properly reference such a column, use double quotes, as in:

```
SELECT "EXCEPTION" INTO exc FROM prog_errors;
```

Since columns are stored in uppercase, the quoted identifier has to be uppercase. You might also use double quotes to include blanks or other delimiters, such as

```
SELECT cr_msg "*** Credit Message ***" FROM messages;
```

although this is more typically used in SQL*Plus for column headings.

COMMENTING YOUR CODE

Good programmers comment their code heavily. The more time they have when writing code, the better their comments tend to be.

You can use comments when first laying out a complex PL/SQL program to indicate various sections. In fact, you can often take your comments directly from the program specifications. Then you can go back to each section and flesh it out with the actual code. For example, use a module header comment that contains some basic information, then organize your declarations by scope and type, as follows:

```
/*
  Program Name: c2f
  Module Name : c2f.sql
  Written By  : Daniel J.. Clamage
  Description : .This module converts Celsius to Fahrenheit.
  Modification: V.001 04-OCT-1997 - djc - Initial release.
*/
...
  -- public global constant variables (shared between modules)
  prog_version CONSTANT VARCHAR2 (25) := 'V.001 04-OCT-1997 - djc';
  prog_name CONSTANT VARCHAR2(30) := 'c2f';
...
  -- public global record types needed
...
  -- public global variables
...
  -- public global cursors needed
...
```

When you compile a saved fundamentalscript with those multiline comments, SQL*Plus echoes them back as a DOC block:

```
SQL> @d:\plsql\library\c2f
DOC>  Program Name: c2f
...
DOC>  Modification: V.001 04-OCT-1997 - djc - Initial release.
DOC>*/
```

This is convenient when you're compiling a whole set of modules, and you're spooling the outcome to a file. It's recommended that you limit the use of multiline comments in the comment header block of a module because they may be echoed during compilation, causing some confusion. If the first multiline comment delimiter is not placed on its own line, then the first comment line doesn't even show up. You can use single-line comments fundamental everywhere else.

DECLARING VARIABLES

In general, there are two forms of variables: scalar and composite. Scalar variables permit only a single value for the variable. Composite variables can contain multiple values of either identical or single data types, depending on the kind of composite variable. You declare only one variable per statement.

Table 28.3 shows a list of scalar data types supported by PL/SQL and their corresponding database types (if any).

TABLE 28.3   SCALAR DATA TYPES (+ AS OF 7.2; ^ AS OF 7.3; # AS OF 8.0.3)

Type	Subtypes	Description	Value Limits	Database Limits
CHAR(s)	CHARACTER STRING ROWID[*] NCHAR[#**]	Fixed length character strings [**]holds NLS data	0–32,767 bytes optional size defaults to 1.	255 bytes [*]holds database ROWID string [**]2,000 bytes
VARCHAR2(s)	VARCHAR STRING[±] NVARCHAR2[#*]	Variable length character strings [*]holds NLS data	0–32,767 bytes optional size defaults to 1.	2,000 bytes [#]4,000 bytes
NUMBER (p, s)	NUMERIC DEC DECIMAL INT[-] INTEGER[*] FLOAT[*] REAL DOUBLE PRECISION SMALLINT[-]	Packed decimal values p = precision (total # of digits) s = scale (where rounding occurs) [*]cannot specify scale	Magnitude range is $1.0E^{-129}$ – $9.99E^{125}$ Precision is 1–38 (default size is the maximum value supported by system). Scale is -84 – 127 (default scale is 0).	Same size as PL/SQL NUMBER

TABLE 28.3 CONTINUED

Type	Subtypes	Description	Value Limits	Database Limits
BINARY INTEGER	NATURAL[*] POSITIVE[**] NATURALN[^-] POSITIVEN[^-] SIGNTYPE[#***]	Signed binary numbers [*] range starts at 0 [**] range starts at 1 - Predefined as NOT NULL; same ranges as above	Magnitude range is $-2^{31}-1$ to $2^{31}-1$; or $\pm2,147,483,647$ [***] limited to $(-1, 0, +1)$ for implementing tri-state logic.	No database type exists (use NUMBER)
PLS INTEGER[^]		Signed binary numbers Fastest machine arithmetic, less storage than NUMBER	Magnitude range is $2^{31}-1$ to $2^{31}-1$; -or $\pm2,147,483,647$.	No database type exists (use NUMBER)
DATE		An internal date value	January 1, 4712 BC —December 31, 4712 AD; time in seconds since midnight (default time is 12:00 midnight)	Same as PL/SQL date
BOOLEAN		Boolean (logical) values	TRUE, FALSE, NULL (unknown value)	No database type exists
LONG		Variable length character strings	0—32,760 bytes (size is not specified)	0–2,147,483,647 bytes
RAW(s)	LONG RAW	Non-interpreted (character set independent) binary data	RAW: 0 -32,767 bytes; LONG RAW: 0—32,760 bytes (same as LONG) (required size must be at least 1)	RAW is 2000 bytes; LONG RAW is 2,147,483,647
REF CURSOR[±]		Cursor variable (pointer to cursor)		No database type exists
LOB (Large Object)	BFILE[*] BLOB[**] CLOB[***] NCLOB[****]	Locator to large, unstructured, or binary data (images, sound, video, documents) stored in the database or in external operating system files	$2^{32}-1$ bytes or 0–4GB [*] external binary files only (read-only) [**] internal/external binary data (read/write) [***] internal/ external single-byte data (read/write) [****] internal/ external fixed width multi-byte data (read/write)	Same as PL/SQL LOBs

Subtypes generally have the same value limits as their main counterparts. Oracle provides them with PL/SQL for compatibility with the column data types found in Oracle and other databases. For example, you can use the alternate NUMBER subtypes when you want something more descriptive. If a type takes an optional size parameter, it is put in parentheses as shown.

This size parameter must be specified with integer literals only (for example, CHAR(3)). For strings, a value of length 0 is the NULL value (unknown value).

Character strings are treated as scalars. In order to access individual characters, you use the Oracle-supplied character functions SUBSTR(), INSTR(), and so on. The maximum size of a CHAR is specified in bytes, not characters. This means that multibyte character sets will require more storage. Note the shift in treatment of the STRING subtype from version 7.1 to 7.2.

Oracle performs a conversion from NUMBER (packed decimal) data types into an internal floating point representation in order to accomplish numeric operations. In contrast, the BINARY_INTEGER and PLS_INTEGER data types already have this internal format. Loops coded with indexes using BINARY_INTEGER, while limited in the range of values, can execute faster because this conversion is not necessary. PLS_INTEGER is even faster than BINARY_INTEGER because it uses native machine arithmetic, while BINARY_INTEGER and NUMBER rely on math library routines. However, BINARY_INTEGER values can be assigned to NUMBER variables to avoid overflow exceptions, while using PLS_INTEGER will not avoid the overflow exception. This slight semantic difference should not concern you very much.

Negative scale rounds to the left of the decimal; for example, -3 rounds to the nearest thousands place (1000, 2000, 3000, ...), while +3 rounds to the nearest thousandth (0.001, 0.002, 0.003, ...).

Looking at this table, you may realize that LONG and RAW PL/SQL types have limited usefulness when interacting with database columns of those types. The PL/SQL LONG RAW is actually shorter than a RAW! They should have called it a RAW LONG. However, there is an Oracle-supplied routine to get a database LONG value into PL/SQL LONG variables.

The other thing you may notice from the table is that the limits of a database data type and that of the corresponding PL/SQL data type may be significantly different (specifically, the character types). Please bear this in mind while programming. Some value errors you may experience are related to this discrepancy (when inadvertently trying to stuff a longer string into a shorter variable).

USING PL/SQL DATA TYPES

Some examples of scalar variable declarations are as follows:

- item_name CHAR(32),—May be padded with trailing spaces
- item_category VARCHAR2(32);—These strings are not padded
- price NUMBER(5,2);—Can hold a number between ± 999.99
- quantity INTEGER(3);—Can hold a number between ± 999
- discountable BOOLEAN;—Can be TRUE, FALSE, or NULL
- discount REAL(3,3);—Any real number between ± 0.999
- run_date DATE;—Date fields take up 7 bytes

Of course, a variable of any data type can hold a NULL value (not just Booleans).

PART

VI

CH

28

One really slick feature is called "basing" variables. Instead of hard-coding a data type, you use the data type of another variable, database column, or table. You do this with the %TYPE and %ROWTYPE attributes. The %TYPE attribute provides the type and length of the desired database column or variable. The %ROWTYPE attribute allows one to define a record variable whose member variables have the correct type and length for every column in the table or cursor. Each member variable in the record is referenced using dot notation. My convention is to suffix a %ROWTYPE variable with _rec to indicate that it is a record variable. For example:

- `quantity orders.qty%TYPE;`—Based on qty column in table orders

- `discount orders.discount%TYPE;`—Based on discount column in table orders

- `orders_rec orders %ROWTYPE;`—A record based on the table orders

Here are some more examples of using types:

```
DECLARE   -- define user variables
  MAX_INT CONSTANT INTEGER := +2147483647;
  MAX_STR VARCHAR2(32767);   -- let's use this for typing only
  notes    MAX_STR%TYPE;       -- based on another variable's type
  items_rec items%ROWTYPE;   -- based on a table in the database
  iname      items.item_name%TYPE;  -- based on a column in a table
  last_id   MAX_INT%TYPE;   -- this must be a constant too
BEGIN   -- executable code
  iname := 'HAMMER';
  items_rec.item_name := iname;  -- compatible data types
  last_id := 0;                  -- Wait! Aagggh! Runtime error!
```

This provides excellent control over data typing problems that occur when a database column or table changes. Because the variable's type is based, rather than explicitly declared, the correct data type and length are already in place. If the table changes, the code need only be recompiled. In this fashion, based variables provide a measure of data independence, minimizing code maintenance. Imagine how much work would be required to modify the code in perhaps dozens of modules when some column's length or type changed, had an explicit data type been used in the code instead. Of course, if the table column's data type changes from a CHAR(5) to a NUMBER(5), you'll still have some rework to do to your PL/SQL code (hey, it's happened to me), for example, inserting TO_CHAR() conversions.

When you use %TYPE, however, you get all the excess baggage. In the preceding example, you see that the programmer erroneously tried to assign a new value to a variable that is based on a constant variable, which makes the based variable a constant as well.

You should especially make use of based variables in subprogram parameter lists and function return declarations, where the types but not the lengths are declared.

DEFINING COMPOSITE DATA TYPES

PL/SQL supports two kinds of composite (a vector, or set of values) data types: RECORD and TABLE. Composite variables can also be created by basing on a table or cursor row type, as above. These have similar semantics as RECORD variables.

To declare a new composite data type, you use the keyword TYPE. TYPE declarations only declare a new data type; they do not define storage. In order to use them, variables must be declared of that type. Here, the convention is to suffix the new data type's name with _TYPE to indicate its use as a data type:

```
DECLARE
  -- user-defined data types
  TYPE MY_STRING_TYPE IS RECORD OF (
    str_len INTEGER := 0,  -- initialized when variable is declared
    str VARCHAR2(32767));  -- defaults to NULL
  TYPE MY_ARRAY_TYPE IS TABLE OF CHAR(8) INDEX BY BINARY_INTEGER;
  -- variables
  str MY_STRING_TYPE;   -- a new composite variable
  arr MY_ARRAY_TYPE;    -- a new 1-D array
```

CREATING YOUR OWN RECORD TYPES   A RECORD type defines a structure that can contain any number of member variables of any data type, including previously defined RECORD or TABLE types. Like a record variable of some table %ROWTYPE, individual members are referenced using dot notation. Any initialization defined for a member occurs at runtime for the based variable.

You can nest RECORD types:

```
DECLARE
  TYPE ZIP_TYPE IS RECORD (
    zip5 VARCHAR(5),
    DASH CONSTANT VARCHAR2(1) := '-',  -- for display purposes perhaps
    plus4 VARCHAR2(4) := '0000');      -- initialized at runtime
  TYPE ADDR_TYPE IS RECORD (
    line1 VARCHAR2(30),
    line2 VARCHAR2(30),
    city  VARCHAR2(20),
    state VARCHAR2(2),
    zip_code ZIP_TYPE);
  TYPE EMPLOYEE_TYPE IS RECORD (
    ssn VARCHAR2(9);
    dob DATE;
    address ADDR_TYPE);
  employee_rec EMPLOYEE_TYPE;  -- actual storage defined
BEGIN
  employee_rec.ssn := '123456789';                 -- someone's SSN#
  employee_rec.address.city := 'Pittsburgh';
  employee_rec.address.zip_code.zip5 := '15210';  -- Pittsburgh's zip
  employee_rec.address.zip_code.plus4 := '3702';  -- Mt. Oliver in Pgh
```

Note the usage of dot notation to reference any sub-component of this nested record. The main saving grace of this form is that a lot of related data of differing data types can be managed more easily. A collection of data can be passed to or returned from a subroutine with a single parameter. It's tidier and more compact than the alternative. Records enable developers to think in terms of clumps of tightly related data.

You can assign one record variable to another only if they are declared to be of the same data type. Variables based on a database table ROWTYPE and those defined as a record type are always incompatible, even if the members match exactly:

```
DECLARE
  TYPE ORDERS_TYPE IS RECORD (  -- looks like the database table
      ord_num  orders.ord_num%TYPE,
      quantity orders.quantity%TYPE,
      ...
      discount orders.discount%TYPE);
  orders_rec orders%ROWTYPE;  -- based on a database table
  new_ords_rec ORDERS_TYPE;
  old_ords_rec ORDERS_TYPE;
BEGIN
  ...  -- do some work
  old_ords_rec := new_ords_rec;  -- this is correct
  new_ords_rec := orders_rec;     -- this is incorrect!
```

When inserting rows into the database table, the VALUES clause must specify each member separately:

```
INSERT INTO orders orders_rec;     -- WRONG!
INSERT INTO orders old_ords_rec;   -- WRONG!
INSERT INTO orders
  (ord_num, qty, ..., discount) VALUES
  (new_ords_rec.ord_num, new_ords_rec.quantity, ...,
  new_ords_rec.discount);          -- CORRECT!
```

CREATING YOUR OWN ARRAYS   A PL/SQL TABLE is a one-dimensional array of any single scalar type. For Oracle Servers before 7.3, TABLE cannot contain a RECORD or another TABLE. For Oracle7.3 and up, a TABLE can contain a user-defined record, but not another TABLE. In Oracle8i, TABLEs are just one of several types of collections.

A PL/SQL TABLE is not like an Oracle database table. It is an unbounded array whose elements do not exist until assigned a value. It is always indexed by BINARY_INTEGER, giving it elements whose indexes range ±2,147,483,647 (okay, not quite unbounded). The programmer can choose to begin indexing the array at offset 0, 1, or anywhere it makes sense. Because an unassigned element does not exist, the array can contain sparsely located values with no additional impact on memory usage. Each element is referenced with an offset in parentheses. You create a PL/SQL table variable by first declaring a table type, then basing a variable on the type. For example, the following code uses only enough memory to store these values:

```
DECLARE
  TYPE STR_TYPE IS TABLE OF VARCHAR2(8)
      INDEX BY BINARY INTEGER;
  arr STR_TYPE;
  i BINARY_INTEGER := 17;  -- Universal Constant of Uncertainty
BEGIN
  arr(-2,147,483,647) := 'smallest';
  arr(0) := 'zero';
  arr(+2,147,483,647) := 'biggest';
  arr(i) := 'UCU';  -- an index variable makes for good loops
```

> In versions earlier than 7.3, a TABLE element is allocated a buffer sized to the data type and size for which it was declared, plus a little overhead. This means that if the table is of VARCHAR2(32767), each string stored in the table requires a 32KB buffer, even if the string is only one byte. Take care not to exhaust memory!

When declaring many long string variables, it would be wise to consider if PL/SQL always allocates a buffer of the size declared for VARCHAR2 variables.

You can also specify that a stored value must not be NULL by declaring the table like this:

```
DECLARE
  TYPE STR_TYPE IS TABLE OF VARCHAR2(8) NOT NULL
       INDEX BY BINARY INTEGER;
  arr STR_TYPE;
BEGIN
  arr(0) := NULL;  -- raises an exception!
```

You can also used a based reference, such as to a database column:

```
DECLARE
  TYPE QTY_TYPE IS TABLE OF items.quantity%TYPE NOT NULL
       INDEX BY BINARY INTEGER;
  qty QTY_TYPE;
BEGIN
  qty(0) := 0;  -- quantity of zero
```

Some of the benefits of using PL/SQL tables include the following:

- They enable you to pass a large amount of data into or out of a subprogram
- They enable performing an operation on a large set of data very quickly
- They can be loaded with a large set of data from a database table and manipulated without the overhead of additional database access
- In Oracle8i, they can be used in a select statement with the new TABLE() operator
- They facilitate performing complex operations that would be difficult with SQL, especially those involving multiple rows within the data set

Additionally, you can bind these PL/SQL tables to arrays in OCI and precompiler programs, allowing very fast data transfer. However, think about the increase in network traffic when moving large amounts of data between PL/SQL tables and these programs.

> You can only bind a one-dimensional host array to a PL/SQL table based on a scalar data type (record-based host arrays are not supported).

You can assign one table variable to another only if they have the same base types. The assignment copies the entire contents, if any, of the table to the other table variable. This technique is also used to clear a table.

PART

VI

CH

28

```
DECLARE
  TYPE ORDITEM_TYPE IS TABLE OF orders.item_no%TYPE
      INDEX BY BINARY INTEGER;
  clr_orditem ORDITEM_TYPE;  -- use ONLY to clear array
  new_orditem ORDITEM_TYPE;  -- new list of order items
  old_orditem ORDITEM_TYPE;  -- old list of order items
BEGIN
  ...  -- fill up new order items array
  old_orditem := new_orditem;  -- copy for safekeeping
  ...  -- modify new order items array and save
  new_orditem := clr_orditem;  -- erase contents for next operation
```

If you try to read an element that has not yet been assigned a value, PL/SQL raises the NO_DATA_FOUND exception. Listing 28.10 illustrates this.

LISTING 28.10 `badref.sql`—REFERENCING AN ARRAY ELEMENT BEFORE IT HAS A VALUE RAISES AN EXCEPTION

```
DECLARE
  SCHAR VARCHAR2(1);  -- we'll use this for typing only
  TYPE SCHAR_TYPE IS TABLE OF SCHAR%TYPE INDEX BY BINARY_INTEGER;
  schar_arr SCHAR_TYPE;
  local_schar SCHAR%TYPE;
BEGIN
  local_schar := schar_arr(0);  -- no value stored!
END;
/
ERROR at line 1:
ORA-01403: no data found
ORA-06512: at line 7
```

In PL/SQL 2.3 (Oracle7.3) and later versions, tables can also be based on database tables and RECORD types you declare. Each record member must be a scalar type. This enables you to load and subsequently manipulate a set of database rows.

REFERENCING ARRAYS OF ROW TYPES   You use dot notation to reference a particular member of a record with the array element:

```
DECLARE
  TYPE ORDERS_TYPE IS TABLE OF orders%ROWTYPE
      INDEX BY BINARY_INTEGER;
  qty orders.quantity%TYPE;  -- local copy of quantity
  orders_tab_rec ORDERS_TYPE;  -- array of table rows
BEGIN
  ...  -- fill the array with database table rows
  qty := orders_tab_rec(i).quantity;
```

PL/SQL TABLE ATTRIBUTES   Tables in PL/SQL 2.3 have attributes to help you manipulate them more easily. COUNT, FIRST, and LAST operate on the table itself. EXISTS, PRIOR, NEXT, and DELETE operate on a specific table element. Table 28.4 lists some of these attributes.

TABLE 28.4   USING PL/SQL TABLE ATTRIBUTES

Attribute	Description	Return Value	Usage
EXISTS	Tests a table element for a value	TRUE/FALSE	tablename.EXISTS (offset)
COUNT	Returns number of entries in table	BINARY_INTEGER	tablename.COUNT
FIRST	Returns the offset of the first table entry	BINARY_INTEGER	tablename.FIRST
LAST	Returns offset of the last table entry	BINARY_INTEGER	tablename.LAST
PRIOR	Returns offset of the previous table entry	BINARY_INTEGER	tablename. PRIOR(offset)
NEXT	Returns offset of the next table entry	BINARY_INTEGER	tablename.NEXT (offset)
DELETE	Removes the specified element, range or all	none	tablename. DELETE([off_m, [off_n]])

When you're already at the FIRST or LAST element, PRIOR and NEXT return NULL, respectively.

DELETE can remove just the specified element, a range of elements, or all elements, using any of these forms:

- tablename.DELETE(m);—Deletes just one element entry
- tablename.DELETE(m, n);—Deletes all elements in the range [m..n] inclusive
- tablename.DELETE;—Deletes all elements in the table

If an offset within a specified range doesn't contain an entry, it's simply skipped (no exception is raised). The range has to be ascending; if *m* > *n*, DELETE does nothing.

VARIABLE ARRAYS AND NESTED TABLES   Oracle8i defines two new types of array-like constructs, or collections: variable arrays, or varrays, and nested tables. They differ from PL/SQL tables, now called "index-by tables" in how they can be used and their primary focus. While index-by tables are PL/SQL constructs, varrays and nested tables focus on the database itself. For instance, they can be stored in a database table as though they were any other column of data, but they cannot be bound to host variables.

CREATING VARIABLE ARRAYS   Creating a varray is similar to creating a PL/SQL TABLE, in that the type is declared and a variable is created of that type. Unlike a PL/SQL TABLE, however, a varray is "dense" as opposed to "sparse"—you don't have "holes" where there is no data, the way you do with a TABLE. What's more, where a PL/SQL TABLE is virtually unbounded, a varray has a very specific limit. When a varray is created, it is NULL, and can be tested for nullity. In order to use it, you must first initialize it using a constructor, as shown in the following code:

PART

VI

CH

28

```
TYPE Performers IS VARRAY(250) OF varchar2(100);
TYPE Contacts is VARRAY(200) OF prospects;
showLineup  Performers('Juggler', 'Singer', 'Fire Swallower');
myContacts  Contacts := Contacts('John', 'Mary', 'Tito');
```

NESTED TABLES Types can also be created in SQL*Plus and used in the database as nested tables. In this case, the database manages the storage.

```
CREATE TYPE act AS OBJECT (
                         act_no number(5),
                 act_name      varchar2(35),
                 act_desc      varchar2(500));

CREATE TYPE performers IS TABLE OF act;

CREATE TABLE schedules (evt_id number(5) PRIMARY KEY,
                              evt_name varchar2(100),
                              evt_date date,
                              evt_location varchar2(100),
                              evt_lineup performers)
NESTED TABLE evt_lineup STORE AS evt_lineup_tab;

INSERT into schedules VALUES (1138, 'Not Quite the Greatest Show On Earth',
sysdate+180, 'Colorado Springs', performers(act('1', 'John', 'Trick Riding'),
 act('2', 'Mary', 'High Wire'),
 act('3', 'Albert the Dog-faced Boy', 'Contortionist')));
```

Manipulating individual elements involves the use of a new operator in Oracle8i, TABLE(). TABLE() returns a variable array, and can be used to allow us to access the data individually, although the syntax is probably not as intuitive as it could be. To add an act to our Colorado Springs show above, see the following code snippet:

```
BEGIN
   INSERT INTO
      TABLE(SELECT evt_lineup FROM schedules WHERE evt_id = 1138)
      VALUES('12', 'The Amazing Rando', 'Magician');
END;
```

Similarly, we can update the information using this snippet:

```
BEGIN
   UPDATE TABLE(SELECT evt_lineup FROM schedules WHERE evt_id = 1138)
      SET act_desc = 'Ruler of the Known Universe'
      WHERE act_no = 12;
END;
```

We can remove Mary's high-wire act using this statement:

```
BEGIN
   DELETE TABLE(SELECT evt_lineup FROM schedules WHERE evt_id = 1138)
      WHERE act_name = 'Mary';
END;
```

And of course pull out the information for viewing using the following:

```
DECLARE
MyAct varchar2(35);
    MyDesc varchar2(500);
BEGIN
```

```
    SELECT act_name, act_desc INTO MyAct, MyDesc
        FROM TABLE(SELECT evt_lineup FROM schedules WHERE evt_id = 1138)
        WHERE act_no = 3;
    ...
END;
```

USING SUBTYPES

User-defined subtypes were introduced in Oracle7.2 with PL/SQL 2.2. Subtypes enable you to provide another, more meaningful name for a type, optionally constrained. They do not define storage, merely another name for a more general data type. For example, the predefined subtypes for NUMBER and CHAR use this facility. You cannot directly constrain a subtype with a fixed length; instead you must use a two-step method involving %TYPE and %ROWTYPE. Here are some examples (right and wrong):

```
SUBTYPE SSN_TYPE IS VARCHAR2;              -- legal (method #1)
emp_ssn SSN_TYPE(9);                       -- legal
SUBTYPE PHONE_TYPE IS VARCHAR2(10);        -- illegal!
big_string VARCHAR2(32767);                -- will be used below
TYPE MAX_STRING_TYPE IS big_string%TYPE;   -- legal (method #2)
dynam_str MAX_STRING_TYPE;                 -- legal
```

Note method #2. This is one way of defining subtypes that are constrained by length. Another method is to base the variable on a constrained database column type. Using this method can help you bounds-check variables based on the subtype. When used judiciously, this method leads to better self-documenting code.

Subtypes based on a database column do not inherit the NOT NULL constraints of the column. The subtype does inherit the NOT NULL constraint of a PL/SQL variable declaration, but not the default assignment:

Tip #82	By basing variable definitions on the database columns whose information they will contain, you will help prevent value errors. If you change a column size or type in a table, your code will still be accurate.

```
small_str VARCHAR2(20) NOT NULL := 'blick';  -- #1
subtype SMALL_TYPE is small_str%TYPE;  -- fails NOT NULL constraint!
tiny_str VARCHAR2(1) := 'T';                  -- #2
subtype TINY_TYPE is tiny_str%TYPE;
tiny TINY_TYPE;  -- does not inherit assignment!
```

Variables based on different unconstrained subtypes are compatible for assignment purposes only if those subtypes are based, in turn, on the same type. For example, DECIMAL and NUMERIC, being subtypes of NUMBER, are interchangeable. If the parent types are different, some sort of conversion must take place.

CHANGING ONE TYPE TO ANOTHER

As with strongly typed languages, sometimes you need to convert one data type to another. This generally occurs when you're assigning a value to a variable or computing an expression. There are two ways to do this: implicitly and explicitly.

PART

VI

CH

28

IMPLICIT TYPE CONVERSION   Implicit type conversion is performed by the PL/SQL compiler, with no effort on your part. For example, given the following:

```
DECLARE
  flt_x FLOAT(3,2)  := 2.25;
  int_y INTEGER(6)  := 100;
  flt_z DOUBLE(10,2);
BEGIN
  flt_z := flt_x + int_y;  -- implicit numeric conversion
END;
/
```

The integer value is implicitly converted up to a floating-point value in order to properly perform the arithmetic. This is typical among compilers. A value is converted to the most generalized type in order to perform the calculation. In PL/SQL, the VARCHAR2 data type is the most generalized type of all.

Table 28.5 illustrates all valid implicit type conversions. If you don't see a conversion listed, you'll have to do an explicit conversion, using a built-in conversion function.

TABLE 28.5   IMPLICIT TYPE CONVERSION

TO FROM	VARCHAR **2**	CHAR	NUMBER	DATE	RAW	ROWID	
BINARY_ INTEGER		√		√	√	√	
CHAR	√		√	√	√	√	√
DATE		√		√		√	
LONG		√			√	√	
NUMBER	√	√		√		√	
RAW		√		√		√	
ROWID		√				√	
VARCHAR2	√	√	√	√	√	√	√

PLS_INTEGER has the same implicit conversion characteristics as BINARY_INTEGER, as well as implicitly converting between each other. The following examples are all valid declarations and assignments:

```
DECLARE
  date_from DATE   := '20-AUG-85'; -- char to date (match NLS format)
  cnt INTEGER(3)   := '0';         -- char to integer (subtype of number)
  loop_control BINARY_INTEGER;
  bin_val RAW(2)   := '1';         -- char to raw
  str VARCHAR2(9) := '26-AUG-60';  -- char to varchar2
  short_num VARCHAR2(3);
BEGIN
  loop_control := cnt + '1';       -- char to number to binary integer
  str := date_from;                -- date to varchar2
  short_num := bin_val;            -- raw to varchar2
  cnt := short_num;                -- varchar2 to integer
```

Anything can be converted implicitly to and from CHAR and VARCHAR2. If you need to convert a RAW to a NUMBER, you could first convert the RAW value to VARCHAR2, say, then to NUMBER. Implicit conversions hold for a data type's subtypes as well.

For DATE, an implicit conversion from CHAR or VARCHAR2 can only successfully occur when the string is in the default NLS format defined for the database. If the string is in a different format, you must perform an explicit conversion and supply a conversion string.

EXPLICIT TYPE Conversion Table 28.6 lists all the PL/SQL functions available to perform explicit data type conversions.

TABLE 28.6   EXPLICIT DATA TYPE CONVERSION

TO FROM	VARCHAR2	CHAR	NUMBER	DATE	RAW	ROWID
VARCHAR2			TO_NUMBER (vc, [fmt [,lang]])	TO_DATE (vc, [fmt [, lang]])	HEXTORAW (vc)	CHARTOROWID (vc)
CHAR			TO_NUMBER (c, [fmt [, lang]])	TO_DATE (c, [fmt [, lang]])	HEXTORAW (c)	CHARTOROWID (c)
NUMBER	TO_CHAR (n, [format [,lang]])	TO_CHAR (n, [format [,lang]])		TO_DATE (n, [fmt [, lang]])		
DATE	TO_CHAR (dt, [format [,lang]])	TO_CHAR (dt, [format [,lang]])				
RAW	RAWTOHEX (raw)	RAWTOHEX (raw)				
ROWID	ROWIDTOCHAR (rowid)	ROWIDTOCHAR (rowid)				

Where:

- fmt is a format string
- lang is an NLS language format string

Actually, TO_CHAR() returns VARCHAR2, but it can be easily used for CHAR because these two types convert implicitly. Note, however, that there are no conversion routines for LONG. To do much with LONG you'd have to first implicitly convert it to VARCHAR2 and then explicitly to some other type.

ASSIGNMENT

Unlike some languages, such as C or Pascal, assignments must be single statements. You can only assign one value to one variable at a clip. You cannot assign a value to a variable inside another statement, such as an IF conditional test.

Most data type mismatch errors are caught at compile-time, as long as the type of the expression can be determined. Value errors are caught at runtime.

One special concern arises when dealing with NULL values. Any mathematical operation involving a NULL value always returns a NULL value; by definition, the result is indeterminate. This does not hold true for string concatenation. For example:

```
DECLARE
  x NUMBER;
  y NUMBER;
  z NUMBER := 10;
  a VARCHAR2(20) := 'Hello, ';
BEGIN
  x := 1/NULL;          -- result is NULL
  y := x * (z - 1);     -- result is NULL
  z := (y - 1)**10;     -- result is NULL
  a := a || NULL || 'World!';  -- result is 'Hello, World!'
```

LOOPING

PL/SQL supports three brands of looping:

- Unconditional Looping (Do-Forever Loops)
- Iterative Looping (FOR Loops)
- Conditional Looping (WHILE Loops)

The simplest kind of loop looks like this:

```
LOOP
  NULL;  -- infinite loop!
END LOOP;
```

Note the LOOP...END LOOP syntax. Oracle won't detect the infinite loop. You have to supply a test to break out of the loop.

There are a few ways of exiting a loop:

- EXIT—An unconditional break of the loop. Use it in an IF test.
- EXIT WHEN—A conditional break when the supplied condition exists.
- GOTO—Jump out of the loop to the outer context.

Obviously, the first two methods involving EXIT are preferred. Here are some examples:

```
DECLARE
  i NUMBER := 0;
BEGIN
  LOOP  -- example #1
    i := i + 1;
    IF (i >= 100) THEN  -- enough iterations
      i := 0;  -- reset
      EXIT;    -- unconditional termination
    END IF;  -- enough iterations
  END LOOP;  -- example #1 done
```

```
LOOP   -- example #2
  i := i + 1;
  EXIT WHEN (i >= 100); -- conditional termination
END LOOP;  -- example #2 done
```

Certainly, the EXIT WHEN syntax is cleaner when all you have to do when the condition is met is to terminate the loop. Use the conditional logic when you have to reset values or do some other kind of work before getting out of the loop.

CONTROLLING YOUR LOOP

You can use the WHILE loop to test for a condition at the beginning of a loop. As long as the condition holds true, the loop continues to iterate. Conversely, if you need to test a condition at the end of a loop, use the LOOP-EXIT WHEN structure instead:

```
WHILE (x < 10) LOOP   -- While loop
...
  x := x + 1;
END LOOP;  -- done
LOOP   -- simulated Repeat-Until (or Do-While) loop
 ...
  EXIT WHEN ...
END LOOP;  -- done
```

It's a good habit to always comment the top and bottom of a loop, especially a long one, so you know what it's for.

PL/SQL does not support a FORTRAN-like CONTINUE statement for branching to the end of a loop, skipping all the code in between. Some people will tell you to modularize your code with conditional logic in this case, causing your code to become hideously indented and more difficult to maintain. However, there is a solution. You can use the GOTO statement to simulate a CONTINUE statement (see Listing 28.11). CONTINUE is a reserved word in SQL, so you can't use it in a statement or label.

LISTING 28.11   contine.sql—SIMULATING

```
DECLARE
  j NUMBER := 0;
BEGIN
  DBMS_OUTPUT.enable;
  LOOP          print even numbers between 0 and 20
    IF (MOD(j, 2) = 1) THEN  -- skip odd numbers
      GOTO CONTINE,  -- the misspelling is an inside joke
    END IF;  -- skipping odd numbers
    DBMS_OUTPUT.put_line(TO_CHAR(j) || ' is even');
    <<CONTINE>>
    EXIT WHEN j = 20;  -- done
    j := j + 1;  -- don't forget to increment the loop counter!
  END LOOP;  -- print even numbers between 0 and 20
END;
/
```

The server responds with the following:

```
0 is even
2 is even
4 is even
6 is even
8 is even
10 is even
12 is even
14 is even
16 is even
18 is even
20 is even
PL/SQL procedure successfully completed.
```

Using GOTO in this manner simplifies the logic within a loop.

ITERATING WITH FOR LOOPS

Another kind of loop performs a specific number of iterations:

```
BEGIN
  FOR i IN 1..100 LOOP  -- do nothing for exactly 100 iterations
    NULL;
  END LOOP;  -- done doing nothing
END;
```

Note the syntax of the FOR loop. The IN clause must specify a range. Now in this case, you do not need to declare the loop control variable (i in this example) because it is created automatically within the scope of the FOR loop. This means you cannot reference it outside the scope of the loop, because it ceases to exist when the loop completes. If you need the value of the loop control variable for something, you must copy it into another variable (see Listing 28.12).

LISTING 28.12 lastodd.sql—CAPTURING THE VALUE OF A LOOP CONTROL VARIABLE

```
DECLARE
  j NUMBER;
BEGIN
  DBMS_OUTPUT.enable;  -- enable output
  FOR i IN 1..100 LOOP  -- do nothing for exactly 100 iterations
    IF (MOD(i, 2) = 1) THEN  -- must be odd
      j := i;
    END IF;  -- capture odd numbers
  END LOOP;  -- done doing nothing
  DBMS_OUTPUT.put_line('last odd number was ' || TO_CHAR(j));
END;
/
```

The server displays the following:

```
last odd number was 99
PL/SQL procedure successfully completed.
```

There is no support for stepping by any value other than one. But you can simulate it! There are a couple of ways; one might be to multiply the loop counter by the step to get the values you want to work with. You can't actually modify the loop control variable because that would be illegal (it's strictly read-only). Another method would be to create another variable and increment it by the desired value; this probably makes more sense with a simple loop, but it's still perfectly valid inside a FOR loop. You might have to adjust the loop range to get the behavior you want. And, of course, you can always use EXIT or EXIT WHEN to prematurely break out of a loop.

You can also do the iteration in reverse, in countdown-wise fashion (see Listing 28.13).

LISTING 28.13   *countdwn.sql*—USING IN A LOOP

```
BEGIN
  FOR j IN REVERSE 1..10 LOOP   -- countdown
    DBMS_OUTPUT.put(TO_CHAR(j) ¦¦ '-');
  END LOOP;   -- countdown
  DBMS_OUTPUT.put_line('Blastoff!');
END;
/
```

And you get the following:

```
10-9-8-7-6-5-4-3-2-1-Blastoff!
PL/SQL procedure successfully completed.
```

USING CURSORS

A cursor is an object that provides row-level control of a SQL statement. The cursor declaration is not that of a variable, but rather a handle to an area of memory used to implement the cursor. The cursor declaration only defines what query will be submitted to the SQL Statement Executor; the management of the query occurs under programmatic control in executable code. The cursor can represent any valid SQL SELECT statement. Cursors are generally the basic building blocks of any PL/SQL application. They provide the looping mechanism for operating on sets of data stored in the database. If you also need to do updates, use the FOR UPDATE clause.

Caution

Be aware that using the FOR UPDATE clause will lock all the rows found by the query. All these rows will remain locked until the cursor is closed.

A cursor may return one or more rows, or none at all. The general sequence of operations is

1. Declare the cursor, as well as a data structure into which to retrieve rows
2. Open the cursor
3. Fetch repeatedly from the cursor into the data structure, until the data set is exhausted
4. Close the cursor

PART

VI

CH

28

DEFINING A CURSOR

In defining a cursor, you will notice a few variations on a theme:

```
DECLARE
  -- gets all orders in database
  CURSOR get_orders IS
    SELECT * FROM orders;
  -- gets a few columns for a specified order number
  CURSOR get_orditem(Pord_num orders.ord_num%TYPE) IS
    SELECT seq_num, quantity, unit_price, extended_price
    FROM orders
    WHERE ord_num = Pord_num;
  -- gets the whole row for a particular item#
  CURSOR get_items(Pitem_no items.item_no%TYPE) RETURN items%ROWTYPE IS
  SELECT * FROM items WHERE item = Pitem;

  -- gets the item name for a particular item#
  CURSOR get_item_name(Pitem_no items.item_no%TYPE)
  RETURN items.item_name%TYPE IS
  SELECT item_name FROM items WHERE item_no = Pitem_no;
```

Even though there are quite a few variants, there are just two basic patterns. A cursor can take parameters, or not. You supply the values for the parameters when you open the cursor. You can define the return type, or not. The return type can be a user-defined record, a database table row type, or individual variables. Whichever way, the columns defined in the SELECT clause must match one for one whatever you use to receive the return values.

Once declared, the cursor can be opened, rows fetched, its state examined, and closed when no longer needed.

A cursor can have any name; in these examples the convention is to suffix the cursor's name with _cur(sor) or _loop, or prefix it with get_ (depending on my mood). Use the name of the table in the cursor name, or otherwise try to make it meaningful (without being long-winded), as in get_addresses or employee_by_dept_cur.

Be aware that the parameter list can only input values, never output them. That is why the parameter flow is not needed nor allowed. The input parameters must also be scalar values.

When a cursor is opened, the SQL is executed and the corresponding data set computed. However, no rows have actually been returned to the program. You use FETCH to get one row at a time. The row fetched remains the current row until another fetch is performed. You can only fetch in the forward direction; there is no control to move back in the data set.

CURSOR ATTRIBUTES

Cursors have the attributes as described in Table 28.7.

TABLE 28.7 CURSOR ATTRIBUTES

Attribute	Return Value	Description
ISOPEN	TRUE/FALSE	Indicates whether a cursor is open or closed
FOUND	TRUE/FALSE	Indicates whether a row was found
NOTFOUND	TRUE/FALSE	Indicates whether a row was not found
ROWCOUNT	NUMBER	The ordinal value of each row retrieved (1st, 2nd, 3rd, ...)

Here are some examples of their use:

```
IF (orders_cur%FOUND) THEN  -- got an order
  OPEN items_cur(orders_cur.orderno);  -- open a related cursor
  LOOP
    FETCH items_cur into order_item;
    EXIT WHEN items_cur%NOTFOUND;  -- break out when done
    -- show how many rows were processed so far
    DBMS_OUTPUT.put_line('On Row #' ¦¦ TO_CHAR(items_cur%ROWCOUNT));
  END LOOP;
END IF;  -- got an order
...
IF (items_cur%ISOPEN) THEN  -- close the cursor
  CLOSE items_cur;
END IF;  -- close an open cursor
```

CURSOR FOR LOOPS

A cursor FOR loop is the simplest way to use cursors. The opening, fetching and closing of the cursor are handled automatically within the scope of the FOR loop. The return record variable is also defined implicitly for you, and cannot be referenced outside the scope of the loop. The cursor can take parameters. You can either declare the cursor in the declaration section or in the body of the cursor FOR loop itself (see Listing 28.14).

LISTING 28.14 cfor1.sql—SIMPLE USE OF CURSOR LOOP

```
DECLARE
  CURSOR get_tables IS
    SELECT * FROM user_tables;
BEGIN
  FOR get_tables_cur IN get_tables LOOP
    DBMS_OUTPUT.put_line(get_tables_cur.table_name);
  END LOOP;
END;
/
```

If you run this as scott/tiger, you would get the following:

```
BONUS
DEPT
EMP
SALGRADE
PL/SQL procedure successfully completed.
```

Lines 2–3 define the cursor.

Line 5 defines the cursor record variable to be used with the cursor.

Line 6 uses dot notation to refer to the column specified in the cursor.

As Listing 28.15 shows, you can be even more concise and yet still get the same results:

LISTING 28.15   `cfor2.sql`—A SIMPLE LOOP, SIMPLER

```
BEGIN
  FOR get_tables_cur IN (SELECT * FROM user_tables) LOOP
    DBMS_OUTPUT.put_line(get_tables_cur.table_name);
  END LOOP;
END;
/
```

The difference is that the cursor is also defined locally to the loop. This is fine for simple programs.

You can also take a parameter and search for a specific table (see Listing 28.16).

LISTING 28.16   `cfor3.sql`—SIMPLE LOOP CURSOR TAKES PARAMETERS

```
DECLARE
  CURSOR get_tables(Powner all_tables.owner%TYPE) IS
    SELECT * FROM all_tables
    WHERE owner = Powner;
  local_owner all_tables.owner%TYPE := 'DEMO';  -- search criteria
BEGIN
  FOR get_tables_cur IN get_tables(local_owner) LOOP
    DBMS_OUTPUT.put_line(get_tables_cur.table_name);
  END LOOP;
END;
/
```

Notice the good use of based variables, especially in the cursor definition, and how the parameter was passed into the cursor. This time you get the following (because now you're looking at only those tables in the schema DEMO that were made visible to scott):

```
CUSTOMER
DEPARTMENT
EMPLOYEE
JOB
LOCATION
SALARY_GRADE
SALES_ORDER
PL/SQL procedure successfully completed.
```

For larger, more complex programs, define your cursor within the scope of the enclosing block (as in the preceding), and control the cursor yourself.

OPENING, FETCHING, AND CLOSING A CURSOR

The longer-winded approach, starting with the last example, looks like Listing 28.17.

LISTING 28.17 `ofc.sql`—CONTROLLING THE CURSOR YOURSELF

```
DECLARE
  -- cursor definitions
  CURSOR get_tables(Powner all_tables.owner%TYPE) IS
    SELECT * FROM all_tables
    WHERE owner = Powner;
  -- record variable definitions
  get_tables_rec get_tables%ROWTYPE;
  -- local variables
  local_owner all_tables.owner%TYPE := 'DEMO';  -- search criteria
BEGIN
  OPEN get_tables(local_owner);           -- compute rows to return
  LOOP  -- find all DEMO tables available to SCOTT
    FETCH get_tables INTO get_tables_rec;  -- try to get a row
    EXIT WHEN get_tables%NOTFOUND;         -- no more rows
    DBMS_OUTPUT.put_line(get_tables_rec.table_name);
  END LOOP;
  CLOSE get_tables;  -- done with this cursor
END;
/
```

You get exactly the same set as before. This time you defined the record variable to receive the rows as based on the cursor. You could have defined a record variable yourself (using TYPE RECORD IS ...). In fact, you could have defined individual variables to FETCH into, but basing a variable on the cursor return type is simpler and easier to maintain. Now if you change the column list for the cursor, you won't have to modify anything else involving the record variable.

After opening the cursor, which computes the rows that the cursor will return (although it hasn't actually returned anything yet), you loop through all rows, fetching one at a time. You need to test for end of set and break out of the loop, as in line 14. When the loop is terminated, line 17 closes the loop. In order to reuse the cursor, you must open it again, perhaps with a new parameter this time.

Suppose you only are interested in one row. Listing 28.18 illustrates the simplest solution.

LISTING 28.18 `onerow.sql`—EXPLICITLY FETCHING ONE ROW

```
DECLARE
  -- cursor definitions
  CURSOR get_tables(Powner all_tables.owner%TYPE) IS
    SELECT * FROM all_tables
    WHERE owner = Powner;
  -- record variable definitions
  get_tables_rec get_tables%ROWTYPE;
  -- local variables
```

continues

LISTING 28.18   CONTINUED

```
  local_owner all_tables.owner%TYPE := 'DEMO';   -- search criteria
BEGIN
  OPEN get_tables(local_owner);                  -- compute rows to return
  FETCH get_tables INTO get_tables_rec;  -- try to get a row
  IF (get_tables%FOUND) THEN               -- got a row
    DBMS_OUTPUT.put_line(get_tables_rec.table_name);
  END IF;
  CLOSE get_tables;  -- done with this cursor
END;
/
```

This time, you get the following:

```
CUSTOMER
PL/SQL procedure successfully completed.
```

Notice that the cursor attribute %FOUND was used to check if you actually fetched something. If nothing had been returned, the record variable would have the same value as it did before the FETCH. In fact, let's prove it (see Listing 28.19).

LISTING 28.19   *badfetch.sql*—ONLY OVERWRITES A RECORD VARIABLE ON SUCCESS

```
DECLARE
  -- cursor definitions
  CURSOR get_tables(Powner all_tables.owner%TYPE) IS
    SELECT * FROM all_tables
    WHERE owner = Powner;
  -- record variable definitions
  get_tables_rec get_tables%ROWTYPE;
  -- local variables
  local_owner all_tables.owner%TYPE := 'BLICK';  -- unknown owner
BEGIN
  get_tables_rec.table_name := 'GARBAGE';  -- initialize to something
  OPEN get_tables(local_owner);                  -- compute rows to return
  FETCH get_tables INTO get_tables_rec;  -- try to get a row
  IF (get_tables%NOTFOUND) THEN          -- got a row
    DBMS_OUTPUT.put_line(get_tables_rec.table_name);
  END IF;
  CLOSE get_tables;  -- done with this cursor
END;
/
```

You get the following:

```
GARBAGE
PL/SQL procedure successfully completed.
```

This was done to prove a point: If the FETCH fails, it does not overwrite what it's fetching into.

USING IMPLICIT CURSORS

Implicit cursors are relatively low maintenance. They are used only when you're expecting to get exactly one row. If zero or more than one row is found, the exception NO_DATA_FOUND or TOO_MANY_ROWS is raised, and you get nothing for your trouble. Listing 28.20 reveals an implicit cursor in action.

LISTING 28.20 *impcur.sql*—A SIMPLE IMPLICIT CURSOR

```
DECLARE
  -- record variable definitions
  get_tables_rec all_tables%ROWTYPE;   -- based on the table
  -- local variables
  local_owner all_tables.owner%TYPE       := 'DEMO';  -- search criteria
  local_table all_tables.table_name%TYPE := 'CUSTOMER';
BEGIN
  SELECT * INTO get_tables_rec  -- looking for a single row
  FROM ALL_TABLES
  WHERE owner = local_owner AND table_name = local_table;
  DBMS_OUTPUT.put_line(get_tables_rec.tablespace_name);
END;
/
```

And you get the following:

```
USER_DATA
PL/SQL procedure successfully completed.
```

This is what happens if you don't construct your search so as to return exactly one row (see Listing 28.21).

LISTING 28.21 *toomany.sql*—THE IMPLICIT CURSOR FAILS WHEN TOO MANY ROWS ARE FOUND

```
DECLARE
  -- record variable definitions
  get_tables_rec all_tables%ROWTYPE;   -- based on table
  -- local variables
  local_owner all_tables.owner%TYPE := 'DEMO';
BEGIN
  SELECT * INTO get_tables_rec FROM ALL_TABLES
  WHERE owner = local_owner;
  DBMS_OUTPUT.put_line(get_tables_rec.tablespace_name);
END;
/
```

The server complains with a meaningful error message:

```
ERROR at line 1:
ORA-01422: exact fetch returns more than requested number of rows
ORA-06512: at line 7
```

Here's what really happened:

1. Oracle opened the cursor and fetched a row.

2. Not satisfied, Oracle tried another fetch and got another row!

3. Since you can't stuff ten pounds of rows in a five-pound variable, Oracle closed the cursor (well, it would have closed it anyway) and generated the exception.

Tip #83	Oracle always does two fetches on an implicit cursor, just to see if it would return another row (and hence fail the requirement of an implicit cursor to return exactly one row). This is an ANSI requirement.

When all you want is one row, and you don't want to mess with exceptions, use an explicit cursor and do the one FETCH yourself. If you want to know if there might be more than one row (or none at all!), and you don't mind handling the exception, then use an implicit cursor. In fact, you can use implicit cursors in single-row lookup routines for just this reason. You need to know if the single-row lookup will actually be exactly one row, or you perceive it as an error. If you only cared about getting the one row, you'd do it more efficiently with an explicit cursor.

Implicit cursors can't be used with an array to handle the extra rows. By definition, all they are supposed to return is a single row.

HANDLING EXCEPTIONS

An exception is a non-fatal event that immediately interrupts normal program execution and causes an unconditional branch to the current block's exception handler. Some exceptions, like NO_DATA_FOUND or TOO_MANY_ROWS, are events that may be considered a normal part of processing. Exceptions like VALUE_ERROR indicate a program bug or some unexpected event. Yet other exceptions indicate a severe problem, such as running out of memory.

If no exception handlers are defined for a block, the exception is returned to the next higher block (if any). The exception "bubbles up" through enclosing blocks until either an exception handler is found for the block, or control is returned to the calling context (in our case here, SQL*Plus).

Your programs will experience exceptions all the time. All you need is an exception handler, to handle them. Refer again to the implicit cursor that blew up last time (see Listing 28.22).

LISTING 28.22   graceful.sql—USING AN EXCEPTION HANDLER

```
DECLARE
  -- record variable definitions
  get_tables_rec all_tables%ROWTYPE;   -- based on table
  -- local variables
  local_owner all_tables.owner%TYPE := 'DEMO';
  status NUMERIC := 0;  -- capture error code (initialize to OK)
```

```
BEGIN
  SELECT * INTO get_tables_rec FROM ALL_TABLES
  WHERE owner = local_owner;
  DBMS_OUTPUT.put_line(get_tables_rec.tablespace_name);
EXCEPTION
  WHEN TOO_MANY_ROWS THEN
    status := SQLCODE;
    DBMS_OUTPUT.put_line('get_tables: ' || SQLERRM(status));
    DBMS_OUTPUT.put_line('get_tables: Exiting gracefully.');
END;
/
```

This time, the server gives you the following:

```
get_tables: ORA-01422: exact fetch returns more than requested number of rows
get_tables: Exiting gracefully.
PL/SQL procedure successfully completed.
```

A variable is defined to store the potential error code on line 6.

A WHEN clause is used in the exception section to specify the exception on line 12.

The error code is trapped in line 13.

The error message associated with the error code is displayed in line 14.

The server now tells you that the program completed successfully. Had the error not occurred, the SQLCODE would have been set to zero, which means okay. SQLCODE is actually a built-in function that returns the SQL status.

Table 28.8 is a list of all the predefined exceptions.

TABLE 28.8   EXCEPTIONS THAT CAN BE EXPLICITLY TESTED FOR IN EXCEPTION BLOCK ()

Exception Name	Oracle Error	Value
CURSOR_ALREADY_OPEN	ORA-06511	-6511
DUP_VAL_ON_INDEX	ORA-00001	-1
INVALID_CURSOR	ORA-01001	-1001
INVALID_NUMBER	ORA-01722	-1722
LOGIN_DENIED	ORA-01017	-1017
NO_DATA_FOUND	ORA-01403	+100
NOT_LOGGED_ON	ORA-01012	-1012
PROGRAM_ERROR	ORA-06501	-6501
STORAGE_ERROR	ORA-06500	-6500
TIMEOUT_ON_RESOURCE	ORA-00051	-51
TOO_MANY_ROWS	ORA-01422	-1422
TRANSACTION_BACKED_OUT	ORA-00061	-61
VALUE_ERROR	ORA-06502	-6502
ZERO_DIVIDE	ORA-01476	-1476

Notice how most of the exceptions have negative SQLCODE values, with NO_DATA_FOUND being the conspicuous exception (no pun intended). This is because the ANSI standard calls for the SQLCODE value to be +100 when no row is found, even as the Oracle error code is negative. Oracle is an ANSI-compliant database. You might say it makes them ANSI (bad pun intended).

If the exception you anticipate is not covered by the above list, or you're not sure which exceptions might occur, or you don't even care except to handle any of them, you can use the WHEN OTHERS THEN clause. This is the catch-all that allows your exception handler to handle any error that might arise.

You can also use any combination of exception names, and end the list with the WHEN OTHERS THEN clause. They act together like an IF... ELSIF... ELSE group of statements. If any one of them is true, its corresponding code is executed, and the block is exited:

```
EXCEPTION
  WHEN NO_DATA_FOUND THEN   -- row not found!
    -- do this and skip to end of block
    ...
  WHEN ZERO_DIVIDE THEN     -- divide by zero!
    -- do that and skip to end of block
    ...
  WHEN VALUE_ERROR THEN     -- 10 lbs of data in a 5lb var
    -- do these and skip to end of block
    ...
  WHEN OTHERS THEN          -- dunno, don't care
    -- do the other and skip to end of block
    ...
END;
```

Tip #84	Always code a WHEN OTHERS clause at the end of your exception handler. Sometimes it'll be the only handler.

AVOIDING AN INFINITE LOOP IN THE EXCEPTION HANDLER

Sometimes, you perform an action inside an exception handler that might itself raise an exception. This can lead to an infinite loop! The trick to avoiding this scenario is to enclose the exception handler in a block and give it its own exception handler. This embedded exception handler need not (nor should it) do anything. Consult the following:

```
EXCEPTION   -- main block handler
  WHEN OTHERS THEN
    BEGIN   -- embedded block
      IF (get_cursor%ISOPEN) THEN  -- cursor left open
        CLOSE get_cursor;  -- close it
      END IF;  -- cursor left open
    EXCEPTION
      WHEN OTHERS THEN
        NULL;  -- don't care
    END;  -- embedded block
END;  -- main block
```

Your exception handler should perform all necessary cleanup, such as closing cursors that might have been open.

Tip #85	Always put an exception handler in the topmost block of any application PL/SQL code. Exceptions should be handled in a graceful manner. The last thing a user needs to see is a terse, technical error message.

DEFINING YOUR OWN EXCEPTIONS

If the list of predefined exceptions seems a little short, you can define more of them by associating a name for any particular Oracle exception number. You can then reference the exception by name in the exception block. To accomplish this, define an exception and a pragma to convey to the compiler that you want to associate the exception with the given error code. A pragma is a compiler directive that is processed at compile time instead of runtime. It specifies how the compiler should handle language-specific information or conditions. All good compilers have them (or something like them). Listing 28.23 is an example of using a pragma.

LISTING 28.23   *excpinit.sql—*USING *EXCEPTION_INIT*

```
SET SERVEROUTPUT ON
DECLARE
  -- exceptions and pragmas (compiler directives)
 INVALID_NUM_FORMAT EXCEPTION;   -- first we define an exception object
 PRAGMA EXCEPTION_INIT (INVALID_NUM_FORMAT, -1481);   -- then associate it with
➥an exception
  -- constants
 NUM_FMT CONSTANT VARCHAR2(3) := 'aaa';  -- an invalid number format
 x NUMBER(10);
BEGIN
  DBMS_OUTPUT.enable;
  SELECT TO_NUMBER('999', NUM_FMT) INTO x FROM DUAL;  -- try to convert
EXCEPTION
WHEN INVALID_NUM_FORMAT THEN
  DBMS_OUTPUT.put_line('Trapped an illegal Number Conversion');
WHEN OTHERS THEN
  DBMS_OUTPUT.put_line('Some other error');
END;
/
```

This time you get the following:

```
Trapped an illegal Number Conversion
PL/SQL procedure successfully completed.
```

Here you see a two-step process; you first define an exception, and then associate an Oracle error code with it. Your next question is, why didn't Oracle pre-define all their error codes? All 24,000 of them? As Richard Bach once wrote, "If you ask the question correctly, it answers itself." Oracle defined just the errors that give you 80% of the problems. After all, these things do take up space in memory.

Another method is defining application-specific exceptions. These have nothing to do with Oracle error codes. These are errors you define for your application. You have to detect a situation that violates a particular business rule, and raise the appropriate user-defined exception. For instance, suppose non-exempt employees who make less than $10 an hour are only allowed raises of 1 to 5 percent. Your buddy, Joe, is an hourly employee making $8 an hour. His boss (who's also his uncle) wants to give him a big raise. Listing 28.24 shows an implementation of this business rule.

LISTING 28.24 *busrule.sql*—TRAPPING BUSINESS RULE VIOLATIONS WITH APPLICATION-SPECIFIC EXCEPTIONS

```
DECLARE
  -- exceptions
  INVALID_ANNUAL_RAISE EXCEPTION;
  -- constants
  HRLY_STATUS CONSTANT VARCHAR2(1)    := 'H';      -- hourly status
  HRLY_WAGE_LIMIT CONSTANT REAL(4,2) := 10.00;    -- upper hourly wage limit
  MIN_HRLY_RAISE CONSTANT REAL(5,4)  := 1.0100;   -- lower hourly raise limit
  MAX_HRLY_RAISE CONSTANT REAL(5,4)  := 1.0500;   -- upper hourly raise limit
  -- info entered by user
  emp_name   VARCHAR2(20) := '&emp_name';         -- employee name
  emp_status VARCHAR2(1)  := '&emp_status';       -- employee status
  hrly_wage  REAL    := &wage;                     -- hourly wage
  ann_raise  REAL    := &annual_raise;            -- annual raise
BEGIN
  IF (emp_status = HRLY_STATUS AND                 -- this is business rule #532
      hrly_wage < HRLY_WAGE_LIMIT AND
      ann_raise NOT BETWEEN MIN_HRLY_RAISE AND MAX_HRLY_RAISE) THEN
    RAISE INVALID_ANNUAL_RAISE;
  ELSIF (FALSE) THEN  -- code other rules here (pertaining to raises)
    NULL;
  ELSE  -- passed the gauntlet
    DBMS_OUTPUT.put_line(emp_name || ' now makes ' ||
                         TO_CHAR(hrly_wage * ann_raise, '$99.99'));
  END IF;
EXCEPTION
WHEN INVALID_ANNUAL_RAISE THEN
  DBMS_OUTPUT.put_line('Don''t give ' || emp_name || ' the raise!');
WHEN OTHERS THEN
  DBMS_OUTPUT.put_line('Some other problem computing ' || emp_name || '''s
increase');
END;
/
```

The server processes Joe's boss' request in this manner:

```
Enter value for emp_name: Joe
old  10:   emp_name   VARCHAR2(20) := '&emp_name'; -- employee name
new  10:   emp_name   VARCHAR2(20) := 'Joe';       -- employee name
Enter value for emp_status: H
old  11:   emp_status VARCHAR2(1)  := '&emp_status'; -- employee status
new  11:   emp_status VARCHAR2(1)  := 'H'; -- employment status
Enter value for wage: 8.00
old  12:   hrly_wage  REAL(4,2)    := &wage;         -- hourly wage
```

```
new  12:   hrly_wage  REAL(4,2)     := 8.00;                -- hourly wage
Enter value for annual_raise: 1.06
old  13:   ann_raise  REAL(5,4)     := &annual_raise;    -- annual raise
new  13:   ann_raise  REAL(5,4)     := 1.06;      -- annual raise
Don't give Joe the raise!
PL/SQL procedure successfully completed.
```

Using application-specific exceptions and raising them in your logic is a basic business rule encoding technique. Design your code for expansion and ease of maintenance by setting up a pattern for everyone to follow.

If you want the same code executed for two or more exceptions, just list them in a Boolean OR condition, such as the following:

```
EXCEPTION
WHEN INVALID_NUMBER OR VALUE_ERROR THEN
  ...
WHEN OTHERS THEN
  ...
END;
```

HANDLING EXCEPTIONS INLINE

A very good habit to get into is to code blocks with exception handlers for all SQL statements. If an exception occurs on the SQL statement, you usually want to continue processing inline (sequentially with the next conceptual program block). This is especially true for loops. If you don't code a block with an exception handler for a SQL statement within a loop, any exception will cause the loop to immediately terminate by jumping to the enclosing block's exception handler (the "bubble up" syndrome). To illustrate the point, look at the following:

```
LOOP  -- get some rows from a master table
  FETCH master_cursor INTO master_rec;
  EXIT WHEN master_cursor%NOTFOUND;
  BEGIN  -- delete some child table rows
    -- master primary key is foreign key in child
    DELETE FROM child_table
    WHERE master_fkey = master_rec.master_pkey;
  EXCEPTION  -- something untoward occurred
    WHEN OTHERS THEN  -- so output a message, say
      status := SQLCODE;  -- always capture error code!
      DBMS_OUTPUT.put_line('during delete: ' || SQLERRM(status));
  END;  -- delete some child table rows
END LOOP;
```

If the enclosing block with an exception handler was not present, an exception (such as no rows found) would immediately bomb out of the loop. The graceful thing you probably wanted to do is to skip this row and go on to the next. Handling the exception inline meets this desire.

USING SUBPROGRAMS

Now you're going to look at subprograms. Subprograms enable you to modularize our code and make it more efficient.

WHAT'S A SUBPROGRAM?

A subprogram is a subroutine that can be called one or more times. I use the term subprogram generically and interchangeably with subroutine. Actually, subprogram is the term Oracle started with, and I just picked up on it.

PL/SQL has two types of subprograms (or subroutines): procedures and functions. In an unnamed PL/SQL block, functions and procedures are declared (giving the name and optional parameters and type) and defined (giving the executable code) in the Declaration section. You can think of them as callable static code fragments; they must be referenced at runtime in order to execute the code they contain. These subprograms, like most blocks, contain declaration (except the subprogram name substitutes for the keyword DECLARE), body and optional exception handler sections, and are terminated with an END statement, optionally labeled with the subroutine name.

FUNCTIONS

A function is a subroutine whose name returns a single value of some one particular data type. You assign this return value to a variable of the same data type, or you use the return value in an expression. Functions often take parameters. When no parameters are passed, no parentheses are used. Some simple and familiar examples are the following:

```
status := SQLCODE;  -- note no parentheses
NL CONSTANT VARCHAR2(1) := CHR(10);  -- ASCII character (newline)
IF (employee_exists('Scaboda')) THEN ...  -- use them in expressions
```

In an unnamed PL/SQL block, you declare and implement them at the same time, in the block's declaration section, following all other declarations. Listing 28.25 some examples of functions.

LISTING 28.25   *boolsub.sql*—FUNCTIONS MAKE REPETITIVE TASKS EASIER

```
DECLARE
  -- local variables
  x NUMBER(3);
  -- local subprograms (must follow all other declarations!)
  FUNCTION is_even(Pnum IN x%TYPE)  -- returns TRUE if number is even
  RETURN BOOLEAN IS
  BEGIN
    RETURN(MOD(Pnum, 2) = 0);  -- test for evenness
  EXCEPTION
  WHEN OTHERS THEN
    RETURN (NULL);  -- indeterminate
  END is_even;
  FUNCTION bool_to_char(Pbool IN BOOLEAN)
  RETURN VARCHAR2 IS
    str VARCHAR2(5);  -- capture string to return
  BEGIN
    IF (Pbool) THEN  -- test Boolean value for TRUE
      str := 'TRUE';
    ELSIF (NOT Pbool) THEN  -- FALSE
      str := 'FALSE';
```

```
      ELSE  -- must be NULL
        str := 'NULL';
      END IF;  -- test Boolean value
      RETURN (str);
  END bool_to_char;
BEGIN  -- executable code
  x := 0;
  DBMS_OUTPUT.put_line('It is ' || bool_to_char(is_even(x)) ||
                       ' that ' || TO_CHAR(x) || ' is even');
  x := 1;
  DBMS_OUTPUT.put_line('It is ' || bool_to_char(is_even(x)) ||
                       ' that ' || TO_CHAR(x) || ' is even');
  x := 2;
  DBMS_OUTPUT.put_line('It is ' || bool_to_char(is_even(x)) ||
                       ' that ' || TO_CHAR(x) || ' is even');
  x := 3;
  DBMS_OUTPUT.put_line('It is ' || bool_to_char(is_even(x)) ||
                       ' that ' || TO_CHAR(x) || ' is even');
  x := 4;
  DBMS_OUTPUT.put_line('It is ' || bool_to_char(is_even(x)) ||
                       ' that ' || TO_CHAR(x) || ' is even');
  DBMS_OUTPUT.put_line(bool_to_char(NULL) || ' is neither TRUE nor FALSE');
END;
/
```

The server's output is the following:

```
It is TRUE that 0 is even
It is FALSE that 1 is even
It is TRUE that 2 is even
It is FALSE that 3 is even
It is TRUE that 4 is even
NULL is neither TRUE nor FALSE
PL/SQL procedure successfully completed.
```

This rather lengthy example illustrates a few properties and restrictions of functions:

- Functions (in fact, all subprograms) must be declared after all types, constants, and variables.

- Variables local to the function are declared between the IS...BEGIN.

- Parameters can be based; when representing database column values, this is the preferred method.

- A RETURN statement must be used to return a value, even in the EXCEPTION clause.

- Function calls can be nested and can, in fact, be in expressions of arbitrary complexity.

- The function's END statement is given a label the same as the function name (although it is optional, I always do it; and it must match).

- Every parameter has a mode, a keyword that specifies whether the parameter is to be treated as a read-only (IN), write-only (OUT), or read-write (IN OUT) variable. If you leave off the mode it defaults to IN.

PART

VI

CH

28

Note the verbose declaration of the function. The scope of parameter variables are strictly local to the function or any nested subprograms within it. You can nest other subprograms, which will exist only when program execution enters the enclosing subprogram, by defining them between the IS... BEGIN portion. This technique of limiting scope to the smallest program unit helps reduce coupling between program routines, which is a good thing.

While it is technically legal to return a value on the parameter list (by specifying OUT or IN OUT for the mode), it is generally frowned upon as a poor programming style. If you feel obliged to do this, you should have a compelling reason and must document the precise usage, raising it to the level of a standard. This avoids abuses and nonstandard coding styles (one could argue that a function returning a value on the parameter list is already an abuse of style).

Tip #86	Most Oracle developers avoid returning values on a function's parameter list. To prevent the proliferation of hideous, unmaintainable code, your organization might want to prohibit this practice altogether.

It is perfectly normal and acceptable to enclose very small chunks of code, even one-liners, in a function. This technique reduces code size and simplifies code maintenance. For example, if later on you wished to add some additional data validation to your function, you would only need to add it in the one place.

PROCEDURES

A procedure is a subroutine that performs a bit of repetitive work, passing values in and out strictly through the parameter list. A procedure is always a single statement; you cannot insert it in an expression. The same scoping rules as for functions apply. The syntax is almost identical to functions, less the return statement.

If no mode is specified, it defaults to IN. As a matter of style, I always specify the mode. The compiler will catch whether a parameter is used inconsistently with its mode. An IN parameter must appear only on the right side of an assignment statement, or in any expression that can be evaluated. An OUT parameter may only appear on the left side of an assignment statement. An IN OUT parameter can appear anywhere.

In general, use the most restrictive mode as needed for the subprogram. This provides the greatest protection from programming errors where variables are inadvertently trashed during a subprogram execution.

When using these modes, the server makes a copy of the variable to work with so that the original value is preserved should an exception occur. Sometimes, however, this is not what you want, and in any case can involve a significant amount of overhead. Oracle8i introduces the NOCOPY modifier, which causes the server to point directly to the original variable by reference. If you insist on using OUT variables and are not worried about preserving the original values, you can get a significant performance increase by going this route.

Try coding all your single row lookup routines as procedures. Follow the same coding style for single-row lookups. Pass in the key values, a return row type record variable, and a status indicator. This style has the advantage of encapsulating the SQL statement or cursor in order to handle exceptions inline, as well as making for reusable code fragments. It is also an easily maintainable style. Listing 28.26 shows an example of this style.

LISTING 28.26 `table.sql`—A STANDARDIZED CODING STYLE LENDS ITSELF TO MAINTAINABLE CODE

```
DECLARE
  -- constants
  TB CONSTANT VARCHAR2(1) := CHR(9);  -- TAB
  -- variables
  status NUMERIC;
  table_rec all_tables%TYPE;
  -- routines
  PROCEDURE get_table(Powner  IN     all_tables.owner%TYPE,
                      Ptable  IN     all_tables.table_name%TYPE,
                      Prec       OUT all_tables%TYPE,
                      Pstatus IN OUT NUMERIC) IS
    -- local cursors
    CURSOR table_cur(Cowner all_tables.owner%TYPE,
                     Ctable all_tables.table_name%TYPE) IS
      SELECT *
      FROM all_tables
      WHERE owner = Cowner AND table_name = Ctable;
    -- local variables
    Lowner all_tables.owner%TYPE;
    Ltable all_tables.table_name%TYPE;
  BEGIN
    Pstatus := 0;  -- OK
    Lowner := UPPER(Powner);
    Ltable := UPPER(Ptable);
    OPEN table_cur(Lowner, Ltable);
    FETCH table_cur INTO Prec;
    IF (table_cur%NOTFOUND) THEN
      RAISE NO_DATA_FOUND;
    END IF;
    CLOSE table_cur;
  EXCEPTION
  WHEN OTHERS THEN
    BEGIN
      Pstatus := SQLCODE;  -- capture error code
      IF (table_cur%ISOPEN) THEN  -- close the open cursor
        CLOSE table_cur;
      END IF;
      Prec := NULL;  -- clear return values and display input values
      DBMS_OUTPUT.put_line('get_table: ' || SQLERRM(Pstatus));
      DBMS_OUTPUT.put_line('OWNER = ' || '<' || Lowner || '>');
      DBMS_OUTPUT.put_line('TABLE = ' || '<' || Ltable || '>');
    EXCEPTION
    WHEN OTHERS THEN
```

continues

LISTING 28.26 CONTINUED

```
      NULL;  -- don't care (avoid infinite loop)
    END;
  END get_table;
BEGIN  -- display storage parameters for a given table
  DBMS_OUTPUT.enable;
  DBMS_OUTPUT.put_line('TABLE'    || TB || 'TABLESPACE'  || TB ||
                       'INITIAL'  || TB || 'NEXT'  || TB || 'MAX');
  DBMS_OUTPUT.put_line(RPAD('-', 43, '-'));  -- just an underline
  get_table('scott', 'dept', table_rec, status);
  IF (status = 0) THEN
    DBMS_OUTPUT.put_line(
      table_rec.table_name       || TB ||
      table_rec.tablespace_name  || TB ||
      table_rec.initial_extent   || TB ||
      table_rec.next_extent      || TB ||
      table_rec.max_extents);
  END IF;
  get_table('scott', 'garbage', table_rec, status);
  IF (status = 0) THEN
    DBMS_OUTPUT.put_line(
      table_rec.table_name       || TB ||
      table_rec.tablespace_name  || TB ||
      table_rec.initial_extent   || TB ||
      table_rec.next_extent      || TB ||
      table_rec.max_extents);
  END IF;
END;
/
```

The server returns the following:

```
TABLE    TABLESPACE        INITIAL NEXT    MAX
-------------------------------------------
DEPT    USER_DATA        10240   10240   121
get_table: ORA-01403: no data found
OWNER = <SCOTT>
TABLE = <GARBAGE>
PL/SQL procedure successfully completed.
```

If you anticipate an exact match using a unique key, manage the cursor yourself and perform exactly one fetch. When detecting no rows, close the cursor in the exception handler, rather than inside the conditional block (it has to be closed in the exception block anyway, so why code it three times?). Note that you must raise the predefined exception NO_DATA_FOUND, because the fetch does not generate one automatically. The input values are converted to uppercase using local variables because the converted values are used in more than one place.

Also take note of the additional information displayed by the exception handler. Why not take the opportunity to show the key values that the exception occurred on? This would be especially valuable when processing a large number of rows. This information could also have been dumped to an error table for post mortem analysis.

You might be thinking, "I can get the same information with a simple SELECT statement. What does all this buy me?" In the larger scheme of things, canned queries are more efficient because they can be found in the shared SQL area and reused. The manual control of the cursor with its single fetch is certainly more efficient, especially when it is run thousands of times over and over. Remember, your goal is to write efficient applications. After you have the row that was found, you can programmatically do anything you want with it. You have total flexibility and control, yet the underlying procedure is coded once and reused.

Listing 28.27 shows another example that implements a binary search on a PL/SQL table containing numeric values.

LISTING 28.27 *bintest.sql*—A BINARY SEARCH ROUTINE MADE EASY TO USE WITH A PROCEDURE

```
SET SERVEROUTPUT ON
DECLARE
  -- constants
  FIXED_TOP CONSTANT NUMBER := 12;  -- fixed # of elements
  -- data types
  TYPE NUMARR_TYPE IS TABLE OF NUMBER INDEX BY BINARY_INTEGER;
  -- global variables
  numarr NUMARR_TYPE;
  isfound BOOLEAN;
  rowout NUMBER;

  -- routines
  PROCEDURE binary_search(   -- binary search on sorted array
      Parr    IN NUMARR_TYPE,
      Pnum    IN NUMBER,
      Pfound OUT BOOLEAN,
      Prow    OUT NUMBER) IS
    local_found BOOLEAN := NULL;
    top BINARY_INTEGER := FIXED_TOP;
    bottom BINARY_INTEGER := 1;
    middle BINARY_INTEGER := NULL;
  BEGIN
    local_found := FALSE;
    LOOP  -- binary search
      middle := ROUND((top + bottom) / 2);  -- find middle
      IF (Parr(middle) = Pnum) THEN  -- exact match
        local_found := TRUE;    -- match succeeded
        EXIT;  -- break
      ELSIF (Parr(middle) < Pnum) THEN  -- GO UP
        bottom := middle + 1;
      ELSE  -- GO DOWN
        top := middle - 1;
      END IF;  -- test for match
      IF (bottom > top) THEN  -- search failed
        IF (Pnum > Parr(middle)) THEN
          middle := middle + 1;    -- MAY BE OUTSIDE ARRAY!
        END IF;  -- insert after
        EXIT;
```

continues

LISTING 28.27 CONTINUED

```
      END IF;  -- failed
    END LOOP;  -- search
    Pfound := local_found;
    Prow := middle;
  EXCEPTION
  WHEN OTHERS THEN
    DBMS_OUTPUT.PUT_LINE(SQLERRM(SQLCODE));
    DBMS_OUTPUT.PUT_LINE(TO_CHAR(middle));
  END binary_search;

  FUNCTION bool_to_char(Pbool IN BOOLEAN)  -- convert Boolean to char
  RETURN VARCHAR2 IS
    str VARCHAR2(5);  -- capture string to return
  BEGIN
    IF (Pbool) THEN  -- test Boolean value for TRUE
      str := 'TRUE';
    ELSIF (NOT Pbool) THEN  -- FALSE
      str := 'FALSE';
    ELSE  -- must be NULL
      str := 'NULL';
    END IF;  -- test Boolean value
    RETURN (str);
  END bool_to_char;
BEGIN  -- bintest executable code
  DBMS_OUTPUT.enable;
  numarr(1) := 100;  -- fill array with numbers in order
  numarr(2) := 103;
  numarr(3) := 104;
  numarr(4) := 108;
  numarr(5) := 110;
  numarr(6) := 120;
  numarr(7) := 121;
  numarr(8) := 122;
  numarr(9) := 130;
  numarr(10) := 140;
  numarr(11) := 145;
  numarr(12) := 149;
  binary_search(numarr, 90, isfound, rowout);
  DBMS_OUTPUT.put_line('FOUND=' || bool_to_char(isfound) ||
                       ', ROW=' || TO_CHAR(rowout) || ' SB=1');
  binary_search(numarr, 150, isfound, rowout);
  DBMS_OUTPUT.put_line('FOUND=' || bool_to_char(isfound) ||
                       ', ROW=' || TO_CHAR(rowout) || ' SB=13');
  binary_search(numarr, 100, isfound, rowout);
  DBMS_OUTPUT.put_line('FOUND=' || bool_to_char(isfound) ||
                       ', ROW=' || TO_CHAR(rowout) || ' SB=1');
  binary_search(numarr, 145, isfound, rowout);
  DBMS_OUTPUT.put_line('FOUND=' || bool_to_char(isfound) ||
                       ', ROW=' || TO_CHAR(rowout) || ' SB=11');
  binary_search(numarr, 108, isfound, rowout);
  DBMS_OUTPUT.put_line('FOUND=' || bool_to_char(isfound) ||
                       ', ROW=' || TO_CHAR(rowout) || ' SB=4');
  binary_search(numarr, 105, isfound, rowout);
  DBMS_OUTPUT.put_line('FOUND=' || bool_to_char(isfound) ||
                       ', ROW=' || TO_CHAR(rowout) || ' SB=4');
END;  -- bintest
/
```

The output from the server is the following:

```
FOUND=FALSE, ROW=1 SB=1
FOUND=FALSE, ROW=13 SB=13
FOUND=TRUE, ROW=1 SB=1
FOUND=TRUE, ROW=11 SB=11
FOUND=TRUE, ROW=4 SB=4
FOUND=FALSE, ROW=4 SB=4
PL/SQL procedure successfully completed.
```

Note the OUT parameter mode, which means output only. This means inside the procedure, this variable can only be written to. If you need to read and write from a parameter variable, declare it as IN OUT.

Does that binary to char conversion routine look familiar? Wouldn't it be nice not to have to paste into every PL/SQL program that needs it?

DEFAULT PARAMETER VALUES

Parameters can receive default values, to be used when the parameter is not provided in the actual call to the subprogram. This makes the subprogram appear as if it can have a variable list of parameters:

```
DECLARE
   ...   -- types, constants, variables
   FUNCTION get_data (Pkey   IN CHAR,
                      Pflag IN BOOLEAN DEFAULT FALSE,
                      Psort IN CHAR DEFAULT ' ')
   RETURN VARCHAR2 IS
   ...   -- function implementation
BEGIN   -- executable code
   IF get_data(key1) THEN   -- valid call (Pflag, Psort defaulted)
     ...
   ELSIF get_data(key2, TRUE)   -- valid call (Psort defaulted)
     ...
   ELSIF get_data(key3, , 'ASCENDING') THEN   -- invalid!
```

Note the use of the keyword DEFAULT. You could also use the assignment operator (:=). As a coding convention, only DEFAULT is used in this context, to distinguish this semantically unusual construction from the more straightforward assignment upon declaration.

Both default parameters can be left off intentionally, so in the first call to get_data the flag parameter is defaulted to FALSE, and the sort parameter is defaulted to spaces. This makes for a very clean coding style where you only specify the parameters of interest to you. Note, however, that you cannot skip a default parameter and provide the next one because this notation for specifying parameters is positional. The positions of the parameters is significant. You cannot try to use a placeholder, such as the extra comma above.

POSITIONAL AND NAMED NOTATION

You can use an alternate notation, however, called *named notation* to specify parameters in any order. You provide the name of the parameter along with the value:

```
ELSIF get_data(key3,
               Psort => 'ASCENDING') THEN   -- valid (Pflag defaulted)
```

You can start off left to right using positional notation, then switch to named notation, which is known as mixed notation. Once you use named notation, you must then stick with it for subsequent parameters. Named notation can be used for any parameter, not just any that were defaulted:

```
ELSIF get_data(key3, Psort => 'ASCENDING',
               Pflag => TRUE) THEN  -- right
    ...
ELSIF get_data(Pkey => key3, 'ASCENDING',
               Pflag => TRUE) THEN  -- wrong!
```

Although this seems convenient and unusual among programming languages, I've never needed it. But if you had a bunch of parameters and nearly every parameter was defaulted and you wanted to have maximum flexibility calling the subroutine, this is practically indispensable. One example is in using Oracle's Web Application Server Developer's Toolkit, where procedures have a lot of parameters, most of which you won't be using at any given time.

BUILT-IN FUNCTIONS

Nearly all the built-in functions and operators you use in SQL can also be used in PL/SQL expressions and procedural statements. There are only a few exceptions to this rule.

You cannot use '= ANY (...)' in an expression. Instead, use the IN operator, as in the following:

```
IF (key IN ('A', 'B', 'C')) THEN  -- acts like an OR conditional
```

You can still use operators such as BETWEEN, IS NULL, IS NOT NULL, LIKE, and so on.

You cannot use DECODE in procedural statements. Also, none of the SQL group functions are allowed in procedural statements. They don't make much sense in this context, either. Of course, there are no such restrictions for SQL statements embedded in PL/SQL.

You have seen how to use SQLCODE to trap the numeric exception error value. SQLERRM (sqlcode) is used to convert the SQLCODE value to the error message string associated with the exception. All the other built-in functions are fair game.

ONLY IN ORACLE8I

Oracle has worked hard to improve performance and usability with every version, and Oracle8i is no exception. In addition to the other enhancements (such as easier use of PL/SQL tables), Oracle has made some of PL/SQL's more powerful features much easier to use, or just plain faster.

NATIVE DYNAMIC SQL

Sometimes you don't know what you'll be looking for until you actually try. For instance, you might not know what tables you'll need to look in or what criteria you'll be using when you do. Developers already had the capability to generate a query on-the-fly, so to speak, but it was an arcane process involving the DBMS_SQL package provided with the RDBMS. With 8i, however, the process has been greatly simplified, as follows:

```
PROCEDURE INSERT_ITEMS (Ptable varchar2, Pprod varchar2, Pdesc varchar2) is
   sql_statement varchar2(500);
BEGIN
   sql_statement := 'insert into '||p_table||' values (:prod_id, :desc)';
   EXECUTE IMMEDIATE sql_statement USING Pprod, Pdesc;
END;
```

To use DBMS_SQL to accomplish the same task would take almost a dozen lines of code! Native dynamic SQL will also give you a significant performance gain.

BULK BINDS

One advantage of using PL/SQL is the fact that you can include a series of statements to be sent to the server in a single group. Even so, each SQL statement embedded within the PL/SQL code requires a context switch as the server moves between the PL/SQL engine and the SQL engine. To take advantage of this new feature, the statement

```
FOR i in 1..10000
LOOP
   INSERT INTO orders VALUES (hold_orders(i).cust_id, hold_orders(i).prod_id);
END LOOP;
```

can be rewritten as

```
FORALL I in 1..10000
  INSERT INTO orders VALUES (hold_orders(i).cust_id, hold_orders(i).prod_id);
```

USING STORED SUBPROGRAMS, PACKAGES, AND THE SUPPLIED PACKAGES

In this chapter

DEFINING STORED SUBPROGRAMS AND PACKAGES

True Oracle8i application development begins when you start building stored subprograms and *packages*, which are persistent code modules that are compiled and stored in the database. They are shareable, re-entrant, and reusable software objects that you design. They are callable from other PL/SQL modules, SQL statements, and client-side applications in languages that support remote procedure calls.

Whenever you compile a stored subprogram or package, the source code, compiled code, compilation statistics, and any compilation errors are stored in the data dictionary. Various data dictionary views help you visualize these entities. You can get information about modules you compile with the USER_ views; you can get some restricted information about modules other folks compiled and granted you access to with the ALL_ views, and you can get all information anyone compiled with the DBA_ views, provided you have DBA rights. These views are listed in Table 29.1 (for simplicity, listed as DBA_ views).

TABLE 29.1   DATA DICTIONARY VIEWS FOR STORED SUBPROGRAMS AND PACKAGES

View Name	Description
DBA_SOURCE	Textual source code for all compiled modules
DBA_ERRORS	Textual listing of any compilation errors for all modules
DBA_OBJECT_SIZE	Statistics for compiled modules, such as validity, source, and object sizes
DBA_OBJECTS	Catalog of compiled modules (stored procedures, functions, packages, package bodies)
DBA_DEPENDENCIES	List of object dependencies, such as tables referenced in packages

No views exist to expose the object code because you don't need to see it. All you need to know is that it's in there and whether it's valid. A compiled module becomes invalid when a dependent object is changed or removed, such as when a column is added or a table dropped. If a stored module becomes invalid, it must be recompiled either automatically by the server or manually by the owner.

BUILDING AND USING STORED PROGRAMS

The syntax for creating stored subprograms is very similar to that for defining subprograms in anonymous PL/SQL blocks. Stored subprograms have all the same features of the subprograms you learned to write in the previous chapter, plus some additional ones. Let's make a stored function out of that bool_to_char function you saw earlier (see Listing 29.1).

LISTING 29.1 **BOOL2CHR.SQL**—STORED SUBPROGRAMS MAKE FOR REUSABLE CODE

```
CREATE OR REPLACE FUNCTION bool_to_char(Pbool IN BOOLEAN)
RETURN VARCHAR2 IS
  str VARCHAR2(5);  -- capture string to return
BEGIN
  IF (Pbool) THEN  -- test Boolean value for TRUE
    str := 'TRUE';
  ELSIF (NOT Pbool) THEN  -- FALSE
    str := 'FALSE';
  ELSE  -- must be NULL
    str := 'NULL';
  END IF;  -- test Boolean value
  RETURN (str);
END bool_to_char;
/
```

The server replies:

```
Function created.
```

That's all you get. The server doesn't execute the program; it compiles the program so that you can execute it later when called from other PL/SQL blocks.

Tip #87

The CREATE OR REPLACE syntax creates a new function or replaces an existing one. This means you don't make incremental recompilations or source changes to stored code; instead, you totally replace them with new versions.

Caution

Good source code management is required when using CREATE OR REPLACE. When you replace a subprogram, the old source is gone forever from the data dictionary. It also means you can only have one object of this name in your schema.

Now, run this newly created stored function using an unnamed PL/SQL block, as shown in Listing 29.2.

LISTING 29.2 **TESTBOOL.SQL** A TEST EXECUTION OF YOUR STORED SUBPROGRAM

```
SET SERVEROUTPUT ON
BEGIN
  DBMS_OUTPUT.enable;
  DBMS_OUTPUT.put_line(bool_to_char(TRUE));
  DBMS_OUTPUT.put_line(bool_to_char(FALSE));
  DBMS_OUTPUT.put_line(bool_to_char(NULL));
END;
/
```

This example pretty much exhausts the possibilities for all possible values returned by the stored function. It is called a Unit Test. For each input, verify the output. The input values should test all boundary conditions (values at and near the limits defined for the inputs, as well as some random values in between). You should always have a Unit Test file for your stored subprograms such as this one so that you can verify and validate the correct functioning of your code. Keep the Unit Test program with the stored subprogram so that when you modify the subprogram, you can test it again.

After running Listing 29.2, the server sends back the following output:

```
TRUE
FALSE
NULL

PL/SQL procedure successfully completed.
```

What happens if you try to pass in something other than a Boolean? Try it and see:

```
BEGIN
  DBMS_OUTPUT.put_line(bool_to_char(0));
END;
/
```

The server responds with the following:

```
ERROR at line 1:
ORA-06550: line 2, column 24:
PLS-00306: wrong number or types of arguments in call to 'BOOL_TO_CHAR'
ORA-06550: line 2, column 3:
PL/SQL: Statement ignored
```

This error message indicates a compilation error. The PL/SQL engine's strong type checking caught the problem and responded with a detailed error message.

Look at another, slightly long-winded example of a stored procedure, shown in Listing 29.3.

LISTING 29.3   SHOWINDX.SQL—A STORED PROCEDURE TO DISPLAY INDEX INFORMATION FOR TABLES

```
CREATE OR REPLACE PROCEDURE show_index(Ptable IN all_indexes.table_name%TYPE
DEFAULT NULL) IS
  -- local cursors
  CURSOR show_index_cur(Ctable all_indexes.table_name%TYPE) IS
    SELECT
      table_owner, table_name, tablespace_name, index_name, uniqueness, status
    FROM all_indexes
    WHERE
      (Ctable IS NULL OR table_name = Ctable)   -- one table or all
    ORDER BY
      table_owner, table_name, index_name;
  -- local constants
  TB CONSTANT VARCHAR2(1) := CHR(9);       -- tab character
  -- local record variables
  show_index_rec show_index_cur%ROWTYPE;   -- based on cursor
  old_index_info show_index_cur%ROWTYPE;   -- used to detect control break
  -- local variables
  status NUMERIC;
```

```
      local_table all_indexes.table_name%TYPE;
BEGIN
  status := 0;
  local_table := UPPER(Ptable);  -- make upper case
  old_index_info.table_owner := 'GARBAGE_OWNER';  -- initialize
  old_index_info.table_name  := 'GARBAGE_TABLE';
  IF (local_table IS NULL) THEN  -- one table or all?
    DBMS_OUTPUT.put_line('User ' || USER || ': Index Information for All
Tables');
  ELSE
    DBMS_OUTPUT.put_line('User ' || USER || ': Index Information for Table ' ||
local_table);
  END IF;  -- one table or all?
  OPEN show_index_cur(local_table);
  LOOP        -- get index information
    FETCH show_index_cur INTO show_index_rec;
    EXIT WHEN show_index_cur%NOTFOUND;
    IF (old_index_info.table_owner != show_index_rec.table_owner OR
        old_index_info.table_name  != show_index_rec.table_name) THEN  -- control
break
      DBMS_OUTPUT.put_line(TB);  -- double spacing between tables
    END IF;
    DBMS_OUTPUT.put_line('Table Owner: ' || show_index_rec.table_owner || TB ||
                        'Table: ' || show_index_rec.table_name);
    DBMS_OUTPUT.put_line('Index: ' || show_index_rec.index_name || TB || ' in '
||
                        show_index_rec.tablespace_name || TB ||
                        show_index_rec.uniqueness || TB ||
show_index_rec.status);
    old_index_info := show_index_rec;  -- copy new values to old
  END LOOP;  -- get index information
  CLOSE show_index_cur;
EXCEPTION
WHEN OTHERS THEN
  BEGIN
    status := SQLCODE;
    DBMS_OUTPUT.put_line('show_index: ' || SQLERRM(status));  -- display error
message
    IF (show_index_cur%ISOPEN) THEN  -- close any open cursors
      CLOSE show_index_cur;
    END IF;
  EXCEPTION
  WHEN OTHERS THEN
    NULL;       don't oaro
  END;
END show_index;
/
```

This time, the server responds with the following:

```
Procedure created.
```

To execute this procedure, you can call it from an anonymous PL/SQL block, or you can use the EXECUTE command for one-liners:

```
EXECUTE show_index('DEPT');
```

Tip #88

> The EXECUTE command can only be used to run one-line statements. If your statement spans two or more lines, you must use an anonymous PL/SQL block (using BEGIN .. END). If you can cram two or more statements onto a single line, you can still use EXECUTE. In fact, EXECUTE expands to a BEGIN .. END block on one line. It's just short-hand.

Following is the output generated by the author's test system:

```
User SYSTEM: Index Information for Table DEPT

Table Owner: SYSTEM      Table: DEPT
Index: DEPT_PRIMARY_KEY  in USER_DATA    UNIQUE   VALID

PL/SQL procedure successfully completed.
```

The first time you run this stored procedure, you might notice a slight pause as you wait for the server to load the procedure into memory. On subsequent calls, running it is much faster because it's already loaded in the database cache.

This particular example shows some fine features you'll want in your own stored procedures. You should always try to be consistent with the organization of local variable declarations, always putting them in the same order. Also, notice the block inside the exception handler to close the cursor in case an error leaves it open. If you don't do this and you do have an exception, the next time you run the stored procedure, you will immediately bomb with the CURSOR_ALREADY_OPEN exception. Your users would have to reconnect in order to clear the open cursor because the cursor remains open for the duration of a session until either the cursor is closed or the session is terminated.

If the user wants all tables and their indexes that are visible, simply drop the single input parameter (and parentheses in this case), as with the following:

```
EXECUTE show_index;
```

You have to put yourself in your users' (in this case, developers') shoes to anticipate the various ways in which they might want to use this tool. Better yet, go ask them. You'll be surprised at the answers you'll get.

CALLING STORED SUBPROGRAMS FROM SQL

Suppose you aren't satisfied with the Oracle8i-supplied TO_NUMBER() built-in function. Your complaint with it might be that when a character-to-number conversion fails because the string doesn't represent a valid number, the SQL fails and terminates abruptly. What you'd prefer is that at the very least, the error is handled gracefully so that processing can continue with the rest of the data set. Try to cure this problem with a stored function, as shown in Listing 29.4.

LISTING 29.4   CHAR2NUM.SQL—CHARACTER-TO-NUMBER CONVERSION

```
CREATE OR REPLACE FUNCTION char_to_number(Pstr IN VARCHAR2, Pformat IN VARCHAR2
DEFAULT NULL)
RETURN NUMBER IS
BEGIN
  IF Pformat IS NULL THEN  -- optional format not supplied
    RETURN (TO_NUMBER(Pstr));
  ELSE
    RETURN (TO_NUMBER(Pstr, Pformat));  -- format supplied
  END IF;  -- test for optional format
EXCEPTION
WHEN OTHERS THEN  -- unknown value
  RETURN (NULL);
END char_to_number;
/
```

You can run this stored function in two ways:

- From a PL/SQL block
- From within a SQL statement

First, try it from a PL/SQL block, as shown in Listing 29.5.

LISTING 29.5   TESTC2N1.SQL—TESTING char_to_number() FROM A PL/SQL BLOCK

```
DECLARE
  v VARCHAR2(1) := 0;
  w VARCHAR2(10) := '999.999';       -- try a floating point number
  x VARCHAR2(11) := '+4294967295';  -- try a big positive number
  y CHAR(11) := '-4294967296';      -- try a big negative number
  z VARCHAR2(10) := 'garbage';       -- this is NOT a number!
BEGIN
  -- stored function returns NULL on error, so convert NULL to error message
  DBMS_OUTPUT.put_line(v || ' is ' || NVL(TO_CHAR(char_to_number(v)), 'NOT A
NUMBER!'));
  DBMS_OUTPUT.put_line(w || ' is ' || NVL(TO_CHAR(char_to_number(w)), 'NOT A
NUMBER!'));
  DBMS_OUTPUT.put_line(x || ' is ' || NVL(TO_CHAR(char_to_number(x)), 'NOT A
NUMBER!'));
  DBMS_OUTPUT.put_line(y || ' is ' || NVL(TO_CHAR(char_to_number(y)), 'NOT A
NUMBER!'));
  DBMS_OUTPUT.put_line(z || ' is ' || NVL(TO_CHAR(char_to_number(z)), 'NOT A
NUMBER!'));
END;
/
```

The server responds with the following:

```
0 is 0
999.999 is 999.999
+4294967295 is 4294967295
-4294967296 is -4294967296
garbage is NOT A NUMBER!

PL/SQL procedure successfully completed.
```

Okay, now try it in a SQL statement, as shown in Listing 29.6.

LISTING 29.6   TESTC2N2,SQL—RUNNING char_to_number() FROM SQL

```
SELECT '0' str,
       NVL(TO_CHAR(char_to_number('0')), ' IS NOT A NUMBER!') num FROM DUAL;
SELECT '999.999' str,
       NVL(TO_CHAR(char_to_number('999.999')), ' IS NOT A NUMBER!') num FROM
➥DUAL;
SELECT '+4294967295' str,
       NVL(TO_CHAR(char_to_number('+4294967295')), ' IS NOT A NUMBER!') num FROM
➥DUAL;
SELECT '-4294967296' str,
       NVL(TO_CHAR(char_to_number('-4294967296')), ' IS NOT A NUMBER!') num FROM
➥DUAL;
SELECT 'garbage' str,
        NVL(TO_CHAR(char_to_number('garbage')), ' IS NOT A NUMBER!') num FROM
➥DUAL;
```

You get the same results as before. It looks kind of goofy converting back to a string when you just got through converting from a string to number, but it still verifies the operation of the stored function, particularly in the last query shown.

CALLING STORED PROGRAMS FROM PL/SQL

You've already seen how to invoke a stored subprogram from a PL/SQL block. What's a high value use for them? Have you ever tried to compose a query that has a 14-table join? Instead, create a bunch of single row lookup routines for each master table whose key you would have used in a join. Then, in a PL/SQL block, code just the minimal tables required to drive a cursor loop. Inside the loop, perform the single row lookups for the attendant data values. Using this technique, you could see speed improvements of up to 100% or more. Queries that previously ran in 20 minutes can be run in 2 minutes or faster using this technique. If you're using some sort of report writer to format the output, you can write the data to a temporary table, which can then be scanned by the reporting tool. Obviously, this slows things down somewhat, but it's still faster than bogging down the Oracle8i Server with a huge, complex query. Plus, it's easier to verify the correctness of the output. If you rigorously test the single row lookup routines, the only facet you'll have to validate is the substantially smaller query.

Now think about how many times you've had to code an outer join in a complex query. In a PL/SQL block, it's a piece of cake to test the single row lookup for no data found and skip to the end of the loop or carry on, as needed. For example, a Claims Processing program might have a loop in it that looks something like this:

```
LOOP  -- process all claims for the period selected
  FETCH claims_cur INTO claims_rec;
  EXIT WHEN claims_cur%NOTFOUND;
  -- get related table info
  get_claimant_info(claims_rec.claimant_ssn, status);
  get_provider_info(claims_rec.provider_id, status);
```

```
  get_approval_info(claims_rec.approvedby, status);
  IF (status != 0) THEN  -- no approval on file!
    GOTO SKIPIT;  -- skip processing claim
  END IF;
  ...  -- more single row lookups, claims processing
  <<SKIPIT>>  -- continue with next claim
END LOOP;  -- process all claims for the period selected
```

In this case, status is passed back the SQLCODE result value of the single row lookup. To make this example really useful, you need to dump information about why the claim wasn't processed (no approval) to some sort of application error table. Even better, inside the lookup routine you could dump the lookup key and error code to an error table of your design. Then, you could later determine the subroutine and key values that caused a claim to go unprocessed. The calling program could then dump additional data (such as context information) to make troubleshooting easier.

Another use for stored procedures is to implement business rules. Then, the rule can be invoked from a trigger, a client program, or another PL/SQL program, as in the following example:

```
CREATE OR REPLACE TRIGGER check_approval_status
  BEFORE INSERT ON claim_disbursal
  DECLARE
    status NUMERIC;
  BEGIN  -- check for approval
    get_approval_info(:new.approvedby, status);
    IF (status != 0) THEN  -- no approval on file!
      RAISE_APPLICATION_ERROR(-20100, 'No approval on file!');
    END IF;
  END;  -- check for approval
END check_approval_status;
```

Here, the application-defined exception causes an INSERT to be rolled back. The business rule is defined by a single stored procedure, which can now be used in many places. Should the rule require modification, it can be changed within the body of the stored procedure. The dependent PL/SQL code would then only need to be recompiled.

DEBUGGING WITH SHOW ERRORS

Up to now, your stored procedures have compiled flawlessly. Unfortunately, you can expect to make mistakes leading to compilation errors. Fortunately, the information to debug them is at hand. However, the feature provided by Oracle8i to observe them has some limitations, given its relative simplicity, but there is a better solution.

When your unnamed PL/SQL blocks failed to compile, the server dumped the error information straight back to SQL*Plus. With stored subroutines, the procedure is a little different. Immediately after the failed compilation, you type the following:

```
SHOW ERRORS
```

Then, every error and the line numbers on which they occurred are displayed for your perusal.

Tip #89	SHOW ERRORS only shows the errors for the last stored subprogram or package submitted for compilation. If you submit two in a row and the first has errors, SHOW ERRORS only shows errors for the second one (if any occurred). However, the error information for both is still available in USER_ERRORS.

Please consider the source code in Listing 29.7, a bug infested procedure:

LISTING 29.7   SHOWERR1.SQL—ERROR FORMATTER PROCEDURE WITH BUGS

```
CREATE OR REPLACE PROCEDURE showerr1(
    Pname   IN user_errors.name%TYPE,
    Ptype   IN user_errors.type%TYPE) IS
  CURSOR get_errors(Cname IN user_errors.name%TYPE,
                    Ctype IN user_errors.type%TYPE) IS
    SELECT * FROM USER_ERRORS
    WHERE name = Cname AND type = Ctype
    ORDER BY SEQUENCE;
  get_errors_rec get_errors%TYPE;
  status NUMERIC := 0;
  Lname   user_errors.name%TYPE;
  Ltype   user_errors.type%TYPE;
BEGIN
  Lname   := UPPER(Pname);
  Ltype   := UPPER(Ptype);
  DBMS_OUTPUT.put_line('Compilation errors for ' ¦¦ Lname);
  OPEN get_errors(Lname, Ltype);
  LOOP   -- display all errors for this object
    FETCH get_errors INTO get_errors_rec;
    EXIT WHEN get_errors%NOTFOUND;
    DBMS_OUTPUT.put_line('At Line/Col: ' ¦¦ get_errors_rec.line ¦¦
                    '/' ¦¦ get_errors_rec.position);
    DBMS_OUTPUT.put_line(get_errors_rec.text);
  END LOOP;   -- display all errors
  CLOSE get_errors;
  DBMS_OUTPUT.put_line('Errors Found: ' ¦¦ TO_CHAR(errs));
EXCEPTION
WHEN OTHERS THEN
  BEGIN
    status := SQLCODE;
    IF (get_errors%ISOPEN) THEN   -- cursor still open
      CLOSE get_errors;
    END IF;
  END;
END showerr1;
/
```

The server sends back this error message:

```
Warning: Procedure created with compilation errors.
```

To get more information, you type in the following command:

```
SHOW ERRORS
```

The output of the SHOW ERRORS command is shown following:

```
Errors for PROCEDURE SHOWERR1:

LINE/COL ERROR
-------- -----------------------------------------------------------
9/18     PLS-00206: %TYPE must be applied to a variable or column, not
         'GET_ERRORS'

9/18     PL/SQL: Item ignored
19/5     PL/SQL: SQL Statement ignored
19/27    PLS-00320: the declaration of the type of this expression is
         incomplete or malformed

21/5     PL/SQL: Statement ignored
21/45    PLS-00320: the declaration of the type of this expression is
         incomplete or malformed

23/5     PL/SQL: Statement ignored
23/26    PLS-00320: the declaration of the type of this expression is
         incomplete or malformed

26/3     PL/SQL: Statement ignored
26/52    PLS-00201: identifier 'ERRS' must be declared
```

> **Note**
>
> The PL/SQL engine strips blank lines from the stored source code. If you sprinkle double spacing throughout your programs for readability, you will discover that the source code stored in USER_SOURCE will quickly become unsynchronized from your source module, making debugging from the original source code file more difficult.

Some of these error messages are fairly informative; others are quite vague. The line number and column where the error occurred are also provided. Unfortunately, the source code line suffering the error is not displayed. You can display the source code with this SQL statement:

```
SELECT line, text
FROM user_source
WHERE name='SHOWERR1' AND line IN (9, 19, 21, 23, 26)
ORDER BY line;
```

The source lines displayed are the following:

```
LINE TEXT
---- ----------------------------------------------------------------
   9 get_errors_rec get_errors%TYPE;
  19 FETCH get_errors INTO get_errors_rec;
  21 DBMS_OUTPUT.put_line('At Line/Col: ' ¦¦ get_errors_rec.line ¦¦
  23 DBMS_OUTPUT.put_line(get_errors_rec.text);
  26 DBMS_OUTPUT.put_line('Errors Found: ' ¦¦ TO_CHAR(errs));
```

Matching up the error messages above, you see the following:

On Line 9, you have to base the record variable on get_errors%ROWTYPE, not %TYPE.

Line 19 failed because get_errors_rec was not defined correctly.

Line 21 failed because get_errors_rec was not defined correctly.

Line 23 failed because get_errors_rec was not defined correctly.

On Line 26, you forgot to declare the variable errs.

You can see how an error can propagate through the code. Fix it in the declaration, and the related errors go away.

Also, notice that some syntax errors were not uncovered during this compilation. For instance, the column named 'type' needs to be capitalized and double quoted because TYPE is actually a reserved word. After the five errors above are cleaned up, this bug appears (try it).

The repaired and enhanced stored procedure is found in Listing 29.8.

LISTING 29.8 SHOWERR.SQL—FINAL VERSION, PL/SQL ERROR FORMATTER PROCEDURE

```
CREATE OR REPLACE PROCEDURE showerr(
    Pname  IN user_errors.name%TYPE,
    Ptype  IN user_errors."TYPE"%TYPE DEFAULT NULL) IS
  CURSOR get_errors(Cname IN user_errors.name%TYPE,
                    Ctype IN user_errors."TYPE"%TYPE) IS
    SELECT
      E.sequence, E.line, E.position, E.text err_text, S.text src_text
    FROM USER_ERRORS E, USER_SOURCE S
    WHERE
      E.name = Cname AND E."TYPE" = Ctype AND
      S.name = E.name AND S."TYPE" = E."TYPE" AND S.line = E.line
    ORDER BY E.sequence;
  get_errors_rec get_errors%ROWTYPE;
  status NUMERIC := 0;
  Lname  user_errors.name%TYPE;
  Ltype  user_errors.type%TYPE;
  errs   NUMERIC := 0;  -- number of errors
  cols   NUMERIC;       -- extra column padding needed for error position
  wspc   VARCHAR2(2) := CHR(20) || CHR(10);  -- trailing whitespace
  dspc   VARCHAR2(1) := CHR(9);              -- double spacing
BEGIN
  Lname  := UPPER(Pname);
  IF (Ptype IS NOT NULL) THEN  -- user supplied type
    Ltype  := UPPER(Ptype);
  ELSE  -- look for 1 object and get the type
    BEGIN
      SELECT object_type INTO Ltype
      FROM user_objects
      WHERE object_name = Lname;
    EXCEPTION
    WHEN OTHERS THEN
      RAISE_APPLICATION_ERROR(-20100, Lname ||
                              ' type ambiguously defined');
```

```
      END;
    END IF;  -- user supplied type
    DBMS_OUTPUT.put_line('Compilation errors for ' ||
                          Ltype || ' ' || Lname);
    OPEN get_errors(Lname, Ltype);
    LOOP  -- display all errors for this object
      FETCH get_errors INTO get_errors_rec;
      EXIT WHEN get_errors%NOTFOUND;
      IF (SUBSTR(get_errors_rec.err_text, 1, 4) = 'PL/S') THEN
        GOTO SKIPIT;  -- ignore the 'PL/SQL: Statement ignored' messages
      END IF;
      cols := LENGTH(TO_CHAR(get_errors_rec.line)) + 3;
      DBMS_OUTPUT.put_line('[' || TO_CHAR(get_errors_rec.line) ||
                           '] ' || RTRIM(get_errors_rec.src_text, wspc));
      DBMS_OUTPUT.put_line(LPAD('^', get_errors_rec.position + cols, '-'));
      DBMS_OUTPUT.put_line('[' || TO_CHAR(get_errors_rec.line) ||
                           '] ' || get_errors_rec.err_text);
      DBMS_OUTPUT.put_line(dspc);  -- double space
      errs := errs + 1;
      <<SKIPIT>>
      NULL;
    END LOOP;  -- display all errors
    CLOSE get_errors;
    DBMS_OUTPUT.put_line('Errors Found: ' || TO_CHAR(errs));
  EXCEPTION
  WHEN OTHERS THEN
    BEGIN
      status := SQLCODE;
      IF (get_errors%ISOPEN) THEN  -- cursor still open
        CLOSE get_errors;
      END IF;
      DBMS_OUTPUT.put_line('showerrs: ' || SQLERRM(status));
    EXCEPTION
    WHEN OTHERS THEN
      NULL;  -- don't care
    END;
END showerr;
/
```

By executing the new procedure, you get something cleaner, more verbose, and hopefully easier to read:

```
oxoouto showerr('showerr1');
Compilation errors for PROCEDURE showerr1
[9]    get errors rec get errors%type,
--------------------^
[9] PLS-00206: %TYPE must be applied to a variable or column,
not 'GET_ERRORS'

[19]    FETCH get_errors INTO get_errors_rec;
------------------------------^
[19] PLS-00320: the declaration of the type of this expression is
incomplete or malformed

[21]    DBMS_OUTPUT.put_line('At Line/Col: ' || get_errors_rec.line ||
------------------------------------------------^
```

```
[21] PLS-00320: the declaration of the type of this expression is
incomplete or malformed

[23]    DBMS_OUTPUT.put_line(get_errors_rec.text);
----------------------------^
[23] PLS-00320: the declaration of the type of this expression is
incomplete or malformed

[26]    DBMS_OUTPUT.put_line('Errors Found: ' ¦¦ TO_CHAR(errs));
----------------------------------------------------^
[26] PLS-00201: identifier 'ERRS' must be declared

Errors Found: 5

PL/SQL procedure successfully completed.
```

You will like this much better. Maybe you want to control how many source lines are printed before and after the afflicted line in order to get the context. I leave that to you as an exercise.

CHECKING THE STATUS OF A STORED PROGRAM OR PACKAGE

Execute the following SQL statement to see the status of all your stored programs:

```
COLUMN object_name FORMAT A30
COLUMN timestamp FORMAT A20
SELECT object_name, object_type, timestamp, status
FROM user_objects
WHERE
  object_type IN ('FUNCTION', 'PROCEDURE', 'PACKAGE', 'PACKAGE BODY')
ORDER BY object_name, object_type;
```

The output of this command, on my system for example, is as follows:

```
OBJECT_NAME                 OBJECT_TYPE    TIMESTAMP             STATUS
--------------------------- -------------  --------------------  -------
CHAR_TO_BOOL                FUNCTION       1997-11-01:16:06:43   VALID
CHAR_TO_NUMBER              FUNCTION       1997-11-01:13:34:26   VALID
SHOWERR                     PROCEDURE      1997-11-05:06:01:31   VALID
SHOWERRS                    PROCEDURE      1997-11-05:05:47:10   VALID
SHOWERR1                    PROCEDURE      1997-11-04:19:51:31   INVALID
SHOW_INDEX                  PROCEDURE      1997-11-01:13:17:37   VALID

6 rows selected.
```

Notice that the procedure SHOWERR1 exists, even though it failed to compile. It's in there, source code and all. But if you try to run it, you get an error.

Tip #90	Changes in table structure can invalidate stored procedures and objects in some cases. You can recompile a specific database object with the ALTER .. COMPILE command as shown in the following example: ALTER PROCEDURE SHOWERRS COMPILE;

Another interesting thing to look at is the code statistics. To view these, run the following statement:

```
SELECT name, "TYPE", source_size, parsed_size, code_size, error_size
FROM user_object_size
WHERE
  "TYPE" IN ('FUNCTION', 'PROCEDURE', 'PACKAGE', 'PACKAGE BODY')
ORDER BY name, "TYPE";
```

The output of this statement on my system looks like this:

```
NAME             TYPE        SOURCE_SIZE PARSED_SIZE CODE_SIZE ERROR_SIZE
---------------- ---------- ----------- ----------- --------- ----------
CHAR_TO_BOOL     FUNCTION    391         841         546       0
CHAR_TO_NUMBER   FUNCTION    375         575         384       0
SHOWERR          PROCEDURE   2587        5725        3598      0
SHOWERRS         PROCEDURE   2227        5035        3073      0
SHOWERR1         PROCEDURE   1149        0           0         495
SHOW_INDEX       PROCEDURE   2408        4221        2629      0

6 rows selected.
```

Notice that SHOWERR1 doesn't have a parsed or code size because it failed to compile. Interestingly, the code and parsed sizes are larger than the source. There really isn't much correlation between source size and parsed and code sizes. It depends on the number of cursors, implicit SQL, subprograms, and so on--things that you might expect to require more storage. The code size gives you an idea how much memory in the SGA each object will occupy.

Tip #91

You can get a quick and dirty view of a particular stored program's parameter list with the DESCRIBE command:

```
DESC SHOWERR
PROCEDURE SHOWERR
 Argument Name                      Type                    In/Out Default?
 ---------------------------------- ----------------------- ------ ----
 ----
 PNAME                              VARCHAR2(30)            IN
 PTYPE                              VARCHAR2(12)            IN     DEFAULT
```

BUILDING AND USING PACKAGES

Packages are collections of programming objects that offer persistence of data, cursors, and other language constructs. When any object within a package is referenced, the entire package is loaded into memory. Although this seems like it would be a huge disk hit, remember that after it's loaded, the code is available to all users. As long as any one user is referencing the package, it will remain in the SGA. All program code inside is now available. The alternative would be to load each one separately as a stored subprogram would. Because the code is re-entrant when loaded, it is available to all users. The first disk hit is mitigated by code re-entrancy. From the point of view of the server, this is extremely efficient, both in memory use and disk access.

Packages also enable subprogram overloading, a feature not available to mere stored subprograms. With overloading, the same subprogram name is repeated with different combinations and numbers of parameter types. If you look at STANDARD.SQL, you'll see several declarations for TO_CHAR, TO_DATE, and TO_NUMBER. Each declaration takes a parameter of differing data type.

The Package Specification and Body

There are two components to a PL/SQL package:

- The package specification (also called a *header*)
- The package body

The package body contains the actual code for any subprograms mentioned in the specification.

The package specification contains all those language constructs you want to expose to the rest of the world. These can be program variables, user-defined data types, cursors, and subprograms. Anything put in the specification is globally accessible. No executable code is found here, just the declaration of subprograms. Listing 29.9 shows an example of a package header, using a few functions you've seen already.

LISTING 29.9 LIBHDR.SQL—Specification for a Proposed Library Package

```
CREATE OR REPLACE PACKAGE lib IS
  -- public global user defined types
  -- public global constants
  MAXINT CONSTANT BINARY_INTEGER := +2147483647;   -- +(2^31 - 1)
  MININT CONSTANT BINARY_INTEGER := -2147483647;   -- -(2^31 - 1)
  MAXDATE CONSTANT DATE := TO_DATE('31-DEC-4712 AD', 'DD-MON-YYYY AD');
  MINDATE CONSTANT DATE := TO_DATE('01-JAN-4712 BC', 'DD-MON-YYYY BC');
  -- public global cursors
  -- public global variables
  -- public global subprograms
  -- convert a BOOLEAN to a STRING ('TRUE', 'FALSE', 'NULL')
  FUNCTION bool_to_char(Pbool IN BOOLEAN)
  RETURN VARCHAR2;
  -- convert a STRING to BOOLEAN (TRUE, FALSE, NULL)
  FUNCTION char_to_bool(Pstr IN VARCHAR2) RETURN BOOLEAN;
  -- safe STRING to NUMBER conversion; returns NUMBER or NULL
  FUNCTION char_to_number(Pstr IN VARCHAR2, Pformat IN VARCHAR2 DEFAULT NULL)
  RETURN NUMBER;
  -- debug flag interface routines
  PROCEDURE debug_on;        -- turns debug on
  PROCEDURE debug_off;       -- turns debug off
  PROCEDURE debug_toggle;    -- toggles debug on/off
  FUNCTION  debug_status     -- is debug on/off?
  RETURN BOOLEAN;
END lib;
/
```

Notice the standard CREATE OR REPLACE syntax you saw in other stored subprogram objects. Now, you don't have to explicitly create subprograms as you did for the stand-alone ones. Instead, you're back to declaring them as you did when they were embedded in blocks, except that in the package header, you only specify a declaration including the subprogram name, its parameters (if any), and return type (if any). Also, notice how the subprograms must follow all other declarations.

Those familiar with the C programming language will recognize this kind of function prototyping. Now that the specification exists, you're free to develop the actual code for these routines and change it as necessary—without disturbing the specification. Developers can begin working on their applications as soon as the specifications are available, even if the body isn't written yet. Because of this separation of specification and implementation, programs using these routines need not be recompiled just because the code was enhanced. Dependent modules only require recompilation if the specification portion changes.

> **Note**
>
> The standard practice for packages is to put the header and body in separate files. This way, if changes to just the code occur (which is more likely when a package is somewhat new yet still in a state of flux), just the body will need be recompiled.
>
> Use any standardized naming convention you want. Some folks like to use different extensions (*.hdr and *.pkg) for header and body. Others prefer to always use the *.sql extension, but still indicate the contents (*hdr.sql, *pkg.sql) for header and body.

The package body contains the actual code for subprograms exposed in the specification, as well as privately defined subprograms, variables, user-defined data types, and cursors. These objects are hidden from the rest of the world. The body can also contain initialization code, which is only executed once, the first time the package is referenced. Although this might appear to have limited usefulness, you can use it to enable output, set various application flags (like Debug On/Off), and gather global user-related data. Although the package body is a distinct object from the package header, the body cannot be successfully compiled until the header has been first compiled.

LISTING 29.10   LIBPKG.SQL—PACKAGE BODY FOR THE PRECEDING SPECIFICATION

```
CREATE OR REPLACE PACKAGE BODY lib_IO
      private global user defined types
   -- private global constants
   -- private global cursors
   -- private global variables
   debug_flag BOOLEAN;
   user_name  VARCHAR(30);    -- application user's login ID
   appl_name  VARCHAR2(30);   -- application currently running
   modl_name  VARCHAR2(30);   -- module (within app) currently running
   context_pt VARCHAR2(30);   -- check-in point within module
   run_date   DATE;           -- when an application was launched
   -- private global subprograms
   -- implementation of exposed subprograms
   -- convert a BOOLEAN to a STRING ('TRUE', 'FALSE', 'NULL')
```

continues

Listing 29.10   Continued

```
FUNCTION bool_to_char(Pbool IN BOOLEAN)
RETURN VARCHAR2 IS
  str VARCHAR2(5);  -- capture string to return
BEGIN
  IF (Pbool) THEN  -- test Boolean value for TRUE
    str := 'TRUE';
  ELSIF (NOT Pbool) THEN  -- FALSE
    str := 'FALSE';
  ELSE  -- must be NULL
    str := 'NULL';
  END IF;  -- test Boolean value
  RETURN (str);
END bool_to_char;
-- convert a STRING to BOOLEAN (TRUE, FALSE, NULL)
FUNCTION char_to_bool(Pstr IN VARCHAR2) RETURN BOOLEAN IS
  Lstr VARCHAR2(32767);  -- max string length
  Lbool BOOLEAN := NULL; -- local Boolean value (default)
BEGIN
  Lstr := UPPER(LTRIM(RTRIM(Pstr)));  -- remove leading/trailing spaces,
uppercase
  IF (Lstr = 'TRUE') THEN
    Lbool := TRUE;
  ELSIF (Lstr = 'FALSE') THEN
    Lbool := FALSE;
  END IF;
  RETURN(Lbool);
END char_to_bool;
-- safe STRING to NUMBER conversion; returns NUMBER or NULL
FUNCTION char_to_number(Pstr IN VARCHAR2, Pformat IN VARCHAR2 DEFAULT NULL)
RETURN NUMBER IS
BEGIN
  IF Pformat IS NULL THEN  -- optional format not supplied
    RETURN (TO_NUMBER(Pstr));
  ELSE
    RETURN (TO_NUMBER(Pstr, Pformat));  -- format supplied
  END IF;  -- test for optional format
EXCEPTION
WHEN OTHERS THEN  -- unknown value
  RETURN (NULL);
END char_to_number;
-- debug flag interface routines
PROCEDURE debug_on IS       -- turns debug on
BEGIN
  debug_flag := TRUE;
END debug_on;
PROCEDURE debug_off IS      -- turns debug off
BEGIN
  debug_flag := FALSE;
END debug_off;
PROCEDURE debug_toggle IS  -- toggles debug on/off
BEGIN
  debug_flag := XOR(debug_flag, TRUE);
END debug_toggle;
FUNCTION  debug_status      -- is debug on/off?
RETURN BOOLEAN IS
```

```
  BEGIN
    RETURN(debug_flag);
  END debug_status;
BEGIN  -- optional package initialization
  DBMS_OUTPUT.enable(1000000);
  debug_flag := FALSE;  -- reset
END lib;
/
```

This object is called the package body in the declaration. The routines are declared just as they would be in an anonymous block. Also, take note that the package body name must be the same as the package header name. Every routine declared in the header must have a corresponding implementation in the package body.

Another thing to watch out for is initializing variables in their declarations. Such initialization is performed only once, when the package is first referenced. This is because these variables are allocated and initialized exactly once and then persist for the duration of the session. I could have reset the debug flag in its declaration and saved a couple of microseconds, but it makes it more explicit and maintainable to do it in the package initialization.

COMPARING PUBLIC AND PRIVATE DECLARATIONS

Any objects declared in the package specification are global in scope. That is, within the present session, any PL/SQL programs can reference and make use of any variables, cursors, and subprograms defined in the specification. In contrast, variables, cursors, and subprograms that are declared only in the package body, although being global to the body itself, are hidden from the outside world. In either case, variables and cursors are persistent. They continue to hold their present values until the package is aged out of memory or the session is terminated.

My recommendation for global variables is that you use them sparingly, if at all. Also, if you hide them in the body, you gain all the benefits of persistence while controlling programmatic access to them. You handle this access by creating globally available subprograms to manipulate them.

The debug interface routines illustrate this standard practice for exposing not a variable itself to the world, but subroutines for manipulating the variable. For example, you don't want the developer modifying and checking the value of the debug_flag variable directly. If the debug flag were public and global, any program could change it with potentially disastrous or at least undesirable results. If, in the future, something needs to be added or changed to the way the Debug feature is implemented, the details are hidden from the developers. This is a common approach in object-oriented programming.

I use very few global variables beyond constants and record variables for various tables. I also like to put the declarations in a standard order, as shown in Listing 29.10. That way, I always know precisely where to look for things.

REFERENCING PACKAGE ELEMENTS

Package contents are referenced by PL/SQL code outside the package using dot notation, as shown in Listing 29.11. Remember, dot notation is required to remove any ambiguity of an object's scope. In order to reference a packaged object, the package name must also be supplied, in the format *package name.package object*. If the code referencing an object is within the same scope, such as within the same package, then the qualifier is unnecessary.

LISTING 29.11   TESTLIB.SQL—TESTING THE EXECUTION OF THE PROPOSED LIBRARY PACKAGE

```
BEGIN
  DBMS_OUTPUT.put_line('DEBUG status is initially: ' ||
                    LIB.bool_to_char(LIB.debug_status));
  LIB.debug_on;
  DBMS_OUTPUT.put_line('DEBUG status is now: ' ||
                    LIB.bool_to_char(LIB.debug_status));
  LIB.debug_off;
  DBMS_OUTPUT.put_line('DEBUG status is now: ' ||
                    LIB.bool_to_char(LIB.debug_status));
  LIB.debug_toggle;
  DBMS_OUTPUT.put_line('DEBUG status is finally: ' ||
                    LIB.bool_to_char(LIB.debug_status));
END;
/
```

To make this a real test, first get completely out of your SQL*Plus session, and then go back in. This will make absolutely sure that your session is truly fresh. Then, SET SERVER-OUTPUT ON, and run the unnamed block shown in Listing 29.11. Notice that this block doesn't enable output; that bit of trivia is performed in the package initialization code. The debug flag, that's value would normally default to NULL, is also reset initially. The server responds with the following:

```
DEBUG status is initially: FALSE
DEBUG status is now: TRUE
DEBUG status is now: FALSE
DEBUG status is finally: TRUE

PL/SQL procedure successfully completed.
Now run it again.
DEBUG status is initially: TRUE
DEBUG status is now: TRUE
DEBUG status is now: FALSE
DEBUG status is finally: TRUE

PL/SQL procedure successfully completed.
```

Notice now that the initial debug flag value is TRUE. The value carried over from one program run to the next. If you reconnect, you effectively have a new session, and the package initialization is performed again. Remember, the code is static in memory, but each user gets a fresh, local set of private variables. Run a second SQL*Plus session and verify this behavior.

ABOUT THE SUPPLIED ORACLE8I DATABASE PACKAGES

Aside from the STANDARD package that gives the Oracle8i Server its basic functionality, such as your basic subtype declarations and data type conversion routines, there is a set of packages intended for use by DBAs and developers. These packages are distinguished by their names, which begin with DBMS_ or UTL_, meaning that they interact with the database or provide general purpose utilities. First, you'll take a quick look at these packages and afterwards examine them more closely.

INTERACTION WITHIN THE SERVER

Most of the Oracle8i supplied packages work on data within the server environment: data dictionary items, user database objects, or objects found solely within the System Global Area, like the shared memory pool. With them, you can manage snapshots, recompile program units, generate asynchronous alerts when database entries change, run jobs, and so on.

Many of these packages interface with functionality built into the database application or extends the database environment with calls to loadable external modules, such as DLLs. It's neither expected nor necessary that you understand or use these module entry points. I'd go so far as to say you're definitely not supposed to try to use them directly, but rather, through the PL/SQL programmatic interface provided.

INTERACTION BEYOND THE SERVER

Some packages give feedback to the calling context or otherwise provide an interface to an external process. The Oracle8i pipe feature, for example, is intended as a method for intersession communication that is strictly memory only—no database objects are used for intermediate storage. As another example, the DBMS_OUTPUT package enables the display of print statements when running PL/SQL programs in SQL*Plus.

GETTING MORE INFORMATION FROM YOUR SERVER

Several packaged routines enable you to obtain additional tuning information about your database server, such as shared memory pool usage, segment space information, running traces, getting general database information, and so on. After you get used to using them, they'll become a standard part of your toolbox

DESCRIBING SUPPLIED PACKAGES

Table 29.2 is a handy, quick reference of some of the important Oracle8i supplied packages and a brief description of what they contain.

TABLE 29.2   SUMMARY OF SUPPLIED PACKAGES

Package Name	Package Header File	Description
DBMS_ALERT	dbmsalrt.sql	Asynchronous handling of database events.
DBMS_APPLICATION_INFO	dbmsutil.sql	Register the name of the application that's currently running (for performance monitoring).
DBMS_AQADM	dbmsaqad.sql	Used with the Advanced Queueing Option.
DBMS_DDL	dbmsutil.sql	Recompile stored subprograms and packages; analyze database objects.
DBMS_DEBUG	dbmspb.sql	Interface to the PL/SQL debugger.
DBMS_DEFER	dbmsdefr.sql	User interface to a remote procedure call facility.
DBMS_DESCRIBE	dbmsdesc.sql	Describe parameters for a stored subprogram.
DBMS_JOB	dbmsjob.sql	Run user-defined jobs at a specified time or interval.
DBMS_LOCK	dbmslock.sql	Manage database locks.
DBMS_OUTPUT	dbmsotpt.sql	Write text lines to a buffer for later retrieval and display.
DBMS_PIPE	dbmspipe.sql	Send and receive data between sessions via a memory "pipe".
DBMS_PROFILER	dbmspbp.sql	Used to profile PL/SQL scripts to identify bottlenecks.
DBMS_REFRESH	dbmssnap.sql	Manage groups of snapshots that can be refreshed together.
DBMS_SESSION	dbmsutil.sql	Perform Alter Session statements programmatically.
DBMS_SHARED_POOL	dbmspool.sql	View and manage the contents of the shared pool.
DBMS_SNAPSHOT	dbmssnap.sql	Refresh, manage snapshots, and purge snapshot logs.
DBMS_SPACE	dbmsutil.sql	Get segment space information.
DBMS_SQL	dbmssql.sql	Perform dynamic SQL and PL/SQL.
DBMS_SYSTEM	dbmsutil.sql	Turn on/off SQL trace for the given session.
DBMS_TRANSACTION	dbmsutil.sql	Manage SQL transactions.

Package Name	Package Header File	Description
DBMS_UTILITY	dbmsutil.sql	Various Utilities: For a given schema, recompile stored subprograms and packages, analyze database objects, format error and call stacks for display, display whether instance is running in parallel server mode, get the current time in 10ms increments, resolve the full name of a database object, convert a PL/SQL table to a comma-delimited string or vv, get a database version/operating system string.
UTL_RAW	utlraw.sql	String functions for RAW data type.
UTL_FILE	utlfile.sql	Read/write ASCII-based operating system files.
UTL_HTTP	utlhttp.sql	Get an HTML-formatted page from a given URL.
DBMS_LOB	dbmslob.sql	Manage Large Objects.

GETTING STARTED WITH THE ORACLE8I-SUPPLIED PACKAGES

In addition to the default packages that come installed with the Oracle8i server, there are many others that come with the optional software that can be installed into the server. The Advanced Queueing option, new for Oracle8i, is an example of that.

Before you can use the routines contained in the Oracle8i-supplied packages, you should first check that they've been installed and are valid. The DBA can run the following query:

```
SELECT object_name, object_type, status
FROM dba_objects
WHERE owner='SYS' AND object_type LIKE 'PACKAGE%'
ORDER BY object_name, object_type;
```

This should give you a list similar to the following:

```
OBJECT NAME                     OBJECT_TYPE   STATUS
------------------------------- ------------- ------
DBMS_ALERT                      PACKAGE       VALID
DBMS_ALERT                      PACKAGE BODY  VALID
DBMS_APPLICATION_INFO           PACKAGE       VALID
DBMS_APPLICATION_INFO           PACKAGE BODY  VALID
DBMS_DDL                        PACKAGE       VALID
DBMS_DDL                        PACKAGE BODY  VALID
DBMS_DESCRIBE                   PACKAGE       VALID
DBMS_DESCRIBE                   PACKAGE BODY  VALID
DBMS_JOB                        PACKAGE       VALID
DBMS_JOB                        PACKAGE BODY  VALID
DBMS_LOCK                       PACKAGE       VALID
DBMS_LOCK                       PACKAGE BODY  VALID
```

```
DBMS_OUTPUT              PACKAGE       VALID
DBMS_OUTPUT              PACKAGE BODY  VALID
DBMS_PIPE                PACKAGE       VALID
DBMS_PIPE                PACKAGE BODY  VALID
DBMS_REFRESH             PACKAGE       VALID
DBMS_REFRESH             PACKAGE BODY  VALID
DBMS_SESSION             PACKAGE       VALID
DBMS_SESSION             PACKAGE BODY  VALID
DBMS_SHARED_POOL         PACKAGE       VALID
DBMS_SHARED_POOL         PACKAGE BODY  VALID
DBMS_SNAPSHOT            PACKAGE       VALID
DBMS_SNAPSHOT            PACKAGE BODY  VALID
DBMS_SPACE               PACKAGE       VALID
DBMS_SPACE               PACKAGE BODY  VALID
DBMS_SQL                 PACKAGE       VALID
DBMS_SQL                 PACKAGE BODY  VALID
DBMS_SYSTEM              PACKAGE       VALID
DBMS_SYSTEM              PACKAGE BODY  VALID
DBMS_TRANSACTION         PACKAGE       VALID
DBMS_TRANSACTION         PACKAGE BODY  VALID
DBMS_UTILITY             PACKAGE       VALID
DBMS_UTILITY             PACKAGE BODY  VALID
```

There will be some other packages not shown above, but don't concern yourself with them here. Most of these additional packages are not intended to be called by user applications, but rather are for internal use only.

LOCATING THE DBMS PACKAGES

The Oracle8i supplied packages are located in %ORACLE_HOME%\RDBMS\ADMIN where ORACLE_HOME is the path to the Oracle Home directory (you can check the system variable of the same name in UNIX or check the Registry entry under Windows NT). You can examine the package header files listed in Table 29.2 for each of these packages to see what routines and global variables are available.

You might also note the existence of files of the form prvt*.sql and prvt*.plb (for example, prvtpipe.sql and prvtpipe.plb). The former are the package bodies for the supplied packages, in ASCII format. The latter are binary compiled versions of the package bodies. The PLB files are recognizable by the PL/SQL engine and result in a valid and executable package body when submitted to the Oracle8i Server. These represent the "release" form of the package bodies.

Caution

Do not attempt to modify the package body of any of the Oracle8i supplied packages for recompilation. You're liable to break something.

MAKING SURE THE PACKAGES ARE INSTALLED CORRECTLY

You'll want to verify two things:

- The packages exist and are valid (as shown by the previous query).
- Users have EXECUTE privilege on them or the ones they intend to use.

A user can check to see if they have the EXECUTE privilege on the Oracle8i supplied packages with the following query:

```
SELECT table_name, grantee
FROM all_tab_privs
WHERE grantor='SYS' and privilege='EXECUTE'
ORDER BY table_name;
```

A typical response might be the following:

```
TABLE_NAME                       GRANTEE
-------------------------------  -------------------------------
DBMS_APPLICATION_INFO            PUBLIC
DBMS_DDL                         PUBLIC
DBMS_DESCRIBE                    PUBLIC
DBMS_JOB                         PUBLIC
DBMS_OUTPUT                      PUBLIC
DBMS_PIPE                        PUBLIC
DBMS_SESSION                     PUBLIC
DBMS_SNAPSHOT                    PUBLIC
DBMS_SPACE                       PUBLIC
DBMS_SQL                         PUBLIC
DBMS_STANDARD                    PUBLIC
DBMS_TRANSACTION                 PUBLIC
DBMS_UTILITY                     PUBLIC
DBMS_REFRESH                     PUBLIC
UTL_FILE                         PUBLIC
```

All the Oracle8i supplied packages should have been granted with EXECUTE to PUBLIC. I used the all_flavor of the data dictionary view to verify this. If any are missing that you intend to use, the DBA can run the appropriate script as SYS. If a package exists but is invalid, the DBA can recompile it with the following:

```
ALTER PACKAGE SYS.<name> COMPILE PACKAGE;
```

name is the name of the invalid package. The clause COMPILE PACKAGE tells Oracle8i to recompile the package specification and body. If just the body needs to be recompiled, instead run the following:

```
ALTER PACKAGE SYS.<name> COMPILE BODY;
```

Tip #92

> Some supplied packages might have dependencies on other packages. If you have to recompile a package header, this invalidates any dependent packages. Check again that other packages are still valid after recompiling. If only the body is recompiled, dependent packages are not invalidated. Any user-written stored subprograms and packages will also likely be affected in this manner.

USING THE ORACLE8I-SUPPLIED PACKAGES

Now it is time for some hands-on work. I'll illustrate some of the more interesting contents of each supplied package with some reasonably simple and useful examples.

MONITORING WITH DBMS_APPLICATION_INFO

This package enables developers to add application tracking information in the views V$sqlarea and V$session. The kind of data that can be tracked is the following:

- A module name (such as the name of the currently running application), a VARCHAR2 string up to 48 bytes, stored in V$sqlarea.module and V$session.module

- The current action (for example, "Update Customer Info," "Verify Credit Limit"), a VARCHAR2 string up to 32 bytes, stored in V$sqlarea.action and V$session.action

- Any client-specific information, a VARCHAR2 string up to 64 bytes, stored in V$session.client_info

Oracle8i doesn't do anything with this information; it's provided for the use of the DBA so she can run statistics against each application and component operations. Strings longer than what's supported are truncated. Listing 29.12 shows a simple example.

LISTING 29.12 APPINFO.SQL—SETTING AND READING APPLICATION INFORMATION

```
DECLARE
  module VARCHAR2(48);   -- application info
  action VARCHAR2(32);
  client VARCHAR2(64);
  ldate  VARCHAR2(30);   -- to capture system date
BEGIN
  DBMS_OUTPUT.enable;
  module := 'CLAIM TRACKING';
  action := 'VERIFY ELIGIBILITY';
  DBMS_APPLICATION_INFO.set_module(module, action);
  DBMS_APPLICATION_INFO.set_client_info(USER);
  DBMS_APPLICATION_INFO.read_module(module, action);
  DBMS_APPLICATION_INFO.read_client_info(client);
  DBMS_OUTPUT.put_line(client || ' is running ' || module || ': ' || action);
  SELECT TO_CHAR(SYSDATE, 'YYYY-MON-DD HH:MI:SS') INTO ldate
  FROM DUAL;
END;
/
```

The response I get is the following:

```
SCOTT is running CLAIM TRACKING: VERIFY ELIGIBILITY
```

While this session is still up, the DBA can check who is doing what with the following:

```
COLUMN module FORMAT A20
COLUMN action FORMAT A20
COLUMN client_info FORMAT A20
SELECT client_info, module, action
FROM V$session
WHERE client_info IS NOT NULL;
```

This gets the following:

```
CLIENT_INFO          MODULE               ACTION
-------------------  -------------------  -------------------
SCOTT                CLAIM TRACKING       VERIFY ELIGIBILITY
```

The DBA can then see the effects of everyone running this module and action with the following:

```
SELECT
  sql_text, SUM(sharable_mem) smem, SUM(persistent_mem) pmem,
  SUM(runtime_mem) rmem, SUM(sorts) sorts, SUM(loads) loads,
  SUM(disk_reads) rdisk, SUM(buffer_gets) bget,
  SUM(rows_processed) prows
FROM V$sqlarea
WHERE module = 'CLAIM TRACKING' AND action = 'VERIFY ELIGIBILITY'
GROUP BY sql_text;
```

The results are pretty interesting:

```
SQL_TEXT
--------------------------------------------------------------------------------
     SMEM      PMEM      RMEM     SORTS     LOADS     RDISK      BGET     PROWS
--------- --------- --------- --------- --------- --------- --------- ---------
SELECT TO_CHAR(SYSDATE,'YYYY-MON-DD HH:MI:SS')     FROM DUAL
     4267       508       792         0         1         0         4         2

SELECT USER    FROM SYS.DUAL
     3596       508       688         0         1         0         4         1

begin dbms_output.get_lines(:lines, :numlines); end;
     4317       592       420         0         1         0         0         1
```

The only query I explicitly made was the first one, but SQL*Plus apparently does some work behind the scenes.

As a module performs different actions, the developers should make the appropriate calls to set_action() to reflect this. In this manner, you can collect some interesting statistics on how badly an application is battering the server by query, by action, by module, by user, or by groups of users.

> **Note**
>
> Even after a user disconnects, entries still exist in V$sqlarea until the related SQL gets aged out of the SGA.

RECOMPILING PACKAGES WITH DBMS_DDL

There are two things you can do with this package:

- Recompile stored subprograms and packages with alter_compile().
- Analyze a table, index, or cluster with analyze_object().

A simple use for alter_compile() would be to find what stored program objects are invalid and then recompile them. Listing 29.13 illustrates this.

LISTING 29.13   `RECOMPIL.SQL`—RECOMPILE INVALID PROGRAM OBJECTS ONLY

```
-- recompile invalid stored program objects
-- CAVEAT: does not take package dependencies
--         into account!
DECLARE
  CURSOR invalid_prog_obj IS
    SELECT object_name, object_type
    FROM user_objects
    WHERE status = 'INVALID';
  rec invalid_prog_obj%ROWTYPE;
  status NUMERIC;
BEGIN
  DBMS_OUTPUT.enable;
  OPEN invalid_prog_obj;
  LOOP  -- recompile each stored program object
    FETCH invalid_prog_obj INTO rec;
    EXIT WHEN invalid_prog_obj%NOTFOUND;
    DBMS_OUTPUT.put('Recompile ' || rec.object_type ||
                            ' ' || rec.object_name);
    DBMS_DDL.alter_compile(rec.object_type, NULL, rec.object_name);
    DBMS_OUTPUT.put_line(' SUCCESSFUL');  -- recompile succeeded
  END LOOP;  -- invalid program objects
  CLOSE invalid_prog_obj;
EXCEPTION
WHEN OTHERS THEN
  BEGIN
    status := SQLCODE;
    DBMS_OUTPUT.put_line(' FAILED with ' || SQLERRM(status));
    IF (invalid_prog_obj%ISOPEN) THEN
      CLOSE invalid_prog_obj;
    END IF;
  EXCEPTION WHEN OTHERS THEN
    NULL;  -- do nothing
  END;
END;
/
```

This might return something similar to the following:

```
Recompile FUNCTION TABLE_EXISTS SUCCESSFUL
1 Program Objects Recompiled
PL/SQL procedure successfully completed.
```

Caution

If a program object fails to recompile successfully, `alter_compile` will *not* tell you! After running `alter_compile`, you should check the status of the package to make sure it compiled successfully.

If you provide a program object name that doesn't exist or you have the type wrong, you get the following:

```
ORA-20000: Unable to compile PACKAGE "BLICK", insufficient privileges or does not
exist
```

You can programmatically analyze (generate statistics) for tables, indexes, and clusters. For example, you could analyze all or selected objects in your schema, as shown in Listing 29.14.

LISTING 29.14 runstats.sql—RUNNING STATISTICS PROGRAMMATICALLY

```
-- analyze all tables, indexes and clusters in your own schema
-- computes exact statistics
SET ECHO OFF
ACCEPT method PROMPT 'ANALYZE Method ([COMPUTE]¦ESTIMATE¦DELETE): '
ACCEPT estrow PROMPT '  IF ANALYZE Method is ESTIMATE, #Rows (0-n) [100]: '
ACCEPT estpct PROMPT '  IF ANALYZE Method is ESTIMATE, %Rows (0-99) [20]: '
DECLARE
  -- application-defined exceptions
  bad_method EXCEPTION;  -- user entered an invalid method
  bad_estrow EXCEPTION;  -- user entered an invalid est. #rows
  bad_estpct EXCEPTION;  -- user entered an invalid est. %rows
  -- cursors
  CURSOR analyze_obj IS
    SELECT object_name, object_type
    FROM user_objects
    WHERE object_type = ANY ('TABLE', 'INDEX', 'CLUSTER');
  -- constants
  METHOD CONSTANT VARCHAR2(30) := NVL(UPPER('&&method'), 'COMPUTE');
  -- variables
  estrow NUMBER := NVL('&&estrow', '100');  -- user input est. #rows
  estpct NUMBER := NVL('&&estpct',  '20');  -- user input est. pct
  rec analyze_obj%ROWTYPE;
  status NUMERIC := 0;
  cnt NUMERIC := 0;
BEGIN
  DBMS_OUTPUT.enable;
  -- validate user input
  IF (METHOD NOT IN ('COMPUTE', 'ESTIMATE', 'DELETE')) THEN
    RAISE bad_method;
  ELSIF (METHOD IN ('COMPUTE', 'DELETE')) THEN  -- ignore est. #/%row
    estrow := NULL;
    estpct := NULL;
  ELSE -- picked ESTIMATE; must provide either est. #rows or %rows
    IF (estrow < 1 AND estpct = 0) THEN
      RAISE bad_estrow;
    ELSIF (estpct NOT BETWEEN 1 AND 99) THEN
      RAISE bad_estpct;
    END IF;
  END IF;  -- validate input
  OPEN analyze_obj;
  LOOP        -- analyze schema objects
    FETCH analyze_obj INTO rec;
    EXIT WHEN analyze_obj%NOTFOUND;
    -- COMPUTE STATISTICS for this schema only
    DBMS_OUTPUT.put('Analyze ' || METHOD || ' ' ||
                    rec.object_type || ' ' || rec.object_name);
    DBMS_DDL.analyze_object(rec.object_type, NULL, rec.object_name, 'COMPUTE');
    DBMS_OUTPUT.put_line(' SUCCESSFUL');
    cnt := cnt + 1;
  END LOOP;  -- analyze schema objects
  CLOSE analyze_obj;
```

continues

LISTING 29.14 CONTINUED

```
    DBMS_OUTPUT.put_line(TO_CHAR(cnt) || ' objects analyzed');
EXCEPTION
WHEN bad_method THEN
  DBMS_OUTPUT.put_line('Invalid Method! Must be COMPUTE, ESTIMATE or DELETE
only');
WHEN bad_estrow THEN
  DBMS_OUTPUT.put_line('Invalid Est. #Rows! Must be >= 1');
WHEN bad_estpct THEN
  DBMS_OUTPUT.put_line('Invalid Est. %Rows! Must be between 1 and 99');
WHEN OTHERS THEN
  BEGIN
    status := SQLCODE;
    DBMS_OUTPUT.put_line(' FAILED with ' || SQLERRM(status));
    IF (analyze_obj%ISOPEN) THEN
      CLOSE analyze_obj;
    END IF;
  EXCEPTION WHEN OTHERS THEN
    NULL;
  END;
END;
/
```

Note all the input validation you have to do. Partly, this is because `analyze_object` does very little of its own. If you provide a row estimate along with the COMPUTE method, for instance, you get the following:

```
Analyze TABLE <table> FAILED with ORA-01490: invalid ANALYZE command.
```

When I compute statistics by picking all the defaults, my run looks like this:

```
ANALYZE Method ([COMPUTE]|ESTIMATE|DELETE):
  IF ANALYZE Method is ESTIMATE, #Rows (1-n)   [1]:
  IF ANALYZE Method is ESTIMATE, %Rows (1-99) [20]:
old  12:    METHOD CONSTANT VARCHAR2(30) := NVL(UPPER('&&method'), 'COMPUTE');
new  12:    METHOD CONSTANT VARCHAR2(30) := NVL(UPPER(''), 'COMPUTE');
old  14:    estrow NUMBER := NVL('&&estrow', '1');          -- user input est.
#rows
new  14:    estrow NUMBER := NVL('', '1');           -- user input est. #rows
old  15:    estpct NUMBER := NVL(TRUNC('&&estpct'), '20');  -- user input est. pct
new  15:    estpct NUMBER := NVL(TRUNC(''), '20');  -- user input est. pct
Analyze COMPUTE TABLE BONUS SUCCESSFUL
Analyze COMPUTE TABLE DEPT SUCCESSFUL
Analyze COMPUTE TABLE EMP SUCCESSFUL
Analyze COMPUTE INDEX PK_DEPT SUCCESSFUL
Analyze COMPUTE INDEX PK_EMP SUCCESSFUL
Analyze COMPUTE TABLE SALGRADE SUCCESSFUL
6 objects analyzed
PL/SQL procedure successfully completed.
```

If you enter in an invalid method, it complains as follows:

```
Invalid Method! Must be COMPUTE, ESTIMATE or DELETE only
```

This is as you desired. Play around with it and see how you like it.

This implementation of the ANALYZE command doesn't do VALID STRUCTURE or LIST CHAINED ROWS. In this respect, it's an incomplete implementation, but it's still pretty useful.

FORMATTING OUTPUT WITH DBMS_OUTPUT

If you've been following along since the tutorial, you're already familiar with the put_line procedure in this package. Here are some details regarding the implementation of the package:

- Each line is terminated with a newline character.
- Each line can only be up to 255 bytes, including the newline character.
- Each line is stored in a private PL/SQL table.
- Nothing is stored unless DBMS_OUTPUT.ENABLE is first called.
- The buffer size specified must be in the range 2,000 to 1,000,000.

You use the procedure enable to turn on the output feature. Put_line calls are ignored if output hasn't first been enabled. When you enable output, you can also specify a buffer size, as with the following:

```
DBMS_OUTPUT.enable(1000000);   -- 1 million bytes is the max
```

Conversely, you can turn output back off with disable, as follows:

```
DBMS_OUTPUT.disable;   -- turn off output
```

You can store a line of text with put_line. It's overloaded to take a DATE, NUMBER, or VARCHAR2. You can also store a line of text without terminating it by using the put procedure (which is overloaded in like manner). This is useful if the line you're building requires some logic, as in the following example:

```
-- excerpt taken from Package rev_eng
IF (Ltable IS NULL) THEN  -- parameter comments
  DBMS_OUTPUT.put('-- ALL TABLES');
ELSE
  DBMS_OUTPUT.put('-- TABLE ' || Ltable);
END IF;
DBMS_OUTPUT.put_line(' FOR OWNER ' || Lowner ||
                     ', TABLESPACE ' || Ltspace);
```

You can terminate text submitted with put by using the new_line procedure. This signals the end of the current line of text with a marker and also stores the length of the text line along with the text (this is completely transparent to the user). Note that if you try to double- or triple-space output lines by sending new lines without first using put, it doesn't work:

```
BEGIN
  DBMS_OUTPUT.put('Hey, ');
  DBMS_OUTPUT.put('Dan!');
  DBMS_OUTPUT.new_line;
  DBMS_OUTPUT.new_line;
  DBMS_OUTPUT.put_line('Time to go to the library!');
end;
/
```

This gives you the following:

```
Hey, Dan!
Time to go to the library!
PL/SQL procedure successfully completed.
```

Please note that it did not print out double-spaced.

You'll get an exception if you attempt to output a string longer than the acceptable 255 bytes before ending it with new_line:

```
ORA-20000: ORU-10028: line length overflow, limit of 255 bytes per line.
```

Why did the folks at Oracle limit the string length to 255? Look back to the example where a PL/SQL table of VARCHAR2 (32767) quickly exhausted available memory (Chapter 28, "PL/SQL Fundamentals," Listing 28.10). In other words, they picked what they considered a reasonable limit.

Strings are returned with get_line. This is what SQL*Plus does to return the strings written with put_line. Unseen, it calls get_line until no more lines are available. You really only need concern yourself with get_line (and its multiple line version, get_lines) if you're writing a 3GL program to receive lines stored with put_line. You can use it in a PL/SQL program if you want, such as to buffer lines and then access them in FIFO manner, perhaps to insert them into a table.

What's the buffer size for? After all, a PL/SQL table can have over four billion elements! Imagine you're writing a C program to receive buffered strings via get_line. It would really be a waste (and not a good idea) to allocate a chunk of memory 4.29 billion×255 bytes. You would need a terabyte of memory! Memory's cheap nowadays, but not that cheap. Instead, you ask the user to specify the buffer size between, say, 2K and 1MB, and that's what you allocate. The package tracks the buffer space usage because your C program expects no more data than what the user specified. Then, you pack the lines returned into this memory area, wasting little or no space. Finally, all the lines are now available to display to the user. This might not seem like a particularly sophisticated scheme, but it's simple and it works.

If you exceed the buffer space size you specified, you'll get the following exception:

```
ORA-20000: ORU-10027: buffer overflow, limit of <buf_limit> bytes.
```

SUMMARY

In this chapter, you learned a wealth of information on how to write your own stored procedures and packages, as well as how to use the packages supplied with the database server. You learned how to debug your stored programs with the SHOW ERRORS command, and you even wrote a script to enhance the output of that command. Lastly, you learned how to check the validity of a stored procedure, and how to recompile one should it become invalid. You should now be able to take the PL/SQL examples in this chapter and be able to enhance them with your own customizations or create new procedures of your own design.

Using Import/Export

In this chapter

Understanding the Purpose and Capabilities of Import/Export

The Oracle8.x Server comes with two important utilities: Import and Export. These two utilities are useful for many important database functions such as backing up data, copying objects among different schemas and databases, and generating object creation scripts. They are also useful in migrating from one version of Oracle to another, and can be used to upgrade your database to Oracle8.x.

The Import and Export utilities provide a wide range of capabilities. The main purpose is to back up and recover data and objects. The objects and data are stored in a binary form that can be read only by Oracle databases. Export and Import can perform the following tasks:

- Back up and recover your databases—Export and Import are frequently used as part of a backup plan. Typically, full or hot backups are used to back up the entire database in the event of a disk or computer failure. However, if just one table in the entire database needs to be recovered, the entire database would have to be recovered on another machine, and the one table would be copied over. This is incredibly time and resource consuming. Import and Export can save you this hassle by providing the capability to export the entire database and import just the tables you need recovered. They can also serve as a backup and recovery mechanism for the entire database, as Point-in-time Recovery is also an option.

- Move data and objects among schemas—You can use import and Export to copy tables, indexes, grants, procedures, and views, among all other object types, from one schema to another. This helps save time and effort because you can just specify those objects you desire to move. Also, moving data can be used as a form of data replication among different Oracle databases.

- Migrate databases from one Oracle version to another—You can upgrade (or downgrade) the version of Oracle by using the Import and Export utilities. You can export an entire Oracle7 database, for example. Then, providing you have the Oracle8 Server installed, the database can be imported, making the data and application function in an Oracle8 environment. This process is called *migration*.

- Defragment a tablespace or the entire database—Fragmentation occurs when objects such as tables and indexes are created, deleted, enlarged, and reduced in size over time. Fragmentation also occurs when object storage parameters are poorly defined. By exporting a tablespace, coalescing space, and importing objects again, you can defragment tablespaces.

- Generate CREATE scripts—You can also use Import and Export to generate CREATE scripts for tables, partitions, views, grants, indexes, constraints, and tablespaces, among all other objects in the database. This proves quite useful for modifying objects and safeguarding the structure of your objects in the event one gets corrupted or deleted.

■ Writing to multiple files in Export—Export supports writing to multiple export files, and Import can read from multiple export files. If, on exporting, you specify a value (byte limit) for the Export FILESIZE parameter, Export will write only the number of bytes you specify to each dump file. On Import, you must use the Import parameter FILESIZE to tell Import the maximum dump file size you specified on Export.

The FILESIZE parameter has a maximum value equal to the maximum value that can be stored in 64 bits.

PART

VI

CH

30

> **Note**
>
> The maximum value that can be stored in 64 bits is dependent on which operating system (OS) you use. You should verify this maximum value in your OS-specific documentation before specifying FILESIZE.

The FILESIZE value can be specified as a number followed by K (number of kilobytes). For example, FILESIZE=2K is the same as FILESIZE=2048. Similarly, M specifies megabytes (1024 × 1024), whereas G specifies gigabytes (1024×1024 ×1024). B remains the shorthand for bytes; the number is not multiplied to get the final file size (FILESIZE=2048b is the same as FILESIZE=2048).

■ Oracle8i enables fine-grained access support—You can export tables with fine-grain access policies enabled. Note, however, to restore the policies, the user who imports from an export file containing such tables must have the appropriate privileges (specifically execute privilege on the DBMS_RLS package so that the tables' security policies can be reinstated). If a user without the correct privileges attempts to import from an export file that contains tables with fine-grain access policies, a warning message will be issued. Therefore, it is advisable for security reasons that the exporter/importer of such tables be the DBA.

■ Oracle8i enables Partition-Level Import—You can import tables, partitions, and subpartitions in the following ways:

• Table-level Import—Imports all data from the specified tables in an Export file.

• Partition-level Import—Imports only data from the specified source partitions or subpartitions. You must set the parameter IGNORE = Y when loading data into an existing table. For information on the parameter IGNORE, see the IGNORE entry later this chapter in the parameters table in the section "Controlling and Configuring Import and Export."

• Oracle8i enables exporting a partial table—Select a subset of rows from a table when doing a table mode export. The value of the query parameter is a string that contains a WHERE clause for a SQL SELECT statement which will be applied to all tables (or table partitions) listed in the TABLE parameter.

For example, if user SCOTT wants to export only those employees in department 10, he could do the following (note that this example is UNIX-based):

```
exp scott/tiger tables=emp query='"where deptno=10"'
```

Note that the value of the QUERY parameter is a quoted string. The use of the single and double quotes at the beginning and end of the string is UNIX-specific. Please see your OS-specific documentation for information about how to pass quoted strings in a command line. When executing this command, Export builds a SELECT statement similar to this:

```
SELECT * FROM EMP where deptno=10;
```

The QUERY is applied to all tables (or table partitions) listed in the TABLE parameter. So, for example,

```
exp scott/tiger tables=emp,dept query='"where deptno=10"'
```

will unload rows in both EMP and DEPT that match the query. Again, the SQL statements that Export executes are similar to these:

```
SELECT * FROM EMP where deptno=10;
SELECT * FROM DEPT where deptno=10;
```

Note

The export file is in a binary format that can only be used with Oracle databases. You cannot export from Oracle and import into a non-Oracle database. Similarly, you cannot import from a non-Oracle database. If you want to copy data to Oracle from another database product such as Microsoft Access, you should use SQL*Loader on a delimited file format of the data, such as CSV (comma-separated values). To transfer data from Oracle to a non-Oracle database, using Oracle tools, you must make a delimited file manually by spooling from within PL/SQL or SQL*Plus.

UNDERSTANDING BEHAVIOR

There are three types of exports:

- FULL export—Exports all objects, structures, and data within the database
- OWNER export—Exports only those objects owned by a particular user account
- TABLE export—Exports only the specified tables and partitions

With dozens of types of structures that can be exported, it is important to distinguish what gets exported with each of the three export categories. Table 30.1 shows which structures are exported with each export option (in the order that Export exports). The following section then describes the syntax of running the exp and imp executables for export and import with Oracle8.

> **Note**
>
> On a Windows NT and UNIX environment, `exp` and `imp` are the commands for the Export and Import utilities.

TABLE 30.1   THE THREE EXPORT OPTIONS AND THEIR OBJECTS

Object/Schema	with FULL=Y option	with OWNER option	with TABLE option
Tablespace	All objects definitions		
Profiles	All objects		
User	All objects definitions		
Roles	All objects		
Resource costs	All objects		
Rollback segment	All objects definitions		
Database links	All objects	Just for owner	
Sequence	All objects numbers	Just for owner	
Directory	All objects aliases		
Foreign function	All objects	Just for owner library names	
Object type	All objects definitions	Just for owner	
Cluster	All objects definitions	Just for owner	Just for table and owner
Tables	All objects	Just for owner	Just for table and owner
Indexes	All objects	Just for owner	Just for table and owner
Referential integrity constraints	all objects	Just for owner	Just for table and owner
Postable actions	All objects	Just for owner	
Synonyms	All objects	Just for owner	Just for table and owner
Views	All objects	Just for owner	
Stored procedures	All objects	Just for owner	
Triggers	All objects	Just for owner	Just for table and owner
Snapshots	All objects	Just for owner	
Snapshot logs	All objects	Just for owner	
Job queues	All objects	Just for owner	
Refresh groups and children	All objects	Just for owner	
User history table	All objects		
Default and system auditing options	All objects		

Caution

> ROWIDs are re-assigned during an import. If a table has a column with ROWID information, the data will become obsolete. Also, ROWID snapshots become obsolete after an import and must be refreshed with the COMPLETE option before they can be automatically refreshed again. In addition, some REF attributes might contain ROWID information, so the REFs might become obsolete during an Import session. To re-create the REF information with proper ROWIDs after importing the data, issue the ANALYZE TABLE owner.table_name VALIDATE REF UPDATE; command.

CONTROLLING AND CONFIGURING IMPORT AND EXPORT

The Import and Export utilities—with the availability of dozens of parameters that can be passed—are extremely flexible. Also, there are two methods of running Import and Export: Interactive mode and Non-interactive mode. With the Interactive mode, you are stepped through a series of prompts to enter the basic information for an import and export session. This method is less flexible; you are prompted for only a few of the dozens of available parameters.

To export with the Interactive mode, just enter **exp** at the command line. You are then prompted for a username and password.

Caution

> To export the entire database, the user account that you export with must have been granted the EXP_FULL_DATABASE system privilege. For accounts with DBA privileges, such as SYSTEM, this privilege is implicitly granted to the user. Otherwise, the export will fail.

Next, you receive a prompt for the *array fetch buffer size*. This is the size of the memory buffer through which rows are exported. This should be larger than the size of the largest record multiplied by the number of rows that you want to fit in the buffer. This size is OS-dependent.

You then receive a prompt for the name of the export file. By default, it is expdat.dmp. Next, a small menu with three options appears:

- If you select Option 1, E(ntire database), you receive a prompt to enter values for grants (Y/N), table data (Y/N), and compress extents (Y/N).
- If you select Option 2, U(sers), you receive a prompt to enter values for grants (Y/N), table data (Y/N), compress extents (Y/N), and user(s) to be exported (keep entering until done, and then enter a single period on the line to finish).
- If you select Option 3, T(ables), you receive a prompt to enter values for export table data (Y/N), compress extents (Y/N), and Table (T) or Partition (T:P) to be exported (keep entering until done, and then enter a single period on the line to finish).

To export in Non-interactive mode, you can either pass all parameters at the command line or through a parameter file. For all possible parameters of the export command, type **exp HELP=Y** in Windows NT, as shown in Figure 30.1.

Figure 30.1
Sample result of "exp HELP=Y", on a Windows NT environment.

You can use 23 parameters during an export session. You can either specify them in the command line or any parameter file that is specified. Table 30.2 describes all the export parameters.

TABLE 30.2   DESCRIPTION OF EXPORT UTILITY PARAMETERS

Parameter	Default Value	Description
BUFFER	OS-Dependent	The size of BUFFER (in bytes) determines the memory buffer through which rows are exported. This should be larger than the size of the largest record multiplied by the number of rows that you want to fit within the buffer.
COMPRESS	Y	If COMPRESS=Y, the INITIAL storage parameter will be set to the total size of all extents allocated for the object. The change takes effect only when the object is imported.

continues

TABLE 30.2 CONTINUED

Parameter	Default Value	Description
CONSISTENT	N	Setting CONSISTENT=Y exports all tables and references in a consistent state. This slows the export because rollback space is used. If CONSISTENT=N, which is the default, and a record is modified during the export, the data becomes inconsistent.
CONSTRAINTS	N	Specifies whether table constraints are exported.
DIRECT	N	If DIRECT=Y, Oracle bypasses the SQL command processing layer, improving the speed of the export. Unfortunately, the new object types common to Oracle8, such as LOBs, will not get exported.
FEEDBACK	0	Oracle displays a period for each group of records inserted. The size of the group is defined by FEEDBACK. By setting FEEDBACK=1000, for example, a period displays for every 1000 records imported. This parameter is useful for tracking the progress of large imports.
FILE	expdat.dmp	By default, expdat.dmp (which stands for export data.dump) will be the name of the file. For a more meaningful filename, change the FILE parameter.
FULL	N	The entire database will be exported if FULL=Y, including tablespace definitions.
FILESIZE		Maximum size of each dump file.
GRANTS	Y	Specifies whether all grant definitions will be exported for the objects being exported.
HELP	N	No other parameters are needed if you specify HELP=Y. A basic help screen displays.
INCTYPE		The valid options for the INCTYPE parameter are COMPLETE, CUMULATIVE, and INCREMENTAL. A COMPLETE export lays down a full export on which the other two options rely for restores of the database. CUMULATIVE exports all tables and other objects that have changed since the last CUMULATIVE or COMPLETE export was taken. If one record in a table has been altered, the entire table is exported. INCREMENTAL exports all tables and objects that have changed since the last INCREMENTAL, CUMULATIVE, or COMPLETE export.

Parameter	Default Value	Description
INDEXES	Y	Specifies whether user-defined indexes are exported. System indexes created with constraints (primary key, unique key), and OID indexes are automatically exported, regardless of the value of the INDEXES parameter.
LOG		The LOG parameter specifies the name of the file to spool the feedback from the export session. Unless otherwise specified, Oracle appends a .LOG extension to the file.
PARFILE		Instead of entering all parameters on the command line, some or all can be kept in a parameter file. The PARFILE parameter specifies which file to use, if desired. This parameter is especially useful for non-interactive import sessions.
POINT_IN_	N	Exports information for a Point-in-time Recovery TIME_RECOVER for the tablespace listed with the TABLESPACES parameter.
QUERY		WHERE clause used to export a subset of a table
RECORD	Y	If using the INCTYPE parameter with RECORD=Y, the SYS data dictionary tables INCEXP, INCFIL, and INCVID are populated with export data such as owner, type of export, and the time of export.
RECORD_LENGTH	OS-Dependent	The RECORDLENGTH parameter is used only when you will import on a machine with a byte count of the file different from on the machine where the export occurs. In most import sessions, the default should be used.
RECOVERY_TABLESPACES		The RECOVERY_TABLESPACES, used in conjunction with the POINT_IN_TIME_RECOVER parameter, specifies which tablespaces can be recovered using Point-in-time Recovery. This is important because imports could not otherwise recover transactions past the time of export.
ROWS	Y	Specifies whether table and object data will be exported. If ROWS=N, only object definitions are exported.
STATISTICS	ESTIMATE	Specifies whether table and index statistics are to be analyzed with COMPUTE or ESTIMATE when imported. Note that only those objects that already have statistics on them will be analyzed during import. Specify NONE if no objects should be analyzed.

continues

PART

VI

CH

30

TABLE 30.2 CONTINUED

Parameter	Default Value	Description
TABLES		Specifies a comma-separated list of all tables to be exported. This parameter should be used in conjunction with the FROMUSER parameter. In a non-UNIX environment, such as Windows NT, you must enclose the table list within parentheses.
TABLESPACES		List of tablespaces to be exported with the POINT_IN_TIME_RECOVER parameter.
USERID		Specifies the username and password of the user conducting the import. The format for the command is *username/password*. You can also use Net8's *@connect_string* format if desired.
VOLSIZE		Number of bytes to write to each tape volume. VOLSIZE specifies the maximum number of bytes in an export file on each volume of tape. The VOLSIZE parameter has a maximum value equal to the maximum value that can be stored in 64 bits.

To use Import with the Interactive mode, just enter **imp** *at the command line. You then receive a prompt for a username and password.*

Caution

> To use Import from a DBA-invoked export, the user account that you import with must have been granted the IMP_FULL_DATABASE system privilege. For accounts with DBA privileges, such as SYSTEM, this privilege is implicitly granted to the user. Otherwise, the import will fail.

You then receive a prompt for the name of the export file from which to import. By default, it is expdat.dmp. Next, you receive a prompt for the array fetch buffer size. This is the size of the memory buffer through which rows are exported.

Next, you are asked whether you want to list the contents of the import file only (Yes/No). The results if you select Yes are described later in this chapter in the section titled "Using the SHOW and INDEXFILE Options." If you select No, you are asked whether to ignore all create errors that might occur due to object existence (Yes/No).

Then, you are asked whether to import grants, table data, and the entire export file. If you select No to import the entire export file, you receive a prompt for the username corresponding to the owner of the objects. This is followed by a repeating prompt to enter all tables and partitions. If you leave the line blank, all objects for the username are assumed. To stop the repeating prompt, enter a single period at the prompt.

To use Import in Non-interactive mode, you can either pass all parameters at the command line or through a parameter file. Type **"imp HELP=Y"** for all possible parameters of the import command, as shown in Figure 30.2.

Figure 30.2
Sample output from "imp HELP=Y" on a Windows NT platform.

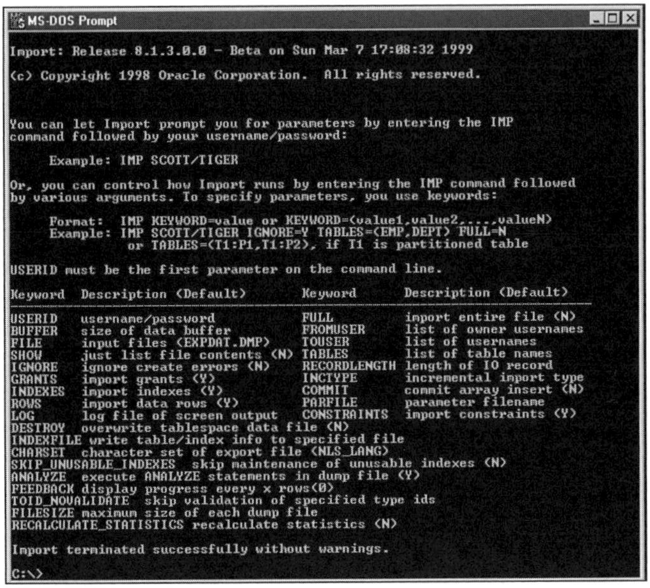

PART

VI

CH

30

You can use 27 parameters during an import session. You can specify them in either the command line or any parameter file that is specified. Table 30.3 describes all the export parameters.

TABLE 30.3   DESCRIPTION OF THE IMPORT UTILITY PARAMETERS

Parameter	Default Value	Description
ANALYZE	Y	Tables that are imported will have their statistics analyzed if ANALYZE is set to Y. Note that only those tables that already had statistics on them during the export will be computed. The tables will be ESTIMATED by default unless the export was performed with the STATISTICS=COMPUTE parameter configuration.
BUFFER	OS-Dependent	The size of BUFFER (in bytes) determines the memory buffer through which rows are imported. This should be larger than the size of the largest record multiplied by the number of rows that you want to fit within the buffer.

continues

TABLE 30.3   CONTINUED

Parameter	Default Value	Description
CHARSET		The CHARSET is an obsolete Oracle6 parameter, indicating whether the export was done in ASCII or EBCDIC. In Oracle7 and Oracle8, this information is processed automatically.
COMMIT	N	By default, a commit occurs after each table, nested table, and partition. If you are importing a large table, the rollback segments might grow large. To improve performance when loading large tables, you should set COMMIT=Y.
DESTROY	N	If you set DESTROY=Y and do a full import, Oracle overwrites any datafiles that exist. If you use raw devices for your datafiles, they will be overwritten during a full import because DESTROY=N does not prevent the overwriting of datafiles! It is always a good practice to back up the database before such an import. Do not use this option unless you know what you are doing.
FEEDBACK	0	Oracle displays a period for each group of records inserted. The size of the group is defined by FEEDBACK. By setting FEEDBACK=1000, for example, a period displays for every 1000 records imported. This parameter is useful for tracking the progress of large imports.
FILE	expdat.dmp	By default, expdat.dmp (which stands for Export Data.Dump) is the name of the file that import will import from. If the file is something other than expdat.dmp, specify it with the FILE parameter.
FILESIZE		Maximum size of each dump file –if importing from multiple files.
FROMUSER		Specifying this parameter imports only those objects owned by the FROMUSER user account.
FULL	N	The entire database will be imported if FULL=Y.
GRANTS	Y	Specifies whether all grants will be created for the objects that were exported.
HELP	N	No other parameters are needed if you specify HELP=Y. A basic help screen displays.

Parameter	Default Value	Description
IGNORE	N	If IGNORE=Y, object creation errors are ignored, and records are inserted into the table. Be aware that duplicate records might result if no unique constraints exist for the table. Note that non-object creation errors will still be reported, such as OS problems.
INCTYPE		If importing an incremental export, tables are dropped and re-created. You must first restore from the last SYSTEM export (specify INCTYPE=SYSTEM). Then, import every incremental export (specify INCTYPE=RESTORE) until the desired changes are applied to the database.
INDEXES	Y	Specifies whether user-defined indexes are imported. System indexes created with constraints (primary key, unique key) and OID indexes are automatically imported, regardless of the value of the INDEXES parameter.
INDEXFILE		The INDEXFILE parameter specifies the name of the file to generate CREATE INDEX statements. Unless otherwise specified, Oracle appends a .SQL extension to the file. You can find the INDEXFILE parameter described in more detail later in this chapter.
LOG		The LOG parameter specifies the name of the file to spool the feedback from the import session. Unless otherwise specified, Oracle appends a .LOG extension to the file.
PARFILE		Instead of entering all parameters on the command line, some or all can be kept in a parameter file. The PARFILE parameter specifies which file to use, if desired. This parameter is especially useful for non-interactive import sessions.
POINT_IN_TIME	N	Performs a Point-in-time Recovery for the tablespace RECOVER exported with the TABLESPACES parameter
RECORDLENGTH	OS-Dependent	The RECORDLENGTH parameter is used only when importing on a machine with a byte count of the file different from on the machine where the export occurred. In most import sessions, the default should be used.

continues

Table 30.3 Continued

Parameter	Default Value	Description
RECALCULATE_STATISTICS	N	Recalculate statistics, which are used by cost based optimizer
SHOW	N	The SHOW parameter displays each SQL statement to the screen and does not modify the database. When used with the FILE parameter, the SQL statements can be viewed and modified. You can find a more detailed description of the SHOW parameter later in this chapter in the section, "Using the SHOW and INDEXFILE Options."
SKIP_UNUSABLE_INDEX	N	The SKIP_UNUSABLE_INDEXES enables you to postpone index INDEXES creation until the record data has been imported. The indexes affected are only those set to an unusable state; all other indexes will be created if INDEXES=Y (which is the default value).
TABLES		Specifies a comma-separated list of all tables to be imported. This parameter should be used in conjunction with the FROMUSER parameter. In a non-UNIX environment, such as Windows NT, you must enclose the table list within parentheses.
TOUSER		The TOUSER parameter specifies the user account into which tables should be imported, if it is desired to be different from the original owner of the tables. This parameter needs to be used in conjunction with the FROMUSER parameter.
TOID_NOVALIDATE		When you import a table that references a type, but a type of that name already exists in the database, Import attempts to verify that the pre-existing type is in fact the type used by the table (rather than a different type that just happens to have the same name). To do this, Import compares the type's unique identifier (TOID) with the identifier stored in the export file and will not import the table rows if the TOIDs do not match. In some situations, you might not want this validation to occur on specified types (for example, if the types were created by a cartridge installation). You can use the TOID_NOVALIDATE parameter to specify types to exclude from TOID comparison.
USERID		Specifies the username and password for the user conducting the import. The format for the command is *username/password*. You can also use Net8's *@connect_string* format if desired.

TAKING WALKTHROUGHS OF IMPORT AND EXPORT SESSIONS

This section steps you through several walkthroughs of Import and Export sessions. These walkthroughs demonstrate some of the powerful features of the two utilities and point out some pitfalls that you should avoid.

IDENTIFYING BEHAVIOR WHEN A TABLE EXISTS

If an import is started that attempts to import a table that already exists in the database, an error occurs. Import skips the table (along with the foreign keys and indexes on that table) and proceeds with the import process, importing all other specified tables and objects, as shown in Figure 30.3.

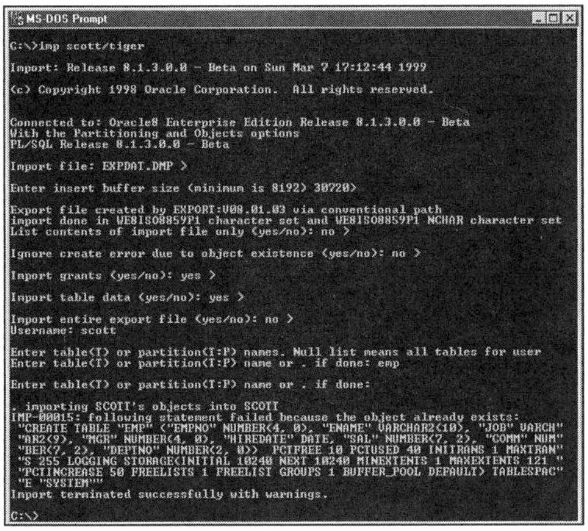

Figure 30.3
Errors resulting from importing a table that already exists in the database.

If you want to import data into a table that already exists, use the IGNORE=Y parameter specification. This causes the data to be appended into the table. If there is a constraint violation, such as duplicate records based on the primary key, those rows that violate the constraint are not loaded. The existence of constraints is helpful in preventing the loading of duplicate records in a table.

Assume, for example, that the EMPLOYEE table, owned by the DEMO user account, has records in the table. An import is started that attempts to load a duplicate record into the table. Figure 30.4 shows the result.

Figure 30.4
Example of attempting to load duplicate records against a table with a unique constraint.

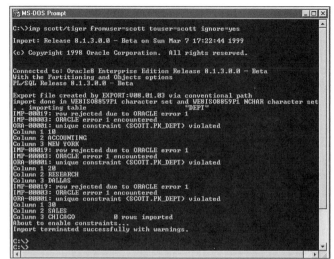

REORGANIZING A FRAGMENTED TABLESPACE

A fragmented tablespace has many blocks of free space that are not contiguous. Fragmentation can cause performance and space problems. Performance is affected because Oracle has to scan across multiple object extents and possibly over multiple physical disk drives. When the data is defragmented, objects can be compressed from many extents into one. This reduces internal Oracle overhead when scanning data.

A fragmented tablespace affects the object storage adversely. With many small blocks of free space spread out across the tablespace, some objects might not be able to be created that otherwise could fit if all the free space were contiguous. By defragmenting the tablespace, the data is reorganized so that all the small free blocks form one free block, as shown in Figure 30.5.

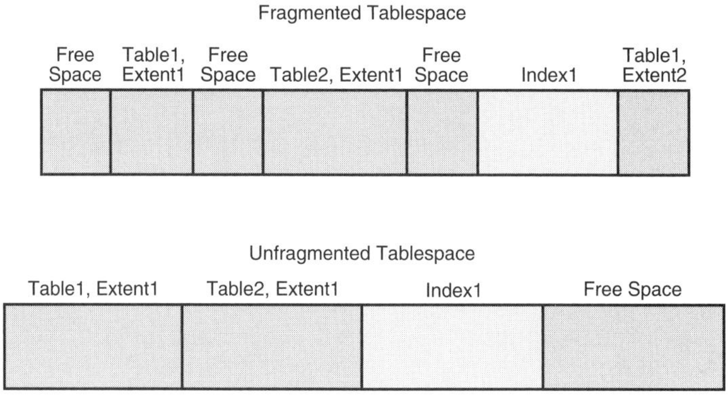

Figure 30.5
Example of a fragmented tablespace and an unfragmented tablespace.

Fragmented Tablespace

Free Space	Table1, Extent1	Free Space	Table2, Extent1	Free Space	Index1	Table1, Extent2

Unfragmented Tablespace

Table1, Extent1	Table2, Extent1	Index1	Free Space

Fragmentation occurs when objects such as tables and indexes are created, deleted, enlarged, and reduced in size over time. Because Oracle can only create an extent of an object within a contiguous free space in the tablespace, pockets of free space might start to appear. When an object is deleted, its free space is likely in an isolated spot within the tablespace, and only another object of the same or lesser size can be created within that free space.

To check for tablespace fragmentation, you can check to see how many segments of free space there are in a given tablespace, along with their sizes. This is done by running CHP30_1.SQL and passing the tablespace name, as shown in Listing 30.1. You can run the script in SQL*Plus, Server Manager, or any third-party product that can connect to the Oracle8 database.

LISTING 30.1   CHP30_1.SQL—SCRIPT TO DETERMINE THE NUMBER AND SIZES OF FREE SPACE WITHIN A TABLESPACE

```
SQL>   START CHP30_1.SQL
SQL>   COLUMN FILE_NAME FORMAT A40
SQL>   SELECT A.TABLESPACE_NAME, B.FILE_NAME, A.BYTES
     2   FROM DBA_FREE_SPACE A, DBA_DATA_FILES B
     3   WHERE  A.TABLESPACE_NAME = '&tablespace_name' AND
     4   A.FILE_ID = B.FILE_ID
     5   ORDER BY BYTES DESC
```

When you run the script, the server will prompt you to enter the name of the tablespace:

```
Enter value for tablespace_name: USERS
```

The server will return the free space information:

```
TABLESPACE_NAME     FILE_NAME                                BYTES
---------------     ----------------------------             -----------
USERS               /u02/oradata/TEST/users01.dbf            32768
USERS               /u02/oradata/TEST/users01.dbf            114688
USERS               /u04/oradata/TEST/users02.dbf            122400
USERS               /u04/oradata/TEST/users02.dbf            101908480SQL>
```

There should be one record for each distinct FILE_NAME. If not, your tablespace is fragmented. The tables contained in the tablespaces will be made unavailable to the users during the export and import process. Before you rely on the export and import tablespace to defragment the tablespace, you should enter the command ALTER TABLESPACE tablespace_name COALESCE and run CHP30_1.SQL again. If two chunks of free space are adjacent to each other, this command makes them into one bigger chunk. If the command does not help, you must use Export and Import to defragment the tablespace.

Another reason to defragment a tablespace is if an object within the tablespace contains multiple extents. In most cases, you should be concerned if the object has more than five extents, after which point performance starts to get noticeably affected. By exporting the tables with COMPRESS=Y specified, Oracle calculates the size of the INITIAL extent so that it encompasses all the data into one extent. This helps to defragment the database as well.

Run CHP30_2.SQL to determine which objects have more than five extents, as shown in Listing 30.2.

LISTING 30.2   CHP30_2.SQL   SCRIPT TO LIST ALL OBJECTS IN THE DATABASE WITH MORE THAN FIVE EXTENTS

```
SQL>    START CHP30_2.SQL
SQL>    COLUMN SEGMENT_NAME FORMAT A25
SQL>    SELECT OWNER, SEGMENT_NAME, EXTENTS
  2     FROM DBA_SEGMENTS
  3     WHERE EXTENTS > 5 AND
  4     OWNER NOT IN ('SYS','SYSTEM')
  5     ORDER BY EXTENTS
```

After running the script, the server returns all objects with more than five extents:

```
OWNER                SEGMENT_NAME               EXTENTS
----------------     ----------------------     ---------

DEMO                 EMPLOYEE                   6
DEMO                 JOB                        9
DEMO                 DEPARTMENT                 12
SQL>
```

Before you do the defragment process, make sure that the people who will be affected are notified because the tables within the tablespace will become unavailable for use during this process. If possible, schedule the process during a time when no one is accessing those tables.

To use Export and Import to defragment a tablespace, follow these steps:

1. Export all the tables contained within the tablespace. Be sure to set COMPRESS=Y option of export. This changes the INITIAL storage parameter of the tables, if necessary, to fit within one extent each.

2. Manually drop all tables from the tablespace.

3. Coalesce the free space in the tablespace. This is done with the ALTER TABLESPACE tablespace_name COALESCE command. All free space should be coalesced into one big chunk or as many chunks as there are datafiles for the tablespace. This is due to having no objects within the tablespace.

4. Import all tables that were contained within the tablespace. Oracle allocates the proper space for each object because COMPRESS=Y was specified during the export. When finished, you have a clean, unfragmented tablespace.

Caution

If you export with COMPRESS=Y, any LOB data that is exported will not be compressed; its original INITIAL and NEXT storage parameters remain unchanged.

The preceding method requires the knowledge of all objects contained within a tablespace. In a more time-consuming approach, you can defragment the entire database. This is done by exporting the entire database, dropping and re-creating the database with the CREATE DATABASE command, and then importing the entire export file.

MOVING DATABASE OBJECTS FROM ONE SCHEMA TO ANOTHER

Many times, it is important to move objects among schemas. This is the case, for example, for a developer who wants to have a set of tables to test with but does not want to affect data in the original schema. This is also useful to copy tables among instances.

First, export all objects for a given user account. Do this by specifying the OWNER parameter of the Export utility. In the example here, you will be copying the DEMO schema into the QUE schema, as shown in Figure 30.6.

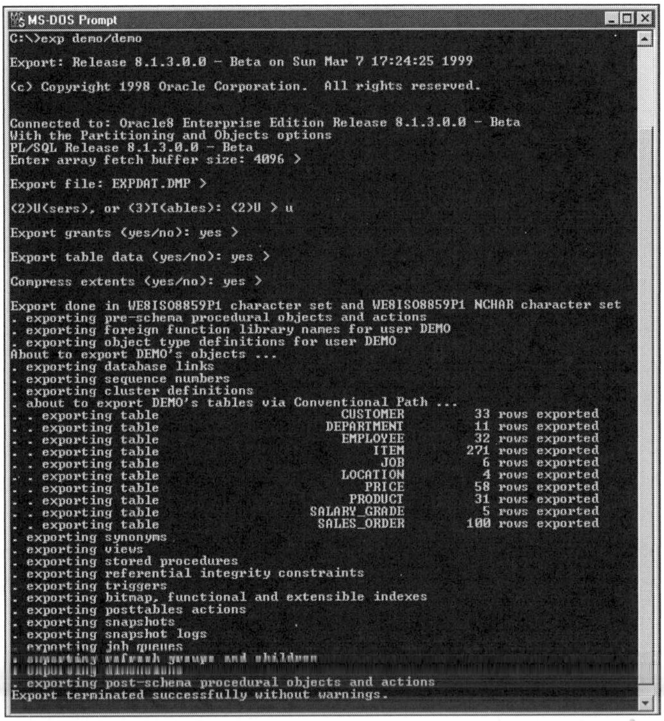

PART

VI

CH

30

Figure 30.6
Copying the DEMO schema to the QUE schema

If any objects being imported are in conflict with existing objects, only the conflicting objects are skipped.

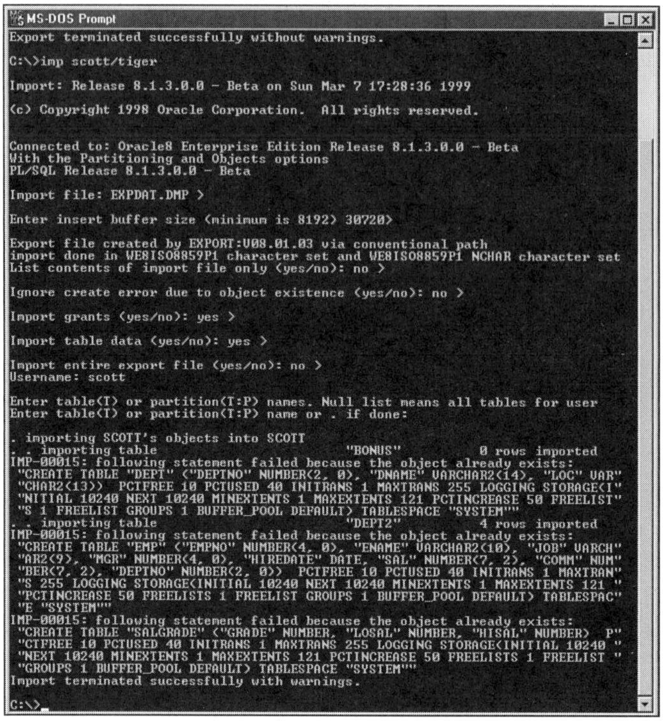

Figure 30.7
Exporting all objects of the *DEMO* user account.

Next, create the user account that will be the new owner, if that account does not already exist. At this point, you can import into the new schema by specifying the FROMUSER and TOUSER parameters with the Import utility, as shown in Figure 30.7.

Tip #93	If you have BFILE datatypes, Oracle stores only pointers to the files themselves. The actual data is external to the database. If you are exporting from one database and importing into another on a different server, be sure to copy all needed external files and place them in the same directory path. Otherwise, Oracle cannot access the associated BFILE files.

MULTIPLE OBJECTS AND MULTIPLE OBJECT TYPES

You need to specify the list of objects in the TABLES parameter specification during the export if you want to move a subset of tables from one schema to another, or for backup purposes. This must be used in conjunction with FROMUSER and TOUSER for the import.

To export a table, specify the owner, followed by a period and the table name, such as *Owner.Table_Name*. To export a partition, specify the owner, followed by a period and the table name, followed by a colon, followed by the partition name, such as *Owner.Table_Name:Partition_Name*.

Figure 30.8
Importing all objects of the *DEMO* user account into the *QUE* user account.

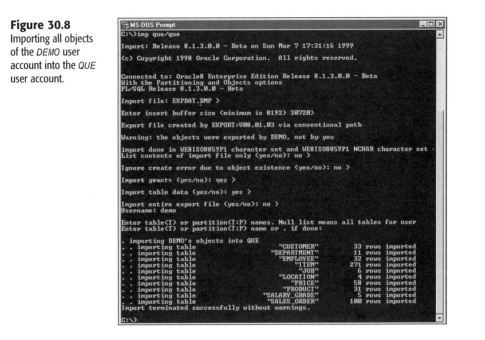

Figure 30.9 shows an example of exporting multiple objects and multiple object types: the PRICE table, along with two of five partitions for the EMP table (LOW_SALARY and MEDIUM_SALARY).

To import the multiple objects and object types into a different user account, import specifying the FROMUSER and TOUSER clauses. If you want to import into the same user, use either the FULL=Y or OWNER parameter specifications.

PARTITION-LEVEL IMPORT

Partition-level Import imports a set of partitions or subpartitions from a source table into a target table.

Note the following points:

Import always stores the rows according to the partitioning scheme of the target table. Partition-level Import lets you selectively retrieve data from the specified partitions or subpartitions in an export file. Partition-level Import inserts only the row data from the specified source partitions or subpartitions. If the target table is partitioned, partition-level Import rejects any rows that fall above the highest partition of the target table. Partition-level Import can be specified only in table mode. Partition-level Export and Import do not provide for splitting a partition.

Figure 30.9
Sample of exporting multiple objects and multiple object types.

IDENTIFYING BEHAVIOR WHEN TABLESPACES DON'T MATCH

When an object is imported, Oracle attempts to create it within the same tablespace from which it was exported. Sometimes, when an export is performed on one database and imported into another database, the tablespaces do not always match. An object from the exported database was stored in the DBA_TOOLS tablespace, for example. In the database to which the object is being imported, there is no DBA_TOOLS tablespace.

In such a scenario, during the import process, the Import utility attempts to create the object in the DBA_TOOLS but fails because there is no such tablespace in the target database. Import then tries to create the table into the default tablespace for the owner of the object. If there is enough space and the owner has an appropriate quota on the tablespace, the object is imported. Otherwise, an error occurs, and the object is not imported.

MOVING DATABASE OBJECTS FROM ONE TABLESPACE TO ANOTHER

By default, Import attempts to create objects in the same tablespace from which they were exported. If the user does not have permission to that tablespace or that tablespace no longer exists, Oracle creates the database objects in the default tablespace for that user account. These properties can be utilized to move database objects from one tablespace to another using Export and Import. To move all objects from *TABLESPACE_A* to *TABLESPACE_B* for *USER_A*, follow these steps:

1. Export all objects in the *TABLESPACE_A* for *USER_A*.

2. Issue REVOKE UNLIMITED TABLESPACE ON *TABLESPACE_A* FROM *USER_A*; to revoke any unlimited tablespace privileges granted to the user account.

3. Issue ALTER USER *USER_A* QUOTA 0 on tablespace_a; to enable no objects to be created in *TABLESPACE_A* by the *USER_A* user account.

4. Drop all objects owned by *USER_A* in *TABLESPACE_A*.

5. Issue ALTER USER *USER_A* DEFAULT TABLESPACE *TABLESPACE_B*; to make *TABLESPACE_B* the default tablespace for the *USER_A* user account. Oracle will try to import the objects into *TABLESPACE_A*, where they were exported from. Notice that the user does not have a quota on *TABLESPACE_A*, and then look to the default tablespace of the user. Before Oracle can import the data into *TABLESPACE_B*, you must give a large enough quota on the tablespace to the *USER_A* user. This is shown in the following step.

6. Issue ALTER USER *USER_A* QUOTA UNLIMITED ON *TABLESPACE_B*;. By giving an unlimited quota, the import will succeed, provided that *TABLESPACE_B* is large enough to handle all the database objects being imported.

7. Import the database objects that were exported. By default, the Import utility attempts to import them into *TABLESPACE_A*. Because the user does not have a quota on that tablespace, however, the objects will be created in the *USER_A* default tablespace, *TABLESPACE_B*.

The preceding steps show how you can use the Import and Export utilities, along with knowledge of SQL, to do powerful operations on data with relative ease. One of the most useful capabilities of the Import and Export utilities is the use of the SHOW and INDEXFILE options, which are described in the following section.

USING THE SHOW AND INDEXFILE OPTIONS

You can use the SHOW parameter to generate all SQL statements used to create the database structure and all objects. This includes creating comments, tablespaces, users, privilege grants, roles and their assignments, quota definitions, rollback segments, sequences, tables, constraints, indexes, packages, procedures, partitions, user-defined datatypes, and so on.

One powerful use of the SHOW parameter is to create a script file that can re-create part or all of the database. The statements are listed in the proper order of dependencies —that is, a table is created before an index, a foreign key that references a primary key is created after the primary key, and so on. Listing 30.3 shows a sample portion of the output from specifying SHOW=Y.

LISTING 30.3   CHP30_3.1st   A SAMPLE PORTION OF IMPORTING WITH SHOW=Y

```
"ALTER SCHEMA = "QUE""
"CREATE UNIQUE INDEX "I_PRICE" ON "PRICE" ("PRODUCT_ID" , "START_DATE" )  PC"
"TFREE 10 INITRANS 2 MAXTRANS 255 STORAGE (INITIAL 10240 NEXT 10240 MINEXTEN"
"TS 1 MAXEXTENTS 121 PCTINCREASE 50 FREELISTS 1) TABLESPACE "USER_DATA" LOGG"
"ING"
"ALTER TABLE "PRICE" ADD  CHECK (PRODUCT_ID IS NOT NULL) ENABLE"
"ALTER TABLE "PRICE" ADD  CHECK (START_DATE IS NOT NULL) ENABLE"
"ALTER TABLE "PRICE" ADD  CHECK (LIST_PRICE IS NULL OR MIN_PRICE IS NULL OR "
"MIN_PRICE <= LIST_PRICE) ENABLE"
"ALTER TABLE "PRICE" ADD  CHECK (END_DATE IS NULL OR START_DATE <= END_DATE)"
" ENABLE"
"ALTER TABLE "PRICE" ADD  PRIMARY KEY ("PRODUCT_ID","START_DATE") ENABLE"
"GRANT SELECT ON "PRICE" TO PUBLIC"
"ALTER SCHEMA = "QUE""
"COMMENT ON TABLE "PRICE" IS  'Prices (both standard and minimum) of product"
"s.  Database tracks both effective dates and expiration dates for prices.'"
"COMMENT ON COLUMN "PRICE"."PRODUCT_ID" IS  'Product number to which price a"
"pplies.  Product name found in table PRICE.'"
"COMMENT ON COLUMN "PRICE"."LIST_PRICE" IS  'Undiscounted price (in U.S.dol"
"lars).'"
"ALTER TABLE "PRICE" ADD FOREIGN KEY ("PRODUCT_ID") REFERENCES "PRODUCT" ("P"
"RODUCT_ID") ENABLE"
```

To make a file from the results, specify the LOG=filename parameter specification. This file can be modified to change almost any aspect of the database. Each line begins and ends with a quotation mark. Be sure to string these quotation marks from the beginning and ending of each line. Additionally, Oracle does not word-wrap lines in the output. This results in having statements with the likelihood of words and numbers being cut in two. To remedy this, you must manually join the lines in each statement. The sample listing, shown in the preceding listing, could be cleaned up to look like Listing 30.4.

LISTING 30.4   CHP30_4.1st   SQL STATEMENTS AFTER CLEANING UP THE
SHOW=Y IMPORT FILE

```
ALTER SCHEMA = "QUE";
CREATE UNIQUE INDEX "I_PRICE" ON "PRICE" ("PRODUCT_ID" , "START_DATE" )
    PCTFREE 10 INITRANS 2 MAXTRANS 255
    STORAGE (INITIAL 10240 NEXT 10240 MINEXTENTS 1 MAXEXTENTS 121
    PCTINCREASE 50 FREELISTS 1)
    TABLESPACE "USER_DATA" LOGGING;
ALTER TABLE "PRICE" ADD  CHECK (PRODUCT_ID IS NOT NULL) ENABLE;
ALTER TABLE "PRICE" ADD  CHECK (START_DATE IS NOT NULL) ENABLE;
ALTER TABLE "PRICE" ADD  CHECK (LIST_PRICE IS NULL OR MIN_PRICE IS NULL
                         OR MIN_PRICE <= LIST_PRICE) ENABLE;
ALTER TABLE "PRICE" ADD  CHECK (END_DATE IS NULL OR START_DATE <= END_DATE)
                         ENABLE;
ALTER TABLE "PRICE" ADD  PRIMARY KEY (PRODUCT_ID,START_DATE) ENABLE;
GRANT SELECT ON "PRICE" TO PUBLIC;
COMMENT ON TABLE "PRICE" IS
    'Prices (both standard and minimum) of products.  Database tracks both
     effective dates and expiration dates for prices.';
```

```
COMMENT ON COLUMN "PRICE"."PRODUCT_ID" IS  'Product number to which price
➥applies.
      Product name found in table PRICE.';
COMMENT ON COLUMN "PRICE"."LIST_PRICE" IS  'Undiscounted price (in U.S.
➥dollars).';
ALTER TABLE "PRICE" ADD FOREIGN KEY (PRODUCT_ID) REFERENCES PRODUCT
➥(PRODUCT_ID) ENABLE;
```

You can use the INDEXFILE parameter to generate CREATE INDEX statements. The value of the INDEXFILE parameter specifies the name of the file to be created. By default, Oracle appends a .SQL extension unless otherwise specified. Generic table creation statements are shown, commented out so they will not execute if the script is run. The INDEXFILE parameter does not generate CREATE primary key or unique key clauses. Listing 30.5 is a portion of the output file X.LOG from an import with INDEXFILE=X.LOG specified. Notice how Oracle word-wraps all lines appropriately and does not add quotation marks before and after each line. This enables immediate use of the index file with no further modifications.

LISTING 30.5   X.LOG   SAMPLE PORTION OF THE X.LOG FILE CREATED BY IMPORTING WITH INDEXFILE=X.LOG

```
REM   CREATE TABLE "QUE"."PRICE" ("PRODUCT_ID" NUMBER(6, 0), "LIST_PRICE"
REM   NUMBER(8, 2), "MIN_PRICE" NUMBER(8, 2), "START_DATE" DATE, "END_DATE"
REM   DATE) PCTFREE 10 PCTUSED 40 INITRANS 1 MAXTRANS 255 LOGGING
REM   STORAGE(INITIAL 10240 NEXT 10240 MINEXTENTS 1 MAXEXTENTS 121
REM   PCTINCREASE 50 FREELISTS 1 FREELIST GROUPS 1) TABLESPACE "USER_DATA" ;
REM   ... 58 rows
CONNECT QUE;
CREATE UNIQUE INDEX "QUE"."I_PRICE" ON "PRICE" ("PRODUCT_ID" ,
"START_DATE" ) PCTFREE 10 INITRANS 2 MAXTRANS 255 STORAGE (INITIAL 10240
NEXT 10240 MINEXTENTS 1 MAXEXTENTS 121 PCTINCREASE 50 FREELISTS 1)
TABLESPACE "USER_DATA" LOGGING ;
```

TRANSPORTABLE TABLESPACES

This feature enables a user to move a subset of an Oracle database into another Oracle database. It is as if the subset were unplugged from the original database and plugged into another one. It is also possible to clone a tablespace in one database and plug it into another, thereby copying the tablespace between databases. Moving data using the transportable tablespace feature can potentially be a lot faster than either export/import or unload/load because it involves only the copying of the datafiles and integrating metadata. In the data warehouse environment, where huge amounts of data flow from the initial OLTP databases into the enterprise data warehouse and on to data marts, this feature presents an opportunity for a faster and more innovative means of data movement. In addition, its use can be extended to the archiving of data.

CHAPTER **31**

SQL*Loader

In this chapter

Running SQL*Loader

Databases today are ever increasing in complexity and size. Gigabyte-sized databases are common and data warehouses are often reaching the terabyte-sized range. With the growth of these databases, the need to populate them with external data quickly and efficiently is of paramount importance. To handle this challenge, Oracle provides a tool called SQL*Loader to load data from external data files into an Oracle database.

SQL*Loader has many functions that include the following capabilities:

- Data can be loaded from multiple input datafiles of differing file types.
- Input records can be of fixed and variable lengths.
- Multiple tables can be loaded in the same run. It can also logically load selected records into each respective table.
- SQL functions can be used against input data before loading into tables.
- Multiple physical records can be combined into a single logical record. Likewise, SQL can take a single physical record and load it as multiple logical records.
- Support for nested columns, nested tables, VARRAYS, and LOBS (large objects, including BLOB, CLOB, NCLOB, and BFILES).

SQL*Loader can be invoked by typing sqlload, sqlldr, or sqlldr80 at the command line. The exact command might differ depending on your operating system (OS). Refer to your Oracle OS-specific manual for the exact syntax. Please note that all listings and server responses in this chapter might differ from your results based on the operating system that you are using. The sqlldr command accepts numerous command-line parameters. Invoking SQL*Loader without any parameters displays help information on all the valid parameters (see Listing 31.1).

LISTING 31.1 SQL*Loader Help Information

```
Invoking SQL*Loader without parameters:
$ sqlldr

The server responds with help information because SQL*Loader was invoked without
parameters:
SQL*Loader: Release 8.1.5.0.0 - Production on Wed Mar 10 7:20:11 1999
(c) Copyright 1999 Oracle Corporation.  All rights reserved.

Usage: SQLLOAD keyword=value [,keyword=value,...]

Valid Keywords:

    userid -- ORACLE username/password
   control -- Control file name
       log -- Log file name
       bad -- Bad file name
      data -- Data file name
   discard -- Discard file name
```

```
    discardmax -- Number of discards to allow          (Default all)
          skip -- Number of logical records to skip     (Default 0)
          load -- Number of logical records to load     (Default all)
        errors -- Number of errors to allow             (Default 50)
          rows -- Number of rows in conventional path bind array or between
                  direct path data saves
                  (Default: Conventional path 64, Direct path all)
      bindsize -- Size of conventional path bind array in bytes  (Default
                  65536)
        silent -- Suppress messages during run
                  (header,feedback,errors,discards,partitions)
        direct -- use direct path                       (Default FALSE)
       parfile -- parameter file: name of file that contains parameter
                  specifications
      parallel -- do parallel load                      (Default FALSE)
      readsize - Size (in bytes) of the read buffer
          file -- File to allocate extents from
skip_unusable_indexes -- disallow/allow unusable indexes or index
  partitions  (Default FALSE)
skip_index_maintenance -- do not maintain indexes, mark affected indexes
  as unusable  (Default FALSE)
commit_discontinued -- commit loaded rows when load is discontinued
                  (Default FALSE)

PLEASE NOTE: Command-line parameters may be specified either by
position or by keywords.  An example of the former case is 'sqlload
scott/tiger foo'; an example of the latter is 'sqlload control=foo
userid=scott/tiger'.  One may specify parameters by position before
but not after parameters specified by keywords.  For example,

'sqlload scott/tiger control=foo logfile=log' is allowed, but
'sqlload scott/tiger control=foo log' is not, even though the
position of the parameter 'log' is correct.
```

COMPONENTS OF SQL*LOADER

SQL*Loader is an Oracle utility that loads data into the database from external data files. Figure 31.1 shows the different components of SQL*Loader.

THE CONTROL FILE

The control file is the nerve center of SQL*Loader. This is the file that controls how data in the external data file is to be mapped into Oracle tables and columns. It should be noted that SQL*Loader input datatypes are totally independent from the database column datatypes into which they are being loaded. Implicit datatype conversions will be done as necessary, and errors will be trapped if the conversion fails. The language used in the control file is the SQL*Loader Data Definition Language (DDL). The control file consists of multiple sections with many parameters, too many to cover in depth for the scope of this chapter. Refer to the Oracle Server Utilities manual for full documentation on all valid syntax and parameters of the control file. Basic syntax is covered in the "Looking at SQL*Loader Examples" section to demonstrate the different uses of SQL*Loader.

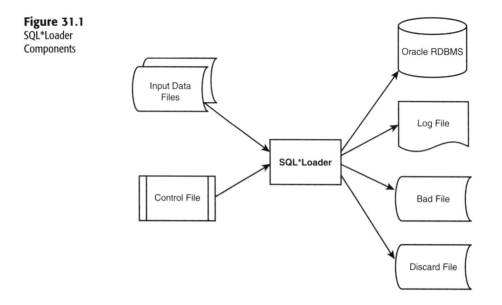

Figure 31.1
SQL*Loader
Components

SQL*LOADER INPUT DATA

SQL*Loader can accept input data files in many different formats. Files can be stored on disk or tape, or the records themselves can be embedded in the control file. Record formats can be of fixed or variable lengths. Fixed length records are records in which every record is the same fixed length and the data fields in each record have the same fixed length, datatype, and position. For example, the PART_NBR data item in a record would always occupy columns 10 to 19, regardless of the actual length of the data. If the part number were 12345, the remaining space in columns 15 to 19 would be blank. With variable length records, the data item would only take up as much space as necessary on each record.

In the PART_NBR example, the data item would only need five bytes with no trailing blanks. Each record in a variable length formatted file can have different space usage for PART_NBR based on its actual length. It is important to note that even though variable length records might use less space in the data file, data items on each record have to have a delimiter to separate the data items.

SQL*LOADER OUTPUTS

The next few sections discusses the various files created by a SQL*Loader session.

ORACLE TABLES AND INDEXES

SQL*Loader can load multiple tables and indexes in an Oracle database in the same loader session. SQL*Loader's behavior in inserting the data and building the indexes will be discussed later in the sections "Using Conventional Path" and "Using Direct Path Loading" later in this chapter.

THE BAD FILE

SQL*Loader goes through a two-stage process in validating data for insertion into the database. The first stage is validating the format of the data according to the specifications in the control file. If the data format or length is inconsistent with the specifications, SQL*Loader writes that record to the bad file. When records pass the first stage of validation, they are passed to the database for insertion.

The second stage of validation then takes place in the database. The database might reject the record for many reasons, some of which could be database check constraints and datatype conversion errors. Second stage validation rejections are also written to the bad file. If the number of rejections reaches a certain threshold (the default is 50), the SQL*Loader session is aborted. This threshold can be set at the command line with the errors parameter. The bad file is written in the same format as the original input data file, which enables the bad file records to be loaded using the same control file after the necessary corrections are made.

THE DISCARD FILE

SQL*Loader writes records to the discard file if there are conditions present in the control file and the record fails all the conditions. For example, a condition in the control file states that records must have an X in column one. Records that do not have an X will not be inserted into the database and will be written to the discard file. Unlike the bad file, the default threshold of discard records is to enable all discards. This threshold can be set lower at the command line with the discardmax parameter.

THE LOG FILE

When SQL*Loader begins execution, it creates a log file. Any situations that prevent this log file from being successfully created terminate the loader session. The default filename for the log file is the control filename with the .log extension. It is important to note that if you do not give it a new name at the command line using the log parameter, the loader session automatically overwrites the last log with the same name. The log file has multiple sections showing the environment at which the loader session ran with results and summary statistics. Listing 31.8 in section "Lookng at SQL*Loader Examples" displays the contents of a log file.

CONTROL FILE SYNTAX

Most control files begin with the following keywords:

LOAD DATA

Other keywords that might precede these are —, which are comments, and options, which enable command-line options previously discussed to be included in the control file.

This is followed by the definition to indicate the source external data file to use for the load:

```
INFILE 'mydata.dat'
```

Multiple data files can be loaded in the same session by specifying multiple INFILE statements:

```
INFILE 'mydata1.dat'
INFILE 'mydata2.dat'
```

If the file extension is not specified, SQL*Loader defaults the extension to .dat. Although it is not required to enclose the data file in single quotes, it is highly recommended to avoid incorrect special character translations when specifying full data paths. The loading method (see Table 31.1) to be used for all tables in the loading session is then specified.

TABLE 31.1   TABLE LOADING METHODS

Method	Description
INSERT	This is the default method. It assumes that the table is empty before loading. If there are still rows within the table, SQL*Loader aborts.
APPEND	This method enables rows to be added to the table without affecting existing rows.
REPLACE	This method deletes existing rows in the table first and then starts loading the new rows. Note that any delete triggers on the table fire when the old rows are deleted.
TRUNCATE	This method uses the SQL command TRUNCATE to remove the old rows before loading. This is much quicker than REPLACE because delete triggers fire and no rollback is generated. TRUNCATE is not a recoverable command. In order to use this method, the table's referential integrity constraints must be disabled, and specific privileges granted.

This is followed by the table definition:

```
INTO TABLE  tablename method
```

In this example, method is the same as described above in Table 31.1, but this method only applies to the table specified on this INTO TABLE line. This gives the user better control when loading multiple tables from the same SQL*Loader session.

What follows after the INTO TABLE keywords are the fields and datatypes specifications. Instead of reviewing all the different options, it is simpler to look at the different examples in the following section.

LOOKING AT SQL*LOADER EXAMPLES

All examples use the following schema consisting of four tables (Listing 31.2). This schema simulates a banking schema with customer, account, and transaction tables. For the purposes of demonstrating loading into a partitioned table, partition_xact table is a duplicate of the transaction table with the data partitioned based on the quarter in which the transaction took place.

LISTING 31.2 LIST1.1—EXAMPLE SCHEMA

```
create table customer (

    cust_nbr        number(7)         not null,
    cust_name       varchar2(100)         not null,
    cust_addr1       varchar2(50),
    cust_addr2       varchar2(50),
    cust_city      varchar2(30),
    cust_state       varchar2(2),
    cust_zip      varchar2(10),
    cust_phone       varchar2(20),
    cust_birthday    date)
/

create table account (

    cust_nbr        number(7)         not null,
    acct_nbr        number(10)        not null,
    acct_name       varchar2(40)          not null)
/

create table transaction (

    acct_nbr        number(10)        not null,
    xact_amt        number(10,2)          not null,
    xact_flag       char             not null,
    xact_date       date             not null)
/

create table partition_xact (

    acct_nbr        number(10)         not null,
    xact_amt        number(10,2)          not null,
    xact_flag       char             not null,
    xact_date       date             not null)

    PARTITION BY RANGE (xact_date)
    (PARTITION P1 VALUES LESS THAN (to_date('01-APR-1999','DD-MON-YYYY')),
     PARTITION P2 VALUES LESS THAN (to_date('01-JUL-1999','DD-MON-YYYY')),
     PARTITION P3 VALUES LESS THAN (to_date('01-OCT-1999','DD-MON-YYYY')),
     PARTITION P4 VALUES LESS THAN (MAXVALUE))
/
```

All examples use the following data files (see Listings 31.3, 31.4, and 31.5).

LISTING 31.3 cust.dat—DESCRIPTION OF THE LISTING

```
0000001BOB MARIN            123 MAIN ST.       TOPEKA           KS12345
999-555-1234     20-APR-55
0000002MARY JOHNSON         18 HOPE LANE       SAN FRANCISCO    CA94054
415-555-1299     32-JAN-69
0000003RICHARD WILLIAMS     1225 DAFFODIL LANE  BOSTON           MA98377
0000004WALTER SIMS          1888 PROSPECT AVE.  BROOKLYN         NY11218
718-555-3420
```

continues

LISTING 31.3 CONTINUED

```
0000005LARRY HATFIELD     TWO FIELDS CT.      SOMERSET          NJ07689
732-555-2454         25-DEC-60
0000006LAURA LAU          25 CHRISTOPHER LN   SAN BRUNO         CA90234
510-555-4834
0000123PRISCILLA WONG     888 FORTUNE COURT   PHILADELPHIA      PA35545
01-JAN-65
0000068SONNY BALRUP       27 KAMA ST.         JACKSON HEIGHTS   NY10199
718-555-9876         07-MAY-61
0023494RUPAL PARIKH       2 FORCE BLVD        NEW YORK          NY10105
212-555-5887         31-DEC-72
0000324CRAIG SILVEIRA     1674 ISLAND ST      SMITHTOWN         NY12467
516-555-5534         27-OCT-74
0000010DANIEL SMITH       35 DIRECT DRIVE     BERGEN            NJ07899
201-555-3734
0011102STEPHEN LEUNG      16 STANFORD CT      STANFORD          CA96688
650-555-1248         05-SEP-76
0011102ALICIA LOWRY       5678 TIMOTHY DR     ATLANTA           GA47730
0002340JENNIFER LEUNG     1 MURRAY HILL       GREENWICH         CT78835
203-555-7564
1003423HORACE MICHAEL     90 MINISTER ST      MINNEAPOLIS       MN77788
18-MAR-65
0000223CHRISTOPHER YEE    9077 MUSIC AVE      DETROIT           MI45345
777-555-7785         22-JUL-75
0009032JAMES BORIOTTI     65 FIREMENS LANE    COLUMBUS          OH37485
904-555-5674
0000088HIREN PATEL        69 CLUB ST.         NEW YORK          NY12445
212-555-7822         12-APR-70
0000100RICHARD JI         1225 STEER ST       KOBE              KS12009
999-555-5824         10-OCT-74
0000046DAVID CHOW         49 HUGO DRIVE       FLUSHING          NY10199
718-555-4367
0000758HENRY WALKER       12 SIGMUND ST.      CHICAGO           IL33890
312-555-5567         09-APR-45
0002993GEORGE BLOOM       28 BRIDGEWATER ST   SAN MATEO         CA90475
650-555-2838         25-MAY-63
0009488LISA JONES         30 MISSION ST       UNITY             FL23899
```

LISTING 31.4   acct.dat—DESCRIPTION OF THE LISTING

```
0000001,459023,SAVINGS
0000001,459024,CHECKING
0000003,211108,SAVINGS
0000003,211123,CHECKING
0000006,23388,SAVINGS
0000123,43992,CHECKING
0000123,50699390,LINE OF CREDIT
0000068,23330,SAVINGS
0023494,433020,SAVINGS
0000010,4566,SAVINGS
0000010,4599,CHECKING
0000223,8887544,SAVINGS
```

LISTING 31.5   xact.dat—DESCRIPTION OF THE LISTING

```
0000459023     123.45D01-FEB-99
0000459023    1233.86C01-MAR-99
0000459023     987.00P01-DEC-99
0000459024      1000C03-JUN-99
0000211108     875.27D23-JUL-99
0000211123   20987.88C30-DEC-99
0000211123   12500.16D10-JAN-99
0000023388       1.75C19-MAY-99
0000043992     350.00C12-MAR-99
0050699390    2899.09D01-SEP-99
0000023330       100D26-JAN-99
0000433020      60.99C20-NOV-99
0000004566     230.23C20-AUG-99
0000004599      14.96D05-JUN-99
0000004599      14.AAD07-JUN-99
0008887544    9999.99D11-JUL-99
```

EXAMPLE 1—LOADING FIXED-LENGTH DATA

This example loads the data in the cust.dat data file into the customer table. Because the data is in fixed-length format, the control file (see Listing 31.6) maps the data to the database by column positions.

LISTING 31.6   load1.ctl—THE CONTROL FILE

```
LOAD DATA
INFILE 'cust.dat'
INTO TABLE customer
    (cust_nbr     POSITION(01:07)    INTEGER EXTERNAL,
     cust_name    POSITION(08:27)    CHAR,
     cust_addr1   POSITION(28:47)    CHAR,
     cust_city    POSITION(48:67)    CHAR,
     cust_state   POSITION(68:69)    CHAR,
     cust_zip     POSITION(70:79)    CHAR,
     cust_phone   POSITION(80:91)    CHAR,
      cust_birthday    POSITION(100:108) DATE "DD-MON-YY" NULLIF cust_
➡birthday=BLANKS)
```

Invoke SQL*Loader using example/expass as the user name and password. The control, log, bad, and discard files are passed to SQL*Loader as command line parameters as previously discussed in the section "SQL*Loader Outputs".

LISTING 31.7   load1.ctl—INVOKING THE SQL*LOADER

```
$ sqlldr example/expass control=load1.ctl log=load1.log bad=load1.bad
                                          discard=load1.dis
```

The following is the server response:

```
SQL*Loader: Release 8.0.3.0.0 - Production on Wed Mar 10 8:10:23 1999
(c) Copyright 1997 Oracle Corporation.  All rights reserved.

Commit point reached - logical record count 23
```

LISTING 31.8 load1.ctl—EXAMPLE 1 LOG FILE CONTENTS

```
SQL*Loader: Release 8.0.3.0.0 - Production on Wed Mar 10 8:11:03 1999

(c) Copyright 1997 Oracle Corporation.  All rights reserved.

Control File:    load1.ctl
Data File:       cust.dat
  Bad File:      load1.bad
  Discard File:  load1.dis
 (Allow all discards)

Number to load: ALL
Number to skip: 0
Errors allowed: 50
Bind array:     64 rows, maximum of 65536 bytes
Continuation:    none specified
Path used:      Conventional

Table CUSTOMER, loaded from every logical record.
Insert option in effect for this table: INSERT

    Column Name                    Position   Len  Term Encl Datatype
------------------------------ ---------- ----- ---- ---- --------------
CUST_NBR                               1:7     7
      CHARACTER
CUST_NAME                              8:27    20             CHARACTER
CUST_ADDR1                            28:47    20             CHARACTER
CUST_CITY                             48:67    20             CHARACTER
CUST_STATE                            68:69     2             CHARACTER
CUST_ZIP                              70:79    10             CHARACTER
CUST_PHONE                            80:91    12             CHARACTER
CUST_BIRTHDAY                       100:108     9             DATE DD-MON-YY

Column CUST_NAME is NULL if CUST_NAME = BLANKS
Column CUST_ADDR1 is NULL if CUST_ADDR1 = BLANKS
Column CUST_CITY is NULL if CUST_CITY = BLANKS
Column CUST_STATE is NULL if CUST_STATE = BLANKS
Column CUST_ZIP is NULL if CUST_ZIP = BLANKS
Column CUST_PHONE is NULL if CUST_PHONE = BLANKS
Column CUST_BIRTHDAY is NULL if CUST_BIRTHDAY = BLANKS

Record 2: Rejected - Error on table CUSTOMER, column CUST_BIRTHDAY.
ORA-01847: day of month must be between 1 and last day of month

Table CUSTOMER:
  22 Rows successfully loaded.
  1 Row not loaded due to data errors.
  0 Rows not loaded because all WHEN clauses were failed.
  0 Rows not loaded because all fields were null.
```

```
Space allocated for bind array:                    9216 bytes(64 rows)
Space allocated for memory besides bind array:        0 bytes

Total logical records skipped:          0
Total logical records read:            23
Total logical records rejected:         1
Total logical records discarded:        0

Run began on Wed Mar 10 8:11:03 1999
Run ended on Wed Mar 10 8:11:03 1999

Elapsed time was:      00:00:00.21
CPU time was:          00:00:00.04
```

Example 1 comments: Record 2 is rejected due to an invalid date and is written to the bad file (load1.bad). This record can then be corrected in the bad file and loaded by doing the following: making changes to the same control file to use the bad file as the input file and adding the keyword APPEND before the keywords INTO TABLE. Also, note the use of the NULLIF clause in the control file. Without this clause, records that had blanks for dates would have failed the database date check.

EXAMPLE 2—LOADING VARIABLE-LENGTH DATA

This example loads the data in the acct.dat data file into the customer table. Because the data is in variable-length format, the control file defines the delimiter used to distinguish between the different data items.

LISTING 31.9   LOAD2.CTL—EXAMPLE 2 CONTROL FILE

```
LOAD DATA

INFILE 'acct.dat'

INTO TABLE account

FIELDS TERMINATED BY ',' OPTIONALLY ENCLOSED BY '"'

    (cust_nbr, acct_nbr, acct_name)
```

Invoking SQL*Loader for Example 2 at the command prompt is done as follows:

```
$ sqlldr example/expass control=load2.ctl log=load2.log bad=load2.bad
                                discard=load2.dis
```

The following is the server response:

```
SQL*Loader: Release 8.0.3.0.0 - Production on Wed Mar 10 8:15:51 1999

(c) Copyright 1997 Oracle Corporation.  All rights reserved.

Commit point reached - logical record count 12
```

LISTING 31.10   EXAMPLE 2 LOG FILE CONTENTS

```
SQL*Loader: Release 8.0.3.0.0 - Production on Wed Mar 10 8:16:03 1999

(c) Copyright 1997 Oracle Corporation.  All rights reserved.

Control File:    load2.ctl
Data File:       acct.dat
  Bad File:      load2.bad
  Discard File:  load2.dis
  (Allow all discards)

Number to load: ALL
Number to skip: 0
Errors allowed: 50
Bind array:     64 rows, maximum of 65536 bytes
Continuation:   none specified
Path used:      Conventional

Table ACCOUNT, loaded from every logical record.
Insert option in effect for this table: INSERT

   Column Name                  Position   Len  Term Encl Datatype
------------------------------ ---------- ----- ---- ---- -------------
CUST_NBR                          FIRST      *    ,   O(") CHARACTER
ACCT_NBR                          NEXT       *    ,   O(") CHARACTER
ACCT_NAME                         NEXT       *    ,   O(") CHARACTER

Table ACCOUNT:
  12 Rows successfully loaded.
  0 Rows not loaded due to data errors.
  0 Rows not loaded because all WHEN clauses were failed.
  0 Rows not loaded because all fields were null.

Space allocated for bind array:                35328 bytes(64 rows)
Space allocated for memory besides bind array:     0 bytes

Total logical records skipped:        0
Total logical records read:          12
Total logical records rejected:       0
Total logical records discarded:      0

Run began on Wed Mar 10 8:16:03 1999
Run ended on Wed Mar 10 8:16:28 1999

Elapsed time was:     00:00:00.23
CPU time was:         00:00:00.04
```

Example 2 comments: All records are successfully loaded. Remember that variable-length data must have delimiters to separate data items within the input data file. When loading delimited character data, it is more efficient to define the maximum length of each char data field. In this example, acct_name char(20) should be used in the control file. If the maximum length is not defined, SQL*Loader uses a default of 255 bytes for the length, which influences how many records are inserted in each execution of the bind array.

EXAMPLE 3—LOADING WITH EMBEDDED DATA

This example shows that data does not have to be in a datafile; it can be directly embedded into the control file. The BEGINDATA keyword indicates that all lines after it are data records to be used as the input source for this control file.

LISTING 31.11 LOAD3.CTL—EXAMPLE 3 CONTROL FILE

```
LOAD DATA
INFILE *
APPEND
INTO TABLE account
FIELDS TERMINATED BY ',' OPTIONALLY ENCLOSED BY '"'
    (cust_nbr, acct_nbr, acct_name)

BEGINDATA

0000324,89073,SAVINGS
0000324,89074,CHECKING
0000075,111,SAVINGS
0011102,800,CHECKING
0000068,23338,CHECKING
```

Invoking SQL*Loader for Example 3 from the command prompt is done as follows:

```
$ sqlldr example/expass control=load3.ctl log=load3.log bad=load3.bad
                                discard=load3.dis
```

The following is the server response:

```
SQL*Loader: Release 8.0.3.0.0 - Production on Wed Mar 10 8:20:11 1999

(c) Copyright 1997 Oracle Corporation.  All rights reserved.

Commit point reached - logical record count 5
```

LISTING 31.12 EXAMPLE 3 LOG FILE CONTENTS

```
SQL*Loader: Release 8.0.3.0.0 - Production on Wed Mar 10 8:21:21 1999

(c) Copyright 1997 Oracle Corporation.  All rights reserved.

Control File:  load3.ctl
Data File:     load3.ctl
  Bad File:      load3.bad
  Discard File: load3.dis
  (Allow all discards)

Number to load: ALL
Number to skip: 0
Errors allowed: 50
Bind array:    64 rows, maximum of 65536 bytes
Continuation:    none specified
Path used:     Conventional
```

continues

LISTING 31.12 CONTINUED

```
Table ACCOUNT, loaded from every logical record.
Insert option in effect for this table: APPEND

    Column Name                     Position   Len  Term Encl Datatype
    ------------------------------- ---------- ---- ---- ---- -------------
CUST_NBR                            FIRST       *    ,   O(") CHARACTER
ACCT_NBR                            NEXT        *    ,   O(") CHARACTER
ACCT_NAME                           NEXT        *    ,   O(") CHARACTER

Table ACCOUNT:

  5 Rows successfully loaded.
  0 Rows not loaded due to data errors.
  0 Rows not loaded because all WHEN clauses were failed.
  0 Rows not loaded because all fields were null.

Space allocated for bind array:                 35328 bytes(64 rows)
Space allocated for memory besides bind array:      0 bytes

Total logical records skipped:          0
Total logical records read:             5
Total logical records rejected:         0
Total logical records discarded:        0

Run began on Wed Mar 10 8:20:11 1999
Run ended on Wed Mar 10 8:20:35 1999

Elapsed time was:     00:00:00.24
CPU time was:         00:00:00.03
```

Example 3 comments: To load data embedded into the control file, use * instead of an input filename after the keyword INFILE. This example also shows the use of the APPEND loading method to add to the account table. If the APPEND keyword is omitted in this control file, the load aborts because SQL*Loader's default loading method is INSERT, which expects the table to be empty before loading.

EXAMPLE 4—LOADING WITH CONDITIONAL CHECKING

This example loads data from the xact.dat file. The control file checks the flag to see if the amount is a debit or credit and loads the data accordingly.

LISTING 31.13 EXAMPLE 4 CONTROL FILE

```
LOAD DATA

INFILE 'xact.dat'
INTO TABLE transaction
WHEN xact_flag = 'D'

    (acct_nbr    POSITION(01:10)    INTEGER EXTERNAL,
     xact_amt    POSITION(11:20)    INTEGER EXTERNAL ":xact_amt * -1",
     xact_flag   POSITION(21:21)    CHAR,
     xact_date   POSITION(22:31)    DATE "DD-MON-YY" NULLIF xact_date=BLANKS)
```

```
INTO TABLE transaction
WHEN xact_flag = 'C'

    (acct_nbr     POSITION(01:10)     INTEGER EXTERNAL,
     xact_amt     POSITION(11:20)     INTEGER EXTERNAL,
     xact_flag    POSITION(21:21)     CHAR,
     xact_date    POSITION(22:31)       DATE "DD-MON-YY" NULLIF xact_date=BLANKS)
```

Invoke SQL*Loader for Example 4 from the command prompt as follows:

```
$ sqlldr example/expass control=load4.ctl log=load4.log bad=load4.bad
                                     discard=load4.dis
```

The following is the server response:

```
SQL*Loader: Release 8.0.3.0.0 - Production on Wed Mar 10 9:20:11 1999

(c) Copyright 1997 Oracle Corporation.  All rights reserved.

Commit point reached - logical record count 16
```

LISTING 31.14   EXAMPLE 4 LOG FILE CONTENTS

```
SQL*Loader: Release 8.0.3.0.0 - Production on Wed Mar 10 9:20:11 1999

(c) Copyright 1997 Oracle Corporation.  All rights reserved.

Control File:   load4.ctl
Data File:      xact.dat
  Bad File:     load4.bad
  Discard File: load4.dis
 (Allow all discards)

Number to load: ALL
Number to skip: 0
Errors allowed: 50
Bind array:     64 rows, maximum of 65536 bytes
Continuation:    none specified
Path used:      Conventional

Table TRANSACTION, loaded when XACT_FLAG = 0X44(character 'D')
Insert option in effect for this table: INSERT

    Column Name                    Position   Len  Term Encl Datatype
    ----------------------------   --------   --    ---- ----------
ACCT_NBR                             1:10     10         CHARACTER
XACT_AMT                             11:20    10         CHARACTER
XACT_FLAG                            21:21    1          CHARACTER
XACT_DATE                            22:31    10         DATE DD-MON-YY

Column XACT_AMT had SQL string
":xact_amt * -1"
 applied to it.
Column XACT_DATE is NULL if XACT_DATE = BLANKS
```

continues

LISTING 31.14 CONTINUED

```
Table TRANSACTION, loaded when XACT_FLAG = 0X43(character 'C')
Insert option in effect for this table: INSERT

    Column Name                    Position   Len  Term Encl Datatype
------------------------------- ---------- ----- ---- ---- -------------
ACCT_NBR                             1:10    10             CHARACTER
XACT_AMT                            11:20    10             CHARACTER
XACT_FLAG                           21:21     1             CHARACTER
XACT_DATE                           22:31    10             DATE DD-MON-YY

Column XACT_DATE is NULL if XACT_DATE = BLANKS

Record 3: Discarded - failed all WHEN clauses.
Record 15: Rejected - Error on table TRANSACTION, column XACT_AMT.
ORA-01722: invalid number

Table TRANSACTION:

  7 Rows successfully loaded.
  1 Row not loaded due to data errors.
  8 Rows not loaded because all WHEN clauses were failed.
  0 Rows not loaded because all fields were null.

Table TRANSACTION:

  7 Rows successfully loaded.
  0 Rows not loaded due to data errors.
  9 Rows not loaded because all WHEN clauses were failed.
  0 Rows not loaded because all fields were null.

Space allocated for bind array:                 7168 bytes(64 rows)
Space allocated for memory besides bind array:     0 bytes

Total logical records skipped:       0
Total logical records read:         16
Total logical records rejected:      1
Total logical records discarded:     1

Run began on Wed Mar 10 9:20:11 1999
Run ended on Wed Mar 10 9:20:46 1999

Elapsed time was:     00:00:00.35
CPU time was:         00:00:00.02
```

Example 4 comments: This example shows how to use the WHEN clause in the control file to do conditional loading. The multiple WHEN clauses load into the same table in this example, but they can also be different tables. The dollar amount is multiplied by –1 before being inserted into the table when the transaction flag equals D. This is an example of being able to apply operators or SQL functions to the data as it is being loaded.

Record 3 is discarded and placed into the discard file because the flag is neither C nor D and thus not satisfying either condition. Record 15 is rejected because the dollar amount is not numeric. These two records show the two stages of checking previously mentioned. Record 3 is discarded by the loader process, whereas record 15 is not rejected until the database tries to insert it into the table.

EXAMPLE 5—LOADING INTO A TABLE PARTITION

This example is a variation of Example 4, in which you load the data from xact.dat file. In this example, you load the data into the partition_xact table, which has four partitions to store the data in by calendar quarter. A single partition or all partitions of a table can be loaded in the same loader session. In this instance, you only load partition P1 for the first quarter.

PART

VI

CH

31

LISTING 31.15   LOAD5.CTL—EXAMPLE 5 CONTROL FILE

```
LOAD DATA

INFILE 'xact.dat'
INTO TABLE partition_xact PARTITION (P1)
WHEN xact_flag = 'D'

     (acct_nbr     POSITION(01:10)     INTEGER EXTERNAL,
      xact_amt     POSITION(11:20)     INTEGER EXTERNAL ":xact_amt * -1",
      xact_flag    POSITION(21:21)     CHAR,
      xact_date    POSITION(22:31)     DATE "DD-MON-YY" NULLIF xact_date=BLANKS)

INTO TABLE partition_xact PARTITION (P1)
WHEN xact_flag = 'C'
     (acct_nbr     POSITION(01:10)     INTEGER EXTERNAL,
      xact_amt     POSITION(11:20)     INTEGER EXTERNAL,
      xact_flag    POSITION(21:21)     CHAR,
      xact_date    POSITION(22:31)      DATE "DD-MON-YY" NULLIF xact_date=BLANKS)
```

Invoking SQL*Loader for Example 5 from the command prompt is done as follows:

```
$ sqlldr example/expass control=load5.ctl log=load5.log bad=load5.bad
                                  discard=load5.dis
```

The following is the server response:

```
SQL*Loader: Release 8.0.3.0.0 - Production on Wed Mar 10 10:20:11 1999
```

```
(c) Copyright 1997 Oracle Corporation.  All rights reserved.
```

```
Commit point reached - logical record count 16
```

LISTING 31.16   EXAMPLE 5 LOG FILE CONTENTS

```
SQL*Loader: Release 8.0.3.0.0 - Production on Wed Mar 10 10:20:11 1999

(c) Copyright 1997 Oracle Corporation.  All rights reserved.

Control File:    load5.ctl
Data File:       xact.dat
  Bad File:      load5.bad
  Discard File:  load5.dis
 (Allow all discards)

Number to load: ALL
Number to skip: 0
Errors allowed: 50
Bind array:     64 rows, maximum of 65536 bytes
Continuation:    none specified
Path used:       Conventional

Table PARTITION_XACT, partition P1, loaded when XACT_FLAG = 0X44(character 'D')
Insert option in effect for this partition: INSERT

    Column Name                   Position   Len  Term Encl Datatype
------------------------------ ---------- ----- ---- ---- -------------
ACCT_NBR                            1:10    10             CHARACTER
XACT_AMT                           11:20    10             CHARACTER
XACT_FLAG                          21:21     1             CHARACTER
XACT_DATE                          22:31    10             DATE DD-MON-YY

Column XACT_AMT had SQL string
":xact_amt * -1"
 applied to it.
Column XACT_DATE is NULL if XACT_DATE = BLANKS

Table PARTITION_XACT, partition P1, loaded when XACT_FLAG = 0X43(character 'C')
Insert option in effect for this partition: INSERT

    Column Name                   Position   Len  Term Encl Datatype
------------------------------ ---------- ----- ---- ---- -------------
ACCT_NBR                            1:10    10             CHARACTER
XACT_AMT                           11:20    10             CHARACTER
XACT_FLAG                          21:21     1             CHARACTER
XACT_DATE                          22:31    10             DATE DD-MON-YY

Column XACT_DATE is NULL if XACT_DATE = BLANKS

Record 3: Discarded - failed all WHEN clauses.
Record 5: Rejected - Error on table PARTITION_XACT, partition P1.
ORA-14401: inserted partition key is outside specified partition
Record 10: Rejected - Error on table PARTITION_XACT, partition P1.
ORA-14401: inserted partition key is outside specified partition
Record 14: Rejected - Error on table PARTITION_XACT, partition P1.
ORA-14401: inserted partition key is outside specified partition
Record 15: Rejected - Error on table PARTITION_XACT, column XACT_AMT.
ORA-01722: invalid number
Record 16: Rejected - Error on table PARTITION_XACT, partition P1.
ORA-14401: inserted partition key is outside specified partition
```

```
Record 4: Rejected - Error on table PARTITION_XACT, partition P1.
ORA-14401: inserted partition key is outside specified partition
Record 6: Rejected - Error on table PARTITION_XACT, partition P1.
ORA-14401: inserted partition key is outside specified partition
Record 8: Rejected - Error on table PARTITION_XACT, partition P1.
ORA-14401: inserted partition key is outside specified partition
Record 12: Rejected - Error on table PARTITION_XACT, partition P1.
ORA-14401: inserted partition key is outside specified partition
Record 13: Rejected - Error on table PARTITION_XACT, partition P1.
ORA-14401: inserted partition key is outside specified partition

Table PARTITION_XACT, partition P1:

  3 Rows successfully loaded.
  5 Rows not loaded due to data errors.
  8 Rows not loaded because all WHEN clauses were failed.
  0 Rows not loaded because all fields were null.

Table PARTITION_XACT, partition P1:

  2 Rows successfully loaded.
  5 Rows not loaded due to data errors.
  9 Rows not loaded because all WHEN clauses were failed.
  0 Rows not loaded because all fields were null.

Space allocated for bind array:                  7168 bytes(64 rows)
Space allocated for memory besides bind array:      0 bytes

Total logical records skipped:        0
Total logical records read:          16
Total logical records rejected:      10
Total logical records discarded:      1

Run began on Wed Mar 10 10:21:39 1999
Run ended on Wed Mar 10 8:22:01 1999

Elapsed time was:     00:00:00.31
CPU time was:         00:00:00.04
```

PART

VI

CH

31

Example 5 comments: To load a partition of a partitioned table, the keyword PARTITION needs to be added after the table name in the control file. Note that the partition name, in this instance P1, must be enclosed in parenthesis. All partitions are loaded if the keyword PARTITION is omitted. All records that are not in the partition range of P1 are written in the bad file.

CONVENTIONAL AND DIRECT PATH LOADING

SQL*Loader provides two methods to load data, conventional and direct path loading. Conventional path loading is the default for SQL*Loader. To enable direct path loading, DIRECT=TRUE must be added to the command-line parameters when invoking SQL*Loader. As seen in Figure 31.2, conventional path loading has additional steps that direct path loading doesn't. These extra steps add additional overhead to the process, making conventional path loading slower than direct path loading. The additional steps of formatting SQL

INSERT statements and going through the buffer cache of the SGA are contending with all other processes that are running concurrently against the database. Although the inclination is to always use direct path loading for its speed, there are restrictions and cases when conventional path loading should be used. This is covered in the following section.

Figure 31.2
Conventional and
Direct Path Loading
Methods

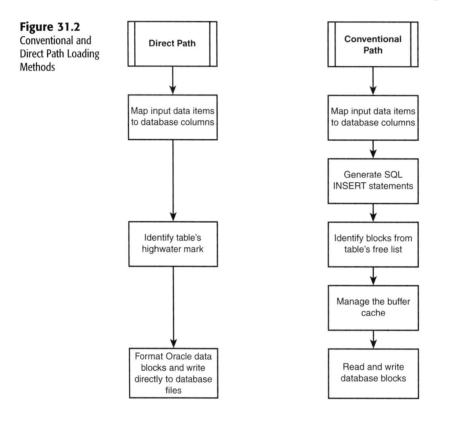

USING CONVENTIONAL PATH LOAD

The conventional path uses SQL INSERT statements and in-memory bond array buffers to load data into Oracle tables. This process competes with all other processes for memory resources within the SGA. This can slow down loader performance if the database already has the overhead of supporting many concurrent processes.

Another overhead of using conventional path loading is that the loader process must scan the database for partially filled blocks of the table being loaded and attempt to fill those blocks. This is efficient for daily transactional processing, but it is an additional overhead that conventional path loading has.

There are cases when conventional path loading is the preferred and sometimes mandatory method over the direct path:

- If the table being loaded is indexed and being accessed concurrently with the load or if inserts and deletes are being run against the table, conventional path loading must be used.

- When applying SQL functions in the control file, SQL functions will not be applied when using the direct path.

- When the table being loaded is a clustered table.

- When loading a small number of rows into a large indexed table or when the table has referential integrity or check constraints. It is explained in the following section, "Using Direct Path Loading," why the conventional path is preferred in this instance.

- When loading is done through SQL*Net or Net8 with heterogeneous platform, both nodes must belong to the same family of computers and be using the same character set to use direct path loading.

USING DIRECT PATH LOADING

Instead of using SQL INSERT statements and bind array buffers, the direct path formats the input data into Oracle data blocks and writes them directly into the database. It is important to note that direct path loading always inserts data above the table's high-water mark. This eliminates the time spent scanning for partially filled blocks. If the direct path is being used and does not complete and if loader is restarted from the beginning, the data that is loaded should be truncated, or the table should be dropped and re-created. Simply deleting the data does not reset the high-water mark, and you will be using more storage than is necessary.

An understanding of what happens to a table's indexes using the direct path method is important to maximize the efficiency of direct path loading. In Oracle8, indexes are marked unusable when the loaded data becomes visible (high-water mark is moved and committed), as this is the point that the indexes are out-of-date in respect to the data that they index. As each index is brought up-to-date, the index unusable state is cleared. This enables queries to take place against the table while direct path loading is in progress. However, a query executing while the load is in the finishing stage (moving the high-water mark and updating indexes) might fail if the query requires an index that is in an unusable state.

During the load, the new index values are written to temporary segments, and at the end of the load, they are sorted and merged with the old index values. At this time the index becomes usable again. This can significantly increase the need for temp space. To avoid the additional need for temporary space to do the sort, you can presort the data in the order of the index and use the keywords SORTED INDEXES in the control file.

In the previous section on conventional path loading, the restrictions were listed that would prevent the use of a direct path. Loading a relatively small number of rows into a large table with indexes and/or referential and check constraints is not a restriction against using direct path loading, but it will probably be more efficient to use the conventional path. In the case of the indexes, it would probably be quicker for the conventional path to update the indexes as it is loading the data, rather than doing a large sort/merge to create the new indexes. With referential and check constraints, direct path loading requires that these constraints be disabled before the load. After all the data is loaded and constraints are re-enabled, the entire data's table is checked against these constraints, not only the data that was loaded.

LOADING NESTED COLUMNS, NESTED TABLES, AND VARRAYS

A nested column object is one in which a column object is inside another column object.

A nested table is a table within another table. This nested table appears as a column in another table. This table can be referenced as a table or as a column within the other table.

A VARRAY is an ordered set of objects called elements. These elements are indexed by their position in the array.

Listing 31.17 displays two nested column-objects, em_contact is nested inside dept_mgr, which is a nested column to TABLE dept.

LISTING 31.17   LOAD6.CTL—EXAMPLE 6 CONTROL FILE

```
LOAD DATA

INFILE 'example6.dat'

INTO TABLE dept

    (deptno        CHAR(5),
    dept_name     CHAR(30),
    dept_mgr      COLUMN OBJECT
        (name     CHAR(30),
        age     INTEGER EXTERNAL(3),
        emp_id    INTEGER EXTERNAL(7),
        em_contact  COLUMN OBJECT
            (name     CHAR(30),
            PHONE     CHAR(25))
        )
    )
```

Example 6 comments: Loading data into a nested table is very similar to loading data into regular tables. Note the differences in the syntax in the preceding example where the nested table appears as a column object.

Listing 31.18 illustrates the use of a VARRAY and a nested table in a control file.

LISTING 31.18   LOAD7.CTL—EXAMPLE 7 CONTROL FILE

```
LOAD DATA

INFILE 'example7.dat'

INTO TABLE dept
```

```
(deptno        CHAR(4),
dept_name      CHAR(30),
emp_count      FILLER INTEGER EXTERNAL(5),
emp_str        VARRAY COUNT(emp_count)
    (name      FILLER CHAR(30),
    emp_str    COLUMN OBJECT
        (name    CHAR(30),
        age     INTEGER EXTERNAL(3),
        emp_id   INTEGER EXTERNAL(7)
        )
    ),
proj_sid    FILLER CHAR(30),
emp_projects    NEXTED TABLE SDF(CONSTANT 'project.txt', "proj1")
        SID(proj_sid) TERMINATED BY ";"
    (project_id    POSITION(1:6) INTEGET EXTERNAL(6),
    project_name    POSITION(7:31) CHAR
    )
)
```

Example 7 comments: Loading data into a VARRAY requires that SQL*Loader know exactly how many rows will be loaded. This is achieved using the COUNT syntax. This COUNT has a parameter that contains the number of elements for the VARRAY. Also note that the parameter field to COUNT appears directly in front of the COUNT syntax.

Note

Each element of a VARRAY needs four bytes of client memory prior to loading into the database. SQL*Loader might need at least twice this space for each VARRAY. For example, if you have a 100 element VARRAY, 400 bytes of client memory will be needed, and SQL*Loader might need over 800 bytes of client memory to process the VARRAY. If you are running out of memory during the load, try a smaller value for BINDSIZE or ROWS, and restart the load.

USING SQL*LOADER TO LOAD LOBS

LOBS, or large objects, fall into two categories, those stored internally in the database and those stored externally. BLOBS, CLOBS, and NCLOBS are stored in tables. Externally stored LOBs are stored in BFILEs. Listing 31.19 illustrates a control file storing an internally defined LOB, Listing 31.20 illustrates a control file storing an internally defined LOB but loading the LOB from a LOBFILE, and listing 31.21 illustrates a control file using BFILEs.

LISTING 31.19   RESUME1.CTL—EXAMPLE 8 CONTROL FILE

```
LOAD DATA

INFILE 'resume1.dat'

INTO TABLE resumes

    (resume_name    POSITION(1:21) CHAR,
    resume          POSITION(22:1000) CHAR
    )
```

Example 8 comments: This loader control file is pretty much straight forward in that the resume_name and the LOB data appear in the same input data file.

LISTING 31.20   RESUME2.CTL—EXAMPLE 9 CONTROL FILE

```
LOAD DATA

INFILE 'resume2.dat'

INTO TABLE resumes

    (resume_name    POSITION(1:21) CHAR,
    "RESUME2"    LOBFILE(CONSTANT 'Resume2' VARCHAR(4,2000)
    )
```

Example 9 comments: This control file contains a secondary data file, or SDF. Note that CONSTANT is the name of the SDF, and also note that the first four positions of this file must contain the length of the LOB. This is specified by VARCHAR(4,2000), where the 4 says that the first four positions of file RESUME2 will contain the length of the LOB.

> **Caution**
>
> When loading LOBs from LOBFILES, if the LOB fails to load, the record containing the LOB will load but contain an empty LOB.

LISTING 31.21   RESUME3.CTL—EXAMPLE 10 CONTROL FILE

```
LOAD DATA

INFILE 'resume3.dat'

INTO TABLE resumes
FIELDS TERMINATED BY ','

    (resume_name    CHAR(3),
    file_name    CHAR(50),
    resume        BFILE(CONSTANT "Resume", file_name)
    )
```

Example 10 comments: The BFILE stores the LOB in OS files. The BFILE column stores the file locator of the external file that actually will contain the LOB. This is convenient for very large LOBS, such as video.

SQL*LOADER PERFORMANCE TIPS

Following are some additional tips on increasing the performance of SQL*Loader:

1. Use positional fields over delimited fields, which require the loader to scan the data to search for the delimiters. Positional fields are quicker because the loader only has to do simple pointer arithmetic.

2. Specify maximum lengths for *terminated by fields* to make each bind array insert more efficient.

3. Pre-allocate enough storage. As data is being loaded and more space is required in the table, Oracle allocates more extents to hold the data. This operation can be expensive if it is being done constantly during the load. Calculating or estimating the storage requirements prior to the load enables you to create the necessary storage up front.

4. Avoid using NULLIF and DEFAULTIF clauses in the control file if possible. Each clause causes the column to be evaluated for every row being loaded.

5. Split data files, and run concurrent conventional path loads.

6. Reduce the number of commits by using the command-line parameter ROWS.

7. Avoid unnecessary character set conversions. Ensure that the client's NLS_LANG environment is the same as the server's.

8. Use direct path loading whenever possible.

9. When using direct path loading, presort data for the largest index of the table and use the SORTED INDEXES clause.

10. When using direct path loading, use the parallel direct path option when possible.

11. Minimize the use of redo logs during direct path loads. There are three ways of doing this with different levels of control:

    - Disable archiving of the database.
    - Use the keyword UNRECOVERABLE in the control file.
    - Alter the table and/or index with the NOLOG attribute.

SQL*LOADER SUMMARY

SQL*Loader is a powerful utility provided by Oracle Corporation. SQL*Loader is capable of loading almost any kind of data from almost any kind of data format, utilizing the Oracle kernel (conventional load) or using an extremely fast data load (direct path load). SQL*Loader eliminates the need to write special data-load type programs.

DESIGNER FOR ADMINISTRATORS

In this chapter

DESIGNER—ORACLE'S POPULAR CASE SOLUTION

The acronym CASE stands for Computer-Aided Software/Systems Engineering. Traditionally, the system development process involved very little planning before programming of the system began, and also the IT group was not in constant communication with the users of the system. This resulted in systems that did not meet user expectations. Today, many organizations rely on a formal methodology to guide their system development tasks wherein the methodology has specific guidelines regarding what is accomplished at specific stages of the project, resulting in better systems. There are an increasing number of organizations that have purchased a CASE tool or are considering purchasing one to assist them with their system development tasks. Oracle's popular CASE solution is the Designer toolset.

SYSTEMS DEVELOPMENT LIFE CYCLE (SDLC)

The idea of a life cycle is to break a large project into smaller units called stages. Each stage consists of many specific tasks that must be completed before the next stage is started. The life cycle begins with the initial idea of the project, followed by planning and design, programming, testing, implementing, and finally, using the system. Usually, the life cycle spends a lot of time in the initial phases where critical data is gathered from the user community and is properly documented. Organizations must understand the importance of this stage; if they rush through this stage, the resulting system might not be what the users expect.

A traditional SDLC consists of a minimum of five stages:

- Strategy—Involves gaining an overall idea of the scope of the project and how the project will proceed.
- Analysis—Involves determining the user requirements for the proposed system and the project planning.
- Design—Involves the database design and programming modules design.
- Implementation—Programming and testing the system.
- Support—The system is put in production, users are trained to use the system, and support is provided for the system.

Oracle Corporation has a customized methodology called Oracle Case Method. Customers can purchase *CASE*Method Tasks and Deliverables*, which details the tasks and outputs of each stage.

Here are some terms that you need to know:

- Application—A logical grouping of software engineering elements. It can represent anything from a high-level conceptual model to a specific system model.
- DES2K repository/instance—An Oracle account that owns a set of database objects. Whenever you create, edit, or delete something in DES2K, the records of underlying tables are modified by DES2K via specific packages.

- Subordinate user—An Oracle account that accesses the repository through synonyms.
- Repository—Consists of the tables and views that are used to interface with the data and the procedures to manage them.

UPPER CASE VERSUS LOWER CASE

A common terminology in use today is whether a given CASE tool is an upper CASE tool or a lower CASE tool. An *upper CASE* tool is used to define system requirements and produce diagrams and documentation that can be reviewed by the users during the early stages of the project. An upper CASE tool is not used to generate the actual database or program modules. *Lower CASE* tools are primarily concerned with the design and building stages of the SDLC. They increase productivity by generating syntax to build databases and programs. On its own, neither tool is sufficient because the upper CASE tool does not increase productivity whereas the lower CASE tool does not provide documentation for verification by the users.

DESIGNER OVERVIEW

Designer provides a complete upper CASE and lower CASE solution and supports the entire SDLC.

The logical model created during the analysis stage becomes the basis of the physical model, which is created during the design stage. Applications are generated using this model and therefore any business change is immediately reflected in the application. Non-Oracle CASE methodology can also be used by customers.

The minimal requirements for installing Designer are listed as follows (client side, then server side).

Client-side requirements include the following:

- Pentium 90MHz processor or higher
- CD-ROM drive
- 300MB-600MB free disk space depending on the options chosen
- 40MB minimum swap space to run the applications
- 32MB available RAM
- 1GB hard disk
- NT 4.0, Windows 95, or Windows 98
- SQL*NET version 2.3.4 (SQL*NET is only required if running against a remote server)
- SQL*Plus 3.3.4 or SQL*Plus 8.0.4 (for Oracle8 databases)
- Net8 client 8.0.4 (for Oracle8 databases)
- Use at least 640x480 settings for your display.

PART

VI

CH

32

Server-side requirements include the following:

- Oracle7 version 7.3.4 or higher
- Shared_pool_size of 18MB minimum
- Recommended optimizer mode is COST-based
- At least 30MB available RAM
- 60MB in the SYSTEM tablespace for the repository PL/SQL packages, procedures, and views
- 70MB in the ROLLBACK tablespace for the installation of the repository
- SQL*Plus 3.3.4 or SQL*Plus 8.0.4 (for Oracle8 databases)
- Net8 client 8.0.4 (for Oracle8 databases)
- For PC-based servers use Windows NT 4.0, Windows 95, or Windows 98
- For UNIX-based servers user SUN Solaris 2.5 or equivalent UNIX system

Note

Refer to the installation manuals to determine storage requirements.

For the latest information on product availability, please contact Oracle Worldwide Customer Support. As of the date of writing this module, the latest release available is Designer R2.1.2 and is certified against the following software:

- Windows NT 4.0, Windows 95, and Windows 98
- Oracle7.3.4 or higher
- Designer Object Extensions (object database designer) R2.1.1
- Developer 2.1 production with the application of October 1998 patch
- Web Server 3.0.1, 3.0.2, and 4.0
- Netscape 3.04 Gold, Netscape 4.0.6, Internet Explorer 3.0.2, and Internet Explorer 4.01
- Visual Basic 4.0 or higher

Note

You should make sure that all the client tools and the repository are operating at the same release level to avoid compatibility problems.

CHANGES FROM DESIGNER/2000 R1.3.2

Designer Release 2.x provides a variety of new features. These features are summarized in the following lists.

Extended server generation includes the following:

- Support for Oracle7, Oracle RdB, and Oracle Web server
- Support for non-Oracle databases: MS SQL Server, Sybase, DB2/2, and Informix
- Support for ODBC databases
- API generation for DML and lock procedures for tables

Client generation includes the following:

- Design reuse: after a module is defined, components can be shared with other modules
- Application logic: store PL/SQL, Visual Basic, and Java code
- Generators integration
- Generation of database triggers based on declarative design information in the repository
- 100% reverse engineering of application logic as well as 100% generation

The Design Editor includes the following:

- A single, fully integrated design and generation environment
- Maximizes ease-of-use by means of wizards, drag-and-drop, edit-in-place, right mouse menus, and synchronized updates

Migration paths to Designer R 2.x include the following:

- Designer R 2.x can perform upgrades on Designer 2000 R1.x repositories.

Application upgrades include the following:

- The Restore facility in the RON (Repository Object Navigator), which is discussed in more detail in the section "Designer Administration," can be used to upgrade a pre-existing Release 1 application or a set of applications to Designer R2.x. A two-step process upgrades the archived applications to be 1.3.2-compliant and then upgrades this to R2.x. The disadvantage of this approach is that if the upgrade process is aborted due to errors, it has to be restarted with the original archive. To prevent this from happening, analyze the data before archiving it.

Co-existence of release 1.x and release 2.0 includes the following:

- 16-bit release 1.x—Yes. Provided that the 16-bit release 1.x and the 32-bit release 2.x are in separate Oracle Homes.
- 32-bit release 1.x—Yes. Installing release 2.x on top of existing release 1.x will not be a problem because the default directory names are different in release 2.x.

PART

VI

CH

32

Cautions include the following:

- The NLS_LANG parameter in the Registry must match the NLS_LANG parameter in the server, otherwise it will cause problems when loading package definitions during install and upgrade.
- A typical upgrade should take 2–3 hours to drop the existing API and another 2–3 hours to load the new API and perform instance conversion and initialization.
- If the RAU (Repository Administration Utility—discussed in more detail in the section "Designer Administration") has invoked the SQL*PLUS, *do not* manually invoke SQL*PLUS; it can lead to process hands and even corruption of the repository.

DESIGNER COMPONENTS

The Designer toolset contains the components in the following lists.

Repository services include the following:

- Repository Object Navigator (RON)
- Matrix Diagrammer
- Repository management facilities
- Process Modeler

The Systems Modeler includes the following:

- Entity Relationship Diagrammer
- Function Hierarchy Diagrammer
- DataFlow Diagrammer

The Systems Designer includes the following:

- Design Editor
- Generators

The Designer components are shown in Figure 32.1.

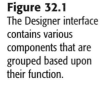

Figure 32.1
The Designer interface contains various components that are grouped based upon their function.

The Designer interface consists of various parts described as follows:

- Modeling System Requirements—The tools in this area can be used to model business processes, create E-R diagrams, and create models of entities, functions and data flow in the system.

- Generating Preliminary Designs—The Database Transformer and Application Transformer in this area can be used to create designs from the models created earlier.

- Designing and Generating—The tools in this area can be used to design a system that represents the system functionality. Both server-side components and client-side applications can be created by using information from the repository.

- Utilities—The tools in this area can be used to manage the repository, write SQL-based queries interactively, and obtain online help.

DESIGN EDITOR

The Design Editor replaces and enhances the functionality of the Data Schema Diagrammer, Module Data Diagrammer, Module Network Diagrammer, Module Logic Navigator, and the Preferences Navigator. The Design Editor is an integrated environment that enables you to perform a variety of tasks at design time (refer to Figures 32.2 and 32.3), including the following:

- Creation of module diagrams
- Creation of data diagrams
- Drag-and-drop features
- Navigator to enable working with the data model outside the context of a diagram

Figure 32.2
Design Editor
Navigator modules.

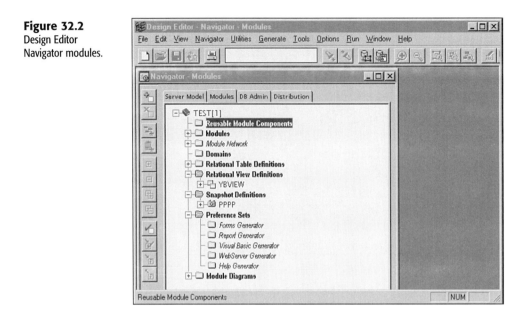

Figure 32.3
Design Editor
Navigator server
model.

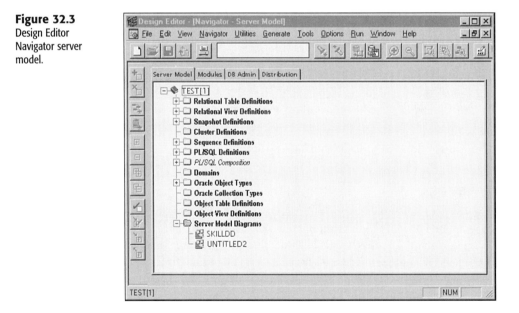

UNDERSTANDING THE REPOSITORY

The heart of the Designer is the repository that records all the information entered into Designer. It is the basis for generation in the implementation stage of the SDLC. Features include the following:

- Repository Object Navigator (RON)—A part of the repository services that enables a highly intuitive method of viewing and manipulating repository objects as shown in Figure 32.4

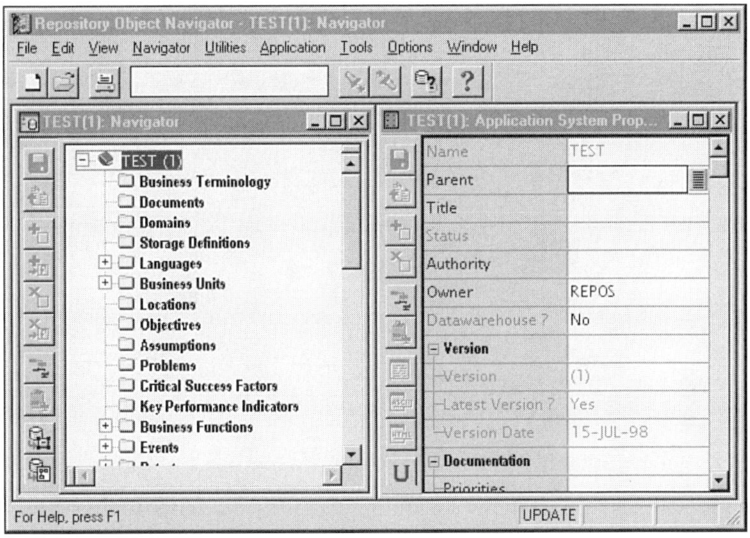

Figure 32.4
Repository Object Navigator components.

- Repository-based—This enables multiuser concurrent access, check in and check out facilities and also enables data access from other products like SQL*PLUS.

- Version control—This enables the development to proceed with the current state of the application frozen. It enables the maintaining of a history of system development over time and also parallel development of the application using one or more versions. For example, an inventory system can be developed for use in both the United States and the UK—one version containing UK-specific details and the other containing US-specific information.

- Quality checks—It provides a variety of quality checks during the initial stages by cross-referencing and checking consistency rules that enable the fixing of errors during the early stages.

- Documentation—It offers an extensive set of reporting options to generate systems documentation. All the information is entered into property sheets and diagrammers as the project progresses; the reports are available easily. There are over a hundred standard reports that can be run.

- National language support—This enables Designer to be run against an Oracle database built in any character set, including multi-byte character sets.

There are several reports that can be obtained from the repository, as shown in figure 32.5.

PART
VI

CH
32

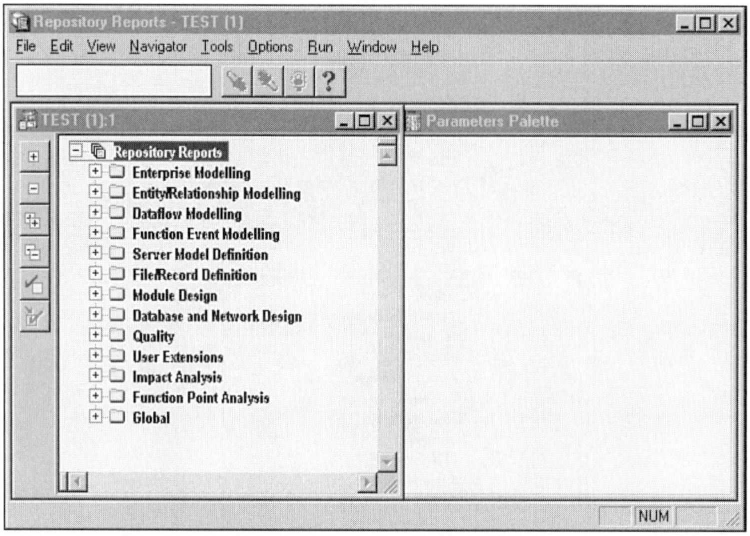

Figure 32.5
The reports available from the repository.

USING THE DIAGRAMMERS

Features common to all the diagrammers of the Designer toolset are as follows:

- Graphical User Interface
- Point-and-click capability
- Pull-down menus
- Context-sensitive help
- Multiple windows
- Integration with the repository
- OLE 2.0 integration
- Hierarchical views

All the diagrammers and utilities provided with DES2K have certain common features, and you can use similar procedures to interface with them. After Designer has been installed, you will see an Oracle Designer icon in the Designer group. Double-click this icon, and log on to the Oracle database where the repository resides. If you are opening an existing application system, choose it at this point. Otherwise, you can create a new application system at this point.

Note

The Designer window can be started from the command line using the following syntax:

`DES2KXX username/password@database /A:apps_system,version /S`

`username/password@database` is the connect string; `/A` specifies the application system and the version, and `/S` is used to suppress the splash screen.

To create a new application system, complete the following steps:

1. Select Repository Object Navigator (RON) from the Design Editor screen, and choose File, New Application.

2. Create a name for the application system.

You can continue working with this application system or change it by choosing a different one from the File menu.

The status line of the different tools and utilities contains valuable information about the current session, such as the application system, version, and logged on user. All the diagrammers have a similar look and feel. They have a Multiple Document Interface (MDI) and enable the user to look at the same object from different views and through different diagrams at the same time.

The diagrammers make extensive use of the mouse to manipulate objects and also respond to dialog boxes. All the standard Windows mouse actions such as drag-and-drop, selecting, double-clicking to change the properties, moving, resizing, and so on are supported. There is a full-featured menu system that enables easy manipulation of the objects and the application systems. A toolbar is also provided as an extension of the menu system and makes the most frequently used functions easily accessible to the developers. The DES2K utilities also have a common look and feel. There are two types of utilities that are used:

- Full-Windows utilities, such as Repository Object Navigator, Repository Administration Utility, Repository Reports, and Matrix Diagrammer, provide an MDI interface similar to the diagrammers. These utilities provide an object navigator and properties window in order to easily manipulate the objects.

- Pop-up Window utilities, such as the generators and reverse engineering utilities, are generally started from another diagrammer or utility.

DIAGRAMMING TECHNIQUES USED BY DESIGNER

During the logical and physical design of a system, diagrams help you to accurately document the proposed system and communicate with the users and other team members. The following Designer diagrammers are commonly used during the logical and physical design of the database:

- Entity Relationship Diagrammer—An ERD models the information needs of an organization. It should involve communication and consensus between the project team and the end users. Entity Relationship Modeling involves identifying the things of importance in an organization (entities), the properties of those things (attributes), and how they relate to each other (relationships). A simple two-entity ERD is shown in Figure 32.6.

Figure 32.6
An example of a two-entity relationship diagram.

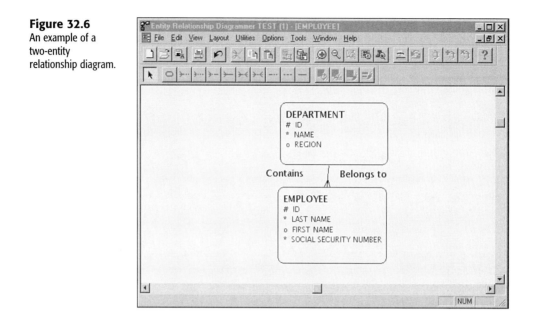

- Function Hierarchy Diagrammer—This identifies everything the company needs to do and shows the functions that the company performs and those that it wants to implement in the future. The function hierarchy begins with an overall mission description and breaks it down into major functions that are further deconstructed until it is not possible to break it further.

- Dataflow Diagrammer—The DFD depicts how information flows in the business and how it also flows between the outside environment and the system interfaces.

- Matrix Diagrammer—The Repository Services of Designer enable the generation of a variety of matrix diagrams for the system. The purpose of the matrix is to identify areas that might have been overlooked during the logical design.

- Process Flow Diagrammer—The process modeler component of Designer supports process modeling techniques that can be used to support Business Process Re-engineering (BPR) or prototyping. It can also act as a visual feedback to the users about the analyst's understanding of the system requirements.

GENERATORS

There are several code generators provided by Designer, and these are repository utilities that enable the generation of complete, bug-free code to be used in the build phase of the System Development Life Cycle. The collection of generators can be classified into two types: Server Code Generator and Front-end Code Generator.

FORMS GENERATOR (FRONT-END CODE GENERATOR)

This is a DES2K component that enables Developer/2000 applications to be built quickly based on repository information. Forms Generator has a lot of features that include the following:

- Generates full-featured and menued forms applications
- Enables generation of applications with GUI items such as buttons, check boxes, radio groups, and so on
- Provides foreign key validation
- Provides implementation of business rules
- Enables reverse engineering of Oracle forms applications and storing them into the repository
- Regenerates forms without losing code enhancements added by developers
- Provides support for VBX controls for 16-bit versions and OCX controls for 32-bit versions
- Provides OLE 2.0 support and integration with Windows-based desktop applications

REPORTS GENERATOR (FRONT-END CODE GENERATOR)

The Reports Generator is a DES2K component that enables Oracle reports applications to be built quickly based on repository information. Its many features include the following:

- Supports multilink reports
- Provides many reporting styles and layouts, including control break, master-detail, and matrix reports
- Provides productivity gains to developers
- Provides templates for standardization
- Enables customization of generator operations
- Provides a variety of summary functions
- Enables reverse engineering from existing reports and creates module definitions that are stored in the repository
- Regenerates reports with changed specifications

SERVER GENERATOR (SERVER CODE GENERATOR)

This is a Designer component that provides for the creation of database objects and PL/SQL modules based on repository information. Its features include the following:

- Generates ANSI standard SQL for database object creation
- Generates check constraints
- Generates and validates PK-FK relationships

- Supports the role-based security of Oracle7
- Generates PL/SQL modules including triggers, procedures, functions, and packages
- Supports snapshots
- Reverse engineers database objects and stores their definitions in the repository

Basically, you define the objects in the repository and then use this generator to specify the object for which you want the script created.

Visual Basic Generator (Front-End Code Generator)

This generator is similar to the Forms Generator. The code from this generator can be loaded into Visual Basic 6.0 and used to create an executable file.

WebServer Generator (Front-End Code Generator)

The WebServer Generator can be used to create Web applications. To create a Web application, follow these steps:

1. Define the modules in the Module Data Diagrammer.
2. Create PL/SQL packages from the modules using WebServer.
3. Run the generated PL/SQL scripts on the Oracle WebServer to create the Web application.

MS Help Generator (Front-End Code Generator)

The MS Help Generator creates help files in MS Help file format that can be used along with Forms and Visual Basic applications. The MS Help Generator puts help text in a file and creates the necessary links and jumps that are needed. You will also need the MS Help compiler, which is a separate product, to generate the WinHelp format files.

C++ Object Layer Generator (Server Code Generator)

This generator enables you to access object-relational databases by creating C++ class definitions and code using the systems modeler tools. It can be used to produce the classes for both the data and the functions that form the object. You will need to compile the generated classes with the rest of the C++ code and also link it with the C++ libraries.

Module Regeneration Strategy

All the post-generation work should be implemented in such a way that module regeneration can take place more or less in a painless manner. The following strategies can be used to accomplish this task:

- Put all the information in the repository.—This method ensures that the changes are automatically applied in the regenerated modules. However, this method results in increased administration of the repository.

- Use multiple templates: a base template and other form-specific templates.—The base template can be used for all the forms in the system, and you can also put form-specific information in the other templates, thereby making it easy to manage the code.

Oracle CASE Exchange

Oracle CASE Exchange is a utility that enables bi-directional exchange of information between Designer and CASE tools from other vendors. This can be very useful for people who have been using CASE tools from other vendors and are now interested in using Designer. It is especially useful if an organization does its analysis using another CASE tool such as LBMS Automate Plus and now wants to finish the project using Designer. One of the limitations of DES2K is that it does not generate 3GL code; using CASE Exchange, you can transfer the information from the repository into another CASE tool and generate 3GL from that tool.

Oracle CASE Exchange supports the CASE tools described in the following lists.

Upper CASE support includes the following:

- ADW/IEW from Knowledgeware
- Excelerator from Intersolv
- Design/1 from Anderson Consulting
- LBMS Automate Plus

Lower CASE support includes the following:

- ASK Ingres 6.0
- Pansophic Telon

Validation checks are provided by CASE Exchange for the following before loading:

- Entities without attributes
- Attributes without an entity
- Entities without relationships
- Entities without unique identifiers
- Compatibility with the target tool

Waterfall Oriented Methodology Using Designer

The Waterfall Methodology is very popular for CASE studies, and it makes use of the following stages: Strategy, Analysis, Design, and Implementation. Various Designer components can be used during this process as shown below:

1. Create an APPLICATION, which will be your work area. Use Repository Object Navigator (choose File, New Application).

2. Using the Entity Relationship Diagrammer, create the entities and their relationships. Use Edit, Domains to enter domains, their valid values, and their defaults. Double-click an entity to enter attributes and specify its domain and relationships. Also add attribute defaults and valid values.

3. Use the Function Hierarchy Diagrammer to create this diagram. Double-click each function, and add additional information to determine whether it will be a module or a form.

4. Using the Matrix Diagrammer, specify the correlation between functions and entity attributes.

5. Use the various reports to examine the quality of your analysis.

6. Use the Properties window to define an area where the database objects will reside.

7. Using the Database Design Transformer, specify all the entities to be translated to tables.

8. Use RON to edit the table definitions.

9. Using RON, add error messages for rule violations.

10. Use the RON check constraint to enforce data integrity constraints.

11. Create Sequence Type columns to delineate a detail table from its master.

12. Using the Data Diagrammer, edit the column definitions.

13. Use the Server Generator to generate DDL.

14. Using the Application wizard from RON, create a GUI model of the application.

15. Edit the module definitions using the Module Data Diagrammer.

16. Use the appropriate generators (Forms, Report, Menu, and so on) to generate the application.

Table 32.1 shows the most common tasks, and the tools that can be used for their purpose.

TABLE 32.1   DESIGNER TOOLS TO USE FOR SPECIFIC TASKS

Task	Tool
Model the process flow	Process Modeler or Dataflow Diagrammer
Create an Entity Relationship Diagram	ER Diagrammer
List entities and processes	Repository Reports
Map entity usages to processes	Matrix Diagrammer
Functional decomposition	Function Hierarchy Diagrammer

Task	Tool
Move from one phase to another	RON (Application versioning) Prototyping/ Generators
Implementing GUI standards	Design Editor
Designing physical database	Database Design Transformer (Refer to Figure 32.11)
Refining of physical design	Data Diagrammer and RON
Application design	Application Design—Transformer (Refer to figure 32.12)
Refining of application design	Module Data Diagrammer, Module Structure Diagrammer, Matrix Diagrammer, RON
Developing application modules	Generators
Database object creation scripts	Data Diagrammer, Server Generator
Sanity check of the design	Matrix Diagrammer
Documentation	Repository Reports
Fixing bugs	Depends on the utility
User and repository management	Repository Object Navigator, Repository Administration Utility

Figure 32.7
Database design transformer components.

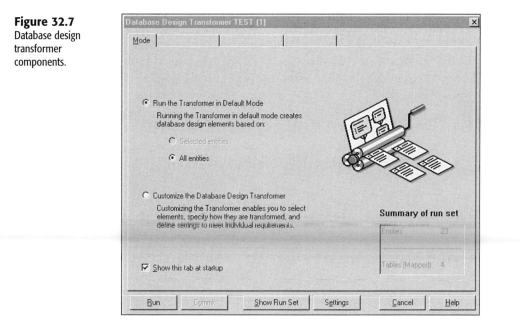

PART

VI

CH

32

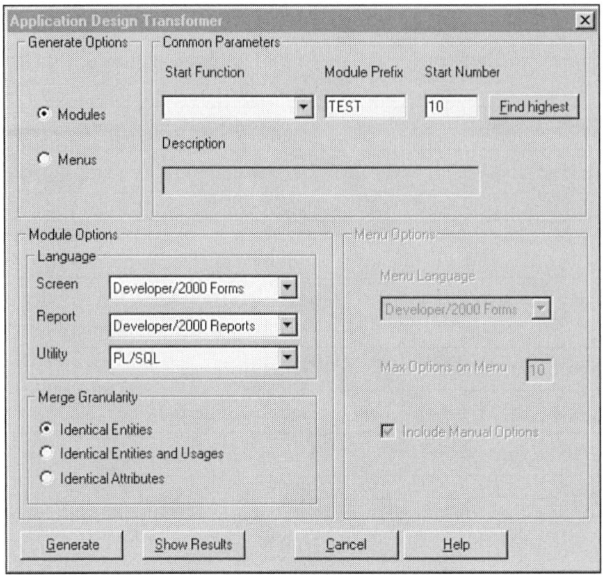

Figure 32.8
Application design
transformer
components.

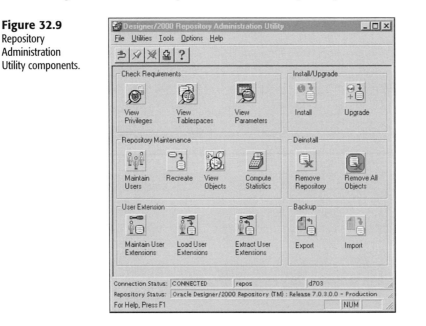

DESIGNER ADMINISTRATION

Designer administration consists of the set of techniques used to monitor and manage a project's data. Tools provided by DES2K to perform these functions are accessible via the File, Utiltity, and Application pull-down menus within the Repository Object Navigator (RON) and the Repository Administration Utility (RAU). Administration tasks include repository setup, granting permissions to repository users, migration, version control, and sharing of data elements. Figure 32.9 shows the Repository Administration Utility interface.

Figure 32.9
Repository
Administration
Utility components.

UNDERSTANDING THE REPOSITORY

The repository is implemented as a standard Oracle database. It consists of tables that store information about the system being analyzed, designed, and generated. Repository users who have sufficient privileges create one or more application systems and grant access at the application system level to other repository users. The creator/owner of the application system can share objects into their application system from another application system in which they are given share access by the owner of that other application system. These shared objects, however, can be modified only in the application system that they are created within.

To use the repository effectively, it is very important to understand its design and the elements that comprise it. There are a few diagrams shipped by Oracle as part of the Designer software that are very helpful in understanding the repository. They can also help you understand why Designer works the way it does. The repository consists of elements, associations between those elements, and the attributes of the elements or associations. There are several types of elements and associations that exist in the repository, such as Entity, Column, Function-Entity, and so on.

There are two groups of repository elements: Primary Access Controlled (PAC) and Secondary Access Controlled (SAC). Primary Access Controlled elements are owned by the application system; deleting a primary access controlled element deletes all its secondary access controlled elements. Examples of PAC include table, function, and module. Secondary Access Controlled elements are owned by a PAC. Some SACs can have detailed SACs of their own. Examples of SAC include attribute, ID, and so on. *Associations* are similar to SACs in the sense that they also need a parent and cannot exist independently; in fact, an association has two parents—the two PACs that it links together. Associations are deleted when any of the two parent PACs are deleted. Examples of associations include function-entity usage and function-business unit usage. The repository model does not enable associations of aassociations.

REPOSITORY SIZING

The Repository Administration Utility has a feature to calculate the repository size as small, medium, or large. The Installation manual provides a chart that can be used to determine the tablespace needed in a repository of that size. The flexibility provided in the allocation of tablespaces and rollback segments should minimize the chances of running out of resources during install and upgrade.

PROTECTING THE DESIGNER REPOSITORY

Access to the Designer repository can be controlled by two main methods:

- Repository level—You can control whether a user has manager or user privilege.
- Application system level—You can control whether a user has read-only, insert, update, delete, share, or administrative privilege to individual applications. The locking capabilities of Designer can be used if finer control is required.

The Maintain Users tab of the Repository Administration Utility (RAU) is used to create new repository users. The RAU is accessible only to the repository owner. This tab contains the following information:

- Oracle Username—Name of the user (in the database) who needs to have access to the repository.
- Username—Description for the Oracle user.
- Type—Manager (can create new application systems within the repository) or user.
- Description—Comments for the user.

Click the RECONCILE button to save the changes.

Use the Repository Object Navigator (RON) to grant repository users access to a particular application system. Only the application system owner of the users with Administrate access to the application system can perform this function. The effect of granting certain privileges by choosing Application, Grant Access is described in the following list:

- Select—Gives the users read-only access to the application system.
- Insert—Enables the users to create new primary access elements within the application system.
- Update—Enables the users to modify primary access elements and create or delete secondary access elements.
- Delete—Enables the users to remove primary access elements.
- Share—Enables the users to share definitions from this application system in another application system.
- Admin—Enables users to control access at the application-system level. Users with this privilege are Application System Administrators and can do almost anything that the application system creator can do. Application system administrators can grant application system access to other users, revoke application system access from other users, set application system level privileges, freeze and unfreeze preferences, remove locks on element sets, and perform many other functions. The only function that the application system owner can do that other administrators cannot is transfer ownership of the application system.

SHARING AND TRANSFERRING OBJECTS

These utilities enable the usage of one definition of an element in more than one application system. Table 32.2 describes the various commands and their usage. For example, if you have a Codes table defined in one application system and this Codes table is required in another application system, you can share the Codes table and ensure that the structure is identical in both of the application systems by using Designer's Design Reuse feature. The application systems that will share the definitions should be in the same repository (see Table 32.3).

TABLE 32.2   SHARING AND TRANSFERRING OBJECTS FROM RON

Commands	Description
Application, Share	The application system states that it will enable another application system to use its objects. Refer to Figure 32.11.
Application, Unshare	An application system states that it will no longer use another application system's element definition.
Application, Transfer Ownership	This moves a primary access element to another application system. Refer to Figure 32.10.

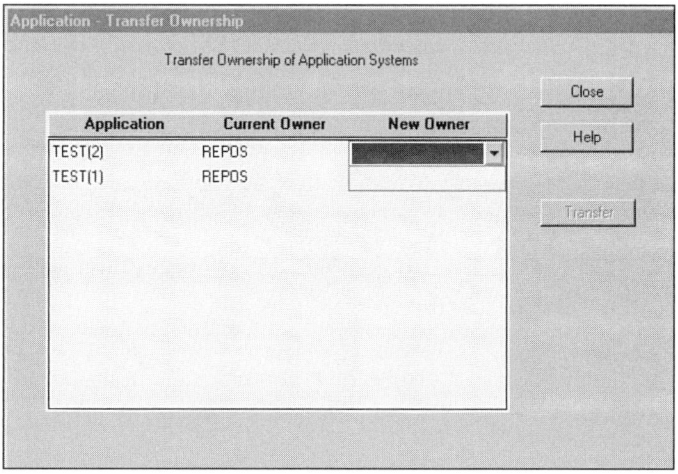

Figure 32.10
Transferring application ownership.

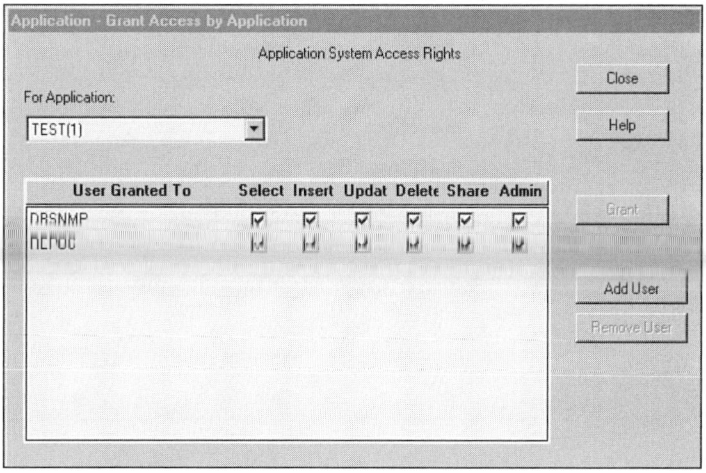

Figure 32.11
Granting access.

TABLE 32.3   CONTROLLING SPECIFICATIONS HELD IN THE REPOSITORY

Commands in RON	Description
Utilities, Unload	Enables the creation of an ASCII file that stores in a proprietary format the definitions of selected primary access control (PAC) objects, the PAC's secondary access control objects, and stub objects associated with the selected objects. Refer to Figure 32.13.
Utilities, Load	Opposite of File, Unload. Enables the loading of information unloaded from another repository or application system. Refer to Figure 32.12.
Utilities, Check Out, Check In, Lock Set, Unlock Set	Like Load and Unload, Check Out and Check In enable the moving of selected elements between application systems in the same or a different repository. Check Out also locks the objects in the source application system, thereby preventing accidental change to the object while it is checked out. Check In unlocks the objects. Refer to Figures 32.14 and 32.15.
Application, Archive	Extracts repository application versions to a special set of temporary archive tables.
Application, Export	Exports the contents of the temporary archived tables into an operating system file.
Application, Restore	Used to load .DMP files into temporary archive tables and then into the repository.
Application, Reset	Flushes the temporary archive tables. The application version in the repository is unchanged.

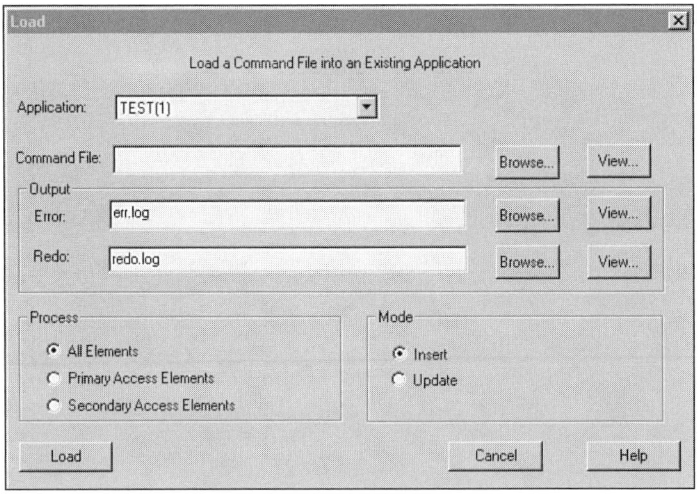

Figure 32.12
Repository Object
Navigator Load utility.

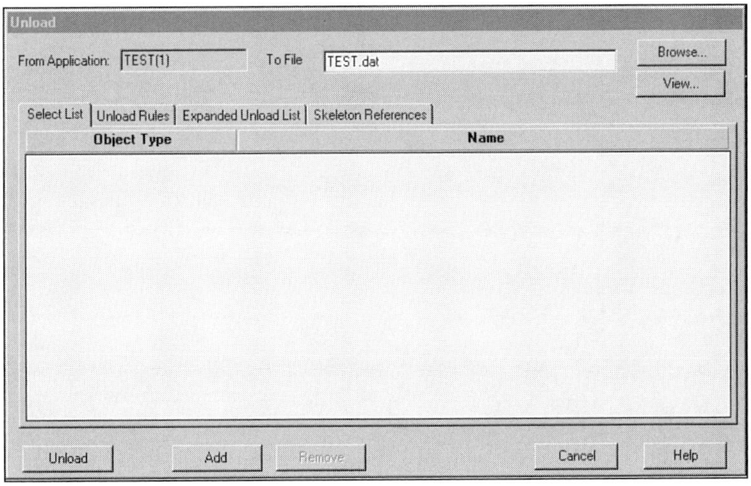

Figure 32.13
Repository Object
Navigator Unload
utility.

Repository Object Navigator Unload utility dialog showing:
- Unload
- From Application: TEST(1)   To File: TEST.dat   Browse...   View...
- Tabs: Select List | Unload Rules | Expanded Unload List | Skeleton References
- Columns: Object Type | Name
- Buttons: Unload   Add   Remove   Cancel   Help

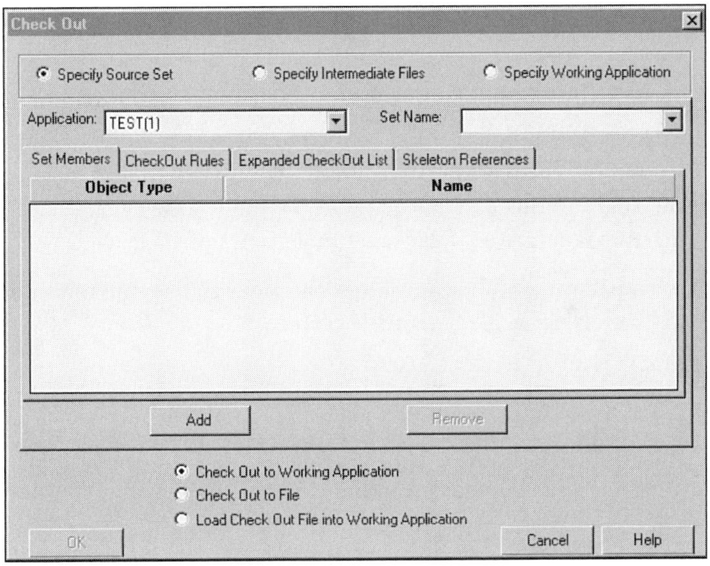

Figure 32.14
Repository Object
Navigator Check Out.

Repository Object Navigator Check Out dialog showing:
- Check Out
- ⊙ Specify Source Set   ○ Specify Intermediate Files   ○ Specify Working Application
- Application: TEST(1)   Set Name:
- Tabs: Set Members | CheckOut Rules | Expanded CheckOut List | Skeleton References
- Columns: Object Type | Name
- Buttons: Add   Remove
- ⊙ Check Out to Working Application
- ○ Check Out to File
- ○ Load Check Out File into Working Application
- Buttons: OK   Cancel   Help

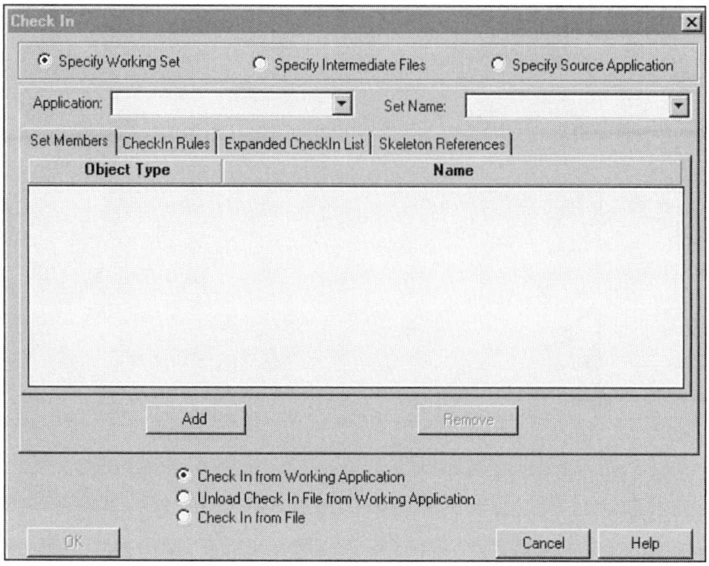

Figure 32.15
Repository Object
Navigator Check In.

REFERENTIAL INTEGRITY USING THE REPOSITORY

Designer R2.x has a utility that can be used to check the referential integrity of data held in the repository. The repository analyzer in the RAU (Utilities menu) removes redundant or invalid data, ensuring data integrity. To run the repository analyzer, the repository owner must be granted the Create Table and Create Index privilege.

Execute the following SQL statement to check the state of the repository. If no rows are returned, the repository is referentially correct:

```
SQL> select count (*)
        from ckaz_actions
        where check_no is not null
        group by check_no, elmt_type, refd_elmt_type, action;
```

To use the cost-based optimizer, compute the statistics for the repository table using the following:

```
SQL> analyze table <repository table> compute statistics;
```

The Oracle server can then use the most efficient path using the statistics for SQL statements that access the analyzed objects.

VERSION AND CHANGE CONTROL

A user with Admin access to the application and Manager type can create a new version of an application. To create a new version of an application, connect to DES2K and from the Design Editor screen, select RON utility and then Application, New Version.

This will result in two versions, one that is frozen and cannot be modified but can be viewed, and the other, which can be modified.

If an application system shares elements with other application systems, a stub application will be created for the other application.

For example if you have two application systems—Inventory (INV) and Items (ITM)—that share objects and if you create a new version of the inventory, a stub application of ITM (01ITM) will be created. Version 1 of INV will be compatible with 01ITM and version 2 of INV will be compatible with ITM. 01ITM is frozen.

To drop a version of an application, you must make sure that its elements are not used by other applications. If there are used elements, you can do one of the following to drop the application:

- Unshare all the shared elements.
- Drop both the applications at the same time.
- Drop the dependent applications (provided there is no inter-dependencies).

Things to consider are the following:

- Version Control is a single-user utility that locks other users out of the system. Do not run it during normal business hours or when others are accessing the system.
- When run, it needs a large rollback space that is proportional to the application size.
- After a new version is created, the application takes approximately twice the space in the database.
- Time required to run the version control utility is proportional to the size of the repository and not the application size.
- An application version can be frozen or unfrozen at any time; however, unfreezing an older version might result in inconsistencies.

MIGRATING APPLICATIONS

The following sections describe methods that can be used to move your software design between applications.

EXPORT/IMPORT OF COMPLETE REPOSITORY

This method involves moving the entire repository from the source to the destination database. The unit of migration is the Oracle account. The needed packages must be created at the destination database.

Complete the following steps:

1. Using the RON, choose Export Repository User from the backup group.
2. Transfer the export file in Binary mode to the destination machine.
3. Create an Oracle user (refer to the installation guide for details).
4. Using the RON utility, import the user into the destination database.
5. Create the packages in the destination database.
6. Recreate the synonyms.

This method is not recommended when you perform the following tasks:

- Move single application systems.
- Move applications into a CASE instance that already has other applications.

UNLOAD/LOAD AN APPLICATION SYSTEM

This method involves moving one or more application systems between repositories. Unit of migration is the application system. It is generally used to move applications between the same versions of DES2K.

Complete the following steps:

1. Access RON as a user with Manager ranking and Admin privileges to the application.
2. Clear the extract tables using Application, Reset.
3. Load the application into the extract tables using Application, Archive.
4. Export the extract tables to a *.DMP file using Application, Export.
5. Transfer the export file in binary to the destination machine.
6. At the destination database, load the *.DMP file into the extract table using Application, Import.
7. Load the extract table into the base table using Application, Restore.

This method is not recommended when you want to perform the following tasks:

- Move all the application systems in an instance.
- Take a backup of your CASE instance.

MOVING PRIMARY ACCESS CONTROLLED (PAC) ELEMENTS

There are two methods that are commonly used to control the movement of PAC elements between CASE repositories: unload/load and check out/check in.

UNLOAD/LOAD PROCESS

This method is designed for fast transfer without many restrictions. The elements are unloaded into an ASCII file with extension .DAT. It also unloads Secondary Access Controlled (SAC) elements while preserving association between elements. If one of the elements in the association is not part of the unloaded set, it creates a skeleton with the name of the element to complete the association. The elements are then loaded from the .DAT file into an application system.

There are two modes of loading that are used for conflict resolution:

- Insert—The element causing conflict is not loaded, and the loading process continues after recording the conflict in a log file.
- Update—The conflict is resolved using the .DAT file information.

CHECK OUT/CHECK IN PROCESS

A *User-defined set* (UDS) is a non-shareable PAC element and it has associations with other PAC elements in the application system. An element can be associated with more than one UDS. A UDS can be locked and unlocked as desired. Operations that can be performed on a locked UDS are copying the element, sharing the element, or updating associations between the element and unlocked elements. Operations that cannot be performed on a locked UDS are transferring ownership of the element, updating the element's properties, or locking another UDS that contains this element.

The process of check out and check in is performed on a UDS. When checked-out, a UDS is automatically locked in the source application system and it is automatically unlocked upon check in. An `.RCO` file is created if a UDS is checked out of a source application system, whereas an `.RCI` file is created if a UDS is checked out of a working application system. These two file formats contain the UDS and its associations.

Table 32.4 compares and contrasts different scenarios where Load/Unload can be used instead of Check Out/Check In.

TABLE 32.4 SCENARIOS FOR USING UNLOAD/LOAD VERSUS CHECK OUT/CHECK IN

Scenario	Unload/Load	Check out/Check in
Single-user environment.	Yes. You don't need to track elements that have been unloaded from an application system.	No.
Multiuser environment.	No.	Yes. You need to keep track of migrated elements. Check out elements will be locked, preventing accidental updates.
Building application system from elements in other application systems.	Yes. It is simpler and the process is done only once so you don't need to define a UDS.	No.
Backing up of an element.	Yes. It is simpler.	No. You don't need to define a UDS or back up the entire application system.
Require tight control over elements.	No. It is very flexible.	Yes. Tight control can be achieved over checked out elements.
Distributed development.	No.	Yes.
Source control is required.	No.	Yes. Elements checked out from the source application system are locked against updates.

PLACING DESIGNER DIAGRAMS IN DOCUMENTS

Designer enables a variety of output methods and provides the capability to capture the output from the different diagrammers into destinations such as word processors and HTML-based tools, such as Netscape Navigator and Microsoft Internet Explorer.

LOADING DIAGRAMS INTO MICROSOFT WORD

This task can be achieved by using three different methods: Object Linking and Embedding (OLE), screen capture, and Print file. These methods are described in greater detail in the following list:

- Using Object Linking and Embedding (OLE)—Designer is V2.0 OLE-compliant and can serve as both an OLE container and an OLE Server. To load an ERD into Word, complete the following steps:

  1. Start MS Word and open a new document.
  2. Choose Insert, Object from the menu and select Entity Relationship Diagrammer.

  To load a Word document into an ERD, complete the following steps:

  1. Start Designer.
  2. From an ERD, choose Edit, Insert New Object and include a word document.

- Using Screen Capture—There are several techniques used to get screen captures, including using Alt+Print Screen, editing and pasting the picture using Paintbrush, or using a third-party tool such as PaintShop Pro to capture the screen.

- Using Print File—The Designer tools print to the default printer unless another printer is chosen. Using the Print Manager, you can change the printer setup so that the printer destination is a file. This file can then be loaded in the document. If the default printer is a fax machine, you can send a fax directly from Designer.

PUTTING DESIGNER REPOSITORY DATA ON THE WORLD WIDE WEB

Putting Designer repository data on the World Wide Web can be done using a third-party driver such as Adobe Exchange, which supports the .PDF file format. Using this driver as the default driver, save the file in .PDF format. The file can then be downloaded on the WebServer and an HTML link established so that the file can be read through the Web using any Web browser, such as Netscape or Microsoft Internet Explorer.

REVERSE ENGINEERING USING DESIGNER

Most organizations have many existing applications that they would like to load into Designer. A variety of methods are available to perform this task. The following methods are popular:

■ Reverse Engineer DDL—This method can be used to take data objects from an existing Oracle7 database and document the elements in the repository. It cannot, however, deduce the constraints that are implemented through the program code. It can reverse engineer data objects from a local or a remote Oracle database. Using this method requires that the repository user have select privileges on tables, views, and snapshots and also have execute privileges on functions, procedures, and packages.

■ Reverse Engineer Forms and Reports—The forms reverse engineering utility extracts the information from a Forms version 5.0 program and puts it in the DES2K module definition and secondary access elements. The reports reverse engineering utility works very similarly to the forms reverse engineering utility and can reverse engineer reports in several languages, including SQL*PLUS reports, Oracle pre-compiler reports, SQL*ReportWriter 1.1 reports, and so on.

Follow these steps to reverse engineer forms and reports:

1. Define the database in the repository.

2. Define primary and foreign key constraints in the repository.

3. Load the forms into the Oracle database and reverse engineer them one batch at a time or one at a time.

4. Manually insert any logic that did not get reverse engineered.

Note

Note that triggers, library attachments, procedures, and procedure calls are not reverse engineered.

■ From RON, Utilities, Table to Entity Retrofit—This utility transforms the physical data model into a logical data model. The efficiency and usage of this method depends on how closely the physical model and the logical model match each other. The most important precaution you can take when using this utility is to make sure that primary and foreign key constraint definitions are defined in the physical database design. It should be noted that this method *does not* convert a bad physical design into a good logical design. In fact, it just converts it as is; therefore, if you want to save a lot of work after the transformation is complete, you must match the physical model as closely as possible to the desired logical model. This method has the following restrictions:

• Constraint definitions should exist, otherwise all columns will become attributes instead of relationships.

• Shared table definitions are not retrofitted.

• The table should not be already mapped to an entity. If it is mapped, you must delete the association or the entity definition.

In order to run the retrofit utility, you can choose Utilities, Table to Entity Retrofit from the RON or the Entity Relationship Diagrammer.

Usually after the Retrofitting has been performed you will have to clean up the logical design that is generated. To do this, complete the following steps:

1. Change the Relationship names to be more meaningful because the names generated due to retrofitting are derived from the foreign key constraint names and are usually not very intuitive.

2. Check the type of relationships and make sure that they are what you really want them to be; for example, mandatory foreign keys become optional/mandatory relationships, whereas optional foreign keys become optional/optional relationships.

3. Rename the attributes to be more meaningful to the users because in the physical design they might have been abbreviated.

4. Do a sanity check of the resulting logical design to make sure that the entities and relationships are really what they are supposed to be because the physical design might have implemented them differently.

DATA ADMINISTRATION CONFIGURATION USING DESIGNER

Data administration involves the monitoring and control of a project's data. Different configurations can be used for this purpose and they each have their advantages and disadvantages. Designer provides features in the RON and the RAU to simplify this function.

Data administration configuration consists of knowing the application configuration that best fits your organization's structure and also knowing the number of repositories that works well with this structure and the number of users that need to be supported.

DETERMINING THE NUMBER OF CASE APPLICATIONS TO USE

There are a number of questions that should be answered to determine the number of CASE applications that are used. These include the following:

- What is the structure of the organization?
- How good is the inter-group communication?
- What is the size of the application?
- Are the designers familiar with CASE techniques?
- What is more important, control or flexibility?

There are several strategies that can be used, and each has its pros and cons.

CENTRALIZED CONFIGURATION   In a *centralized configuration*, all the data is owned by one application, and the others share this data.

The advantages to this strategy include the following:

- Ease of administration because there is only one set of access rights to maintain.
- Needs no element transfer because all the elements are owned by one application.
- Version control is simplified.

The disadvantages to this strategy include the following:

- Requires all the users to access one database (single point of failure).
- Requires greater communication between groups because they all share the same data and therefore have to agree on a lot of things.
- Results in larger systems and therefore utilities take longer to run.

DECENTRALIZED CONFIGURATION *Decentralized configuration* means that each application owns its own data and can grant privileges on its elements to other applications as needed.

The advantages to this strategy include the following:

- Greater flexibility than the centralized approach.
- Migration and version control of application systems can be done independently.
- Results in smaller applications and therefore utilities run faster.
- The number of development teams that can access the applications increases without increasing the likelihood of locking each other.

The disadvantages to this strategy include the following:

- If applications are not well-partitioned, it can result in a lot of sharing and transferring of elements.
- Care must be taken to ensure there is no redundancy.
- Boundaries and objectives of individual applications have to be established well in advance for this approach to be successful.

COMBINED CONFIGURATION In *combined configuration*, there is a master application that owns elements that are common to more than one application and shares these with applications that need them. There are also applications that contain application-specific data that is not shared with others.

The advantages to this strategy include the following:

- Takes the best of both worlds by enabling the sharing of elements as well as individual application system development.
- Results in manageable applications.

The disadvantages to this strategy include the following:

- If not planned properly, it can result in complex version control and migration tasks at a later stage.
- Requires a lot of administrative effort due to the flexibility it provides.

DETERMINING THE NUMBER OF REPOSITORIES

There are several things to consider when determining the number of repositories. These include the following:

- The number of and inter-relationships between the applications.
  - If you have more than one application and they share elements, they should all reside in the same repository, because sharing between repositories is not supported.
  - An application should exist only in one instance; otherwise, it will result in a lot of merging at a later stage.
  - Applications that have nothing in common should be placed in separate instances in order to have a better control over them.
- The expected number of users.
  - Certain utilities, such as Versioning, run in a single-user mode, and if such a utility is to be run concurrently by different application systems, it might worthwhile to place the applications in separate instances.
  - Multiple instances should be considered if the physical limits of the hardware are reached.
  - Each CASE user needs a certain amount of RAM, swap space, and so on. In some cases, it will be beneficial to consider a client-server solution.

Using multiple instances can have its advantages and disadvantages:

- It can result in a fault-tolerant system.
- It does not require all the users to access the same database.

The pros and cons of using the different configurations is summarized in Table 32.5.

TABLE 32.5   PROS AND CONS OF USING DIFFERENT CONFIGURATIONS

Factor to Consider	Centralized	Decentralized	Mixed
Time to administer access privileges	low	low	medium
Ease of version control	high	low	medium
Support for parallel system development	low	high	medium
Performance on frequently versioned systems	low	high	medium
Need to use multiple instances	low	high	medium
Interdependency of applications	high	low	medium

ENHANCING THE PERFORMANCE OF DESIGNER

The installation guide for Designer has a number of hardware and software requirements that should be met. The following discussion provides suggestions that can improve the performance of Designer. (Use them with caution because it might also affect other Windows applications.)

OPTIMIZING THE CLIENT MACHINE

A client-server configuration works quite well with Designer. A minimum of a 386 machine is required, and there is no notable difference between using one hardware manufacturer or another. 32MB of memory is the minimum, although 64MB is recommended. Optimize memory usage in your system with some of the following tips:

- Use a hard disk optimizer to remove fragmentation from hard disk on a periodic basis.
- Do not put your working directory on the LAN.
- Clear the Temp directory periodically.
- Designer requires a 40MB swap file minimum.
- Rearranging the order of loading programs and drivers can help minimize fragmentation.
- Disable screensavers.
- Unload unused fonts.

PART

VI

CH

32

OPTIMIZING THE NETWORK

The network performance can affect the overall system performance and should be carefully monitored.

Get SQL*NET trace files or put sniffers to determine the network performance and where the degradation is present. Use dead connection detection by setting `sqlnet.expire_time=<time_in_minutes>` in sqlnet.ora. This will enable the listener to check after every time period specified in the preceding setting to make sure that there are no dead connections.

OPTIMIZING DESIGNER

There are several things that can be done to optimize Designer:

- Rebuild CASE indexes.
- Rearrange the repository data to use the correct configuration for your environment.
- Determine the number of repositories used.
- Determine whether the elements are properly shared between the application systems.
- Get diagnostic information to make sure that the SQL statements are used optimally.
- The repository is stored in its own tables in the database, and therefore, database optimization techniques such as removing fragmentation can be applied to Designer.

OPTIMIZING THE DATABASE SERVER

Database optimizing is an art and has to be constantly performed on the database due to changing conditions in the database. *Tuning Oracle* by Oracle Press is a very good book on different tips that can be used to optimize the database performance. The following tips can be helpful (also refer to Chapters 16 through 20 of this book for more information on tuning the database server):

- Use the correct optimizer mode (COST based is recommended for R2.x).
- Truncate RM$HASH_ELMS.
- Reduce fragmentation by pinning objects properly and not using a large sort_area_size.
- Reduce disk I/O.
- Reduce contention, and maintain a high hit ratio.
- Set LOG_CHECKPOINT_INTERVAL to be greater than the redo log size so that checkpoint occurs only at a log switch.
- Set the DB_BLOCK_BUFFERS to the correct value to prevent the repository from going to the disk for the API.
- Increase the number and size of the redo logs.
- Make sure that the data files and the swap file are on separate disks.
- Create the repository indexes on a different disk from the one that contains the data files.
- Place redo logs and rollback segments on a disk other than the one containing the swap file.
- Pin the API in the shared pool.

APPLICATION PROGRAMMING INTERFACE

As you are developing your applications using Designer, you will realize that there are some activities that you want to do that are not easily done using even the most sophisticated tools it provides. The user extensibility feature of DES2K can be helpful in putting the extensions you created in the repository. The API opens the repository by enabling you to input and output information from the repository as well as the user extensibility features that you create. The API basically enables you to manipulate the repository in any way you want and thus bypass any limitation that you might encounter with the DES2K functionality. The API will also enable you to customize certain functionality according to your project needs instead of being forced to use the DES2K functionality. This results in a direct increase in productivity and higher percentage of generation. It is important to understand that working with API will require creating program code and that there will be a learning curve. It is therefore important to be sure that the functionality you are looking for is really not provided by DES2K. In the long run, it will help to identify the best method of getting your task accomplished.

USING THE API

API is a set of database views and PL/SQL packages in the repository owner's schema that enable safe manipulation of the repository. The repository consists of a set of tables and the relationship between these tables is not documented. The API consists of several important views of these tables and PL/SQL packages that enable you to perform DML on these tables without using the DES2K interface.

A good SQL and PL/SQL knowledge is recommended to be able to use the API in an effective manner. It will be useful to have a thorough understanding of the elements and properties that you intend to manipulate. After you know which elements and properties you want to work with, look through the API documentation, including the online help and the meta-model diagrams that ship with the product, to get a better understanding of all the API that you can use. The meta-model diagrams that ship with Designer are very useful and show the API views and their relationships. These diagrams are grouped into subsets:

- Business Planning Model
- Business Requirement Model
- Database Administration Model
- Database Design Model
- Module Design Model

Use the appropriate model based on what you want to achieve. When the details about the element and the API to use have been understood, the next step is to create PL/SQL procedure and packages to do the needed manipulation.

API VIEWS AND PACKAGES

The repository base tables have names with the prefix SDD_ and CDI_. The API views have names with the prefix CI_. All the repository views have some important columns, such as the following:

- CREATED_BY and CHANGED_BY, which can be queried to find out when an element definition was inserted or updated
- An ID column that uniquely identifies the element in the repository
- Columns that correspond to the attributes of the element they represent
- NAME column that holds the name that is seen in the RON

The online help system is very powerful in the determination of the view descriptions.

API packages are prefixed with CIO and there are over 300 PL/SQL packages that comprise the API, one package for each type of repository element. These packages contain procedures with the following prefixes:

- INS (Insert)
- UPD (Update)

- DEL (Delete)
- SEL (Select)

The online help system provides useful information about the packages as well. In addition to the API calls mentioned previously, there are API calls that implement a set of statements instead of individual statements, thereby acting as a transaction model. The transaction model temporarily disables constraint checking until the transaction is complete. As a result of this, complex relationships can be established, and the constraint checking is deferred until the end of when the transaction is committed. The CDAPI package is mostly responsible for handling the transaction model.

The following steps can be used to implement the transaction model:

1. Declare the application system and version you will be using.

2. Open the transaction.

3. Load the value of record variable.

4. Load the indicator of record variable.

5. Perform the DML and validate it.

6. If the previous steps are successful, commit the transaction or else rollback the transaction.

API LIMITATIONS

Even though you have seen that the API is a powerful and flexible feature, it has some limitations. For example, you cannot manipulate text types such as Notes, Descriptions, PL/SQL blocks, and where clauses. This text can be queried from the CDI_TEXT table, but performing DML on these texts is not recommended. The structure of the CDI_TEXT table is described in Table 32.6.

TABLE 32.6   STRUCTURE OF THE CDI_TEXT TABLE

Column Name	Null?	Type	Comments
TXT_REF	Not Null	NUMBER(38)	Element ID
TXT_SEQ	Not Null	NUMBER(6)	Line number for the record
TXT_TYPE	Not Null	VARCHAR2(6)	The type of text
TXT_TEXT	Null	VARCHAR2(240)	The text

Another limitation of the API is that it cannot be called directly from Oracle Forms.

TROUBLESHOOTING DESIGNER

Although Designer is "perfect", there are times when non-user errors occur, and you need to determine the cause of the error and resolve it. This section discusses several common errors and also different strategies that can be used to diagnose Designer errors.

CHECKING COMMON ERRORS

During the install, the Repository Administration Utility checks its work and stops if there is a problem. Common errors include the following:

- `ORA-4030: out of process memory when trying to allocate <x> bytes.`

  This is an Operating System problem because the server has run out of memory to allocate to the Process Global Area.

  Solution: Increase the available swap or real memory, or reduce the number of processes running on the server.

- `ORA-4031: unable to allocate <x> bytes of shared memory.`

  The SGA on the server has run out of memory.

  Solution: Execute the following: `ALTER SYSTEM FLUSH SHARED_POOL`; if this does not work, increase `shared_pool_size` (check the recommended values).

- `ORA-3113 or ORA-3114: no longer connected to the database.`

  Possibly a network error. Check the alert log on the server for more details.

- `Warning: Package Body created with compilation errors.`

  Type the following text: **`SQL>show errors package body <package>`**

USING DIAGNOSTICS AND TRACING

There are several things that can be used to diagnose Designer components to find the underlying SQL that is causing the problem or generating a trace file that will be needed by Oracle support. Table 32.7 summarizes different trace levels to be used, depending on the information that is desired.

TABLE 32.7 TRACE LEVELS USED FOR DIAGNOSING PROBLEMS

Level	Description and Use
0	No tracing and no diagnostic output
1	Generates SQL trace
2	Displays SQL statements as a number to narrow down to the relevant code
3	Displays bound variables of relevant SQL statements
4	Execution thread
5	Execution thread with function arguments

> **Note**
>
> Not all the DES2K components support all the preceding levels. In other words, some levels are not valid in some of the components.

Table 32.8 contains `oracle.ini` variables per Designer components to be placed in the section `[Designer]`.

TABLE 32.8 `oracle.ini` VARIABLES PER DESIGNER COMPONENTS

Component	Variable
Process Modeler	DES2_BPMOD_DIAG_LEVEL
Entity Relationship	DES2_SYSMOD20_ERD_DIAG_LEVEL
Function Hierarchy	DES2_SYSMOD20_FHD_DIAG_LEVEL
Dataflow Diagrammer	DES2_SYSMOD20_DFD_DIAG_LEVEL
Matrix Diagrammer	DES2_REPADM10_MD_DIAG_LEVEL
Data Diagrammer	DES2_SYSDES10_DD_DIAG_LEVEL
Forms Generator	DES2_CGENF45_DIAG_LEVEL
Reports Generator	DES2_CGENR25_DIAG_LEVEL
RON	DES2_REPADM10_RON_DIAG_LEVEL
Repository Administrator	DES2_REPADM10_RAU_DIAG_LEVEL
Repository Reports	DES2_REPADM10_REP_DIAG_LEVEL
Repository Utilities	DES2_REPADM10_UTL_DIAG_LEVEL
Visual Basic Generator	DES2_VBGEN10_DIAG_LEVEL
C++ Generator	DES2_CPPGEN10_DIAG_LEVEL
DB Design Wizard	DES2_DATWIZ55_DIAG_LEVEL

For example, if you receive the message `ora-1422 exact fetch returns more than requested number of rows` when using Data Flow Diagrammer, you should edit your `oracle.ini`—setting the level to 4—and reproduce the error. Examine the trace file for additional clues related to the error.

The following applies to Win95/NT only:

- Tracing RON sessions—The Registry can be modified to enable RON sessions to put trace information in a file. Be *very* careful when making changes to the Registry; always back up the Registry before making any changes. Using REGEDIT or REGEDT32, create the following keys under `\HKEY_LOCAL_MACHINE\SOFTWARE\ORACLE\REPADM10` node:
- `DES2_REPADM10_RON_TRACE_FILE`—Provide the location and filename for the trace file.
- `DES2_REPADM10_RON_DIAG_LEVEL`—Set this value to a trace level based on what you want to trace. Refer to Table 32.9 for a full listing.

TABLE 32.9   RON TRACE LEVELS

Type of Trace	Trace Value and Meaning
SQL Area	1=SQL Trace 2=SQL Statement Locations 4=SQL Statements
Messages	16=Fatal Messages 32=Non-Fatal Messages 64=All Messages
Dispatch	128=API Dispatch Calls
External Calls	512=WinExec Command 1024=Utility Parameters
General	2048=Function Trace 4096=Version Information

These trace levels can be used cumulatively. For example, if you want to trace SQL Trace and SQL Statement Locations for all the fatal error messages, use the setting of 19 (1+2+16). Figure 32.16 shows some diagnostic events that can be set.

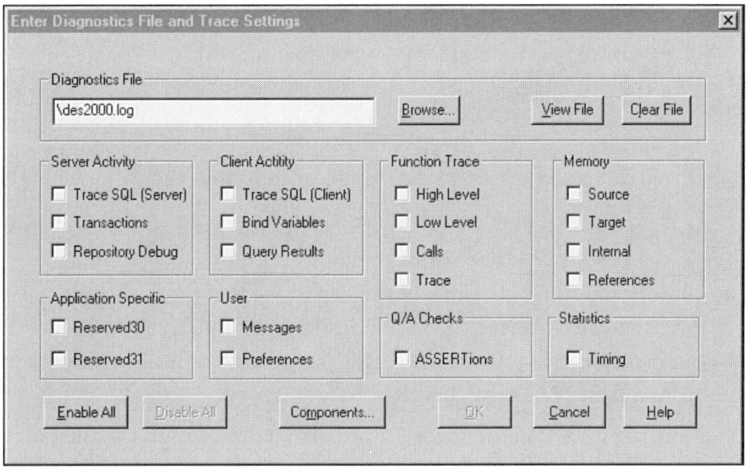

Figure 32.16
Diagnostic event settings.

TIPS TO EFFICIENTLY GENERATE DEVELOPER APPLICATIONS FROM DESIGNER

Developer is a family of products that can be used to develop client-server applications. Developer consists of the following main components:

- Oracle Forms—Used for building forms-based applications
- Oracle Reports—Used for designing reports
- Oracle Graphics—Used to build queries that generate business graphics
- Procedure Builder—Used to design and manage PL/SQL code

The Forms Generator uses the repository in ways that are not very obvious from the documentation. Several tips on taking the pain out of generating applications from Designer are demonstrated in the following list. These tips can help an administrator/developer to use Designer to build applications effectively:

- Training at the right time—If people are trained a long time before they start using the system, they will forget a lot of what they learned by the time they have to start using it. On the other hand, if they are trained after they have started developing the system, they will have figured things out on their own through tutorials and other books and might be using an approach that is not the best method to get the job done.

- Build users interface prototype and get it approved by the users—This is very important because it can take a lot of effort after the generation to make changes in the user interface. A prototype will convey to the user what the designers have really understood about the user requirements and also what the users should expect from the end product. User interface design can have an impact on the overall system design and at times even on the physical layout of the data. Things to consider during user interface design include but are not limited to the following: toolbar design, colors, fonts, single or multiple windows, menu system, screen layout, and so on.

- Use of domains makes it easy to maintain columns—Domains should be used in the following cases:
  - Attributes that appear in more than one entity
  - PK-FK attributes
  - Column definitions that can be standardized
  - Columns with a few distinct sets of enabled values
  - Usage of domains will make it easy to propagate changes to all the affected columns in one step.

- Understand the limitations of the design—Do not promise an interface to the users that cannot be achieved with the design that is being used. A lot of money and effort can be spent trying to fix the forms post-generation if the design does not reflect the ultimate vision held by the users.

- Normalize the data design—A normalized data design is easier to maintain and also is more responsive to changes in requirement. However, a normalized data design is not intuitive to the users. For example, a normalized data design will eliminate data redundancy and place it in separate tables, but users want to see everything in the same table.

There are three different alternatives to resolve this problem:
  - Normalize the physical designs and denormalize the user presentation—A "normal" presentation of the data is not always intuitive to the users, and therefore, users will push for a non-normal representation of the data. This approach basically always strives for a normal form but can result in a high maintenance system. Whenever this approach is taken, it results in post-generation modifications, such as creation of a lot of views (de-normalized presentation), to reconcile the differences.

- Educate the users regarding the usage of normalization—This approach is probably the best if the users can be convinced of the approach of data normalization. Also, the users need to be more aware of database-specific things, such as primary-foreign keys. They might or might not be willing to understand such things.

- Denormalize the physical designs and match the presentation with that of the user expectations—This approach has the advantage of higher generation (lower post-generation modifications). It however is less flexible to change in user requirements. It becomes very important to understand the user requirements at the onset of the project, and hopefully, these don't change a lot during the application development.

Keep in mind that the project is being created to benefit the users. Therefore, it is very important to the success of the project that the users are convinced and happy with the end result. The first approach generally involves a lot of post-generation maintenance because the user's expectations are not met by the design; therefore, changes are made in the forms or views created to reconcile the differences. The second approach is very helpful, provided the users are willing to be educated about the process, and this changes from one organization to another. The third approach involves very little post-generation effort, but it is difficult to incorporate changes in the original requirements. It is not an easy choice, but if the development team and the users are in constant communication with each other, the process becomes more manageable.

- Use views to reconcile post-generation differences—Usually developers are afraid to use views because views are extra objects to maintain and can be less efficient than directly querying tables. However, keep in mind that views are just stored `select` statements, and they can be used post-generation for the minor changes requested by the users, such as new reports or security changes to the application.

- Before the creation of modules, make sure that the "Default" data is entered—Before modules are created, default data should be entered in the table definitions. The following defaults can be verified for every table: display datatype, display sequence, format, prompt, hint, default order sequence, display length, and display width. This will save a lot of time when modules need to be redeveloped.

- Display meaningful error messages—When users enter invalid information in fields, it is better to provide meaningful error messages to them that indicate what the valid values are than to give them meaningless system-generated errors.

- Enforce standards—Standardization in development can lead to increased development efficiency, reduction of maintenance, and reduction in learning curve for new developers. Designer provides many reports that enforce standards. It also provides an API that consists of a set of views against the repository tables and a set of PL/SQL packages that enable the repository to be updated. The API can be used to generate reports that list/fix the violations in the standard.

- Learn about the generation preferences of forms and reports—The time spent in understanding the preferences during generation pays off at the end by reducing post-generation efforts.

- Set the default preferences for the application—Become familiar with the preferences that can be set at the application level and should be left unchanged for the generated modules. There are other preferences that can be used for each generated module as needed to conform to the design standards.

- Learn and use the forms and reports generators—Many developers like to use the Designer generators to generate a skeleton form or report and do most of their development using Developer/2000. However, the DES2K generators are quite useful, and if you take the time to understand their capabilities, it will result in a high percentage of generation.

- Involve users up to a certain extent of the project—It definitely helps to get user approval for the prototype, and constant communication is essential with the users. However, after a certain point, the users should not be allowed to make suggestions; otherwise, the system will be constantly changing, and the user expectations can become very high.

- Post-generation should start after all the modules are generated—If post-generation is started at an early stage, major changes in data design will be difficult to incorporate in the final modules.

- Document post-generation steps—Use the DES2K repository to store a detailed description of post-generation steps so that the developers can easily reapply these steps if there is (and usually there is) a need to reapply the steps. You can use the module's text fields, such as "notes," or create your own custom text fields to store this information.

- Customize the templates—DES2K provides a number of templates that can be customized to implement specific needs.

- PL/SQL should be placed in library functions, procedures, and packages—This will simplify code maintenance of the modules. The template code can access these libraries and therefore, if there is any change to the code in the library, the modules will immediately reflect the changes without recompilation.

DESIGNER AND ORACLE8I

The introduction of Oracle8i has taken the databases and the applications built on those databases to a whole new level, both in the amount of data stored and the number of users supported. Designer provides a complete set of modeling and generation tools for the relational and object constructs of Oracle8i.

Designer 2.x provides support for all the Oracle8i scalability features, including the following:

- Partitioning of tables
- BLOBs (binary large objects) and CLOBs (character large objects)
- Index organized tables (IOTs)
- Deferred constraint checking

- Type tables
- Collections
- Object views (which represent a relational structure as though it were a type)
- Embedded types
- VARRAYS (multi-valued columns)
- Nested tables (tables embedded within other tables)
- References (directly reference one object from another)

Designer's schema modeler has been extended to use the scalability and object features of Oracle8i without compromising ease of use. It enables you to design database schema or load existing schema definitions into its repository. The Server Generator then translates the graphical representation into the appropriate SQL DDL to implement it. Designer uses unified modeling language (UML), an emerging open standard from the Object Management Group (OMG), to represent its type models.

Table 32.10 details the Designer supported-versions list (Please contact Oracle WorldWide Support for an updated list for Designer R2.x).

TABLE 32.10   DESIGNER SUPPORTED VERSIONS

Designer 2.1.2	Component version
Platform	Windows NT 4.0 or Windows 95 or Windows 98
Oracle server version	7.3.4 or higher
Designer Repository Administrator	2.0.20.5.0
Designer Design Editor	2.0.20.5.0
Designer Server Generator	7.0.20.5.0
Designer Form Generator	5.0.20.11.0
Designer Report Generator	3.0.20.6.0
Designer Library Generator	2.0.20.5.0
Designer MS Help Generator	2.0.20.5.0
Designer Visual Basic Generator	2.0.20.5.0
Designer Web Server Generator	2.0.20.6.0
Oracle Installer	3.3.0.1.3
SQL*Plus	8.0.4.0.0
Oracle Net8 products	8.0.4.0.0
Reports Runtime	3.0.5.8.0

PART **VII**

ORACLE NETWORKING

ORACLE NETWORKING FUNDAMENTALS

In this chapter

UNDERSTANDING ORACLE NETWORKING PRODUCT FEATURES

Oracle network products—SQL*Net in the Oracle7 environment and Net8 in Oracle8—are Oracle's networking solution for transparent client-to-server and server-to-server application connectivity. These products contain a rich core of network services including data transport, network naming, security, and transaction monitoring. These Oracle network products form an abstraction layer, insulating users and user applications from the physical network, allowing heterogeneous, distributed computing across computers regardless of vendor, operating system, hardware architecture, or network topology. Applications will work as written on an AS-400 with LU6.2 network protocol, on a Token-Ring network, or on an HP-9000 with TCP/IP network protocol on an ethernet network. Oracle SQL*Net is available on virtually every platform supported by Oracle, from PCs to mainframes, and supports almost every network transport protocol including TCP/IP, Novell SPX/IPX, IBM LU6.2, NetBIOS, DECNet, and AppleTalk.

> **Note**
>
> Net8 now allows applications to connect to an Oracle database directly from a browser using IIOP or HTTP protocols. In addition it supports Internet technologies such as iFS (Internet file system), Enterprise Java Beans and the Internet-standard SSL (Secure Socket Layer) protocol to provide added security to network connections.

The Oracle Network architecture offers excellent performance for all it does. In Oracle7, SQL*Net supports network load balancing and fault tolerance. When multiple paths to the database server exist, SQL*Net determines which route is the most efficient and establishes the connection accordingly. Additionally, during connection setup, SQL*Net detects any component failures on the primary path and automatically switches to an alternative route if possible, using secondary network interfaces or network software protocol stacks. SQL*Net also detects a broken connection and releases all server resources, cleaning up failed connections.

Oracle8 and Net8 surpass the SQL*Net family in performance and scalability through two new features: *connection pooling* and *session multiplexing*. These technologies reduce the amount of server-system resources needed to support network connections, allowing a single database server to support increasing numbers of users. In Oracle8 Enterprise Edition, a new middleware application called Oracle Connection Manager takes advantage of the multiplexing feature to act as a high-speed proxy to a database server. As a proxy, the Oracle Connection Manager acts as a firewall controlling network-level access to the database server for enhanced network security.

In addition to connection pooling and session multiplexing, a connection load balancing feature was added in Oracle8i. When multiple dispatchers and listeners are involved, Net8 has the capability to balance the load between these dispatchers and listeners.

It consists of two components:

- Client load balancing in order to distribute client connections between listeners
- Connection load balancing in order to distribute client connections among multiple instances and their handlers

Other standard features available in all Oracle Network Products include

- Support for multiple protocols running simultaneously on a single machine.
- Support for transaction processing monitors such as Encina and Tuxedo.
- Open interfaces to third-party applications through open interfaces and Oracle's SQL*Net/Net8 OPEN application programming interface.
- Open database interfaces using Oracle's SQL*Net/Net8 Open Database Connectivity (ODBC) drivers for Microsoft Windows, and Oracle Transparent Gateway technology for third-party database access. Net8 provides interfaces for JavaSoft's JDBC specification for Java applications.
- Multiple protocols in a single connection when using the Oracle MultiProtocol Interchange. The Oracle MultiProtocol Interchange runs on a computer loaded with two or more protocols. This computer provides transparent protocol bridging so clients running one protocol can connect with a server running a different one.
- Because each database instance is registered with the listener, the instance can now do connection load balancing because it has information on all remote listeners. Connection load balancing balances the number of active connections among various instances and dispatchers for the same service. This enables listeners to make their routing decisions based on how many connections each dispatcher has and on how loaded the nodes are that the instances run.

UNDERSTANDING THE ADMINISTRATION AND MANAGEMENT COMPONENTS

Oracle Network Products include a comprehensive set of administration and management components. SQL*Net's graphical management facility, Oracle Network Manager for Oracle7 and Net8 Assistant for Oracle8, are powerful tools for creating and managing an Oracle network. Oracle Net8 Assistant and Net8 Easy Config supersedes Oracle Network Manager by providing a Java based tool that is driven by a wizards interface. The administrator can configure all components of the Oracle SQL*Net family, including database servers, gateways, clients, and Oracle MultiProtocol Interchanges, either centrally or in a distributed fashion using these tools. Oracle Net8 Assistant runs on most desktop and UNIX operating systems, but Oracle Network Manager is only for desktop systems.

Oracle Names, the Oracle global naming service, is also fully administered and maintained through the preceding tools. Oracle Names allows administrators to define network entities (such as service addresses, database aliases, and so on).

PART

VII

CH

33

SQL*Net and Net8 include support for the Simple Network Management Protocol (SNMP). The Oracle7 and Oracle8 servers (as well as Network Listener, MultiProtocol Interchange, and Oracle Names) can be monitored by SNMP-based network management consoles, such as Oracle Enterprise Manager and HP OpenView. This allows existing network operation centers in a company to include Oracle systems in their proactive monitoring.

Other administrative components and features include

- Client registration services give SQL*Net 2.3 and Net8 administrators access to registration information about who is accessing the database, including username and resource usage.

- Comprehensive diagnostic error and trace logging at the client and the server. Oracle Trace in Oracle7 Release 7.3 and Oracle Trace Assistant in Net8 are diagnostic and performance analysis tools to help administrators interpret trace information generated.

- Native naming services allow the leveraging of existing enterprise-wide directory services, such as Sun NIS/Yellow Pages, Novell NetWare Directory Services (NDS), Banyan StreetTalk, and OSF DCE Cell Directory Service. This Advanced Networking Option integrates Oracle clients and servers into the native name environment.

- Network configuration and route testing tools, including the Network Test (NetTest), for testing connections to remote databases across the network and TNSPing for testing connections to servers, without need for a service name, username, and password. TNSPing also allows full diagnostic tracing to a trace file, and measures round-trip time for the client-to-server connection.

- In Oracle8.1.x, the database instances register themselves with the listener when started. In previous releases the information about the database instance had to be manually configured in the LISTENER.ORA file. Now database instance registration is done through service registration, which provides the listener with instance information, such as database service names and instance names.

NETWORK NAMING CONVENTIONS

One of the challenges in a large organization is producing unique names for all network resources. The common flat model naming system, where objects are given a single unique name, often falls short in the enterprise. For this reason, Oracle supports naming network resources using a domain hierarchy. In a domain model, network resources are named according to the group they fall in or the purpose they serve. For example, the marketing department in the Oracle Corporation might belong to the marketing.oracle.com domain. TNS resources belonging to the marketing department would be named using this domain—for example, prod01.marketing.oracle.com for a production database or listener01.marketing.oracle.com for a listener.

In version 7.3 of the Oracle database, TNS resources are placed in the world domain if no domain is created for them. This ensures that network applications expecting a domain name always have one, even if the organization has implemented a flat naming hierarchy.

> **Note**
>
> Oracle tools expect the full network resource name, including the domain, unless a default domain is specified in the `sqlnet.ora` configuration file. The `names.default_domain` parameter specifies what domain should be automatically added to any network resource name when resolving the resource name.

For most installations, using a flat naming model (implemented with the `.world` default domain) is sufficient. Adding domains to your network topology should be done out of need, not simply because it can be done. Managing an Oracle network with multiple domains adds complexity to the installation and configuration.

UNDERSTANDING THE OPTIONAL SECURITY EXTENSIONS

The final set of Oracle Network Products include several optional security extensions that make up the Oracle Advanced Networking Option. These include

- High speed global data encryption using RSA RC4 or DES encryption algorithms. This encrypts all network traffic with either a 56-bit or exportable 40-bit encryption key.
- Single sign-on using Kerberos and SESAME authentication servers, Security Dynamics ACE/Server token system, and Identix TouchNet II fingerprint ID system.
- Integration with OSF/DCE and the DCE security system.
- RADIUS (Remote Authentication Dial-In User Service) authentication method

RADIUS is a lightweight, open protocol for user authentication, authorization, and accounting between a network client and an authentication server. The RADIUS authentication method enables authentication with Radius-compliant devices such as token cards. In addition, RADIUS support enables challenge-response mechanism and accounting. Net8 provides integration to RADIUS services.

PART
VII

CH
33

SQL*NET AND NET8 ARCHITECTURES

With the introduction of Oracle8, Oracle has renamed the current SQL*Net Network Product group to Net8. As mentioned previously, Oracle has introduced some new network performance and scalability features in the updated Net8 product. All other components and features in Net8 remain relatively unchanged from SQL*Net 2.3.3, the latest SQL*Net release for Oracle7 Release 7.3. In this discussion of Oracle Networking Fundamentals, functions of SQL*Net will be described. TCP/IP and ethernet will be used in most examples because this is the predominate network architecture. To make things as simple as possible, all jargon will be described and analogies will be used where possible.

In most of the current SQL*Net architecture diagrams, SQL*Net is shown as the central building block, tightly integrating network transport (Oracle Protocol Adapters), network naming (Naming Adapter), and security services (Oracle Advanced Networking Option) at the network level. User-client applications ride on top of this SQL*Net layer to access Oracle7 servers, transparent gateways to third-party database servers, procedural gateways to other applications, or the Oracle Web Server.

NETWORKING PROTOCOL STACKS

In this section, you will look closely at the network transport services, the native local area network (LAN), and wide area network (WAN) protocol stacks that make up the core of networking. You will also touch on native network naming services as they apply to the native network protocols. Native network naming services are used to map "English" names and aliases for computers with their network addresses. Oracle Names are used to map English names and aliases to Oracle databases. Oracle Names often take advantage of native network naming services by allowing the administrator to specify server host names rather than network addresses in the Oracle Names database.

As promised, jargon will be defined as it comes up. Start with *network architectures* and *protocol stacks*. A network architecture is a collection of modular components that are combined to form an effective, synergistic solution. Each component provides a "service" to the whole. By choosing and combining a subset of the available component technologies, a network architecture is built. It is this ability to mix and match components that underlies the principle of open systems and interoperability.

Without some type of reference *blueprint* for the assembly of components, and a set of standards governing their construction, these pieces would not be plug and play. This environment exists for native network transports. These standards are often called *protocols*, and the reference blueprint is called a *stack*. The reference blueprint describes the network framework as a stack of service layers, much like a layer cake. Each layer has a specific, clearly defined responsibility within the stack and provides service to the layer above until all the stack of components is working together.

For the native network transport, the reference model is the International Organization for Standardization's (ISO) Open Systems Interconnection reference model. Standards are developed and maintained by the American National Standards Institute (ANSI) and the Institute for Electronic and Electrical Engineers (IEEE) 802 committee. The Oracle networking layers and protocols above the native network transport follow Oracle's SQL*Net architecture.

The current SQL*Net architecture blueprint is missing some important protocol layer detail needed to understand how SQL*Net works. It is missing the core network protocol of SQL*Net, Oracle's Transparent Network Substrate (TNS) peer-to-peer networking application. It is the TNS that provides the primary abstraction layer, or a common application interface, to many of the network products that make Oracle applications hardware and network *transparent*—thus the name Transparent Network Substrate. TNS provides the service layer to access the native network transport, Oracle Names, and various security and naming services. The Oracle Network Listener is a TNS application that runs on an Oracle server to establish connections between clients and the server. The TNS layer is responsible for most of the client error messages as the TNS- prefix on these error messages reveals.

There are five fundamental protocol layers that make up the SQL*Net Architecture (see Figure 33.1):

■ Network-Specific Protocol Stack—The foundation is the native network transport supported by the computer and the local area network (LAN) or wide area network (WAN). The most commonly used LAN protocol, and the one used in examples, is the TCP/IP protocol stack, although SPX/IPX, NetBIOS, DECNet, LU6.2, AppleTalk, Banyan Vines, MaxSix, Named Pipes, OSI, and X.25 protocols are also supported.

■ Oracle Protocol Adapter—The *connector* between the function calls of the TNS protocol and the native network transport protocol stack. The adapters are specific to the exact native stack used.

■ Transparent Network Substrate (TNS)—The peer-to-peer networking protocol, very similar to NetBIOS that forms universal transport for all Oracle network products.

■ SQL*Net—Layers on top of TNS to offer a set of functions needed to authenticate and communicate with a distributed database.

■ User Programmatic Interface (UPI)—Sits on top and is the application programming interface connector between SQL*Net and the client application.

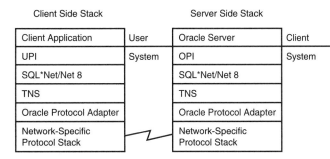

Figure 33.1
The client side and server side SQL*Net and Net8 protocol stacks.

ORACLE PROTOCOL ADAPTERS

The Oracle Protocol Adapters are the interfaces between specific native protocol stack implementations and the Transparent Network Substrate (TNS). The Oracle Protocol Adapters perform a function similar to the interfaces in the native network transport, mapping the standard functionality to TNS with those functions found in the native stack. Oracle Protocol Adapters are specific to the exact vendor's implementation of the native protocol stack.

TRANSPARENT NETWORK SUBSTRATE (TNS)

As stated earlier, the TNS is a peer-to-peer networking protocol developed by Oracle. It provides the means for establishing network connections, and delivering a "pipe" through which to pass SQL*Net, application messages, and data. The most critical TNS application is the Network Listener.

The Network Listener is a protocol-independent application listener, or daemon, that receives TNS connections for any TNS application running on the Oracle server. SQL*Net connections are identified by the listener, based on a SQL*Net-specific port or socket identified in the ADDRESS portion of the *connect descriptor* in the TNSNAMES.ORA file or Oracle Names database. While a session is established with the listener, a dedicated server process is established (or assigned) to handle the communication session.

USING THE OPEN SYSTEMS INTERCONNECTION REFERENCE MODEL

As the foundation for both TNS and SQL*Net, your local area network (LAN) protocols must be working properly before anything layered on top will work. Understanding proper LAN operation, therefore, is a prerequisite to understanding Oracle Networking. As I describe the native network protocol stack, I will emphasize the concepts needed for troubleshooting and proper design.

As previously mentioned, the reference blueprint for the native network transport is the ISO's seven layer Open Systems Interconnection (OSI) reference model. In the late 1970s the ISO organized a subcommittee of computer professionals to establish standards to encourage interoperability among computer and data communication vendors. The resulting OSI blueprint organizes network communication into the following seven layers:

> Layer 1—Physical Layer
>
> Layer 2—Data Link Layer
>
> Layer 3—Network Layer
>
> Layer 4—Transport Layer
>
> Layer 5—Session Layer
>
> Layer 6—Presentation Layer
>
> Layer 7—Application Layer

This reference blueprint is much too detailed for your purposes. For your purposes, I will describe a simplified reference blueprint (see Figure 33.2) beginning with the foundation, the interfaces, and the protocol stacks.

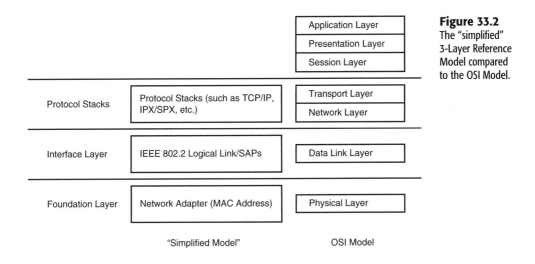

Figure 33.2
The "simplified"
3-Layer Reference
Model compared
to the OSI Model.

THE FOUNDATION

Nothing can be built without a strong foundation. The same is true of networks. This layer consists of the physical cabling and electronics required to electrically transmit data between computers. This world is governed by the Electronics Industries Association (EIA), Telecommunication Industries Association (TIA), and the Institute of Electrical and Electronic Engineers (IEEE). The joint EIA/TIA standards committee has worked toward the development of cabling standards and standard practices. These standards harmonize the wiring necessary for telephone and data. The adoption of EIA/TIA-568A standard in the wiring industry has driven most LANs to a star-wired design using telephone-type cable called unshielded twisted-pair (UTP). Shielded twisted-pair (IBM Type1 Token-Ring) and fiber optic cabling are also recommended in the 568A standard.

IEEE standards exist for most of the popular network technologies including ethernet, Token-Ring, FDDI, 100BASE-T, ATM, and Gigabit ethernet.

Why should you care about this layer? There are two very good reasons. First, the MAC address (sometimes called the DLC address) is a critical addressing component for almost every protocol stack. Individual workstations can be identified and tracked based on this number. The other reason is that this layer is the most unreliable layer in the network. It is often quoted that 80% of network faults occur in the wiring. These faults are not only due to bad or loose wiring connections. Wiring faults can also be due to wrongly configured electronics.

Tip #94	With ethernet, one main source of failure comes from excessive packet collisions. The causes for this can be attributed to an excessive number of repeaters between stations (more than three), ethernet transceivers connected to repeaters with SQE turned on (SQE should never be turned on in this instance), and failing ethernet adapters not listening before sending.

THE INTERFACE

On top of the foundation is an interface. The main interface for LAN protocols is the IEEE 802.2 Logical Link Control protocol. It creates a simple and standard means, called Service Access Points (SAPs), for accessing the wire. This is not a very important layer for troubleshooting, but you probably should remember that SAPs are the methods used to access the foundation, because this term comes up occasionally.

THE PROTOCOL STACK

Above the interface is the protocol stack. The protocol stack encompasses the network and transport layer of the OSI model. Multiple protocol stacks can share the same wire, while the same protocol stack uses different wires. The network layer of the stack handles the routing of messages through the network, or through the multiple connected wires. The transport layer of the stack provides error-free transmission of data, data flow control, error recovery, and receipt acknowledgment. TCP/IP has established itself as the standard protocol stack. Other protocol stacks include IPX/SPX, NetBIOS, DECNet, LU6.2, AppleTalk, Named Pipes, Banyan Vines, and so on.

The protocol stack is very complicated. A lot goes on in the stack, and each stack is very different from others. Protocol stacks often have another addressing scheme different from the MAC address. These addressing schemes often break a network up into *subnetworks* or *subnets*, also called *zones* or *areas* in some stacks. Much like an area code is needed when dialing a long-distance telephone number, special subnet addressing is used to communicate with another subnet. Specialized devices, called routers, are placed at the intersections of adjacent subnets to inspect messages and deliver them to the correct subnet.

THE TCP/IP PROTOCOL STACK

TCP/IP is most popular protocol stack used for SQL*Net and client/server connections. Developed in the 1960s by the U.S. military and a group of West Coast American universities, TCP/IP was developed for the original Internet, called the ARPAnet. Core to the design of TCP/IP was the capability to "self-heal" in case of the loss of a portion of the network. This was important to a Cold War era military, concerned about command-and-control during a nuclear attack. It is also a good design for a huge network without any central control—the Internet.

The TCP/IP stack can run over almost every type of foundation, including ethernet, Token-Ring, Frame Relay, and ATM. This flexibility accounts for much of TCP/IP's success. The TCP/IP protocol implements two protocols, IP and ICMP, to handle the routing of messages through the network.

INTERNET CONTROL MESSAGE PROTOCOL (ICMP)

ICMP is a very important protocol for troubleshooting, as it provides error and other control information for testing of routes through a network. Some of the most useful ICMP messages include

- Echo Request / Echo Reply—A TCP/IP utility, called PING, uses echo request and reply to determine whether a specified address can be reached. The PING command sends an echo request to the remote node. If the protocol stack is working, it replies to the request with an ICMP echo reply. When PING receives the reply, it calculates the elapsed time required for the round trip. It also indicates whether a reply is missing, indicating a busy network. This tool is indispensable.

- Destination Unreachable—If a route between networks or subnets cannot be accessed, the ICMP reports the error. Again, the PING tool reports an unreachable destination, indicating some type of routing misconfiguration or network failure.

- Time Exceeded—ICMP reports back to the sender when the message's time-to-live (TTL) counter expires. The TTL counter is normally set to 20 when a message is first broadcast on the network. Each time a message passes through a router moving from one network or subnet to another, the TTL counter is decremented by 1. When the counter is decremented to 0, ICMP sends the message back to the sender providing the name of the last router or *hop*. This stops messages from getting into infinite loops, and provides the name of the offending router.

Another indispensable tool for TCP/IP uses this feature to trace the route a message takes to get to its destination. The TRACEROUTE tool begins by sending a message with a TTL of one. This first router expires its counter and sends back the message. The address of this router is then recorded by TRACEROUTE. A message with a TTL of 2 is now sent to discover the second router, and so on until the destination is found. In Windows 95, this standard Microsoft utility is called TRACERT.EXE.

Tip #95

A super, free combination PING and TRACEROUTE tool called Sub-O-Tronic is available for Windows 95 from Virgin Interactive at http://subspace.vie.com on their download page. It is a diagnostic tool for use with their SubSpace Internet game to identify network bottlenecks hurting the performance of their client/server game. It works just as well looking for network problems and bottlenecks in your network. A must have!

Another area of concern for most administrators is correct IP addressing and configuration. For the IP protocol to correctly route your messages across the network, several parameters must be set up correctly.

IP ADDRESSING

The IP address is expressed in 4-byte, dotted-decimal notation. In decimal notation, a byte can have a value between 0 and 255, so a 4-byte, dotted-decimal notation looks like an address between 0.0.0.0 and 255.255.255.255. As mentioned earlier, the IP address refers to both a specific network or subnet and a specific host. These address are divided into classes:

- Class A—The first byte of a Class A address is a number starting with 1 to 126. Class A addresses use the first byte to designate the network address and the last three bytes to designate the host address. Class A addresses are reserved networks with a huge number of hosts.

- Class B—The first byte of a Class B address is a number starting with 128 to 191. Class B addresses use the first two bytes to designate the network address and the last two bytes to designate the host address. Class B addresses are normally reserved for Internet service providers.

- Class C—The first byte of a Class C address is a number starting with 192 to 223. Class C addresses use the first three bytes to designate the network address and the last byte to designate the host address. Only 254 hosts can be in any Class C network.

- Class D—The first byte of a Class D address is a number starting with 224 to 247. These addresses are reserved for multicasting and should not be used for IP addressing.

Some IP addresses are reserved or have special meanings. Some important ones include

- An address of all 0s or all 255s is not allowed, for example, 0.0.0.0 or 255.255.255.255.

- The host portion of the IP address cannot be all 0s because this is used to designate the network itself and is a reserved address.

- The host portion of the IP address cannot be all 255s. This address is used for broadcast traffic that is received by all nodes on a network.

- The address 127.0.0.1 is a loopback testing address. When you ping the address 127.0.0.1, your TCP/IP stack replies, indicating that the stack is working.

- IP addresses with a first byte starting with 248 to 254 have special purposes and are not be used for IP addressing.

Tip #96

The 10.x.x.x network has been set aside for sites wanting to use an unregistered IP address scheme. The routers within the Internet ignore messages with a 10.x.x.x network address. It is highly recommended to use this scheme at most sites.

IP SUBNET MASK

Another level of complexity added to IP network addressing is subnet masking. Subnet masking is used to expand the number of networks due to the 4-byte limitation of IP's addressing field. Bits can be robbed from the host number to allow additional subnets to be defined. For example, if you choose to use the 10.x.x.x Class A network number for your unregistered network, you can use a subnet mask to create additional networks using this address. The subnet mask specifies which bits of the IP address designate network addresses and which bits designate host numbers. The bit is given the value 1 if it designates network addresses and 0 for hosts. A Class A address, therefore, would have all 1s in the first eight bits because the first byte is the network address. The decimal value for a byte of all 1s is 255. Therefore a Class A address would have a standard mask of 255.0.0.0.

Now say you want to use the second byte of your 10.x.x.x address for subnet addresses. Now the first two bytes are being used for the network address, so the mask would be 255.255.0.0. This will give you 254 subnets with 65,534 hosts in each.

DEFAULT ROUTER

Another configuration needed to make the IP portion of TCP/IP route correctly over the network is to specify a default route. This is the IP address of a router in your network with connections to other networks. If you are sending a message to an address on another network and your node doesn't know the address of the next "hop" on its way to the destination, IP sends your message to the default route host. It is assumed this router knows how to handle your message. If it fails, the message comes back with a "network unreachable" error.

DOMAIN NAME SERVER (DNS) PROTOCOL

Another important piece of the TCP/IP protocol stack is DNS protocol. In very static networks, host names and their corresponding IP addresses can be entered into a host table and stored on each client computer. As the network grows, this becomes impossible to maintain. The DNS service, like the Oracle Names service, delivers the correct IP address to a client from a centralized names database. DNS also has the capability to learn names by querying other DNS servers, and caching the results. Implementing DNS is important if connection to the Internet is important to your organization. DNS is the basis of all Internet addressing and address resolution. DNS design and configuration is a complex topic outside the scope of this chapter.

DYNAMIC HOST CONFIGURATION PROTOCOL

The Dynamic Host Configuration Protocol (DHCP) provides easy, automatic administration of IP addresses. Any NT Server, InterNetWare server, and most UNIX servers can be configured as DHCP servers. The DHCP server is configured with the network address of the network for which it will be granting IP addresses. This configuration is called a DHCP scope. The range of address that will be "leased" is also specified in the scope definition. DHCP can also supply your clients with the correct subnet mask, the default route, and DNS server address while supplying the IP address. DHCP is a very powerful protocol and should be implemented on any network with Windows 95 or Windows NT clients.

UNDERSTANDING SQL*NET OPERATIONS

SQL*Net provides three general operations that are used with Oracle products and databases that use SQL*Net for distributed processing. These functions provided by SQL*Net operate in the background and are not visible to the user:

Connect Operations   A client application initiates a request for a connection to a remote database by providing the database alias name for the desired destination database. This alias name, called a *service name*, is mapped to a network address contained in the connect descriptor stored in the TNSNAMES.ORA network configuration file or in a database serviced by Oracle Names.

Data Operations   The client and server can send and receive data between each other. Oracle supports both synchronous (single-threaded, ping/pong) requests and asynchronous (multi-threaded, windowed) requests.

Exception Operations   SQL*Net supports several exception functions such as breaking, resynchronizing, and testing a SQL*Net connection.

INSTALLING AND CONFIGURING SQL*NET

All installation information applies to SQL*Net version 2.3.3, refer to your operating system specific Net8 Installation Manual for assistance in installing Net8.

PLANNING THE NETWORK DESIGN

Before installing SQL*Net, some planning needs to be done up front. Decisions to be made include the following:

- The network layout and use of LAN protocols
- Centralization or decentralization of Oracle network management
- Naming of network and database components
- Use of the Oracle Network Manager tool

The most critical network layout decision is whether more than one LAN protocol needs to be used. Using multiple protocols greatly increases the complexity of the Oracle network and increases the number of point of failure. If possible, use only one LAN protocol.

The second issue to confront is the centralization of Oracle network management. As with most things, the more fingers in the pie, the more problems that occur. Some sites are so big that decentralization is necessary. If possible, centralize network management.

Many things in an Oracle network require names. Each protocol type used in the Oracle network is called a *community* and is given a *community name*. Regions of a company can be broken up for decentralized management reasons. These regions are called *domains*. By default, Oracle Network Manager names the core domain .WORLD. Additionally, all network listener nodes, database *service names*, MultiProtocol *Interchanges*, and Oracle Name servers need names. Document a scheme and stick with it. Consistency counts! See Chapter 34, "The Advanced Security Option," for more information on naming.

As you have probably figured out by now, the Oracle Network Manager is the tool for naming and configuring all these network pieces.

OVERVIEW OF CONFIGURATION FILES

Client and server machines require configuration files for proper operation. Client machines typically have three configuration files that are created by the Oracle Network Manager program, and one optional file that must be created manually. These files provide configuration information regarding network destinations, network navigation, and diagnostics such as tracing and logging:

TNSNAMES.ORA—This file contains network destination information used by the client. Information contained in this file includes database "service names" and connect descriptors. With Net8, another section was added to this file to handle the failover mode of the Oracle Parallel Server Option where multiple instances can access the same database. Different parameters can be used in this section: BASIC, PRECONNECT, SELECT, SESSION, and NONE. A better understanding of these parameters can be found in Oracle's Parallel Server manual. Without Oracle Names, a client requires this file to expand short service names into fully qualified connections. This file can be generated by Oracle Network Manager or Oracle Net8 Assistant. Although it's not recommended by Oracle, experienced users who are familiar with the proper syntax can edit this file manually with success. It would be good practice to back up this file if you do intend to do this.

For example, A sample TNSNAMES.ora would look like the following:

```
# D:\ORANT\NETWORK\ADMIN\TNSNAMES.ORA Configuration
File:D:\ORANT\NETWORK\ADMIN\tnsnames.ora
# Generated by Oracle Net8 Assistant
EXTPROC_CONNECTION_DATA.US.ORACLE.COM =
  (DESCRIPTION =
    (ADDRESS_LIST =
      (ADDRESS = (PROTOCOL = IPC)(KEY = EXTPROC0))
    )
    (CONNECT_DATA =
      (SID = PLSExtProc)
      (PRESENTATION = RO)
    )
  )
ORCL.US.ORACLE.COM =
  (DESCRIPTION =
    (ADDRESS_LIST =
      (ADDRESS = (PROTOCOL = TCP)(HOST = pxsharma-lap)(PORT = 1521))
    )
    (CONNECT_DATA =
      (SERVICE_NAME = orcl.world)
    )
  )
```

Note: ORCL is the name of database instance

SQLNET.ORA—This file contains optional diagnostic parameters and client information about Oracle Names. This file is created by Network Manager but can also contain node-specific parameters that require manual editing.

PART

VII

CH

33

For Example:

```
# D:\ORANT\NETWORK\ADMIN\SQLNET.ORA Configuration
File:D:\ORANT\network\admin\sqlnet.ora
# Generated by Oracle Net8 Assistant
            NAMES.DEFAULT_DOMAIN = us.oracle.com
SQLNET.AUTHENTICATION_SERVICES= (NTS)
```

TNSNAV.ORA—This file is used in multiprotocol (community) networks using one or more Oracle MultiProtocol Interchanges. It lists network navigation information such as communities and the names and addresses of Interchanges to reach these other communities. This file is created by Network Manager and should never be edited manually.

PROTOCOL.ORA—This file contains protocol-specific options for LAN protocols that require them (for example, Async and APPC/LU6.2). If needed, this file must be created manually. The database server machine will also contain a configuration file for the TNS Listener. This file is appropriately called LISTENER.ORA.

LISTENER.ORA—This file contains the names and addresses of all listeners on a machine, the system identifiers (SIDs) of the databases, and control parameters used by the Listener Control Utility.

For Example:

```
# D:\ORANT\NETWORK\ADMIN\LISTENER.ORA Configuration
File:D:\ORANT\network\admin\listener.ora
# Generated by Oracle Net8 Assistant
LISTENER =
  (ADDRESS_LIST =
    (ADDRESS = (PROTOCOL = TCP)(HOST = pxsharma-lap)(PORT = 1521))
    (ADDRESS = (PROTOCOL = IPC)(KEY = EXTPROC0))
  )
SID_LIST_LISTENER =
  (SID_LIST =
    (SID_DESC =
      (SID_NAME = PLSExtProc)
      (ORACLE_HOME = D:\ORANT)
      (PROGRAM = extproc)
    )
    (SID_DESC =
      (SID_NAME = orcl3)
    )
  )
```

PREPARING TO INSTALL SQL*NET

The Oracle Installer product is used for installing all client Oracle products, including all networking products. The Oracle Installer also includes the Oracle Client Software Manager (OCSM) to allow you to install 16-bit (Windows 3.x) applications on a shared file server for use by any Windows client platform. This does not imply that you can't run the standard installation of Oracle products from a shared, server directory—you can! OCSM goes beyond a shared directory, by supporting the delivery file updates directly to the client hard drive.

Not all SQL*Net configurations are created equal. There are two distinct versions of Oracle Network Products and Oracle Applications. There is a 16-bit version that supports Windows 3.1 clients. There are also 32-bit versions for Windows 95 and Windows NT. The 16-bit and 32-bit versions have very different sets of DLLs, and applications and tools compiled for the 16-bit SQL*Net do not work with the 32-bit versions.

There is good news, however. The 16-bit and 32-bit versions of Oracle Network Products can be installed on the same PC. Two separate Oracle Homes can exist and will not conflict with each other. This will be described in more detail shortly.

It is important to note here that there are two different 32-bit versions of Oracle Installer and Oracle products: one 32-bit Installer for Windows 95 and one 32-bit Installer for Windows NT. You must run the correct installer for the operating system you are using. Windows 95 installer can be found in the Oracle Product Media's \WIN95 directory, while Windows NT installer is found in the \WIN32 directory.

Another big difference between the 16-bit and 32-bit versions is maturity. The following tools are provided in the 16-bit version but are missing in the 32-bit version:

- GUI TNSPing application for testing the TNS protocol stack and the Network Listener. The 32-bit SQL*Net offers only DOS command-line TNSPing.
- The Network Test tool for testing database access via the SQL*Net protocol.
- The Client Status Monitor, a simple GUI tool that displays client software and configuration parameter settings in a summarized and printable form.
- The SQLNET.ORA editor that allows setting important trace and log parameters.
- The Oracle Client Software Manager (OCSM). OCSM does not currently support the shared installation of 32-bit applications for Windows 95 and Windows NT.
- The Oracle Home Switcher tool for switching between multiple Oracle homes.

PART

VII

CH

33

One major difference between the 16-bit version and the 32-bit version is the location of client configuration information. The 16-bit version of SQL*Net stores its configuration information in a file named ORACLE.INI. The location of this file is referenced by a parameter, ORA_CONFIG, in Windows's WIN.INI file under the [Oracle] section. The 32-bit version stores all configuration information in the Windows Registry.

DETERMINING YOUR ORACLE HOME LOCATION

The most critical decision to be made when installing SQL*Net on your client PC is the choice of your Oracle Home. This is the location of all Oracle Networking and Application products. It also includes important client and network configuration files. For non-OCSM installations, the two predominate schemes are to install your Oracle home on the primary hard drive of the client PC or to install your Oracle home into a common, shared file server directory. The former scheme offers the highest performance possible and greatest simplicity with a loss of centralized configuration control, whereas the latter is just the opposite.

Because performance and simplicity are a lot to give up for centralized configuration control, why bother? Aside from being able to deploy updates and patches quickly to a central, shared Oracle home, there are the group of four critical configuration files stored in the in the \ORAWIN\NETWORK\ADMIN directory of the Oracle home:

TNSNAMES.ORA

SQLNET.ORA

TNSNAV.ORA

PROTOCOL.ORA

Because these files are manipulated using Oracle Network Manager, they get changed every time a new database *service name* or server name gets added or changed. Having these files in one central location is very advantageous.

CHOOSING STANDALONE, NON-OCSM ORACLE HOME

If you choose to install Oracle to your local hard drive, remember that you need to copy the *.ORA files from a central repository of network configuration files. These files should be copied into the \ORAWIN\NETWORK\ADMIN directory.

CHOOSING SHARED, NON-OCSM ORACLE HOME

There are several steps and caveats to take care of if you choose to load files to a shared network drive, a configuration I will call a shared non-OCSM Oracle home.

1. During installation of the Oracle products, some DLL files are written to the \WINDOWS and \WINDOWS\SYSTEM directories. These files have to be identified and copied to each user. A quick way to identify these files is to turn off the archive bit on all files in the Windows and System directory using the ATTRIB command:
   ATTRIB C:\WINDOWS*.* -A /S

2. After running the install, search for files with their archive bits turned on. These files have been written to during the install.

3. Copy the ORACLE.INI file to the C: drive and put it in the Windows directory.

4. Edit WIN.INI in the C:\WINDOWS directory so that there exists an [Oracle] section and the key ORA_CONFIG=C:\WINDOWS\ORACLE.INI exists. Change the key to point to the location of your ORACLE.INI file.

5. Add the path to the \ORAWIN\BIN directory to your search path. This is normally done in the network login script.

The previous steps aid in having a smooth install of the configuration files to a shared network drive.

Choosing Local DLL/EXE with Shared, Non-OCSM Oracle Home

This is an improvement over the previous configuration. In this configuration, a copy of the shared `\ORAWIN\BIN` directory is made on the local `C:` drive. Change the path from the shared directory to the local directory in your `AUTOEXEC.BAT` file or network login script. This local bin directory needs to be updated each time the shared bin directory is updated.

Installing 32-bit SQL*Net

This description assumes that you will install a local version of 32-bit SQL*Net on a local hard drive. If you are running Windows 95/98 or Windows NT, your PC will probably autorun the installer for the appropriate 32-bit version of SQL*Net for your operating system. If the Oracle Installer is autorun, skip to step 2. Otherwise, start with step 1 to install 32-bit SQL*Net:

1. Start the Oracle Installer. The install directory on the CD-ROM for the 32-bit version is called `\WIN95` for Windows 95 and `\WIN32` for Windows NT. Be sure to pick the correct directory. Change to this directory and run the program `SETUP.EXE`.

   To start Oracle Installer under Windows 95 and Windows NT 4.0, click Start, Run from the Taskbar and type the following (substituting your CD-ROM drive letter for D): **D:\WIN95\SETUP.EXE** for Windows 95 and **D:\WIN32\SETUP.EXE** for Windows NT. Confirm the selection by clicking OK.

   To start Oracle Installer under Windows NT 3.51 (or greater), click File, Run from Program Manager and type the following (again substituting your CD-ROM drive letter for D): **D:\WIN32\SETUP.EXE**. Confirm by clicking OK.

2. Select Oracle Installation Settings.

3. Next you are prompted for the language being used for the installation. After choosing a language and selecting OK, you are presented with an Oracle Installation Settings dialog box.

4. The selection of your Oracle Home is important. Think about this before selecting the default. In this example you are again installing to the local hard drive. The default path for Oracle Home is `C:\ORAWIN95` for the 32-bit Windows95 version and `C:\ORANT` for the 32-bit Windows NT version.

5. The next screen is a wizard to automate installing products such as Oracle Networking, SQL*Plus, Documentation, and so on.

> **Caution**
>
> If you have a previous installation of SQL*Net, Oracle recommends that you remove all the components first before installing an upgraded version. This is done by selecting Custom Installation and removing all components on the right side of the screen

6. For a new install, select Oracle Networking to quickly install all the components necessary for SQL*Net and TNS. Pick the correct underlying network protocol and the correct stack vendor and let Oracle install the rest. For Windows 95 this will be

under Winsock stacks. Pick the configuration for Microsoft Windows 95 if you're using the native TCP/IP stack. If the Installer finds any duplicate DLL files in the path, the installer asks you to rename them so they will not conflict with older versions. If you answer no, Installer creates a file listing the duplicates found.

7. When the installation is complete, you are left at the two-panel Oracle Installer screen.

The core SQL*Net files installed are shown on the right side of the Oracle Installer screen, while available applications are shown on the left. If you will work with older versions of Oracle databases, you need to load the Required Support Files (RSFs) for these versions. The 7.3 RSFs are already installed. If you might use Oracle 7.2, install these RSFs too. It is good to install SQL*Plus for support and testing reasons as well. If support for Oracle 7.1 or 7.0 is needed, you need to get an older Oracle CD-ROM to find these older RSFs.

To install specific product components, double-click the desired product in the Products Available list and then select the specific component to install. Click Install to begin product installation.

Tip #97	Update the Windows Registry to add the key USERNAME to the HKEY_Local_Machine/Software/Oracle section and the HKEY_Local_Machine/Software/Oracle/Oracle_Homes/Oracle1 section. The value for this key should be the user's name. This value is used when a SQL*Net connection is made to the Oracle server. This value is displayed on the server for your connection. This aids releasing connections to shut down the database.

Tip #98	Two other changes to the registry should be considered. Add the key CNTL_BREAK=ON to the HKEY_Local_Machine/Software/Oracle and HKEY_Local_Machine/Software/Oracle/Oracle_Homes/Oracle1 sections of the Windows Registry. This key allows a Ctrl+C keypress to stop a long query. Also, changing the value for NLS_LANG in both sections can improve the order data is sorted using the ORDER BY clause. PeopleSoft software running against Oracle requires the US7ASCII character set be used. Use the following syntax in the ORACLE.INI file: NLS_LANG=AMERICAN_AMERICA.US7ASCII.

Using the Oracle Client Software Manager (OCSM) Component

Oracle Client Software Manager is a new feature to the Oracle Windows Installer. It allows the administrator to install 16-bit applications on a shared file server directory for use by any Windows client platform, including Windows 95 and Windows NT. Installation is centralized and updates to software on client workstations are automatic, using the intelligence built into Oracle Installer.

The Oracle Client Software Manager (OCSM) can be used to deliver 16-bit client software bundled with Oracle7 Workgroup and Enterprise servers including SQL*Net.

Runtime and development versions of Oracle Developer /2000, Oracle Office, and the Oracle Applications suite can also be installed with OCSM. It is also a critical delivery tool for the GUI version of Oracle Financials.

Caution

Two notable omissions to the applications delivered by the Oracle7 OCSM are the Oracle ODBC driver and the 7.1 and 7.0 Required Support Files. This is no longer the case with Net8.

Oracle Windows Installer creates the Oracle Client Software Manger directory and loads the selected software into this shared network directory. Oracle Windows Installer configures the administrator's PC to run the Oracle Client Software Administrator, a utility that allows the administrator to set up client configurations. The exact suite of products needed by a group of users is associated to a configuration. Users are then assigned the appropriate configuration to perform their job. Optionally, the administrator can give the user a suite of products to pick from and install for themselves.

The Client Software Administrator has other options such as installation conflict resolution, and the ability for the administrator to decide the location of executables. A client can be configured to use Oracle applications in three ways:

- In shared mode directly from the file server
- In EXE/DLL download mode when only the executables and DLLs are loaded locally on the client PC for performance improvements
- In full download mode, when a complete installation is made on the client machine

The user portion of OCSM is the Oracle Client Software Agent. This small executable is loaded onto the client PC and is run in the Windows StartUp group. The Agent monitors the server for changes and automatically updates the client using the Oracle Window Installer engine.

PART

VII

CH

33

INSTALLING SQL*NET USING THE ORACLE CLIENT SOFTWARE MANAGER

If you are running Windows 95 or Windows NT, your PC will probably autorun the installer for the appropriate 32-bit version of SQL*Net for your operating system. Because you are installing, and OCSM works only with the 16-bit version of the Oracle Network Products, cancel out of this installation if autorun is enabled on your PC. Use the following steps to install SQL*Net using the Oracle Client Software Manager.

Tip #99

Autorun can be disabled by holding down the Shift key while loading the CD-ROM.

1. Start the Oracle Installer. The install directory on the CD for the 16-bit version of Oracle Network Products is called \WINDOWS. Change to this directory. Find and run the program SETUP.EXE with a /SHARED option using File, Run in Windows 3.1

and Windows NT 3.51 or the Start, Run dialog box in Windows 95 and Windows NT 4.0. Type the following (substituting your CD-ROM drive letter for D): **D:\WINDOWS\SETUP.EXE /SHARED**.

2. Select Oracle Installation Settings.

3. Next you are prompted for the language being used for the installation. After choosing a language and selecting OK, you are presented with an Oracle Installation Settings dialog box. Type your company name in the Company Name field and then specify the location of the shared Oracle Home in the Oracle Home field.

> **Note**
>
> In Oracle8.1.x, the installation is done by running `d:\setup.bat` where `d:` is your CD-ROM drive.
>
> In Oracle8.1.x, the networking components installation is merged with the Oracle8.1.x database installation.
>
> For Windows NT, the networking files such as `tnsnames.ora` reside in the directory %ORAHOME%\net80\admin.

> **Caution**
>
> You must be careful in specifying the Oracle Home for the shared installation. This path should be on a network file server drive that all Oracle users can access. This should *not* be on your local hard drive.

4. You are then prompted for the /BIN directory setting in your Autoexec.bat file. You see the Oracle Client Software Manager Administrator Information dialog box. Type the administrator's username, and click OK. The standard Software Asset Manager dialog box now appears.

5. Install the Oracle Installer, Oracle Client Software Manager Administrator, and the Oracle Client Software Manager Agent to the shared Oracle Home by first highlighting them on the left pane and then clicking Install. When complete, install all other required applications, such as SQL*Net and the appropriate Oracle Protocol Adapter. Pick any other applications needed in the shared Oracle Home.

6. Exit the installer.

As the Software Manager Administrator, the Administration program is installed on your PC. You need to use the PC to make changes to the shared configuration.

> **Caution**
>
> You can't be the Software Manger Administrator *and* a user running the Manager Agent. You probably should pick a machine you do not use for development or production as your Administrator machine. You should pick an alias name as your administrator name so it will not conflict with your username if you install Oracle products on the computer at your desk.

SUMMARY

Net8 (previously known as SQL*Net) is Oracle's standard networking software layer which is used to allow communications from client to server. Net8 needs to be installed on both the client and server. The listener process needs to be started at the server before clients can connect to it. Main files required for Net8 to function properly are `SQLNET.ORA`, `TNSNAMES.ORA`, and `LISTENER.ORA`.

THE ADVANCED SECURITY OPTION

In this chapter

The database world has changed with the advent of the Internet and Web-based applications, and Oracle has provided a new option to meet the new security challenges.

The Advanced Security Option (ASO) provides all the tools needed to create a highly secure environment. A secure environment is defined as being Confidential and having Integrity and Availability; this is the foundation. ASO will help you meet each one of these tenets of security.

FOUNDATIONS OF A STRONG SECURITY POLICY

ASO has many options to provide a strong secured database environment. This means that known vulnerabilities of the computing architecture is strengthened by using this product. Security should always start with a plan. A security plan is usually based on a company security policy. This policy foundation is based on the perceived threat to the computing resource and the associated risk of not protecting the resource. The foundation for computer security policy is based on Confidentiality, Integrity, and Availability. Confidentiality of the transaction includes authentication of the user and or server that the transaction has originated from this makes sure that it is an authorized transaction. Authentication is established by integrating authentication support in ASO. This authentication extends to users, databases, and Web servers.

A user is authenticated using a password, whereas Web servers and databases can be authenticated using digital signatures.

Encryption of the data ensures that the data stays private. ASO supports all different levels of encryption algorithms.

WHY DO WE NEED A HIGHLY SECURE ENVIRONMENT?

The database must be kept secured from computer vandals. In the past the database was kept in a secure internal network; breaches of security were uncommon due to the inaccessibility of the database to the outside world. The database administrator (DBA) would perform appropriate security due diligence, which would include

- Making sure all the external database structures are protected with the appropriate operating system file level security
- Restrict access to the database server by limiting who has the operating system super user password and who is authorized to sign on to the database server
- Physically restrict the placement of the server to a secured room with appropriate fire protection

Tip #100	The database server that is used for Internet processing must be secured like all other production servers (see Chapter 23, "Security Management"). Then, using ASO, additional security can be implemented to handle the needs of the Internet database.

The security challenge facing the DBA today is a daunting one, because the advent of Web-based computing and electronic commerce. The network is no longer an internal secure zone, it is the Internet, a virtual world that has now allowed access to the corporation data crown jewels to anyone who has an Internet logon.

THE INTERNET USES A THREE-TIERED APPLICATION DESIGN

The users are using a thin client that connects to a Web server, then the Web server connects to the database (see Figure 34.1). The Web server then becomes the client to the database, where the non-Internet database has a typical client–to–database server two-tier configuration (see Figure 34.2). Later in this chapter, configuration of the client is discussed. The client can be a Web server or a traditional client PC.

Figure 34.1
Three-tiered
application design.

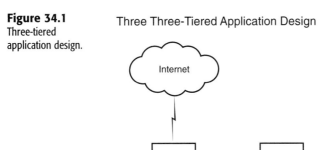

Three Three-Tiered Application Design

Figure 34.2
Two-tiered application
design.

Two-Tiered Application Design

THE INTERNET CAN POSE A THREAT TO YOUR COMPANY

The Internet can pose a very real threat to your company. The computer vandal is alive and well and does not work a typical nine-to-five workday. Computer vandals have their own conferences that they can attend to learn how to be better at what they do, just like a normal computing professional. They have Web sites to share information and even a magazine that is published and available at the larger book chains. The threat is very real and the newspapers cover only a very small percentage of the actual computer break-ins that occur. The hackers have tools to probe your network in order to determine the number and type of database servers that are in use. They also have tools to guess passwords, read network data packets, and emulate the IP address of the Web server to make your database think it is talking to an official computer on your network (see Figure 34.3). Internet access to a company's production database requires special security considerations and even then a computer vandal can still strike. The typical attack tries to defeat one or more of the tenets of security. A network sniffer that can scan data packets might compromise the confidentiality of your data. A network sniffer is available with the Windows NT 4.0 operating system, so even the trusted employee might discover new ways to exploit the network. The data could be credit card numbers or information about the customers that do business with you.

Figure 34.3
Computing vandal emulating a Web server.

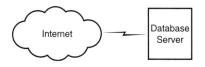
Computer Vandal Emulating a Web Server

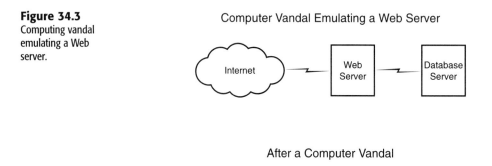
After a Computer Vandal

FIREWALLS: WHAT THEY ARE AND WHAT THEY ARE NOT

Firewalls are designed to isolate a potentially hostile environment from a secure environment. The typical architecture for a firewall is to have the Internet connect to a Web server, and then have the Web server pass data through a firewall to a database server (see Figure 34.4). A firewall acts as a portal from the Web server to the database server.

Figure 34.4
Web server using a firewall

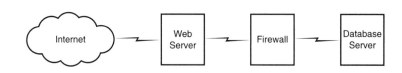
Web Server Using a Fire Wall

The goals of firewall use are as follows:

- Lock down ports on the computing resource
- Restrict network traffic from one computing resource to another
- Restrict the direction of the traffic, meaning to allow network traffic to only go one way
- Limit the type of interactions between the Web server and the database

LOCKING DOWN PORTS ON THE COMPUTING RESOURCE

A computer vandal looks for ways into a network; an open port on computer system is the first invitation. SQL*Net needs port 1521 available to allow SQL*Net traffic; other ports might be needed for different operating systems and Oracle gateways. If the port is just opened up, all types of network traffic can use this port, not just SQL*Net traffic.

This allows the computer vandal to exploit the seven layers of the network protocol stack. The challenge is to open the port that is used by SQL*NET in a secure manner: this is what a firewall is designed to do.

RESTRICT NETWORK TRAFFIC FROM ONE COMPUTING RESOURCE TO ANOTHER

The Internet database is being accessed by thousands of users who might or might not want to harm your company. The firewall allows isolation of the database server or network that the database resides on.

RESTRICT THE DIRECTION OF THE TRAFFIC

The firewall can open a port to allow network traffic to be only inbound or outbound. Figure 34.5 shows two firewalls at work in a typical Internet configuration. Firewall A allows inbound and outbound traffic on a specific port. Firewall B allows only outbound traffic on a specific port. This prevents access to anything on the network that is being protected by firewall B. The production network can place items onto the Internet network but won't allow any inbound traffic. This prevents computer vandals from trying to probe the production network and keep them from compromising the corporation crown jewels.

LIMIT THE WEB SERVER AND DATABASE INTERACTIONS

The types of transactions between the Web-enabled database and the company's production computing resources should be limited to only the bare essentials of computing services. For example the Network File System (NFS) service should be turned off; this service has been exploited in computer vandal circles for many years.

Figure 34.5
Typical Internet
Configuration

Database Server Being Isolated by Firewalls

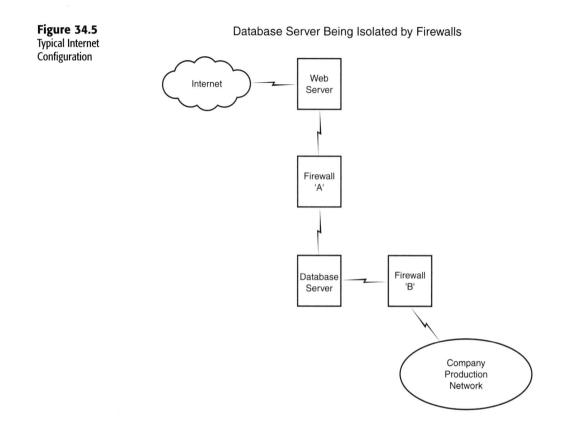

Tip #101

While testing your Internet database, turn off all optional services, such as mail, FTP, and NFS. Then try running your database, you might be surprised at how little services your database needs to function. Each service you can shut down is one fewer area a computer vandal can exploit.

How the firewall is implemented is based on the security policy of the company. This policy determines what the firewall is supposed to do and what type of firewall is used. The policy is based on a risk analysis that shows to what level the company computing resources are put at risk and what is considered an acceptable risk.

Tip #102

The most secure way of protecting your internal network is to have a completely separate network for your Internet servers.

TYPES OF FIREWALLS

There are three main types of firewalls: a screening router, proxy gateway, or a guard.

SCREENING ROUTER

A host/server uses a router to direct the network traffic to a specific network. A screening router allows rules to be enforced at the data packet level. The rules must not be too complex or the router will become a significant bottleneck on the network. The screening router can look only at packet header information and can check the address of the host where the packet originated from, although this can be forged. A screening router can be configured to block traffic from a specific network. It can also be used to control traffic at an application level by restricting the port usage. For example, File Transfer Protocol (FTP) uses port 21. If the FTP application were to be turned off, a screening router could close port 21 or allow FTP traffic to flow only one way.

PROXY GATEWAY

A screening router reviews only the header of the data packet allowing damaging transactions to occur as long as they pass the screening rules. A proxy gateway acts as a true middleman between the Internet application and the internal application that the Internet is trying to interact with. Electronic mail, when used by the Internet, connects to the company's mail server (see Figure 34.6). The proxy gateway allows the Internet to connect to the gateway and the Internet thinks it has connected to the mail application. This allows the proxy gateway to screen all commands that come through and execute only the ones that have been defined as allowed. This activity is transparent to both the mail server and the Web server.

Figure 34.6
Electronic mail connecting to the proxy gateway

Electronic Mail Connecting to the Internet

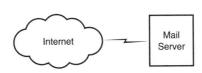

PART

VII

CH

34

GUARD TYPE OF FIREWALL

A guard firewall incorporates all the features of the proxy firewall, while adding rules that can be computable for a given activity. These rules can be complex and must be tested for error. If an error is introduced, the company computing resources can be compromised.

Tip #103	The more advanced firewalls now have proxies for SQL*Net; this means that when a port is opened for SQL*Net traffic, only SQL*Net traffic is allowed through the port. In the past when the port was opened for SQL*Net traffic, a computer vandal could exploit this as a vulnerability and use this port to probe the network for exposure.

USING THE ADVANCED SECURITY OPTION

The Oracle Advanced Security Option encompasses a range of tools that provide a level of data security and integrity not found in the standard Oracle networking tool set. Although some of the features are enabled in the Oracle software, the majority of the functionality comes from integrating Oracle networking with other third-party security and authentication products.

The functions provided by the Advanced Security Option are

- Data Encryption and Checksumming—Using the Advanced Security Option, you can ensure data security over network lines by enabling encryption of the data stream while in transit between the client and server. You can also safeguard against modification of data as it moves between the client and database server by enabling the transmission of checksum packets with data packets.

- Authentication and Single Sign-on—The Advanced Security Option allows you to integrate your Oracle environment with other authentication or single sign-on solutions that can be in place at your site. Net8 supports adapters for Kerberos, CyberSAFE, Identix TouchNet II, and SecurID. Also, the new Oracle Security Server will provide authentication services for your Oracle resources. Digital certificates X.509V3 can be used with Secured Sockets Layers (SSL).

- Integration with DCE Environments—Using the Advanced Security Option, you can integrate your Oracle network and resources with OSF's Distributed Computing Environment (DCE).

- Remote Authentication Dial-In User Service (RADIUS) protocol—This allows all devices that comply with the RADIUS standard to be used by ASO.

- Secured Sockets Layer (SSL)—SSL is one of the Internet standards that is now easier to integrate with ASO.

- Oracle wallets—Help manage Public Key Infrastructure (PKI).

Configuring the third-party authentication adapters and the DCE adapter are beyond the scope of this book. For information on configuring these items, refer to the Oracle Advanced Security Option Administrator's Guide, as well as the documentation specific to the adapter you are trying to install.

Note

There are two versions of the Oracle Advanced Security Option: one is for domestic use (USA and Canada) which can use the highest level of encryption currently available, the other is for other countries. The latter is referred to as the Export Use version. The export version must use the lowest level of encryption; this is required by law. Check with your Oracle vendor to determine which is the appropriate software for your site.

Enabling Data Encryption and Checksums

ASO encrypts your data using RSA Data Security's RC4 or the Data Encryption Standard (DES). A randomly generated key for Net8 sessions provides the security for all network traffic. This encryption works with all NET8 networks including gateways.

To enable data stream encryption or the data checksums, you must set several parameters in the client and server's sqlnet.ora file. There is one set of parameters for the client and one set for the server. Note that if a database server also acts as a client, both the client and server parameters must be set. You can configure sqlnet.ora by editing the file with a text editor or by using Network Manager or Net8 Assistant to edit the default Profile.

The SQLNET.ENCRYPTION_SERVER and SQLNET.ENCRYPTION_CLIENT parameters specify whether a connection is encrypted or not. The value of both the server and client machine evaluated together decides the session configuration. The valid values are

- ACCEPTED—The machine does not encrypt the session unless the other machine requests it.
- REJECTED—The machine does not encrypt, even if the other side wants to. If the other machine REQUIRES an encrypted session, the two machines will not connect.
- REQUESTED—The machine attempts to encrypt the session, but still connects if the other machine will not encrypt.
- REQUIRED—The machine accepts only encrypted connections.

The SQLNET.ENCRYPTION_TYPES_SERVER and SQLNET.ENCRYPTION_TYPES_CLIENT parameters specify the encryption algorithms the client or server machine can use. If more than one algorithm is specified, the machine attempts each one, starting from the first to the last. The actual algorithm used in the session is determined from the negotiation between the client and server. If an algorithm can't be negotiated because the server and the client do not have an algorithm in common, the connection fails.

Valid encryption types are

- RC4_40—RSA RC4 (40-bit key size) Domestic and international
- RC4_56—RSA RC4 (56-bit key size) Domestic only
- RC4_128—RSA RC4 (128-bit key size) Domestic only
- DES—Standard DES (56-bit key size) Domestic only

PART
VII

CH
34

- DES40—DES40 (40-bit key size) Domestic and international
- 3DES (triple DES using SSL)

To specify the checksum behavior, the SQLNET.CRYPTO_CHECKSUM_SERVER and SQLNET.CRYPTO_CHECKSUM_CLIENT parameters are used. Like the encryption parameters, these parameters accept ACCEPTED, REJECTED, REQUESTED, and REQUIRED as valid values, and behave in the same way when negotiating a connection.

There is one final set of parameters: SQLNET.CRYPTO_CHECKSUM_TYPES_SERVER and SQLNET.CRYPTO_CHECKSUM_TYPES_CLIENT. These parameters specify the type of algorithm used to produce the checksum values. Currently, only MD5 is supported as a valid value for these parameters.

Finally, the SQLNET.CRYPTO_SEED parameter is configured on the client computer to seed the cryptographic keys. This is an alphanumeric value from 10 to 70 characters long. The longer and more random this series of digits is, the stronger the checksum key is. You must specify a value for this parameter when using encryption or checksums.

RADIUS PROTOCOL DEVICE SUPPORT IN ASO

Support for the RADIUS protocol means more authentication vendors can work with Oracle, giving you more choice in implementing your security plan. The Oracle server acts as a radius client and authenticate to the RADIUS server (see Figure 34.7). The client using ASO logs in to the Oracle8i database, the database requests from the RADIUS server authentication of the request, the RADIUS server either accepts or denies the request. This answer is given to the Oracle8i server and then it performs the appropriate action. The Oracle8i server is really performing a transparent proxy authentication. ASO can provide customizable Java classes so that you can customize your security policy. The RADIUS option can be implemented in your Internet strategy by using a firewall that acts as a RADIUS client (see Figure 34.8). The authorization server can be any RADIUS protocol complaint server such as ActivCard, SecureId, Kerberos, Biometrics, and so on.

Figure 34.7
Oracle using RADIUS protocol

Oracle Using Radius Protocol

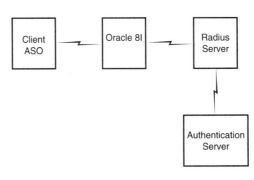

Figure 34.8
Firewall as RADIUS
client

Database Server Using Radius Architecture

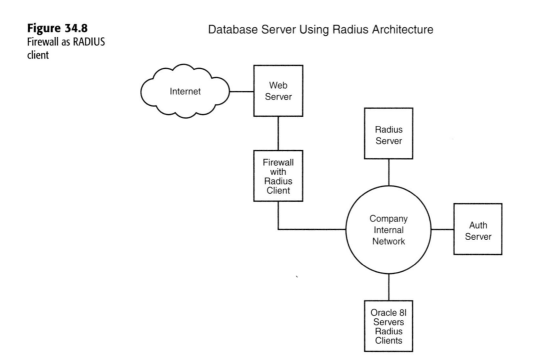

The advanced features of ASO for RADIUS include challenge-response authentication and accounting and contain the following steps:

1. The application server is challenged by the RADIUS server.
2. The challenge is passed on to the client.
3. The end user is presented with the challenge.
4. The user then provides a response to the challenge.
5. The response is passed through to the RADIUS server.
6. The RADIUS server then validates the response and sends a message either rejecting or accepting the end user.

RADIUS accounting provides the ability to create audit reports, that can be used for security, and resource usage.

SECURE SOCKETS LAYER (SSL) PROTOCOL

Secure Sockets Layer support is incorporated into the Oracle8i database and ASO. SSL is one of the Internet standards and is now easier to integrate with ASO. SSL provides authentication using X.509 digital certificates and encrypts network traffic. When all components of an Internet session uses SSL, you have an industrial strength security solution. The requirements are that all tiers of the Internet session support SSL. This includes the client tier, the Web server tier, and the database tier. SSL works with Net8 connections and uses protocols IIOP and Enterprise JavaBeans (EJB). Ensuring the integrity of the data is handled by cipher suites. The client and server each have a set of cipher suites and they negotiate which suite to use for the transaction. See Figure 34.9 showing the SSL architecture.

Figure 34.9
SSL architecture.

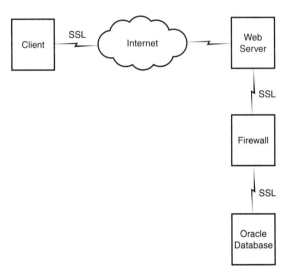

SSL Architecture

SUPPORT FOR ORACLE WALLETS

Support for Oracle Wallets helps manage Public Key Infrastructure (PKI). The Oracle Wallet Manager will allow users and administrators to manage the contents of wallets. A wallet can contain user certificates and trust points (certificate authorities that are trusted). When configured, the wallet can be placed in an Internet directory that is protected by a password. This password would be communicated to the user in a way that would not use the computing resource. This is done to achieve a secure way of only allowing the user to know the password.

A wallet can be configured with common trust points for the company and can be managed using a centralized administration plan. The process of using a wallet follows:

1. The Oracle Wallet is installed.

2. The password for the wallet is requested.

3. The password is used to create a public and private key. The private key is stored in the wallet.

4. The Oracle Wallet Manager requests certificate (this can be from a Oracle or non-Oracle CA).

5. The certificate gets downloaded and stored in the wallet.

6. The SSL connection is initiated.

7. The identity of the user is retrieved using SSL and the server validates the identity.

UNDERSTANDING THE MULTITHREADED SERVER

By default, users connect to the Oracle database server through the use of dedicated server processes. This means that for each user connection, an associated process handles the work for that user process, such as loading requested data from the datafiles into the data block buffer and returning the results of database queries to the user. This is the fastest and simplest way to provide connectivity into the database. However, in situations where hundreds or even thousands of users are connected simultaneously, the overhead involved in maintaining these dedicated server processes is prohibitive. Also, the dedicated server processes consume the same amount of resources on the database server whether they are active or idle. If, as in many cases, you have a large population of users connected to the database but actually access data from the database infrequently, the server resources tied up in maintaining these dedicated server processes are wasted. It is here that the Multithreaded Server (MTS) can save the day.

In simplest terms, the Multithreaded Server allows many user sessions to share a group of server processes, thereby reducing the overhead resources necessary to support a large simultaneous user base. This structure also allows you to reduce the overall idle time among these server sessions. For example, if you have 100 simultaneous user connections, but on average 10 are active at any one time, you can maximize your resources by allocating 10 server processes for the users to use. This keeps 10 server processes active at all times, rather than 10 active and 90 idle processes when using dedicated server processes.

MULTITHREADED SERVER ARCHITECTURE

When MTS is used, there are several differences in the architecture that need to be understood. Recall, from Chapter 6, "The Oracle Instance Architecture," that when connecting to an Oracle database using dedicated server processes, the Listener connects the user session with a dedicated server process, which manages the user's connection to the Oracle database. In an MTS environment, the Listener's actions are slightly different. Instead of spawning and connecting the User session to a dedicated Server process, it passes the User process to one or more Dispatcher processes. These Dispatcher processes are responsible for placing the User processes commands into the Request Queue, as well as retrieving the results of User processes commands from the Response Queue. The Request and Response Queues are both held in the SGA.

The Shared Server processes do not communicate directly with the Dispatcher or the Server processes. Rather, they monitor the Request queue. When a new command is placed in the queue they read the command, process it by reading appropriate data blocks in the data block buffer and submitting the command to the database, then place the results in the

Dispatcher's Response Queues. All Dispatchers place their requests into one Request Queue. Each Dispatcher also has its own Response queue. The Shared Server processes ensure that the results of User commands are placed in the correct Response Queue for the Dispatcher that issued the command. In this way, the Shared Server processes can work very efficiently together by handling the requests from all User sessions, while the Dispatcher's only have to retrieve and manipulate data for User sessions being handled by them.

Usage of the Multithreaded Server also changes the allocation of memory to the SGA. Because there are no dedicated server processes, user session data and cursor state information is stored in the SGA, rather than the PGA. The SGA should be adjusted accordingly because of this. Note that this is not an additional cost of running MTS, but an adjustment of where the data is held in memory.

CONFIGURING THE MULTITHREADED SERVER

The Multithreaded Server is configured largely through parameters contained in each database's init.ora file. The following are the parameters you configure to enable MTS:

MTS_SERVICE	The name of the service the Dispatcher processes associate themselves with. The Listener passes requests for a service to the appropriate Dispatcher based on the value of this parameter. Usually set to the value of the database name (db_name init.ora parameter value).
MTS_SERVERS	Specifies the number of shared server processes to create at instance startup.
MTS_MAX_SERVERS	Specifies the maximum number of shared server processes that run at any one time. Shared server processes are allocated and destroyed depending on need, but their number will never be greater than this number, or lower than the value of MTS_SERVERS.
MTS_DISPATCHERS	Defines the protocol and number of dispatchers to allocate at instance startup. To specify multiple dispatchers with different protocols, specify each protocol with separate MTS_DISPATCHERS parameters.
MTS_MAX_DISPATCHERS	Specifies the maximum number of dispatcher processes that run at any one time. Dispatcher processes are allocated and destroyed based on system load.
MTS_LISTENER_ADDRESS	The address at which the dispatcher processes listens. This is the same as the Listener address.

The MTS parameters from a sample init.ora file are shown in Listing 34.1.

LISTING 34.1   INIT.ORA

```
MTS_SERVICE = PROD01        # Database name is PROD01.
MTS_SERVERS = 3                      # Start 3 shared server processes at
instance start.
MTS_MAX_SERVERS = 10        # Never start more than 10 shared server processes.
MTS_DISPATCHERS = "tcp,3"   # Start 3 dispatchers that use the TCP/IP protocol.
MTS_DISPATCHERS = "spx,1"   # Start 1 dispatcher that uses SPX.
MTS_MAX_DISPATCHERS = 10    # Never start more than 10 dispatcher processes.
MTS_LISTENER_ADDRESS = "(address=(protocol=tcp)(address=dbserver)(port=1521))"
MTS_LISTENER_ADDRESS = "(address=(protocol=spx)(service=novellserver))"
```

In addition to configuring the dispatchers and shared server processes, you can also control MTS behavior on the client. Because certain jobs cannot be run using a shared server process (such as direct load exports and SQL*Loader executions) and certain jobs perform much better using dedicated servers (such as batch or processing intensive jobs), you might want to force the usage of a dedicated server. You can do this globally on the client by setting the sqlnet.ora parameter USE_DEDICATED_SERVER to TRUE. This forces all SQL*Net connections made by the client to use a dedicated server. To specify the usage of a dedicated server for an individual TNS alias, set the tnsnames.ora file SERVER parameter to DEDICATED. For example, Listing 34.2 specifies two TNS aliases that connect to the same database. However, the second alias uses a dedicated server, while the first uses a shared.

LISTING 34.2   TWO TNS ALIASES CONNECTED TO THE SAME DATABASE

```
PROD_MTS =
(DESCRIPTION =
    (ADDRESS_LIST =
        (ADDRESS =
(COMMUNITY = tcp.world)
(PROTOCOL = tcp)
(HOST = dbprod)
        (PORT = 1521)
        )
    )
    (CONNECT_DATA = (SID = PROD01)
    )
 )

PROD_BATCH =
(DESCRIPTION =
    (ADDRESS_LIST =
        (ADDRESS =
(COMMUNITY = tcp.world)
(PROTOCOL = tcp)
(HOST = dbprod)
        (PORT = 1521)
        (SERVER = DEDICATED)
        )
    )
    (CONNECT_DATA = (SID = PROD01)
    )
    )
```

PART

VII

CH

34

ADMINISTERING THE MULTITHREADED SERVER

During normal operation, the Oracle server starts and stops shared server and dispatcher processes as they are needed. This is based on the load placed on the processes. However, it might be necessary to manually administer MTS operation or monitor for performance problems. For this reason, there are several data dictionary views available that display information relating to the MTS workings. V$DISPATCHERS and V$SHARED_SERVERS display run-time information on the dispatcher and shared server processes. V$MTS displays overall statistics such as the maximum number of MTS connections, the number of servers started, the number of servers killed, and the high-water mark for servers. V$QUEUE displays information on the Request and Response queues. Finally, V$CIRCUIT shows information on user connections using dispatchers or servers. These performance views allow you to check on your MTS configuration and make adjustments or refinements where necessary.

You can adjust the number of shared server and dispatcher processes while the instance is running by using the appropriate ALTER SYSTEM commands. You can increase or decrease the number of processes with the appropriate command. Note that if you attempt to terminate servers or dispatchers, the Oracle server only terminates them as the User sessions using them are closed.

The following examples show how these commands are used:

```
ALTER SYSTEM SET MTS_DISPATCHERS = 'spx,10';
```

This starts or stops SPX dispatchers until 10 are running.

```
ALTER SYSTEM SET MTS_SERVERS = 5;
```

This starts or stops shared server processes until five are running.

USING THE ORACLE CONNECTION MANAGER

The Oracle Connection Manager is a new Net8 option that is supplied with the Enterprise version of Oracle8. It provides enhanced services for handling connection pooling, access control, and multiple protocol support. It is ideal for environments with hundreds or thousands of simultaneous connections and provides similar benefits as the Multithreaded Server.

To configure the Connection Manager, use the Network Manager or Net8 Assistant. Alternatively, the Connection Manager can be configured by directly editing the cman.ora file.

CONFIGURING CONNECTION MULTIPLEXING

Multiplexing connections (or Concentration, as it is referred to in Oracle documentation) is the process of routing multiple discrete connections over a single network connection. When connections are multiplexed, fewer resources are consumed by the server, because the multiplexed connections only use the overhead of a single connection. Concentration can be enabled in environments configured to use MTS.

In an Oracle Names environment configured with Dynamic Discovery, concentration occurs automatically when the Connection Manager is brought online. To manually enable concentration, you must place the address and port where the Connection Manager is listening in the `tnsnames.ora` file.

To configure where Connection Manager will listen, add the following line to `cman.ora`

```
cman=(address=(protocol=tcp)(host=HOSTNAME)(port=PORT)))
```

where *HOSTNAME* is the hostname of the computer Connection Manager is running on, and *PORT* is the port Connection Manager should listen to. By default, Connection Manager listens on port 1600.

To configure the client to use Connection Manager pooling, specify the Connection Manager information in the address list and set the `SOURCE_ROUTE` parameter to yes. For example,

```
(description =
   (address_list =
      (address = (protocol=tcp)(host=conman)(port=1600))
      (address = (protocol=tcp)(host=dbserver)(port=1580))
   )
   (connect_data=(sid=db1))
(source_route = yes))
```

Note

> The `SOURCE_ROUTE` parameter indicates the client must travel through multiple destinations to get to the final destination. Used with Connection Manager, it indicates the client must first go to the Connection Manager machine before traveling on to the actual database.

CONFIGURING MULTIPLE PROTOCOL SUPPORT

The Multiple Protocol Support of Connection Manager takes the place of the Multiprotocol Exchange of Oracle7. To enable Connection Manager to handle multiple protocols, install all the protocols on the machine where Connection Manager is run. Connection Manager routes the requests automatically depending on the configuration of the client's `tnsnames.ora` file. A source route address that indicates the protocols being traversed in the `tnsnames.ora` file is all that is required to enable multiprotocol communications. For example,

```
(description =
   (address_list =
      (address = (protocol = spx)(service=conmansrvc))
      (address = (protocol = tcp)(host = dbserver)(port = 1580))
   (connect_data = (sid = db))
   (source_route = yes))
```

A CASE STUDY

A company was just beginning to use the Internet, so they set up a Web server that was connected to the Internet and allowed the Web server to communicate with a database server though a firewall. This was a standalone network and was not connected to the company's internal network (see Figure 34.10). This provided some real problems to the administration staff. Because the database was not connected to the internal network, remote administration of the database became quite difficult. The backup and recovery of the database would not fit their current corporate model and additional hardware and procedures had to be developed. The security team and the database team had a meeting to determine whether it was feasible to connect the database to the internal network. The security team was quick to point out that if computer vandals compromised the internal network, they could do great damage to the company, so the risk was deemed to be very high. On further review of the diagram a number of alternatives were discussed. The alternative chosen required an additional firewall that would go between the database server that services the Internet application and the company's internal network. This firewall would only allow port 1521 access to the internal network and only SQL*Net traffic (see Figure 34.11). Digital certificates will also be used to verify that the SQL*Net traffic originated from the company's own database server and not a computer vandal. This solution allowed the DBAs to administer the database in an efficient manner while not compromising the security of the company.

Figure 34.10
Case study.

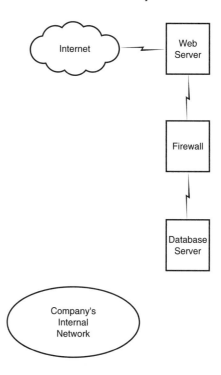

Case Study

Figure 34.11
Case study–alternative implementation.

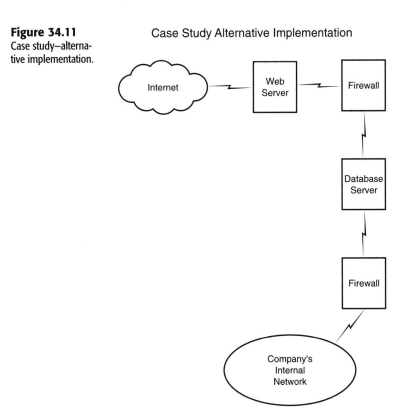

Case Study Alternative Implementation

SUMMARY

The Advanced Security Option (ASO) provides a very complete list of tools to secure your database. Security should always start with a plan and include many checks and balances to achieve the results of the plan. ASO is extremely versatile in its ability to integrate with industry standards for security. The Internet has changed everything; you now have the possibility of computer vandals striking at the very heart of the company's computing resources, and you have given them the doorway into your electronic fortress. The business demands that you allow Internet access to facilitate business, but sound judgement based on a risk analysis of any given Internet system must prevail. ASO has given us the tools, but now you must use them to build a pyramid of security that will protect the company's infrastructure.

ORACLE APPLICATION SERVER

CHAPTER 35

ORACLE APPLICATION SERVER (OAS)

In this chapter

INTRODUCING THE ORACLE APPLICATION SERVER

The Internet burst into the consciousness of most people in the 1995–1996 time frame. It was seized on by the media and computer users as something new, unlike any computing innovation that preceded it.

The Internet has also added some new standards to the computing environment. With the nearly universal addressing scheme offered by the Internet and TCP/IP, the standard mail and other protocols offered by the Internet services, and an easy, cross-platform hypertext display standard in HTML, the Internet provides a way to integrate dissimilar computers across the world.

Oracle has been a leader in providing database technology for more than 15 years, and because the Internet is a gigantic network for exchanging data, it makes sense that Oracle products should play a role in the retrieval and dissemination of data over the Internet and through Internet-based applications.

The Oracle Application Server (OAS) is currently the basis for Oracle's use of the Internet. However, it is also much more than just a way to use the Internet. The OAS is a key piece of Oracle's strategy for "Internet Computing", which is, in turn, the blueprint for the implementation of a completely distributed application system. Internet-based applications are a type of distributed application, so the OAS is ideally suited for Web-based applications as well. The rest of this chapter introduces you, at a high level, to the Oracle Application Server. The rest of this book helps you create systems that are implemented over the Internet or an intranet and use the services of the Oracle Application Server and the Oracle8 RDBMS.

UNDERSTANDING INTERNET COMPUTING

Internet Computing is a framework that can be used to create open, distributed application systems. To understand Internet Computing, it helps to take a look at the evolution of the computing infrastructure over the past few years.

Ten years ago, virtually all applications were deployed on a single monolithic machine with users connected to the machine by dumb terminals. Different software components running on the machine were used to implement systems, such as database management systems and application programs, but all the components communicated with each other through shared resources, such as disk and memory, or at worst over an internal communication bus.

As personal computers began to enter the computing landscape, the client/server model began to be used for application systems. Client/server computing featured PCs as clients, with enough power to support the graphical user interfaces demanded by users, as well as the execution of application logic, connected over a local area network (LAN) to a database server. It took several years for developers and the tools that they used to appropriately support the client/server architecture and reduce the impact of the bottlenecks imposed by limited network bandwidth.

The client/server computing architecture was widely favored by users, but the distribution of computing resources over a wide number of client machines created its own set of problems for application developers and system administrators. Whenever applications changed, new client components had to be distributed to all client machines, and the growing complexity of application logic began to strain the limits of the computing power on PC clients. To address both of these issues, a three-tier computing model evolved, where application logic was run on a server machine that acted as an intermediary between the client and the database server.

Internet Computing extends the three-tier model into a multitier model. It provides a standard interface that can be used by a variety of components, which are self-contained units of functionality that can act as client components, application logic components, or data components. Internet Computing also includes a standardized communication protocol so that the different cartridges in an application can communicate with each other. The basic structure of Internet Computing as it is implemented by Oracle Application Server is illustrated in Figure 35.1. Internet Computing is also ideally suited for applications that need to be accessed for many diverse locations. A Web client, in the form of a browser, can use the framework to interact with other application components. The same components can be used as cartridges within a more traditional client/server architecture, or even with dumb terminals connected to a monolithic computer. By clearly defining the ways that client, logic, and data cartridges interact, Internet Computing allows virtually unlimited flexibility in creating and deploying application systems.

Figure 35.1
The Internet Computing architecture provides a framework for distributed computing.

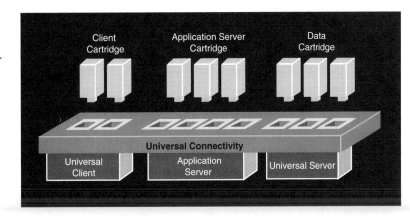

UNDERSTANDING THE ORACLE APPLICATION SERVER

The Oracle Application Server plays a key role in Internet Computing and acts as the focal point for the management of component services and the communication between components, or cartridges.

An *application* is a collection of business logic, which can be composed of multiple cartridge servers. A *cartridge server* is a code module that interacts with the OAS through a standard

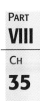

interface. The basic function of the OAS is to manage the interaction of cartridges, or more accurately, cartridge instances. To accomplish this, the OAS manages the creation of application logic cartridges, the communication between client cartridges and application logic cartridges, and the inter-cartridge communication between application logic cartridges. The OAS also provides the basic services to components that are necessary to implement robust applications through a CORBA 2.0-compliant Object Request Broker (ORB).

The Oracle Application Server is composed of the following three layers:

- The HTTP Listener layer, which handles communication between clients and the Application Server layer through standard Internet protocols.

- The Oracle Application Server layer, which manages the creation of cartridge server processes and cartridge instances; load balancing between multiple instances of individual cartridges; and services to cartridges, such as transaction services, inter-cartridge communication services, persistent storage services, and authentication services.

- The Application layer, where specific cartridges are used to implement specific application functionality.

This layered architecture gives OAS two basic advantages. First of all, it allows each component to be designed to best address the needs of its particular function, instead of trying to handle all the tasks of a server. For instance, the HTTP Listener must be ready to receive all HTTP messages, so it should be a small application to be as responsive as possible. The ORB, which ties all three layers together, on the other hand, will potentially have to handle many different types of requests, so it will have to be capable of managing multiple tasks, requiring a more robust application.

The OAS can support multiple instances of individual cartridges, which makes applications that use these cartridges highly scalable. This scalability is enhanced by the capability to add additional resources where you need them, without affecting the rest of the components. For instance, you can have multiple listeners to handle high volume traffic or spawn additional cartridge servers and instances if a particular cartridge's functionality is heavily taxed.

The second advantage comes from having a well-defined application program interface (API) between the different components. This interface makes OAS an open system to which you can add your own custom components to create your system. For instance, you can substitute some other HTTP listener for the Oracle Web Listener and still use the other components of the Oracle Application Server. Even more importantly, the open architecture of OAS allows you to write your own cartridges to support any development environment in most common programming languages, and to deliver any type of functionality you need in your Web applications.

Figure 35.2
The architecture of
the Oracle Application
Server handles the
assignment of tasks to
Web request engines.

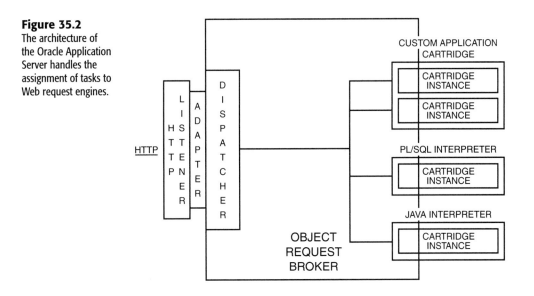

THE HTTP LISTENER LAYER

The HTTP Listener, as the name implies, listens for HTTP requests coming to the IP address of the server machine. When the HTTP Listener gets a request, it attempts to translate the URL into a physical entity, such as an HTML file or a CGI script. If it cannot, it passes the request on to the Dispatcher, which, along with the ORB, ties the listener in to the Oracle Application Server layer. Part of the Dispatcher is the Virtual Path Manager. If the Virtual Path Manager receives the request, it likely corresponds to an application cartridge. The application logic is executed and the results are returned to the listener for retrieval by the browser.

THE ORACLE APPLICATION SERVER LAYER

The Oracle Application Server layer is the glue that holds everything together, as well as the location of basic services such as authentication, logging, failure recovery, transaction control, and load balancing. With the ORB, it also allows for a distributed system, where applications, listeners, and data can be located on different physical machines, but still configured and managed from a centralized interface.

THE APPLICATION LAYER

What's under the hood of the Oracle Application Server layer? When a request comes in for a particular application, the Dispatcher passes the request to the appropriate cartridge server. Each cartridge server is a multithreaded process, and each cartridge instance has its own thread. This saves the overhead of starting a process for each request. You can have more than one cartridge server for an application (as long as they are of the same type) and specify the maximum and minimum number of threads for the service, so the Dispatcher performs dynamic load balancing between multiple services.

PART

VIII

CH

35

Each cartridge server has its own execution engine and uses a shared library. The Object Request Broker communicates with components through three basic API calls to initialize a service, shut down the service, and pass requests to the service.

CARTRIDGES

Oracle Web Application Server comes with the following six predefined cartridges:

- The PL/SQL cartridge, which can call stored PL/SQL packages and procedures
- The JWeb cartridge, which provides a runtime Java execution environment on the server
- The Perl cartridge, which can call Perl scripts, eliminating the need to start the Perl interpreter for every request
- The ODBC cartridge, which provides access to a variety of data sources using the Open Database Connection interface
- The C Web cartridge (formerly the WRB API, this is called simply the C Cartridge on Windows NT), which allows you to write your own server side applications in C
- The LiveHTML cartridge to work with server-side includes

The PL/SQL, JWeb, and C Web cartridges include additional functions that extend the capability of the cartridge to perform extended processing, such as writing HTML back to a browser.

Oracle has also delivered Oracle Developer Server, a Web cartridge interface for applications developed with Oracle Developer. The Developer Server allows any application created with Oracle Developer or Oracle Designer to be recompiled and deployed over the Web with a Java applet acting as a user interface on the client and the application itself running on a Web server.

The OAS uses an open API, so you can design your own cartridges in C. You can create *system cartridges*, which execute a predefined function, or *programmable cartridges*, which can be used to interpret runtime applications. Third-party developers can also develop cartridges for specific purposes. Any new cartridge can be easily integrated into the open OAS environment by registering the cartridge in the OAS configuration file.

JCORBA AND ENTERPRISE JAVA BEANS

In Oracle Application Server 4.0, you have the ability to write not only cartridge-based applications, but also JCORBA objects—CORBA objects written in Java. JCORBA objects can be accessed via IIOP in the same way that any CORBA object can be accessed and by any appropriate client, such as a browser or even a cartridge-based application.

There is also support for Enterprise Java Beans (EJBs), which allows you to more easily reuse your own Java code or to purchase functionality from other vendors to cut your development time.

PROVIDING BASIC SERVICES WITH THE ORACLE APPLICATION SERVER

The OAS provides some basic services that can be used by any cartridge. There are four basic categories of services provided by the Oracle Application Server:

- Transaction services
- Inter-Cartridge Exchange services
- Persistent storage services
- Authentication services

In addition, the Oracle Web Application Server provides a log server to log requests to the Oracle Application Server and a log analyzer, which helps to understand the server logs.

TRANSACTION SERVICES

The Oracle Application Server provides *transaction* services to all cartridges. A transaction is a clearly defined unit of work. If a transaction is committed, all changes implemented by the transaction are applied to the relevant data stores. If a transaction is rolled back, which means that the data is returned to the state it was in prior to the start of the transaction, the data stores are left in the same state they were in prior to the start of the transaction. Since the Web is an inherently stateless medium, each page is normally a transaction in and of itself. By providing transaction services, the Oracle Application Server allows you to overcome the problems faced by the stateless nature of HTTP communication by enabling the transactions to span multiple requests.

INTER-CARTRIDGE EXCHANGE SERVICES

The Oracle Application Server provides Inter-Cartridge Exchange services, which allows different cartridges to communicate with each other.

In Release 3.0 of the Oracle Web Application Server, the internal communications between cartridges were handled by an internal communication protocol that was compliant with the *Common Object Request Broker Architecture*, also known as *CORBA*. The CORBA standard is an open protocol that is supported by a wide variety of hardware and software vendors.

Release 4.0 of Oracle Application Server extends the use of the CORBA standard for Inter-Cartridge Exchange so the independently developed CORBA components are capable of transparently interacting with cartridges through the use of the OAS.

PERSISTENT STORAGE SERVICES

The OAS includes a set of application programming interfaces that allow developers to read and write data objects, create data objects, and delete data objects and their data. These APIs can be used to write data to either the Oracle8 database or to native files on the server platform.

PART

VIII

CH

35

These APIs are built on a schema that includes attributes such as content type, author, and creation date. The persistent storage services allow all cartridges to operate through a common interface whenever data has to be stored on disk or for future reference within an application.

AUTHENTICATION SERVICES

Release 4.0 of the Oracle Application Server gives developers a variety of extensible authentication schemes that can be used in their applications including basic, digest, domain, and database authentication. In addition, Release 4.0 allows you to authenticate through an LDAP server.

The authentication services give developers the flexibility to implement security in the way that is best suited to the needs of their particular application.

ORACLE APPLICATION SERVER COMPONENTS

In this chapter

EXAMINING THE HTTP LISTENER LAYER

The Oracle Application Server (OAS) uses a Web Listener to wait for incoming requests for services. Typically, such a listener would set up an address that serves as an electronic signpost to tell all wayfaring packets of data "I'm open for business." Of course, the listener must tell Oracle Application Server its address before opening for business. When OAS has this address registered, it can build a road from the listener. This way, when a client issues a request, the listener can route the message on to the application server, which then can execute the appropriate service (see Figure 36.1).

Figure 36.1
The Oracle Application Server is made up of three conceptual layers that work together.

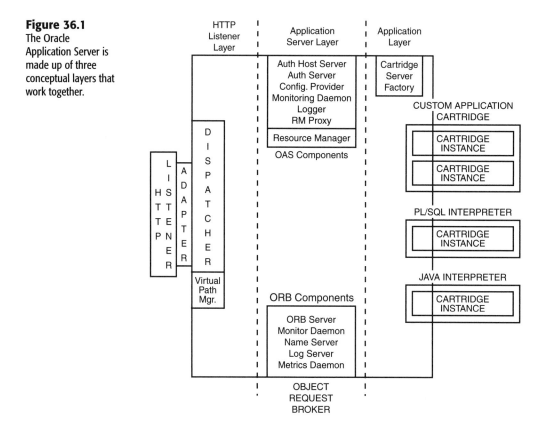

GETTING INTO MORE DETAILS

The HTTP Listener processes one or many simultaneous requests, in which case the remote server or browser is acting as a client. For requests to be issued from a remote server, you must make sure that the Object Request Broker (ORB) has been instantiated first. Otherwise, the remote listener won't exist and client requests can't be issued remotely.

Fortunately, the ORB will always be running as long as the listener is up because the listener can't be started unless the ORB is running, and the ORB can't be shut down if the listener is running. This is because the listener must register itself with the Dispatcher. The Dispatcher, a component of the Oracle Application Server layer, connects the listener to the application server by hooking into the ORB.

An important part of the Dispatcher is the Virtual Path Manager. When the listener receives a request, it is in the form of a "virtual path," the latter part of a URL. The VPM is responsible for translating that virtual path into a physical entity. If that physical entity is a cartridge-based application, the request is routed through the ORB, which coordinates its execution and returns the results to the listener. In the case of static files and CGI scripts, the request is routed back to the listener, which creates the response itself and sends it back to the client.

Listeners are created and managed through the Node Manager, a Web-based interface that allows you to manage all pieces of the Oracle Application Server. The node manager is started automatically by the installer, but you can start it later using the command line utility:

```
owsctl start -nodemgr
```

For more information on the Node Manager, see Chapter 37, "Installing and Configuring the OAS."

UNDERSTANDING THE HTTP LISTENER'S ARCHITECTURE

Although multithreaded processing is a must in today's mission-critical client/server environment, some IS technicians have overused and abused this technology. What they neglect to understand—and it's easy to do—is that each process needs memory and resources allocated to it. Without the appropriate memory and resource allocation, system performance can slow as more threads are opened, especially where processes handle requests synchronously. Therefore, you need to put a lot of thought into implementing multithreaded architectures.

Oracle designed the HTTP Listener with this in mind. The listener's only tasks are to accept incoming client requests, route them to the Application Server layer, and return the results to the browser. Therefore, only two processes are needed—one to listen, and one to talk, so to speak. The HTTP Listener also handles requests asynchronously, meaning that when it receives a request, the listener doesn't need the client for further processing.

MEMORY MAPPING OF FILES

If a file won't be permanently cached in memory, the HTTP Listener uses a dynamic memory address mapping scheme in which more than one client connection can access common files. As a result, file access is sped up as duplicate disk reads are avoided. And because a file is mapped in memory, the operating system can retrieve the next memory segment of such a file while another file is being sent to a client. This performance-enhancing strategy works well even where there is only one connection.

DIRECTORY MAPPING

An important concept in the object-oriented circles is the idea of *encapsulation* or *data hiding*. Here, you don't care what an object does, you just want it to perform the way you expect. Likewise, the HTTP Listener, in a sense, encapsulates how it stores URL path-names. That is, you might see the same URL every time you go to a Web site, but it might correspond to different physical files over time. OAS administrators are responsible for correctly mapping the URL directories that users see to the actual physical directory in the machine's file system.

RESOLVING THE DOMAIN NAME

Domain name server resolution ensures that the client user's request is sent to the proper network address/URL. When this is happening, the IP address of the client machine is recorded by the HTTP server through which the request for an HTML form is being routed.

The Domain Name Service (DNS) serves as a reference for the conversion of a client's IP address into an ASCII hostname. More than one machine may be involved in this resolution process, meaning that you might consider listening to your favorite CD while waiting for the address to be resolved.

The HTTP Listener offers you, as the Oracle Application Server administrator, four methods for handling DNS tasks:

- Resolving IP addresses on connection
- Resolving IP addresses when needed
- Resolving IP addresses when needed by a CGI script or application cartridge
- Never resolving IP addresses

With DNS resolution, the results of this process are cached in memory as many connections may occur within the same time window, possibly from the same client. For performance reasons, the default configuration for DNS resolution is to never resolve IP addresses.

HTTP LISTENER CONFIGURATION PARAMETERS

The configuration parameters for the HTTP Listener are stored in a configuration file, which is read when the listener is initially started. You can start the listener using the command-line utility. The utility has changed in each version of Oracle Application Server, and version 4.0 is no exception. To start the listener itself from the command line, use the following:

```
owsctl start -l myListener
```

The Node Manager, which can be accessed by any forms-capable Web browser, eliminates the need for you to edit the listener configuration file manually, in most cases, and provides explanatory help text on the individual parameters. This section documents the parameters in the configuration file for completeness in the event an administrator wants to edit the file manually.

The Web Listener configuration file is divided into sections that start with a section name in brackets for example, [NetInfo]. You set individual configuration parameters by name = value pairs, with the configuration parameter to the left (the lvalue) of the equal sign and the value to the right (the rvalue). For example, look at the following section of a typical configuration file:

```
;
[NetInfo]
MaxConnectCount     = 338
;    The maximum number of connections.  338 is an OS limitation
;      based on the number of filehandlesa single process can handle.
DNSResolution = NEVER
ServerPID = /u01/app/oracle/admin/ows/website40/httpd_csac07/myweb/myweb.pid
;
[LogParams]
TimeStyle = GMT
AdminFile = /u01/app/oracle/admin/ows/website40/httpd_csac07/myweb/myweb.err
;
[Server]
InitialFile        = wwwIndex.html
;    The "default" file accessed when no file is specified,
;    ie "http://www.csac.com/" would return
;    http://www.csac.com/wwwIndex.html.  Note that while
;    wwwIndex.html is the default for OAS,
;    most sites use "index.html" as their default.
DefaultMIMEType    = application/octet-stream
DefaultCharset     = iso-8859-1
PreferredLanguage  = en
ImageMap           = map
UseDirIndexing     = FALSE
CGITimeout         = 900
;
[SecureInfo]
UserID        = root
GroupID       = dba
;    Only applicable on UNIX systems.  Note that if you are
;    listening on a port under 1024, the process must run as root.
;
[DirMaps]
;Physical Directory               Flag          Virtual Path shown in URL
;    The flag specifies whether content is Non-CGI, CGI, or Win-CGI,
;    and whether thedesignation is Recursive or Non-Recursive.
/u01/app/oracle/product/8.0.4/ows/4.0/doc/        NR          /
/u01/app/oracle/product/8.0.4/ows/4.0/admin/doc/ NR          /ows-adoc/
/u01/app/oracle/product/8.0.4/ows/4.0/admin/img/ NR          /ows-aimg/
/u01/app/oracle/product/8.0.4/ows/4.0/bin/        CN          /ows-bin/
/u01/app/oracle/product/8.0.4/ows/4.0/doc/        NR          /ows-doc/
/u01/app/oracle/product/8.0.4/ows/4.0/admin/img/ NR          /ows-img/
/u01/app/oracle/product/8.0.4/ows/4.0/classes/    NR          /ows-vbclasses/
/u08/htdocs/                                      NR          /soaig/
;
```

continues

```
continued    [LangExt]
             en                      iso-8859-1              eng
             en                      unicode-1-1            engU                    uc
             fr-CA                   iso-8859-1              frc
             fr-FR                   iso-8859-1              fr
             jp-JP                   iso-2022-jp             jp
             jp-JP                   unicode-1-1-utf-8       jpU
             ;       Used by NLS functions.
             ;
             [MIMETypes]
             text/html           htm                     html
             image/jpeg          jpg                     jpeg
             image/gif           gif
             appl/text           doc
             text/plain          txt                     ksh                     lst
             application/pdf     pdf
             application/postscript ps
             model/vrml          wrl                     vrml
             video/mpeg          mpeg                    mpg                     mpe
             ;
             [Encodings]
             compress            Z
             gzip                gz
             ;
             [DynApps]
             /u01/app/oracle/product/8.0.4/ows/4.0/lib/ndwfss.so oracle_adp_init
             ;       Directs the listener to the Adapter.
             ;
             [MultiPort]
             ; IP address     TCP Port       Encryption        Host Name     Base Directory
                    LogInfo Directory      Client Autentication
             ANY                 80                     NORM                   csac07.csac.com    /
             ➥/u01/app/oracle/admin/ows/website40/httpd_csac07/myListener/ NONE
             ANY                 443                    SSL                    csac07.csac.com    /
             ➥/u01/app/oracle/admin/ows/website40/httpd_csac07/myListener/ NONE
             ;       A single listener can listen on multiple ports and multiple IP addresses,
             ;       and can direct logging for each IP/port combination to a different
             ➥directory.
```

THIRD-PARTY HTTP LISTENERS

Because the HTTP listener speaks to the ORB with the Dispatcher as an intermediary, you are not limited to the Oracle HTTP Listener. You can use any HTTP listener as long as you have the appropriate adapter (see Figure 36.2).

To use a third-party HTTP listener with the Oracle Application Server, you need to "register" it. From the OAS Welcome page, choose "OAS Utilities" and expand the main menu on the left. From there, expand the "External Listener" node, and the "Register" node to reveal the available adapters. Click the appropriate adapter and follow the menus to register your external listener.

Figure 36.2
Register an external
listener.

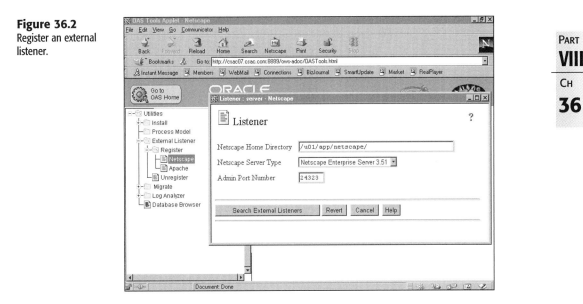

Version 4.0.7 ships with adapters for Netscape and Apache (on UNIX) and Microsoft
Internet Information Server (on Windows NT).

EXAMINING THE APPLICATION SERVER LAYER

After the HTTP listener successfully receives incoming messages from clients, it passes the
baton to the Application Server layer. Of all the Oracle Application Server components, the
Application Server layer (formerly known as the Web Request Broker or WRB) is the most
pivotal because the listeners and application cartridges broker their messages through it.

WRB incorporates a multithreaded and multiprocess architecture, resulting in increases in
machine productivity as more requests can be processed almost simultaneously. The WRB
also supports asynchronous independent processing, so client and server resources aren't
forced unnecessarily to wait for result sets or other messages to be returned.

When the dispatcher notifies the ORB that it needs a new execution instance of a cartridge,
the Resource Manager component (RM), checks for an available cartridge instance. If none
are available, it instructs an existing cartridge server to create one. If all existing cartridge
servers are at their maximum number of instances, the RM instructs the cartridge factory to
create a new cartridge server. If the number of cartridge servers is at its maximum, the
request is queued.

> **Note**
>
> Interobject message communications follow the Common Object Request Broker Architecture (CORBA). In a nutshell, systems that support the CORBA model have objects that can carry out the role of client, agent, or server, each of which help pass messages from an end user's machine to some local or remote server.

THE WRB DISPATCHER

You've just digested quite a bit of information; now it's time to delve a little deeper. After Web Listener sends a message to WRB, WRB's dispatcher determines the type of object the client requested. In detail, this dispatcher looks into the WRB configuration file, which helps the dispatcher determine the relationship between virtual directories and WRB services. If the dispatcher finds no relationship to suit the client's request, it returns the request back to Web Listener, which continues the message life cycle.

When the Dispatcher receives a request for a cartridge-based application, the request needs to be routed to a cartridge instance, which runs as a thread in a cartridge server. If the Dispatcher knows of an available cartridge instance, it uses the ORB to send the request on to that instance. If not, it contacts the Application Server layer to request a new instance. The reference is returned to the Dispatcher, which stores it in its object cache for current and future use.

Quite naturally, with this architecture you can distribute processing loads between service object instances dynamically. This helps minimize network contention and optimize Oracle Application Server performance. As administrator of Oracle Application Server, you have to keep an eye out for potential resource drains and performance degradation when using multiple processes (or service instances, for those of you on NT). You can specify minimum and maximum numbers of cartridge servers (processes) for each application. You can also specify the minimum and maximum numbers of cartridge instances (threads) within those servers.

> **Note**
>
> Not all applications can be multithreaded. For instance, the PL/SQL cartridge is considered to be "stateful" instead of "stateless," so each cartridge server can have a maximum of one cartridge instance.

In a nutshell, each object has an interface that provides essential methods (functions) to deliver a "product" to the client. In object-oriented terms, this acceptance of service responsibility and the resulting delivery of the service is called a *binding contract*. Further, as some client/server experts have noted, "the location of the object should be transparent to the client and object implementation."

In this situation, OAS is defined along the ORB model, and in fact uses CORBA for interobject communication. As with CORBA, the main idea behind ORB is that an object, acting as an agent on the behalf of some client object, handles the requesting of remote services. The ORB, then, provides clients the capability to invoke object methods on service objects transparently across a network or on your machine. This means that you don't need to concern yourself with the physical location or operating system platform of the objects providing the services you need. This lends itself to *data hiding* or *encapsulation*, as well as distributed installations, where functionality can be spread over multiple machines or nodes.

IPC SUPPORT

The transport-independent ORB protocol handles all interprocess communications (IPC). Oracle Application Server supports standard IPC mechanisms. IPC is the heart and soul of client/server architecture for UNIX platforms. However, IPC isn't the easiest client/server tool suite to use, especially when it comes to developing multitiered, multiprocess applications. My hunch is that Oracle provided this support because of its heavy background in UNIX-based platforms.

Oracle Application Server 4.0 supports other mechanisms in addition to IPC, such as OMX, Oracle's CORBA-compliant ORB. The idea here is that services may be implemented together as industry-standard distributed objects, thus enabling distribution and scalability across multiple nodes.

APPLICATION SERVER LAYER COMPONENTS

The components of this layer can be separated into two categories: ORB components and Application Server components.

ORB COMPONENTS

We refer to the ORB as a single object, but it actually consists of five processes that work in concert. (Process names end in "40" on Windows NT.)

- Monitoring Daemon (mnmon40)—Brings up and monitors the other ORB components
- Log Server (mnlogsrv)—Logs status and error messages
- Metrics Daemon (mnorbmet)—Used by the WRB Monitor process to collect statistics about applications
- Name Server (mncnmsrv)—The ORB Server, all Application Server components, all listeners (except the Node Manager), and all cartridges register with the Name Server.
- ORB Server (mnorbsrv)—Handles requests from and to distributed objects

APPLICATION SERVER COMPONENTS

The ORB merely facilitates communication. Requests are actually processed by the Application Server components. These processes run in one of two modes: collapsed and non-collapsed. In non-collapsed mode, all the following processes are visible and controllable. In collapsed mode, several of the processes below show up as the process "oassrv".

- Authentication Server (wrbasrv) and Authentication Host Server (wrbahsrv)—Using one broker and server authentication providers, these processes handle authentication for listeners and cartridges.

- Configuration Provider (wrbcfg)—All configuration information is contained in a single file, the wrb.app file, even for remote nodes. The configuration provider reads this file and supplies the appropriate information.

- Logger (wrblog)—Logs application server messages, errors, warnings, etc. to a central location. This may be a file or a database.

- Monitoring Daemon (wrbmon)—Monitors application server processes and objects.

- Resource Manager (wrbroker)—Exists only on the primary node, this process takes care of load management, keeping track of the number of cartridge servers and instances.

- RM Proxy (wrbrmpxy)—Maintains object references to JCORBA and EJB objects.

Examining the Application Layer

You have a myriad of options for building applications in the Oracle Application Server. You can build PL/SQL procedures, migrate your Perl CGI scripts, build Java servlets or JCORBA objects, and even use Enterprise Java Beans.

Using the PL/SQL Cartridge

With the PL/SQL Cartridge, you can develop your Web applications by using Oracle stored procedures. Oracle assures its customers that interacting with database objects is much easier in PL/SQL than any other language. Quite obviously, because Oracle Application Server is more mature with Oracle databases, your safest bet for portability and scalability issues is to incorporate PL/SQL.

In terms of speed, the PL/SQL Cartridge has made serious improvements since the first versions of Oracle Application Server. This improvement comes from the fact that each PL/SQL Agent instance stays connected to your Oracle database between incoming requests rather than disconnecting after it returns its results. The idea here is that there's no need to establish a new database per stored procedure execution. You should use the latest version of PL/SQL after doing isolation testing to make sure that you experience no side effects.

The PL/SQL Agent executes two tasks that allow your stored procedures to create dynamic HTML pages:

- It invokes a parameterized procedure and passes in the essential parameters shipped with the HTTP request. The Web Application Server must perform a translation of an HTTP request to PL/SQL.

- It provides a method for your stored procedure to send data as returns to the caller. The low-level details here are seamless to you.

For non-hardcore programmers, this is more information than you really need. The main advantage of the PL/SQL cartridge is that it hides the complexity of interacting with the database. Basically, when it receives a request, the cartridge server logs in to the database, executes a stored procedure, and returns any results to the browser.

In addition to performing these tasks, the OAS includes the PL/SQL Toolkit—a collection of packaged procedures, functions, and utilities to enhance productivity and ensure valid HTML output. The Toolkit includes PL/SQL versions of all HTML 3.2 tags (in the htp package), as well as utilities to help you perform more advanced tasks.

The important thing to remember is that calling a stored procedure from the browser is identical to calling it from a tool such as SQL*Plus. Any inserts, updates, deletes, etc. will be performed in the same way, with one important distinction: unless you are using transactions, as soon as your request is completed, the cartridge instance will log out of the database, and changes will be committed.

LISTING 36.1 SAMPLE PL/SQL PROCEDURE

```
procedure demo_htp (the_user varchar2) is
    user_host          varchar2(150);
    cnt                integer;
begin
    htp.htmlOpen;
    htp.headOpen;
        htp.title(the_user||'s Page');
        — Takes the value of "the_user" from the input parameters
    htp.headClose;
    htp.bodyOpen;

    user_host := owa_util.get_cgi_env('REMOTE_HOST');
    — Gets the value of the "remote host" CGI environment variable.  You
    — can use any environment variable

    insert into user_history (web_user, web_host, web_time)
        values (the_user, user_host, sysdate);
        — This will be inserted as if the procedure was executed from SQL*Plus

    htp.p('Good morning, '||the_user||'!<P>');
    — htp.p() can be used to out put any arbitrary text to the browser,

    — including HTML tags

    select count(*) into cnt from user_history;
    htp.p('There have been '||cnt||' visits to this page so far.');
    — You can easily integrate information from the database into your pages.
    — This could just as easily have been names, times, anything stored in the

    — database.

    htp.bodyClose;
    htp.htmlClose;

end;
```

To execute this procedure from the browser, you would set your browser to:

```
http://www.yourhost.com/myApp/plsql/demo_htp?the_user=Nick
```

This assumes that you have assigned the virtual path "myApp/plsql" to point to the PL/SQL cartridge.

To help get a handle on how this works, try experimenting by logging in to SQL*Plus and checking the contents of the table before and after calling this page, then inserting a row into the table manually, committing the changes, and calling the page again.

You cannot use positional notation for parameters; your names must match exactly, and every parameter comes in as a varchar2, because it's part of the URL text. On the bright side, if you overload the procedures in your packages, they can all have the same parameter types, as long as the names are distinct.

Tip #104	You can check the output of your procedures from SQL*Plus using:
| | ```
set serveroutput on
exec myprocedure;
exec owa_util.showpage
``` |

Oracle has included dozens of utilities to make your life easier. Check the documentation for the Toolkit packages before you reinvent the wheel!

Note	Oracle has implemented Java stored procedures to be callable as though they were PL/SQL stored procedures, so they should be callable from the browser in the same way.

For you hard-core programmers out there, Oracle has continued support for C language programs, incorporating it into an actual cartridge, called the C Web cartridge on UNIX and simply the C cartridge on Windows NT.

SON OF THE WRB SDK: THE C WEB CARTRIDGE

In version 2.0, Oracle introduced the Web Request Broker Software Developer's Kit, or WRB SDK. This open API encouraged customers and solution providers to extend the server in ways that Oracle had not necessarily envisioned. The applications they built were called "cartridges" but are now simply "applications." These applications are written in C, and can do anything a C program can do, such as integrating with a payment system. They run as a shared library and are dynamically loaded and cached at runtime.

If you have written C cartridges for previous versions, you will need to upgrade them using the OAS utilities in the Node Manager, but they will still work. Older API's are still being supported, but will be removed in a future release.

WRB APPLICATION PROGRAM INTERFACE

You can use the WRB API to register three essential callback functions with the ORB:

- Initialization
- Request handler
- Shutdown
```

These methods taken together follow the typical class structure in which you can initialize objects, send and receive messages when the object is initialized, and destroy objects when you're finished using them. This structure lends itself quite easily to the object-oriented approach to system development.

The WRB API can be quite extensive in terms of auxiliary methods or functions it contains. Some of these methods are discussed later in this chapter. These methods may be invoked directly from the three basic callbacks mentioned earlier.

Oracle's open approach to product development means that customers and solution providers/partners are jointly developing the WRB API. This cooperative effort means that the API should provide maximum openness and interoperability between Oracle Application Server and third-party applications.

UNDERSTANDING CARTRIDGES AND ICX

ICX, which stands for *Inter-Cartridge Exchange*, is a mechanism supported by the Oracle Application Server that facilitates communications between cartridges. It permits communications across different machines, especially when using a Java-based cartridge.

WRB CARTRIDGES

Each cartridge follows an architecture/model type. Cartridge developers should be aware of only three such design models:

- Request-response
- Session
- Transaction

THE REQUEST-RESPONSE MODEL   Almost as if in a knee-jerk reaction, WRB cartridge instances process individual client requests and issue a request per expected response. After the expected response is dispatched, the cartridge instance has "amnesia," where no data is associated with the client and the request is not persistently stored anywhere. If you're familiar with the lack of state information tracked by regular HTTP requests, this should be quite familiar. So, your cartridge's Exec method would receive the request as an argument and return relevant information without keeping track of any state data.

THE SESSION MODEL   A session is established between a client and a particular cartridge instance in execution. A cartridge, then, uses the sessions mechanism to maintain a persistent association between the two. You determine how long this association persists by setting the timeout period. The cartridge's Exec method would then state information related to the client that initiated the request. The Exec method stores this state information in the context structure of the application that owns the instance of the cartridge, that is, the application responsible for creating an instance of the cartridge (instantiating the cartridge instance, the runtime object copy of the designtime cartridge).

> **Note**
>
> For more information on the differences between a cartridge's designtime architecture and its runtime architecture, refer to works on object-oriented methodologies by Grady Booch, Jim Rumbaugh, or Ivar Jacobson.

The sessions mechanism makes sure that there's an association between a client and an executed cartridge instance. This association provides the cartridge a specialized focus between itself and a client. This instance specialization is where the differences between runtime and designtime architectures make sense. At any given time, many instances of a cartridge can be in execution, each containing state and data specific to a particular client. That is, if you have a cartridge that managed many checking accounts for a particular bank branch, one instance of a cartridge might have a balance of $5,000, another might have $230.98, another might have $1,209, and so on, all in execution as tellers reconcile their batches at the end of the day. Data integrity isn't compromised because each cartridge instance is concerned only with the information related to one account. You would then save the state information related to each account in the application context structure so that such information survives the current user session.

> **Note**
>
> In version 3.0, each cartridge instance ran in its own process space. In version 4.0, instances can share process space (in the cartridge server process).

THE TRANSACTION MODEL   If, in your analysis and design, you realize that your cartridge will need to concentrate on handling database transactions, the transaction model is for you. The Exec method would assume the role of a transaction processor. Several states are normally involved in the implementation of this model:

- Cartridge is receiving a request
- Cartridge is beginning a transaction
- Cartridge is performing incremental updates within the transaction context
- If everything is okay, cartridge is committing a transaction
- If everything isn't okay, cartridge is issuing a rollback on the transaction (state of transaction: ended)
- Cartridge is sending a response to the client (acknowledgement or error)

Transactions don't necessarily have to be made in one call (invocation of Exec method). Some transactions can span several invocations of the cartridge's Exec method. The caveat here is that the cartridge's Exec method must determine which of the preceding states applies to the current scenario. This model allows you to support requests independent of any transaction if your design calls for this feature. (For more information, refer to your WRB Transaction Service API Reference on designing cartridges.)

If you were savvy enough to purchase the Enterprise version of Oracle Application Server, you can get additional API help from the Transaction Service library. (These services aren't included in the Basic version of Oracle Application Server.) With this library, you or your development staff can perform any number of database transactions from your cartridge. Oracle based the WRB Transaction Service on the TX interface as it was defined by the X/Open Company.

> **Note**
>
> If you want more information on the background of this helpful feature, refer to X/Open's *Distributed Transaction Processing: The TX (Transaction Demarcation) Specification.*

With advanced transaction services, your cartridge can perform database transactions that span several HTTP requests. The actual access to the database is established through database-access APIs such as OCI or ProC, in addition with the transaction service. Transaction functions such as `commit` and `rollback` aren't done through these services. To make the transaction services accessible to your cartridge, you'll have to enable the `TRANSACTION` service for it. Refer to your Transaction Service documentation for more details.

Looking at ICX

The WRB Intercartridge Exchange Service API allows one WRB cartridge to issue HTTP requests to another WRB cartridge.

Using ICX helps system architects design cartridges that provide specialized behavior for an application or enterprise domain. ICX permits cartridges to be located on different machines, thus improving the performance of Oracle Application Server and providing valuable load-balancing for the network. This also means increased storage space (all the application's components don't reside on one machine) and a more scalable architecture. Coupled with good class and object models, ICX makes maintaining many interactive cartridges relatively easier.

Table 36.1 shows all the methods in the WRB Intercartridge Exchange Service API.

TABLE 36.1   THE ICX API METHODS

Method	Description
`WRB_ICXcreateRequest()`	Creates a request object
`WRB_ICXdestroyRequest()`	Destroys a request object
`WRB_ICXfetchMoreData()`	Gets more data when `WRB_ICXmakeRequest()` returns the structure `WRB_MOREDATA`
`WRB_ICXgetHeaderVal()`	Gets the value of a specific response header
`WRB_ICXgetInfo()`	Gets information about a request
`WRB_ICXgetParsedHeader()`	Gets response headers

continues

TABLE 36.1   CONTINUED

Method	Description
WRB_ICXmakeRequest()	Issues a request
WRB_ICXsetAuthInfo()	Sets the authorization headers for a specific request
WRB_ICXsetContent()	Sets the content data for a specific request
WRB_ICXsetHeader()	Sets the headers for a specific request
WRB_ICXsetMethod()	Sets the HTTP method to use in a specific request
WRB_ICXsetNoProxy()	Specifies domains for which the proxy server shouldn't be used
WRB_ICXsetProxy()	Specifies a proxy server
WRB_ICXsetWalletInfo()	Sets the ICX request to use SSL certificates for authentication

Two enumerated types are also supported in the ICX API:

- WRBInfoType
- WRBMethod

The following sections describe each method.

WRB_ICXcreateRequest()   This method allocates and returns a handle to an opaque request object, which encodes the request specified by a given URL. Listing 36.2 shows the code necessary to create a request object.

LISTING 36.2   CREATING A REQUEST OBJECT WITH WRB_ICXcreateRequest()

```
dvoid *
WRB_ICXcreateRequest(void *WRBCtx,
text *url);
Parameters
Return Values
WRB_ICXcreateRequest() returns a handle to the newly created request object.
WRB_ICXcreateRequest() returns NULL on failure.
```

Beyond creating request objects, you might want to also issue requests. The process for issuing requests is as follows:

1. Call WRB_ICXcreateRequest().
2. Call WRB_ICXmakeRequest().
3. Issue the request.
4. If something goes wrong, abort the request by calling the WRB_ICXdestroyRequest() method. This call frees resources the WRB allocated for the request.

*WRBCtx is a pointer to the opaque WRB context object that the WRB application engine passed to your cartridge method. text*url is a pointer to the URL of the request.

WRB_ICXdestroyRequest()   This method frees resources WRB allocated for a specified request. It's good programming practice to free resources allocated to objects no longer in use. Listing 36.3 shows you how to destroy the request object after you're finished with it.

LISTING 36.3   DESTROYING A REQUEST OBJECT WITH WRB_ICXdestroyRequest()

```
WAPIReturnCode
WRB_ICXdestroyRequest(void *WRBCtx,
dvoid *hRequest);
Parameters
Return Values
WRB_ICXdestroyRequest() returns a value of type WAPIReturnCode.
```

After a request is satisfied, you must invoke WRB_ICXdestroyRequest(). As long as you don't use WRB_ICXmakeRequest() to issue a request, you can use WRB_ICXdestroyRequest() to cancel a request that was created by WRB_ICXcreateRequest().

*WRBCtx is a pointer to the opaque WRB context object that the WRB application engine passed to your cartridge method. dvoid *hRequest identifies the request to be destroyed. The method WRB_ICXcreateRequest() would return this handle.

WRB_ICXfetchMoreData()   WRB_ICXfetchMoreData() retrieves the requested number of bytes when a previous call to WRB_ICXmakeRequest() returns WRB_MOREDATA. If this requested number is more than is available, this method returns the number of bytes available. Listing 36.4 shows this method in detail.

LISTING 36.4   GETTING MORE DATA WITH WRB_ICXfetchMoreData()

```
WRBAPIReturnCode
WRB_ICXfetchMoreData(dvoid *WRBCtx,
dvoid *hRequest,
dvoid **response,
ub4 *responseLength,
ub4 chunkSize);
Parameters
Return Values
WRB_ICXfetchMoreData() returns a value of type WAPIReturnCode.
```

*WRBCtx is a pointer to the opaque WRB context object that the WRB application engine passed to your cartridge method. dvoid *hRequest identifies the request to be destroyed.

dvoid **response is a pointer to the location to which the method is to store a pointer to the response data. ub4 * responseLength is a pointer to the location to which the function is to store the length (in bytes) of the response data. If ub4 chunkSize has a non-zero value, the size of the request response in bytes will be restricted to this value. In such situations, you'll need to invoke the WRB_ICXfetchMoreData() method repeatedly until you've received the entire response. If ub4 chunkSize is zero, no data is returned.

If a call to `WRB_ICXmakeRequest()` returns `WRB_MOREDATA`, you can invoke this method as many times as necessary to get `chunkSize` additional bytes of the request response. This would need to be done until all response data has been received.

WRB_ICXgetHeaderVal()   Before using this method, you must invoke the `WRB_ICXmakeRequest()` method, which issues a request. `WRB_ICXgetHeaderVal()` uses the response to this request to return the value of a specified HTTP header (see Listing 36.5).

LISTING 36.5   GETTING THE VALUE OF A SPECIFIC RESPONSE HEADER WITH `WRB_ICXgetHeaderVal()`

```
text *
WRB_ICXgetHeaderVal(void *WRBCtx,
dvoid *hRequest,
text *name);
Parameters
Return Values
WRB_ICXgetHeaderVal() returns the value of the specified header.
WRB_ICXgetHeaderVal() returns NULL on failure.
```

`WRB_ICXgetHeaderVal()` returns the pointer to the value of a specified HTTP header from the response to a request issued by `WRB_ICXmakeRequest()`. The pointer can be quite valuable for retrieving response data that response headers contain.

`*WRBCtx` is a pointer to the opaque WRB context object that the WRB application engine dispatched to your cartridge method. `dvoid *hRequest` identifies the request for which the WRB extracts header value from the response. `text * name` is a pointer to the name of the header that you want.

WRB_ICXgetInfo()   This method returns a character string containing information about a specified request. You can specify the kind of information you want back. Listing 36.6 details this method.

LISTING 36.6   GETTING INFORMATION ABOUT A REQUEST WITH `WRB_ICXgetInfo()`

```
text *
WRB_ICXgetInfo(void *WRBCtx,
dvoid *hRequest,
WRBInfoType infoType);
Parameters
Return Values
WRB_ICXgetInfo() returns a pointer to the requested information as a character
string. WRB_ICXgetInfo() returns NULL on failure.
```

When an ICX request is complete, you invoke `WRB_ICXgetInfo()` to get information about the request. The event that triggers this completion state is the completion and return of `WRB_ICXmakeRequest()`. The usefulness here is that you get the realm name in cases when WRB reissues the request with the proper authentication information.

*WRBCtx is a pointer to the opaque WRB context object that the WRB application engine passed to your cartridge function. dvoid *hRequest identifies the request about which you want information. Together, infoType and WRBInfoType represent a code that identifies the type of information you want. The infoType parameter specifies the kind of information to be returned.

WRB_ICXgetInfo() accepts an argument of type WRBInfoType that specifies the kind of request information to return to the caller. Listing 36.7 shows the structure of this type.

LISTING 36.7   THE **WRBInfoType** ENUMERATED TYPE

```
typedef enum _WRBInfoType
{
STATUSCODE,
HTTPVERSION,
REASONPHRASE,
REALM
} WRBInfoType;
WRBInfoType Values
```

STATUSCODE represents the HTTP response code. HTTPVERSION represents the version of the HTTP protocol used in the response. REASONPHRASE represents the reason text string that corresponds to the HTTP response code. REALM represents the name of the authentication realm specified in the response.

WRB_ICXgetParsedHeader()   Before using this method, you must invoke WRB_ICXmakeRequest(), which issues a request. WRB_ ICXgetParsedHeader() uses the response to this request to return the value of a specified header. Listing 36.8 shows this method.

LISTING 36.8   GETTING RESPONSE HEADERS WITH **WRB_ICXgetParsedHeader()**

```
WAPIReturnCode
WRB_ICXgetParsedHeader(void *WRBCtx,
dvoid *hRequest,
WRBpBlock *hPblock);
Parameters
Return Values
WRB_ICXgetParsedHeader() returns a value of type WAPIReturnCode.
```

This method returns in the location pointed to by hPblock a parameter block containing the header values of the response to an ICX request issued by WRB_ICXmakeRequest(). The usefulness here is that you can retrieve response data that the response headers contain.

*WRBCtx is a pointer to the opaque WRB context object that the WRB application engine passed to your cartridge function. dvoid *hRequest identifies the request. WRBpBlock * hPblock is a pointer to the location to which the function is to store the parameter block containing the parsed header data.

WRB_ICXmakeRequest()   This method issues the specified request. Listing 36.9 shows this method.

LISTING 36.9   ISSUING A REQUEST WITH WRB_ICXmakeRequest()

```
WAPIReturnCode
WRB_ICXmakeRequest(void *WRBCtx,
dvoid *hRequest,
void **response,
ub4 *responseLength,
ub4 chunkSize,
ub1 sendToBrowser);
Return Values
WRB_ICXmakeRequest() returns a value of type WAPIReturnCode.
```

After you call `WRB_ICXcreateRequest()` to create a request and other ICX API functions such as `WRB_ICXsetHeader()` and `WRB_ICXsetContent()` to prepare the request, you can call `WRB_ICXmakeRequest()` to issue the request.

`*WRBCtx` is a pointer to the opaque WRB context object that the WRB application engine passed to your cartridge function. `dvoid *hRequest` identifies the request to be issued.

`void **` `response` is a pointer to the location in which the function is to store a pointer to the response data. `ub4 *` `responseLength` is a pointer to the location to which the function is to store the length in bytes of the response data.

If `chunkSize` `ub4` has a non-zero value, the size of the request response in bytes will be restricted to this value. In such situations, you'll need to invoke the `WRB_ICXfetchMoreData()` method repeatedly until you've received the entire response. If `ub4` `chunkSize` is zero, no data is returned. If `ub1` `sendToBrowser` is non-zero, WRB will send the response directly to the originating browser; in this case, the response parameter will contain `NULL` on return.

WRB_ICXsetAuthInfo()   This method sets the authentication header data to accompany the specified request (see Listing 36.10).

LISTING 36.10   SETTING THE AUTHORIZATION HEADER FOR A SPECIFIC REQUEST WITH WRB_ICXsetAuthInfo()

```
WAPIReturnCode
WRB_ICXsetAuthInfo(void *WRBCtx,
dvoid *hRequest,
text *username,
text *password,
text *realm);
Parameters
Return Values
WRB_ICXsetAuthMethod() returns a value of type WAPIReturnCode.
```

If your cartridge issues requests to another cartridge that in turn requires that your cartridge authenticate itself, you should invoke the WRB_ICXsetAuthInfo() method. Doing so sets the authentication header data per request to the other cartridge.

*WRBCtx is a pointer to the opaque WRB context object that the WRB application engine passed to your cartridge method. dvoid *hRequest identifies the request for which authentication is to be established. WRB_ICXcreateRequest() returns this handle. text * username is a pointer to a user name for request authentication. The username must be defined in the specified realm. text * password points to the password for the username. text * realm points to the name of the authentication realm that defines the username.

WRB_ICXsetContent()   WRB_ICXsetContent() sets request content for a specified request (see Listing 36.11).

LISTING 36.11   SETTING CONTENT DATA FOR A SPECIFIC REQUEST WITH WRB_ICXsetContent()

```
WAPIReturnCode
WRB_ICXsetContent(void *WRBCtx,
dvoid *hRequest,
WRBpBlock hPBlock);
Parameters
Return Values
WRB_ICXsetContent() returns a value of type WAPIReturnCode.
```

To establish content data for a particular request, perform the following steps:

1. Invoke WRB_createPBlock() to allocate a parameter block containing the content data.
2. Pass the parameter block to WRB_ICXsetContent(). You specify the request by passing the request handle returned by WRB_ICXcreateRequest().
3. Set the content data.

*WRBCtx points to the opaque WRB context object that the WRB application engine passed to your cartridge function. dvoid *hRequest identifies the request for which content is to be specified. This should be a handle returned by WRB_ICXcreateRequest(). WRBpBlock hPBlock represents the parameter block containing the request content.

WRB_ICXsetHeader()   WRB_ICXsetHeader() is responsible for setting HTTP header data for a specified request (see Listing 36.12).

LISTING 36.12   SETTING HEADERS FOR A SPECIFIC REQUEST WITH WRB_ ICXsetHeader()

```
WAPIReturnCode
WRB_ICXsetHeader(void *WRBCtx,
dvoid *hRequest,
WRBpBlock hPBlock,
boolean useOldHdr);
Parameters
Return Values
WRB_ICXsetHeader() returns a value of type WAPIReturnCode.
```

Invoking this method requires that certain calls have been made first. The sequence of calls involved are as follows:

1. Invoke WRB_createPBlock() to allocate a parameter block and contain the header data.

2. Pass the parameter block to WRB_ICXsetHeader(). You specify the request by passing the request handle that WRB_ICXcreateRequest() returned.

3. Set header data for a request.

*WRBCtx points to the opaque WRB context object that the WRB application engine passed to your cartridge function. dvoid *hRequest identifies the request for which headers are to be set. WRB_ICXcreateRequest() returns the dvoid *hRequest handle. WRBpBlock *hPBlock represents the parameter block that contains the header information. If boolean useOldHdr is set to TRUE, the ICX request incorporates header data from the original request, in addition to the data defined by the parameter block. If useOldHdr is FALSE, only header data from the parameter block is used.

WRB_ICXsetMethod() WRB_ICXsetMethod() is responsible for setting the request method, such as GET or POST, for a specified request (see Listing 36.13).

LISTING 36.13 SETTING THE HTTP METHOD TO USE IN A SPECIFIC REQUEST WITH WRB_ICXsetMethod()

```
WAPIReturnCode
WRB_ICXsetMethod(void *WRBCtx,
dvoid *hRequest,
WRBMethod method);
Parameters
Return Values
WRB_ICXsetMethod() returns a value of type WAPIReturnCode.
```

The assumption here is that you invoked the WRB_ICXcreateRequest() method to create a request. Invoke WRB_ICXsetMethod() to specify a request method for the request. The default request method is GET.

*WRBCtx points to the opaque WRB context object that the WRB application engine passed to your cartridge function. dvoid *hRequest identifies the request for which the method is to be set. WRB_ICXcreateRequest() returns this handle.

WRB_ICXsetMethod() takes an argument of type WRBMethod that represents the request method to be used for a request (see Listing 36.14).

LISTING 36.14 THE WRBMethod ENUMERATED TYPE

```
typedef enum _WRBMethod
{
OPTIONS,
GET,
HEAD,
```

```
POST,
PUT,
DELETE,
TRACE
} WRBMethod;
```

For more information on this enumerated type, refer to your documentation on Web Request Broker.

WRB_ICXsetNoProxy()   This method builds a list of DNS domains for which the proxy server (specified by WRB_ICXsetProxy()) should not be used. This ensures that any request URLs originally intended for the given proxy server are rejected. Listing 36.15 shows how to implement this method.

LISTING 36.15   SPECIFYING DOMAINS FOR WHICH THE PROXY SERVER SHOULD NOT BE USED WITH WRB_ICXsetNoProxy()

```
WAPIReturnCode
WRB_ICXsetNoProxy(void *WRBCtx,
text *noProxy);
Parameters
Return Values
WRB_ICXsetNoProxy() returns a value of type WAPIReturnCode.
```

If your cartridge calls WRB_ICXsetProxy() to set up proxy server request translation but you don't want requests to all DNS domains to use the proxy server, use WRB_ICXsetNoProxy() to specify a comma-separated list of domains to which requests should be sent directly, without proxy server intervention.

*WRBCtx points to the opaque WRB context object that the WRB application engine passed to your cartridge function. *noProxy points to a comma-separated list of DNS domains to which requests should be sent directly.

WRB_ICXsetProxy()   This method tells cartridges which proxy server to use in making future ICX requests that must be routed outside a firewall. Listing 36.16 shows how to specify a proxy server.

LISTING 36.16   SPECIFYING A PROXY SERVER WITH WRB_ICXsetProxy()

```
WAPIReturnCode
WRB_ICXsetProxy(void *WRBCtx,
text *proxyAddress);
Parameters
Return Values
WRB_ICXsetProxy() returns a value of type WAPIReturnCode.
```

Invoking this method is useful when your intranet-based cartridge needs to dispatch ICX requests to servers outside the firewall. The cartridge would reference the address set by this method.

*WRBCtx points to the opaque WRB context object that the WRB application engine passed to your cartridge function. *proxyAddress represents the proxy address in character-string form.

THE WRB LOGGER API

Given Oracle Application Server's tight coupling with the Oracle database, you should become more familiar with the WRB APIs related to database connections. The WRB Logger API functions offers such routines:

- WRB_LOGopen()—Opens a file or establishes a database connection.
- WRB_LOGwriteMessage()—Writes a system message to persistent storage. Persistent storage can be either a database or flat file where the log data lives persistently beyond the life of the server application.

Note

WRBLogMessage() is supported in an earlier version of the Oracle Application Server. In Oracle Application Server 4.0, you should use WRB_LOGwriteMessage() instead.

- WRB_LOGwriteAttribute()—Writes a client-defined attribute to persistent storage.
- WRB_LOGclose()—Closes a file or shuts down a database connection.

Listing 36.17 shows the WRB_LOGopen method's implementation.

LISTING 36.17 THE SYNTAX FOR THE WRB_LOGopen() METHOD

```
WAPIReturnCode WRB_LOGopen( dvoid *WRBCtx,
ub4 *logHdl,
WRBLogType type,
WRBLogDestType dest,
text *MyFileName );
Parameters
Return Values
[Returns WAPIReturnCode]
```

Invoke this method from your cartridge component to open a file or initiate a database connection. The WRB application engine passes the WRBCtx pointer to your calling method in your cartridge. WRBCtx points to the WRB context object. LogHdl is a handle that indicates the type of object contained in the connection object: file or database. type indicates the type of entry in the log. The entry can be a client attribute or a message. dest indicates whether to log the transaction in a flat file or a database. MyFileName is the string name of the file. It can also be NULL when you're logging information to the database.

The method in Listing 36.18 writes a system message to the persistent storage specified by the value of logHdl.

LISTING 36.18   WRB_LOGwriteMessage() METHOD SYNTAX

```
WAPIReturnCode WRB_LOGwriteMessage( dvoid *WRBCtx,
ub4 logHdl,
text *component,
text *msg,
sb4 severity);
Parameters
Return Values
Returns WAPIReturnCode.
```

Invoke this method from your cartridge to write a system message to the persistent storage specified by the value in logHdl. The WRB application engine passes the WRBCtx pointer to your calling method in your cartridge. WRBCtx points to the WRB context object. logHdl is a handle that indicates the type of object contained in the connection object: file or database. type indicates the type of entry in the log. It can be a client attribute or a message. component points to the text description to identify the type of cartridge, such as "java". msg is the text you want to log. Messages can't exceed 2K in length. The backquote character (`) is used as a delimiter; if you need to incorporate this character in your message, you must specially tag it with a backslash (that is, \`). severity is just the severity of the message.

The code in Listing 36.19 writes a client-defined attribute to the storage specified by logHdl.

LISTING 36.19   THE WRB_LOGWriteAttribute() METHOD SYNTAX

```
WAPIReturnCode WRB_LOGWriteAttribute( dvoid *WRBCtx,
ub4 logHdl,
text *component,
text *name,
text *value);
Parameters
Return Values
Returns WAPIReturnCode.
```

Invoke this method from your cartridge to write client-defined attributes to the persistent storage specified by the value in logHdl. The information that is stored is useful for seeing how your custom cartridge responds to system messages. Tracking error and exception handling is critical when developing components. The WRB application engine passes the WRBCtx pointer to your calling method in your cartridge. WRBCtx points to the WRB context object. logHdl is a handle that indicates the type of object contained in the connection object: file or database. type indicates the type of entry that is in the log. It can be a client attribute or a message. component points to the text description to identify the type of cartridge, such as "ODBC". msg is the text you want to log. name is a text item that identifies a particular attribute you want to log. value provides additional text to qualify the attribute you named. See Listing 36.20 for the syntax for WRB_LOGclose() method.

LISTING 36.20   THE `WRB_LOGclose()` METHOD SYNTAX

```
WAPIReturnCode WRB_LOGclose( dvoid *WRBCtx, ub4 logHdl);
Parameters
Return Values
Returns WAPIReturnCode.
```

Invoke the `WRB_LOGclose()` method from a method in your cartridge to close the file or shut down a database connection as specified by the value in `logHdl`.

The WRB application engine passes the `WRBCtx` pointer to your calling method in your cartridge. `WRBCtx` points to the WRB context object. `logHdl` is a handle that indicates the type of object contained in the connection object: file or database. This handle was created in the `WRB_LOGopen()` method.

USING THE JWEB CARTRIDGE

The JWeb cartridge, formerly called the Java cartridge, was a source of some confusion. The JWeb cartridge does not have anything to do with Java applets. A Java applet is a small program downloaded and run in the browser. Essentially a Java virtual machine, the JWeb cartridge runs a Java application on the server and returns straight HTML to the browser. The browser needs no special capabilities because it is not being asked to do anything but interpret HTML.

Oracle has also provided pl2java, a utility that allows you to call PL/SQL from a Java application, and the Java Toolkit, which allows you to write PL/SQL and WRB functionality into Java applications.

ADDING A JAVA APPLICATION

Before you can run a Java application, you will need to let the OAS know where and what it is.

1. Access the Node Manager.
2. Click OAS Manager.
3. Expand the main menu on the left and click Applications.
4. On the right, add a new application by clicking the + sign.
5. Under Application Type, choose JWeb. Make sure the radio button is set to configure manually. Click the Apply button (see Figure 36.3).
6. Fill in the Application Name (that is, Hello World) and Display Name (that is helloworld). These are how your applications will appear in the list of applications and the menu, respectively. Choose an appropriate version number, such as 1.0. Click the Add Cartridge to this Application button.

Figure 36.3
Adding a JWeb
application.

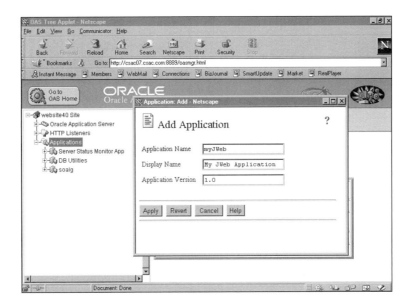

7. Enter the cartridge and display name. These will be used to display information in the Node Manager.

8. Enter the location of the directory where you will put your compiled class files and a virtual path, such as /java/myTest, and click Apply. This directory must be part if your CLASSPATH environment variable.

9. Reload the Application Server. Click Oracle Application Server on the left, and then choose All and Reload, which looks like a VCR Rewind button.

You have now created the "Hello World" application with one cartridge.

Tip #105

If you already have applications written in PL/SQL, don't feel obligated to convert them to Java. Oracle has structured their support for Java so that one can be called from the other. Don't rewrite your PL/SQL, just call it from your new Java code.

BUILDING A PAGE IN JAVA

You are now ready to create your actual Java application. This is a little different from normal Java programming where you might have one or several classes, but where the user basically starts the application with the main() method and sticks with it until he or she is through. During this time, what the user sees may be controlled by many different methods. When creating Java applications for OAS, keep in mind that every single page is its own class, and that the OAS will always be calling the main method to display it. Let's take a look at a sample application:

LISTING 36.21   SAMPLE JWEB APPLICATION

```
import oracle.html.*; // This is the Java Toolkit
class showJavaPage {
        public static void main (String args[]) {
            HtmlHead h = new HtmlHead("My Java App");
            // Just creates the HTML for the <HEAD> and <TITLE> tags
            HtmlBody b = new HtmlBody();
            b.addItem("This text was generated by my Java Application.");
            // Add text to the body
            HtmlPage p = new HtmlPage(h, b);
            // Creates the page object and adds the head and body objects
            p.printHeader();
            // All pages must have HTTP headers.
            p.print();
            // The page prints itself.
        } // main
} // class
```

You must compile this into a *.class file before it can be accessed by the application server. The JWeb cartridge uses Java 1.1.4, NOT 1.2 or even 1.1.6, so be certain to watch what features you add. Oracle recommends choosing a compiler that uses the same version. Oracle also has its own Java tool, JDeveloper.

After the class is compiled and tested, copy it to the directory you referenced when creating the application. To see it in your browser, go to the following URL:

```
http://www.yourmachine.com/java/myTest/showJavaPage
```

Note that www.yourmachine.com is your machine, and /java/myTest is the virtual path you entered when you created the application. Note that even though your application is called "Hello World", nowhere do you actually see that text. The name of the application is an arbitrary choice and is needed only for administration of your application through the Node Manager.

Using the JWeb cartridge, you have access to the same WRB services that you would by using the CWeb cartridge. They are contained in the oracle.* packages.

Tip #106

In version 4.0, the oracle.owas.wrb.services.logger package was deprecated. Use oracle.OAS.Services.Logger instead.

For those of you who have been around for awhile, LiveHTML is just Oracle's name for Server Side Includes, or SSI. SSI was one of the Web's earliest ways to provide dynamic information in a page. It allows the developer to create a static HTML page, but "embed" dynamic information, such as the date, or another HTML page, within the content. When the server receives a request for one of these pages, it parses the page, adds the additional information, and sends the whole thing back to the browser. Looking at the HTML source gives no indication that this has happened. LiveHTML can be separated into two categories. The first is SSI.

In SSI, commands are embedded in the syntax:

```
<!--#command var=values-->
config:  Determines how subsequent information will be displayed
<!--#config cmdecho=on-->
 include:  Includes the contents of a file.
     Can be an absolute or virtual path, so you can include dynamic information
<!--#include file="/u08/webdocs/motd.txt"-->
<!--#include virtual="/soaig/plsql/register.reg_page"-->
 echo:  Prints an environment variable
<!--#echo var="DATE_LOCAL"-->
 fsize:  Prints the size of a file -- not necessarily the file that
     includes this command
<!--#fsize file="pic3.jpg">
 flastmod:  Same as fsize, but prints the last time the file was modified
<!--#flastmod file="index.html">
 exec:  Executes a script.  This could be a CGI script or a shell script.
     Administrators can disable this tag, since it does constitute a security
     risk.  Note that to see the results of a cmd execution, you must use
     config to set cmd=on.
<!--#exec cgi="/cgi-bin/counter.pl">
<!--#exec cmd="/home/nick/scripts/myscript.sh">
 request:  Allows you to access the ICX by calling on another cartridge.  Most
     commonly used to get the results of a PL/SQL, Perl or Java request, but
     can be used to call on another machine altogether, and even allows access
     to protected URL's by allowing for a username and password to be included.
<!--#request url="http://user:pass@www.mymachine.com/java/user_info?day=Sunday-->
```

Tip #107	You can use LiveHTML's SSI capabilities to allow users to change content, say in a text file that's INCLUDEed, without touching the interface itself.

LiveHTML on OAS, however, has been extended way beyond just including the date or the contents of another file. Oracle has, in fact, included functionality similar to Microsoft's Active Server Pages. Instead of being based on VisualBasic, however, server-side scripting has been based on Perl. This has several advantages. Oracle has provided several standard "Web Application Objects" that allow advanced functionality and even access to CORBA objects.

Embedded scripting takes one of three syntax forms, similar to ASPs:

```
<% %> : Encapsulates a script
<%= %> : Prints the value of an expression
<SCRIPT RUNAT=SERVER> </SCRIPT> :  Also encapsulates a script,
but if "RUNAT=SERVER" is left off, the script text will be provided to
and run by the browser.
```

You also have the option of accessing variables supplied to the page. For instance, let's say you call the page

```
http://www.myserver.com/scriptpages/hellopage.asp?user=Nick&numstuff=3
```

and the text of that pages includes

```
Let me guess. Your name is

<% $Response->write($user) %>
, right?
<% $Response->write(" Let's see.  You own ");
      for ($countem = 1; $countem >= $numstuff; $countem++) { %>
 <%= $countem %>,
 <% } ;
      $Response->write(" computers.")%>
```

The output would be

```
Let me guess. Your name is Nick, right? Let's see. You own 1, 2, 3, computers.
```

> **Note**
>
> You also have the option to specify a language using `<SCRIPT Language="lan-guage">` but for now, the only language supported is Perl. Oracle plans to add support for other languages in the future.

Using the Perl Cartridge

Before the advent of application servers, most CGI scripts were written in either C or Perl. We've dealt with C applications with CWeb, and now we're going to deal with Perl. Perl scripts are much easier to write than C applications, but running them as a CGI has it's drawbacks. For one thing, like any CGI script, every time a user makes a request, the interpreter needs to be started because Perl is an interpreted language. This can be a serious resource and performance drain.

OAS solves this problem with the Perl cartridge, which is basically a version of the Perl interpreter that stays resident in memory and waits for requests, and then executes them. Depending on the operating system, the cartridge is implemented as a shared object (UNIX, `libperlctx.so`) or a dynamic linked library (NT, `perlnt40.dll`). Migrating your Perl scripts to the OAS is a simple process—basically re-mapping your virtual path to point to the cartridge server instead of the CGI.

To create a Perl application, follow the same steps as for a JWeb application, selecting Perl instead of JWeb. Your location of files does not need to be part of any particular environment variable.

Some things to keep in mind about the Perl cartridge:

- The interpreter is based on Perl 5.003.
- Standard I/O and STDERR have been redirected to the browser and to the WRB Logger, respectively.
- You cannot use "fork". Use "system" instead, but be aware that output has been redirected to the browser.

ENTERPRISE JAVA BEANS AND JCORBA

Both Enterprise Java Beans (EJB) and JCORBA involve writing CORBA objects in Java. The EJB specification was created by JavaSoft, and the JCORBA specification is an Oracle proprietary specification written by Oracle prior to EJB and finalized by JavaSoft. Both are designed to encapsulate objects and to allow you to send messages to and from other CORBA objects. Which you choose will depend on what development you have already done and what you will be trying to accomplish. Keep the following in mind:

TABLE 36.2   CHOOSING AN OBJECT MODEL

Objects	EJB	JCORBA
Existing objects	extend java.rmi.Remote	extend org.omg.CORBA.Object
Passing objects by	value	reference
Clients written in	Java only	Java or other languages

You will also want to use EJB if you plan on using third-party beans.

SUMMARY

The early sites on the Web consisted of nothing but static information without even the benefit of graphics. Things have certainly come a long way since then! Today, not only has the Web progressed to much more sophisticated fare, but Web-type applications are increasingly surfacing in all aspects of business. Fortunately, technology is keeping up. You can use Oracle Application Server not only to Web-enable your existing PL/SQL applications, but to keep up with the move to Java and even to create applications that would not normally have been considered content for the Web using the C cartridge. With the benefit of the Application Server architecture, no matter what comes next, it is likely that you will be able to build your application using Oracle Application Server or its descendants.

INSTALLING AND CONFIGURING THE OAS

In this chapter

INSTALLING THE ORACLE APPLICATION SERVER FOR SUN SOLARIS

Oracle Application Server (OAS) has come a long way since it was simply a Hypertext Transfer Protocol (HTTP) server that included a tightly integrated Oracle7x server. This database server component enabled you to create dynamic Hypertext Markup Language (HTML) documents from data stored in an Oracle database in addition to static, or unchanging, data.

The HTTP listener, which is integrated with a new "application server layer," determines whether a client request from a browser is for a static or a dynamic document. The HTTP listener directly services static document requests as well as traditional Common Gateway Interface (CGI) requests, and passes everything else off to the application server layer. The application server layer then handles the request and passes the output back to the listener.

HARDWARE AND SOFTWARE REQUIREMENTS

To even think about installing OAS on Solaris, you need to meet a few minimum machine requirements (see Tables 37.1, 37.2, and 37.3).

TABLE 37.1 HARDWARE REQUIREMENTS

Hardware	Requirement
CPU	A SPARC processor
Memory	128M
Disk space	300M
Swap space	256M
CD-ROM device	RockRidge format

TABLE 37.2 SOFTWARE REQUIREMENTS

Software	Requirement
Operating system	Solaris 2.5.1 with the following patches: 103640-08 (or later) 103566-08 (or later) 103582-08 (or later)
Browser	Netscape Communicator: 4.04 (with JDK 1.1 patch) 4.05 (International version only) 4.06 or higher

Source: Oracle Corp.

TABLE 37.3   CERTIFIED SOFTWARE

Software Item	Version
>HTTP listener	Oracle 40 bit (v2.14)
	Oracle 128 bit (v2.14)
	Netscape Enterprise Server 2.01, 3.0, 3.51
	Netscape Fastrack Server 2.01, 3.0, 3.51
	Apache 1.2.5
Oracle	7.3.2x
	7.3.4
	8.0.3
	8.0.4
	8.0.5
Java Development Kit (JDK)	1.1.4

Source: Oracle Corp.

PART

VIII

CH

37

> **Note**
>
> Oracle's documentation does not require the exclusive use of an Oracle database in the application server. However, Oracle Application Server is most mature with an Oracle database.

RELINKING YOUR EXECUTABLES AFTER INSTALLATION

In addition to hardware and software requirements, you might find it necessary to relink your executables. *Linking* is the process of combining compiled programs and libraries into an executable program. Relinking an executable is necessary because Oracle Application Server handles some of the duties an operating system would normally handle. In addition, Oracle Application Server has its own header files that you need to incorporate into any executables that require the services of the application server. Typically, any relinking that is necessary is handled by the installer itself. Nevertheless, if you choose to relink the executable after doing the installation, Oracle Application Server requires that you install the following files, libraries, and utilities:

- Oracle library files, which have the .a extension
- Oracle make files, which have the .mk extension
- Oracle object files, which have the .o extension
- Networking system libraries
- The ar library manipulation utility
- The ld utility
- The make utility
- X libraries
- Motif libraries

It might be in your best interest to do a full recompile of your executables if time permits. That way, you can isolate any upgrade/migration-related anomalies before they come back to haunt you.

IMPLEMENTING PRE-INSTALLATION TASKS

Before installing Oracle Application Server for Solaris, you must perform some duties to ensure a smooth installation process. These duties include the following:

- Choose a network port for the Node Manager Listener (formerly called the admin listener). This port number makes it possible for the Web listener to receive incoming client requests. The number should be at least 1024 but no higher than 65535. The default, as installed, is 8889 on UNIX.

- On UNIX, you must set the following environment variables: ORACLE_TERM, ORACLE_HOME, ORAWEB_HOME, and ORACLE_SID. You also need to know the name of your machine. This is the machine name you normally use to access files and services. For instance, for HTTP Web machines, your machine name might be www.csac.com or something similar. If you're not sure, ask the person responsible for creating domain names and assigning TCP/IP addresses in your company or group.

- Create your admin password. This is the password that is requested by your browser when you connect to the Web-based configuration pages.

- You need to have an operating system user account to actually have ownership over the Web listener's UNIX account. For security reasons, it's not a good idea to use the Oracle owner account as the owner of these processes because it could create a serious breach of database security. Similar concerns arise from using the root, or superuser account, but in many situations it can't be avoided. For instance, the default port for HTTP servers is 80, but only root can start a process on ports less than 1024. Because you can start your listener from the command line, however, you might opt to run your Node Manager Listener as another user, such as the low-privileged nobody, for added safety. There is a useradd command to help you create such an account.

The following installation duties require that you log on using the built-in Oracle user account. Because it is assumed that you are an administrative user with the authorization to install such a system, no password is necessary.

SETTING PRELIMINARY ENVIRONMENT VARIABLES

Specifying initial values for your server environment variables helps your operating system communicate with Oracle Application Server. Certain environment variables need to be set before installation, and some of them need to be set whenever you start or manage the application server. You need to place the necessary environment variable values in the startup file of the built-in Oracle account. This is advisable when possible. Of course, if you don't set them in the startup file, specify the values in the .PROFILE or .LOGIN file of the Oracle account. You can also set variables specific to the current shell session as the shell prompt is displayed (see Table 37.4).

TABLE 37.4   INITIAL ENVIRONMENT VARIABLE VALUES

Environment Variable	Sample Value
ORACLE_HOME	/u01/app/oracle/product/8.0.3
ORACLE_BASE	/u01/app/oracle
ORACLE_SID	MyID
ORACLE_TERM	xsun5
ORAWEB_HOME	$ORACLE_HOME/ows/4.0
ORAWEB_SITE	website40
TNS_ADMIN	$ORACLE_HOME/network/admin
LD_LIBRARY_PATH	$ORACLE_HOME/orb/4.0. lib:$ORAWEB_HOME/lib
CLASSPATH	$ORAWEB_HOME/classes: $ORAWEB_HOME/admin
PATH	.:$ORAWEB_HOME/bin: $ORACLE_HOME /bin:/opt/bin:/bin:/usr/bin: /usr/ccs/bin:/GNU/bin/make: $ORACLE_HOME/orb/4.0/bin: $ORACLE_HOME/orb/4.0/admin/cgi :$ORAWEB_HOME/admin/cgi
TMPDIR	/var/tmp
TWO_TASK	Must be undefined while installing software

For instance, you set the ORACLE_SID value using the C shell as follows:

setenv ORACLE_SID MyID

In Bourne, it would be the following:

ORACLE_SID=MyID; export ORACLE_SID

When setting environment variables, keep the following in mind:

■ Version 3.0 enables you to use the same ORACLE_HOME as your database, but Oracle Application Server 4.0 must be installed to a different ORAOLE_HOME. (The only exceptions are Oracle8.0.4, providing you are willing to rebuild Server Manager and SQL *Plus afterwards and Oracle8.0.5.)

■ If ORACLE_BASE is set, the installer performs an OFA (Oracle Flexible Architecture) installation. If you don't want an OFA installation, make sure that ORACLE_BASE is not set before installing.

SETTING PERMISSION CODES FOR CREATING FILES

You set permission codes in the startup files. The umask variable holds the necessary permission code you need. Before changing the value of umask, look at its contents by entering the following at the prompt:

```
$ umask
```

If the value of umask is not 022, change it to this value. This value tells the server what groups or users have READ and EXECUTE permissions; the WRITE permission is not affected. To set umask to 022, do the following:

- For Bourne or Korn shell, enter umask 022 in .profile.
- For C shell, enter umask 022 in .login.

Finally, you should check the various user startup files just to be sure the umask variable is set to 022.

UPDATING YOUR ENVIRONMENT FROM A STARTUP FILE

As your environment situation changes (that is, you install new nodes and so on), you have to upgrade your environment information. To update environment variables, load the startup file into memory or some persistent medium as follows:

```
Bourne/Korn shell: $ . .profile
C shell: % source .login
```

Note that if you update these variables in a nonpersistent media such as memory (at the prompt), their values are not stored after you exit your current shell session. If you store them in a persistent object such as a file, you must execute the startup file to make the values effective.

INSTALLING ORACLE APPLICATION SERVER ON WINDOWS NT

Installing Oracle products on Windows NT is generally much simpler than installing on UNIX, but the essential concepts are the same (see Tables 37.5, 37.6, 37.7).

HARDWARE AND SOFTWARE REQUIREMENTS

TABLE 37.5 HARDWARE REQUIREMENTS

Hardware	Requirement
CPU	An Intel compatible 486 or higher processor
Memory	128M
Disk space	200M
Swap space	256M

TABLE 37.6   SOFTWARE REQUIREMENTS

Software	Requirement
Operating system	Windows NT 4.0 Service Pack 3
Browser	Netscape Communicator: 4.04 (with JDK 1.1 patch) 4.05 (International version only) 4.06 or higher Microsoft Internet Explorer 4.01 with Service Pack 1

Source: Oracle Corp.

TABLE 37.7   CERTIFIED SOFTWARE

Software Item	Version
>HTTP listener	Oracle 40 bit (v2.14) Oracle 128 bit (v2.14) Netscape Enterprise Server 2.01, 3.0, 3.51 Netscape Fastrack Server 2.0.1, 3.0, 3.51 Microsoft Internet Information Server 3.0, 4.0
Oracle	7.3.2x 7.3.4 8.0.3 8.0.4 8.0.5
Java Development Kit (JDK)	1.1.4

Source: Oracle Corp.

Before you start the Oracle Installer, be sure to stop all Oracle services, such as the database itself and MSDTC.

To start the installer, put the CD-Rom in your drive and if the auto run feature is supported, the installer will start automatically. If not, locate G:\ NT_X86\Install\SETUP.EXE, where G: is your CD-ROM.

UNDERSTANDING ORACLE APPLICATION SERVER'S LATEST INSTALLATION FEATURES

To help make your installation a little easier, Oracle has incorporated several installation enhancements to Oracle Application Server 4.0. These features include the following:

- Installation components—Oracle provides several installation products, including an HTTP listener, the Web Request Broker, a CORBA-based Object Request Broker, logging utilities, and several different programming language environments in the form of cartridge servers.

- The owsctl utility—This utility provides centralized control of each of the application server's listeners and related Object Request Broker (ORB) processes. In an improvement over version 3.0, the HTTP listener used by the administration pages is now separate from the Web Application Server layer. Where previously the Web Request Broker had to be started before any administration could be done, you can now start the Node Manager listener independently.

- Flexible upgrading and migrating options—If your previous Internet server was Oracle WebServer 2.x or Oracle Web Application Server 3.x, Oracle Application Server now helps ease your migration migraines. If it was a Netscape server, Oracle Application Server can also help. However, unfortunately, it does not look like it offers any assistance with migrating from Microsoft's Internet Information Server.

- Single or multi-node install options—If your domain requires only one network node, you can choose the single-node option. If it requires more than one, you have the flexibility to customize the install to recognize more than one node.

- Flexible Oracle Application Server location variable (ORAWEB_HOME)—Back in version 2.x, when Oracle Application Server was still called WebServer, the location of the system was tied to the home location specified in the ORACLE_HOME environment variable. In version 3.0 and 4.0, you can now have a location that is not tied to this environment variable. Each installation, then, would have its own environment domain called ORAWEB_HOME.

IDENTIFYING PRODUCT DEPENDENCIES

You need to consider what products you must have in place for Oracle Application Server to be useful. If you plan to use Oracle Application Server only as a stand-alone Internet server, you don't need to concern yourself with this section. However, if you plan to implement Oracle Application Server as a server within your overall Oracle environment, you should read the list in this section. To make sure your environment has all the necessary components, you should go through the following list, which includes the software component and its respective release:

- Oracle7 Server, 7.1.6
- PL/SQL, 2.1.6
- SQL*Net, 2.1.6
- TCP/IP Protocol, 2.1.6
- Server Manager, 2.1.3

DESIGNING THE DIRECTORY STRUCTURE

Identifying your needs for a directory structure in some ways resembles the principles of object-oriented design. You must know your base objects and any derived objects descending from these base objects. Implementing the wrong hierarchy can cause confusion later and lead to redundant effort. For directories, this is especially true when server software upgrades become necessary as older versions become archaic. Many domains have a policy in place for creating and maintaining complex directory structures. Oracle offers the Optimal Flexible

Architecture (OFA) to ease the management and maintenance duties associated with directories. Listing 37.1 shows the recommended directory structure for the primary node.

LISTING 37.1 ORACLE-RECOMMENDED DIRECTORY STRUCTURE

```
ORACLE_BASE
     product
          oracle
               8.0.4 ($ORACLE_HOME)
                    rdbms
                    ows
                         cartx
                              plsql

                              java
                         4.0
                              bin
                              lib
     admin
          MyDBName
          ows
               MySite1
                    httpd_MyMachine1
                         owl.cfg
                         admin
                              svadmin.cfg
                              svadmin.pid

                    log
                         wrb.log
                         plsql.log
                    wrb
<
                    wrb.app
                              site.app
```

This directory structure conforms to the Optimal Flexible Architecture directory structure. OFA separates data files from configuration files and executables so that you can run more than one version of any of Oracle's products, including Oracle Application Server.

INSTALLING THE ORACLE APPLICATION SERVER

To install the Oracle Application Server, follow these steps.

1. Start the Oracle Installer.

2. After you answer initial questions about your database system (preferably the Oracle8x database), choose to install the Oracle Application Server.

3. Specify the hostname and network port for the Oracle Application Server Node Manager. This is the listener that serves the pages that you use to configure the application server later. The default is 8889 on UNIX, and 8888 on Windows NT.

4. Specify a port for the `admin` listener. Unlike previous versions, this is not the listener that administers your server, but instead it serves the samples. The default is 10000 on UNIX and 8889 on Windows NT.

5. Specify the password for the Oracle Application Server Administrator account. The username of the Oracle Application Server Administrator is `admin`.

6. On UNIX systems, log in as root, and run the `$ORACLE_HOME/orainst/oasroot.sh` shell script. This step is very important because it adjusts important file ownerships and permissions and starts the Node Manager. On Windows NT systems, reboot your machine.

7. Start the Oracle Application Server. To do this, open your browser and go to `http://www.yourdomain.com:8889` (or whatever hostname and port you chose). Click OAS Manager. In the right-hand pane, you see a list of all the nodes on your system. Select the radio button next to the primary node and click the start button. This is the triangular icon above the list of nodes that looks like a VCR "Play" button. The individual processes are listed in a separate window where you should check for any errors.

Tip #108

The OAS is very sensitive to DNS resolution issues when installing. Make sure that your DNS is running before you start.

USING THE ORACLE APPLICATION SERVER NODE MANAGER

In version 3.0 of Oracle Application Server, all HTTP listeners required that the application server layer, then called the Web Request Broker, be running when they were started—including the Administration Utility. Of course, that meant that if there was a problem with the WRB, there was no easy way to fix it. While the Web Request Broker is still present—albeit in altered form—Oracle has solved this problem in version 4.0 with the Node Manager, a simple HTTP listener that does not require the application server to be running.

The Node Manager enables management of the entire Oracle Application Server. The administrative tasks that are possible through these pages include the following:

- Startup and shutdown of Oracle databases
- Startup and shutdown of Web listeners
- Startup and shutdown of all system components
- Creation of new Oracle Web listeners and modification of existing ones
- Creation and modification of PL/SQL or other applications

The node manager is automatically started when you run the `oasroot.sh` script after installation. It can be started or stopped later from the command line using the `owsctl` utility or with the OracleStartOAS 4.0(`ORACLE_HOME,website_name`) service on Windows NT. To start it, type: `owsctl start -nodemgr`. To access the Administration Utility, open your browser and go to the following URL (unless you chose a different port during the installation process):

```
UNIX:  http://www.yourdomain.com:8889

NT:  http://www.yourdomain.com:8888
```

Note that unlike in previous versions, this is *not* the `admin` listener, although this is just a name change. It still performs the fuction that the admin listener did.

CREATING AN HTTP LISTENER

The first step in any Web page request is contacting the HTTP listener. Because the HTTP listener plays such an important role in Application Server operations, you should understand the various configuration parameters that the Web listener needs.

To create a new HTTP listener, follow these steps:

1. Go to the OAS Welcome Page, normally at http://www.yourdomain.com:8889 (`UNIX`) or http://www.yourdomain.com:8888 (`NT`).
2. Choose OAS Manager.
3. When the applet on the left side of the window appears, double-click to expand the main menu.
4. Choose HTTP Listeners. This brings up a list of all existing HTTP listeners on the right side of the window. Add a new listener by clicking the + sign on the right side. Choose the appropriate node, and click Apply. (See Figure 37.1)
5. Fill in the appropriate values, and click **Submit**.

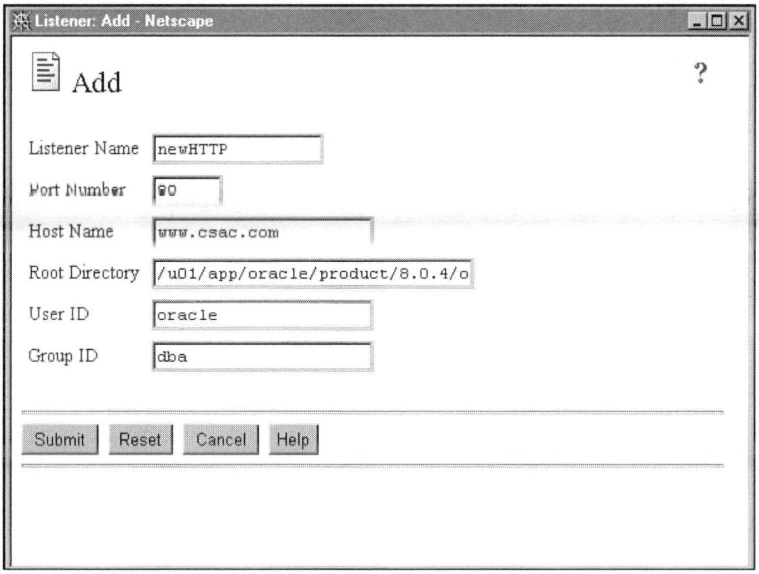

Figure 37.1
Creating an HTTP listener

Table 37.5 Web Listener Configuration Parameters

Parameter Name	Default Value	Description
Listener Name	none	Unique identifier for this listener.
Port Number	80	The TCP port it listens on. If this port number is less than 1024, you need root access to start the listener.
Host Name	from install	The "Internet name" by which this listener will be known, such as www.csac.com.
Root Directory	$ORAWEB_HOME/doc	The default location where the HTTP listener will try to find your files. For instance, using previous examples, http://www.csac.com/index.html will be found in this directory.
User ID	www	The operating system user who owns the listener process (UNIX only).
Group ID	dba	The operating system group the listener runs under (UNIX only).

Installing the PL/SQL Toolkit

The easiest way to get information from an Oracle database to a Web browser is with the PL/SQL cartridge server component of the Oracle Application Server. To do this, you simply write stored PL/SQL procedures and functions that make calls to the PL/SQL toolkit. In previous versions, unless you planned carefully, you wound up with copies of the toolkit for every schema accessed by the Web. Version 4.0, however, installs the toolkit into a single schema and makes it available publicly to other schemas. To install the PL/SQL Toolkit, follow these steps:

1. Connect to the Oracle Application Server Administrative Server, and click the OAS Utilities link.
2. Expand the **Utilities** menu on the left, and then the **Install** menu.
3. Click **PL/SQL Toolkit**.
4. If you are installing the Toolkit to a local database, use **ORACLE_SID**. Otherwise, use **Connect String**.
5. Enter the **sys** user password. The application uses this database user because it creates the user OAS_PUBLIC, grants it privileges, and creates public synonyms. If you don't have this password, you have to find someone who does. Fortunately, you only have to do this once per database.
6. Click the **Apply** button. (See Figure 37.2)

Figure 37.2
Installing the PL/SQL toolkit.

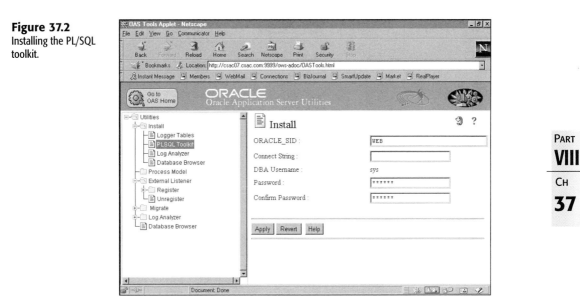

CREATING A NEW PL/SQL CARTRIDGE

The PL/SQL cartridge is a direct descendent of the original "Oracle Web Agent", a CGI script that logged into the database and passed the output of a stored procedure back to the browser. In version 4.0, however, it resembles OWA as much as modern man resembles the caveman. These days, it is a full-fledged multithreaded application that doesn't even have to be on the same node as the HTTP listener.

Of course, with capability can come complexity. Creating a new PL/SQL cartridge is not as straightforward as it could be. You must do the following:

1. Access the Node Manager.
2. Click OAS Manager.
3. Expand the main menu on the left, and click Applications.
4. On the right, add a new application by clicking the + sign.
5. Under Application Type, choose PL/SQL. Make sure the radio button is set to configure manually. Click the Apply button.
6. Fill in the Application Name and Display Name. These entries are how your application will appear in the list of applications and the menu, respectively. Choose an appropriate version number, such as "1.0" (see Figure 37.3). Click Apply, then the Add cartridge to this application button.

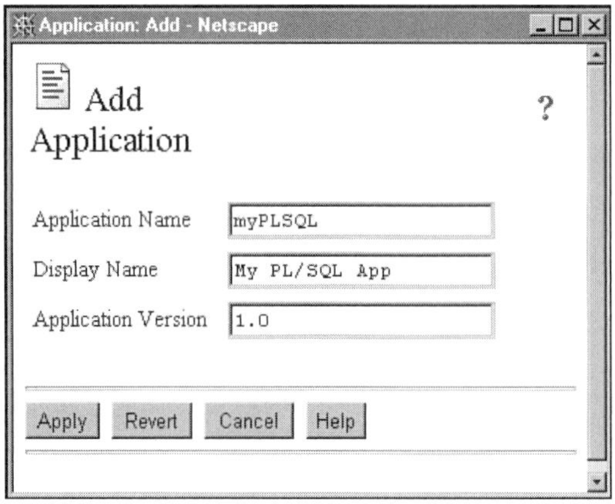

Figure 37.3
Adding a PL/SQL
cartridge.

7. Before the cartridge can access the database, it needs to know what database it's accessing. This information is stored in the Database Access Descriptor (DAD), a largely conceptual component that stores information such as the username and password, service name, or ORACLE_SID. Click the **Create New Dad** button (See Figure 37.4).

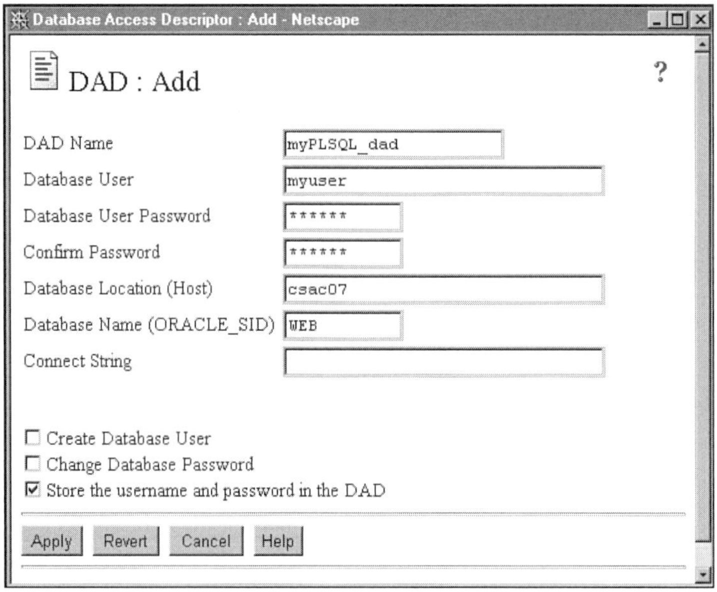

Figure 37.4
Creating a new
Database Access
Descriptor.

8. Fill in the appropriate identifying information. The username and password is what the application will use when accessing the database. Note the box on the bottom marked "Store the username and password in the DAD". You can opt *not* to store it in the DAD. If you do so, when the user attempts to access a page stored in the database, their browser pops up a window asking for a username and password and stating that this is what the application will use. Click the Apply button.

9. Now that you have created your application, you will add a cartridge to it. Again, the Cartridge Name and Display Name determine how your cartridge will appear in the administration utility. The Virtual Path determines how your application looks to a browser. For instance, it might be mycart/plsql, as in version 3.0, or mycart/owa, as in versions 1.0 and 2.0, but it could just as easily be simply mycart. Leave the physical path as the default, $ORAWEB_HOME/bin. Click **Apply**. (See Figure 37.5.)

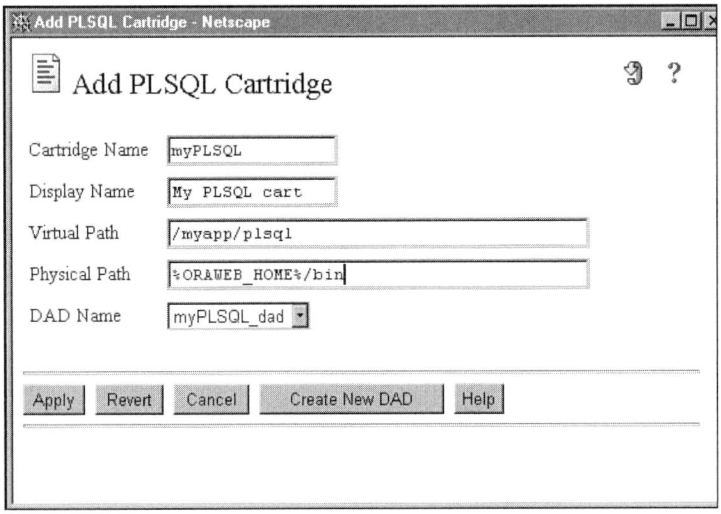

Figure 37.5
Applying a PL/SQL
cartridge.

10. Reload the Application Server. Click **Oracle Application Server** on the left, and then choose **all** and the reload button, which looks like a VCR Rewind button.

To test your new cartridge, create the following stored procedure:

```
create or replace procedure hello_world is
begin
    htp.p('Hello World!');
end;
```

Access it by setting your browser to
http://www.yourmachine.com/yourvirtualpath/hello_world.

TROUBLESHOOTING

Because Oracle Application Server 4.0 is pretty new to the market, you can expect to run into numerous problems. Other users have encountered several and so have users on the Internet and at Oracle. The following paragraphs include information culled from personal experience, Oracle's online manual, and other sources on the Internet.

PROBLEM

Node Manager is not running.

SOLUTION

Make certain that `$ORACLE_HOME/orainst/root.sh` shell script has been run by the root user. You can use the `$ORAWEB_HOME/bin/owsctl` utility as an alternative method for starting the Node Manager. Use the following:

```
<C1>owsctl start -nodemgr
```

PROBLEM

HTTP listener is not starting.

SOLUTION

Make certain that it was configured to listen on a different port from the Node Manager.

If it is on a part less than 1024, make sure you have root access.

Make sure you are using the new 4.0 syntax. For example, to start the listener `mylistener`, use the following:

```
owsctl start -l mylistener
```

PROBLEM

You receive "URL Not Found" when trying to access a new cartridge.

SOLUTION

Make sure you've reloaded the Oracle Application Server.

PROBLEM

You receive the error message `OWS-05526: Service OWA_DEFAULT_SERVICE submission failed due to error 1034.`

SOLUTION

Start up the Oracle8x database before attempting to create a service.

OTHER HELPFUL NOTES ON INSTALLATION

Just when you were ready to turn on the television and unwind, you've got more things to learn. The following list represents some helpful suggestions and warnings found on the Web. They deal with installing parts of the Oracle Application Server. Oracle Application Server provides a simplified, extremely basic default installation process that you might need to modify often. Check out the following suggestions:

- To get the latest Solaris patches, go to the URL
  `ftp://sunsolve1.sun.com/pub/patches/patches.html`.

- You might be using secondary HTTP listeners. In this case, for every listener, you might want to map URL aliases to the Oracle Application Server home site. You also might want to incorporate aliases for the services.

PART IX

PARALLEL AND DISTRIBUTED ENVIRONMENTS

PARALLEL QUERY MANAGEMENT

In this chapter

INTRODUCTION

Large systems with significant memory and CPU resources were available for decades. However, these systems were available only with proprietary operating systems and were not very cost effective. Multiple CPU machines with the UNIX open system architecture were available in the early '90s. These machines had significant hardware resources and were comparatively inexpensive. Oracle introduced Parallel Query Option (PQO)in Oracle version 7.1 to effectively use the hardware resources available in these systems. Oracle Parallel Query Option enables long-running SQL operations, mainly queries, to be spread among the multiple CPUs in a coordinated fashion. This enables the system to reduce the elapsing time for execution of resource-intensive SQL operations.

The Parallel Query Option enables certain operations to be performed in parallel by multiple server processes. One process, known as the Query Coordinator, dispatches the execution of a statement to several servers, coordinates the results from all the servers, and sends the results back to the user.

Although the feature is generally referred as PQO (Parallel Query Option), it also includes the following:

- Parallel Load
- Parallel Recovery
- Parallel Replication
- Parallel SQL

PARALLEL LOAD

The SQL*Loader direct path enables you to load data into the same table or partition simultaneously using multiple SQL*Loader sessions, as in the following example:

```
sqlload saledba/saledba control=sales1.ctl parallel=TRUE direct=TRUE
sqlload saledba/saledba control=sales2.ctl parallel=TRUE direct=TRUE
sqlload saledba/saledba control=sales3.ctl parallel=TRUE direct=TRUE
```

Tip #109

Use the keywords `parallel` and `direct` in the SQL*Loader command line to perform parallel data load operations.

Note the use of keywords `parallel` and `direct` in the command line. Also note the use of three different input data files for each of the sessions. Important features of parallel load are:

- Each SQL*Loader session allocates a new extent and loads data into it. To optimize the I/O performance of the system, it is highly recommended to control the location and size of the new extent by using the FILE and STORAGE keywords of the OPTIONS clause. A FILE keyword can be specified in the command line or in the control file. However, a storage clause can only be specified in the control file.

- Parallel load requires that there be no local and global indexes. If any index is present, it causes an error message and aborts the load operation. You need to manually drop the index before the load and rebuild the index when the load is completed.

- Each loading session acquires a shared lock on the table.

- Each loading session is independent, and there is no communication between the loading sessions.

- When a session finishes loading, Oracle joins the loaded extents with the existing extents. The unused blocks from the last loaded extents are returned back as free extents. This results in nonstandard sizes of the extents after the load. Truncating takes place even if you specify the extent size through a storage clause via options in the loader control file.

As mentioned previously, each parallel load session loads data into new extents and does not use any existing extents, even if they do not contain any data. Thus, the initial extent of a table that is loaded by parallel loads only is never used.

Tip #110	To optimize disk space usage, you can either create a very small initial extent or put data in the initial extent by loading it without the parallel load option.

PARALLEL RECOVERY

Oracle's basic read-write unit is a data block. Whenever changes are made to a block, Oracle records these changes in the form of a redo log so the block can be reconstructed using these logs if needed. Due to media failure or for any other reasons, if the contents of the present data files are lost, the files are restored from a suitable backup copy, and then recovery is done. The recovery process involves the following steps:

1. Read the log file and obtain the series of changes done to the data blocks.
2. Determine which data blocks need the changes to be applied.
3. Read these data blocks in the buffer cache.
4. Apply the desired changes to these data blocks, from the redo log.
5. Write the modified blocks back to the disk.

To perform recovery in parallel, you can set the initialization parameter RECOVERY_PARALLELISM. Alternatively, you can use the PARALLEL clause of the RECOVER command. During parallel recovery, the Server Manager or SQLDBA session reads the redo log file and passes on the changes to the parallel server processes. These processes then read the corresponding data files and apply the changes.

Tip #111

> When an Oracle instance is restarted after a crash, Oracle transparently performs the crash recovery before the instance is made available to the users. Set the initialization parameter RECOVERY PARALLELISM if you want the instance crash recovery to be performed in parallel mode.

PARALLEL PROPAGATION (REPLICATION)

Replication enables you to maintain multiple images of one or more database objects in multiple databases. Oracle Server transfers data over database links among these databases to propagate changes made to the replicated objects. The SNP background processes perform the data replication. However, if the data volume to be replicated is significantly large, it might take longer to synchronize the objects. Oracle8 enables parallel replication, whereby multiple parallel server processes can be used to propagate transactions.

PARALLEL SQL EXECUTION

An Oracle database is a collection of physical data files that are manipulated through various processes. A set of such background processes and a shared memory segment, collectively called Oracle Instance, enable concurrent users to interface with the database. When a user wants to use (select, insert, update, or delete) the data in the database, she needs to connect to the database. On most of the UNIX systems, Oracle uses a two-task architecture. In this scheme, when a user connects to the database, an additional process, frequently referred to as the shadow process, foreground, and so on, is forked. The shadow process accesses the shared memory segment and the data files on behalf of the user.

Note

> In a multithreaded server (MTS) environment, when a user logs on to the database, a shared server process is used instead of the shadow process. During Parallel Query Operation this shared server process acts as the query coordinator.

Oracle stores the data in the data files in blocks. A data block is the Oracle's basic data input/output unit. When a user needs data, the corresponding data block is read by the shadow process in the Oracle's buffer cache (part of the shared memory segment). The block in the buffer cache can then be modified by the user shadow process. Modified data blocks (dirty buffers) are written back to the disk by the DBWR process. Thus a shadow process does the major part of the work required by the user. Operations like parsing the SQL statement, sorting the data, and so on, are also done by the shadow process.

This works very well in an OLTP system where the amount of data manipulated by a user is relatively small. However, in a DSS environment where a user generally processes a huge amount of data, the shadow process might take a while to do the required work. While the shadow process is working long and hard to manipulate the data, it might be quite possible that system has idle CPU and memory resources. This is where Oracle's Parallel Query

Option comes in handy. With this option, Oracle can divide a user's large data processing request into multiple, comparatively smaller units of work which are then concurrently executed by different processes. It uses a set of dedicated background processes, known as Parallel Query Slaves (servers), to do the work. The shadow process gets promoted to a management role and is called the Query Coordinator. It is the responsibility of the Query Coordinator to do the following:

1. Break down the functions into parallel pieces.
2. Ensure that the sufficient number of parallel query slaves are available.
3. Initialize the slave process for the given work and assign the work among the PQO server's processes.
4. Gather the output from the slave processes and return the output.
5. When the desired work is finished, the query slave processes are freed and are available for other work.

Under favorable conditions, parallel execution reduces the execution time by as many factors as the number of query slaves it uses. However, it does not reduce the total CPU time consumed by the SQL statement. Parallel execution uses more memory than serial execution, so if the machine does not have enough CPU and memory resources, it might not yield the desired scalability.

PART

IX

CH

38

SQL Operations that Can Be Parallelized

When a SQL statement is submitted, it is first parsed and then executed. After parsing and before executing, the optimizer builds the execution plan. The Query Coordinator process examines the operations in the execution plan to determine whether the individual operations can be parallelized.

Prior to version 8, Oracle could parallelize only SQL statements having queries or DDL operations, such as create index, create table, as select, and so on, whose execution plan involved a full scan of an existing table. In version 8, Oracle introduced parallel execution for insert, update, and delete operations.

The *Oracle8 Server Concepts Manual* mentions that Oracle8 enables the following operations to be parallelized:

- Table scan
- Nested loop join
- Sort merge join
- Hash join
- "Not in"
- Group by
- Select distinct

- Union and union all
- Aggregation
- PL/SQL functions called from SQL
- Order by
- Create table as select
- Create index
- Rebuild index
- Move partition
- Split partition
- Update
- Delete
- Insert...select
- Enable constraint(the table scan is parallelized)
- Star transformation

In addition to these operations Oracle8i can also parallelize `cube` and `rollup` operations.

As a rule of thumb, you can say that Oracle can parallelize any operation that involves a full table (partition) scan. Consider the following SQL statement:

```
select cust_id, sales_amt from sales_97 order by sales_amt;
```

The execution plan consists of a full-table scan of the `sales_97` table, assuming there is no index on these columns, followed by a sort on the `sales_amt` column. As shown in Figure 38.1, the scan and sort operations are divided and given to multiple processes. Both scanning and sorting are done simultaneously by different processes. Thus, PQO not only enables an operation to be done by multiple processes, but it also enables multiple operations in the same SQL statement to be executed simultaneously rather than one after another. It is possible because of the creator and consumer nature of these operations. In the example, the rows fetched by the table scan operation are given to sort operation without waiting for scan to finish.

Figure 38.1
Parallel execution involving a full-table scan followed by a sort.

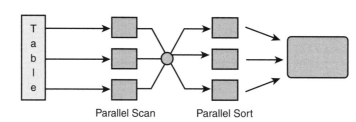

Parallel Scan   Parallel Sort

PART

IX

CH

38

Note

Dividing a SQL operation among multiple server processes is generally referred to as *intra-operation parallelism*, whereas executing multiple operations (from the same SQL statement) concurrently is known as *inter-operation parallelism*.

In the previous example, scan and sort operations have their own server processes. Thus, inter-operation parallelism assigns different sets of servers to each operation. Oracle can execute two operations simultaneously, in parallel, for a SQL statement. If the SQL statement has three or more operations that can be parallelized, the third operation waits until the first one finishes. The query slaves used by the first operation are then recycled and used by the third operation.

UNDERSTANDING THE DEGREE OF PARALLELISM

The number of parallel query slaves a SQL operation can use is called the *degree of parallelism*. Oracle determines the degree of parallelism considering various user inputs, instance initialization parameters, number of data files the table resides on, number of CPU in the system, and so on.

DETERMINING THE DEGREE OF PARALLELISM

The degree of parallelism for a given SQL statement is decided from the following, in the given order:

1. SQL statement level—The SQL statement can specify the degree of parallelism through the use of a parallel hint as follows:

   ```
   select /*+ PARALLEL (sales_97, 3) */
   cust_id, sales_amt from sales_97 order by sales_amt;
   ```

   In this example, Oracle uses three query slaves to perform the full table scan operation. The sort operation requires another three slaves. Thus, the SQL statement uses seven processes—six parallel query slaves and one shadow process—in all.

2. Object level—You set the degree of parallelism associated with a table, cluster, partition, and so on through the corresponding create and alter commands. You can query the degree of parallelism of an existing object from the data dictionary from USER_TABLES view's degree column, as follows:

   ```
   Alter table sales_97 parallel(degree,3);
   select degree from user_tables where table_name='SALES_97';
   ```

   The first statement sets the degree of parallelism for the table sales_97 to three. The second SQL statement queries the degree of parallelism for the sales_97 table. If multiple tables are involved in a SQL operation and each of them has a different degree of parallelism, the highest degree of parallelism becomes the degree of parallelism for that SQL operation. In the following example, the SQL operation is performed with a parallel degree of five:

```
alter table sales_97 parallel (degree 3);
alter table warehouse parallel (degree 5);
select /*+ parallel(s) parallel(w) */
w.location, s.sales_date, s.sales_value
from warehouse w, sales_97 s
where c.w_id = s.w_id
order by s.sales_value, w.location ;
```

3. Instance level—If Oracle fails to get the degree of parallelism in the previous two steps (that is, if the degree of parallelism is not specified by the user), it uses the default degree of parallelism.

The process of determining the default degree of parallelism has changed with version 7.3. In version 7.3 and above, Oracle uses the number of available CPU and number of disk drives (files, if it can not determine the disk affinity) to determine the default degree of parallelism, as follows:

```
Default degree of parallelism = Min (#CPU in the system, #disk drives the tables
is spread on)
```

If you are using RAID disk and OS striping so that a data file is striped across multiple disks, Oracle does not know of the underlying disk striping and assumes the file to be on one disk.

In 7.1 and 7.2, Oracle uses the default degree of parallelism as the minimum of the following:

```
Table size in number of blocks / PARALLEL_DEFAULT_SCANSIZE
```

```
PARALLEL_DEFAULT_MAX_SCANS (init.ora parameter)
```

The degree of parallelism you should use is dependent on your machine resources (which include CPU, memory, and the I/O bandwidth of your system), how the data is spread, the number of SQL statements executed concurrently, and other loads on your system. You need to give considerable thought when deciding the degree of parallelism. It is important that you have enough system resources for the given degree of parallelism, otherwise you might introduce problems, such as excessive paging, I/O bottlenecks, and so on, that might be counterproductive.

WHEN ENOUGH QUERY SLAVES ARE NOT AVAILABLE

When the degree of parallelism for a SQL operation is decided, Query Coordinator tries to enlist the available (already created but idle) servers. If available servers are not sufficient, it creates them. If it cannot create the required query slaves due to the MAX_PARALLEL_SERVERS limit, it creates as many as possible and uses the available slaves for parallel execution.

> **Note**
>
> In versions older than version 7.3, Oracle executes the parallel operation with as many query slaves as possible, and if no query slaves are available, the query is executed by the shadow process itself, that is, serially.

With version 7.3 you can specify the minimum number of slaves required to execute the query by using the `init.ora` parameter `PARALLEL_MIN_PERCENT`. The default value of this parameter is `0`, which simulates behavior prior to 7.3. Any integer value from `0` to `100` can be specified for this parameter. When this parameter is set to a nonzero value, Oracle determines the minimum number of query slaves required for an operation as follows:

```
Minimum slaves required = Parallel_min_pecent * Degree of parallelism /100
```

An error is signaled to the user and the SQL operation is aborted when Oracle cannot get the requisite number of query slaves as determined by the previous formula.

UNDERSTANDING THE QUERY SERVER PROCESSES

When an Oracle instance is started, it also starts the number of parallel query servers as defined by the `PARALLEL_MIN_SERVERS` initialization parameter. If you have multiple Oracle instances running on a system, each instance has its own set of independent parallel query slaves. Similarly, in an Oracle parallel server environment, each instance has its own set of parallel query slaves. If at any time the instance requires more query servers, it creates them. However, the maximum number of parallel query slaves created at any time cannot exceed the `PARALLEL_MAX_SERVERS` initialization parameter. Idle servers are shut down after they have been idle for the time designated by `PARALLEL_SERVER_IDLE_TIME`, which is specified in minutes. However, the minimum number of servers active at any time does not go below `PARALLEL_MIN_SERVERS`.

In the Oracle parallel server environment, a SQL operation can execute on multiple instances. The maximum number of instances that can participate in a parallel SQL execution is determined by the `PARALLEL_MAX_INSTANCE` `init.ora` parameter at the instance where the execution is started. The Query Coordinator also resides on the same instance where the SQL statement is started.

ANALYZING OBJECTS TO UPDATE STATISTICS

Oracle uses a cost-based optimizer during parallel execution. If it finds the statistics associated with a table in the data dictionary, it uses them. If the statistics are not present, it collects them on-the-fly. If the statistics present with an object are outdated, Oracle might use the wrong execution plan. You should regularly analyze the objects to keep the latest data dictionary's statistics. Also, after any major data manipulation operation on a table, you should reanalyze the table.

UNDERSTANDING THE 9,3,1 ALGORITHM

Oracle uses various algorithms for parallel execution. Prior to version 8, it mainly parallelized operations based on a full-table scan. The simple scheme of parallelizing a table scan involves the following:

1. Determining the degree of parallelism as described in the previous section.

2. Finding out the high water mark for the table and thus detecting the total number of occupied data blocks in the table.

3. Dividing the blocks to be scanned into equal parts by dividing the total blocks with available query servers. Now you are almost ready to assign equal work to each query slave. However, if the data is not evenly distributed or access to part of the data is slower, some slaves might finish their work earlier than others. To address this problem and optimize the performance, Oracle uses the 9,3,1 algorithm.

4. Oracle further divides each work partition into three chunks. The first part is 9/13 of the whole. The second and third are 3/13 and 1/13 of the whole. Thus the whole table is divided into Degree of parallelism * 3 partitions.

5. The Query Coordinator now assigns all the 9/13 parts to each of the query slaves. The 3/13 and 1/13 parts are assigned subsequently, when the query slaves finish their earlier assigned work. This ensures the almost equal use of all the slaves.

Please note that 9,3,1 is one of the basic algorithms Oracle uses for parallel execution. Oracle parallel execution takes into consideration various other factors, as follows:

1. In the Oracle parallel server environment, the Oracle work division algorithm also takes into account the disk affinity and so on.

2. Oracle8 parallelizes by partitions when parallelizing partitioned indexes and tables.

UNDERSTANDING PARALLEL DML

As noted earlier, Oracle8 can also parallelize insert, update, and delete operations. To execute an insert, update, or delete operation in parallel, you need to issue the following command:

```
alter session enable parallel dml ;
```

If you do not issue this command, the DML operation is executed in serial, even if the SQL statement contains explicit hints or parallel clauses to parallelize it.

Update and delete operations can be parallelized only across partitions. However, an insert operation can be parallelized within a partition. Thus, for an update and delete operation, the maximum degree of parallelism can not be greater than the number of partitions. Thus, the following SQL statement deletes all the sales transactions of less than $100 from the table sales_97, which has three partitions:

```
delete /*+ parallel (s,3) */
from sales_97 s where sales_value < 100 ;
```

The following are hints related to Parallel Query and parallel DML Operations:

- **PARALLEL** You can use a PARALLEL hint to specify the degree of parallelism in a SQL operation. Oracle7 enables you to control the degree of parallelism for a table scan operation with PARALLEL hints. In Oracle8, you can use hints to control the degree of parallelism for INSERT, UPDATE, and DELETE operations, in addition to a table scan operation. The syntax of parallel hint is

  PARALLEL (<table_name>, *m*,*n*)

  m equals the number of parallel servers desired for a SQL operation, and *n* equals the number of instances that should execute the SQL operation. It is useful only in an OPS environment.

- **NOPARALLEL** If you want to ignore the parallel degree associated with an object and want the SQL operation to be performed in serial mode, use the NOPARALLEL hint.

- **APPEND** You can use the APPEND hint to control the parallel execution during an INSERT operation. It is the default mode of the parallel insert operation, and it uses new free blocks for the inserted data; existing free space in the blocks is not used.

- **NOAPPEND** This hint enables you to use existing free space in the blocks before allocating new blocks for the inserted data.

- **PARALLEL_INDEX** Oracle8 enables parallel execution for index range scanning of a partitioned index. You can use the PARALLEL_INDEX hint to this effect. Its syntax is similar to the PARALLEL hint.

PARALLEL EXECUTION IN OPS ENVIRONMENT

Oracle enables multiple Oracle Parallel Server (OPS) instances to participate in parallel execution of a SQL operation. If there are four Oracle instances and you execute the parallel operation with degree of parallelism equal to two, two parallel query slaves are used at each instance.

You can control the number of participating instances by using the following:

- Parallel hint
- Parallel instance group

INSTANCE_GROUPS enable you to group instances in the desired manner. The PARALLEL_INSTANCE_GROUP parameter defines the default group on which the instance's parallel operation is executed. PARALLEL_INSTANCE_GROUP is a dynamic parameter, and you can change the value of the PARALLEL_INSTANCE_GROUP parameter at the session or system level by using ALTER SESSION/SYSTEM... command. When a parallel operation is started, all the instances belonging to the INSTANCE_GROUP defined by the PARALLEL_INSTANCE_GROUP parameter are involved in the execution.

Consider a four-instance OPS configuration with the following initialization parameter:

```
Instance 1 -> INSTANCE_GROUPS = g_12, g_13, g_14, g_123
PARALLEL_INSTANCE_GROUP = g_12

Instance 2 -> INSTANCE_GROUPS = g_12, g_23, g_24, g_123
PARALLEL_INSTANCE_GROUP = g_123

Instance 3 -> INSTANCE_GROUPS = g_13, g_23, g_34
PARALLEL_INSTANCE_GROUP = g_34

Instance 4 -> INSTANCE_GROUPS = g_14, g_24, g_34
PARALLEL_INSTANCE_GROUP = g_12
```

When a user logs on the first instance and executes a parallel SQL operation (without issuing an alter session set `parallel_instance_group` command), the operation is executed by parallel server processes from instances 1 and 2. However, if the user executes

```
alter session set parallel_instance_group g_123 ;
```

before issuing the SQL statement, the operation is executed on instances 1, 2, and 3.

CHANGES IN ORACLE8I

Oracle has made several changes in Oracle8i with respect to the parallel query option. However, these changes do not impact the technique for the parallel execution. Most of the changes have been made to automate the determination of the degree of parallelism and the tuning process. Oracle's objective behind this is to make this feature as transparent to the user as possible. The objective is to free the DBA from spending too much time on tuning the parallel operations and let Oracle do the job on-the-fly taking into consideration the system resources that are available at the start of the query.

Tip #112	Set PARALLEL_AUTOMATIC_TUNING= TRUE, when you want Oracle to determine the behavior of parallel execution. Also set PARALLEL_ADAPTIVE_MULTI_USER=TRUE, for Oracle to consider the free system resources to determine the degree of parallelism at the start of the parallel operation.

TUNING PARALLEL QUERY

Parallel Query Option is a very powerful tool, and if used effectively, it can reduce the processing time by several orders. However, it is very resource-consuming and the achieved performance gain is highly dependent on the data distribution. You should have enough CPU and memory resources to support the active parallel query slaves. Also, plan your data appropriately so that you do not have I/O bottleneck during parallel processing.

TROUBLESHOOTING

How does Oracle decide the degree of parallelism for a parallel operation?

Normally, Oracle determines the degree of parallelism as follows:

1. A Parallel Clause or the Hint in SQL statement is given the first consideration.

2. An object's (table/index) degree of parallelism from its definition in the data dictionary is used as the next criterion.

3. Oracle uses the number of available CPUs and number of disk drives the object is spread on to determine the default degree of parallelism. (Refer the section "Determining the Default Degree of Parallelism" for more details.)

4. In Oracle8i, if the parameter PARALLEL_ADAPTIVE_MULTI_USER is set to TRUE, Oracle can reduce the degree of parallelism depending on the CPU and disk resources available at the start of the query.

Is it necessary to analyze the tables before performing parallel operations on them?

Oracle parallel query operations always use a cost based optimizer. If the table statistics are not present, Oracle collects the statistics on-the-fly. However, if the statistics are present, Oracle uses them. You should ensure that the tables are re-analyzed to update the statistics in the dictionary after any major DML operations. Outdated statistics may lead to an inefficient execution plan.

Presently, a table contains very few rows as compared to what it had in the past; do the operations still using parallel query take more (or the same) time?

A parallel query operation always scans the table up to its present HWM, high water mark, (the highest formatted block which contained data). Deleting rows from the table does not lower the high water mark and hence does not improve the performance of parallel SQL operations involving the table. It is advisable to rebuild a table after a massive delete operation to lower the HWM.

CHAPTER 39

PARALLEL SERVER MANAGEMENT

In this chapter

UNDERSTANDING THE BENEFITS OF PARALLEL SERVER

Oracle Parallel Server is useful for two basic types of applications: those that need high availability and those that can be scaled along with the underlying hardware. In order for parallel instances to run, they need more components than a single instance database. In this chapter, you will find out what these additional components are and how you can use them to manage your Parallel Server database.

Parallel Server is an option that allows two or more instances to mount the same database concurrently. With multiple instances, you increase the number or the net size of a number of resources available to the database. These resources include

- System global area, containing shared pool space and database buffer cache
- Background processes such as database writer (DBWR), log writer (LGWR), and parallel processing slaves
- User processes
- SQL*Net or Net8 listeners

Figure 39.1 shows how these resources multiply with parallel instances. As you can imagine, these increases allow the database to process more work for more users, and this is the primary benefit most people attribute to Parallel Server. As you add more hardware nodes, you can also start extra instances, providing you with a long-term scalability strategy.

Tip #113	Parallel Server can help you increase the number of tasks you are doing without increasing the duration of each task or reducing the overall time taken by concurrent tasks for the same number of users. This is achieved if the work can be spread around the available instances to avoid contention on the available resources.

You can configure the various instances running in a Parallel Server database with different initialization parameters. This allows you to tune some instances for users who perform heavy transaction processing and tune others to best support batch report programs and optimize online decision support activities, depending on your user requirements. You might also need to configure your instances differently if they are running on nodes with dissimilar capacity, such as memory size, number of CPUs, or CPU power.

Additionally, the extra instances can provide a security blanket for the users and for the database administrator. There are a number of events, scheduled and unscheduled, that can cause an Oracle instance to stop running. In a single instance database, a stopped instance closes all access to the database for the users and their applications. With parallel instances, the users who were working on a stopped instance can reconnect to a still-running instance. For users of Oracle8, the reconnection can be automatic if the application uses special Oracle Call Interface (OCI) calls and the Net8 configuration files have the correct entries. You can design your system with Parallel Server to include one or more spare instances to support all your users if their primary instances are unavailable.

Figure 39.1
Single instance versus Parallel Server instances and resources.

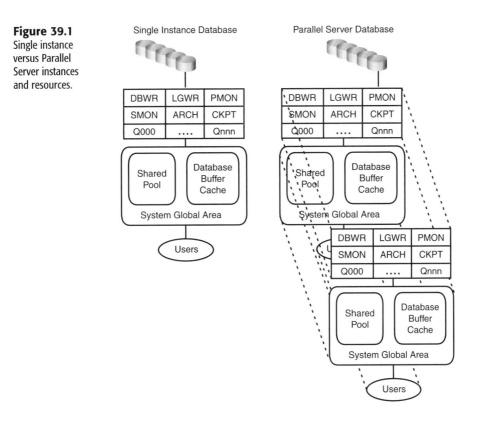

If your hardware can support sufficient nodes, you can make use of the scalability features as well as the failover capability of Parallel Server in the same database. You simply have to reserve instances on one or more nodes for use in a failover situation rather than using them all concurrently for performance gains. It is important when planning a multi-instance database to make a clear distinction between these two functions. Shifting work onto an instance being kept free for failover reasons is going to cause contention and performance problems when it is needed by users from a failed instance.

SINGLE INSTANCE VERSUS PARALLEL SERVER DATABASES

To fully understand how a parallel database is structured, you need to have a good grasp of the distinction between *databases* and *instances*. A database consists of a set of files stored on disk; these include datafiles, redo log files, and control files. An instance comprises a set of memory structures and processes. The major structure is called the System, or Shared Global Area (SGA), and the required background processes are the database writer (DBWR), redo log writer (LGWR), system monitor (SMON), and process monitor (PMON). If you are running Oracle8, Version 8.0 or 8.1, the CKPT process is also a mandatory background process. There are a number of optional processes that you can initiate, typically by setting parameters in the initialization file.

Oracle Parallel Server requires additional background processes. Some of these are started with initialization parameters and others start automatically like the mandatory processes for non-parallel instances. Which processes you need and can control with initialization parameters depends on the version of Oracle you are running, but you will always require at least one lock (LCK) process that is responsible for managing inter-instance locking. Later in this chapter, you will look at the details of the differences between Oracle Parallel Server versions and the parameters used to control the special background processes.

Tip #114	You should be prepared to modify the init.ora parameters you have used for a single instance database so that the multiple instances used by Parallel Server can interact successfully. Some parameters must be set identically in each instance and others may need to reflect the use of each individual instance.

You will also need to know how to start up an instance in parallel mode. A normal, exclusive Oracle instance locks the control file for use by any other instance when it starts up. To avoid setting this lock, the instance must be opened in parallel, or shared, mode. In Version 7.3, you do this by including the either of the keywords, PARALLEL or SHARED, in the STARTUP statement in command mode, or by using the SHARED radio button on the instance management screens of the GUI database management tools. In Oracle8, you need to set the parameter, PARALLEL_SERVER, to TRUE in your initialization file.

Note	The instance management GUI screens are part of Oracle's Enterprise Manager product that runs only on NT platforms. Special Parallel Server management GUI tools also exist but they are also limited to NT platforms. However, these tools can be used for databases using other operating systems by configuring the NT platforms as clients for the database server.

VENDOR INTERFACES

Parallel Server runs a single database using two or more concurrent instances. The hardware must support this configuration by allowing independent nodes to share the disks where the database is stored. Many vendors support multiple nodes in UNIX clusters and a number are already providing two or four node clusters under NT. Some vendors support clusters using proprietary operating systems. In all cases, the vendor has to provide software to manage the cluster and the access to the shared disks. This might be part of a proprietary operating system or be one or more additional products. Oracle certifies Parallel Server on platforms where it can successfully interface with these software functions. In some cases, Oracle might limit the number of nodes on which Parallel Server can be run, even though the vendor might be able to configure more.

In order for the various instances to talk with each other, they have to make use of the hardware's internode connectivity and disk management software. The interface between the Oracle code and the vendor code has changed over time. In Version 7.3, Oracle required the hardware vendor to provide a Distributed Lock Manager (DLM) to provide a mechanism for Oracle to pass messages between the instances on different nodes. This architecture is shown in Figure 39.2. In some cases, Oracle worked closely with the vendor to write the required code for the DLM, other vendors already had cluster management software that could talk to Oracle without much modification. In the case of NT platforms, the Version 7.3 Parallel Server option was not released until the Oracle8 product was well along in its development. Consequently, to avoid rewriting the code for the new release, the NT version of Parallel Server was based on the Oracle8 architecture.

Figure 39.2
Version 7.3 Parallel Server interface to the DLM.

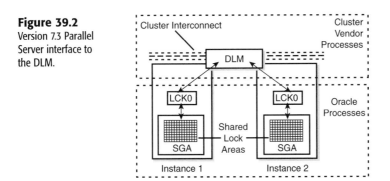

In Oracle8, Version 8.0, Oracle integrated the DLM into its own code. The Integrated DLM (IDLM) talks to the vendor's software through a series of services collectively known as Group Membership Services (GMS). These are responsible for managing the cluster, handling shared disk access, and passing messages between the nodes on behalf of the IDLM. Some vendors even provided startup and shutdown interfaces so that Oracle could start and stop the GMS along with the instances on each node. A diagram of a Version 8.0 configuration is shown in Figure 39.3.

Figure 39.3
Version 8.0 Parallel Server interface to GMS.

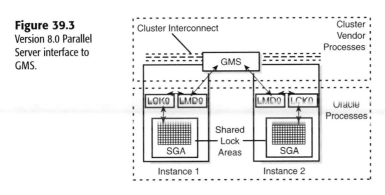

In order to improve the performance and the capability of Oracle to identify and diagnose problems, the architects decided to incorporate most of the GMS functionality into the kernel when they developed Oracle8i, version 8.1, Parallel Server. This required adding code to the background process, LMON, the monitoring process for the IDLM. The functions

PART

IX

CH

39

performed by GMS that were not incorporated into the IDLM remain as Cluster Group Services (CGS) and are still provided by the cluster vendor. This improvement reduced the reliance of Oracle on the vendor's code and cluster implementation details to a bare minimum while providing a more seamless product to manage. Figure 39.4 shows a diagram of Oracle8*i*, version 8.1, architectural components for cluster access.

Figure 39.4
Version 8.1 Parallel
Server Interface to
Cluster Group
Services.

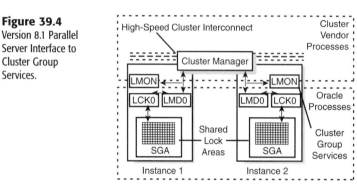

No matter which release you are using, the details of the Oracle/vendor interface depend on the vendor's architecture. You will need to read the Oracle Parallel Server installation manual related to your particular hardware, software, and Oracle release to find out the details of this configuration. There might be some special vendor-supplied code you have to run, and you will have to set parameters in your initialization file to configure the background jobs required by your specific release.

There is one final note for you to consider when planning for Parallel Server if you are running on a UNIX or NT operating system. On these platforms, you will have to put your database files into raw partitions in order for them to be shared successfully by multiple instances. This includes the datafiles, control files, and online redo log files. In some cases, this might be beneficial because of some performance improvements in disk writes, but raw devices are generally more difficult for the system administrator to manage. In addition to the operating system documentation for your system, you can also find details about raw devices in the Oracle Installation and Configuration guide for your specific database release, usually in a chapter named "Raw Devices."

USING THE PARALLEL CACHE MANAGEMENT LOCK PROCESS

Parallel Server uses Parallel Cache Management (PCM) locks to control access to database blocks by the various instances. An instance is only allowed to access a block if it has the necessary PCM lock in the correct mode. In order to change the contents of a block with an INSERT, UPDATE, or DELETE operation, the instance must hold the PCM lock that covers the block in exclusive mode. To query the contents of a block, the instance is required to hold the requisite PCM lock in shared mode. PCM locks are passed between the instances on an as needed basis. As you might guess from the mode names, an exclusive mode can only be held by one instance at a time, whereas shared locks can be held by multiple instances concurrently. PCM locks are completely independent of row level locks, which Oracle continues to use in the same way as in a single instance database to ensure that only one user can change the contents of a row at a time.

Each parallel instance controls an LCK process to track the status of the PCM locks for that instance and to communicate lock requests between the instance and the DLM. Every PCM lock has a status with respect to each instance

- NULL when the lock is not in use
- SHARED when the lock is held in shared mode
- EXCLUSIVE when the instance currently owns the lock for its own use alone

The status of each lock is stored in a special area of the SGA known as the shared lock area. When a user needs a lock that is not currently owned or is owned in a SHARED mode but is required in EXCLUSIVE mode, the LCK process is responsible for posting the request for the lock status change to the DLM. Similarly, when the DLM receives a request for a lock status change, it sends a request to relinquish the lock to the LCK process on the instance where the PCM lock is currently held.

The DLM is responsible for the global allocation of locks across all instances and manages requests for locks made by the various instances. The DLM can allocate unused locks or recall locks from another instance to pass them on to a requesting instance. The DLM also maintains the current status of all locks, whether they are assigned to an instance or not. Prior to Oracle8, the DLM code was provided by either the operating system vendor or by Oracle, depending on the platform. Consequently, the commands you use to start and stop the DLM, and any files or parameters you need to configure it, will differ from platform to platform. A sample Oracle7 DLM configuration file is shown in Listing 39.1.

PART

IX

CH

39

LISTING 39.1 SAMPLE DLM CONFIGURATION FILE

```
                                                   SERVICE
#NODE NAME   IP ADDRESS       NODE ID    DOMAIN    PORT NUMBER
apple        123.45.678.001   1          0         1544
orange       123.45.678.002   2          0         1544
pear         123.45.678.003   3          0         1544
```

Whether you are using the Oracle7 with a separate DLM or Oracle8 with the IDLM, you need to confer with your platform-dependent Oracle installation/configuration guide for specific configuration information for the DLM. In Oracle7, the options tend to be very platform dependent because the DLM is provided by the vendor, whereas the IDLM is configured completely with parameters in your initialization file. The parameters are necessary to size the two background processes used by the DLM, LMD0, and LMON.

Assignment of PCM locks to the database data files is a critical task for the administrator of a multi-instance database. Too many locks cause performance degradation due to the memory requirements of the shared lock area and the DLM structures. If you don't assign sufficient locks, you can incur substantial block *pinging*.

IDENTIFYING AND PREVENTING EXCESSIVE BLOCK PINGING

Block pinging occurs when one instance needs a PCM lock that is currently held by another instance in EXCLUSIVE mode. Before releasing the lock, the owning instance wakes up its DBWR process to inspect the blocks covered by the lock. DBWR looks for any blocks that contain changes not yet flushed to disk and writes them back to the database files. This process of writing dirty blocks as part of the down conversion of the PCM lock is known as pinging. As you increase the number of blocks covered by a single lock, you also increase the likelihood that another instance might want the lock and thus introduce the potential for more block pings.

At the other end of the ping is the instance that requested the lock. On receiving the lock, this instance must read any blocks it needs into its buffer cache. It cannot rely on images of these blocks already held in its cache because the other instance could have changed the block while it held the exclusive lock. If the receiving instance needs all the blocks that were pinged to disk, the pings are considered to be *true pings*. However, if the receiving instance needed none or only some of the blocks pinged to disk, the unneeded block writes are considered to be *false pings*. See Figure 39.5 for a diagram of how these different types of ping occur.

Figure 39.5
How pinging occurs between instances.

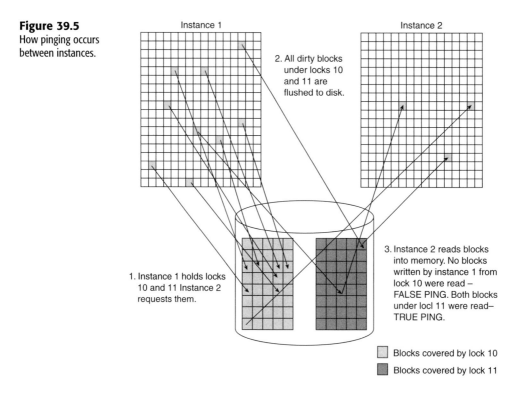

Instance 1

Instance 2

2. All dirty blocks under locks 10 and 11 are flushed to disk.

1. Instance 1 holds locks 10 and 11 Instance 2 requests them.

3. Instance 2 reads blocks into memory. No blocks written by instance 1 from lock 10 were read – FALSE PING. Both blocks under locl 11 were read– TRUE PING.

☐ Blocks covered by lock 10

■ Blocks covered by lock 11

While true pings might be unavoidable if the instances need access to exactly the same blocks on a regular basis, false pings constitute unnecessary overhead and need to be detected and decreased. The amount of pinging and false pinging you experience depends on your database design and on the settings of the PCM lock parameters in your initialization file.

Note

Pinging is not bad, but a necessary component of the Parallel Server architecture. Excessive pinging is a problem because it degrades performance. As you read this chapter, you will learn how to design a database that maintains an acceptable level of pinging.

For those of you who are using or plan to use Oracle8i, version 8.1, a new feature—Cache Fusion, Phase I—will help reduce pinging. When the Oracle8i, version 8.1, DLM receives a request for a shared PCM lock and it can easily construct the read-consistent block image needed by the requesting instance, it can avoid the ping. Rather than writing the block to disk for the other instance to read, the instance owning the exclusive PCM lock will use its Block Server Process (BSP) background process to build the required block image. It will use any of its rollback information required to make the block image consistent to the point in time at which the requesting instance contacted the IDLM. The BSP will then transmit that block image directly to the requesting instance across the high-speed node interconnect. Not only does this avoid a resource-intensive disk write and read, but the block image copy can be transferred without requiring the IDLM to change the exclusive status of the lock on the original instance. Figure 39.6 illustrates how Cache Fusion works in Oracle8i, version 8.1.

Figure 39.6
How Cache Fusion, Phase I, avoids pings.

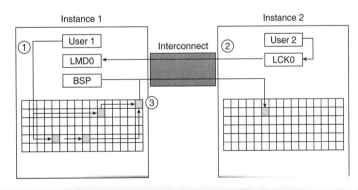

1. User1 on Instance 1 changes a block and related rollback blocks under an Exclusive PCM lock.
2. User2 requests the block for a query on Instance 2 and the LCK0 process contacts the LMD0 process on Instance 2 to downgrade the PCM to Shared status.
3. Instead of converting the lock, the BSP process builds an undo block in the buffer cache of Instance 1, using any necessary rollback information, and sends the completed block to Instance 1 directly over the interconnect.

USING PARALLEL CACHE MANAGEMENT LOCK PARAMETERS

You use a set of global cache management parameters to define the PCM lock environment for your instances. The global cache parameter names are prefixed with the string GC. Reflecting the architectural changes discussed earlier in each release of Oracle Parallel Server, these parameters differ slightly between versions. Table 39.1 lists the parameter names and descriptions and indicates in which version(s) they are valid.

TABLE 39.1   PCM LOCK MANAGEMENT PARAMETERS

Parameter Name	Description	7.3	8.0	8.1
GC_DB_LOCKS	Number of hash PCM locks	X(3)		
GC_DEFER_TIME	Time (1/100 seconds) to wait before responding to a ping request	X(3)	X(4)	
GC_FILES_TO_LOCKS	Allocates PCM locks to datafiles	X(3)	X(4)	X(5)
GC_FREELIST_GROUPS	Number of hash locks for freelist group header blocks	X(3)		
GC_LATCHES	Number of locks reserved for latch management (only in 8.0.4)	X(3)		
GC_LCK_PROCS	Number of lock processes (LCK0, LCK1, etc.) to	X(3)	X(4)	
	start			
GC_RELEASABLE_LOCKS	Number of fine grain PCM locks	X(3)	X(4)	X(5)
GC_ROLLBACK_ LOCKS	Number locks for rollback segments (just hash locks for header blocks prior Version 8.0) to	X(3)	X(4)	X(5)
GC_ROLLBACK_ SEGMENTS	Number of hash locks for rollback segment undo blocks	X(3)		
GC_SAVE_ROLLBACK__ LOCKS	Number of hash locks for deferred rollback segment blocks	X(3)		
GC_SEGMENTS	Number of hash locks for header blocks other than rollback segments	X(3)		
GC_TABLESPACES	Number of hash locks for tablespace ALTER ONLINE/ OFFLINE commands	X(3)		

You can leave many of these parameters at their default values, as do many DBAs. Of course, you need to monitor your database performance to ensure that you are not creating unnecessary overhead that could be avoided by changing these values. But the most serious performance problems with Parallel Server tend to result from excessive pinging and lock conversions caused by choosing inopportune values for the GC_RELEASABLE_LOCKS and GC_FILES_TO_LOCKS parameters. Further, each lock consumes space within the DLM as well as in the shared lock area of each instance's SGA. If you define too many locks, you can use memory for PCM lock management for which other database operations need to compete.

As you can see from Table 39.1, there are two types of PCM locks: hash locks and fine grain locks, also known as data block address (dba) locks. These two types of locks have one important difference. When a hash PCM lock is acquired by an instance, it is not released back to the DLM unless it is required by another instance. It is possible, therefore, for an instance to obtain a hash lock and never to release it until the instance shuts down. However, a fine grain lock is only held by the instance while it is using the block(s) being managed by the lock. After that, the lock is returned to the DLM for use by another or even the same instance, if it is needed.

In general, you should use hash locks for query-intensive applications because instances can acquire the same locks in shared mode. As long as the blocks are not updated by any instance, these locks will be held indefinitely by every instance performing queries. You can define these hash locks to span many blocks, which reduces the total number of locks and hence memory needed for the instance. If you also define the locks to cover contiguous blocks, you will improve the performance of full table scans that read sets of adjacent blocks. In transaction-intensive databases you should consider fine grain locks. Each of these locks covers a single block or possibly a very few related blocks. Consequently, the possibility for pinging, especially false pinging, is greatly reduced.

PART

IX

CH

39

Caution

You should not automatically use fine grain locks unless you expect severe contention for PCM locks between instances. Fine grain locks cause additional overhead because they are released automatically when an instance is done with the related blocks, even if another instance is not in need of them.

Of course, if you are using Parallel Server on a two node system for *failover* purposes, where only one instance will have active users at any time, you can use a minimal number of hash locks regardless of the type of database activity. Locks do not serve their usual interinstance function in a parallel environment used solely for failover.

How do you set values for the GC_RELEASABLE_LOCKS and GC_FILES_TO_LOCKS parameters to achieve the required PCM lock distribution? First, you should be aware that in Oracle7, as opposed to Oracle8 and Oracle8i, the default behavior is slightly different. In Oracle7, Version 7.3, the default mechanism is hash locking and the parameter GC_DB_LOCKS determines how many hash locks are available for files which don't have PCM locks assigned to them with the GC_FILES_TO_LOCKS parameter. Files not listed in this parameter will have unassigned locks distributed evenly across them. Figure 39.7 illustrates how a database configured with only 10 hash locks—not that such a database is likely to exist outside of this example—would have those 10 locks assigned by the default behavior. Figure 39.7 is simplified for the purpose of this illustration. The first block in a datafile is not necessarily covered by the lowest numbered PCM lock assigned to it, but by using a hash algorithm.

Figure 39.7
Default allocation of hashed PCM locks.

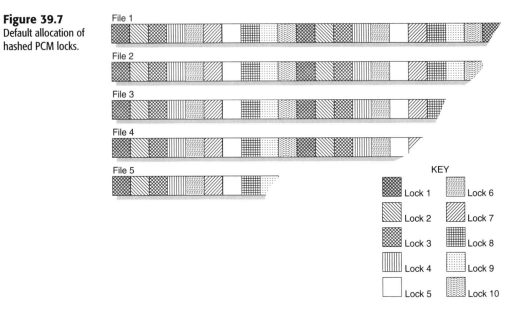

As of Oracle8, version 8.0, the default locking mechanism is fine grain locking, with the number of releasable locks being the same as your DB_BLOCK_BUFFERS value. By default, an Oracle8 and Oracle8*i* database has no locks preassigned to the datafiles. Whenever a block is needed by an instance, one of the fine grain locks from the releasable pool is assigned to cover it. When the block is no longer needed, the lock is released and becomes available for the next block that needs it.

When assigning PCM locks, you do not need to assign any locks to tablespaces in the following categories:

- READ ONLY mode
- TEMPORARY mode
- Contains only rollback segments
- Contains only temporary segments

Leave the file ID numbers for these tablespaces out of the GC_FILES_TO_LOCKS parameter to avoid assigning unnecessary locks.

Tip #115

> By placing all your read-only segments into their own tablespaces, you can alter these tablespaces to be read only and thus reduce the number of PCM locks needed. Similarly, you can decrease the number of locks you have to assign by using the TEMPORARY keyword when defining tablespaces for your temporary segments. This prevents any other types of segment from being created in these tablespaces, so you can safely assign zero PCM locks to their datafiles.
>
> Additionally, you should reserve tablespaces to contain only rollback segments because you will not need to assign PCM locks to the related datafiles, just to the rollback segments themselves. However, there is no special keyword to ensure these tablespaces are kept free of other types of segments.

PCM Locks in Version 7.3

If you define hash locks with the GC_DB_LOCKS parameter in Version 7.3, they will be assigned evenly across the datafiles (refer to Figure 39.7). You will almost certainly want to override this default organization and allocate these locks to your datafiles in the proportions best suited to your applications and database design. You will use the GC_FILES_TO_LOCKS parameter in your initialization file to accomplish this. You must leave some locks unassigned so that Oracle has a pool of spare locks to allocate to datafiles not identified in this parameter, or to datafiles you might need to add. The GC_FILES_TO_LOCKS parameter has the following syntax:

```
GC_FILES_TO_LOCKS =
➥"file_list=locks:file_list=locks:file_list=locks"
where

file_list    is a file id number, or multiple file id numbers separated by
commas forindividual files, or dashes for inclusive sets
    locks        is the number of locks.
```

You can include as many different file lists as you need, with a colon separating each file list and lock count value. Note that the complete set of entries must be enclosed in double quotation marks and there cannot be blank spaces in the entry. Here is an example of a valid parameter that assigns a total of 1,005 locks.

```
GC FILES TO LOCKS = "1=100:2-5=500:6,8,12=400:7,9-11=5"
```

File 1 receives 100 locks, files 2–5 share another 500, files 6, 8, and 12 share 400 more locks, and files 7, 9, 10, and 11 share 5 locks. Figure 39.8 shows how the five locks on files 7, 9, 10, and 11 could be allocated to these files, with the first lock in each file being dependent on the hashing algorithm. Any files that are not listed in the parameter will be covered by spare locks. This will be the balance of the locks assigned by GC_DB_LOCKS but not allocated by GC_FILES_TO_LOCKS. In the preceding case, there would be GC_DB_LOCKS minus 1,005 spare locks which could be allocated to files in the default round-robin fashion as shown earlier in Figure 39.7.

PART

IX

CH

39

Figure 39.8
Allocation of hash PCM locks where GC_FILES_TO_LOCKS="...7,9-11=5".

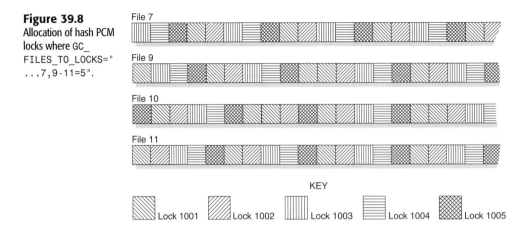

If you want the locks to cover contiguous sets of blocks, you can use the grouping operator, the exclamation point (!), to indicate the number of blocks per group. For example, to cover 10 blocks with each hash lock on files 7, 9, 10, and 11 from the previous example, you would rewrite the parameter as

```
GC_FILES_TO_LOCKS = "1=100:2-5=500:6,8,12=400:7,9-11=5!10"
```

Figure 39.9 shows you how these locks are allocated to the first few blocks in each of these files.

Figure 39.9
Allocation of hash PCM locks where GC_FILES_TO_LOCKS="...7,9-11=5!10".

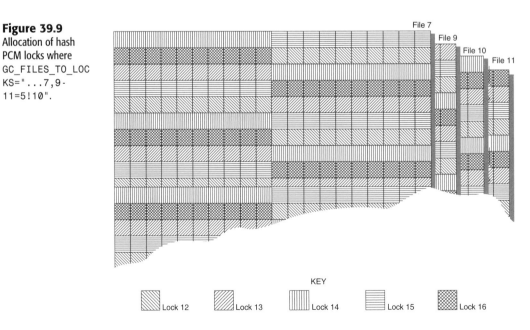

Another option that saves you typing and to shortens the length of the parameter string is to use the keyword EACH. This allocates the same number of locks to each of the files in a file list. Rewriting the preceding example as

```
GC_FILES_TO_LOCKS = "1=100:2-5=500:6,8,12=400EACH:7,9-11=5!10"
```

you would allocate a total of 1,805 locks, with files 6, 8, and 12 each obtaining 400 locks.

If you would prefer to use releasable locks in your Version 7.3 database, you need to modify the global cache parameters slightly from their defaults. First you need to set the number of fine grain locks required with the GC_RELEASABLE_LOCKS parameter. This must be set no less than the value for your DB_BLOCK_BUFFERS parameter, and can be higher if you want. Next decide if you want to use all fine grain locks or if you want to mix fine grain with hash locks. The former is accomplished by setting GC_DB_LOCKS to 0. The second option requires setting the individual parameters for each of the lock categories after setting both GC_DB_LOCKS and GC_RELEASABLE_LOCKS to non-zero values.

To use fine grain locks instead of hash locks on a particular category of locks, set the related parameter to 0. The parameters and lock categories you can control are shown in Table 39.1. You can also assign fine grain locks to your database segments by allocating zero locks to them in the GC_FILES_TO_LOCKS parameter. Listing 39.2 is an extract from a parameter file that sets fine grain locking on all segment header blocks as well as on files 13–17.

LISTING 39.2   SAMPLE ENTRIES FROM AN ORACLE7 PARALLEL INSTANCE PARAMETER FILE

```
DB_BLOCK_BUFFERS = 1000        # Total block buffers
GC_DB_LOCKS = 500                  # Total hash locks
GC_RELEASABLE_LOCKS = 1000     # Total fine grain locks
                      # Assign fine grain locks to:
GG_SEGMENTS = 0               # (a) segment header blocks
GC_FREELIST_GROUPS = 0        # (b) freelist header blocks
GC_ROLLBACK_SEGMENTS = 0      # (c) rollback segment header blocks
GC_FILES_TO_LOCKS = "13-17=0"  # (d) datafiles 13 through 17
GC_ROLLBACK_BLOCKS = 200         # Assign hash locks to rollback blocks
```

The datafiles not included in Listing 39.2 will share hash locks. There are slightly more than 500 hash locks available because Oracle uses an internal algorithm to increase the number beyond the value you set in GC_DB_LOCKS. Of these, 200 are assigned to the rollback segment undo blocks, leaving just over 300 to be allocated to the unlisted files in the normal round robin fashion.

Fine grain locks might not be your best option for segment header blocks, as used in Listing 39.2, unless you have a very busy database with lots of active instances, such as a massively parallel processing (MPP) platform running an online transaction processing (OLTP) system. However, the default number of hash locks assigned to certain lock categories might be inadequate. The two you should probably change are GC_SEGMENTS and GC_ROLLBACK_SEGMENTS. The former should be set to the total number of tables and indexes you have in your database and the latter to the number of rollback segments.

In Version 7.3, you can assign fine grain PCM locks to cover contiguous sets of blocks as discussed earlier with respect to hash locks. To set the grouping character for fine grain locks in GC_FILES_TO_LOCKS, you must use the value of 0 for the number of locks or else the files will revert to hash locking. The following line is taken from a parameter file where both hash and fine grain locks are used, some with and some without the grouping option. The zeroes on the right side of the equals signs enforce fine grain locking on files 9–14 and 18; and the ! causes locks to be grouped on sets of 20 contiguous blocks in files 9–14 and sets of 10 blocks in files 19–22.

```
GC_FILES_TO_LOCKS = "1=50:5-8=100EACH:9-14=0!20:15,18=0:16-17,19-22=1000!10"
```

PCM LOCKS IN ORACLE8

As you can see from Table 39.1, you have less global cache parameters to deal with in a database using Oracle8 compared to an Oracle7 database. Nevertheless, you actually have many additional options on how to assign locks. First, you should note that the default locking mechanism is fine grain rather than hash and that since version 8.0, Oracle has assumed the responsibility for assigning the locks to many lock categories. Second, hash locks can behave as they did in Oracle 7.3 or they can assume some of the characteristics of fine grain locks. Third, the locks on rollback segment undo blocks are assigned using similar syntax to the GC_FILES_TO_LOCKS parameter. After a particular type of lock is assigned to a lock or set of locks, it will behave just as it would in Version 7.3. A non-releasable hash lock, the default type, will not be relinquished by an instance unless requested to do so by the DLM on behalf of another instance; a fine grain or releasable hash lock will be released as soon as the instance finishes working with it.

The new parameter, GC_DEFER_TIME, introduced in Oracle8, Version 8.0, can help reduce pinging if set correctly. In Oracle7, or with GC_DEFER_TIME set to its default value of 0, requests made by an instance for PCM locks are satisfied as quickly as they can be processed. In some cases, two instances trying to use the same block, or a set of few blocks, at the same time, will each issue requests for the necessary PCM locks over and over again just to get a single transaction completed. The resulting lock conversions and block pings prevent either instance from completing work in a timely fashion. By setting the GC_DEFER_TIME to a positive number, indicating a number of 100ths of a second, you allow an instance to wait for that period of time before satisfying a DLM request to release a PCM lock. This can give the instance time to complete its work under the lock before releasing it, and any changed blocks, to the requesting instance.

The other changes in the Oracle8 parameters listed in Table 39.1 are not obvious from the table. First, there is a new option, mentioned earlier, that allows you to identify which hash locks you want to be releasable. This requires you to include the letter R to identify these locks, either by itself or as a prefix to the EACH keyword, in the GC_FILES_TO_LOCKS parameter. The entry in the following example shows the valid uses of this new feature.

```
GC_FILES_TO_LOCKS = "1=100:4-6=500R:7,9=200REACH"
```

Tip #116

Use the R (releasable) option for hash locks if you want to reduce the time it takes for an instance to start or restart following a planned or unplanned instance shut down. This can help you meet service level agreements. However, you should realize that the initial acquisition of each releasable hash lock on behalf of a user process will take longer and so there will be a slight performance degradation compared to hash locks acquired in the default manner.

You can see that the 500 hash locks shared by files 4–6 are releasable, as are the 400 locks assigned to files 7–9, each of which have 200 locks.

Using the R (releasable) option for hash locks does not cause the locks to behave exactly as fine grain releasable locks. Once acquired, the locks are not released, but are retained for the life of the instance and passed between instances just like any other hashed PCM lock. The purpose of the option is to allow the locks to be acquired only when first needed rather than during instance start up.

Caution

The R and EACH options must be combined in the order shown if both are needed. The expression EACHR is not valid.

The syntax for the other options in GC_FILES_TO_LOCKS remains unchanged between all current production releases of Oracle, Version 7.3, 8.0, and 8.1.

The second parameter that takes on a new form in Oracle8 is GC_ROLLBACK_LOCKS. Instead of providing a single number for the value, you need to use a format similar to GC_FILES_TO_LOCKS to assign different numbers of locks to each rollback segment. There is a stipulation that rollback segments cannot share locks, so when using this parameter you must include the EACH option if you specify ranges of rollback segments, as shown in this example:

```
GC_ROLLBACK_LOCKS = "1=50:2=100:3-10=200EACH:11-15=30EACH"
```

In this parameter, the values on the left of the equals signs are the ID numbers of the rollback segments, not file ID numbers as in GC_FILES_TO_LOCKS. You can correlate the ID numbers to the names of the rollback segments in your database by querying either DBA_ROLLBACK_SEGMENTS or GV$ROLLNAME. Both of these sources will show the undo segment number (USN) or the rollback segment ID number along with the segment name.

The final change to an existing global cache parameter, introduced in Oracle8, version 8.0, is to GC_RELEASABLE_LOCKS. This minor change allows you to set the value to be less than DB_BLOCK_BUFFERS. You can now set the parameter value to be the same in each instance even if the DB_BLOCK_BUFFERS value is not the same in all of them in order to reduce lock overhead.

Caution

Setting GC_RELEASABLE_LOCKS less than DB_BLOCK_BUFFERS is not recommended unless you are certain you don't need all the locks. There are only two types of situations where this is likely to be possible. First, if you have defined all the releasable locks with GC_FILES_TO_LOCKS to cover multiple blocks that will be needed in memory simultaneously and, second, if the balance of blocks in the buffer cache will always be ones covered by hash locks. If you don't have sufficient releasable locks available, applications will be forced to wait for a lock to become available if they are all in use, even if there is space in the buffer cache for the blocks requiring the locks.

PARALLEL SERVER INITIALIZATION PARAMETERS

As well as the global cache (GC_) parameters discussed in the previous section, you might need to use a few additional parameters in your init.ora file in order to manage your parallel database successfully. Table 39.2 shows in which release you can use these parameters.

TABLE 39.2 PCM LOCK MANAGEMENT PARAMETERS

Parameter Name	Version		
	7.3	**8.0**	**8.1**
ALLOW_PARTIAL_SN_RESULTS			X(4)
CACHE_SIZE_THRESHOLD		X(3)	X(4)
DELAYED_LOGGING_BLOCK_CLEANOUTS	X(2)	X(3)	X(4)
DML_LOCKS	X(2)	X(3)	X(4)
FREEZE_DB_FOR_FAST_INSTANCE_RECOVERY		X(3)	X(4)
IFILE	X(2)	X(3)	X(4)
INSTANCE_GROUPS		X(3)	X(4)
INSTANCE_NAME			X(4)
INSTANCE_NUMBER	X(2)	X(3)	X(4)
LM_LOCKS		X(3)	X(4)
LM_PROCS		X(3)	X(4)
LM_RESS		X(3)	X(4)
MAX_COMMIT_PROPAGATION_DELAY	X(2)	X(3)	X(4)
OPS_ADMIN_GROUP			X(4)
PARALLEL_DEFAULT_MAX_INSTANCES		X(3)	X(4)
PARALLEL_INSTANCE_GROUP		X(3)	X(4)
PARALLEL_SERVER		X(3)	X(4)

Parameter Name	Version		
	7.3	8.0	8.1
PARALLEL_SERVER_INSTANCES			X(4)
PARALLEL_TRANSACTION_RESOURCE_TIMEOUT		X(3)	
SERVICE_NAMES			X(4)
THREAD	X(2)	X(3)	X(4)

ALLOW_PARTIAL_SN_RESULTS

If set to TRUE this allows a query of the global transaction tables to complete even if not all the group's instances are online. If set to FALSE, a query that cannot access one or more instances in the queried group will fail. This should be set to TRUE to access global views (GV$_) in batch programs so that they will not fail. Set it to FALSE to use these views interactively to receive an alert should any instance fail.

CACHE_SIZE_THRESHOLD

The maximum number of blocks from any table to be cached in a single instance's database buffer cache. The default setting of 1/10 of DB_BLOCK_BUFFERS is generally the preferred value.

DELAYED_LOGGING_BLOCK_CLEANOUTS

When a transaction commits, the blocks changed by the transaction have to be updated to indicate the completion of the transaction in a process known as a *block cleanout*. In some situations the cleanout and the generation of the associated redo information is delayed until the blocks are accessed again. When such delayed cleanout occurs, the blocks are *dirtied* and require an exclusive PCM and potential ping to disk if another instance needs the blocks. By setting DELAYED_LOGGING_BLOCK_CLEANOUTS to TRUE, you prevent queries from performing delayed block cleanout. Therefore, only DML commands, which need exclusive PCM locks, and which dirty the block anyway, will perform the delayed cleanout. If you set the parameter to FALSE, queries can perform delayed block cleanout and thus generate potential pings.

DML_LOCKS

This parameter controls enqueues on tables being modified by concurrent transactions. Setting the value to 0 on all instances will improve performance, but the following statements will be disabled: DROP TABLE, CREATE INDEX, and explicit lock statements (LOCK TABLE). Assign a value of 0 when there is no requirement to use the preceding commands.

FREEZE_DB_FOR_FAST_INSTANCE_RECOVERY

This parameter controls whether all the instances are frozen while instance recovery for a failed instance is being processed. If set to TRUE, Oracle prevents all disk reads and writes except those associated with the recovery processing. This allows the recovery to complete faster but will effectively freeze all user activity until recovery completes. When set to FALSE, users can continue to work on parts of the database unaffected by the instance failure, but they will be competing for disk access with the recovery processing. Oracle chooses the default value for this parameter based on the ratio of files covered by hash versus fine grain locks, with FALSE being the default if all the online datafiles use hash locks.

IFILE

The IFILE parameter identifies another parameter file to be included within the current file. Use this parameter to include a common file containing all the parameters that need to be identical across all instances. Your release-specific documentation will identify which parameters must have the same value on all nodes. Ideally, keep this file on a shared file system so that every instance can read a single copy.

> **Caution**
>
> The included parameter file will be logically inserted where the IFILE parameter is included in the current init.ora file. If a parameter in the included file is repeated later in the current file, the instance will use the value from the current file rather than the included file because it will be the last one read.
>
> It is therefore best to place the IFILE parameter at the end of the instance's init.ora file. If you have organized your parameter file using some logical arrangement of parameters, such as by function, alphabetically, or by date of change, you might want to include the IFILE parameter twice; once in its logical location with a comment that it is repeated at the end of the file and again as the last entry in the file.

INSTANCE_GROUPS

INSTANCE_GROUPS names one or more instance groups to which the instance will be assigned. The group names can be identified, explicitly or implicitly, in the PARALLEL_INSTANCE_GROUP parameter. Only instances named by PARALLEL_INSTANCE_GROUP, whether set in init.ora or with an ALTER SYSTEM or ALTER SESSION command, will be selected to execute parallel operations.

INSTANCE_NAME

This parameter sets the name of the instance that is used in Net8 connections when you want to specify exactly which instance you want to connect to. It defaults to the instance identifier (SID) set in the operating system. See the SERVICE_NAMES parameter description for further information on connection options.

INSTANCE_NUMBER

INSTANCE_NUMBER associates the instance with the freelists in manually allocated extents and in specific freelist groups assigned to tables and indexes. If a table or index has fewer freelist groups assigned than the INSTANCE_NUMBER value, modulo arithmetic is applied to identify the freelist group to be used. The default value is 0 in which case an instance number is assigned at startup based on the order in which the instance starts relative to other instances.

LM_LOCKS

This parameter specifies the number of locks to be used by the IDLM. This value should be no less than:

RESOURCES + (RESOURCES × (NODES − 1)) / NODES

If your applications freeze while trying to execute DML, you might need to add more locks for the DLM by increasing this parameter above the suggested minimum value.

Tip #117

> The Oracle8 and Oracle8i Parallel Server Concepts and Administration manuals contain detailed explanations on the calculations needed to compute a reasonable value for the LM_LOCKS and the other IDLM parameters (LM_). They also provide sample worksheets you can use in performing these calculations.

LM_PROCS

LM_PROCS controls the number of Oracle processes that can use the lock management service. This value should be at least (Processes + *number of active instances*).

LM_RESS

LM_RESS defines the number of resources used by the DLM layer. This value should be

```
2 * ( ENQUEUE_RESOURCES + GC_FILES_TO_LOCKS
      GC_RELEASABLE_LOCKS + GC_ROLLBACK_LOCKS)
```

You are advised to not reduce the value below the result of this formula. If you don't know the value of one or more of the parameters needed for the calculation, you should start one instance and query the V$PARAMETER table for the values you need.

MAX_COMMIT_PROPAGATION_DELAY

This parameter sets the maximum length of time that any pair of instances will take before synchronizing their system change numbers (SCNs). You can choose to reduce the inter-instance overhead by reducing the frequency of such synchronization, but you risk instances seeing changes committed in one instance as being uncommitted in another if you do this. This is because the SCN is used to determine whether a query began before or after a change occurred. Generally, the default value is sufficient and should be used unless queries are failing to see sufficiently current changes required by the application. Faster propagation rates can hurt overall performance.

OPS_ADMIN_GROUP

Use this parameter to assign an instance group name to the instance to allow subsets of instances to be identified for administrative and reporting purposes. A query using a GV$_ view will only return results from instances with the same group name as the current instance.

PARALLEL_DEFAULT_MAX_INSTANCES

This parameter specifies the default number of instances to be employed by a query coordinator performing a parallel query when query is processed in parallel with an INSTANCES value of DEFAULT. The parameter's default value is derived from various operating system values and is optimal for most databases.

PARALLEL_INSTANCE_GROUP

PARALLEL_INSTANCE_GROUP identifies the group of instances that will be used by an operation executed in parallel across multiple instances. Only slave processes in the requested group, as set by the INSTANCE_GROUPS parameter, will be used for performing the parallel operations. This parameter is useful when the database is partitioned into subsets of related instances, but it can be overridden with the ALTER SYSTEM or ALTER SESSION commands if needed, to specify an alternative instance group.

PARALLEL_SERVER

This parameter identifies the instance as one that will be opened in parallel with other instances. It replaces the keyword PARALLEL, or optionally SHARED, of the STARTUP command in Version 7.3. Set to FALSE, the instance will be exclusive and must be the only one running against the database.

PARALLEL_SERVER_INSTANCES

Set this parameter to the total number of instances you expect to run in parallel against the database. Oracle uses this value to size the SGA appropriately for this number which, in many cases, makes better use of memory than leaving it at the default value.

PARALLEL_TRANSACTION_RESOURCE_TIMEOUT

This parameter sets the number of seconds for which an operation, being performed in parallel, will wait for a PCM lock or other shared resource to be released or downgraded to a compatible level by another instance. The operation will time out if the resource is not acquired in the specified time and such time outs are indicative of inter-instance contention, including potential deadlocks. You can assign a value of 0 to this parameter, which effectively sets the time out value to unlimited, preventing such time outs from occurring.

SERVICE_NAMES

Service names are used by Net8 to help balance the user load across multiple instances. This parameter identifies one or more service names to be associated with an instance. A user requests a Net8 connection to one of the available service names rather than to a specific instance. Net8 will assign the user's connection to one of the instances associated with the named service, using an algorithm to decide which of the available instances is least loaded.

THREAD

THREAD assigns the number of the redo log thread to be used by the instance. If the number is 0, the instance will attempt to acquire a free public thread of redo. If the number is non-zero, the instance will try to acquire the redo thread of that number, whether it is enabled as a private or a public thread. If a required thread is available, the instance will acquire it for its exclusive use; otherwise the instance will fail to open. A discussion of redo threads and the private and public options follows in a later section.

ROLLBACK SEGMENT CONSIDERATIONS FOR PARALLEL SERVER

A parallel instance will share the system rollback segment with the other instances operating against the database. You will need to add at least one additional rollback segment for each instance to use exclusively or else the instance will not start. After creating your database, which you have to do in an exclusive instance, you should use that instance to add the required rollback segments. Of course, you can add more than one rollback segment for each instance, following the same guidelines you would in a single instance database.

When creating rollback segments for Parallel Server, you can use private or public segments. Although they require a little more work initially, private rollback segments give you more control and are easier to manage in the long run. If you use private rollback segments, which are the default type, you will need to list their names in the ROLLBACK_SEGMENTS parameter of their associated initialization file. For public rollback segments, you need the PUBLIC keyword in the CREATE ROLLBACK SEGMENT command. You also need to set the two parameters, TRANSAC-TIONS and TRANSACTIONS_PER_ROLLBACK_SEGMENT, to the required values. These can easily be set identically for all instances using an included parameter file if you need the same number of rollback segments for each instance. You can also control the number of public rollback segments each individual instance will try to acquire. Oracle computes the ratio of two different parameters, TRANSACTIONS and TRANSACTIONS_PER_ROLLBACK_SEGMENT, and determines the number of rollback segments the instance should obtain for its exclusive use by rounding the result up to the next largest integer (the CEILING function). The formula is

```
Number of public rollback segments required =
CEILING ( TRANSACTIONS / TRANSACTIONS_PER_ROLLBACK_SEGMENT )
```

Take care when using public rollback segments that you create a sufficient number for each instance to acquire the number it requested. As long as at least one rollback segment is available, an instance can start. This can result in an instance acquiring less rollback segments than you expect, which leads to a poorly performing instance. If there are no free rollback segments available because some instances acquire more than expected, one or more instances will not be capable of starting.

This propensity of instances to be capable of starting with less than the required number of active rollback segments is one reason that private segments are preferred. Because you must name private segments, your instances will only start if they can acquire their designated rollback segments. If you accidentally name the same one in two different parameter files, only the first instance to start will acquire it. The second instance will fail to start rather than run without the rollback segment assigned to it.

The second reason for preferring private rollback segments is their location. When you create rollback segments, you can assign them to a particular tablespace. It might be useful to place the rollback segments for each instance in their own tablespace or set of tablespaces. This makes it easy to identify which instance(s) might be affected if the underlying disk drives become unavailable. Also, when using non-shared architectures, you should place the rollback segments on disks that are local to instance. If you use public rollback segments, you have no control over whether an instance will acquire rollback segments on a local disk or a non-local disk.

> **Caution**
>
> There are some rare Oracle Parallel Server implementations where only public rollback segments are supported. Your platform-specific documentation will indicate if you are using such a system.

REDO LOGS AND PARALLEL SERVER INSTANCES

Every instance in a parallel server environment runs its own LGWR process. On most platforms, these processes write to their own set of online redo log files. There are a couple of architectures where the log writers send their output to a centralized process that interleaves them into a single set of log files. These are rare platforms and you can easily determine if yours is one of them from the installation guide. The remainder of this section addresses only instances that write their own redo log files.

A set of log files used by an instance is called a *thread*. As with rollback segments, you can make your threads either public or private. Also, like rollback segments, public threads of redo are acquired by an instance at startup from the pool of available resources and you have no control over which thread is acquired by which instance. Hence, the same concerns that relate to public rollback segments apply also to public threads of redo.

When using public redo threads, for example, you will not necessarily know which is being written by which instance, making it difficult to identify which users will be affected if you suffer disk failure. Also, you might not enable enough public threads for all your instances during database expansion and, consequently, less instances than you intended will be capable of starting. If you are using Parallel Server on a shared-nothing platform, you should use private redo threads in order to place the associated log files on disks local to each instance's node.

You have to create and enable your threads of redo in an active instance. The commands to achieve this are options of the ALTER DATABASE command as exemplified in Listing 39.3. You should note that a thread of redo must be created and enabled before its associated instance can be started. Choose a unique thread number for each instance's redo logs. Note that you must assign redo log group numbers that are unique across the whole database, not just unique within each thread.

LISTING 39.3 DEFINE A THREAD OF REDO AND MAKE IT ACCESSIBLE

```
SQL> ALTER DATABASE ADD LOGFILE THREAD 2
  2     GROUP 3 ('/ora/testdb/redo1/redo3a.log','/ora/testdb/redo2/redo3b.log')
  3           SIZE 1M
  4     GROUP 4 ('/ora/testdb/redo1/redo4a.log','/ora/testdb/redo2/redo4b.log')
           SIZE 1M;

Database altered.

SQL> ALTER DATABASE ENABLE PUBLIC THREAD 2;

Database altered.
```

Unlike rollback segments, the option to make a thread public or private is part of the ALTER command rather than the CREATE command. To enable a thread privately, leave out the PUBLIC keyword from the ALTER DATABASE command. If you need to change the status of an enabled thread, for example to turn it from a public to a private thread, you will first have to shut down any instance that is currently using the thread and make the change from a different instance. The change itself consists of executing the ALTER DATABASE command twice, first with the DISABLE THREAD option, and then with the required ENABLE THREAD option.

You do not have to make all your threads identical if the instances will not be doing similar work. For example, you can have larger and more redo logs in a thread for an instance that will be processing many transactions and fewer, smaller redo logs in a thread for a read-intensive instance. If you decide to use such a variety of redo structures, you will have to enable the threads privately to ensure that each instance acquires the proper thread. Also, if you intend your instances to act as failover instances for each other, you should consider using identical redo threads for each instance.

USING FREELIST GROUPS TO AVOID CONTENTION

Freelists are used by Oracle to identify which blocks in a segment contain space for new rows to be stored during an INSERT operation. The first available block in a freelist is identified by an entry in the header block of the segment. The other blocks are linked by pointers from each block to the next in the freelist. By default, all freelists for a segment are started from the same header block. When a segment contains multiple freelist groups, an additional, special, header block is created for the segment. Each of these header blocks contains the starting pointer to the blocks on the freelists belonging to a specific freelist group.

> **Caution**
>
> Although most discussions of freelists note their use for INSERT operations, you should be aware that UPDATEs can also require access to a freelist. If the row no longer fits in its original block due to an increase in the size of one or more columns, it will be migrated to a different block. If there are no blocks yet allocated to the segment for such migrated rows, an empty one will have to be found from a freelist.

There are two main reasons for using multiple freelist groups with Parallel Server. The first is to avoid contention for freelist access. Only one user at a time can control a freelist and in a multiuser database, multiple freelists are needed to allow concurrent inserts into the same segment. There is an upper limit to the number of freelists that can be assigned to a segment, based on the database block size. For very active databases and segments, you might need to add more freelists by including multiple freelist groups, each with multiple freelists.

Freelist contention also occurs because the freelist information for a normal segment is stored in the segment's header block. As blocks are added and dropped from the freelists, this information must be updated. The overhead introduced by this activity when there are frequent freelist changes on different instances can cause serious performance degradation due to the pinging of the header block.

The second reason to use freelist groups is to control which blocks are used by an instance for inserts. If two or more instances share freelists, they are likely to attempt to put new rows onto the same blocks as each other. Once more, this will introduce excessive pinging as the blocks at the head of each freelist are transferred between the instances. By using freelist groups, you can explicitly or implicitly assign sets of blocks to a specific set of freelists and ensure that those blocks are covered by different PCM locks. Each instance will then only execute inserts on blocks in its own freelist group's freelists and avoid using blocks assigned to another instance.

The first method uses a table in which extents are manually allocated and assigned to an instance number, which implicitly associates them to a freelist group. When looking for available blocks, each instance will use the freelist group associated with the instance number it acquires on startup. The inserts for any specific instance will be pointed to blocks on a specific extent. By placing these extents in separate datafiles, you can ensure that a different PCM lock will be used for each instance's extents with your GC_FILES_TO_LOCKS parameter. As a result, the PCM locks and blocks will not have to be shared between instances and the related blocks will not need to be pinged. An example of a table built this way with four freelist groups is shown in Figure 39.10.

In order to use this method of freelist group allocation, you should build the table using the STORAGE clause's FREELIST GROUPS option and add the instance-specific extents with the ALTER TABLE...ALLOCATE EXTENT command. This command gives you the capability to assign each allocated extent to a specific datafile and instance number. You need to monitor space usage in this scenario to ensure that Oracle does not allocate new extents dynamically because you can't control the datafile in which they are built, and they will be assigned to the generic freelists stored in the main table header block. You should also use a minimal initial extent because you don't want records inserted into this common part of the table and you should separate this extent from the instance specific extents. Figure 39.11 shows an example of a table built to support just two instances doing inserts against two freelist groups. Note that the initial extent is not only in its own datafile, but uses fine grain locks to reduce contention should the two instances need access to this extent.

Figure 39.10
A table with four freelist groups.

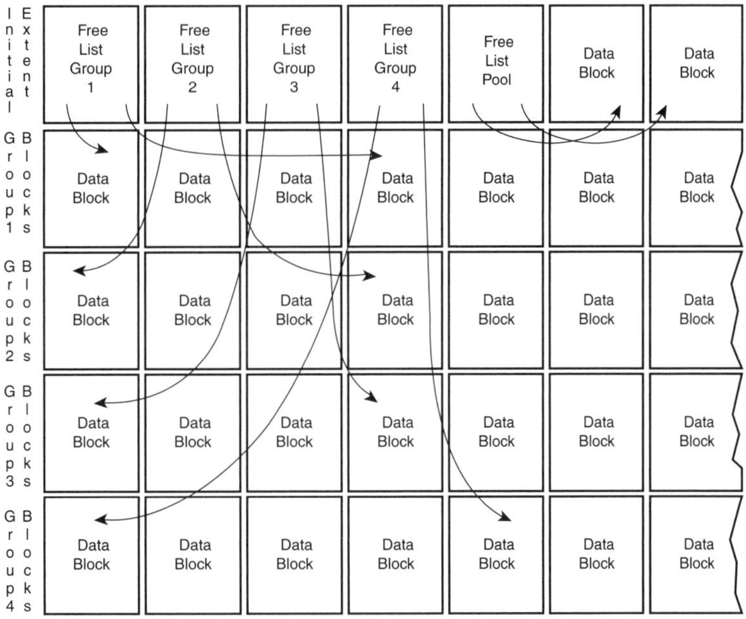

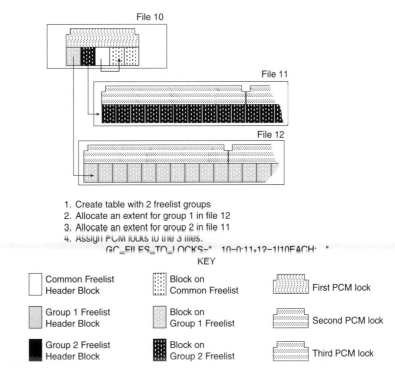

Figure 39.11
Manual allocation of freelist groups.

File 10

File 11

File 12

1. Create table with 2 freelist groups
2. Allocate an extent for group 1 in file 12
3. Allocate an extent for group 2 in file 11
4. Assign PCM locks to the 3 files.
   GC_FILES_TO_LOCKS=" 10=0:11,12=1!10EACH; "

KEY

Common Freelist Header Block	Block on Common Freelist	First PCM lock
Group 1 Freelist Header Block	Block on Group 1 Freelist	Second PCM lock
Group 2 Freelist Header Block	Block on Group 2 Freelist	Third PCM lock

In order to avoid contention for the blocks that you have not specifically assigned to a freelist group, you might consider following these guidelines:

1. Create the initial extent only just large enough to hold the segment header block and the freelist header blocks.

2. Use the STORAGE clause to restrict the number of extents to the initial extent plus one extent for each instance/freelist.

3. Allocate only one extent per instance in its own datafile.

4. Monitor space usage and only increment the MAXEXTENTS storage clause when you need more space for an instance; in this case, add 1 (one) to MAXEXTENTS and immediately allocate an instance-specific extent.

In Listing 39.4, you can see how to build the table initially and add one extent for each of two instances.

LISTING 39.4 CREATING A TABLE FOR TWO INSTANCES TO SHARE

```
CREATE TABLE my_table (id NUMBER(10), . . .)
  TABLESPACE user_data
  STORAGE (INITIAL 10K MAXEXTENTS 3 FREELIST GROUPS 2);

ALTER TABLE my_table
  ALLOCATE EXTENT (SIZE 1M DATAFILE 'user_data_instance1_01.dbf' INSTANCE 1);

ALTER TABLE my_table
  ALLOCATE EXTENT (SIZE 1M DATAFILE 'user_data_instance2_01.dbf' INSTANCE 2);
```

The second method you can use to allocate blocks used for inserts to different instances and PCM locks is to use the grouping option on fine grain locks. To understand this, you need some background information. As Oracle inserts entries into a segment, it has to move the *high water mark*, a pointer in the segment header block, to the last used block in the segment. This is done to reduce the number of blocks that have to be tracked by freelists; any block beyond the high water mark is logically not available for use and so does not have to be on a freelist. Generally, Oracle moves the high water mark five blocks at a time.

However, if you have assigned fine grain locks to a datafile and a segment has been allocated multiple freelist groups, Oracle changes its default behavior. When the current high water mark is reached and needs to be moved, Oracle moves it by the number of blocks defined in the GC_FILES_TO_LOCKS parameter for that datafile. Additionally, it assigns a single releasable PCM lock to the instance's freelist group that covers all the blocks added beyond the high water mark. This guarantees that these blocks can be seen and used only by the instance to which they were assigned.

Another instance needing space in the table will have to move the high water mark again, a process that will acquire the same number of additional blocks for its freelist group and a single releasable lock to cover them. This movement of the high water mark for each instance, with the concomitant freelist and PCM lock assignment, ensures that inserts will only occur on blocks related to the specific instance's freelist group header block and already-allocated PCM lock. This behavior is show in Figure 39.12, again restricted to a two-instance database.

Figure 39.12
Automatic allocation of freelist groups and PCM locks.

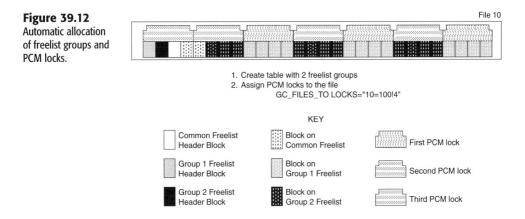

1. Create table with 2 freelist groups
2. Assign PCM locks to the file
   GC_FILES_TO_LOCKS="10=100!4"

KEY

Common Freelist Header Block	Block on Common Freelist	First PCM lock
Group 1 Freelist Header Block	Block on Group 1 Freelist	Second PCM lock
Group 2 Freelist Header Block	Block on Group 2 Freelist	Third PCM lock

It is not safe to assume that a block will always *belong* to just one instance when using freelist groups. After a block is allocated to a freelist group, it will stay on its associated freelist until it fills to its PCTFREE value, the same as any other block. If the space used in the block subsequently falls to its PCTUSED value, the block will be returned to the freelist group of the instance that makes the change. This instance might not necessarily be the one that originally had the block on one of its freelists. Similarly, if you export and then import the rows from a segment with multiple freelist groups, the rows will all be placed on blocks from the freelist group belonging to the instance performing the import. They will not necessarily, therefore, return to their original freelists.

DETERMINING WHEN PARALLEL SERVER CAN SOLVE A BUSINESS NEED

To determine if Parallel Server is a good fit for your failover needs, you need to compare its costs and complexity with other options. If you need your database to be available on a 24 hours per day and 365 days per year basis, you might be a candidate for Parallel Server. While at least one instance remains active, your users can continue to access your database. You should also consider Parallel Server as a means to grow your applications, database size, or user community.

The following two sections highlight the work needed to build available and scalable applications on Parallel Server. By working through the steps described in either section, you should be able to decide if your environment is suited for Parallel Server. You will probably find some issues that fit well with the architecture and some that mitigate against it. In order to make the best decision, you should complete a similar analysis of the alternative strategies and compare the pros and cons of them all.

PART
IX

CH
39

DESIGNING A PARALLEL DATABASE FOR FAILOVER

The simplest failover setup consists of a two-node cluster with an Oracle instance running on each node against a database stored on a shared disk system. The users all connect to the same instance by default, with a secondary path to the alternative database. In client/server situations, SQL*Net or Net8,(depending on your Oracle version), can be configured to provide the alternative, failover address. In three- or *n*-tiered architectures, a TP-style monitor can route the users to the active instance.

While this model can be extended to include multiple active nodes and instances with one failover instance, there is a point at which a single node and instance may not offer sufficient protection against failures. If two instances fail at the same time—an increasingly likely occurrence as the number of nodes increases—a single failover instance might not be capable of handling the workload from both. Deciding which users to move to which failover node is a subset of the partitioning activity you need to undertake for scaling your applications as discussed in the section "Designing a Parallel Database for Scalability."

Whether you have one or many failover instances, you still have to build your TNSNAMES.ORA file to identify the primary and failover instances or else code the routing scheme in a middle tiered component, such as a TP monitor. To achieve the former option, you should use the best options allowed to you by your Oracle version. On the simplest level, available in all releases, you will need to use an ADDRESS_LIST in the DESCRIPTION clause of TNSNAMES.ORA and instances with the same name. This is exemplified by the entry from a TNSNAMES.ORA file shown in Listing 39.5.

LISTING 39.5   IDENTIFYING PRIMARY AND FAILOVER NODES IN A TNSNAMES.ORA ENTRY

```
PROD.world=
    (DESCRIPTION=
        (ADDRESS_LIST=
            (ADDRESS=
                (COMMUNITY=tcp.world)
                (PROTOCOL=TCP)
                (HOST=apple)
                (PORT=1521)
            )
            (ADDRESS=
                (COMMUNITY=tcp.world)
                (PROTOCOL=TCP)
                (HOST=pear)
                (PORT=1521)
            )
        )
        (CONNECT_DATA=
            (SID=PROD)
        )
    )
```

Oracle8 adds to the failover capability of Parallel Server. First, you have the option of starting a parallel, dummy connection on the failover instance for each user connection on the primary database. If the primary fails, the reconnection to the standby is faster than if the pre-spawned connection has not been created. You should consider this option if you don't intend to allow any other connections to the standby instance while the primary is running.

Second, the Oracle Call Interface (OCI) language has been extended to allow a user disconnected from the primary instance—because it fails—to be connected to the failover instance automatically. In addition, if the user were in the process of executing a query, the query could be restarted for them following such an automatic reconnection. The TNSNAMES.ORA file contains a FAILOVER_MODE clause to identify what type of auto-reconnection is required. The new keywords are shown in Table 39.3.

TABLE 39.3   KEYWORDS FOR TNSNAMES.ORA TO PROVIDE RECONNECTION OPTIONS

Keyword Name	Function
BASIC	Do not use pre-created connections on the alternative instance
PRECONNECT	Use an existing connection when switching to the alternative instance
SELECT	Continue any interrupted query after reconnecting to the alternative instance
SESSION	Reconnect to the alternative instance following instance failure
NONE	Do not attempt an automatic reconnection following primary instance failure

Listing 39.6 shows you how you can build a TNSNAMES.ORA file for Net8 to provide for automatic failover from a failed to an alternative instance.

LISTING 39.6   DEFINING FAILOVER NODES IN TNSNAMES.ORA

```
(DESCRIPTION=
        (ADDRESS=
                (PROTOCOL=TCP)
                (HOST=apple)
                (PORT=1521)
        )
        (CONNECT_DATA=
                (SIDGRP=fruit_group)
                (SERVER=DEDICATED)
        )
        (FAILOVER_MODE=
                (TYPE=select)
                (METHOD=basic)
        )
)
```

If you decide to take advantage of the failover options offered by OCI, you should be aware that they can also be used to implement a soft failover. If you need to bring down an instance, you can move the active connections to their failover instance transparently to the user. Use the command

```
SHUTDOWN FAILOVER
```

to stop the current transactions and alert the application of the shutdown with an error message. As with unplanned failover, this technique relies on the OCI program to trap an error message and invoke the failover connection. You can also failover a single connection using the command

```
ALTER SYSTEM DISCONNECT SESSION 'sid,serial#' POST-TRANSACTION;
```

Again, this command will signal the application with an error that is trapped and managed by the OCI code, causing the user to reconnect to the failover instance when the current transaction completes.

Other than setting up the components necessary to redirect connections to the alternative instance, there is no need to make any database design changes to support a simple failover option. With only one node active at a time, you do not have to plan for the sharing of blocks and the PCM locks required to do this. A single lock for the whole database would, in theory, be sufficient. Due to internal algorithms, however, you will never be able to reduce the number of locks quite this much. By setting the parameters as follows

```
GC_DB_LOCKS = 1
GC_RELEASABLE_LOCKS = 0
```

and leaving GC_FILES_TO_LOCKS at its default value of a null string, you will enable Oracle to assign the minimal number of locks possible.

DESIGNING A PARALLEL DATABASE FOR SCALABILITY

Scalability refers to the capability of a system to grow as demands grow, whether they are for supporting more users, handling more data, or performing more complex tasks. The primary goal of the design phase of a scalable system is to ensure that there will be minimal contention between instances. This is an easy issue for query intensive Oracle databases because all PCM locks can be acquired concurrently by all the instances that need them in shared mode. For transaction intensive databases, particularly OLTP systems, the challenge is greater. You have to partition the database so that each instance typically uses one subset of blocks while the other instances use their own different and distinct subsets. A secondary goal is to spread the workload across the instances as evenly as possible so that you are not overworking the resources of one server while under utilizing those on another.

You have a number of options as to how you can partition your database. These include application, functional, departmental/line of business, physical table, and transaction partitioning. The following sections examine these options.

APPLICATION AND FUNCTIONAL PARTITIONING

Application partitioning and functional partitioning are very similar approaches with the significant difference being the business level at which you begin the partitioning.

Application partitioning involves running different applications, such as Financials and Manufacturing, on different instances. Generally, applications use completely different sets of tables, so there is little need to combine them in the same database. If you do have some data in common between applications, you might want to run both in the same database. To design a database of this nature for Parallel Server, you will use the same approach as for functional partitioning.

Functional partitioning involves separating the distinct functions of an application. For example, you could separate a human resource application into four functions—Recruitment, Employment History, Payroll, and Benefits. Such an application might need to be run on a Parallel Server if the company is large and offers its employees and recruits telephone and Web access to its database, which results in a large database with high transaction rates.

For both application and functional partitioning, you need to consider the data implications rather than the functional definitions. This requires that you analyze how each table in the database will be used by each application or function. To simplify this task you can record your findings in tables. Using the human resource example, you can proceed as follows. First, create a table similar to Table 39.4 that identifies which tables are used by each function.

TABLE 39.4 PARTITIONING TABLES—TABLE USE BY FUNCTION

Recruitment	Employment History	Payroll	Benefits
Table 1	Table 1	Table 1	Table 1
Table 2	Table 2	Table 3	Table 2
Table 3	Table 4	Table 5	Table 4
	Table 6	Table 7	Table 5

Next record the *common* tables—those tables that are used by more than instance. To simplify the example, only the Payroll and Benefits sets of tables will be considered. The next iteration of the table is shown in Table 39.5

TABLE 39.5 PARTITIONING TABLES—COMMON TABLES BY FUNCTION

Payroll	Tables	Common Benefits
Payroll	**Common Tables**	**Benefits**
Table 3	Table 1	Table 2
Table 7	Table 5	Table 4

If you discover many common tables in your application, you might want to re-examine the table definitions to determine if they can be redefined. Your objective should be to minimize the number of tables in the Common Tables column. If you are fortunate enough to have no common tables, you have a perfectly partitionable application. In this case, place the tables for the different functions into separate tablespaces and assign single hash locks to each of the files involved, or even a single hash lock to the set of files associated with each function's tablespace or tablespaces. Users of each function will connect to their appropriate instance.

For any tables that remain in the Common column, your next step is to examine and record the types of activity that each instance performs on the table and the frequency of the accesses. In Table 39.6, the values for the Human Resource example are inserted.

TABLE 39.6 PARTITIONING TABLES—COMMON TABLE ACTIVITY

Common Table Name	Payroll Access and Volumes		Benefits Access and Volumes	
Table 1	SELECT	100/second	SELECT	300/second
Table 5	SELECT	200/second	SELECT	10/second
	INSERT	10/second	INSERT	0
	UPDATE	20/second	UPDATE	200/second

You should now be ready to design your tablespaces to reduce PCM lock contention and block pinging. The database tables that are not common to multiple instances can be placed in their own tablespaces and only need minimal PCM locks. The files in these tablespaces can be covered with hash locks rather than fine grain locks because their contents will not be shared with other instances.

The tables in the Common Table column that are read only—that is, they only have queries performed on them by all instances—can also be placed in their own tablespace(s). You should alter these tablespaces to be read only after loading the data because Oracle does not need to use any PCM locks for data that cannot be updated. Leave datafiles for read-only tablespaces out of the GC_FILES_TO_LOCKS parameter to avoid assigning locks unnecessarily.

You now have to deal with the tables that are used by one or more functions and modified in at least one of them. First, you should categorize these into low, medium, and high activity tables. Based on the range of your transaction rates, you should be able to define which tables fall into which category. For example, if your busiest table has 100 inserts per second and 600 updates per second, it has a transaction rate of 700 operations per second. If your least volatile table has 40 operations per second, your transaction range is 660 operations (700–40). Dividing this into three equal ranges of 220 operations, you would classify them as follows:

- Tables with up to 260 transactions per second (40+220) as low activity tables
- Tables with 261 to 480 transactions per second as medium activity tables
- Tables with 481 to 700 transactions per second as high activity tables

For high activity tables, you should use tablespaces to which you assign either many hash locks or fine grain locks. If the only activity is the insertion of new rows, you should use multiple freelist groups on the table and index segments. Then assign either hash locks in conjunction with manually allocated extents or assign fine grain locks with a grouping factor in the GC_FILES_TO_LOCKS parameter for the associated datafiles. You should separate the medium and low activity tables into their own tablespaces with hash locks on the related datafiles.

Although you might need to perform some fine tuning later, you should initially choose three simple values to compute the number of locks you apply to datafiles where you want to use hash locks. These values will represent the granularity of the hash locks and should be chosen based on some simple ratios. For example, you can use a ratio of 1 through 10 for high activity datafiles to medium activity datafiles, and the same ratio for medium activity to low activity datafiles. These granularity numbers are divided into the number of blocks in a datafile to compute the number of hash locks needed to cover the file. Using the ratios mentioned, you can select a granularity of 10 for high activity files, 100 for medium activity files, and 1,000 for low activity files.

For any given datafile, divide the number of blocks in the file by the granularity number appropriate to the activity level of the contents of the file. Table 39.7 shows the lock counts for some sample files of different sizes for each level of granularity using the values from the previous paragraph.

TABLE 39.7 HASH LOCK ASSIGNMENTS BASED ON ACTIVITY LEVEL AND DATAFILE SIZE

| | Number of Hash Locks | | |
| Number of Blocks | High Activity | Medium Activity | Low Activity |
	Granularity =10	Granularity =100	Granularity =1,000
1,000,000	100,000	10,000	1,000
5,000	500	50	5
1,000	100	10	1

If you still need a large number of locks to cover the datafiles using the preceding approach, you have other options to try to reduce them. You can use releasable locks for the datafiles belonging to the tablespaces for the medium activity as well as the high activity tables or for all the common tables. You can also try a different partitioning scheme or apply an additional type of partitioning to the functional partitions you already have. You will definitely have to use one of these techniques if you have more locks than your system can handle or too many for it to be capable of starting up your instances in a reasonable amount of time.

You may also want to test your instance recovery time if you increase the number of PCM and related DLM locks. The greater the number of locks, the longer the DLM reconfiguration can take, particularly if an entire node fails, stopping both the instance and the DLM processing on that node.

If your users have a maximum time during which they can afford to be idle following a failure, you might need to reduce the number of locks you assign in order to meet their recovery time requirements.

DEPARTMENT AND LINE OF BUSINESS PARTITIONING

Department and Line of Business (LOB) partitioning works if you have groups of users who tend to access their own subsets of data even if they are in the same tables. To extend the human resources example from the previous section, the company might have a number of offices where the personnel are handled by a local human resource department, or there may be an HR group for native employees and another for international workers.

You can use a different instance for each department or LOB if such natural partitioning exists. Because of the nature of this partitioning scheme, it is likely that the users on each instance will perform practically all the DML as well as the queries for their own data. Consequently, you should only need a few PCM locks for each shared table. The best way to accomplish this is to use multiple freelist groups and allocate extents for each instance in its own datafile or set of datafiles. Then you only need to assign a very few hash PCM locks to each of these datafiles. In some cases, you might find that a single lock is all you need on some files, although if any of the rows are occasionally shared by other instances, this may not provide sufficiently good performance.

PHYSICAL TABLE PARTITIONING

If you don't have any natural subsets of users and one or more critical tables that they all need to modify, you might need to resort to physical partitioning of the table. This is not as elegant of a solution as departmental or LOB partitioning because you also have to control how the users connect to the database. With departmental or LOB partitions, the users are already working in different locations or different administrative units. A new user will belong to one of these groups and can be assigned to the appropriate instance. To enforce physical partitioning, you need a mechanism to ensure that a user connects to the correct instance, depending on what part of the data they need to access.

An example of physical partitioning is the creation of multiple employee tables instead of a single table. For a four-instance database, you might have a table for employees whose last names start with letters in the range A–E, a table for F–J, one for K–Q, and one for R–Z. You can place these tables in separate datafiles, even in different tablespaces. In Oracle7, you need to use partition views and completely separate tables to implement physical partitioning. In Oracle8, you can take advantage of the Partition Option and build a single table with multiple partitions, although partition views and logically partitioned tables are still available to you.

If your users can be partitioned with the same partition boundaries as the table, you might be able to implement this scheme easily; it is very similar to department or LOB partitioning. This would be the case if different human resource department employees were responsible for employees based on last name. A partitioning scheme similar to the one just discussed would work. The only major difference between this case and LOB partitioning is when a query needs to report on all employees or at least employees in more than one partition. Oracle8 solves this problem if you use its Partitioning Option because you only have to query the single table. Prior to Oracle8, you would need to use partition views created with a UNION or UNION ALL operator to retrieve all the records.

Queries against physical partitions can be very efficient if you have configured your Parallel Server database to use slave processes on multiple instances when running such queries. The Partition Option also allows you to perform parallel DML commands across all the partitions using slaves on multiple instances. Prior to Oracle8, Version 8.0, you could not execute parallel DML.

If you cannot partition your users on the same criteria as your tables, you will need your application to route the user to the correct instance based on the data being processed. This might even require that the users make a new connection for each transaction so that they will always work on the desired instance based on the record of interest. While this might be impractical in a standard client/server architecture, it is possible to build applications around this model using three or more tiered architectures. In multitier architectures, a Transaction Processing (TP) monitor sits between the users and the database server and controls the routing of the clients' SQL statements and the return of information back to the users. TP monitors can also assist in load balancing when a request is not instance-specific and route requests to alternative nodes in cases of individual instance failures.

If you can implement a physical table partitioning approach, you will also probably be able to apply a hash PCM locking scheme. The initial storage and all subsequent operations on a row should be performed by the same instance so you can use a single lock on the datafiles containing the partitions for the instance. Additionally, you should not need multiple instance groups, as only one instance will be creating new rows. As with department or LOB partitioning, however, you might need more locks if there are occasional requirements for rows to be used by another instance.

PART

IX

CH

39

TRANSACTION PARTITIONING

If you cannot find a way to manually partition your applications or your tables as discussed in the previous sections, you might need to attempt transaction partitioning. Transaction partitioning requires very complex applications probably used in conjunction with a TP monitor. The approach requires that each transaction is routed to the best instance to process it based on the nature of the transaction and the tables involved. If all the tables are covered by locks assigned to one instance, the coding is fairly simple; but when a transaction involves tables that are assigned to locks on different instances, the decision tree can be very complex. This requirement makes the approach a difficult and expensive option.

One benefit to transaction partitioning is that there is no need to make changes to the table structure should you need to add more instances to support growth. With the other partitioning schemes, there is typically a need to repartition either the tables or the users when a new instance is added. With transaction partitioning, you modify the code not the database. While this may sound like an onerous task, the time required to move large amounts of data around can be sufficient to exceed service level agreements for availability. However, with transaction partitioning, code changes can be made in anticipation of a new instance in a test environment and can be implemented with minimum downtime.

INDEXES AND SCALABILITY CONSIDERATIONS

While determining the best partitioning option for your database tables, you also need to plan for any indexes you might need. To reduce disk contention, it is generally recommended that you place your indexes in separate tablespaces from their parent tables, employing different disks for their datafiles. Accomplishing this in a Parallel Server environment, with multiple tablespaces already employed to allow table partitioning, can make for an administrative headache. It might be beneficial, therefore, to place a table and its indexes in the same tablespace in some cases. The Oracle Partitioning Option also offers good reasons to store the partitions of a table and their locally partitioned indexes in the same tablespaces as each other. This way, the related table and index partitions are either available or offline concurrently.

Another problem you need to anticipate with index processing in multi-instance databases is associated with the use of linearly increasing primary keys. This is typically a numeric key that is provided through an Oracle sequence generator or some other mechanism that uses an increasing integer value. If two or more instances insert records into a table using such a primary key mechanism, they will also need to insert entries into the same index leaf block, causing continual pinging of that block. To avoid this problem, you have a number of available strategies.

You can create instance specific ranges of values by modifying the value with a multiplier based on the instance number. You can use a formula such as the following for this purpose:

```
instance_number * 10000000 + sequence_number
```

This option requires changes in the statements that you code in order to access rows using the index. The same conversion operation you apply to the data when you add the row has to be applied when you try to retrieve it. This may not be as simple as it sounds if instances other than the one that create the entry try to retrieve it.

A second option is to use a different sequence for each instance. There are a number of methods to define such sequence generators, although they all have their own particular drawbacks. The two simplest approaches involve using generators with different lower and upper bounds or different starting values and a non-unity step size for each instance. For example, consider a four-instance database.

In the first case, Instance 1 could be assigned the range 1–1,000,000, Instance 2 the range 1,000,001–2,000,000, Instance 3 the next 1,000,000 numbers, and Instance 4 the numbers from 4,000,001 and up. In the second case, Instance 1 could use a sequence generator defined to start with 1 and increment by 4, thus it would be assigned the numbers 1, 5, 9, 13, and so on. Similarly, Instance 2 would have its generator begin with 2 and increment by 4, giving it the values 2, 6, 10, 14,and so on. Although this approach will not run out of numbers for the existing instances, it is hard to incorporate an additional instance if one is ever required as the application grows and needs an additional instance.

Tip #118

If you want to use sequences with different starting values, but also want to plan for additional instances, you can make the step size larger than the number of current instances. For example, in our four-instance example, you could increment each of the four sequences by 10. Instance 1 would now generate the values 1, 11, 21, and so on. Similarly, the other instances would, between them, use the values 2, 3, 4, 12, 13, 14, 22, 23, 24, and so. This leaves the values 5 through 10, and their increments of 10, available for new instances.

A final option is to use the reverse key index feature of Oracle8, which will reverse the bytes in each column of your index. The benefit to this approach is that you can still use the original value from the column in the predicate of a SQL statement because the optimizer knows the structure of the index. Create a reverse key index using the keyword REVERSE as shown in the following example:

```
CREATE INDEX busy_table_ix ON busy_table (id) REVERSE;
```

Caution

Although the reversal of the bytes in the indexed column will distribute the index entries throughout the index leaf blocks and avoid contention for the rightmost leaf block among the instances, the distribution of the values is not completely random. If numbers are cached 100 at a time by each instance, the last binary digit can be the same for two different instances retrieving the values available to them from their cached values. For example, the final byte of the internal representation of the number 4022 is 27, which is exactly the same as the final byte for the number 4122. If two instances add their values, 4022 and 4122 respectively, to the table at the same time, they will also both need to update the same leaf block if they use a reverse key index.

You should use reverse key indexes to help reduce the frequency of index rebuilds—the purpose for which they were designed—and not in the hope they will avoid contention in Parallel Server databases. You could allocate PCM locks inappropriately otherwise, and be disappointed with your database performance.

SEQUENCE GENERATORS AND MULTIPLE INSTANCES

If you decide to use sequence generators in a Parallel Server database, you need to be aware of a couple of limitations. One of the ways sequence generators can speed up processing is through their capability to keep a few numbers cached in the SGA of an instance. This allows most transactions that need a sequence number to find it already available in memory rather than having to perform a disk read. The cache also avoids the need to lock a resource while the next number is generated and saved.

The ORDER option for sequence generators ensures that the numbers be assigned in sequential order. This means that the first process to request a number will be given the lowest unused number. You may use this feature in a Parallel Server database, but Oracle will only be able to provide this capability by assigning each number from the data dictionary on disk. It cannot use number caching because the instances do not have the capability to transfer cached numbers between themselves. Also, a failed instance cannot transmit its cached numbers to another instance. Consequently, if you define a sequence generator with both the CACHE and the ORDER option, Oracle will ignore the CACHE option when you start an instance in parallel mode. This is likely to reduce the efficiency of the sequence generator.

SPECIAL CONSIDERATIONS FOR PARALLEL SERVER CREATION

Whether you are building your parallel database to support failover or scalability, you need to pay attention to various options regarding the basic structure. By the time you are ready to build your database, you should have already decided how many instances you will need and how you are going to partition your data, if needed. You will also have to consider the other options for the database structure that are part of any Oracle database design, such as the number of redo log groups you will need, whether you will use the database in ARCHIVELOG or NOARCHIVELOG mode, and what character set you will need to support all required character sets. When you have determined these design issues, you can build your database using the CREATE DATABASE command.

In Table 39.8, the options for the CREATE DATABASE command are listed along with the issues you should consider when building your database.

TABLE 39.8   CREATE DATABASE COMMAND OPTIONS

Option	Description and Usage
CONTROLFILE REUSE	Only needed if you plan to overwrite an existing control file. You are advised not to use this option because it can destroy a good control file accidentally if you should start the instance with the wrong init.ora parameter file.
LOGFILE	As with a single instance database, this parameter lets you create as many redo log file groups as you want, each containing your preferred number of multiplexed copies. The groups you create with this option will all belong to the first thread of redo and will be automatically enabled as a public thread. You can disable this thread and re-enable it as a private thread, if you want, after you have started a different instance and shut this one down.
MAXLOGFILES	Sets the maximum number of redo log groups you will be able to create for the database. This number should, therefore, be the sum of the redo log groups from all the instances you intend to create. You might want to set the value large enough to support additional log groups in case you need to add redo to one or more instances and to support additional instances, if they become available.

Option	Description and Usage
MAXLOGMEMBERS	Sets the maximum number of multiplexed redo log files that can be assigned to any one redo log group. Generally, the number of log members will be the same for the redo on all instances, but if not, you should set this to the highest number you will need for a log group.
MAXLOGHISTORY	Determines the number of archive log file entries that will be stored in the control file. When this number is reached, the oldest entries are replaced as the new entries are added. These entries contain information about the archive log names and contents and are used by the automatic media recovery option to identify which archive log files it needs to apply. If you intend to use automatic media recovery, you should set this parameter value to at least the number of archive log files that will be created by all instances during a single backup cycle.
MAXDATAFILES	Sets the maximum number of datafiles that you will be able to create for the database. This will typically be a higher number than for single instance databases because of the need for partitioning tables and indexes to avoid inter-instance conflicts for blocks. As with MAXLOGFILES, you should consider making this value sufficiently large to accommodate future growth or further partitioning requirements.
MAXINSTANCES	Specifies the maximum number of instances that can simultaneously access the database. If you are using one or more instances for failover, you need to include these in this total, even though you will not have users connecting to them under normal circumstances. This is another parameter that you might want to set with consideration for future growth.
[NO]ARCHIVELOG	Allows you to determine whether the database is placed in ARCHIVELOG mode at the time of creation. Although ARCHIVELOG mode is recommended for most production databases, it is generally not necessary to place it in this mode immediately. The default value is NOARCHIVELOG.
EXCLUSIVE	This is an optional keyword and will become obsolete in Oracle8. It reinforces the fact that the initial instance cannot be opened in shared or parallel mode. You are advised to leave it out.
CHARACTER SET	Specifies the character set to be used by the database to store data. This parameter has no particular characteristics specific to Parallel Server.
DATAFILE	Names the datafile or datafiles that will initially comprise the SYSTEM tablespace. This parameter has no particular characteristics specific to Parallel Server. Similarly, the AUTOEXTEND options for the named datafiles work identically in single and multi-instance database.

You might want to build a SQL script file to contain this command along with the other commands you need to customize the database for Parallel Server use. These include, among others, commands to perform the following steps:

- Add at least one rollback segment for each instance
- Add a redo thread for each additional instance
- Enable the redo threads
- Run the `catparr.sql` script

HOW TO MONITOR AND TUNE PARALLEL SERVER

You will need to know about some special dynamic performance tables in order to monitor the performance of a parallel database. These tuning tools and tuning steps have to be used in addition to the standard tuning approaches you need for any Oracle database.

A number of dynamic performance tables that are particularly useful for tuning Oracle Parallel Server are created using a script called `catparr.sql`. Run this script as the user SYS to create the tables and to update them as you add new segments or extents you want to track. You will also need to run this script after Oracle has dynamically added extents you might want to monitor in order for the database to map the extent locations to the views.

Tip #119	You should get into the habit of routinely running this script as a matter of course before beginning any monitoring or tuning work. This way, you can be assured of seeing the most current information when you examine the various dynamic performance tables you need.

In Oracle8, each of the tables discussed in the following sections, as well as most of the other dynamic performance tables, has a global version that shows the individual values for all the active instances. An instance number column identifies for which instance the data is being reported. To use one of these global tables, you need to include a g in front of the name. Listing 39.7 shows a query against the global view of V$VERSION.

LISTING 39.7   QUERYING A GLOBAL DYNAMIC PERFORMANCE TABLE

```
SQL> SELECT * FROM gv$version;

INSTANCE_ID BANNER
----------- ---------------------------------------------------------------
          1 CORE Version 4.0.2.0.0
          1 NLSRTL Version 3.3.0.0.0
          1 Oracle8 Server Release 8.0.3.0.0
          1 PL/SQL Release 3.0.2.0.0
          1 TNS for Solaris: Version 3.0.2.0..0
          2 CORE Version 4.0.2.0.0
          2 NLSRTL Version 3.3.0.0.0
          2 Oracle8 Server Release 8.0.3.0.0
          2 PL/SQL Release 3.0.2.0.0
          2 TNS for Solaris: Version 3.0.2.0.0
```

V$LOCK_ACTIVITY

The first table you need to monitor is V$LOCK_ACTIVITY. This table shows the number and types of lock conversions that have occurred in a single instance since it started up. Although the actual numbers are not meaningful in themselves because each system will handle locks and related activity at different speeds, you can use them to compare the performance of different instances and to compare the behavior of a specific instance at different times. A query against the V$LOCK_ACTIVITY table will produce an output similar to the one shown in Listing 39.8.

LISTING 39.8 QUERYING V$LOCK_ACTIVITY

```
FROM TO    ACTION                                              COUNTER
----  ---- -------------------------------------------------- -------
NULL  S    Lock buffers for read                                 3595
NULL  X    Lock buffers for write                                8111
S     NULL Make buffers CR (no write)                            2763
S     X    Upgrade read lock to write                            1046
X     NULL Make buffers CR (write dirty buffers)                   92
X     S    Downgrade write lock to read (write dirty buffers)    1220
X     SSX  Write transaction table/undo blocks                    907
SSX   NULL Transaction table/undo blocks (write dirty buffers)      0
SSX   S    Make transaction table/undo block available share        0
SSX   X     Rearm transaction table write mechanism               907
```

Listing 39.8 shows each of the different types of PCM lock conversions that can occur in an instance along with the number of the times such conversions have occurred. The entries in the FROM and TO columns show the mode of the locks:

- NULL—Not currently assigned to the instance
- S—Shared mode
- X—Exclusive mode
- SSX—Sub-shared exclusive mode

Shared locks are used for querying table and index blocks; exclusive locks are used when the block contents need to be changed. Rollback segments use the sub-shared exclusive locks. Because each rollback segment is acquired by an instance at startup and only that instance can write to it, there is no need for the instance to give up its exclusive capability to write to its rollback segment blocks. However, other instances might need to read rollback information and sub-shared exclusive locks are used to cover rollback segment blocks on the owning instance while these reads are in progress. You should see that the two counters for conversions from X to SSX and SSX to X contain the same values because any rollback block *loaned* to another instance for read purposes has to be returned to the owning instance. You can ignore the entries for SSX to NULL and SSX to S conversions as they result from operations performed during system startup or tablespace management activity.

If you suspect that PCM lock conversions and pinging are causing performance problems, or if you want to be proactive and monitor the behavior of the PCM locks on a regular basis, the V$LOCK_ACTIVITY table is where you should begin. You will always see some lock conversion activity because an instance owns all PCM locks in NULL status at instance startup and must convert any of them it needs before it can do any work. You should concentrate on the values of the lock conversions that return locks to a NULL status and on the values for rollback segment lock activity. Conversions to a NULL status only occur when a lock is needed by a different instance than the one you are monitoring. This means that some form of pinging is occurring. If the counter for these conversions is high and continually increasing, you should suspect pinging as one cause of any degraded database performance. You will need to examine the other Parallel Server dynamic performance tables to determine which blocks and segments are involved.

The paired conversions between X to SSX and SSX to X indicate that rollback segment data is being pinged. If these numbers are high, you should consider increasing the number of rollback locks using GC_ROLLBACK_LOCKS, possibly switching to fine grain locks if the problem persists.

V$BH

The V$BH table shows you the current contents of the database buffer cache of the instance. It provides the file and block identification numbers for the block in each buffer along with the status of the PCM lock on the block. A query, along with the partial listing, is shown in Listing 39.9.

LISTING 39.9 QUERYING THE V$BH TABLE

```
SQL> SELECT file#, block#, class#, status, xnc FROM v$bh;

FILE# BLOCK# CLASS# STATUS XNC
----- ------ ------ ------ ---
    8    438      1 XCUR     0
    8    467      1 SCUR     0
    8    468      1 SCUR     0
    8    468      1 SCUR     0
    9    192      1 CR       0
    9    198      1 CR       2
    9    201      1 XCUR    10
. . .
```

The status column has one of seven values, described in Table 39.9. You will typically only see the rows with XCUR, SCUR, or CR values after your instance has been running for a while. By then, all the buffers will have been used at least once and any media or instance recovery should be complete. Occasionally you may catch a buffer that is currently being loaded with data being read from a datafile.

TABLE 39.9 BUFFER STATUS AS REPORTED IN V$BH

STATUS	EXPLANATION
FREE	The buffer is not currently in use
XCUR	The block in the buffer is covered by an exclusive PCM lock

STATUS	EXPLANATION
SCUR	The block in the buffer is covered by a shared PCM lock
CR	The block in the buffer is covered by an XCUR or SCUR lock that was downgraded
READ	A block is being read into the buffer from disk
MREC	The block in the buffer is in media recovery mode
IREC	The block in the buffer is in instance recovery mode

Tip #120

If you find buffers with the MREC or IREC status, you should exit from the database immediately. You can learn no useful information about your database performance when buffers are in either of these recovery states. Further, your session is almost certainly competing for resources that are better used by the recovery process to complete its work in a timely manner

You will usually find that the cache contains many buffers in CR status when there is excessive X to NULL or X to S conversion counts in V$LOCK_ACTIVITY. The XNC column shows the X to NULL conversion count for a particular block. Rows with non-zero values in this column represent blocks that are actually being pinged. You can identify which blocks are involved from the FILE# and BLOCK# columns. By comparing the blocks held in the buffer cache's of the other instances, using their V$BH tables or the Oracle8 GV$BH table, you can determine which blocks are being pinged and between which instances. In some cases, you will not find the same blocks in any other instance's cache. This indicates that false pings are taking place because the lock is being released but the blocks themselves were not needed.

To solve real or false pinging problems, it is useful to know which tables and even which values in those tables are involved. You can look at the blocks involved by querying tables using the ROWID pseudo-column. The query in Listing 39.10 is an example of such a query in a Version 7.3 database. Index entries cannot be found by this method, the best you can do is identify the name of the index.

LISTING 39.10   EXAMINING ROW CONTENTS OF SPECIFIC BLOCKS

```
SQL> SELECT * FROM DEPT
  2    WHERE SUBSTR(rowid,1,8) = '00000201'    -- the block id number
  3    AND SUBSTR(rowid,15,4) = '0009';         -- the file id number

DEPTNO NAME                   LOCATION    MGR_ID
------ --------------------   ----------- ------
    14 Human Resources        Fairview       198
    22 International Sales     New York      1356
. . .
```

To find the name of the segments associated with specific blocks identified in V$BH, you can query the DBA_EXTENTS view but, more easily, you can use the V$CACHE or V$PING views.

V$CACHE AND V$PING

The two dynamic performance tables, V$CACHE and V$PING, are based on the same buffer information as the V$BH view, but they include three additional columns. In Listing 39.11, you can see these columns in the output from a query against V$CACHE. The columns identify the name, type, and owner ID number of the segment to which the block in the buffer belongs. These views will not contain segment information for newly added extents unless catparr.sql has been run since their creation. If the NAME, KIND, and OWNER# columns contain nulls, run the script again to populate them with the new information.

LISTING 39.11 QUERYING V$CACHE

```
SQL> SELECT name, kind, owner#, file#, block#, status, xnc FROM v$cache;

NAME            KIND          OWNER# FILE# BLOCK# CLASS# STATUS XNC
--------------- ------------- ------ ----- ------ ------ ------ ---
EMP             TABLE             14     8    438      1 XCUR     0
EMP             TABLE             14     8    467      1 SCUR     0
EMP             TABLE             14     8    468      1 SCUR     0
EMP             TABLE             14     8    468      1 SCUR     0
DEPT            TABLE             14     9    192      1 CR       0
DEPT            TABLE             14     9    198      1 CR       2
DEPT            TABLE             14     9    201      1 XCUR    10
. . .
```

The difference between V$CACHE and V$PING is that the former contains an entry for every buffer in the cache whereas V$PING only contains a row for each buffer that has potentially been pinged. This is determined by the buffer having a non-zero value in the XNC column, indicating at least one X to NULL conversion for the block it contains.

You may also use the V$FALSE_PING dynamic performance table to identify potential false pings. This table contains the same columns as V$PING but only contains rows for blocks that are highly likely to have been pinged falsely a large number of times. However, Oracle does not guarantee that every block listed in this table is undergoing false pinging or that the table will include every block that has been falsely pinged. You should still check the other instances' caches to find definitive evidence of false pinging as discussed previously. You can easily do this using the global versions of the views discussed.

TUNING STRATEGY FOR PARALLEL SERVER

The basic tuning strategy for the parallel instance components of a multi-instance database consists of the following four steps:

1. Determine if there is excessive pinging
2. Identify what is being pinged
3. Resolve whether the pinging is true or false
4. Solve the pinging problem

By using the Parallel Server dynamic performance tables discussed previously, you can find the amount of pinging, the objects being pinged, and whether the same blocks are being pinged by one or more instances. What should you do with this information?

As with all tuning activities, you only need to tune if the database performance is not at the level required by users. By monitoring the values in V$LOCK_ACTIVITY over time, you can tell if increases in any of the values are inversely proportional to the response time of the transactions. If they are, you need to find the blocks responsible from VBH, VCACHE, or V$PING.

Caution

Be careful when using the dynamic performance tables only when response time, or related issues, are at a peak. If you look at the values now, they will almost certainly be larger than they were an hour ago because Oracle accumulates the statistics over the life of the instance. Any time the database does useful work, a number of its performance statistics will increase to reflect this. You need to employ a monitoring strategy for your multiple instances just as you would for a single instance database. This involves collecting statistics over fixed periods of time so that you can monitor the rate of change for specific periods rather than relying on instantaneous values.

Tip #121

Collection of statistics related to all your instances is made much easier through the global dynamic performance tables if you are using Oracle8. If you are migrating from an Oracle7 database to Oracle8, you might want to revise any scripts you have been using to query the V$_ tables and have them query the GV$_ tables instead.

PART

IX

CH

39

If you find true pinging from the dynamic performance tables, you have a number of options. First, if only two instances are involved, you might consider combining their workload and their users into just one instance. If this is not possible due to resource limitations or if more than one instance is involved, you might need to consider the partitioning options discussed earlier. Your objective should be to find a means to restrict the majority of the access on a given block to only one instance. This might require examining the values of the rows on the pinged blocks to identify partitioning options.

If you find false pinging is occurring, your simplest solution would be to add more hash locks or to convert to fine grain locks for the datafiles involved. The former may involve creating too many locks for your current memory to handle, in which case you would have to use fine grain locks. If these additional fine grain locks in conjunction with existing hash locks still constitute too many locks for your system to manage, you will need to try reassigning some of the datafiles covered by hash locks to fine grain locks.

If you cannot solve the pinging problems using these methods, it might mean that your database is not properly designed and you might need to return to the drawing board and use the design techniques discussed earlier to find a better design. Earlier releases of Oracle, prior to Version 7.3, which didn't offer fine grain locks and the related benefits, made some databases inappropriate for Parallel Server. Now, with fine grain locking, the use of TP monitors and the additional features of Oracle8, such as the global views and reverse key indexes, you should be capable of building and monitoring a multi-instance database for either failover or scalable purposes, if not both.

ADDITIONAL TIPS AND CAUTIONS

Unless you are using one of a very few operating systems, such as nCUBE and derivations of DEC's VAXCluster systems, you must locate your Oracle Parallel Server database on raw disks. With the release of Oracle8*i* the control files are no longer fixed in size. Entries about the status of archived redo log files are accumulated for use by Oracle's Recovery Manager, even if you don't use that tool for backup and recovery. You can reduce the number of entries stored by setting the initialization parameter, CONTROL_FILE_RECORD_KEEP_TIME, to a low number.

You can still change the size of the control file, however, with your own actions. For example, you can set your instance's parameter files to include a value for DB_FILES which is greater than the value for MAXDATAFILES, set in the CREATE DATABASE command. If you add more files to your database than was requested with MAXDATAFILES, your control files will grow to accommodate them. You should ensure that you place your control files on sufficiently large raw partitions, therefore, to hold a larger control file than the CREATE DATABASE command produces. This is particularly critical if your disk management system allows the contents of a raw partition to grow larger than the partition size.

Although Cache Fusion, Phase I, reduces the overhead of passing blocks between instances for use in queries, you should not conclude that you can avoid the process of partitioning your data by instance. There is still a cost involved in sending blocks to requesting instances. The Integrated Distributed Lock Manager still has to pass lock requests between the instances and the cluster interconnect has to pass blocks images, not just short messages, between instances. If your design requires too many blocks to be passed across the interconnect, you can exceed its bandwidth and thus reduce the efficiency of the system.

Also, there are some vendors who do not provide an interconnect that Oracle can use for passing block images. You should check your Installation and Configuration manual before expecting to use Cache Fusion.

If you have a database design that doesn't require users to log on to a specific instance, you can use the new option of defining a service in your Net8 files. A service comprises two or more instances and its name is used in the Net8 connection string instead of an individual instance name. Statistics maintained by the listener processes for each of the instances related to the service will be used by Net8 to identify the least busy instance and a user's log on request will be routed to that instance. This allows you to maintain a balanced work load across your instances. If you are running a number of instances, you can, of course, create multiple services, each covering a subset of your instances. This allows you to provide load balancing for different sets of users and instances.

DISTRIBUTED DATABASE MANAGEMENT

In this chapter

Understanding Distributed Databases

Distributed databases are systems that act as a single database but are located in different locations. These locations can be anywhere, from in the next office to the other side of the world. In a networked environment with various nodes connected together, distributed databases act as a single system. In order to fully understand how a distributed system works, the DBA must have a knowledge and understanding of multiple hardware systems, networking, client/server technology, and database management.

There is little information concerning the management of distributed database systems. The use of distributed databases dramatically changes with the release of Oracle8i and the further development of data warehouses. Many DBAs have not had the opportunity to manage such systems and might not be familiar with what they are.

This chapter describes each type of distributed system, how they are used, and how to manage them. Oracle8i provides a simple, no-nonsense method of creating several distributed systems. However, not all companies have the capability of supporting a GUI environment; or in the event of remote support, the line mode on the server might be the only option. For this reason, the processes described in this chapter do not address the GUI portion of the distributed option. It does address what happens after the mouse is clicked and how to manage a system without a GUI environment. Oracle8 and Oracle8i come with a GUI tool named Oracle Enterprise Manager for managing distributed databases. In Oracle8, the Enterprise Manager was available on Windows NT. In Oracle8i, Enterprise Manager is a Java-based tool and can be run from all major platforms.

Describing Each Type of Database

Distributed databases are actually two types of systems:

- Distributed databases with remote queries, data manipulation, and two-phase commit
- Replicated databases through data managed methods such as snapshots and triggers, or other non-database managed methods (such as the COPY in SQL*PLUS)

A *distributed database*, in the purest form, is a series of independent databases logically linked together through a network to form a single view. *Replicated databases* contain information from other remote databases copied through a network connection.

Replicated databases are most easily classified by the method used to pass information between them. The following are the two primary methods for this copy process (most commonly referred to as *propagation*):

- Distributed transactions
- Snapshot refreshes

The *distributed transaction* is the process wherein a user's updates to one site and changes are sent to another site by means of triggers and procedures. *Snapshots* are copies of a table (or subset) that are propagated to each of the remote sites from a master site.

In distributed database systems where it might be necessary to join tables across systems, poor data access techniques can cause user data flow between database servers to be a major factor in overall performance. In order to determine the best access technique for an optimum execution plan, the optimizer must first be capable of determining a sufficient number of alternative paths. The remote join enhancements in Oracle8i present more options, allowing for better execution plans to be generated with a corresponding performance increase.

DATABASE NAMING CONVENTIONS

Access to the Internet and Internet-based databases are beginning to have a greater influence on the way databases are named, accessed, and managed. Oracle recommends that the naming convention of databases and their links follow standard Internet domain-naming conventions. This convention can have several parts, and each is divided by dots like the ones in an IP address.

The name of the database is read from right to left. This naming convention can have several parts, with the first (rightmost) being the base or root domain. By default, the domain is world. This is not required in Net8 but for consistency, it might be best to include it in order to support older versions of SQL*Net.

The domain name can be based on the structure of the company or location. For example, the naming convention for the database in Germany can be done in a few ways. In the simplest form, the name can be GERMANY.WORLD. If the database name is based on location, the name would be GERMANY.BWC with BWC being the domain. One other way would be to expand the location to continents, and then the name would be GERMANY.EUROPE.BWC. Whatever the naming convention, it must be easily understood for future maintainability yet remain transparent to programmers and users.

> **Caution**
>
> There are some limitations when naming a domain and database. In addition to normal Oracle naming conventions, (no spaces, no special characters, and so on), the size of the name may be limited by the operating system or network. Refer to the Oracle specific documentation for name length limitations.

ACHIEVING TRANSPARENCY

It is important that when providing names to the tables and objects on remote systems, the naming convention allows the programmer and user of the system to access the table as they would if it were local. *Transparency* is the concept that all objects are accessible and look the same for the DBA and user alike.

Oracle, through the use of SQL*Net and transparent gateways, enables the development of a system that looks the same regardless of database vendor, type, and location. For more information concerning data transparency, refer to Chapter 34, "The Advanced Security Option."

The purpose of transparency is to provide seamless access to all databases. For example, users should be able to access any table (provided they have security) in the same method. A table located on a SYBASE database should be accessible with the same SQL syntax as a local table. A table located on an Oracle database in Germany should be accessible with the same syntax as a local table in Detroit. For more information concerning transparent gateways, read Oracle8i documentation on the gateway desired. For example, through the use of a transparent gateway, the SYBASE system will now look like an Oracle database and can be referenced by using a database link.

Heterogeneous service (HS) agents have been made multithreaded in Oracle8i. This new feature will reduce the amount of system resources consumed when there are large numbers of user sessions concurrently accessing the same non-Oracle system. This more efficient use of system resources allows a greater number of concurrent user sessions.

The following is an example of what a heterogeneous environment can look like:

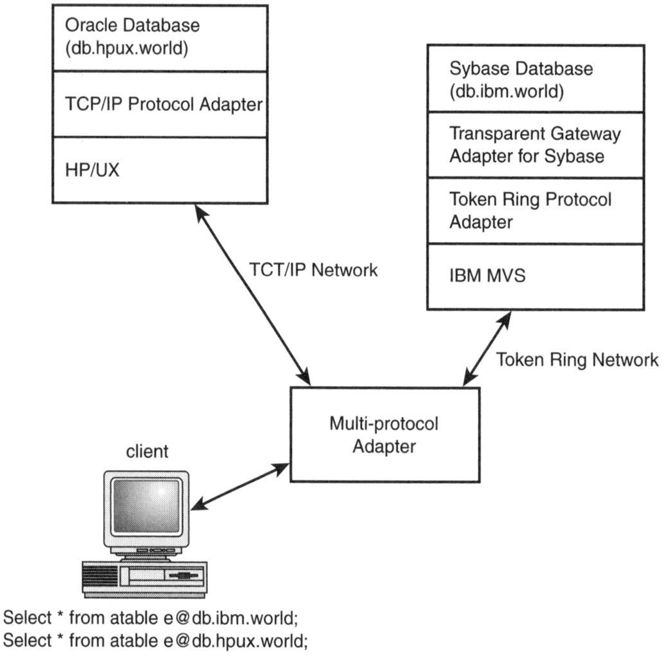

Figure 40.1
A distributed hetero-
geneous environment.

```
Select * from atable e@db.ibm.world;
Select * from atable e@db.hpux.world;
```

There must be a methodology in place to propagate any changes of database addresses to other distributed sites. This is ultimately the responsibility of the DBA. Many sites place the TNSNAMES.ORA and SQLNET.ORA on a centralized application server, which enables management of TNSNAMES in a less painful manner. However, this may not always be an optimal solution. In a distributed environment, each site might have other independent databases (such as testing databases, other databases specific to that site, and so on) and cannot have a localized TNSNAMES. If this is the case, the company might decide to use Oracle Names rather than Net8 as the method of managing connectivity. Schema names, userIDs, and passwords must also be managed when creating a distributed environment. For example, if the password is included in the creation of a link, the password cannot change, or if it does, this must be communicated to the DBA responsible for maintaining the links affected by that schema.

> **Note**
>
> If Net8 is used, communication between sites is important. There should be a formalized methodology for moving distributed database IP addresses or renaming databases.

Agent self-registration was introduced in Oracle8.0. It reduces or eliminates the need for DBA intervention in configuring heterogeneous services. In Oracle8i, code has been rewritten to make the self-registration process more efficient.

New in Oracle8i is an agent-specific, shared library for HS object files, other than drivers, that is substituted when linking agent executables. While the benefits from this change are platform-specific, they can improve scalability by using a single agent library for all types of agents (`extproc`, `hsalloci`, `hssqlpss`, `hsdepxa`, and `hsots`). Also, memory requirements might be reduced because agent executables become quite small.

USING ORACLE SECURITY SERVER AND GLOBAL USERS

Oracle Security Server is a product that will enable the DBA or security administrator to manage security in a global environment. The Security Server enables the administrator to create a user that utilizes a personal certificate rather than a password for authentication. This certificate is like the one required when accessing sites that support electronic commerce. One such certifying agency is VeriSign.

When logging in to certain sites, an error is issued that warns users they must have a personal certificate prior to entering the site. Their certificate identifies them by name, address, and other required information that uniquely identifies the person. It can be issued only once, and great care must be taken to secure this certificate. Release 1 of Oracle Security Server issues certificates only for Web servers. In Release 2, this capability is improved to include Net8 clients and servers. According to Oracle documentation, the certificates issued by the Oracle Security Server are in compliance with the international standard for electronic commerce (X.509).

To ensure that only those people with the proper authorization access the database, Oracle has created a two-tiered level of security. The DBA must create the user with the Oracle Security Server and also in the database as a global user. Without both the userID and the certificate, access is denied. Care must be taken in creating the global user. A userID cannot be both global and local.

SQL*NET

The DBA must have a strong understanding of how to effectively set up and use Net8 in order to manage a distributed system. Net8 and its management are addressed Chapter 33, "Oracle Networking Fundamentals."

In conjunction with the system administrator and the network administrator, the DBA will have to establish what servers will be capable of supporting the distributed systems. A server that controls the mail or intranet system will be an unlikely target for the distributed databases. Network traffic has a direct impact on the performance of any database, particularly the distributed system.

USING A DISTRIBUTED DATABASE

The distributed database is made up of several databases that are linked by database links and network connections. Management of these systems can vary greatly. In large, highly decentralized companies, each location may have its own DBA. In a highly centralized company, one DBA may be responsible for databases located in different states, and in some cases, countries. The management and tuning of these databases are the same as of autonomous databases, with the exception of the links and the views that reference them.

There are several reasons to utilize a distributed database system. The following are some of them:

- Application design—Certain software designs evolve into a distributed system. Companies that have multiple locations with separate IT/IS departments or databases will utilize the same or similar software. Each locality will maintain data that is unique to its own environment. As the company evolves, each locality will require access to data located at the other sites. This will eventually develop into a distributed system.

- Improved performance—Local databases will be smaller than a larger centralized database. As a result, queries and other transactions on the database will be faster. Network activity will be significantly reduced, improving the overall system.

- Smaller, less expensive hardware requirements—By reducing the total number of users on each system, the hardware required to support such a system can be considerably smaller (depending on the actual number of users on each site). For example, each local database might be capable of running on a single CPU NT server rather than a large mainframe.

- Improved reliability and availability—By distributing the data over several sites, the system is more likely to be up. While one site might be down, the rest of the system will still be up and accessible. This can be improved by distributing not only the data, but the software as well. The distribution of software adds another dimension of reliability. By having sites that are software copies, each can be a mirror site in the support of a disaster recovery plan.

- Improved mass deployment support and front office applications

In release 8.1 (8i), Oracle is providing its advanced replication to back office types of applications and front office applications. Back office applications require near real-time replication of data. The front office applications area is a growing market, particulary for mass deployment where the advanced replication functionality has many advantages.

These features can be useful for companies. For example, suppose Big Widget Company (BWC) is a large, international widget maker with offices in Detroit, Michigan; Milan, Italy; and Frankfurt, Germany. BWC has started an aggressive R&D program to develop a new type of widget for international use. Because of each country's standards, the widget specification for each country is slightly different. These differences are kept in a separate table named SITE_SPECIFICATION. Because this is an R&D project, the changes to the specifications are highly dynamic, and each country requires occasional access to the other's specifications; so there is a need for a distributed database.

SETTING UP A DISTRIBUTED SYSTEM

The setup of a distributed system might be dependent on the application. If the software utilizes the distributed database, many of the tasks performed by the DBA, such as the creation of database links, might be performed automatically during the installation of the software. However, in the case of BWC, the responsibility of setting up the distributed database is the DBAs. Because this is an R&D project, BWC has decided to invest the funds in the development side of the project. As a result, the responsibility for maintaining the databases relies on one DBA.

Each database will be installed as an autonomous database. The setup should be based on the number of concurrent users on the database in each country. Other factors to consider when installing the database as follows:

- Overall use of the database
- Other applications using the database
- Standard DBA tuning techniques
- Type of network protocol for connectivity.
- How dynamic the data is, and how it will affect the network traffic
- Current level of network traffic and what the new databases will do to affect it

PART

IX

CH

40

Note Remote users should be included in determining concurrent users if a system is heavily accessed.

USING DATABASE LINKS

Database links comprise the method used by Oracle to access a remote database object. There are three types of database links:

- Public
- Private
- Global

A public database link is similar to a public synonym; when referenced, it is accessible to all users. Private links are accessible by the owner (schema) of the link. A global link is created automatically when using Oracle Names. Oracle Names is explained in detail in Chapter 33.

There are some significant additions in the syntax of the Oracle8 database link. The syntax for creating a public or private database link is essentially the same:

```
CREATE
[SHARED]
[PUBLIC]
DATABASE LINK dblink
[authenticated clause]¦[CONNECT TO [CURRENT_USER¦user

IDENTIFIED BY password] [authenticated clause] USING '{connect string}';
```

There are several differences between Oracle8 and Oracle7 for this syntax. A new process has been added and another has been altered.

SHARED is an entirely new process. In order to use this process, the database must be using a multithreaded server. This enables the creation of a database link that can use existing connections, if available. This should not be used unless the DBA fully understands the concept behind shared database links and the multithreaded server. If set up improperly, the performance of the system can be severely affected. For more information concerning shared database links and how to effectively use them, read Chapter 2, "Distributed Database Administration—Shared Database Links," in *Oracle8 Server Distributed Database Systems*.

The authenticated clause is associated with the SHARED portion of the database link. This must be used when using SHARED. The following is the syntax for the authentication clause:

AUTHENTICATED BY *username* IDENTIFIED by *PASSWORD*

This does not perform any action by the user in the authentication clause; it requires that the username be a valid user and password on the remote server. The DBA can create a dummy account specifically for this purpose.

CURRENT_USER uses the new Oracle8 global user type. This powerful new feature enables the creation of a user that can access any database on a node (server) with the use of a single login. This is not to be confused with a local user. This user must be created using the Oracle8 Security Server.

Using the BWC example, the following code would create a simple public link in the Germany database from Detroit:

```
CREATE PUBLIC DATABASE LINK germany.bwc.com
USING 'GERMANY';
```

Note that the database name is case-sensitive. If not defined by Oracle Names, the name GERMANY must appear, either as an alias or as the actual name in TNSNAMES.ORA. The TNSNAMES.ORA must be on the client and server. With this syntax, the user must have a current login on both Germany's and Detroit's database. Assuming that the schema name is the same for both Germany and Detroit, the syntax for accessing the table SITE_SPECIFICATION would be the following:

```
SELECT * FROM SITE_SPECIFICATION@GERMANY.BWC.COM;
```

Note	The link within the SQL statement is not case-sensitive.

Tip #122	To ensure transparency, create a synonym or view to hide the database link from the users: `CREATE SYNONYM germany_specification` `FOR site_specification@germany.bwc.com;`

Creating a database link can be as simple or as complex as the DBA chooses to make it. For example, a link can be created establishing a connection to Europe. This could be advantageous in the event that BWC expands to other countries in Europe. The database link for both Milan and Frankfurt would be

```
CREATE DATABASE LINK europe using 'EUROPE.BWC';
```

This initial connect would not work, however, when creating a synonym; the DBA could then expand on the name by adding the country:

```
CREATE SYNONYM germany_specification FOR site_specification@europe@germany;
```

PART

IX

CH

40

Note	As in previous versions of Oracle, Oracle8 does not support selecting a LONG datatype from a remote database.

DEFERRED TRANSACTIONS   Deferred transactions are transactions that will occur at a later time. For example, changes made at a primary site are stored in a queue and are deferred until the replication mechanism takes the changes and applies them to a remote site(refer to Table 40.1).

USING INITIALIZATION PARAMETERS FOR DISTRIBUTED SYSTEMS

In addition to the parameters specified in the distributed database section, more parameters are in Table 40.1.

TABLE 40.1   PARAMETERS AFFECTED BY DEFERRED TRANSACTION DATABASE

Parameter	Description
COMMIT_POINT_STRENGTH (0–255)	This parameter is used to set the commit point site in the two-phased commit. The site with the highest commit point strength will be the commit point site. Each of the sites using this as the commit point site must be on the same node. The factors determining which database should be the commit point site should be ownership (driver) of data, criticality of data, and availability of the system. Information concerning the status of the commit is located on the commit point site. It is recommended that not all sites have the same value or only one with a higher value. This ensures that in the event of a failure, other sites can record this data. This parameter's defaults are operating system-specific. Refer to your operating system-specific Oracle8 documentation for these values.
DISTRIBUTED_TRANSACTIONS (0–TRANSACTIONS)	Limits the number of concurrent distributed transactions. If set to 0, the process RECO (Oracle's recovery process) is not activated, and distributed capabilities of the database are disabled.
GLOBAL_NAMES	If set to TRUE, the name referenced in the link must match the name of the database and not the alias. This must be used in order to utilize advanced replication features of Oracle8.
DML_LOCKS (20–unlimited)	Limits the number of DML locks in a single transaction.
ENQUEUE RESOURCES (10–65535)	Allows several concurrent processes to share resources. To determine whether this value is set appropriately, enqueue_waits in the v$sysstat table. If this is a non-zero value, increase the enqueue resources.
MAX_TRANSACTION BRANCHES (1–32)	The maximum value for this parameter has been increased from 8 to 32. Branches are the numbers of different servers (or server groups) that can be accessed in a single distributed transaction. Reducing this number might decrease the amount of shared pool use.
OPEN_LINKS (0–255)	The number of concurrent open connections to other databases by one session. In a distributed environment, care must be taken to ensure that this value is not less than the number of remote tables that can be referenced in a single SQL statement. If the value is set to 0, there can be no distributed transactions.
OPEN_LINKS_PER INSTANCE (0–UB4MAXVAL)	This is new to Oracle8. It limits the number of open links created by an external transaction manager. For more information, refer to your Oracle8i documentation.

IDENTIFYING POTENTIAL PROBLEMS WITH A DISTRIBUTED SYSTEM

System changes are the biggest problem in managing a simple distributed system. It is similar to managing a single, autonomous database, but the difference is that each database can see objects in other databases. This creates a system that depends on continuity. Following are the changes within a system that must be coordinated within a distributed system.

■ Structural changes—Procedures and triggers used to update or replicate specific remote tables will fail when the remote table is structurally altered or removed. Database links that reference a dropped table will fail.

Note

If a user drops a table that is referenced by links from another system, there will not be a referential integrity warning. These warnings occur only when the table contains elements that are referenced.

■ Schema changes—In addition to tables being removed, the privileges of a user referenced in a database link must have the proper privileges. Changes to profiles and roles must be coordinated to ensure that they will not affect the rest of the distributed system. This includes passwords!

■ Changes to the SQL*Net objects—Files such as TNSNAMES, PROTOCOL, and TNSNAV will affect the distributed database system.

■ System outages—Coordination between outages is crucial, particularly to systems that depend on distributed updates, snapshots, or replication. In many cases, if this process is broken, manual intervention must occur in order to repair the problem. Unless a DBA is informed that a database or network is down, the integrity of the distributed system is jeopardized.

Communication between organizations is extremely important, particularly among developers and the DBA. A change in the structure of one database or IP address can affect the entire company and the integrity of the distributed system. This coordination usually is in the hands of the DBA.

Another problem can occur if the connection between databases is lost. The responsibility in determining what has happened if connectivity is lost begins with the DBA. The DBA must be able to easily identify error messages, particularly associated with SQL*Net or Net8. For more information concerning troubleshooting connection problems, refer to Chapter 33 of this book.

TUNING A DISTRIBUTED SYSTEM

Tuning methods for a distributed database should be the same as those for an autonomous database. Please refer to Part IV, "Performance Tuning," and keep the following rules in mind:

■ Poorly written SQL will still perform poorly if distributed.

■ Remote tables that are partitioned are not seen as partitioned by the local cost-based optimizer.

■ Avoid using multiple database links in a single SQL statement.

PART
IX

CH
40

USING DISTRIBUTED TRANSACTIONS

When referring to a distributed transaction and the two-phased commit, there is a complexity that might seem overwhelming. Keep in mind one primary idea: Oracle7 and Oracle8i manage the distributed transaction *automatically*. Most DBAs will not have the opportunity to actually see a two-phase commit because they are trigger-based processes. The following example illustrates a two-phased commit.

BWC has a specifications tables (SPEC_TABLE) that is dependent on the regulations table within the U.S. (US_REG). When new data is inserted or updated in the US_REG table, the application updates and inserts data into SPEC_TABLE at sites in Germany, Italy, and Detroit.

Figure 40.2
A two-phased commit.

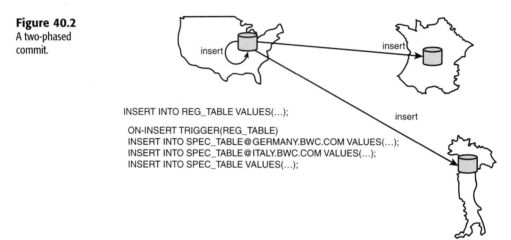

```
INSERT INTO REG_TABLE VALUES(...);

ON-INSERT TRIGGER(REG_TABLE)
INSERT INTO SPEC_TABLE@GERMANY.BWC.COM VALUES(...);
INSERT INTO SPEC_TABLE@ITALY.BWC.COM VALUES(...);
INSERT INTO SPEC_TABLE VALUES(...);
```

UNDERSTANDING TWO-PHASED COMMIT

A two-phased commit occurs with all data manipulation language (DML), and as the name implies, it is made up of two distinct phases. In order to ensure consistency in the explanation, the DML used in this section is an update.

The first phase of a two-phased commit is called the *prepare phase*. The initiating database is known as the *global coordinator*; it sends a message to all the other databases informing them that an update is about to occur. This message does not have the actual update, just a small amount that enables the other databases to know what is to be updated. The receiving databases will respond to the global coordinator if the update can occur. The receiving databases can respond in three ways:

- Prepared—Ready for update.
- Read-only—No preparation necessary.
- Abort—The child cannot perform the update.

> **Note**
>
> The global coordinator will determine the order of the databases to be updated.

The receiving databases must also perform some system checks, including sending a prepare statement to any of its own coordinating databases. This includes placing locks (if not read-only) on the row to be updated. After all the receiving databases have responded, the global coordinator places the transaction in-doubt. If all the children respond with prepared or read-only, the global coordinator determines the commit point site.

The DBA determines which database should be a commit point site by the stability of the databases. For example, a database on a UNIX server is more stable than a database on a PC. The primary goal is to pick a database that will not create a lock due to an in-doubt transaction. A transaction that is rolled back or committed is referred to as an in-doubt transaction.

The DBA assigns commit point sites by the value COMMIT_POINT_STRENGTH in the parameter file. The higher value in the distributed tree determines the commit point strength. If the system is highly distributed, more than one database should be assigned as the commit point site. This is also applicable if transactions affect different databases. The commit point site is the first database to be committed. Then it keeps up with the status of the transaction until all transactions have been completed.

The second phase, or the commit phase, is the process of committing the data. After all the receiving databases have successfully committed and communicated their success to the global coordinator, the global coordinator sends a message to the commit point site. The commit point site removes the status as in-doubt. Each of the children will commit and release the row-level lock on the record.

When the child responds with an abort message, the entire transaction is rolled back. The transaction is an all-or-nothing process. In order to ensure data consistency, all the children must either commit or roll back the master transaction. The DBA must be able to identify and correct an unsuccessful commit to effectively manage this type of distributed system.

PART

IX

CH

40

> **Note**
>
> When a commit is unsuccessful, the program or person performing the update must be notified that an error has occurred. This notification should occur by design.

> **Note**
>
> If a transaction fails to commit on one of the nodes of a distributed system, the transaction is rolled back on all nodes. When creating rollback segments, all the hosts (nodes) in the distributed system must be capable of accommodating the largest transaction anticipated on the distributed system.

Dealing with In-Doubt Transactions

Network problems will be the most likely cause of in-doubt transactions. Just as in the management of the two-phased commit, Oracle7 and Oracle8i automatically manage any problems detected during a network failure. As it is easier to allow the automatic recover in the disaster recovery process, Oracle recommends that the DBA allow the automatic recover of an in-doubt transaction. There are some exceptions to this recommendation. Problems can occur because of row-level locks placed on in-doubt transactions during the network failure. This can make data inaccessible for other users trying to access the rows in question during the failure. A DBA might need to manually manage the transaction in order to remove these locks. The process of managing the transactions is referred to as forcing a transaction.

In the event of a network loss, it will most likely be evident to not only the DBA but also the entire user community affected by that network. Other users with databases not affected by the downed network will continue to work. Users will notice a problem when they try to perform DDL on the inaccessible database. The problem that a DBA will have to address is the lock. DBAs with experience on earlier versions of SQL*Net are familiar with the daemon locks that occur when a connection is dropped. This is the same type of scenario that occurs when the network drops during a distributed transaction. The primary difference is that if left alone, the distributed transaction will correct itself when the network is back up. If a network is going to be down for a long period of time, the DBA should be prepared to force any outstanding transactions that are causing locks.

The actual process of forcing the transaction to either rollback or commit is simple. The problem is that the DBA (or DBAs) must force the transaction locally. This can mean that if one DBA is responsible for managing several databases, each transaction will have to be manually investigated. For example, a user in Detroit has updated a row in a table that is to update the same table in Milan and Frankfurt. If the transaction failed prior to writing to any system, the DBA should log on to each computer and force the transaction at each site. The force can be in either the form of a commit or a rollback. Although cumbersome, this should not be something that will have to be done frequently.

Great care should be taken when manually forcing a transaction. This should be done as an all-or-nothing solution. When performed, the DBA should either coordinate with other DBAs to ensure that the modification matches the other environments or validate the consistency on all databases by hand. This means querying each database affected and ensuring that the data is exactly the same on each site. If this is not done, inconsistencies of the data can occur. The steps to manually force a transaction are as follows:

1. Follow that transaction to where it failed or started to fail.

2. If possible, find a transaction that has completed, either by rolling the transaction back or committing.

3. Use this transaction as the template to force the other transactions. A logical place to start is the commit point site.

4. Query the DBA_2PC_PENDING table. In the column TRAN_COMMENT, there might be information on where the transaction started and what was being done. For example

```
COMMIT COMMENT 'transaction name';
```

The single quotes are required, and the transaction name is case-sensitive

There might also be information in the ADVICE column. This indicates to the DBA where the transaction was. For example

```
ALTER SESSION ADVISE COMMIT;
```

The column GLOBAL_TRAN_ID in the DBA_2PC_PENDING table provides the DBA with the transaction ID. This ID is the same on all databases involved in the distributed transaction. If the database is the global coordinator, the last part of the GLOBAL_TRAN_ID will match LOCAL_ID in the DBA_2PC_PENDING table.

5. Look at the DBA_2PC_NEIGHBORS. The table looks like this:

LOCAL_TRAN_ID—The local transaction ID for this distributed transaction.

IN_OUT—Indicates whether the transaction is IN or OUT.

DATABASE—If the transaction is IN, this is the name of the database sending the transaction. If the transaction is OUT, this is the name of the database link to the database to which the transaction is being sent.

DBUSER_OWNER—If the transaction is IN, this is the name of the local user. If the transaction is OUT, this is the owner of the database link.

INTERFACE—C for commit request, N if in prepare or read-only state.

DBID—Oracle unique identifier for the connecting database.

SESS#—Session ID of the connection.

BRANCH—Transaction ID for this branch.

6. Using the information in this table (the database and LOCAL_TRAN_ID), follow this thread to the next database.

7. Query the DBA_2PC_PENDING table. If LOCAL_TRAN_ID and GLOBAL_TRAN_ID match, this is the global coordinator. This is where the DBA should start to follow the transaction thread. If during this tracing process the DBA encounters a resolved transaction, use this as the template for the outstanding transactions.

8. To force a transaction, use the TRANSACTION_ID in the DBA_2PC_PENDING table, as in the following:

```
Commit force 'transaction id';
Rollback force 'transaction_id';
```

The single quotes are required.

9. If in doubt, always roll the transaction back. Then communicate this rollback to the user community. As an added precaution, check the status of the tables affected to ensure data consistency. Although cumbersome, this will happen infrequently and will always ensure the integrity of the database.

UNDERSTANDING READ-ONLY SNAPSHOTS

A snapshot is a copy of a master table (or a subset) replicated to other child sites at specified intervals. The read-only snapshot is a faster solution than the distributed query (a select statement referencing a remote table). In addition to removing the network overhead, the hits on the remote table are significantly reduced. The snapshot can be one of the best methods of providing information to other remote sites, if the information needed does not have to be in real-time. The snapshots are normally refreshed on a predetermined schedule. Each snapshot or set of snapshots can have its own update schedule. Snapshots can be replicated to different locations depending on the requirements of each site. In addition to scheduled refreshes, the DBA can manually refresh a snapshot. This is done using the DBMS_REFRESH procedure. The syntax for such a refresh is

```
EXECUTE DBMS_REFRESH.REFRESH ('Snapshotname');
```

> **Note**
>
> In this format, the refresh will use the default of FAST. If a COMPLETE is desired, this must be added to the procedure call.

The purposes for providing snapshots are the same as those of a simple distributed system. The following are specific reasons to use snapshots rather than dynamic database links:

■ Improved performance—A snapshot is actually a local object. A user can query the snapshot without the overhead associated with the network.

■ Greater reliability—If the master site is down, access to the object is not restricted.

For example, BWC has determined that because of increased reliance on the U.S. widget specifications, the distributed databases no longer support the business. Snapshots of the widget specifications are established. For business reasons, BWC has decided that Italy and Germany do not need to know what the other country's specifications are, but the United States needs to know what the widget specifications are for the other two countries. All the widget designs are kept in separate tables, so you don't need to combine the tables. The owner of the tables is the same worldwide to reduce confusion.

CREATING A SNAPSHOT AT THE COLUMN LEVEL

Updatable snapshots can now be subset horizontally (selected rows) or vertically (selected columns). The previous release allows vertical subsetting only.

Vertical partitioning allows the deployment of the minimum amount of data needed by a remote site, thus reducing connection time. It also protects snapshot sites from changes to their associated masters. A column can be added to a master site without impacting the snapshot site, or a column can be deleted and not impact the snapshot site if the snapshot site does not currently reference that column.

SETTING UP A SNAPSHOT

Creating snapshots is as simple as creating a table. Actually, this is what the DBA is doing—creating a copy of a table. The difference is that the copy becomes an automated process rather than a manual one. Then after the table is copied, it is updated on a regular schedule to reflect the changes. The layout of the snapshot should be based on the same principles used to create a table.

The syntax for creating a snapshot is as follows:

```
CREATE SNAPSHOT [schema.]SNAPSHOT [Physical attributes *]
[TABLESPACE tablespace]
[LOB_storage_clause]
[CACHE¦NOCACHE]
[CLUSTER (cluster column{,})]
[table partition clause]
[parallel clause]
[USING INDEX physical attributes clause [LOGGING¦NOLOGGING]TABLESPACE tablespace]
[FAST¦COMPLETE¦FORCE]
[START WITH date]
[NEXT date]
[WITH PRIMARY KEY¦ROWID]
[USING DEFAULT {MASTER¦LOCAL}] ROLLBACK SEGMENT]
[LOCAL¦MASTER ROLLBACK SEGMENT rollback_segment]
FOR UPDATE AS select_command;
```

For example, the following creates a simple snapshot:

```
CREATE SNAPSHOT milan_specification
REFRESH FORCE START WITH SYSDATE next SYSDATE + 7 ;
```

START WITH and NEXT of the CREATE SNAPSHOT command is based on SYSDATE. A whole number represents a single date. In the preceding example, the next refresh rate is exactly 7 days from the first refresh. If next is not used, the snapshot will never refresh. If the refresh is to occur on a segment of time, such as an hour or half-hour, it will be in fractions. For example, a refresh rate of an hour will be SYSDATE + 1/24. A refresh rate of a half-hour will be 1/10, every 15 minutes would be 1/64, and so on. If the refresh should always occur on a Monday, the syntax is a bit more complicated, such as the following:

```
NEXT_DAY(TRUNC(SYSDATE), 'MONDAY')+3/24
```

NEXT_DAY is specified instead of SYSDATE. The 3 of the 24 represents 3 a.m. in the morning.

Using Index allows the creation of an index which can improve performance when selecting from the snapshot.

PART

IX

CH

40

FORCE/FAST/COMPLETE of the CREATE SNAPSHOT command is the method of replication. COMPLETE is the most time-intensive. This is recreating the snapshot and is done by performing an INSERT INTO ...AS SELECT *. COMPLETE is also what is used to create the initial snapshot. If a table is a significant size, this option should be avoided after the initial creation.

FAST is the default. It uses the log to compare the two snapshots and only adds what is in the log.

Note

> In a Version 7 database if a fast refresh fails, the snapshot refresh becomes broken and cannot be repaired without manual intervention. In Version 8, if the FAST refresh fails, a complete refresh will be performed. FAST refresh will work only if the snapshot has a snapshot log.

FORCE performs a FAST refresh unless it is incapable of doing so (for example, a broken refresh). This option is removed in Version 8.

The management of snapshots does not change significantly between Version 7 and 8. The biggest change is in the addition of options within the create clause. Most of these changes are not directly related to the snapshot process. They are due to the addition of new object types, new create table commands, and new create index commands. The differences include the following:

LOB_STORAGE_CLAUSE is related to the Large Object Definition. For more information on large objects, please refer to *Oracle8i Server Application Developer's Guide*.

LOGGING/NOLOGGING specifies whether redo log information is to be written when creating an index. This is similar to the CREATE INDEX NO RECOVER command. It also affects direct loading and direct load inserts. This can significantly affect the index during recovery. For more information read the GREAT INDEX command in the Oracle8i SQL documentation.

CACHE/NOCACHE specifies whether the snapshot will be kept in memory after a full table scan. For more information, read the *Oracle8i Concepts Guide* concerning memory structures, cache, and the LRU algorithm.

WITH PRIMARY KEY is a default in Oracle8i. By specifying the creation of a primary key snapshot, the master table can be reorganized without impacting a fast refresh. There are some limitations concerning utilizing a PRIMARY KEY snapshot

- There must be a primary key in the table referenced. This must be by using the PRIMARY KEY constraint of the CREATE TABLE command.
- All columns within the primary key must be used.

Caution

> If the primary key is not used with the create snapshot command, the record's rowid will be used. This can create potential problems if the master table is recovered due to a database recovery. The recovery will change the rowid values and can potentially invalidate the snapshot. To ensure that this is not a problem, refresh snapshots using the complete option after any database recovery.

USING DEFAULTMASTER | LOCAL specifies the type of rollback segment. DEFAULT will enable Oracle to choose; MASTER will use the rollback segment at the remote site; and LOCAL will use the rollback segments in the local database.

USING SNAPSHOT REFRESH GROUPS

Many snapshots, although associated with different master tables, might have the same refresh rate, making them candidates for grouping. Although Oracle8i enables a point-and-click method for creating these snapshots, it is important to know what happens behind the mouse.

Oracle refers to this capability as *API calls*. The manipulations of replicated objects are not performed via standard SQL commands. The calls are performed through the use of procedures. For more information concerning procedures, their syntax and how they are used, refer to the *Oracle8i™ Application Developer's Guide*.

FASTER SNAPSHOT REFRESH

Snapshot refresh has been optimized to support large refresh groups. There is improved support for subquery snapshots, and for null refresh (no changes to the master tables since the last refresh). A single refresh group can now contain 400 snapshots, and the number of roundtrips required to refresh snapshots in a refresh group has been reduced. (This feature was first added in release 8.0.5.)

IDENTIFYING POTENTIAL PROBLEMS WITH A SNAPSHOT

As with any database management process, proactive management is the most appropriate method. To proactively manage the snapshot process, the DBA must be able to identify potential problems and design the system in order to prevent them from occurring. This section identifies some of these problems.

SIZING

There is one pitfall to avoid during the creation of a snapshot. Although it is query only, the snapshot is not a static table. Sizing should be based on the update rate of the table copied, not the snapshot itself. For example, if the table GERMANY_SPECS is highly dynamic, it should have a larger percent used (PCTUSED) to accommodate the updates. The table should be sized to ensure that fragmentation does not occur.

DROPPING OBJECTS INADVERTENTLY

Some of the snapshots are in refresh groups. To find the job numbers associated with them, query the DBA_REFRESH_CHILDREN table. These groups can be dropped; however, care must be taken to ensure that the objects are not also dropped. For this reason, the method for dropping any type of replication group should be performed via SQL code and not the Enterprise Manger. The Enterprise Manager enables the DBA to drop the objects by clicking on them. The way to drop refresh groups is to use this procedure:

```
execute DBMS_REPCAT.DROP_SNAPSHOT_REPGROUP(gname=>'[name of group]'
```

The drop_contents defaults to FALSE; when using procedures, they must be entered as a single line or they will not be invoked.

| Caution | If you set drop_contents to TRUE, the tables associated with the group are also dropped. |

LOSING SNAPSHOT REFRESHES

When a master database cannot complete the refresh of a snapshot, it will try 16 more times before the refresh attempts stop. The 16 times does not mean 16 refresh intervals. The first time a refresh fails, the snapshot process will wait one minute and try again. If that fails, the time doubles to two minutes then four minutes, and the time span grows exponentially until it reaches or exceeds the actual refresh interval. When that occurs, it will continue at the refresh rate. After 16 times, Oracle will update the column BROKEN in the tables USER_REFRESH and USER_REFRESH_CHILDREN. The BROKEN column indicates that something has gone wrong with the snapshot refresh. This will not only be reflected in this table, but the Oracle SNP process will also indicate a refresh problem in trace files and alert.log.

One way to reduce the possibility of a broken snapshot is to create the snapshot with the FORCE option rather than FAST. FORCE will choose FAST unless something has occurred to prevent a successful FAST refresh; then it will perform a complete refresh instead. One drawback to using this option is in the event of a very large table. If the refresh takes a long time, problems might occur if the current refresh is still going when the next refresh is scheduled to occur.

After the DBA has determined that the refresh is broken and has rectified the problems that broke the snapshot, the snapshot can be manually refreshed. Oracle8i provides several methods of refreshing manually. One way is to execute the job defined as the snapshot. To determine this, log in at the child site and perform the following query:

```
SELECT RNAME,JOB FROM DBA_REFRESH;
```

The results will be similar to this:

```
RNAME           JOB
GERMANY SPECS   142
```

Run the job that has the broken snapshot. The job name will be the same as the snapshot (local/child). To perform this, use the following procedure:

```
Execute DBMS_JOB.RUN(142);
```

The response will be the following:

```
PL/SQL procedure successfully completed.
```

When this has been completed, verify that the BROKEN status of the USER_REFRESH and USER_REFRESH_CHILDREN tables is no longer Y. If the BROKEN status remains at Y, repeat the process again. If this does not fix the problem, ensure that there are not other problems (such a loss of connectivity,) which is preventing this refresh from occurring.

To proactively monitor the refresh process and prevent another broken snapshot, compare the snapshot time and the time in the snapshot logs. These should match; if they do not, it might indicate that the problem causing the initial loss of the snapshot has not been completely resolved.

At the master site, use the following query:

```
SELECT MASTER,SUBSTR
(TO_CHAR
(CURRENT_SNAPSHOTS,'MM-DD-YYYY HH:MI:SS'),
1,20)
TIME FROM DBA_SNAPSHOT_LOGS;
```

From the local/child site, use the following query:

```
SELECT NAME,SUBSTR
(TO_CHAR
(LAST_REFRESH,'MM-DD-YYYY HH:MISS'),
1,20)
TIME FROM DBA_SNAPSHOTS;
```

These times should match. If they do not, the snapshots will require manual management until the problem has been completely resolved.

CONTROLLING SNAPSHOT LOG GROWTH

Snapshot logs contain the DML changes of the master snapshot. This determines what should be sent to the remote sites. The log is purged after *all* the snapshots using this log have been completed. However, if there is a problem with the snapshot or one of the snapshots is refreshed infrequently, the snapshot log can grow uncontrollably. This can present a problem in two ways. The DBA should size the logs to enable a certain amount of growth. If the stability of the snapshot is mission-critical, the use of unlimited extents is recommended. This removes the possibility of reaching the max extents and fills the tablespace where the log resides. The DBA should periodically check this log to ensure that this does not occur. If the size of the log is becoming unmanageable, the DBA should purge the logs. This can be done via the enterprise management tool, or the DBA can perform this with the stored procedure or API call DBMS_SNAPSHOT.PURGE_LOG. The syntax for this is as follows:

```
Execute dmbs_snapshot.purge_log('[master table name]',number,'flag');
```

number is the number of historical snapshots to remove. If the DBA wants to remove all the logs in the snapshot log, this number should be very high. Care must be taken when using this. If all the logs are removed, the snapshot will have to be completely refreshed. This can be a problem if the table is very large.

> **Note**
>
> The flag is an override value. If set to DELETE, or even if the number is set to 0, the logs will be deleted from the least recently refreshed snapshot.

UNDERSTANDING LIMITATIONS OF SNAPSHOTS

The initial creation of a snapshot of a large table might be beyond the capabilities of the system. For example, if a snapshot of a large table with several million rows of data has to be replicated over unstable communication lines, it might be better to perform an offline instantiation. To perform this, several steps must be taken. This must be done carefully and if possible, in a test environment with a great deal of storage space. Use these steps:

1. In the production database, create a snapshot log for each of the master tables (the tables that will have snapshots in the remote site).

2. Using a new schema and in the test database, create a snapshot referencing the production database containing the master table. The name must be unique. Ideally, it should be the name that will be used at the remote site.

3. If this process must be done in the production database (not recommended), the link in the CREATE SNAPSHOT statement will refer to the current database. Oracle refers to this capability as a *loopback link*.

4. Export the new schema. The same schema as the owner of the new snapshots should perform the export.

5. Drop the newly created snapshots. Be sure that this is done by hand (using API calls). If not, ensure that only the snapshots and not the corresponding objects are created.

To create a snapshot at the remote site:

1. Create an empty snapshot group. This is necessary to support the procedure call in the next step.

2. Use the following procedure:
```
DBMS_OFFLINE_SNAPSHOT.BEGIN_LOAD
(gname='[groupname]'.sname=>'snapshotname',)
```
This will create a snapshot "shell" for the data about to be imported.

3. Import the snapshot base table. This is identified by the preface SNAP$ table.

4. After the import is complete, use the procedure DBMS_OFFLINE_SNAPSHOT.END_LOAD to indicate to the system that the import is complete. The easiest way to visualize this process is the hot backup process, where the command ALTER TABLESPACE BEGIN BACKUP is issued.

Note

Just as tables cannot be created using `select` on a LONG datatype, snapshots cannot support this `select` statement.

TUNING SNAPSHOTS

Complex snapshots consisting of multiple table joins can severely degrade performance. It is imperative that the query used to create a snapshot be thoroughly tested and tuned.

This includes utilizing `explain plan` and `TKPROF` prior to creating the snapshot. If required, create several single table snapshots at the child site, and then create a view locally based on the physical snapshots. Performance will be significantly enhanced and network traffic will be reduced.

In order to keep the packages used to refresh a database in the library cache, it helps to pin these packages in memory. This helps prevent the package from being removed from memory. To pin a package, call the package, and then use the package `DBMS_SHARED_POOL`. Prior to pinning a package, it must be referenced. The easiest way to reference a package is to recompile it. The syntax follows:

```
ALTER PACKAGE DBMS_SNAPSHOT.I_AM_A_REFRESH COMPILE;
```

There will be a response:

```
Package altered.
```

Now, pin the package with the following statement:

```
Execute DBMS_SHARED_POOL.KEEP('DBMS_SNAPSHOT');
```

The response will be

```
PL/SQL procedure successfully completed.
```

This will improve performance, but might not significantly enhance it. However, it does help—particularly with those snapshots that are frequently refreshed.

Other packages that can be pinned for performance are

- DBMS_REFRESH
- DBMS_REPUTIL
- DBMS_REPCAT
- DBMS_DEFER

For more information on these packages, refer to the *Oracle8i Server Replication—Replication Manager API Reference*.

INTERNALIZATION OF REPLICATION PACKAGES

Significant performance gains are realized by the internalization of PL/SQL replication packages and by optimizations to the snapshot refresh.

Continuing the trend started with release 8.0, more replication code has been moved into the database engine. The PL/SQL generated packages used to apply replicated transactions at a remote site have been internalized. This allows replicated transactions to be more efficiently applied at remote sites and because packages are not generated, a site can be more quickly instantiated. Internal packages are also more secure because they are tamper proof.

PART
IX

CH
40

USING INITIALIZATION PARAMETERS FOR SNAPSHOTS

The init.ora table contains several parameters that directly impact the snapshot process. These parameters are defined in Table 40.2.

TABLE 40.2   INITIALIZATION PARAMETERS FOR SNAPSHOTS

Parameter	Description
JOB_QUEUE_INTERVAL (1–3600)	The interval that the snapshot process wakes up. Care must be taken to ensure that this is not set so high as to interfere with the interval of the snapshot itself.
JOB_QUEUE_PROCESSES (0–36)	Limits the number of processes for the snapshot process. Normally, one should be sufficient unless there are several snapshots or large snapshots that might interfere with the snapshot process.

REPLICATION MANAGEMENT

In this chapter

What Is Replication?

Replication is the process of maintaining copies of tables in a distributed database environment. Inserts, updates, and deletes are stored locally and applied to the distributed environment. Replicated objects include tables, indexes, database triggers, packages, and views that exist on more than one machine. Oracle supports full copies of replicated objects and partial copies of replicated objects. Oracle uses replication groups to ease the administration of the replication process. Oracle has implemented various methods of replication as well. When a database environment such as Oracle supports the update capability of the replicated sites, there might be conflicts in the data between the replicated objects. This multiple-site update capability is known as the advanced replication environment. Oracle provides several methods of dealing with conflict resolution.

Tip #123	Oracle8 supports the replication of partitioned tables and indexes.

Oracle Replication utilizes the Master site/Snapshot site scenario. A Master Site contains all of the objects (tables, indexes, views, etc) that are to be replicated with other sites. A Master Group contains a grouping of objects that are to be replicated across many sites. A snapshot site is directly related to one and only one master site. It can contain all of the objects in the master site but usually contains just a subset of objects.

Job processes are an important part of the replication process. You need one job process per master site. Snapshot sites need from one to three job processes. These job processes are necessary for user-defined jobs, purging, and the scheduling link. These jobs need to be initiated periodically. The `job_queue_intervals` mechanism controls how often these jobs are started and is recorded in seconds. `job_queue_intervals` controls the timing of the jobs.

Note

Make sure the following `INIT.ORA` parameters are set prior to attempting replication setup for a master site environment with five other master sites, replicating once per minute:

```
global_names= True
job_queue_processes = 7
job_queue_intervals = 60
```

Multiple Master Replication

Replication can also be performed via multiple masters. This will be discussed in the following sections by focusing on the concepts of master groups and snapshot groups.

MASTER GROUPS

Master groups are a collection of replicated objects. The master sites store all the objects and all the data. There is always a *master definition site*, or one master site that contains the definition of the objects being replicated and acts as a control point for the other master sites. This master definition site is where any DDL changes are applied and where replication is started and stopped. The changes to the data are then pushed from one master site to another. This is known as n-way replication.

When replication groups are placed on multiple machines, they are referred to as *multi-master groups*. Multi-master groups must contain the same number of replicated objects at each location. These multi-master groups perform true peer-to-peer replication in that each group contains the same objects and the same data. Figure 41.1 illustrates a multiple master replication scheme. Note the replication groups and the objects are the same at each node. Also, note that masters can only share data with a neighbor site. This gives Oracle a two-master update approach. If all master sites could update all other master sites at the same time, the potential conflicts would be impossible to predict, let alone manage.

Figure 41.1
Multiple master site replication example.

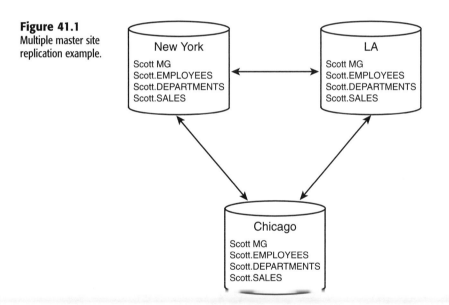

To set up a master site for replication, follow the steps outlined in Figure 41.2. Follow the steps in Figure 41.3 to set up master groups.

> **Note**
>
> Multiple master replication is only supported in Oracle8i Enterprise Edition.

Tip #124

Make sure you are logged in as `SYSTEM` before attempting to create a master site.

Figure 41.2
Steps to set up a master site.

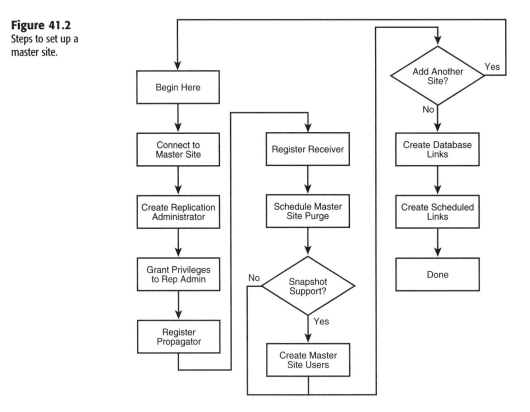

SNAPSHOT GROUPS

A *snapshot* is a subset of a master object. A snapshot contains either a complete copy or a subset of the objects in the master group. Snapshots can contain a subset of the master data, but they must contain all the columns. Snapshot groups are similar to master groups in that they are a convenient way to maintain the replication. Snapshot groups are only related to a single master group. Snapshots can be updatable. Figure 41.4 illustrates a multiple master/snapshot replication group configuration. Note that the snapshot group is only capable of sharing data with a single master group.

Figure 41.3
Steps to set up master groups.

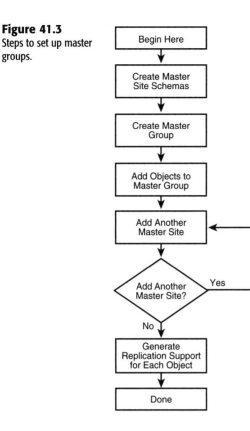

Now look at a more complex model containing master groups and snapshot groups in Figure 41.5. Note that the home office group is the master definition site as well. The home office group has three snapshot groups off of it, one updatable snapshot for each department that is responsible for the data within its control. The home office master contains all the objects. The San Francisco and New York City master group sites are sales offices. They, too, contain all the replicated objects, but their snapshot groups only contain the sales data and employee data related to that particular office.

Figure 41.4
Multiple master/
snapshot replication.

Figure 41.5
Complex master
group/snapshot
group example.

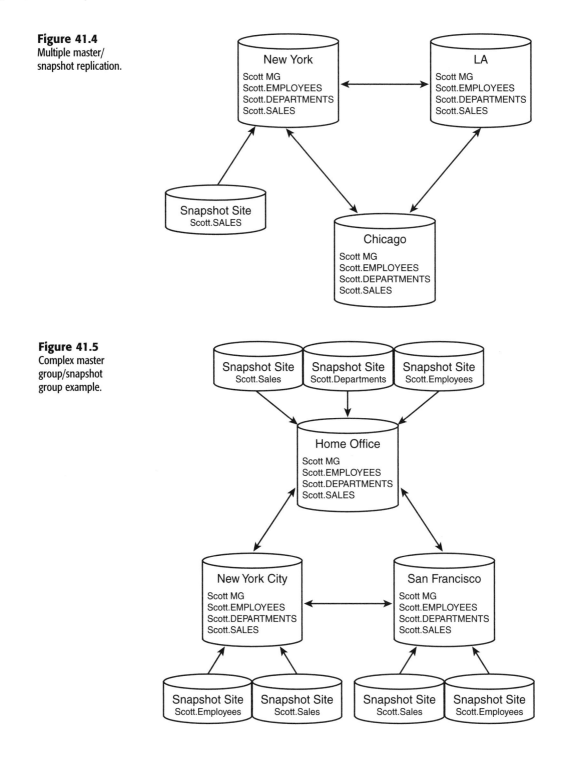

Snapshot sites are also easy to set up. Follow the steps outlined in Figure 41.6 to set up snapshot sites. After this step is done, follow the steps in Figure 41.7 to set up snapshot groups.

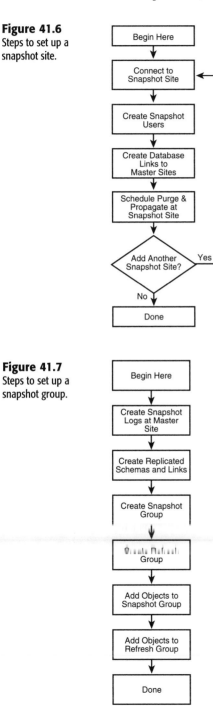

Figure 41.6
Steps to set up a snapshot site.

Figure 41.7
Steps to set up a snapshot group.

TYPES OF PROPAGATION

Changes to the master groups are pushed from one master site to another. Changes are then pulled from the master site to its snapshot sites. Changes to snapshot sites are pushed back to their coordinating master sites.

ASYNCHRONOUS PROPAGATION

Asynchronous propagation, also known as deferred transactions, is when changes are deferred or queued at the site where they occur and are pushed to the other sites at timed intervals. This push can be manually started as well. This method is known as the store-and-forward method. Figure 41.8 illustrates the use of Oracle triggers and queues in an advanced replication scheme between two master sites. This same configuration can be used to propagate changes in an asynchronous manner between snapshot sites and master sites as well.

Figure 41.8
Oracle triggers and queues between two master sites.

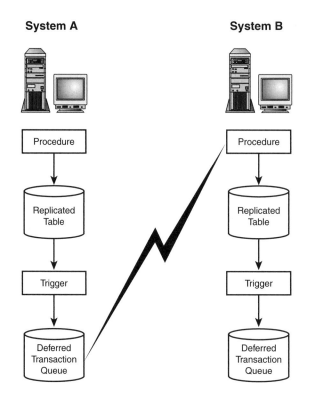

The use of triggers in an advanced replication scheme is essential. Oracle manages this propagation scheme using Oracle's job queue mechanism and deferred transactions. Internal Oracle triggers build RPCs that are used to replicate data changes on the master or snapshot sites. These RPCs are what actually get stored for later propagation. Jobs in the job queue in a typical advanced replication scheme include jobs to push the transactions, jobs to purge the completed transactions, and so on.

Asynchronous propagation has a high degree of availability. Users can continue to work even though the replicated sites might not be available. This method of propagation also performs better in that the users do not have to wait for the change to be applied to other sites before continuing with their work. Data conflicts can occur, however. The data being replicated is not immediately available to the other sites, and the asynchronous propagation environment is more complex to administrate.

SYNCHRONOUS PROPAGATION

Synchronous propagation, or real-time propagation, is when the changes are applied to the local replication and to all the other master and snapshot replication sites in a single transaction. This method of propagation is much easier to configure but is very dependent on the network and system resources being available all the time. Figure 41.9 illustrates the few processes involved in synchronous propagation.

Figure 41.9
Synchronous
Propagation
Processes

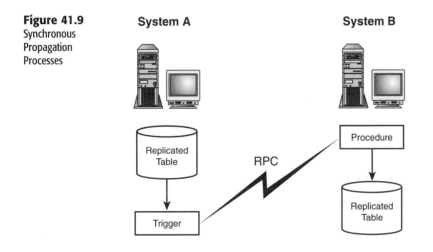

Advantages to synchronous propagation include having no data conflicts, having data immediately available to all replicated sites, and being much easier to administrate. Generally, synchronous propagation environments are less efficient as users have to wait for the changes to be made throughout the replication scheme.

> **Note**
>
> If any of the replicated sites are unavailable in a synchronous propagation environment, changes cannot be made to *any* site!

PART
IX

CH
41

TYPES OF REPLICATION

There are four main types of replication available in the Oracle8 and Oracle8i replication environments: row-level (or direct interface), serial, parallel, and procedural.

ROW-LEVEL REPLICATION

Row-level, or direct interface, replication enables applications to update the local replicas with standard DML statements. Automatic conflict detection is built in, and you can use the built-in conflict resolution routines.

Row-level replication is easier to implement because Oracle creates the necessary code for the actual propagation and conflict detection. This method is also more flexible as changes are propagated no matter what tool is being used to make the data changes.

Generated objects for row-level replication include the following:

- *<table name>*$RT—This trigger fires for each DML statement and puts the changes on the deferred log queue (Oracle7 only).

- *<table name>*$TP—This trigger is used with the $RT trigger when synchronous propagation is being utilized (Oracle7 only).

- *<table name>*$RP—This package is used to perform the DML statements at the destination environments. This package also contains conflict detection (Oracle8).

- *<table name>*$RR—This package works with the $RP package and performs the necessary conflict resolution (Oracle8).

Figure 41.10 contains the steps necessary to implement row-level replication.

Figure 41.10
Steps for row-level
replication.

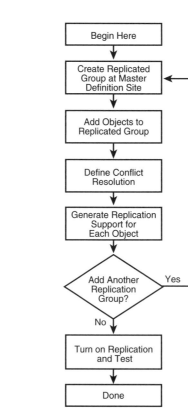

SERIAL PROPAGATION

Oracle propagates changes to the replicated sites in the exact order of the commits to the originating site of the change.

PARALLEL PROPAGATION

Oracle asynchronously updates the replicated sites using the same parallel mechanism that Oracle uses for parallel query, load, recovery, and so on.

PROCEDURAL REPLICATION

Procedural replication is known as the wrapper interface as developers write the procedures necessary for the data manipulations, and Oracle writes a wrapper to handle the propagation. There is no automatic conflict detection provided, and no built-in conflict routines can be used. This method is faster than row-level replication because the developer controls the data being replicated.

Tip #125	Procedural replication is ideal for batch jobs because applications can change large amounts of data in a single transaction. The data isn't really being replicated. The update code is sent and executed at each site.

Figure 41.11 contains the steps necessary to implement procedural replication.

Figure 41.11
Steps for procedural replication.

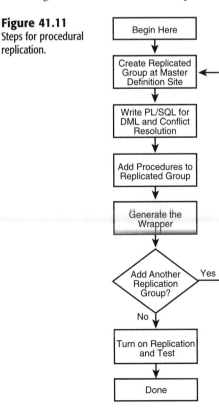

CONFLICT RESOLUTION

Whenever you can update the same row in multiple environments, there is the chance of a data conflict. The DBA or developer must consider what to do if transactions from different sites try to update the same record at approximately the same time.

Most conflicts can be avoided through proper application design. Applications such as airline reservations cannot have conflicts. Other types of applications, such as sales-oriented applications, can have local updates through local ownership of the data. There are applications that do require that data be able to be updated at many sites. When this is the case, you need to design the application in such a way as to handle the data conflicts should they arise.

TYPES OF CONFLICTS

There are three types of conflicts:

- Update conflicts result when two or more sites are trying to update the same row at approximately the same time.

- Uniqueness conflicts occur when an update causes a primary key or uniqueness constraint to be violated.

- Delete conflicts occur when one transaction has deleted a row that another transaction has updated.

Figure 41.12 illustrates how multiple site updates can cause data integrity conflicts. In this example, the New York site updates a department code at roughly the same time the LA site is updating the department name of the same record.

Figure 41.12
Multiple site UPDATE
Conflicts

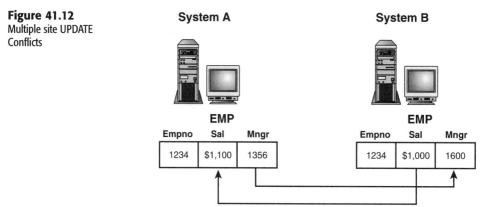

System A   System B

EMP   EMP

Empno	Sal	Mngr		Empno	Sal	Mngr
---	---	---		---	---	---
1234	$1,100	1356		1234	$1,000	1600

AVOIDING CONFLICTS

The first recommendation for avoiding conflicts is to limit the number of sites that have update capabilities to the same data. This can be achieved through primary site ownership. In this scenario, only one site can update the data; all other sites only have read permissions to specific data. More granular forms of control can be implemented by allowing only certain sites to be able to update certain columns of data. *Dynamic ownership*, or token passing, differs from primary ownership as the ability to update the data moves from site to site. This is useful in those workflow-type applications. In this scenario, the application should be designed to automatically change the ownership as needed.

Whenever a row is to be updated, you do the following:

- Locate the current owner of the row.
- Lock the row to prevent updates while the ownership is changing.
- Change the ownership of the row (update the owner field).
- Perform the update.

Figure 41.13 illustrates how this might be implemented in an application.

Figure 41.13
Dynamic Ownership Example

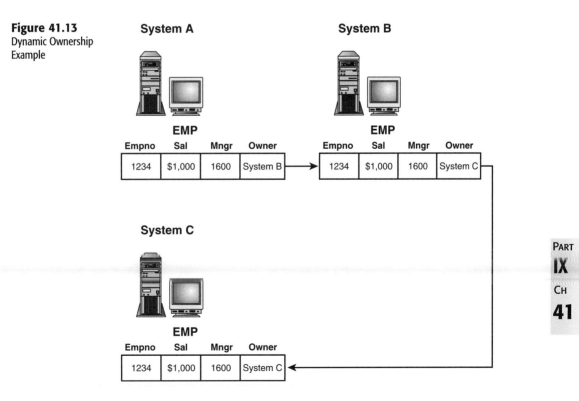

PART

IX

CH

41

Creating a series of unique sequence numbers per replicated site can help to avoid unique-ness conflicts across the replicated sites. Another idea is to implement a local sequence number that becomes part of the composite key.

Delete conflicts can be avoided by not using the DELETE DML statement. Applications that need the ability to delete records can mark the rows for deletion and purge them periodi-cally using procedural replication.

Update conflicts in an advanced replication environment can be difficult to avoid. Try to understand all possible conflict scenarios, and configure the replication environment to auto-matically handle the conflicts. At a minimum, provide an alert process so that the conflict can be researched and corrected.

IDENTIFYING CONFLICTS

Oracle needs to be able to identify and match corresponding rows at the different replicated sites. Oracle does this with the primary key. If the primary key needs to be updated, an alternative key needs to be identified.

Tip #126	Do not allow applications to alter the primary key values of replicated objects.

RESOLVING CONFLICTS

If data conflicts cannot be avoided, you should use Oracle's automatic conflict resolution to correct conflicts when they occur. If data conflicts are not resolved, the inconsistencies can create more inconsistencies. If Oracle's automatic conflict resolution is not implemented, the data conflicts are simply logged and have to be dealt with manually. This manual method, especially if not done in a timely manner, can lead to additional data inconsistencies.

You can use column groups to detect and resolve update type conflicts. A column group is a set of one or more columns. These columns are identified at the master definition site by first creating column groups and then assigning columns to these column groups. Figure 41.14 illustrates the steps necessary in creating column groups. A column group enables you to con-figure different resolution methods for different data conflicts. Be careful that resolution methods do not conflict with one another.

If uniqueness conflicts are unavoidable, you can assign resolution methods to a PRIMARY KEY or UNIQUE constraint to resolve these types of conflicts when they occur. Again, delete con-flicts should be avoided. To resolve these kinds of conflicts, you have to write your own conflict resolution methods, as Oracle does not provide any.

Column groups offer five Oracle prebuilt conflict resolution methods for update-type data conflicts: overwrite and discard value, minimum and maximum value, earliest and latest timestamp value, additive and average value, and priority groups and site priority.

Figure 41.14
Steps for column groups.

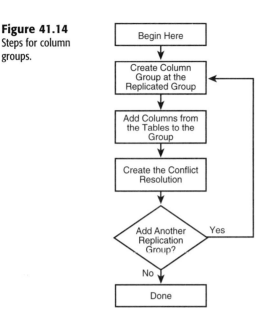

The overwrite and discard prebuilt resolution method can ignore the values from either the originating site or the destination site. This method was intended for a single master site with several snapshot sites. Overwrite and discard can be set up to force the master site change onto the snapshot site.

The minimum and maximum value prebuilt resolution method compares the values from the originating site and the destination site and uses either the less of the two values or the greater of the two values to create data convergence.

The earliest and latest timestamp prebuilt resolution method is the same as the previously mentioned minimum and maximum value resolution method except that it applies to DATE data fields.

The additive and average prebuilt resolution method is used with column groups that have only a single numeric field. The additive part of this method adds the difference between the old value and new value of the originating column to the current value of the column at the destination site. The average part of this method averages the new value of the originating column onto to that of the current value at the destination site. This average method should only be used in single master site configurations.

Priority groups and site priority enable you either to assign priority values to column values for priority groups or to assign priorities for site preference. Oracle uses the lower priority to resolve the conflict. Figure 41.15 illustrates five sales-status field values and their associated priority. When resolving a conflict, Oracle updates the site that has the lower priority column value with the data from the higher priority column value. The site priority works the same way except the various sites are given a priority value.

PART
IX

CH
41

Figure 41.15
Priority group
example.

	Priority Group	Priority		Value
...	site-priority	1	...	System A
...	site-priority	2	...	System B
...	Sales	1	...	Qualified
...	Sales	2	...	Trial
...	Sales	3	...	Contract

There are three Oracle prebuilt conflict resolution methods for uniqueness conflicts. The following methods can be assigned to the PRIMARY KEY or UNIQUE constraints: append site name to duplicate value, append sequence number to duplicate value, or discard duplicate value.

Note

Oracle does not have any prebuilt resolution methods for delete-type conflicts or PRIMARY KEY field updates.

In addition to the previously mentioned prebuilt resolution methods, Oracle supports multiple conflict resolution methods for a column group. This is useful when one conflict resolution fails to correct the conflict. Figure 41.16 illustrates how multiple conflict resolution methods can be implemented.

You should always assign more than one method to resolve a particular conflict. For example, if the time stamp is unable to resolve a conflict, Oracle can still resolve the conflict if the site priority is configured.

Figure 41.16
Multiple conflict reso-
lution example.

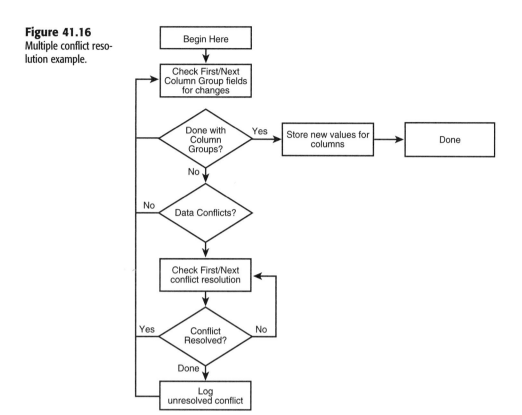

SNAPSHOTS

A *snapshot* is a copy of a master site table. Multiple master site tables are updated from other master sites, whereas snapshots are updated from a single master site (see Figure 41.17) with the use of a refresh. Think of a refresh as a batch job. Snapshots can contain subsets of data from the master site with the use of a WHERE clause. This is useful when it is not neces- sary to maintain complete sets of data at each remote site. Changes to snapshots are pushed to a single master site. These changes can then be propagated to other master sites as previ- ously discussed. Changes to the master site are pulled to the snapshot site. These changes can be asynchronously or synchronously maintained. This asynchronous method does not need a dedicated network connection, which makes refreshing data from a salesperson's laptop possible when the salesperson connects into the network.

Figure 41.17
Snapshots updated from a single master site.

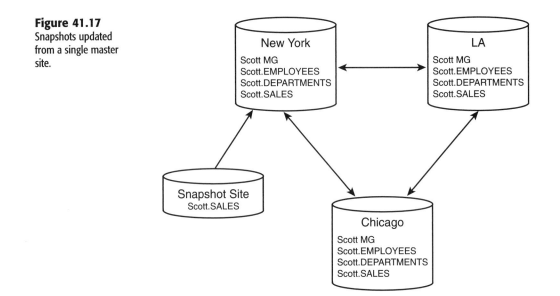

Snapshots can be used to reduce network traffic. When using the asynchronous propagation method, the network traffic can be controlled by the timing of the propagation.

Snapshot architecture is rather straightforward, depending on whether the snapshot is updatable (see Figure 41.18) or if the snapshot is read-only (see Figure 41.19). If the snapshot is updatable, as illustrated in Figure 41.18, there is a snapshot log that contains the primary key and/or the ROWID of the rows affected by an update. A refresh can either be a *fast refresh*, where just the contents of the snapshot log are applied, or a *complete refresh*, where the entire snapshot table is recopied or refreshed. The snapshot log can also contain filter information on snapshots that are a subset of the master site.

Note

If the snapshot is dependent on ROWIDS and the master table is truncated or reorganized, the fast refresh feature of the snapshot log cannot be used.

There are three types of snapshots available: primary key snapshots, ROWID snapshots, and complex snapshots.

Primary key snapshots are the normal type of snapshot in an Oracle8 environment. Changes are logged and propagated based on just the primary key.

ROWID snapshots are maintained for compatibility with Oracle7.

A complex snapshot contains a SELECT statement with a distinct or other aggregate function, a CONNECT BY clause, or a set operation (UNION, INTERSECT, or MINUS). Complex snapshots cannot use the fast refresh technology and should be avoided if a large amount of data is being propagated.

Figure 41.18
Updateable snapshot example.

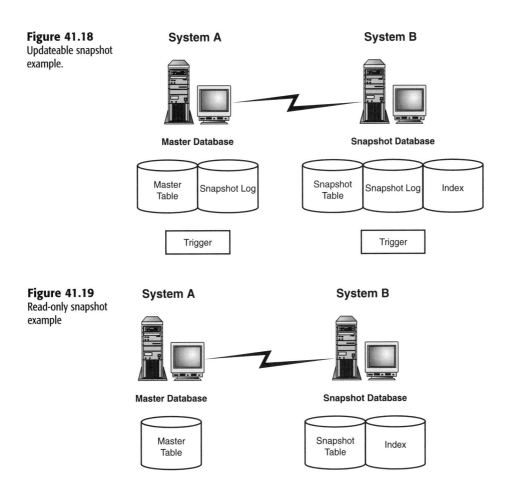

Figure 41.19
Read-only snapshot example

Figure 41.20 illustrates the differences between a simple and a complex snapshot. The simple snapshot query performance is acceptable, and this snapshot scenario can use the fast refresh. The complex snapshot already has the data joined, so query performance will be better but at the cost of having to do a complete refresh. If refreshing is infrequent, use the complex snapshot. If refresh speed and efficiency are required, use the simple snapshot. A snapshot index is always created based on the primary key of the master site. The index name is I_SNAP$_snapshot_name. The snapshot log is only created for updatable snapshots.

Read-only snapshots use many of the same maintenance mechanisms, but they do not need to belong to a snapshot group. A read-only snapshot is read-only because the FOR UPDATE clause is left off the CREATE SNAPSHOT syntax.

Using the WHERE clause to create snapshots with subsets of data from master sites reduces network traffic on refreshes (meaning better refresh performance), reduces snapshot data storage requirements, and can be used to provide users with just the data they need. This last method can be used as a security measure in that only sensitive data that needs to be accessed at a site is actually stored at the site.

Figure 41.20
Simple and complex snapshot example.

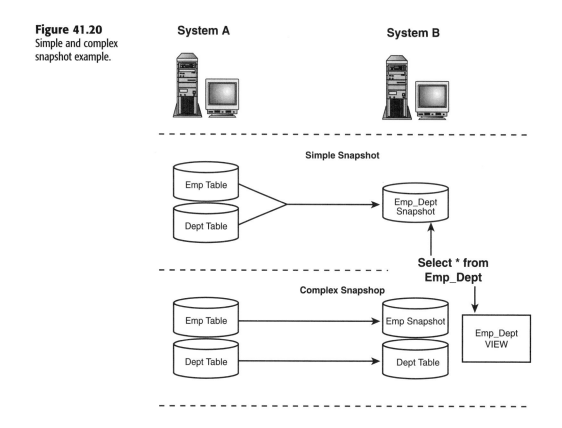

Oracle supports snapshots of master site columns containing the following data types: NUMBER, DATE, VARCHAR2, CHAR, NVARCHAR2, NCHAR, RAW, ROWID, LOBs, BLOBs, and CLOBs.

Note

LOB datatypes are *not* supported in the mixed environment of Oracle8i and Oracle7 version 7.3.

DEPLOYMENT TEMPLATES

Deployment templates make the installation of snapshots in a distributed environment both easy and secure for the DBA. A deployment template can be as simple as a single snapshot or as complex as necessary. Deployment templates give the DBA control over the installation, the capability to repeatedly run the installation at various sites, and assistance with security via an authorized user list.

Figure 41.21 illustrates the steps necessary to build a deployment template.

Figure 41.21
Steps for a
Deployment Template

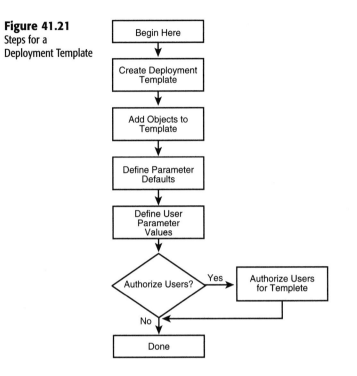

After building a deployment template, you need to create a script that executes the steps necessary to install the deployment script. This is known as *instantiation*. Instantiation can either be ONLINE or OFFLINE. The difference between the ONLINE and the OFFLINE instantiation is that the OFFLINE script contains both the DDL to create the snapshot objects and the DML to populate the snapshot. The ONLINE instantiation only contains the DDL, as the normal refresh mechanisms populate the snapshot.

Figure 41.22 illustrates the steps necessary to offline-instantiate a master site. Figure 41.23 illustrates the steps necessary to offline instantiate a snapshot site.

Figure 41.22
Offline-instantiation of
a master site
example.

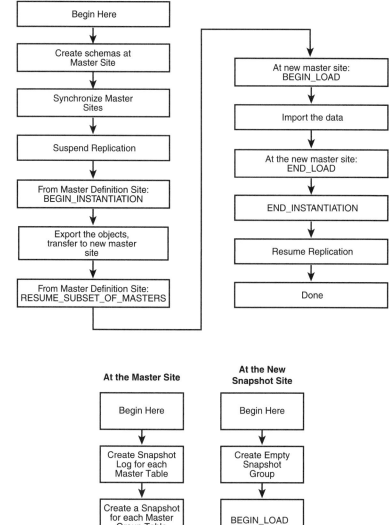

Figure 41.23
Offline-instantiation of
a snapshot site
example.

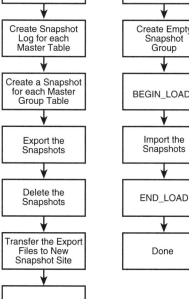

SOME USEFUL UTILITIES

The following is a list of the packages used to create and maintain the Advanced Replication option:

DBMS_REPCAT_AUTH	This package is used to grant and revoke SYS privileges for administrator accounts.
DBMS_REPCAT_ADMIN	This package creates replication administrator accounts, granting and revoking roles and so on.
DBMS_REPCAT	This package is the workhorse of the advanced replication model, performing many types of operations. This package adds masters to the replication group, creates the master and snapshot groups, enables and disables propagation, generates the packages, triggers, and procedures, and so on.
DBMS_REPUTIL	This utility enables and disables replication at the session level.
DBMS_OFFLINE_OG	This utility enables the user to instantiate sites, copying data from the master site to the replicated site and so on.
DBMS_RECTIFIER_DIFF	This utility compares two replicated tables and enables you to synchronize them if differences are found.
DBMS_DEFER_SYS	This utility enables the DBA to schedule, execute, and delete queued transactions.
DBMS_DEFER	This utility is used to build deferred calls.
DBMS_DEFER_QUERY	This utility provides access to parameters passed to deferred calls and can be used for diagnostic reporting as well.
DBMS_SNAPSHOT	This utility enables the DBA to maintain snapshots and snapshot logs.
DBMS_OFFLINE_SNAPSHOT	This package is useful to instantiate snapshots, particularly large snapshots.
DBMS_REFRESH	This utility initiates a refresh of snapshot groups at a snapshot site. It is useful for remote, disconnected PCs when they connect to the network and want to access their data

NEW FEATURES OF ORACLE8 AND ORACLE8I

Oracle8 introduced a host of performance enhancements and new replication features. These will be discussed in the remainder of this chapter.

ORACLE8 REPLICATION NEW FEATURES

Oracle enhanced performance and several features itemized below with version 8.0. Oracle also added was support for LOB replication in the Oracle8 replication model.

Feature	Description
Parallel Propagation of Deferred Transactions	This feature dramatically improves performance by paralleling the synchronous and asynchronous propagation of data.
Internalized Replication Triggers	This improvement reduces overhead, requires less administration, and improves response-time performance.
Reduced Data Propagation	This feature reduces the amount of data being propagated over the network.
Snapshot Subsets Based on Subqueries	Certain types of subqueries can now be fast-refreshed.
LOB Support	Oracle8 now supports the replication of BLOBs, CLOBs, and NCLOBs.
Primary Key Snapshots	Oracle8 continues to support the ROWID snapshot, but this new feature will be the default snapshot model. This feature also allows you to reorganize the master tables and maintain the fast-refresh feature and the consistency of the master snapshot logs.
Partitioned Tables and Indexes	Oracle8 supports the replication of partitioned tables and indexes.
Enhanced Security Model	Oracle8 improves consistency in both the synchronous and asynchronous environments. Transactions are less likely to fail due to the lack of privileges.

ORACLE8I REPLICATION NEW FEATURES

The following list includes some of the new replication features of Oracle8i.

Feature	Description
Internal Apply Packages	Continuing with the Oracle8 trend to internalize triggers and needed functions, Oracle8i internalized the PL/SQL-generated packages used to apply changes to remote sites.
Refresh Groups	This technique results in faster snapshot refreshes. A single refresh group can now contain 400 snapshots.
Parameterized Snapshot Deployment Templates	This feature will facilitate the deployment of very large applications, such as sales force automation, world wide support organizations, and so on.
Column Level Snapshot Subsetting	Oracle always supported limiting the number of rows at a snapshot site, but Oracle8i now supports limiting the number of columns at a snapshot site as well.

SUMMARY

Replication is definitely one of Oracle's strengths and Oracle continues to support and enhance its replication model. This chapter introduces you to the entire Oracle Replication model in addition to all the terms and architecture of the various components. An understanding of each replication option as well as potential contention issues promotes efficient management of the Advanced Replication feature of Oracle.

APPENDIXES

Oracle on Solaris

In this chapter

Oracle exists on many platforms, primarily on UNIX (in most of its incarnations), VMS, NT, and Novell. Oracle has also been moving into the relational mainframe market, which has always been dominated by DB2/MVS. However, Oracle's presence has always been, and still remains, strongest on UNIX. Hence, here is this UNIX-specific appendix.

SOLARIS

Currently, Solaris is the number one UNIX platform to which Oracle ports. Solaris, the modern Sun operating system, is the successor to SunOS. Since Solaris 2.0, Solaris has been predominantly System V Release 4 (SVR4)–based and compliant with numerous UNIX standards that proliferated in the early 90s. At the time of this writing, Solaris is currently up to version 2.6. SunOS, on the other hand, a long-time favorite of the academic and scientific communities, was Berkeley Systems Distribution (BSD)–based. Most modern UNIX operating systems today are largely SVR4-based, except for some particularly proprietary High Performance Computing (HPC), Massively Parallel Processor (MPP) machines, BSD itself, and some shareware operating systems such as Linux. This means that, believe it or not, UNIX has become more standardized over the years. This is good news because UNIX has long been largely divided along the major System V and BSD fronts, further divided down vendor lines, and further still divided by the actual shells (command interpreters). Aside from some of the rarer exceptions, today the shell differences are what an Oracle DBA worries about most often. Because it is currently the market-leading UNIX operating system and Oracle's number one port, this appendix uses mainly Solaris examples to illustrate the general UNIX issues.

A UNIX PRIMER FOR ORACLE DBAS

Before launching too quickly into the more advanced Oracle on UNIX topics, it is useful to review some UNIX basics that are often used by Oracle DBAs working on UNIX platforms. Skip this section if you are a UNIX veteran; otherwise, please read it before continuing.

SHELLS AND PROCESS LIMITS

There are three main UNIX command interpreters, or shells, you will run across in the SA and DBA setup: Bourne, Korn, and C. These shells are not only interactive command interpreters, but are also used to write noninteractive programs called *scripts*. The Bourne shell was the first UNIX shell, and its backward compatibility makes it the shell of choice for portability. However, it lacks several important features, such as job control and command-line history. Next came the C shell, which was developed with the BSD UNIX. It offered a simplified command C-like language, job control, and other features. Last came the Korn shell, which is a superset of the Bourne shell. Hence, Korn can run any Bourne or Korn shell script. Korn also incorporated many C shell features, such as job control. C shell remains the predominant user choice of interactive shells, although administrators tend to use Bourne more often. Korn, however, gained some popularity with the POSIX standard.

In any case, because Oracle runs so many UNIX processes, many Oracle environment configurations are shell-specific. A good example is *process limits*. Processes are limited in the C shell by using the `limit` and `unlimit` commands. In Korn and Bourne, processes are limited by using the `ulimit` command.

> **Note**
>
> Remember, use the `limit` and `ulimit` commands when logged in as the user oracle, not as some other user, such as your ordinary login.

For example, in C shell, you might want to unlimit the number of file descriptors by doing the following:

```
% limit -f
% 1024
% limit -f unlimited
% limit -f
% unlimited
```

This is similar in the Korn and Bourne shells, except you use a different command (`ulimit`) and different options. See the man pages for `csh`, `ksh`, or `sh` for further information.

SOFT AND HARD LINKS

A *link* in UNIX is a filename that contains nothing more than a pointer to the actual file. That is, a link is an alternative name for the same file. With a hard link, you see only the filenames and cannot tell if indeed two files are the same unless you inspect the inodes:

```
% ls
% file1
% ln file1 file2
% ls -l file2
% -rwxr-xr-x     user1     group1 10000     file2
% ls -f
% 1234 file1 1234 file2
```

With a soft link, on the other hand, you can see the link you make:

```
% ls
% file1 file2
% ln -s file1 file3
% ls -l file3
% lrwxrwxrwx    user1     group1 10000     file3 -> file1
```

In general, for this reason, it is better to use soft links because unless your system is well-documented, you will likely forget what files are hard-linked. It's not that you can't figure it out again, but the maintenance of doing so outweighs almost any benefit as your system size increases. See the man pages for `ls` for further information.

NAMED PIPES AND COMPRESSION

A *pipe* in UNIX is a program that has its standard output connected to file descriptor #1, `stdout`, and its standard input connected to file descriptor #0, `stdin`. Hence, multiple commands can be "piped" together to form a pipeline. In the following example, the ls (list directory contents) command is run first and then piped to lp (the print client process) to print it:

```
% ls
% file1 file2 file3
% ls ¦ lp
% standard input accepted by printerque1
```

Notice that to pipe programs together, you use a vertical bar (¦). A *named pipe* in UNIX is a user-defined filename that's purpose is to accept input to stdin and produce output to stdout. It is a passthrough with a name. The named pipe is memory-resident. For Oracle DBAs, the most useful example is the following:

```
% mknod pipe1 p
% export file=pipe1 &
% dd if=pipe1 ¦ compress ¦ tar cvf /dev/rmt/0
```

This series of commands creates the pipe pipe1. It starts an export to that file in the background, and then it reads the pipe, compresses it, and sends it to tape. You can, of course, export directly to tape (or first to a file), compress it, and then go to tape, but this is the only way to get a compressed file to tape *without having to store it first on disk*. With regard to Oracle, this is extremely useful for people who must export very large tables to tape and have little extra disk space to use as a staging area.

TEMPORARY DIRECTORIES

In UNIX, there are at least three kinds of temporary directories: *system volatile*, *user-defined volatile*, and *system nonvolatile*. The /tmp directory is system volatile, any tmpfs directory is user-defined volatile, and the /var/tmp directory is system nonvolatile. The commonly known one is /tmp. The directory /tmp is mounted to the UNIX virtual memory area known as *swap*. It is a special kind of temporary file system (tmpfs), known as swapfs. Its contents are cleaned out on reboot. An SA might create other nonswap directories that are tmpfs. These are memory-based file systems. As mentioned, they are volatile. That is, their contents are lost at shutdown or power loss. However, these special file systems offer increased I/O because the information that is written to and read from these directories is less than that required, per file, for normal UNIX file systems (UFS). Performance is further enhanced because you are reading from and writing to either main memory or virtual memory at any given time. Obviously, main memory is fastest, but virtual memory is faster overall than ordinary disk because it is cached in memory. One last type of temporary directory in UNIX is /var/tmp (Solaris), which is sometimes /usr/tmp. This directory is typically smaller than /tmp, but is nonvolatile. That is, it does not lose its contents at shutdown or power loss. The /var/tmp directory is used for many things. For example, it is the default sorting location for the UNIX sort program, and it stores temporarily buffered editor (vi) files. The main thing is that it retains its contents unless a program cleans up after itself.

Oracle uses these directories for various purposes. For example, SQL*Net listener files are found in /var/tmp/oracle, and temporary installation files are sometimes stored in the /tmp directory.

THE SA AND DBA CONFIGURATION ON UNIX

The DBA should actually know quite a bit about UNIX System Administration (SA) in order to effectively manage an Oracle RDBMS and instance/database on a UNIX system. In many companies, the SA and DBA are one and the same. For example, I was a UNIX SA, Sybase DBA, and an Oracle DBA. Other companies, more often than not, separate the SA and DBA jobs. Although this provides more jobs and truly does enable technical people to specialize fully in one position or the other, it also winds up being a largely segregated working situation, especially if the SA and DBA work for different bosses. In this type of situation, clear, concise, and timely communication is of the utmost importance. In any case, I encourage DBAs to learn as much as possible about their particular variant of the UNIX operating system, specifically basic SA tasks. This means having *root* access. You should be able to almost act as a backup for the SA! This extra effort will reward you in being able to take full advantage of your operating system with the Oracle RDBMS. Many of the following issues are covered in your *Operating System Specific Installation and Configuration Guide (ICG)* or *Server Administrator's Reference Guide (SARG)*. These are the purple-striped hard-copy books. You can also use the online documentation.

SETTING UP THE dba GROUP AND OPS$ LOGINS

In UNIX, in order to Connect Internal (in svrmgrl), you must be a member of the UNIX dba group specified in /etc/group. An example entry in /etc/group might look like this:

```
dba:*:500:oracle, jdoe, jsmith, bfong, ppage
```

In order to add this group, you must be the root user. When done, to connect with DBA privileges *without a password*, you might do either of the following:

```
SVRMGRL> CONNECT INTERNAL;
```

```
SVRMGRL> CONNECT / AS SYSDBA;
```

The latter is preferred and the former is obsolete, although both currently work. A related mechanism for any Oracle user accounts is OPS$. This enables the user to use the same login that he has at the UNIX level for the Oracle account. A recommendation is to set the init.ora parameter OS_AUTHENT_PREFIX="" (the null string) so that you can use names such as jdoe and not OPS$jdoe. Remember, on UNIX, everything is case-sensitive, so use the same case everywhere. To create your Oracle user, do the following:

```
SQL> CREATE USER jdoe
  2> IDENTIFIED EXTERNALLY;
```

Of course, you would probably specify tablespace defaults, quotas, and maybe a profile. If the user already exists, use an ALTER rather than a CREATE. There are some SQL*Net catches, however. OPS$ logins are not supported by default. To enable them, set the init.ora parameter REMOTE_OS_AUTHENT=TRUE. Also, the *daemon* user must exist in /etc/passwd, and it must *not* be an OPS$ login.

USING THE oratab FILE AND dbstart/dbshut SCRIPTS

When you finish running the install, one of the most important postinstallation steps is running the root.sh script (as root, of course). When complete, you have a /var/opt/oracle/oratab (or /etc/oracle/oratab) file, which is a list of ORACLE SID entries and some other information. An installation with two (instance) entries might look like this:

```
SID1:/dir1/dir2/dir3/oracle:Y
SID2:/dir1/dir2/dir3/oracle:N
```

The Y specifies yes, start this instance (SID) up when dbstart is run. The dbstart and dbshut programs are Oracle-supplied UNIX shell scripts. You must create your own script to wrap around these scripts and run as Oracle at boot time for dbstart and at shutdown for dbshut. Create a Bourne shell script like the following:

```
#! /bin/sh
# ora.server
ORACLE_HOME=/dir1/dir2/dir3/oracle
# start
case "$1" in
'start')
su - oracle $ORACLE_HOME/bin/dbstart &
# stop
'stop')
su - oracle $ORACLE_HOME/bin/dbshut &
;;
esac
```

Save this file to the /etc/init.d directory. Then (soft) link this ora.server script like so:

```
# ln -s /etc/init.d/ora.server /etc/rc0.d/K99ora.server
# ln -s /etc/init.d/ora.server /etc/rc2.d/S99ora.server
```

At boot or reboot (# init 6) time, Solaris calls all the S* scripts in the /etc/rc?.d directories, including S99ora.server, and passes each *start* as the $1 parameter. Similarly, at shutdown (# init 0), all the K* scripts are called, including K99ora.server, and passed each *stop* as the $1 parameter.

USING THE (c)oraenv SCRIPTS AND GLOBAL LOGINS

Oracle supplies an oraenv shell script for Bourne and Korn shells and a coraenv shell script for C shell. When placed in the user's startup file or read interactively into the current shell, they set the proper Oracle environment for that user, in particular the SID value. Add the (c)oraenv file to a user's startup file. The user's startup file depends on the shell used. If using the Bourne or Korn shells, add the following lines to the user's .profile file (or alternatively, the ENV file for Korn):

```
ORAENV_ASK=NO
. /opt/bin/oraenv
ORANEV_ASK=
```

For C shell, add the following lines to the user's .login (or .cshrc if preferred):

```
set ORAENV_ASK=NO
source /opt/bin/coraenv
unset ORAENV_ASK
```

Notice that the (c)oraenv files are located in the /opt/bin directories. This is true for Solaris. For other machines, it might be /usr/local/bin. There are a few variations on this setup. Adding these lines to each user's *local* login (and maintaining them) can be tedious. An alternative is to add them to the *global* login files. For Bourne and Korn shells, this is /etc/profile, and for C shell, this is /etc/.login. When a user logs in, the global login file is read first and then the user's local login. Hence, local overrides global. By adding these lines to the global login files, you need only add them to, at most, two files, rather than to all users' files. In addition, you are guaranteed a common Oracle environment for all users unless users override it. It's a policy question as to whether different users might need different environments. A last variation exists on using the (c)oraenv files: If you have multiple instances and have the need to change the SID at login time, simply don't set the ORAENV_ASK variable before reading the (c)oraenv. Each user is then asked what SID she wants, for example:

```
ORACLE_SID = [ SID1 ] ?
```

Then you can enter another SID to override the default SID, SID1 in this case. Further, after login, each user can rerun the (c)oraenv to change to another instance, by doing the following:

```
. /opt/bin/oraenv for Bourne or Korn shells, or
source /opt/bin/coraenv for C shell.
```

CONFIGURING SHARED MEMORY AND SEMAPHORES

Shared memory is, of course, memory that is shared among many processes or threads. An Oracle instance's SGA resides in shared memory. If your total SGA size exceeds that which you configure for your UNIX OS, your instance cannot start. Shared memory is segmented and can be allocated according to three models: one segment, contiguous multisegment, or noncontiguous multisegment. Oracle tries to allocate the SGA memory requested in the order of these models as listed. If all three possible models fail to allocate enough shared memory for the requested Oracle SGA, Oracle raises an ORA error, and the instance fails to start. The values that control the SGA size, of course, are mostly DB_BLOCK_SIZE, DB_BLOCK_BUFFERS, SHARED_POOL_SIZE, and LOG_BUFFER. Sorting parameters affect SGA and nonSGA memory, too. Please refer to Chapter 21, "Managing Database Storage," for more sorting configuration information.

The Solaris (and most SVR4 systems) shared memory parameters that you set are the following:

SHMMAX	Maximum size (bytes) of a single segment
SHMSEG	Maximum number of segments for a single process
SHMMNI	Maximum number of segments, systemwide

The most critical of these are SHMMAX and SHMSEG. Work through the following example and set the init.ora and UNIX parameters. Your system supports one instance, and the machine has 1GB of main memory. There are no other really competing applications with Oracle and especially none that would use shared memory. In other words, this is a "dedicated" database (hardware) server. You could start with 1/2 or 3/4 main memory. Start with 3/4, or 768MB, main memory. Your init.ora parameters might look like the following:

```
DB_BLOCK_SIZE=16384              # 16KB
DB_BLOCK_BUFFERS=45056           # x 16KB = 704MB
SHARED_POOL_SIZE= 16777216       # 16MB
LOG_BUFFER= 8388608              # 8 MB = size of 1 redo log
```

The database buffer cache (704MB), plus the shared pool (16 MB), plus the log_buffer (8MB) take up 728MB, which is 40MB shy of 768MB. Now, set your shared memory to exactly 768MB. Your Solaris shared memory parameters might be set as follows (in the file /etc/system):

```
set shmsys:shminfo_shmmax= 805306368
set shmsys:shminfo_shmseg=10
```

As long as Oracle is starting up with no competition from other applications for the shared memory, it allocates exactly one shared memory segment of something less than 768MB—and uses most of it.

In addition, you might relocate the starting address of your shared memory segments. Download the free white papers from www.sun.com, which detail how this is done in Solaris for Oracle. This might be necessary to obtain all the shared memory you request in one segment.

Semaphores are global (shared) memory locking mechanisms. They are "true" locks in that they are made up of a "gate" and a queue. Sometimes they are referred to as *queued locks*, as opposed to nonqueued ones, such as latches or spin locks. Oracle uses at least one semaphore per Oracle process. Set your maximum number of UNIX semaphores greater than your PROCESSES parameter in init.ora for all your instances combined if you have multiple instances running concurrently. Suppose you expect to have no more than 100 concurrent users; add your Oracle background processes (these can vary considerably, depending on the other init.ora parameters and RDBMS options that you run) to this number. Suppose you have 15 Oracle background processes. You might set the following in your init.ora to have a little room for error:

```
PROCESSES=120
```

In Solaris (and most SVR4 systems), you might then set the following in the /etc/system file to be safely higher than 120:

```
set semsys:seminfo_semmsl=150
```

SEMMSL sets the maximum number of semaphores per set. As shared memory is allocated in segments, semaphores are allocated in sets. Two other parameters you can also set, but which are not as critical as the previous ones, are the following:

SEMMNI   Maximum number of sets, systemwide

SEMMNS   Maximum number of semaphores, systemwide

There are other Solaris (SVR4) kernel parameters, which can also be set in the `/etc/system` kernel file, that affect shared memory, semaphores, and other memory-based structures. Please refer to the Solaris system configuration reference manuals for further details.

UNDERSTANDING THE OFA

The Optimal Flexible Architecture (OFA), offered by Oracle with the release of version 7, provides a set of installation recommendations and guidelines. The OFA was developed with UNIX in mind. The OFA white paper is free and downloadable from `www.oracle.com`. Remember, these aren't requirements. Further, suggested naming conventions are just that: suggestions, not requirements. Hence, the OFA is flexible in this respect, too. Primarily, though, the flexibility the OFA gives is the capability of coping with large installations, many instances, and many versions. Also, OFA helps when you have instances moving through many stages, or phases, such as development, integration, testing, and production.

Maintaining separate environments can be a challenge, but using an OFA-like setup can help ease the administration of your implementation. The OFA offers more than just directory and file organization and naming suggestions; it also deals with tablespace naming and separation, for example. In any case, an example of a two-version, two-instance (production and development) configuration might have the following environment variable settings and OFA structure:

`$ORACLE_BASE=/u01/oracle`

`$ORACLE_HOME=$ORACLE_BASE/product/7.3.3` for the production SID

`$ORACLE_HOME=$ORACLE_BASE/product/8.0.3` for the development SID

`$TNS_ADMIN=$ORACLE_HOME/network/admin`; note that, like `$ORACLE_HOME`, this can only belong to one instance at a time

`oratab` is located in `/var/opt` or `/etc`

`(c)oraenv` files are located in `/opt/bin` or `/usr/local/bin`

datafiles, control files, redo log files, and rollback datafiles are located in `/u0` `[1-n]/oracle/<sid>` subdirectories, where *n* represents the number of root `/` `u0` directories; soft links can be used as necessary

administrative files are stored in `$ORACLE_BASE/admin/ssid`, such as `bdump`, `cdump`, `udump`, `pfile`, and `exp` subdirectories.

Please refer to the OFA white paper for further details on its guidelines. Even though OFA grew out of Oracle on UNIX, it can be retrofitted for NT, Netware, VMS, and other platforms. Figure A.1 shows a graph of the sample OFA structure, using DEV as the name of the development SID and PROD for production.

Figure A.1
An OFA directory structure for the two-version, two-instance configuration

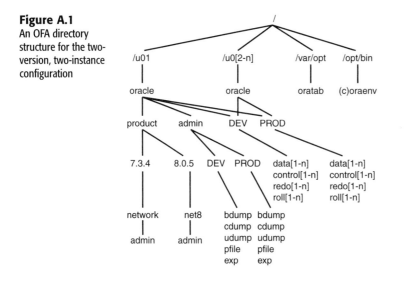

COMPARING RAW DISK AND UFS

The comparison of Raw Disk and UFS is a classic debate between Oracle and other RDBMS DBAs that has no resolution. In other words, there is no blanket statement anyone can make that holds true for all applications. A *raw partition* in UNIX is a disk partition on which a UNIX file system (UFS) is *not* created. Hence, there is no file system (or general UNIX I/O) buffering for that partition. In fact, aside from its device filename at the UNIX level, UNIX otherwise has nothing to do with a raw partition. Why use raw partitions? If nearly random I/O is the characteristic usage pattern of your application type (for example, OLTP), raw partition can help by bypassing the UNIX buffer. If your application type involves heavy sequential I/O (for example, DSS and DW), buffering helps minimize the electromechanical disadvantage. In other words, the UNIX (read-ahead) buffer outperforms raw partitioned access when I/O is the bottleneck. However, other factors come into play, such as think time and computational time. Think time is the time a user needs between interactions in an interactive system such as OLTP. Computational time is the batch analogy of think time. It is the time a program uses in computing between significant functional tasks. In either case, if think or computational time is high under heavy I/O, the benefit of the UNIX buffering might be negated, and hence, a raw partition could yield better results. Following are some of the major advantages and disadvantages of using raw partitions.

The advantages are as follows:

- Decreased I/O overhead (no UNIX buffer/file system buffer)
- Increased performance for random I/O or heavy think/computational time
- Writes guaranteed (Oracle -> disk instead of Oracle -> UNIX -> disk)

The disadvantages are as follows:

- Decreased performance for heavy sequential I/O
- Decreased performance (less than file system) if used improperly
- Harder to manage

Briefly look at the last disadvantage because there are many inherent administrative problems with using raw partitions, including the following three:

- To create or change one partition requires a complete disk dump/reload. For example, suppose you have set up your raw partitions and your database. Then, you see the need to increase the size of one of the raw partitions. If no others are available and you must increase a particular one, you have to dump the entire disk contents, repartition, and reload.

- There are fewer I/O utilities (only dd), especially for backup. The dd utility can back up only one partition at a time and cannot span tapes. (It is not a multivolume utility.) Also, dd cannot sense the end of a tape, so you must be sure that your raw partition can fit. You don't want to find out it didn't when you are in the middle of a recovery.

- The allocation of datafiles is less flexible, and you potentially wasted space, especially cumulatively over time. Suppose you need to move datafiles around for performance-tuning reasons (that is, to balance I/O). This would not be too complicated using file system files. However, moving two raw partitions, unless they are the same size, can require the complete dumping and reloading of the two disks on which they reside.

Final notes: If opting to use raw disks, before you do so, complete disk checks (bad sector checks) on all disks that might be used. Make sure you have enough disk space—plus some. Make all your raw partitions the same size, or choose three or four fixed raw partition sizes, such as 256MB, 512MB, 768MB, and 1024MB (1GB), and this mitigates the inflexibility of managing them. This latter solution of using a few classes of sizes is better for most installations. For example, it increases the likelihood of your having a properly sized partitions at the expense of some internal fragmentation (wasted space). Even so, this is nearly unavoidable when using raw disks.

> **Caution**
>
> When formatting your raw disks, always skip cylinder 0 to leave room for the disk label. Otherwise, the Oracle RDBMS will likely overwrite it at the worst possible time. By comparison, the high-level UFS I/O access routines have the knowledge to skip it built in.

ADDITIONAL UNIX PERFORMANCE TUNING TIPS

USE ASYNCHRONOUS I/O

Normally, a DBWR/LGWR process must write, wait, write, wait, and so forth. Although buffer transfers are involved, this is not real-time. It is however, synchronous (serial) I/O.

Asynchronous (parallel) I/O (AIO) reduces wait times between buffered read/write acknowledgments. AIO works for either UFS or raw disks. If supported, use KAIO, which is an additional enhancement of AIO residing within the kernel, rather than above it. Hence, it is even faster. Ensure that the following init.ora parameters, enabled by default, are set:

```
ASYNC_WRITE=TRUE
ASYNC_READ=TRUE
or ASYNC_IO=TRUE in place of the previous two for some platforms.
```

USE MULTIPLE DATABASE WRITERS (DBWRs)

If you are not using AIO, set the following init.ora parameter:

```
DB_WRITERS=<the number of distinct disks containing datafiles>
```

Increase this up to twice the number of distinct disks containing datafiles as necessary. This parallelizes I/O without using asynchronous I/O because I/O is synchronous by default for each DBWR. Use KAIO first, AIO second, and multiple DBWRs last, but none of these together.

USE THE readv() SYSTEM CALL

For heavy sequential I/O, readv() reduces buffer-to-buffer transfer times. The readv() system call is disabled by default. Enable it by setting the following:

```
USE_READV=TRUE
```

USE OUTER DISK CYLINDERS FIRST

Because of the Zone Bit Recording (ZBR) technology used by Sun, outer cylinders tend to outperform inner cylinders. The outer cylinders are cylinders 0, 1, and 3, as opposed to 4, 5, 6, and 7.

> **Caution**
>
> Remember, don't use cylinder 2, the overlap cylinder, because it retains the total size of the disk. Some programs are baffled when this cylinder gets changed.

USE THE ORACLE POSTWAIT DRIVER

If available on your platform, the Oracle postwait driver provides a substitute mechanism for using semaphores that is faster and provides the same functionality of semaphores for Oracle usage.

MONITOR SHARED MEMORY AND SEMAPHORES WITH ipcs OR tstshm

To monitor shared memory, use the UNIX interprocess communication status (ipcs) command with the -mb option, or use the Oracle shared memory utility (tstshm) if you have it. To monitor semaphores, use ipcs -sb. These utilities help you determine how much shared memory and how many semaphores are being used. They can also help you determine the fragmentation of your shared memory. See the man page on `ipcs` for further details. Here is one sample run of each utility:

```
# ipcs -mb
IPC status from <running system> as of Tue Nov 18 11:59:34 1997
T    ID    KEY       MODE      OWNER    GROUP    SEGSZShared Memory:
m    500   0x0898072d   --rw-r-----   oracle   dba      41385984
m    301   0x0e19813f   --rw-r-----   oracle   dba      38871040
m    200   0x0e3f81dc   --rw-r-----   oracle   dba      45301760

hostname:oracle> tstshm
Number of segments gotten by shmget() = 50
Number of segments attached by shmat() = 10
Segments attach at lower addresses
Maximum size segments are not attached contiguously!
Segment separation = 4292345856 bytes
Default shared memory address = 0xeed80000
Lowest shared memory address = 0xfff00000
Highest shared memory address = 0xeed80000
Total shared memory range = 4010278912
Total shared memory attached = 20971520
Largest single segment size = 2097152
Segment boundaries (SHMLBA) = 8192 (0x2000)

# ipcs -sb
IPC status from <running system> as of Tue Nov 18 11:59:39 1997
T    ID     KEY          MODE         OWNER    GROUP    NSEMS
Semaphores:
s    327680   00000000    --ra-r-----   oracle   dba      25
s    327681   00000000    --ra-r-----   oracle   dba      25
s    196610   00000000    --ra-r-----   oracle   dba      20
s    400000   00000000    --ra-r-----   oracle   dba      25
s    500000   00000000    --ra-r-----   oracle   dba      25
```

USE DIRECT I/O

Some UNIX systems support direct I/O with UFS, effectively bypassing the UNIX buffer caches. This negates the need to use raw partitions as an option. Enable this facility if your platform supports it. Use it in place of raw partitions.

DON'T USE PROCESSOR BINDING OR CHANGE THE SCHEDULING CLASSES

Because SMP machines have most of the market share of Oracle database servers, I make this recommendation. Programs written to run on SMP machines are most efficient when their processes are processor-independent, hence the *S* for *Symmetric* in SMP. Available facilities exist (`tcpctl`, `pbind`, `nice/renice`, and `prioctl`) that enable reformulation of processor affinity and process priority. In general, on SMP machines, it is a bad idea to mess with these parameters for Oracle system (background) processes.

DON'T MODIFY THE BUFFER CACHE

Don't modify the general UNIX buffer cache or the file system buffer unless you have a really good idea of what you're doing. In general, modifying these UNIX kernel and UFS parameters has little effect on Oracle performance. For example, the kernel parameter bufhwm is the maximum KB that can be used by the general UNIX I/O buffers. By default, the UNIX buffer grows to up to 2 percent of available memory. The program tunefs controls the UFS logical block (or buffer), which is 8KB by default. Be careful in changing these. Have a good reason for doing so. For example, if you have heavy sequential I/O and are using UFS, you can increase bufhwm in /etc/system.

KEEP YOUR UFS FILE SYSTEMS BELOW 90 PERCENT FULL

Unless you changed it, your minfree for each of your UFS is 10 percent. At less than 90 percent capacity, a UFS is speed-optimized. At greater than or equal to 90 percent, the UFS optimization strategy switches to space optimization. Hence, attempt to keep your UFS housing Oracle datafiles and other Oracle components at 89 percent or less.

ORACLE ON WINDOWS NT

In this chapter

This appendix covers Oracle's relationship with Microsoft's Windows NT operating system platform. For references to non–platform-specific Oracle database issues, please refer to the rest of the book. Because this publication is dedicated to providing information on the latest and most used versions of software, the information provided in this section is specific to version 8.0.x.x of the Oracle Relational Database and mainly version 4.0 of the Windows NT 4.0 Server operating system.

Table B.1 lists the supported versions (for versions 7.3.x.x and 8.0.x.x only) for Windows NT Server, as published and released by Oracle Worldwide Customer Support in January of 1999 (the most recent at the time this book went to press).

TABLE B.1 VERSION AVAILABILITY

Oracle Version	Windows NT 3.1	Windows NT 3.5	Windows NT 3.51	Windows NT 4.0
7.3.2.1.1	no	no	yes	yes
7.3.2.2.1	no	no	yes	yes
7.3.2.3.1	no	no	yes	yes
7.3.3.0.0	no	no	no	yes
7.3.4.0.0	no	no	yes	yes
8.0.4.0.0	no	no	no	yes
8.0.5.0.0	no	no	no	yes
8.1.5.0.0	no	no	no	yes

The latest 7.3.x.x version of Oracle released on Windows NT to date is version 7.3.4.0.0. A version 7.4 will not likely be released. Oracle8 was released instead. The most recent version of Oracle8 for Windows NT available (as of March 30 , 1999) is version 8.1.5.

WHY CHOOSE ORACLE ON WINDOWS NT?

There is no doubt that businesses today are looking for less expensive alternatives to provide quality-service information systems. As a result, a market has grown for an operating system that is capable of supporting a small to midsize business. Smaller businesses don't necessarily want or need to put out the money for large platforms when their needs don't require all the options of a larger system. Microsoft Windows NT was created to provide this exact service.

Windows NT is becoming more and more robust every day, which enables consumers to consider Windows NT as a viable platform consideration. Because consumers are interested in cutting costs wherever possible, Windows NT is taking over a bigger and bigger share of the operating system market. Oracle has seen the growth of this particular operating system and has moved Windows NT up to its developmental platform level. This means that

Oracle is developing its software on Windows NT at the same level as Sun Solaris, HP/UX, and other developmental platforms.

Oracle on Windows NT is a fully functional RDBMS (Relational Database Management System). The Oracle software on Windows NT is a single process with multiple operating system threads. This is different from some versions of UNIX. Because of its development level status, Oracle has been integrated tightly with the Windows NT operating system, including relationships between Oracle and Windows NT's Performance Monitor, Event Viewer, and Registry. NT also provides security capabilities, which is a much desired option in the database world. Of course, the added advantage of Oracle's single point-of-control GUI (Graphical User Interface) administration tool—Oracle Enterprise Manager (OEM) (see Chapter 27, "Oracle Enterprise Manager")—is also an added user-friendly product.

Release 8.1 contains several features to make it easier to develop Oracle-based applications with Microsoft products. The Oracle Data Server makes NT a highly available, scalable, and secure platform for application deployment.

The main concern on most DBAs' minds is Windows NT's capability to handle large, DSS (Decision Support System) or OLTP (Online Transaction Processing) databases. Windows NT has come a tremendously long way with its capabilities to handle multiple users and large amounts of data. There is no doubt that it is incapable of handling the multiuser, ter-abyte-sized systems that are being handled by large UNIX platforms at present. Oracle is only being limited by NT's limitations. However, NT's capabilities are growing every day, and eventually it will be a serious competitor for the current large systems. In the mean-time, Windows NT provides a cheaper and often satisfactory solution for many situations that arise in small to midsize businesses. Given the speed of its development at Microsoft, it is useful to note that several years down the road, NT might possibly be the solution of choice.

NEW FEATURES IN ORACLE8I FOR WINDOWS NT

Oracle8i includes two new features specifically for the Windows NT platform: The Oracle Application Generator for Microsoft Visual C++ and Oracle Objects For OLE.

ORACLE APPLICATION GENERATOR FOR MICROSOFT VISUAL C++

The Oracle Application Wizard (AppWizard) provides developers with a GUI tool with which to quickly and seamlessly create a C++ application that provides connectivity and data access to an Oracle database. A developer can use this tool to generate an Oracle database-enabled application that compiles, links, and runs without writing a single line of code.

AppWizard is thoroughly integrated with the Visual Studio IDE, which is the most popular IDE for developing C++ applications on the Windows NT/95 platform. It enables ISVs, VARs, and other users to easily build applications that leverage Oracle database technology in the Visual Studio IDE.

The wizard can be invoked whenever a developer decides to create a new project in Visual Studio. AppWizard guides the developer through a two-step process. First, the wizard prompts the user with questions about the programming task that is about to be undertaken: connection string, username, and password to the Oracle database. Then, the user is enabled to select the specific tables and columns from which the application will retrieve data.

Second, based on the developer's responses, AppWizard generates a Visual Studio project and source code that provide the developer with a custom-tailored application framework from which to start developing immediately. The generated C++ code framework consists of a mixture of MFC and OracleObjects for OLE (OO4O). The MFC code provides the basic GUI application code, and the OO4O classes provide the connectivity and data access to Oracle databases.

ORACLE OBJECTS FOR OLE

Oracle Objects for OLE (OO4O) is a COM-based database connectivity tool that provides seamless and optimized access to Oracle databases. OO4O can be used in environments ranging from the typical two-tiered client/server applications to application servers deployed in n-tiered environments and Web servers, such as Microsoft IIS or MTS. It can be used from virtually any programming or scripting language that supports the Microsoft COM Automation technology, such as Visual Basic, Visual C++, VBA in Excel, VBScript, and JavaScript in IIS Active Server Pages. OO4O consists of an in-process COM Automation Server, a C++ class library, and the Oracle Data Control.

The release 8.1 version of OO4O will enable developers that use COM/DCOM-based development tools to have seamless access to all Oracle8 specific features that are presently inaccessible from other ODBC or OLE DB-based components, such as ADO.

WINDOWS NT FILE SYSTEMS

Before installing the Windows NT operating system, the administrator needs to decide which file system is going to be appropriate for the database server. The Windows NT operating system provides two systems: FAT (File Allocation Table) and NTFS (NT File System). This section provides both the advantages and disadvantages of each file system so that you can make an educated decision on which file system will be appropriate for your particular situation.

FAT FEATURES

The File Allocation Table (FAT) is a file system that has been used on DOS, Windows 3.x, OS2, and Windows 95 and Windows98 PCs. Table B.2 lists the features of FAT.

TABLE B.2   FILE ALLOCATION TABLE (FAT) FEATURES

Feature	Details
Operating systems that can access FAT	Windows NT, Windows 95, Windows98, MS DOS, OS/2
Partition size limit	4GB
Filename length limit	255 characters
File size limit	4GB*
File types	Read Only, Archive, System, Hidden
Local security	None
File compression capability	None

APP

B

* For Windows98, which uses the FAT32 file system, the file size can go up to 2 terabyte (TB).

ADVANTAGES

The main advantage to the FAT16 file system is that the system overhead is very low (less than 1MB per partition). This is a good choice for drives/partitions that are less than 400MB. Also, because FAT16 has been present on previous operating systems (as listed in the introduction to this table), FAT is backwards compatible and capable of performing multiple operating system boots.

For FAT32 systems, the advantage of overhead is diminished since it requires more space and manipulation of the FAT. However, partition sizes are larger (4GB). It is not recommended for drives smaller than 512MB.

DISADVANTAGES

Security is the main issue with the FAT file system (both FAT16 and FAT32) . The only security on FAT is directory-level sharing. Outside of that, FAT has no local security. Even the directory-level sharing enables users that log on locally to gain access to the physical directories. This is a serious issue for databases that contain sensitive information. Another issue with the FAT16 file system is that once the drives/partitions grow to greater than 400MB, file access becomes much slower and database performance decreases significantly. This is due to the fact that FAT16 uses a linked list folder structure. Therefore, as a file gets larger and larger—as a result of inserts and updates, for example—it becomes fragmented on the hard disk. These issues are fixed in the FAT32 file system which is faster then FAT16.

NTFS FEATURES

The NT File System (NTFS) can only be accessed by the Windows NT operating system, enabling for higher security. Table B.3 lists the features for the NTFS file system.

TABLE B.3   NT FILE SYSTEM (NTFS) FEATURES

Feature	Detail
Operating systems that can access NTFS	Windows NT
Partition size limit	2 terabytes actually, (16 exabytes, theoretically)
Filename length limit	255 characters
File size limit	4GB–64GB actually, (16 exabytes, theoretically)
File types	Further extended, extensible
Local security	Yes
Compression capability	Yes: on files, on folders and on drives

ADVANTAGES

NTFS is a much more robust file system than FAT mainly because of its security features. Local security is required. NTFS provides for file-level (versus directory-level) security. This gives the administrator the capability to control access to all the information stored in the file system. Also, security is added because the NTFS file system can only be accessed by Windows NT; therefore, someone cannot start the computer with any other operating system and access information on the NTFS partition. In addition to its security features, NTFS is a better choice for drives/partitions larger than 400MB due to performance advantages over the FAT16 file system dealing with larger drives/partitions.

DISADVANTAGES

The overhead for an NTFS drive ranges from 1MB–5MB(or more) depending on the size of the partition. This is fine for large volumes, but for smaller volumes (smaller than 400MB), the overhead is a disadvantage.

Tip #128	Make sure that you install Service Pack 4 for Windows NT. This works out a lot of kinks with the operating system, one of which being the Windows Explorer tool. Without the service pack, Explorer can give you misleading file size numbers if you are pushing file size limits. You can download this service pack from the Microsoft Web site at www.microsoft.com.

UNDERSTANDING WINDOWS NT ADMINISTRATION

Administering Oracle from a Windows NT machine can be an easy task when the administrator is familiar with the NT environment. There are a number of tools and utilities that NT provides that are integrated with the Oracle software. In this section, you will find some basic information about the NT operating system as it pertains to Oracle that will provide the administrator with a clear mapping of the interaction between an NT server and an Oracle database.

ASSOCIATED WINDOWS NT TOOLS

There are many ways to access and monitor your Oracle database using Windows NT tools, including creating, editing, and starting Oracle services and instances, user management, backup utilities, and Oracle Performance Monitor. In this section, you will find descriptions of the Windows NT tools that you will be using as an Oracle DBA.

CONTROL PANEL

The Windows NT Control Panel is found by going to the Start menu and selecting Settings, Control Panel. The screen that appears looks like Figure B.1.

Figure B.1
Control Panel is the Windows NT computer configuration interface.

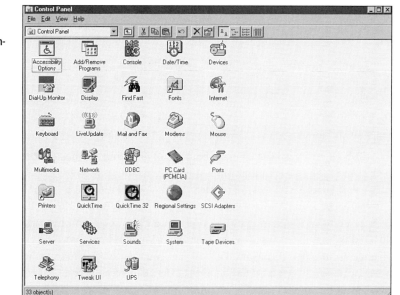

You will find several tools within this panel. A tool used often in conjunction with Oracle is the Services tool. NT Services includes both a listing of executables on the NT server that is identified in the Registry (for example, FTP, third-party backup software, Oracle instances, and so on) and their availability status on the machine. Look to this chapter's section "Windows NT Services and Oracle Instances" for more information regarding the definition of an NT Service. (See Figure B.7.)

USER MANAGER FOR DOMAINS

User Manager is Windows NT's administrative tool for managing user, group, and network security (see Figure B.2). It is important to note that user security on the Windows NT Server can be mapped to Oracle security. This tool is opened by going to the Start menu and selecting Programs, Administration Tools, User Manager for Domains.

Figure B.2
User Manager for Domains is Windows NT Server's administrative tool for managing user, group, and network security.

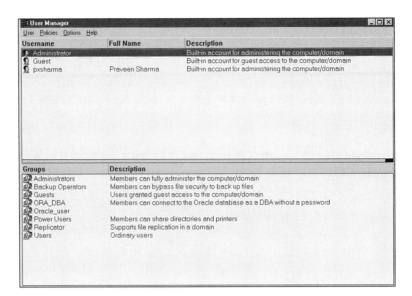

WINDOWS NT BACKUP

NT's Backup utility is used to make backups of anything residing on the machine (see Figure B.3). Windows NT Backup is good for making cold physical backups of the Oracle database. It enables you to select which drives you want to back up and where you want to send the backup, and it offers verification upon completion of the backup. This tool is activated by going to the Start menu and selecting Programs, Administration Tools, Backup. NT Backup can also be used at the command-line level in a batch file. This is useful to schedule regular backups using the NT "at" command. Oracle must be shutdown in order to perform a cold backup of the database (this can also be accomplished using Server Manager in line mode). Also, the command-line version allows only selections at the directory level. You cannot select individual files.

For example, to backup all the files in the directory f:\rdbms_ts and to write out a log file, I used the following command:

```
ntbackup backup f:\rdbms_ts /l "f:\backup.log"
```

ORACLE DATABASE CONFIGURATION ASSISTANT (FORMERLY NAMED WINDOWS NT INSTANCE MANAGER)

Until Oracle7.3.x, the Windows NT Instance Manager was used to create a SID (also called system identifier, SID, or instance name), Service, Database, and Data Dictionary for Oracle. In Oracle8i, the Instance Manager is replaced by the Oracle Database Configuration Assistant (see Figure B.4).

Figure B.3
Backup utility is the Windows NT Server's tool for performing cold physical back-ups.

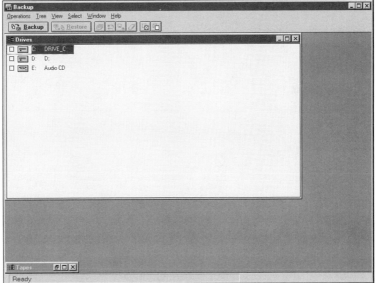

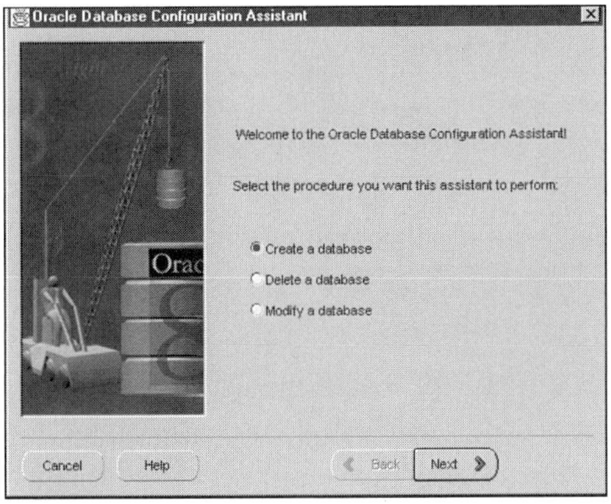

Figure B.4
Oracle Database Configuration Assistant main screen.

In Oracle8i, the Database Assistant is further divided into the Oracle Database Configuration Assistant and the Oracle Migration Assistant. You will examine the Configuration Assistant here. The Migration Assistant will be examined later in this chapter.

THE ORACLE DATABASE CONFIGURATION ASSISTANT The Configuration Assistant helps you to create, modify, and delete databases. The Configuration Assistant is a graphical tool with a wizard interface that enables you to create a database. You can also modify or delete an existing database. Windows NT enables you to have multiple Oracle databases running simultaneously on your machine. Each database must have a unique database name. The Oracle Database Assistant creates a unique Windows NT service for each database. You can manage each service using the Services applet within the Windows Control Panel (see Figure B.5).

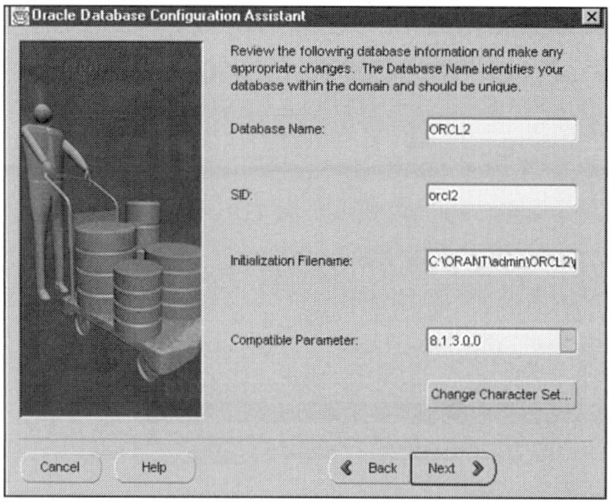

Figure B.5
Oracle Database
Configuration
Assistant Options
Screen

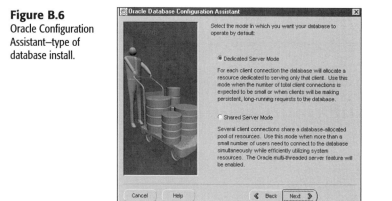

When creating a new database with the help of the Database Configuration Assistant, the assistant gives various options as to which type of database you wish to create (See Figure B.6).

Figure B.6
Oracle Configuration
Assistant—type of
database install.

WINDOWS NT SERVICES AND ORACLE INSTANCES

When working with Oracle on Windows NT, you, the Oracle DBA, might find that the difference between a Windows NT service and an Oracle instance is very confusing. This section clears up that confusion.

A *service* in Windows NT is an executable that was installed in the Windows NT Registry. The NT Registry tracks security information for each service created. An Oracle *instance* is a word used to describe a unique SGA (System Global Area) paired with an Oracle service.

At least one Oracle service is created for each specific database: one that runs the database and a possible other that starts the database whenever the operating system itself is started. When an Oracle service is created, it can be found under Control Panel/Services and is named in the format OracleService*sid* (see Figure B.7). The *sid* (system identifier) identifies which instance the service refers to. Also, you might find the OracleStart*sid* service if the service was created in AUTO start mode by the NT Instance Manager.

APP

B

Tip #129

When Oracle is installed, there are also services created for the Oracle Listener for NamedPipes (nmp) and the Oracle Listener for TCP/IP (tcp). An Oracle Listener literally acts like an ear on the Oracle server that listens for clients who want to contact the Oracle server.

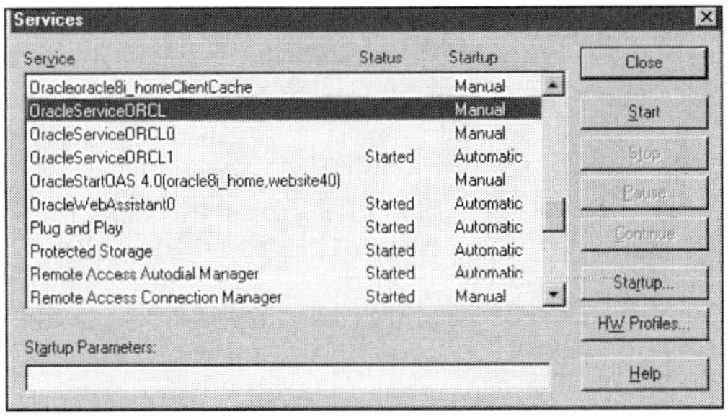

Figure B.7
Windows NT Services screen.

When you first install Oracle on NT, you will find that the installation already has created an Oracle instance named *orcl*. The *orcl* instance is the default database provided by Oracle. If you open up Services in the Control Panel, you will find two things: the Oracle service OracleServiceorcl and another service called OracleStartorcl. You'll also notice that next to the name of the service, it identifies the service as being AUTOMATIC. There are three different start modes for a service, as described in Table B.4.

TABLE B.4   NT SERVICE MODES

Mode	Description
AUTOMATIC	Service starts automatically every time the operating system is started
MANUAL	Service can be started manually, by a user, or by a dependent service
DISABLED	Service cannot be started

Tip #130

If there is an OracleStart*sid* service, the Oracle database service will not only be started, but the actual database will open as if a startup command had been issued as the database's internal user. The OracleStart*sid* service creates a `strtsid.cmd` file in the `ORANT\DATABASE\` directory. Therefore, when the operating system starts the database is also started and there is no need to start each separately.

Caution

> As always, make sure to shut down the database first before shutting down the operating system, for this will not be done automatically.

INSTALLING ORACLE SERVER ON THE WINDOWS NT SERVER

There are some things you must consider when you install Oracle on the Windows NT Server. Previous lessons with other software might have taught you to be prepared for any new installation on a computer. Well, Oracle is, by far, no exception. In the following sections you will find some basic installation checklists.

BEFORE INSTALLING

Before you install Oracle on the Windows NT Server, it is important to use the following as a basic checklist:

- Make sure to read through the Installation Guides and Readme files that Oracle provides with its software. This information will prevent you from making some wrong turns in the process. Also read the online documentation provided in the install CD.
- Install and Test all network hardware and software, if necessary.
- Make sure you have enough disk space for the software and a CD-ROM drive.
- Perform post-installation tasks.
- Back up the Windows NT Registry using regedit (select the Registry, Export menu option).
- Also if any repository is required (such as one for Oracle Enterprise Manager), create it.

INSTALLATION INSTRUCTIONS

Installation begins by putting the Oracle8i Server CD into the CD-ROM drive. The Oracle Installer should start up immediately; if it doesn't, go to Windows Explorer (or My Computer) and select the CD-ROM drive and then select SETUP.bat. After that, simply follow the directions, and enter information as you are prompted for it. It is highly suggested that you choose the defaults during installation. If you decide to use your own selection instead of a default, make sure to take note and be aware of the effect it might have on a successful installation. Some of things you should remember while installing Oracle8.1.x are as follows:

- Log on to your Windows NT server as a member of the Administrators group.
- Stop all Oracle applications (if any are running).
- Stop all Oracle services (if any are running).

The default installation directory for Oracle8.1.x is C:\Oracle\ora81. If you have existing Oracle homes created with a pre-8.1 release, the default is C:\orant. Change C:\orant to C:\Oracle\ora81.

Available products are the following:

- Oracle8 Enterprise Edition 8.1.x
- Oracle8 Client 8.1.x
- Programmer/2000 8.1.x

> **Note**
>
> To view a description of a component, click the plus sign (+) next to New Installations to make the component names appear, and then move your mouse pointer over the component name.

The Oracle Protocol Support screen appears if a Custom installation has been chosen. Select the protocol for which you want to install Oracle Protocol support. You must have the native software for this protocol installed on your computer.

> **Note**
>
> After the selected products have been installed, the Configuration Tools screen appears and Net8 Configuration Assistant and Oracle Database Configuration Assistant are started automatically in succession.

> **Tip #131**
>
> If Oracle Universal Installer detects an earlier version of an Oracle database on your hard drive, it asks if you want to migrate your database to Oracle8 Enterprise Edition Release 8.1.x. If you select Yes, Oracle Data Migration Assistant starts at the end of installation and migrates your database to Oracle8 Enterprise Edition 8.1.x.

BEFORE UPGRADING

Oracle8i comes with the Oracle Data Migration Assistant, which helps you to migrate from an Oracle7.1.x, 7.2.x, 7.3.x, or Oracle8.0.x to an Oracle8i database. (see Figure B.8).

Figure B.8
Oracle Data Migration
Assistant Main Screen

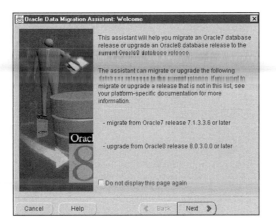

The migration utility will prompt users for specific requirements for migration (see Figure B.9).

Figure B.9
Oracle Data Migration Assistant—List of valid databases that can be migrated

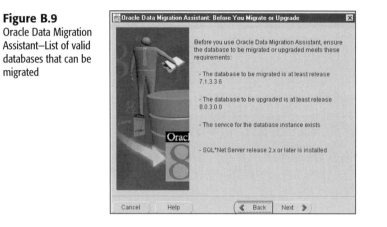

Now that you have prepared for installation, you can enter the installation phase.

UPGRADE INSTRUCTIONS

The primary advantages of using the Oracle8i migration utility are speed and ease of use. The migration utility takes significantly less time than Export/Import, and its use entails a standardized series of specific, easy steps. In addition, the time required to migrate a database with the migration utility depends less on the size of the database than on the number of objects in the data dictionary. The migration utility is especially useful for quickly migrating an entire source database. Unlike Export/Import, the migration utility cannot selectively migrate specific data files. However, for databases with large amounts of data, large datatypes, and some other version 7 features, the migration utility might be the only practical tool for migration to version 8. The migration utility requires only enough temporary space in the SYSTEM tablespace to hold both the version 7 (source) and version 8 (target) data dictionaries simultaneously. The migration utility converts the entire database, including database files, rollback segments, and the control files.

At any point before actually migrating the version 7 database, you can open and access data with the version 7 instance. However, after the migration utility has migrated the version 7 source database to version 8, you can go back to version 7 only by restoring a full backup of the version 7 source database. The migration utility cannot perform direct migrations on release 7.0 databases nor on databases below a specific 7.1 release. The specific release 7.1 requirement is operating-system–specific. For example, on some operating systems, the migration utility can migrate only release 7.1.4 or higher databases to version 8. If you are using a release below the release supported by the migration utility on your operating system, you first must migrate or upgrade your database to a supported version 7 release before using the migration utility to migrate to version 8.

USING MIGRATION UTILITY TO MIGRATE TO ORACLE8.1.X

The Migration utility converts the data dictionary and structures of a version 7 database into version 8 format. To migrate the database, the DBA first installs and runs the version 8 Migration Utility on the version 7 database. Then, the DBA executes a series of ALTER DATABASE commands on the new version8 database. The completion of these procedures results in the conversion of the following version 7 structures into structures that can be used in version 8: Data files (file header only), the data dictionary, control file(s) and Rollback segment(s).

Tip #132	The version 8 Migration Utility cannot migrate a database to a computer system that has a different operating system. For example, it cannot migrate a database from version 7 on Solaris to version 8 on Windows NT. However, you normally can use Export/Import to migrate a database to a different operating system.

Tip #133	On some operating systems, the Migration Utility can migrate only release 7.1.4 and later databases, and cannot migrate a release lower than release 7.1.4 (such as release 7.0 or release 7.1.3). If your database release number is lower than the release supported by the Migration Utility on your operating system, upgrade or migrate the database to the required release or use Export/Import.

CREATING AN INSTANCE ON WINDOWS NT

Although Oracle provides a default instance (ORCL), it is suggested that you create an instance that is specially designed for your database's needs. The following section shows you how.

CREATING INITsid.ora

When creating a new instance, the first thing you need to do is determine all the parameters you need to delineate the shape and size of your database. The parameter file, called the INITsid.ora file (where sid is the name of the instance), is used to start up the database with all the proper configurations. The simplest way to create your new INITsid.ora file is by making a copy of the INITorcl.ora file and modifying it. This file is the parameter file for the default database created on installation. You can find the INITorcl.ora file in the \ORANT\DATABASE directory. Make sure to rename the copy to INITnsid.ora (where nsid is the name this section will use for the new instance) and change, at the very least, the following parameters:

- Set DB_NAME = nsid
- Specify the new names for your control files by altering the filenames next to the CONTROL_FILES parameter. If you don't rename them, you will overwrite the control files for the ORCL instance, which will destroy the ORCL instance.

You can alter all the other parameters in the file also, but the two noted above are mandatory changes that must be made. In addition, make sure the INIT*nsid*.ora file is in the \ORANT\DATABASE directory before making a service for the new instance.

CREATING A SERVICE

After the completion of the INIT*nsid*.ora file, it is necessary to create a Windows NT service for the new instance (for a description of a Windows NT service, see the previous section "Windows NT Services and Oracle Instances"). You can create a service by using either the Oracle Database Configuration Assistant or using line mode.

USING ORACLE DATABASE CONFIGURATION ASSISTANT

To open Oracle Database Configuration Assistant, go to Start, choose Programs, Oracle for Windows NT , Oracle Enterprise Manager, Database Administration Applications, Oracle Database Configuration Assistant. Do the following:

- Select Create new database.
- Enter the instance name.
- Follow the default selections.

USING LINE MODE

To use line mode, you need to open a DOS command prompt. Go to Start and choose Programs, MS-DOS Prompt. Type the following at the prompt:

```
> oradim -new -sid NSID -intpwd ORACLE -startmode AUTO -pfile
c:\ORANT\DATABASE\INITnsid.ora
```

NSID is the name of the new instance, and ORACLE is the internal password for that instance.

After you are done creating the instance, open Server Manager. Connect internal and try to start the database as follows:

```
>CONNECT INTERNAL/ORACLE@2:NSID
>STARTUP PFILE=C:\ORANT\DATABASE\INITnsid.ora
```

> **Note**
>
> oradim is a line mode utility used to create an instance. Oracle8i provides the Oracle Database Configuration Assistant to create the database. Also note that oradim73 is replaced by oradim.

This will verify that the instance has been created.

TUNING AND OPTIMIZING ORACLE ON WINDOWS NT

Hopefully, if your database is properly designed, it will need little or no tuning and optimizing. However, more often than not, unexpected situations arise, causing your database to need some tweaking. In the following sections you will find several causes and solutions for adjusting your database into a well-oiled machine.

ADJUSTING WINDOWS NT CONFIGURATIONS

There are several default configurations of a Windows NT server that can be adjusted if necessary. The following are some examples:

- If you are using raw partitions to improve I/O performance, Oracle recommends that you make all raw disk partitions the same size.

- For optimal performance, you want to make sure that your machine has enough memory to accommodate the entire SGA (System Global Area) and still have some memory left for the operating system to perform well.

- Check the paging file size by opening the System Control Panel applet. Select the Performance Tab and then the Change button under Virtual Memory. The logical drives are listed with the paging file size for each. The block titled "Total Paging File Size For All Drives" shows a recommended and totally allocated amount across all drives. The administrator should ensure that the size meets the recommended number or some other optimal number and that it's on a drive that will have that much space available, if necessary.

- Windows NT optimizes its server, by default, for file sharing. You can change this optimization if your machine is mainly for database usage by going to the Control Panel and opening Network and Server. Change optimization from Sharing to Maximize Throughput for Network Applications. You will have to restart the machine in order for these changes to take place. (This is according to "Performance Tuning Tips for Oracle7 RDBMS on Microsoft Windows NT," released by Oracle Desktop Performance Group, February 1995.)

- On the average machine (32MB of RAM), Windows NT allocates 4MB of memory to its system cache. However, the system cache can be set with the configuration LargeSystemCache (located in the registry under \HKEY_LOCAL_MACHINE\SYSTEM\ CONTROL\SESSION MANAGER\MEMORY MANAGEMENT) equal to zero in order to favor the working set size of the Oracle7 process over that of the system cache.

- The Oracle8 server is integrated with the Windows NT Performance Monitor. (The integrated tool can be found by choosing Start, Programs, and Oracle for Windows NT—Oracle8 Performance Monitor.) See Figure B.10 for a picture of the Windows NT Performance Monitor. This can be used to monitor Oracle-related statistics like library cache and Oracle8 sorts info.

- You can also use the Windows NT performance monitor, which can be found in Start Programs, Administrative Tools, Performance Monitor, to evaluate where the system has bottlenecks. This tool enables you to monitor the Windows NT uses process boundaries to separate different subsystems. If you want to monitor a user's application, use the Performance Monitor's breakdown of CPU usage for the user process. If the percent user time is high, the system is doing well.

■ Other useful statistics, such as memory and CPU usage, can be obtained from the Windows NT Task Manager

Figure B.10
The Windows NT
Performance Monitor

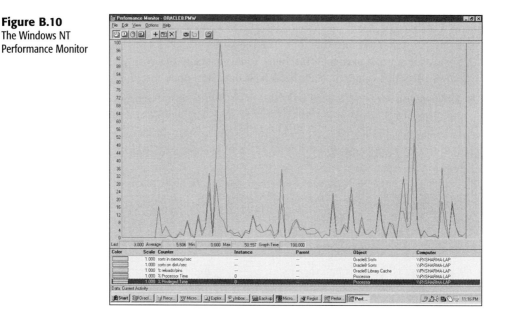

As mentioned before, there is a new Oracle-specific Performance Monitor, which monitors Oracle-specific performance parameters. (See Figure B.11 for the Oracle Performance Monitor.)

Other useful statistics like memory and CPU usage can be obtained by using the Windows NT Task Manager.

STORING ORACLE CONFIGURATIONS

Configurations for Oracle are stored in the Windows NT Registry. To open the Registry, go to the Start menu, choose Run, and then type regedt32. You can find all the information for Oracle stored under the registry key \HKEY_LOCAL_MACHINE\SOFTWARE\ORACLE. In order for the changes to take place, the Oracle services and instances must be restarted.

Some configurations to consider are as follows:

■ Mainly for OLTP purposes, Oracle has set the ORACLE_PRIORITY to normal priority class. You can change the priority class for each background process to higher priorities according to your unique situation. This might cause some instability problems, however. If so, change back to the default value. Oracle recommends that all threads be set at the same priority level. (This is according to "Performance Tuning Tips for Oracle7 RDBMS on Microsoft Windows NT," released by Oracle Desktop Performance Group, February 1995.)

- If DBA_AUTHORIZATION is set to "BYPASS", there is no password required when logging as the user internal. This might be okay during development, but you might want to increase security in a production system. To require a password to be entered upon logging in as internal, set DBA_AUTHORIZATION to "" (a zero-length string).

- If your system has more than one database instance, you might want the default database to be set to a particular instance. You can specify this with the ORACLE_SID value. Oracle sets this value to ORCL (the default database) upon installation.

- You can also set ORACLE_HOME to whatever directory you prefer. For desktop, Oracle sets this configuration to C:\ORANT (or whichever drive Oracle was installed on).

For more Performance Tuning Tips, please refer to Chapter 16, "Performance Tuning Fundamentals," found earlier in this book.

APP

B

Figure B.11
The Oracle
Performance Monitor

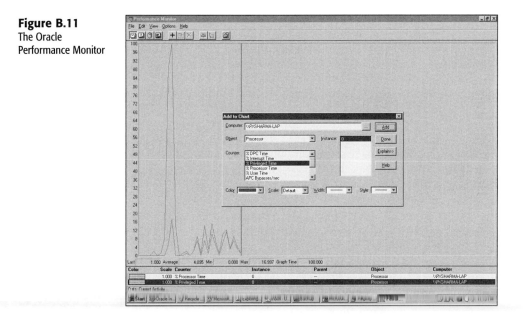

LEARNING FROM ORACLE WINDOWS NT

I have often found that the most valuable information is that learned from previous experiences. In the following sections, I have listed some of my personal encounters and struggles with Oracle on Windows NT.

KNOWING THE LIMITATIONS

It is important to be aware of any limitations that might affect your database design. Oracle often puts this information in obscure places, so for your convenience I have added some of the limitations that I've run across:

- The maximum DB_BLOCK_SIZE in Oracle version 8.1.x.x for Windows NT is 32KB.
- The maximum size for any extent (initial, next, optimal, and so on) is less than 2GB in Oracle version 8.1.x.x for Windows NT.

INSTALLING ENTERPRISE MANAGER

When installing Enterprise Manager on the server (realize Enterprise Manager is mainly used for remote administration), make sure that your Windows NT server has the TCP/IP option installed. If you don't install TCP/IP, set to NETBUI and make sure Oracle's Bequeth is identified with a unique alias.

ACCESSING LARGE FILE SIZES ON WINDOWS NT

Oracle is capable of working around Windows NT in order to access files larger than 4GB. However, you need to note that the backup utility provided by Windows NT will most likely have trouble backing these files up. You might need to obtain a third-party software package (such as Seagate, Arcserve, and so on) to use for backup, or you can make several smaller files to replace the one large file.

THE UTL_FILE PACKAGE

The UTL_FILE package was first introduced in version 7.3x.x of the Oracle database. This package provides capabilities for PL/SQL programs to access files and write output to them. It also has its own error handling and debugging. The UTL_FILE package is not automatically installed on the system during installation, but the script is included with Oracle8.1.x and can be found in the \ORANT\RDBMS\ADMIN directory. The documentation for this package can be found in the *Oracle8 Server Application Developer's Guide* (which is provided as a part of the Oracle server documentation).

If you choose to use this package, make sure you put the name of the directories in the INITsid.ora file. This requirement ensures security in accessing files. To set the directory (and you can put in multiple directories) in the parameter file, use the following:

```
UTL_FILE_DIR = directory name
```

Make sure the directory name does not end in a / because it will cause a UTL_FILE.INVALID_PATH error. Also make sure to give the Oracle owner permissions in the UTL_FILE directories in order to provide security against overwriting system files. Remember that in order for the database to recognize any change in the INITsid.ora file, the database must be shut down and restarted.

The following sample code shows a message being written to a log file:

```
DECLARE
  al UTL_FILE.FILE_TYPE;
  linebuff VARCHAR2(80);
BEGIN
  al := UTL_FILE.FOPEN('C:\LOG','dbproc.log','w');
  linebuff := 'SUCCESSFUL COMPLETION  '¦¦TO_CHAR(SYSDATE,'mm/dd/yyyy hh:mi:ss');
  UTL_FILE.PUT_LINE(al,linebuff);
  UTL_FILE.FCLOSE(al);
END;
```

App

B

The maximum buffer size for a UTL_FILE.PUT_LINE or UTL_FILE.GET_LINE is 1,023 bytes. The file size limit is dependent on the operating system (see the section "Windows NT File Systems" at the beginning of this appendix).

Although it does provide a much needed programming capability, there is a bug in the UTL_FILE package

You cannot, at least not in Windows NT, use the UTL_FILE package to write files across a network. This has been reported as a problem, and there is no fix to date. There is no workaround. The only solution is to write the file to the local machine and use some other tool or programming language to transport it across the network.

Hopefully, the above information has provided you with knowledge that you will be able to use in the future, if not today. Remember, no software package is bullet-proof.

SUPPORTING ORACLE8 ON WINDOWS NT

Oracle version 8 on Windows NT promises to make the database more enterprising by making many of its sizing limits much bigger. Support for Oracle7 will continue until at least December 31, 1999 (this is according to Oracle's World Wide Customer Support Services announcement by Randy Baker, in August, 1997). Version 8.05 of the Oracle database is the most current release for the Windows NT platform as of September, 1997.

INDEX

Other Related Titles

Working with Oracle Cartridges
Steve Shiflett
ISBN: 0-7897-1417-5
$39.99 US/
$59.95 CAN

OCP Training Guide: Oracle DBA
Willard Baird
ISBN: 1562-05891-6
$59.99 US/
$89.95 CAN

Special Edition Using SAP R/3, Third Edition
World Consultancy, LTD.
ISBN: 0-7897-1821-9
$75.00 US/
$95.00 CAN

Using Oracle8
David Austin
ISBN: 0-7897-1653-4
$29.99 US/
$44.95 CAN

www.quecorp.com

REGISTER FOR THE ORACLE TECHNOLOGY NETWORK

Oracle Technology Network (OTN) is the primary technical resource for developers building Oracle-based applications. As an OTN member, you will be part of an online community with access to technical papers, code samples, product documentation, self-service technical support, free software, OTN-sponsored Internet developer conferences, and discussion groups on up-to-date Oracle technology. Membership is FREE! Register for OTN on the World Wide Web at `http://technet.oracle.com/register/oracle8i_pe.htm`.

IMPORTANT PRE-INSTALLATION CONSIDERATIONS

SYSTEM REQUIREMENTS

This section lists the system requirements for each product provided on the Oracle8i Personal Edition CD-ROM.

Note

Important:

The hard disk requirement for each Oracle8i product includes 15MB, which is required to install Java Runtime Environment (JRE) and Oracle Universal Installer on the partition in which the operating system is installed.

If you choose to install Oracle online documentation (HTML), you need an additional 140MB hard disk space.

If you choose to install a starter database, you need an additional 320MB hard disk space.

ORACLE8I PERSONAL EDITION FOR WINDOWS NT

Oracle8i Personal Edition can be installed *only* on Windows NT. The following system configuration is required:

Requirement	Details
Processor	Minimal processor: Pentium 133 or Pentium 166. Recommended processor: Pentium 200
RAM	Typical installation: 96MB (128MB recommended). Minimal installation: 64MB (96MB recommended). Note: You can complete installation on a 64MB machine, but you cannot run Oracle Universal Installer and the database assistants during the same installation session. To run the assistants on a 64MB machine, complete installation, and when asked if you want to create a database, answer No. After installation is completed and Oracle Universal (interMedia, Spatial, and so on) are not installed during a minimal installation. If you want to install any of the options, do so after completing a minimal installation. Custom installation: depends on components selected for installation.

continues

Requirement	Details
Hard disk	Typical installation: 702MB*. Minimal installation: 586MB**. Custom installation: depends on components selected for installation.
Web browser	Frames and Java-enabled
Video	16 color
Microsoft Visual C++ 5.0 or 6.0	If you plan to use the Oracle AppWizard for Microsoft Visual C++

A starter database and the online documentation are included in this calculation.

*** If a starter database is installed.*

By opening this package, you are agreeing to be bound by the following agreement:

You may not copy or redistribute the entire CD-ROM as a whole. Copying and redistribution of individual software programs on the CD-ROM is governed by terms set by individual copyright holders.

The installer and code from the author(s) are copyrighted by the publisher and the author(s).

This software is sold as-is, without warranty of any kind, either expressed or implied, including but not limited to the implied warranties of merchantability and fitness for a particular purpose. Neither the publisher nor its dealers or distributors assumes any liability for any alleged or actual damages arising from the use of this program. (Some states do not allow for the exclusion of implied warranties, so the exclusion may not apply to you.)

Oracle8i Personal Edition © 1999, Oracle Corporation. All rights reserved.